THE PRENTICE-HALL SERIES IN MARKETING

Philip Kotler, Series Editor

Prentice Hall, Englewood Cliffs, New Jersey 07632

8^{TH EDITION}

Marketing Management

ANALYSIS, PLANNING, IMPLEMENTATION, AND CONTROL

Philip Kotler

Northwestern University

Library of Congress Cataloging-in-Publication Data

KOTLER, PHILIP.
    Marketing management : analysis, planning, implementation, and
control / Philip Kotler. —8th ed.
       p.   cm.
    Includes bibliographical references and indexes.
    ISBN 0-13-722851-1
    1. Marketing—Management. I. Title.
HF5415.13.K64 1994   93-16057
658.8— dc20   CIP

Eighth Edition
MARKETING MANAGEMENT
Analysis, Planning, Implementation, and Control
PHILIP KOTLER

Editor-in-Chief: **Valeria Ashton**
Acquisition Editor: **Sandra M. Steiner**
Editorial and production supervision: **Esther S. Koehn**
Copy Editor: **Donna Mulder**
Design Director: **Patricia Wosczyk**
Interior design: **Maureen Eide**
Cover design: **Donna M. Wickes**
Cover art: *Peeling Globe* by David Shannon. Photo courtesy of British Telecommunications.
Manufacturing buyers: **Trudy Pisciotti/Patrice Fraccio**
Assistant Marketing Editor: **Wendy Sue Goldner**
Marketing Manager: **Carol Carter**
Editorial Assistants: **Cathi Profitko, Renée Pelletier**

Printed in the United States of America
10 9 8 7 6 5 4 3 2 1

ISBN 0-13-722851-1

Prentice-Hall International (UK) Limited, *London*
Prentice-Hall of Australia Pty. Limited, *Sydney*
Prentice-Hall Canada Inc., *Toronto*
Prentice-Hall Hispanoamericana, S.A., *Mexico*
Prentice-Hall of India Private Limited, *New Delhi*
Prentice-Hall of Japan, Inc., *Tokyo*
Simon & Schuster Asia Pte. Ltd., *Singapore*
Editora Prentice-Hall do Brasil, Ltda., *Rio de Janeiro*

This book is dedicated to my wife and best friend, Nancy, with love

About the Author

Philip Kotler is one of the world's leading authorities on marketing. He is the S. C. Johnson & Son Distinguished Professor of International Marketing at the Kellogg Graduate School of Management, Northwestern University. He received his master's degree at the University of Chicago and his Ph.D. degree at M.I.T., both in economics. He did postdoctoral work in mathematics at Harvard and behavioral science at the University of Chicago.

Dr. Kotler is the author of *Principles of Marketing* and *Marketing: An Introduction*. His *Strategic Marketing for Nonprofit Organizations*, now in its fourth edition, is the best seller in that specialized area. Dr. Kotler's other books include *The New Competition; Marketing Professional Services; Marketing for Health Care Organizations; Strategic Marketing for Educational Institutions; High Visibility; Social Marketing; Marketing Places; Marketing for Congregations;* and *Marketing Models*.

In addition, he has written over 90 articles for leading journals, including the *Harvard Business Review, Sloan Management Review, Business Horizons, California Management Review, Journal of Marketing, Journal of Marketing Research, Management Science, Journal of Business Strategy,* and *Futurist*. He is the only three-time winner of the coveted Alpha Kappa Psi award for the best annual article published in the *Journal of Marketing*.

Dr. Kotler has served as chairman of the College on Marketing of The Institute of Management Sciences (TIMS); a director of the American Marketing Association; a trustee of the Marketing Science Institute; a director of The MAC Group (Gemini), and an advisor to Yankelovich Partners. He has consulted many major U.S. and foreign companies—AT&T, Bank of America, Ford, General Electric, IBM, Merck, Marriott, Montedison, and so on—on marketing strategy.

In 1978, Dr. Kotler received the *Paul D. Converse Award* given by the American Marketing Association to honor "outstanding contributions to science in marketing." In 1983, he received the *Steuart Henderson Britt Award* as Marketer of the Year. In 1985, he was named the first recipient of the *Distinguished Marketing Educator Award*, a new award established by the American Marketing Association. In the same year, the Academy for Health Services Marketing established the *Philip Kotler Award for Excellence in Health Care Marketing* and nominated him as the first recipient. He also received the *Prize for Marketing Excellence* awarded by the European Association of Marketing Consultants and Sales Trainers. In 1989, he received the *Charles Coolidge Parlin Award* which each year honors an outstanding leader in the field of marketing. He has received honorary doctorate degrees from DePaul University and the University of Zurich.

Brief Contents

Part IV Developing Marketing Strategies

Part V Planning Marketing Programs

Part VI Organizing, Implementing, and Controlling Marketing Effort

Contents

Part VI ORGANIZING, IMPLEMENTING, AND CONTROLLING MARKETING EFFORT

Exhibits

Marketing Strategies

Marketing Concepts and Tools

Marketing Environment and Trends

Global Marketing

Companies and Industries

Socially Responsible Marketing

Preface

Today's companies must urgently and critically rethink their business mission and marketing strategies. Instead of operating in a marketplace of fixed and known competitors and stable customer preferences, today's companies work in a war zone of rapidly changing competitors, technological advances, new laws, managed trade policies, and diminishing customer loyalty. Companies find themselves competing in a race where the road signs and rules keep changing, where there is no finish line, no permanent "win." They simply must keep racing, hopefully in a direction where the public wants them to go.

In the days when it was "business as usual," companies could succeed by producing their products and supporting them with hard selling and heavy advertising. This was called "marketing." This is still a widespread "man-in-the-street" view of marketing. Unfortunately some company presidents also think marketing is whipping up the sales troops to go out and sell whatever the company makes. But this view of marketing is a recipe for disaster.

Consider the fact that today's customers face a plentitude of products in every category. Consider that customers exhibit varying and diverse requirements for product/service combinations and prices. Consider that they have high and rising expectations of quality and service. In the face of their vast choices, customers will gravitate to the offerings that best meet their individual needs and expectations. They will buy on the basis of their perception of value.

Therefore it is not surprising that today's winning companies are those who succeed best in satisfying, indeed delighting, their target customers. These companies see marketing as a company-wide philosophy, not a separate function. They want their marketing people to help define which customer groups and needs the company can profitably serve and how to serve them more effectively than competitors. These companies dedicate themselves to being the best in meeting the needs of their target markets. They don't settle for being number 3 or 4. If they cannot bring something special to their target market, they will not last long. These companies are market-focused and customer-driven, rather than solely product-focused or cost-driven. They pay extreme attention to quality and service—to meeting and even exceeding customer expectations. They compete vigorously, and at the same time they cooperate smartly with their strategic partners in their supply and distribution chain. They pursue efficiency and yet are responsive and flexible.

What is the work of marketing like in these winning companies? Marketing is seen as more than a department. Marketers get involved in management decision making long before any product is designed and they continue their work long after the product is sold. Marketers identify customer needs that represent profitable opportunities; they participate in the design of the product and service mix; they heavily influence the pricing of the offerings; they work hard to communicate and promote the company's products, services, and image; they monitor customer satisfaction; and they constantly improve the company's offerings and performance on the basis of market feedback.

Today's winning companies are moving from viewing the company as a set of departments to viewing it as a *system* for managing core business processes. Companies must manage and master such basic processes as new product realization, order generation, and order fulfilment. Each process involves several steps and requires inputs from several departments. Companies are establishing cross-functional teams to manage each process smoothly and swiftly. Marketing personnel are interfacing increasingly with personnel from research and development, purchasing, manufacturing, logistics, and finance.

Today's winning companies create a culture where all members of the organization are "market-conscious" and "customer- conscious." As Ted Levitt of Harvard observed, "if you are not thinking customer, you are not thinking." Every employee can potentially improve or damage customer perceptions and preferences. The accountant who sends cryptic invoices to customers; the receptionist who looks bored; the telephone operator who sends the customer on a wild-goose chase; all these employees are creating negative "moments of truth."

The marketing discipline is undergoing fresh reappraisal in the light of the vast global, technological, economic, and social challenges facing today's companies. Mass markets are fragmenting into micromarkets; multiple distribution channels are replacing single channels; customers are buying direct through catalogs, telemarketing, and home video shopping; price discounting and sales promotion are rampant and are eroding brand loyalty; conventional advertising media are delivering less and costing more. These and other seismic marketplace changes mean that companies must reexamine their foundational concepts and even reverse the very premises on which they built their successful businesses.

The marketing discipline is redeveloping its assumptions, concepts, skills, tools, and systems for making sound business decisions. Marketers must know when to cultivate large markets and when to niche; when to launch new brands and when to extend existing brand names; when to push products through distribution and when to pull them through distribution; when to protect the domestic market and when to penetrate aggressively into foreign markets; when to add more benefits to the offer and when to reduce the price; and when to expand and when to contract their budgets for salesforce, advertising, and other marketing tools.

Perhaps the basic change in marketing thinking is the paradigm shift from *pursuing a sale* to *creating a customer*. Past marketing has been largely transaction oriented; today it is more relationship oriented. In addition to designing the best marketing mix "to make a sale," there is growing emphasis on designing the best relationship mix for winning and keeping customers. Good customers are an asset which, when well managed and served, will return a handsome lifetime income stream to the company. In the intensely competitive marketplace, the company's first order of business is to retain customer loyalty through continually satisfying their needs in a superior way.

Relationship marketing is not only a company drive to bond better with their consumers. Winning companies also develop mutually profitable relationships with their suppliers and distributors. If the company squeezes its suppliers' profits unduly, if it forces too much product on its distributors, if it wins by making its partners in the supply chain lose, the company will fail. Smart companies partner with their suppliers and distributors in the drive to better serve their ultimate customers.

And marketing, at its best, goes beyond meeting existing customer needs. Akio Morita, chairman of Sony, put it well: "I create markets." Good companies will meet needs; great companies will create markets. Market leadership is gained by envisioning new products, services, lifestyles, and ways to raise living standards. There is a vast difference between companies that offer me-too products and those that create new product and service values not even imagined by the marketplace. Ultimately, marketing at its best is about value creation and raising the world's living standards.

The Nature of This Book

Marketing thinking obviously isn't easy or it would be applied more successfully. *Although it only takes a semester to learn marketing, it takes a lifetime to master it.* Marketing problems, it turns out, do not exhibit the neat quantitative properties of many problems in the production, accounting, and finance areas. Psychological forces play a large role; marketing expenditures affect demand and costs simultaneously; marketing plans shape and interact with other business function plans. Marketing decisions must be made in the face of insufficient information about processes that are dynamic, lagged, stochastic, interactive, and downright difficult. However, this is not an argument for intuitive decision making. Rather it is an argument for improved marketing theory and tools of analysis.

Marketing Management has several major features:

1. *A managerial orientation:* This book focuses on the major decisions that marketing managers and top management face in their efforts to harmonize the objectives, core competences, and resources of the organization with the needs and opportunities in the marketplace.

2. *An analytical approach:* This book presents a framework for analyzing recurrent problems in marketing management. Actual company cases are introduced throughout the text to illustrate the marketing principles, strategies, and practices.

3. *A basic disciplines perspective:* This book draws on economics, behavioral science, management theory, and mathematics. *Economics* provides fundamental concepts and tools for seeking optimal results in the use of scarce resources. *Behavioral science* provides fundamental concepts and tools for understanding consumer and organizational buying behavior. *Management theory* provides a framework for identifying the issues facing managers and guidelines for their satisfactory resolution. *Mathematics* provides an exact language for expressing relationships among important variables.

4. *A universal approach:* This book applies marketing thinking to products and services, consumer and business markets, profit and nonprofit organizations, domestic and foreign companies, small and large firms, manufacturing and middlemen businesses, and low-tech and high-tech industries.

5. *Comprehensive and balanced coverage:* This book covers all the topics that an informed marketing manager needs to know. It covers the main issues faced in strategic, tactical, and administrative marketing.

This eighth edition of *Marketing Management* is organized into six parts. *Part I* develops the societal, managerial, and strategic underpinnings of marketing theory and practice. *Part II* presents concepts and tools for analyzing any market and marketing environment to discern opportunities. *Part III* presents principles for measuring and forecasting markets and carrying out market segmentation and market targeting. *Part IV* examines issues in designing marketing strategies for companies in different market positions, global positions, and stages in the product life cycle. *Part V* deals with tactical marketing and how companies handle, or should handle, each element of the marketing mix—product, price, place, and promotion. Finally, *Part VI* examines the administrative side of marketing, namely, how firms organize, implement, and control marketing efforts.

Changes in the Eighth Edition

The eighth edition has the following objectives:

1. To highlight the most recent trends and developments in the global marketing environment
2. To emphasize the importance of teamwork between marketing and all the other functions of the firm
3. To introduce new perspectives in successful strategic market planning
4. To present additional company examples of creative market- focused and customer-driven action
5. To describe a host of new developments in marketing planning, organization, implementation, and control
6. To underscore the growing importance of computers, telecommunications, and other new technologies in improving marketing planning and performance
7. To emphasize the critical importance of marketers acting in an ethical and socially responsible way.

These objectives led to the following distinctive features in the new eighth edition:

1. A new Chapter 2, "Building Customer Satisfaction Through Quality, Service, and Value." Further emphasis throughout the book on the importance of offering quality, service, and value.
2. The addition of considerable new global marketing material throughout the book in addition to a revised Chapter 16, "Designing Strategies for the Global Marketplace."
3. The addition of substantial material dealing with socially responsible and ethical marketing.
4. New material bearing on the importance of managing business processes and core competences, not just departmental functions.
5. A greatly expanded section on "brand development" as one of the keys to successful marketing in the 1990s.
6. New exhibits have been added and color-coded into six groups: Marketing Strategies, Marketing Concepts and Tools, Marketing Environment and Trends, Companies and Industries, Global Marketing, and Socially Responsible Marketing. In addition, parts of several chapters have been substantially revised. Writing has been made smoother and tighter.
7. New and expanded material has been added on relationship marketing, value-added marketing, customer loyalty, brand equity, frequency marketing, club marketing, guarantee marketing, customer satisfaction tracking, core competences and capabilities, marketing pioneer advantages, theatrical retailing, superpower retailers, competitive benchmarking, virtual reality, integrated marketing communications, word-of-mouth marketing, and marketing engineering,

Improved Pedagogical Aids

Pedagogical aids for this edition of *Marketing Management* include:

1. A comprehensive, extensively revised Instructor's Manual, created by Bruce Wrenn and Slimen Saliba, contains teaching formats, suggested syllabi, and video case exercises, as well as a complete section on integrating supplementary material into the course such as cases, casebooks, readings, videos, and computer-based material. It is available to adopters on request.

2. A Test Item File containing over 2,500 questions, authored by Marsha Griffin, incorporates designations for level of difficulty and page reference for each question. A computerized version in IBM PC 3.5 and 5.25 and compatible formats is also available. Both are available to adopters on request.

3. A Cooperative Learning Guide by Mary Nicastro and David Jones is a teaching handbook designed to meet the needs of marketing instructors who wish to incorporate active (nonlecture-based) forms of learning in the classroom. Available to instructors upon adoption.

4. Transparency acetates highlight important concepts in *Marketing Management*. Each full-color transparency is accompanied by teaching and integration notes that ties the concept to the text material it represents. Compiled and annotated by Lewis Hershey, these transparencies are also available electronically on Powerpoint software.

5. ABC News/PH Video Library for *Marketing Management,* Eighth Edition, provides the most dynamic of all the supplements you can use to enhance your class. The quality of the video material and how well it relates to your course can make the difference. For these reasons, Prentice Hall and ABC News worked together to bring you the best and most comprehensive video ancillaries available in the college market.

    Through its wide variety of award-winning programs—Nightline, Business World, On Business, This Week with David Brinkley, World News Tonight, and Health Show—ABC offers a resource for feature and documentary-style videos related to text concepts and applications. The programs have extremely high production quality, present substantial content, and are hosted by well-versed, well-known anchors. Prentice Hall, its authors, and editors have selected videos on topics that will work well with this course and text and give you teaching notes on how to use them in the classroom.

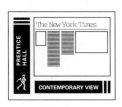

6. The *New York Times* and Prentice Hall offer **A Contemporary View**, a program designed to enhance student access to current information of relevance in the classroom.

    Through this program, the core subject matter provided in the text is supplemented by a collection of time-sensitive articles from one of the world's most distinguished newspapers, the *New York Times*. These articles demonstrate the vital, ongoing connection between what is learned in the classroom and what is happening in the world around us. Prentice Hall and the *New York Times* are proud to co-sponsor **A Contemporary View**. We hope it will make the reading of both this text and the *Times* a more dynamic, involving process. To enjoy the wealth of information of the *New York Times* daily, a reduced, subscription rate is available. For information, call toll-free: 1-800-631-1222.

Acknowledgments

The eighth edition bears the imprint of many persons. My colleagues and associates at the Kellogg Graduate School of Management at Northwestern University continue to have an important impact on my thinking: James C. Anderson, Robert Blattberg, Bob J. Calder, Greg Carpenter, Richard M. Clewett, Anne T. Coughlan, Dawn Iacobucci, Dipak C. Jain, Jill Klein, Sidney J. Levy, Ann McGill, John F. Sherry, Jr., Louis W. Stern, Brian Sternthal, Alice Tybout, and Andris A. Zoltners.

I benefited from the excellent secretarial assistance of Mary Novak and Nancy Singer. I want to thank the S. C. Johnson family for the generous support of my chair at the Kellogg School. Completing the Northwestern team is my dean and longtime friend, Donald P. Jacobs, whom I want to thank for his continuous support of my research and writing efforts.

I am also indebted to the following colleagues at other universities who reviewed this edition and the previous edition and provided insightful suggestions.

Hiram Barksdale
University of
Georgia

Boris Becker
Oregon State
University

Sunil Bhatla
Case Western Reserve
University

John Burnett
Texas A&M
University

Surjit Chhabra
DePaul University

John Deighton
University of
Chicago

Ralph Gaedke
University of
California

David Georgoff
Florida Atlantic
University

Dennis Gensch
University of
Wisconsin–
Milwaukee

Arun Jain
State University of
New York–Buffalo

H. Lee Matthews
Ohio State University

Mary Ann McGrath
Loyola University–
Chicago

Pat Murphy
University of Notre
Dame

Nicholas Nugent
Boston College

Donald Outland
University of
Texas–Austin

Albert Page
University of
Illinois–Chicago

Christopher Puto
Arizona State
University

Robert Roe
University of
Wyoming

Dean Siewers
Rochester Institute
of Technology

My thanks also go to my foreign-edition coauthors for their suggestions on the contents of the eighth edition:

- ◆ Friedhelm W. Bliemel—Universitat Kaiserslautern (Germany)
- ◆ Bernard Dubois—Centre d'Enseignement Superieur des Affaires (France)
- ◆ Peter Fitzroy and Robin Shaw—Monash University (Australia)
- ◆ Walter Georgio Scott—Catholic University (Italy)
- ◆ Ronald E. Turner—Queen's University (Canada)

The talented staff at Prentice Hall deserves praise for their role in shaping this edition. My editor, Sandra Steiner, offered excellent advice and direction for the eighth edition. I also want to acknowledge the fine editorial work of Esther Koehn, production editor; the creative graphic design of Maureen Eide; the computer work and assistance of Maureen Gilchrist; and the marketing research work of Carol Carter.

My overriding debt is to my wife, Nancy, who provided me with the time, support, and inspiration needed to prepare this edition. It is truly our book.

PHILIP KOTLER
Evanston, Illinois

Professors!

Bring Dr. Philip Kotler into your classroom through his video series,

◆ PHILIP KOTLER ON COMPETITIVE MARKETING ◆

The fundamentals of marketing for the '90s come to life with:

- *case studies on Lexus, Bank One, Dell Computer, Forester Products, and the San Jose Sharks*
- *a panel of marketing professionals from Motorola, Johnson's Wax, IBM, Northwest Airlines, and the Illinois Lottery*
- *discussions with Kevin Clancy and Al Reis about why organizations fail and how they must adapt to succeed*
- *classic television commercials that illustrate the key differentiators of best selling products*
- *practical guidance from Philip Kotler on how to become not just market driven, but market drivers*

This two part video series brings the real world into your classroom. Call or fax today and use it tomorrow.

◆ PHILIP KOTLER ON COMPETITIVE MARKETING ◆
Part 1: Segmenting & Targeting
Part 2: Differentiating & Positioning

In the United States, each part, $995; both parts, $1,692. Shipping and applicable taxes will be added. For information and pricing outside the United States, call Video Arts Ltd.

Video Arts Inc.
8614 West Catalpa Avenue
Chicago, IL 60656

From USA and Canada:
Tel No. 800-553-0091
Fax No. 312-693 7030

Video Arts Ltd.
Dumbarton House
68 Oxford Street
London, W1N 9LA

London: Tel No. 071-637 7228
         Fax No. 071-580 8103
Birmingham: Tel No. 021-666-6998
             Fax No. 021-666-7515

Understanding the Critical Role of Marketing in Organizations and Society

Marketing is so basic that it cannot be considered a separate function. It is the whole business seen from the point of view of its final result, that is, from the customer's point of view. . . . Business success is not determined by the producer but by the customer.

PETER DRUCKER

Marketing consists of all activities by which a company adapts itself to its environment — creatively and profitably.

RAY COREY

Marketing's job is to convert societal needs into profitable opportunities.

ANONYMOUS

Every decade calls upon company management to think freshly about its objectives, strategies, and tactics. Rapid changes can easily make obsolete yesterday's winning principles for conducting business. Henry Ford kept producing black Model T Fords when car buyers started clamoring for more variety. General Motors responded and overtook Ford. Later, General Motors kept producing large automobiles when customers started clamoring for smaller cars, something Volkswagen and the Japanese began to hear. Still later, customers began to insist on quality, and the Japanese responded with better cars. No wonder management guru Peter Drucker observed that a company's winning formula in the last decade will probably undo it in the next decade.

What are the new challenges in the 1990s? With the Cold War over, companies and countries are confronting a new set of problems. They are wrestling today with increased global competition, environmental deterioration, infrastructure neglect, economic stagnation, low labor skills, and a host of other economic, political, and social problems.

Yes, these are problems; but they are also opportunities. The globalized market means that domestic companies can count on a much larger market potential for their goods and services; the bad news is that they will face a greater number of competitors. Environmental deterioration presents countless opportunities to companies that can create more effective means of cleaning up the environment. Infrastructure neglect will provide huge opportunities for companies in the construction, transportation, and communication industries. Economic stagnation and recession will favor companies that are good at "lean production and lean marketing." Low labor skills will challenge educational and training companies to design more effective programs for upgrading human skills.

The problems plaguing a society are only one source of business opportunities. Consider the opportunities presented by the multiplying scientific and technological advances in genetic engineering, multisensory robotics, artificial intelligence, micromechanics, molecular designing, superconductors, and dozens of other scientific areas.

Doing Business in a Rapidly Changing Global Economy

Let's look deeper into some specific challenges that are facing today's businesses.

The Globalized Economy

The world economy has undergone a radical transformation in the last two decades. Basically, geographical and cultural distances have shrunk significantly with the advent of jet airplanes, fax machines, global computer and telephone linkups, and world television satellite broadcasting. This shrinkage of distance has permitted companies to widen substantially their geographical markets as well as their supplier sources. In the past, a U.S. company such as Chrysler would build its cars from components mostly sourced in the United States and would sell most of its cars in the U.S. marketplace. Today, Chrysler orders its components from suppliers in Japan, Korea, Germany, and a dozen other countries and also sells its cars in other parts of the world. One is no longer sure that Chrysler-labeled cars were primarily made by Chrysler.

Companies in various industries are also developing their products using a global assembly line. Consider the following:[1]

◆ In the past, most American clothing was made and sold in America. Much cutting and sewing were done in New York and New England "sweatshops" by immigrant labor working long hours. The workers joined unions and raised wages. Searching for lower labor costs, many clothing manufacturers moved to Southern states. More recently, many U.S. companies moved their manufacturing to Asia. Today, Bill Blass, one of America's top fashion designers, will examine woven cloth made from Australian wool with printed designs prepared in Italy. He will design a dress and fax the drawing to a Hong Kong agent who will place the order with a mainland China factory. The finished dresses will be airfreighted to New York where they will be redistributed to department stores that had placed orders. Not surprisingly, as a result of the lower foreign manufacturing costs, more than 400,000 apparel jobs have been lost in the United States.

◆ Is the Boeing 767 an American plane? Boeing's staff in Seattle designed the plane and manufactured the wings and cockpit. The nose tip and certain wing parts were manufactured in Italy, the rear section in Canada, the front windshields and engines in England, and the fusilage and high-tech components in Japan. Altogether, 29 countries participated in producing this plane.

◆ Most books appearing in U.S. bookstores normally would have been developed and printed in the United States with U.S. equipment and supplies. Today, the author is probably typing on a computer made in Taiwan with software developed in California. The printing would be done on a German printing press with ink obtained from Korea and paper from Canada. The pages may have been shipped for binding in Mexico with the final books shipped back to the United States and other English-speaking markets. A good part of the book's price of say $45 will have ended up as income paid to people in other countries.

The point is that many domestically purchased goods and services are "hybrid" in that the design, materials, manufacture, and assembly have taken place in various countries. This fact has apparently escaped the notice of those U.S. companies who want to wage a "Buy American Campaign." If Americans decided to "buy American," they would buy a Dodge Colt that was actually made in Japan and they would avoid buying a Honda, which was essentially manufactured and assembled in the United States!

U.S. companies are not only increasingly sourcing their components, supplies, and goods from abroad; they are also trying to sell more of their locally made goods abroad. But they are recognizing that to do this well, they cannot do it alone. So they are forming strategic alliances with foreign companies who serve as suppliers, distributors, technological partners, joint venture partners, even competitors. In the last case, we see surprising alliances formed between competitors such as Ford and Mazda, General Electric and Matsushita, and AT&T and Olivetti. Even the largest U.S. companies, instead of competing in the world marketplace on their own, are building extensive *global business networks* to extend their global reach. Winning companies in the 1990s will be those that have built the most effective global business networks.

At the same time that global markets are expanding, so are regional trade blocs emerging. The United States signed a Free Trade Agreement with Canada and is considering signing one with Mexico. Eventually the American hemisphere may act as one trading bloc giving preferential treatment to goods made in this area. The

European Common Market consists of twelve countries with 340 million consumers that is eliminating internal trade barriers and setting common standards and regulations. It now represents a larger market than the United States. Meanwhile, Japan and other Far East nations are organizing a possible trade bloc in that region of the world, which happens to have the highest economic growth rate. Clearly, the world economic map is changing rapidly.

The Income Gap

A large part of the world has grown poorer, not richer, in the last few decades. Although wages may have risen, real purchasing power has declined, especially for the less skilled members of the workforce. In the United States, many households managed to maintain their purchasing power chiefly because wives entered the workforce. Many other workers lost their jobs as U.S. manufacturers "downsized" their workforce to cut their costs. Company workforces in the computer, steel, auto, textile, and other industries shrunk to a fraction of their former size. In January 1993, the U.S. unemployment rate reached 7.1%, with the result that over 9 million workers were unemployed.

A U.S. recession slows down other economies. "When America sneezes, other countries catch a cold." Western Europe tumbled into a recession, and this reduced European imports from the Far East, which subsequently dampened business activity in the Far East. All this underscores the complex interdependency of the global economy.

Meanwhile, Eastern European countries are attempting to convert to market economies and are finding this difficult. Instead of worker conditions improving, they are worsening. Western governments are making loans and investments in Eastern-bloc countries but their resources are too limited to make a sufficient impact.

In the meantime, Third World countries in Africa, South America, and other regions complain about the attention that Eastern Europe is getting when their own economies are stagnating. The gap between the rich and poor nations is growing wider. The poor nations pressure the richer nations to open their markets to their cheaper goods but the rich nations maintain tariffs and quotas to protect their local industries and employment.

Unfortunately, people's needs are greater than ever but they lack the means to pay for the needed goods. Meanwhile factories in the industrial nations operate at half capacity because they cannot find enough buyers for their goods. This is the tragedy of "poverty amidst plenty." Markets, after all, consist of people with needs *and* purchasing power, but the latter is lacking.

Two solutions partly address the income gap. The first is *countertrade*, namely that the poor pay for needed goods by exchanging other goods and services. Thus, Russia takes Pepsi Cola and pays for it with vodka. General Electric builds a lamp factory in Hungary and gets paid in light bulbs. Although countertrade is less efficient than hard cash transactions, it nevertheless permits consumers, companies, and countries lacking hard cash to obtain some of the goods they need.

The other solution is providing "more for less" in place of "more for more." America's largest retailer, Wal-Mart, rose to market leadership on two principles emblazoned in large letters on every Wal-Mart store: "Satisfaction Guaranteed" and "We Sell for Less." The customer enters a Wal-Mart store, is welcomed by a friendly greeter, and finds a huge assortment of good quality merchandise at "everyday low prices." The same principle explains the burgeoning growth of factory outlet malls and discount chain stores, namely that customers want to be smart shoppers and buy on value. This applies even to buying a luxury automobile, as when Toyota launched its luxury Lexus automobile against Mercedes with the headline: "Perhaps The First Time In History That Trading A $72,000 Car For A $36,000 Car Could Be Considered Trading Up."

The Environmental Imperative

A third new factor in today's business climate is that companies must accept increasing responsibility for their environmental impacts. In the past, a chemical company could belch out factory smoke that polluted the air and dispose of chemicals that polluted the water and soil without much accountability. The chemical company was not deliberately trying to hurt the environment; it was simply trying to keep its costs low. Starting in the 1970s, environmental laws were passed that required companies to install pollution control equipment of all kinds. As the air quality in major cities worsened, automobile manufacturers were held to increasingly stricter standards for catalytic converters. All of this raised costs for American manufacturers who felt they were being put at a disadvantage against global competitors who operated under weaker or nonexistent environmental regulations.

If anything, the environmental movement will become more uncompromising over time. The West was not only shocked by the Chernobyl nuclear disaster in 1986 but by further revelations after the fall of Communism about how negligently the former Eastern Bloc governments had handled the environment. In many East European cities, the air is terrible, the water is polluted, and the soil is poisoned by chemical dumping. In June 1992, the Earth Summit was held in Rio de Janiero and attended by representatives from over 100 countries to consider how to handle such problems as the destruction of rain forests, global warming, endangered species, and other environmental threats. Clearly, companies will be increasingly held accountable for their effluents, packaging material, waste handling, and other environmental fallouts from their manufacturing and marketing activities.

Other Issues

Many other critical changes have occurred in consumer and business markets. Consumer markets are often characterized by an aging population; an increasing number of working women; later marriage, more divorce, and smaller families; the emergence of distinct ethnic consumer groups and needs; and the proliferation of more varied consumer lifestyles. Business markets are also changing. Business firms demand higher product quality from their suppliers, faster delivery, better service, and lower prices. Business firms need to speed up their product-development process because of shorter product life cycles. They need to find better ways to distribute and promote their products at lower cost.

The New View of the Firm

The last decade taught a humbling lesson to business firms everywhere. Domestic companies can no longer ignore foreign competitors, foreign markets, and foreign sources of supply. Companies cannot allow their wage and material costs to get far out of line with the rest of the world. Companies cannot ignore emerging technologies, materials, equipment, and new ways of organizing and marketing.

U.S. companies are a case in point. In the 1970s, the most powerful U.S. companies included General Motors, Sears, RCA, and IBM. Today, all four are struggling to remain profitable. They all failed at marketing. Each company failed to understand its changing marketplace and customers and the need to provide competitive value. In 1992, General Motors suffered a $23.5-billion loss—the largest in history—and is still trying to figure out why German and Japanese automobiles are more preferred than GM cars in most of the world. Mighty Sears in 1992 laid off 60,000 employees and closed 11 stores; it was caught between fashionable department stores and boutiques at one end and discount mass merchandisers at the other. RCA, inventor of so many new patents, never quite mastered the art of marketing, and now puts its brand name on products largely imported from Japan and South Korea. IBM, one of the world's great sales-driven companies, experienced its first loss ever in 1992—$4.96 billion—because it continued to focus on selling mainframes, while the market was moving inexorably toward newer needs, such as microcomputing, computer networking, and computer work stations.

In view of all this "marketing myopia,"[2] it is not surprising that companies have been treated to a flood of books offering fresh prescriptions on how to run their businesses in the new environment. In the 1960s, "theory Y" was the rage, calling for companies to treat their employees not as cogs in a machine but as individuals whose creativity can be released through enlightened management practice. In the 1970s, "strategic planning" offered a way of thinking about building and managing the company's portfolio of businesses in a turbulent environment. In the 1980s, "excellence and quality" received major attention as the new formulas for success. All of these themes will continue to inspire our business thinking.

In the 1990s, companies finally may be ready to acknowledge the critical importance of being "customer-oriented and driven" in conducting all of their activities. It is not enough to be product-driven or technology-driven; too many companies still design their products without customer input, only to find them rejected in the marketplace. And too many companies forget the customers after the sale, only to lose them to competitors through benign neglect. Not surprisingly, we are witnessing a flood of books with such titles as *The Customer-Driven Company*, *Keep the Customer*, *Customers for Life*, *Total Customer Service: The Ultimate Weapon*, and *The Only Thing That Matters: Bringing the Power of the Customer into the Center of Your Business*.[3] All said, a new view of the firm's winning platform for the 1990s is emerging, and much of it rests on a market-based view of business success.

Plan of this Chapter

One marketing scholar defined *marketing* as "the creation and delivery of a standard of living." We take this as an inspired and insightful view of the purpose of marketing. This chapter will present the major concepts and philosophies underlying modern marketing thinking and practice. We will address the following questions:

- ◆ What are the core concepts that underlie the discipline of marketing?
- ◆ What are the basic tasks performed by marketing managers?
- ◆ What is the marketing philosophy, and how does it contrast with other philosophies of doing business?
- ◆ What role does marketing play in different industries, in nonprofit organizations, and in different countries?

The Core Concepts of Marketing

Marketing has been defined in various ways.[4] We like the following definition of marketing:

❖ Marketing *is a social and managerial process by which individuals and groups obtain what they need and want through creating, offering, and exchanging products of value with others.*

This definition of marketing rests on the following core concepts: *needs, wants, and demands; products; value, cost, and satisfaction; exchange, transactions, and relationships; markets;* and *marketing and marketers*. These concepts are illustrated in Figure 1-1 and discussed below.

Needs, Wants, and Demands

Marketing thinking starts with the fact of human needs and wants. People need food, air, water, clothing, and shelter to survive. Beyond this, people have a strong desire for recreation, education, and other services. They have strong preferences for particular versions and brands of basic goods and services.

There is no doubt that people's needs and wants today are staggering. In a given year, 249 million Americans might consume or use 67 billion eggs, 2 billion chickens, 5 million hair dryers, 133 billion domestic air travel passenger miles, and over 4 million lectures by college English professors. These consumer goods and services create a demand for more than 150 million tons of steel, 4 billion tons of cotton, and many other industrial goods. These are a few of the demands that get expressed in a $5.7 trillion economy.

A useful distinction can be drawn between needs, wants, and demands. *A human need is a state of felt deprivation of some basic satisfaction* People require food, clothing, shelter, safety, belonging, esteem, and a few other things for survival. These needs are not created by their society or by marketers; they exist in the very texture of human biology and the human condition.

Wants are desires for specific satisfiers of these deeper needs. An American needs food and wants a hamburger, needs clothing and wants a Pierre Cardin suit, needs esteem and buys a Mercedes. In another society, these needs are satisfied differently: Australian aborigines satisfy their hunger with kiwis, their clothing needs with a loincloth, their esteem with a shell necklace. Although people's needs are few, their wants are many. Human wants are continually shaped and reshaped by social forces and institutions, such as churches, schools, families, and business corporations.

Demands are wants for specific products that are backed by an ability and willingness to buy them. Wants become demands when supported by purchasing power. Many people want a Mercedes; only a few are able and willing to buy one. Companies must therefore measure not only how many people want their product but, more important, how many would actually be willing and able to buy it.

These distinctions shed light on the frequent charge by marketing critics that "marketers create needs" or "marketers get people to buy things they don't want." Marketers do not create needs; needs preexist marketers. Marketers, along with other influencers in the society, influence wants. They promote the idea that a Mercedes would satisfy a person's need for social status. Marketers, however, do not create the need for social status. Marketers influence demand by making the product appropriate, attractive, affordable, and easily available to target consumers.

FIGURE 1-1 The Core Concepts of Marketing

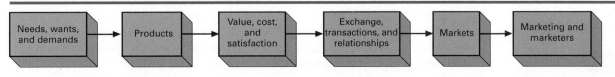

Products

People satisfy their needs and wants with goods and services. We will use the term *products* to cover both. We will define a product as *anything that can be offered to satisfy a need or want*. The importance of physical products lies not so much in owning them as in obtaining the services they render. We don't buy a car to look at but because it supplies transportation service. We don't buy a microwave oven to admire but because it supplies a cooking service. Thus physical products are really vehicles that deliver services to us.

In fact, services are also supplied by other vehicles, such as *persons, places, activities, organizations,* and *ideas*. If we are bored, we can attend a comedy club and watch a comedian (person); travel to a warm vacationland like Bermuda (place); engage in some physical exercise (activity); join a lonely hearts club (organization); or adopt a different philosophy about life (idea). Therefore, we will use the term *product* to cover physical products, service products, and other vehicles that are capable of delivering satisfaction of a want or need. Occasionally we will use other terms for product, such as *offerings, satisfiers,* or *resources*.

Manufacturers often make the mistake of paying more attention to their physical products than to the services produced by these products. They see themselves as selling a product rather than providing a solution to a need. Yet a woman isn't buying lipstick; she is buying "hope." A carpenter isn't buying a drill; he is buying a "hole." A physical object is a means of packaging a service. The marketer's job is to sell the benefits or services built into physical products rather than just describe their physical features. Sellers who concentrate their thinking on the physical product instead of the customer's need are said to suffer from "marketing myopia."

Value, Cost, and Satisfaction

How do consumers choose among the many products that might satisfy a given need? Suppose Tom Jones needs to travel three miles to work each day. A number of products could satisfy this need: roller skates, a bicycle, a motorcycle, an automobile, a taxicab, and a bus. These alternatives constitute his *product choice set*. Assume that Jones would like to satisfy several additional needs in traveling to work, namely speed, safety, ease, and economy. We call these his *need set*. Now each product has a different capacity to satisfy his various needs. Thus a bicycle will be slower, less safe, and more effortful than an automobile, but it will be more economical. Somehow Tom Jones has to decide which product will deliver the most total satisfaction.

The guiding concept is *customer value*. Tom Jones will form an estimate of the capacity of each product to satisfy his set of needs. He might rank the products from the most need-satisfying to the least need-satisfying. Value is the consumer's estimate of the product's overall capacity to satisfy his or her needs.

We can ask Jones to imagine the characteristics of an *ideal product* for this task. Jones might answer that the *ideal product* would get him to his place of work in a split second with absolute safety, no effort, and zero cost. Then the value of each actual product would depend on how close it came to this ideal product.

Suppose Jones is primarily interested in the speed and ease of getting to work. If Jones were offered any of these products at no cost, we would predict that he would choose the automobile. But now comes the rub. Since each product involves a *cost*, he will not necessarily buy the automobile. The automobile costs substantially more than, say, a bicycle. Jones will have to give up more of other things (represented by the cost) to obtain the car. Therefore, he will consider the product's value and price before making a choice. He will choose the product that will produce the most value per dollar.

Today's consumer-behavior theorists have gone beyond narrow economic assumptions of how consumers form value judgments and make product choices. We will look at modern theories of consumer-choice behavior in Chapter 7. These theories are important to marketers because the whole marketing plan rests on assumptions about how customers make choices. Therefore, the concepts of value, cost, and satisfaction are crucial to the discipline of marketing.

Exchange, Transactions, and Relationships

The fact that people have needs and wants and can place value on products does not fully define marketing. Marketing emerges when people decide to satisfy needs and wants through exchange. Exchange is one of four ways people can obtain products.

The first way is *self-production*. People can relieve hunger through hunting, fishing, or fruit gathering. They need not interact with anyone else. In this case, there is no market and no marketing.

The second way is *coercion*. Hungry people can wrest or steal food from others. No benefit is offered to the others except that of not being harmed.

The third way is *begging*. Hungry people can approach others and beg for food. They have nothing tangible to offer except gratitude.

The fourth way is *exchange*. Hungry people can approach others and offer a resource in exchange, such as money, another good, or a service.

Marketing arises from this last approach to acquiring products. *Exchange is the act of obtaining a desired product from someone by offering something in return.* Exchange is the defining concept underlying marketing. For exchange to take place, five conditions must be satisfied:

1. There are at least two parties.
2. Each party has something that might be of value to the other party.
3. Each party is capable of communication and delivery.
4. Each party is free to accept or reject the offer.
5. Each party believes it is appropriate or desirable to deal with the other party.

If these conditions exist, there is a potential for exchange. Whether exchange actually takes place depends upon whether the two parties can agree on *terms of exchange* that will leave them both better off (or at least not worse off) than before the exchange. This is the sense in which exchange is described as a *value-creating process*; that is, exchange normally leaves both parties better off than before the exchange.

Exchange must be seen as a process rather than as an event. Two parties are said to be engaged in exchange if they are negotiating and moving toward an agreement. If an agreement is reached, we say that a *transaction* takes place. Transactions are the basic unit of exchange. *A transaction consists of a trade of values between two parties.* We must be able to say: A gave X to B and received Y in return. Jones gave $400 to Smith and obtained a television set. This is a classic *monetary transaction*. Transactions, however, do not require money as one of the traded values. A *barter transaction* would consist of Jones giving a refrigerator to Smith in return for a television set. A barter transaction can also consist of the trading of services instead of goods, as when lawyer Jones writes a will for physician Smith in return for a medical examination.

A transaction involves several dimensions: at least two things of value, agreed-upon conditions, a time of agreement, and a place of agreement. Usually a legal system arises to support and enforce compliance on the part of the transactors.

Transactions can easily give rise to conflicts based on misinterpretation or malice. Without a "law of contracts," people would approach transactions with some distrust, and everyone would lose.

Businesses maintain records of their transactions and sort them by item, price, customer, location, and other variables. Sales analysis is the act of analyzing where the company's sales are coming from by product, customer, territory, and so on.

A *transaction* differs from a *transfer*. In a transfer, A gives X to B but does not receive anything tangible in return. When A gives B a gift, a subsidy, or a charitable contribution, we call this a transfer, not a transaction. It would seem that marketing should be confined to the study of transactions and not transfers. However, transfer behavior can also be understood through the concept of exchange. Typically, the transferer has certain expectations upon giving a gift, such as receiving gratitude or seeing good behavior in the recipient. Professional fund raisers are acutely aware of the "reciprocal" motives underlying donor behavior and try to provide benefits to the donors, such as thank-you notes, donor magazines, and special invitations to events. Marketers have recently broadened the concept of marketing to include the study of transfer behavior as well as transaction behavior.

In the most generic sense, the marketer is seeking to elicit a *behavioral response* from another party. A business firm wants a response called buying, a political candidate wants a response called voting, a church wants a response called joining, a social-action group wants a response called adopting the idea. Marketing consists of actions undertaken to elicit desired responses to some object from a target audience.

To effect successful exchanges, the marketer analyzes what each party expects to give and get. Simple exchange situations can be mapped by showing the two actors and the wants and offers flowing between them. Suppose Caterpillar, the world's largest manufacturer of earth-moving equipment, researches the benefits that a typical construction company wants in buying earth-moving equipment. These benefits are listed at the top of the exchange map in Figure 1-2. A construction company wants high-quality equipment, a fair price, on-time delivery, good financing, and good service. This is the buyer's *want list*. The wants are not all equally important and may vary from buyer to buyer. One of Caterpillar's tasks is to discover the importance of these different wants of the buyer. At the same time, Caterpillar has a want list that is shown below the Caterpillar arrow in Figure 1-2. Caterpillar wants a good price for the equipment, on-time payment, and good word of mouth. If there is a sufficient match or overlap in the want lists, there is a basis for a transaction. Caterpillar's task is to formulate an offer that motivates the construction company to buy Caterpillar equipment. The construction company might in turn make a counteroffer. The process of trying to arrive at mutually agreeable terms is called *negotiation*. Negotiation leads to either mutually acceptable terms or a decision not to transact.

So far, we have explained the nature of *transaction marketing*. Transaction marketing is part of a larger idea, that of *relationship marketing*. Smart marketers try

FIGURE 1-2
Two-Party Exchange Map Showing Want Lists of Both Parties

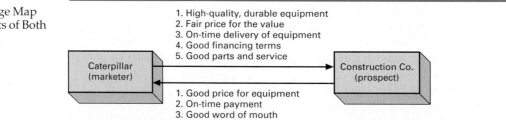

1. High-quality, durable equipment
2. Fair price for the value
3. On-time delivery of equipment
4. Good financing terms
5. Good parts and service

Caterpillar (marketer) → Construction Co. (prospect)

1. Good price for equipment
2. On-time payment
3. Good word of mouth

FIGURE 1-3
A Simple Marketing System

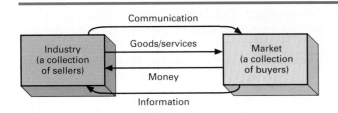

to build up long-term, trusting, "win-win" relationships with valued customers, distributors, dealers, and suppliers. That is accomplished by promising and delivering high quality, good service, and fair prices to the other parties over time. It is accomplished by building strong economic, technical, and social ties with the other parties. Relationship marketing cuts down on transaction costs and time; in the best cases, transactions move from being negotiated each time to being routinized.

The ultimate outcome of relationship marketing is the building of a unique company asset called a *marketing network*. A marketing network consists of the company and its suppliers, distributors, and customers, with which it has built solid, dependable business relationships. Increasingly, marketing is shifting from trying to maximize the profit on each individual transaction to maximizing mutually beneficial relationships with other parties. The operating principle is to build good relationships, and profitable transactions will follow.

Markets

The concept of exchange leads to the concept of a market.

❖ *A* market *consists of all the potential customers sharing a particular need or want who might be willing and able to engage in exchange to satisfy that need or want.*

Thus the size of the market depends upon the number of persons who exhibit the need, have resources that interest others, and are willing to offer these resources in exchange for what they want.

Originally the term *market* stood for the place where buyers and sellers gathered to exchange their goods, such as a village square. Economists use the term *market* to refer to a collection of buyers and sellers who transact over a particular product or product class; hence the housing market, the grain market, and so on. Marketers, however, see the sellers as constituting the *industry* and the buyers as constituting the market. The relationship between the industry and the *market* is shown in Figure 1-3. The sellers and the buyers are connected by four flows. The sellers send goods and services and communications to the market; in return they receive money and information. The inner loop shows an exchange of money for goods; the outer loop shows an exchange of information.

Businesspeople use the term *markets* colloquially to cover various groupings of customers. They talk about *need markets* (such as the diet-seeking market); *product markets* (such as the shoe market); *demographic markets* (such as the youth market); and *geographic markets* (such as the French market). Or they extend the concept to cover noncustomer groupings as well, such as *voter markets, labor markets,* and *donor markets*.

The fact is that modern economies operate on the principle of division of labor where each person specializes in the production of something, receives payment, and buys needed things with this money. Thus modern economies abound in markets. The basic kinds of markets and the flows connecting them are shown in Figure

FIGURE 1-4
Structure of Flows in a
Modern Exchange Economy

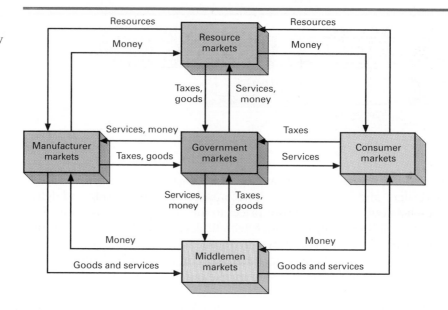

1-4. Essentially, manufacturers go to resource markets (raw-material markets, labor markets, money markets, and so on), buy resources, turn them into goods and services, sell them to middlemen, who sell them to consumers. The consumers sell their labor, for which they receive money income to pay for the goods and services they buy. The government is another market that plays several roles. It buys goods from resource, manufacturer, and middlemen markets; it pays them; it taxes these markets (including consumer markets); and it returns needed public services. Thus each nation's economy and the whole world economy consist of complex interacting sets of markets that are linked through exchange processes.

Marketing and Marketers

The concept of markets brings us full circle to the concept of marketing. Marketing means human activity taking place in relation to markets. Marketing means working with markets to actualize potential exchanges for the purpose of satisfying human needs and wants.

If one party is more actively seeking an exchange than the other party, we call the first party a *marketer* and the second party a *prospect. A marketer is someone seeking a resource from someone else and willing to offer something of value in exchange.* The marketer is seeking a response from the other party, either to sell something or to buy something. The marketer, in other words, can be a seller or a buyer. Suppose several persons want to buy an attractive house that has just become available. Each prospective buyer will try to market himself or herself to be the one the seller selects. These buyers are doing the marketing! In the event that both parties actively seek an exchange, we say that both of them are marketers and call the situation one of reciprocal marketing.

In the normal situation, the marketer is a company serving a market of end users in the face of competitors (see Figure 1-5). The company and the competitors send their respective products and messages directly and/or through marketing intermediaries (middlemen and facilitators) to the end users. Their relative effectiveness is influenced by their respective suppliers as well as major environmental forces (demographic, economic, physical, technological, political/legal, social/cul-

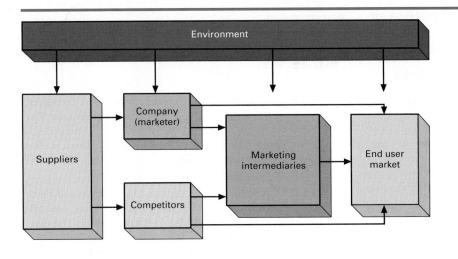

FIGURE 1-5
Main Actors and Forces in a
Modern Marketing System

tural). Thus Figure 1-5 represents the main elements in a modern marketing system.

Having reviewed these concepts, we are ready to define marketing: *marketing is a social and managerial process by which individuals and groups obtain what they need and want through creating, offering, and exchanging products of value with others.*

Meeting customer needs at a profit.

Marketing Management

Coping with exchange processes calls for a considerable amount of work and skill. *Marketing management* takes place when at least one party to a potential exchange gives thought to objectives and means of achieving desired responses from other parties. We will use the following definition of marketing (management) approved in 1985 by the American Marketing Association:

❖ *Marketing (management) is the process of planning and executing the conception, pricing, promotion, and distribution of goods, services, and ideas to create exchanges with target groups that satisfy customer and organizational objectives.*[5]

This definition recognizes that marketing management is a process involving analysis, planning, implementation, and control; that it covers goods, services, and ideas; that it rests on the notion of exchange; and that the goal is to produce satisfaction for the parties involved.

Marketing management can occur in an organization in connection with any of its markets. Consider an automobile manufacturer. The vice-president of personnel deals in the *labor market*; the vice-president of purchasing, the *raw-materials market*; and the vice-president of finance, the *money market*. They must set objectives and develop strategies for achieving satisfactory results in these markets. Traditionally, however, these executives have not been called marketers, nor have they trained in marketing. At best, they are "part-time" marketers.[6] Instead, marketing management is historically identified with tasks and personnel dealing with the *customer market*. We will follow this convention, although what we say about marketing applies to all markets.

Marketing work in the customer market is formally carried out by *sales managers, salespeople, advertising and promotion managers, marketing researchers, customer-*

Demand States and Marketing Tasks

1. *Negative demand:* A market is in a state of negative demand if a major part of the market dislikes the product and may even pay a price to avoid it. People have a negative demand for vaccinations, dental work, vasectomies, and gall bladder operations. Employers feel a negative demand for ex-convicts and alcoholics as employees. The marketing task is to analyze why the market dislikes the product and whether a marketing program consisting of product redesign, lower prices, and more positive promotion can change the market's beliefs and attitudes.

2. *No demand:* Target consumers may be uninterested or indifferent to the product. Thus, farmers may not be interested in a new farming method, and college students may not be interested in foreign-language courses. The marketing task is to find ways to connect the benefits of the product with the person's natural needs and interests.

3. *Latent demand:* Many consumers may share a strong need that cannot be satisfied by any existing product. There is a strong latent demand for harmless cigarettes, safer neighborhoods, and more fuel-efficient cars. The marketing task is to measure the size of the potential market and develop effective goods and services that would satisfy the demand.

4. *Declining demand:* Every organization, sooner or later, faces declining demand for one or more of its products. Churches have seen their membership decline, and private colleges have seen their applications fall. The marketer must analyze the causes of market decline and determine whether demand can be restimulated by finding new target markets, changing the product's features, or developing more effective communication. The marketing task is to reverse the declining demand through creative remarketing of the product.

5. *Irregular demand:* Many organizations face demand that varies on a seasonal, daily, or even hourly basis, causing problems of idle capacity or overworked capacity. In mass transit, much of the equipment is idle during the off-peak hours and insufficient during the peak

---

service managers, product and brand managers, market and industry managers, and the marketing vice-president. Each job carries well-defined tasks and responsibilities. Many of these jobs involve managing particular *marketing resources* such as advertising, salespeople, or marketing research. On the other hand, product managers, market managers, and the marketing vice-president manage *programs.* Their job is to analyze, plan, and implement programs that will produce a desired level and mix of transactions with target markets.

The popular image of the marketing manager is someone whose task is primarily to stimulate demand for the company's products. However, this is too limited a view of the diversity of marketing tasks performed by marketing managers. *Marketing management has the task of influencing the level, timing, and composition of demand in a way that will help the organization achieve its objectives.* Marketing management is essentially *demand management.*

The organization presumably forms an idea of a *desired level of transactions* with a target market. At times, the *actual demand level* may be below, equal to, or above the *desired demand level.* That is, there may be no demand, weak demand, adequate demand, excessive demand, and so on, and marketing management has to cope with these different states. Marketing Concepts and Tools 1-1 distinguishes eight different states of demand and the corresponding tasks facing marketing managers.

Marketing managers cope with these tasks by carrying out *marketing research, planning, implementation, and control.* Within marketing planning, marketers must make decisions on target markets, market positioning, product development, pricing, distribution channels, physical distribution, communication, and promotion. These marketing tasks will be analyzed in subsequent chapters of the book.

travel hours. Museums are undervisited on weekdays and overcrowded on weekends. Hospital operating rooms are overbooked early in the week and underbooked toward the end of the week. The marketing task, called *synchromarketing*, is to find ways to alter the same pattern of demand through flexible pricing, promotion, and other incentives.

6. *Full demand:* Organizations face full demand when they are pleased with their volume of business. The marketing task is to maintain the current level of demand in the face of changing consumer preferences and increasing competition. The organization must maintain or improve its quality and continually measure consumer satisfaction to make sure it is doing a good job.

7. *Overfull demand:* Some organizations face a demand level that is higher than they can or want to handle. Thus, the Golden Gate Bridge carries a higher amount of traffic than is safe, and Yosemite National Park is terribly overcrowded in the summertime. The marketing task, called *demarketing*, requires finding ways to reduce the demand temporarily or permanently. General demarketing seeks to discourage overall demand and consists of such steps as raising prices and reducing promotion and service. Selective demarketing consists of trying to reduce the demand coming from those parts of the market that are less profitable or less in need of the service. Demarketing aims not to destroy demand but only to reduce its level, temporarily or permanently.

8. *Unwholesome demand:* Unwholesome products will attract organized efforts to discourage their consumption. Unselling campaigns have been conducted against cigarettes, alcohol, hard drugs, handguns, X-rated movies, and large families. The marketing task is to get people who like something to give it up, using such tools as fear communication, price hikes, and reduced availability.

SOURCE: For a fuller discussion, see Philip Kotler, "The Major Tasks of Marketing Management," *Journal of Marketing*, October 1973, pp. 42–49; and Philip Kotler and Sidney J. Levy, "Demarketing, Yes, Demarketing," *Harvard Business Review*, November–December 1971, pp. 74–80.

Company Orientations Toward the Marketplace

We have described marketing management as the conscious effort to achieve desired exchange outcomes with target markets. Now we ask what philosophy should guide these marketing efforts? What weights should be given to the interests of the *organization*, the *customers*, and *society*? Very often these interests conflict. Clearly, marketing activities should be carried out under a well-thought-out philosophy of efficient, effective, and responsible marketing.

There are five competing concepts under which organizations conduct their marketing activity.

The Production Concept

The production concept is one of the oldest concepts guiding sellers.

❖ *The* production concept *holds that consumers will favor those products that are widely available and low in cost. Managers of production-oriented organizations concentrate on achieving high production efficiency and wide distribution coverage.*

The assumption that consumers are primarily interested in product availability and low price holds in at least two types of situations. The first is where the demand for a product exceeds supply, as in many Third World countries. Here consumers are more interested in obtaining the product than in its fine points. The suppliers will concentrate on finding ways to increase production. The second situation is where the product's cost is high and has to be brought down through increased productivity to expand the market. Texas Instruments provides a contemporary example of the production concept:

> Texas Instruments is the leading American exponent of the "get-out-production, cut-the-price" philosophy that Henry Ford pioneered in the early 1900s to expand the automobile market. Ford put all of his talent into perfecting the mass production of automobiles to bring down their costs so that Americans could afford them. Texas Instruments puts all of its efforts in building production volume and improving technology in order to bring down costs. It uses its lower costs to cut prices and expand the market size. It strives to achieve the dominant position in its markets. To Texas Instruments, marketing primarily means one thing: bringing down the price to buyers. This orientation has also been a key strategy of many Japanese companies.

Some service organizations also follow the production concept. Many medical and dental practices are organized on assembly-line principles, as are some government agencies such as unemployment offices and license bureaus. While it results in handling many cases per hour, this management orientation is open to charges of impersonality and poor service quality.

The Product Concept

Other sellers are guided by the product concept.

❖ *The* product concept *holds that consumers will favor those products that offer the most quality, performance, or innovative features. Managers in these product-oriented organizations focus their energy on making superior products and improving them over time.*

These managers assume that buyers admire well-made products and can appraise product quality and performance. These managers are caught up in a love affair with their product and fail to appreciate that the market may be less "turned on." Marketing management becomes a victim of the "better-mousetrap" fallacy, believing that a better mousetrap will lead people to beat a path to its door.[7] Consider the following example:

> In 1972, Du Pont researchers invented Kevlar, which it considers its most important new fiber since nylon. Kevlar has the same strength as steel with only one-fifth the weight. Du Pont asked its divisions to find applications for this new miracle fiber. Du Pont's executives imagined a huge number of applications and a billion-dollar market. Now, years later, Du Pont is still waiting for the bonanza. True, Kevlar is a very good fiber for bulletproof vests, but there isn't a big demand for bulletproof vests, so far. Kevlar is a promising fiber for sails, cords, and tires, and manufacturers are beginning to nibble. Eventually Kevlar may prove to be a miracle fiber, but it is taking longer than Du Pont expected.[8]

Product-oriented companies often design their products with little or no customer input. They trust that their engineers will know how to design or improve the product. Too often they will not even examine competitors' products because "they were not invented here." A General Motors executive said years ago: "How can the public know what kind of car they want until they see what is available?" GM's designers and engineers would develop plans for a new car. Then manufacturing would make it. Then the finance department would price it. Finally, marketing and sales would try to sell it. No wonder the car required such hard selling by the dealers! GM failed to ask customers what they wanted and never brought in the marketing people at the beginning to help figure out what kind of car would sell.

The product concept leads to "marketing myopia," a focus on the product rather than on the customer's need. Railroad management thought that users wanted trains rather than transportation and overlooked the growing challenge of the airlines, buses, trucks, and automobiles. Slide-rule manufacturers thought that engineers wanted slide rules rather than the calculating capacity and overlooked the challenge of pocket calculators. Churches, department stores, and the post office all assume that they are offering the public the right product and wonder why their sales falter. These organizations too often are looking into a mirror when they should be looking out of the window.

The Selling Concept

The selling concept (or sales concept) is another common approach many firms take to the market.

❖ *The* selling concept *holds that consumers, if left alone, will ordinarily not buy enough of the organization's products. The organization must therefore undertake an aggressive selling and promotion effort.*

The concept assumes that consumers typically show buying inertia or resistance and have to be coaxed into buying, and that the company has available a whole battery of effective selling and promotion tools to stimulate more buying.

The selling concept is practiced most aggressively with "unsought goods," those goods that buyers normally do not think of buying, such as insurance, encyclopedias, and funeral plots. These industries have perfected various sales techniques to locate prospects and hard-sell them on the product benefits.

Hard selling also occurs with sought goods, such as automobiles:

> From the moment the customer walks into the showroom, the auto salesperson "psychs him out." If the customer likes the floor model, he may be told that there is another customer about to buy it and that he should decide now. If the customer balks at the price, the salesperson offers to talk to the manager to get a special concession. The customer waits ten minutes and the salesperson returns with "the boss doesn't like it but I got him to agree." The aim is to "work up the customer" and "close the sale."[9]

The selling concept is also practiced in the nonprofit area by fund raisers, college admissions offices, and political parties. A political party will vigorously sell its candidate to the voters as being a fantastic person for the job. The candidate stomps through voting precincts from early morning to late evening shaking hands, kissing babies, meeting donors, making breezy speeches. Countless dollars are spent on radio and television advertising, posters, and mailings. Any flaws in the candidate are concealed from the public because the aim is to make the sale, not worry about postpurchase satisfaction. After the election, the new official continues to take a sales-oriented view toward the citizens. There is little research into what the public wants and a lot of selling to get the public to accept policies that the politician or party wants.[10]

Most firms practice the selling concept when they have overcapacity. *Their aim is to sell what they make rather than make what the market wants.* In modern industrial economies, productive capacity has been built up to a point where most markets are buyer markets (i.e., the buyers are dominant), and sellers have to scramble hard for customers. Prospects are bombarded with television commercials, newspaper ads, direct mail, and sales calls. At every turn, someone is trying to sell something. As a result, the public identifies marketing with hard selling and advertising.

Therefore, people are surprised when they are told that the most important part of marketing is not selling! Selling is only the tip of the marketing iceberg. Peter Drucker, one of the leading management theorists, puts it this way:

> *There will always, one can assume, be need for some selling.* But the aim of marketing is to make selling superfluous. *The aim of marketing is to know and understand the customer so well that the product or service fits him and sells itself. Ideally, marketing should result in a customer who is ready to buy. All that should be needed then is to make the product or service available. . . .*[11]

Thus, selling, to be effective, must be preceded by several marketing activities such as needs assessment, marketing research, product development, pricing, and distribution. If the marketer does a good job of identifying consumer needs, developing appropriate products, and pricing, distributing, and promoting them effectively, these products will sell very easily. When Sony designed its Walkman, when Nintendo designed a superior video game, and when Mazda introduced its RX-7 sports car, these manufacturers were swamped with orders because they had designed the "right" product based on careful marketing homework.

Indeed, marketing based on hard selling carries high risks. It assumes that customers who are coaxed into buying the product will like it; and if they don't, they won't bad-mouth it to friends or complain to consumer organizations. And they will possibly forget their disappointment and buy it again. These are indefensible assumptions to make about buyers. One study showed that dissatisfied customers may bad-mouth the product to ten or more acquaintances; bad news travels fast.[12]

The Marketing Concept

The marketing concept is a business philosophy that challenges the previous concepts. Its central tenets crystallized in the mid–1950s.[13]

❖ *The* marketing concept *holds that the key to achieving organizational goals consists in determining the needs and wants of target markets and delivering the desired satisfactions more effectively and efficiently than competitors.*

The marketing concept has been expressed in many colorful ways:

- ◆ "Meeting needs profitably."
- ◆ "Find wants and fill them."
- ◆ "Love the customer, not the product."
- ◆ "Have it your way." (Burger King)
- ◆ "You're the boss." (United Airlines)
- ◆ "To do all in our power to pack the customer's dollar full of value, quality and satisfaction." (J. C. Penney)

Theodore Levitt drew a perceptive contrast between the selling and marketing concepts.

> *Selling focuses on the needs of the seller; marketing on the needs of the buyer. Selling is preoccupied with the seller's need to convert his product into cash; marketing with the idea of satisfying the needs of the customer by means of the product and the whole cluster of things associated with creating, delivering and finally consuming it.*[14]

The marketing concept rests on four main pillars, namely *target market, customer needs, coordinated marketing, and profitability.* These are shown in Figure 1-6,

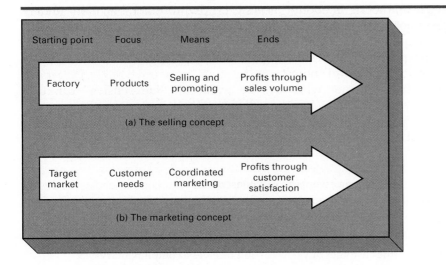

FIGURE 1-6
The Selling and Marketing
Concepts Contrasted

where they are contrasted with a selling orientation. The selling concept takes an *inside-out* perspective. It starts with the factory, focuses on the company's existing products, and calls for heavy selling and promoting to produce profitable sales. The marketing concept takes an *outside-in* perspective. It starts with a well-defined market, focuses on customer needs, coordinates all the activities that will affect customers, and produces profits through creating customer satisfaction.

Here we examine how each pillar of the marketing concept contributes to more effective marketing.

TARGET MARKET ❖ No company can operate in every market and satisfy every need. Nor can it even do a good job within one broad market: Even mighty IBM cannot offer the best solution for every information processing need. Companies do best when they define their target market(s) carefully and prepare a tailored marketing program:

> An auto manufacturer can think of designing passenger cars, station wagons, sports cars, and luxury cars. But this thinking is less precise than defining a customer target group. One Japanese car maker is designing a car for the career woman, and it will have many features that male-dominated cars don't have. Another Japanese car maker is designing a car for the "town man," the young person who needs to get about town and park easily. In each case, the company has clarified a target market, and this will greatly influence the car design.

CUSTOMER NEEDS ❖ A company can define its target market but fail to fully understand the customers' needs. Consider the following example:

> A major chemical company invented a new substance that hardened into a marble-like material. Looking for an application, the marketing department decided to target the bathtub market. The company created a few model bathtubs and exhibited them at a bathroom trade show. They hoped to convince bathtub manufacturers to produce bathtubs with the new material. Although bathtub manufacturers thought the new bathtubs were attractive, none signed up. The reason became obvious. The bathtub would have to be priced at $2,000; for this price, consumers could buy bathtubs made of real marble or onyx. In addition, the bathtubs were so heavy that homeowners would have to reinforce their floors. Furthermore, most bathtubs sold in the $500 range, and few people would spend $2,000. The chemical company chose a target market but failed to understand the customers.

Although marketing is about "meeting needs profitably," actually understanding customer needs and wants is not always a simple task. Customers speak in a code that requires some interpretation. What does it mean when the customer asks for an "inexpensive" car, a "powerful" lawn mower, a "fast" lathe, an "attractive" bathing suit, or a "restful" hotel?

Consider the customer who says he wants an "inexpensive" car. Unfortunately, we would not know how he will judge whether a car is really inexpensive. At the very least, the marketer must probe further. The fact is that the customer has not stated all of his or her needs. We can distinguish among five types of needs:

1. *Stated needs:* (the customer wants an inexpensive car)
2. *Real needs:* (the customer wants a car whose operating cost, not its initial price, is low)
3. *Unstated needs:* (the customer expects good service from the dealer)
4. *Delight needs:* (the customer buys the car and receives a complimentary U.S. road atlas)
5. *Secret needs:* (the customer wants to be seen by friends as a value-oriented savvy consumer)

Responding to the customer's stated need often shortchanges the customer. Consider a carpenter who enters a hardware store and asks for a sealant to seal windows to frames. This carpenter is stating a *solution*, not a need. The need is to affix glass to a wooden frame. The hardware store salesperson might suggest a better solution than a sealant, namely using a tape. The tape has the additional advantage of zero curing time. In this case, the salesperson has aimed to meet the customer's real need, not the stated need.

Customer-oriented thinking requires the company to define customer needs from the *customer point of view.* Every buying decision involves tradeoffs, and management cannot know what these are without researching customers. Thus a car buyer would like a safe, attractive, reliable high-performance car under $10,000. Since all of these desirable features cannot be combined in one car, the car designers must make hard choices based on knowing customer trade-offs.

In general, a company can respond to customers' requests by giving customers what they want, or what they need, or what they really need. Each level involves more probing, but the end result will be more appreciative customers. The key to professional marketing is to meet the customers' *real needs* better than any competitor can.

Why is it supremely important to satisfy the target customer? Basically because a company's sales each period come from two groups: *new customers* and *repeat customers.* It always costs more to attract new customers than to retain current customers. Therefore, *customer retention* is more critical than *customer attraction.* The key to customer retention is *customer satisfaction.* A satisfied customer:

- Buys more and stays "loyal" longer
- Buys additional products as the company introduces and upgrades its products
- Talks favorably about the company and its products
- Pays less attention to competing brands and advertising and is less price sensitive
- Offers product/service ideas to the company
- Costs less to serve than new customers because transactions are routinized

In describing the success of the Lexus automobile, one Japanese Toyota executive told the author: "My company's aim goes beyond satisfying the customer.

Our aim is to *delight* the customer." This is a higher quest and may be the secret of great marketers. Delighted customers are more effective advertisers than all the paid advertisements placed in the media.

Thus a company would be wise to regularly measure customer satisfaction. The company would phone a sample of recent buyers and inquire how many are *highly satisfied, somewhat satisfied, indifferent, somewhat dissatisfied*, and *highly dissatisfied.* It would also find out the major factors in customer satisfaction and dissatisfaction. The company would use this information to improve its performance in the next period.

Some companies think that they are getting a measure of customer satisfaction by tallying the number and types of *customer complaints* each period. But in fact, 95% of dissatisfied customers don't complain; many may just stop buying.[15] The best thing a company can do is to make it *easy for the customer to complain.* Suggestion forms found in hotel rooms and company "hot lines" such as run by Procter & Gamble and General Electric serve this purpose (see Marketing Concepts and Tools 18-2, pp. 479). These companies hope that customers will call them with suggestions, inquiries, and even complaints. 3M claims that over two thirds of its product-improvement ideas come from listening to their customers.

Listening is not enough. The company must respond constructively to the complaints.

> *Of the customers who register a complaint, between 54 and 70% will do business again with the organization if their complaint is resolved. The figure goes up to a staggering 95% if the customer feels that the complaint was resolved quickly. Customers who have complained to an organization and had their complaints satisfactorily resolved tell an average of five people about the treatment they received.[16]*

When a company realizes that a loyal customer may account for a substantial sum of revenue over the years, it seems foolish to risk losing the customer by ignoring a grievance or quarreling over a small amount. For example, IBM requires every salesperson to write a full report on each lost customer and all the steps taken to restore satisfaction.

A customer-oriented company would track its customer-satisfaction level each period and set improvement goals. For example, Citibank aims to achieve a 90% customer satisfaction level. If Citibank continues to increase its customer satisfaction level, it is on the right track. On the other hand, if its profits rise but its customer satisfaction falls, it is on the wrong track. Profits could change in a particular year for many reasons, including rising costs, falling prices, major new investments, and so on, but the ultimate sign of a healthy company is that its customer-satisfaction index is high and keeps rising. Customer satisfaction is the best indicator of the company's future profits. (See Marketing Strategies 1-1.)

COORDINATED MARKETING ❖ Unfortunately, not all company employees are trained and motivated to work for the customer. An engineer complained that the salespeople were "always protecting the customer and not thinking of the company's interest"! He went on to blast customers for "asking for too much." The following situation highlights the coordination problem:

> The marketing vice-president of a major airline wants to increase the airline's traffic share. Her strategy is to build up customer satisfaction through providing better food, cleaner cabins, and better trained cabin crews. Yet she has no authority in these matters. The catering department chooses food that keeps down food costs; the maintenance department uses cleaning services that keep down cleaning costs; and the personnel department hires people without regard to whether they are friendly and

Marketing Strategies 1-1

The Secret of L. L. Bean's Profitability: Customer Satisfaction

One of the most successful mail-order houses is L. L. Bean, Inc., of Freeport, Maine, which specializes in clothing and equipment for rugged living. L. L. Bean has carefully blended its external and internal marketing programs. To its customers, it offers the following:

100% GUARANTEE

All of our products are guaranteed to give 100% satisfaction in every way. Return anything purchased from us at any time if it proves otherwise. We will replace it, refund your purchase price or credit your credit card, as you wish. We do not want you to have anything from L. L. Bean that is not completely satisfactory.

To motivate its employees to serve the customers well, it displays the following poster prominently around its offices:

What Is a Customer?

A Customer is the most important person ever in this office . . . in person or by mail.

A Customer is not dependent on us . . . we are dependent on him.

A Customer is not an interruption of our work . . . he is the purpose of it. We are not doing a favor by serving him . . . he is doing us a favor by giving us the opportunity to do so.

A Customer is not someone to argue or match wits with. Nobody ever won an argument with a Customer.

A Customer is a person who brings us his wants. It is our job to handle them profitably to him and to ourselves.

SOURCE: Brochure and poster material from L. L. Bean, Inc., Freeport, Maine.

---

inclined to serve other people. Since these departments generally take a cost or production point of view, she is stymied in creating a high level of customer satisfaction.

Coordinated marketing means two things. First, the various marketing functions — salesforce, advertising, product management, marketing research, and so on — must be coordinated among themselves. Too often the salesforce is mad at the product managers for setting "too high a price" or "too high a volume target"; or the advertising director and a brand manager cannot agree on the best advertising campaign for the brand. These marketing functions must be coordinated from the customer point of view.

Second, marketing must be well coordinated with the other company departments. Marketing does not work when it is merely a department; it only works when all employees appreciate the impact they have on customer satisfaction. As David Packard of Hewlett Packard put it: "Marketing is too important to be left to the marketing department!" IBM goes so far as to include in every one of its job descriptions an explanation of how that job impacts on the customer. IBM factory managers know that customer visits to the factory can help sell a potential customer if the factory is clean and efficient. IBM accountants know that customer attitudes toward IBM are affected by the billing accuracy and their promptness in returning customer calls.

For this reason, the marketing concept requires the company to carry out *internal marketing* as well as *external marketing*. Internal marketing is the task of successfully hiring, training, and motivating able employees who want to serve the customers well. In fact, internal marketing must precede external marketing. It makes no sense to promise excellent service before the company's staff is ready to provide excellent service. A story is told about how Bill Marriott, Jr., chairman of the Marriott hotels, interviews prospective managers:

> Bill Marriott tells the job candidate that the hotel chain wants to satisfy three groups: *customers, employees,* and *stockholders.* Although all the groups are important, he asks in which order the groups should be satisfied. Most candidates say first satisfy the customers. Bill Marriott, however, reasons differently. First, the company must satisfy its employees. If the employees love their work and feel a sense of pride in the hotel, they will serve the customers well. The satisfied customers will return frequently to the Marriott. This repeat business will in turn yield high profits for the stockholders.

Bill Marriott still believes that the customer is the key to profitability. He and some other company presidents consider the typical organization chart—a pyramid with the president at the top, management in the middle, and front-line people (sales and service people, telephone operators, receptionists) at the bottom — to be obsolete. Master marketing companies know better; they invert the chart, as shown in Figure 1-7. At the top of the organization are the customers. Next in importance are the front-line people who meet, serve, and satisfy the customers. Under them are the middle managers whose job it is to support the front-line people so they can serve the customers well. And finally, at the base is top management whose job it is to support the middle managers so that they can support the front-line people who make all the difference in whether the customers feel satisfied with the company. We have added customers along the sides of the figure to indicate that all the managers in the company are personally involved in knowing, meeting, and serving customers.

PROFITABILITY ❖ The purpose of the marketing concept is to help organizations achieve their goals. In the case of private firms, the major goal is profit; in the case of nonprofit and public organizations, it is surviving and attracting enough funds to perform their work. Now the key is not to aim for profits as such but to achieve them as a byproduct of doing the job well. The General Motors executive who said, "We're in the business of making money, not cars," is misplacing the emphasis. A company makes money by satisfying customer needs better than competitors can.

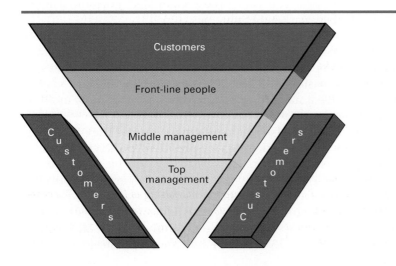

FIGURE 1-7
The "Correct" View of the Chart Company Organization

Perdue Farms is a $1.2-billion chicken business whose margins are substantially above the industry average and whose market shares in its major markets reach 50%. And the product is chicken—a commodity if there ever was one! Yet its colorful founder, Frank Perdue, does not believe that "a chicken is a chicken is a chicken," nor do his customers. His theme is, "It takes a tough man to make a tender chicken," and he offers a money-back guarantee to dissatisfied customers. He is so devoted to producing quality chickens that his customers pay a price premium to buy them. His attitude is that if one offers superior product quality and business integrity, high profits, market share, and growth will follow.

Nevertheless, marketers must be involved in analyzing the profit potential of different marketing opportunities. The following story illustrates this:

An American shoe company sent its financial officer to a Pacific island to see if the company could sell its shoes there. In a few days, the officer wired back: "The people here don't wear shoes. There is no market."

The shoe company decided to send its best salesman to the country to verify this. After a week, the salesman wired back: "The people here don't wear shoes. There is a tremendous market!"

The shoe company next sent the marketing vice-president to assess the situation. After two weeks, the marketing vice-president wired back: "The people here don't wear shoes. However, they have bad feet and could benefit from wearing shoes. We would need to redesign our shoes, however, because they have smaller feet. We would have to educate the people about the benefits of wearing shoes. We would need to gain the tribal chief's cooperation. The people don't have any money, but they grow great pineapples. I've estimated the sales potential over a three-year period and all of our costs, including selling the pineapples to a European supermarket chain, and concluded that we could make a 30% return on our money. I say that we should go ahead."

Clearly, the marketing vice-president not only wore a marketing hat—he noticed a need and a way to satisfy it—but also wore a financial hat. He is in the business of creating profitable customers.

How many companies actually practice the marketing concept? Unfortunately, too few. Only a handful of companies really stand out as master marketers: Procter & Gamble, Apple, Disney, Nordstrom's, Wal-Mart, Milliken, Limited, McDonald's, Marriott Hotels, Delta Airlines, and several Japanese companies (Sony, Toyota, Canon) and European companies (Ikea, Club Med, Ericsson, Bang & Olufsen, Marks & Spencer). (See Marketing Strategies 1-2.)

These companies focus on the customer and are organized to respond effectively to changing customer needs. Not only do they have well-staffed marketing departments, but their other departments—manufacturing, finance, research and development, personnel, purchasing—all accept the concept that the customer is king. These organizations have a marketing culture that has deep roots in all of their departments and divisions.

Most companies have not arrived at full marketing maturity. They *think* they have marketing because they have a marketing vice-president, product managers, a salesforce, advertising budgets, and so on. *But a marketing department does not assure a market-oriented company.* The company has marketing operations, but this does not mean that it is a *market-focused and customer-driven company*. The question is whether it is finely tuned to changing customer needs and competitive strategies. Formerly great companies—General Motors, Singer, Zenith, Sears—all lost substantial market shares because they failed to adjust their marketing strategies to the changing marketplace.

Marketing Strategies 1-2

How Jan Carlzon "Marketized" SAS Airlines

When Jan Carlzon took over as president of SAS, now Scandinavian Airlines, in 1980, the airline was losing money. In previous years, management had faced this problem by cutting costs. Carlzon saw that as the wrong solution: the airline needed to find new ways to compete and build its revenue. SAS had been pursuing all travelers with no focus and no superior advantage to offer to anyone; in fact, it was seen as one of the least punctual carriers in Europe. Competition had increased so much that Carlzon had to figure out:

- *Who are our customers?*
- *What are their needs?*
- *What must we do to win their preference?*

Carlzon decided that the answer was to focus SAS's services on *frequent-flying business people* and their needs. But he recognized that other airlines were trying to attract the same segment. They were offering wider seats, free drinks, and other amenities. SAS had to find a way to do this better if it was to be the preferred airline. The starting point was market research to find out what frequent business travelers wanted and expected in the way of airline service. His goal was to find ways to be 1% better in 100 details rather than 100% better in only one detail.

The market research showed that the number-one priority of business travelers was on-time arrival. Business travelers also wanted to check in fast and be able to retrieve their luggage fast. Carlzon appointed dozens of task forces to come up with ideas for improving these and other services. They came back with hundreds of proposals, of which 150 were selected at an implementation cost of $40 million.

One of the key projects was to train a total cus-tomer orientation into all SAS's employees. Carlzon figured that the average passenger came into contact with five SAS employees on an average trip. Each interaction created "a moment of truth" about SAS. Given the 5 million passengers per year flying SAS, this amounted to 25 million moments of truth where the airline either satisfied or dissatisfied its customers. To create the right customer attitudes within the company, the airline sent 10,000 front-line staff to service seminars for two days and 25,000 managers to three-week courses. Carlzon regarded the front-line people who met the customers as the most important people in the company. As for managers, their role was to help the front-line people do their job well. And his role as president was to help the managers support the front-line employees.

The result: within four months, SAS achieved the record as the most punctual airline in Europe. Check-in systems are much faster, including a service where travelers who are staying at Scandinavian Airlines hotels can have their luggage sent directly to the airport and airplane for loading. Scandinavian Airlines does a much faster job of unloading luggage upon landing. Another innovation is that it sells all tickets as business class unless the traveler wants economy class. The airline's improved reputation among business flyers led to an increase in its European full-fare traffic of 8% and its full-fare intercontinental travel of 16%, quite an accomplishment considering that price cutting and zero growth were taking place in the air travel market.

Carlzon's impact on Scandinavian Airlines illustrates the customer satisfaction and profits that a corporate leader can achieve when he or she creates a vision and mission for the company that excites and gets the employees to all swim in the same direction—namely toward satisfying the target customers.

Most companies do not really grasp or embrace the marketing concept until driven to it by circumstances. Any of the following developments might prod them:

- *Sales decline:* When companies experience falling sales, they panic and look for answers. For example, newspapers are experiencing declining circulation as more people turn to television news. Some publishers now realize that they know little about why people read newspapers. These publishers are commissioning consumer research and attempting to redesign newspapers to be contemporary, relevant, and interesting to readers.

- *Slow growth:* Slow sales growth will lead some companies to cast about for new markets. They realize that they need marketing know-how if they are to identify and select new opportunities. Dow Chemical, wanting new sources of revenue, decided to enter consumer markets and invested heavily in acquiring consumer marketing expertise to perform well in these markets.

- *Changing buying patterns:* Many companies operate in markets characterized by rapidly changing customer wants. These companies need more marketing know-how if they are to continue producing value for buyers.

- *Increasing competition:* Complacent companies may suddenly be attacked by powerful marketing companies and forced to learn marketing to meet the challenge. Thus, AT&T was a regulated, marketing-naive telephone company until the 1970s when other companies were suddenly allowed to sell telecommunications equipment to AT&T's customers. At this point, AT&T plunged into the marketing waters and hired the best marketers it could find to help it compete.[17]

- *Increasing marketing expenditures:* Companies may find their expenditures for advertising, sales promotion, marketing research, and customer service getting out of hand. Management then decides it is time to undertake a *marketing audit* and to improve its marketing.[18]

In the course of converting to a market-oriented company, a company will face three hurdles—organized resistance, slow learning, and fast forgetting.

ORGANIZED RESISTANCE ❖ Some company departments, often manufacturing, finance, and R&D, do not like to see marketing built up because it threatens their power in the organization. The nature of the threat is illustrated in Figure 1-8. Initially, the marketing function is seen as one of several equally important business functions in a check-and-balance relationship (Fig. 1-8[a]). A dearth of demand then leads marketers to argue that their function is somewhat more important than the others (Fig. 1-8[b]). A few marketing enthusiasts go further and say marketing is the major function of the enterprise, for without customers, there would be no company. They put marketing at the center, with other business functions serving as support functions (Fig. 1-8[c]). This view incenses the other managers, who do not want to think of themselves as working for marketing. Enlightened marketers clarify the issue by putting the customer rather than marketing at the center of the company (Fig. 1-8[d]). They argue for a *customer orientation* in which all functions work together to sense, serve, and satisfy the customer. Finally, some marketers say that marketing still needs to command a central company position if customers' needs are to be correctly interpreted and efficiently satisfied (Fig. 1-8[e]).

The marketer's argument for the business concept shown in Figure 1-8(e) is as follows:

1. The company's assets have little value without the existence of customers.
2. The key company task is therefore to attract and retain customers.
3. Customers are attracted through competitively superior offers and retained through satisfaction.
4. Marketing's task is to develop a superior offer and deliver customer satisfaction.
5. Customer satisfaction is affected by the performance of the other departments.
6. Marketing needs to influence these other departments to cooperate in delivering customer satisfaction.

In spite of this argument, marketing is still resisted in many quarters. The resistance is especially strong in industries where marketing is being introduced for

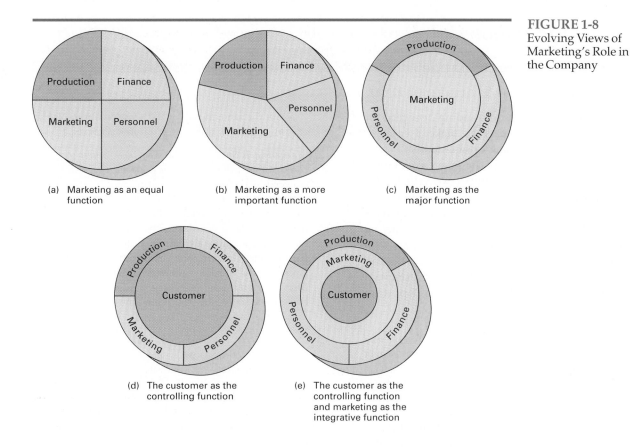

FIGURE 1-8
Evolving Views of Marketing's Role in the Company

(a) Marketing as an equal function

(b) Marketing as a more important function

(c) Marketing as the major function

(d) The customer as the controlling function

(e) The customer as the controlling function and marketing as the integrative function

the first time, for instance, in law offices, colleges, hospitals, or government agencies. Colleges have to face the hostility of professors, and hospitals have to face the hostility of doctors, because each group thinks that "marketing" their service would be degrading. In the newspaper industry, publisher hostility is shown by one newspaper editor who wrote a diatribe entitled "Beware the 'Market' Thinkers."[19] This editor warned newspapers not to let marketers in because they do not understand that the function of newspapers is to "print news."

SLOW LEARNING ❖ In spite of some resistance, many companies manage to introduce some marketing into their organization. The company president establishes a marketing department; outside marketing talent is hired; key managers attend marketing seminars; the marketing budget is substantially increased; marketing planning and control systems are introduced. Even with these steps, the learning as to what marketing really is comes slowly. (Companies and Industries 1-1 describes the five stages through which bank marketing passed.)

FAST FORGETTING ❖ Even after installing marketing, management must fight a strong tendency to forget basic marketing principles. Management tends to forget marketing principles in the wake of marketing success. For example, a number of major American companies entered European markets in the 1950s and 1960s expecting to achieve outstanding success with their sophisticated products and marketing capabilities. A number of them failed because they forgot the marketing maxim: *Know your target market and how to satisfy them.* American companies introduced their current products and advertising programs instead of adapting them. For example, General Mills introduced its Betty Crocker cake mixes in Britain only to withdraw a short time later. Their angel cake and devil's food cake sounded too

Five Stages in the Slow Learning of Bank Marketing

Years ago, bankers had little understanding or regard for marketing. Bankers did not have to make a case for checking accounts, savings, loans, or safe-deposit boxes. The bank building was created in the image of a Greek temple, calculated to impress the public with the bank's importance and solidity. The interior was austere, and the tellers rarely smiled. One lending officer arranged his office so that a prospective borrower would sit across from his massive desk on a lower chair. The office window was located behind the officer's back, and the sun would pour in on the hapless client, who tried to explain why he or she needed a loan. This was the bank's posture before the age of marketing.

1. *Marketing Is Advertising, Sales Promotion, and Publicity:* Marketing came into banks not in the form of the "marketing concept" but in the form of the "advertising and promotion concept." Banks were facing increased competition for savings. A few banks started to do heavy advertising and sales promotion. They offered umbrellas, radios, and other "come-ons" and attracted new customer accounts. Their competitors were forced

to adopt the same measures and scurried out to hire advertising agencies and sales-promotion experts.

2. *Marketing Is Smiling and a Friendly Atmosphere:* The banks learned that attracting people to a bank is easy; converting them into loyal customers is hard. These banks began to formulate programs to please the customer. Bankers learned to smile. The bars were removed from the tellers' windows. The bank interior was redesigned to produce a warm, friendly atmosphere. Even the outside Greek-temple architecture was changed. Competitors quickly launched similar programs of friendliness training and decor improvement. Soon all banks were so friendly that friendliness lost its decisiveness as a factor in bank choice.

3. *Marketing Is Segmentation and Innovation:* Banks found a new competitive tool when they began to segment their markets and innovate new products for each target segment. Citibank, for example, today offers more than 500 financial products to customers. Financial services, however, are easily copied, and specific advantages are short-lived. But if the same bank invests in continuous innovation, it can stay ahead of the

---

exotic for British homemakers. And many Britons felt that the perfect-looking cakes pictured on the Betty Crocker packages must be hard to make. American marketers failed to appreciate the major cultural variations between and even within European countries.

The Societal Marketing Concept

In recent years, some have questioned whether the marketing concept is an appropriate philosophy in an age of environmental deterioration, resource shortages, explosive population growth, world hunger and poverty, and neglected social services.[20] Are companies that do an excellent job of satisfying individual consumer wants necessarily acting in the best long-run interests of consumers and society? The marketing concept sidesteps the potential conflicts between *consumer wants,* *consumer interests,* and *long-run societal welfare.*

Consider the following criticisms:

The fast-food hamburger industry offers tasty but not nutritious food. The hamburgers have a high-fat content, and the restaurants promote fries and pies, two products high in starch and fat. The products are wrapped in convenient packaging, but this leads to much packaging waste material. In satisfying consumer wants, these restaurants may be hurting consumer health and causing environmental problems.

other banks. Bank One of Columbus, Ohio is an example of a market leader whose rapid growth is based on an uncanny ability to continuously innovate new retail bank products.

4. *Marketing Is Positioning:* What happens when all banks advertise, smile, segment, and innovate? Clearly they begin to look alike. They are forced to find a new basis for competition. They begin to realize that no bank can offer all products and be the best bank for all customers. A bank must examine its opportunities and "take a position" in the market.

   Positioning goes beyond image making. The image-making bank seeks to cultivate an image in the customer's mind as a large, friendly, or efficient bank. It often develops a symbol, such as a lion (Harris Bank in Chicago) or kangaroo (Continental Bank in Chicago) to dramatize its personality in a distinctive way. Yet the customer may see the competing banks as basically alike, except for the chosen symbols. Positioning is an attempt to distinguish the bank from its competitors along real dimensions in order to be the preferred bank for certain market segments. Positioning aims to help customers know the real differences between competing banks, so that they can match themselves to the bank that can satisfy their needs best.

5. *Marketing Is Marketing Analysis, Planning, and Control:* There is a higher concept of bank marketing. The issue is whether the bank has installed effective systems for marketing analysis, planning, implementation, and control. One large bank, which had achieved sophistication in advertising, friendliness, segmentation, innovation, and positioning, nevertheless lacked good systems of marketing planning and control. Each fiscal year, commercial loan officers submitted their volume goals, usually 10% higher than the previous year's goals. They also requested a budget increase of 10%. No rationale or plans accompanied these submissions. Top management was satisfied with the officers who achieved their goals. One loan officer, judged to be a good performer, retired and was replaced by a younger man, who proceeded to increase the loan volume 50% the following year! The bank painfully learned that it had failed to conduct marketing research to measure the potentials of its various markets, to require marketing plans, to set quotas, and to develop appropriate management incentive systems.

The American auto industry traditionally caters to the American desire for large automobiles, but meeting this desire results in high fuel consumption, heavy pollution, more fatal accidents to those in small cars, and higher auto purchase and repair costs.

The soft-drink industry has catered to the American desire for convenience by increasing the share of one-way disposable bottles. However, the one-way bottle represents a great waste of resources in that approximately seventeen bottles are necessary where formerly one two-way bottle made seventeen trips before it was damaged; many one-way bottles are not biodegradable; and these bottles often litter the environment.

The detergent industry caters to the American passion for whiter clothes by offering a product that pollutes rivers and streams, kills fish, and injures recreational opportunities.

These situations call for a new concept that enlarges the marketing concept. Among the proposals are "the human concept," "the intelligent consumption concept," and "the ecological imperative concept," all of which get at different aspects of the same problem.[21] We propose calling it the societal marketing concept.

❖ *The* societal marketing *concept holds that the organization's task is to determine the needs, wants, and interests of target markets and to deliver the desired satisfactions more effectively and efficiently than competitors in a way that preserves or enhances the consumer's and the society's well-being.*

The societal marketing concept calls upon marketers to balance three considerations in setting their marketing policies, namely, *company profits, consumer want satisfaction,* and *public interest.* Originally, companies based their marketing decisions on maximizing short-term company profit. Then they began to recognize the long-run importance of satisfying consumer wants, and this introduced the marketing concept. Now they are beginning to factor in society's interests in their decision making. A number of companies have achieved notable sales and profit gains through adopting and practicing the societal marketing concept. Here are two examples:

In 1976, Anita Roddick opened *The Body Shop* in Brighton, England and she now operates over 700 stores in 41 countries. The Body Shop's annual sales growth rate has been between 60 and 100%, reaching $196 million in 1991, with pretax profits of $34 million. Her company manufactures and sells natural ingredient-based cosmetics in simple and appealing recyclable packaging. The ingredients are largely plant-based and often sourced from developing countries to aid in their economic development. All the products are formulated without any animal testing. Her company donates a certain percentage of profits each year to animal rights groups, homeless shelters, Amnesty International, Save the Rainforest, and other social causes. Many customers patronize The Body Shop because they share these social concerns. Her employees and franchise owners are also very dedicated to social causes. According to Roddick: "I thought it was very important that my business concern itself not just with hair and skin preparations, but also with the community, the environment, and the big wide world beyond cosmetics."[22]

In the late 1970s, two guys from Vermont —Ben Cohen and Jerry Greenfield— formed a company to produce a superpremium ice cream which they branded Ben & Jerry's Homemade. Their sales, which were $9.8 million in 1985, climbed to $97 million by 1991. Their share of the superpremium ice cream category is now 36%, and climbing further. Why the appeal? First they are masters at creating innovative "mix-in" ice cream flavors, such as Rainforest Crunch, Blueberry Cheesecake, and Chocolate Chip Cookie Dough. Second, they espouse a concept of "fair pay," holding down their top executive pay to seven times the average for their workers. Third, they believe in contributing a percentage of their profits to alleviate social and environmental problems. Their corporate concept is that of "caring capitalism" which focuses equally on a product, social, and economic mission. Although it is hard to tell howmuch customer loyalty arises from their superrich ice cream versus their social cause advocacy, there is no doubt that Ben & Jerry's customers are extraordinarily loyal.[23]

These companies are practicing *cause-related marketing,* a version of the societal marketing concept, and it is one major factor in their success.[24]

The Rapid Adoption of Marketing Management

Marketing management today is a subject of growing interest in all types of organizations within and outside the business sector in all kinds of countries.

In the Business Sector

In the business sector, marketing entered the consciousness of different companies at different times. General Electric, General Motors, Procter & Gamble, and Coca-Cola were among the early leaders. Marketing spread most rapidly in consumer packaged-goods companies, consumer durables companies, and industrial-equipment companies —in that order. Producers of commodities like steel, chemicals, and paper came later to marketing consciousness, and many still have a long way to go. Within the past decade, consumer-service firms, especially airlines and banks, have moved toward modern marketing. Marketing is beginning to attract the interest of insurance and stock-brokerage companies, although they also have a long way to go in applying marketing effectively.

The most recent business groups to take an interest in marketing are professional service providers, such as lawyers, accountants, physicians, and architects.[25] Professional societies used to prohibit their members from engaging in price competition, client solicitation, and advertising. But the U.S. antitrust division ruled that these restraints are illegal. Accountants, lawyers, and other professional groups can now advertise and price aggressively.

> *The fierce competition . . . is forcing accounting firms into aggressive new postures. . . . The accountants insist on referring to their efforts to drum up business as "practice development." But many of the activities . . . are dead ringers for what is called "marketing" in other fields. . . . Accountants speak of "positioning" their firms and of "penetrating" unexploited new industries. They compile "hit lists" of prospective clients and then "surround" them by placing their firms' partners in close social contact with the top executives of the target companies.*[26]

In the Nonprofit Sector

Marketing is increasingly attracting the interest of nonprofit organizations such as colleges, hospitals, churches, and performing arts groups.[27] Consider the following developments:

> Facing falling enrollments and rising costs, many private colleges are using marketing to compete for students and funds. They are defining their target markets better, improving their communication and promotion, and responding better to student wants and needs.[28]

> As hospital costs soar, many hospitals face underutilization and have turned to marketing. They are developing product-line plans, improved emergency-room service, better physician services, advertising programs, and sales calls on corporations.[29]

> Many of America's 300,000 churches are in trouble, losing members and failing to attract enough financial support. Churches need to better understand member needs as well as competitive institutions and activities if they hope to revive their role in their communities.[30]

> Many performing arts groups need to attract larger audiences. Even those that have seasonal sellouts, such as the Lyric Opera Company of Chicago, face huge operating deficits each year, which they must cover by more aggressive donor marketing.[31]

> Many longstanding nonprofit organizations—the YMCA, the Salvation Army, the Girl Scouts, and the Woman's Christian Temperance Union—have lost members and are now modernizing their mission and "product" to attract more members and donors.[32]

These organizations have marketplace problems. Their administrators are struggling to sustain these organizations in the face of rapidly changing consumer attitudes and diminishing financial resources. They are turning to marketing. Over half of U.S. hospitals now have a marketing director. Even U.S. government agencies such as the U.S. Postal Service, Amtrak, and the U.S. Army are implementing marketing plans. Various government and private nonprofit agencies are also launching *social marketing campaigns* to discourage cigarette smoking, excessive drinking, hard-drug usage, and unsafe sex practices.[33]

In the International Sector

Multinational companies are investing heavily to improve their global marketing skills. In fact, several European and Japanese multinationals —Nestlé, Benetton, Unilever, Toyota, Sony— have in many cases understood marketing better and outperformed their U.S. competitors. Multinationals have introduced and spread modern marketing practices throughout the world. This trend has prodded smaller domestic companies in various countries to strengthen their marketing muscle so they can compete effectively with the multinationals.

In the former socialist economies, marketing had a bad name, even though some public-sector agencies carried on limited marketing research and advertising. Today these economies are undertaking a major effort to convert to market-driven economies. The challenge is enormous and this conversion will take years if not decades to achieve. Countries in the West and the Far East are giving economic aid, and multinationals are exploring the potentially large market opportunities that lie in trading and investing in the East Bloc countries.

SUMMARY ❖

Companies cannot survive today by simply doing a good job. They must do an excellent job if they are to succeed in the increasingly competitive global marketplace. Consumer and business buyers face an abundance of suppliers seeking to satisfy their every need. Recent studies have demonstrated that the key to profitable company performance is knowing and satisfying target customers with competitively superior offers. And marketing is the company function charged with defining customer targets and the best way to satisfy their needs and wants competitively and profitably.

Marketing has its origins in the fact that humans are creatures of needs and wants. Since many products can satisfy a given need, product choice is guided by the concepts of value, cost, and satisfaction. These products are obtainable in several ways: self-production, coercion, begging, and exchange. Most modern societies work on the principle of exchange. People specialize in producing particular products and trade them for the other things they need. They engage in transactions and relationship building. A market is a group of people who share a similar need. Marketing encompasses those activities involved in working with markets, that is, in trying to actualize potential exchanges.

Marketing management is the conscious effort to achieve desired exchange outcomes with target markets. The marketer's basic skill lies in influencing the level, timing, and composition of demand for a product, service, organization, place, person, or idea.

Five alternative philosophies can guide organizations in carrying out their marketing work. The production concept holds that consumers will favor products that are affordable and available, and therefore management's major task is to improve production and distribution efficiency and bring down prices. The product concept holds that consumers favor quality products that are reasonably priced, and therefore little promotional effort is required. The selling concept holds that consumers will not buy enough of the company's products unless they are stimulated through a substantial selling and promotion effort. The marketing concept holds that the main task of the company is to determine the needs, wants, and preferences of a target group of customers and to deliver the desired satisfactions. Its four principles are target market, customer needs, coordinated marketing, and profitability. The societal marketing concept holds that the main task of the company is to generate customer satisfaction and long-run consumer and societal well-being as the key to satisfying organizational goals and responsibilities.

Interest in marketing is intensifying as more organizations in the business sector, the nonprofit sector, and the international sector recognize how marketing contributes to improved performance in the marketplace.

NOTES ❖

1. The following three illustrations were reported in the television documentary, "Made In America?" narrated by Robert Reich and aired on public television channels on May 26–27, 1992.

2. See Theodore Levitt's classic article, "Marketing Myopia," *Harvard Business Review,* July–August 1960, pp. 45–56.

3. Richard C. Whiteley, *The Customer-Driven Company* (Reading, MA: Addison-Wesley, 1991); Robert L. Desatnick, *Keep the Customer* (Boston: Houghton Mifflin Co., 1990); Charles Sewell, *Customers for Life: How to Turn the One-Time Buyer Into a Lifetime Customer* (New York: Pocket Books, 1990); William H. Davidow and Bro Uttal, *Total Customer Service: The Ultimate Weapon* (New York: Harper & Row Publishers, 1989); and Karl Albrecht, *The Only Thing That Matters: Bringing the Power of the Customer into the Center of Your Business* (New York: HarperBusiness, 1992).

4. For various definitions with a management flavor, see note 5.

5. Here are some other useful definitions of marketing (management):
   ❖ *Marketing* is the process by which an organization relates creatively, productively, and profitably to the marketplace.
   ❖ *Marketing* is the art of creating and satisfying customers at a profit.
   ❖ *Marketing* is getting the right goods and services to the right people at the right places at the right time at the right price with the right communications and promotion.

6. Evert Gummesson, "Marketing-Orientation Revisited: The Crucial Role of the Part-Time Marketer," *European Journal of Marketing,* Vol. 25, No. 2, 1991, pp. 60–75.

7. Emerson originated this advice: "If a man . . . makes a better mousetrap . . . the world will beat a path to his door." Several companies, however, have built better mousetraps—one was a laser mousetrap costing $1,500––and most of these companies failed. People do not automatically learn about new products, believe in their superiority, or willingly pay a higher price.

8. See Lee Smith, "A Miracle in Search of a Market," *Fortune,* December 1, 1980, pp. 92–98.

9. See Irving J. Rein, *Rudy's Red Wagon: Communication Strategies in Contemporary Society* (Glenview, IL: Scott, Foresman, 1972).

10. See Bruce I. Newman and Jagdish N. Sheth, *Political Marketing: Readings and Annotaed Bibliography,* (Chicago: American Marketing Association, 1985).

11. Peter Drucker, *Management: Tasks, Responsibilities, Practices* (New York: Harper & Row, 1973), pp. 64–65.

12. See Karl Albrecht and Ron Zemke, *Service America!* (Homewood, IL: Dow-Jones-Irwin, 1985), pp. 6–7.

13. See John B. McKitterick, "What Is the Marketing Management Concept?" *The Frontiers of Marketing Thought and Action* (Chicago: American Marketing Association, 1957), pp. 71–82; Fred J. Borch, "The Marketing Philosophy as a Way of Business Life," *The Marketing Concept: Its Meaning to Management,* marketing series, no. 99 (New York: American Management Association, 1957), pp. 3–5; and Robert J. Keith, "The Marketing Revolution," *Journal of Marketing,* January 1960, pp. 35–38.

14. Levitt, "Marketing Myopia," p. 50.

15. See *Technical Assistance Research Programs* (TARP), U.S. Office of Consumer Affairs Study on Complaint Handling in America, 1986.

16. Albrecht and Zemke, *Service America!,* p. 6–7.

17. See Bro Uttal, "Selling Is No Longer Mickey Mouse at AT&T," *Fortune,* July 17, 1978, pp. 98–104.

18. See Thomas V. Bonoma and Bruce H. Clark, *Marketing Performance Assessment* (Boston: Harvard Business School Press, 1988).

19. William H. Hornby, "Beware the 'Market' Thinkers," *The Quill,* 1976, pp. 14 ff.

20. See Lawrence P. Feldman, "Societal Adaptation: A New Challenge for Marketing," *Journal of Marketing,* July 1971, pp. 54–60; Martin L. Bell and C. William Emery, "The Faltering Marketing Concept," *Journal of Marketing,* October 1971, pp. 37–42; and Franklin S. Houston, "The Marketing Concept: What It Is and What It Is Not," *Journal of Marketing,* April 1986, pp. 81–87.

21. Leslie M. Dawson, "The Human Concept: New Philosophy for Business," *Business Horizons,* December 1969, pp. 29–38; James T. Rothe and Lissa Benson, "Intelligent Consumption: An Attractive Alternative to the Marketing Concept," *MSU Business Topics,* Winter 1974, pp. 29–34; and George Fisk, "Criteria for a Theory of Responsible Consumption," *Journal of Marketing,* April 1973, pp. 24–31.

22. See Anita Roddick, *Body and Soul* (New York: Crown Publishing Group, 1991); and Bo Burlingham, "This Woman Has Changed Business Forever," *INC.,* June 1990, pp. 34–45.

23. See "Life's Just a Bowl of Cherry Garcia for Ben & Jerry's," *The Wall Street Journal,* July 15, 1992, B2.

24. See P. Rajan Varadarajan and Anil Menon, "Cause-Related Marketing: A Coalignment of Marketing Strategy and

Corporate Philanthropy," *Journal of Marketing,* July 1988, pp. 58–74.

25. See Philip Kotler and Paul Bloom, *Marketing Professional Services* (Englewood Cliffs, NJ: Prentice-Hall, 1984).

26. Deborah Rankin, "How C.P.A.'s Sell Themselves," *The New York Times,* September 25, 1977.

27. See Philip Kotler and Alan R. Andreasen, *Strategic Marketing for Nonprofit Organizations,* 4th ed., (Englewood Cliffs, NJ: Prentice Hall, 1991).

28. See Philip Kotler and Karen Fox, *Strategic Marketing for Educational Institutions* (Englewood Cliffs, NJ: Prentice-Hall, 1985).

29. Philip Kotler and Roberta N. Clarke, *Marketing for Health Care Organizations* (Englewood Cliffs, NJ: Prentice-Hall, 1987)

30. Norman Shawchuck, Philip Kotler, Bruce Wren, and Gustave Rath, *Marketing for Congregations: Choosing to Serve People More Effectively* (Nashville, TN: Abingdon Press, 1993).

31. Bradley G. Morrison and Julie Gordon Dalgleish, *Waiting in the Wings: A Larger Audience for the Arts and How to Develop It* (New York: ACA Books, 1987).

32. Kotler and Andreasen, *Strategic Marketing for Nonprofit Organizations,* 4th ed.

33. Philip Kotler and Eduardo Roberto, *Social Marketing: Strategies for Changing Public Behavior* (New York: Free Press, 1990).

2

Building Customer Satisfaction Through Quality, Service, and Value

Our goal as a company (Wal-Mart) is to have customer service that is not just the best, but legendary.

SAM WALTON

The only job security anybody has in this company (Chrysler) comes from quality, productivity, and satisfied customers.

LEE IACOCCA

Perhaps the reason so many people are satisfied with our automobiles is because we aren't. . . . Our purpose is to make products with pleasure, that we can sell with pleasure and that our customers can use with pleasure.

HONDA

Today's companies are facing their toughest competition in decades. And it will only get worse. We argued in Chapter 1 that companies can confront their competition better if they can move from a *product and selling philosophy* to a *customer and marketing philosophy*. In this chapter, we want to spell out in more detail how companies can go about winning customers and outperforming competitors. We believe that the answer lies in doing a better job of *meeting and satisfying customer needs*.

In shortage economies and near monopoly markets, companies don't expend any special effort to please customers. Today in Eastern Europe, millions of consumers stand sullenly in line for hours to obtain poorly made clothes, toiletries, and appliances. Their dissatisfaction with the available goods and services is of little concern to the producers and retailers. The sellers pay relatively little attention to marketing theory and practice.

In buyer markets, on the other hand, customers can choose from a large array of goods and services. Here sellers must deliver acceptable product quality or rapidly lose customers to competitors. Even today's acceptable quality and service levels may not be acceptable tomorrow. Today's consumers are much more educated and demanding. Their quality expectations have been elevated by the practices of superior manufacturers (Toyota, Sony) and retailers (Marks & Spencer, Nordstrom, L. L. Bean). The shrinkage of many industries in the United States—autos, cameras, machine tools, consumer electronics—offers dramatic evidence that firms offering average quality lose their consumer franchise when attacked by superior competitors.

Companies wanting to win, let alone survive, need a new philosophy. Only customer-centered companies will win, those that can deliver superior value to their target customers. These companies will be adept in *building customers*, not just *building products*. They will be skillful in *market engineering*, not just *product engineering*.

Too many companies think that it is the marketing/sales department's job to procure customers. If they cannot, the conclusion is drawn that the company's marketing people aren't very good. But one of the fundamental new insights is that marketing cannot do this job alone. In fact, marketing can only be a partner in the company's task of attracting and keeping customers. The best marketing department in the world cannot sell products which are poorly made or which fail to meet anyone's need. The marketing department can only be effective in companies whose departments and employees have successfully teamed to design and implement a competitively superior *customer value-delivery system*.

Take the example of McDonald's. People do not swarm to the world's 11,000 McDonald's outlets because they love the hamburger. Some other restaurants make better-tasting hamburgers. They are flocking to a system, not a hamburger. It is a fine-tuned system that delivers throughout the world a high standard of what McDonald's calls QSCV—quality, service, cleanliness, and value. McDonald's is only effective to the extent that it partners with its suppliers, franchise owners, employees, and others to jointly deliver exceptionally high value to its customers.

In this chapter, we will describe and illustrate the philosophy of the customer-focused firm and *value marketing*.[1] We will address the following questions:

- What is customer value and satisfaction?
- How do leading companies organize to produce and deliver high customer value and satisfaction?
- How can companies retain customers as well as attract customers?
- How can companies determine customer profitability?
- How can companies practice total quality marketing?

Defining Customer Value and Satisfaction

Over 35 years ago, Peter Drucker insightfully observed that a company's first task is "to create customers." But today's customers face a vast array of product and brand choices, prices, and suppliers. This is the question: How do customers make their choices?

We believe that customers estimate which offer will deliver the most value. Customers are value-maximizers, within the bounds of search costs and limited knowledge, mobility, and income. They form an expectation of value and act on it. Then they learn whether the offer lived up to the value expectation and this affects their satisfaction and their repurchase probability.

Here we will examine more carefully the concepts of customer value and customer satisfaction.

Customer Value

Our premise is that buyers will buy from the firm that they perceive to offer the highest *customer delivered value*. We define this as follows (see Figure 2-1):

❖ *Customer delivered value* is the difference between *total customer value* and *total customer cost*. And *total customer value* is the bundle of benefits customers expect from a given product or service.

We can explain customer delivered value in terms of an example. The buyer for a large construction company wants to buy a tractor. He will buy it from either Caterpillar or Komatsu. The competing salespeople carefully describe their respective offers to the buyer.

Now the buyer has a particular tractor application in mind, namely employing the tractor in residential construction work. He would like the tractor to deliver certain levels of reliability, durability, and performance. Suppose he evaluates the two tractors and judges that Caterpillar has a higher product value based on perceived reliability, durability, and performance. He perceives differences in the accompanying services—delivery, training, and maintenance—and judges that Caterpillar provides better service. He also perceives Caterpillar personnel to be more knowledgeable and responsive. Finally, he places higher value on Caterpillar's corporate image. He adds all the values from these four sources—*product*, *services*, *personnel*, and *image*—and perceives Caterpillar as offering more *total customer value*.

Does he buy the Caterpillar tractor? Not necessarily. He also examines the *total customer cost* of transacting with Caterpillar versus Komatsu. The total customer cost consists of more than the *monetary cost*. As Adam Smith observed over two centuries ago, "The real price of anything is the toil and trouble of acquiring it." It includes the buyer's anticipated time, energy, and psychic costs. The buyer evaluates these costs along with the monetary cost to form a picture of total customer cost.

FIGURE 2-1
Determinants of Customer
Added Value

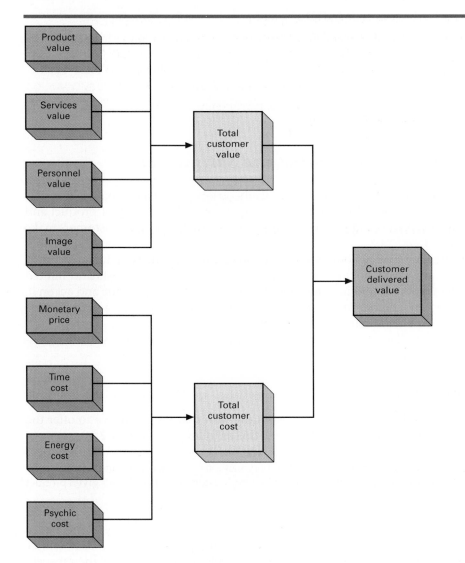

The buyer now considers whether Caterpillar's total customer cost is too high in relation to Caterpillar's total customer value. If it is, the buyer might buy the Komatsu tractor. The buyer will buy from whomever offers the highest delivered value.

Now let's use this theory of buyer decision making to help Caterpillar succeed in selling its tractor to this buyer. Caterpillar can improve its offer in three ways. First, Caterpillar can augment total customer value by improving product, services, personnel, and/or image benefits. Second, Caterpillar can reduce the buyer's nonmonetary costs by lessening the buyer's time, energy, and psychic costs. Third, Caterpillar can reduce its monetary cost to the buyer.

Suppose Caterpillar carries out a *customer value assessment* and concludes that the buyer sees Caterpillar's offer as worth $20,000. Further, suppose Caterpillar's cost of producing the tractor is $14,000. This means that Caterpillar's offer potentially generates $6,000 ($20,000 − $14,000) of *total added value*.

Caterpillar needs to charge a price between $14,000 and $20,000. If it charges less than $14,000, it won't cover its costs. If it charges more than $20,000, it would exceed the buyer's perception of total value. The price Caterpillar charges will determine how much of the *total added value* will be delivered to the buyer and how much will flow to Caterpillar. For example, if Caterpillar charges $19,000, it is granting $1,000 of total added value to the customer and keeping $5,000 for itself as profit. The lower Caterpillar sets its price, the higher is the delivered value and, therefore, the customer's *incentive to purchase* from Caterpillar. Delivered value should be looked at as the "profit" to the customer.

Given that Caterpillar wants to win the sale, it must offer more delivered value than does Komatsu. Delivered value can be measured either as a difference or a ratio. If total customer value is $20,000 and total customer cost is (say) $16,000, then the delivered value is $4,000 (measured as a difference) or 1.25 (measured as a ratio). When ratios are used to compare offers, they are often called *value/price ratios*.[2]

Some marketers might argue that this is too rational a theory of how buyers choose suppliers. They will cite examples where buyers did not choose the offer with the highest delivered value. Consider the following situation:

> The Caterpillar salesperson convinces the buyer that taking into account the purchase price and the benefits in use and disposal, Caterpillar's tractor offers a higher delivered value to the buyer's company. The Caterpillar salesperson also points out that the Caterpillar tractor uses less fuel and has fewer breakdowns. Yet the buyer decides to buy the Komatsu tractor.

How can we explain this appearance of nonvalue-maximizing behavior? Here are three possible explanations:

1. The buyer might be under company orders to buy at the lowest price. The buyer is explicitly prevented from making a choice based on delivered value. The Caterpillar salesperson's task is to convince the buyer's management that buying on price will damage the customer's long-run profitability.

2. The buyer will retire before the company realizes that the Komatsu tractor is more expensive to operate than the Caterpillar tractor. The buyer will look good in the short run and is maximizing personal benefit and placing no weight on company benefit. The salesperson's task is to convince other members of the customer company that Caterpillar's offer creates greater delivered value.

3. The buyer enjoys a long-term friendship with the Komatsu salesperson. Caterpillar's salesperson needs to show the buyer that the Komatsu tractor will draw complaints from the tractor operators when they discover the high fuel cost and frequent repairs associated with this tractor.

Clearly, buyers operate under various constraints and furthermore make occasional choices that give more weight to their personal benefit than to the company benefit. However, we feel that delivered-value maximization is a useful interpretative framework that applies to many situations and that yields rich insights. Here are its implications. First, the seller must assess the total customer value and total customer cost associated with the offer of each competitor to know where his or her own offer will stand. Second, the seller who is at a delivered-value disadvantage has two alternatives. This seller can try to increase total customer value or decrease total customer cost. The former calls for strengthening or augmenting the product, services, personnel, and/or image benefits of the offer. The latter calls for reducing the buyer's costs. The seller can reduce the price, simplify the ordering and delivery process, or absorb some buyer risk by offering a warranty.

Customer Satisfaction

Thus, we assert that the buyer forms a judgment of value and acts on it. Whether the buyer is satisfied after purchase depends upon the offer's performance in relation to the buyer's expectations. Here is our definition of customer satisfaction:

❖ Satisfaction is the level of a person's felt state resulting from comparing a product's perceived *performance* (or outcome) in relation to the person's *expectations*.

Thus the satisfaction level is a function of the difference between *perceived performance* and *expectations*. A customer could experience one of three broad levels of satisfaction. If the performance falls short of expectations, the customer is dissatisfied. If the performance matches the expectations, the customer is satisfied. If the performance exceeds expectations, the customer is highly satisfied, pleased, or delighted.

But how do buyers form their expectations? Expectations are formed on the basis of the buyer's past buying experience, statements made by friends and associates, and marketer and competitor information and promises. If marketers raise expectations too high, the buyer is likely to be disappointed. For example, Holiday Inn ran a campaign a few years ago called "No Surprises." But hotel guests still encountered a host of problems and Holiday Inn had to withdraw this campaign. On the other hand, if the company sets expectations too low, it won't attract enough buyers although it will satisfy those who buy.

Some of today's most successful companies are raising expectations and delivering performances to match. These companies are aiming for TCS—Total Customer Satisfaction.

> Xerox, for example, guarantees "total satisfaction" and will replace at its expense any dissatisfied customer's equipment for a period of three years after purchase with the same or comparable product. Cigna advertises "We'll never be 100% satisfied until you are, too." And Honda's ad says: "One reason our customers are so satisfied is that we aren't."

These companies are aiming high because customers who are *just satisfied* will still find it easy to switch suppliers when a better offer comes along. In one consumer packaged-goods category, 44% of those reporting satisfaction subsequently switched brands. Those who are *highly satisfied* are much less ready to switch. One study showed that 75% of Toyota buyers were highly satisfied and about 75% said they intended to buy a Toyota again. The fact is that high satisfaction or delight creates an emotional affinity with the brand, not just a rational preference, and this creates high customer loyalty.

The challenge is to create a company culture such that everyone within the company aims to delight the customer. Unisys, the computer company, recently introduced the term "customerize" in its ads, and defined it as follows: "To make a company more responsive to its customers and better able to attract new ones." Unisys sees this as a matter of extending information system capabilities to field locations and other points of customer contact and support. But "customerizing" a company calls for more than providing good information to customer contact employees. Ultimately it may require linking staff pay to customer satisfaction. The company's staff must be "converted" to practicing a strong customer orientation. Anita Roddick, founder of The Body Shop, wisely observes: "Our people (employees) are my first line of customers."

Companies seeking to win in today's markets must track their customers' expectations, perceived company performance, and customer satisfaction. They need to monitor this for their competitors as well. Consider the following:

A company was pleased to find that 80% of its customers said they were satisfied. Then the CEO found out that its leading competitor attained a 90% customer satisfaction score. He was further dismayed when he learned that this competitor was aiming to reach a 95% satisfaction score.

Marketing Concepts and Tools 2-1 describes how companies can track customer satisfaction.

For customer-centered companies, customer satisfaction is both a goal and a marketing tool. Companies that achieve high customer satisfaction ratings make sure that their target market knows it. The Honda Accord has received the number-one rating in customer satisfaction from J. D. Powers for several years, and their advertising of this fact has helped sell more Accords. Dell Computer's meteoric growth in the personal computer industry is partly attributable to achieving and advertising its number-one rank in customer satisfaction.

Although the customer-centered firm seeks to create high customer satisfaction, it is not out to *maximize* customer satisfaction. First, the company can increase customer satisfaction by lowering its price or increasing its services, but this may result in lower profits. Second, the company might be able to increase its profitability in other ways, such as by improving its manufacturing or investing more in R&D. Third, the company has many stakeholders including employees, dealers, suppliers, and stockholders. Spending more to increase customer satisfaction would divert funds from increasing the satisfaction of other "partners." Ultimately, the company must operate on the philosophy that it is trying to deliver a high level of customer satisfaction subject to delivering at least acceptable levels of satisfaction to the other stakeholders within the constraints of its total resources.

Marketing Concepts and Tools 2-1

Methods of Tracking and Measuring Customer Satisfaction

A company's tools for tracking and measuring customer satisfaction range from the primitive to the sophisticated. Companies use the following methods to measure how much customer satisfaction they are creating.

Complaint and Suggestion Systems

A customer-centered organization would make it easy for its customers to deliver suggestions and complaints. Many restaurants and hotels provide forms for guests to report their likes and dislikes. A hospital could place suggestion boxes in the corridors, supply comment cards to exiting patients, and hire a patient advocate to handle patient grievances. Some customer-centered companies — P&G, General Electric, Whirlpool — establish "customer hot lines" with toll-free 800 telephone numbers to maximize the ease with which customers can inquire, make suggestions, or complain. These information flows provide these companies with many good ideas and enable them to act more rapidly to resolve problems.

Customer Satisfaction Surveys

A company must not conclude that it can get a full picture of customer satisfaction and dissatisfaction by simply running a complaint and suggestion system. Studies show that customers are dissatisfied with one out of every four purchases and less than 5% of dissatisfied customers will complain. Customers may feel that their complaints are minor, or that they will be made to feel stupid, or that no remedy will be offered. Most customers will buy less or switch suppliers rather than complain. The result is that the company has needlessly lost customers.

Therefore, companies cannot use complaint levels as a measure of customer satisfaction. Responsive companies obtain a direct measure of customer satisfaction by conducting periodic surveys. They send questionnaires or make telephone calls to a random sample of their recent customers to find out how they feel about various aspects of the company's performance. They will also solicit buyers' views on their competitors' performances.

Customer satisfaction can be measured in a number of ways. It can be measured directly by asking: "Indicate how satisfied you are with *service x* on the following scale: highly dissatisfied, dissatisfied, indifferent, satisfied, highly satisfied" *(directly reported satisfaction)*. Respondents can be asked as well to rate how much they expected of a certain attribute and also how much they experienced *(derived dissatisfaction)*. Still another method is to ask respondents to list any problems they have had with the offer and to list any improvements they could suggest *(problem analysis)*. Finally, companies could ask respondents to rate various elements of the offer in terms of the importance of each element and how well the organization performed each element *(importance/performance ratings)*. This last method helps the company to know if it is underperforming on important elements and overperforming on relatively unimportant elements (see Chapter 18, Marketing Concepts and Tools 18-1, p. 478).

While collecting customer satisfaction data, it would also be useful to ask additional questions to measure the customer's *repurchase intention;* this will normally be high if the customer's satisfaction is high. According to John Young, Hewlett-Packard's former CEO:

> Fully nine out of 10 customers in our surveys who rank themselves as highly satisfied say they would definitely or probably buy from HP again. This satisfaction translates into profitability because it costs five times more to gain a new customer than it does to keep an existing one.

It would also be useful to measure the customer's likelihood or willingness to recommend the company and brand to other persons. A high positive word-of-mouth score indicates that the company is producing high customer satisfaction.

Ghost Shopping

Another useful way to gather a picture of customer satisfaction is to hire persons to pose as potential buyers to report their findings on strong and weak points they experienced in buying the company's and competitors' products. These ghost shoppers can even pose certain problems to test whether the company's sales personnel handle the situation well. Thus, a ghost shopper can complain about a restaurant's food to test how the restaurant handles this complaint. Not only should companies hire ghost shoppers, but managers themselves should leave their office from time to time, enter company and competitor sales situations where they are unknown, and experience firsthand the treatment they receive as "customers." A variant of this is for managers to phone their own company with different questions and complaints to see how the call is handled.

Lost Customer Analysis

Companies should contact customers who have stopped buying or who have switched to another supplier to learn why this happened. When IBM loses a customer, they mount a thorough effort to learn where they failed—is their price too high, their service deficient, their products unreliable, and so on. Not only is it important to conduct *exit interviews* but also to monitor the *customer loss rate*, which, if it is increasing, clearly indicates that the company is failing to satisfy its customers.

Some Cautions in Measuring Customer Satisfaction

When customers rate their satisfaction with an element of the company's performance, say delivery, we need to recognize that customers will vary in how they define good delivery: it could mean early delivery, on-time delivery, order completeness, and so on. Yet if the company had to spell out every element in detail, customers would face a huge questionnaire. We must also recognize that two customers can report being "highly satisfied" for different reasons. One may be easily satisfied most of the time and the other might be hard to please but was pleased on this occasion.

Companies should also note that managers and salespersons can manipulate their ratings on customer satisfaction. They can be especially nice to customers just before the survey. They can also try to exclude unhappy customers from being included in the survey.

One danger is that if customers know that the company will go out of its way to please customers, some customers may want to express high dissatisfaction (even if satisfied) in order to receive more concessions.

Marketing Concepts and Tools 2-2

Observations on Customer Satisfaction

Professor Claes Fornell of the University of Michigan is engaged in a major project to create an index for measuring customer satisfaction on an industry and national basis. A Customer Satisfaction Barometer would yield information not supplied by Gross National Product (GNP) measures. It is possible, for example, for an industry's or nation's output to increase while customer satisfaction falls. The measured value of industrial output is not necessarily a measure of customer satisfaction with that output. Here are some of Professor Fornell's findings on the industry level:

♦ Customer satisfaction will be lower in industries where the industry offers a homogeneous product to a heterogeneous market. On the other hand, industries that sup-

ply a high-quality homogeneous product to a homogeneous market will register high satisfaction.

♦ Customer satisfaction is lower in industries where repeat buyers face high switching costs. They have to buy from the supplier even though their satisfaction is low.

♦ Industries which depend upon repeat business generally create a higher level of customer satisfaction.

♦ As a company increases its market share, customer satisfaction can fall. This is because more customers with heterogeneous demands are drawn into buying a fairly homogeneous product.

SOURCE: Claes Fornell, "A National Customer Satisfaction Barometer: The Swedish Experience," *Journal of Marketing*, January 1992, pp. 6–21.

Additional observations on customer satisfaction are described in Marketing Concepts and Tools 2-2 above.

Delivering Customer Value and Satisfaction

Given the importance of customer value and satisfaction, what does it take to produce and deliver it? To answer this, we need to introduce the concepts of a *value chain* and *value-delivery systems*.

Value Chain

Michael Porter of Harvard proposed the *value chain* as a company tool for identifying ways to create more customer value (see Figure 2-2).[3] Every firm is a collection of activities that are performed to design, produce, market, deliver, and support its product. The value chain identifies nine strategically relevant activities that create value and cost in a specific business. The nine value-creating activities consist of five primary activities and four support activities.

The primary activities represent the sequence of bringing materials into the business, operating on them, sending them out, marketing them, and servicing them. The support activities occur throughout all of these primary activities. Thus, procurement represents the purchasing of various inputs for each primary activity, only a fraction of which are handled by the purchasing department. Technology development occurs in every primary activity, only a fraction of which is done in the R&D department. Human-resource management also occurs in all departments. The firm's infrastructure covers the overhead of general management, planning, finance, accounting, legal, and government affairs that are borne by all the primary and support activities.

CHAPTER 2
Building Customer
Satisfaction Through Quality,
Service, and Value

The firm's task is to examine its costs and performance in each value-creating activity and to look for improvements. The firm should estimate its competitors' costs and performances as benchmarks. To the extent that it can perform certain activities better than its competitors, it can achieve a competitive advantage.

The firm's success depends not only on how well each department performs its work but also on how well the various departmental activities are coordinated. Too often, company departments act to maximize their department's interests rather than the company's and customers' interests. A credit department may take a long time to check a prospective customer's credit so as not to incur bad debts; meanwhile, the customer waits and the salesperson is frustrated. A traffic department chooses to ship the goods by rail to save the department money and again the customer waits. Each department has erected walls that slow down the delivery of quality customer service.

The answer to this problem is to place more emphasis on the smooth management of *core business processes*, most of which involve cross-functional inputs and cooperation. Among the core business processes are:

◆ New *product realization process:* all the activities involved in identifying, researching, developing, and successfully launching new products with speed, high quality, and target cost attainment

◆ *Inventory management process:* all the activities involved in developing and managing the right inventory locations of raw materials, semifinished materials, and finished goods so that adequate supplies are available while avoiding the costs of high overstocks

◆ *Order-to-remittance process:* all the activities involved in receiving orders, approving them, shipping the goods on time, and collecting payment

◆ *Customer service process:* all the activities involved in making it easy for customers to reach the right parties within the company and receive quick and satisfactory service, answers, and resolutions of problems

Strong companies are those that develop *superior capabilities* in managing these *core processes*. For example, one of Wal-Mart's great strengths is its superefficiency in arranging goods to move from suppliers to its individual stores. As Wal-Mart stores sell their goods, sales information flows not only to Wal-Mart's headquarters but to Wal-Mart's suppliers who ship replacement merchandise to the Wal-Mart stores almost at the rate they move off the shelf. Various commentators have noted the competitive edge achieved by companies that have mastered the management of certain core business processes.[4]

Value-Delivery System

The firm also needs to look for competitive advantages beyond its own value chain, into the value chains of its suppliers, distributors, and ultimately customers. More companies today are turning to partnering with the other members of the *supply chain* to improve the performance of the customer value-delivery system. For example:

> Procter & Gamble has assigned twenty of its employees to live and work at Wal-Mart's headquarters to improve the speed and reduce the costs of supplying P&G goods to Wal-Mart's branch stores.

> Campbell Soup operates a qualified supplier program where it sets up high standards and chooses the few suppliers who are willing to meet its stringent requirements for quality, on-time delivery, and continuous improvement. Campbell's assigns its own experts to work with its suppliers to constantly improve their joint performance.

An excellent example of a value-delivery system is the one that connects Levi Strauss, the famous maker of blue jeans, with its suppliers and distributors (see Figure 2-3). One of Levi's major retailers is Sears. Every night, thanks to electronic data interchange (EDI), Levi's learns the sizes and styles of its blue jeans that sold through Sears and other major outlets. Levi's then electronically orders more fabric for next day delivery from the Milliken Company, its fabric supplier. Milliken, in turn, relays an order for more fiber to Du Pont, the fiber supplier. In this way, the partners in the supply chain use the most current sales information to manufacture what is selling, rather than to manufacture for a forecast that may be at variance with current demand. This is known as a *quick response system*. The goods are pulled by demand, rather than pushed by supply. And Levi's performance against another jeans maker—say Wrangler—will depend upon the teamwork quality of Levi's *strategic network* against Wrangler's strategic network. Companies no longer compete—strategic networks do.

As companies struggle to become more competitive, they are turning, ironically, to practicing more cooperation. Companies formerly viewed their suppliers and distributors as cost centers, and in some cases, as adversaries. But today, they are carefully selecting their partners and attempting to work out mutually profitable strategies. In structuring customer value-delivery systems, the new competition is no longer between individual competitors but between the relative effectiveness of competing value-delivery systems organized by these competitors. Thus, if Levi's has built a more potent value-delivery system than its competitor, it will win more share and profit in this marketplace.

The implication, then, is that marketing can no longer be thought of as only a selling department. That view of marketing would only give it responsibility for formulating a promotion-oriented marketing mix without much to say about product features, costs, and so on. The new view of marketing is that it is responsible for *designing and managing a superior value-delivery system to reach target customer segments*. Today's marketing executives must think not only about selling today's products but about how to stimulate the development of improved company products, working actively with other departments in managing core business processes, and building stronger external partnerships.

FIGURE 2-3
Levi Strauss' Value Delivery
System

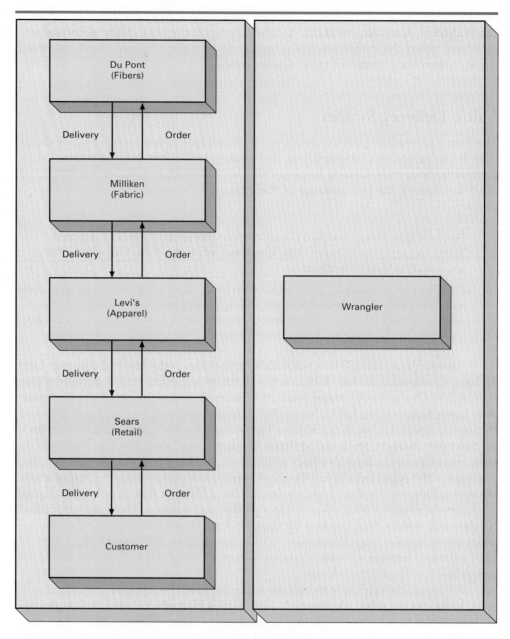

COMPETITION IS BETWEEN *NETWORKS*, NOT *COMPANIES*!
THE WINNER IS THE COMPANY WITH THE BETTER NETWORK!

Retaining Customers

Companies are not only seeking to improve their relations with their partners in the supply chain. Today they are intent on developing stronger bonds and loyalty with their ultimate customers. In the past, many companies took their customers for granted. Their customers either did not have many alternative suppliers, or the other suppliers were just as deficient in quality and service, or the market was growing so fast that the company did not worry about fully satisfying its customers. The company could lose 100 customers a week and gain another 100 customers and consider its sales to be satisfactory. But this is a condition of high *customer churn* and it involves a higher cost than if the company retained all 100 customers and acquired no new ones. Such a company is operating on a "leaky bucket" theory of its business, namely, that there will always be enough customers to replace the defecting ones.

The Cost of Lost Customers

Today's companies need to pay closer attention to their customer defection rate and undertake steps to reduce it. There are four steps. First the company must define and measure its retention rate. For a magazine, it would be the renewal rate; for a college, it could be the first- to second-year retention rate, or the class graduation rate.

Second, the company must distinguish the various causes of customer attrition and identify those that can be managed better. Not much can be done about customers who leave the region or who go out of business. But much can be done about customers who leave because of poor service, shoddy products, excessive pricing, and so on. The company needs to prepare a frequency distribution showing the percentage of customers who defect for different reasons.

Third, the company needs to estimate how much profit it loses when it loses customers unnecessarily. In the case of an individual customer, this is the same as the *customer's lifetime value*, namely the profit that would have been yielded by the customer if he had continued purchasing for the normal number of years. For the case of a group of lost customers, a major transportation carrier estimated the profit loss as follows:

- The company had 64,000 accounts.
- The company lost 5% of its accounts this year specifically due to poor service, namely 3,200 accounts ($.05 \times 64,000$).
- The average lost account represented a $40,000 loss in revenue. Therefore, the company lost $128,000,000 in revenue ($3,200 \times \$40,000$).
- The company's profit margin is 10%. Therefore, the company lost $12,800,000 unnecessarily ($.10 \times \$128,000,000$).

Fourth, the company needs to figure out how much it would cost to reduce the defection rate. As long as the cost is less than the lost profit, the company should spend that amount. Thus if the transportation carrier can spend less than $12,800,000 to retain all of these accounts, it would pay.

The Need for Customer Retention

Today's companies are going all out to retain their customers. They are struck by the fact that the cost of attracting a new customer may be five times the cost of keeping a current customer happy. Offensive marketing typically costs more than defensive marketing because it requires much effort and cost to induce satisfied customers to switch away from their current suppliers.

Unfortunately, classic marketing theory and practice center on the art of attracting new customers rather than retaining existing ones. The emphasis has been on creating *transactions* rather than *relationships*. Discussion has focused on *presale activity* and *sale activity* rather than on *postsale activity*. Today, however, more companies are recognizing the importance of retaining current customers. According to Reichheld and Sasser, companies can improve profits anywhere from 25% to 85% by reducing customer defections by 5%.[5] Unfortunately, companies' accounting systems fail to show the value of loyal customers.

We can work out an example to support the case for emphasizing customer retention. Suppose a company researches its *new customer acquisition cost*. It finds:

Cost of an average sales call (including salary, commission, benefits, and expenses)	$300
Average number of sales calls to convert an average prospect into a customer	× 4
Cost of attracting a new customer	$1,200

This is an underestimate because we are omitting the cost of advertising and promotion, operations, planning, and so on.

Now suppose the company estimates the probable average *customer lifetime value*:

Annual customer revenue	$5,000
Average number of loyal years	× 2
Company profit margin	× .10
Customer lifetime value (undiscounted)	$1,000

Clearly this company is spending more to attract new customers than they are worth. Unless this company can sign up customers with fewer sales calls, spend less per sales call, increase new customer annual spending, retain customers longer, or sell them higher-margined products, the company is headed for bankruptcy.

Given that customer retention is the first imperative, there are two ways to accomplish it. One is to erect high switching barriers. Customers are less inclined to switch to another supplier when this would involve high capital costs, high search costs, the loss of loyal-customer discounts, and so on.

A better approach to customer retention is to deliver high customer satisfaction. Then it would be harder for a competitor to overcome barriers by simply offering lower prices or switching inducements. The task of creating strong customer loyalty is called *relationship marketing*.

Customer Relationship Marketing: The Key

How much should a company invest in relationship marketing, given the extra cost and effort that it involves? To answer this, we need to distinguish five different levels of relating to customers:

- *Basic:* The salesperson sells the product but does not contact the customer again (example: the auto salesperson just sells the car).

- *Reactive:* The salesperson sells the product and encourages the customer to call if he or she has any questions or complaints.

- *Accountable:* The salesperson phones the customer a short time after the sale to check whether the product is meeting the customer's expectations. The salesperson also solicits from the customer any product improvement suggestions and any specific disappointments. This information helps the company continuously improve its offering.

- *Proactive:* The company salesperson phones the customer from time to time with suggestions about improved product use or helpful new products.

- *Partnership:* The company works continuously with the customer to discover ways to effect customer savings or help the customer perform better.

Most companies will practice *basic* marketing if their markets contain numerous customers and if their unit profit margins are small (see Figure 2-4). Thus the Heinz Company is not going to phone each ketchup buyer to express appreciation. At best, Heinz will be reactive by setting up a customer answering service. At the other extreme, in markets with few customers and high margins, most sellers will

FIGURE 2-4
Levels of Relationship
Marketing

	HIGH MARGIN	MEDIUM MARGIN	LOW MARGIN
Many customers/distributors	Accountable	Reactive	Basic or reactive
Medium number of customers/distributors	Proactive	Accountable	Reactive
Few customers/distributors	Partnership	Proactive	Accountable

move toward partnership marketing. Boeing, for example, will work closely with United Airlines in designing and insuring that Boeing airplanes fully satisfy United's requirements. In between these two extreme situations, other levels of relationship marketing are appropriate.

What specific marketing tools can a company use when it wants to develop stronger customer bonding and satisfaction? Berry and Parasuraman have distinguished three customer value-building approaches.[6] The first relies primarily on adding *financial benefits* to the customer relationship. Thus, airlines sponsor frequent-flyer award programs, hotels give upgrades to their frequent guests, supermarkets may give patronage refunds, and so on. Although these reward programs build customer preference, they are easily imitated by competitors and therefore often fail to permanently differentiate the company's offer. (However, see Marketing Strategies 2-1.)

The second approach is to add *social benefits* as well as financial benefits. Here company personnel work on increasing their social bonds with customers by learning their individual needs and wants and individualizing and personalizing their service (see Table 2-1). They turn their *customers* into *clients*. Donnelly, Berry, and Thompson draw this distinction:

> *Customers may be nameless to the institution; clients cannot be nameless. Customers are served as part of the mass or as part of larger segments; clients are served on an individual*

TABLE 2-1
Social Actions Affecting
Buyer-Seller Relationships

GOOD THINGS	BAD THINGS
Initiate positive phone calls	Make only callbacks
Make recommendations	Make justifications
Candor in language	Accommodative language
Use phone	Use correspondence
Show appreciation	Wait for misunderstandings
Make service suggestions	Wait for service requests
Use "we" problem-solving language	Use "owe-us" legal language
Get to problems	Only respond to problems
Use jargon/shorthand	Use long-winded communications
Personality problems aired	Personality problems hidden
Talk of "our future together"	Talk about making good on the past
Routinize responses	Fire drill/emergency responsiveness
Accept responsibility	Shift blame
Plan the future	Rehash the past

Source: Reprinted by permission of the *Harvard Business Review.* An exhibit from Theodore Levitt, "After the Sale is Over," *Harvard Business Review* (September–October 1983, p. 119). Copyright © 1983 by the President and Fellows of Harvard College.

Strategies for Building Customer Loyalty: Frequency Marketing Programs and Clubs

As companies move from a transaction-oriented view of their customers to a relationship-building view, they will create and sponsor programs to keep their customers coming back, buying more, and staying loyal. The challenge is to develop a special relationship with the company's "best customers" in which they experience good two-way communication and see themselves as receiving special privileges and awards. Among the most promising programs are *frequency marketing programs* and *club marketing programs.*

Frequency Marketing Programs

Frequency marketing programs (FMP) are designed to provide rewards to customers who buy frequently and/or in substantial amounts. *Colloquy,* a quarterly frequency marketing newsletter, defines frequency marketing as the effort "to identify, maintain, and increase the yield from Best Customers, through long-term, interactive, value-added relationships." Frequency marketing is an acknowledgment of the Pareto principle — that 20% of a company's customers might account for 80% of its business.

American Airlines was one of the first companies to pioneer a frequency marketing program when they decided to offer free mileage credit to their customers in the early 1980s. A customer simply has to join the AAdvantage program at no cost. After accumulating sufficient mileage credits, the customer can turn them in for an airline seat upgrade, free ticket, or other benefits. As more flyers switched to American, the other air carriers were compelled to offer the same program.

Hotels next adopted FMP, with Marriott taking the lead with its Honored Guest Program, soon followed by Hyatt with its Gold Passport Program, and other hotel and motel chains. Frequent guests receive room upgrades or free rooms after earning so many points. Shortly thereafter, car rental firms sponsored FMPs. Then credit card companies began to offer points based on their cards' usage level; for example, Sears offers rebates to their Discover cardholders on charges made against the card.

Typically, the first company to introduce an FMP gains the most benefit, especially if competitors are slow to respond. After competitors respond, FMPs can become a burden to all the offering companies. By this time, most customers belong to most of the FMPs and accumulate credit with whomever they patronize. The companies find that they are giving away many flights, rooms, and so on. The winning companies, if any, are those who run their programs most efficiently, or attract the most business based on their program's distinctive benefits, or who build a sophisticated database system to design and present cogent and relevant offers to specific customers.

A criticism leveled against FMPs is that they might diminish the company's focus on delivering a superior level of customer service. That is, these programs attempt to produce repeat business on the basis of an economic incentive. European airlines, on the other hand, claim to rely on offering superior service to attract repeat business.

Club Marketing Programs

Many companies have created club concepts around their product. Club membership may be offered automatically upon purchase or promised purchase of a certain amount, or by paying a fee. Some clubs have been spectacularly successful:

> Shiseido, the Japanese cosmetic company, has enrolled over ten million members in its Shiseido Club, which provides a Visa card, discounts at theaters, hotels, and retailers, and also "frequent buyer" points. Its members receive a free magazine containing interesting articles on personal grooming.

> Nintendo, the Japanese video game company, has enrolled two million members in its Nintendo Club. For $16 a year, they receive a monthly magazine, *Nintendo Power,* previewing and reviewing Nintendo games, providing tips on winning, and so on. They have also set up a "game counselor" phone number that kids can call with questions or problems.

> Burger King sponsors the Burger King Kids Club which now numbers over 1.6 million members. Kids receive free membership, a secret code name, a newsletter, and premiums such as Ninja Turtles and other figurines. Other companies targeting kids through clubs include Kraft, LEGO, and Toys "Я" Us.

Waldenbooks sponsors a Preferred Reader Program which has attracted over four million members each paying $10 who receive mailings about new books, a 10% discount on book purchases, toll-free ordering, and a number of other services.

Harley-Davidson sponsors the Harley Owners Group (HOG) that now numbers 127,000 members. The first-time buyer of a Harley-Davidson motorcycle gets a free one-year membership with annual renewal costing $35. HOG benefits include a magazine (*Hog Tales*), a touring handbook, an emergency pick-up service, a specially designed insurance program, theft reward service, discount hotel rates, and a Fly & Ride program enabling members to rent Harleys while on vacation.

Lladro, maker of fine porcelain figurines, sponsors a "Collectors Society" with an annual membership fee of $35. Members receive a free subscription to a quarterly magazine, a bisque plaque, free enrollment in the Lladro Museum of New York, and member-only tours to visit the company and Lladro family in Valencia, Spain.

Apple Computer has worked with many User Groups in various cities who get together and exchange information. Apple sends them newsletters and general information. Each User Group will contain several Special Interest Groups (SIGs).

Gateway Federal, a Cincinnati thrift bank, sponsors The Statesman's Club for customers who maintain a minimum deposit of $10,000. Their 10,000 current members receive over 26 benefits including free checking, money orders and travelers' checks; social gatherings and guest lecturers; and complimentary refreshments. Members can reserve the club room for private receptions after regular hours and have access to IBM computers and other equipment.

Wolf Camera & Video stores operate a Frequent User Club whose members receive upon turning film in for development either a 25% discount on film development, a free roll of film, or a free second set of prints. Members also receive a 10% discount on picture frames and other store purchases. The cost of membership is $9.95 a year, except for senior citizens who receive membership privileges free!

In developing a club or frequency program, a company must make decisions in seven areas. First, what are the program's *objectives*? Is the aim to increase average order size or order frequency, to build goodwill, to prevent brand switching, to attract new customers, to prepare customized mailings, and so on? Each objective might lead to designing a different customer loyalty program.

Second, who is the *target group*? Neiman Marcus, the upscale department store, limits its InCircle Program to customers spending more than $3,000 a year. American Express offers its Platinum Card (in contrast to its Green and Gold cards) "By Invitation Only" to its best customers, entitling them to attend extraordinary cultural, culinary, and artistic events available only to platinum cardmembers.

Third, the company needs to define the *benefit bundle*. Will the benefits consist of "soft" benefits amounting to special services (such as room upgrades, free delivery, gift wraps, consultations, magazine), or "hard" benefits amounting to awards (such as free air travel, rooms, merchandise, cash, or other prizes)? For example, Neiman Marcus offers the following benefits to its InCircle customers: a toll-free hotline, special travel privileges, complimentary magazine subscriptions, a cookbook, members-only newsletters, and complimentary perfume.

Fourth, the company needs to develop an effective *communications strategy* to promote its program. The program can be mass-communicated or promoted through mail or telemarketing to specific customers or noncustomers.

Fifth, the company needs to develop a *funding program*. Should the program be supported by a membership fee? Should co-sponsors be drawn in who pay for the privilege of sending specific communications or offers to club members?

Sixth, the company needs an *implementation strategy* to make sure that its personnel are well trained and ready to run the program.

Seventh, the company needs to measure and continuously improve *program performance* to make sure that the program is achieving its objectives at a reasonable cost.

Clearly, companies will continuously invent and refine new programs to build and deepen customer loyalty in this era of intense competition.

basis. . . . Customers are served by anyone who happens to be available; clients are served . . . by the professional . . . assigned to them.[7]

The third approach is to add *structural ties* as well as financial and social benefits. For example, the company may supply customers with special equipment or computer linkages which help customers manage their orders, payroll, inventory, and so on. A good example is McKesson Corporation, a leading pharmaceutical wholesaler, which invested millions of dollars in *electronic data interchange* (*EDI*) capabilities to help small pharmacies manage their inventory, order entry, and shelf space. Another example is Milliken which provides proprietary software programs, marketing research, sales training, and sales leads to its loyal customers. (For more on relationship marketing, see Chapter 25, pp. 711–13.)

Customer Profitability: the Ultimate Test

Ultimately, marketing is the art of attracting and keeping *profitable customers*. Yet companies often discover that between 20 to 40% of their customers may be unprofitable. Further, many companies report that their most profitable customers are not their largest customers but their mid-size customers. The largest customers demand considerable service and receive the deepest discounts, thus reducing the company's profit level. The smallest customers pay full price and receive minimal service but the costs of transacting with small customers reduce their profitability. The mid-size customers receive good service and pay nearly full price and in many cases are the most profitable. This helps explain why many large firms which formerly targeted only large customers are now invading the middle market.

A company should not pursue and satisfy every customer. For example, if business customers of Courtyard (which is Marriott Hotels' less expensive motel) start asking for Marriott-level business services, Courtyard should say "no." Acceding to this would only confuse the respective positioning of the Marriott and Courtyard systems. Lanning and Phillips make this point well:

> *Some organizations . . . try to do anything and everything customers suggest . . . Yet, while customers often make many good suggestions, they also suggest many courses of action that are unactionable or unprofitable. Randomly following these suggestions is fundamentally different from market-focus — making a disciplined choice of which customers to serve and which specific combination of benefits and price to deliver to them (and which to deny them).*[8]

What makes a profitable customer? We define a profitable customer as follows:

❖ A profitable customer is a person, household, or company that yields a revenue stream over time, exceeding by an acceptable amount the company cost stream of attracting, selling, and servicing that customer.

Note that the emphasis is on the lifetime stream of revenue and cost, not on the profit from a particular transaction. Here are a few dramatic illustrations of *customer lifetime value*:

Stew Leonard, who operates a highly profitable supermarket, says that he sees $50,000 flying out of his store every time he sees a sulking customer. Why? Because his average customer spends $100 a week, shops for 50 weeks a year, and remains in the area for ten years. So if this customer has an unhappy experience, and switches to another supermarket, Stew Leonard has lost $50,000 in revenue. This understates the loss if the disappointed customer bad-mouths the store and causes other customers to defect. So Stew Leonard has his employees follow two rules:

- *Rule #1:* The customer is always right.
- *Rule #2:* If the customer is wrong, see Rule #1.

Tom Peters, noted author of several books on "managerial excellence," runs a business which involves spending $1,500 a month on Federal Express service. He spends this amount 12 months a year and expects to remain in business for another ten years. Therefore, he expects to spend $180,000 on future Federal Express service. If Federal Express makes a 10% profit margin, his lifetime business will contribute $18,000 to Federal Express's profits. All this is at risk if he starts getting poor service from the Federal Express driver or if a competitor offers better service.

Most companies fail to measure individual customer profitability. For example, banks claim that this is hard to do since a customer uses different banking services and the transactions are logged in different departments. Banks which have succeeded in linking customer transactions have been appalled by the number of unprofitable customers in their customer base. Some banks report losing money on over 45% of their retail customers. It is not surprising that banks are increasingly charging fees for various services that they supplied free in the past.

A useful type of profitability analysis is shown in Figure 2-5.[9] Customers are arrayed along the columns and products along the rows. Each cell contains a symbol for the profitability of selling that product to that customer. We observe that customer 1 is very profitable in that he buys three profit-making products, namely P_1, P_2, and P_4. Customer 2 yields a picture of mixed profitability; he buys one profitable product and one unprofitable product. Customer 3 represents a losing customer because he buys one profitable product and two unprofitable products. What can the company do about this? (1) It can raise the price of its less profitable products, or eliminate them. (2) It can also try to cross-sell its profit-making products to these

Products		Customers			
		C_1	C_2	C_3	
	P_1	++		+	Highly profitable product
	P_2	+	+		Profitable product
	P_3		−	−	Losing product
	P_4	+		−	Mixed-bag product
		High profit customer	Mixed-bag customer	Losing customer	

FIGURE 2-5
Customer/Product Profitability Analysis

CHAPTER 2
Building Customer Satisfaction Through Quality, Service, and Value

The Malcolm Baldrige National Quality Award: A Spur to Higher Quality

Competition is no longer local; for a growing number of companies, it is global. And as long as national markets remain open, foreign goods will arrive that are either cheaper, better, or both. Therefore, a nation's companies must strive to produce goods that are competitive or superior on world markets. This has led some countries to establish a national prize that is awarded to companies that exemplify the best quality practices and improvements.

Japan was the first country to award a national quality prize, the Deming prize, named after the American statistician who taught the importance of quality to postwar Japan. In the mid-1980s, the United States established the Malcolm Baldrige National Quality Award in honor of the late Secretary of Commerce. The Award encourages U.S. companies to implement explicit quality practices and when results justify it, companies are encouraged to submit applications and evidence for an award. The Board of Examiners may give up to two awards each year in three categories: manufacturing companies, service companies, and small businesses. The award criteria consist of seven measures, whose dynamic relationships are shown in the accompanying figure.

Each of the seven measures carries a certain number of award points, the total of which adds to 1,000 points. Of these measures, customer focus and satisfaction gets the most points, namely 300. The 300 points are further broken down into points for understanding customer expectations, managing customer relationships well, determining customer satisfaction, and so on.

Thus far, Baldrige awards have gone to such companies as Xerox, Motorola, Federal Express, IBM, AT&T, Texas Instruments, Cadillac division of General Motors, Ritz-Carlton Hotel, and a few other companies. One company that is currently competing for a Baldrige National Quality Award in the category of small business is a marketing research firm, Custom Research Incorporated (CRI), headquartered in Minneapolis. In 1990, CRI began using the Baldrige criteria as a framework for developing its quality system. It applied for the award in 1991 and received verbal feedback that led to further improvements. In 1992, CRI was selected to receive a site visit. CRI believes that it earned a site visit because it manages the company according to the following principles:

1. Pursue a strategy of focusing on building major client relationships.

2. Organize into cross-functional, client-centered teams.

3. Develop processes and procedures to get work done, then measure the results.

4. Explicitly ask clients what they expect from a partnering relationship.

5. Seek client feedback on individual projects and the overall relationship.

6. Hire the best people and invest in their development.

7. Stay flexible, agile, fast moving—and empower everyone in the company to "just do it."

8. Have fun with hoopla and recognition.

9. Build quality continuously.

10. Never be satisfied.

This is an excellent statement of modern business and marketing thinking that all companies will do well to emulate.

---

unprofitable customers. If these unprofitable customers choose to defect, it may be for the good. One could even argue that the company would benefit by encouraging its unprofitable customers to switch to their competitors.

Implementing Total Quality Marketing

A company's marketing will not be effective if it is only entrusted to the marketing department. The greatest marketing department in the world cannot compensate for deficient products or service. The customer who cannot understand the company's written product instructions, or who cannot reach the right manager, or who

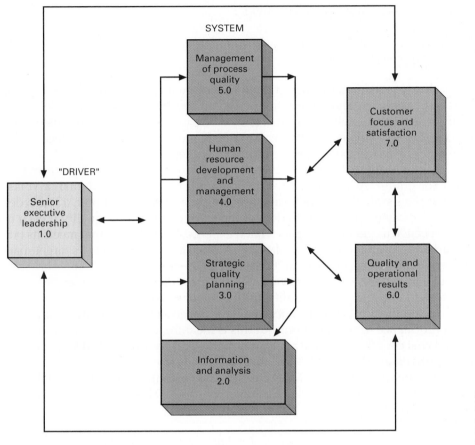

BALDRIGE AWARD CRITERIA FRAMEWORK
Dynamic Relationships

SYSTEM

Management of process quality 5.0

Human resource development and management 4.0

Strategic quality planning 3.0

Information and analysis 2.0

"DRIVER"

Senior executive leadership 1.0

Customer focus and satisfaction 7.0

Quality and operational results 6.0

GOAL

Customer satisfaction

Customer satisfaction relative to competitors

Customer retention

Market share gain

MEASURES OF PROGRESS

Product & service quality

Productivity improvement

Waste reduction/elimination

Supplier quality

SOURCE: 1993 Award Criteria, Malcolm Baldrige National Quality Award brochure, U.S. Department of Commerce, Technology Administration, National Institute of Standards and Technology, Gaithersburg, MD.

receives an incorrect invoice will understandably downgrade the company in his or her mind. The company will lose "company equity" in the customer's mind.

Today's top executives view the task of improving product and service quality to be their top priority. Many global successes of Japanese companies are due to their building exceptional quality into their products. Most customers will no longer accept or tolerate average-quality performance. Companies today have no choice but to adopt *total quality management* (TQM) if they want to stay in the race, let alone be profitable. According to G.E.'s Chairman, John F. Welch, Jr.: "Quality is our best assurance of customer allegiance, our strongest defense against foreign competition, and the only path to sustained growth and earnings."[10] (See Marketing Environment and Trends 2-1 above.)

There is an intimate connection between product and service quality, customer satisfaction, and company profitability. Higher levels of quality result in higher levels of customer satisfaction, while at the same time supporting higher prices and often lower costs. Therefore, *quality improvement programs* (QIP) normally will increase profitability. The well-known PIMS studies show a high correlation between relative product quality and company profitability.[11]

But first let us define quality. Quality has been variously defined by experts as "fitness for use," "conformance to requirements," "freedom from variation," and so on.[12] We will use the definition propounded by the American Society for Quality Control that has been adopted worldwide:[13]

❖ Quality *is the totality of features and characteristics of a product or service that bear on its ability to satisfy stated or implied needs.*

This is clearly a customer-centered definition of quality. Customers have a set of needs, requirements, and expectations. We can say that the seller has delivered quality whenever the seller's product and service meets or exceeds the customers' expectations. A company that manages to satisfy most of its customers' needs most of the time is a *quality company* (see Marketing Strategies 2-2).

It is important to distinguish between conformance quality and performance quality (or grade). A Mercedes provides higher *performance quality* than a Volkswagen: it rides smoother, goes faster, lasts longer, and so on. Yet both a Mercedes and a Volkswagen can be said to deliver the same conformance quality if each of their respective target markets gets what it expects. A $70,000 car that meets its target market's requirements is a quality car. A $15,000 car that meets its target market's requirements is a quality car. But if Mercedes cars vary in the smoothness of their ride, or if Volkswagen cars vary in their fuel efficiency, then both cars have failed to deliver conformance quality and customer satisfaction.

At the same time, conformance quality is not enough. The product may have high conformance to specifications but this is meaningless if the specifications are wrong. What counts in the final analysis is market-driven quality (MDQ), not engineering-driven quality (EDQ).

Total quality is the key to value creation and customer satisfaction. Total quality is everyone's job, just as marketing is everyone's job. This was expressed well by Daniel Beckham:

> Marketers who don't learn the language of quality improvement, manufacturing, and operations will become as obsolete as buggy whips. The days of functional marketing are gone. We can no longer afford to think of ourselves as market researchers, advertising people, direct marketers, strategists—we have to think of ourselves as customer satisfiers—customer advocates focused on whole processes.[14]

Marketing management has two responsibilities in a quality-centered company. First, marketing management must participate in formulating strategies and policies designed to help the company win through total quality excellence. Second, marketing must deliver marketing quality besides production quality. Each marketing activity—marketing research, sales training, advertising, customer service, and so on—must be performed to high standards.

One study, however, reported that marketing and salespeople were responsible for more customer complaints than any other department (35%). The marketing errors included cases where the salesforce ordered something special for the customer but failed to notify manufacturing of the changes, where incorrect order processing resulted in the wrong product being made and shipped, and where customer complaints were not adequately resolved.[15]

Marketing Strategies 2-2

Observations on Pursuing a Total Quality Marketing Strategy

A growing number of companies have appointed a "Vice-President of Quality" to spearhead TQM. TQM requires recognizing the following premises about quality improvement:

1. *Quality Must Be Perceived by Customers.* Quality work must begin with the customers' needs and end with the customers' perceptions. If customers want more reliability, durability, or performance, then these constitute quality in the eyes of the customers. Quality improvements are only meaningful when they are perceived by customers. According to Hauser: "To assure that customers perceive products to be of high quality, manufacturers must deploy the voice of the customer throughout design, engineering, manufacturing, and distribution."[1]

2. *Quality Must Be Reflected in Every Company Activity, Not Just in Company Products.* Leonard A. Morgan of GE said: "We are not just concerned with the quality of the product, but with the quality of our advertising, service, product literature, delivery, after-sales support, and so on."[2]

3. *Quality Requires Total Employee Commitment.* Quality can only be delivered by companies in which all employees are committed to quality and motivated and trained to deliver quality. Successful companies are those which have removed the barriers between departments. Their employees work as a team to carry out core business processes and desired outcomes. Employees are intent to satisfy their internal customers as well as external customers.

4. *Quality Requires High-Quality Partners.* Quality can only be delivered by companies whose value-chain partners are also committed to quality. Therefore, the quality-driven company has a responsibility to find and ally with high-quality suppliers and distributors.

5. *Quality Can Always Be Improved.* The best companies believe in *kaizen,* "continuous improvement of everything by everyone." The best way to improve quality is to benchmark the company's performance against the "best-of-class" competitors and strive to emulate them or even "leapfrog" over them. For example, Alcoa meas- ured the best-of-class competitors and then set a goal of closing the gap by 80% within two years.

6. *Quality Improvement Sometimes Requires Quantum Leaps.* Although quality should be continuously improved, it pays for a company to sometimes target a quantum improvement. Small improvements are often obtainable through working harder. But large improvements call for fresh solutions, for working smarter. For example, John Young of Hewlett Packard did not ask for a 10% reduction in defects; he asked for a tenfold reduction, and got it.

7. *Quality Does Not Cost More.* Philip Crosby argues that "quality is free."[3] The old idea was that achieving more quality would cost more and slow down production. But quality is really improved by learning ways to "do things right the first time." Quality is not inspected in; it must be designed in. When things are done right the first time, many costs are eliminated such as salvage and repair, not to mention losses in customer goodwill. Motorola claims that its quality drive has saved $700 million in manufacturing costs during the last five years.

8. *Quality Is Necessary But May Not Be Sufficient.* Improving a company's quality is absolutely necessary because buyers are becoming more demanding. At the same time, higher quality may not confer a winning advantage, especially as competitors increase their quality to more or less the same extent. For example, Singapore Airlines enjoyed the reputation as the world's best airline. However, competitor airlines have recently been attracting a larger share of passengers as they have narrowed the perceived gap between their service quality and Singapore's service quality.

9. *A Quality Drive Cannot Save a Poor Product.* Pontiac could not save its Fiero automobile simply by launching a quality drive since the car lacked a sports engine. A quality drive cannot compensate for product deficiencies.

SOURCES: 1. John R. Hauser and Don Clausing, "The House of Quality," *Harvard Business Review,* May–June 1988, pp. 63–73. 2. Leonard A. Morgan, "The Importance of Quality," in *Perceived Quality of Products, Services and Stores,* ed. Jacob Jacobi and Jerry Olson (New York: Lexington Books, 1984), p. 61. 3. Philip B. Crosby, *Quality Is Free* (New York: McGraw-Hill, 1979).

At the same time, ironically, marketers must play several major roles in helping their company define and deliver high-quality goods and services to target customers. First, marketers bear the major responsibility for correctly identifying the customers' needs and requirements. Second, marketers must communicate customer expectations correctly to product designers. Third, marketers must make

Winning Through Value in a Market Made Up of Humdrum Household Products: Rubbermaid

Can a company prosper that sells unexciting, "low-involvement" convenience products in a mature market? Can it command a price premium although it is competing with more than 150 other companies making similar products? And can such a company score success with nine out of ten new product introductions in such a market? Yes, if your name is Rubbermaid.

Rubbermaid, Inc., headquartered in Wooster, Ohio, produces and distributes a utilitarian line of plastic and rubber houseware products, including dish drainers, microwave utensils, and plate scrapers. It sells these in over 120,000 retail outlets as well as to commercial and institutional buyers. Its sales and earnings growth have been phenomenal, with sales reaching over $1.6 billion in 1991. Rubbermaid is able to charge 5% to 10% more than competitors, has an 8.3% margin, and a return on average shareholder's equity of 19.7%. Anyone investing $10,000 in Rubbermaid stock in 1980 would have realized $180,000 in 1990. And Rubbermaid continues to be cited as one of America's ten most admired corporations in *Fortune* magazine's annual survey. In fact, it again ranked second, next to Merck, in *Fortune's* 1993 survey.

Stanley Gault took over as Rubbermaid's CEO in 1980 with a goal of seeking a 15% average annual increase in sales, profits, and earnings per share in an industry where household growth was limping along at 2% a year. To achieve this goal, Gault did not resort to standard growth strategies such as price cutting or aggressive acquisition and diversification into unrelated industries. Rubbermaid's stellar success is in large part the result of effective marketing planning, implementation, and control to achieve competitive advantage as the "premium quality, premium price" company in its field.

Rubbermaid's success formula reads like a marketing textbook:

1. *Market and customer feedback.* Rubbermaid is serious about market research and listening to customers' needs. It continuously monitors market trends to spot new needs. Thus, the trend toward smaller households led Rubbermaid to introduce a successful line of space-saving products. Rubbermaid runs focus groups to test color and style preferences and confirms the preferences by carrying out surveys in shopping malls. Its executives personally read letters and listen to complaints to learn how to improve product and service quality.

2. *Focus on target markets.* Rubbermaid is organized in six divisions, each containing separate strategic business units that focus on specific product markets.

3. *Customer satisfaction orientation.* Rubbermaid makes good on every customer complaint, replacing its products free. Even when the complaint is about a product wrongly thought to be Rubbermaid's, the company will send a free Rubbermaid replacement product to illustrate its superiority.

4. *Quality obsession.* Rubbermaid insists on delivering product and service quality to both trade customers and

sure that the customers' orders are filled correctly and on time. Fourth, marketers must check that customers have received proper instructions, training, and technical assistance in the use of the product. Fifth, marketers must stay in touch with customers after the sale to make sure that they are satisfied and remain satisfied. And sixth, marketers must gather and convey customer ideas for product and service improvements to the appropriate company departments. When marketers do all this, they are making their specific contributions to total quality management and customer satisfaction.

An implication is that marketing people must spend time and effort not only to improve external marketing, but also to improve internal marketing. The marketer must complain like the customer complains when the product or the service is not right. Marketing must be the customer watchdog or guardian. Marketing must constantly hold up the standard of "giving the customer the best solution" (see Companies and Industries 2-1).

end users. In making its products, Rubbermaid uses a thicker-gauge plastic and the best resins to insure high durability for its products.

5. *Innovation.* Rubbermaid's product line has grown from a few hundred to over 2,000 products, with 30% of its sales coming from new products introduced in the last five years. Rubbermaid launched 360 new products in 1992, averaging one each day of the year. Its products are launched with record speed, sometimes within 20 weeks of the birth of the idea. New-product cross-functional teams manage the entire process from spotting a need to product introduction. They skip test marketing because of their careful homework with customers to develop the right product, and the wish to avoid exposing their new product to competitors. Rubbermaid achieves the unheard-of new-product success rate of 90%.

6. *Process teamwork.* Rubbermaid organizes its employees into small project and process teams who carry considerable authority, feel a sense of ownership and pride, and who are rewarded for achieving objectives.

7. *Trade partnership.* Rubbermaid works closely with its major retailers such as Wal-Mart and K mart and offers strong reseller support in the form of jointly designed displays, merchandising plans, promotions, and logistics. Rubbermaid has substantially expanded its manufacturing and distribution locations to keep up with its growing volume and to improve delivery time and service to its trade partners.

8. *Strong communication programs.* Rubbermaid engages in extensive advertising to inform target customer segments about its new products and its high quality. It also sponsors co-op ads with retailers that focus on promotions.

9. *Green consciousness.* Rubbermaid uses recyclable plastic when possible and designs its containers for easy recycling. It innovated a litterless lunchbox that can carry food and drink without the need for throw-away sandwich wrappings, paper bags, and juice containers.

10. *Globalization.* Rubbermaid now operates in several countries and has localized its products where necessary to meet each country's varying needs.

In addition to these marketing touchstones for success, Rubbermaid works continuously on productivity improvement. It divested some losing businesses and reorganized others into fewer divisions. Rubbermaid carefully monitors oil prices because of their impact on plastic costs. Rubbermaid continuously invests in state-of-the-art equipment in order to remain the low-cost producer.

SOURCES: See Alex Taylor III, "Why the Bounce at Rubbermaid?" *Fortune,* April 13, 1987, pp. 77–78; James Braham, "The Billion-Dollar Dustpan," *Industry Week,* August 1, 1988, pp. 46–48; Zachary Schiller, "At Rubbermaid, Little Things Mean A Lot," *Business Week,* November 11, 1991, p. 126; and Seth Lubove, "Okay, Call Me A Predator," *Forbes,* February 15, 1993.

SUMMARY ❖

Today's customers face a growing range of choice in the products and services they can buy. They are making their choice on the basis of their perceptions of quality, service, and value. Companies need to understand the determinants of customer value and satisfaction. Customer-delivered value is the difference between total customer value and total customer cost. Customers will normally choose the offer that maximizes the delivered value.

Customer satisfaction is the outcome felt by buyers who have experienced a company performance that has fulfilled expectations. Customers are satisfied when their expectations are met and delighted when their expectations are exceeded. Satisfied customers remain loyal longer, buy more, are less price sensitive, and talk favorably about the company.

CHAPTER 2
Building Customer
Satisfaction Through Quality,
Service, and Value

To create customer satisfaction, companies must manage their value chain as well as the whole value-delivery system in a customer-centered way. The company's goal is not only to get customers but even more importantly, to retain customers. Customer relationship marketing provides the key to retaining customers and involves providing financial and social benefits as well as structural ties to the customers. Companies must decide how much relationship marketing to invest in different market segments and individual customers, from such levels as basic, reactive, accountable, proactive, to full partnership. Much depends on estimating customer lifetime value against the cost stream required to attract and retain these customers.

Total quality management is seen today as a major approach to providing customer satisfaction and company profitability. Companies must understand how their customers perceive quality and how much quality they expect. Companies must then strive to offer relatively higher quality than their competitors. This involves total management and employee commitment as well as measurement and reward systems. Marketers play an especially critical role in their company's drive toward higher quality.

NOTES ❖

1. See, for example, "Value Marketing: Quality, Service, and Fair Pricing Are the Keys to Selling in the '90s," *Business Week*, November 11, 1991, pp. 132–40.

2. See Irwin P. Levin and Richard D. Johnson, "Estimating Price-Quality Tradeoffs Using Comparative Judgments," *Journal of Consumer Research*, June 11, 1984, pp. 593–600.

3. Michael E. Porter, *Competitive Advantage: Creating and Sustaining Superior Performance* (New York: Free Press, 1985).

4. See George Stalk, "Competing on Capability: The New Rules of Corporate Strategy," *Harvard Business Review*, March–April 1992, pp. 57–69; and Benson P. Shapiro, V. Kasturi Rangan, and John J. Sviokla, "Staple Yourself to an Order," *Harvard Business Review*, July–August 1992, pp. 113–22.

5. Frederick F. Reichheld and W. Earl Sasser, Jr., "Zero Defections: Quality Comes to Services," *Harvard Business Review*, September–October 1990, pp. 301–07.

6. Leonard L. Berry and A. Parasuraman, *Marketing Services: Competing Through Quality* (New York: The Free Press, 1991), pp. 136–42.

7. James H. Donnelly, Jr., Leonard L. Berry, and Thomas W. Thompson, *Marketing Financial Services—A Strategic Vision* (Homewood, IL: Dow Jones-Irwin, 1985), p. 113.

8. Michael J. Lanning and Lynn W. Phillips, "Strategy Shifts Up a Gear," *Marketing*, October 1991, p. 9.

9. See Thomas M. Petro, "Profitability: The Fifth 'P' of Marketing," *Bank Marketing*, September 1990, pp. 48–52; and Petro, "Who Are Your Best Customers?" *Bank Marketing*, October 1990, pp. 48–52.

10. "Quality: The U.S. Drives to Catch Up," *Business Week*, November 1982, pp. 66–80, here p. 68. For a recent assessment of progress, see "Quality Programs Show Shoddy Results," *The Wall Street Journal*, May 14, 1992, Section B, p. 1.

11. Robert D. Buzzell and Bradley T. Gale, *The PIMS Principles: Linking Strategy to Performance* (New York: The Free Press, 1987), Chapter 6.

12. See "The Gurus of Quality: American Companies Are Hearing the Quality Gospel Preached by Deming, Juran, Crosby, and Taguchi," *Traffic Management*, July 1990, pp. 35–39.

13. The International Organization for Standardization recently propagated a set of standards known as ISO 9000, which is rapidly being adopted by European companies. Unfortunately, U.S. firms know little about ISO 9000 and few have registered. This portends a possible future handicap when U.S. companies try to sell in European Community countries. See Cyndee Miller, "U.S. Firms Lag in Meeting Global Quality Standards," *Marketing News*, February 15, 1993.

14. J. Daniel Beckham, "Expect the Unexpected in Health Care Marketing Future," *The Academy Bulletin*, July 1992, p. 3.

15. Kenneth Kivenko, *Quality Control For Management* (Englewood Cliffs, NJ: Prentice-Hall, Inc., 1984). Also see Kate Bertrand, "Marketing Discovers What 'Quality' Really Means," *Business Marketing*, April 1987, pp. 58–72.

3

Laying the Groundwork Through Market-Oriented Strategic Planning

If we don't change our direction, we are likely to end up where we are headed.

OLD CHINESE PROVERB

There are five types of companies: those who make things happen; those who think they make things happen; those who watch things happen; those who wonder what happened; and those that did not know that anything had happened.

ANONYMOUS

In Chapters 1 and 2, we raised the question: "What makes a company excellent?" We found that a large part of the answer is that the company's managers and employees are committed to creating satisfied customers. We can now add a second part to the answer, namely that excellent companies know how to adapt to a continuously changing marketplace. They practice the art of *market-oriented strategic planning.*

❖ Market-oriented strategic planning *is the managerial process of developing and maintaining a viable fit between the organization's objectives, skills, and resources and its changing market opportunities. The aim of strategic planning is to shape and reshape the company's businesses and products so that they yield target profits and growth.*

Strategic planning and its set of special concepts and tools emerged in the 1970s as a result of a succession of shock waves—the energy crisis, double-digit inflation, economic stagnation, Japanese competitive victories, deregulation of key industries—that hit American industry. No longer could U.S. companies rely on simple growth projections in planning their production, sales, and profits. Conventional long-range planning needed to be converted into strategic planning.

The aim of strategic planning is to help a company select and organize its businesses in a way that would keep the company healthy in spite of unexpected upsets occurring in any of its specific businesses or product lines.

Three key ideas defined strategic planning. The first called for managing a company's businesses as an *investment portfolio,* for which it would be decided which business entities deserve to be *built, maintained, phased down* (harvested, milked), or *terminated.* Each business has a different profit potential, and the company's resources should be allocated according to each business's profit potential.

The second key idea is to assess accurately the *future profit potential* of each business by considering the market's growth rate and the company's position and fit. It is not sufficient to use current sales or profits as a guide. For example:

> If the Ford Motor Company used current profits as a guide to investment in the seventies, it would have continued to pour money into large cars, since that was where it made its money. But Ford's analysis showed that the profits on large cars would dry up, and therefore Ford needed to reallocate its funds to improving its compact cars, even though the company was losing money on compact cars at the time.

The third key idea underlying strategic planning is that of *strategy.* For each business, the company must develop a "game plan" for achieving its long-run objectives. Furthermore, there is no one strategy that is optimal for all competitors in that business. Each company must determine what makes the most sense in the light of its *industry position* and its *objectives, opportunities, skills,* and *resources.* Thus, in the rubber-tire industry:

> Goodyear is pressing for *cost reduction*; Michelin is pursuing *innovation*; and Bridgestone is pressing for market share. Each strategy can be successful under the right circumstances.

Marketing plays a critical role in the company's strategic-planning process. According to a strategic-planning manager at General Electric:

> . . . the marketing manager is the most significant functional contributor to the strategic-planning process, with leadership roles in defining the business mission; analysis of the environmental, competitive, and business situations; developing objectives, goals, and strategies; and defining product, market, distribution, and quality plans to implement the business's strategies. This involvement extends to the development of programs and operating plans that are fully linked with the strategic plan.[1]

To understand strategic planning, we need to recognize that most large companies consist of four organizational levels: the *corporate level*, *division level*, *business level*, and *product level*. Corporate headquarters is responsible for designing a *corporate strategic plan* to guide the whole enterprise into a profitable future; it makes decisions on how much resource support to allocate to each division as well as which businesses to start or eliminate. Each division establishes a *division plan* covering the allocation of funds to each business unit within the division. Each business unit in turn develops a *business unit strategic plan* to carry that business unit into a profitable future. Finally, each product level (product line, brand) within a business unit develops a *marketing plan* for achieving its objectives in its product market. These plans are then implemented at the various levels of the organization, results are monitored and evaluated, and corrective actions are taken. The whole planning, implementation, and control cycle is shown in Figure 3-1.

In this chapter, we will first examine the nature of a *high-performance business* and then examine the major concepts and tools for carrying out *corporate strategic planning* and *business strategic planning*. In the next chapter, we will focus on marketing planning and the overall marketing management process.

The Nature of High-Performance Businesses

The major challenge facing today's companies is how to build and maintain viable businesses in the face of the rapidly changing marketplace and environment. At one time, the answer was thought to lie in increasing production efficiency. Later companies sought growth and profits through vigorous acquisition and diversification programs. They saw their businesses as constituting an investment portfolio to which they added promising businesses and removed faltering businesses. Still later, companies were told to "stick to their knitting" and stay in businesses they knew well and where they had superior core competences.

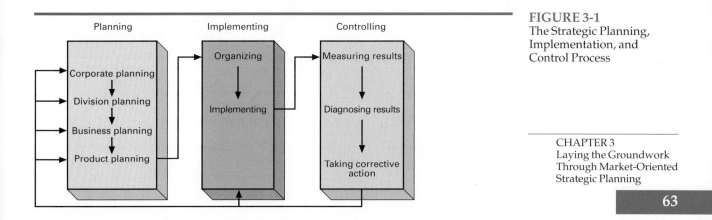

CHAPTER 3
Laying the Groundwork
Through Market-Oriented
Strategic Planning

63

Recently, the consulting firm of Arthur D. Little proposed a model of the characteristics of a *high-performance business*. They pointed to the four factors shown in Figure 3-2.[2] We will review these factors here.

Stakeholders

The starting point for any business is to define the stakeholders and their needs. Traditionally, most businesses primarily nourished their stockholders. Today's businesses, however, are increasingly recognizing that unless other stakeholders—customers, employees, suppliers, distributors—are nourished, the business may never earn sufficient profits for the stockholders. Thus, if General Motors' employees, customers, dealers, and suppliers are unhappy, profits will not be achieved. This leads to the principle that a business must at least strive to satisfy the minimum expectations of each stakeholder group.

At the same time, the company can aim to deliver satisfaction levels above the minimum for different stakeholders. The company can deliver to any stakeholder a *threshold level*, a *performance level*, or an *excitement level* of satisfaction. Thus, the company might aim to delight the customers, to perform well for the employees, and to deliver a threshold level of satisfaction to the suppliers, at least in the coming planning period. In setting these levels, the company must be careful not to violate the sense of fairness among stakeholders about the relative treatment they are getting.

There is a dynamic relationship connecting the stakeholder groups. This is shown in Figure 3-3. The progressive company creates a high level of employee satisfaction which leads employees to work on continuous improvements as well as breakthrough innovations. The result is higher-quality products and services which create high customer satisfaction. Their satisfaction leads to repeat business and therefore higher growth and profits, both of which deliver high stockholder satisfaction. This cycles back and permits building a still higher-quality environment for employees.

Processes

A company can only accomplish its satisfaction goals through managing work processes. Company work is traditionally carried on by departments. But departmental organization poses some problems. Departments typically operate to maximize their own objectives, not necessarily the company's objectives. Walls come up

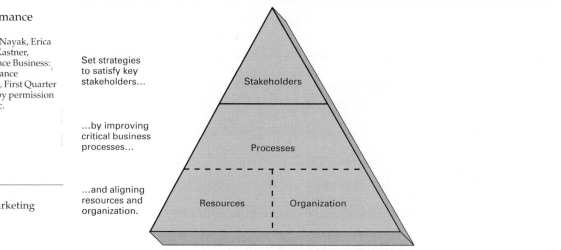

FIGURE 3-2
The High-Performance
Business
Source: P. Ranganath Nayak, Erica Drazen, and George Kastner, "The High-Performance Business: Accelerating Performance Improvement," *Prism,* First Quarter 1992, p. 6. Reprinted by permission of Arthur D. Little, Inc.

Set strategies
to satisfy key
stakeholders...

Stakeholders

...by improving
critical business
processes...

Processes

...and aligning
resources and
organization.

Resources | Organization

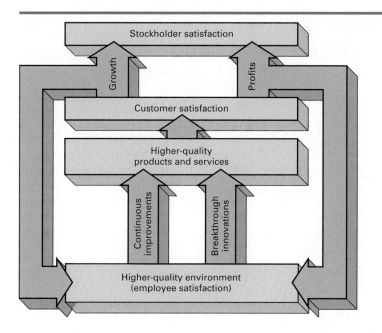

FIGURE 3-3
Dynamic Relationships
Among Stakeholder Groups
in a High-Performance
Business
Source: Ray Stata, "Organizational
Learning: The Key to Success in the
1990s," *Prism,* Fourth Quarter 1992,
p. 102.

between departments and there is usually less than ideal cooperation. Work is slowed down and plans often are altered as they pass from department to department.

Companies are increasingly refocusing their attention on the need to manage processes even more than departments. They are studying how tasks pass from department to department and the impediments to effective output. They are now building cross-functional teams that manage core business processes. They believe that superior competitors will be those who achieve excellent capabilities in managing core business processes.

Resources

To carry out processes, a company needs resources such as manpower, materials, machines, and information. These resources can be owned, leased, or rented. Traditionally, companies sought to own and control most of the resources that entered their business. But now this is changing. Companies are finding that some resources under their control are not performing as well as those that they could obtain from outside. They could access certain outside resources at a lower cost. More companies today have decided to *outsource* less critical resources. On the other hand, they appreciate the need to own and nurture those core resources and competences that make up the essence of their business. Smart companies are identifying their core competences and using them as the basis for their strategic planning of future products and businesses.

Organization

The organizational side of a company consists of its structure, policies, and culture, all of which tend to become dysfunctional in a rapidly changing economy. While structure and policies can be changed, albeit with difficulty, the company's culture is the hardest to change and yet is often the key to change. Companies must work hard to align their organization's structure, policies, and culture to the changing requirements of business strategy.

Corporate Strategic Planning

Corporate headquarters has the responsibility for setting into motion the whole planning process. By preparing statements of mission, policy, strategy, and goals, headquarters establishes the framework within which the divisions and business units prepare their plans. Some corporations give a lot of freedom to their business units to set their own sales and profit goals and strategies; others set goals for their business units but let them develop their own strategies; still others set the goals and get heavily involved in the strategies of the individual business units.[3]

We will now examine four planning activities that all corporate headquarters must undertake:

- Defining the corporate mission
- Establishing strategic business units (SBUs)
- Assigning resources to each SBU
- Planning new businesses

Defining the Corporate Mission

An organization exists to accomplish something: to make cars, lend money, provide a night's lodging, and so on. Its specific mission or purpose is usually clear at the beginning. Over time some managers may lose interest in the mission, or the mission may lose its relevance in the light of changed market conditions. Or the mission may become unclear as the organization adds new products and markets. Recently, American Can sold its original business, canning; clearly American Can is redefining its mission.

When management senses that the organization is drifting, it must renew its search for purpose. According to Peter Drucker, it is time to ask some fundamental questions.[4] *What is our business? Who is the customer? What is value to the customer? What will our business be? What should our business be?* These simple-sounding questions are among the most difficult the company will ever have to answer. Successful companies continuously raise these questions and answer them thoughtfully and thoroughly.

The company's mission is shaped by five elements. The first is its *history*. Every company has a history of aims, policies, and achievements. The organization must not depart too radically from its past history. It would not make sense for Harvard University, for example, to open two-year junior colleges, even if these colleges represented a growth opportunity. The second consideration is the *current preferences* of the owners and management. If Zenith's current management wants to get out of the television-receiver business, this is going to influence Zenith's mission statement. Third, *the market environment* influences the organization's mission. The Girl Scouts of America would not recruit successfully in today's market environment with their former purpose, "to prepare young girls for motherhood and wifely duties." Fourth, the organization's *resources* determine which missions are possible. Singapore Airlines would be deluding itself if it adopted the mission to become the world's largest airline. Finally, the organization should base its mission on its *distinctive competences*. McDonald's could probably enter the solar energy business, but that would not use its core competence—providing low-cost food and fast service to large groups of customers. (See Marketing Strategies 3-1.)

Organizations develop mission statements in order to share them with their managers, employees, and in many cases, customers and other publics. A well-worked-out mission statement provides company employees with a shared sense of purpose, direction, and opportunity. The company mission statement acts as an

Marketing Strategies 3-1

Should a Company Focus on Its Core Competence or Its End Products?

Professors Gary Hamel and C. K. Prahalad wrote an insightful article pointing out that the Japanese have outsmarted U.S. companies by leveraging their *core competences* while U.S. companies have been systematically abandoning their core competences. They define a core competence as one that provides a potential access to a wide variety of markets, makes a significant contribution to the perceived customer benefits of the end product, and is difficult for competitors to imitate.

Chrysler, for example, no longer makes its own engines, preferring to outsource them from Mitsubishi. How can an automobile company compete in the long run when it no longer commands the core skills to make something as basic to a car as its engine? Many other U.S. companies no longer even make the end products on which they put their name: Apple's laptop computer, Magnavox's video recorder, and RCA's fax machine are simply U.S. company names put on outsourced products made by Japanese, South Korean, and other Far Eastern companies. All of this portends a "hollowing out" of U.S. technology and manufacturing skills.

In contrast, Japan's Honda has nurtured its major core competence, namely making engines. Its skill at designing and improving engines has been the basis of its move into such end products as motorcycles, automobiles, lawnmowers, snowmobiles, power tillers, and outboard motors. Similarly, Canon's skills in fine optics, precision mechanics, and microelectronics are the basis for its success with such products as copy machines, video cameras, printers, and Fax machines.

Prahalad and Hamel dramatize the contrasting strategies by offering the metaphor of a tree in which the roots are *core competences* (basic skills in making engines), the trunk is *core products* (such as engines), the branches are *business units* (cars, motorcycles, and so on), and the leaves are *end products* (Accord, Civic, and so on). Companies that only work at the business unit and/or end products levels will increasingly be at the mercy of those who work at the roots and trunk level of the "tree."

The message is clear. A company must sharply distinguish between what it can afford to buy on the outside and what it must master and produce for itself. Thus Xerox can safely buy paper stock and glass from outside vendors, but it would make a mistake if it gave up its research strength in material science, mechanics, and optics.

SOURCE: C. K. Prahalad and Gary Hamel, "The Core Competence of the Corporation," *Harvard Business Review*, May–June 1990, pp. 79–91.

"invisible hand" that guides geographically dispersed employees to work independently and yet collectively toward realizing the organization's goals.

Writing a formal mission statement is not easy. Some organizations spend a year or two trying to prepare a satisfactory statement about their company's purpose. In the process, they generally discover a lot about themselves and their potential opportunities.

Good mission statements embody a number of characteristics. They should focus on a limited number of *goals*. The statement "We want to produce the highest-quality products, offer the most service, achieve the widest distribution, and sell at the lowest prices" claims too much. It fails to supply guidelines when management faces difficult decisions.

The mission statement should define the major *competitive scopes* within which the company will operate.

- *Industry scope:* The range of industries that the company will consider. Some companies will operate in only one industry, some in only a set of related industries, some in only industrial goods, consumer goods, or services, and finally some in any industry. For example, Du Pont prefers to operate in the industrial market, whereas Dow is willing to operate in the industrial and consumer markets. 3M will get into almost any industry where it can make money.

CHAPTER 3
Laying the Groundwork
Through Market-Oriented
Strategic Planning

- *Products and applications scope:* The range of products and applications in which the company will participate. Thus, a steel manufacturer might limit itself to products for the construction industry.

- *Competencies scope:* The range of technological and other core competencies that the company will master and leverage. Thus, Japan's NEC has built its core competencies in computing, communications, and components; and these support its production of laptop computers, television receivers, hand-held telephones, and so on.

- *Market-segment scope:* The type of market or customers the company will serve. Some companies will serve only the upscale market. For example, Porsche makes only expensive cars, sunglasses, and other accessories, and Gerber primarily serves the baby market.

- *Vertical scope:* The number of channel levels from raw material to final product and distribution in which the company will engage. At one extreme are companies with a large vertical scope; at one time Ford owned its own rubber plantations, sheep farms, glass manufacturing plants, and some steel foundries. At the other extreme are corporations with low or no vertical integration, such as the "hollow corporation" or "pure marketing company," which consists of a person with a phone, fax, computer, and desk who contracts outside for every service including design, manufacture, marketing, and physical distribution.[5]

- *Geographical scope:* The range of regions, countries, or country groups where the corporation will operate. At one extreme are companies that operate in a specific city or state; at the other extreme are multinationals like Unilever or Caterpillar, which operate in almost every one of the world's 150-plus countries.

The company's mission statement should be *motivating.* Employees need to feel that their work is significant and contributes to people's lives. Contrast IBM and Apple Computer's missions. When IBM sales were $50 billion, President John Akers said that IBM's goal was to become a $100 billion company by the end of the century. Meanwhile Apple's long-term goal has been to put computer power into the hands of every person. Apple's mission is much more motivating than IBM's mission. A company's mission should not be stated as making more sales or profits. Profits are a reward to risk takers for investing in a useful activity.

Missions are at their best when they are guided by a *vision,* an almost "impossible dream." Sony's president, Akio Morita, wanted everyone to have access to "personal portable sound," and his company created the Walkman. Fred Smith wanted to deliver mail anywhere in the United States before 10:30 A.M. the next day, and he created Federal Express. Thomas Monaghan wanted to deliver hot pizza to any home within thirty minutes, and he created Domino's Pizza.

The corporate mission statement should stress major *policies* that the company wants to honor. Policies define how employees should deal with customers, suppliers, distributors, competitors, and other important groups. Policies narrow the range of individual discretion, so that employees act consistently on important issues.

The company's mission statement should provide a vision and direction for the company for the next ten to twenty years. Missions are not revised every few years in response to every new turn in the economy. On the other hand, a company must redefine its mission if that mission has lost credibility or no longer defines an optimal course for the company.[6]

Establishing Strategic Business Units

Most companies operate several businesses. However, they often fail to define them carefully. Companies too often define their businesses in terms of products. They are in the "auto business" or the "slide-rule business." But Levitt argued that market definitions of a business are superior to product definitions.[7] A business must be viewed as a *customer-satisfying process*, not a *goods-producing process*. Products are transient, but basic needs and customer groups endure forever. A horse-carriage company will go out of business soon after the automobile is invented, unless it switches to making cars. Levitt encouraged companies to redefine their business in terms of needs, not products. Several examples are given in Table 3-1.

Management, of course, should avoid a market definition that is too narrow or too broad. Consider a lead-pencil manufacturer. If it sees itself as a *writing-instruments company*, it might expand into the production of pens. If it sees itself as a *writing-equipment company*, it might consider making word processors. The broadest concept of its business is that it is a *communication company*, but this would be stretching things too far for a lead-pencil manufacturer.

> Holiday Inns, Inc., the world's largest hotel chain with over 300,000 rooms, fell into this trap. Some years ago it broadened its business definition from the "hotel business" to the "travel industry." It acquired Trailways, Inc., the nation's second largest bus company, and Delta Steamship Lines, Inc. But Holiday Inns did not manage these companies well and later divested these properties. Holiday Inns decided to "stick close to its knitting," and concentrate on the "hospitality industry".[8]

A business can be defined, according to Abell, in terms of three dimensions: *customer groups*, *customer needs*, and *technology*.[9] Consider, for example, a small company that designs incandescent lighting systems for television studios. Its customer group is television studios; the customer need is lighting; and the technology is incandescent lighting. The company's *business domain* is defined by the floating cell in Figure 3-4. This diagram gives a very clear picture of the company's business.

The company might want to expand into additional businesses. For example, it could make lighting for other customer groups, such as homes, factories, and offices. Or it could supply other services needed by television studios, such as heating, ventilation, or air conditioning. Or it could design other lighting technologies for television studios, such as infrared or ultraviolet lighting. Each business is defined by the intersection of the three dimensions. If this company expands into other cells, we say that it has widened its business domain.

Companies have to identify their businesses in order to manage them strategically. General Electric went through this grueling exercise some years ago and identified 49 *strategic business units* (SBUs). An SBU has three characteristics:

1. It is a single business or collection of related businesses that can be planned separately from the rest of the company.
2. It has its own set of competitors.
3. It has a manager who is responsible for strategic planning and profit performance and who controls most of the factors affecting profit.

TABLE 3-1
Product-Oriented Versus Market-Oriented Definitions of a Business

COMPANY	PRODUCT	MARKET DEFINITION
Revlon	We make cosmetics.	We sell hope.
Missouri-Pacific Railroad	We run a railroad.	We are a people-and-goods mover.
Xerox	We make copying equipment.	We help improve office productivity.
Standard Oil	We sell gasoline.	We supply energy.
Columbia Pictures	We make movies.	We market entertainment.
Encyclopedia Britannica	We sell encyclopedias.	We distribute information.
Carrier	We make air conditioners and furnaces.	We provide climate control in the home.

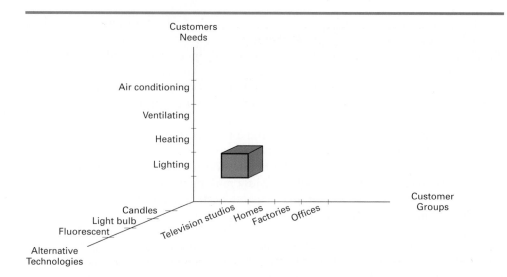

Assigning Resources to Each SBU

The purpose of identifying the company's strategic business units is to assign to these units strategic-planning goals and appropriate funding. These units send their plans to company headquarters, which approves them or sends them back for revision. Headquarters reviews these plans in order to decide which of its SBUs to *build, maintain, harvest*, and *divest*. Senior management knows that its portfolio of businesses includes a number of "yesterday's has-beens" as well as "tomorrow's breadwinners." But it cannot rely just on impressions; it needs analytical tools for classifying its businesses by profit potential. Two of the best known business portfolio evaluation models are the Boston Consulting Group model and the General Electric model.[10]

BOSTON CONSULTING GROUP APPROACH ❖ The Boston Consulting Group (BCG), a leading management consulting firm, developed and popularized the *growth-share matrix* shown in Figure 3-5. The eight circles represent the current sizes and positions of eight businesses making up a hypothetical company. The dollar-volume size of each business is proportional to the circle's area: thus, the two largest businesses are 5 and 6. The location of each business indicates its market growth rate and relative market share.

Specifically, the *market growth rate* on the vertical axis indicates the annual growth rate of the market in which the business operates; in the figure, it ranges from 0% to 20%, although a larger range could be shown. A market growth rate above 10% is considered high.

The horizontal axis, *relative market share*, refers to the SBU's market share relative to that of the largest competitor. It serves as a measure of the company's strength in the relevant market. A relative market share of 0.1 means that the company's sales volume is only 10% of the leader's sales volume; and 10 means that the company's SBU is the leader and has ten times the sales of the next-strongest company in that market. Relative market share is divided into high and low share, using 1.0 as the dividing line. Relative market share is drawn in log scale, so that equal distances represent the same percentage increase.

The growth-share matrix is divided into four cells, each indicating a different type of business:

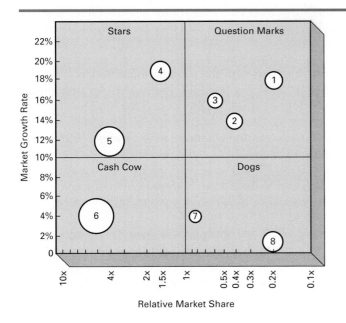

FIGURE 3-5
The Boston Consulting
Group's Growth-Share
Matrix
Source: B. Heldey, "Strategy and the
Business Portfolio," *Long Range
Planning*, February 1977, p. 12.
Reprinted with permission from
Long Range Planning, copyright ©
1977, Pergamon Press, Ltd.

◆ *Question marks:* Question marks are company businesses that operate in high-growth markets but have low relative market shares. Most businesses start off as a question mark in that the company tries to enter a high-growth market in which there is already a market leader. A question mark requires a lot of cash, since the company has to add plants, equipment, and personnel to keep up with the fast-growing market, and additionally, it wants to overtake the leader. The term *question mark* is well chosen because the company has to think hard about whether to keep pouring money into this business. The company in Figure 3-5 operates three question-mark businesses, and this may be too many. The company might be better off investing more cash in one or two of these businesses instead of spreading its cash thinly over all three businesses.

◆ *Stars:* If the question-mark business is successful, it becomes a star. A star is the market leader in a high-growth market. This does not necessarily mean that the star produces a positive cash flow for the company. The company must spend substantial funds to keep up with the high market growth and fight off competitors' attacks. Stars are usually profitable and become the company's future cash cows. In the illustration, the company has two stars. The company would justifiably be concerned if it had no stars.

◆ *Cash cows:* When a market's annual growth rate falls to less than 10%, the star becomes a cash cow if it still has the largest relative market share. A cash cow produces a lot of cash for the company. The company does not have to finance a lot of capacity expansion because the market's growth rate has slowed down. And since the business is the market leader, it enjoys economies of scale and higher profit margins. The company uses its cash-cow businesses to pay its bills and support the stars, question marks, and dogs, which tend to be cash hungry. In the illustration, however, the company has only one cash-cow business and is therefore highly vulnerable. In the event this cash cow starts losing relative market share, the company has to pump enough money back into its cash cow to maintain market leadership. If instead it uses the throw-off cash to support its other businesses, its strong cash cow may transform into a dog business.

◆ *Dogs:* Dogs describe company businesses that have weak market shares in low-growth markets. They typically generate low profits or losses, although they may throw off some cash. The company in the illustration manages two dog businesses, and this may be two too many. The company should consider whether it is holding on to these dog businesses for good reasons (such as an expected turnaround in the market growth rate or a new chance at market leadership) or for sentimental reasons. Dog businesses often consume more management time than they are worth and need to be phased down or out.

Having plotted its various businesses in the growth-share matrix, the company then determines whether its business portfolio is healthy. An unbalanced portfolio would have too many dogs or question marks and/or too few stars and cash cows.

The company's next task is to determine what objective, strategy, and budget to assign to each SBU. Four alternative objectives can be pursued:

- *Build:* Here the objective is to increase the SBU's market share, even foregoing short-term earnings to achieve this objective. "Building" is appropriate for question marks whose shares have to grow if they are to become stars.
- *Hold:* Here the objective is to preserve the SBU's market share. This objective is appropriate for strong cash cows if they are to continue to yield a large positive cash flow.
- *Harvest:* Here the objective is to increase the SBU's short-term cash flow regardless of the long-term effect. This strategy is appropriate for weak cash cows whose future is dim and from whom more cash flow is needed. Harvesting can also be used with question marks and dogs.
- *Divest:* Here the objective is to sell or liquidate the business because resources can be better used elsewhere. That is appropriate for dogs and question marks that are acting as a drag on the company's profits.

As time passes, SBUs change their position in the growth-share matrix. Successful SBUs have a life cycle. They start as question marks, become stars, then cash cows, and finally dogs toward the end of their life cycle. For this reason, companies should examine not only the current positions of their businesses in the growth-share matrix (as in a snapshot) but also their moving positions (as in a motion picture). Each business should be reviewed as to where it was in past years, and where it will probably move in future years. If the expected trajectory of a given business is not satisfactory, the company should ask its business's manager to propose a new strategy and the likely resulting trajectory. Thus, the growth-share matrix becomes a planning framework for the strategic planners at company headquarters. They use it to try to assess each business and assign the most reasonable objective.

Although the portfolio in Figure 3-5 is basically healthy, wrong objectives or strategies could be assigned. The worst mistake would be to require all the SBUs to aim for the same growth rate or return level; the very point of SBU analysis is that each business has a different potential and requires its own objective. Additional mistakes would include

1. Leaving cash-cow businesses with too little in retained funds, in which case they grow weak; or leaving them with too much in retained funds, in which case the company fails to invest enough in new growth businesses.

2. Making major investments in dogs hoping to turn them around but failing each time.

3. Maintaining too many question marks and underinvesting in each; question marks should either receive enough support to achieve segment dominance or be dropped.

GENERAL ELECTRIC APPROACH ❖ The appropriate objective to assign to an SBU cannot be determined solely on the basis of its position in the growth-share matrix. If additional factors are introduced, the growth-share matrix can be seen as a special case of a multifactor portfolio matrix that General Electric (GE) pioneered. This model is shown in Figure 3-6(a), and seven businesses of a disguised company are plotted. This time the size of the circle represents the size of the relevant market rather than the size of the company's business. And the shaded part of the circle represents that business's market share. Thus, the company's clutch business operates in a moderate-size market and enjoys approximately a 30% market share.

Each business is rated in terms of two major dimensions, *market attractiveness* and *business strength*. These two factors make excellent marketing sense for rating a business. Companies will be successful to the extent that they go into attractive markets and possess the required business strengths to succeed in those markets. If one or the other is missing, the business will not produce outstanding results. Neither a strong company operating in an unattractive market nor a weak company operating in an attractive market will do very well.

The real issue, then, is to measure these two dimensions. To do so, the strategic planners must identify the factors underlying each dimension and find a way to measure them and combine them into an index. Table 3-2 illustrates sets of factors making up the two dimensions. (Each company has to decide on its list of factors.) Thus, market attractiveness varies with the market's size, annual market growth rate, historical profit margins, and so on. And competitive position varies with the company's market share, share growth, product quality, and so on. Note that the two BCG factors, market growth rate and market share, are subsumed under the two major variables of the GE model. The GE model leads strategic planners to look at more factors in evaluating an actual or potential business than the BCG model.

TABLE 3-2
Factors Underlying Market Attractiveness and Competitive Position in GE Multifactor Portfolio Model: Hydraulic-Pumps Market

		WEIGHT	RATING (1 – 5)	VALUE
Market Attract-iveness	Overall market size	0.20	4.00	0.80
	Annual market growth rate	0.20	5.00	1.00
	Historical profit margin	0.15	4.00	0.60
	Competitive intensity	0.15	2.00	0.30
	Technological requirements	0.15	4.00	0.60
	Inflationary vulnerability	0.05	3.00	0.15
	Energy requirements	0.05	2.00	0.10
	Environmental impact	0.05	3.00	0.15
	Social/political/legal	Must be acceptable		
		1.00		3.70

		WEIGHT	RATING (1 – 5)	VALUE
Business Strength	Market share	0.10	4.00	0.40
	Share growth	0.15	2.00	0.30
	Product quality	0.10	4.00	0.40
	Brand reputation	0.10	5.00	0.50
	Distribution network	0.05	4.00	0.20
	Promotional effectiveness	0.05	3.00	0.15
	Productive capacity	0.05	3.00	0.15
	Productive efficiency	0.05	2.00	0.10
	Unit costs	0.15	3.00	0.45
	Material supplies	0.05	5.00	0.25
	R&D performance	0.10	3.00	0.30
	Managerial personnel	0.05	4.00	0.20
		1.00		3.40

Source: Slightly modified from La Rue T. Hosmer, *Strategic Management* (Englewood Cliffs, NJ: Prentice-Hall, 1982), p. 310.

FIGURE 3-6
Market Attractiveness—
Portfolio Classification and
Strategies
Source: Slightly modified and
adapted with permission from
*Analysis for Strategic Marketing
Decisions* by George S. Day
(St. Paul, MN: West Publishing,
1986), pp. 202 and 204.

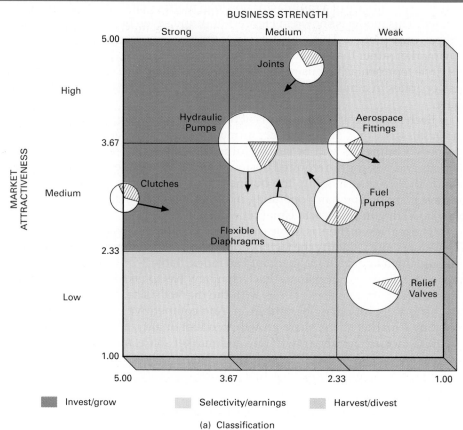

(a) Classification

BUSINESS STRENGTH

	Strong	Medium	Weak
High	**PROTECT POSITION** • invest to grow at maximum digestible rate • concentrate effort on maintaining strength	**INVEST TO BUILD** • challenge for leadership • build selectively on strengths • reinforce vulnerable areas	**BUILD SELECTIVELY** • specialize around limited strengths • seeks ways to overcome weaknesses • withdraw if indications of sustainable growth are lacking
Medium	**BUILD SELECTIVELY** • invest heavily in most attractive segments • build up ability to counter competition • emphasize profitability by raising productivity	**SELECTIVITY/MANAGE FOR EARNINGS** • protect existing program • concentrate investments in segments where profitability is good and risks are relatively low	**LIMITED EXPANSION OR HARVEST** • look for ways to expand without high risk; otherwise, minimize investment and rationalize operations
Low	**PROTECT AND REFOCUS** • manage for current earnings • concentrate on attractive segments • defend strengths	**MANAGE FOR EARNINGS** • protect position in most profitable segments • upgrade product line • minimize investment	**DIVEST** • sell at time that will maximize cash value • cut fixed costs and avoid investment meanwhile

MARKET ATTRACTIVENESS

(b) Strategies

Table 3-2 shows a hypothetical rating for the hydraulic-pumps business. Management rates each factor from 1 (very unattractive) to 5 (very attractive) to reflect how the business stands on that factor. In the illustration, the hydraulic-pumps business is rated 4.00 on overall market size, indicating that the market size is pretty large (a 5.00 would be very large). Clearly, these factors require data and assessment from marketing and other company personnel. The ratings are then multiplied by weights reflecting the factors' relative importance to arrive at the values, which are summed for each dimension. The hydraulic-pumps business scored a 3.70 on market attractiveness and a 3.40 on business strength, out of a maximum possible score of 5.00 for each. The analyst places a point in the multifactor matrix in Figure 3-6(a) representing this business and draws a circle around it whose size is proportional to the size of the relevant market. The company's market share of approximately 14% is shaded in. Clearly, the hydraulic-pumps business is in a fairly attractive part of the matrix.

In fact, the GE matrix is divided into nine cells, which in turn fall into three zones. The three cells at the upper left indicate strong SBUs in which the company should *invest/grow*. The diagonal cells stretching from the lower left to the upper right indicate SBUs that are medium in overall attractiveness: The company should pursue *selectivity/earnings*. The three cells at the lower right indicate SBUs that are low in overall attractiveness: The company should give serious thought to *harvest/divest*. For example, the relief-values business represents an SBU with a small market share in a fair-size market that is not very attractive and in which the company has a weak competitive position: It is a fit candidate for harvest/divest.[11]

Management should also forecast the expected position of each SBU in the next three to five years given the current strategy. This involves analyzing where each product is in its product life cycle, as well as expected competitor strategies, new technologies, economic events, and so on. The results are indicated by the length and direction of the vectors in Figure 3-6(a). For example, the hydraulic-pumps business is expected to decline slightly in market attractiveness, and the clutches business is expected to decline strongly in the company's business strength.

The final step is for management to decide what it wants to do with each business. Figure 3-6(b) outlines plausible strategy options for businesses in each cell. The strategy for each business has to be discussed and debated. The intent is for business and corporate management to agree on the objectives and strategies for each business and the funds necessary to achieve these objectives.

Marketing managers will discover that their objective is not always to build sales in each SBU. Their job might be to maintain the existing demand with fewer marketing dollars or to take cash out of the business and allow demand to fall. *Thus, the task of marketing management is to manage demand or revenue to the target level negotiated with the corporate management*. Marketing contributes to assessing each SBU's sales and profit potential, but once the SBU's objective and budget are set, marketing's job is to carry out the plan efficiently and profitably.

CRITIQUE OF PORTFOLIO MODELS ❖ Other portfolio models have been developed and used, particularly the Arthur D. Little model and the Shell directional-policy model.[12] The use of portfolio models has produced a number of benefits. The models have helped managers to think more futuristically and strategically, to understand the economics of their businesses better, to improve the quality of their plans, to improve communication between business and corporate management, to pinpoint information gaps and important issues, and to eliminate weaker businesses and strengthen their investment in more promising businesses.

On the other hand, portfolio models must be used cautiously. They may lead the company to place too much emphasis on market-share growth and entry into high-growth businesses, to the neglect of managing the current businesses well. The results are sensitive to the ratings and weights and can be manipulated to produce a desired location in the matrix. Furthermore, since an averaging process is occurring, two or more businesses may end up in the same cell position but differ greatly in the underlying ratings and weights. A lot of businesses will end up in the middle of the matrix owing to compromises in ratings, and this makes it hard to know what the appropriate strategy should be. Finally, the models fail to delineate the synergies between two or more businesses, which means that making decisions for one business at a time might be risky. There is a danger of terminating a losing business unit that actually provides an essential core competence needed by several other business units. Overall, however, portfolio models have improved the analytical and strategic capabilities of managers and permitted them to make tough decisions on a more data-oriented and hard-nosed basis than mere impressions would permit.

Planning New Businesses

The company's plans for its existing businesses will allow it to project total sales and profits. Often, however, projected sales and profit will be less than what corporate management wants to achieve over the planning horizon. After all, the portfolio plan will include divesting some businesses, and these will need replacement. If there is a gap between future desired sales and projected sales, corporate management will have to develop or acquire new businesses to fill this strategic planning gap.

Figure 3-7 illustrates this strategic-planning gap for a major manufacturer of cassette tape called Musicale (name disguised). The lowest curve projects the expected sales over the next ten years from the company's current portfolio of businesses. The highest curve describes the corporation's desired sales over the next ten years. Evidently the company wants to grow much faster than its current businesses will permit; in fact, it wants to double its size in ten years. How can it fill the strategic-planning gap?

A company can fill the gap in three ways. The first is to identify further opportunities to achieve growth within the company's current businesses *(intensive growth opportunities)*. The second is to identify opportunities to build or acquire businesses that are related to the company's current businesses *(integrative growth opportunities)*. The third is to identify opportunities to add attractive businesses that

FIGURE 3-7
The Strategic-Planning Gap

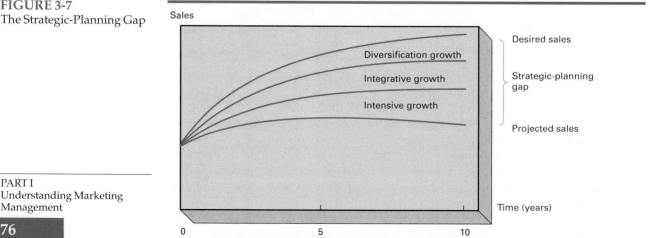

INTENSIVE GROWTH	INTEGRATIVE GROWTH	DIVERSIFICATION GROWTH
• Market penetration • Market development • Product development	• Backward integration • Forward integration • Horizontal integration	• Concentric diversification • Horizontal diversification • Conglomerate diversification

TABLE 3-3
Major Classes of Growth Opportunities

are unrelated to the company's current businesses *(diversification growth opportunities)*. The specific opportunities within each broad class are listed in Table 3-3 and discussed next.

INTENSIVE GROWTH ❖ Corporate management should first review whether there are any further opportunities for improving the performance of its existing businesses. Ansoff has proposed a useful framework for detecting new intensive growth opportunities. Called a *product/market expansion grid*, it is shown in Figure 3-8.[13] Management first considers whether it could gain more market share with its current products in their current markets *(market-penetration strategy)*. Next it considers whether it can find or develop new markets for its current products *(market-development strategy)*. Then it considers whether it can develop new products of potential interest to its current markets *(product-development strategy)*. (Later it will also review opportunities to develop new products for new markets—*diversification strategy*.) Let us examine the three major intensive growth strategies further.

Market-Penetration Strategy. Here management looks for ways to increase the market share of its current products in their current markets. There are three major approaches. Musicale could try to encourage its current customers to buy more cassette tapes per period. This could work if its customers were infrequent buyers of tape and could be shown the benefits of using more tape for music recording or dictation. Or Musicale could try to attract the competitors' customers to switch to its brand. This could work if Musicale noticed major weaknesses in the competitors' product or marketing program. Finally, Musicale could try to convince nonusers of cassette tapes who resemble current users to start using tapes. This could work if there were still many people who did not own tape recorders or tape players.

Market-Development Strategy. Management should also look for new markets whose needs might be met by its current products. First, Musicale might try to identify potential user groups in the current sales areas whose interest in cassette tapes might be stimulated. If Musicale had been selling cassette tapes only to consumer markets, it might go after office and factory markets. Second, the company might seek additional distribution channels in its present locations. If it has been selling its tape only through stereo-equipment dealers, it might add mass-merchandising

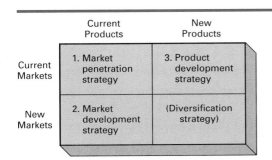

FIGURE 3-8
Three Intensive Growth Strategies: Ansoff's Product/Market Expansion Grid
Source: Adapted from Igor Ansoff, "Strategies for Diversification," *Harvard Business Review,* September–October 1957, p. 114.

channels. Third, the company might consider selling in new locations here or abroad. Thus, if Musicale sold only in the eastern part of the United States, it could consider entering the western states or Europe.

Product-Development Strategy. Next, management should consider new-product possibilities. It could develop new cassette-tape features, such as a longer-playing tape and a tape that buzzes at the end of its play. It could develop different quality levels of tape, such as a higher-quality tape for fine-music listeners and a lower-quality tape for the mass market. Or it could research an alternative technology to cassette tape such as compact discs and digital audio tape.

By examining these three intensive growth strategies, management will hopefully discover several ways to grow. Still, that may not be enough, in which case management must also examine integrative growth opportunities.

INTEGRATIVE GROWTH ❖ Often a business's sales and profits can be increased through integrating backward, forward, or horizontally within that business's industry. Figure 3-9 shows Musicale's core marketing system. Musicale might acquire one or more of its suppliers (such as plastic-material producers) to gain more profit or control *(backward integration)*. Or Musicale might acquire some wholesalers or retailers, especially if they are highly profitable *(forward integration)*. Finally, Musicale might acquire one or more competitors, provided that the government does not bar this move *(horizontal integration)*.

Through investigating possible integration moves, the company may discover additional sources of sales-volume increases over the next ten years. These new sources may still not deliver the desired sales volume. In that case, the company must consider diversification moves.

DIVERSIFICATION GROWTH ❖ Diversification growth makes sense when good opportunities can be found outside the present businesses. A good opportunity, of course, is one where the industry is highly attractive and the company has the mix of business strengths to be successful. Three types of diversification can be considered. The company could seek new products that have technological and/or marketing synergies with existing product lines, even though the products may appeal to a new class of customers *(concentric diversification strategy)*. For example, Musicale might start a computer-tape manufacturing operation based on knowing how to manufacture audio cassette tape, well aware that it will be entering a new market and selling to a different class of customers. Second, the company might search for new products that could appeal to its current customers though technologically unrelated to its current product line *(horizontal diversification strategy)*. For example, Musicale might produce cassette-holding trays, even though they require a different manufacturing process. Finally, the company might seek new businesses that have no relationship to the company's current technology, products, or markets *(conglomerate diversification strategy)*. Musicale might want to consider such new-business areas as fax machines, franchising, or diet products.

FIGURE 3-9
Core Marketing-System Map for a Cassette-Tape Manufacturer

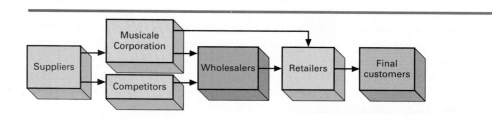

FIGURE 3-10   **The Business Strategic -Planning Process**

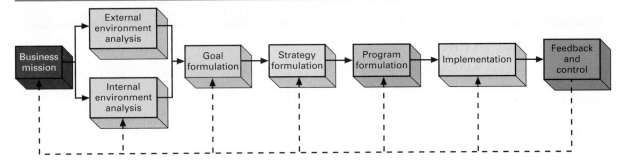

Thus, we see that a company can systematically identify new business opportunities by using a marketing-systems framework, first looking at ways to intensify its position in current product markets, then considering ways to integrate backward, forward, or horizontally in relation to its current businesses, and finally searching for profitable opportunities outside of its current businesses.

Business Strategic Planning

Having examined the strategic-planning tasks of company management, we can now examine the strategic-planning tasks facing business unit managers. The business unit strategic-planning process consists of the eight steps shown in Figure 3-10. We shall now examine these steps.

Business Mission

Each business unit needs to define its specific mission within the broader company mission. Thus, the television-lighting-equipment company described earlier in Figure 3-4 must define its various scopes more specifically: its products and applications, competences, market segments, vertical positioning, and geography. It must also define its specific goals and policies as a separate business.

External Environment Analysis (Opportunity and Threat Analysis)

The business manager now knows the parts of the environment to monitor if the business is to achieve its goals. For example, the television-lighting-equipment company needs to watch the growth rate in the number of television studios; its financial health; current and new competitors; new technological developments; laws and regulations that might affect equipment design or marketing; and distribution channels for selling lighting equipment.

In general, a business unit has to monitor key *macroenvironment forces* (demographic/economic, technological, political/legal, and social/cultural) and significant *microenvironment actors* (customers, competitors, distribution channels, suppliers) that will affect its ability to earn profits in this marketplace. The business unit should set up a *marketing intelligence system* to track trends and important developments. For each trend or development, management needs to identify the implied opportunities and threats.

CHAPTER 3
Laying the Groundwork
Through Market-Oriented
Strategic Planning

Marketing Strategies 3-2

Who Should Produce an Electric Car?

Suppose General Motors, General Electric, and Sears all became interested in developing and marketing an electric car. Which firm would enjoy the greatest competitive advantage?

First consider the success requirements. The key success requirements would include (1) having good relations with suppliers of engines, batteries, metal, plastic, glass, and other materials needed to produce an automobile; (2) having skill at mass production and mass assembly of complicated pieces of equipment; (3) having a strong distribution capacity to store, show, and sell automobiles; and (4) having the confidence of buyers that the company is able to produce and service a good electric automobile.

General Motors has distinctive competences in all four areas. General Electric has distinctive competences in (1) supply and (2) production but not in (3) distribution or (4) automobile reputation. It does have great know-how in electrical and electronic technology. Sears's major distinctive competence is its extensive retailing system, which includes servicing cars, selling auto parts, and financing purchases. General Motors would probably enjoy the greatest total competitive advantage in producing and marketing electric cars.

OPPORTUNITIES ❖ A major purpose of environmental scanning is to discern new opportunities. We define a marketing opportunity as follows:

❖ A marketing opportunity *is an area of need in which a company can perform profitably.*

Opportunities can be listed and classified according to their *attractiveness* and the *success probability*. The company's success probability depends on whether its *business strengths* not only match the *key success requirements* for operating in the target market but also exceed those of its competitors. Mere competence does not constitute a competitive advantage. The best-performing company will be the one that can generate the *greatest customer value and sustain it over time* (see Marketing Strategies 3-2).

Looking at Figure 3-11, the best opportunities facing the TV-lighting-equipment company would be listed in the upper-left cell; and management should prepare plans to pursue these opportunities. The opportunities in the lower-right cell are too minor to consider. The opportunities in the upper-right cell and lower-left cell should be monitored in the event that any of them improve in their attractiveness and success probability.

FIGURE 3-11
Opportunity Matrix

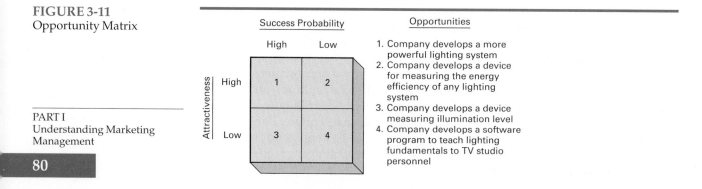

Success Probability

Opportunities

1. Company develops a more powerful lighting system
2. Company develops a device for measuring the energy efficiency of any lighting system
3. Company develops a device measuring illumination level
4. Company develops a software program to teach lighting fundamentals to TV studio personnel

THREATS ❖ Some developments in the external environment represent threats. We define an environmental threat as follows:

❖ *An* environmental threat *is a challenge posed by an unfavorable trend or development that would lead, in the absence of defensive marketing action, to sales or profit deterioration.*

Threats should be classified according to their *seriousness* and *probability of occurrence*. Figure 3-12 illustrates the location of several threats facing the TV-lighting-equipment company. The threats in the upper-left cell are major threats, since they can seriously hurt the company and have a high probability of occurrence. For these threats, the company needs to prepare contingency plans that spell out what changes the company can make before or during the threat's occurrence. The threats in the lower-right cell are very minor and can be ignored. The threats in the upper-right and lower-left cells do not require contingency planning but need to be carefully monitored in the event they grow more critical.

By assembling a picture of the major threats and opportunities facing a specific business unit, it is possible to characterize its overall attractiveness. Four outcomes are possible. An *ideal business* is high in major opportunities and low in major threats. A *speculative business* is high in both major opportunities and threats. A *mature business* is low in major opportunities and threats. Finally, a *troubled business* is low in opportunities and high in threats.

Internal Environment Analysis (Strengths/Weaknesses Analysis)

It is one thing to discern attractive opportunities in the environment; it is another to have the necessary competencies to succeed in these opportunities. Each business needs to evaluate its strengths and weaknesses periodically. This can be done by using a form such as shown in Figure 3-13. Management—or an outside consultant—reviews the business's marketing, financial, manufacturing, and organizational competencies. Each factor is rated as to whether it is a major strength, minor strength, neutral factor, minor weakness, or major weakness. A company with strong marketing capability would show up with the ten marketing factors all rated as major strengths. By connecting the ratings vertically for a specific business, we can easily profile the business's major strengths and weaknesses.

In examining its pattern of strengths and weaknesses, clearly the business does not have to correct all of its weaknesses nor gloat about all of its strengths. The big question is whether the business should limit itself to those opportunities where it now possesses the required strengths or should consider better opportunities where it might have to acquire or develop certain strengths. For example, managers in Texas Instruments (TI) split between those who want TI to stick to

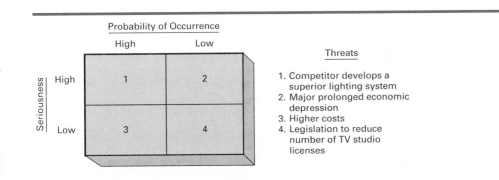

Threats

1. Competitor develops a superior lighting system
2. Major prolonged economic depression
3. Higher costs
4. Legislation to reduce number of TV studio licenses

FIGURE 3-12
Threat Matrix

FIGURE 3-13
Strengths/Weaknesses
Analysis

	Performance					Importance		
	Major Strength	Minor Strength	Neutral	Minor Weakness	Major Weakness	Hi	Med	Low

Marketing

1. Company reputation
2. Market share
3. Product quality
4. Service quality
5. Pricing effectiveness
6. Distribution effectiveness
7. Promotion effectiveness
8. Salesforce effectiveness
9. Innovation effectiveness
10. Geographical coverage

Finance

11. Cost/availability of capital
12. Cash flow
13. Financial stability

Manufacturing

14. Facilities
15. Economies of scale
16. Capacity
17. Able dedicated workforce
18. Ability to produce on time
19. Technical manufacturing skill

Organization

20. Visionary capable leadership
21. Dedicated employees
22. Entrepreneurial orientation
23. Flexible/responsive

industrial electronics where it had clear strength and those who want the company to continue introducing consumer electronic products where it lacks some required marketing strengths.

Sometimes a business does poorly not because its departments lack the required strengths but because they do not work together as a team. In one major electronics company, the engineers look down upon the salespeople as "engineers who couldn't make it," and the salespeople look down upon the service people as "salespeople who couldn't make it." It is therefore critically important to assess interdepartmental working relationships as part of the internal environmental audit.

Every year, Honeywell asks each of its departments to rate its own strengths and weaknesses and those of the other departments with which it interacts. The notion is that each department is a "supplier" to some departments and a "customer" of other departments. Thus, if Honeywell engineers always underestimate the cost and completion time of new products, their "internal customers" (manufacturing, finance, and sales) will all be hurt. Once each department's weaknesses are identified, work can be undertaken to correct them.

George Stalk, a leading BCG consultant, suggests that winning companies are those which have achieved superior *in-company capabilities*, not just *core compe-*

tences.[14] Every company must manage some basic processes, such as *new-product re-alization, raw materials to finished products, sales leads to orders, customer orders to cash realization, customer problems to resolution time,* and so on. Each process creates value and each process requires interdepartmental teamwork. Although each department may possess a core competence, the challenge is to develop superior competitive capability in managing these processes. Stalk calls this *capabilities-based competition.*

Goal Formulation

After the business unit has defined its mission and examined its external and internal environments, it can proceed to develop specific objectives and goals for the planning period. This stage is called *goal formulation.*

Very few businesses pursue only one objective. Most business units pursue a mix of objectives including *profitability, sales growth, market-share improvement, risk containment, innovativeness, reputation,* and so on. The business unit sets these objectives and *manages by objectives.* For this system to work, the business unit's various objectives should be hierarchical, quantitative, realistic, and consistent.

The business unit should strive to arrange its objectives *hierarchically,* from the most to the least important. An excellent example is provided by a business unit of Interstate Telephone (name disguised). The business unit's mission is to provide good service to customers. Its current major objective is to increase its return on investment. From this objective follows a hierarchy of further objectives (see Figure 3-14). Thus a major business objective can be ultimately translated into specific objectives for all employees.

Where possible, objectives should be stated *quantitatively.* The objective "increase the return on investment (ROI)" is not as satisfactory as "increase ROI to 15%" or, even better, "increase ROI to 15% within two years." Managers use the

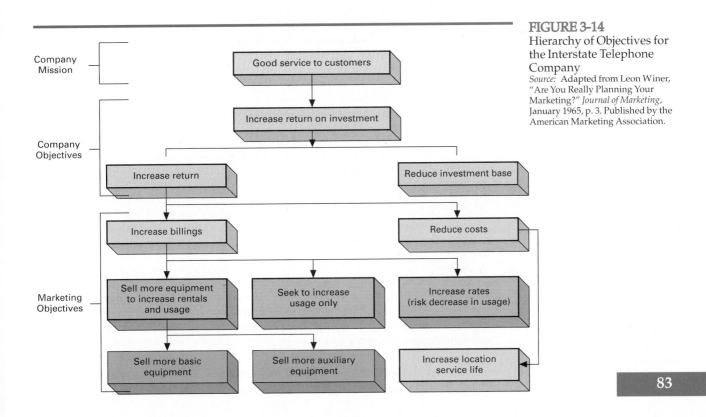

FIGURE 3-14
Hierarchy of Objectives for the Interstate Telephone Company
Source: Adapted from Leon Winer, "Are You Really Planning Your Marketing?" *Journal of Marketing,* January 1965, p. 3. Published by the American Marketing Association.

term *goals* to describe objectives that are specific with respect to *magnitude* and *time*. Turning objectives into measurable goals facilitates management planning, implementation, and control.

A business should set *realistic* goals. The levels should arise from an analysis of the business unit's opportunities and strengths, not from wishful thinking.

Finally, the company's objectives need to be *consistent*. It is not possible to "maximize both sales and profits," or "achieve the greatest sales at the least cost," or "design the best product in the shortest possible time." These objectives are in a *tradeoff* relationship. Here are some important tradeoffs:

- High profit margins versus high market share
- Deep penetration of existing markets versus developing new markets
- Profit goals versus nonprofit goals
- High growth versus low risk

When goals are not consistent, there will be confusion. Too often American CEOs tell their managers to invest for "long-run market-share growth" and then put pressure on them to achieve "high current profits." Meanwhile Japanese CEOs clearly tell their managers to pursue higher market shares and worry about profits later. Each choice in the preceding set of goal tradeoffs will call for quite a different marketing strategy.

Strategy Formulation

Goals indicate what a business unit wants to achieve; strategy answers how to get there. Every business must tailor a strategy for achieving its goals. Although one can list many types of strategies, Michael Porter has condensed them into three generic types that provide a good starting point for strategic thinking:[15]

- *Overall Cost Leadership:* Here the business works hard to achieve the lowest production and distribution costs, so that it can price lower than its competitors and win a large market share. Firms pursuing this strategy must be good at engineering, purchasing, manufacturing, and physical distribution and need less skill in marketing. Texas Instruments is a leading practitioner of this strategy. The problem with this strategy is that other firms will usually emerge with still lower costs (from the Far East, for example) and hurt the firm that rested its whole future on being low cost. The real key is for the firm to achieve the lowest costs among those competitors adopting a similar differentiation or focus strategy.

- *Differentiation:* Here the business concentrates on achieving superior performance in an important customer benefit area valued by a large part of the market. It can strive to be the service leader, the quality leader, the style leader, the technology leader, and so on; but it is hardly possible to be all of these things. The firm cultivates those strengths that will give it a competitive advantage in one or more benefits. Thus the firm seeking quality leadership must make or buy the best components, put them together expertly, inspect them carefully, and so on. This has been Canon's strategy in the copy-machine field.

- *Focus:* Here the business focuses on one or more narrow market segments rather than going after a large market. The firm gets to know the needs of these segments and pursues either cost leadership or a form of differentiation within the target segment. Thus Armstrong Rubber has specialized in making superior tires for farm-equipment vehicles and recreational vehicles and keeps looking for new niches to serve.

According to Porter, those firms pursuing the same strategy directed to the same market or market segment constitute a *strategic group*. The firm that carries off that strategy best will make the most profits. Thus the lowest-cost firm among those pursuing a low-cost strategy will do the best. Porter suggests that firms that do not pursue a clear strategy—"middle-of-the-roaders"—do the worst. Thus Chrysler and International Harvester both came upon hard times because in their respective industries neither stood out as lowest in cost, highest in perceived value, or best in serving some market segment. Middle-of-the-roaders try to be good on all strategic dimensions, but since strategic dimensions require different and often inconsistent ways to organize the firm, these firms end up being not particularly excellent at anything. (See Marketing Concepts and Tools 3-1.)

Marketing Concepts and Tools 3-1

Strategic Groups in the Truck-Manufacturing Industry

The role of generic strategies and strategic groups can be illustrated by William Hall's research in the truck-manufacturing industry. The accompanying figure is called a *competitive map*. It shows how seven U.S. truck manufacturers were positioned some years ago in terms of their *relative delivered cost* (i.e., being a low-cost firm) and their *relative performance* (i.e., offering the most differentiated product). The percentages in the figure represent each manufacturer's ROI at the time.

Ford clearly has the lowest relative delivered cost, followed by General Motors. Ford's low-cost leadership gives it the highest ROI (i.e., 25%) in its strategic group. Paccar, on the other hand, is the leader in the high-performance truck strategic group and commands a 31% ROI, compared with Mack's 20%.

At the other extreme is White Motor, whose trucks were below average in performance and high in relative cost. Not surprisingly, its rate of return was a low 4.7%, and White was subsequently purchased by Volvo, whose intent is to reposition it.

The four companies in the middle box are "middle-of-the-roaders" that try to be good at performance and cost but are not superior at either. Their ROIs lag behind those of the two leading firms, Ford and Paccar. Freightliner was subsequently purchased by Mercedes, and International Harvester's truck line was later reborn as Navistar.

In order for a middle-of-the-roader to improve its ROI, the company must make a clearer commitment to one of the three winning strategies. For example, International Harvester (IH) had three options. IH could invest in a more modern plant in a drive to become the low-cost firm. In this case, its major competitors would be Ford and General Motors, both of which make up the strategic group pursuing cost leadership. Alternatively, IH could try to improve the quality of its trucks

and services so that it competed with Paccar and Mack, the strategic group pursuing profitability through product differentiation. This would be harder for IH because it takes years to build a better product and reputation, and Paccar is too well entrenched. Finally, IH might go after multiple niches within the trucking industry (this cannot be shown in the figure), becoming a leader in each niche through either low costs, product differentiation, or both. As it turned out, IH adopted the third strategy, and it has been successful.

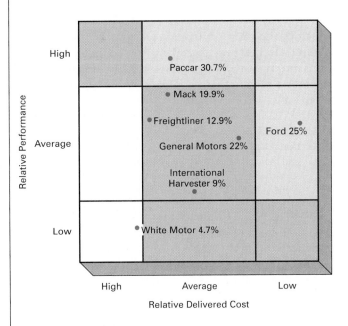

Companies are also discovering that the most effective strategy may require their finding *strategic partners*. Even giant companies—AT&T, IBM, Philips, Siemens—often cannot achieve leadership in single countries or globally without forming *strategic alliances* with domestic and/or multinational companies that complement or leverage their capabilities and resources. Just to do business in another country may require the firm to license its product, form a joint venture with a local firm, buy from local suppliers to meet "domestic content" requirements, and so on. The result is that firms are rapidly building *strategic networks*. And victory is going to those who build the better network (see Companies and Industries 3-1).[16]

Program Formulation

Once the business unit has developed its principal strategies, it must work out supporting programs. Thus if the business has decided to attain technological leadership, it must run programs to strengthen its R&D department, gather technology intelligence, develop leading-edge products, train the technical sales force, develop ads to communicate its technological leadership, and so on. We will say more about these programs later.

Implementation

Even a clear strategy and well-thought-out supporting programs may not be enough. The firm may fail at implementation. Strategy is only one of seven ele-

Companies and Industries 3-1

Companies Join Together in Strategic Alliances and Joint Ventures

Much of the work of strategic planners involves determining the best way to expand the company's operations into new markets. Suppose a U.S. company wants to enter a foreign market. The company can do this in three ways:

1. *Establish a foreign subsidiary:* This has been the traditional way in which companies such as IBM, Xerox, 3M and others have entered foreign markets. Setting up the subsidiary is costly and time-consuming but it gives full control to the parent firm. Even then, some subsidiaries over time become relatively independent of the parent firm in setting their policies. For example, Opel, General Motors' European subsidiary, operates fairly independently of General Motors in the United States.

2. *Acquire competitors and other businesses:* This is the most expensive way of entering another market and is subject to all the pitfalls of trying to select and integrate an acquisition. Porter reported that of more than 2,000 acquisitions made by 33 large companies between 1950–1980, over half were divested by 1986. McKinsey reported in another study that only 23% of the acquisitions studied earned financial returns exceeding the cost of the funds spent to acquire them. Bridgestone, the

Japanese tire manufacturer, saw its profits plummet after it acquired Firestone. Relatively few companies—Federal Express, Cooper Industries, Stanley Tools—have shown considerable success in picking and managing their acquisitions.

3. *Form alliances and joint ventures:* Although forming and managing strategic alliances is fairly complex, it has the advantage of much lower cost and speedier consummation than start-ups or acquisitions. Alliances are undertaken for many reasons: to gain access to new technologies, to enter "blocked" markets, to reduce required investment, to gain access to a brand name or customer group, or to achieve more global coverage. The number of joint ventures has risen steeply in the last few decades. Yet they are subject to such problems as partner disagreements on further investment, different expectations of return, inability to change with changing market conditions, cultural communication barriers, and difficulties in integrating the two companies' accounting and information systems. Some studies show that as many as 70% of alliances may come to an unsatisfactory ending.

Within alliances, there are four types of *marketing alliances:*

ments, according to the McKinsey Consulting Firm, that the best-managed companies exhibit.[17] The McKinsey 7-S framework is shown in Figure 3-15. The first three elements—strategy, structure, and systems—are considered the "hardware" of success. The next four—style, staff, skills, and shared values—are the "software."

The first "soft" element, *style*, means that employees in that company share a common way of behaving and thinking. Thus everyone at McDonald's smiles at the customer, and employees of IBM are very professional in their customer dealings. The second, *skills*, means that the employees have the skills needed to carry out the company's strategy. The third, *staffing*, means that the company has hired able people, trained them well, and assigned them to the right jobs. The fourth, *shared values*, means that the employees share the same guiding values and missions. When these "soft" elements are present, companies are usually more successful at implementation.[18]

Feedback and Control

As it implements its strategy, the firm needs to track the results and monitor new developments in the environment. Some environments are fairly stable from year to year. Other environments evolve slowly in a fairly predictable way. Still other environments change rapidly in major and unpredictable ways. The company can count on one thing: that the environment will change. And when it does, the company will need to review and revise its implementation, programs, strategies, or even objectives. Consider what happened at GE's vacuum-tube division:

1. *Product and/or service alliances:* These can range from one company licensing another to produce its product; to two companies jointly marketing their complementary products (Apple PC's joined with Digital Vax computers); to two companies co-designing, manufacturing, and marketing a new product (Mazda and Ford's joint production of the Escort). A marketing alliance can also be formed between a product and a service company (Citibank's new credit card grants rebate points for buying a Ford). Finally, two service companies can form a marketing alliance (H&R Block and Hyatt Legal Services).

2. *Promotional alliances:* One company may agree to carry a promotion for another company's product or service. For example, the Teenage Mutant Ninja Turtle videocassette series included Pizza Hut dinner coupons. Pathe Entertainment and Bantam Books got together and co-promoted the movie and book *The Russia House*. A fine restaurant may agree to display on its walls paintings from a local art gallery.

3. *Logistic alliances:* Here one company offers logistical support services for the product of another company. For example, Federal Express warehouses the parts of many companies that it guarantees to deliver anywhere

in the United States the next day for any order received by the previous evening. Abbott Laboratories has an alliance with 3M where it warehouses and delivers all of 3M's medical and surgical products to hospitals across the United States.

4. *Pricing collaborations:* Here one or more companies join in a special pricing collaboration. It is common for hotel chains and rental car companies to offer mutual price discounts.

Companies need to give more creative thought to finding partners who might complement their strengths or offset their weaknesses. Alliances, when well-managed, permit companies to obtain a greater sales impact at less cost. The main risk is that the partners may reach disagreements about present responsibilities or future directions.

SOURCE: Adapted, with permission of the publisher, from *The 6 Imperatives of Marketing: Lessons from the World's Best Companies*, Chapter 4, copyright ©1992, Allan J. Magrath. Published by AMACOM, a division of the American Management Association. All rights reserved.

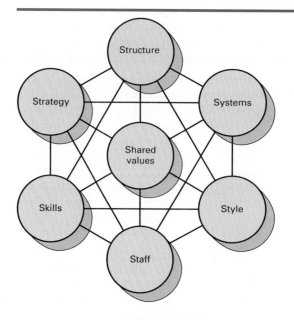

FIGURE 3-15
McKinsey 7-S Framework
Source: Thomas J. Peters and Robert H. Waterman, Jr., *In Search of Excellence: Lessons from America's Best Run Companies.* Copyright © 1982 by Thomas J. Peters and Robert H. Waterman, Jr. Reprinted by permission of Harper & Row, Publishers.

Some years ago, General Electric's president called in the general manager of the vacuum-tube division. The general manager expected to be congratulated because he had increased vacuum-tube sales by 20%. Instead, he was berated for keeping GE too long in the wrong business. GE's sales had risen because some competitors had left the vacuum-tube business, not because of GE's competitive edge. In addition, transistor technology was making headway against vacuum tubes and bringing in new players such as Texas Instruments and Fairchild. In fact, the total market for devices that amplified weak electrical signals had grown by 30% during the period, which meant that GE's market share of the total market had actually fallen. The manager was guilty of marketing myopia, focusing on vacuum tubes instead of the total range of technologies competing to serve the particular need. Some businesses are dead without management's really knowing it.

A company's *strategic fit* with the environment will inevitably erode because the market environment almost always changes faster than the company's 7-S's. Thus it is possible for a company to remain efficient while it becomes ineffective. Peter Drucker pointed out that it is more important *to do the right thing* (being effective) than *to do things right* (being efficient). Excellent companies excel at both.

Once an organization starts losing its market position through failure to respond to a changed environment, it becomes increasingly harder to retrieve leadership:

General Motors was slow in recognizing the rapidly growing U.S. market for small cars. Small cars were a new opportunity for U.S. car manufacturers in a mature market. A new opportunity is a *strategic window* that stays open for only a short time.[19] As Volkswagens and small Japanese cars increased their market share, GM finally responded with a poorly made car called the Vega. GM's blindness was the result of operating in the 1970s and 1980s with the leftovers of 1960s' strategy, structure, systems, style, staff, skills, and shared values. GM's management needed to realize that competitiveness requires drastic steps, including reducing bloated management and labor costs, sourcing parts from abroad, partnering with foreign car manufacturers, and improving product quality and dealer service.[20]

Organizations, especially large ones, have much inertia. They are set up as efficient machines, and it is difficult to change one part without adjusting everything else. Yet organizations can be changed through leadership, probably in advance of a crisis but certainly in the midst of a crisis. The key to organizational health is the organization's willingness to examine the changing environment and to adopt appropriate new goals and behaviors. Adaptable organizations continuously monitor the environment and attempt through flexible strategic planning to maintain a viable fit with the evolving environment.

SUMMARY ❖

Excellent companies know how to adapt and respond to a continuously changing marketplace through the practice of market-oriented strategic planning. They know how to develop and maintain a viable fit between their objectives, resources, skills, and opportunities. They carry out the strategic-planning process at the corporate level, business level, and product level. The objectives developed at the corporate level move down to lower levels where business strategic plans and marketing plans are prepared to guide the company's activities. Strategic planning involves repeated cycles of analysis, planning, implementation, and control.

Corporate strategic planning involves four planning activities. The first is developing a clear sense of the company's mission in terms of its industry scope, products and applications scope, competences scope, market-segment scope, vertical scope, and geographical scope. A well-developed mission statement provides employees with a shared sense of purpose, direction, and opportunity.

The second activity calls for identifying the company's strategic business units (SBUs). A business is defined by its customer groups, customer needs, and technologies. SBUs are business units that can benefit from separate planning, face specific competitors, and be managed as profit centers.

The third activity calls for allocating resources to the various SBUs based on their market attractiveness and company business strength. Several portfolio models, including those by the Boston Consulting Group and General Electric, are available to help corporate management determine the SBUs that should be built, maintained, harvested, or divested.

The fourth activity calls for expanding present businesses and developing new ones to fill the strategic-planning gap. The company can identify opportunities by considering intensive growth (market penetration, market development, and product development); integrative growth (backward, forward, and horizontal integration); and diversification growth (concentric, horizontal, and conglomerate diversification).

Each SBU conducts its own business strategic planning, which consists of eight steps: defining the business mission, analyzing the external environment, analyzing the internal environment, choosing business objectives and goals, developing business strategies, preparing programs, implementing programs, and gathering feedback and exercising control. All of these steps keep the SBU close to its environment and alert to new opportunities and problems. Furthermore, the SBU strategic plan provides the context for preparing market plans for specific products and services, which we will examine in the next chapter.

NOTES ❖

1. Steve Harrell, in a speech at the plenary session of the American Marketing Association's Educators' Meeting, Chicago, August 5, 1980.

2. See Tamara J. Erickson and C. Everett Shorey, "Business Strategy: New Thinking for the '90s," *Prism*, Fourth Quarter 1992, pp. 19–35.

3. See "The New Breed of Strategic Planning," *Business Week,* September 7, 1984, pp. 62–68.

4. See Drucker, *Management: Tasks, Responsibilities and Practices* (New York: Harper & Row, 1973), Chap. 7.

5. See "The Hollow Corporation," *Business Week,* March 3, 1986, pp. 57–59.

6. For more discussion, see Laura Nash, "Mission Statements—Mirrors and Windows," *Harvard Business Review,* March–April 1988, pp. 155–56.

7. Theodore Levitt, "Marketing Myopia," *Harvard Business Review,* July–August 1960, pp. 45–56.

8. See "Holiday Inns: Refining Its Focus to Food, Lodging and More Casinos," *Business Week,* July 21, 1980, pp. 100–104.

9. Derek Abell, *Defining the Business: The Starting Point of Strategic Planning* (Englewood Cliffs, NJ: Prentice-Hall, 1980), Chap. 3.

10. See Roger A. Kerin, Vijay Mahajan, and P. Rajan Varadarajan, *Contemporary Perspectives on Strategic Planning* (Boston: Allyn & Bacon, 1990).

11. A hard decision must be made between harvesting and divesting a business. Harvesting a business will strip it of its long-run value, in which case it will be difficult to find a buyer. Divesting, on the other hand, is facilitated by maintaining a business in a fit condition in order to attract a buyer.

12. See Peter Patel and Michael Younger, "A Frame of Reference for Strategy Development," *Long Range Planning,* April 1978, pp. 6–12; and S.J.Q. Robinson et al., "The Directional Policy Matrix—Tool for Strategic Planning," *Long Range Planning,* June 1978, pp. 8–15

13. The same matrix can be expanded into nine cells by adding modified products and modified markets. See S. C. Johnson and Conrad Jones, "How to Organize for New Products," *Harvard Business Review,* May–June 1957, pp. 49–62.

14. George Stalk, Philip Evans, and Lawrence E. Shulman, "Competing Capabilities: The New Rules of Corporate Strategy," *Harvard Business Review,* March–April 1992, pp. 57–69.

15. See Michael E. Porter, *Competitive Strategy: Techniques for Analyzing Industries and Competitors* (New York: Free Press, 1980), Chap. 2.

16. For readings on strategic alliances, see Peter Lorange and Johan Roos, *Strategic Alliances: Formation, Implementation and Evolution* (Cambridge, MA: Blackwell Publishers, 1992), and Jordan D. Lewis, *Partnerships for Profit: Structuring and Managing Strategic Alliances* (New York: The Free Press, 1990).

17. See Thomas J. Peters and Robert H. Waterman, Jr., *In Search of Excellence: Lessons from America's Best-Run Companies* (New York: Harper & Row, 1982), pp. 9–12. The same framework is used in Richard Tanner Pascale and Anthony G. Athos, *The Art of Japanese Management: Applications for American Executives* (New York: Simon and Schuster, 1981).

18. See Terrence E. Deal and Allan A. Kennedy, *Corporate Cultures: The Rites and Rituals of Corporate Life* (Reading, MA: Addison-Wesley, 1982); "Corporate Culture," *Business Week,* October 27, 1980, pp. 148–60; Stanley M. Davis, *Managing Corporate Culture* (Cambridge, MA: Ballinger, 1984); and John P. Kotter and James L. Heskett, *Corporate Culture and Performance* (New York: Free Press, 1992).

19. See Derek F. Abell, "Strategic Windows," *Journal of Marketing,* July 1978, pp. 21–26.

20. For a brilliant account of how one outside leader would have changed GM, read Ross Perot, "How I Would Turn Around GM," *Fortune,* February 15, 1988, pp. 44–48.

4

Managing the Marketing Process and Marketing Planning

Plans are nothing; planning is everything.

DWIGHT D. EISENHOWER

Marketing strategy is a series of integrated actions leading to a sustainable competitive advantage.

JOHN SCULLY

W e saw in Chapters 1, 2, and 3 that successful modern companies are driven by a *market orientation* and *strategic planning*. The company's strategic plan, however, is only the starting point for planning. It serves as a guide to the development of sound subplans to accomplish the organization's objectives. These subplans, or *business plans*, must be prepared for each division, strategic business unit, product category, product, and important target market.

The business plan has three purposes. First, it serves to develop a strategy and communicate it to higher levels of management. Second, it serves as the justification of the budget request. Third, it provides an instrument for monitoring ongoing progress and making corrections during the plan's implementation.

A crucial part of every business plan is the *marketing plan*. The marketing plan operates at two levels. The *strategic marketing plan* develops the broad marketing objectives and strategy based on an analysis of the current market situation and opportunities. The *tactical marketing plan* outlines the specific marketing tactics for the period, including advertising, merchandising, pricing, channels, service, and so on.

On the basis of the marketing plan, the other components of the business plan can be developed, namely support plans for R&D, purchasing, manufacturing, personnel, and finance. This is not to suggest that marketing sets the marketing game plan by itself. Business planning is increasingly conducted with inputs and signoffs from every important function. Today's plans are team-developed, not developed by any individual or function.

The marketing plan is the central instrument for directing and coordinating the marketing effort. Companies that want to improve their marketing effectiveness and efficiency must learn how to create and implement sound marketing plans. Our discussion of marketing planning will seek to answer these questions:

♦ What are the major steps in the marketing process?
♦ What are the major contents of a marketing plan?
♦ What are the main theoretical tools for describing how various types of marketing efforts affect the company's sales and profits?

The Marketing Process

To understand the *marketing process*, we must first look at the *business process*. The task of any business is to deliver value to the market at a profit. But there are at least two views of the *value-delivery process*.[1] The traditional view is that the firm proceeds to make something and then to sell it (Figure 4-1). For example, Thomas Edison invents the phonograph and then hires salespeople to sell it. In this view, marketing takes place in the second half of the value-delivery process. The traditional view assumes that the company knows what to make and the market will buy enough units to produce profits for the company.

This traditional view has the best chance of succeeding in economies of

FIGURE 4-1   Contrasting Two Views of Creating Value

Source: Michael J. Lanning and Edward G. Michaels, "A Business Is a Value Delivery System," McKinsey staff paper, no. 41, June 1988. (McKinsey & Co., Inc.).

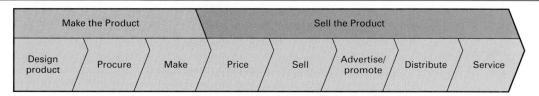

(a) Traditional Physical Process Sequence

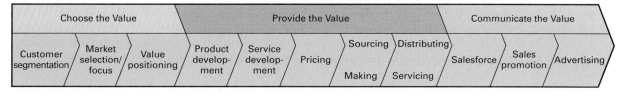

(b) The Value Creation and Delivery Sequence

scarcity. Thus consumers in Eastern Europe are desperate for goods and will buy whatever is made. They are not fussy about quality, features, or style. But this view of the business process will not work in more competitive economies where people face abundant choices and exercise discrimination. The "mass market" is splintering into many *micromarkets*, each with its own wants, perceptions, preferences, and buying criteria. The smart competitor therefore must design the offer for well-defined *target markets*.

This view is incorporated in Figure 4-1(b), which now places marketing at the beginning of the business planning process. Instead of a make/sell view, the business process consists of choosing the value, providing the value, and communicating the value.

The first phase, *choosing the value*, represents the "homework" that marketing must carry out before any product exists. The marketing staff proceeds to *segment* the market, select the appropriate *market target*, and develop the offer's *value positioning*. The formula—segmentation, targeting, positioning (STP)—is the essence of *strategic marketing*.

Once the business unit has chosen the value to deliver to the target market, it is ready to *provide the value*. The tangible product and service must be specified in detail, a target price must be established, and the product must be made and distributed. Developing specific product features, prices, and distribution occur at this stage and are part of *tactical marketing*.

The task in the third stage is to *communicate the value*. Here further tactical marketing occurs in utilizing the salesforce, sales promotion, advertising, and other promotional tasks to inform the market about the offer. All said, Figure 4-1(b) demonstrates that the marketing process begins before there is a product and continues while it is being developed and after it becomes available.

The Japanese have further developed this view of the value-creation and value-delivery processes by adding the following concepts:

- ◆ *Zero Customer Feedback Time:* Customer feedback should be continuously collected after purchase to learn how to improve the product and its marketing.

- *Zero Product-Improvement Time*: The company should evaluate all the customers' improvement ideas, as well as employee ideas, and introduce the most valued and feasible improvements as soon as possible.
- *Zero Purchasing Time:* The company should receive the required parts and supplies continuously through just-in-time arrangements with suppliers. By lowering its inventories, the company can reduce its costs.
- *Zero Setup Time:* The company should be able to manufacture any of its products as soon as they are ordered, without facing high setup costs or time.
- *Zero Defects:* The products should be of high quality and free of flaws.

Thus the first step in business planning is the marketing step, where the target market and product-positioning strategy are defined and sales goals and needed resources are established for achieving these goals. The role of the finance, purchasing, manufacturing, physical distribution, and personnel departments is to make sure that the proposed marketing plan can be supported with enough money, materials, machines, and personnel.

To carry out their responsibilities, marketing managers go through a marketing process. We define it as follows:

❖ *The* marketing process *consists of analyzing marketing opportunities, researching and selecting target markets, designing marketing strategies, planning marketing programs, and organizing, implementing, and controlling the marketing effort.*

These steps are listed in Figure 4-2, along with the chapters in this book that will describe each step in detail. The steps will be illustrated here in connection with the following situation:

> Zeus, Inc. (name disguised) operates in several industries, including chemicals, energy, typewriters, and some consumer goods. Each area is organized as an SBU. Corporate management is considering what to do with its Atlas typewriter division. At present, Atlas produces standard office electric typewriters. The market for standard electric typewriters is declining. On a growth-share matrix, this business would be called a dog. Zeus's corporate management wants Atlas's marketing group to produce a strong turnaround plan. Marketing management has to come up with a convincing marketing plan, sell corporate management on the plan, and then implement and control it.

Analyzing Market Opportunities

The first task facing Atlas's marketing management is to analyze the long-run opportunities in this market for improving its performance as a business division of Zeus, Inc. These managers recognize the abundance of opportunities in the burgeoning business-office-equipment field. The *office of the future* is a major investment frontier in the coming decades. The U.S. economy is increasingly becoming a service economy, and there are more office workers than factory workers. Yet offices are often poorly organized for such elementary tasks as typing, filing, storing, and transmitting information, especially in terms of the latest available technologies. Many manufacturers are active in this market and are seeking to provide integrated systems of microcomputers, copying and duplicating equipment, telecommunications equipment, fax machines, and the like. Among them are IBM, Xerox, Olivetti, and several Japanese companies. They are all engaged in developing office hardware and software that will increase office productivity. Xerox, in fact, sees itself not as a copying-machine company but as an office-productivity-improvement company.

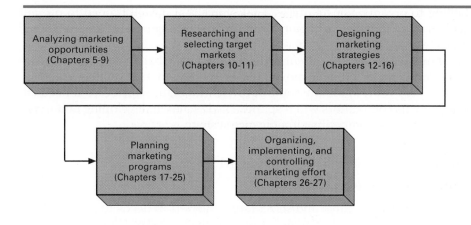

FIGURE 4-2
The Marketing Management
Process

Atlas's long-run goal is to become a complete office-equipment manufacturer. At the present, however, it must come up with a plan for an improved product line. Even within typewriters, there are still some opportunities. Atlas can scale down its office typewriter to a version for the home market and advertise it as an "office-quality" home typewriter. Or it can design an electronic or "smart" typewriter. Atlas can also consider designing a word processor, which would have more memory and text-editing capability than an electronic typewriter. Or Atlas can develop a computer work station that performs a large number of functions. Ultimately, Atlas can work on voice-activated typewriters, which only require oral dictation.

To evaluate its opportunities, Atlas needs to operate a reliable marketing information system (Chapter 5). Marketing research is an indispensable marketing tool, in that companies can serve their customer markets well only by researching their needs and wants, their locations, their buying practices, and so on. At the very least, Atlas needs a good internal accounting system that reports current sales by typewriter model, customer, industry and size, customer location, salesperson, and channels of distribution. In addition, Atlas's executives should be collecting continuous market intelligence on customers, competitors, dealers, and so on. The marketing people should conduct formal research in secondary sources; running focus groups; and conducting telephone, mail, and personal surveys. If the collected data are well analyzed using advanced statistical methods and models, the company will probably gain useful information on how sales are influenced by various marketing forces.

The purpose of Atlas's research is to gather significant information about Atlas's marketing environment (Chapter 6). Atlas's *microenvironment* consists of all the players who affect the company's ability to produce and sell typewriters, namely, suppliers, marketing intermediaries, customers, competitors, and publics of various sorts. Atlas's *macroenvironment* consists of demographic, economic, physical, technological, political/legal, and social/cultural forces that affect its sales and profits.

To the extent that Atlas considers manufacturing writing equipment for the home, it needs to understand *consumer markets* (Chapter 7). It needs to know: How many households plan to buy typewriters or computers? Who buys and why do they buy? What are they looking for in the way of features and prices? Where do they shop? What are their images of different brands?

Atlas also sells to *business markets*, including large corporations, professional firms, retailers, and government agencies (Chapter 8). Large organizations use purchasing agents or buying committees who are skilled at evaluating equipment.

Selling to organizations requires a salesforce that is well trained to present product benefits. Atlas needs to gain a full understanding of how organizational buyers buy.

Atlas must also pay close attention to competitors (Chapter 9). Atlas must anticipate its competitors' possible moves and know how to react quickly and decisively. Atlas may want to initiate some surprise moves, in which case it needs to anticipate how its competitors will respond. The key lies in developing and maintaining an up-to-date competitive intelligence system.

Researching and Selecting Target Markets and Positioning the Offer

Atlas is now ready to research and select target markets. It needs to know how to measure and forecast the attractiveness of any given market (Chapter 10). This requires estimating the market's overall size, growth, profitability, and risk. Marketers must understand the major techniques for measuring market potential and forecasting future demand. Each technique has certain advantages and limitations that must be understood by marketers to avoid their misuse.

These market measures and forecasts become key inputs into deciding which markets and new products to focus on. Modern marketing practice calls for dividing the market into major market segments, evaluating them, and selecting and targeting those market segments that the company can best serve (Chapter 11).

Market segmentation can be done in a number of ways. Figure 4-3 shows the typewriter market segmented by two broad variables, namely, customer groups and customer needs. This particular framework is called a *product/market grid*. Marketing management can estimate for each cell the degree of market segment attractiveness and the company's degree of business strength. Atlas seeks to determine which product/market cells, if any, best match the company's objectives and resources.

Designing Marketing Strategies

Suppose Atlas decides to target the "home customer, electronic typewriter market" (see shaded cell in Figure 4-3). It needs to develop a *differentiating* and *positioning strategy* for that target market (Chapter 12). Should Atlas be the "Cadillac" firm offering a superior product at a premium price with excellent service that is well ad-

FIGURE 4-3
Product/Market Grid
for Typewriters

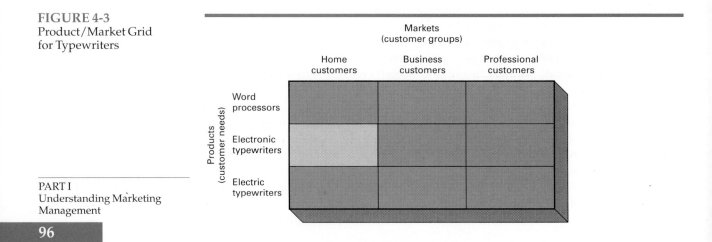

vertised and aimed at more affluent homeowners? Or should Atlas build a simple low-price electronic typewriter aimed at the more price-conscious homeowners? Atlas can develop a *product-positioning map* (Figure 4-4) to describe the positions of four competitors currently selling to this market. The four competitors, A, B, C, and D, differ in sales volume as reflected by the circle sizes. A occupies the high-quality/high-price position in this market. B is perceived to produce an average-quality product at an average price. C sells a slightly below-average-quality product for a low price. D is perceived as a "rip-off artist" because it sells a low-quality product for a high price.

Where should Atlas position itself? It normally would not make sense to position at A because it would be fighting a well-established company. However, if A is rendering poor service, Atlas may decide to attack A. Atlas might give serious consideration to positioning itself in the high-quality/medium-price quadrant (shown by the dotted circle). In this way, it would be "filling a hole" in the market. It must satisfy itself on three points, however. First, Atlas must find out from its engineers if they can build a high-quality typewriter that could sell at a medium price and make money. Second, Atlas must check whether there is a sufficient number of buyers who want a high-quality machine at a medium price. Finally, Atlas must be able to convince buyers that its typewriter's quality and service are comparable to A's. Many buyers do not believe that medium-price units can be as good as higher-priced units, so heavy promotional expenditures may be required.

Once Atlas decides on its product positioning, it must initiate new-product development, testing, and launching (Chapter 13). The art of new-product development calls for organizing this process effectively and using distinct decision tools and controls at each stage of the process.

After launch, the new product's strategy will have to be modified at the different stages in the product life cycle: introduction, growth, maturity, and decline (Chapter 14). Furthermore, strategy choice will depend on whether the firm plays the role of market leader, challenger, follower, or nicher (Chapter 15). Finally, strategy will have to take into account changing global opportunities and challenges (Chapter 16).

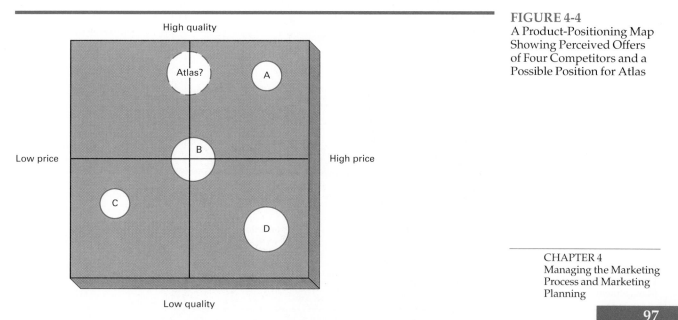

FIGURE 4-4
A Product-Positioning Map Showing Perceived Offers of Four Competitors and a Possible Position for Atlas

Planning Marketing Programs

Marketing strategy must be transformed into marketing programs. This is accomplished by making basic decisions on marketing expenditures, marketing mix, and marketing allocation.

Atlas must decide what level of *marketing expenditures* is necessary to achieve its marketing objectives. Companies typically establish their marketing budget at a conventional percentage of the sales goal. Companies try to learn what the *marketing budget-to-sales ratio* is for competitors. A particular company may spend more than the normal ratio in the hope of achieving a higher market share. Ultimately the company should analyze the marketing work required to attain a given sales volume or market share and then cost out this work; the result is the required marketing budget.

The company also has to decide how to divide the total marketing budget among the various tools in the *marketing mix*. Marketing mix is one of the key concepts in modern marketing theory.

❖ Marketing mix *is the set of marketing tools that the firm uses to pursue its marketing objectives in the target market.*

There are literally dozens of marketing-mix tools. McCarthy popularized a four-factor classification of these tools called the four Ps: *product, price, place* (i.e., distribution), and *promotion.*[2] The particular marketing variables under each *P* are shown in Figure 4-5.

The company's marketing mix at time *t* for a particular product can be represented by $(P_1, P_2, P_3, P_4)_t$. If Atlas develops product quality at 1.2 (with 1.0 = average), prices its product at $1,000, and spends $30,000 a month on distribution and $20,000 a month on promotion, its marketing mix at time *t* can be represented as $(1.2, \$1,000, \$30,000, \$20,000)_t$.

One can see that a marketing mix is selected from a great number of possibilities. If product quality could take on one of two values, and product price is con-

FIGURE 4-5
The Four Ps of
the Marketing Mix

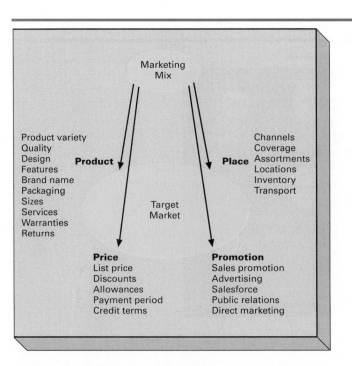

FIGURE 4-6 Marketing-Mix Strategy

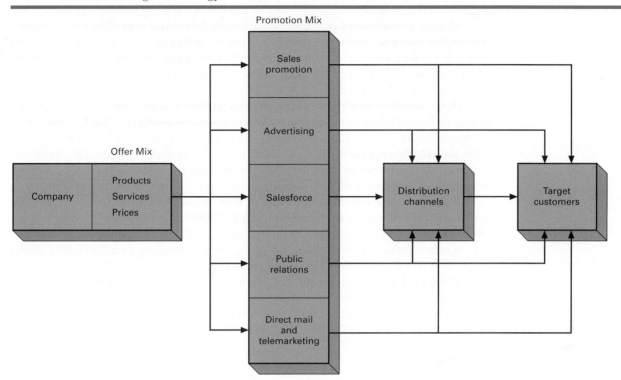

strained to lie between $500 and $1,500 (to the nearest $100), and distribution and advertising expenditures are constrained to lie between $10,000 and $50,000 (to the nearest $10,000), then 550 ($=2\times11\times5\times5$) marketing-mix combinations are posssible.

To complicate matters further, marketing-mix decisions must be made for both the distribution channels and the final consumers. Figure 4-6 shows the company preparing an *offer mix* of products, services, and prices, and utilizing a *promotion mix* of sales promotion, advertising, salesforce, public relations, direct mail, and telemarketing to reach the distribution channels and the target consumers.

Not all marketing-mix variables can be adjusted in the short run. Typically, the firm can change its price, salesforce size, and advertising expenditures in the short run. It can only develop new products and modify its distribution channels in the long run. Thus the firm typically makes fewer period-to-period marketing-mix changes in the short run than the number of marketing-mix variables suggest.

Finally, marketers must decide on the *allocation* of the marketing dollars to the various products, channels, promotion media, and sales areas. How many dollars should support Atlas's electric versus electronic typewriters? Direct versus distributor sales? Direct-mail advertising versus trade-magazine advertising? East Coast markets versus West Coast markets? We can represent a distinct allocation in the following way: Suppose management sets product quality at 1.2, price at $1,000, a monthly distribution budget of $5,000, and a monthly advertising budget of $10,000 for product i selling to customer-type j in area k at time t. This is represented by $(1.2, \$1,000, \$5,000, \$10,000)_{i,j,k,t}$.

To make these allocations, marketing managers use the notion of *sales-response functions* that show how sales would be affected by the amount of dollars put in each possible application.

The most basic marketing-mix tool is *product*, which stands for the firm's tangible offer to the market, including the product quality, design, features, branding,

CHAPTER 4
Managing the Marketing
Process and Marketing
Planning

and packaging (Chapter 17). Atlas also provides various services, such as delivery, repair, and training, as well as running an equipment-leasing business (Chapter 18).

A critical marketing-mix tool is *price*, namely, the amount of money that customers have to pay for the product (Chapter 19). Atlas has to decide on wholesale and retail prices, discounts, allowances, and credit terms. Its price should be commensurate with the perceived value of the offer or buyers will turn to competitors in choosing their products.

Place, another key marketing-mix tool, stands for the various activities the company undertakes to make the product accessible and available to target customers (Chapters 20 and 21). Atlas must identify, recruit, and link various middlemen and marketing facilitators so that its products and services are efficiently supplied to the target market. It must understand the various types of retailers, wholesalers, and physical-distribution firms and how they make their decisions.

Promotion, the fourth marketing-mix tool, stands for the various activities the company undertakes to communicate and promote its products to the target market (Chaps. 22–25). Thus Atlas has to hire, train, and motivate salespeople. It has to set up communication and promotion programs consisting of advertising, direct marketing, sales promotion, and public relations.

Note that the 4Ps represent the sellers' view of the marketing tools available for influencing buyers. From a buyer's point of view, each marketing tool is designed to deliver a customer benefit. Robert Lauterborn suggested that the 4Ps correspond to the customers' 4Cs:

4Ps	4Cs
Product	Customer needs and wants
Price	Cost to the customer
Place	Convenience
Promotion	Communication

Thus, winning companies will be those who can meet customer needs economically and conveniently and with effective communication.[3]

Organizing, Implementing, and Controlling the Marketing Effort

The final step in the marketing process is organizing the marketing resources and implementing and controlling the marketing plan. The company must build a marketing organization that is capable of *implementing* the marketing plan (Chapter 26). In a small company, one person might carry out all the marketing tasks: marketing research, selling, advertising, customer servicing, and so on. In a large company such as Atlas, several marketing specialists will be found, such as salespeople, sales managers, marketing researchers, advertising personnel, product and brand managers, market-segment managers, and customer-service personnel.

Marketing organizations are typically headed by a marketing vice-president, who performs two tasks. The first is to coordinate the work of all of the marketing personnel. Atlas's marketing vice-president must make sure, for example, that the advertising manager works closely with the salesforce manager in timing promotions for gathering new sales-prospects leads. The marketing vice-president's other task is to work closely with the other functional vice-presidents. Thus if Atlas's marketing people advertise its new electronic typewriter as a quality product, but R&D does not design a quality product or manufacturing fails to manufacture it carefully, then marketing will not deliver on its promise. The marketing department's effectiveness also depends on how well its personnel are selected, trained, directed, motivated, and evaluated. There is a vast difference in the performance of a "turned-on" versus "turned-off" marketing group. Managers must meet with their subordinates periodically to review their performance, praise their strengths, point out their weaknesses, and suggest ways to improve.

There are likely to be many surprises and disappointments as marketing plans are implemented. The company needs feedback and control procedures (Chapter 27). Three types of marketing controls can be distinguished: annual-plan control, profitability control, and strategic control.

Annual-plan control is the task of making sure that the company is achieving its sales, profits, and other goals. First, management must state well-defined goals in the annual plan for each month or quarter. Second, management must measure its ongoing performance in the marketplace. Third, management must determine the underlying causes of any serious performance gaps. Fourth, management must choose corrective actions to close gaps between goals and performance.

Profitability control is the task of measuring actual profitability of products, customer groups, trade channels, and order sizes. This is not a simple task. A company's accounting system is seldom designed to report the real profitability of different marketing entities and activities. *Marketing profitability analysis* is the tool used to measure the profitability of different marketing activities. *Marketing efficiency studies* are also needed to study how various marketing activities could be carried out more efficiently.

Strategic control is the task of evaluating whether the company's marketing strategy is still appropriate to the market conditions. Because of the rapid changes in the marketing environment, each company needs to reassess periodically its marketing effectiveness through a control instrument known as the *marketing audit*.

Figure 4-7 presents a grand summary of the marketing process and the forces

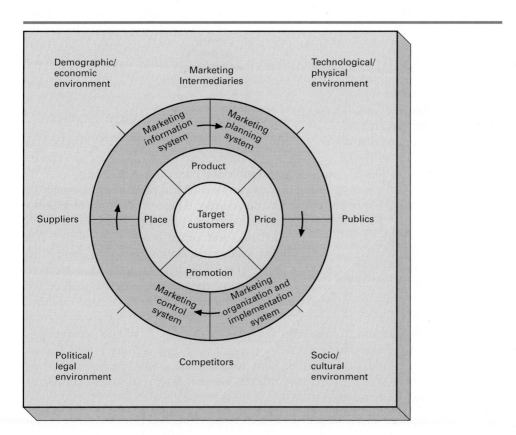

FIGURE 4-7
Factors Influencing Company Marketing Strategy

shaping the company's marketing strategy. Through the systems shown in Figure 4-7, the company monitors and adapts to the marketing environment. The company adapts to its microenvironment consisting of marketing intermediaries, suppliers, competitors, and publics. And it adapts to the macroenvironment consisting of demographic/economic forces, political/legal forces, technological/physical forces, and social/cultural forces. The company takes into account the actors and forces in the marketing environment in developing its strategy to serve the target market. All this applies as much to managing a small domestic business as well as to managing a global corporation (see Global Marketing 4-1).

Global Marketing 4-1

Marketing Engineering Comes to the Aid of Global Marketing Management

Multinational companies face the twin problems of managing complexity and diversity. Complexity exists to the extent that the company operates in different geographical areas with different segments, sales channels, and products. Diversity exists to the extent that there are pronounced differences among the geographical areas in market segments, channels, and products.

Consider the Phoenix Company (name and business disguised), a major chemicals manufacturer operating in over 50 countries. It operates in nine markets, with an average of five segments per market. Well over 5,000 Phoenix products address the needs of these 45 types of buyers.

The following challenges face management: How can headquarters know what is happening throughout the world with all its products in all of the market segments? How can the company assess its best market opportunities for investing money for future research, plant, and equipment? How can headquarters put some order in this diversity to build significant competitive advantages and achieve its long run growth goals? How can marketing managers in one part of the world learn from their counterparts in other countries who have faced similar marketing challenges?

Unless a company can *micromanage* its worldwide businesses, it cannot hope to optimize its results. To solve these problems, Phoenix hired the CRG Marketing Group of Washington, D.C., which specializes in databased strategic planning systems for marketing management. CRG staff worked with Phoenix's worldwide commercial team, executive council, and MIS department to achieve common definitions of markets, segments, and data sources. The resulting product was a Strategic Marketing Planning System (SMPS) consisting of data-driven market planning routines

which enable managers throughout the world to track and forecast product sales by market and segment based upon analysis of market dynamics, customer segment needs, and competitor success factors. The system also incorporates recommended short-term tactics and long-term strategies to capture added revenue above baseline trend.

With SMPS, this company is now able to micromanage its businesses in over fifty countries. Systems such as this are changing marketing from a "conceptual system" to an "engineering science." To the extent that this is achieved, marketing will be able to influence the company's R&D budgets, manufacturing schedules, and financial requirements rather than the other way around.

How Marketing Engineering Works

To understand how marketing engineering works, consider a Phoenix marketing manager located in Germany who is responsible for preparing a marketing plan for selling his company's chemical products to German automotive manufacturers. These products include industrial chemicals, electronic products, lubricant additives, flame retardants, and other product categories. The marketing manager turns on his PC which displays five regions of the world. He clicks on to the European region, then Germany, then the automotive market, and then the OEM segment which uses industrial chemicals in its manufacturing process. This important segment of manufacturers has its own requirements, perceptions, competitor preferences, and purchasing power, that are different from other manufacturing segments in the automotive market, like parts and accessories manufacturers.

The Nature and Contents of a Marketing Plan

We have seen that one of the most important outputs of the marketing process is the *marketing plan*. We now ask: What does a marketing plan look like?

Marketing plans will have several sections, such as those listed in Table 4-1. The plan sections will be illustrated with the following case:

> Jane Melody is the product manager of Zenith's line of modular stereo systems, called the Allegro line. Each system consists of an AM-FM tuner/amplifier plus phono-

The marketing manager in Germany can review the number of such manufacturers; the sales of various products to these businesses; his company's historical market share, prices, and revenue, and so on. He can retrieve a profile of this segment's key success factors in making its product purchase selections, and how his company and each major competitor stand in relation to these success factors. He can develop a strategy to outperform competitors by repositioning existing products and product groups to more closely meet heavily weighted success factors in customer purchase behavior. He can estimate the added revenue from such repositioning within this segment, along with costs and margins.

In addition, he can identify new customer needs, and new product developments which respond to these needs, as well as estimate their added value above baseline forecasts. Then he can estimate how this segment rates as an opportunity in relation to other automotive segments. This will help him decide on the proper strategic direction and investment to make within each segment in this market.

Beyond the structured framework for data-driven decision making, the system also offers a second benefit to the German marketing manager. He may have heard that his counterpart in Japan has been very successful selling to the same segment. By clicking to the Far East, Japan, and automobiles, he can examine his counterpart's data and strategy. He may gain some important insights in reviewing his counterpart's data and strategy in selling to this segment in Japan. He may want to phone his counterpart to discuss their strategies further.

Finally, from a global perspective, worldwide marketing managers are now able to review the recommendations and strategies of their counterparts across the world in a common format and to make critical management decisions in an informed and interactive manner.

Uses and Benefits of Marketing Engineering Systems

Here are several benefits which can be obtained with relational databased global marketing planning systems:

- Better segment-level planning within a country.
- Better performance in identifying cross-country niches and opportunities.
- Better cross-country communication about winning strategies and tactics within the market segment.
- Better financial discipline for deciding among competing R&D investments.
- Better training of marketing skills and thinking as a result of providing a common marketing paradigm and mindset.
- Better worldwide tracking of significant competitors.
- Better archival memory for new managers who take over segment responsibility.
- Better headquarters control of worldwide investment as a result of built-in cost estimates.

All said, marketing engineering means that the company has converted itself into a learning organization which continuously and flexibly zeroes in on the best opportunities in the marketplace.

SOURCE: From a draft by Nelson Rosenbaum, Milton Kotler, and Philip Kotler, CRG Marketing Group, Washington, D.C., 1993.

TABLE 4-1
Contents of a Marketing Plan

SECTION	PURPOSE
I. Executive summary	Presents a brief overview of the proposed plan for quick management skimming.
II. Current marketing situation	Presents relevant background data on the market, product, competition, distribution, and macroenvironment.
III. Opportunity and issue analysis	Identifies the main opportunities/threats, strengths/weaknesses, and issues facing the product.
IV. Objectives	Defines the goals the plan wants to reach in the areas of sales volume, market share, and profit.
V. Marketing strategy	Presents the broad marketing approach that will be used to achieve the plan's objectives.
VI. Action programs	Answers: *What* will be done? *Who* will do it? *When* will it be done? *How much* will it cost?
VII. Projected profit-and-loss statement	Forecasts the expected financial outcomes from the plan.
VIII. Controls	Indicates how the plan will be monitored.

graph plus tape deck and separate speakers. Zenith offers several different models that sell in the $150–$400 range. Zenith's main goal is to increase its market share and profitability in the modular-stereo-system market. As product manager, Jane Melody has to prepare a marketing plan to improve the performance of the Allegro line.

Executive Summary

The planning document should open with a short summary of the plan's main goals and recommendations. Here is an abbreviated example:

> The 1994 Allegro marketing plan seeks to generate a significant increase in company sales and profits over the preceding year. The profit target is $1.8 million. The sales-revenue target is $18 million, which represents a planned 9% sales gain over last year. This increase is seen as attainable through improved pricing, advertising, and distribution. The required marketing budget will be $2,290,000, a 14% increase over last year. . . . [More details follow.]

The executive summary permits higher management to grasp quickly the plan's major thrust. A table of contents should follow the executive summary.

Current Marketing Situation

This section presents relevant background data on the market, product, competition, distribution, and macroenvironment. The data will be drawn from a *product fact book* maintained by the product manager.

MARKET SITUATION ❖ Here data are presented on the target market. The size and growth of the market (in units and/or dollars) are shown for several past years in total and by market and geographical segments. Data are also presented on customer needs, perceptions, and buying-behavior trends.

> The modular stereo market accounts for approximately $400 million, or 20% of the home stereo market. Sales are expected to be stable over the next few years. . . . The primary buyers are middle-income consumers, ages 20 to 40, who want to listen to good music but do not want to invest in expensive stereo component equipment. They want to buy a complete system produced by a name they can trust. They want a system with good sound and whose looks fit the decor primarily of family rooms.

PRODUCT SITUATION ❖ Here the sales, prices, contribution margins, and net profits are shown for each major product in the line for several past years (see Table 4-2):

Row 1, in Table 4-2, shows the total industry sales in units growing at 5% annually until 1993, when demand declined slightly. Row 2 shows Zenith's market share hovering around 3%, although it reached 4% in 1989. Row 3 shows the average price for an Allegro stereo rising about 10% per year except the last year, when it rose 4%. Row 4 shows variable costs—materials, labor, energy—rising each year. Row 5 shows that the gross contribution margin per unit—the difference between price (row 3) and unit variable cost (row 4)—rose the first few years and remained at $100 in the latest year. Rows 6 and 7 show sales volume in units and dollars, and row 8 shows the total gross contribution margin, which rose until the latest year, when it fell. Row 9 shows that overhead remained constant during 1990 and 1991 and increased to a high level during 1992 and 1993, owing to an increase in manufacturing capacity. Row 10 shows net contribution margin, that is, gross contribution margin less overhead. Rows 11, 12, and 13 show marketing expenditures on advertising and promotion, salesforce and distribution, and marketing research. Finally, row 14 shows net operating profit after marketing expenses. The picture is one of increasing profits until 1993, when they fell to about one third of the 1992 level. Clearly Zenith's product manager needs to find a strategy for 1994 that will restore healthy growth in sales and profits to the product line.

COMPETITIVE SITUATION ❖ Here the major competitors are identified and are described in terms of their size, goals, market share, product quality, marketing strategies, and other characteristics that are needed to understand their intentions and behavior.

Zenith's major competitors in the modular-stereo-system market are Panasonic, Sony, Magnavox, General Electric, and Electrophonic. Each competitor has a specific strategy and niche in the market. Panasonic, for example, offers 33 models covering the whole price range, sells primarily in department stores and discount stores, and is a heavy advertising spender. It plans to dominate the market through product proliferation and price discounting. . . . [Similar descriptions are prepared for the other competitors.]

TABLE 4-2 Historical Product Data

VARIABLE	ROWS	1990	1991	1992	1993
1. Industry sales (units)		2,000,000	2,100,000	2,205,000	2,200,000
2. Company market share (%)		0.03	0.03	0.04	0.03
3. Average price per unit ($)		200	220	240	250
4. Variable cost per unit ($)		120	125	140	150
5. Gross contribution margin per unit ($)	(3−4)	80	95	100	100
6. Sales volume (units)	(1×2)	60,000	63,000	88,200	66,000
7. Sales revenue ($)	(3×6)	12,000,000	13,860,000	21,168,000	16,500,000
8. Gross contribution margin ($)	(5×6)	4,800,000	5,985,000	8,820,000	6,600,000
9. Overhead ($)		2,000,000	2,000,000	3,500,000	3,500,000
10. Net contribution margin ($)	(8−9)	2,800,000	3,985,000	5,320,000	3,100,000
11. Advertising and promotion ($)		800,000	1,000,000	1,000,000	900,000
12. Salesforce and distribution ($)		700,000	1,000,000	1,100,000	1,000,000
13. Marketing research ($)		100,000	120,000	150,000	100,000
14. Net operating profit ($)	(10−11−12−13)	1,200,000	1,865,000	3,070,000	1,100,000

DISTRIBUTION SITUATION ❖ This section presents data on the size and importance of each distribution channel.

> Modular stereo sets are sold through department stores, radio/TV stores, appliance stores, discount stores, furniture stores, music stores, audio specialty stores, and mail order. Zenith sells 37% of its sets through appliance stores, 23% through radio/TV stores, 10% through furniture stores, 3% through department stores, and the remainder through other channels. Zenith dominates in channels that are declining in importance, while it is a weak competitor in the faster-growing channels, such as discount stores. Zenith gives about a 30% margin to its dealers, which is similar to what other competitors give.

MACROENVIRONMENT SITUATION ❖ This section describes broad macroenvironment trends —demographic, economic, technological, political/legal, socio/cultural— that bear on this product line's future.

> About 50% of U.S. households now have stereo equipment. As the market approaches saturation, effort must be turned to convincing consumers to upgrade their equipment.... The economy is expected to be weak, which means people will postpone consumer-durables purchases.... The Japanese have designed new and more compact audio systems that pose a challenge to conventional stereo systems.

Opportunity and Issue Analysis

Now the product manager proceeds to identify the major *opportunities/threats, strengths/weaknesses*, and *issues* facing the product line.

OPPORTUNITIES/THREATS ANALYSIS ❖ Here the manager identifies the main opportunities and threats facing the business. The main *opportunities* facing Zenith's Allegro line are as follows:

- ◆ Consumers are showing increased interest in more compact modular stereo systems, and Zenith should consider designing one or more compact models.
- ◆ Two major national department store chains are willing to carry the Allegro line if we will give them extra advertising support.
- ◆ A major national discount chain is willing to carry the Allegro line if we will offer a special discount for their higher purchase volume.

The main *threats* facing Zenith's Allegro line are as follows:

- ◆ An increasing number of consumers are buying their sets in mass-merchandise and discount stores, in which Allegro has weak representation.
- ◆ An increasing number of upscale consumers are showing a preference for component systems, and we do not have an audio component line.
- ◆ Some of our competitors have introduced smaller speakers with excellent sound quality, and consumers are favoring these smaller speakers.
- ◆ The federal government may pass a more stringent product-safety law, which would entail product redesign work.

STRENGTHS/WEAKNESSES ANALYSIS ❖ The manager needs to identify product strengths and weaknesses. The main *strengths* of Zenith's Allegro line are as follows:

- ◆ Zenith's name has excellent brand awareness and an image of high quality.
- ◆ Dealers who sell the Allegro line are knowledgeable and well trained in selling.

♦ Zenith has an excellent service network, and consumers know they will get quick repair service.

The main *weaknesses* of Zenith's Allegro line are as follows:

♦ Allegro's sound quality is not demonstrably better than that of competing sets, and yet sound quality can make a big difference in brand choice.

♦ Zenith is budgeting only 5% of its sales revenue for advertising and promotion, while some major competitors are spending twice that level.

♦ Zenith's Allegro line is not clearly positioned compared with Magnavox ("quality") and Sony ("innovation"). Zenith needs a *unique selling proposition*. The current advertising campaign is not particularly creative or exciting.

♦ Zenith's brand is priced higher than other brands without being supported by a real perceived difference in quality. The pricing strategy should be reevaluated.

ISSUES ANALYSIS ❖ In this section, the company uses the previous findings to define the main issues that must be addressed in the plan. Zenith must consider the following basic *issues*:

♦ Should Zenith stay in the stereo-equipment business? Can it compete effectively? Or should it harvest or divest this product line?

♦ If Zenith stays in, should it continue with its present products, distribution channels, and price and promotion policies?

♦ Should Zenith switch to high-growth channels (such as discount stores), and can it do this and yet retain the loyalty of its current channel partners?

♦ Should Zenith increase its advertising and promotion expenditures to match competitors' expenditures?

♦ Should Zenith pour money into R&D to develop advanced features, sound, and styling?

Objectives

At this point, the product manager must decide on the plan's objectives. Two types of objectives must be set: financial and marketing.

FINANCIAL OBJECTIVES ❖ Zenith's management wants each business unit to deliver a good financial performance. The product manager sets the following financial objectives for the Allegro line:

♦ Earn an annual rate of return on investment over the next five years of 15% after taxes.

♦ Produce net profits of $1,800,000 in 1994.

♦ Produce a cash flow of $2,000,000 in 1994.

MARKETING OBJECTIVES ❖ The financial objectives must be converted into marketing objectives. For example, if the company wants to earn $1,800,000 profit, and its target profit margin is 10% on sales, then it must set a goal of $18 million in sales revenue. If the company sets an average price of $260, it must sell 69,230 units. If it expects total industry sales to reach 2.3 million units, that is a 3% market share. To maintain this market share, the company will have to set certain goals for consumer awareness, distribution coverage, and so on. Thus the *marketing objectives* might read:

♦ Achieve total sales revenue of $18,000,000 in 1994, which represents a 9% increase from last year.

- Therefore, achieve a unit sales volume of 69,230, which represents an expected market share of 3%.
- Expand consumer awareness of the Allegro brand from 15% to 30% over the planning period.
- Expand the number of distribution outlets by 10%.
- Aim for an average realized price of $260.

Marketing Strategy

The product manager now outlines the broad marketing strategy or "game plan":

Zenith's basic strategy for Allegro is to aim at the upscale family, with particular emphasis on the woman buyer. The product line will be expanded by adding lower-price and higher-price units. The average price of the line will be raised 4%. A new and intensified advertising campaign will be developed to increase the perceived reliability of our brand in the consumer's mind. We will launch a strong sales-promotion program to attract increased consumer and dealer attention to our line. We will expand distribution to cover department stores but will avoid discount stores. We will put more funds into restyling the Allegro line so that it projects an image of high-quality sound and reliability.

The same strategy can be presented in list form:

Target market:	Upscale households, with particular emphasis on female buyer.
Positioning:	The best-sounding and most reliable modular stereo system.
Product line:	Add one lower-price model and two higher-price models.
Price:	Price somewhat above competitive brands.
Distribution outlets:	Heavy in radio/TV stores and appliance stores; increased efforts to penetrate department stores.
Salesforce:	Expand by 10% and introduce a national account-management system.
Service:	Widely available and quick service.
Advertising:	Develop a new advertising campaign that supports the positioning strategy; emphasize higher-price units in the ads; increase the advertising budget by 20%.
Sales promotion:	Increase the sales-promotion budget by 15% to develop a point-of-purchase display and to participate to a greater extent in dealer trade shows.
Research and development:	Increase expenditures by 25% to develop better styling of Allegro line.
Marketing research:	Increase expenditures by 10% to improve knowledge of consumer-choice process and to monitor competitor moves.

In developing the strategy, the manager needs to discuss it with the purchasing and manufacturing people to make sure they are able to buy enough material and produce enough units to meet the targeted sales-volume levels, the sales manager to obtain the planned salesforce support, and the financial officer to make sure enough advertising and promotion funds will be available.

Action Programs

The strategy statement represents the broad marketing thrusts to achieve the business objectives. Each marketing strategy element must now be elaborated to answer: *What* will be done? *When* will it be done? *Who* will do it? *How much* will it cost? Consider the sales-promotion action program:

> Zenith's sales-promotion program will consist of two parts, one directed at dealers and the other at consumers. The dealer-promotion program will consist of:
>
> *April.* Zenith will participate in the Consumer Electronics Trade Show in Chicago. Robert Jones, dealer promotion director, will make the arrangements. The expected cost is $14,000.
>
> *August.* A sales contest will be conducted, which will award three Hawaiian vacations to the three dealers producing the greatest percentage increase in sales of Allegro units. The contest will be handled by Mary Tyler at a planned cost of $13,000.

The consumer promotion program will consist of:

> *February.* Zenith will advertise in the newspapers that a free Barbra Streisand record album will be given to everyone buying an Allegro unit this month. Ann Morris, consumer promotion director, will handle this project at a planned cost of $5,000.
>
> *September.* A newspaper advertisement will announce that consumers who attend an Allegro store demonstration in the second week of September will have their names entered in a sweepstakes, the grand prizes to be ten Allegros. Ann Morris will handle this project at a planned cost of $6,000.

Projected Profit-and-Loss Statement

The action plans allow the product manager to build a supporting budget. On the revenue side, it shows the forecasted sales volume in units and the average realized price. On the expense side, it shows the cost of production, physical distribution, and marketing, broken down into finer categories. The difference is projected profit. Higher management will review the budget and approve or modify it. If the requested budget is too high, the product manager will have to make some cuts. Once approved, the budget is the basis for developing plans and schedules for material procurement, production scheduling, employee recruitment, and marketing operations.

Controls

The last section of the plan outlines the controls for monitoring the plan's progress. Typically the goals and budget are spelled out for each month or quarter. Higher management can review the results each period and spot businesses that are not attaining their goals. Managers of lagging businesses must explain what is happening and the actions they will take to improve plan fulfillment.

Some control sections include contingency plans. A contingency plan outlines the steps that management would take in response to specific adverse developments, such as price wars or strikes. The purpose of contingency planning is to encourage managers to give prior thought to difficulties that might lie ahead (see Marketing Concepts and Tools 4-1).

What's Marketing Planning Like in the 1990s?

In 1990, the Conference Board surveyed marketing executives working in major consumer, industrial, and service companies to gather their views on the current state of marketing planning. A number of changes had occurred since their last study in 1981. They found that more companies rediscovered the marketing concept and saw the central purpose of their enterprise to be that of acquiring and satisfying customers rather than producing goods or services. Business plans had become more customer and competitor-oriented and they were better reasoned and more realistic. The plans drew more inputs from all the functions and were essentially team-developed. Marketing executives increasingly saw themselves as professional managers first, and specialists second. Senior management was becoming more involved in making and/or approving marketing decisions. And planning was becoming a continual process throughout the year to respond to rapidly changing market conditions.

At the same time, marketing planning procedures and content varied considerably among companies. The plan was variously called a business plan, a marketing plan, and sometimes an operating plan. Most marketing plans covered one year, but some covered a few years. The plans varied in their length from under ten pages to over 50 pages. Some companies took their plans very seriously and others saw them as only a rough guide to action.

When marketing executives were asked about shortcomings of current marketing plans, the most cited criticisms were the lack of realism, insufficient competitive analysis, and the short-run focus.

SOURCE: Howard Sutton, *The Marketing Plan in the 1990s* (New York: The Conference Board, 1990).

SUMMARY ❖

Marketing plans focus on a product/market and consist of the detailed marketing strategies and programs for achieving the product's objectives in a target market. Marketing plans are the central instrument for directing and coordinating the marketing effort.

The marketing planning process consists of five steps: analyzing market opportunities; researching and selecting target markets; designing marketing strategies; planning marketing programs; and organizing, implementing, and controlling the marketing effort.

Marketing planning results in a document that contains the following sections: executive summary, current market situation, opportunity and issue analysis, objectives, marketing strategy, action programs, projected profit-and-loss statement, and controls.

To plan effectively, marketing managers must understand the key relationship between types of marketing-mix expenditures and their sales and profit consequences. These relationships are explained in the appendix to Chapter 4.

NOTES ❖

1. Michael J. Lanning and Edward G. Michaels, "A Business Is a Value Delivery System," McKinsey staff paper, no. 41, June 1988 (McKinsey & Co., Inc.).

2. E. Jerome McCarthy, *Basic Marketing: A Managerial Approach* (Homewood, IL: Richard D. Irwin, 1981), now in its ninth edition. Two alternative classifications are worth noting. Frey proposed that all marketing-decision variables could be categorized into two factors: the *offering* (product, packaging, brand, price, and service) and *methods and tools* (distribution channels, personal selling, advertising, sales promotion, and publicity). See Albert W. Frey, *Advertising*, 3rd ed. (New York: Ronald Press, 1961), p. 30. Lazer and Kelly proposed a three-factor classification: *goods and service mix, distribution mix*, and *communications mix*. See William Lazer and Eugene J. Kelly, *Managerial Marketing: Perspectives and Viewpoints*, rev. ed. (Homewood, IL: Richard Irwin, 1962), p. 413.

3. Robert Lauternborn, "New Marketing Litany: Four P's Passe; C-Words Take Over," *Advertising Age*, October 1, 1990, p. 26.

APPENDIX

The Theory of Effective Marketing-Resource Allocation

Having examined how actual marketing plans are constructed, we will now describe important tools and concepts that managers can use to improve their marketing planning. Planning can now be done on microcomputers using tailored computer programs and spreadsheets. At companies such as Quaker Oats and General Mills, brand managers use computers to develop and estimate the revenue and cost of different marketing strategies. These computer programs utilize equations that describe how sales and profits respond to different marketing-mix expenditures. We will illustrate in the following paragraphs the type of equations used.

The Profit Equation

Every marketing-mix strategy will lead to a certain level of profit. The profit can be estimated through a profit equation. Profits (Z) by definition are equal to the product's revenue (R) less its costs (C):

$$Z = R - C \tag{4-1}$$

Revenue is equal to the product's net price (P') times its unit sales (Q):

$$R = P'Q \tag{4-2}$$

But the product's net price (P') is equal to its list price (P) less any allowance per unit (k) representing freight allowances, commissions, and discounts:

$$P' = P - k \tag{4-3}$$

The product's costs can be conveniently classified into unit variable non-marketing costs (c), fixed costs (F), and marketing costs (M):

$$C = cQ + F + M \tag{4-4}$$

Substituting equations (4-2), (4-3), and (4-4) into (4-1) and simplifying,

$$Z = [(P - k) - c]Q - F - M \tag{4-5}$$

where:

Z = total profits
P = list price
k = allowance per unit (such as freight allowances, commissions, discounts)
c = production and distribution variable cost (such as labor costs, delivery costs)
Q = number of units sold
F = fixed costs (such as salaries, rent, electricity)
M = discretionary marketing costs (such as advertising, sales promotion)

The expression $[(P-k)-c]$ is the *gross contribution margin per unit*—the amount the company realizes on the average unit after deducting allowances and the variable costs of producing and distributing the average unit. The expression $[(P-k)-c]Q$ is the *gross contribution margin*—the net revenue available to cover the fixed costs, profits, and discretionary marketing expenditures.

The Sales Equation

In order to use the profit equation for planning purposes, the product manager needs to develop a model of the variables affecting sales volume (Q). The relation of sales volume to these variables is specified in a sales equation (also called the *sales-response function*):

$$Q = f(X_1, X_2 \ldots, X_n, Y_1, Y_2, \ldots, Y_m) \qquad (4\text{-}6)$$

where:

$(X_1, X_2, \ldots, X_n)$ = sales variables under the control of the firm
$(Y_1, Y_2, \ldots, Y_m)$ = sales variables not under the control of the firm

Y variables include the size of the target market, its income, competitors' prices, and so on. As these variables change, so does the market's buying rate. The manager has no influence over the Y variables but needs to estimate them for forecasting purposes. We will assume that the manager has estimated Y variables and their effect on sales volume, which is conveyed by

$$Q = f(X_1, X_2, \ldots, X_n \mid Y_1, Y_2, \ldots, Y_m) \qquad (4\text{-}7)$$

which says that sales volume is a function of the X variables, for given levels of the Y variables.

The X variables are the variables that the manager can set to influence the sales level. The X variables include the list price (P), allowances (k), variable cost (c) (to the extent that high variable costs reflect improved product quality, delivery time, and customer service), and marketing expenditures (M). Thus sales, as a function of the manager's controllable variables, are described by

$$Q = f(p, k, c, M) \qquad (4\text{-}8)$$

We can make one additional refinement. The marketing budget, M, can be spent in several ways, such as advertising (A), sales promotion (S), salesforce (D), and marketing research (R).

The sales equation is now

$$Q = f(P, k, c, A, S, D, R) \qquad (4\text{-}9)$$

where the elements in the parentheses represent the *marketing mix*.

Profit-Optimization Planning

Suppose the manager wants to find a marketing mix that will maximize profits in the coming year. This requires having an idea of how each element in the marketing mix will affect sales. We will use the term *sales-response function* to describe the relationship between sales volume and a particular element of the marketing mix. Specifically, *the sales-response function forecasts the likely sales volume during a specified time period associated with different possible levels of a marketing-mix element, holding constant the other marketing-mix elements.* It should not be thought of as describing a relationship over time between the two variables. To the extent that managers have a good intuition for the relevant sales-response functions, they are in a position to formulate more effective marketing plans.

What are the possible shapes of sales-response functions? Figure 4A-1 shows several possibilities. Figure 4A-1(a) shows the well-known relationship between price and sales volume, known as the law of demand. The relationship states that more sales will occur, other things being equal, at lower prices. The illustration shows a curvilinear relationship, although a linear relationship is also possible.

Figure 4A-1(b) shows four possible functional relationships between sales volume and marketing expenditures. Marketing expenditure function (*A*) is the least plausible: It states that sales volume is not affected by the level of marketing expenditures. It would mean that the number of customers and their purchasing rates are not affected by sales calls, advertising, sales promotion, or marketing research. Marketing expenditure function (*B*) states that sales volume grows linearly with marketing expenditures. In the illustration, the intercept is 0, but this is inaccurate if some sales would take place even in the absence of marketing expenditures.

Marketing expenditure function (*C*) is a concave function showing sales volume increasing throughout at a decreasing rate. It is a plausible description of sales response to salesforce-size increases. The rationale is as follows: If a field salesforce consisted of one sales representative, that representative would call on the best prospects, and the marginal rate of sales response would be highest. A second sales rep would call on the next best prospects, and the marginal rate of sales response would be somewhat less. Successively hired sales reps would call on successively less responsive prospects, resulting in a diminishing rate of sales increase.

Marketing expenditure function (*D*) is an **S**-shaped function showing sales volume initially increasing at an increasing rate and then increasing at a decreasing rate. It is a plausible description of sales response to increasing levels of advertising expenditure. The rationale is as follows: Small advertising budgets do not buy enough advertising to create more than minimal brand awareness. Larger budgets can produce high brand awareness, interest, and preference, all of which might lead to increased purchase response. Very large budgets, however, may not produce much additional response because the target market becomes highly familiar with the brand.

The relation of eventually diminishing returns to increases in marketing ex-

FIGURE 4A-1
Sales-Response Functions

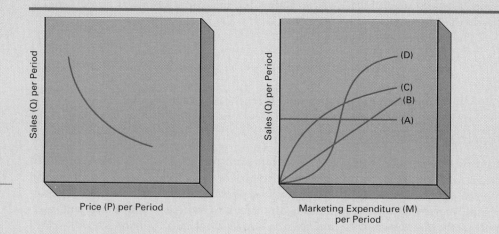

(a) Price function

(b) Market expenditure functions

penditures is plausible for the following reasons. First, there is an upper limit to the total potential demand for any particular product. The easier sales prospects buy almost immediately, leaving the more recalcitrant sales prospects. As the upper limit is approached, it becomes increasingly expensive to attract the remaining buyers. Second, as a company steps up its marketing effort, its competitors are likely to do the same, with the net result that each company experiences increasing sales resistance. And third, if sales were to increase at an increasing rate throughout, natural monopolies would result. A single firm would take over each industry. Yet we do not see this happening.

How can marketing managers estimate the sales-response functions that apply to their business? Three methods are available. The first is the *statistical method*, where the manager gathers data on past sales and levels of marketing-mix variables and estimates the sales-response functions through statistical techniques. Several researchers have used this method with varying degrees of success, depending on the quantity and quality of available data and the stability of the underlying relationships.[1] The second is the *experimental method*, which calls for varying the marketing expenditure and mix levels in matched samples of geographical or other units and noting the resulting sales volume.[2] The experimental method produces the most reliable results but is not used extensively because of its complex requirements, high cost, and inordinate level of management resistance. The third is the *judgmental method*, where experts are asked to make intelligent guesses about the needed magnitudes. This method requires a careful selection of the experts and a defined procedure for gathering and combining their estimates, such as the Delphi method.[3] The judgmental method is often the only feasible one and can be quite useful. We believe that using the estimates of experts is better than forgoing formal analysis of profit optimization.

In estimating sales-response functions, some cautions have to be observed. The sales-response function assumes that other variables remain constant over the range of the function. Thus the company's price and competitors' prices are assumed to remain unchanged no matter what the company spends on marketing. Since this assumption is unrealistic, the sales-response function has to be modified to reflect competitors' probable responses. The sales-response function also assumes a certain level of company efficiency in spending marketing dollars. If the spending efficiency rises or falls, the sales-response function has to be modified. Also, the sales-response function has to be modified to reflect delayed impacts of expenditures on sales beyond one year. These and other characteristics of sales-response functions are spelled out in more detail elsewhere.[4]

Profit Optimization

Once the sales-response functions are estimated, how are they used in profit optimization? Graphically, we introduce some further curves to find the point of optimal marketing expenditure. The analysis is shown in Figure 4A-2. The sales-response function shown here is **S** shaped, although the same analysis applies to any shape. First, the manager subtracts all nonmarketing costs from the *sales-response function* to derive the *gross profit function*. Next, the marketing expenditure function is represented as a straight line starting at the origin and rising at the rate of one dollar of marketing expenditure for every ten dollars of the vertical axes. The marketing expenditure function is then subtracted from the *gross profit curve* to derive the *net profit curve*. The net profit curve shows positive net profits with marketing expenditures between M_L and M_U, which could be defined as the rational range of marketing expenditure. The net profit curve reaches a maximum of M. Therefore the marketing expenditure that would maximize net profit is M.

The graphical solution can also be carried out numerically or algebraically; in-

FIGURE 4A-2
Relationship between Sales Volume, Marketing Expenditures, and Profits

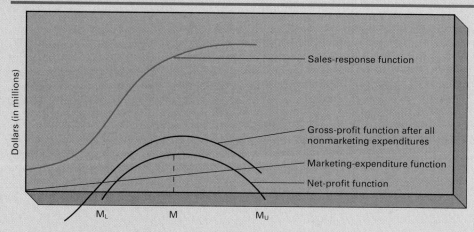

deed it has to be if sales volume is a function of more than one marketing-mix variable. Here we will present a numerical example of how it is done.

A NUMERICAL EXAMPLE ❖ Jane Melody, the Allegro product manager at Zenith, also handles a small phonograph-record-cleaning machine that sells for $16. For some years, she has been using a low-price, low-promotion strategy. Last year she spent $10,000 on advertising and another $10,000 on sales promotion. Sales were 12,000 units, and profits were $14,000. Her boss thinks more profits could be made on this item. Ms. Melody is anxious to find a better strategy to increase profits.

Her first step is to visualize some alternative marketing-mix strategies. She imagines the eight strategies shown in the first three columns of Table 4A-1 (the first strategy is the current one). They were formed by assuming a high and a low level for each of three marketing variables and elaborating all the combinations $(2^3 = 8)$.

Her next step is to estimate the likely sales that would be attained with each marketing mix. She feels that the needed estimates are unlikely to be found through fitting historical data or through conducting experiments. She decides to ask the sales manager for his estimates, since he has shown an uncanny ability to be on target. Suppose he provides the sales estimates shown in the last column in Table 4A-1.

The final step calls for determining which marketing mix maximizes profits,

TABLE 4A-1
Marketing Mixes and Estimated Sales

MARKETING MIX NO.	PRICE (P)	ADVERTISING (A)	PROMOTION (S)	SALES (Q)
1	$16	$10,000	$10,000	12,400
2	16	10,000	50,000	18,500
3	16	50,000	10,000	15,100
4	16	50,000	50,000	22,600
5	24	10,000	10,000	5,500
6	24	10,000	50,000	8,200
7	24	50,000	10,000	6,700
8	24	50,000	50,000	10,000

assuming the sales estimates are reliable. This calls for introducing a profit equation and inserting the different marketing mixes into this equation to see which maximizes profits.

Suppose fixed costs, F, are $38,000; unit variable costs, c, are $10; and the contemplated allowance off list price, k, is $0. Then profit equation (4-5) reads:

$$Z = (P-10)Q - 38{,}000 - A - S \qquad (4\text{-}10)$$

Thus profits are a function of the chosen price, advertising, and sales-promotion budgets.

At this point, the manager can insert each marketing mix and estimated sales level (from Table 4A-1) into this equation. The resulting profits are #1($16,400), #2($13,000), #3(−$7,400), #4(−$2,400), #5($19,000), #6($16,800), #7(−$4,200), and #8($2,000). Marketing mix #5, calling for a price of $24, advertising of $10,000, and promotion of $10,000, yields the highest expected profits ($19,000).

The manager can take one more step. Some marketing mix not shown might yield a still higher profit. To check that possibility, the product manager can fit a sales equation to the data shown in Table 4A-1. The sales estimates can be viewed as a sample from a larger universe of expert judgments concerning the sales equation $Q = f(P,A,S)$. A plausible mathematical form for the sales equation is the multiple exponential:

$$Q = bP^{p}A^{a}S^{s} \qquad (4\text{-}11)$$

where:

b = a scale factor
p, a, s = price, advertising, and promotion elasticity, respectively

Using least-squares regression estimation (not shown), the manager finds the fitted sales equation to be

$$Q = 100{,}000P^{-2}A^{1/8}S^{1/4} \qquad (4\text{-}12)$$

This fits the sales estimates in Table 4A-1 extremely well. Price has an elasticity of -2; that is, a 1% reduction in price, other things being equal, tends to increase unit sales by 2%. Advertising has an elasticity of $\frac{1}{8}$, and promotion has an elasticity of $\frac{1}{4}$. The coefficient 100,000 is a scale factor that translates the dollar magnitudes into sales-volume units.

The product manager now substitutes this sales equation for Q in the profit equation (4-10). This yields, when simplified:

$$Z = 100{,}000\,A1^{1/8}S^{1/4}[P^{-1} - 10P^{-2}] - 38{,}000 - A - S \qquad (4\text{-}13)$$

Profits are shown to be strictly a function of the chosen marketing mix. The manager can insert any marketing mix (including those not shown in Table 4A-1) and derive an estimate of profits. To find the profit-maximizing marketing mix, she applies standard calculus. The optimal marketing mix (P,A,S) is ($20, $12,947, $25,894). Twice as much is spent on promotion as on advertising because its elasticity is twice as great. The product manager would forecast a sales volume of 10,358 units and profits of $26,735. While other marketing mixes can produce higher sales, no other marketing mix can produce higher profits. Using this equation, the product manager has solved not only the optimum marketing mix but also the optimum marketing budget $(A + S = $38,841)$.

Marketing-Mix Optimization

Now we want to examine more closely how to divide the marketing budget among the marketing mix tools. The tools are partially substitutable. A company seeking increased sales can lower the price or increase the salesforce, advertising budget, or promotion budget. The challenge is to find the optimal marketing mix.

Suppose that the marketer wants to divide the marketing budget between advertising and sales promotion. In principle, there is an infinite number of possible divisions. This is shown in Figure 4A-3(a). If there are no constraints on the level of advertising and sales promotion, then every point in the $A - S$ plane shown in Figure 4A-3(a) is a possible marketing mix. An arbitrary line drawn from the origin, called a constant-mix line, shows the set of all marketing mixes where the two tools are in a fixed ratio but where the budget varies. Another arbitrary line, called a constant-budget line, shows a set of varying mixes that would be affordable with a fixed marketing budget.

Associated with every possible marketing mix is a resulting sales level. Three sales levels are shown in Figure 4A-3(a). The marketing mix (A_1S_2)—calling for a small budget divided approximately equally between advertising and sales promotion—is expected to produce sales of Q_1. The marketing mix (A_2S_1) involves the same budget with more expenditure on advertising than on sales promotion; this is expected to produce slightly higher sales, Q_2. The mix (A_3S_3) calls for a larger budget but a relatively equal splitting between advertising and sales promotion and is expected to yield Q_3. Given the many possibilities, the marketer's job is to find the sales equation that predicts the different levels of Q.

For a given marketing budget, the money should be divided among the various marketing tools in a way that gives the same marginal profit on the marginal dollar spent on each tool. A geometrical version of the solution is shown in Figure 4A-3(b). Here we are looking down at the $A - S$ plane shown in Figure 4A-3(a). A constant-budget line is shown, indicating all the alternative marketing mixes that could be achieved with this budget. The curved lines are called *iso-sales curves*. An iso-sales curve shows the different mixes of advertising and sales promotion that

FIGURE 4A-3 The Sales Function Associated with Two Marketing-Mix Elements

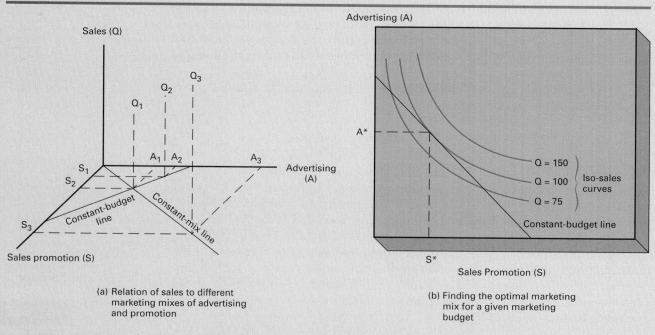

(a) Relation of sales to different marketing mixes of advertising and promotion

(b) Finding the optimal marketing mix for a given marketing budget

Marketing-Mix Interactions Need To Be Watched

Marketing managers carry beliefs in their heads about how specific pairs of marketing variables interact. Here are some of the more popular beliefs:

- Higher advertising expenditures reduce buyers' price sensitivity. Thus a company wishing to charge a higher price should spend more on advertising.
- Advertising expenditures have a greater sales impact on low-price products than on high-price products.
- Higher advertising expenditures reduce the total cost of selling. The advertising expenditures presell the customer, and sales representatives can concentrate their time on answering objections and closing the sale.
- Higher perceived product quality allows the company to charge a disproportionately higher price.
- Higher quality does not cost more to produce, and often costs less than lower quality.
- Higher prices lead buyers to impute higher product quality.
- Tighter credit terms require greater selling and advertising effort to move the same volume of goods.

Marketing-mix variables also interact with nonmarketing variables. Japanese companies are especially sensitive to these interactions. The price they can charge depends upon the company's productivity, which is influenced by personnel policies as well as capital investments. Similarly, product quality is influenced by production reliability and technology, which in turn are influenced by personnel management and R&D investment. Thus marketers must not take price and product for granted but must influence their company to drive down costs and produce higher-quality products.

would produce a given level of sales. It is a projection into the $A - S$ plane of the set of points resulting from horizontal slicing of the sales function shown in Figure 4A-3(a) at a given level of sales. Figure 4A-3(b) shows iso-sales curves for three different sales levels: 75, 100, and 150 units. Given the budget line, it is not possible to attain sales of more than 100 units. The optimum marketing mix is shown at the point of tangency between the budget line and the last-touching iso-sales curve above it. Consequently, the marketing mix $(A*S*)$, which calls for somewhat more advertising than promotion, is the sales-maximizing (and in this case profit-maximizing) marketing mix.

This analysis could be generalized to more than two marketing tools. Ferber and Verdoorn stated that "In an optimum position the additional sales obtained by a small increase in unit costs are the same for all nonprice instruments. . . ."[5]

Dorfman and Steiner went further and formalized the conditions under which price, promotion, and product quality would be optimized.[6] More recently, marketing scientists have investigated how various marketing-mix variables interact in their impact on sales (Marketing Concepts and Tools 4A-1).

Marketing-Allocation Optimization

A final issue is to optimally allocate a given marketing budget to the various *target markets* (TMs). The TMs could be different sales territories, customer groups, or other market segments. Even with a given marketing budget and mix, it may be possible to increase sales and profits by shifting funds among different markets.

Most marketing managers allocate their marketing budgets to the various TMs on the basis of some percentage of actual or expected sales. Consider the following example:

The marketing manager at the Guardian Oil Company (name disguised) estimates total gasoline sales volume (which combines regular and premium gasoline) and

CHAPTER 4
Managing the Marketing
Process and Marketing
Planning

adds premium sales volume back to this figure to yield "profit gallons" (thus giving double weight to premium gasoline sales). The manager then takes the ratio of the advertising budget to the profit gallons to establish a figure for advertising dollars per profit gallon. This is called the prime multiplier. Each market receives an advertising budget equal to its previous year's profit gallons sold multiplied by the prime multiplier. Thus the advertising budget is allocated largely on the basis of last year's company sales in the territory.[7]

Unfortunately, size rules for allocating funds lead to inefficient allocations. They confuse "average" and "marginal" sales response. Figure 4A-4(a) illustrates the difference between the two and indicates that there is no reason to assume they are correlated. The two dots in the figure show current marketing expenditures and company sales in two TMs. The company spends $3 million on marketing in both TMs. Company sales are $40 million in TM 1 and $20 million in TM 2. The average sales response to a dollar of marketing effort is thus greater in TM 1 than in TM 2; it is 40/3 as opposed to 20/3, respectively. It might seem desirable to shift funds from TM 2 to TM 1, where the average response is greater. Yet the real issue is one of the marginal response. The marginal response is represented by the *slope* of the sales function through the points. A higher slope has been drawn for TM 2 than for TM 1. The respective slopes show that another $1 million in marketing expenditure would produce a $10 million sales increase in TM 2 and only a $2 million sales increase in TM 1. Clearly marginal response, not average response, should guide the allocation of marketing funds.

Marginal response is indicated along the sales-response function for each territory. Assume that a company is able to estimate TM sales-response functions. Suppose the sales-response functions for two TMs are those shown in Figure 4A-4(b). The company wishes to allocate a budget of B dollars between the two TMs to maximize profits. When costs are identical for the two TMs, then the allocation that will maximize profits is the one that will maximize sales. The funds are optimally allocated when they exhaust the budget and the marginal sales response is the same in both TMs. Geometrically, this means that the slopes of the tangents to the two sales-response functions at the optimal allocations will be equal. Figure 4A-4(b) shows that a budget of $6 million would be allocated in the amounts of approximately $4.6 million to TM 1 and $1.4 million to TM 2 to produce maximum sales of approximately $180 million. The marginal sales response would be the same in both TMs.

The principle of allocating funds to TMs to equalize the marginal response is

---

FIGURE 4A-4 Sales-Response Functions in Two Target Markets (TMs)

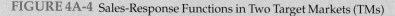

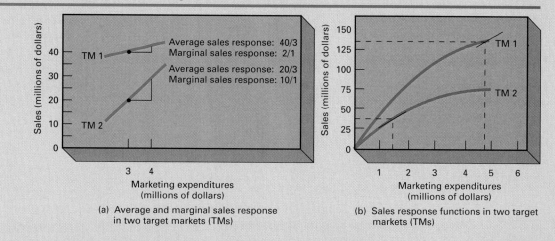

(a) Average and marginal sales response in two target markets (TMs)

(b) Sales response functions in two target markets (TMs)

BUDGET (M)	MARKETING PLAN	SALES FORECAST (Q)
$1,400,000	Maintain sales and market share in the short term by concentrating sales effort on largest chain stores, advertising only on TV, sponsoring two promotions a year, and carrying on only limited marketing research.	60,000 units
$2,000,000	Implement a coordinated effort to expand market share by contacting 80% of all retailers, adding magazine advertising, adding point-of-purchase displays, and sponsoring three promotions during the year.	70,000 units
$2,600,000	Seek to expand market size and share by adding two new product sizes, enlarging the salesforce, increasing marketing research, and expanding the advertising budget.	90,000 units

used in the planning technique called *zero-based budgeting*.[8] The manager of each TM is asked to formulate a marketing plan and estimate the expected sales for (say) three levels of marketing expenditure, such as 30% below the normal level, the normal level, and 30% above the normal level. An example is shown in Table 4A-2, outlining what the Zenith marketing manager would do with each budget level and her estimate of Allegro sales volume. Then higher management reviews this response function against those of other product managers and gives serious consideration to shifting funds from TMs with low marginal responses to TMs with higher marginal responses.

Measuring sales-response functions can lead to substantial shifts in company marketing strategy. A major oil company had located its service stations in every large U.S. city.[9] In many markets, it operated only a small percentage of the total stations. Company management began to question this broad location strategy. It decided to estimate how the company's market share in each city varied with its percentage share of marketing expenditures in each city (as measured by the share of outlets). A curve was fitted showing the share of outlets and share of markets in different cities. The resulting curve was **S** shaped (see Figure 4A-5). This showed

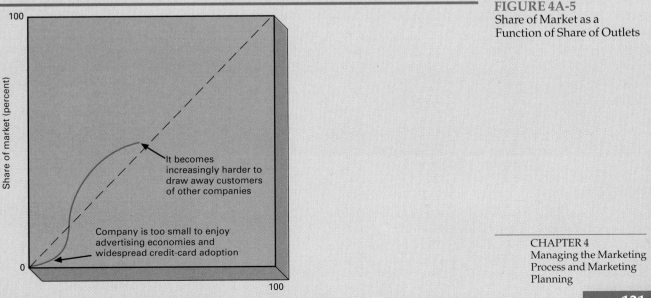

FIGURE 4A-5
Share of Market as a
Function of Share of Outlets

that having a low percentage of stations in a city yielded an even lower percentage of market volume. The practical implication was clear: The company should either withdraw from its weak markets or build them up to, say, 15% of the competitive outlets. Instead of establishing a few outlets in each of many cities, the oil company should establish a large number of outlets in a smaller number of cities. In fact, that is what is happening. Most of the major oil companies in the past tried to be present throughout the United States. Today, each is concentrating geographically and trying to be the regional leader.

NOTES ❖

1. For examples of empirical studies using fitted sales-response functions, see Doyle L. Weiss, "Determinants of Market Share," *Journal of Marketing Research*, August 1968, pp. 290–95; Donald E. Sexton, Jr., "Estimating Marketing Policy Effects on Sales of a Frequently Purchased Product," *Journal of Marketing Research*, August 1970, pp. 338–47; and Jean-Jacques Lambin, "A Computer On-Line Marketing Mix Model," *Journal of Marketing Research*, May 1972, pp. 119–26. More recent studies are reviewed in Dominique M. Hanssens, Leonard J. Parsons, and Randall L. Schultz, *Market Response Models: Econometric and Time Series Analysis* (Boston: Kluwer Academic Publishers, 1990), Chap. 6.

2. See Russell Ackoff and James R. Emshoff, "Advertising Research at Anheuser-Busch," *Sloan Management Review*, Winter 1975, pp. 1–15.

3. See Philip Kotler, "A Guide to Gathering Expert Estimates," *Business Horizons*, October 1970, pp. 79–87.

4. See Gary L. Lilien, Philip Kotler and K. Sridhar Moorthy, *Marketing Models* (Englewood Cliffs, NJ: Prentice-Hall, 1992).

5. Robert Ferber and P. J. Verdoorn, *Research Methods in Economics and Business* (New York: Macmillan, 1962), p. 535.

6. Robert Dorfman and Peter O. Steiner, "Optimal Advertising and Optimal Quality," *American Economic Review*, December 1954, pp. 826–36.

7. Donald C. Marschner, "Theory versus Practice in Allocating Advertising Money," *Journal of Business*, July 1967, pp. 286–302.

8. See Paul J. Stonich, *Zero-Base Planning and Budgeting: Improved Cost Control and Resource Allocation* (Homewood, IL: Dow-Jones-Irwin, 1977).

9. See John J. Cardwell, "Marketing and Management Science —A Marriage on the Rocks?" *California Management Review*, Summer 1968, pp. 3–12.

5

Marketing Information Systems and Marketing Research

A wise man recognizes the convenience of a general statement, but he bows to the authority of a particular fact.

OLIVER WENDELL HOLMES, JR.

To manage a business well is to manage its future; and to manage the future is to manage information.

MARION HARPER

We have emphasized the importance of starting marketing and strategic planning with an outside-inside point of view. Management needs to monitor the larger forces in the marketing environment if it is to keep its products and marketing practices current. But how can management learn about changing customer wants, new competitor initiatives, changing distribution channels, and so on? The answer is clear: Management must develop and manage information.

In the long history of business, management devoted most of its attention to managing *money, materials, machines,* and *men.* Today, management has recognized the critical importance of a fifth resource: *information.* But many managers are dissatisfied with the available information. Their complaints include not knowing where critical information is located in the company; getting too much information that they can't use and too little that they really need; getting important information too late; and doubting the accuracy of the information. Here is one example:

> A computer salesperson wanted to prepare a quote for a customer who wanted to buy an upgraded computer system. The customer was planning to choose between her company and a major competitor. The salesperson, however, couldn't locate the prices for some components on her computer and in other cases got contradictory prices. It took her three days to prepare the quote. Meanwhile her major competitor prepared the quote in one day and was working to close the sale.

The irony is that this salesperson's company was installing computer information systems in other companies but lacked a well-run computer information system of its own.

Many companies have not yet adapted to the intensified information requirements for effective marketing in the 1990s. Three developments render the need for marketing information greater than at any time in the past:

- ◆ *From local to national to global marketing:* As companies expand their geographical market coverage, their managers need more market information than ever before.
- ◆ *From buyer needs to buyer wants:* As buyers' incomes increase, they become more selective in their choice of goods. Sellers find it harder to predict buyers' response to different features, styles, and other attributes, unless they turn to marketing research.
- ◆ *From price to nonprice competition:* As sellers increase their use of branding, product differentiation, advertising, and sales promotion, they require information on the effectiveness of these marketing tools.

The explosive information requirements have been met on the supply side by impressive new information technologies. The past 30 years have witnessed the emergence of the computer, microfilming, cable television, copy machines, fax machines, tape recorders, video recorders, videodisc players, and other devices that have revolutionized information handling. Nevertheless, most business firms lack information sophistication. Many firms do not have a marketing research department. Many other firms have small marketing research departments whose work is limited to routine forecasting, sales analysis, and occasional surveys. Some firms have developed advanced marketing information systems that provide company

Marketing Environment and Trends 5-1

Marketing Researchers Know the Smallest Details about Consumers

Large companies know the whats, wheres, hows, and whens of their consumers. They figure out all sorts of things about us that we don't even know ourselves. To marketers, this isn't trivial pursuit—knowing all about the customer is the cornerstone of effective marketing.

Coke knows that we put 3.2 ice cubes in a glass, see 69 of its commercials every year, and prefer cans to pop out of vending machines at a temperature of 35 degrees. One million of us drink Coke with breakfast every day. Did you know that 38% of Americans would rather have a tooth pulled than take their car to a dealership for repairs? We each spend $20 a year on flowers; Arkansas has the lowest consumption of peanut butter in the United States; 51% of all males put their left pants leg on first, whereas 65% of women start with the right leg; and if you send a husband and a wife to the store separately to buy beer, there is a 90% chance they will return with different brands.

Nothing about our behavior is sacred. Procter & Gamble once conducted a study to find out whether most of us fold or crumple our toilet paper; another study showed that 68% of consumers prefer their toilet paper to unwind over the spool rather than under. Abbott Laboratories figured out that one in four of us has "problem" dandruff, and Kimberly Clark, which makes Kleenex, has calculated that the average person blows his or her nose 256 times a year.

It's not that Americans are all that easy to figure out. Hoover had to hook up timers and other equipment to vacuum cleaners in people's homes to learn that we spend about 35 minutes each week vacuuming, sucking up about 8 pounds of dust each year and using six bags to do so. Banks know that we write about 24 checks a month, and pharmaceutical companies know that all of us together take 52 million aspirins and 30 million sleeping pills a year. In fact, almost everything we swallow is closely monitored by someone. Each year, we consume 156 hamburgers, 95 hot dogs, 283 eggs, 5 pounds of yogurt, 9 pounds of cereal, 2 pounds of peanut butter, and 46 quarts of popcorn. We spend 90 minutes a day preparing our food and 40 minutes a day munching it. And as a nation, we down $650 million of antacid a year to help digest the food we eat.

Thus, most big marketing companies have answers to all the what, where, when, and how questions about their consumers' buying behavior. Seemingly trivial facts add up quickly and provide important input for designing marketing strategies. But to influence consumer behavior, marketers need the answer to one more question: Beyond knowing the whats and wherefores of behavior, they need to know the *whys*—what *causes* our buying behavior? That's a much harder question to answer.

SOURCES: John Koten, "You Aren't Paranoid If You Feel Someone Eyes You Constantly," *The Wall Street Journal*, March 29, 1985, pp. 1, 22; and "Offbeat Marketing," *Sales & Marketing Management*, January 1990, p. 35; and Erik Larson, "Attention Shoppers: Don't Look Now But You Are Being Tailed," *Smithsonian Magazine*, January 1993, pp. 70–79.

---

management with incredible up-to-date detail about buyer behavior (see Marketing Environment and Trends 5-1 and Global Marketing 5-1).

Concept and Components of a Marketing Information System

Every firm must organize the flow of marketing information to its marketing managers. Companies are studying their managers' information needs and designing *marketing information systems* (MIS) to meet these needs. We define a marketing information system as follows:

❖ *A marketing information system (MIS) consists of people, equipment, and procedures to gather, sort, analyze, evaluate, and distribute needed, timely, and accurate information to marketing decision makers.*

What Are Europeans Made Of?

Although there is much talk about a single European market, the truth is that Europeans vary tremendously in their food and other preferences. This is all the more reason that marketers selling in Europe must at least think "countries," and better yet, "localities." They must put a microscope on consumers and research their target markets carefully. How many of the following questions can you answer about European country consumption differences:

On a per capita basis, in what European country do the people . . . .

1. consume the most chocolate?
2. eat the most cheese?
3. drink the most wine?
4. eat the most breakfast cereal?
5. drink the most tea?
6. spend the most on hair care products?
7. smoke the most cigarettes?
8. have the lowest consumption of toilet tissue?
9. spend the most on male fragrances

Answers:

1. Switzerland 2. Greece 3. France 4. United Kingdom 5. Ireland 6. Austria 7. Austria 8. Portugal 9. France

SOURCE: From *Consumer Europe 1993*, a publication of Euromonitor, pnc. London: Tel. +4471 251 8021; U.S. offices: (312) 541–8024.

The marketing-information-system concept is illustrated in Figure 5-1. The marketing managers, in order to carry out their analysis, planning, implementation, and control responsibilities (shown at the far left), need information about developments in the marketing environment (shown at the far right). The role of the MIS is to assess the manager's information needs, develop the needed information, and distribute the information in a timely fashion to the marketing managers. The

FIGURE 5-1 The Marketing Information System

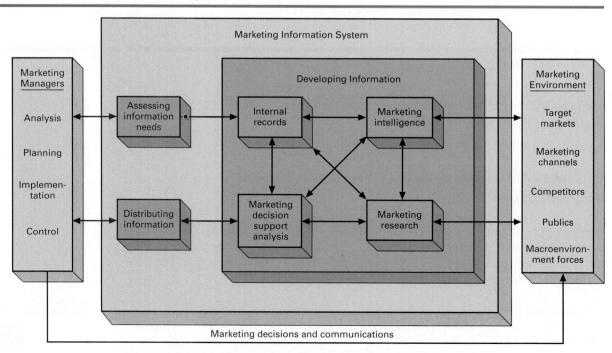

Marketing Research at Hewlett-Packard

If marketing information is the key to marketing performance, then the way a company organizes, manages, and uses its marketing research department will critically affect its performance. One company that believes strongly in the importance of marketing research is the $14 billion Hewlett-Packard company that produces technical products for business.

Marketing information is handled by the Market Research & Information Center (MRIC) located at HP headquarters. It is a shared resource for all the HP divisions worldwide. Consisting of 30 professionals, MRIC also uses outside research supplier partners of proven quality. HP divisions annually contract for a share of MRIC's staff and library resources. Business units are responsible for funding the incremental expenses of projects they request.

MRIC is divided into three groups: Market Information Center, Decision Support Teams, and Regional Satellites. The Market Information Center provides background information on industries, markets, and competitors using syndicated and other information services. Decision Support Teams provide research consulting to sponsoring entities. Regional Satellites are established in specific locales worldwide to support regional HP initiatives.

MRIC sees the research process as consisting of gathering intelligence, testing proposals, and tracking results. Intelligence is gathered to identify market opportunities and to stimulate creative solutions. Testing is the stage when specific decisions on product features, price changes, and advertising programs are pretested with potential buyers. Testing is done using quantitative choice modeling and behavioral experimentation. Tracking is carried on to assess the results and interpret the causal factors.

MRIC has contributed to HP's profitability by identifying market opportunities, improving product offerings, recommending appropriate prices, and enhancing the quality of marketing communications.

SOURCE: See William R. BonDurant, "Research: the 'HP Way'," *Marketing Research*, June 1992, pp. 28–33.

---

needed information is developed through internal company records, marketing intelligence activities, marketing research, and marketing decision support analysis. We will now describe each major subsystem of the company's MIS (see Companies and Industries 5-1).

Internal Records System

The most basic information system used by marketing managers is the internal records system. Included are reports on orders, sales, prices, inventory levels, receivables, payables, and so on. By analyzing this information, marketing managers can spot important opportunities and problems.

The Order-to-Remittance Cycle

The heart of the internal records system is the *order-to-remittance cycle*. Sales representatives, dealers, and customers dispatch orders to the firm. The order department prepares invoices and sends copies to various departments. Out-of-stock items are back ordered. Shipped items are accompanied by shipping and billing documents that are also multicopied and sent to various departments.

Today's companies need to perform these steps quickly and accurately. Customers favor those firms that can deliver their goods on time. Sales representatives need to send in their orders every evening, in some cases immediately. The order-fulfillment department must process these orders quickly. The warehouse must send the goods out as soon as possible. And bills should go out promptly. Alert firms are now applying *total quality-improvement programs* to improve the speed and accuracy of workflows between departments, and many report substantial gains in efficiency.

Sales Reporting Systems

Marketing managers need up-to-date reports of their current sales. Consumer packaged-goods companies can receive reports of retail sales every two months. Auto executives wait about ten days for their sales reports. Many marketing executives complain that sales are not reported fast enough in their company.

Here are three companies that have designed fast and comprehensive sales-reporting systems:

- *Baxter:* Baxter has supplied hospital purchasing departments with computers so that the hospitals could dispatch orders directly to Baxter. The timely arrival of orders enables Baxter to cut inventories, improve customer service, and obtain better terms from suppliers for higher volumes. Baxter achieved a great advantage over competitors, and their market share soared.

- *Wrangler Womenswear:* Sales people at Wrangler Womenswear can connect their laptop computers to the corporate computer. The salesforce can send and retrieve messages, enter orders, and receive up-to-the-minute sales information. A salesperson can enter the average order in about half the time involved in writing out an order on paper.

- *Mead Paper:* Mead sales representatives can obtain on-the-spot answers to customers' questions about paper availability by dialing Mead Paper's computer center. The computer determines whether paper is available at the nearest warehouse and when it can be shipped; if it is not in stock, the computer checks the inventory at nearby warehouses until one is located. If the paper is nowhere in stock, the computer determines where and when the paper can be produced. The sales representative gets an answer in seconds and thus has an advantage over competitors.

Designing a User-Oriented Reports System

In designing an advanced sales information system, the company should avoid certain pitfalls. First, it is possible to create a system that delivers too much information. The managers arrive at their offices each morning to face voluminous sales statistics, which they either ignore or spend too much time reading. Second, it is possible to create a system that delivers information that is too current! Managers may end up overreacting to minor sales reversals.

The company's marketing information system should represent a cross between what managers think they need, what managers really need, and what is economically feasible. A useful step is the appointment of an *internal marketing-information-systems committee*, which interviews a cross section of marketing executives—product managers, sales managers, sales representatives, and so on—to discover their information needs. A useful set of questions is shown in Table 5-1. The MIS committee will want to pay special attention to strong desires and complaints. At the same time, the committee will wisely discount some of the information requests. The information planning committee must take another step, that of determining what managers *need to know* to be able to make responsible decisions. For example, what do brand managers need to know in order to set the size of the advertising budget? They need to know the degree of market saturation, the rate of sales decay in the absence of advertising, and the spending plans of competitors. The information system should be designed to provide the data needed for making each key marketing decision.

TABLE 5-1
Questionnaire for
Determining Marketing
Information Needs

1. What types of decisions are you regularly called upon to make?
2. What types of information do you need to make these decisions?
3. What types of information do you regularly get?
4. What types of special studies do you periodically request?
5. What types of information would you like to get that you are not getting now?
6. What information would you want daily? Weekly? Monthly? Yearly?
7. What magazines and trade reports would you like to see routed to you on a regular basis?
8. What specific topics would you like to be kept informed of?
9. What types of data-analysis programs would you like to see made available?
10. What do you think would be the four most helpful improvements that could be made in the present marketing information system?

Marketing Intelligence System

While the internal records system supplies *results data*, the marketing intelligence system supplies *happenings data*. We define a marketing intelligence system as follows:

❖ A marketing intelligence system *is a set of procedures and sources used by managers to obtain their everyday information about pertinent developments in the marketing environment.*

Managers scan the environment in four ways:

- *Undirected viewing:* General exposure to information where the manager has no specific purpose in mind
- *Conditioned viewing:* Directed exposure, not involving active search, to a more or less clearly identified area or type of information
- *Informal search:* A relatively limited and unstructured effort to obtain specific information or information for a specific purpose
- *Formal search:* A deliberate effort — usually following a preestablished plan, procedure, or methodology — to secure specific information[1]

Marketing managers carry on marketing intelligence mostly on their own by reading books, newspapers, and trade publications; talking to customers, suppliers, distributors, and other outsiders; and talking with other managers and personnel within the company. Yet this system is casual, and valuable information could be lost or arrive too late. Managers might learn of a competitive move, a new-customer need, or a dealer problem too late to make the best response.

Well-run companies take additional steps to improve the quality and quantity of marketing intelligence. First, they train and motivate the salesforce to spot and report new developments. Sales representatives are the company's "eyes and ears." They are in an excellent position to pick up information missed by other means. Yet they are very busy and often fail to pass on significant information. The company must "sell" its salesforce on their importance as intelligence gatherers. The salesforce should be provided with easy reports to fill out. Sales representatives should know which types of information to send to different managers.

Second, the company motivates distributors, retailers, and other middlemen to pass along important intelligence. Consider the following example:[2]

Parker Hannifin Corporation, a major fluid-power-products manufacturer, has arranged with each distributor to forward to Parker's marketing research division a copy of all the invoices containing sales of their products. Parker analyzes these invoices to learn about end-user characteristics and to help its distributors improve their marketing programs.

Some companies appoint specialists to gather marketing intelligence. They send "ghost shoppers" to monitor the presentations of their dealers or branches. They learn about competitors through purchasing their products; attending open houses and trade shows; reading competitors' published reports; attending their stockholders' meetings; talking to their former employees and present employees, dealers, distributors, suppliers, and freight agents; collecting competitors' ads; and reading *The Wall Street Journal*, The *New York Times*, and trade association papers.

Third, the company purchases information from outside suppliers such as the A. C. Nielsen Company and Information Resources, Inc. (see Table 5-4, part D, p. 134). These research firms can gather store and consumer-panel data at much less cost than if each company carried on its own panel operations.

Fourth, some companies have established an internal *marketing information center* to collect and circulate marketing intelligence. The staff scans major publications, abstracts relevant news, and disseminates a news bulletin to marketing managers. It collects and files relevant information and assists managers in evaluating new information. These services greatly improve the quality of information available to marketing managers.

Marketing Research System

Marketing managers often commission formal research studies of specific problems and opportunities. They may need a market survey, a product-preference test, a sales forecast by region, or an advertising-effectiveness study. Managers normally do not have the skill or time to obtain this information. They need to commission formal marketing research. We define *marketing research* as follows:

❖ Marketing research *is the systematic design, collection, analysis, and reporting of data and findings relevant to a specific marketing situation facing the company.*

Suppliers of Marketing Research

A company can obtain marketing research in a number of ways. Small companies can engage students or professors at a local college to design and carry out the project, or they can hire a marketing research firm. Most large companies, on the other hand, have their own marketing research departments.[3] The marketing research manager normally reports to the marketing vice-president and acts as a study director, administrator, company consultant, and advocate.

> Procter & Gamble assigns marketing researchers to each product operating division to conduct research for existing brands. There are two separate in-house research groups, one in charge of overall company advertising research and the other in charge of market testing. The staff of each group consists of marketing research managers, supporting specialists (survey designers, statisticians, behavioral scientists), and in-house field representatives to conduct and supervise interviewing. Each year, Procter & Gamble calls or visits over one million people in connection with about 1,000 research projects.

Companies normally budget marketing research at anywhere from 1 to 2% of company sales. Between 50% to 80% of this money is spent directly by the department, and the remainder is spent in buying the services of outside marketing research firms. Marketing research firms fall into three groups:

- *Syndicated-service research firms:* These firms gather periodic consumer and trade information, which they sell for a fee to clients. Examples: A. C. Nielsen, SAMI/Burke.
- *Custom marketing research firms:* These firms are hired to carry out specific research projects. They participate in designing the study, and the report becomes the client's property.
- *Specialty-line marketing research firms:* These firms provide a specialized research service to others. The best example is the field-service firm, which sells field interviewing services to other firms.

The Scope of Marketing Research

Marketing researchers have steadily expanded their activities and techniques. Table 5-2 lists 36 marketing research activities and the percentage of companies carrying on each activity. These activities have benefited from increasingly sophisticated techniques. Many research techniques — such as questionnaire construction and area sampling — came along early and were quickly and widely applied by marketing researchers. Others — such as motivation research and mathematical methods — came in uneasily, with prolonged and heated debates among practitioners over their practical usefulness. But they, too, settled in the corpus of marketing research methodology.

The Marketing Research Process

Effective marketing research involves the five steps shown in Figure 5-2. We will illustrate these steps with the following situation:

> American Airlines is constantly looking for new ways to serve the needs of air travelers. One manager came up with the idea of offering phone service to passengers. The other managers got excited about this idea and agreed that it should be researched further. The marketing manager volunteered to do some preliminary research. He contacted a major telecommunications company to find out the cost of providing this service on B-747 coast-to-coast flights. The telecommunications company said that the device would cost the airline about $1,000 a flight. The airline could break even if it charged $25 a phone call and at least 40 passengers made calls during the flight. The marketing manager then asked the company's marketing research manager to find out how air travelers would respond to this new service.

DEFINING THE PROBLEM AND RESEARCH OBJECTIVES ❖ The first step calls for the marketing manager and marketing researcher to define the problem carefully and agree on the research objectives. An old adage says, "A problem well defined is half solved."

Management must steer between defining the problem too broadly or too narrowly. If the marketing manager tells the marketing researcher, "Find out everything you can about air travelers' needs," the manager will get much unneeded information. On the other hand, if the marketing manager says, "Find out if enough passengers aboard a B-747 flying between the East Coast and West Coast would be willing to pay $25 to make a phone call so that American Airlines would break even on the cost of offering this service," this is too narrow a view of the problem. The marketing researcher could say: "Why does a call have to be priced at $25? Why does American have to break even on the cost of the service? The new service might attract enough new passengers to American so that even if they don't make enough phone calls, American will make money on the extra tickets."

TABLE 5-2
Research Activities of 587
Companies

TYPE OF RESEARCH		PERCENT DOING
A. Business/Economic and Corporate Research	1. Industry/market characteristics and trends	83
	2. Acquisition/diversification studies	53
	3. Market-share analyses	79
	4. Internal employee studies (morale, communication, etc.)	54
B. Pricing	5. Cost analysis	60
	6. Profit analysis	59
	7. Price elasticity	45
	8. Demand analysis:	
	a) market potential	74
	b) sales potential	69
	c) sales forecasts	67
	9. Competitive pricing analyses	63
C. Product	10. Concept development and testing	68
	11. Brand name generation and testing	38
	12. Test market	45
	13. Product testing of existing products	47
	14. Packaging design studies	31
	15. Competitive product studies	58
D. Distribution	16. Plant/warehouse location studies	23
	17. Channel performance studies	29
	18. Channel coverage studies	26
	19. Export and international studies	19
E. Promotion	20. Motivation research	37
	21. Media research	57
	22. Copy research	50
	23. Advertising effectiveness	65
	24. Competitive advertising studies	47
	25. Public image studies	60
	26. Salesforce compensation studies	30
	27. Salesforce quota studies	26
	28. Salesforce territory structure	31
	29. Studies of premiums, coupons, deals, etc.	36
F. Buying Behavior	30. Brand preference	54
	31. Brand attitudes	53
	32. Product satisfaction	68
	33. Purchase behavior	61
	34. Purchase intentions	60
	35. Brand awareness	59
	36. Segmentation studies	60

Source: Thomas C. Kinnear and Ann R. Root, eds., *1988 Survey of Marketing Research: Organization, Functions, Budget, Compensation* (Chicago: American Marketing Association, 1989), p. 43.

In working further on the problem, the managers discovered another issue. If the new service was successful, how fast could other airlines copy it? Airline marketing competition is replete with examples of new services that were so quickly copied by competitors that no airline gained a sustainable competitive advantage. How important is it to be first and how long could the lead be sustained?

The marketing manager and marketing researcher agreed to define the problem as follows: "Will offering an in-flight phone service create enough incremental preference and profit for American Airlines to justify its cost against other possible

FIGURE 5-2
The Marketing Research
Process

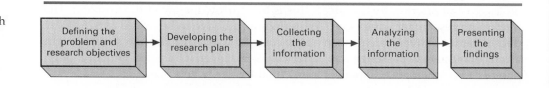

investments that American might make?" They then agreed on the following specific research objectives:

1. What are the main reasons why airline passengers might place phone calls while flying?
2. What kinds of passengers would be the most likely to make phone calls?
3. How many passengers are likely to make phone calls, given different price levels?
4. How many extra passengers might choose American because of this new service?
5. How much long-term goodwill will this service add to American Airlines's image?
6. How important will phone service be relative to other factors such as flight schedules, food quality, and baggage handling?

Not all research projects can be made this specific in their objectives. Three types of research projects can be distinguished. Some research is *exploratory*— that is, to gather preliminary data to shed light on the real nature of the problem and suggest possible hypotheses or new ideas. Some research is *descriptive*—that is, to ascertain certain magnitudes, such as how many people would make an in-flight phone call at $25 a call. Some research is *causal*—that is, to test a cause-and-effect relationship, such as that passengers would make more calls if the phone was next to their seat rather than having to stand where the phone was located.

DEVELOPING THE RESEARCH PLAN ❖ The second stage of marketing research calls for developing the most efficient plan for gathering the needed information. The marketing manager cannot simply say to the marketing researcher, "Find some passengers and ask them if they would use an in-flight phone service if it were available." The marketing researcher has the skills to design the research approach. The marketing manager should know enough about marketing research to evaluate the research plan and the findings.

The marketing manager needs to know the cost of the research plan before approving it. Suppose the company estimates that launching the in-flight phone service without doing any marketing research would yield a long-term profit of $50,000. The manager believes that the research would lead to an improved promotional plan and a long-term profit of $90,000. In this case, the manager should be willing to spend up to $40,000 on this research. If the research would cost more than $40,000, it would not be worth doing.[4]

Table 5-3 shows that designing a research plan calls for decisions on the *data sources, research approaches, research instruments, sampling plan*, and *contact methods*.

Data Sources. The research plan can call for gathering secondary data, primary data, or both. Secondary data consist of information that already exists somewhere, having been collected for another purpose. Primary data consist of original information gathered for the specific purpose.

SECONDARY DATA. Researchers usually start their investigation by examining secondary data to see whether their problem can be partly or wholly solved without

		TABLE 5-3
Data Sources:	Secondary data, primary data	Constructing the Research Plan
Research Approaches:	Observation, focus groups, survey, experiment	
Research Instruments:	Questionnaire, mechanical instruments	
Sampling Plan:	Sampling unit, sample size, sampling procedure	
Contact Methods:	Telephone, mail, personal	

collecting costly primary data. Table 5-4 shows the rich variety of secondary-data sources available in the United States.[5]

Secondary data provide a starting point for research and offer the advantages of low cost and ready availability. On the other hand, the data needed by the researcher might not exist, or the existing data might be dated, inaccurate, incom-

TABLE 5-4
Secondary Sources of Data

A. Internal Sources	Internal sources include company profit-loss statements, balance sheets, sales figures, sales-call reports, invoices, inventory records, and prior research reports.
B. Government Publications	*Statistical Abstract of the U.S.*, updated annually, provides summary data on demographic, economic, social, and other aspects of the American economy and society.
	County and City Data Book, updated every three years, presents statistical information for counties, cities, and other geographical units on population, education, employment, aggregate and median income, housing, bank deposits, retail sales, etc.
	U.S. Industrial Outlook provides projections of industrial activity by industry and includes data on production, sales, shipments, employment, etc.
	Marketing Information Guide provides a monthly annotated bibliography of marketing information.
	Other government publications include the *Annual Survey of Manufacturers; Business Statistics; Census of Manufacturers; Census of Population; Census of Retail Trade, Wholesale Trade, and Selected Service Industries; Census of Transportation; Federal Reserve Bulletin; Monthly Labor Review; Survey of Current Business*; and *Vital Statistics Report*.
C. Periodicals and Books	*Business Periodicals Index*, a monthly, lists business articles appearing in a wide variety of business publications.
	Standard and Poor's Industry Surveys provides updated statistics and analyses of industries.
	Moody's Manuals provide financial data and names of executives in major companies.
	Encyclopedia of Associations provides information on every major trade and professional association in the U.S.
	Marketing journals include the *Journal of Marketing, Journal of Marketing Research*, and *Journal of Consumer Research*.
	Useful trade magazines include *Advertising Age, Chain Store Age, Progressive Grocer, Sales and Marketing Management*, and *Stores*.
	Useful general business magazines include *Business Week, Fortune, Forbes, The Economist*, and *Harvard Business Review*.
D. Commercial Data	*A.C. Nielsen Company* provides data on products and brands sold through retail outlets (Retail Index Services), supermarket scanner data (Scantrack), data on television audiences (Media Research Services), magazine circulation data (Neodata Services, Inc.), and others.
	MRCA Information Services provides data on weekly family purchases of consumer products (National Consumer Panel) and data on home food consumption (National Menu Census).
	Information Resources, Inc., provides supermarket scanner data (InfoScan) and data on the impact of supermarket promotions (PromotioScan).
	SAMI/Burke provides reports on warehouse withdrawals to food stores in selected market areas (SAMI reports) and supermarket scanner data (Samscam).
	Simmons Market Research Bureau (MRB Group) provides annual reports covering television markets, sporting goods, and proprietary drugs, giving demographic data by sex, income, age, and brand preferences (selective markets and media reaching them).
	Other commercial research houses selling data to subscribers include the *Audit Bureau of Circulation; Arbitron, Audits and Surveys; Dun and Bradstreet; National Family Opinion; Standard Rate & Data Service*; and *Starch*.

plete, or unreliable. In this case, the researcher will have to collect primary data at greater cost and longer delay but probably with more relevance and accuracy.

PRIMARY DATA. Most marketing research projects involve some primary-data collection. The normal procedure is to interview some people individually and/or in groups to get a preliminary sense of how people feel about air carriers and services and then develop a formal research instrument, debug it, and carry it into the field.

Research Approaches. Primary data can be collected in four ways: observation, focus groups, surveys, and experiments.

OBSERVATIONAL RESEARCH. Fresh data can be gathered by observing the relevant actors and settings. The American Airlines researchers meander about around airports, airline offices, and travel agencies to hear how travelers talk about the different carriers. The researchers can fly on American and competitors' planes to observe the quality of in-flight service. This exploratory research might yield some useful hypotheses about how travelers choose their air carriers.

FOCUS-GROUP RESEARCH. A focus group is a gathering of six to ten persons who are invited to spend a few hours with a skilled moderator to discuss a product, service, organization, or other marketing entity. The moderator needs objectivity, knowledge of the issue, and knowledge of group dynamics and consumer behavior. The participants are normally paid a small sum for attending. The meeting is typically held in pleasant surroundings (a home, for example), and refreshments are served to increase the informality.

In the American Airlines example, the moderator might start with a broad question, such as "How do you feel about air travel?" Questions then move to how people regard the different airlines, different services, and in-flight telephone service. The moderator encourages free and easy discussion, hoping that the group dynamics will reveal deep feelings and thoughts. At the same time, the moderator "focuses" the discussion, and hence the name *focus-group interviewing*. The discussion is recorded through note taking or on audio or video tape and is subsequently studied to understand consumer beliefs, attitudes, and behavior.

Focus-group research is a useful exploratory step to take before designing a large-scale survey. It yields insights into consumer perceptions, attitudes, and satisfaction that help define the issues to be researched more formally. Consumer-goods companies have been using focus groups for many years, and an increasing number of newspapers, law firms, hospitals, and public-service organizations are discovering their value. Yet however useful they are, researchers must avoid generalizing the reported feelings of the focus-group participants to the whole market, since the sample size is too small and the sample is not drawn randomly.[6]

SURVEY RESEARCH. Survey research stands midway between observational and focus-group research, on the one hand, and experimental research on the other hand. Observation and focus groups are best suited for exploratory research, surveys are best suited for descriptive research, and experiments are best suited for causal research. Companies undertake surveys to learn about people's knowledge, beliefs, preferences, satisfaction, and so on, and to measure these magnitudes in the population. Thus American Airlines researchers might want to survey how many people know American, have flown it, prefer it, and so on. We will say more about survey research when we move to research instruments, sampling plans, and contact methods.

EXPERIMENTAL RESEARCH. The most scientifically valid research is experimental research. Experimental research calls for selecting matched groups of subjects, subjecting them to different treatments, controlling extraneous variables, and checking whether observed response differences are statistically significant. To the extent that extraneous factors are eliminated or controlled, the observed effects can be related to the variations in the treatments. The purpose of experimental research is to capture cause-and-effect relationships by eliminating competing explanations of the observed findings.

For example, American Airlines might introduce in-flight phone service on one of its regular flights from New York to Los Angeles at a price of $25 a phone call. On the same flight the following day, it announces the availability of this service at $15 a phone call. If the plane carried the same number and type of passengers on each flight, and the day of the week made no difference, then any significant difference in the number of calls made could be related to the price charged. The experimental design could be elaborated further by trying other prices, replicating the same price on a number of flights, and including other routes in the experiment. To the extent that the design and execution of the experiment eliminate alternative hypotheses that might explain the results, the research and marketing managers can have confidence in the conclusions.

Research Instruments. Marketing researchers have a choice of two main research instruments in collecting primary data: the questionnaire and mechanical devices.

QUESTIONNAIRES. The questionnaire is by far the most common instrument in collecting primary data. A questionnaire consists of a set of questions presented to respondents for their answers. The questionnaire is very flexible in that there are any number of ways to ask questions. Questionnaires need to be carefully developed, tested, and debugged before they are administered on a large scale. One can usually spot several errors in a casually prepared questionnaire (see Marketing Concepts and Tools 5-1).

In preparing a questionnaire, the professional marketing researcher carefully chooses the questions and their form, wording, and sequence.

A common type of error occurs in the *questions asked*, that is, in including questions that cannot, would not, or need not be answered and in omitting questions that should be answered. Each question should be checked to determine whether it

Marketing Concepts and Tools 5-1

A "Questionable" Questionnaire

Suppose an airline asked passengers the following questions. What do you think of each question? (Answer before reading the comment in *each box.*)

1. What is your income to the nearest hundred dollars?
   People don't necessarily know their income to the nearest hundred dollars, nor do they want to reveal their income that closely, if at all. Furthermore, a questionnaire should never open with such a personal question.

2. Are you an occasional or a frequent flyer?
   How do you define frequent versus occasional flying?

3. Do you like this airline?
   Yes ( )   No ( )
   "Like" is a relative term. Besides, will people answer this honestly? Furthermore, is yes-no the best way to allow a re-

sponse to the question? Why is the question being asked in the first place?

4. How many airline ads did you see on television last April? This April?
   Who can remember?

5. What are the most salient and determinant attributes in your evaluation of air carriers?
   What are "salient" and "determinant" attributes? Don't use big words on me.

6. Do you think it is right for the government to tax air tickets and deprive a lot of people of the chance to fly?
   Loaded question. How can one answer this biased question?

contributes to the research objectives. Questions that are merely interesting should be dropped because they lengthen the time required and exhaust the respondent's patience.

The *form of the question* can influence the response. Marketing researchers distinguish between closed-end and open-end questions. *Closed-end questions* prespecify all the possible answers, and respondents make a choice among them. Table 5-5, section A, shows the most common forms of closed-end questions.

Open-end questions allow respondents to answer in their own words. These questions take various forms; the main ones are shown in Table 5-5, section B. Generally speaking, open-end questions often reveal more because respondents are not constrained in their answers. Open-end questions are especially useful in the exploratory stage of research where the researcher is looking for insight into how people think rather than in measuring how many people think a certain way. Closed-end questions, on the other hand, provide answers that are easier to interpret and tabulate.

Care should be exercised in the *wording of questions*. The researcher should use simple, direct, unbiased wording. The questions should be pretested with a sample of respondents before they are used.

Care should also be exercised in the *sequencing of questions*. The lead question should create interest when possible. Difficult or personal questions should be asked toward the end of the interview so that respondents do not become defensive. The questions should flow in a logical order. Questions on the respondent's demographics come last because they are more personal and less interesting to the respondent.

MECHANICAL INSTRUMENTS. Mechanical devices are used less frequently in marketing research. Galvanometers measure the subject's interest or emotions aroused by an exposure to a specific ad or picture. The tachistoscope flashes an ad to a subject with an exposure interval that may range from less than one-hundredth of a second to several seconds. After each exposure, the respondent describes everything he or she recalls. Eye cameras study respondents' eye movements to see where their eyes land first, how long they linger on a given item, and so on. The audiometer is attached to television sets in participating homes to record when the set is on and to which channel it is tuned.[7]

Sampling Plan. The marketing researcher must design a sampling plan, which calls for three decisions:

1. *Sampling Unit:* This answers: *Who is to be surveyed?* The marketing researcher must define the target population that will be sampled. In the American Airlines survey, should the sampling unit be business travelers, vacation travelers, or both? Should travelers under age 21 be interviewed? Should both husbands and wives be interviewed? Once this unit is determined, a sampling frame must be developed, so that everyone in the target population has an equal or known chance of being sampled.

2. *Sample Size:* This answers: *How many people should be surveyed?* Large samples give more reliable results than small samples. However, it is not necessary to sample the entire target population or even a substantial portion to achieve reliable results. Samples of less than 1% of a population can often provide good reliability, given a credible sampling procedure.

3. *Sampling Procedure:* This answers: *How should the respondents be chosen?* To obtain a representative sample, a probability sample of the population should be drawn. Probability sampling allows the calculation of confidence limits for sampling error. Thus one could conclude after the sample is taken that "the interval five to seven trips per year has 95 chances in 100 of containing the true number of trips taken annually by air travelers in the Southwest." Three types of probability sampling are described in

TABLE 5-5 Types of Questions

A. CLOSED-END QUESTIONS

Name	Description	Example
Dichotomous	A question with two possible answers.	"In arranging this trip, did you personally phone American?" Yes ☐ No ☐
Multiple choice	A question with three or more answers.	"With whom are you traveling on this flight?" No one ☐ Children only ☐ Spouse ☐ Business associates/ Spouse and friends/relatives ☐ children ☐ An organized tour group ☐
Likert scale	A statement with which the respondent shows the amount of agreement/ disagreement.	"Small airlines generally give better service than large ones." Strongly disagree Disagree Neither agree nor disagree Agree Strongly agree 1 ☐ 2 ☐ 3 ☐ 4 ☐ 5 ☐
Semantic differential	A scale connecting two bipolar words, where the respondent selects the point that represents his or her opinion.	American Airlines Large _ _ _ _ _ _ _ _ _ _ Small Experienced _ _ _ _ _ _ _ _ Inexperienced Modern _ _ _ _ _ _ _ _ _ _ Old-fashioned
Importance scale	A scale that rates the importance of some attribute.	"Airline food service to me is" Extremely important Very important Somewhat important Not very important Not at all important 1___ 2___ 3___ 4___ 5___
Rating scale	A scale that rates some attribute from "poor" to "excellent."	"American's food service is" Excellent Very good Good Fair Poor
Intention-to-buy scale	A scale that describes the respondent's intention to buy.	"If an inflight telephone was available on a long flight, I would" Definitely buy Probably buy Not sure Probably not buy Definitely not buy 1___ 2___ 3___ 4___ 5___

Table 5-6, section A. When the cost or time involved in probability sampling is too high, marketing researchers will take nonprobability samples. Table 5-6, section B describes three types of nonprobability sampling. Some marketing researchers feel that nonprobability samples can be very useful in many circumstances, even though the sampling error cannot be measured.

Contact Methods.   This answers: *How should the subject be contacted?* The choices are mail, telephone, or personal interviews.

The *mail questionnaire* is the best way to reach individuals who would not give personal interviews or whose responses might be biased or distorted by the interviewers. On the other hand, mail questionnaires require simple and clearly worded questions, and the response rate is usually low and/or slow.

Telephone interviewing is the best method for gathering information quickly; the interviewer is also able to clarify questions if they are not understood. The response rate is typically higher than in the case of mailed questionnaires. The two main drawbacks are that only people with telephones can be interviewed, and the interviews have to be short and not too personal.

Personal interviewing is the most versatile of the three methods. The interviewer can ask more questions and can record additional observations about the respondent, such as dress and body language. Personal interviewing is the most expensive method and requires more administrative planning and supervision. It is also subject to interviewer bias or distortion.

B. OPEN-END QUESTIONS

Name	Description	Example
Completely unstructured	A question that respondents can answer in an almost unlimited number of ways.	"What is your opinion of American Airlines?"
Word association	Words are presented, one at a time, and respondents mention the first word that comes to mind.	"What is the first word that comes to your mind when you hear the following?" Airline _____ American _____ Travel _____
Sentence completion	An incomplete sentence is presented and respondents complete the sentence.	"When I choose an airline, the most important consideration in my decision is _____
Story completion	An incomplete story is presented, and respondents are asked to complete it.	"I flew American a few days ago. I noticed that the exterior and interior of the plane had very bright colors. This aroused in me the following thoughts and feelings." Now complete the story.
Picture completion	A picture of two characters is presented, with one making a statement. Respondents are asked to identify with the other and fill in the empty balloon.	
Thematic Apperception Test (TAT)	A picture is presented and respondents are asked to make up a story about what they think is happening or may happen in the picture.	

Personal interviewing takes two forms, *arranged interviews* and *intercept interviews*. In arranged interviews, respondents are randomly selected and are either telephoned or approached at their homes or offices and asked to grant an interview. Often a small payment or incentive is presented to respondents in appreciation of their time. Intercept interviews involve stopping people at a shopping mall or busy street corner and requesting an interview. Intercept interviews have the drawback of being nonprobability samples, and the interviews must be quite short.

COLLECTING THE INFORMATION ❖ The researcher must now collect the data. This phase is generally the most expensive and the most liable to error. In the case of surveys, four major problems arise. Some respondents will not be at home and must be recontacted or replaced. Other respondents will refuse to cooperate. Still others will give biased or dishonest answers. Finally, some interviewers will occasionally be biased or dishonest.

In the case of experimental research, the researchers have to worry about matching the experimental and control groups, not influencing the participants by their presence, administering the treatments in a uniform way, and controlling for extraneous factors.

Data-collection methods are rapidly improving thanks to modern computers and telecommunications. Some research firms interview from a centralized location. Professional interviewers sit in booths and draw telephone numbers at random from somewhere in the nation. When the phone is answered, the interviewer

TABLE 5-6
Types of Probability and
Nonprobability Samples

A. PROBABILITY SAMPLE	Simple random sample	Every member of the population has a known and equal chance of selection.
	Stratified random sample	The population is divided into mutually exclusive groups (such as age groups), and random samples are drawn from each group.
	Cluster (area) sample	The population is divided into mutually exclusive groups (such as blocks), and the researcher draws a sample of the groups to interview.
B. NONPROBABILITY SAMPLE	Convenience sample	The researcher selects the most accessible population members from which to obtain information.
	Judgment sample	The researcher uses judgment to select population members who are good prospects for accurate information.
	Quota sample	The researcher finds and interviews a prescribed number of people in each of several categories.

asks the person a set of questions, reading them from a monitor. The interviewer types the respondents' answers into a computer. This procedure eliminates editing and coding, reduces the number of errors, saves time, and produces all the required statistics.

Other research firms have set up *interactive terminals* in shopping centers. Persons willing to be interviewed sit at a terminal, read the questions from the monitor, and type in their answers. Most respondents enjoy this form of "robot" interviewing.[8] Marketing Concepts and Tools 5-2 describes an even more recent and revolutionary breakthrough in electronic marketing research.

ANALYZING THE INFORMATION ❖ The next step in the marketing research process is to extract pertinent findings from the data. The researcher tabulates the data and develops one-way and two-way frequency distributions. Averages and measures of dispersion are computed for the major variables. The researcher will also apply some advanced statistical techniques and decision models in the hope of discovering additional findings (see pp. 145–48).

PRESENTING THE FINDINGS ❖ The researcher should not try to overwhelm management with lots of numbers and fancy statistical techniques — this will lose them. The researcher should present major findings that are relevant to the major marketing decisions facing management. The study is useful when it reduces management's uncertainty concerning the right move to make.

Suppose the main survey findings for the American Airlines case show that:

1. The chief reasons for using in-flight phone service are emergencies, urgent business deals, mix-ups in flight times, and so on. Making phone calls to pass the time would be rare. Most of the calls would be made by businesspeople on expense accounts.

2. About five passengers out of every 200 would make in-flight phone calls at a price of $25 a call; and about 12 would make calls at $15. Thus a charge of $15 would produce more revenue ($12 \times \$15 = \$180$) than $25 a call ($5 \times \$25 = \$125$). Still, that is far below the in-flight break-even cost of $1,000.

3. The promotion of in-flight phone service would win American about two extra passengers on each flight. The net revenue from these two extra passengers would be about $620, but that still would not help meet the break-even cost.

4. Offering in-flight service would strengthen the public's image of American Airlines as an innovative and progressive airline. However, it would cost American about $200 per flight to create this extra goodwill.

The Marketer's Dream: Measuring Marketing Impact Through Single-Source Data

Several technical advances have recently permitted marketers to test the sales impact of ads and sales promotions. The advances include (1) the universal bar code on packages, (2) optical scanners, (3) electronic cash registers, (4) smart cards, (5) cable television, and (6) television viewing monitors. Here is how they work in concert.

A research firm, Information Resources, Inc., recruits a panel of supermarkets equipped with optical scanners and electronic cash registers. The store clerk passes the customer's goods over a light beam that reads the *universal code* on each package and records the brand, size, and price. Meanwhile the research firm has also recruited a panel of customers of these stores who have agreed to charge their grocery purchases with a special Shopper's Hotline ID card that not only has their name and bank account number but also personal information on household characteristics, lifestyle, income, and so on. These customers have also agreed to let their television-viewing habits be monitored by a black box in their television sets that records what is being watched, when, and by whom. All consumer panelists receive their programs through cable television. Information Resources controls the advertising messages being sent out to the consumer-panel members. The company can beam different messages, headlines, or promotions to different panel members. The research firm can then capture through the store purchase data which ads led to more purchasing and by what kinds of consumers. This research service makes it possible to evaluate consumer responses to various marketing stimuli with greater precision than ever.

Aside from this advanced service for advertisers, the retailers have also benefited from using optical scanner equipment. Retailers can more quickly analyze the movement of goods for the purposes of improved inventory control and shelf space allocation, thus helping them improve the profitability of their store operations.

For further reading see Joanne Lipman, "Single-Source Ad Research Heralds Detailed Look at Household Habits," *The Wall Street Journal*, February 16, 1988, p. 39; Joe Schwartz, "Back to the Source," *American Demographics*, January 1989, pp. 22–26; and Magid H. Abraham and Leonard M. Lodish, "Getting the Most Out of Advertising and Promotion," *Harvard Business Review*, May–June 1990, pp. 50–60.

These findings, of course, could suffer from sampling error, and management may want to study the issues further. However, it looks as if in-flight phone service would add more cost than long-term revenue and should not be implemented at the present time. Thus a well-defined marketing research project has helped American's managers make a better decision than would probably have come out of "seat-of-the-pants" decision making.

Characteristics of Good Marketing Research

We can now highlight six characteristics of good marketing research.

SCIENTIFIC METHOD ❖ Effective marketing research uses the principles of the scientific method: careful observation, formulation of hypotheses, prediction, and testing. An example follows.

A mail-order house was suffering from a high rate (30%) of returned merchandise. Management asked the marketing research manager to investigate the causes. The marketing researcher examined the characteristics of returned orders, such as the geographical locations of the customers, the sizes of the returned orders, and the merchandise categories. One hypothesis was that the longer the customer waited for ordered merchandise, the greater the probability of its return. Statistical analysis confirmed this hypothesis. The researcher estimated how much the return rate would

CHAPTER 5
Marketing Information Systems
and Marketing Research

drop for a specified speed up of service. The company did this, and the prediction proved correct.[9]

RESEARCH CREATIVITY ❖ At its best, marketing research develops innovative ways to solve a problem. A classic example of research creativity follows:

> When instant coffee was first introduced, housewives complained that it did not taste like real coffee. Yet in blindfold tests, many housewives could not distinguish between cups of instant and real coffee. This indicated that much of their resistance was psychological. The researcher decided to design two almost identical shopping lists, the only difference being that regular coffee was on one list and instant coffee on the other. The regular-coffee list was given to one group of housewives and the instant-coffee list was given to a different but comparable group. Both groups were asked to guess the social and personal characteristics of the woman whose shopping list they saw. The comments were pretty much the same with one significant difference: a higher proportion of the housewives whose list contained instant coffee described the subject as "lazy, a spendthrift, a poor wife, and failing to plan well for her family." These women obviously were imputing to the fictional housewife their own anxieties and negative images about the use of instant coffee. The instant-coffee company now knew the nature of the resistance and could develop a campaign to change the image of the housewife who serves instant coffee.[10]

MULTIPLE METHODS ❖ Competent marketing researchers shy away from overreliance on any one method, preferring to adapt the method to the problem rather than the other way around. They also recognize the desirability of gathering information from multiple sources to give greater confidence.

INTERDEPENDENCE OF MODELS AND DATA ❖ Competent marketing researchers recognize that the facts derive their meaning from models of the problem. These models guide the type of information sought and therefore should be made as explicit as possible.

VALUE AND COST OF INFORMATION ❖ Competent marketing researchers show concern for estimating the value of information against its cost. Value/cost helps the marketing research department determine which research projects to conduct, which research designs to use, and whether to gather more information after the initial results are in. Research costs are typically easy to quantify, while the value is harder to anticipate. The value depends on the reliability and validity of the research findings and management's willingness to accept and act on its findings.

HEALTHY SKEPTICISM ❖ Competent marketing researchers will show a healthy skepticism toward glib assumptions made by managers about how the market works (see Marketing Concepts and Tools 5-3).

ETHICAL MARKETING ❖ Most marketing research benefits both the sponsoring company and its consumers. Through marketing research, companies learn more about consumers' needs, and are able to supply more satisfying products and services. However, the misuse of marketing research can also harm or annoy consumers (see Socially Responsible Marketing 5-1).

Management's Use of Marketing Research

In spite of the rapid growth of marketing research, many companies still fail to use it sufficiently or correctly. Several factors stand in the way of its greater utilization.

Marketing Concepts and Tools 5-3

Marketing Researchers Challenge Conventional Marketing Wisdom

Kevin Clancy and Robert Shulman, former principals of Yankelovich Clancy Shulman, a leading marketing research firm, criticized American marketers for practicing "death-wish" marketing. Noting that over 80% of new packaged-goods introductions fail, and average brands keep losing market share, the authors conclude that there must be something wrong with marketing thinking.

Clancy and Shulman charge that too many companies build their marketing plans on "marketing myths." Webster's dictionary defines a myth as "an ill-founded belief held uncritically, especially by an interested group." The authors list the following myths that have led marketing management down the wrong path:

1. *A brand's best prospects are the heavy buyers in the category:* Although most companies pursue heavy buyers, they may not be the best target. Many heavy users are highly committed to specific competitors and those who are not are often deal prone. Even if the company wins them today, they may lose them tomorrow when a competitor makes a better offer.

2. *The more appealing a new product is, the more likely it will be a success:* This philosophy can lead the company to give away too much to the customer and result in lower profitability. New-product appeal and profitability are curvilinearly related.

3. *The effectiveness of advertising is revealed by how memorable and persuasive it is:* Actually, the best "testing" ads, when measured by recall and persuasion scores, are not necessarily the most effective. A much better predictor is the buyer's attitude toward the advertising, specifically whether the buyer feels he or she received useful information and whether the buyer liked the advertising.

4. *A company is wise to spend the major portion of its research budget on focus groups and qualitative research:* Focus groups and qualitative research are useful but the major part of the research budget should be spent on quantitative research and surveys.

Clancy and Shulman list several other myths which they think cloud the thinking of many marketers. Some marketers will undoubtedly present counterexamples where the "so-called" myths have yielded positive results. Nevertheless, the authors deserve credit for forcing marketers to rethink some of their basic assumptions.

SOURCE: See Kevin J. Clancy and Robert S. Shulman, *The Marketing Revolution: A Radical Manifesto for Dominating the Marketplace* (New York: Harper Business, 1991).

- *A narrow conception of marketing research:* Many managers see marketing research as only a fact-finding operation. The marketing researcher is supposed to design a questionnaire, choose a sample, conduct interviews, and report results, often without being given a careful definition of the problem or of the decision alternatives facing management. As a result, some fact finding fails to be useful. This reinforces management's idea of the limited usefulness of some marketing research.

- *Uneven caliber of marketing researchers:* Some managers view marketing research as little better than a clerical activity and reward it as such. Less-able marketing researchers are hired, and their weak training and deficient creativity lead to unimpressive results. The disappointing results reinforce management's prejudice against expecting too much from marketing research. Management continues to pay low salaries, perpetuating the basic difficulty.

- *Late and occasional erroneous findings by marketing research:* Managers want quick results that are accurate and conclusive. But good marketing research takes time and money. Managers become disappointed, and they lower their opinion of the value of marketing research. This is especially a problem in conducting marketing research in foreign countries (see Global Marketing 5-2).

- *Intellectual differences:* Intellectual divergences between the mental styles of line managers and marketing researchers often get in the way of productive relationships. The marketing researcher's report may seem abstract, complicated, and tentative, while

Issues in the Use of Marketing Research

Two public policy and ethical concerns posed by marketing research are intrusions on consumer privacy and the misuse of research findings.

Intrusions on Consumer Privacy

Most consumers feel positively about the purpose of marketing research and some actually enjoy being interviewed. However, others strongly resent or even mistrust marketing research. A few consumers fear that researchers might use sophisticated techniques to probe their deepest feelings, and then use this knowledge to manipulate their buying. Others may have been taken in by previous "research surveys" that actually turned out to be attempts to sell them something. Still other consumers confuse legitimate marketing research studies with telemarketing or database development efforts and say "no" before the interviewer can even begin.

Increasing consumer resentment has become a major problem for the research industry and this has led to lower survey response rates in recent years—one study found that 36% of Americans now refuse to be interviewed in an average survey. The industry is considering several options for responding to this problem. One is to expand its "Your Opinion Counts" program to educate consumers about the benefits of legitimate marketing research and to distinguish it from telephone selling and database building. Another option is to provide a toll-free number that respondents can call to verify that a survey is legitimate. The industry has also considered adopting broad standards, perhaps based on Europe's International Code of Marketing and Social Research Practice. This code outlines researchers' responsibilities to respondents and to the general public. For example, it specifies that researchers should make their names and addresses available to participants, and it bans companies from representing activities like database compilation or sales and promotional pitches as research.

Misuse of Research Findings

Research studies can be powerful tools of persuasion — companies often use study results as claims in their advertising and promotion. Today, however, many research studies appear to be little more than vehicles for pitching the sponsor's products. In fact, in some cases, the research surveys appear to have been designed to subtly produce the intended effect. Consider the following examples:

> A study by Chrysler contends that Americans overwhelmingly prefer Chrysler to Toyota after test driving both. However, the study included just 100 people in each of two tests. More importantly, none of the people surveyed owned a foreign car, so they appear to be favorably predisposed to U.S. cars.

> A poll sponsored by the disposable diaper industry asked: "It is estimated that disposable diapers account for less than 2% of the trash in today's landfills. In contrast, beverage containers, third-class mail, and yard waste are estimated to account for about 21% of the trash in landfills. Given this, in your opinion, would it be fair to ban disposable diapers?" Again, not surprisingly, 84% said no.

Thus, subtle manipulations of the study's sample, or the choice or wording of questions, can substantially affect the conclusions reached.

In other cases, so-called "independent" research studies are actually paid for by companies with an interest in the outcome. Two studies sponsored by the cloth-diaper industry conclude that cloth diapers are more environmentally friendly. Not surprisingly, two other studies sponsored by the paper-diaper industry conclude just the opposite. Yet both appear to be correct *given* the underlying assumptions used.

Recognizing that surveys can be abused, several associations—including the American Marketing Association and the Council of American Survey Research Organizations—have developed codes of research ethics and standards of conduct. Each company must accept responsibility for policing the conduct and reporting of its own marketing research to protect consumers' best interests and its own.

Sources: Excerpts from Cynthia Crossen, "Studies Galore Support Products and Positions, but Are They Reliable?" *The Wall Street Journal*, November 14, 1991, pp. A1, A9. Also see Betsy Spethmann, "Cautious Consumers Have Surveyors Wary," *Advertising Age*, June 10, 1991, p. 34.

Global Marketing 5-2

Problems in Global Marketing Research

As companies expand into foreign markets, they need reliable data on which to base their marketing decisions and plans. They need to know the potential size of a foreign market, buyer attitudes and preferences, characteristics of channels of distribution, and other pieces of information. They cannot simply enter the foreign market and sell their product or service in the same way as in the home country.

Unfortunately, much data on foreign markets—particularly less economically developed countries—is nonexistent, unreliable, or very costly to collect. Consider the problems with secondary data. Many countries estimate their population by asking local authorities to estimate the local population; they will get back numbers that are pure guesses or just extrapolations of past numbers. The national income estimate may be based on tax returns but no allowance is made for widespread unreported or underreported income.

Collection of primary data is also saddled with problems. Survey research suffers from a lack of sampling lists, few or unqualified interviewers, poor language translation of questions, respondent refusals to be interviewed, or less than truthful responses. Researchers have to be aware that the target respondent may have to change depending upon whether the husband, wife, or child is influential in the purchasing decisions in that country. And if the husband has several wives, as in some Moslem and African countries, who is to be interviewed? Furthermore, the questionnaire will contain words such as "high quality," "colorful," "expensive," which will have varying meanings from country to country.

In many countries, the researcher cannot send a mailed questionnaire because of low population literacy or poor postal service; and telephone interviews are infeasible where telephone ownership or service is poor. This means that researchers must rely primarily on personal interviewing, focus group interviewing, and observational research to arrive at a fair picture of the marketplace. While they can gain a lot of insight into the market from these methods, they cannot know how representative the findings are.

Thus companies going abroad face a problem: they need reliable data because they know little about other countries' cultures, distribution, and economics; yet the data often are poor for making key international decisions. Over time, as more companies move toward "borderless marketing," the marketing research infrastructures in these countries will hopefully improve.

For further reading, see Susan P. Douglas and C. Samuel Craig, *International Marketing Research* (Englewood Cliffs, N.J.: Prentice-Hall, 1983).

---

the line manager wants concreteness, simplicity, and certainty. Yet in the more progressive companies, marketing researchers are increasingly being included as members of the product management team, and their influence on marketing strategy is growing.

Marketing Decision Support System

A growing number of organizations have added a fourth information service — a *marketing decision support system (MDSS)* — to help their marketing managers make better decisions. Little defines an MDSS as:

> . . . a coordinated collection of data, systems, tools and techniques with supporting software and hardware by which an organization gathers and interprets relevant information from business and environment and turns it into a basis for marketing action.[11]

Figure 5-3 illustrates the concept of an MDSS. Suppose a marketing manager needs to analyze a problem and take action. The manager puts questions to the ap-

FIGURE 5-3
Marketing Decision Support System

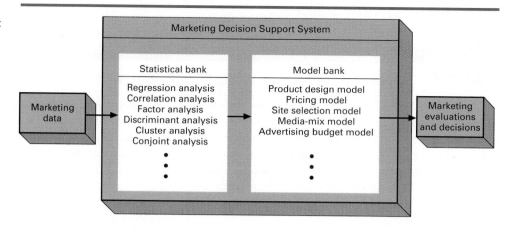

The figure shows a Marketing Decision Support System with Marketing data flowing into a Statistical bank (Regression analysis, Correlation analysis, Factor analysis, Discriminant analysis, Cluster analysis, Conjoint analysis) and a Model bank (Product design model, Pricing model, Site selection model, Media-mix model, Advertising budget model), leading to Marketing evaluations and decisions.

propriate model in the MDSS. The model draws up data which are analyzed statistically. The manager can then use a program to determine the optimum course of action. The manager takes this action and the action, along with other forces, affect the environment and result in new data. (Table 5-7 describes the major statistical tools, models, and optimization routines that comprise a modern MDSS.)

Marketing managers in a growing number of companies now have available *computer marketing work stations*. These work stations are to marketing managers what the cockpit controls are to airline pilots — arming managers with the means of "flying" the business in the right direction.[12]

New software programs regularly appear to help marketing managers analyze, plan, and control their operations. *Marketing News*, April 27, 1992, lists over 92 different marketing and sales software programs. They provide support for designing marketing research studies, segmenting markets, setting prices and advertising budgets, analyzing media, planning salesforce activity, and so on. Here are examples of decision models that have been used by marketing managers:

BRANDAID: A flexible marketing-mix model focused on consumer packaged goods whose elements are a manufacturer, competitors, retailers, consumers, and the general environment. The model contains submodels for advertising, pricing, and competition. The model is calibrated with a creative blending of judgment, historical analysis, tracking, field experimentation, and adaptive control.[13]

CALLPLAN: A model to help salespeople determine the number of calls to make per period to each prospect and current client. The model takes into account travel time as well as selling time. The model was tested at United Airlines with an experimental group that managed to increase its sales over a matched control group by 8 percentage points.[14]

DETAILER: A model to help salespeople determine which customers to call on and which products to represent on each call. This model was largely developed for pharmaceutical detailpeople calling on physicians where they could represent no more than three products on a call. In two applications, the model yielded strong profit improvements.[15]

GEOLINE: A model for designing sales and service territories that satisfies three principles: the territories equalize sales workloads; each territory consists of adjacent areas; and the territories are compact. Several successful applications were reported.[16]

MEDIAC: A model to help an advertiser buy media for a year. The media planning model includes market segment delineation, sales potential estimation, diminishing marginal returns, forgetting, timing issues, and competitor media schedules.[17]

STATISTICAL TOOLS

1. **Multiple regression.** A statistical technique for estimating a "best fitting" equation showing how the value of a dependent variable varies with changing values in a number of independent variables.
Example: A company can estimate how unit sales are influenced by changes in the level of company advertising expenditures, salesforce size, and price.

2. **Discriminant analysis.** A statistical technique for classifying object or persons into two or more categories. Example: A large retail chain store can determine the variables which discriminate between successful and unsuccessful store locations.[1]

3. **Factor analysis.** A statistical technique used to determine the few underlying dimensions of a larger set of intercorrelated variables.
Example: A broadcast network can reduce a large set of TV programs down to a small set of basic program types.[2]

4. **Cluster analysis.** A statistical technique for separating objects into a specified number of mutually exclusive groups such that the groups are relatively homogeneous.
Example: A marketing researcher might want to classify a miscellaneous set of cities into four groups of similar cities.

5. **Conjoint analysis.** A statistical technique whereby the ranked preferences of respondents for different offers are decomposed to determine the person's inferred utility function for each attribute and the relative importance of each attribute.
Example: An airline can determine the total utility delivered by different combinations of passenger services.

6. **Multidimensional scaling.** A variety of techniques for representing objects as points in a multidimensional space of attributes where their distance from each other is a measure of dissimilarity.
Example: A computer manufacturer wants to see where his brand is positioned in relation to competitive brands.

MODELS

1. **Markov-process model.** This model shows the probability of moving from a current state to any new state.
Example: A branded packaged-goods manufacturer can determine the period-to-period switching and staying rates for his brand and, if the probabilities are stable, the brand's ultimate brand share.

2. **Queuing model.** This model shows the waiting times and queue lengths that can be expected in any system, given the arrival and service times and the number of service channels.
Example: A supermarket can use the model to predict queue lengths at different times of the day given the number of service channels and service speed.

3. **New-product pretest models.** This model involves estimating functional relations between buyer states of awareness, trial, and repurchase based on consumer preferences and actions in a pretest situation of the marketing offer and campaign. Among the well-known models are ASSESSOR, COMP, DEMON, NEWS and SPRINTER.[3]

4. **Sales-response models.** This is a set of models which estimate functional relations between one or more marketing variables—such as salesforce size, advertising expenditure, sales-promotion expenditure, etc.—and the resulting demand level.

OPTIMIZATION ROUTINES

1. **Differential calculus.** This technique allows finding the maximum or minimum value along a well-behaved function.

2. **Mathematical programming.** This technique allows finding the values that would optimize some objective function that is subject to a set of constraints.

3. **Statistical decision theory.** This technique allows determining the course of action that produces the maximum expected value.

4. **Game theory.** This technique allows determining the course of action in the face of the uncertain behavior of one or more competitors, or nature, that will minimize the decision maker's maximum loss.

5. **Hueristics.** This involves using a set of rules of thumb that shorten the time or work required to find a reasonably good solution in a complex system.

1. S. Sands, "Store Site Selection by Discriminant Analysis," *Journal of the Market Research Society*, 1981, pp. 40–51.

2. V. R. Rao, "Taxonomy of Television Programs Based on Viewing Behavior," *Journal of Marketing Research*, August 1975, pp. 355–58.

3. For references, see Chapter 13, note 1 in Marketing Concepts and Tools 13-7, p. 343.

Marketing Strategies 5-1

The 1990s Marketing Manager Uses Information Power

Envision the working day of a 1990s marketing manager. On arriving at work, the manager turns on his computer and reads messages that arrived during the night, reviews the day's schedule, checks the status of an ongoing computer conference, reads several intelligence alerts, and browses through abstracts of relevant articles from the previous day's business press. To prepare for a late-morning meeting of the new-products committee, the manager retrieves a recent marketing research report from the computer's memory, reviews relevant sections, edits them into a short report, and sends copies electronically to other committee members. Before leaving for the meeting, the manager uses the computer to make lunch reservations at a favorite restaurant for an important distributor and to buy airline tickets for next week's sales meeting in Chicago.

The afternoon is spent preparing sales and profit forecasts for the new product. The manager obtains test market data from company data banks and information on market demand, sales of competing products, and expected economic conditions from external data bases to which the company subscribes. These data are used as inputs for the sales forecasting model stored in the company's model bank. The manager "plays" with the model to see how different assumptions affect predicted results.

At home later that evening, the manager uses his laptop computer to get back on the information network, prepare a report on the product, and send copies to the computers of other involved managers, who can read them first thing in the morning. When the manager logs off, the computer automatically sets an alarm clock for a wake-up call the next morning.

Some newer models now claim to duplicate the way expert marketers normally make their decisions. Here are examples of recent "expert system" models:

PROMOTER evaluates sales promotions by determining baseline sales (what sales would have been without promotion) and measuring the increase over baseline associated with the promotion.[18]

ADCAD recommends the type of ad (humorous, slice of life, and so on) to use given the marketing goals and characteristics of the product, target market, and competitive situation.[19]

COVERSTORY examines a mass of syndicated sales data and writes an English-language memo reporting the highlights.[20]

The 1990s will usher in further software programs and decision models.[21] Those companies that supply superior information power to their marketing managers will gain a competitive edge. Marketing Strategies 5-1 describes a day in the life of the mid-1990s marketing manager.

SUMMARY ❖

Marketing information is a critical element in effective marketing as a result of the trend toward national and international marketing, the transition from buyer needs to buyer wants, and the transition from price to nonprice competition. All firms operate a marketing information system, but the systems vary greatly in their sophistication. In too many cases, information is not available or comes too late or cannot be trusted. An increasing number of companies are now taking steps to improve their marketing information system.

A well-designed market information system consists of four subsystems. The first is the internal records system, which provides current data on sales, costs, inventories, cash flows, and accounts receivable and payable. Many companies have developed advanced computer-based internal records systems to allow for speedier and more comprehensive information.

The second is the marketing intelligence system, which supplies marketing managers with everyday information about developments in the external marketing environment. Here a well-trained salesforce, purchased data from syndicated sources, and an intelligence office can improve the marketing intelligence available to company marketing managers.

The third system is marketing research, which involves collecting information that is relevant to a specific marketing problem facing the company. The marketing research process consists of five steps: defining the problem and research objectives, developing the research plan, collecting the information, analyzing the information, and presenting the findings. Good marketing research is characterized by the scientific method, creativity, multiple methodologies, model building, cost/benefit measures of the value of information, healthy skepticism, and ethical marketing.

The fourth system is the marketing decision support system, which consists of statistical techniques and decision models to assist marketing managers in making better decisions.

NOTES ❖

1. Francis Joseph Aguilar, *Scanning the Business Environment* (New York: Macmillan, 1967).

2. James A. Narus and James C. Anderson, "Turn Your Industrial Distributors into Partners," *Harvard Business Review*, March–April 1986, pp. 66–71.

3. See *1988 Survey of Marketing Research*, eds. Thomas Kinnear and Ann Root (Chicago: American Marketing Association, 1988).

4. For a discussion of the decision-theory approach to the value of research, see Donald R. Lehmann, *Market Research and Analysis*, 3rd ed. (Homewood, IL: Richard D. Irwin, 1989), Chap. 2.

5. For an excellent annotated reference to major secondary sources of business and marketing data, see Gilbert A. Churchill, Jr., *Marketing Research: Methodological Foundations*, 5th ed. (Chicago: The Dryden Press, 1991), pp. 287–303.

6. Thomas L. Greenbaum, *The Handbook for Focus Group Research* (New York: Lexington Books, 1993).

7. An overview of mechanical devices is presented in Roger D. Blackwell, James S. Hensel, Michael B. Phillips, and Brian Sternthal, *Laboratory Equipment for Marketing Research* (Dubuque, IA: Kendall/Hunt Publishing Co., 1970), pp. 7–8. For newer devices, see Wally Wood, "The Race to Replace Memory," *Marketing and Media Decisions*, July 1986, pp. 166–67.

8. Selwyn Feinstein, "Computers Replacing Interviewers for Personnel and Marketing Tasks," *The Wall Street Journal*, October 9, 1986, p. 35.

9. Horace C. Levinson, "Experiences in Commercial Operations Research," *Operations Research*, August 1953, pp. 220–39.

10. Mason Haire, "Projective Techniques in Marketing Research," *Journal of Marketing*, April 1950, pp. 649–56.

11. John D. C. Little, "Decision Support Systems for Marketing Managers," *Journal of Marketing*, Summer 1979, p. 11.

12. See "Information Power: How Companies Are Using New Technologies to Gain a Competitive Edge," *Business Week*, October 14, 1985, pp. 108–14; and Valerie Free, "Ready, Aim, Computer . . . The Marketing War Gets Automated," *Marketing Communications*, June 1988, p. 41 ff.

13. John D. C. Little, "BRANDAID: A Marketing Mix Model, Part I: Structure; Part II: Implementation," *Operations Research*, Vol. 23, 1975, pp. 628–73.

14. Leonard M. Lodish, "CALLPLAN: An Interactive Salesman's Call Planning System," *Management Science*, December 1971, pp. 25–40.

15. David B. Montgomery, Alvin J. Silk, and C. E. Zaragoza, "A Multiple-Product Sales Force Allocation Model," *Management Science*, December 1971, pp. 3–24.

16. S. W. Hess and S. A. Samuels, "Experiences with a Sales Districting Model: Criteria and Implementation," *Management Science*, December 1971, pp. 41–54.

17. John D. C. Little and Leonard M. Lodish, "A Media Planning Calculus," *Operations Research*, January/February 1969, pp. 1–35.

18. Magid M. Abraham and Leonard M. Lodish, "PROMOTER: An Automated Promotion Evaluation System," *Marketing Science*, Spring 1987, pp. 101–23.

19. Raymond R. Burke, Arvind Rangaswamy, Jerry Wind and Jehoshua Eliashberg, "A Knowledge-Based System for Advertising Design," *Marketing Science*, Vol. 9, no. 3, 1990, pp. 212–29.

20. John D. C. Little, "Cover Story: An Expert System to Find the News in Scanner Data," Sloan School, MIT Working Paper, 1988.

21. For further reading, see Gary L. Lilien, Philip Kotler, and K. Sridhar Moorthy, *Marketing Models* (Englewood Cliffs, NJ, Prentice-Hall, 1992).

6

Analyzing the Marketing Environment

It is useless to tell a river to stop running; the best thing is to learn how to swim in the direction it is flowing.

ANONYMOUS

The future ain't what it used to be.

YOGI BERRA

We have repeatedly emphasized that excellent companies take an *outside-inside* view of their business. They recognize that the marketing environment is constantly spinning out new opportunities and threats. These companies recognize the vital importance of continuously monitoring and adapting to the changing environment.

Too many other companies, unfortunately, fail to think of change as opportunity. They ignore or resist critical changes until it is almost too late. Their strategies, structures, systems, and business culture grow increasingly obsolete and dysfunctional. Corporations as mighty as General Motors, IBM, and Sears are brought down to their knees for ignoring macroenvironmental changes too long.

To a company's marketers falls the major responsibility for identifying significant changes in the environment. They, more than any other group in the company, must be the trend trackers and opportunity seekers. Although every manager in an organization needs to observe the outside environment, marketers have two special aptitudes. They have disciplined methods—marketing intelligence and marketing research—for collecting information about the marketing environment. They also normally spend more time in the customer and competitor environment. By conducting systematic environmental scanning, marketers are able to revise and adapt marketing strategies to meet new challenges and opportunities in the marketplace.

In this and the next three chapters, we examine the *external environment* of the firm—*macroenvironment forces, consumer markets, business markets, and competitors*—and consider how to monitor and analyze these forces and agents. In this chapter, we focus on the macroenvironment and address two questions: What are the key methods for tracking and identifying opportunities in the macroenvironment? What are the key developments worth noting in the way of demographic, economic, natural, technological, political, and cultural forces?

Analyzing Needs and Trends in the Macroenvironment

Successful companies are those that can recognize and respond profitably to unmet needs and trends in the macroenvironment. *Unmet needs* always exist. Companies could make a fortune if they could solve any of these problems: a cure for cancer; chemical cures for mental diseases; desalinization of seawater; nonfattening tasty nutritious food; practical electric cars; voice-controlled computers; and affordable housing.

Even in slow-growth economies, some enterprising individuals and companies manage to create new solutions to unmet needs. The 1970s and 1980s saw marvelous new businesses spring up. Club Mediterranee emerged to meet the needs of single people for exotic vacations; the Walkman was created for active people who wanted to listen to personal music; Nautilus was created for men and women who

Faith Popcorn Points to Ten Trends in the Economy

Faith Popcorn runs a marketing consultancy firm called BrainReserve, which she started in 1974. Her clients include AT&T, Citibank, Black & Decker, Hoffman-La Roche, Nissan, Rubbermaid, and many others. Her firm offers several services: Brand Renewal, which attempts to breathe new life into fading brands; BrainJam, which uses a list of trends to generate new ideas; FutureFocus, which develops marketing strategies and concepts that create long-term competitive advantages; and TrendBank, which is a proprietary database made up of culture monitoring and consumer interviews. Popcorn and her associates have identified ten major trends:

1. *Cashing Out:* Cashing out is the impulse to change one's life to a slower but more rewarding pace. It is manifested by career persons who suddenly quit their hectic urban jobs and turn up in Vermont or Montana running a small newspaper, managing a bed-and-breakfast establishment, or joining a band. They don't think the office stress is worth it. There is a nostalgic return to small-town values with clean air, safe schools, and plain-speaking neighbors.

2. *Cocooning:* Cocooning is the impulse to stay inside when the outside gets too tough and scary. More people are turning their home into a nest. They are becoming "couch potatoes," glued to watching TV movies, ordering goods from catalogs, redecorating their homes, using their answering machine to filter out the outside world. In reaction to increased crime, AIDS, and other social problems, Armored Cocoon people are *burrowing in,* building bunkers. Self-preservation is the underlying theme. Also manifest are Wandering Cocoons, people eating in their cars and phoning from their cars. Socialized Cocooning describes the forming of a small group of friends who frequently get together for conversation, for "saloning."

3. *Down-Aging:* Down-aging is the tendency to act and feel younger than one's age. The sexy heroes today are Cher (age 45), Paul Newman (over 65), Elizabeth Taylor (over 60). Older people are spending more on youthful clothes, hair coloring, and facial plastic surgery. They are engaging in more playful behavior, willing to act in ways not normally found in their age group. They buy adult toys, attend adult camps, and sign up for adventurous vacations.

4. *Egonomics:* Egonomics is the desire of persons to develop an individuality so that one is seen and treated as different than anyone else. It is not egomania but simply the wish to individualize oneself through one's possessions and experiences. People are increasingly subscribing to narrow-interest magazines; joining small groups with a narrow mission; buying customized clothing, cars, and cosmetics. Egonomics provides marketers with a competitive opportunity to succeed by offering customized goods, services, and experiences.

5. *Fantasy Adventure:* Fantasy adventure meets the growing needs of people for emotional escapes to offset their daily routines. People express this need through seeking

wanted to tone their bodies; and Federal Express was created to meet the need for next-day mail delivery.

Opportunities are also found by identifying *trends*. *A trend is a direction or sequence of events which have some momentum and durability*. For example, one major trend is the "increasing participation of women in the workforce." This trend has profound implications for economic growth, family life, business life, political power, and goods-and-service preferences. Identifying a trend, ferreting out the likely consequences, and determining company opportunities are critical skills.

We need to draw a distinction between a fad, a trend, and a megatrend. A fad is "unpredictable, short-lived, and without social, economic, and political significance."[1] A company can cash in on a fad such as Pet Rocks or Cabbage Patch dolls, but this is more a matter of luck and good timing than anything else.

Trends on the other hand are more predictable and durable. A trend reveals the shape of the future. Friedrich von Schiller said: "In today already walks tomorrow." A trend, according to futurist Faith Popcorn, has longevity, is observable across several market areas and consumer activities, and is consistent with other significant indicators occurring or emerging at the same time.[2] Popcorn has identi-

vacations, eating exotic foods, going to Disneyland and other fantasy parks, redecorating their homes with a Sante Fe look, and so on. For marketers, this is an opportunity to create new fantasy products and services or add fantasy touches to their current products and services.

6. *99 Lives:* 99 Lives is the desperate state of people who must juggle many roles and responsibilities—think of SuperMom, who has a full-time career, must manage the home and the children, do the shopping, and so on. People feel time-poor and attempt to solve this by using fax machines and car phones, eating at fast food restaurants, and so on. Marketers can address this need by creating *cluster marketing enterprises,* which are all-in-one service stops, such as "Video Town Laundrette" which, in addition to its laundry facilities, includes a tanning room, an exercise bike, copying and fax machines, and 6,000 video titles to rent.

7. *S.O.S. (Save Our Society):* S.O.S. is the drive on the part of a growing number of people to make society more socially responsible along the three critical Es: Environment, Education, and Ethics. These individuals are joining groups to promote more social responsibility on the part of companies and other citizens. Marketers are urging their own companies to practice more socially responsible marketing, along the lines of The Body Shop, Ben & Jerry's, and other socially concerned companies.

8. *Small Indulgences:* This describes the need on the part of stressed-out consumers for occasional emotional fixes. They might not be able to afford a BMW car but might buy a BMW motorcycle. They might eat healthfully during the week and then indulge themselves with a pint of superpremium Haagen-Dazs ice cream. They won't take a two-week vacation to Europe but instead a three-day minicruise in the Caribbean. Marketers should be aware of the deprivations felt by many consumers and the opportunity to offer them small indulgences for an emotional lift.

9. *Staying Alive:* Staying alive is about people's drive to live longer and better lives. They now know that their lifestyle can kill them—eating the wrong foods, smoking, breathing bad air, using hard drugs. People are ready to take responsibility for their own health and choose better foods, exercise more regularly, relax more often. Marketers can meet this need by designing healthier products and services for consumers.

10. *The Vigilante Consumer:* Vigilante consumers are those who will no longer tolerate shoddy products and inept service. They want companies to be more humane. They want automobile companies to take back "lemons" and fully refund their money. They subscribe to the *National Boycott News* and *Consumer Reports,* join MADD (Mothers Against Drunk Driving), and look for lists of good companies and bad companies. Marketers must be the conscience of their company in bringing about more humane standards in the goods and services they provide.

SOURCE: This summary is drawn from various pages of Faith Popcorn's *The Popcorn Report* (New York: Harper Business, 1992).

---

fied ten major trends and their implications for business decision making (see Marketing Environment and Trends 6-1).

John Naisbitt, another futurist, prefers to talk about *megatrends,* which are "large social, economic, political and technological changes [that] are slow to form, and once in place, they influence us for some time — between seven and ten years, or longer." Whereas Popcorn's trends are more psychological and mood-oriented, Naisbitt's megatrends are more societal in their scope. (Naisbitt's megatrends are described in Marketing Environment and Trends 6-2.)

These trends and megatrends merit close attention by marketers. A new product or marketing program is likely to be more successful if it is in line with strong trends rather than opposed to them. At the same time, detecting a new market opportunity does not guarantee its success, even if it is technically feasible. For example, it is possible to offer people a customized daily newspaper appearing on their computer covering only items they are interested in. But there may not be a sufficient number of people interested in it or willing to pay the required price. This is where market research must be undertaken to determine the profit potential of hypothetical opportunities.

John Naisbitt's Megatrends

For many years, John Naisbitt has been publishing *Trend Report*, and several major corporations each pay over $15,000 a year to receive these reports. Naisbitt and his staff spot the trends through content analysis, namely, by counting the number of times hard-news items bearing on different topics appear in major newspapers. The items fall into 13 broad categories and over 200 subcategories. In 1982, Naisbitt published *Megatrends*, listing ten megatrends:

1. *Industrial Society → Information Society:* The economy is undergoing a "megashift" from an industrial to an information-based society.

2. *Forced Technology → High Tech/High Touch:* As technology increases, there will be a need to supply high-touch features.

3. *National Economy → World Economy:* National economies are increasingly affected by global interdependence.

4. *Short Term → Long Term:* Companies will begin to start thinking more about the long-term implications of their short-term moves.

5. *Centralization → Decentralization:* Companies are increasingly decentralizing power and initiative.

6. *Institutional Help → Self-Help:* There is an increasing emphasis on self-reliance instead of institutional dependence.

7. *Representative Democracy → Participatory Democracy:* Workers and consumers are demanding a greater voice in government, business, and the marketplace.

8. *Hierarchies → Networking:* The computer is making it possible to share ideas over networks, instead of relying on hierarchical lines of communication.

9. *North → South:* People are showing a preference for moving from the North and Northeast to the South and Southwest.

10. *Either/Or → Multiple Options:* People are demanding variety instead of "one size for all."

In his book, *Megatrends 2000,* Naisbitt describes ten new trends:

1. The Booming Global Economy of the 1990s
2. A Renaissance in the Arts
3. The Emergence of Free-Market Socialism
4. Global Lifestyles and Cultural Nationalism
5. The Privatization of the Welfare State
6. The Rise of the Pacific Rim
7. The Decade of Women in Leadership
8. The Age of Biology
9. The Religious Revival of the New Millennium
10. The Triumph of the Individual

SOURCE: John Naisbitt, *Megatrends: Ten New Directions Transforming Our Lives* (New York: Warner Books, 1982); and John Naisbitt and Patricia Aburdene, *Megatrends 2000* (New York: Avon Books, 1990).

Deciphering and Responding to the Major Macroenvironment Forces

Companies and their suppliers, marketing intermediaries, customers, competitors, and publics all operate in a larger macroenvironment of forces and trends that shapes opportunities and poses threats. These forces represent "noncontrollables," which the company must monitor and respond to. Among the new social forces are the green movement, the women's movement, gay rights, and so on. Among the economic forces is the increasing impact of global competition. Companies and consumers are increasingly impacted by global forces (see Global Marketing 6-1). Within the rapidly changing global picture, the firm must monitor six major forces, namely, *demographic, economic, natural, technological, political,* and *cultural* forces.

Demographic Environment

The first environmental force to monitor is population because people make up markets. Marketers are keenly interested in the size and growth rate of population in different cities, regions, and nations; age distribution and ethnic mix; educational levels; household patterns; and regional characteristics and movements. We will examine the major demographic characteristics and trends and illustrate their implications for marketing planning.

WORLDWIDE EXPLOSIVE POPULATION GROWTH ❖ The world population is showing "explosive" growth. It totaled 5.4 billion in 1991 and is growing at 1.7% per year. At this rate, the world's population will reach 6.2 billion by the year 2000.[3]

The world population explosion has been a major concern of governments and various groups throughout the world. Two factors underlie this concern. The first is the possible finiteness of the earth's resources to support this much human life, particularly at living standards that represent the aspiration of most people. *The Limits to Growth* presented an impressive array of evidence that unchecked population growth and consumption would eventually result in insufficient food supply, depletion of key minerals, overcrowding, pollution, and an overall deterioration in the quality of life.[4] One of its strong recommendations is the worldwide *social marketing* of family planning.[5]

The second cause for concern is that population growth is highest in countries and communities that can least afford it. The less-developed regions of the world currently account for 76% of the world population and are growing at 2% per year, whereas the population in the more-developed regions of the world is growing at only 0.6% per year. In less-developed economies, the death rate has been falling as a result of modern medicine, while the birthrate has remained fairly stable. For these countries to feed, clothe, and educate the children and also provide a rising standard of living is out of the question. Furthermore, the poorer families have the

Global Marketing 6-1

Forces and Trends in the Global Marketing Environment

The global market environment is being shaped by the following major forces:

- The substantial speedup of international transportation, communication, and financial transactions, leading to the rapid growth of world trade and investment, especially tri-polar trade (North America, Western Europe, Far East).

- The gradual erosion of U.S. international dominance and competitiveness and the rising economic power of Japan and several Far Eastern countries in world markets.

- The rising trade barriers put up by countries and economic regions to protect their markets against foreign competition.

- The severe debt problems of several Latin American and Eastern European countries, along with the increasing fragility of the international financial system.

- The increasing use of barter and countertrade to support international transactions.

- The growing move toward market economies in formerly socialist countries along with rapid privatization of publicly-owned companies.

- The rapid dissemination of global lifestyles resulting from the growth of global communications.

- The gradual opening of major new markets, namely China, India, Eastern Europe, and the Arab countries.

- The increasing tendency of multinationals to transcend their locational and national characteristics and become transnational firms, along with the growth of global brands in autos, food, clothing, electronics, and so on.

- The increasing number of cross-border corporate strategic alliances — for example, General Motors and Toyota, GTE and Fujitsu, and Corning and Ciba-Geigy.

- The increasing regional tensions and conflicts resulting from the ending of the Cold War.

most children, and this reinforces the cycle of poverty. The explosive world population growth has major implications for business. A growing population means growing human needs, but it does not mean growing markets unless there is sufficient purchasing power. If the growing population presses too hard against the available food supply and resources, costs will shoot up and profit margins will decline.

POPULATION AGE MIX DETERMINES NEEDS ❖ National populations vary in their age mix. At one extreme is Mexico, a country with a very young population and rapid population growth. At the other extreme is Japan, a country with one of the world's oldest populations. Products of high importance in Mexico would be milk, diapers, school supplies, and toys, whereas Japan's population will consume many more adult products.

A population can be subdivided into six age groups: *preschool, school-age children, teens, young adults age 25–40; middle-aged adults age 40–65; and older adults age 65 and up*. The age groups that will experience the most rapid growth in the United States will be teens, middle-aged adults, and older adults. For marketers, this signals the kinds of products and services that will be in high demand for the next several years. For example, the increasing segment of older adults will lead to increased demand for assisted living communities, small-portion items, and medical equipment and appliances. Stores catering to senior citizens will need stronger lighting, larger print signs, and safe restrooms.

Marketers are increasingly identifying age groups within age groups as possible target markets. They bear such acronyms as:

- SKIPPIES: School Kids with Income and Purchasing Power
- MOBYS: Mother Older, Baby Younger
- DINKS: Double Income, No Kids
- DEWKS: Dual Earners with Kids
- PUPPIES: Poor Urban Professionals
- WOOFS: Well-Off Older Folks

Each group has a known range of product and service needs and media and retail preferences, which helps marketers fine-tune their market offers.

ETHNIC MARKETS ❖ Countries vary in their ethnic and racial makeup. Japan is at one extreme where almost everyone is Japanese; and the United States is at the other extreme, with people from virtually all nations. The United States was originally called a "melting pot" but there are increasing signs that the melting didn't occur. Now people call the United States a "salad bowl" society with ethnic groups maintaining their ethnic differences, neighborhoods, and cultures. The U.S. population (249 million in 1990) is 80% white; blacks constitute another 12%, and Asians 3%. The Hispanic population constitutes 9% and has been growing fast, with the largest subgroups Mexicans (5.4%), Puerto Ricans (1.1%), and Cubans (0.4%), in that order. The Asian population has also burgeoned, the Chinese constituting the largest group, followed by the Filipinos, Japanese, Asian Indians, and Koreans, in that order. Hispanic and Asian consumers are concentrated in the far western and southern parts of the country, although some dispersal is taking place. Each population group has certain specific wants and buying habits. Several food, clothing, and furniture companies have directed their products and promotions to one or more of these groups.[6]

EDUCATIONAL GROUPS ❖ The population in any society falls into five educational groups: illiterates, high school dropouts, high school degrees, college degrees, and professional degrees. In Japan, 99% of the population are literate, whereas in the United States, 10%–15% of the population may be functionally illiterate. On the other hand, the United States has one of the world's highest percentages of college-educated citizenry, around 20%. The high number of educated people in the United States spells a high demand for quality books, magazines, and travel.

Nations are increasingly realizing that the ultimate wealth of a nation lies not in its natural resources but in its human resources. People with little education have few job opportunities other than manual and domestic work. Countries that aspire to be world-class competitors must invest in providing their people with world-class education and job training.

HOUSEHOLD PATTERNS ❖ The traditional household is thought to consist of a husband, wife, and children (and sometimes grandparents). In the United States today, the traditional household is no longer the dominant household pattern. Today's households include *single live-alones, adult live-togethers of one or both sexes, single-parent families, childless married couples,* and *empty nesters.* Behind the growth of nontraditional households is the fact that people are choosing not to marry, or marrying later, or marrying without the intention to have children, and divorcing and separating more frequently. Each group has a distinctive set of needs and buying habits. For example, the SSWD group (single, separated, widowed, divorced) need smaller apartments; inexpensive and smaller appliances, furniture, and furnishings; and food packaged in smaller sizes. Marketers must increasingly consider the special needs of nontraditional households, since they are now growing more rapidly than traditional households.

GEOGRAPHICAL SHIFTS IN POPULATION ❖ The 1990s is a period of great migration movements between countries and within countries. As a result of the collapse of Soviet Eastern Europe, nationalities are reasserting themselves and trying to form independent countries. The new countries are making certain ethnic groups unwelcome (such as Russians in Latvia, or Muslims in Serbian Yugoslavia), and many of these groups are migrating to safer areas. As foreign groups enter other countries for political sanctuary, some of the local groups start protesting. In the United States, there has been opposition to the influx of immigrants from Mexico, the Caribbean, and certain Asian nations.

Population movement also occurs in normal times as people migrate from rural to urban areas, and then to suburban areas. People's location makes a difference in their goods-and-service preferences. For example, the movement to the Sunbelt states will lessen the demand for warm clothing and home heating equipment and increase the demand for air conditioning. Those who live in large cities such as New York, Chicago, and San Francisco account for most of the sales of expensive furs, perfumes, luggage, and works of art. These cities also support the opera, ballet, and other forms of "high culture." On the other hand, Americans living in the suburbs lead more casual lives, do more outdoor living, and have greater neighbor interaction, higher incomes, and younger families. Suburbanites buy station wagons, home workshop equipment, outdoor furniture, lawn and gardening tools, and outdoor cooking equipment. There are also regional differences: for example, people in Seattle buy more toothbrushes per capita than any other U.S. city; people in Salt Lake City eat more candy bars; folks from New Orleans use more ketchup, and those in Miami drink more prune juice.

SHIFT FROM A MASS MARKET TO MICROMARKETS ❖ The effect of all these changes is to fragment the *mass market* into numerous *micromarkets*, differentiated by age, sex, ethnic background, education, geography, lifestyle, and so on. Each group has strong preferences and consumer characteristics and is reached through increasingly targeted communication and distribution channels. Companies are abandoning the "shotgun" approach that aimed at a mythical "average" consumer and are increasingly designing their products and marketing programs for specific micromarkets.

Demographic trends are highly reliable for the short and intermediate run. There is little excuse for a company's being suddenly surprised by demographic developments. The Singer Company should have known for years that its sewing machine business would be hurt by smaller families and more working wives; yet it was slow in responding. Companies need to list the major demographic trends, their probable impacts, and what actions they should take.

Economic Environment

Markets require purchasing power as well as people. The available purchasing power in an economy depends on current income, prices, savings, debt, and credit availability. Marketers must pay close attention to major trends in income and consumer-spending patterns.

INCOME DISTRIBUTION ❖ Nations vary greatly in the level and distribution of income. A major determinant is the nation's *industrial structure*. Four types of industrial structures can be distinguished:

1. *Subsistence Economies:* In a subsistence economy, the vast majority of people engage in simple agriculture. They consume most of their output and barter the rest for simple goods and services. They offer few opportunities for marketers.

2. *Raw-Material-Exporting Economies:* These economies are rich in one or more natural resources but poor in other respects. Much of their revenue comes from exporting these resources. Examples are Zaire (rubber) and Saudi Arabia (oil). These countries are good markets for extractive equipment, tools and supplies, materials-handling equipment, and trucks. Depending on the number of foreign residents and wealthy native rulers and landholders, they are also a market for Western-style commodities and luxury goods.

3. *Industrializing Economies:* In an industrializing economy, manufacturing begins to account for between 10 to 20% of the country's gross national product. Examples include India, Egypt, and the Philippines. As manufacturing increases, the country relies more on imports of raw materials, steel, and heavy machinery and less on imports of finished textiles, paper products, and processed foods. The industrialization creates a new rich class and a small but growing middle class, both demanding new types of goods, some of which can be satisfied only by imports.

4. *Industrial Economies:* Industrial economies are major exporters of manufactured goods and investment funds. They buy manufactured goods from each other and also export them to other types of economies in exchange for raw materials and semifinished goods. The large and varied manufacturing activities of these industrial nations and their sizable middle class make them rich markets for all sorts of goods.

Income distribution is related to a country's industrial structure but is also affected by the political system. The marketer distinguishes countries with five different income-distribution patterns: (1) *very low incomes*, (2) *mostly low incomes*, (3) *very low, very high incomes*, (4) *low, medium, high incomes*, and (5) *mostly medium incomes*. Consider the market for Lamborghinis, an automobile costing more than $100,000. The market would be very small in countries with type 1 or 2 income patterns. One of the largest single markets for Lamborghinis turns out to be Portugal (income pattern 3), one of the poorest countries in Western Europe, but one with enough wealthy families to afford them.

Real income per capita in the United States has not advanced in the last two decades, saved only by the growing number of dual- income households. There is some evidence that the rich have grown richer, the middle class has shrunk, and the poor have remained poor. This is leading to a two-tier U.S. market with affluent people buying expensive goods and working-class people spending more carefully, shopping at discount stores and factory outlet malls, and selecting less expensive store brands. Conventional retailers who offer medium-price goods are the most vulnerable to these changes.

SAVINGS, DEBT, CREDIT AVAILABILITY ❖ Consumer expenditures are affected by consumer savings, debt, and credit availability. The Japanese, for example, save about 18% of their income while U.S. consumers save about 6%. The result has been that Japanese banks could loan out money to Japanese companies at a much lower interest rate than could U.S. banks, and this access to cheaper capital helped Japanese companies expand faster. U.S. consumers also have a high debt-to-income ratio, which retards further expenditures on housing and large-ticket items. Credit is very available in the United States but at fairly high interest rates, especially to lower-income borrowers. Marketers must pay careful attention to any major changes in incomes, cost of living, interest rates, savings, and borrowing patterns because they can have a high impact, especially on companies whose products have high income and price sensitivity.

Natural Environment

The deteriorating condition of the natural environment is bound to be one of the major issues facing business and the public in the 1990s. In many world cities, air and water pollution have reached dangerous levels. There is great concern about industrial chemicals creating a hole in the ozone layer that will produce a "greenhouse effect," namely, a dangerous warming of the earth. In Western Europe, "green" parties have vigorously pressed for public action to reduce industrial pollution. In the United States, several thought leaders—including Kenneth Boulding, the Erlichs, the Meadowses, and Rachel Carson—documented the amount of ecological deterioration, while watchdog groups such as the Sierra Club and Friends of the Earth carried these concerns into political and social action (see Marketing Environment and Trends 6-3).

Marketers need to be aware of the threats and opportunities associated with four trends in the natural environment.

SHORTAGE OF RAW MATERIALS ❖ The earth's materials consist of the infinite, the finite renewable, and the finite nonrenewable. An *infinite resource*, such as air, poses no immediate problem, although some groups see a long-run danger. Environmental groups have lobbied for a ban of certain propellants used in aerosol cans because of their potential damage to the ozone layer of air. Water is already a major problem in some parts of the world.

Finite renewable resources, such as forests and food, have to be used wisely. Forestry companies are required to reforest timberlands in order to protect the soil and to ensure sufficient wood to meet future demand. Food supply can be a major problem in that the amount of arable land is relatively fixed, and urban areas are constantly encroaching on farmland.

Finite nonrenewable resources—oil, coal, platinum, zinc, silver—will pose a serious problem as their time of depletion approaches. Firms making products that

Impact of Environmentalism on Marketing Decision Making

Environmentalism is an organized movement of concerned citizens and government to protect and enhance people's living environment. Environmentalists are concerned with strip mining, forest depletion, factory smoke, billboards, and litter; with the loss of recreational opportunity; and with the increase in health problems caused by bad air, water, and chemically sprayed food.

Environmentalists are not against marketing and consumption; they simply want businesses and consumers to operate on more ecological principles. They think the goal of the marketing system should be to maximize life quality. And *life quality* means not only the quantity and quality of consumer goods and services but also the quality of the environment.

Environmentalists want environmental costs factored into producer and consumer decision making. They favor taxes and regulations to limit the social costs of antienvironmental behavior. Requiring business to invest in antipollution devices, taxing nonreturnable bottles, and banning high-phosphate detergents are viewed as necessary to induce businesses and consumers to act in environmentally sound ways.

Environmentalism has hit certain industries hard. Steel companies and public utilities have had to invest billions of dollars in pollution-control equipment and costlier fuels. The auto industry has had to introduce expensive emission controls in cars. The soap industry has had to increase biodegradability in its products. The gasoline industry has had to formulate low-lead and no-lead gasolines. These industries resent environmental regulations, especially when imposed too rapidly to allow the companies to make the proper adjustments. These companies have absorbed large costs and have passed them on to customers.

Companies have questioned how many people are willing to pay more for "green" products. A 1991 Simmons report shows U.S. consumers falling into five groups:

1. *Premium greens (22%):* Higher income, recycle regularly, favor boycotts, willing to pay green premiums
2. *Red, white, and greens (20%):* Similar to premium greens but lower willingness to pay green premiums
3. *No-cost ecologists (28%):* Limited resources, believe in recycling but do not practice it
4. *Convenient greens (11%):* Lower-income group, some will pay for green solutions if convenient
5. *Unconcerned (19%):* Lower-income group, least informed about environment

This demonstrates that there are significant consumer groups who are willing to support green products and initiatives.

At the very least, companies must check into the environmental consequences of their products, packag-

require these increasingly scarce minerals face substantial cost increases. They may not find it easy to pass these cost increases on to customers. Firms engaged in research and development face an excellent opportunity to develop new substitute materials.

INCREASED COST OF ENERGY ❖ One finite nonrenewable resource, oil, has created serious problems for the world economy. Oil prices shot up from $2.23 a barrel in 1970 to $34.00 a barrel in 1982, creating a frantic search for alternative energy forms. Coal became popular again, and companies searched for practical means to harness solar, nuclear, wind, and other forms of energy. In the solar energy field alone, hundreds of firms introduced first-generation products to harness solar energy for heating homes and other uses. Other firms searched for ways to make a practical electric automobile, with a potential prize of billions going to the winner.

The development of alternative sources of energy and more efficient ways to use energy led to a decline in oil prices by 1986. Lower prices had an adverse effect

ing, and production processes. They must avoid the temptation of using "green" appeals such as "recyclable" or "environmentally safe" if these claims are not authentic. Smart companies have appointed an environmental manager to develop and implement environmental criteria throughout the company's decision making. They have directed their R&D staff to develop ecologically superior products to establish a competitive advantage. Sears developed and promoted a phosphate-free laundry detergent; Pepsi-Cola developed a one-way, plastic biodegradable soft-drink bottle; and American Oil pioneered no-lead and low-lead gasolines.

Several companies have done an outstanding job of meeting their environmental responsibilities. 3M runs a *Pollution Prevention Pays* program, which has led to substantial pollution and cost reduction. Dow built a new ethylene plant in Alberta that uses 40% less energy and releases 97% less wastewater. AT&T uses a software program to choose the least harmful materials, cut hazardous waste, reduce energy use, and improve product recycling. McDonald's has eliminated its polystyrene cartons and now uses smaller paper boxes and paper napkins.

Committed "green" companies pursue not only environmental cleanup but also pollution prevention. They aim to produce "high value/high virtue" products by improving "front-of-pipe" technology as well as "end-of-pipe" technology. They recognize that shipping pollutants to landfills or incinerators does not provide a permanent solution. True "green" work requires companies to practice the 3Rs of waste management: reducing, reusing, and recycling waste.

Du Pont's chairman, Edward Woolard, Jr., recently announced that Du Pont would take an activist position in environmental affairs. "The real environmental challenge is not one of responding to the next regulatory proposal. Nor is it making the environmentalists see things our way. Nor is it educating the public to appreciate the benefits of our products and thus to tolerate their environmental impacts. . . . I'm calling for corporate environmentalism, which I define as an attitude and a performance commitment that places corporate environmental stewardship fully in line with public desires and expectations."

SOURCES: Francoise L. Simon, "Marketing Green Products in the Triad," *The Columbia Journal of World Business,*" Fall & Winter 1992, pp. 268–85; Jacquelyn A. Ottman, *Green Marketing: Responding to Environmental Consumer Demands* (Lincolnwood, IL: NTC Business Books, 1993); Patrick Carson and Julia Moulden, *Green is Gold: Business Talking to Business About the Environmental Revolution* (Toronto: Harper Business, 1991); and Edward Woolard, Jr., "Environmental Stewardship," *Chemical and Engineering News,* May 29, 1989.

on the oil-exploration industry but considerably improved the income of oil-using industries and consumers. Companies need to pay close attention to any major changes in oil and energy prices.

INCREASED LEVELS OF POLLUTION ❖ Some industrial activity will inevitably damage the quality of the natural environment. Consider the disposal of chemical and nuclear wastes, the dangerous mercury levels in the ocean, the quantity of DDT and other chemical pollutants in the soil and food supply, and the littering of the environment with nonbiodegradable bottles, plastics, and other packaging materials.

The public's concern creates a marketing opportunity for alert companies. It creates a large market for pollution-control solutions, such as scrubbers, recycling centers, and landfill systems. It leads to a search for alternative ways to produce and package goods that do not cause environmental damage. Smart companies, instead of dragging their feet, are initiating environment-friendly moves to show their concern with the future of the world's environment.

CHANGING ROLE OF GOVERNMENTS IN ENVIRONMENT PROTECTION ❖ Governments vary in their concern and efforts to promote a clean environment. On the one hand, the German government is vigorous in its pursuit of environmental quality, partly because of the strong green movement and partly because of the experience of seeing the ecological devastation in former East Germany. On the other hand, many poor nations are doing little about pollution largely because the funds or the political will is lacking. It is in the interest of the richer nations to subsidize the poorer nations to control their pollution but even the richer nations today lack the necessary funds. The major hope is that companies around the world accept more social responsibility and also that less expensive devices are found to control and reduce pollution.

Technological Environment

The most dramatic force shaping people's lives is technology. Technology has released such wonders as penicillin, open-heart surgery, and the birth-control pill. It has released such horrors as the hydrogen bomb, nerve gas, and the submachine gun. It has also released such mixed blessings as the automobile, video games, and white bread. One's attitudes toward technology depend on whether one is more enthralled with its wonders or its horrors.

Every new technology is a force for "creative destruction." Transistors hurt the vacuum-tube industry, xerography hurts the carbon-paper business, autos hurt the railroads, and television hurts the newspapers. Instead of old industries moving into the new, many fought or ignored them, and their businesses declined.

The economy's growth rate is affected by how many major new technologies are discovered. Unfortunately, technological discoveries do not arise evenly through time—the railroad industry created a lot of investment, and then there was a dearth until the auto industry emerged; later radio created a lot of investment, and then there was a dearth until television appeared. In the time between major innovations, the economy can stagnate. Some economists believe that the current economic flatness of the global economy will continue until a sufficient number of new major innovations emerge.

In the meantime, minor innovations fill the gap. Freeze-dried coffee probably made no one happier, and antiperspirant deodorants probably made no one more attractive, but they do create new markets and investment opportunities.

Each technology creates major long-run consequences that are not always foreseeable. The contraceptive pill, for example, led to smaller families, more working wives, and larger discretionary incomes—resulting in higher expenditures on vacation travel, durable goods, and other things.

The marketer should watch the following trends in technology.

ACCELERATING PACE OF TECHNOLOGICAL CHANGE ❖ Many of today's common products were not available 30 years ago. John F. Kennedy did not know personal computers, digital wristwatches, video recorders, or facsimile machines. Alvin Toffler, in his *Future Shock*, sees an accelerative thrust in the invention, exploitation, and diffusion of new technologies.[7] More ideas are being worked on; the time lag between new ideas and their successful implementation is decreasing rapidly; and the time between introduction and peak production is shortening considerably. Ninety percent of all the scientists who ever lived are alive today, and technology feeds upon itself.

In Toffler's later book, *The Third Wave*, he forecasts the emergence of the *electronic cottage* as a new way that work and play will be organized in society.[8] The advent of personal computers and facsimile machines make it possible for people to telecommute, that is work at home instead of traveling to offices that may be 30 or more minutes away. As seen by Toffler, the electronic-cottage revolution will reduce auto pollution, bring the family closer together as a work unit, and create more home-centered entertainment and activity. It will have substantial impact on consumption patterns and marketing systems.

UNLIMITED INNOVATIONAL OPPORTUNITIES ❖ Scientists today are working on a startling range of new technologies that will revolutionize our products and production processes. The most exciting work is being done in biotechnology, solid-state electronics, robotics, and material sciences.[9] Scientists today are working on AIDS cures, happiness pills, pain killers, household robots, totally safe contraceptives, and nonfattening tasty nutritious foods. In addition, scientists also speculate on fantasy products, such as small flying cars, three-dimensional television, and space colonies. The challenge in each case is not only technical but commercial, namely, to develop affordable versions of these products.

VARYING R&D BUDGETS ❖ The United States leads the world in annual R&D expenditures ($74 billion) but nearly 60% of these funds are still earmarked for defense. There is a need to transfer more of this money into researching material science, biotechnology, and micromechanics. Meanwhile Japan is increasing its R&D expenditures much faster and is now spending $30 billion, mostly nondefense, with a good portion exploring fundamental problems in physics, biophysics, and computer science.[10]

A growing portion of U.S. R&D expenditures is going into the development side of R&D, raising concerns about whether the United States can maintain its lead in basic science. Many companies are pursuing minor product improvements rather than gambling on major innovations. Even basic-research companies such as Du Pont, Bell Laboratories, and Pfizer are proceeding cautiously. Many companies are content to put their money into copying competitors' products and making minor feature and style improvements. Much of the research is defensive rather than offensive. Increasingly, research directed toward major breakthroughs is being conducted by consortiums of companies rather than by single companies.

INCREASED REGULATION OF TECHNOLOGICAL CHANGE ❖ As products become more complex, the public needs to be assured of their safety. Consequently, government agencies have expanded their powers to investigate and ban potentially unsafe products. Thus the Federal Food and Drug Administration had issued elaborate regulations on testing new drugs, with the result that industry-research costs are higher, the time between idea and introduction has been lengthened from five to about ten years, and much drug research has been driven to countries with fewer regulations. Only recently have changes been made to accelerate new drug approvals. Safety and health regulations have also increased in the areas of food, automobiles, clothing, electrical appliances, and construction. Marketers must be aware of these regulations when proposing, developing, and launching new products.

Technological change is opposed by those who see it as threatening nature, privacy, simplicity, and even the human race. Various groups have opposed the construction of nuclear plants, high-rise buildings, and recreational facilities in national parks. They have called for *technological assessment* of new technologies before allowing their commercialization.

Marketers need to understand the changing technological environment and how new technologies can serve human needs. They need to work closely with R&D people to encourage more market-oriented research. They must be alert to undesirable side effects of any innovation that might harm the users and create consumer distrust and opposition.

Political Environment

Marketing decisions are strongly affected by developments in the political environment. This environment is composed of *laws, government agencies, and pressure groups* that influence and limit various organizations and individuals in society. A discussion of the main political trends and their implications for marketing management follows.

SUBSTANTIAL AMOUNT OF LEGISLATION REGULATING BUSINESS

❖ Legislation affecting business has steadily increased over the years. The European Commission has been active in establishing a new framework of laws covering competitive behavior, product standards, product liability, and commercial transactions for the 12 member nations of the European Community. With the demise of the Soviet bloc, ex-Soviet nations are rapidly passing laws to promote

TABLE 6-1 Milestone U.S. Legislation Affecting Marketing

Sherman Antitrust Act (1890)	Prohibits (a) "monopolies or attempts to monopolize" and (b) "contracts, combinations, or conspiracies in restraint of trade" in interstate and foreign commerce.
Federal Food and Drug Act (1906)	Forbids the manufacture, sale, or transport of adulterated or fraudulently labeled foods and drugs in interstate commerce. Supplanted by the Food, Drug, and Cosmetic Act, 1938; amended by Food Additives Amendment, 1958, and the Kefauver-Harris Amendment, 1962. The 1962 amendments deal with pretesting of drugs for safety and effectiveness and labeling of drugs by generic name.
Meat Inspection Act (1906)	Provides for the enforcement of sanitary regulations in meat-packing establishments and for federal inspection of all companies selling meats in interstate commerce.
Federal Trade Commission Act (1914)	Establishes the commission, a body of specialists with broad powers to investigate and to issue cease-and-desist orders to enforce Section 5, which declares that "unfair methods of competition in commerce are unlawful."
Clayton Act (1914)	Supplements the Sherman Act by prohibiting certain specific practices (certain types of price discrimination, tying clauses and exclusive dealing, intercorporate stockholdings, and interlocking directorates) "where the effect . . . may be to substantially lessen competition or tend to create a monopoly in any line of commerce." Provides that violating corporate officials could be held individually responsible; exempts labor and agricultural organizations from its provisions.
Robinson-Patman Act (1936)	Amends the Clayton Act. Adds the phrase "to injure, destroy, or prevent competition." Defines price discrimination as unlawful (subject to certain defenses) and provides the FTC with the right to establish limits on quantity discounts, to forbid brokerage allowances except to independent brokers, and to prohibit promotional allowances or the furnishing of services or facilities except where made available to all "on proportionately equal terms."
Miller-Tydings Act (1937)	Amends the Sherman Act to exempt fair-trade (price-fixing) agreements from antitrust prosecution. (The McGuire Act, 1952, reinstates the legality of the nonsigner clause.)
Wheeler-Lea Act (1938)	Prohibits unfair and deceptive acts and practices regardless of whether competition is injured; places advertising of foods and drugs under FTC jurisdiction.
Antimerger Act (1950)	Amends Section 7 of the Clayton Act by broadening the power to prevent intercorporate acquisitions where the acquisition may have a substantially adverse effect on competition.
Automobile Information Disclosure Act (1958)	Prohibits car dealers from inflating the factory price of new cars.
National Traffic and Safety Act (1958)	Provides for the creation of compulsory safety standards for automobiles and tires.

and regulate an open market economy. The United States has many laws on its books covering such issues as competition, product safety and liability, fair trade and credit practices, packaging and labeling, and so on (see Table 6-1). Several countries have gone further than the United States in passing strong consumerist legislation. Norway bans several forms of sales promotion—trading stamps, contests, premiums—as being inappropriate or "unfair" instruments for promoting products. Thailand requires food processors selling national brands to market low-price brands also so that low-income consumers can find economy brands on the shelves. In India, food companies need special approval to launch brands that duplicate what already exists on the market, such as another cola drink or brand of rice.

Business legislation has a number of purposes. The first is to *protect companies* from each other. Business executives all praise competition but try to neutralize it when it touches them. If threatened, some engage in hard-ball pricing or promotion

Fair Packaging and Labeling Act (1966)	Provides for the regulation of the packaging and labeling of consumer goods. Requires manufacturers to state what the package contains, who made it, and how much it contains. Permits industries' voluntary adoption of uniform packaging standards.
Child Protection Act (1966)	Bans sale of hazardous toys and articles. Amended in 1969 to include articles that pose electrical, mechanical, or thermal hazards.
Federal Cigarette Labeling and Advertising Act (1967)	Requires that cigarette packages contain the statement: "Warning: The Surgeon General Has Determined that Cigarette Smoking is Dangerous to Your Health."
Truth-in-Lending Act (1968)	Requires lenders to state the true costs of a credit transaction, outlaws the use of actual or threatened violence in collecting loans and restricts the amount of garnishments. Establishes a National Commission on Consumer Finance.
National Environmental Policy Act (1969)	Establishes a national policy on the environment and provides for the establishment of the Council on Environmental Quality. The Environmental Protection Agency was established by "Reorganization Plan No. 3 of 1970."
Fair Credit Reporting Act (1970)	Ensures that a consumer's credit report will contain only accurate, relevant, and recent information and will be confidential unless requested for an appropriate reason by a proper party.
Consumer Product Safety Act (1972)	Establishes the Consumer Product Safety Commission and authorizes it to set safety standards for consumer products as well as exact penalties for failure to uphold the standards.
Consumer Goods Pricing Act (1975)	Prohibits the use of price maintenance agreements among manufacturers and resellers in interstate commerce.
Magnuson-Moss Warranty/ FTC Improvement Act (1975)	Authorizes the FTC to determine rules concerning consumer warranties and provides for consumer access to means of redress, such as the class-action suit. Also expands FTC regulatory powers over unfair or deceptive acts or practices.
Equal Credit Opportunity Act (1975)	Prohibits discrimination in a credit transaction because of sex, marital status, race, national origin, religion, age, or receipt of public assistance.
Fair Debt Collection Practice Act (1978)	Makes it illegal to harass or abuse any person and make false statements or use unfair methods when collecting a debt.
Toy Safety Act (1984)	Gives the government the power to recall dangerous toys quickly when they are found.

or attempts to tie up distribution. So laws are passed to define and prevent unfair competition.

The second purpose of government regulation is to *protect consumers* from unfair business practices. Some firms, if left alone, would adulterate their products, tell lies in their advertising, deceive through their packages, and bait through their prices. Unfair consumer practices have been defined and are enforced by various agencies. Many managers see purple with each new consumer law, and yet a few have said that consumerism may be the best thing that has happened.

The third purpose of government regulation is to *protect the interests of society* against unbridled business behavior. It is possible for a nation's gross national product to rise and the quality of life to fall. A major purpose of new legislation and/or enforcement is to charge businesses with the social costs created by their production processes or products.

The real issue raised by business legislation is: Where is the point reached when the costs of regulation exceed the benefits? The laws are not always administered fairly by those responsible for enforcing them. The regulators and enforcers may be overzealous and capricious. The agencies are dominated by lawyers and economists who often lack a practical sense of how business and marketing work. They may hurt many legitimate business firms and discourage new investment and market entry. Tough antitrust laws have been criticized as hampering U.S. firms' ability to compete internationally. They may also increase consumer costs. Although each new law may have a legitimate rationale, their totality may sap initiative and retard economic growth.

Nevertheless, it is incumbent upon marketers to have a good working knowledge of the major laws protecting competition, consumers, and society. Companies generally establish legal review procedures and promulgate ethical standards to guide their marketing managers. Yet some marketers complain that too many marketing decisions are being shaped by the legal department and that they would like a little more decision latitude.

GROWTH OF PUBLIC-INTEREST GROUPS ❖ The number and power of public-interest groups have increased during the past three decades. Political-action committees (PACs) lobby government officials and pressure business executives to pay more attention to consumer rights, women's rights, senior citizen rights, minority rights, gay rights, and so on. Many companies have established public-affairs departments to deal with these groups and issues. (See Marketing Environment and Trends 6-4.)

New laws and growing numbers of pressure groups have put more restraints on marketers. Marketers have to clear their plans with the company's legal, public-relations, and public-affairs departments. Private marketing transactions have moved into the public domain. Salancik and Upah put it this way:

> There is some evidence that the consumer may not be king, nor even queen. The consumer is but a voice, one among many. Consider how General Motors makes its cars today. Vital features of the motor are designed by the U. S. government; the exhaust system is redesigned by certain state governments; the production materials used are dictated by suppliers who control scarce material resources. For other products, other groups and organizations may get involved. Thus, insurance companies directly or indirectly affect the design of smoke detectors; scientific groups affect the design of spray products by condemning aerosols; minority activist groups affect the design of dolls by requesting representative figures. Legal departments also can be expected to increase their importance in firms, affecting not only product design and promotion but also marketing strategies. At a minimum, marketing managers will spend less time with their research departments asking, "What does the consumer want?" and more and more time with their production and legal people asking, "What can the consumer have?"[11]

Cultural Environment

The society that people grow up in shapes their basic beliefs, values, and norms. People absorb, almost unconsciously, a world view that defines their relationship to themselves, to others, to nature, and to the universe. Here are some of the main cultural characteristics and trends of interest to marketers.

CORE CULTURAL VALUES HAVE HIGH PERSISTENCE ❖ The people living in a particular society hold many core beliefs and values that tend to persist. Thus most Americans still believe in work, in getting married, in giving to charity, and in being honest. Core beliefs and values are passed on from parents to children and are reinforced by major social institutions — schools, churches, business, and government.

People's secondary beliefs and values are more open to change. Believing in the institution of marriage is a core belief; believing that people ought to get married early is a secondary belief. Family-planning marketers could make more headway arguing that people should get married later than that they should not get married at all. Marketers have some chance of changing secondary values but little chance of changing core values.

EACH CULTURE CONSISTS OF SUBCULTURES ❖ Each society contains subcultures, that is, various groups with shared values emerging from their special life experiences or circumstances. Episcopalians, teen-agers, and Hell's Angels all represent subcultures whose members share common beliefs, preferences, and behaviors. To the extent that subcultural groups exhibit different wants and consumption behavior, marketers can choose subcultures as their target markets.

SECONDARY CULTURAL VALUES UNDERGO SHIFTS THROUGH TIME ❖ Although core values are fairly persistent, cultural swings do take place. The advent in the 1960s of "hippies," the Beatles, Elvis Presley, *Playboy* magazine, and other cultural phenomena had a major impact on young people's hair styles, clothing, sexual norms, and life goals. Today's young people are influenced by new heroes and fads: Michael Jordan, Madonna, Bruce Springsteen. One of the major new symbols is the "yuppies"—young urban professionals, who represent the much more careerist and conservative leanings of today's youth.

Marketers have a keen interest in spotting cultural shifts that might augur new marketing opportunities or threats. Several firms offer social/cultural forecasts in this connection. One of the best known is the Yankelovich Monitor. The Monitor interviews 2,500 people each year and tracks 35 social trends, such as "antibigness," "mysticism," "living for today," "away from possessions," and "sensuousness." It describes the percentage of the population who share the attitude as well as the percentage who are antitrend. For example, the percentage of people who value physical fitness and well-being has risen steadily over the years, especially in the under-thirty group, the young women and upscale group, and people living in the West. Marketers of health foods and exercise equipment cater to this trend with appropriate products and communications.

The major cultural values of a society are expressed in people's views of themselves, others, organizations, society, nature, and the cosmos.

People's Views of Themselves. People vary in the relative emphasis they place on self-gratification. The move toward self-gratification was especially strong in the United States during the 1960s and 1970s. *Pleasure seekers* sought fun, change, and escape. Others sought *self-realization* and joined therapeutic or religious groups.

Impact of Consumerism on Marketing Practices

Starting in the 1960s, American business firms found themselves the target of a growing consumer movement. Consumers had become better educated; products had become increasingly complex and hazardous; discontent with American institutions was widespread; influential writings by John Kenneth Galbraith, Vance Packard, and Rachel Carson accused big business of wasteful and manipulative practices; John Kennedy's presidential message of 1962 declared that consumers had the right to safety, to be informed, to choose, and to be heard; congressional investigations of certain industries proved embarrassing; and, finally, Ralph Nader appeared on the scene to dramatize many of the issues.

Since these early stirrings, many private consumer organizations have emerged, several pieces of consumer legislation have been passed, and several state and local offices of consumer affairs have been created. Furthermore, the consumer movement has acquired an international character, with much strength in Scandinavia and the Low Countries and a growing presence in France, Germany, and Japan.

But what is consumerism? *Consumerism is an organized movement of citizens and government to strengthen the rights and power of buyers in relation to sellers.* Consumerists' groups seek to increase the amount of consumer information, education, and protection.

Consumerists have advocated—and in many cases won—such proposals as the right to know the true interest cost of a loan (*truth-in-lending*), the true cost per standard unit of competing brands (*unit pricing*), the basic ingredients in a product (*ingredient labeling*), the nutritional quality of food (*nutritional labeling*), the freshness of products (*open dating*), and the true benefits of a product (*truth-in-advertising*). They want the government to check on the safety of products that are potentially hazardous and to penalize companies that are careless. Some consumerists want companies to elect consumer representatives to their boards to introduce consumer considerations into business decision making.

The most successful consumer group is Ralph Nader's *Public Citizen*. Nader lifted consumerism into a major social force, first with his successful attack on unsafe automobiles (resulting in the passage of the National Traffic and Motor Vehicle Safety Act of 1962), and then through investigations into meat processing (resulting in the passage of the Wholesome Meat Act of 1967), truth-in-lending, auto repairs, insurance, and X-ray equipment.

At first a number of companies balked at the consumer movement. They resented the power of strong consumer leaders to point an accusing finger at their products and cause their sales to plummet, as when

The marketing implications of a "me society" were many. People bought products, brands, and services as a means of self-expression. They bought "dream cars" and "dream vacations." They spent more time in health activities (jogging, tennis), in introspection, and in arts and crafts. The leisure industry (camping, boating, arts and crafts, sports) benefited from the growing number of self-gratifiers. Today, as a contrast, people are adopting more conservative behaviors and ambitions. They have witnessed harder times and can rely less on continuous employment and rising real income. They are more cautious in their spending pattern and more "value-driven" in their purchases.

People's Views of Others. Some observers have pointed to a countermovement from a "me society" to a "we society." People are concerned about the homeless, about crime and victims, and other social problems. They would like to live in a more humane society. At the same time, people are seeking out their "own kind" and avoiding strangers. People hunger for serious and long-lasting relationships with a few others. This portends a growing market for "social support" products and services that promote direct relations between human beings, such as health

Ralph Nader called the Corvair automobile unsafe, when Robert Choate accused breakfast cereals of providing "empty calories," and when Herbert S. Denenberg published a list showing the wide variation in premiums that different insurance companies were charging for the same protection. Businesses resented consumer proposals that appeared to increase business costs more than they helped the consumer. They also felt that most consumers would not pay attention to unit pricing or ingredient labeling and that the doctrines of advertising substantiation, corrective advertising, and counteradvertising would stifle advertising creativity.

Many other companies took no stand and simply went about their business. A few companies undertook a series of bold initiatives to show their endorsement of consumer aims. For example:

> Whirlpool Corporation responded by adopting a number of measures to improve customer information and services. They installed a toll-free corporate phone number for consumers to use if dissatisfied with Whirlpool equipment or service. Whirlpool expanded the coverage of its product warranties and rewrote them in basic English.

Several companies took the initiative in showing "we care" and in several cases enjoyed increased profits.

Competitors were forced to emulate them without, however, achieving the same impact achieved by these firms.

Currently, most companies have accepted consumerism in principle. They recognize the consumers' right to information and protection. Those who take a leadership role recognize that consumerism involves a total commitment by top management, new company policy guidelines, and training programs for all personnel. Several companies have established consumer-affairs departments to help formulate policies and deal with "consumerist" problems.

Product managers today have to spend more time checking product ingredients and product features for safety, preparing safe packaging and informative labeling, substantiating their advertising claims, reviewing their sales promotion, developing clear and adequate product warranties, and so on. They have to work more closely with company lawyers.

Consumerism is actually the ultimate expression of the marketing concept. It compels company marketers to consider things from the consumers' point of view. It suggests consumer needs and wants that may have been overlooked by the firms in the industry. The resourceful manager will look for the positive opportunities created by consumerism rather than brood over its restraints.

clubs, cruises, and religious activity. It also suggests a growing market for "social surrogates," things that allow people who are alone to feel that they are not, such as television, home video games, and computers.

People's Views of Organizations. People vary in their attitudes toward corporations, government agencies, trade unions, and other organizations. Most people are willing to work for these organizations, although they may be critical of particular ones. There is a decline in *organizational loyalty*. The massive wave of company downsizing and delayering along with flat incomes have built more cynicism and distrust of companies. Many see work not as a source of satisfaction but as a necessary pursuit to earn the means to enjoy their nonwork hours.

Several marketing implications follow from this outlook. Companies need to find new ways to win back consumer and employee confidence. They need to review their various activities to make sure they are "good corporate citizens." They need to review their advertising communications to make sure their consumer messages are honest. More companies are turning to *social audits* and *public relations* to improve their image performance with their publics.

People's Views of Society. People vary in their attitudes toward their society, from those who defend it (preservers), to those who run it (makers), to those who take what they can from it (takers), to those who want to change it (changers), to those who are looking for something deeper (seekers), to those who want to leave it (escapers).[12] Often peoples' consumption patterns will reflect their social attitude. Makers are high achievers, who eat, dress, and live well, while changers live more frugally by driving smaller cars, wearing simpler clothes, and so on. Escapers and seekers are a major market for movies, music, surfing, and camping.

People's Views of Nature. People vary in their attitude toward the natural world. Some feel subjugated by it, others feel harmony with it, and still others seek mastery over it. A long-term trend has been people's growing mastery over nature through technology and the attendant belief that nature is bountiful. More recently, however, people have awakened to nature's fragility and finite supplies. People recognize that nature can be spoiled and destroyed by human activities.

People's love of nature is leading to more camping, hiking, boating, and fishing. Business has responded with hiking boots, tenting equipment, and other gear for nature enthusiasts. Tour operators are packaging more tours to wilderness areas. Food producers have found growing markets for "natural" products, such as natural cereal, natural ice cream, and health foods. Marketing communicators are using more scenic backgrounds in advertising their products.

People's Views of the Universe. People vary in their beliefs about the origin of the universe and their place in it. Most Americans are monotheistic, although their religious conviction and practice have been waning through the years. Church attendance has fallen steadily, with the exception of certain evangelical movements that reach out to bring people back into organized religion. Some of the religious impulse has not been lost but has been redirected into an interest in Eastern religions, mysticism, the occult, and the human-potential movement.

As people lose their religious orientation, they seek more of the "good life" here on earth. Self-fulfillment and immediate gratification are rising cultural values. At the same time, every trend seems to breed a countertrend, as indicated by a worldwide rise of religious fundamentalism. From time to time, we can expect "futurists" to identify new trends that warrant attention.

SUMMARY ❖

The company's macroenvironment is the place where the company must start its search for opportunities and possible threats. It consists of all the actors and forces that affect the company's operations and performance. Companies need to understand the trends and megatrends characterizing the current environment.

The company's macroenvironment consists of six major forces: demographic, economic, natural, technological, political, and cultural. The demographic environment shows a worldwide explosive population growth, a changing age, ethnic, and educational mix, new types of households, geographical population shifts, and the splintering of mass markets into micromarkets. The economic environment shows a slowdown in real-income growth, low savings and high debt, and changing consumer-expenditure patterns. The natural environment shows potential shortages of certain raw materials, unstable cost of energy, increased pollution levels, and a growing "green" movement to protect the environment. The technological environment exhibits accelerating technological change, unlimited innovational opportunities, high R&D budgets, concentration on minor improvements rather than on major discoveries, and increased regulation of technological change. The political environment shows substantial business regulation, strong government agency enforcement, and the growth of public-interest groups. The cultural environment shows long-run trends toward self-fulfillment, immediate gratification, and a more secular orientation.

NOTES ❖

1. Gerald Celente, *Trend Tracking* (New York: Warner Books, 1991).

2. See Faith Popcorn, *The Popcorn Report* (New York: Harper Business, 1992).

3. Much of the statistical data in this chapter are drawn from the *World Almanac and Book of Facts*, 1993.

4. Donella H. Meadows, Dennis L. Meadows, Jorgen Randers, and William W. Behrens III, *The Limits to Growth* (New York: New American Library, 1972), p. 41.

5. Philip Kotler and Eduardo Roberto, *Social Marketing: Strategies for Changing Public Attitudes* (New York: Free Press, 1989).

6. For descriptions on the buying habits and marketing approaches to African Americans and Hispanics, see Chester A. Swenson, *Selling to a Segmented Market: The Lifestyle Approach* (Lincolnwood, IL: NTC Business Books, 1992).

7. Alvin Toffler, *Future Shock* (New York: Bantam Books, 1970), pp. 25–30.

8. Alvin Toffler, *The Third Wave* (New York: Bantam Books, 1980).

9. See "White House to Name 22 Technologies It Says Are Crucial to Prosperity, Security," *The Wall Street Journal,* April 26, 1991, p. 2.

10. See "R&D Scoreboard: On A Clear Day You Can See Progress," *Business Week,* June 29, 1992, pp. 104–25.

11. Gerald R. Salancik and Gregory D. Upah, "Directions for Interorganizational Marketing" (paper, School of Commerce, University of Illinois, Champaign, August 1978).

12. Arnold Mitchell of the Stanford Research Institute, private publication.

Analyzing Consumer Markets and Buyer Behavior

There is an old saying in Spain: To be a bullfighter, you must first learn to be a bull.

ANONYMOUS

The aim of marketing is to meet and satisfy target customers' needs and wants. But "knowing customers" is never simple. Customers may state their needs and wants but act otherwise. They may not be in touch with their deeper motivations. They may respond to influences that change their mind at the last minute.

Nevertheless, marketers must study their target customers' wants, perceptions, preferences, and shopping and buying behavior. Such study will provide clues for developing new products, product features, prices, channels, messages, and other marketing-mix elements. This chapter will explore the buying dynamics of consumers, and the next chapter will explore the buying dynamics of business buyers.

A Model of Consumer Behavior

In earlier times, marketers could understand consumers through the daily experience of selling to them. But the growth in the size of companies and markets has removed many marketing managers from direct contact with customers. Increasingly, managers have had to rely on consumer research for answers to the following key questions about any market:

Who constitutes the market?	Occupants
What does the market buy?	Objects
Why does the market buy?	Objectives
Who participates in the buying?	Organizations
How does the market buy?	Operations
When does the market buy?	Occasions
Where does the market buy?	Outlets

The starting point for understanding the buyer is the stimulus-response model shown in Figure 7-1. Marketing and environmental stimuli enter the buyer's consciousness. The buyer's characteristics and decision process lead to certain purchase decisions. The marketer's task is to understand what happens in the buyer's consciousness between the arrival of outside stimuli and the buyer's purchase decisions. We will address two questions:

- How do the buyer's characteristics— cultural, social, personal, and psychological— influence buying behavior?
- How does the buyer make purchasing decisions?

Major Factors Influencing Buying Behavior

Figure 7-2 presents a detailed model of the factors influencing a consumer's buying behavior. We will illustrate these influences for a hypothetical consumer named

FIGURE 7-1
Model of Buyer Behavior

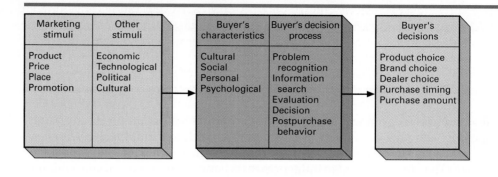

Linda Brown. Linda Brown is 35, married, and a regional sales manager in a leading chemical company. She travels a lot and wants to acquire a laptop computer. She faces a great number of brand choices: IBM, Apple, Dell, Compaq, and so on. Her choice will be influenced by many factors.

Cultural Factors

Cultural factors exert the broadest and deepest influence on consumer behavior. We will look at the role played by the buyer's culture, subculture, and social class.

CULTURE ❖ Culture is the most fundamental determinant of a person's wants and behavior. The growing child acquires a set of values, perceptions, preferences, and behaviors through his or her family and other key institutions. A child growing up in America is exposed to the following values: achievement and success, activity, efficiency and practicality, progress, material comfort, individualism, freedom, external comfort, humanitarianism, and youthfulness.[1]

Linda Brown's interest in computers reflects her upbringing in a technological society. Linda knows what computers are and she knows that the society values computer expertise. In another culture, say a remote tribe in central Africa, a computer would mean nothing. It would simply be a curious piece of hardware, and there would be no buyers.

FIGURE 7-2
Detailed Model of Factors
Influencing Behavior

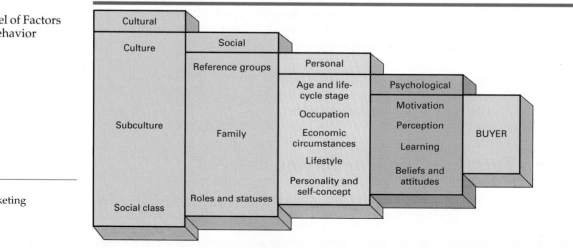

SUBCULTURE ❖ Each culture consists of smaller subcultures that provide more specific identification and socialization for its members. Subcultures include nationalities, religions, racial groups, and geographical regions. Many subcultures make up important market segments, and marketers often design products and marketing programs tailored to their needs (see Marketing Environment and Trends 7-1). Linda Brown's buying behavior will be influenced by her subculture identifications. They will influence her food preferences, clothing choices, recreation, and career aspirations. She may come from a subculture that places a high value on being an "educated person," and this helps explain her interest in computers.

Marketing Environment and Trends 7-1

Marketers Target Three Important Market Segments: Hispanics, Blacks, Seniors

When subcultures grow large and affluent enough, companies often design special marketing programs to serve their needs. Here are examples of three such important subculture groups.

HISPANIC CONSUMERS ❖ For years, marketers have viewed the Hispanic market—Americans of Mexican, Cuban, and Puerto Rican descent—as small and poverty-stricken, but these perceptions are badly out of date. Expected to number 40 million by the year 2000, Hispanics are the second largest and fastest-growing U.S. minority. Annual Hispanic purchasing power totals $134 billion. Over half of all Hispanics live in one of six metropolitan areas—Los Angeles, New York, Miami, San Antonio, San Francisco, and Chicago. They are easy to reach through the growing selection of Spanish-language broadcast and print media that cater to Hispanics. Hispanics have long been a target for marketers of food, beverages, and household care products. But as the segment's buying power increases, Hispanics are now emerging as an attractive market for pricier products such as computers, financial services, photography equipment, large appliances, life insurance, and automobiles. Hispanic consumers tend to be brand conscious and quality conscious—generics don't sell well to Hispanics. Perhaps more important, Hispanics are very brand loyal, and they favor companies who show special interest in them. Many companies are devoting larger ad budgets and preparing special appeals to woo Hispanics. Because of the segment's strong brand loyalty, companies that get the first foothold have an important head start in this fast-growing market.

BLACK CONSUMERS ❖ If the U.S. population of 31 million black Americans—with a total purchasing power of $218 billion annually—were a separate nation, their buying power would rank twelfth in the free world. The black population in the United States is growing in affluence and sophistication. Blacks spend relatively more than whites on clothing, personal care, home furnishings, and fragrances; and relatively less on food, transportation, and recreation. Although more price conscious, blacks are also strongly motivated by quality and selection. They place more importance than other groups on brand names, are more brand loyal, do less "shopping around," and shop more at neighborhood stores. In recent years, many large companies—Sears, McDonald's, Procter & Gamble, Coca-Cola—have stepped up their efforts to tap this lucrative market. They employ black-owned advertising agencies, use black models in their ads, and place ads in black consumer magazines. Some companies develop special products, packaging, and appeals for the black consumer market.

MATURE CONSUMERS ❖ As the U.S. population ages, "mature" consumers—those 65 and older—are becoming a very attractive market. The seniors market will grow to over 40 million consumers by the year 2000. Seniors are better off financially, spending about $200 billion each year, and they average twice the disposable income of consumers in the under-35 group. Mature consumers have long been the target of the makers of laxatives, tonics, and denture products. But many marketers know that not all seniors are poor and feeble. Most are healthy and active, and they have many of the same needs and wants as younger consumers. Because seniors have more time and money, they are an ideal market for exotic travel, restaurants, high-tech home entertainment products, leisure goods and services, designer furniture and fashions, financial services, and life- and health-care services. Their desire to look as young as they feel makes seniors good candidates for specially designed cosmetics and personal-care products, health foods, home physical fitness products, and other items that combat aging. Several companies are hotly pursuing the seniors market. For example, Sears 40,000-member "Mature Club" offers older consumers 25% discounts on everything from eyeglasses to lawnmowers. Southwestern Bell publishes the "Silver Pages," crammed full of ads offering discounts and coupons to 20 million seniors in 90 markets. To appeal more to mature consumers, McDonald's employs older folks as hosts and hostesses in its restaurants and casts them in its ads. And GrandTravel of Chevy Chase, Maryland, sponsors barge trips through Holland, safaris to Kenya, and other exotic vacations for grandparents and their grandchildren. As the seniors segment grows in size and buying power, and as the stereotypes of seniors as doddering, creaky, impoverished shut-ins fade, more and more marketers will develop special strategies for this important market.

SOURCES: For more on marketing to Hispanics, blacks, mature consumers, and Asians, see Jon Berry, "Special Report: Hispanic Marketing," *Adweek*, July 9, 1990, pp. 28–34; Thomas Exter, "One Million Hispanic Club," *American Demographics*, February 1991, p. 59; Gary L. Berman, "The Hispanic Market: Getting Down to Cases," *Sales & Marketing Management*, October 1991, pp. 65–74; Judith Waldrop, "Shades of Black," *American Demographics*, September 1990, pp. 30–34; Melissa Campanelli, "The African-American Market: Community, Growth, and Change," *Sales & Marketing Management*, May 1991, pp. 75–81; Maria Mallory, "Waking Up to a Major Market," *Business Week*, March 23, 1992, pp. 70–73; Milinda Beck, "The Geezer Boom," in "The 21st Century American Family," a special issue of *Newsweek*, Winter/Spring 1990, pp. 62–67; Melissa Campanelli, "The Senior Market: Rewriting the Demographics and Definitions," *Sales & Marketing Management*, February 1991, pp. 63–70; and Maria Shao, "Suddenly, Asian-Americans Are a Marketer's Dream," *Business Week*, June 17, 1991, pp. 54–55.

SOCIAL CLASS ❖ Virtually all human societies exhibit social stratification. Stratification sometimes takes the form of a caste system where the members of different castes are reared for certain roles and cannot change their caste membership. More frequently, stratification takes the form of social classes. *Social classes are relatively homogeneous and enduring divisions in a society, which are hierarchically ordered and whose members share similar values, interests, and behavior.* Social scientists have identified the seven social classes shown in Table 7-1.

Social classes have several characteristics. First, persons within each social class tend to behave more alike than persons from two different social classes. Second, persons are perceived as occupying inferior or superior positions according to their social class. Third, a person's social class is indicated by a number of variables, such as occupation, income, wealth, education, and value orientation, rather than by any single variable. Fourth, individuals can move from one social class to another—up or down—during their lifetime. The extent of this mobility varies according to the rigidity of social stratification in a given society.

Social classes show distinct product and brand preferences in such areas as clothing, home furnishings, leisure activities, and automobiles. Some marketers focus their efforts on one social class. Thus the Four Seasons restaurant in upper Manhattan focuses on upper-class customers whereas Joe's Diner in lower Manhattan focuses on lower-class customers. The social classes differ in their media preferences, with upper-class consumers preferring magazines and books and lower-class consumers preferring television. Even within a media category such as TV, upper-class consumers prefer news and drama, and lower-class consumers prefer soap operas and quiz shows. There are also language differences among the social classes. The advertiser has to compose copy and dialogue that ring true to the targeted social class.

Linda Brown comes from a middle-class background. Her family places high

TABLE 7-1
Characteristics of Seven
Major American Social
Classes

1. **Upper Uppers**
   (less than 1%)

   Upper uppers are the social elite who live on inherited wealth and have well-known families. They give large sums to charity, run the debutante balls, maintain more than one home, and send their children to the finest schools. They are a market for jewelry, antiques, homes, and vacations. They often buy and dress conservatively, not being interested in ostentation. While small as a group, they serve as a reference group for others to the extent that their consumption decisions trickle down and are imitated by the other social classes.

2. **Lower Uppers**
   (about 2%)

   Lower uppers are persons who have earned high income or wealth through exceptional ability in the professions or business. They usually come from the middle class. They tend to be active in social and civic affairs and seek to buy the symbols of status for themselves and their children, such as expensive homes, schools, yachts, swimming pools, and automobiles. They include the nouveau riche, whose pattern of conspicuous consumption is designed to impress those below them. The ambition of lower uppers is to be accepted in the upper-upper stratum, a status that is more likely to be achieved by their children than themselves.

3. **Upper Middles (12%)**

   Upper middles possess neither family status nor unusual wealth. They are primarily concerned with "career." They have attained positions as professionals, independent businesspersons, and corporate managers. They believe in education and want their children to develop professional or administrative skills so that they will not drop into a lower stratum. Members of this class like to deal in ideas and "high culture." They are joiners and highly civic minded. They are the quality market for good homes, clothes, furniture, and appliances. They seek to run a gracious home, entertaining friends and clients.

4. **Middle Class (32%)**

   The middle class are average-pay white- and blue-collar workers who live on "the better side of town" and try to "do the proper things." Often, they buy products that are popular "to keep up with the trends." Twenty-five percent own imported cars, while most are concerned with fashion, seeking "one of the better brand names." Better living means "a nicer home" in "a nice neighborhood on the better side of town" with "good schools." The middle class believes in spending more money on "worthwhile experiences" for their children and aiming them toward a college education.

5. **Working Class (38%)**

   Working class consists of average-pay blue-collar workers and those who lead a "working-class lifestyle," whatever their income, school background, or job. The working class depends heavily on relatives for economic and emotional support, for tips on job opportunities, for advice on purchases, and for assistance in times of trouble. A working-class vacation means "staying in town," and "going away" means to a lake or resort no more than two hours away. The working class maintains sharp sex-role division and stereotyping. Car preferences include standard size and larger cars, rejecting domestic and foreign compacts.

6. **Upper Lowers (9%)**

   Upper lowers are working, not on welfare, although their living standard is just above poverty. They perform unskilled work and are very poorly paid, although they are striving toward a higher class. Often, upper lowers are educationally deficient. Although they fall near the poverty line financially, they manage to "present a picture of self-discipline" and "maintain some effort at cleanliness."

7. **Lower Lowers (7%)**

   Lower lowers are on welfare, visibly poverty stricken, and usually out of work or have "the dirtiest jobs." Some are not interested in finding a permanent job and most are dependent on public aid or charity for income. Their homes, clothes, and possessions are "dirty," "raggedy," and "broken-down."

Source: Richard P. Coleman, "The Continuing Significance of Social Class to Marketing," *Journal of Consumer Research,* December 1983, pp. 265–80; and Richard P. Coleman and Lee P. Rainwater, *Social Standing in America: New Dimension of Class* (New York: Basic Books, 1978).

value on education and becoming a professional, such as a manager, lawyer, accountant, or physician. As a result, Linda has acquired good verbal and mathematical skills and is not daunted by computers, as someone from a less-educated background might be.

Social Factors

A consumer's behavior is also influenced by such social factors as reference groups, family, and social roles and statuses.

REFERENCE GROUPS ❖ Many groups influence a person's behavior. A person's *reference groups* consist of *all the groups that have a direct (face-to-face) or indirect influence on the person's attitudes or behavior*. Groups having a direct influence on a person are called *membership groups*. These are groups to which the person belongs and interacts. Some are *primary groups*, such as family, friends, neighbors, and coworkers, with which the person interacts fairly continuously. Primary groups tend to be informal. A person also belongs to *secondary groups*, such as religious, professional, and trade-union groups, which tend to be more formal and require less continuous interaction.

People are also influenced by groups in which they are not members. Groups to which a person would like to belong are called *aspirational groups*. For example, a teenager may hope one day to play basketball for the Chicago Bulls. A *dissociative group* is one whose values or behavior an individual rejects. The same teenager may want to avoid any relationship with the Hare Krishna cult group.

Marketers try to identify the reference groups of their target customers. People are significantly influenced by their reference groups in at least three ways. Reference groups expose an individual to new behaviors and lifestyles. They also influence the person's attitudes and self-concept because he or she normally desires to "fit in." And they create pressures for conformity that may affect the person's actual product and brand choices.

The level of reference-group influence varies among products and brands. Hendon asked 200 consumers to specify which product and brand choices were strongly influenced by others.[2] Reference groups strongly influenced product and brand choice in the case of automobiles and color television. Reference groups strongly influenced brand choice only in such items as furniture and clothing. And reference groups strongly influenced product choice only in such items as beer and cigarettes.

Reference-group influence changes as products pass through the product life cycle. When a product is first introduced, the decision to buy it is heavily influenced by others, but the brand chosen is less influenced by others. In the market growth stage, group influence is strong on both product and brand choice. In the product maturity stage, brand choice but not product choice is heavily influenced by others. In the decline stage, group influence is weak in both product and brand choice.

Manufacturers of products and brands where group influence is strong must determine how to reach and influence the *opinion leaders* in these reference groups. Opinion leaders are found in all strata of society, and a person can be an opinion leader in certain product areas and an opinion follower in other areas. The marketer tries to reach opinion leaders by identifying demographic and psychographic characteristics associated with opinion leadership, identifying the media read by opinion leaders, and directing messages at the opinion leaders.

Group influence is strong for products that are visible to others whom the buyer respects. Linda Brown's interest in a laptop computer and her attitudes toward various brands will be strongly influenced by some of her membership groups. Her coworkers' attitudes and brand choices will influence her. The more cohesive the group, the more effective its communication process, and the higher the person esteems it, the more the group will shape the person's product and brand choices.[3]

FAMILY ❖ Family members constitute the most influential primary reference group. We can distinguish between two families in the buyer's life. The *family of orientation* consists of one's parents. From parents a person acquires an orientation toward religion, politics, and economics and a sense of personal ambition, self-worth, and love.[4] Even if the buyer no longer interacts very much with parents, the parents' influence on the buyer's behavior can be significant. In countries where parents live with their grown children, their influence can be substantial.

A more direct influence on everyday buying behavior is one's *family of procreation*, namely, one's spouse and children. The family is the most important consumer-buying organization in society, and it has been researched extensively.[5] Marketers are interested in the roles and relative influence of the husband, wife, and children in the purchase of a large variety of products and services. This will vary widely in different countries and social classes. The marketer as always has to research the specific patterns in the particular target market.

In the United States, husband-wife involvement varies widely by product category. The wife has traditionally acted as the family's main purchasing agent, especially for food, sundries, and staple-clothing items. This is changing with the increased number of working wives and the husbands doing more family shopping. Convenience-goods marketers would make a mistake to think of women as the main or only purchasers of their products.

In the case of expensive products and services, husbands and wives engage in more joint decision making. The marketer needs to determine which member normally has the greater influence in choosing various products. Often it is a matter of who has more power or expertise. Here are typical product patterns:

- ◆ *Husband dominant:* Life insurance, automobiles, television
- ◆ *Wife dominant:* Washing machines, carpeting, furniture, kitchenware
- ◆ *Equal:* Vacation, housing, outside entertainment

A family member's influence can vary with different subdecisions made within a product category. Davis found that the decision of "when to buy an automobile" is influenced primarily by the husband in 68% of the cases, primarily by the wife in 3% of the cases, and equally in 29% of the cases.[6] The decision on "what color automobile to buy" was influenced primarily by the husband in 25% of the cases, by the wife in 25% of the cases, and equally in 50% of the cases. An automobile company would need to research the varying decision roles in designing and promoting its cars (see Marketing Environment and Trends 7-2).

In the case of Linda Brown's purchase of a laptop computer, her husband may play an influencer role. He may have initiated the suggestion. He may offer advice on the brand and features. His influence will depend on the strength of his opinions and how much Linda values his opinion.

ROLES AND STATUSES ❖ A person participates in many groups throughout life—family, clubs, organizations. The person's position in each group can be defined in terms of *role* and *status*. With her parents, Linda Brown plays the role of daughter; in her family, she plays wife; in her company, she plays sales manager. A role consists of the activities that a person is expected to perform. Each of Linda's roles will influence some of her buying behavior.

Each role carries a status. A Supreme Court justice has more status than a sales

Women Become a More Important Market for Car Buying

Laurie Ashcraft recently made the following observations at a Midwest marketing and research conference:

Women in car ads have typically been shown sitting on the hood rather than behind the wheel. . . . It seems Detroit is always trying to catch up to changes in consumer demands. . . . And now, they're trying to catch up in their marketing to women. In 1980, women influenced 80% of new-car purchases and actually made 40% of these purchases. And the increase in car ownership by women has been a steady trend, jumping to 40% from 21% in 1972. . . . Some auto manufacturers are frantically trying to change their advertising to reflect the reality that women do more than pick out the color of the upholstery. . . . A study . . . revealed that 47% of women feel they are not being communicated with effectively in car ads. The

women said car ads assume women to be primarily interested in appearance, underestimate women's car sense, and overestimate male influence on women drivers. . . . For example, 60% of service contracts are bought by women, and surveys have found that they should be approached differently than men, since women are interested in aspects such as safety to a greater degree.

Detroit and other top management suffer from inertia and cannot be easily persuaded that change is occurring. . . . Marketing decision makers are bringing too much of their own mind-set to the party.

SOURCES: Laurie Ashcraft, "Marketers Miss Their Target When They Eschew Research," *Marketing News*, January 7, 1983, p. 10. Also see J. Gilbert, "Marketing Cars to Women," *Madison Avenue*, August 1985, pp. 52–56.

---

manager, and a sales manager has more status than an office clerk. People choose products that communicate their role and status in society. Thus company presidents drive Mercedes, wear expensive suits, and drink Chivas Regal Scotch. Marketers are aware of the *status symbol* potential of products and brands. However, status symbols vary for social classes and also geographically. Status symbols that are "in" in New York are jogging to work, fish and fowl, and cosmetic surgery for men; in Chicago buying through catalogs, croissants and tacos, and car telephones; in San Francisco sky diving, freshly made pasta, and Izod shirts.[7]

Personal Factors

A buyer's decisions are also influenced by personal characteristics, notably the buyer's age and life-cycle stage, occupation, economic circumstances, lifestyle, and personality and self-concept.

AGE AND LIFE-CYCLE STAGE ❖ People buy different goods and services over their lifetime. They eat baby food in the early years, most foods in the growing and mature years, and special diets in the later years. People's taste in clothes, furniture, and recreation is also age related.

Consumption is also shaped by the stage of the *family life cycle*. Nine stages of the family life cycle are listed in Table 7-2, along with the financial situation and typical product interests of each group. Marketers often choose life-cycle groups as their target market.

Some recent work has identified *psychological life-cycle stages*. Adults experience certain *passages* or *transformations* as they go through life.[8] Marketers pay close attention to changing life circumstances — divorce, widowhood, remarriage — and their effect on consumption behavior.

TABLE 7-2
An Overview of the Family
Life Cycle and Buying
Behavior

STAGE IN FAMILY LIFE CYCLE	BUYING OR BEHAVIORAL PATTERN
1. Bachelor stage: young, single people not living at home	Few financial burdens. Fashion opinion leaders. Recreation oriented. Buy: basic kitchen equipment, basic furniture, cars, equipment for the mating game, vacations.
2. Newly married couples: young, no children.	Better off financially than they will be in near future. Highest purchase rate and highest average purchase of durables. Buy: cars, refrigerators, stoves, sensible and durable furniture, vacations.
3. Full nest I: youngest child under six.	Home purchasing at peak. Liquid assets low. Dissatisfied with financial position and amount of money saved. Interested in new products. Like advertised products. Buy: washers, dryers, TV, baby food, chest rubs and cough medicines, vitamins, dolls, wagons, sleds, skates.
4. Full nest II: youngest child six or over.	Financial position better. Some wives work. Less influenced by advertising. Buy larger-size packages, multiple-unit deals. Buy: many foods, cleaning materials, bicycles, music lessons, pianos.
5. Full nest III: older married couples with dependent children.	Financial position still better. More wives work. Some children get jobs. Hard to influence with advertising. High average purchase of durables. Buy: new, more tasteful furniture, auto travel, unnecessary appliances, boats, dental services, magazines.
6. Empty nest I: older married couples, no children living with them, head in labor force.	Home ownership at peak. Most satisfied with financial position and money saved. Interested in travel, recreation, self-education. Make gifts and contributions. Not interested in new products. Buy: vacations, luxuries, home improvements.
7. Empy nest II: older married. No children living at home, head retired.	Drastic cut in income. Keep home. Buy: medical appliances, medical-care products that aid health, sleep, and digestion.
8. Solitary survivor, in labor force.	Income still good but likely to sell home.
9. Solitary survivor, retired.	Same medical and product needs as other retired group; drastic cut in income. Special need for attention, affection, and security.

Sources: William D. Wells and George Gubar, "Life-Cycle Concepts in Marketing Research," *Journal of Marketing Research*, November 1966, pp. 355–63, here p. 362. Also see Patrick E. Murphy and William A. Staples, "A Modernized Family Life Cycle," *Journal of Consumer Research*, June 1979, pp. 12–22; and Frederick W. Derrick and Alane E. Linfield, "The Family Life Cycle: An Alternative Approach," *Journal of Consumer Research*, September 1980, pp. 214–17.

OCCUPATION ❖ A person's occupation also influences his or her consumption pattern. A blue-collar worker will buy work clothes, work shoes, lunch boxes, and bowling recreation. A company president will buy expensive suits, air travel, country club membership, and a large sailboat. Marketers try to identify the occupational groups that have above-average interest in their products and services. A company can even specialize their products for certain occupational groups. Thus computer software companies will design different computer software for brand managers, engineers, lawyers, and physicians.

ECONOMIC CIRCUMSTANCES ❖ Product choice is greatly affected by one's economic circumstances. People's economic circumstances consist of their *spendable income* (its level, stability, and time pattern), *savings and assets* (including

Marketing Concepts and Tools 7-1

How Lifestyles Are Identified

Researchers have worked hard to develop a lifestyle classification based on *psychographic* measurements. A number of classifications have been proposed, two of which will be described here, namely, the AIO framework and the VALS framework.

THE AIO FRAMEWORK ❖ In this approach, respondents are presented with long questionnaires seeking to measure their activities, interests, and opinions (AIO). The following table shows the major dimensions used to measure the AIO elements, as well as respondents' demographics.

ACTIVITIES	INTERESTS	OPINIONS	DEMOGRAPHICS
Work	Family	Themselves	Age
Hobbies	Home	Social issues	Education
Social events	Job	Politics	Income
Vacation	Community	Business	Occupation
Entertainment	Recreation	Economics	Family size
Clubs	Fashion	Education	Dwelling
Community	Food	Products	Geography
Shopping	Media	Future	City size
Sports	Achievements	Culture	Stage in cycle

Source: Joseph T. Plummer, "The Concept and Application of Life-Style Segmentation," *Journal of Marketing*, January 1974, p. 34.

Many of the questions are in the form of agreeing or disagreeing with such statements as

- ◆ I would like to become an actor.
- ◆ I enjoy going to concerts.
- ◆ I usually dress for fashion, not for comfort.
- ◆ I often have a cocktail before dinner.

The data are analyzed on a computer to find distinctive lifestyle groups. Using this approach, the Chicago-based advertising agency of Needham, Harper and Steers identified several major lifestyle groups. Here are the five male groups:

- ◆ Ben, the self-made businessman (17%)
- ◆ Scott, the successful professional (21%)
- ◆ Dale, the devoted family man (17%)
- ◆ Fred, the frustrated factory worker (19%)
- ◆ Herman, the retiring homebody (26%)

When developing an advertising campaign, the marketers state the target lifestyle group, and the ad people develop an ad appealing to the AIO characteristics of the group(s).

THE VALS FRAMEWORK ❖ The Stanford Research Institute's Values and Lifestyles (VALS) program

---

the percentage that is liquid), *debts, borrowing power*, and *attitude toward spending versus saving*. Linda Brown can consider buying a laptop computer if she has enough spendable income, savings, or borrowing power and prefers spending to saving. Marketers of income-sensitive goods pay constant attention to trends in personal income, savings, and interest rates. If economic indicators point to a recession, marketers can take steps to redesign, reposition, and reprice their products so they continue to offer value to target customers.

LIFESTYLE ❖ People coming from the same subculture, social class, and occupation may lead quite different lifestyles. Linda Brown, for example, can choose to live a "belonging" lifestyle, which is reflected in wearing conservative clothes, spending a lot of time with her family, helping her church. Or she can choose an "achiever" lifestyle, marked by working long hours on major projects and playing hard when it comes to travel and sports.

A person's *lifestyle* is the person's *pattern of living in the world as expressed in the person's activities, interests, and opinions* (see Marketing Concepts and Tools 7-1). Lifestyle portrays the "whole person" interacting with his or her environment. Marketers will search for relationships between their products and lifestyle groups.

classifies the American public into nine value lifestyle groups based on analyzing the answers of 2,713 respondents to over 800 questions. The nine groups are:

- *Survivors* (4%) are disadvantaged people who tend to be "despairing, depressed, withdrawn."
- *Sustainers* (7%) are disadvantaged people who are valiantly struggling to get out of poverty.
- *Belongers* (33%) are people who are conventional, conservative, nostalgic, and unexperimental, and who would rather fit in than stand out.
- *Emulators* (10%) are ambitious, upwardly mobile, and status conscious; they want to "make it big."
- *Achievers* (23%) are the nation's leaders, who make things happen, work within the system, and enjoy the good life.
- *"I-am-me"* (5%) are people who are typically young, self-engrossed, and given to whim.
- *Experientials* (7%) are people who pursue a rich inner life and want to experience directly what life has to offer.
- *Societally conscious* (9%) people have a high sense of social responsibility and want to improve conditions in society.
- *Integrateds* (2%) are people who have fully matured psychologically and combine the best elements of inner directedness and outer directedness.

The classification is based on the idea that individuals pass through a number of developmental stages, with each stage affecting the person's attitudes, behavior, and psychological needs. People pass from a need-driven stage (survivors and sustainers) into either an outer-directed hierarchy of stages (belongers, emulators, and achievers) or an inner-directed hierarchy of stages (I-am-me, experientials, societally conscious), with a few reaching an integrated stage.

Marketers pay little attention to need-driven segments of the population because they lack economic resources. The other groups are of greater interest and have distinct demographic, occupational, and media characteristics. Thus a manufacturer of expensive luggage will want to know more about the characteristics of achievers and how to advertise to them; a manufacturer of hot tubs will want to focus on the experientials. A manufacturer of garbage disposals will direct different appeals to belongers and societally conscious people. Many corporations subscribe to VALS and use the data to reach lifestyle groups more effectively.

Recently VALS was revised into VALS 2. For a description and criticisms, see Michael R. Solomon, *Consumer Behavior* (Needham Heights: Allyn and Bacon, 1992), pp. 500–506.

A computer manufacturer might find that most computer buyers are achievement oriented. The marketer may then aim the brand more clearly at the achiever lifestyle. Ad copywriters can then draw on symbols that appeal to achievers:

He lives in one of those modern high-rise apartments and the rooms are brightly colored. He has modern, expensive furniture, but not Danish modern. He buys his clothes at Brooks Brothers. He owns a good hi-fi. He skis. He has a sailboat. He eats Limburger and any other prestige cheese with his beer. He likes and cooks a lot of steak and would serve a filet mignon to company. His liquor cabinet has Jack Daniels bourbon, Beefeater gin, and a good Scotch.[9]

Lifestyle segmentation schemes are by no means universal. McCann-Erickson London, for example, identified the following British lifestyles: Avant-Gardians (interested in change), Pontificators (traditionalists, very British), Chameleons (follow the crowd), and Sleepwalkers (contented underachievers).

PERSONALITY AND SELF-CONCEPT ❖ Each person has a distinct personality that will influence his or her buying behavior. By *personality*, we mean the *person's distinguishing psychological characteristics that lead to relatively consistent and enduring responses to his or her environment*. Personality is usually described in terms of such traits as self-confidence, dominance, autonomy, deference, sociability, defensiveness, and adaptability.[10] Personality can be a useful variable in analyzing consumer behavior provided that personality types can be classified and that strong correlations exist between certain personality types and product or brand choices. For example, a computer company might discover that many prospects have high self-confidence, dominance, and autonomy. This suggests using these appeals in advertising computers.

Many marketers use a concept related to personality—a person's *self-concept* (or self-image). Linda Brown may see herself as highly accomplished and deserving the best. She will favor a computer that projects the same qualities. If the Compaq computer is promoted and priced for those who want the best, then its brand image will match her self-image. Marketers try to develop brand images that match the target market's self-image.

The theory, admittedly, is not that simple. Linda's *actual self-concept* (how she views herself) differs from her *ideal self-concept* (how she would like to view herself) and from her *others-self-concept* (how she thinks others see her). Which self will she try to satisfy in choosing a computer? Because this is less clear, self-concept theory has had a mixed record of success in predicting consumer responses to brand images.[11]

Psychological Factors

A person's buying choices are further influenced by four major psychological factors—motivation, perception, learning, and beliefs and attitudes.

MOTIVATION ❖ A person has many needs at any given time. Some needs are *biogenic*. They arise from physiological states of tension such as hunger, thirst, discomfort. Other needs are *psychogenic*. They arise from psychological states of tension such as the need for recognition, esteem, or belonging. Most psychogenic needs are not intense enough to motivate the person to act on them immediately. A need becomes a motive when it is aroused to a sufficient level of intensity. A motive (or drive) is a need that is sufficiently pressing to drive the person to act. Satisfying the need reduces the felt tension.

Psychologists have developed theories of human motivation. Three of the best known—the theories of Sigmund Freud, Abraham Maslow, and Frederick Herzberg—carry quite different implications for consumer analysis and marketing strategy.

Freud's Theory of Motivation Freud assumes that the real psychological forces shaping people's behavior are largely unconscious. Freud sees the person as repressing many urges in the process of growing up and accepting social rules. These urges are never eliminated or perfectly controlled; they emerge in dreams, in slips of the tongue, in neurotic behavior.

Thus a person cannot fully understand his or her own motivations. If Linda Brown wants to purchase a laptop computer, she may describe her motive as wanting to work more efficiently when traveling. At a deeper level, she may be purchasing a computer to impress others. At a still deeper level, she may be buying the computer because it helps her feel smart and sophisticated.[12]

When Linda examines specific brands, she will react not only to their stated capabilities but also to other cues. Each computer's shape, size, weight, material, color, and brand name can all trigger certain associations and emotions. Manufacturers, in designing computers, should be aware of the impact of visual, auditory, and tactile elements in triggering consumer emotions that could stimulate or inhibit purchase.

The leading modern exponent of Freudian motivation theory was Ernest Dichter, who for over three decades interpreted buying situations and product choices in terms of underlying unconscious motives. Dichter called his approach *motivational research*, and it consisted of collecting "in-depth interviews" with a few dozen consumers to uncover their deeper motives triggered by the product. He used various "projective techniques" to throw the ego off guard—techniques such as word association, sentence completion, picture interpretation, and role playing.[13]

Motivation researchers have produced interesting and occasionally bizarre hypotheses as to what may be in the buyer's mind regarding certain products. They have suggested that

- Consumers resist prunes because prunes are wrinkled looking and remind people of old age.
- Men smoke cigars as an adult version of thumb sucking. They like their cigars to have a strong odor in order to prove their masculinity.
- Women prefer vegetable shortening to animal fats because the latter arouse a sense of guilt over killing animals.
- A woman is very serious when baking a cake because unconsciously she is going through the symbolic act of giving birth. She dislikes easy-to-use cake mixes because the easy life evokes a sense of guilt.

Maslow's Theory of Motivation Abraham Maslow sought to explain why people are driven by particular needs at particular times.[14] Why does one person spend considerable time and energy on personal safety and another on pursuing the esteem of others? His answer is that human needs are arranged in a hierarchy, from the most pressing to the least pressing. Maslow's hierarchy of needs is shown in Figure 7-3. In their order of importance, they are physiological needs, safety needs, social needs, esteem needs, and self-actualization needs. A person will try to satisfy

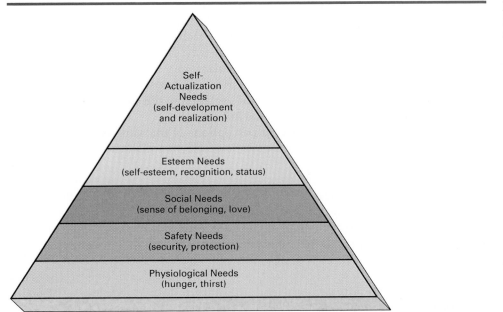

FIGURE 7-3
Maslow's Hierarchy of Needs

the most important needs first. When a person succeeds in satisfying an important need, it will cease being a current motivator, and the person will try to satisfy the next-most-important need.

For example, a starving man (need 1) will not take an interest in the latest happenings in the art world (need 5), nor in how he is viewed or esteemed by others (need 3 or 4), nor even in whether he is breathing clean air (need 2). But as each important need is satisfied, the next-most-important need will become salient.

Maslow's theory helps the marketer understand how various products fit into the plans, goals, and lives of potential consumers. What light does Maslow's theory throw on Linda Brown's interest in buying a computer? We can guess that Linda has satisfied her physiological, safety, and social needs. Her computer interest might come from a strong need for more esteem from others or from a higher need for self-actualization.

Herzberg's Theory of Motivation   Frederick Herzberg developed a "two-factor theory" of motivation, which distinguishes dissatisfiers (factors that cause dissatisfaction) and satisfiers (factors that cause satisfaction).[15] For example, if an Apple computer did not come with a warranty, that would be a dissatisfier. Yet the presence of a product warranty would not act as a satisfier or motivator of Linda's purchase, since it is not a source of intrinsic satisfaction with the Apple computer. The Apple computer's fine color graphics would be a satisfier and enhance Linda's enjoyment of the computer.

This theory of motivation has two implications. First, sellers should do their best to avoid dissatisfiers such as a poor training manual or a poor service policy. While these things will not sell the computer, they might easily unsell the computer. Second, the manufacturer should identify the major satisfiers or motivators of purchase in the computer market and supply them. These satisfiers will make the major difference as to which computer brand the customer buys.

PERCEPTION   ❖   A motivated person is ready to act. How the motivated person actually acts is influenced by his or her perception of the situation. Linda Brown might see a fast-talking computer salesperson as aggressive and insincere. Another shopper might see the same salesperson as intelligent and helpful.

Why do people perceive the same situation differently? The fact is that we apprehend a stimulus object through *sensations* that flow through our five senses: sight, hearing, smell, touch, and taste. However, each of us attends, organizes, and interprets these sensory data in an individual way. *Perception* is defined as "the process by which an individual selects, organizes, and interprets information inputs to create a meaningful picture of the world."[16] Perception depends not only on the physical stimuli but also on the stimuli's relation to the surrounding field (the Gestalt idea) and on conditions within the individual.

People can emerge with different perceptions of the same object because of three perceptual processes: selective attention, selective distortion, and selective retention.

Selective Attention   People are exposed to a tremendous amount of daily stimuli. For example, the average person may be exposed to over 1,500 ads a day. A person cannot possibly attend to all of these stimuli. Most stimuli will be screened out. The real challenge is to explain which stimuli people will notice. Here are some findings:

◆ *People are more likely to notice stimuli that relate to a current need:* Linda Brown will notice computer ads because she is motivated to buy one; she will probably not notice stereo-equipment ads.

- *People are more likely to notice stimuli that they anticipate:* Linda Brown is more likely to notice computers than radios in a computer store because she did not expect the store to carry radios.

- *People are more likely to notice stimuli whose deviations are large in relation to the normal size of the stimuli:* Linda Brown is more likely to notice an ad offering $100 off the list price of an Apple computer than one offering $5 off the list price.

Selective attention means that marketers have to work hard to attract consumer attention. Their messages will be lost on most people who are not in the market for the product. Even people who are in the market may not notice a message unless it stands out from the surrounding sea of stimuli. Ads that are larger in size or that use four colors or are novel and provide contrast are more likely to be noticed.

Selective Distortion Even noted stimuli do not necessarily come across in the predicted way. Each person fits incoming information into his or her existing mindset. Selective distortion describes the tendency of people to twist information into personal meanings. Thus Linda Brown may hear the salesperson mention good and bad points about an IBM computer. If Linda has a strong leaning toward IBM, she is likely to discount the negative statements in order to justify buying an IBM. People interpret information in a way that will support rather than challenge their preconceptions.

Selective Retention People will forget much that they learn. They will tend to retain information that supports their attitudes and beliefs. Because of selective retention, Linda is likely to remember good points mentioned about the IBM and forget good points mentioned about competing computers. She remembers IBM's good points because she "rehearses" them more whenever she thinks about choosing a computer.

These perceptual factors—selective exposure, distortion, and retention—mean that marketers have to work hard to get their messages across. That explains why marketers use drama and repetition in sending messages to their target market.

LEARNING ❖ When people act, they learn. *Learning* describes *changes in an individual's behavior arising from experience.* Most human behavior is learned.

Learning theorists say that a person's learning is produced through the interplay of *drives*, *stimuli*, *cues*, *responses*, and *reinforcement*.

Presumably Linda Brown has a drive toward self-actualization. A *drive* is defined as a strong internal stimulus impelling action. Her drive becomes a *motive* when it is directed toward a particular drive-reducing *stimulus object*, in this case a computer. Linda's response to the idea of buying a computer is conditioned by the surrounding cues. *Cues* are minor stimuli that determine when, where, and how the person responds. Her husband's support, seeing a computer in a friend's home, seeing computer ads and articles, hearing about a special sales price are all cues that can influence Linda's response to her interest in buying a computer.

Suppose Linda buys a computer and chooses an IBM. If her experience is *rewarding*, her response to computers will be reinforced.

Later on, Linda may want to buy a copier. She notices several brands, including one by IBM. Since she knows that IBM makes good computers, she may infer that IBM also makes good copiers. We say that she *generalizes* her response to similar stimuli.

A countertendency to generalization is *discrimination*. When Linda examines a copier made by Sharp, she sees that it is lighter and more compact than IBM's copier. Discrimination means she has learned to recognize differences in sets of similar stimuli and can adjust her responses accordingly.

Learning theory teaches marketers that they can build up demand for a product by associating it with strong drives, using motivating cues, and providing positive reinforcement. A new company can enter the market by appealing to the same drives that competitors use and providing similar cue configurations because buyers are more likely to transfer loyalty to similar brands than to dissimilar brands (generalization). Or the company might design its brand to appeal to a different set of drives and offer strong cue inducements to switch (discrimination).

BELIEFS AND ATTITUDES ❖ Through doing and learning, people acquire beliefs and attitudes. These in turn influence their buying behavior.

A *belief* is *a descriptive thought that a person holds about something*. Linda Brown may believe that an IBM computer has a large memory, stands up well under rugged usage, and costs $2,000. These beliefs may be based on knowledge, opinion, or faith. They may or may not carry an emotional charge. For example, Linda Brown's belief that an IBM laptop computer is heavier than an Apple might not matter to her decision.

Manufacturers, of course, are very interested in the beliefs that people carry in their heads about their products and services. These beliefs make up product and brand images, and people act on their images. If some beliefs are wrong and inhibit purchase, the manufacturer will want to launch a campaign to correct these beliefs (see Global Marketing 7-1).[17]

An *attitude* describes a person's *enduring favorable or unfavorable cognitive evaluations, emotional feelings, and action tendencies toward some object or idea*.[18] People have attitudes toward almost everything: religion, politics, clothes, music, food, and so on. Attitudes put them into a frame of mind of liking or disliking an object, moving toward or away from it. Thus Linda Brown may hold such attitudes as, "Computers are an essential tool for professional workers," "Buy the best," and "IBM makes the best computers in the world." The IBM computer is therefore salient to Linda because it fits well into her preexisting attitudes. A computer company can benefit greatly from researching the attitudes people hold toward the product and the company's brand.

Attitudes lead people to behave in a fairly consistent way toward similar objects. People do not have to interpret and react to every object in a fresh way. Attitudes economize on energy and thought. For this reason, attitudes are very difficult to change. A person's attitudes settle into a consistent pattern, and to change a single attitude may require major adjustments in other attitudes.

Thus a company would be well advised to fit its product into existing attitudes rather than to try to change people's attitudes. There are exceptions, of course, where the great cost of trying to change attitudes might pay off.

> Honda entered the U.S. motorcycle market facing a major decision. It could either sell its motorcycles to a small number of people already interested in motorcycles or try to increase the number interested in motorcycles. The latter would be more expensive because many people held negative attitudes toward motorcycles. They associated motorcycles with black leather jackets, switchblades, and crime. Nevertheless, Honda took the second course and launched a major campaign based on the theme "You meet the nicest people on a Honda." Its campaign worked and many people adopted a new attitude toward motorcycles.

We can now appreciate the many forces acting on consumer behavior. A person's purchase choice is the result of the complex interplay of cultural, social, personal, and psychological factors. Many of these factors cannot be influenced by the

Global Marketing 7-1

Judging Products by Their "Country of Origin"

Buyers make distinct evaluations of brands based on their "country of origin." A product's "country of origin" can have a positive, neutral, or negative effect on prospective buyers. For example, most buyers in the world are favorably disposed to apparel bearing the label "Made in Italy." They would also expect high quality and reliability from automobiles and consumer electronics made in Japan. At the other extreme, a car or stereo set produced in Poland would be negatively viewed. In between are those products, often raw materials and natural resources such as oil from Nigeria or timber from Canada, whose image is not much affected by knowing its country of origin.

Consumers form their preferences based on their personal background, experiences, and national stereotypes about different nations' quality, reliability, and service. Thus buyers will assume that a new printing machine made in Germany would carry higher quality than one made in Bulgaria. Several "country-of-origin" studies have found the following:

- The impact of country of origin varies with the type of product. Consumers would want to know where a car was made but not where the lubricating oil came from.
- Consumers in highly industrialized countries tend to rate their domestic goods high, whereas consumers in the developing world tend to rate foreign goods more favorably.
- Campaigns to persuade people to favor domestic products rarely succeed when these products are perceived to be inferior to foreign products. Furthermore, a "Buy American" campaign may end up favoring foreign jobs, as when a town board voted to buy a John Deere excavator which turned out to be made in Japan instead of a Komatsu excavator which was built in the United States.
- Certain countries enjoy a strong reputation for certain goods: Japan for automobiles and consumer electronics;

United States for high-tech innovations, soft drinks, toys, cigarettes, and jeans; and France for wine, perfumes, and luxury goods.

- The more favorable a country's image, the more prominently the "made-in label" should be displayed in promoting the brand.
- Attitudes toward "country of origin" can change over time. Note how Japan greatly improved its quality image in comparison to pre-World War II days.

What can a company do when its products are competitively equal or superior but its "place of origin" turns off consumers? The company can consider *co-production* with a foreign company that has a better name. Thus South Korea makes a fine leather jacket which it sends to Italy for finishing. The final jacket is then exported with a "Made in Italy" label and commands a much higher price. Another strategy is to hire a well-known *local celebrity* to endorse the product. Thus when Mazda was less known in the United States, Mazda hired the American actor James Garner to tout the Mazda in U.S. commercials. And Nike used America's best-known professional basketball star, Michael Jordan, to promote its footware in Europe. Another strategy is to achieve *world-class quality* in the local industry as is the case with Belgian chocolates, French wine, Irish whiskey, Polish ham, Columbian coffee, and German beer.

SOURCES: Johny K. Johansson, "Determinants and Effects of the Use of 'Made In' Labels," *International Marketing Review* (UK), Vol. 6 Iss. 1, 1989, pp. 47–58; Warren J. Bilkey and Erik Nes, "Country-of-Origin Effects on Product Evaluations," *Journal of International Business Studies*, Spring-Summer 1982, pp. 89–99; and P. J. Cattin et al., "A Cross-Cultural Study of 'Made-In' Concepts," *Journal of International Business Studies*, Winter 1982, pp. 131–41.

marketer. They are useful, however, in identifying the buyers who might have the most interest in the product. Other factors are subject to marketer influence and clue the marketer on how to develop product, price, place, and promotion to attract strong consumer response.

The Buying Decision Process

Marketers have to go beyond the various influences on buyers and develop an understanding of how consumers actually make their buying decisions. Marketers must identify who makes the buying decision, types of buying decisions, and the steps in the buying process.

Buying Roles

For many products, it is easy to identify the buyer. Men normally choose their shaving equipment, and women choose their pantyhose. Other products involve a *decision-making unit* consisting of more than one person. Consider the selection of a family automobile. The teenage son may have suggested buying a new car. A friend might advise the family on the kind of car to buy. The husband might choose the make. The wife might have definite desires regarding the car's size and interior. The husband might make the financial offer. The wife might use the car more often than her husband.

Thus we can distinguish five roles people might play in a buying decision:

- *Initiator:* A person who first suggests the idea of buying the particular product or service
- *Influencer:* A person whose view or advice influences the decision
- *Decider:* A person who decides on any component of a buying decision: whether to buy, what to buy, how to buy, or where to buy
- *Buyer:* The person who makes the actual purchase
- *User:* A person who consumes or uses the product or service

A company needs to identify these roles because they have implications for designing the product, determining messages, and allocating the promotional budget. If the husband decides on the car make, then the auto company will direct advertising to reach husbands. The auto company might design certain car features to please the wife. Knowing the main participants and their roles helps the marketer fine-tune the marketing program.

Types of Buying Behavior

Consumer decision making varies with the type of buying decision. There are great differences between buying toothpaste, a tennis racket, a personal computer, and a new car. Complex and expensive purchases are likely to involve more buyer deliberation and more participants. Assael distinguished four types of consumer buying behavior based on the degree of buyer involvement and the degree of differences among brands.[19] The four types are named in Table 7-3 and described in the following paragraphs.

TABLE 7-3
Four Types of Buying Behavior

	HIGH INVOLVEMENT	LOW INVOLVEMENT
Significant Differences between Brands	Complex buying behavior	Variety-seeking buying behavior
Few Differences between Brands	Dissonance-reducing buying behavior	Habitual buying behavior

Source: Modified from Henry Assael, *Consumer Behavior and Marketing Action* (Boston: Kent Publishing Co., 1987), p. 87. Copyright © 1987 by Wadsworth, Inc. Printed by permission of Kent Publishing Co., a division of Wadsworth, Inc.

COMPLEX BUYING BEHAVIOR ❖ Consumers go through complex buying behavior when they are highly involved in a purchase and aware of significant differences among brands. Consumers are highly involved when the product is expensive, bought infrequently, risky, and highly self-expressive. Typically the consumer does not know much about the product category and has much to learn. For example, a person buying a personal computer may not know what attributes to look for. Many of the product features carry no meaning: "16K memory," "disc storage," "screen resolution," and so on.

This buyer will pass through a learning process characterized by first developing beliefs about the product, then attitudes, and then making a thoughtful purchase choice. The marketer of a high-involvement product must understand the information-gathering and evaluation behavior of high-involvement consumers. The marketer needs to develop strategies that assist the buyer in learning about the attributes of the product class, their relative importance, and the high standing of the company's brand on the more important attributes. The marketer needs to differentiate the brand's features, use mainly print media and long copy to describe the brand's benefits, and motivate store sales personnel and the buyer's acquaintances to influence the final brand choice.

DISSONANCE-REDUCING BUYING BEHAVIOR ❖ Sometimes the consumer is highly involved in a purchase but sees little difference in the brands. The high involvement is again based on the fact that the purchase is expensive, infrequent, and risky. In this case, the buyer will shop around to learn what is available but will buy fairly quickly because brand differences are not pronounced. The buyer may respond primarily to a good price or to purchase convenience. For example, carpet buying is a high-involvement decision because it is expensive and self-expressive; yet the buyer may consider most carpet brands in a given price range to be the same.

After the purchase, the consumer might experience dissonance that stems from noticing certain disquieting features of the carpet or hearing favorable things about other carpets. The consumer will be alert to information that might justify his or her decision. In this example, the consumer first acted, then acquired new beliefs, and ended up with a set of attitudes. Here marketing communications should aim to supply beliefs and evaluations that help the consumer feel good about his or her brand choice.

HABITUAL BUYING BEHAVIOR ❖ Many products are bought under conditions of low consumer involvement and the absence of significant brand differences. Consider the purchase of salt. Consumers have little involvement in this product category. They go to the store and reach for the brand. If they keep reaching for the same brand, it is out of habit, not strong brand loyalty. There is good evidence that consumers have low involvement with most low-cost, frequently purchased products.

Consumer behavior in these cases does not pass through the normal belief/attitude/behavior sequence. Consumers do not search extensively for information about the brands, evaluate their characteristics, and make a weighty decision on which brand to buy. Instead, they are passive recipients of information as they watch television or see print ads. Ad repetition creates *brand familiarity* rather than *brand conviction*. Consumers do not form a strong attitude toward a brand but select it because it is familiar. After purchase, they may not even evaluate the choice because they are not highly involved with the product. So the buying process is brand beliefs formed by passive learning, followed by purchase behavior, which may be followed by evaluation.

Marketers of low-involvement products with few brand differences find it effective to use price and sales promotions to stimulate product trial, since buyers are not highly committed to any brand. In advertising a low-involvement product, a number of things should be observed. The ad copy should stress only a few key points. Visual symbols and imagery are important because they can easily be remembered and associated with the brand. The ad campaigns should go for high repetition with short-duration messages. Television is more effective than print media because it is a low-involvement medium that is suitable for passive learning.[20] Advertising planning should be based on classical conditioning theory where the buyer learns to identify a certain product by a symbol that is repeatedly attached to it.

Marketers can try to convert the low-involvement product into one of higher involvement. This can be accomplished by linking the product to some involving issue, as when Crest toothpaste is linked to avoiding cavities. Or the product can be linked to some involving personal situation, for instance, by advertising a coffee brand early in the morning when the consumer wants to shake off sleepiness. Or the advertising might seek to trigger strong emotions related to personal values or ego defense. Or an important product feature might be added to a low-involvement product, such as by fortifying a plain drink with vitamins. These strategies at best raise consumer involvement from a low to a moderate level; they do not propel the consumer into highly involved buying behavior.

VARIETY-SEEKING BUYING BEHAVIOR ❖ Some buying situations are characterized by low consumer involvement but significant brand differences. Here consumers are often observed to do a lot of brand switching. An example occurs in purchasing cookies. The consumer has some beliefs, chooses a brand of cookies without much evaluation, and evaluates it during consumption. But next time, the consumer may reach for another brand out of boredom or a wish for a different taste. Brand switching occurs for the sake of variety rather than dissatisfaction.

The marketing strategy is different for the market leader and the minor brands in this product category. The market leader will try to encourage habitual buying behavior by dominating the shelf space, avoiding out-of-stock conditions, and sponsoring frequent reminder advertising. Challenger firms will encourage variety seeking by offering lower prices, deals, coupons, free samples, and advertising that presents reasons for trying something new.

Researching the Buying Decision Process

Smart companies will research the buying decision process involved in their product category. They will ask consumers when they first became acquainted with the product category and brands, what their brand beliefs are, how involved they are with the product, how they make their brand choices, and how satisfied they are after purchase.

Consumers, of course, vary in the way they buy any given product. In buying a personal computer, some consumers will spend much time seeking information and making comparisons; others will go straight to a computer store and buy any recommended brand. Thus consumers can be segmented in terms of *buying styles*—for instance, deliberate versus impulsive buyers—and different marketing strategies can be directed at each segment.

How can marketers learn about the typical stages in the buying process for any given product? They can introspect about their own probable behavior (*introspective method*). They can interview a small number of recent purchasers, asking them to recall the events leading to their purchase (*retrospective method*). They can locate consumers who plan to buy the product and ask them to think out loud about going through the buying process (*prospective method*). Or they can ask consumers to describe the ideal way to buy the product (*prescriptive method*). Each method yields a consumer picture of the steps in the buying process.

Table 7-4 shows a retrospective report by a consumer who bought a computer. The marketing researcher should collect reports from several consumers and identify one or more typical buying processes for that product.[21]

Stages in the Buying Decision Process

Figure 7-4 shows a "stage model" of the buying process. The consumer passes through five stages: *problem recognition*, *information search*, *evaluation of alternatives*, *purchase decision*, and *postpurchase behavior*. Clearly the buying process starts long before the actual purchase and has consequences long after the purchase.[22]

This model implies that consumers pass through all five stages in buying a product. But this is not the case, especially in low-involvement purchases. Consumers may skip or reverse some stages. Thus a woman buying her regular brand of toothpaste goes directly from the need for toothpaste to the purchase decision, skipping information search and evaluation. However, we will use the model in Figure 7-4 because it captures the full range of considerations that arise when a consumer faces a highly involving new purchase. We will allude again to Linda Brown and try to understand how she became interested in buying a laptop computer and the stages she went through to make her final choice.

NEED RECOGNITION ❖ The buying process starts when the buyer recognizes a problem or need. The buyer senses a difference between his or her actual state and a desired state. The need can be triggered by internal or external stimuli. In the former case, one of the person's normal needs — hunger, thirst, sex— rises to a threshold level and becomes a drive. From previous experience, the person has learned how to cope with this drive and is motivated toward a class of objects that will satisfy the drive.

Or a need can be aroused by an external stimulus. A person passes a bakery and sees freshly baked bread that stimulates her hunger; she admires a neighbor's new car; or she watches a television commercial advertising a Hawaiian vacation. All these stimuli can trigger a problem or need.

The marketer needs to identify the circumstances that trigger a particular need. In Linda Brown's case, she might answer that her "busy season" was peaking or that she was impressed with a coworker's laptop. By gathering information from

---

3/17	My neighbor just bought a computer. He says he finds it challenging. It would be nice to have a computer; I could keep my financial records on it.
3/19	Here's an ad for an Apple computer showing several applications that I would find interesting.
4/2	I don't have any plans this evening. I'll go over to Computerland and learn something about these computers. Here comes a salesperson. He's very helpful. I'm pleased that he is not pressuring me to buy one. I don't think I can afford a computer. How much would it cost a month if I finance it? I can afford it. My wife also wants me to buy one. I'm impressed with the Apple. I'll buy it and take it home.
4/5	I didn't realize how much time it takes to master. I wish the screen was larger.
4/6	Here's the new IBM advertised. It looks like it has some neat features.
4/8	My other neighbor wants to buy a computer. I told him the good and bad points about the Apple.
4/11	I phoned the computer salesperson for some information about a sticky key. He wasn't helpful. He told me to call the service department.

TABLE 7-4
Report of a Particular Consumer's Involvement in Buying a Computer

FIGURE 7-4
Five-Stage Model of the
Buying Process

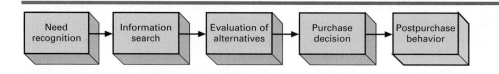

| Need recognition | Information search | Evaluation of alternatives | Purchase decision | Postpurchase behavior |

a number of consumers, the marketer can identify the most frequent stimuli that spark an interest in a product category. The marketer can then develop marketing strategies that trigger consumer interest.

INFORMATION SEARCH ❖ An aroused consumer will be inclined to search for more information. We can distinguish between two levels. The milder search state is called *heightened attention*. Here Linda Brown simply becomes more receptive to information about computers. She pays attention to computer ads, computers purchased by friends, and conversation about computers.

Or Linda may go into *active information search* where she looks for reading material, phones friends, and engages in other activities to learn about computers. How much search she undertakes depends upon the strength of her drive, the amount of information she initially has, the ease of obtaining additional information, the value she places on additional information, and the satisfaction she gets from search. Normally the amount of consumer search activity increases as the consumer moves from situations of *limited problem solving* to *extensive problem solving*.

Of key interest to the marketer are the major information sources that the consumer will turn to and the relative influence each will have on the subsequent purchase decision. *Consumer information sources fall into four groups*:

- *Personal sources:* Family, friends, neighbors, acquaintances
- *Commercial sources:* Advertising, salespersons, dealers, packaging, displays
- *Public sources:* Mass media, consumer-rating organizations
- *Experiential sources:* Handling, examining, using the product

The relative amount and influence of these information sources vary with the product category and the buyer's characteristics. Generally speaking, the consumer receives the most information exposure about a product from commercial sources, that is, marketer-dominated sources. On the other hand, the most effective exposures come from personal sources. Each information source performs a somewhat different function in influencing the buying decision. Commercial information normally performs an informing function, and personal sources perform a legitimizing and/or evaluation function. For example, physicians often learn of new drugs from commercial sources but turn to other doctors for evaluation information.

Through gathering information, the consumer learns about competing brands and their features. The first box in Figure 7-5 shows the *total set* of brands available to the consumer. Linda Brown will come to know only a subset of these brands (*awareness set*). Some brands will meet Linda's initial buying criteria (*consideration set*). As Linda gathers more information, only a few will remain as strong choices (*choice set*). The brands in the choice set might all be acceptable. Linda makes her final choice from this set.[23]

Therefore a company must "strategize" to get its brand into the prospect's awareness set, consideration set, and choice set. Otherwise it loses its opportunity to sell to the customer. Furthermore, the company must identify the other brands in the consumer's choice set so that it can plan its competitive appeals.

As for the consumer's information sources, the marketer should identify them and evaluate their relative importance. Consumers should be asked how they

FIGURE 7-5 Successive Sets Involved in Consumer Decision Making

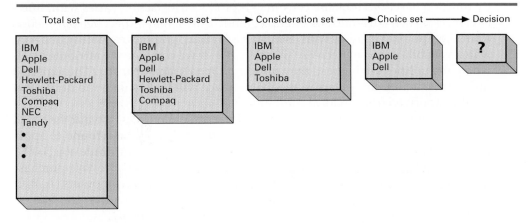

Total set ⟶ Awareness set ⟶ Consideration set ⟶ Choice set ⟶ Decision

Total set	Awareness set	Consideration set	Choice set	Decision
IBM	IBM	IBM	IBM	?
Apple	Apple	Apple	Apple	
Dell	Dell	Dell	Dell	
Hewlett-Packard	Hewlett-Packard	Toshiba		
Toshiba	Toshiba			
Compaq	Compaq			
NEC				
Tandy				

first heard about the brand, what information came in later, and the relative importance of the different information sources. The answers will help the company prepare effective communications for the target market.

EVALUATION OF ALTERNATIVES ❖ How does the consumer process the competitive brand information and make a final judgment of value? It turns out that there is no simple and single evaluation process used by all consumers or even by one consumer in all buying situations. There are several decision evaluation processes. Most current models of the consumer evaluation process are cognitively oriented—that is, they see the consumer as forming product judgments largely on a conscious and rational basis.

Certain basic concepts will help us understand consumer evaluation processes. We see the consumer as trying to satisfy a *need*. The consumer is looking for certain *benefits* from the product solution. The consumer sees each product as a *bundle of attributes* with varying capabilities of delivering the sought benefits and satisfying this need. The attributes of interest to buyers vary by product:

- *Cameras:* Picture sharpness, camera speeds, camera size, price
- *Hotels:* Location, cleanliness, atmosphere, cost
- *Mouthwash:* Color, effectiveness, germ-killing capacity, price, taste/flavor
- *Tires:* Safety, tread life, ride quality, price

Consumers differ as to which product attributes they see as relevant or salient. They will pay the most attention to the ones that will deliver the sought benefits. The market for a product can often be segmented according to the attributes that are salient to different consumer groups.

The most salient attributes may not be the most important ones. Some may be salient because the consumer was recently exposed to an ad mentioning them. Furthermore, nonsalient attributes might include some that the consumer forgot but whose importance would be recognized when mentioned. Marketers should be more concerned with the importance of attributes than with their salience. They should measure the *importance weights* that consumers attach to the various attributes.[24]

The consumer is likely to develop a set of *brand beliefs* about where each brand stands on each attribute. The brand beliefs make up the *brand image*. The consumer's brand beliefs will vary with his or her experiences and the effect of selective perception, selective distortion, and selective retention.

The consumer is assumed to have a *utility function* for each attribute. The utility function describes how the consumer's product satisfaction varies with different levels of each attribute. For example, Linda Brown may expect her satisfaction from a computer to increase with its memory capacity, graphics capability, and software availability; and to decrease with its price. If we combine the attribute levels where the utilities are highest, they make up Linda's *ideal computer*. The expected utility from actual computers in the marketplace will be less than the utility that would be derived from an ideal computer.

The consumer arrives at attitudes (judgments, preferences) toward the brand alternatives through an *evaluation procedure*. Consumers have been found to apply different evaluation procedures to make a choice among multiattribute objects.[25]

We will illustrate these concepts in connection with Linda Brown's purchase of a computer. Suppose she has narrowed her choice set to four computers (A, B, C, D). Assume that she is interested in four attributes: memory capacity, graphics capability, software availability, and price. Table 7-5 shows her beliefs about how each brand rates on the four attributes. Linda rates brand A as follows: memory capacity, 10 on a 10-point scale; graphics capability, 8; software availability, 6; and price, 4 (somewhat expensive). Similarly, she has beliefs about how the other three computers rate on these attributes. The marketer would like to be able to predict which computer Linda will buy.

Clearly, if one computer dominated the others on all the criteria, we could predict that Linda would choose it. But her choice set consists of brands that vary in their appeal. If Linda wants the best memory capacity, she should buy A; if she wants the best graphics capability, she should buy B; and so on. Some buyers will buy on only one attribute, and we can easily predict their choice.

Most buyers will consider several attributes but place different weights on them. If we knew the importance weights that Linda Brown attached to the four attributes, we could more reliably predict her computer choice.

Suppose Linda assigned 40% of the importance to the computer's memory capacity, 30% to its graphics capability, 20% to its software availability, and 10% to its price. To find Linda's perceived value for each computer, her weights are multiplied by her beliefs about each computer. This leads to the following perceived values:

$$\text{Computer A} = 0.4(10) + 0.3(8) + 0.2(6) + 0.1(4) = 8.0$$
$$\text{Computer B} = 0.4(8) + 0.3(9) + 0.2(8) + 0.1(3) = 7.8$$
$$\text{Computer C} = 0.4(6) + 0.3(8) + 0.2(10) + 0.1(5) = 7.3$$
$$\text{Computer D} = 0.4(4) + 0.3(3) + 0.2(7) + 0.1(8) = 4.7$$

We would predict that Linda will favor computer A.

This model is called the *expectancy-value model* of consumer choice.[26] It is one of several possible models describing how consumers evaluate alternatives.[27]

TABLE 7-5
A Consumer's Brand Beliefs about Computers

COMPUTER	ATTRIBUTE			
	Memory Capacity	Graphics Capability	Software Availability	Price
A	10	8	6	4
B	8	9	8	3
C	6	8	10	5
D	4	3	7	8

Note: Each attribute is rated from 0 to 10, where 10 represents the highest level on that attribute. Price, however, is indexed in a reverse manner, with a 10 representing the lowest price, since a consumer prefers a low price to a high price.

Suppose most computer buyers form their preferences using the expectancy-value process. Knowing this, a computer manufacturer can do a number of things to influence buyer decisions. The marketer of computer C, for example, could apply the following strategies to influence people like Linda Brown to show a greater interest in brand C:

- *Modify the computer:* The marketer could redesign brand C so that it offers more memory or other characteristics that the buyer desires. This is called *real repositioning*.
- *Alter beliefs about the brand:* The marketer could try to alter buyers' beliefs about where the brand stands on key attributes. This tactic is especially recommended if buyers underestimate brand C's qualities. It is not recommended if buyers are accurately evaluating brand C; exaggerated claims would lead to buyer dissatisfaction and bad word-of-mouth. Attempting to alter beliefs about the brand is called *psychological repositioning*.
- *Alter beliefs about the competitors' brands:* The marketer could try to change buyers' beliefs about where competitive brands stand on different attributes. That would make sense where buyers mistakenly believe a competitor's brand has more quality than it actually has. It is called *competitive depositioning* and is often accomplished by running a comparison ad.
- *Alter the importance weights:* The marketer could try to persuade buyers to attach more importance to the attributes in which the brand excels. The marketer of brand C can tout the benefits of choosing a computer with great software availability, since C is superior in this attribute.
- *Call attention to neglected attributes:* The marketer could draw the buyer's attention to neglected attributes. If brand C is a more ruggedly made computer, the marketer might tout the benefit of ruggedness.
- *Shift the buyer's ideals:* The marketer could try to persuade buyers to change their ideal levels for one or more attributes. The marketer of brand C might try to convince buyers that computers with a large memory are more likely to jam and that a moderate-size memory is more desirable.[28]

PURCHASE DECISION ❖ In the evaluation stage, the consumer forms preferences among the brands in the choice set. The consumer may also form a purchase intention to buy the most preferred brand. However, two factors can intervene between the purchase intention and the purchase decision. These factors are shown in Figure 7-6.[29]

The first factor is the *attitudes of others*. Suppose Linda Brown's close colleague recommends strongly that Linda should buy the lowest-priced computer (D). As a result, Linda's "purchase probability" for computer A will be somewhat reduced and for computer D will be somewhat increased. The extent to which another person's attitude reduces one's preferred alternative depends upon two things: (1) the intensity of the other person's negative attitude toward the consumer's preferred alternative and (2) the consumer's motivation to comply with the other person's

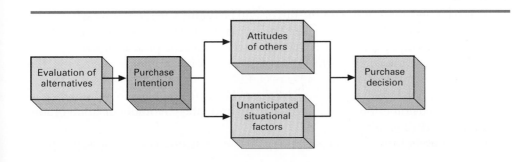

wishes.[30] The more intense the other person's negativism, and the closer the other person is to the consumer, the more the consumer will adjust his or her purchase intention. The converse is also true: A buyer's preference for a brand will increase if someone he or she likes favors the same brand. The influence of others becomes complex when several people close to the buyer hold contradictory opinions and the buyer would like to please them all.

Purchase intention is also influenced by *unanticipated situational factors*. The consumer forms a purchase intention on the basis of such factors as expected family income, expected price, and expected product benefits. When the consumer is about to act, *unanticipated situational factors* may erupt to change the purchase intention. Linda Brown might lose her job, some other purchase might become more urgent, a friend might report disappointment in that computer brand, or a store salesperson may affect her negatively. Thus preferences and even purchase intentions are not completely reliable predictors of purchase behavior.

A consumer's decision to modify, postpone, or avoid a purchase decision is heavily influenced by *perceived risk*. Expensive purchases involve some *risk taking*.[31] Consumers cannot be certain about the purchase outcome. This produces anxiety. The amount of perceived risk varies with the amount of money at stake, the amount of attribute uncertainty, and the amount of consumer self-confidence. A consumer develops certain routines for reducing risk, such as decision avoidance, information gathering from friends, and preference for national brand names and warranties. The marketer must understand the factors that provoke a feeling of risk in consumers and provide information and support that will reduce the perceived risk.

In executing a purchase intention, the person may make up to five *purchase subdecisions*. Thus Linda Brown will make a *brand decision* (brand A), *vendor decision* (dealer 2), *quantity decision* (one computer), *timing decision* (weekend), and *payment-method decision* (credit card). On the other hand, purchases of everyday products involve fewer decisions and less buyer deliberation. In buying sugar, Linda gives little thought to the vendor or payment method. We deliberately chose a product that involved extensive problem solving—here personal computers —to illustrate the full range of behavior that might arise in buying something.

POSTPURCHASE BEHAVIOR ❖ After purchasing the product, the consumer will experience some level of satisfaction or dissatisfaction. The consumer will also engage in postpurchase actions and product uses of interest to the marketer. The marketer's job does not end when the product is bought but continues into the postpurchase period.

Postpurchase Satisfaction   After purchasing a product, a consumer may detect a flaw. Some buyers will not want the flawed product, others will be indifferent to the flaw, and some may even see the flaw as enhancing the value of the product.[32] Some flaws can be dangerous to consumers. Companies making automobiles, toys, and pharmaceuticals must quickly recall any product that has the slightest chance of injuring users.

What determines whether the buyer will be highly satisfied, somewhat satisfied, or dissatisfied with a purchase? The buyer's satisfaction is a function of the closeness between the buyer's product *expectations* and the product's *perceived performance*.[33] If the product's performance falls short of customer expectations, the customer is *disappointed*; if it meets expectations, the customer is *satisfied*; if it exceeds expectations, the customer is *delighted*. These feelings make a difference in whether the customer buys the product again and talks favorably or unfavorably about the product to others.

Consumers form their expectations on the basis of received messages from sellers, friends, and other information sources. If the seller exaggerates the benefits, consumers will experience *disconfirmed expectations*, which lead to dissatisfaction. The larger the gap between expectations and performance, the greater the consumer's dissatisfaction. Here the consumer's coping style comes into play. Some consumers magnify the gap when the product is not perfect, and they are highly dissatisfied. Other consumers minimize the gap and are less dissatisfied.[34]

This theory suggests that the seller must make product claims that faithfully represent the product's likely performance so that buyers experience satisfaction. Some sellers might even understate performance levels so that consumers experience higher-than-expected satisfaction with the product. A seller may create more satisfaction by promising delivery by 4 P.M. and actually delivering by 2 P.M. than if he promised delivery by 11 A.M. and didn't deliver until 12 P.M.

Festinger and Bramel believe that most nonroutine purchase will involve some postpurchase dissonance:

> When a person chooses between two or more alternatives, discomfort or dissonance will almost inevitably arise because of the person's knowledge that while the decision he has made has certain advantages, it also has some disadvantages. That dissonance arises after almost every decision, and further, the individual will invariably take steps to reduce this dissonance.[35]

Postpurchase Actions   The consumer's satisfaction or dissatisfaction with the product will influence subsequent behavior. If the consumer is satisfied, he or she will exhibit a higher probability of purchasing the product again.

> Data on automobile brand choice show a high correlation between being *highly satisfied* with the last brand bought and the intention to rebuy the brand. For example, 75% of Toyota buyers were highly satisfied and about 75% intended to buy a Toyota again; 35% of Chevrolet buyers were highly satisfied and about 35% intended to buy a Chevrolet again.

The satisfied customer will also tend to say good things about the brand to others. Marketers say: "Our best advertisement is a satisfied customer."[36]

A dissatisfied consumer responds differently. The dissatisfied consumer will try to reduce the dissonance because a human being strives "to establish internal harmony, consistency, or congruity among his opinions, knowledge, and values."[37] Dissonant consumers will resort to one of two courses of action. They may try to reduce the dissonance by *abandoning* or *returning* the product, or they may try to reduce the dissonance by seeking information that might *confirm* its high value (or avoiding information that might confirm its low value). In the case of Linda Brown, she might return the computer, or she might seek information that would make her feel better about the computer.

Marketers should be aware of the full range of ways consumers handle dissatisfaction (see Figure 7-7). Consumers have a choice between taking and not taking any action. If the former, they can take public action or private action. Public actions include complaining to the company, going to a lawyer, or complaining to other groups that might help the buyer get satisfaction, such as business, private, or government agencies. Or the buyer might simply stop buying the product (*exit option*) or warn friends (*voice option*).[38] In all these cases, the seller loses in having done a poor job of satisfying the customer.[39]

Marketers can take steps to minimize the amount of consumer postpurchase dissatisfaction. Computer companies can send a letter to new computer owners congratulating them on having selected a fine computer. They can place ads showing satisfied brand owners. They can solicit customer suggestions for improvements and list the location of available services. They can write instruction booklets

FIGURE 7-7

How Customers Handle
Dissatisfaction

Source: Ralph L. Day and E. Laird
Landon, Jr., "Toward a Theory of
Consumer Complaining Behavior,"
in *Consumer and Industrial Buying
Behavior*, eds. Arch G. Woodside,
Jagdish N. Sheth, and Peter D.
Bennett (New York: Elsevier North-
Holland, 1977), p. 432.

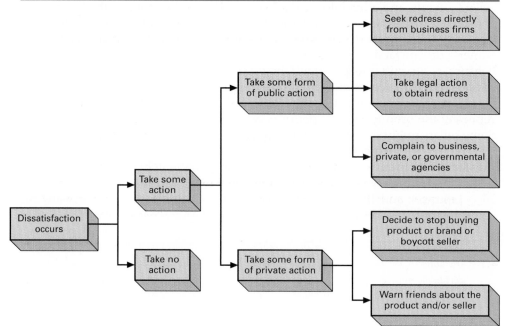

that are intelligible. They can send owners a magazine containing articles describing new computer applications. Postpurchase communications to buyers have been shown to result in fewer product returns and order cancellations.[40] In addition, they can provide good channels for customer complaints and for speedy redress of customer grievances. In general, companies should provide consumers with maximum channels for venting complaints to the company. Smart companies will welcome customer feedback as a way to continually improve their offer and performance.

Postpurchase Use and Disposal. Marketers should also monitor how the buyers use and dispose of the product (see Figure 7-8). If consumers find new uses for the

FIGURE 7-8

How Customers Use
or Dispose of Products

Source: Jacob Jacoby, Carol K.
Berning, and Thomas F. Dietvorst,
"What about Disposition?" *Journal
of Marketing*, July 1977, p. 23.

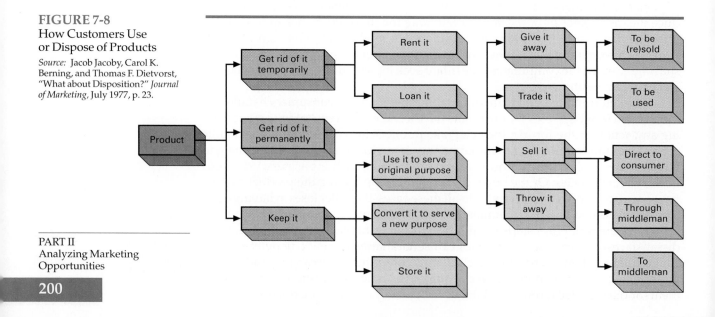

product, these should interest the marketer because these uses can be advertised. If consumers store the product in their closet, this indicates that the product is not very satisfying, and word-of-mouth would not be strong. If they sell or trade the product, new-product sales will be depressed. If they throw the product away, the marketer needs to know how they dispose of it, especially if it can hurt the environment, as is the case with beverage containers and disposable diapers. All said, the marketer needs to study product use and disposal for clues to possible problems and opportunities.[41]

Understanding consumer needs and buying processes is essential to building effective marketing strategies. By understanding how buyers go through need recognition, information search, evaluation of alternatives, the purchase decision, and postpurchase behavior, marketers can pick up clues as to how to meet buyer needs. By understanding the various participants in the buying process and the major influences on their buying behavior, marketers can design effective marketing programs for their target markets.

SUMMARY ❖

Consumer markets and consumer buying behavior have to be understood before sound marketing plans can be developed.

The consumer market buys goods and services for personal consumption. It is the ultimate market for which economic activities are organized. In analyzing a consumer market, one needs to know the occupants, the objects, and the buyers' objectives, organization, operations, occasions, and outlets.

The buyer's behavior is influenced by four major factors: cultural (culture, subculture, and social class), social (reference groups, family, and roles and statuses), personal (age and life-cycle stage, occupation, economic circumstances, lifestyle, and personality and self-concept), and psychological (motivation, perception, learning, and beliefs and attitudes). All of these provide clues as to how to reach and serve buyers more effectively.

Before planning its marketing, a company needs to identify its target consumers and their decision processes. Although many buying decisions involve only one decision maker, other decisions may involve several participants, who play such roles as initiator, influencer, decider, buyer, and user. The marketer's job is to identify the other buying participants, their buying criteria, and their influence on the buyer. The marketing program should be designed to appeal to and reach the other key participants as well as the buyer.

The amount of buying deliberateness and the number of buying participants increase with the complexity of the buying situation. Marketers must plan differently for four types of consumer buying behavior: complex buying behavior, dissonance-reducing buying behavior, habitual buying behavior, and variety-seeking buying behavior. These four types are based on whether the consumer has high or low involvement in the purchase and whether brands exhibit many or few significant differences.

In complex buying behavior, the buyer goes through a decision process consisting of need recognition, information search, evaluation of alternatives, purchase decision, and postpurchase behavior. The marketer's job is to understand the buyer's behavior at each stage and what influences are operating. This understanding allows the marketer to develop an effective and efficient marketing program for the target market.

NOTES ❖

1. See Leon G. Schiffman and Leslie Lazar Kanuk, *Consumer Behavior*, 3rd ed. (Englewood Cliffs, NJ: Prentice-Hall, 1987), pp. 495–503.

2. See Donald W. Hendon, "A New Empirical Look at the Influence of Reference Groups on Generic Product Category and Brand Choice: Evidence from Two Nations," in *Proceedings of the Academy of International Business: Asia-Pacific Dimension of International Business* (Honolulu: College of Business Administration, University of Hawaii, December 18–20, 1979), pp. 752–61.

3. See Linda L. Price and Lawrence F. Feick, "The Role of Interpersonal Sources in External Search: An Informational Perspective," in *Advances in Consumer Research*, vol. 11, ed. Thomas C. Kinnear (Ann Arbor, MI: Association for Consumer Research, 1984), p. 250; and David Brinberg and Linda Plimpton, "Self-Monitoring and Product Conspicuousness on Reference Group Influence," in *Advances in Consumer Research*, vol. 13, ed. Richard Lutz (1986), pp. 297–300.

4. George Moschis, "The Role of Family Communication in Consumer Socialization of Children and Adolescents," *Journal of Consumer Research*, March 1985, pp. 898–913.

5. See Rosann L. Spiro, "Persuasion in Family Decision Making," *Journal of Consumer Research*, March 1983, pp. 393–402; Lawrence H. Wortzel, "Marital Roles and Typologies as Predictors of Purchase Decision Making for Everyday Household Products: Suggestions for Research," in *Advances in Consumer Research*, vol. 7, ed. Jerry C. Olson (1980), pp. 212–15.

6. See Harry L. Davis, "Dimensions of Marital Roles in Consumer Decision-Making," *Journal of Marketing Research*, May 1970, pp. 168–77.

7. See "Flaunting Wealth: It's Back in Style," *U.S. News & World Report*, September 21, 1981, pp. 61–64; John Brooks, *Showing Off in America: From Conspicuous Consumption to Parody Display* (Boston: Little, Brown, 1978).

8. See Lawrence Lepisto, "A Life Span Perspective of Consumer Behavior," in *Advances in Consumer Research*, ed. Elizabeth Hirshman and Morris Holbrook, vol. 12 (Provo, UT: Association for Consumer Research, 1985), p. 47.

9. Sidney J. Levy, "Symbolism and Life Style," in *Toward Scientific Marketing*, ed. Stephen A. Greyser (Chicago: American Marketing Association, 1964), pp. 140–50.

10. See Harold H. Kassarjian and Mary Jane Sheffet, "Personality and Consumer Behavior: An Update," in *Perspectives in Consumer Behavior*, ed. Harold H. Kassarjian and Thomas S. Robertson (Glenview, IL: Scott, Foresman, 1981), pp. 160–80.

11. See M. Joseph Sirgy, "Self-Concept in Consumer Behavior: A Critical Review," *Journal of Consumer Research*, December 1982, pp. 287–300.

12. A technique called *laddering* can be used to trace a person's motivations from the stated instrumental ones to the more terminal ones. Then the marketer can decide at what level to develop the message and appeal. See Thomas J. Reynolds and Jonathan Gutman, "Laddering Theory, Method, Analysis, and Interpretation," *Journal of Advertising Research*, February-March 1988, pp. 11–34.

13. See Ernest Dichter, *Handbook of Consumer Motivations* (New York: McGraw-Hill, 1964).

14. Maslow, *Motivation and Personality* (New York: Harper & Row, 1954), pp. 80–106.

15. See Herzberg, *Work and the Nature of Man* (Cleveland: William Collins, 1966); and Henk Thierry and Agnes M. Koopman-Iwerna, "Motivation and Satisfaction," in *Handbook of Work and Organizational Psychology*," ed. P. J. Drenth (New York: John Wiley, 1984), pp. 141–42.

16. Bernard Berelson and Gary A. Steiner, *Human Behavior: An Inventory of Scientific Findings* (New York: Harcourt Brace Jovanovich, 1964), p. 88.

17. See Alice M. Tybout, Bobby J. Calder, and Brian Sternthal, "Using Information Processing Theory to Design Marketing Strategies," *Journal of Marketing Research*, February 1981, pp. 73–79.

18. See David Krech, Richard S. Crutchfield, and Egerton L. Ballachey, *Individual in Society* (New York: McGraw-Hill, 1962), Chap. 2.

19. See Henry Assael, *Consumer Behavior and Marketing Action* (Boston: Kent, 1987), Chap. 4.

20. Herbert E. Krugman, "The Impact of Television Advertising: Learning without Involvement," *Public Opinion Quarterly*, Fall 1965, pp. 349–56.

21. See James R. Bettman, *Information Processing Theory of Consumer Behavior* (Reading, MA: Addison-Wesley, 1979).

22. Marketing scholars have developed several models of the consumer buying process. See John A. Howard and Jagdish N. Sheth, *The Theory of Buyer Behavior* (New York: John Wiley, 1969); and James F. Engel, Roger D. Blackwell, and Paul W. Miniard, *Consumer Behavior*, 7th ed. (New York: Dryden Press, 1993).

23. See Chem L. Narayana and Rom J. Markin, "Consumer Behavior and Product Performance: An Alternative Conceptualization," *Journal of Marketing*, October 1975, pp. 1–6.

24. James H. Myers and Mark L. Alpert, "Semantic Confusion in Attitude Research: Salience vs. Importance vs. Determinance," in *Advances in Consumer Research*, Proceedings of the Seventh Annual Conference of the Association of Consumer Research, October 1976, pp. 106–10.

25. See Paul E. Green and Yoram Wind, *Multiattribute Decisions in Marketing: A Measurement Approach* (Hinsdale, IL: Dryden Press, 1973), Chap. 2; Leigh McAlister, "Choosing Multiple Items from a Product Class," *Journal of Consumer Research*, December 1979, pp. 213–24.

26. This model was developed by Martin Fishbein in "Attitudes and Prediction of Behavior," in *Readings in Attitude Theory and Measurement*, ed. Martin Fishbein (New York: John Wiley, 1967), pp. 477–92. For a critical review, see Paul W. Miniard and Joel B. Cohen, "An Examination of the Fishbein-Ajzen Behavioral-Intentions Model's Concepts and Measures, *Journal of Experimental Social Psychology*, May 1981, pp. 309–39.

27. Here are some other models. The *ideal-brand model* assumes that a consumer compares actual brands to her ideal brand and chooses the brand that comes closest to her ideal brand. The *conjunctive model* assumes that a consumer sets minimum acceptable levels on all the attributes and considers

only the brands that meet all the minimum requirements. The *disjunctive model* assumes that a consumer sets minimum acceptable levels on only a few attributes and eliminates those brands falling short. For a discussion of these and other models, see Green and Wind, *Multiattribute Decisions in Marketing.*

28. See Harper W. Boyd, Jr., Michael L. Ray, and Edward C. Strong, "An Attitudinal Framework for Advertising Strategy," *Journal of Marketing*, April 1972, pp. 27–33.

29. See Jagdish N. Sheth, "An Investigation of Relationships among Evaluative Beliefs, Affect, Behavioral Intention, and Behavior," in *Consumer Behavior: Theory and Application*, eds. John U. Farley, John A. Howard, and L. Winston Ring (Boston: Allyn & Bacon, 1974), pp. 89–114.

30. See Fishbein, "Attitudes and Prediction."

31. See Raymond A. Bauer, "Consumer Behavior as Risk Taking," in *Risk Taking and Information Handling in Consumer Behavior*, ed. Donald F. Cox (Boston: Division of Research, Harvard Business School, 1967); and James W. Taylor, "The Role of Risk in Consumer Behavior," *Journal of Marketing*, April 1974, pp. 54–60.

32. See Philip Kotler and Murali K. Mantrala, "Flawed Products: Consumer Responses and Marketer Strategies," *Journal of Consumer Marketing*, Summer 1985, pp. 27–36.

33. See Priscilla A. La Barbera and David Mazursky, "A Longitudinal Assessment of Consumer Satisfaction / Dissatisfaction: The Dynamic Aspect of the Cognitive Process," *Journal of Marketing Research*, November 1983, pp. 393–404.

34. See Ralph L. Day, "Modeling Choices among Alternative Responses to Dissatisfaction," in *Advances in Consumer Research*, vol. 11 (1984), pp. 496–99.

35. Leon Festinger and Dana Bramel, "The Reactions of Humans to Cognitive Dissonance," in *Experimental Foundations of Clinical Psychology*, ed. Arthur J. Bachrach (New York: Basic Books, 1962), pp. 251–62.

36. See Barry L. Bayus, "Word of Mouth: The Indirect Effects of Marketing Efforts," *Journal of Advertising Research*, June/July 1985, pp. 31–39.

37. Leon Festinger, *A Theory of Cognitive Dissonance* (Stanford, CA: Stanford University Press, 1957), p. 260.

38. See Albert O. Hirschman, *Exit, Voice, and Loyalty* (Cambridge, MA: Harvard University Press, 1970).

39. See Mary C. Gilly and Richard W. Hansen, "Consumer Complaint Handling as a Strategic Marketing Tool," *Journal of Consumer Marketing*, Fall 1985, pp. 5–16.

40. See James H. Donnelly, Jr. and John M. Ivancevich, "Post-Purchase Reinforcement and Back-Out Behavior," *Journal of Marketing Research*, August 1970, pp. 399–400.

41. See Jacob Jacoby, Carol K. Berning, and Thomas F. Dietvorst, "What about Disposition?" *Journal of Marketing*, July 1977, p. 23.

8

Analyzing Business Markets and Business Buying Behavior

Companies don't make purchases; they establish relationships.

CHARLES S. GOODMAN

Treat the customer as an appreciating asset.

TOM PETERS

Business organizations not only sell; they also buy vast quantities of raw materials, manufactured parts, installations, accessory equipment, supplies, and business services. There are 13 million buying organizations in the United States alone. Companies that sell steel, computers, nuclear-power plants, and other goods to buying organizations need to understand their needs, resources, policies, and buying procedures. They must take into account several considerations not normally found in consumer marketing.

- Organizations buy goods and services to satisfy a variety of goals: making profits, reducing costs, meeting employee needs, and satisfying legal obligations.
- More persons typically participate in organizational buying decisions than in consumer buying decisions, especially in procuring major items. The decision participants usually represent different departments and apply different criteria to the purchase decision.
- The buyers must heed the formal purchasing policies, constraints, and requirements established by their organizations.
- The buying instruments, such as requests for quotations, proposals, and purchase contracts, add another dimension not typically found in consumer buying.

Webster and Wind define *organizational buying* as "the decision-making process by which formal organizations establish the need for purchased products and services and identify, evaluate, and choose among alternative brands and suppliers."[1] Although no two companies buy in the same way, the seller hopes to identify enough buying uniformities to improve its marketing strategy planning.

In this chapter, we will look at business markets and briefly at institutional and government markets. We will examine five questions: *Who is in the market? What buying decisions do buyers make? Who participates in the buying process? What are the major influences on the buyers? How do buyers make their buying decisions?*

The Business Market

Who Is in the Business Market?

The *business market* consists of all the organizations that acquire goods and services to use in the production of other products or services that are sold, rented, or supplied to others. The major industries making up the business market are agriculture, forestry, and fisheries; mining; manufacturing; construction; transportation; communication; public utilities; banking, finance, and insurance; distribution; and services.

More dollars and items are involved in sales to business buyers than to consumers. To produce and sell a simple pair of shoes, hide dealers must sell hides to tanners, who sell leather to shoe manufacturers, who sell shoes to wholesalers, who sell shoes to retailers, who finally sell them to consumers. Each party in the supply chain has to buy many other goods and services, and this explains why there is more business buying than consumer buying.

Business markets have several characteristics that contrast sharply with consumer markets.[2]

FEWER BUYERS ❖ The business marketer normally deals with far fewer buyers than does the consumer marketer. Goodyear Tire Company's fate depends critically on getting an order from one of the big three U.S. automakers. But when Goodyear sells replacement tires to consumers, it faces a potential market of 171 million American car owners.

LARGER BUYERS ❖ Many business markets are characterized by a high buyer-concentration ratio: a few large buyers do most of the purchasing. In such industries as motor vehicles, cigarettes, aircraft engines, and organic fibers, the top four manufacturers account for over 70% of total production.

CLOSE SUPPLIER-CUSTOMER RELATIONSHIP ❖ Because of the smaller customer base and the importance and power of the larger customers, we observe close relationships between customers and suppliers in business markets. Suppliers are frequently expected to customize their offerings to individual business customer needs. Contracts go to those suppliers who cooperate with the buyer on technical specifications and delivery requirements. Suppliers are expected to attend special seminars held by the business customer to become familiar with the buyer's quality and procurement requirements.

GEOGRAPHICALLY CONCENTRATED BUYERS ❖ More than half of U.S. business buyers are concentrated in seven states: New York, California, Pennsylvania, Illinois, Ohio, New Jersey, and Michigan. Industries such as petroleum, rubber, and steel show an even greater geographical concentration. Most agricultural output comes from a relatively few states. This geographical concentration of producers helps to reduce selling costs. At the same time, business marketers need to monitor regional shifts of certain industries, as when textiles moved out of New England to the southern states.

DERIVED DEMAND ❖ The demand for business goods is ultimately derived from the demand for consumer goods. Thus animal hides are purchased because consumers buy shoes, purses, and other leather goods. If the demand for these consumer goods slackens, so will the demand for all the business goods entering into their production. For this reason, the business marketer must closely monitor the buying patterns of ultimate consumers.[3]

INELASTIC DEMAND ❖ The total demand for many business goods and services is not much affected by price changes. Shoe manufacturers are not going to buy much more leather if the price of leather falls. Nor are they going to buy much less leather if the price of leather rises unless they can find satisfactory leather substitutes. Demand is especially inelastic in the short run because producers cannot make quick changes in their production methods. Demand is also inelastic for business goods that represent a small percentage of the item's total cost. For example, an increase in the price of metal eyelets for shoes will barely affect the total demand for metal eyelets. At the same time, producers may switch their eyelets supplier in response to price differences.

FLUCTUATING DEMAND ❖ The demand for business goods and services tends to be more volatile than the demand for consumer goods and services. This is especially true of the demand for new plant and equipment. A given percentage increase in consumer demand can lead to a much larger percentage increase in the demand for plant and equipment necessary to produce the additional output. Economists refer to this as the *acceleration principle*. Sometimes a rise of only 10% in consumer demand can cause as much as a 200% rise in business demand in the next period; and a 10% fall in consumer demand may cause a complete collapse in the demand for investment goods. This sales volatility has led many business marketers to diversify their products and markets to achieve more balanced sales over the business cycle.

PROFESSIONAL PURCHASING ❖ Business goods are purchased by trained purchasing agents, who spend their professional lives learning how to buy better. Many belong to the National Association of Purchasing Managers (NAPM), which seeks to improve the effectiveness and status of professional buyers. Their professional approach and greater ability to evaluate technical information leads to more cost-effective buying. This means that business marketers have to provide and master greater technical data about their product and competitors' products.

SEVERAL BUYING INFLUENCES ❖ More people typically influence business buying decisions than consumer buying decisions. Buying committees consisting of technical experts and even senior management are common in the purchase of major goods. Consequently, business marketers have to send well-trained sales representatives and often sales teams to deal with the well-trained buyers. Although advertising, sales promotion, and publicity play an important role in the business promotional mix, personal selling serves as the main marketing tool.

MISCELLANEOUS CHARACTERISTICS ❖ Here are additional characteristics of business buying:

- *Direct Purchasing:* Business buyers often buy directly from manufacturers rather than through middlemen, especially those items that are technically complex and/or expensive, such as mainframes or aircraft.
- *Reciprocity:* Business buyers often select suppliers who also buy from them. An example would be a paper manufacturer who buys chemicals from a chemical company that buys a considerable amount of its paper.
- *Leasing:* Many industrial buyers lease their equipment instead of buying it. This happens with computers, shoe machinery, packaging equipment, heavy-construction equipment, delivery trucks, machine tools, and company automobiles. The lessee gains a number of advantages: conserving capital, getting the seller's latest products, receiving better service, and gaining some tax advantages. The lessor often ends up with a larger net income and the chance to sell to customers who could not afford outright purchase.[4]

What Buying Decisions Do Business Buyers Make?

The business buyer faces many decisions in making a purchase. The number of decisions depends on the type of buying situation.

MAJOR TYPES OF BUYING SITUATIONS ❖ Robinson and others distinguish three types of buying situations, which they call *buyclasses*.[5] They are the straight rebuy, modified rebuy, and new task.

Straight Rebuy. The straight rebuy describes a buying situation where the purchasing department reorders on a routine basis (e.g., office supplies, bulk chemicals). The buyer chooses from suppliers on its "approved list," giving weight to its past buying satisfaction with the various suppliers. The "in-suppliers" make an effort to maintain product and service quality. They often propose automatic reordering systems so that the purchasing agent will save reordering time. The "out-suppliers" attempt to offer something new or to exploit dissatisfaction so that the business buyer will consider buying some amount from them. Out-suppliers try to get a small order and then enlarge their "purchase share" over time.

Modified Rebuy. The modified rebuy describes a situation where the buyer wants to modify product specifications, prices, delivery requirements, or other terms. The modified rebuy usually involves additional decision participants on both the buyer and seller sides. The in-suppliers become nervous and have to protect the account. The out-suppliers see an opportunity to propose a "better offer" to gain some business.

New Task. The new task describes a purchaser buying a product or service for the first time (e.g., office building, new weapon system). The greater the cost and/or risk, the larger the number of decision participants, the greater their information gathering, therefore the longer the time to decision completion.[6] The new-task situation is the marketer's greatest opportunity and challenge. The marketer tries to reach as many key buying influencers as possible and provide helpful information and assistance. Because of the complicated selling involved in the new task, many companies use a *missionary salesforce* consisting of their best salespeople.

New-task buying passes through several stages. Ozanne and Churchill identified the stages as *awareness, interest, evaluation, trial*, and *adoption*.[7] They found that communication tools varied in effectiveness at each stage. Mass media were most important during the initial awareness stage; salespeople had their greatest impact at the interest stage; and technical sources were the most important during the evaluation stage. Marketers needed to employ different tools at each stage of the new-task buying process.

MAJOR SUBDECISIONS INVOLVED IN THE BUYING DECISION ❖
The business buyer makes the fewest decisions in the straight-rebuy situation and the most in the new-task situation. In the new-task situation, the buyer has to determine *product specifications, price limits, delivery terms and times, service terms, payment terms, order quantities, acceptable suppliers*, and the *selected supplier*. Different decision participants influence each decision, and the order varies in which these decisions are made.

THE ROLE OF SYSTEMS BUYING AND SELLING ❖ Many business buyers prefer to buy a total solution to their problem from one seller. Called *systems buying*, it originated in government purchasing of major weapons and communication systems. The government would solicit bids from prime contractors, who would assemble the package or system. The winning prime contractor would be responsible for bidding and assembling the subcomponents. The prime contractor would thus provide a *turnkey solution*, so called because the buyer simply had to turn one key to get the job done.

Sellers have increasingly recognized that buyers like to purchase in this way and have adopted *systems selling* as a marketing tool. Systems selling can take different forms. The supplier might sell a set of interlocking products; thus a supplier of glue sells not only glue but glue applicators and dryers as well. The supplier might sell a system of production, inventory control, distribution, and other services to meet the buyer's need for a smooth-running operation. Another variant is *systems contracting* where a single supply source provides the buyer with his or her entire requirement of MRO (maintenance, repair, operating) supplies. The customer benefits from reduced costs as the inventory is maintained by the seller. Savings also result from reduced time spent on supplier selection and from price protection over the term of the contract. The seller benefits from lower operating costs because of a steady demand and reduced paperwork.[8]

Systems selling is a key industrial marketing strategy in bidding to build large-scale industrial projects, such as dams, steel factories, irrigation systems, sanitation systems, pipelines, utilities, and even new towns. Project engineering firms such as Bechtel and Fluor must compete on price, quality, reliability, and other attributes to win awards. The award often goes to the firm that best meets the customer's total needs. Consider the following:

> The Indonesian government requested bids to build a cement factory near Jakarta. An American firm made a proposal that included choosing the site, designing the cement factory, hiring the construction crews, assembling the materials and equipment, and turning over the finished factory to the Indonesian government. A Japanese firm, in outlining its proposal, included all of these services plus hiring and training the workers to run the factory, exporting the cement through their trading companies, using the cement to build needed roads out of Jakarta, and also using it to build new office buildings in Jakarta. Although the Japanese proposal involved more money, its appeal was greater, and they won the contract. Clearly, the Japanese viewed the problem not just as one of building a cement factory (the narrow view of systems selling) but as one of contributing to Indonesia's economic development. They saw themselves not as an engineering project firm but as an economic development agency. They took the broadest view of the customer's needs. This is true systems selling.

Who Participates in the Business Buying Process?

Who does the buying of the trillions of dollars' worth of goods and services needed by business organizations? Purchasing agents are influential in straight-rebuy and modified-rebuy situations, whereas other department personnel are more influential in new-buy situations. Engineering personnel usually have major influence in selecting product components, and purchasing agents dominate in selecting suppliers.[9] Thus in new-buy situations, the business marketer must first direct product information to the engineering personnel. In rebuy situations and at supplier-selection time, communications should be directed primarily to the purchasing agent.

Webster and Wind call the decision-making unit of a buying organization the *buying center*, defined as "all those individuals and groups who participate in the purchasing decision-making process, who share some common goals and the risks arising from the decisions."[10] The buying center includes all members of the organization who play any of six roles in the purchase decision process.[11]

- *Users:* Users are those who will use the product or service. In many cases, the users initiate the buying proposal and help define the product specifications.
- *Influencers:* Influencers are persons who influence the buying decision. They often help define specifications and also provide information for evaluating alternatives. Technical personnel are particularly important as influencers.
- *Deciders:* Deciders are persons who decide on product requirements and/or on suppliers.
- *Approvers:* Approvers are persons who authorize the proposed actions of deciders or buyers.
- *Buyers:* Buyers are persons who have formal authority to select the supplier and arrange the purchase terms. Buyers may help shape product specifications, but they play their major role in selecting vendors and negotiating. In more complex purchases, the buyers might include high-level managers participating in the negotiations.

◆ *Gatekeepers:* Gatekeepers are persons who have the power to prevent sellers or information from reaching members of the buying center. For example, purchasing agents, receptionists, and telephone operators may prevent salespersons from contacting users or deciders.

Within any organization, the buying center will vary in the number and type of participants for different classes of products. More decision participants will be involved in buying a computer than in buying paper clips. The business marketer has to figure out: *Who are the major decision participants? What decisions do they influence? What is their level of influence? What evaluation criteria do they use?* Consider the following example:

> Baxter sells nonwoven disposable surgical gowns to hospitals. It tries to identify the hospital personnel who participate in this buying decision. They include the vice-president of purchasing, the operating-room administrator, and the surgeons. Each participant plays a different role. The vice-president of purchasing analyzes whether the hospital should buy disposable gowns or reusable gowns. If the findings favor disposable gowns, then the operating-room administrator compares various competitors' products and prices and makes a choice. This administrator considers the gown's absorbency, antiseptic quality, design, and cost and normally buys the brand that meets the functional requirements at the lowest cost. Finally, surgeons influence the decision retroactively by reporting their satisfaction with the particular brand.

When a buying center includes many participants, the business marketer will not have the time or resources to reach all of them. Small sellers concentrate on reaching the *key buying influencers.* Larger sellers go for *multilevel in-depth selling* to reach as many buying participants as possible. Their salespeople virtually "live" with their high-volume customers.

Business marketers must periodically review their assumptions on the roles and influence of different decision participants. For years, Kodak's strategy for selling X-ray film to hospitals was to sell to lab technicians. The company did not notice that the decision was increasingly being made by professional administrators. As its sales declined, Kodak finally grasped the change in buying practices and hurriedly revised its market targeting strategy.

What Are the Major Influences on Business Buyers?

Business buyers are subject to many influences when they make their buying decisions. Some marketers assume that the most important influences are economic. They see the buyers as favoring the supplier who offers the lowest price, or best product, or most service. This view suggests that business marketers should concentrate on offering strong economic benefits to buyers.

Other marketers see buyers responding to personal factors such as favors, attention, or risk avoidance. A study of buyers in ten large companies concluded that

> . . . corporate decision-makers remain human after they enter the office. They respond to "image"; they buy from companies to which they feel "close"; they favor suppliers who show them respect and personal consideration, and who do extra things "for them"; they "over-react" to real or imagined slights, tending to reject companies which fail to respond or delay in submitting requested bids.[12]

Business buyers actually respond to both economic and personal factors. Where there is substantial similarity in supplier offers, business buyers have little basis for rational choice. Since they can satisfy the purchasing requirements with any supplier, these buyers will place more weight on the personal treatment they receive. Where competing offers differ substantially, business buyers are more accountable for their choice and pay more attention to economic factors.

Webster and Wind have classified the various influences on business buyers into four main groups: environmental, organizational, interpersonal, and individual.[13] These groups are shown in Figure 8-1 and described next.

ENVIRONMENTAL FACTORS ❖ Business buyers are heavily influenced by factors in the current and expected economic environment, such as the level of primary demand, the economic outlook, and the cost of money. In a recession economy, business buyers reduce their investment in plant, equipment, and inventories. Business marketers can do little to stimulate total demand in this environment. They can only fight harder to increase or maintain their share of demand.

Companies that fear a shortage of key materials are willing to buy and hold large inventories. They will sign long-term contracts with suppliers to ensure a steady flow of materials. Du Pont, Ford, Chrysler, and several other major companies regard *supply planning* as a major responsibility of their purchasing managers.

Business buyers are also affected by technological, political, and competitive developments in the environment. The business marketer has to monitor all of these forces, determine how they will affect buyers, and try to turn problems into opportunities.

ORGANIZATIONAL FACTORS ❖ Each buying organization has specific objectives, policies, procedures, organizational structures, and systems. The business marketer has to be familiar with them. Such questions arise as: How many people are involved in the buying decision? Who are they? What are their evaluation criteria? What are the company's policies and constraints on the buyers?

Business marketers should be aware of the following organizational trends in the purchasing area:

◆ *Purchasing-department upgrading:* Purchasing departments commonly occupy a low position in the management hierarchy, in spite of managing often more than half of the company's costs. However, recent competitive pressures have led many companies to

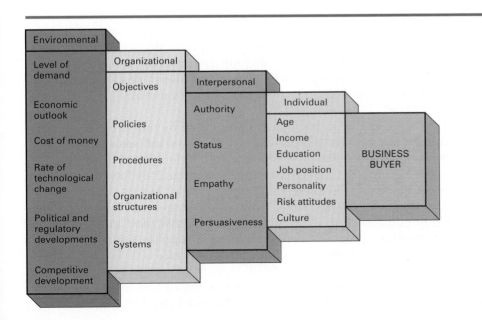

FIGURE 8-1
Major Influences on
Industrial Buying Behavior

CHAPTER 8
Analyzing Business Markets
and Business Buying Behavior

upgrade their purchasing departments and elevate their administrators to vice-presidential status. These departments have been changed from old-fashioned *purchasing departments* with their emphasis on buying at the lowest cost to *procurement departments* with their mission to seek the best value from fewer and better suppliers. Some multinationals have elevated them into *strategic materials departments* with responsibility for sourcing around the world and working with strategic partners. At Caterpillar, functions such as purchasing, inventory control, production scheduling, and traffic have been combined in one department. Many companies are looking for top talent and offering higher compensation. This means that business marketers must correspondingly upgrade their sales personnel to match the higher caliber of the business buyers.

◆ *Centralized purchasing:* In multidivisional companies, most purchasing is carried out by separate divisions because of their differing needs. Recently companies have started to recentralize some of the purchasing. Headquarters identifies materials purchased by several divisions and buys them centrally. The company thereby gains more purchasing clout. The individual divisions can buy from another source if they can get a better deal, but in general, centralized purchasing produces substantial savings for the company. For the business marketer, this development means dealing with fewer and higher-level buyers. Instead of the business marketer's salesforces selling at separate plant locations, the marketer may use a *national account salesforce* to deal with large corporate buyers. National account selling is challenging and demands a sophisticated salesforce and marketing planning effort.[14]

◆ *Long-term contracts:* Business buyers are increasingly initiating or accepting long-term contracts with reliable suppliers. Thus General Motors wants to buy from fewer suppliers, who are willing to locate close to its plants and produce high-quality components. In addition, business marketers are supplying *electronic order-interchange* (EDI) systems to their customers. The customer can enter orders directly on the computer and they are automatically transmitted to the supplier. Many hospitals order directly from Baxter in this way, and many bookstores order from Follett's in this way.

◆ *Purchasing-performance evaluation:* More companies are setting up incentive systems to reward purchasing managers for good buying performance, in much the same way that sales personnel receive bonuses for good selling performance. These systems will lead purchasing managers to increase their pressure on sellers for the best terms.

The emergence of just-in-time production systems promises to have a major impact on organizational purchasing policies. Its ramifications are described in Marketing Strategies 8-1 on pages 214–15.

INTERPERSONAL FACTORS ❖ The buying center usually includes several participants with differing interests, authority, and persuasiveness. The business marketer is not likely to know what kind of group dynamics will take place during the buying decision process, although whatever information he or she can discover about the personalities and interpersonal factors would be useful.

INDIVIDUAL FACTORS ❖ Each participant in the buying process has personal motivations, perceptions, and preferences. These are influenced by the participant's age, income, education, professional identification, personality, attitudes toward risk, and culture (see Global Marketing 8-1 on page 216). Buyers definitely exhibit different buying styles. There are "keep-it-simple" buyers, "own-expert" buyers, "want-the-best" buyers, and "want-everything-done" buyers. Some younger, highly educated buyers are "computer whizzes" and make rigorous analyses of competitive proposals before choosing a supplier. Other buyers are "tough guys" from the "old school" and play off the sellers:

A good example of a cagey buyer is [the] vice-president in charge of purchasing for Rheingold's big New York brewery. . . . Using the leverage of hundreds of millions of cans a year, like many other buyers, he takes punitive action when one company slips in quality or fails to deliver. "At one point American started talking about a price rise," he recalls. "Continental kept its mouth shut. . . . American never did put the price rise into effect, but anyway, I punished them for talking about it." For a three-month period he cut the percentage of cans he bought from American.[15]

Business marketers must know their customers and adapt their tactics to known environmental, organizational, interpersonal, and individual influences on the buying situation.

How Do Business Buyers Make Their Buying Decisions?

Business buyers do not buy goods and services for personal consumption or utility. They buy goods and services to make money, or to reduce operating costs, or to satisfy a social or legal obligation. A steel company will add another furnace if it sees a chance to make more money. It will computerize its accounting system to reduce the costs of doing business. It will add pollution-control equipment to meet legal requirements. To buy the needed goods, business buyers move through a purchasing or procurement process. Robinson et al. have identified eight stages of the industrial buying process and called them *buyphases*.[16] These stages are shown in Table 8-1. All eight phases apply to a new-task buying situation, and some of them to the other two types of buying situations. This model is called the *buygrid* framework. We will describe the eight steps for the typical new-task buying situation.

PROBLEM RECOGNITION ❖ The buying process begins when someone in the company recognizes a problem or need that can be met by acquiring a good or a service. Problem recognition can occur as a result of internal or external stimuli. Internally, the most common events leading to problem recognition are the following:

- The company decides to develop a new product and needs new equipment and materials to produce this product.
- A machine breaks down and requires replacement or new parts.
- Purchased material turns out to be unsatisfactory, and the company searches for another supplier.
- A purchasing manager senses an opportunity to obtain lower prices or better quality.

Externally, the buyer may get new ideas at a trade show, or see an ad, or receive a call from a sales representative who offers a better product or a lower price.

		BUYCLASSES		
		New Task	Modified Rebuy	Straight Rebuy
BUYPHASES	1. Problem recognition	Yes	Maybe	No
	2. General need description	Yes	Maybe	No
	3. Product specification	Yes	Yes	Yes
	4. Suppliers' search	Yes	Maybe	No
	5. Proposal solicitation	Yes	Maybe	No
	6. Supplier selection	Yes	Maybe	No
	7. Order-routine specification	Yes	Maybe	No
	8. Performance review	Yes	Yes	Yes

TABLE 8-1
Major Stages (Buyphases) of the Industrial Buying Process in Relation to Major Buying Situations (Buyclasses)

Source: Adapted from Patrick J. Robinson, Charles W. Faris, and Yoram Wind, *Industrial Buying and Creative Marketing* (Boston: Allyn & Bacon, 1967), p. 14.

Lean Production Changes the Face of Business Buying

Business marketers developed their marketing strategies during the era of mass production. Mass production, which followed the earlier period of craft production, was perfected in the auto industry by Henry Ford and Alfred Sloan. The key concepts were: assembly lines which operated continuously to produce products ahead of demand; workers who carried out simple and repetitive tasks; and the system designed down to the last detail by the company's engineers without the benefit of worker, supplier, or dealer input or participation.

Today, however, manufacturing customers are moving toward a whole new way of manufacturing called *lean production*. Lean production enables a company to produce a greater variety of products at less cost, in less time, using less labor, achieving higher quality, and with less adverse impacts on workers. It permits making more rapid model changes and performance improvements. It also permits entering markets that are typically one-quarter of the size needed by mass production operations. It helps explain how a company like Mazda can design and introduce a small volume car such as the Miata and still make a large profit doing this. All said, lean production seems to combine the best of craft production and mass production, without the limitations of either.

Lean production is changing business customers' attitude toward the selection and management of suppliers. It is imperative that business-to-business marketers recognize and adapt to the changes implied by lean production. Much of the credit for developing the system of lean production belongs to the Toyota company. Lean production contains the following central ideas:

1. Instead of each worker specializing in some repetitive task, workers are organized in teams that take full responsibility for some production activity. The team members can handle various tasks. They have job security and are paid according to their seniority, not by what job they are currently doing. They form quality circles and strive continuously to improve the product and the process. Guided by high quality standards, workers will stop production of their component at any time an error occurs, instead of hiding the error and letting it get embedded in the final product, only to be later corrected at great expense. The workers use the error as an occasion to unearth the error's fundamental cause so that it doesn't happen again.

2. The factory is designed to make it economical to produce small lots of a particular component or product. The setup can be changed quickly to make other products as demand changes. Inventories are kept low and suppliers refill them only at a rate equal to what is being used up.

3. The company carefully selects the suppliers and intends to involve them in a long term relationship. No longer does the company keep switching among suppliers, choosing the lowest bidder each time. The company involves the approved suppliers in the designing of the components. For example, a brake supplier might be told the dimensions and performance qualities needed in a braking system, and the supplier then proposes and designs the braking system. The suppliers remain independent and yet are part of the "company's family." Suppliers willingly invest in the latest equipment because of the assurance of a steady relation with the manufacturer.

4. The dealers also participate in the company's development of products based on their experience in hearing what customers want. Dealers are not forced to take and carry a certain number of cars in inventory. Instead they send in customer orders every evening and the company then produces the car, shipping it within a week of receiving the order.

5. The dealers keep detailed records on every customer (e.g., the car they bought, ages of family members, family income and occupation, and so on). This enables the dealer to know when the customer or a family member will most likely be ready to buy a new car. The dealer's salesperson makes an appointment to visit the customer's home and describe the new cars, and do marketing research in the process. Customers are assumed to be permanently loyal to the brand because of the company's ability to keep improving the product with new features and performances desired by customers.

Thus lean production represents a constellation of new organizational relationships both inside and outside the company, consisting of a different way to view workers, suppliers, dealers, and customers, and a different way to view quality and improvement. Clearly, many manufacturers will find the transition from mass to lean production to be difficult, just as the transition from craft to mass production was difficult. But several elements of lean production thinking are now finding their way into some major American and European manufacturing enterprises. The major elements of lean production that companies are now adopting are:

1. *Just-in-time (JIT) production:* The goal of JIT is zero inventory with 100% quality. It means that materials arrive at the customer's factory exactly when needed. It calls for a synchronization between supplier and customer production schedules so that inventory buffers are unnecessary. Effective implementation of JIT should result in reduced inventory and increased quality, productivity, and adaptability to changes.

2. *Strict Quality Control:* Maximum cost savings from JIT are achieved if the buyer receives perfect goods from the supplier without the need to inspect them. This means that the suppliers apply strict quality-control procedures such as SPC (statistical process control) or TQC (total quality control).

3. *Frequent and Reliable Delivery:* Daily delivery is frequently the only way to avoid inventory buildup. Increasingly, customers are specifying delivery dates rather than shipping dates with penalties for not meeting them. Apple even penalizes for early delivery, while Kasle Steel makes around-the-clock deliveries to the General Motors plant in Buick City. This means that suppliers must develop reliable transportation arrangements.

4. *Closer Location:* Suppliers should locate close to their important customers because this will result in more reliable delivery. Kasle Steel set up its blanking mill within Buick City to serve the General Motors plant there. This means that suppliers will have to make large commitments to major customers.

5. *Telecommunication:* New communication technologies permit suppliers to establish computerized purchasing systems with their customers. One large customer requires that suppliers make their inventory levels and prices available on the system. It allows for just-in-time on-line ordering as the computer searches for the lowest prices. This reduces transaction costs but puts pressure on business marketers to keep their prices competitive.

6. *Stable Production Schedules:* Customers provide their production schedule to the supplier so that the delivery is made on the day the materials are required. Navistar provides one of its suppliers a six-month forecast and a firm 20-day order. If any last minute changes are made, Navistar is billed for the additional costs. This helps reduce the uncertainty and costs faced by the suppliers.

7. *Single Sourcing and Early Supplier Involvement:* JIT implies that the buying and selling organizations work closely together to reduce costs. Business buyers realize that suppliers are experts in their field and should be brought into the design process. The business customer often awards a long-term contract to only one supplier. The payoff is high for the winning supplier, and it is very difficult for other competitors to subsequently get the contract. Contracts are almost automatically renewed provided the supplier has met delivery schedules and quality standards. Harley Davidson reduced its supplier base from 320 to 180 in two years.

8. *Value Analysis:* Value analysis (VA) is a tool for reducing costs and improving quality. Some large manufacturers hold VA seminars for their suppliers. Suppliers with a strong VA program have a competitive edge.

9. *Close Relationship:* All these features help to forge a closer relationship between the business customer and the business marketer. Because of the time invested by the parties, joint location decisions, and telecommunication hookups, switching costs are high. A major implication is that business marketers must improve their skill in *relationship marketing* as compared with *transaction marketing.* Business marketers must plan for profit maximization over the entire relationship period rather than over each transaction.

SOURCES: See James P. Womack, Daniel T. Jones, and Daniel Roos, *The Machine that Changed the World* (New York: Macmillan, 1990); G. H. Manoochehri, "Suppliers and the Just-In-Time Concept," *Journal of Purchasing and Materials Management,* Winter 1984, pp. 16–21; Somerby Dowst, "Buyers Say VA Is More Important Than Ever," *Purchasing,* June 26, 1986, pp. 64–83; Ernest Raia, "Just-in-Time USA," *Purchasing,* February 13, 1986, pp. 48–62; Eric K. Clemons and F. Warren McFarlan, "Telecom: Hook Up or Lose Out," *Harvard Business Review,* July–August 1986, pp. 91–97; and Somerby Dowst and Ernest Raia, "Design Team Signals for More Supplier Involvement," *Purchasing,* March 27, 1986, pp. 76–83.

Global Marketing 8–1

Adapting to the Business Style of the Host Country

Imagine an American salesman, Harry Slick, starting out on his overseas business trip. The following events occur on his trip:

1. In England, he phones a long-term customer and asks for an early breakfast business meeting so that he can fly to Paris at noon.
2. In Paris, he invites a business prospect to have dinner at La Tour d'Argent and greets him with "Just call me Harry, Jacques."
3. In Germany, he arrives ten minutes late for an important meeting.
4. In Japan, he accepts the business cards of his hosts and, without looking at them, puts them in his pocket.

How many orders is Harry Slick likely to get? Probably none, but his company will face a pile of bills.

International business success requires that the businessperson understand and adapt to the local business culture and norms. Here are some rules of social and business etiquette that managers should understand when doing business in other countries.

France — Dress conservatively, except in the south where more casual clothes are worn. Do not refer to people by their first names—the French are formal with strangers.

Germany — Be especially punctual. An American businessman invited to someone's home should present flowers, preferably unwrapped, to the hostess. During introductions, greet women first and wait until, or if, they extend their hands before extending yours.

Italy — Whether you dress conservatively or go native in a Giorgio Armani suit, keep in mind that Italian businesspeople are style conscious. Make appointments well in advance. Prepare for and be patient with Italian bureaucracies.

United Kingdom — Toasts are often given at formal dinners. If the host honors you with a toast, be prepared to reciprocate. Business entertaining is done more often at lunch than at dinner.

Saudi Arabia — Although men will kiss each other in greeting, they will never kiss a woman in public. An American woman should wait for a man to extend his hand before offering hers. If a Saudi offers refreshment, accept—it is an insult to decline it.

Japan — Don't imitate Japanese bowing customs unless you understand them thoroughly—who bows to whom, how many times, and when. It's a complicated ritual. Presenting business cards is another ritual. Carry many cards, present them with both hands so your name can be easily read, and hand them to others in descending rank. Expect Japanese business executives to take time making decisions and to work through all of the details before making a commitment.

SOURCES: Adapted from Susan Harte, "When in Rome, You Should Learn to Do What the Romans Do," *The Atlanta Journal-Constitution*, January 22, 1990, pp. D1, D6. Also see Lufthansa's *Business Travel Guide/Europe*.

Business marketers can stimulate problem recognition by developing ads, calling on prospects, and so on.

GENERAL NEED DESCRIPTION ❖ Having recognized a need, the buyer proceeds to determine the general characteristics and quantity of the needed item. For standard items, this is not much of a problem. For complex items, the buyer will work with others—engineers, users, and so on—to define the general characteristics. They will want to establish the importance of reliability, durability, price, and other attributes desired in the item. The business marketer can render assistance to the buyer in this phase by describing the various criteria to consider in meeting this need.

PRODUCT SPECIFICATIONS ❖ The buying organization next develops the item's technical specifications. A *product-value-analysis* engineering team is assigned to the project. *Product value analysis* is *an approach to cost reduction in which components are carefully studied to determine if they can be redesigned or standardized or made by cheaper methods of production*. The team will examine the high-cost components in a given product—usually 20% of the parts account for 80% of the costs. The team will also identify overdesigned product components that last longer than the product itself. The team will decide on the optimal product characteristics. Tightly written specifications will allow the buyer to refuse merchandise that fails to meet the specified standards.

Suppliers, too, can use product-value analysis as a tool for positioning themselves to win an account. By getting in early and influencing buyer specifications, the supplier has a good chance of being chosen in the supplier-selection stage.

SUPPLIER SEARCH ❖ The buyer now tries to identify the most appropriate suppliers. The buyer can examine trade directories, do a computer search, phone other companies for recommendations, watch trade advertisements, and attend trade shows.[17] The supplier's task is to get listed in major directories, develop a strong advertising and promotion program, and build a good reputation in the marketplace. Suppliers who lack the required production capacity or suffer from a poor reputation will be rejected. Those who qualify may be visited to examine their manufacturing facilities and meet their personnel. The buyer will end up with a short list of qualified suppliers.

PROPOSAL SOLICITATION ❖ The buyer will now invite qualified suppliers to submit proposals. Some suppliers will send only a catalog or a sales representative. Where the item is complex or expensive, the buyer will require a detailed written proposal from each qualified supplier. The buyer will eliminate some and invite the remaining suppliers to make formal presentations.

Thus business marketers must be skilled in researching, writing, and presenting proposals. Their proposals should be marketing documents, not just technical documents. Their oral presentations should inspire confidence. They should position their company's capabilities and resources so that they stand out from the competition.

Consider the hurdles that the Campbell Soup Company has set up in qualifying suppliers:

The Campbell Qualified Supplier Program requires a would-be supplier to pass through three stages: that of a *qualified supplier*, an *approved supplier*, and a *select supplier*. To become qualified, the supplier has to demonstrate technical capabilities, financial health, cost effectiveness, high quality standards, and innovativeness. Assuming that the supplier satisfies these criteria, the supplier applies for approval based on attending a Campbell Vendor seminar, accepting an implementation team visit, agreeing to make certain changes and commitments, and so forth. Once approved, the supplier becomes a select supplier when he demonstrates high product uniformity, continuous quality improvement, and just-in-time delivery capabilities.

SUPPLIER SELECTION ❖ Campbell's program represents the approach that business customers will increasingly use in selecting suppliers. Marketers will have to understand and manage this process if they are to succeed in becoming suppliers to major business customers. The buying center will specify desired supplier attributes and indicate their relative importance. The buying center will rate suppliers against these attributes and identify the most attractive suppliers. They often use a supplier-evaluation model such as the one shown in Table 8-2.

Lehmann and O'Shaughnessy found that the relative importance of different attributes varies with the type of buying situation.[18] For *routine-order products*, they

TABLE 8-2
An Example of Vendor
Analysis

ATTRIBUTES	RATING SCALE				
	Unacceptable (0)	Poor (1)	Fair (2)	Good (3)	Excellent (4)
Technical and production capabilities					x
Financial strength			x		
Product reliability					x
Delivery reliability			x		
Service capability					x
Total score: 4 + 2 + 4 + 2 + 4 = 16					
Average score: 16/5 = 3.2					

Note: This vendor shows up as strong, except on two attributes. The purchasing agent has to decide how important the two weaknesses are. The analysis could be redone using importance weights for the five attributes.

Source: Adapted from Richard Hill, Ralph Alexander, and James Cross, *Industrial Marketing*, 4th ed. (Homewood, IL: Richard D. Irwin, Copyright 1975), pp. 101–104.

found that delivery reliability, price, and supplier reputation are highly important. For *procedural-problem products*, such as a copying machine, the three most important attributes are technical service, supplier flexibility, and product reliability. Finally, for *political-problem products* that stir rivalries in the organization, such as a computer system, the most important attributes are price, supplier reputation, product reliability, service reliability, and supplier flexibility.

The buying center may attempt to negotiate with the preferred suppliers for better prices and terms before making the final selection. The marketer can counter the request for a lower price in a number of ways. The marketer can cite the value of the services the buyer now receives, especially where these services are superior to those offered by competitors. The marketer may be able to show that the "life-cycle cost" of using its product is lower than that of competitors, even if its purchase price is higher. Other more innovative ways may also be used to counter intense price pressure. Consider the following example:

> Lincoln Electric has instituted the Guaranteed Cost Reduction Program for its distributors. Whenever a customer requests a distributor to lower prices on Lincoln equipment to match Lincoln's competitors, the company and the particular distributor guarantee that, during the coming year, they will find cost reductions in the customer's plant that meet or exceed the price difference between Lincoln's products and the competition's. Lincoln sales representative and the distributor then get together and, after surveying the customer's operations, identify and propose specific customer cost savings. If an independent audit at the end of the year does not reveal the promised cost savings, Lincoln Electric and the distributor compensate the customer for the difference, with Lincoln paying 70% and the distributor paying the rest.[19]

Buying centers must also decide how many suppliers to use. Many businesses prefer multiple suppliers so that they will not be totally dependent on one supplier and also to be able to compare the prices and performances of competing suppliers. The buyer will normally place most of the order with a prime supplier. For example, a buyer may buy 60% from the prime supplier and 30% and 10% respectively, from two other suppliers. The *prime supplier* will make an effort to protect its prime position, while the *secondary suppliers* will try to expand their supplier share. In the meantime, *out-suppliers* will seek to get their foot in the door by offering an especially low price and then work hard to increase their share of the customer's business.

ORDER-ROUTINE SPECIFICATION ❖ The buyer now negotiates the final order with the chosen supplier(s), listing the technical specifications, the quantity needed, the expected time of delivery, return policies, warranties, and so on. In the case of MRO items (maintenance, repair, and operating items), buyers are increasingly moving toward *blanket contracts* rather than *periodic purchase orders*. Writing a new purchase order each time stock is needed is expensive. Nor does the buyer want to write fewer and larger purchase orders because that means carrying more inventory. A blanket contract establishes a long-term relationship where the supplier promises to resupply the buyer as needed on agreed price terms over a specified period of time. The stock is held by the seller; hence the name *stockless purchase plan*. The buyer's computer automatically sends an order to the seller when stock is needed. Blanket contracting leads to more single-source buying and ordering of more items from that single source. This locks the supplier in tighter with the buyer and makes it difficult for out-suppliers to break in unless the buyer becomes dissatisfied with the in-supplier's prices, quality, or service.[20]

PERFORMANCE REVIEW ❖ In this stage, the buyer reviews the performance of the particular supplier(s). Three methods are used. The buyer may contact the end users and ask for their evaluations. Or the buyer may rate the supplier on several criteria using a weighted score method. Or the buyer might aggregate the cost of poor performance to come up with adjusted costs of purchase, including price.[21] The performance review may lead the buyer to continue, modify, or drop the supplier. The supplier should monitor the same variables that are used by the buyers and end users of the product.

We have described the buying stages that would operate in a new-task buying situation. In the modified-rebuy or straight-rebuy situation, some of these stages would be compressed or bypassed. For example, in a straight-rebuy situation, the buyer normally has a favorite supplier or a ranked list of suppliers. Each stage represents a narrowing of the number of supplier alternatives. Cardozo has used the buying stages to come up with a model to yield the probability that a particular supplier will get the order for a particular product from a particular buyer.[22]

The eight-stage buyphase model represents the major steps in the business buying process. The business marketer needs to map the flow of work, and this *buyflow* can provide many clues to the marketer. A buyflow map for the purchase of a packaging machine in Japan is shown in Figure 8-2. The numbers within the icons are defined at the right. The italicized numbers between icons show the flow of events. Over 20 people in the purchasing company were involved, including the production manager and staff, new-product committee, company laboratory, the marketing department, and the department for market development. The entire decision-making process took 121 days.

Clearly, business marketing is a challenging area. The key is to know the user's needs, the buying participants, the buying criteria, and the buying procedures. With this knowledge, the business marketer can design marketing plans for selling to different types of customers.

Institutional and Government Markets

Our discussion thus far has concentrated largely on the buying behavior of profit-seeking companies. Much of what we said also applies to the buying practices of institutional and government organizations. However, we want to highlight certain special features found in these latter markets.

The institutional market consists of schools, hospitals, nursing homes, prisons, and other institutions that must provide goods and services to people in their care. Many of these institutions are characterized by low budgets and captive clien-

FIGURE 8-2
Organizational Buying
Behavior in Japan:
Packaging-Machine
Purchase Process
Source: "Japanese Firms Use Unique
Buying Behavior," *The Japan
Economic Journal,* December 23, 1980,
p. 29. Reprinted by permission.

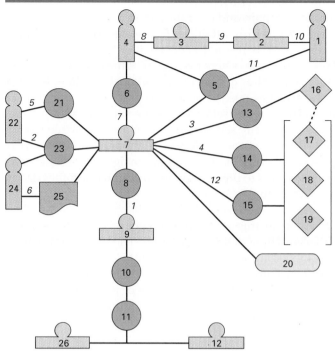

1 President
2 Financial Dept.
3 Sales headquarters
4 Production chief
5 Decision
6 Discussion of production
  and sales plans
7 Production Dept.
8 Production of packing
  process plan
9 New Products Development
  Committee
10 Request for consultation
11 Production of new product
  marketing plan
12 Product Development Dept.
13 Discussion of design of
  prototype machines
14 Prototype machine
15 Placement of orders
16 Makers design and technical
  staff
17 Supplier A
18 Supplier B
19 Supplier C
20 Overseas machine exhibitions
21 Request for testing of
  prototype machines
22 Research staff
23 Production of basic design
24 Foreman
25 Production of draft plans
26 Marketing Dept.

teles. A hospital purchasing agent has to decide what quality of food to buy for the patients. The buying objective is not profit, since the food is provided to the patients as part of the total service package. Nor is cost minimization the objective because patients served with poor food will complain to others and hurt the hospital's reputation. The hospital purchasing agent has to search for institutional-food vendors whose quality meets or exceeds a certain minimum standard and whose prices are low.

Many food vendors set up a separate division to sell to institutional buyers because of their special buying needs and characteristics. Thus Heinz will produce, package, and price its ketchup differently to meet the different requirements of hospitals, colleges, and prisons.

These institutions may have different sponsors and seek different objectives. A Humana hospital is run for profit, a Sisters of Charity Hospital is run as a nonprofit, and a Veterans Hospital is run as a government hospital. The organization's sponsor and objectives will make a difference in how it buys.

In most countries, government organizations are a major buyer of goods and services. Government purchasing has certain characteristics. Because their spending decisions are subject to public review, government organizations require considerable paperwork on the part of suppliers. Suppliers complain about excessive paperwork, bureaucracy, needless regulations, decision-making delays, and frequent shifts in procurement personnel. Suppliers have to master the system and find ways to "cut through the red tape." Most governments provide would-be suppliers with detailed guides describing how to sell to the government.

Another characteristic is that government organizations typically require suppliers to submit bids, and normally they award the contract to the lowest bidder. In some cases, the government unit will make allowance for the supplier's superior quality or reputation for completing contracts on time. Governments will also buy on a negotiated contract basis primarily in the case of complex projects involving major R&D costs and risks, and in cases where there is little effective competition.

A third characteristic is that government organizations tend to favor domestic suppliers over foreign suppliers. A major complaint of multinationals operating in Europe is that each country shows favoritism toward its own nationals in spite of superior offers that might be made by foreign firms. The European Economic Commission is trying to eliminate this bias.

Many companies that sell to the government have not manifested a marketing orientation—for a number of reasons. The government's procurement policies have emphasized price, leading the suppliers to invest considerable effort in bringing their costs down. Where the product's characteristics are carefully specified, product differentiation is not a marketing factor. Nor are advertising and personal selling of much consequence in winning bids.

Several companies, however, have established separate government marketing departments. Rockwell, Kodak, and Goodyear are examples. These companies anticipate government needs and projects, participate in the product specification phase, gather competitive intelligence, prepare bids carefully, and produce stronger communications to describe and enhance their companies' reputations.[23]

SUMMARY ❖

Business markets consist of individuals and organizations that buy goods for purposes of further production, resale, or redistribution. Businesses (including government and nonprofit organizations) are a market for raw and manufactured materials and parts, installations, accessory equipment, and supplies and services.

The industrial market buys goods and services for the purpose of increasing sales, cutting costs, or meeting social and legal requirements. Compared with the consumer market, the industrial market consists of fewer buyers, larger buyers, and more geographically concentrated buyers; the demand is derived, relatively inelastic, and more fluctuating; and the purchasing is more professional, and more buying influences are involved. Industrial buyers make decisions that vary with the buying situation or buyclass. Buyclasses consist of three types: straight rebuys, modified rebuys, and new tasks. The decision-making unit of a buying organization, the buying center, consists of persons who play any of six roles: users, influencers, buyers, deciders, approvers, and gatekeepers. The industrial marketer needs to know: Who are the major participants? In what decisions do they exercise influence? What is their relative degree of influence? and What evaluation criteria does each decision participant use? The industrial marketer also needs to understand the major environmental, organizational, interpersonal, and individual influences operating in the buying process. The buying process itself consists of eight stages called buyphases: problem recognition, general need description, product specification, supplier search, proposal solicitation, supplier selection, order-routine specification, and performance review. As industrial buyers become more sophisticated, industrial marketers must upgrade their marketing capabilities.

The institutional and government markets share many practices with the business market and have some additional characteristics. Institutional buyers are less concerned with profit than with other considerations when they define the products and services to buy for the people under their care. Government buyers tend to require many forms and favor open bidding and their own nationals when they choose their suppliers. Suppliers must be prepared to adapt their offers to the special needs and procedures found in institutional and government markets.

NOTES ❖

1. Frederick E. Webster, Jr., and Yoram Wind, *Organizational Buying Behavior* (Englewood Cliffs, NJ: Prentice-Hall, 1972), p. 2.

2. However, for an argument that consumer and industrial marketing do not differ substantially, see Edward F. Fern and James R. Brown, "The Industrial/Consumer Marketing Dichotomy: A Case of Insufficient Justification," *Journal of Marketing*, Spring 1984, pp. 68–77.

3. See William S. Bishop, John L. Graham, and Michael H. Jones, "Volatility of Derived Demand in Industrial Markets and Its Management Implications," *Journal of Marketing*, Fall 1984, pp. 95–103.

4. See Russell Hindin, "Lease Your Way to Corporate Growth," *Financial Executive*, May 1984, pp. 20–25.

5. Patrick J. Robinson, Charles W. Faris, and Yoram Wind, *Industrial Buying and Creative Marketing* (Boston: Allyn & Bacon, 1967).

6. See Peter Doyle, Arch G. Woodside, and Paul Mitchell, "Organizational Buying in New Task and Rebuy Situations," *Industrial Marketing Management*, February 1979, pp. 7–11.

7. Urban B. Ozanne and Gilbert A. Churchill, Jr., "Five Dimensions of the Industrial Adoption Process," *Journal of Marketing Research*, 1971, pp. 322–28.

8. Marsha A. Schiedt, Fredrick T. Trawick, and John E. Swan, "Impact of Purchasing Systems Contracts on Distributors and Producers," *Industrial Marketing Management*, October 1982, pp. 283–89.

9. See Donald W. Jackson, Jr., Janet E. Keith, and Richard K. Burdick, "Purchasing Agents' Perceptions of Industrial Buying Center Influence: A Situational Approach," *Journal of Marketing*, Fall 1984, pp. 75–83.

10. Webster and Wind, *Organizational Buying Behavior*, p. 6.

11. Ibid., pp. 78–80.

12. See Murray Harding, "Who Really Makes the Purchasing Decision?" *Industrial Marketing*, September 1966, p. 76. Also see Ernest Dichter, "Industrial Buying Is Based on Same 'Only Human' Emotional Factors that Motivate Consumer Market's Housewife," *Industrial Marketing*, February 1973, pp. 14–16.

13. Webster and Wind, *Organizational Buying Behavior*, pp. 33–37.

14. See Thomas H. Stevenson and Albert L. Page, "The Adoption of National Account Marketing by Industrial Firms," *Industrial Marketing Management* 8 (1979), 94–100; and Benson P. Shapiro and Rowland T. Moriarty, *National Account Management: Emerging Insights* (Cambridge, MA: Marketing Science Institute, March 1982).

15. Walter Guzzardi, Jr., "The Fight for 9/10 of a Cent," *Fortune*, April 1961, p. 152.

16. Robinson, Faris, and Wind, *Industrial Buying*.

17. See William A. Dempsey, "Vendor Selection and the Buying Process," *Industrial Marketing Management*, 7 (1978), 257–67.

18. See Donald R. Lehmann and John O'Shaughnessy, "Difference in Attribute Importance for Different Industrial Products," *Journal of Marketing*, April 1974, pp. 36–42.

19. See James A. Narus and James C. Anderson, "Turn Your Industrial Distributors into Partners," *Harvard Business Review*, March-April 1986, pp. 66–71.

20. See Leonard Groeneveld, "The Implications of Blanket Contracting for Industrial Purchasing and Marketing," *Journal of Purchasing*, November 1972, pp. 51–58; and H. Lee Mathews, David T. Wilson, and Klaus Backhaus, "Selling to the Computer Assisted Buyer," *Industrial Marketing Management* 6 (1977), 307–15.

21. See C. David Wieters and Lonnie L. Ostrom, "Supplier Evaluation as a New Marketing Tool," *Industrial Marketing Management* 8 (1979), 161–66.

22. See Richard N. Cardozo, "Modelling Organizational Buying as a Sequence of Decisions," *Industrial Marketing Management* 12 (1983), 75–81.

23. See Warren H. Suss, "How to Sell to Uncle Sam," *Harvard Business Review*, November–December 1984, pp. 136–44; and Don Hill, "Who Says Uncle Sam's a Tough Sell?" *Sales and Marketing Management*, July 1988, pp. 56–60.

9

Analyzing Industries and Competitors

Marketing is merely a civilized form of warfare in which most battles are won with words, ideas, and disciplined thinking.

ALBERT W. EMERY

An opponent is our helper.

EDMUND BURKE

Understanding one's customers is not enough. The nineties will be a decade of intensified competition, foreign and domestic. Many national economies are deregulating and encouraging market forces to operate. The European Common Market is removing trade barriers between Western European countries. Multinationals are aggressively moving into new markets and practicing global marketing. The result is that companies have no choice but to cultivate "competitiveness." They must start paying as much attention to their competitors as to their target customers.

This explains the current talk about "marketing warfare," "competitive intelligence systems," and similar themes.[1] Yet not all companies are investing enough in monitoring their competitors. Some companies think they know all about their competitors because they compete with them. Other companies think they can never know enough about their competitors, so why bother? Sensible companies, however, design and operate systems for gathering continuous intelligence about their competitors.

Knowing one's competitors is critical to effective marketing planning. A company must constantly compare its products, prices, channels, and promotion with its close competitors. In this way, it can identify areas of competitive advantage and disadvantage. The company can launch more precise attacks on its competitors as well as prepare stronger defenses against attacks.

Companies need to know five things about competitors: *Who are our competitors? What are their strategies? What are their objectives? What are their strengths and weaknesses? What are their reaction patterns?* We will examine how this information helps the company shape its marketing strategy.

Identifying the Company's Competitors

Normally, it would seem a simple task for a company to identify its competitors. Coca-Cola knows that Pepsi-Cola is its major competitor; and Sony knows that Matsushita is a major competitor.[2] But the range of a company's actual and potential competitors is much broader. Companies must avoid "competitor myopia." A company is more likely to be "buried" by its latent competitors than by its current ones. Here are two vivid examples:

> Eastman Kodak, in its film business, has been worrying about the growing competition from Fuji, the Japanese film maker. But Kodak faces a much greater threat from the recent invention of the "filmless camera." This camera, sold by Canon and Sony, takes video still pictures that can be shown on a TV receiver, turned into hard copy, and even erased. What greater threat is there to a film business than a filmless camera!

> Unilever and other detergent manufacturers are nervous about research being done on an ultrasonic washing machine. If perfected, this machine would wash clothes in water without any detergent. So far, it can clean only certain kinds of dirt and fabrics. What greater threat to the detergent business than an ultrasonic washing machine!

We can distinguish four levels of competition, based on the degree of product substitution:

1. *Brand competition:* A company can see its competitors as other companies offering a similar product and services to the same customers at similar prices. Thus Buick might see its major competitors to be Ford, Toyota, Honda, Renault, and other manufacturers of moderate-price automobiles. But it would not see itself as competing with Mercedes, on the one hand, or Yugo automobiles, on the other.

2. *Industry competition:* A company can see its competitors more broadly as all companies making the same product or class of products. Here Buick would see itself as competing against all other automobile manufacturers.

3. *Form competition:* A company can see its competitors even more broadly as all companies manufacturing products that supply the same service. Here Buick would see itself competing against not only other automobile manufacturers but also manufacturers of motorcycles, bicycles, and trucks.

4. *Generic competition:* A company can see its competitors still more broadly as all companies that compete for the same consumer dollars. Here Buick would see itself competing with companies that sell major consumer durables, foreign vacations, and new homes.

More specifically, we can identify a company's competitors from an *industry* point of view and a *market* point of view.

Industry Concept of Competition

An *industry* is defined as *a group of firms that offers a product or class of products that are close substitutes for each other*. We talk about the auto industry, the oil industry, the pharmaceutical industry, and so on. Economists define *close substitutes* as products with a *high cross-elasticity of demand*. If the price of one product rises and causes the demand for another product to rise, the two products are close substitutes. If the price of Japanese cars rises and people switch to American cars, the two are close substitutes.

Economists have formulated the framework shown in Figure 9-1 to understand industry dynamics. Essentially, analysis starts with understanding the basic conditions underlying *demand and supply*. These conditions in turn influence the *industry structure*. Industry structure in turn influences *industry conduct* in such areas as product development, pricing, and advertising strategy. Industry conduct then shapes *industry performance*, for instance, the industry's efficiency, technological progress, profitability, and employment.

Here we will focus on the main factors determining industry structure.

NUMBER OF SELLERS AND DEGREE OF DIFFERENTIATION ❖ The starting point for describing an industry is to specify whether there are one, few, or many sellers and whether the product is homogeneous or highly differentiated. These characteristics are extremely important and give rise to five well-known industry structure types, those shown in Marketing Concepts and Tools 9-1.

The competitive structure of an industry can change over time. Consider the case when Sony innovated the Walkman. Sony started as a monopolist, but soon many other companies entered and offered different versions of the product, leading to a monopolistically competitive structure. When demand growth slows down, a "shakeout" occurs, and the industry structure evolves into a differentiated oligopoly. Eventually buyers might see the offers as highly similar with price being the only differentiating characteristic; the industry then approaches a pure oligopoly.

FIGURE 9-1
A Model of Industrial-
Organization Analysis
Source: Adapted from F. M. Scherer,
Industrial Market Structure and Economic Performance, 2nd ed. (Boston:
Houghton Mifflin, 1980), p. 4.

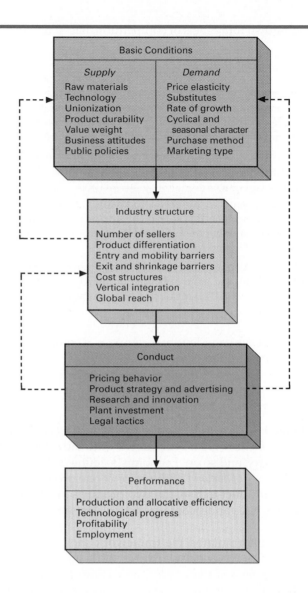

ENTRY AND MOBILITY BARRIERS ❖ Ideally, firms should be free to enter industries that show attractive profits. Their entry would lead to more supply and ultimately bring down profits to a normal rate of return. Ease of entry prevents current firms from extracting long-run excess profits. However, industries differ greatly in their ease of entry. It is easy to open a new restaurant but difficult to enter the auto industry. The major *entry barriers* include *high capital requirements; economies of scale; patents and licensing requirements; scarce locations, raw materials, or distributors; reputational requirements; and so on.* Some barriers are intrinsic to certain industries, and others are erected by the single or combined actions of the incumbent firms. Even after a firm enters an industry, it might face *mobility barriers* when it tries to enter more attractive market segments.

EXIT AND SHRINKAGE BARRIERS ❖ Ideally, firms should be free to leave industries in which profits are unattractive, but they often face *exit barriers*.[3] Among the exit barriers are *legal or moral obligations to customers, creditors, and employees; government restrictions; low-asset salvage value due to overspecialization or obsolescence; lack*

Five Industry Structure Types

- *Pure monopoly:* A pure monopoly exists when only one firm provides a certain product or service in a certain country or area (U.S. Post Office, local electricity company). This monopoly might be the result of a regulatory edict, a patent, license, scale economies, or other factors. An unregulated monopolist that sought to maximize profits would charge a high price, do little or no advertising, and offer minimal service, since customers have to buy its product in the absence of close substitutes. If there are partial substitutes and some danger of imminent competition, the pure monopolist might invest in more service and technology to act as entry barriers to new competition. A regulated monopoly, on the other hand, would be required to charge a lower price and provide more service as a matter of public interest.

- *Pure oligopoly:* A pure oligopoly consists of a few companies producing essentially the same commodity (oil, steel, and so on). A company would find it hard to charge anything more than the going price unless it can differentiate its services. If the competitors match on services, then the only way to gain a competitive advantage is through achieving lower costs. Lower costs are achieved through pursuing a higher volume strategy.

- *Differentiated oligopoly:* A differentiated oligopoly consists of a few companies producing partially dif-

ferentiated products (autos, cameras, and so on). The differentiation can occur along lines of quality, features, styling, or services. Each competitor may seek leadership along one of these major attributes, attract the customers favoring that attribute, and charge a price premium for that attribute.

- *Monopolistic competition:* A monopolistic competitive industry consists of many competitors able to differentiate their offers in whole or part (restaurants, beauty shops). Many of the competitors focus on market segments where they can meet customer needs in a superior way and command a price premium.

- *Pure competition:* A pure competitive industry consists of many competitors offering the same product and service (stock market, commodity market). Since there is no basis for differentiation, competitors' prices will be the same. No competitor will advertise unless advertising can create psychological differentiation (cigarettes, beer); in this case, it would be more proper to describe the industry as monopolistically competitive. Sellers will enjoy different profit rates only to the extent that they achieve lower costs of production or distribution.

---

of alternative opportunities; *high vertical integration*; *emotional barriers*; and so on. Many firms persevere in an industry as long as they cover their variable costs and some or all of their fixed costs. Their continued presence, however, dampens profits for everyone. Companies that want to stay in the industry should lower the exit barriers for others. They can offer to buy competitors' assets, meet customer obligations, and so on. Even if some firms will not exit, they might be induced to shrink their size. Here, too, there are *shrinkage barriers* that the more aggressive competitors can try to reduce.[4]

COST STRUCTURES ❖ Each industry will have a certain cost mix that will drive much of its strategic conduct. For example, steelmaking involves heavy manufacturing and raw-material costs, whereas toy manufacture involves heavy distribution and marketing costs. Firms will pay the greatest attention to their greatest costs and will "strategize" to reduce these costs. Thus the steel company with the most modern plant will have a great advantage over other steel companies.

VERTICAL INTEGRATION ❖ In some industries, companies will find it advantageous to integrate backward and/or forward. A good example is the oil industry where major oil producers carry on oil exploration, oil drilling, oil refining, and chemical manufacture as part of their operation. Vertical integration often effects lower costs and also more control over the value-added stream. In addition, these firms can manipulate their prices and costs in different segments of their business to earn profits where taxes are lowest. Firms that are not able to integrate vertically operate at a disadvantage.

GLOBAL REACH ❖ Some industries are highly local (such as lawn care) and others are *global industries* (such as oil, aircraft engines, cameras). Companies in global industries need to compete on a global basis if they are to achieve economies of scale and keep up with the latest advances in technology.[5] Consider, for example, how U.S. forklift manufacturers lost their market leadership:

> Less than 20 years ago, five companies dominated the U.S. forklift market—Clark Equipment, Caterpillar, Allis and Chalmers, Hyster, and Yale. By 1992, debt-burdened Clark prepared to sell its assets for a mere $95 million, and Caterpillar was the minor partner in an 80%–20% venture with Mitsubishi. Only Hyster held on to its market share while Japanese manufacturers ate into the forklift market. By speeding up product development, concentrating on low-end models, and moving some production to job-hungry Ireland, Hyster was able to compete against Nissan, Toyota, and Komatsu. Hyster also filed an antidumping suit against Japanese models and won the case. Meanwhile, Clark invested in some expensive features on new models that buyers did not want. Caterpillar made the mistake of trying to sell its forklifts through its heavy earth-moving equipment dealers who really did not have an enthusiasm for selling the low-margin forklifts. Clark and Catepillar moved some production to South Korea but encountered even higher costs because Korean labor costs rose sharply and because of the need to carry larger inventories at home due to shipment delays. In failing to think globally—recognizing important market shifts, accurately assessing competitors' intentions and strategies, planning for the long-run—American management lost market leadership.

Market Concept of Competition

Instead of looking at companies making the same product (the industry approach), we can look at companies that satisfy the same customer need. A personal computer manufacturer normally sees its competition as other computer manufacturers. From a customer-need point of view, however, the customer really wants "writing ability." This need can be satisfied by pencils, pens, typewriters, and so on. In general, the market concept of competition opens the company's eyes to a broader set of actual and potential competitors and stimulates more long-run strategic market planning.

The key to identifying competitors is to link industry and market analysis through mapping the *product/market battlefield*. Figure 9-2 illustrates the product/market battlefield in the toothpaste market according to product types and customer age groups. We see that P&G and Colgate-Palmolive occupy nine segments; Lever Brothers, three; Beecham, two; and Topol, two. If Topol wanted to enter other segments, it would need to estimate each segment's market size, competitors' market shares in each segment, and their competitors' capabilities, objectives, and strategies as well as the entry barriers in each segment.

Identifying the Competitors' Strategies

A company's closest competitors are those pursuing the same target markets with the same strategy. A *strategic group* is *a group of firms following the same strategy in a given target market.*[6]

FIGURE 9-2

Product/Market Battlefield
Map for Toothpaste
Source: William A. Cohen, *Winning
on the Marketing Front: The Corporate
Manager's Game Plan* (New York:
John Wiley & Sons, Inc., 1986), p. 63.

Product segmentation		Children/Teens	Age 19-35	Age 36+
Plain toothpaste		Colgate-Palmolive Procter & Gamble	Colgate-Palmolive Procter & Gamble	Colgate-Palmolive Procter & Gamble
Toothpaste with fluoride		Colgate-Palmolive Procter & Gamble	Colgate-Palmolive Procter & Gamble	Colgate-Palmolive Procter & Gamble
Gel		Colgate-Palmolive Procter & Gamble Lever Bros.	Colgate-Palmolive Procter & Gamble Lever Bros.	Colgate-Palmolive Procter & Gamble Lever Bros.
Striped		Beecham	Beecham	
Smoker's toothpaste			Topol	Topol

Customer segmentation

To illustrate, suppose a company wants to enter the major appliance industry. Suppose the two important strategic dimensions of this industry are *quality image* and *vertical integration*. It develops the chart shown in Figure 9-3 and discovers that there are four strategic groups. Strategic group A consists of one competitor (Maytag). Strategic group B consists of three major competitors (General Electric, Whirlpool, and Sears). Strategic group C consists of four competitors, and strategic group D consists of two competitors.

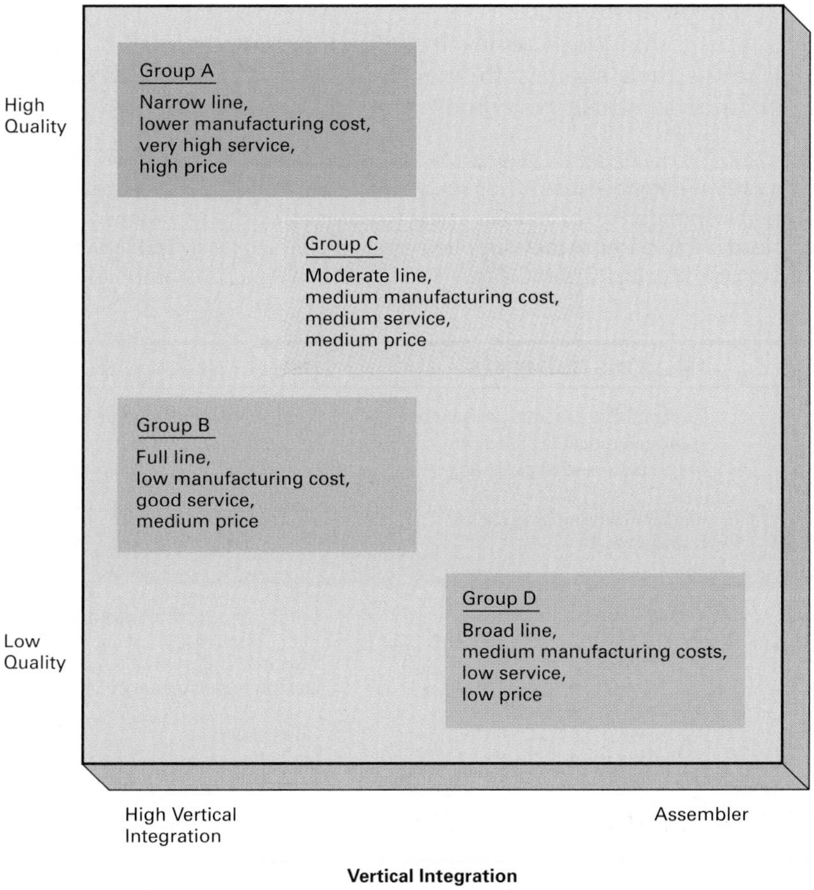

FIGURE 9-3
Strategic Groups in the
Major Appliance Industry

High
Quality

Group A
Narrow line,
lower manufacturing cost,
very high service,
high price

Group C
Moderate line,
medium manufacturing cost,
medium service,
medium price

Group B
Full line,
low manufacturing cost,
good service,
medium price

Group D
Broad line,
medium manufacturing costs,
low service,
low price

Low
Quality

High Vertical
Integration

Assembler

Vertical Integration

Important insights emerge from this strategic-group identification. First, the height of the entry barriers differs for each strategic group. A new company would find it easier to enter group D because it requires minimal investment in vertical integration and in quality components and reputation. Conversely, the company would find it hardest to enter group A or group B. Second, if the company successfully enters one of the groups, the members of that group become its key competitors. Thus if the company enters group B, it will need strength primarily against General Electric, Whirlpool, and Sears. It needs to enter with some competitive advantage if it hopes to succeed.

Although competition is most intense within a strategic group, there is also rivalry between the groups as well. First, some strategic groups may appeal to overlapping customer groups. For example, major appliance manufacturers with different strategies might nevertheless all go after apartment home builders. Second, the customers might not see much difference in the offers. Third, each group might want to expand its market segment scope, especially if the companies are fairly equal in size and power and the mobility barriers between groups are low.

Figure 9-3 used only two dimensions to identify strategic groups within an industry. Other dimensions would include level of technological sophistication, geographical scope, manufacturing methods, and so on. In fact, each competitor should be more fully profiled than the two dimensions would suggest. Table 9-1 contrasts two major electronics firms, Texas Instruments and Hewlett-Packard. Clearly, each has a different strategic makeup and therefore appeals to somewhat different customer segments. A company needs even more detailed information about each competitor. It should know each competitor's product quality, features, and mix; customer services; pricing policy; distribution coverage; salesforce strategy; advertising and sales-promotion programs; and R&D, manufacturing, purchasing, financial, and other strategies.

A company must continuously review its competitors' strategies. Resourceful competitors will revise their strategy through time. Consider how strategy has evolved in the automobile industry over the years:

Ford was an early winner because it was successful at *low cost*. Then GM surpassed Ford because it responded to the market's new wish for *variety*. Later Japanese companies took leadership because they supplied cars with *fuel economy*. The Japanese next moved into producing cars with *high reliability*. When American automakers

TABLE 9-1
Comparison of Strategic Profiles of Texas Instruments and Hewlett-Packard

	TEXAS INSTRUMENTS	HEWLETT-PACKARD
Business Strategy	Competitive advantage in large standard markets based on long-run low-cost position	Competitive advantage in selected, small markets based on unique, high-value products
Marketing	High volume/low price Rapid growth	High value/high price Controlled growth
Manufacturing	Experience curve cost-driven Vertical integration	Delivery and quality Limited vertical integration
R&D	Design to cost	Features and quality Design to performance
Financial	Aggressive Full utilization	Conservative No debt
Human Resources	Competitive Individual incentives	Cooperative Companywide incentives

just about caught up in quality, the Japanese automakers shifted to *sensory qualities*, namely the look and feel of the car and its various components. A former Ford engineer explained: "It's the turn-signal lever that doesn't wobble . . . the speed of the power window up and down . . . the feel of a climate-control knob . . . this is the next nuance of customer competition."[7]

Clearly companies must be alert to changes in what customers want and to how competitors are revising their strategy to meet these emerging wants.

Determining the Competitors' Objectives

Having identified the main competitors and their strategies, we must ask: What is each competitor seeking in the marketplace? What drives each competitor's behavior?

A useful initial assumption is that competitors strive to maximize their profits. Even here, companies differ in the weights they put on short-term versus long-term profits. Furthermore, some companies orient their thinking around "satisficing" rather than "maximizing." They set target profit goals and are satisfied in achieving them, even if more profits could have been produced by other strategies and exertions.

An alternative assumption is that each competitor pursues a mix of objectives. We would want to know the relative weights a competitor places on current profitability, market-share growth, cash flow, technological leadership, service leadership, and so on. Knowing a competitor's weighted mix of objectives allows us to know whether the competitor is satisfied with its current financial results, how it might react to different types of competitive attack, and so on. For example, a competitor pursuing low-cost leadership will react more strongly to a manufacturing process breakthrough by a competitor than to an advertising budget increase by the same competitor.

That competitors' goals can differ sharply is well illustrated by contrasting U.S. and Japanese firms:

> U.S. firms operate largely on a short-run profit-maximization model, largely because their current performance is judged by stockholders who might lose confidence, sell their stock, and cause the company's cost of capital to rise. Japanese firms operate largely on a market-share-maximization model. They need to provide employment for more than 100 million people in a resource-poor country. Japanese firms have lower profit requirements because most of the capital comes from banks that seek regular interest payments rather than high returns at somewhat higher risks. Japanese firms' cost of capital is much lower than American firms' cost of capital, and therefore they can wait longer for the same payback. As a result, Japanese firms can charge lower prices and show more patience in building and penetrating markets. Thus competitors who are satisfied with lower profits have an advantage over their opponents.

A competitor's objectives are shaped by many things, including its size, history, current management, and economics. If the competitor is part of a larger company, it would be important to know whether it is being run for growth or cash or being milked by the parent firm. If the competitor is not critical to the larger company, it could be attacked more readily. Rothschild contends that the worst competitor to attack is the one for whom this is the only business and who has a global operation.[8] The situation is illustrated in the product/market battlefield map in

	Domestic	Quasi-International	Multinational Corporations
Specialist			IBM DEC
Quasi-Specialist			Honeywell Fujitsu
Multi-Industry	Zenith		Sperry Hitachi Siemens Toshiba

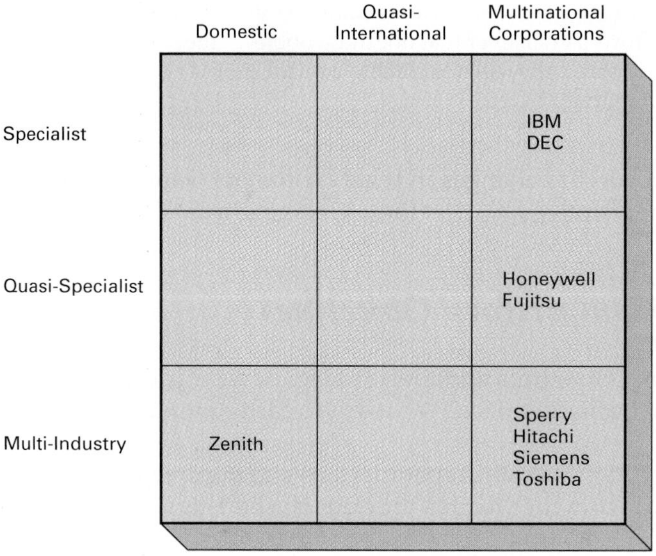

Figure 9-4. Clearly IBM will not easily give up its position in the microcomputer marketplace because it is a specialist multinational firm. On the other hand, Zenith may be an easier target because it is in several businesses and is primarily domestic.

A company must also monitor its competitors' expansion plans. Figure 9-5 shows a product/market battlefield map for the personal computer industry. It appears that Dell, which currently sells personal computers to individual users, plans to add hardware accessories and also to sell to commercial and industrial buyers. The other incumbents in these segments (not shown) are therefore forewarned and, it is hoped, forearmed.

FIGURE 9-5
A Competitor's Expansion Plans

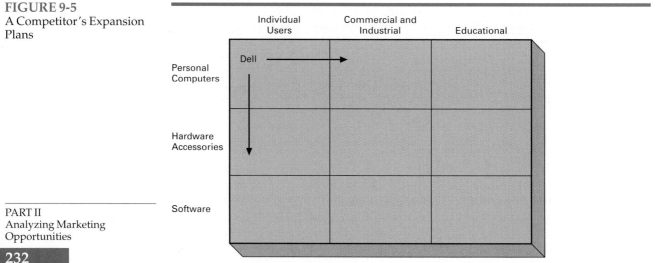

Assessing the Competitors' Strengths and Weaknesses

Can a company's competitors carry out their strategies and reach their goals? That depends on each competitor's resources and capabilities. The company needs to identify each competitor's strengths and weaknesses. As a first step, a company should gather recent data on each competitor's business, particularly *sales, market share, profit margin, return on investment, cash flow, new investment,* and *capacity utilization.* Some information will be difficult to collect. For example, industrial-goods companies find it hard to estimate competitors' market shares because they do not have syndicated data services that are available to consumer-packaged-goods companies. Nevertheless, any information will help them form a better estimate of each competitor's strengths and weaknesses. This kind of information helped a company decide who to attack in the programmable-controls market:

> A company made a decision to enter the programmable-controls market. It faced three entrenched competitors, Allen Bradley, Texas Instruments, and Gould. Its research showed that Allen Bradley had an excellent reputation for technological leadership; Texas Instruments had low costs and engaged in bloody battles for market share; and Gould did a good job but not a distinguished job. The company concluded that its best target was Gould.

Companies normally learn about their competitors' strengths and weaknesses through secondary data, personal experience, and hearsay. They can augment their knowledge by conducting primary marketing research with customers, suppliers, and dealers. A growing number of companies are turning to *benchmarking* as the best guide to improving their competitive standing (see Marketing Concepts and Tools 9-2).

Table 9-2 shows the results of a company asking customers to rate its three competitors, A, B, and C, on five attributes. Competitor A turns out to be well known and viewed as producing high-quality products sold by a good salesforce. However, competitor A is poor in providing product availability and technical assistance. Competitor B is good across the board and excellent in product availability and salesforce. Competitor C rates poor to fair on most attributes. This information suggests that our company could attack competitor A on product availability and technical assistance and competitor C on almost anything, but competitor B has no glaring weakness.

The research findings summarized in Table 9-2 need to be expanded. First, the company's own strengths and weaknesses must be included in the ratings. Second, the cell ratings should show more detail. Obviously, not every customer thought competitor B had good quality. Behind it might lie the finding that 20% said excellent, 40% said good, 30% said fair, and 10% said poor. It would be interesting to know which customer types did not share the general view of competitor B's product quality. Third, customers should also rate other variables, such as price, management quality, and manufacturing capability.

There are three other variables that every company should monitor:

♦ *Share of Market:* The competitor's sales share in the target market.

♦ *Share of Mind:* The percentage of customers who named the competitor in responding to the statement, "Name the first company that comes to mind in this industry."

♦ *Share of Heart:* The percentage of customers who named the competitor in responding to the statement, "Name the company from whom you would prefer to buy the product."

How Benchmarking Helps Improve Competitive Performance

Benchmarking is the art of finding out how and why some companies can perform tasks much better than other companies. There can be as much as a tenfold difference in the quality, speed, and cost performance of an average company versus a world-class company.

The aim of a benchmarking company is to imitate or improve upon the best practices of other companies. The Japanese used benchmarking assiduously in the post-World War II period, copying many American products and practices. Xerox in 1979 undertook one of the first U.S. major benchmarking projects. Xerox wanted to learn how Japanese competitors were able to produce more reliable copiers and charge a price below Xerox's production costs. By buying Japanese copiers and analyzing them through "reverse engineering," Xerox learned how to greatly improve their own copiers' reliability and costs. Xerox didn't stop there. The company went on to ask further questions: Are Xerox scientists and engineers among the best in their respective specialties? Are Xerox marketing, salespeople, and practices among the best in the world? These questions required identifying world-class "best practices" companies and learning from them. Although benchmarking originally focused on studying other companies' products and services, its scope expanded to include benchmarking work processes, staff functions, organizational performance, and the entire value-delivery process.

Another early benchmarking pioneer was Ford. Ford was losing sales to Japanese and European automakers. Don Peterson, then chairman of Ford, instructed his engineers and designers to build a new car that combined the 400 features that Ford customers said were the most important. If Saab made the best seats, then Ford should copy Saab's seats, and so on. Peterson went further: he asked his engineers to "better the best" where possible. When the new car (the highly successful *Taurus*) was finished, Peterson claimed that his engineers had improved upon, not just copied, most of the best features found in competitive automobiles.

In another project, Ford discovered that it employed 500 people to manage its accounts payable operation while its partly owned Japanese partner, Mazda, managed to handle the same task with only ten people. After studying Mazda's system, Ford moved to an "invoiceless system" and reduced its staff to 200 and is still pursuing further improvements.

Today many companies such as AT&T, IBM, Kodak, Du Pont, and Motorola use benchmarking as a standard tool. Some companies benchmark only the best companies in their industry. Others choose to benchmark against the "best practices" in the world. In this sense, benchmarking goes beyond "standard competitive analysis." Motorola, for example, starts each benchmarking project with a search for "best of breed" in the world. According to one of their executives, "The further away from our industry we reach for comparisons, the happier we are. We are seeking competitive superiority, after all, not just competitive parity."

As an example of seeking "best of breed," Robert C. Camp, Xerox's benchmarking expert, flew to Freeport, Maine to visit L. L. Bean, the "outdoors" catalogue company, to find out how Bean's warehouse workers managed to "pick and pack" items three times

TABLE 9-2
Customer's Ratings of Competitors on Key Success Factors

	CUSTOMER AWARENESS	PRODUCT QUALITY	PRODUCT AVAILABILITY	TECHNICAL ASSISTANCE	SELLING STAFF
Competitor A	E	E	P	P	G
Competitor B	G	G	E	G	E
Competitor C	F	P	G	F	F

Note: E = excellent, G = good, F = fair, P = poor.

There is an interesting relationship among these three measures. Table 9-3 shows these numbers for the three competitors listed in Table 9-2. Competitor A enjoys the highest market share, but it is falling. A partial explanation is provided by the fact that its mind share and its heart share are also falling. This slip in customer aware-

as fast as Xerox. As a noncompetitor, Bean was happy to describe its practice, and Xerox ended up redesigning its warehouses and software system. On later occasions, Xerox benchmarked American Express for its billing expertise and Cummins Engine for its production scheduling expertise.

Benchmarking involves the following seven steps: (1) determine which functions to benchmark; (2) identify the key performance variables to measure; (3) identify the best-in-class companies; (4) measure performance of best-in-class companies; (5) measure the company's performance; (6) specify programs and actions to close the gap; and (7) implement and monitor results.

Once a company commits to benchmarking, it may try to benchmark every activity. It may set up a benchmarking department to promote the practice and train departmental personnel in the techniques. Yet there is a time and cost constraint. A company should focus primarily on those critical tasks that deeply affect customer satisfaction and company cost and where substantially better performance is known to exist.

How can a company identify "best-practice" companies? A good starting point is asking customers, suppliers, and distributors who they rate as doing the best job. Also major consulting firms can be contacted because they have built voluminous files of "best practices." An important point is that benchmarking can be done without resorting to industrial espionage.

After the "best practice" companies are identified, the company needs to collect metrics on their performance with respect to cost, time, and quality. For example, a company studying its supply management process found that its purchasing cost was four times higher, its supplier selection time was four times longer, and its delivery lateness was 16 times worse than world-class competitors.

In the meantime, criticisms have been levied against too much reliance on benchmarking. It might hamper real creativity since it takes other companies' performances as a starting point. It might lead to a marginally better product or practice when other companies are leapfrogging ahead. Too often, the studies take many months, and by that time, best practices may have emerged elsewhere. It might cause the company to focus too much on competitors while losing touch with consumers' changing needs. It might distract from making further improvements in the company's core competences.

Nevertheless, a company would be amiss to look only inside when it is trying constantly to improve its performance. The enemy of benchmarking is NIH— "not invented here." Benchmarking remains one of the best sources of ideas for improving quality and competitive performance.

SOURCES: Robert C. Camp, *Benchmarking: The Search for Industry-Best Practices that Lead to Superior Performance* (White Plains, NY: Quality Resources, 1989); Michael J. Spendolini, *The Benchmarking Book* (New York: AMACOM, 1992); Jeremy Main, "How to Steal the Best Ideas Around," *Fortune*, October 19, 1992; and A. Steven Walleck, et al., "Benchmarking World Class Performance," *McKinsey Quarterly*, No. 1, 1990, pp. 3–24.

	MARKET SHARE			MIND SHARE			HEART SHARE			TABLE 9-3
	1991	1992	1993	1991	1992	1993	1991	1992	1993	Market Share, Mind Share, and Heart Share
Competitor A	50%	47%	44%	60%	58%	54%	45%	42%	39%	
Competitor B	30%	34%	37%	30%	31%	35%	44%	47%	53%	
Competitor C	20%	19%	19%	10%	11%	11%	11%	11%	8%	

ness and preference is probably because competitor A, although providing a good product, is not providing good product availability and technical assistance. Competitor B, on the other hand, is steadily gaining in market share, and that is probably due to strategies that are increasing its mind share and heart share. Competitor C seems to be stuck at a low level of market share, mind share, and heart share, given its poor product and marketing attributes. We could generalize as follows: *Companies that make steady gains in mind share and heart share will inevitably make gains in market share and profitability.* What is important, then, is not whether the company made high or low profits in a particular year (so many factors could affect this) but *whether the company has been steadily building up customer awareness and customer preference over time.*

Finally, in searching for competitors' weaknesses, we should identify any assumptions they make about their business and the market that are no longer valid. Some companies believe they produce the best quality in the industry when it is no longer true. Many companies are victims of conventional wisdom like "Customers prefer full-line companies," "The salesforce is the only important marketing tool," "Customers value service more than price." If we know that a competitor is operating on a major wrong assumption, we can take advantage of it.

Estimating the Competitors' Reaction Patterns

A competitor's objectives and strengths/weaknesses go a long way toward indicating its likely moves and reactions to company moves such as a price cut, a promotion step-up, or a new-product introduction. In addition, each competitor has a certain philosophy of doing business, a certain internal culture, and certain guiding beliefs. One needs a deep understanding of a given competitor's mind-set to have hope of anticipating how the competitor might act.

Here are common reaction profiles of competitors:

1. *The Laid-Back Competitor:* Some competitors do not react quickly or strongly to a given competitor move. They may feel their customers are loyal; they may be milking the business; they may be slow in noticing the move; they may lack the funds to react. The firm must try to assess the reasons for the competitors' laid-back behavior.

2. *The Selective Competitor:* A competitor might react only to certain types of attacks and not to others. It might respond to price cuts in order to signal that they are futile. But it might not respond to advertising expenditure increases, believing them to be less threatening. Knowing what a key competitor reacts to gives the company a clue as to the most feasible lines of attack.

3. *The Tiger Competitor:* This company reacts swiftly and strongly to any assault on its terrain. Thus P&G does not let a new detergent come easily into the market. A tiger competitor is signaling that another firm had better not attack because the defender will fight to the finish. It is always better to attack a sheep than a tiger.

4. *The Stochastic Competitor:* Some competitors do not exhibit a predictable reaction pattern. Such a competitor might or might not retaliate on a particular occasion, and there is no way to foretell this based on its economics, history, or anything else.

Some industries are characterized by relative accord among the competitors, and others by constant fighting. Bruce Henderson thinks that much depends on the industry's "competitive equilibrium." Here are some of his observations about the likely state of competitive relations:[9]

1. *If competitors are nearly identical and make their living in the same way, then their competitive equilibrium is unstable:* There is likely to be perpetual conflict in industries where competitive ability is at parity. This would describe "commodity industries" where sellers have not found any major way to differentiate their costs or their offers. In such cases, the competitive equilibrium would be upset if any firm lowers its price—a strong temptation, especially for a competitor with overcapacity. This explains why price wars frequently break out in these industries.

2. *If a single major factor is the critical factor, then competitive equilibrium is unstable:* This would describe industries where cost-differentiation opportunities exist through economies of scale, advanced technology, experience curve learning, and so on. In such industries, any company that achieves a cost breakthrough can cut its price and win market share at the expense of other firms who could only defend their market shares at great cost. Price wars frequently break out in these industries as a result of cost breakthroughs.

3. *If multiple factors may be critical factors, then it is possible for each competitor to have some advantage and be differentially attractive to some customers. The more the multiple factors that may provide an advantage, the more the number of competitors who can coexist. Competitors all have their competitive segment, defined by the preference for the factor tradeoffs that they offer:* This would describe industries where many opportunities exist to differentiate quality, service, convenience, and so on. If customers place different values on these factors, then many firms can coexist through niching.

4. *The fewer the number of competitive variables that are critical, the fewer the number of competitors:* If only one factor is critical, then no more than two or three competitors are likely to coexist. Conversely, the larger the number of competitive variables, the larger the number of competitors, but each is likely to be smaller in its absolute size.

5. *A ratio of 2 to 1 in market share between any two competitors seems to be the equilibrium point at which it is neither practical nor advantageous for either competitor to increase or decrease share.*

Henderson gives the following advice to a firm. Be sure that the rival is fully aware of what would be gained through cooperation and what otherwise would be lost. Convince the rival that you are emotionally dedicated to your position and completely convinced that it is reasonable. Avoid actions that will arouse your competitor's emotions.

Designing the Competitive Intelligence System

We have described the main types of information that company decision makers need to know about their competitors. This information must be collected, interpreted, disseminated, and used. While the cost in money and time of gathering competitive intelligence is high, the cost of not gathering it is higher. Yet the company must design its competitive intelligence system to be cost-effective. There are four main steps:

1. *Setting up the System:* The first step calls for identifying vital types of competitive information, identifying the best sources of this information and assigning a person who will manage the system and its services.

2. *Collecting the Data:* The data are collected on a continuous basis from the field (salesforce, channels, suppliers, market research firms, trade associations) and from published data (government publications, speeches, articles). The company has to develop effective ways of acquiring needed information about competitors without violating legal or ethical standards (see Marketing Concepts and Tools 9-3).

3. *Evaluating and Analyzing:* The data are checked for validity and reliability, interpreted, and organized in an appropriate way.

4. *Disseminating and Responding:* Key information is sent to relevant decision makers, and managers' inquiries about competitors are answered.

With this system, company managers will receive timely information about competitors through phone calls, bulletins, newsletters, and reports. Managers can also contact the department when they need an interpretation of a sudden move by

Marketing Concepts and Tools 9-3

Intelligence Gathering: Snooping on Competitors

Competitive intelligence gathering has grown dramatically as more companies need to know what their competitors are doing. An article in *Fortune* lists over 20 techniques companies use to collect their intelligence. The techniques fall into four major categories.

◆ *Getting Information from Recruits and Competitors' Employees:* Companies can obtain intelligence through job interviews or from conversations with competitors' employees. Companies send engineers to conferences and trade shows to question competitors' technical people. They sometimes advertise and hold interviews for jobs that don't exist in order to pump competitors' employees for information. Companies hire key executives from competitors to find out what they know.

◆ *Getting Information from People Who Do Business with Competitors:* Key customers can keep the company informed about competitors—they might even be willing to request and pass along information on competitors' products. Companies may provide their engineers free of charge to customers. The close, cooperative relationship that the engineers on loan cultivate with the customer's design staff often enables them to learn what new products competitors are pitching.

◆ *Getting Information from Published Materials and Public Documents:* Keeping track of seemingly meaningless published information can provide competitor intelligence. For example, the types of people sought in help-wanted ads can indicate something about a competitor's technological thrusts and new-product development. Although it is illegal for a company to photograph a competitor's plant from the air, aerial photos often are on file with the U.S. Geological Survey or Environmental Protection Agency.

◆ *Getting Information by Observing Competitors or Analyzing Physical Evidence:* Companies increasingly buy competitors' products and take them apart to determine costs of production and even manufacturing methods. Some companies even buy their competitors' garbage. Once it has left the competitor's premise, refuse is legally considered abandoned property.

Though most techniques are legal, many involve questionable ethics. The company should take advantage of publicly available information, but responsible companies avoid practices that might be considered illegal or unethical. A company does not have to break the law or violate accepted codes of ethics to collect intelligence, and the benefits gained from using such techniques are not worth the risks.

SOURCE: Based on Steven Flax, "How to Snoop on Your Competitors," *Fortune*, May 14, 1984, pp. 29–33.

a competitor, or when they need to know a competitor's weaknesses and strengths or how a competitor will respond to a contemplated company move.

In smaller companies that cannot afford to set up a formal competitive intelligence office, a useful step would be to assign specific executives to watch specific competitors. Thus a manager who used to work for a competitor would closely follow that competitor and act as the "in-house" expert on that competitor. In this way, any manager who needs to know the thinking of a specific competitor could contact the corresponding in-house expert.

Selecting Competitors to Attack and Avoid

Given good competitive intelligence, managers will find it easier to formulate their competitive strategies. They will have a better sense of whom they can effectively compete with in the market. The manager must decide which competitors to compete against most vigorously. This manager's choice is aided by conducting a *customer value analysis*, which will reveal the company's strengths and weaknesses relative to various competitors (see Marketing Concepts and Tools 9-4). The company can focus its attack on one of the following several classes of competitors.

STRONG VERSUS WEAK COMPETITORS ❖ Most companies aim their shots at their weak competitors. This requires fewer resources and time per share point gained. But in the process, the firm may achieve little in the way of improved capabilities. The firm should also compete with strong competitors to keep up with the state of the art. Furthermore, even strong competitors have some weaknesses, and the firm may prove to be a worthy competitor.

CLOSE VERSUS DISTANT COMPETITORS ❖ Most companies compete with competitors who resemble them the most. Thus Chevrolet competes with Ford, not with Jaguar. At the same time, the company should avoid trying to "destroy" the close competitor. Porter cites two examples of counterproductive "victories":

> Bausch and Lomb in the late 1970s moved aggressively against other soft lens manufacturers with great success. However, this led each weak competitor to sell out to larger firms, such as Revlon, Johnson & Johnson, and Schering-Plough, with the result that Bausch and Lomb now faced much larger competitors.

> A specialty rubber manufacturer attacked another specialty rubber manufacturer and took away share. The damage to the other company allowed the specialty divisions of the large tire

Marketing Concepts and Tools 9-4

Customer Value Analysis: The Key to Competitive Advantage

In the search for competitive advantage, one of the most important steps is to carry out a *customer value analysis.* The aim of a customer value analysis is to determine the benefits that customers in a target market segment want and how they perceive the relative value of competing suppliers' offers. The major steps in customer value analysis follow.

1. *Identify the major attributes that customers value:* Customers are asked what functions and performance levels they look for in choosing a product and vendors. Different customers will mention different features/benefits. If the list gets overly long, the researcher can remove redundant attributes.

2. *Assess the quantitative importance of the different attributes:* Customers are asked to supply their ratings or rankings of the importance of the different attributes. If the customers diverge much in their ratings, they should be clustered into different customer segments.

3. *Assess the company's and competitors' performances on the different customer values against their rated importance:* The customers are asked where they see the company's

and each competitor's performance on each attribute. Ideally, the company's performance should be rated high on the attributes the customers value most and low on the attributes customers value least.

4. *Examine how customers in a specific segment rate the company's performance against a specific major competitor on an attribute-by-attribute basis:* The key to gaining competitive advantage is to take each customer segment and examine how the company's offer compares to that of its major competitor. If the company's offer exceeds the competitor's offer on all important attributes, the company can charge a higher price, thereby earning higher profits, or it can charge the same price and gain more market share.

5. *Monitor customer values over time:* Although customer values are fairly stable in the short run, they will most probably change as technologies and features change and as customers face different economic climates. The company must periodically redo its studies of customer values and competitors' standings if it wants to be strategically effective.

companies to move more quickly into specialty rubber markets, using them as a dumping ground for excess capacity.[10]

In each case, the company's success in hurting its close rivals brought in tougher competitors.

"GOOD" VERSUS "BAD" COMPETITORS ❖ Porter argues that every industry contains "good" and "bad" competitors.[11] A company would be smart to support the good competitors and attack the bad competitors. Good competitors have a number of characteristics: They play by the industry's rules; they make realistic assumptions about the industry's growth potential; they set prices in a reasonable relation to costs; they favor a healthy industry; they limit themselves to a portion or segment of the industry; they motivate others to lower costs or improve differentiation; and they accept the general level of their share and profits. Bad competitors violate the rules: They try to buy share rather than earn it; they take large risks; they invest in overcapacity; and in general, they upset the industrial equilibrium. For example, IBM finds Cray Research to be a good competitor because it plays by the rules, sticks to its segment, and does not attack IBM's core markets; but IBM finds Fujitsu a bad competitor because it attacks IBM in its core markets with subsidized prices and little differentiation. The implication is that the "good" companies should try to configure their industry to consist of only good competitors. Through careful licensing, selective retaliation, and coalitions, they can shape the industry so that the competitors are not seeking to destroy each other and behave irrationally; they follow the rules; each differentiates somewhat; and they each try to earn share rather than buy it.

Behind this is the more fundamental point that a company benefits from good competitors. Competitors confer several strategic benefits: they lower the antitrust risk; they increase total demand; they lead to more differentiation; they share the cost of market development and legitimatize a new technology; they improve bargaining power vis-à-vis labor unions or regulators; and they may serve less attractive segments.

Balancing Customer and Competitor Orientations

We have stressed the importance of a company's watching its competitors closely. Is it possible to spend too much time and energy tracking competitors? The answer is yes! A company can become so competitor-centered that it loses its customer focus.[12]

A *competitor-centered company* is one whose moves are basically dictated by competitors' actions and reactions. The company tracks competitors' moves and market shares on a market-by-market basis. It sets its course as follows:

COMPETITOR-CENTERED COMPANY

Situation

- ◆ Competitor W is going all out to crush us in Miami.
- ◆ Competitor X is improving its distribution coverage in Houston and hurting our sales.
- ◆ Competitor Y has cut its price in Denver, and we lost three share points.
- ◆ Competitor Z has introduced a new service feature in New Orleans, and we are losing sales.

Reactions

◆ We will withdraw from the Miami market because we cannot afford to fight this battle.

◆ We will increase our advertising expenditure level in Houston.

◆ We will meet competitor Y's price cut in Denver.

◆ We will increase our sales-promotion budget in New Orleans.

Now this mode of strategy planning has some pluses and minuses. On the positive side, the company develops a fighter orientation. It trains its marketers to be on a constant alert, watching for weaknesses in its own position, and watching for competitors' weaknesses. On the negative side, the company exhibits too much of a reactive pattern. Rather than formulating and executing a consistent customer-oriented strategy, it determines its moves based on its competitors' moves. It does not move toward its own goal. It does not know where it will end up, since so much depends on what the competitors do.

A *customer-centered company* would focus more on customer developments in formulating its strategies. It would pay attention to the following developments:

CUSTOMER-CENTERED COMPANY

Situation

◆ The total market is growing at 4% annually.

◆ The quality-sensitive segment is growing at 8% annually.

◆ The deal-prone customer segment is also growing fast, but these customers do not stay with any supplier very long.

◆ A growing number of customers have expressed an interest in a 24-hour hotline, which no one in the industry offers.

Reactions

◆ We will focus more effort on reaching and satisfying the quality segment of the market; we will buy better components, improve quality control, and shift our advertising theme to quality.

◆ We will avoid cutting prices and making deals because we do not want the kind of customer that buys this way.

◆ We will install a 24-hour hotline if it looks promising.

Clearly, the customer-centered company is in a better position to identify new opportunities and set a strategy course that makes long-run sense. By monitoring customer needs, it can decide which customer groups and emerging needs are the most important to serve, given its resources and objectives.

In practice, today's companies must watch both customers and competitors. Figure 9-6 shows that companies have moved through four orientations over the years. In the first stage, companies paid little attention to either customers or competitors (*product oriented*). In the second stage, they started to pay attention to customers (*customer oriented*). In the third stage, they started to pay attention to competitors (*competitor oriented*). In today's stage, they need to pay balanced attention to both (*market oriented*).

FIGURE 9-6
Shifting Company
Orientations

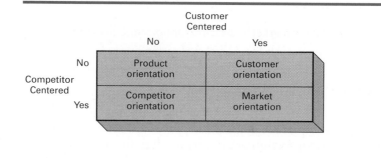

SUMMARY ❖

To prepare an effective marketing strategy, a company must study its competitors as well as its actual and potential customers. That is especially necessary in slow-growth markets because sales can be gained only by winning them away from competitors.

A company's closest competitors are those seeking to satisfy the same customers and needs and making similar offers. A company should also pay attention to its latent competitors, who may offer new or other ways to satisfy the same needs. The company should identify its competitors by using both an industry and a market-based analysis.

A company needs to gather information on competitors' strategies, objectives, strengths/weaknesses, and reaction patterns. The company needs to know each competitor's strategies in order to identify its closest competitors and take the proper steps. The company should know the competitor's objectives in order to anticipate further moves and reactions. Knowing the competitor's strengths and weaknesses permits the company to refine its strategy to take advantage of the competitor's limitations while avoiding engagements where the competitor is strong. Knowing the competitor's typical reaction pattern helps the company choose and time its moves.

Competitive intelligence needs to be collected, interpreted, and disseminated continuously. Company marketing executives should be able to obtain full and reliable information about any competitor that has a bearing on a decision.

As important as a competitive orientation is in today's markets, companies should not overdo their focus on competitors. Companies are more likely to be hurt by changing customer needs and latent competitors than by their existing competitors. Companies that manage a good balance of consumer and competitor considerations are practicing a true market orientation.

NOTES ❖

1. See Al Ries and Jack Trout, *Marketing Warfare* (New York: McGraw-Hill, 1986); William L. Sammon, Mark A. Kurland, and Robert Spitalnic, *Business Competitor Intelligence* (New York: Ronald Press, 1984); and Leonard M. Fuld, *Monitoring the Competition* (New York: John Wiley, 1988).

2. See Hans Katayama, "Fated to Feud: Sony versus Matsushita," *Business Tokyo*, November 1991, pp. 28–32.

3. See Kathryn Rudie Harrigan, "The Effect of Exit Barriers upon Strategic Flexibility," *Strategic Management Journal* 1 (1980), pp. 165–76.

4. See Michael E. Porter, *Competitive Advantage* (New York: Free Press, 1985), pp. 225, 485.

5. See Michael E. Porter, *Competitive Strategy* (New York: Free Press, 1980), Chap. 13.

6. Porter, *Competitive Strategy*, Chap. 7.

7. "The Hardest Sell," *Newsweek*, March 30, 1992, p. 41.

8. William E. Rothschild, *How to Gain (and Maintain) the Competitive Advantage* (New York: McGraw-Hill, 1984), Chap. 5.

9. The following has been drawn from various Bruce Henderson writings, including "The Unanswered Questions, The Unsolved Problems" (paper delivered in a speech at Northwestern University in 1986); *Henderson on Corporate Strategy* (New York: Mentor, 1982); and "Understanding the Forces of Strategic and Natural Competition," *Journal of Business Strategy*, Winter 1981, pp. 11–15.

10. Porter, *Competitive Advantage*, pp. 226–27.

11. Ibid., Chap. 6.

12. See Alfred R. Oxenfeldt and William L. Moore, "Customer or Competitor: Which Guidelines for Marketing?" *Management Review*, August 1978, pp. 43–48.

10

Measuring and Forecasting Market Demand

Forecasting is difficult, especially about the future.

VICTOR BORGE

Forecasting is like trying to drive a car blindfolded and following directions given by a person who is looking out of the back window.

ANONYMOUS

Having examined the tools for analyzing customer markets and competitive forces, we are now ready to consider how the company can choose *attractive markets* and develop *winning strategies* in these markets. Companies face many market opportunities and must carefully evaluate them before choosing their target markets. They need skill in measuring and forecasting the size, growth, and profit potential of competing market opportunities.

Once in a market, the company needs to prepare accurate sales forecasts. These forecasts are used by finance to raise the needed cash for investment and operations; by the manufacturing department to establish capacity and output levels; by purchasing to acquire the right amount of supplies; and by personnel to hire the needed number of workers. Marketing is responsible for making these estimates. If their forecast is far off the mark, the company either will be saddled with excess capacity and inventory or will have lost money because it was out of stock.

This chapter will address three broad questions: *What are the main concepts in demand measurement and forecasting? How can current demand be estimated? How can future demand be forecasted?*

Major Concepts in Demand Measurement

Managers need to define carefully what they mean by market demand. We will present several distinctions that will help managers talk more precisely about market demand.

A Multitude of Measures of Market Demand

As part of their ongoing planning, companies prepare a great number of market-size estimates. Figure 10-1 shows 90 different types of demand estimates that a company can make. Demand can be measured for six different *product levels*, five different *space levels*, and three different *time levels*.

Each demand measure serves a specific purpose. A company might forecast short-run demand for a particular product item for the purpose of ordering raw materials, planning production, and borrowing cash. It might forecast regional demand for its major product line to decide whether to set up regional distribution.

Which Market to Measure?

Marketers talk about *potential markets, available markets, served markets,* and *penetrated markets*. To clarify these terms, let us start with the notion that a *market* is *the set of all actual and potential buyers of a product*. The *size* of a market then hinges on the number of buyers who might exist for a particular market offer. Potential buyers would have three characteristics: *interest, income,* and *access*.

Consider the consumer market for motorcycles. We would first estimate the number of consumers who have a potential *interest* in owning a motorcycle. We would pose the following questions to a sample of consumers: "Would you have an interest in buying and owning a motorcycle?" If one person out of every ten says

FIGURE 10-1
90 Types of Demand
Measurement ($6 \times 5 \times 3$)

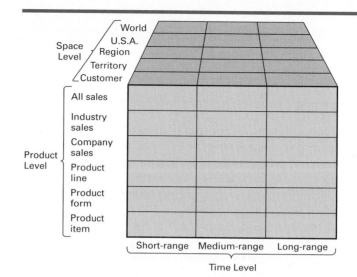

yes, we can assume that 10% of the total number of consumers would constitute the potential market for motorcycles. The *potential market* is the set of consumers who profess a sufficient level of interest in a defined market offer.

Consumer interest is not enough to define a market. Potential consumers must have enough *income* to afford the product. They must be able to answer the following question positively: "Can you afford to purchase a motorcycle?" The higher the price, the fewer the number of people who can answer this question positively. The size of a market is a function of both interest and income.

Access barriers further reduce market size. If motorcycles are not distributed in certain areas, potential consumers in those areas are not available to marketers. The *available market* is the set of consumers who have interest, income, and access to a particular market offer.

For some market offers, the company or government may restrict sales to certain groups. A particular state might ban motorcycle sales to anyone under 21 years of age. The remaining adults constitute the *qualified available market*—the set of consumers who have interest, income, access, and qualifications for the particular market offer.

The company now has the choice of going after the whole qualified available market or concentrating on certain segments. The *served market* (also called the *target market*) is the part of the qualified available market the company decides to pursue. The company, for example, might decide to concentrate its marketing and distribution effort on the East Coast. The East Coast becomes its served market.

The company and its competitors will end up selling a certain number of motorcycles in its served market. The *penetrated market* is the set of consumers who have already bought the product.

Figure 10-2 brings the preceding concepts together with some hypothetical numbers. The bar on the left illustrates the ratio of the potential market—all interested persons—to the total population, here 10%. The bar on the right illustrates several breakdowns of the potential market. The available market—those who have interest, income, and access—is 40% of the potential market. The qualified available market—those who can meet the legal requirements—is 20% of the potential market (or 50% of the available market). The company is concentrating its efforts on 10% of the potential market (or 50% of the qualified available market). Finally, the company and its competitors have already penetrated 5% of the potential market (or 50% of the served market).

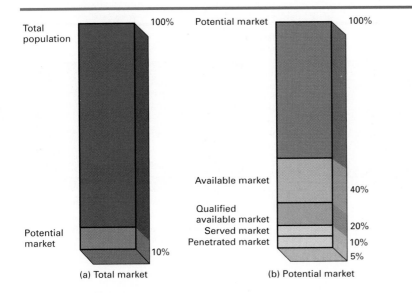

FIGURE 10-2
Levels of Market Definition

These market definitions are a useful tool for market planning. If the company is not satisfied with its current sales, it can take a number of actions. It can try to attract a larger percentage of buyers from its served market. It can lower the qualifications of potential buyers. It can expand its available market by opening distribution on the West Coast or lowering its price. Ultimately, the company can try to expand the potential market by advertising motorcycles to uninterested consumers, as Honda did when it ran its successful campaign, "You meet the nicest people on a Honda."

A Vocabulary for Demand Measurement

Company managers talk of forecasts, estimates, projections, sales goals, and quotas. Many of these terms are redundant. The major concepts in demand measurement are *market demand* and *company demand*. Within each, we distinguish between a *demand function*, a *forecast*, and a *potential*.

MARKET DEMAND ❖ In evaluating marketing opportunities, the first step is to estimate total market demand. It is not a simple concept, however, as the following definition makes clear:

❖ Market demand *for a product is the* total volume *that would be* bought *by a defined* customer group *in a defined* geographical area *in a defined* time period *in a defined* marketing environment *under a defined* marketing program.

We can see that total market demand is not a fixed number but a function of stated conditions. For this reason, it can be called the *market demand function*. The dependence of total market demand on underlying conditions is illustrated in Figure 10-3(a). The horizontal axis shows different possible levels of industry marketing expenditure in a given time period. The vertical axis shows the resulting demand level. The curve represents the estimated market demand associated with varying levels of industry marketing expenditure. Some base sales (called the *market minimum*) would take place without any demand-stimulating expenditures. Higher levels of industry marketing expenditures would yield higher levels of demand, first at an increasing rate, then at a decreasing rate. Marketing expenditures

FIGURE 10-3   Market Demand

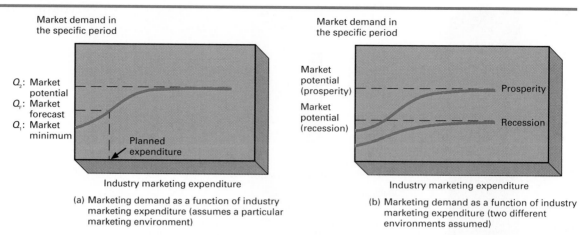

(a) Marketing demand as a function of industry
marketing expenditure (assumes a particular
marketing environment)

(b) Marketing demand as a function of industry
marketing expenditure (two different
environments assumed)

beyond a certain level would not stimulate much further demand, thus suggesting an upper limit to market demand called the *market potential*.

The distance between the market minimum and the market potential shows the overall *marketing sensitivity of demand*. We can think of two extreme types of markets, the *expansible* and the *nonexpansible*. An expansible market, such as the market for racquetball playing, is quite affected in its total size by the level of industry marketing expenditures. In terms of Figure 10-3(a), the distance between Q_1 and Q_2 is relatively large. A nonexpansible market, for example, the market for opera, is not much affected by the level of marketing expenditures; the distance between Q_1 and Q_2 is relatively small. Organizations selling in a nonexpansible market can accept the market's size (the level of *primary demand*) and direct their marketing resources to winning a desired market share (the level of *selective demand*).

It is important to emphasize that the *market demand function* is *not* a picture of market demand over *time*. Rather, the curve shows alternative current forecasts of market demand associated with alternative possible levels of industry marketing effort in the current period.

MARKET FORECAST ❖ Only one level of industry marketing expenditure will actually occur. The market demand corresponding to this level is called the *market forecast*.

MARKET POTENTIAL ❖ The market forecast shows expected market demand, not maximum market demand. For the latter, we have to visualize the level of market demand for a very "high" level of industry marketing expenditure, where further increases in marketing effort would have little effect in stimulating further demand. *Market potential is the limit approached by market demand as industry marketing expenditures approach infinity, for a given environment.*

The phrase "for a given environment" is crucial in the concept of market potential. Consider the market potential for automobiles in a period of recession versus a period of prosperity. The market potential is higher during prosperity. In other words, market demand is income elastic. The dependence of market potential on the environment is illustrated in Figure 10-3(b). The market analyst distinguishes between the position of the market demand function and movement along it. Companies cannot do anything about the position of the market demand function; that is determined by the marketing environment. However, companies influence their particular location on the function when they decide how much to spend on marketing.

COMPANY DEMAND ❖ We are now ready to define company demand. *Company demand* is the company's *share of market demand*. In symbols:

$$Q_i = s_i Q \qquad\qquad (10\text{-}1)$$

where:

$$Q_i = \text{company } i\text{'s demand}$$
$$s_i = \text{company } i\text{'s market share}$$
$$Q = \text{total market demand}$$

The company's share of market demand depends on how its products, services, prices, communications, and so on are perceived relative to the competitors. If other things are equal, the company's market share would depend on the size and effectiveness of its market expenditures relative to competitors. Marketing model builders have developed and measured *sales-response functions* to show how a company's sales are affected by its marketing expenditure level, marketing mix, and marketing effectiveness.[1]

COMPANY FORECAST ❖ Company demand describes estimated company sales at alternative levels of company marketing effort. It remains for management to choose one of the levels. The chosen level of marketing effort will produce an expected level of sales, called the company sales forecast.

❖ *The* company sales forecast *is the expected level of company sales based on a chosen marketing plan and an assumed marketing environment.*

The company sales forecast is represented graphically in the same way as the market forecast was in Figure 10-3(a): substitute company sales for the vertical axis and company marketing effort for the horizontal axis.

Too often the sequential relationship between the company forecast and the company marketing plan is confused. One frequently hears that the company should develop its marketing plan on the basis of its sales forecast. The forecast-to-plan sequence is valid if *forecast* means an estimate of national economic activity or if company demand is nonexpansible. The sequence is not valid, however, where market demand is expansible, or where *forecast* means an estimate of company sales. The company sales forecast does not establish a basis for deciding what to spend on marketing; quite the contrary, the sales forecast is the *result* of an assumed marketing expenditure plan.

Two other concepts are worth mentioning in relation to the company forecast.

❖ *A* sales quota *is the sales goal set for a product line, company division, or sales representative. It is primarily a managerial device for defining and stimulating sales effort.*

Management sets sales quotas on the basis of the company forecast and the psychology of stimulating its achievement. Generally, sales quotas are set slightly higher than estimated sales to stretch the salesforce's effort.

The other concept is a *sales budget*.

❖ *A* sales budget *is a conservative estimate of the expected volume of sales and is used primarily for making current purchasing, production, and cash-flow decisions.*

The sales budget considers the sales forecast and the need to avoid excessive risk. Sales budgets are generally set slightly lower than the sales forecast.

COMPANY POTENTIAL ❖ Company sales potential is *the limit approached by company demand as company marketing effort increases relative to competitors*. The absolute limit of company demand is, of course, the market potential. The two would be equal if the company achieved 100% of the market. In most cases, company sales potential is less than market potential, even when company marketing expenditures increase considerably relative to competitors. The reason is that each competitor has a hard core of loyal buyers who are not very responsive to other companies' efforts to woo them away.

Estimating Current Demand

We are now ready to examine practical methods for estimating current market demand. Marketing executives will want to estimate *total market potential, area market potential*, and *total industry sales and market shares*.

Total Market Potential

Total market potential is the maximum amount of sales that might be available to all the firms in an industry during a given period under a given level of industry marketing effort and given environmental conditions. A common way to estimate it is as follows:

$$Q = nqp \qquad\qquad (10\text{-}2)$$

where:

Q = total market potential
n = number of buyers in the specific product/market under the given assumptions
q = quantity purchased by an average buyer
p = price of an average unit

Thus if 100 million people buy books each year, and the average book buyer buys three books a year, and the average price is $10, then the total market potential for books is $3 billion ($= 100{,}000{,}000 \times 3 \times \$10$). The most difficult component to estimate in (10-2) is n, the number of buyers in the specific product/market. One can always start with the total population in the nation, say 250 million people. This can be called the *suspect pool*. The next step is to eliminate groups that obviously would not buy the product. Let us assume that illiterate people, children under twelve, and persons with poor eyesight do not buy books, and they constitute 20% of the population. Then only 80% of the population, or 200 million people, would be in the *prospect pool*. We might do further research and find that persons of low income and low education do not read books, and they constitute over 30% of the prospect pool. Eliminating them, we arrive at a *hot prospect pool* of approximately 140,000,000 book buyers. We would use this number of potential buyers in formula (10-2) for calculating total market potential.

A variation on formula (10-2) is known as the *chain-ratio method*. This method involves multiplying a base number by several adjusting percentages. Suppose a brewery is interested in estimating the market potential for a new light beer. An estimate can be made by the following calculation:[2]

$$\left.\begin{array}{l} \textit{Demand} \\ \textit{for the} \\ \textit{new} \\ \textit{light} \\ \textit{beer} \end{array}\right\} \text{-----} \left\{\begin{array}{l} \text{Population} \times \text{personal discretionary income per} \\ \text{capita} \times \text{average percentage of discretionary} \\ \text{income spent on food} \times \text{average percentage} \\ \text{of amount spent on food that is spent on} \\ \text{beverages} \times \text{average percentage of amount} \\ \text{spent on beverages that is spent on} \\ \text{alcoholic beverages} \times \text{average percentage of} \\ \text{amount spent on alcoholic beverages that is} \\ \text{spent on beer} \times \text{expected percentage of amount} \\ \text{spent on beer that will be spent on light beer.} \end{array}\right.$$

Area Market Potential

Companies face the problem of selecting the best territories and allocating their marketing budget optimally among these territories. Therefore they need to estimate the market potential of different cities, states, and nations (see Global Marketing 10-1). Two major methods are available: the *market-buildup method*, which is used primarily by business marketers, and the *multiple-factor index method*, which is used primarily by consumer marketers.

MARKET-BUILDUP METHOD ❖ The market-buildup method calls for identifying all the potential buyers in each market and estimating their potential purchases. It is straightforward if we have a list of all potential buyers *and* a good estimate of what each will buy. Unfortunately, one or both are usually lacking.

Consider a machine-tool company that wants to estimate the area market potential for its wood lathe in the Boston area.

The first step is to identify all potential buyers of wood lathes in the Boston area. The buyers consist primarily of manufacturing establishments that have to shape or ream wood as part of their operation.

The company could compile a list from a directory of all manufacturing establishments in the Boston area. Then it might estimate the number of lathes each industry might purchase based on the number of lathes per thousand employees or per $1 million of sales in that industry.

An efficient method of estimating area market potentials makes use of the Standard Industrial Classification System (SIC) developed by the U.S. Bureau of the Census. The SIC classifies all manufacturing into 20 major industry groups, each having a two-digit code. Thus number 25 is furniture and fixtures, and number 35 is machinery except electrical. Each major industry group is further subdivided into about 150 industry groups designated by a three-digit code (number 251 is household furniture, and number 252 is office furniture). Each industry is further subdivided into approximately 450 product categories designated by a four-digit code (number 2521 is wood office furniture, and number 2522 is metal office furniture). For each four-digit SIC number, the Census of Manufacturers provides the number of establishments subclassified by location, number of employees, annual sales, and net worth.

To use the SIC, the lathe manufacturer must first determine the four-digit SIC codes that represent products whose manufacturers are likely to require lathe machines. For example, lathes will be used by manufacturers in SIC number 2511 (wood household furniture), number 2521 (wood office furniture), and so on. To get a full picture of all four-digit SIC industries that might use lathes, the company can use three methods. It can determine the SIC codes of past customers. It can go through the SIC manual and check off all the four-digit industries that, in its judgment, would have an interest in lathes. It can mail questionnaires to a wide range of companies inquiring about their interest in wood lathes.

Global Marketing 10-1

Kentucky Fried Chicken Finds More Potential in Asia than in the United States

Kentucky Fried Chicken's success in Asia dramatizes the case for becoming a global firm. Had PepsiCo's KFC Corporation remained a domestic U.S. business, its fortunes would have continued to slide. In 1991, its U.S. sales fell 5% as other fast-food competitors moved up and Americans continued to reduce their intake of "fried" food with its heart-disease implications.

Not so in Asia. KFC, not McDonald's, is the fast-food leader in China, South Korea, Malaysia, Thailand, and Indonesia, and is second to McDonald's in Japan and Singapore. Its 1,470 outlets average $1.2 million per store, about 60% more than its average U.S. store. In Tiananmen Square, KFC operates its busiest outlet, a 701-seat restaurant serving 2.5 million customers a year. No wonder KFC plans to double its number of Asian outlets in the next five years.

Why is KFC so successful in Asia? First, many of the large Asian cities have a growing concentration of young middle-class urban workers with rising incomes. Fast-food outlets represent a step up from buying food at hawker's stalls, and Asians are willing to pay more for the quality and comfort of sitting in a well-decored American-style restaurant. Second, women have been entering the labor force in large numbers, leaving less time for cooking meals at home. Third, chicken is more familiar to the Asian palate than pizza, and more available than beef. Nor does chicken face the religious strictures that beef faces in India or pork faces in Muslim countries.

KFC basically serves its standard chicken, mashed potatoes, and cole slaw throughout Asia but has offered a few adaptations, such as Hot Wings, a spicier chicken in Thailand, and chicken curry in Japan.

Clearly, companies must increasingly view the world as their market, and identify those areas that promise the greatest potential sales and profit growth.

SOURCE: See Andrew Tanzer, "Hot Wings Take Off," *Forbes,* January 18, 1993, p. 74.

The company's next task is to determine an appropriate base for estimating the number of lathes that will be used in each industry. Suppose customer industry sales are the most appropriate base. For example, in SIC number 2511, ten lathes may be used for every $1 million worth of sales. Once the company estimates the rate of lathe ownership relative to the customer industry's sales, it can compute the market potential.

Table 10-1 shows a hypothetical computation for the Boston area involving two SIC codes. In number 2511 (wood household furniture), there are six establishments with annual sales of $1 million and two establishments with annual sales of $5 million. It is estimated that ten lathes can be sold in this SIC code for every $1 million in customer sales. Since there are six establishments with annual sales of $1 million, they account for $6 million in sales, which is a potential of 60 lathes (6 × 10). The other figures in the table are similarly computed. Altogether, it appears that the Boston area has a market potential for 200 lathes.

The company can use the same method to estimate the market potential for other areas in the country. Suppose the market potentials for all the markets add up to 2,000 lathes. Then the Boston market contains 10% of the total market potential. This might warrant the company's allocating 10% of its marketing expenditures to the Boston market. In practice, the lathe manufacturer needs additional information about each market, such as the extent of market saturation, the number of competitors, the market growth rate, and the average age of existing equipment.

If the company decides to sell lathes in Boston, it must know how to identify the best-prospect companies. In the old days, sales reps called on companies door to door; this was called *bird-dogging* or *smokestacking*. "Cold calls" are far too costly

TABLE 10-1
Market-Buildup Method
Using SIC Codes
(Hypothetical Lathe
Manufacturer—
Boston Area)

SIC	ANNUAL SALES IN MILLIONS $ (1)	NUMBER OF ESTABLISH-MENTS (2)	POTENTIAL NUMBER OF LATHE SALES PER $1 MILLION CUSTOMER SALES (3)	MARKET POTENTIAL $(1 \times 2 \times 3)$
2511	$1	6	10	60
	5	2	10	100
2521	1	3	5	15
	5	1	5	25
				200

today. The company should get a list of Boston companies and qualify them by direct mail or telemarketing to identify the best prospects. The lathe manufacturer can access *Dun's Market Identifiers*, which lists 27 key facts for over 9,300,000 business locations in the United States and Canada.

MULTIPLE-FACTOR INDEX METHOD ❖ Consumer companies also have to estimate area market potentials. Because their customers are so numerous, they cannot list them. The method most commonly used is a straightforward *index method*. A drug manufacturer, for example, might assume that the market potential for drugs is directly related to population size. If the state of Virginia has 2.28% of the U.S. population, the company might assume that Virginia will be a market for 2.28% of total drugs sold.

A single factor, however, is rarely a complete indicator of sales opportunity. Regional drug sales are also influenced by per capita income and the number of physicians per 10,000 people. This makes it desirable to develop a multiple-factor index with each factor assigned a specific weight.

One of the best-known multiple-factor indices of area demand is the "Annual Survey of Buying Power" published by *Sales and Marketing Management*.[3] The index reflects the relative consumer buying power in the different regions, states, and metropolitan areas. *Sales and Marketing Management*'s index of the relative buying power of an area is given by:

$$B_i = 0.5y_i + 0.3r_i + 0.2p_i$$

where:

B_i = percentage of total national buying power found in area i
y_i = percentage of national disposable personal income originating in area i
r_i = percentage of national retail sales in area i
p_i = percentage of national population located in area i

For example, suppose Virginia has 2.00% of the U.S. disposable personal income, 1.96% of U.S. retail sales, and 2.28% of U.S. population. The buying-power index for Virginia would be

$$0.5(2.00) + 0.3(1.96) + 0.2(2.28) = 2.04$$

Thus 2.04% of the nation's drug sales might be expected to take place in Virginia.

The manufacturer recognizes that the weights used in the buying-power index are somewhat arbitrary. They apply mainly to consumer goods that are neither low-priced staples nor high-priced luxury goods. Other weights can be assigned if more appropriate. Furthermore, the manufacturer would want to adjust the market potential for additional factors, such as competitors' presence in that market, local promotional costs, seasonal factors, and local market idiosyncrasies.

Many companies will compute additional area indices as a guide to allocating marketing resources. Suppose the company is reviewing the six cities listed in Table 10-2. The first two columns show the percentage of U.S. brand and category sales, respectively, in these six cities. Column 3 shows the *brand development index (BDI)*, which is the index of brand sales to category sales. Seattle, for example, has a BDI of 114 because the brand is relatively more developed than the category in Seattle. On the other hand, Portland has a BDI of 65, which means that the brand in Portland is relatively underdeveloped. Normally, the lower the BDI, the higher the *market opportunity*, in that there is room to grow the brand. Other marketers would argue the opposite, that marketing funds should go into the brand's strongest markets where it might be easy to capture more brand share. Clearly other factors have to be considered.[4]

After the company decides on the city-by-city allocation of its budget, it can refine each city allocation down to *census tracts* or *ZIP-code centers*. Census tracts are small areas about the size of a neighborhood, and ZIP-code centers (which were designed by the U.S. Post Office Department) are larger areas, often the size of small towns. Information on population size, median family income, and other characteristics is available for these geographical units. Marketers have found these data extremely useful for identifying high-potential retail areas within large cities or for buying mailing lists to use in direct-mail campaigns. Marketing Concepts and Tools 10-1 describes how U.S. Census data are now incorporated into geodemographic coding systems for improved customer identification and targeting.

Estimating Industry Sales and Market Shares

Besides estimating total potential and area potential, a company needs to know the actual industry sales taking place in its market. This means identifying its competitors and estimating their sales.

The industry's trade association will often collect and publish total industry sales, although not listing individual company sales separately. In this way, each company can evaluate its performance against the whole industry. Suppose a company's sales are increasing 5% a year, and industry sales are increasing 10%. This company is actually losing its relative standing in the industry.

Another way to estimate sales is to buy reports from a marketing research firm that audits total sales and brand sales. For example, A. C. Nielsen Company audits retail sales in various product categories in supermarkets and drug stores and sells this information to interested companies. In this way, a company learns total product-category sales as well as brand sales. It can compare its performance

TABLE 10-2
Calculating the Brand Development Index (BDI)

TERRITORY	PERCENT OF U.S. BRAND SALES (1)	PERCENT OF U.S. CATEGORY SALES (2)	BDI $(1 \div 2) \times 100$
Seattle	3.09	2.71	114
Portland	6.74	10.41	65
Boston	3.49	3.85	91
Toledo	.97	.81	120
Chicago	1.13	.81	140
Baltimore	3.12	3.00	104

Geodemographic Analysis: A New Tool for Identifying Micromarket Targets

In recent years, several new business information services that link U.S. census data with lifestyle patterns have arisen. These help market planners to better refine their estimates of market potential down to the ZIP-code level. The underlying assumption is, "Tell me where a person lives and I will tell you what the person is like." Among the leading services are PRIZM (by Claritas), ClusterPlus (by Donnelley Marketing Information Services), and Acorn (C.A.C.I., Inc.). These data services can help marketing planners find the best ZIP-code areas in which to concentrate their marketing efforts. We shall look at the PRIZM system to show how geodemographic analysis works.

The PRIZM designers have picturesquely classified the over 500,000 U.S. neighborhoods into forty clusters, such as "blue-blood estates," "money and brains," "furs and station wagons," "shotguns and pick-ups," "tobacco roads," and "grey power." The clusters were formed by manipulating eight household characteristics. For example, "blue-blood estates" neighborhoods are suburban areas populated mostly by active, college-educated, successful managers and professionals. They include some of America's wealthiest neighborhoods, areas characterized by low household density, highly homogeneous residents, a heavy family orientation, and mostly single-unit housing. On the other hand, the cluster "single-city blues" is characterized by a high household density, city location, mixed population, white with minorities, many singles and couples, some college, white/blue-collar mix, and multiunit housing. Each of the other 38 clusters has a unique combination of characteristics.

To illustrate how geodemographic analysis works, we can draw from a recent publication of the Seventh Day Adventists, who are seeking to identify the best ZIP-code areas for attracting new members to their religious denomination. Their working hypothesis is that they would have the best chance attracting new members in ZIP-code areas that resemble the ones that now contain the most current members. Using the members' home addresses, the researchers coded all current Seventh Day Adventists into the 40 ZIP-code clusters. The researchers found that the "Hispanic-mix" cluster had the highest *index of concentration* of Seventh Day Adventists. Specifically, while the "Hispanic-mix" cluster accounted for only 3.39% of the U.S. population, it accounted for 12.70% of all Seventh Day Adventists. By dividing the latter number by the former and multiplying by 100, they found that the "Hispanic-mix" cluster had an index of concentration of 375. This suggests that Hispanic-mix ZIP-code areas have a high potential for further members and warrant focused marketing, including the opening in these areas of new Seventh Day Adventist churches, door-to-door recruitment, and direct-mail campaigns. On the other hand, the cluster with the lowest potential for Seventh Day Adventist recruitment was "nonmobile married couples, old homes, farm areas," whose index of concentration was only 16. Using this methodology, all 40 clusters could be ranked, and those whose index of concentration exceeded 100 would point to the most attractive ZIP-code areas for recruitment.

The cluster types are also linked with other data banks showing product, brand, and media preferences. For example, the "Hispanic-mix" cluster contains above average purchasers of chili, children's vitamins, baby shampoo, and bus travel. They are heavy users of television (especially boxing matches) but light readers of magazines. This information can help the religious marketers choose the types of events and communications that will best help attract each cluster that ranks high on Seventh Day Adventist concentration.

We have deliberately illustrated geodemographic analysis in an unusual application: religious recruitment. More normally, this analysis is used by manufacturers, retailers, and others to identify the best clusters and areas to target for their particular product or service. For example, Helene Curtis used PRIZM in marketing its Suave shampoo. It found that potential demand is highest in neighborhoods with high concentrations of young working women. These women responded best to advertising messages that Suave is inexpensive, yet will make their hair "look like a million."

SOURCES: See Michael J. Weiss, *The Clustering of America* (New York: Harper & Row, 1988); and "Marketing Firm Slices U.S. into 240,000 Parts to Spur Clients' Sales," *The Wall Street Journal*, November 3, 1986, p. 1. The illustration was taken from "The North American Division Marketing Program, Vol. 1: Profiling Adventist Members and Baptisms," published in mimeograph form, 1986.

to the total industry and/or any particular competitor to see whether it is gaining or losing share.

Business-goods marketers typically have a harder time estimating industry sales and market shares. They have no Nielsens to rely on. Distributors typically will not supply information about how much of competitors' products they are selling. Business-goods marketers therefore operate with less knowledge of their market-share results. Some business-goods marketers simply want to know their share relative to their leading competitor rather than relative to the whole market. They can then concentrate on estimating only their leading competitor's sales and comparing results.

Estimating Future Demand

We are now ready to examine methods of estimating future demand. Very few products or services lend themselves to easy forecasting. Cases of easy forecasting generally involve a product whose absolute level or trend is fairly constant and where competition is nonexistent (public utilities) or stable (pure oligopolies). In most markets, total demand and company demand are not stable, and good forecasting becomes a key factor in company success. Poor forecasting can lead to overly large inventories, costly price markdowns, or lost sales due to out-of-stock conditions. The more unstable the demand, the more critical is forecast accuracy, and the more elaborate is forecasting procedure.

Companies commonly use a three-stage procedure to prepare a sales forecast.

Marketing Concepts and Tools 10-2

Methods of Macroenvironmental Forecasting

The key to organizational survival and growth is the firm's ability to adapt its strategies to a rapidly changing environment. This puts a large burden on management to anticipate future events correctly. The damage can be enormous when a mistake is made. For example, Montgomery Ward lost its leadership in the department store field after World War II because its chairman, Sewell Avery, bet on a stagnant economy while its major competitor, Sears, bet on an expanding economy. That is why a growing number of companies carry out *macroenvironmental forecasting.*

How do firms develop macroenvironmental forecasts? Large firms have planning departments that develop long-run forecasts of key environmental factors affecting their markets. General Electric, for example, has a forecasting staff who study worldwide forces that affect its operations. GE makes its forecasts available to GE divisions and also sells certain forecasts to other firms.

Smaller firms can buy forecasts from several types of suppliers. *Marketing research firms* can develop a forecast by interviewing customers, distributors, and other knowledgeable parties. *Specialized forecasting firms* produce long-range forecasts of particular macroenvironmental components, such as the economy, the population, natural resources, or technology. Finally, there are *futurist research firms* that produce speculative scenarios. Among the latter are the Hudson Institute, the Futures Group, and the Institute for the Future.

Here are some methodologies for producing macroenvironmental forecasts:

EXPERT OPINION ❖ Knowledgeable people are selected and asked to assign importance and probability ratings to possible future developments. The most refined version, the Delphi method, puts experts through several rounds of event assessment, where they keep refining their assumptions and judgments.

TREND EXTRAPOLATION ❖ Researchers fit best-fitting curves (linear, quadratic, or S-shaped

They prepare a *macroeconomic forecast*, followed by an *industry forecast*, followed by a *company sales forecast*. The macroeconomic forecast calls for projecting inflation, unemployment, interest rates, consumer spending, business investment, government expenditures, net exports, and other magnitudes (see Marketing Concepts and Tools 10-2). The end result is a forecast of *gross national product*, which is then used, along with other environmental indicators, to forecast industry sales. Then the company derives its sales forecast by assuming that it will win a certain market share.

All forecasts are built on one of three information bases: *what people say, what people do,* or *what people have done*. The first basis—*what people say*—involves surveying the opinions of buyers or those close to them, such as salespeople or outside experts. It encompasses three methods: surveys of buyer's intentions, composites of salesforce opinions, and expert opinion. Building a forecast on *what people do* involves another method, that of putting the product into a test market to measure buyer response. The final basis—*what people have done*—involves analyzing records of past buying behavior or using time-series analysis or statistical demand analysis.

Survey of Buyers' Intentions

Forecasting is the art of anticipating what buyers are likely to do under a given set of conditions. This suggests that the buyers should be surveyed. Surveys are especially valuable if the buyers have clearly formulated intentions, will carry them out, and will describe them to interviewers.

In regard to *major consumer durables*, several research organizations conduct

growth curves) through past time series to use for extrapolation. This method can be very unreliable in that new developments can completely alter the future direction.

TREND CORRELATION ❖ Researchers correlate various time series in the hope of identifying leading and lagging indicators that can be used for forecasting. The National Bureau of Economic Research has identified twelve of the best leading economic indicators, and their values are published monthly in the *Survey of Current Business.*

ECONOMETRIC MODELING ❖ Researchers build sets of equations that describe the underlying system. The coefficients in the equations are fitted statistically. Econometric models containing more than 300 equations, for example, are used to forecast changes in the U.S. economy.

CROSS-IMPACT ANALYSIS ❖ Researchers identify a set of key trends (those high in importance and/or probability). The question is then put: "If event A occurs, what will be its impact on other trends?" The results are then used to build sets of "domino chains," with one event triggering others.

MULTIPLE SCENARIOS ❖ Researchers build pictures of alternative futures, each internally consistent and having a certain probability of occurring. The major purpose of the scenarios is to stimulate management to think about and plan for contingencies.

DEMAND/HAZARD FORECASTING ❖ Researchers identify major events that would greatly affect the firm. Each event is rated for its *convergence* with several major trends taking place in society. It is also rated for its *appeal* to each major public in the society. The higher the event's convergence and appeal, the higher its probability of occurring. The highest-scoring events are then researched further.

periodic surveys of consumer buying intentions. These organizations ask questions like the following:

Do you intend to buy an automobile within the next six months?					
0.00	0.20	0.40	0.60	0.80	1.00
No chance	Slight Possibility	Fair Possibility	Good Possibility	High Probability	Certain

This is called a *purchase probability scale*. In addition, the various surveys inquire into the consumer's present and future personal finances and their expectations about the economy. The various bits of information are combined into a *consumer sentiment measure* (Survey Research Center of the University of Michigan) or a *consumer confidence measure* (Sindlinger and Company). Consumer durable-goods producers subscribe to these indices in the hope of anticipating major shifts in consumer buying intentions so that they can adjust their production and marketing plans accordingly.

In the realm of *business buying*, various agencies carry out buyer intention surveys regarding plant, equipment, and materials. The better known are McGraw-Hill Research and Opinion Research Corporation. Their estimates tend to fall within a 10% error band of the actual outcomes.

Various industrial firms carry on their own surveys of customer buying intentions:

> *National Lead's marketing researchers would periodically visit a carefully selected sample of 100 companies. They would ask the customer's technical director about the rate of incorporation of titanium in the manufacturer's various products; the sales manager would be questioned about the sales outlook; and the purchasing director would be queried about the total amount of titanium his company plans to purchase. National's marketing researchers would estimate the market demand for titanium and prepare a "most favorable" forecast and a "least favorable" forecast. There are additional benefits in that National would learn about new developments; the visits promoted National's image; and the method yielded disaggregate estimates by territory and industry.*[5]

In summary, the value of a buyer intention survey increases to the extent that the buyers are few, the cost of reaching them is small, they have clear intentions, they implement their intentions, and they willingly disclose their intentions. Buyer-intention surveys are useful in estimating demand for industrial products, consumer durables, product purchases where advanced planning is required, and new products.

Composite of Salesforce Opinions

Where buyer interviewing is impractical, the company will ask its sales representatives for estimates. Each sales representative estimates how much each current and prospective customer will buy of each product made by the company. Few companies use their salesforce's estimates without making some adjustments. Sales representatives might be pessimistic or optimistic, or they might go from one extreme to another because of a recent sales setback or success. Furthermore, they are often unaware of larger economic developments and do not know how their company's marketing plans will influence future sales in their territory. They might deliberately underestimate demand so that the company will set a low sales quota or they might lack the time to prepare careful estimates or might not consider it worthwhile.

The company could supply certain aids or incentives to the salesforce to encourage better estimating. The sales representatives might receive a record of their past forecasts compared with their actual sales and also a description of company assumptions on the business outlook, competitor behavior, marketing plans, and so on.

A number of benefits can be gained by involving the salesforce in forecasting. Sales representatives might have better insight into developing trends than any other single group. Through participating in the forecasting process, the sales representatives might have greater confidence in their sales quotas and more incentive to achieve them.[6] Also, a "grassroots" forecasting procedure provides estimates broken down by product, territory, customer, and sales representatives.

Expert Opinion

Companies can also obtain forecasts from experts. Experts include dealers, distributors, suppliers, marketing consultants, and trade associations. Thus auto companies survey their dealers periodically for their forecasts of short-term demand. Dealer estimates, however, are subject to the same strengths and weaknesses as salesforce estimates.

Many companies buy economic and industry forecasts from well-known economic-forecasting firms, such as Data Resources, Wharton Econometric, and Chase Econometric. These forecasting specialists are able to prepare better economic forecasts than the company because they have more data available and more forecasting expertise.

Occasionally companies will invite a group of experts to prepare a forecast. The experts exchange views and produce a group estimate (*group-discussion methods*). Or they supply their estimates individually, and the analyst combines them in a single estimate (*pooling of individual estimates*). Or they supply individual estimates and assumptions that are reviewed by the company, revised, and followed by further rounds of estimating (*Delphi method*).[7]

Market-Test Method

Where buyers do not plan their purchases carefully or experts are not available or reliable, a direct market test is desirable. A direct market test is especially desirable in forecasting new-product sales or established product sales in a new distribution channel or territory. Market testing is discussed in Chapter 13.

Time-Series Analysis

Many firms prepare their forecasts on the basis of past sales. Past sales (Q) are analyzed into four major components.

The first component, *trend* (T), is the result of basic developments in population, capital formation, and technology. It is found by fitting a straight or curved line through past sales.

The second component, *cycle* (C), captures the wavelike movement of sales. Many sales are affected by swings in general economic activity, which tends to be somewhat periodic. The cyclical component can be useful in intermediate-range forecasting.

The third component, *season* (S), refers to a consistent pattern of sales movements within the year. The term *season* broadly describes any recurrent hourly, weekly, monthly, or quarterly sales pattern. The seasonal component may be related to weather factors, holidays, and trade customs. The seasonal pattern provides a norm for forecasting short-range sales.

The fourth component, *erratic events* (*E*), includes strikes, blizzards, fads, riots, fires, war scares, and other disturbances. These erratic components are unpredictable and should be removed from past data to discern the more normal behavior of sales.

After the past sales series, *Q*, is decomposed into the components, *T*, *C*, *S*, and *E*, these components are recombined to produce the sales forecast. Here is an example:

> An insurance company sold 12,000 new ordinary life-insurance policies this year. It would like to predict next year's December sales. The long-term trend shows a 5% sales growth rate per year. This suggests sales next year of 12,600 ($= 12,000 \times 1.05$). However, a business recession is expected next year and will probably result in total sales achieving only 90% of the expected trend-adjusted sales. Sales next year will more likely be 11,340 ($= 12,600 \times 0.90$). If sales were the same each month, monthly sales would be 945 ($= 11,340/12$). However, December is an above-average month for insurance-policy sales, with a seasonal index standing at 1.2. Therefore December sales may be as high as 1,134 ($= 0.945 \times 1.2$). No erratic events, such as strikes or new insurance regulations, are expected. Therefore the best estimate of the number of new policy sales next December is 1,134.

For a company that has hundreds of items in its product line and wants to produce efficient and economical short-run forecasts, a newer time-series technique called *exponential smoothing* is available. In its simplest form, exponential smoothing requires only three pieces of information: this period's actual sales, Q_t; this period's smoothed sales, $\bar{Q}_t$; and a smoothing parameter, α. The sales forecast for next period's sales is given by

$$\bar{Q}_{t+1} = \alpha Q_t + (1-\alpha)\bar{Q}_t$$

where:

$\bar{Q}_{t+1}$ = sales forecast for next period
α = the smoothing constant, where $0 \le \alpha \le 1$
Q_t = current sales in period t
$\bar{Q}_t$ = smoothed sales in period t

Suppose the smoothing constant is 0.4, current sales are $50,000, and smoothed sales are $40,000. Then the sales forecast is

$$\bar{Q}_{t+1} = 0.4(\$50,000) + 0.6(\$40,000) = \$44,000$$

In this method, the sales forecast will always be between current sales and smoothed sales. The relative influence of current and smoothed sales depends on the smoothing constant, here 0.4. Thus the sales forecast "tracks" actual sales. The method can be refined to reflect seasonal and trend factors by adding two more constants.[8]

Statistical-Demand Analysis

Time-series analysis treats past and future sales as a function of time rather than of any real demand factors. Yet numerous real factors affect the sales of any product. *Statistical-demand analysis* is a set of statistical procedures designed to discover the most important real factors affecting sales and their relative influence. The factors most commonly analyzed are price, income, population, and promotion.

Statistical-demand analysis consists of expressing sales (Q) as a dependent variable and trying to explain sales as a function of a number of independent demand variables ($X_1, X_2, \ldots, X_n$); that is,

$$Q = f(X_1, X_2, \ldots, X_n)$$

Using multiple-regression analysis, various equation forms can be statistically fitted to the data in search of the best predicting variables and equation.

For example, Palda found that the following demand equation gave a fairly good fit to the historical sales of Lydia Pinkham's Vegetable Compound between the years 1908 and 1960:[9]

$$Q = -3649 + 0.665X_1 + 1{,}180 \log X_2 + 774X_3 + 324X_4 - 2.83X_5 \qquad (10\text{-}5)$$

where:

Q = yearly sales in thousands of dollars
X_1 = yearly sales (lagged one year) in thousands of dollars
X_2 = yearly advertising expenditures in thousands of dollars
X_3 = a dummy variable, taking on the value of 1 between 1908 and 1925 and 0 from 1926 on
X_4 = year (1908 = 0, 1909 = 1, and so on)
X_5 = disposable personal income in billions of current dollars

The five independent variables on the right account for 94% of the yearly variation in the sale of Lydia Pinkham's Vegetable Compound between 1908 and 1960. To forecast a future year's sales, it would be necessary to insert estimates for the five independent variables.

Computers have rendered statistical-demand analysis an increasingly useful approach to forecasting. The user, however, should be wary of several problems that might diminish the validity or usefulness of a statistical-demand equation: too few observations, too much correlation among the independent variables, violation of normal curve assumptions, two-way causation, and emergence of new variables not accounted for.

SUMMARY ❖

To carry out their responsibilities, marketing managers need estimates of current and future demand. Quantitative measurements are essential for analyzing market opportunity, planning marketing programs, and controlling marketing effort. The firm usually prepares several types of demand estimates, varying in the level of product aggregation, the time dimension, and the space dimension.

A market consists of the set of actual and potential purchasers of a market offer. The size of the market depends on how many people have interest, income, and access to the market offer. Marketers must know how to distinguish between the potential market, available market, qualified available market, served market, and penetrated market.

Marketers must also distinguish between market demand and company demand, and within these, between potentials and forecasts. Market demand is a function, not a single number, and as such is highly dependent on the level of other variables.

A major task is estimating current demand. Total demand can be estimated through the chain-ratio method, which involves multiplying a base number by successive percentages. Area market demand can be estimated by the market-buildup method (for business markets) and the multiple-factor index method (for consumer markets). In the latter case, geodemographic coding systems are proving a boon to marketers. Estimating industry sales requires identifying the relevant competitors and estimating their individual sales. Finally, companies are interested in estimating their competitors' market shares to judge their relative performance.

For estimating future demand, the company can use several major forecasting methods: buyer's intention surveys, composites of salesforce opinion, expert opinion, market tests, time-series analysis, and statistical-demand analysis. These methods vary in their appropriateness with the purpose of the forecast, the type of product, and the availability and reliability of data.

NOTES ❖

1. For further discussion, see Gary L. Lilien, Philip Kotler, and K. Sridhar Moorthy, *Marketing Models* (Englewood Cliffs, NJ: Prentice-Hall, 1992).

2. See Russell L. Ackoff, *A Concept of Corporate Planning* (New York: Wiley-Interscience, 1970), pp. 36–37.

3. For a helpful exposition on using this survey and three other surveys published by *Sales and Marketing Management*, see "Putting the Four to Work," *Sales Management*, October 28, 1974, pp. 13ff.

4. For suggested strategies related to the market area's *BDI* standing, see Don E. Schultz, Dennis Martin, and William P. Brown, *Strategic Advertising Campaigns* (Chicago: Crain Books, 1984), p. 338.

5. Adapted from *Forecasting Sales*, business policy study no. 106 (New York: National Conference Board, 1963), pp. 31–32.

6. See Jacob Gonik, "Tie Salesmen's Bonuses to Their Forecasts," *Harvard Business Review*, May–June 1978, pp. 116–23.

7. See Norman Dalkey and Olaf Helmer, "An Experimental Application of the Delphi Method to the Use of Experts," *Management Science*, April 1963, pp. 458–67. Also see Roger J. Best, "An Experiment in Delphi Estimation in Marketing Decision Making," *Journal of Marketing Research*, November 1974, pp. 447–52.

8. See S. Makridakis and S. C. Wheelwright, *The Handbook of Forecasting* (New York: John Wiley, 1987).

9. Kristian S. Palda, *The Measurement of Cumulative Advertising Effects* (Englewood Cliffs, NJ: Prentice-Hall, 1964), pp. 67–68.

Identifying Market Segments and Selecting Target Markets

Small is beautiful. Less is more.

E. F. SCHUMACHER

Small opportunities are often the beginning of great enterprises.

DEMOSTHENES

A company that decides to operate in a broad market recognizes that it normally cannot serve all customers in that market. The customers are too numerous, dispersed, and varied in their buying requirements. Some competitors will be in a better position to serve particular customer segments of that market. The company, instead of competing everywhere, needs to identify the most attractive market segments that it can serve effectively.

The heart of modern *strategic marketing* can be described as *STP* marketing—*segmenting*, *targeting*, and *positioning*. This does not obviate the importance of *LGD* marketing—lunch, golf, and dinner—but rather provides the broader framework for strategic success in the marketplace.

Sellers have not always held this view of marketing strategy. Their thinking passed through three stages:

♦ *Mass Marketing:* Here the seller engages in the mass production, mass distribution, and mass promotion of one product for all buyers. This market strategy was epitomized by Henry Ford, who offered the Model T Ford to all buyers. They could have the car "in any color as long as it is black." The traditional argument for mass marketing is that it will lead to the lowest costs and prices and create the largest potential market.

♦ *Product-Variety Marketing:* Here the seller produces several products that exhibit different features, styles, qualities, sizes, and so on. They are designed to offer variety to buyers rather than to appeal to different market segments. General Motors practices this market strategy in that many of its cars go under different names—Pontiac, Buick, Oldsmobile—and exhibit only slight differences in features and style. The traditional argument for product-variety marketing is that customers have different tastes and their tastes change over time. Customers seek change and variety.

♦ *Target Marketing:* Here the seller distinguishes the major market segments, targets one or more of these segments, and develops products and marketing programs tailored to each selected segment. Hyundai, Mercedes, and Porsche have targeted clear automobile-customer segments. Ford, with its larger product line, nevertheless creates concept cars—such as the Mustang and Thunderbird—that are often targeted to specific types of customers. Target marketing is increasingly taking on the character of *micromarketing* where marketing programs are tailored to the needs and wants of customer groups on a *local* basis (trading area, neighborhood, even individual stores). Thus Ford may change the features on Mustangs destined for Miami versus Seattle versus Phoenix. The ultimate form of target marketing is *customized marketing*, where the product and marketing program is adapted to the needs and wants of a distinct consumer or buying organization.

Today's companies are finding it increasingly unrewarding to practice mass marketing or product-variety marketing. Mass markets are becoming "demassified." They are dissolving into hundreds of *micromarkets* characterized by different buyers pursuing different products in different distribution channels and attending to different communication channels.

Companies are increasingly embracing target marketing. Target marketing helps sellers identify marketing opportunities better. The sellers can develop the right offer for each target market. They can adjust their prices, distribution channels, and advertising to reach the target market efficiently. Instead of scattering

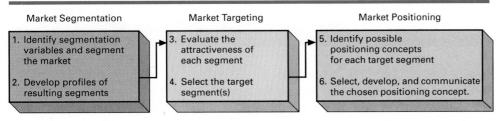

FIGURE 11-1
Steps in Market
Segmentation, Targeting,
and Positioning

their marketing effort ("shotgun" approach), they can focus on the buyers whom they have the greatest chance of satisfying ("rifle" approach).

Target marketing calls for three major steps (Figure 11-1). The first is *market segmentation*, the act of identifying and profiling distinct groups of buyers who might require separate products and/or marketing mixes. The second step is *market targeting*, the act of selecting one or more market segments to enter. The third step is *market positioning*, the act of establishing and communicating the products' key distinctive benefits in the market. This chapter will discuss market segmentation and targeting and the next chapter will discuss positioning.

Market Segmentation

Markets consist of buyers, and buyers differ in one or more respects. They may differ in their wants, purchasing power, geographical locations, buying attitudes, and buying practices. Any of these variables can be used to segment a market.

The General Approach to Segmenting a Market

Figure 11-2(a) shows a market of six buyers. Each buyer is potentially a separate market because of unique needs and wants. A seller might design a separate product and/or marketing program for each buyer. For example, Boeing manufactures

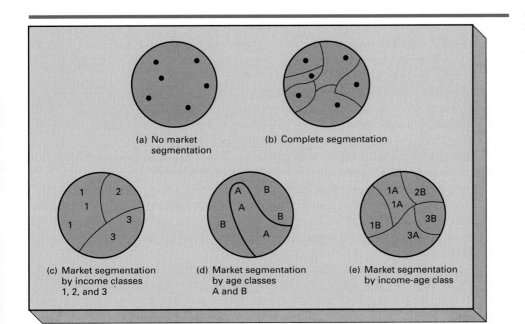

FIGURE 11-2
Different Segmentations of a
Market

(a) No market segmentation

(b) Complete segmentation

(c) Market segmentation by income classes 1, 2, and 3

(d) Market segmentation by age classes A and B

(e) Market segmentation by income-age class

Customized Marketing: It's Coming Back

In early markets, many sellers designed their goods for each customer. Tailors made garments for the specific man and woman; and shoemakers custom made shoes. These craftspeople did not produce for inventory but for order, because they did not know in advance what sizes or materials their customers would require. Even today, some people order customized suits, shirts, and shoes to fit their individual requirements. But generally, the advent of mass production led producers to produce standard size goods for inventory.

Today, customized marketing is coming back, in a form that Stanley Davis calls *mass customization*. This is a strange oxymoron, like "jumbo shrimp" or "permanent change," but it well describes new marketing possibilities opened up by advances in manufacturing and information technology. *Mass customization is the ability to prepare on a mass basis individually designed products to meet each customer's requirements.*

According to Arnold Ostle, chief designer for Mazda, "Customers will want to express their individuality with the products they buy." Not surprisingly, marketers are now experimenting with new systems for providing custom-made products ranging from cars and bicycles to furniture and clothing. One such system, already installed in 18 stores across the country, consists of a camera linked to a computer that calculates a customer's measurements and prints out a custom-fitted

pattern for a bathing suit. The video screen shows the bedazzled and delighted buyer how the new suit will look from the front, side, and rear. The buyer chooses the fabric from about 150 samples, the custom-made design is sent to the producer's tailors, and the suit is stitched up.

Another example is a Japanese bicycle manufacturer that uses flexible manufacturing to turn out large numbers of bikes specially fitted to the needs of individual buyers. Customers visit their local bike shop where the shopkeeper measures them on a special frame and faxes the specifications to the factory. At the factory, the measurements are punched into a computer, which creates blueprints in three minutes that would take a draftsman 60 times that long. The computer then guides robots and workers through the production process. The factory is ready to produce any of 11,231,862 variations on 18 bicycle models in 199 color patterns and about as many sizes as there are people. The price is steep—between $545 and $3,200—but within two weeks the buyer is riding a custom-made, one-of-a-kind machine.

Customization permits people to participate in producing exactly what they want. That people enjoy this is demonstrated in a number of situations. Salad bars are becoming increasingly popular in restaurants because they permit people to "compose" their own sal-

airplanes for a limited number of airline customers and customizes its product for each. This ultimate degree of market segmentation, called *customized marketing*, is illustrated in Figure 11-2(b). (Also see Marketing Strategies 11-1).

Most sellers will not find it profitable to "customize" their product for each buyer. Instead the seller identifies classes of buyers who differ in their broad product requirements and/or marketing responses. For example, the seller might discover that income groups differ in their wants. In Figure 11-2(c), a number (1, 2, or 3) is used to identify each buyer's income class. Lines are drawn around buyers in the same income class. Segmentation by income results in three segments, the most numerous segment being income class 1.

On the other hand, the seller might discover pronounced differences between the needs of younger and older buyers. In Figure 11-2(d), a letter (A or B) is used to indicate each buyer's age. Segmentation by age class results in two segments, each with three buyers.

Now both income and age might influence the buyer's behavior toward the product. In this case, the market can be divided into five segments: 1A, 1B, 2B, 3A, and 3B. Figure 11-2(e) shows that segment 1A contains two buyers, and the other segments each contain one buyer.

ads. Similarly, certain ice-cream parlors allow people to make their own ice-cream concoctions.

Services as well as products can be customized. Jack Whittle predicts the following scenario for financial services:

> The customer will enter an institution, sit down at a selling module, and be counseled by a highly qualified professional. . . . The counselor and the customer will work together from a computer terminal to build and price a financial relationship. For example, the customer might inquire about opening up a deposit relationship. The counselor asks a number of basic questions: Does the customer want to earn interest? Write checks? Transfer money between accounts occasionally? Obtain a loan? Depending on the customer's responses, the desired services will be configured and priced based upon the customer's individualized needs.

Business-to-business marketers are more familiar with customization. A Motorola salesperson, using a hand-held computer, will custom-design a pager following a customer's wishes. The design data is transmitted to the Motorola factory, and production starts within 17 minutes. The customized product will be ready for shipment within two hours. The Oshkosh Truck Corporation designs standard and custom-designed vehicles for municipal and military markets. The Becton-Dickinson Company, a major medical supplier, offers the following options to hospitals: custom-designed labeling; bulk-packaging option; customized quality-control recommendations; customized computer software; and customized billing program.

Even when a business offers a *standard product*, it is probably not making a *standard marketing offer*. The customer is probably able to choose a tailored *offering mix* of elements such as optional product features, delivery conditions, training, financing alternatives, technical service options, and so on. We can conclude that in many cases, the marketing offer is customized, even if the product isn't.

In general, as the cost of customization falls and approaches the cost of segmentation, more companies will turn to customized marketing. Someone suggested that customization should be renamed "customer-ization."

SOURCES: See Stanley M. Davis, *Future Perfect* (Reading, MA: Addison-Wesley, 1987); B. Joseph Pine, *Mass Customization* (Boston: Harvard Business School Press, 1993); Susan Moffat, "Japan's New Personalized Production," *Fortune*, October 22, 1990, pp. 132–35; Page Hill Starzinger, "Fashion Clips," *Vogue*, December 1989, p. 76; and Jack W. Whittle, "Beyond Segmentation: Customized Products for Individuals," *American Banker*, January 22, 1986, p. 4; and Jagannath Dubashi, "Designer Trucks," *Financial World*, May 19, 1987, pp. 35–36.

Markets, Market Segments, and Niches

Figure 11-2 shows that every market can be broken down into market segments, niches, and, ultimately, individuals. *Market segments* are large identifiable groups within a market, such as car buyers seeking basic transportation, car buyers seeking high performance, car buyers seeking safety. A *niche* is a more narrowly defined group that may seek a special combination of benefits. As the seller subdivides a market by introducing more defining characteristics, the segments tend to devolve into a set of niches.

Market segments normally attract several competitors, whereas a niche attracts one or only a few competitors. Niche marketers presumably understand their niches' needs so well that their customers willingly pay a price premium. For example, Porsche obtains a high price for its cars because its loyal buyers feel that no other auto company comes close to offering the product-service-membership bundle desired by these customers.

An attractive niche could be characterized as follows: *The customers in the niche have a distinct and somewhat complex set of needs; they will pay a premium to the firm best satisfying their needs; the niche marketer would need to specialize its operations to be successful; and the niche leader is not easily attacked by other competitors.*

Smart companies are rapidly moving into niche marketing. Marriott now offers Marriott hotels, Marriott Suite hotels, Residence Inns, Courtyards by Marriott, and Fairfield Inns, each targeted to a different customer group. American Express offers not only green cards but gold cards, corporate cards, and even platinum cards aimed at different customer groups. Nike makes different athletic shoes for each athletic activity—jogging, walking, basketball, tennis—with further breakdowns within each. An advertising agency executive observed: "There will be no market for products that everybody likes a little, only for products that somebody likes a lot."[1] A chemical company executive predicted that chemical company winners in the future will be those that can identify niches and specialize their chemicals to serve each niche's needs.[2] According to Linneman and Stanton, nichepickers will find riches in niches and companies will have to niche or be niched.[3]

Patterns of Market Segmentation

Earlier, we segmented a market by income and age, resulting in different *demographic segments*. Suppose, instead, we ask buyers how much they want of two product attributes (say, *sweetness* and *creaminess* in the case of ice cream). The aim is to identify different *preference segments*. Three different patterns can emerge.

- *Homogeneous Preferences:* Figure 11-3(a) shows a market where all the consumers have roughly the same preference. The market shows no *natural segments*. We would predict that existing brands would be similar and cluster in the center.

- *Diffused Preferences:* At the other extreme, consumer preferences may be scattered throughout the space [Figure 11-3(b)], showing that consumers vary greatly in their preferences. The first brand to enter the market is likely to position in the center to appeal to the most people. A brand in the center minimizes the sum of total consumer dissatisfaction. A second competitor could locate next to the first brand and fight for market share. Or it could locate in a corner to attract a customer group that was not satisfied with the center brand. If several brands are in the market, they are likely to position throughout the space and show real differences to match consumer-preference differences.

- *Clustered Preferences:* The market might reveal distinct preference clusters, called *natural market segments* [Figure 11-3(c)]. The first firm in this market has three options. It might position in the center hoping to appeal to all groups (undifferentiated marketing). It might position in the largest market segment (concentrated marketing). It might develop several brands, each positioned in a different segment (differentiated marketing). Clearly, if the first firm developed only one brand, competitors would enter and introduce brands in the other segments.

FIGURE 11-3
Basic Market-Preference
Patterns

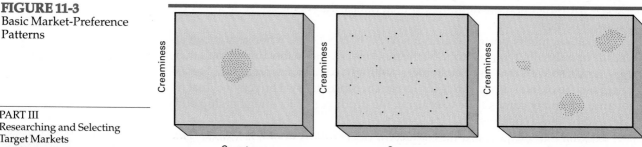

(a) Homogeneous preferences (b) Diffused preferences (c) Clustered preferences

Market-Segmentation Procedure

We have seen that market segments and niches can be identified by applying successive variables to subdivide a market. As an illustration:

> An airline is interested in attracting nonflyers (segmentation variable: *user status*). Nonflyers consist of those who fear flying, those who are indifferent, and those who are positive toward flying (segmentation variable: *attitude*). Among those who feel positive are people with higher incomes who can afford to fly (segmentation variable: *income*). The airline may decide to target higher-income people who have a positive attitude toward flying but simply have not flown.

The question arises: Is there a formal procedure for identifying the major segments in a market? Here is one common approach used by marketing research firms. The procedure consists of three steps:

1. *Survey Stage:* The researcher conducts exploratory interviews and focus groups to gain insight into consumer motivations, attitudes, and behavior. Using these findings, the researcher prepares a formal questionnaire to collect data on:
   - Attributes and their importance ratings
   - Brand awareness and brand ratings
   - Product-usage patterns
   - Attitudes toward the product category
   - Demographics, psychographics, and mediagraphics of the respondents

2. *Analysis Stage:* The researcher applies *factor analysis* to the data to remove highly correlated variables. Then the researcher applies *cluster analysis* to create a specified number of maximally different segments.

3. *Profiling Stage:* Each cluster is now profiled in terms of its distinguishing attitudes, behavior, demographics, psychographics, and media-consumption habits. Each segment can be given a name based on a dominant distinguishing characteristic. Thus in a study of the leisure market, Andreasen and Belk found six market segments:[4] passive homebody; active sports enthusiast; inner-directed self-sufficient; culture patron; active homebody; and socially active. They found that performing arts organizations could sell the most tickets by targeting culture patrons and socially active people.

This market-segmentation procedure must be reapplied periodically because market segments change. For example, Henry Ford assumed that only price mattered. General Motors subsequently outpaced Ford by introducing car brands aimed at different income segments. Later, Volkswagen and the Japanese auto makers recognized the growing importance of small car size and fuel economy as consumer-choice attributes. Still later, the Japanese recognized the growing segment of car buyers seeking quality and reliability. Very often, a new company breaks into an entrenched market by discovering new segmentation possibilities in the market.

One way to discover new segments is to investigate the *hierarchy of attributes* that consumers look at on their way to choosing a brand. In the 1960s, most car buyers first decided on the manufacturer and then on one of its car divisions. This is shown in Figure 11-4(a) as a *brand-dominant hierarchy*. Thus a buyer might favor General Motors cars and, within this set, Pontiac. Today, many buyers decide first on the nation from which they want to buy a car [see Figure 11-4(b) for a *nation-dominant hierarchy*]. Thus a growing number of buyers first decide that they want to buy a Japanese car, and then they may have a second-level preference for, say, Toyota followed by a third-level preference for the Cressida model of Toyota. The lesson is that a company must monitor changes in the consumers' hierarchy of attributes and adjust to changing consumer priorities.

FIGURE 11-4 Hierarchy of Attributes in the Auto Market

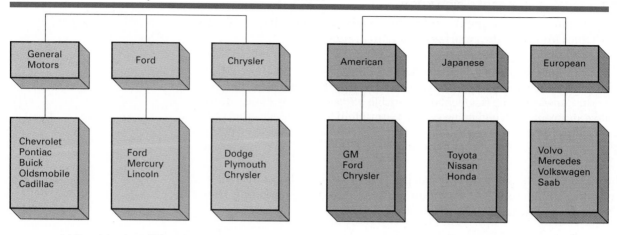

(a) Brand-dominated hierarchy (1960s)   (b) Nation-dominant hierarchy (1980s)

The hierarchy of attributes also reveals customer segments. Those buyers who first decide on price are price dominant; those who first decide on the type of the car (e.g., sports, passenger, station wagon) are type dominant; those who first decide on the car brand are brand dominant; and so on. One can go further and identify those who are type/price/brand dominant, in that order, as making up a segment; those who are quality/service/type dominant as making up another segment; and so on. Each segment may have distinct demographics, psychographics, and mediagraphics. This reasoning is called *market-partitioning theory*. The Hendry Corporation of New York has built a brand-choice forecasting system based on identifying the primary partitioning attributes used by buyers.[5]

Bases for Segmenting Consumer Markets

Different variables are used to segment consumer markets (later we will look at business markets). The variables fall into two broad groups. Some researchers try to form segments by looking at *consumer characteristics*. They commonly use geographic, demographic, and psychographic characteristics. Then they examine whether these customer segments exhibit different needs or product responses. For example, they might examine the differing attitudes of "professionals," "blue collars," and other groups toward, say, "safety" as a car benefit.

Other researchers try to form segments by looking at *consumer responses* to benefits sought, use occasions, or brands. Once the segments are formed, the researcher sees whether different consumer characteristics are associated with each consumer-response segment. For example, the researcher might examine whether people who want "quality" versus "low price" in buying an automobile differ in their geographic, demographic, and psychographic makeup.

The major segmentation variables are shown in Table 11-1, and their use is described next.

GEOGRAPHIC SEGMENTATION ❖ Geographic segmentation calls for dividing the market into different geographical units such as nations, states, regions, counties, cities, or neighborhoods. The company can decide to operate in one or a few geographic areas or operate in all but pay attention to local variations in geographic needs and preferences. For example, General Foods's Maxwell House ground cof-

VARIABLE	TYPICAL BREAKDOWN
GEOGRAPHIC	
Region	Pacific, Mountain, West North Central, West South Central, East North Central, East South Central, South Atlantic, Middle Atlantic, New England
City or Metro size	Under 5,000; 5,000–20,000; 20,000–50,000; 50,000–100,000; 100,000–250,000; 250,000–500,000; 500,000–1,000,000; 1,000,000–4,000,000; 4,000,000 or over
Density	Urban, suburban, rural
Climate	Northern, southern
DEMOGRAPHIC	
Age	Under 6, 6–11, 12–19, 20–34, 35–49, 50–64, 65+
Gender	Male, female
Family size	1–2, 3–4, 5+
Family life cycle	Young, single; young, married, no children; young, married, youngest child under 6; young, married, youngest child 6 or over; older, married, with children; older, married, no children under 18; older, single; other
Income	Under $10,000; $10,000–$15,000; $15,000–$20,000; $20,000–$30,000; $30,000–$50,000; $50,000–$100,000; $100,000 and over
Occupation	Professional and technical; managers, officials, and proprietors; clerical, sales; craftspeople, foremen; operatives; farmers; retired; students; housewives; unemployed
Education	Grade school or less; some high school; high school graduate; some college; college graduate
Religion	Catholic, Protestant, Jewish, Muslim, Hindu, other
Race	White, black, Asian
Nationality	American, British, French, German, Italian, Japanese
PSYCHOGRAPHIC	
Social class	Lower lowers, upper lowers, working class, middle class, upper middles, lower uppers, upper uppers
Lifestyle	Straights, swingers, longhairs
Personality	Compulsive, gregarious, authoritarian, ambitious
BEHAVIORAL – (Lifestyles)	
Occasions	Regular occasion, special occasion
Benefits	Quality, service, economy, speed
User status	Nonuser, ex-user, potential user, first-time user, regular user
Usage rate	Light user, medium user, heavy user
Loyalty status	None, medium, strong, absolute
Readiness stage	Unaware, aware, informed, interested, desirous, intending to buy
Attitude toward product	Enthusiastic, positive, indifferent, negative, hostile

TABLE 11-1
Major Segmentation Variables for Consumer Markets

fee is sold nationally but flavored regionally. Its coffee is flavored stronger in the West than the East. Campbell Soup Company recently appointed *local area market managers* and gave them budgets to study local markets and to adapt Campbell's products and promotions to local conditions.[6] Some companies even subdivide major cities into smaller geographic areas:

> R. J. Reynolds Company has subdivided Chicago into three distinct submarkets. In the North Shore area, Reynolds promotes its low-tar brands because residents are better educated and concerned about health. In the blue-collar southeast area, Reynolds promotes Winston because this area is conservative. In the black South Side, Reynolds promotes the high menthol content of Salem, using the black press and billboards heavily.

DEMOGRAPHIC SEGMENTATION ❖ Demographic segmentation consists of dividing the market into groups on the basis of demographic variables such as age, gender, family size, family life cycle, income, occupation, education, religion, race, and nationality. Demographic variables are the most popular bases for distinguishing customer groups. One reason is that consumer wants, preferences, and usage rates are often highly associated with demographic variables. Another is that demographic variables are easier to measure than most other types of variables. Even when the target market is described in nondemographic terms (say, a personality type), the link back to demographic characteristics is necessary in order to know the size of the target market and the media for reaching it efficiently.

Here we will illustrate how certain demographic variables have been used in market segmentation.

Age and Life-Cycle Stage. Consumer wants and capacities change with age. Alabe Products, a toy manufacturer, realized this and designed different toys for babies as they move through various stages from three months to one year. Crib Jiminy is designed for babies when they begin to reach for things, Talky Rattle when they first grasp things, and so on. This segmentation strategy means that parents and gift buyers can more easily find the appropriate toy by considering the baby's age.

General Foods applied age-segmentation strategy to dog food. Many dog owners know that their dog's food needs change with age. So General Foods formulated four types of canned dog food: Cycle 1 for puppies, Cycle 2 for adult dogs, Cycle 3 for overweight dogs, and Cycle 4 for older dogs. General Foods managed to grab a large market share through this age-segmentation strategy.

Nevertheless, age and life cycle can be tricky variables. For example, the Ford Motor Company used buyers' ages in developing its target market for its Mustang automobile; the car was designed to appeal to young people who wanted an inexpensive sporty automobile. But Ford found that the car was being purchased by all age groups. It then realized that its target market was not the chronologically young but the psychologically young.

The Neugartens' research indicates that age stereotypes need to be guarded against:

> Age has become a poor predictor of the timing of life events, as well as a poor predictor of a person's health, work status, family status, and therefore, also, of a person's interests, preoccupations, and needs. We have multiple images of persons of the same age: there is the 70-year-old in a wheelchair and the 70-year-old on the tennis court. Likewise, there are 35-year-olds sending children off to college and 35-year-olds furnishing the nursery for newborns, producing in turn, first-time grandparenthood for persons who range in age from 35 to 75.[7]

Gender. Gender segmentation has long been applied in clothing, hairdressing, cosmetics, and magazines. Occasionally other marketers will notice an opportunity for gender segmentation. Consider the cigarette market where most brands are smoked by men and women alike. Increasingly, however, feminine brands like Eve and Virginia Slims have been introduced, accompanied by appropriate flavor, packaging, and advertising cues to reinforce the female image. Today it is as unlikely that men will smoke Eve as it is that women will smoke Camels. Another industry that is beginning to recognize gender segmentation is the automobile industry. In the past, cars primarily were designed to appeal to males. With more women car owners, however, some manufacturers are designing certain cars to appeal to women, although stopping short of advertising them explicitly as women's cars.

Income. Income segmentation is another longstanding practice in such product and service categories as automobiles, boats, clothing, cosmetics, and travel. However, income does not always predict the best customers for a given product. Blue-collar workers were among the first purchasers of color television sets; it was cheaper for them to buy these sets than to go to movies and restaurants. Coleman drew a distinction between the "underprivileged" segments and the "overprivileged" segments of each social class.[8] The most economical cars are not bought by the really poor, but rather by "those who think of themselves as poor relative to their status aspirations and to their needs for a certain level of clothing, furniture, and housing which they could not afford if they bought a more expensive car." On the other hand, medium-price and expensive cars tend to be purchased by the overprivileged segments of each social class.

Multiattribute Demographic Segmentation. Most companies will segment a market by combining two or more demographic variables. For example, a major bank segments its retail customers by age and income (see Figure 11-5). The age breakdowns of course could be finer: People in their early forties can differ substantially from those in their late fifties with respect to financial needs. Also, the customers' profit potential would depend on their assets. Some retired people have low incomes but high assets, and others have high incomes but low assets. Nevertheless, this demographic segmentation provides a starting point for the bank to create different offers and programs for different customer groups.

The "young, high-income" segment would include the "yuppies," namely *young urban professionals.* Defined demographically, yuppies are age 25 to 39, high-income, upscale professional, city address. Defined psychographically, they are thought to favor tennis, skiing, and sailing as sports; gourmet foods and wines; fashion, art, and cultural events; and foreign travel. However, demographics and psychographics are not always tightly linked. Many yuppies living in the Midwest favor golf, hunting, and fishing; prefer "junk" food and beer; and score low in art and cultural interests. Thus a bank would have to decide whether it wants to reach demographically defined yuppies or psychographically defined yuppies; it makes a big difference in the bank's offer-and-communication mix. To add further distinctions, yuppies have been subclassified into *buppies* (black yuppies), *guppies* (gay yuppies), *huppies* (Hispanic yuppies), and *muppies* (middle-aged yuppies).

PSYCHOGRAPHIC SEGMENTATION ❖ In psychographic segmentation, buyers are divided into different groups on the basis of social class, lifestyle, and/or personality. People within the same demographic group can exhibit very different psychographic profiles.

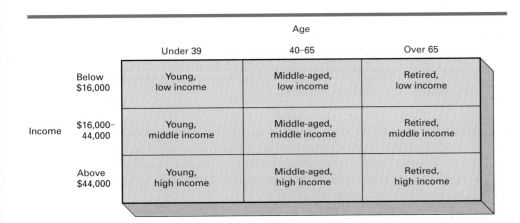

		Age		
		Under 39	40–65	Over 65
Income	Below $16,000	Young, low income	Middle-aged, low income	Retired, low income
	$16,000– 44,000	Young, middle income	Middle-aged, middle income	Retired, middle income
	Above $44,000	Young, high income	Middle-aged, high income	Retired, high income

FIGURE 11-5
Age and Income Segmentation of a Bank's Retail Customers

Social Class. We described the seven American social classes in Chapter 7, p. 177, and showed that social class has a strong influence on the person's preference in cars, clothing, home furnishings, leisure activities, reading habits, retailers, and so on. Many companies design products and/or services for specific social classes.

Lifestyle. We also saw in Chapter 7 that people's product interests are influenced by their lifestyles. In fact, the goods they consume express their lifestyles. Marketers are increasingly segmenting their markets by consumer lifestyles.

> Volkswagen has designed lifestyle automobiles: a car for "the good citizen" emphasizing economy, safety, and ecology; and a car for the "car freak" emphasizing handling, maneuverability, and sportiness. A research firm classified auto buyers into six types: "auto philes," "sensible centrists," "comfort seekers," "auto cynics," "necessity drivers," and "auto phobes."

> Manufacturers of women's apparel are following Du Pont's advice and designing different clothes for the "plain woman," the "fashionable woman," and the "manly woman."

> Cigarette companies develop brands for the "defiant smoker," the "casual smoker," and the "careful smoker."

> The President's Commission on American Outdoors divided Americans into five recreational lifestyle clusters: "health-conscious sociables," "get-away actives," "excitement-seeking competitives," "fitness driven," and "unstressed and unmotivated."

Companies making cosmetics, alcoholic beverages, and furniture are seeking opportunities in lifestyle segmentation. At the same time, lifestyle segmentation does not always work; Nestlé introduced a special brand of decaffeinated coffee for "late nighters," and it failed.

Personality. Marketers have used personality variables to segment markets. They endow their products with *brand personalities* that correspond to *consumer personalities*. In the late fifties, Fords and Chevrolets were promoted as having different personalities. Ford buyers were identified as "independent, impulsive, masculine, alert to change, and self-confident, while Chevrolet owners were conservative, thrifty, prestige-conscious, less masculine, and seeking to avoid extremes."[9] Westfall found evidence of personality differences between the owners of convertibles and nonconvertibles, with owners of the former appearing to be more active, impulsive and sociable.[10] Currently, Nike is using the personality of certain athletes, such as basketball star Michael Jordan, as a brand identifier to attract Michael Jordan fans to Nike shoes.

BEHAVIORAL SEGMENTATION ❖ In behavioral segmentation, buyers are divided into groups on the basis of their knowledge, attitude, use, or response to a product. Many marketers believe that behavioral variables are the best starting point for constructing market segments.

Occasions. Buyers can be distinguished according to occasions when they develop a need, purchase a product, or use a product. For example, air travel is triggered by occasions related to business, vacation, or family. An airline can specialize in serving people for whom one of these occasions dominates. Thus charter airlines serve people who fly for group vacation.

Occasion segmentation can help firms expand product usage. For example, orange juice is most usually consumed at breakfast. An orange juice company can try to promote drinking orange juice on other occasions—lunch, dinner, midday. Certain holidays—Mother's Day and Father's Day, for example—were promoted partly to increase the sale of candy and flowers. The Curtis Candy Company promoted the "trick-or-treat" custom at Halloween, with every home ready to dispense candy to eager little callers knocking at their doors.

In addition to product-specific occasions, a company can consider critical events that mark life's passages to see whether they are accompanied by certain needs that can be met by product and/or service bundles. The occasions include marriage, separation, divorce; acquisition of a home; injury or illness; change in employment or career; retirement; and death of a family member. Among the providers that have emerged to offer services on these critical occasions are marriage, employment, and bereavement counselors.

Benefits. A powerful form of segmentation is to classify buyers according to the different benefits they seek from the product. One of the most successful benefit segmentations was reported by Haley, who studied the toothpaste market (see Table 11-2). Haley's research uncovered four benefit segments: economy, medicinal, cosmetic, and taste. Each benefit-seeking group had particular demographic, behavioristic, and psychographic characteristics. For example, decay-prevention seekers had large families, were heavy toothpaste users, and were conservative. Each segment also favored certain brands. A toothpaste company can use these findings to focus its current brand better and to launch new brands. Thus Procter & Gamble launched Crest toothpaste offering the benefit of "anticavity protection" and became extremely successful. "Anticavity protection" became its *unique selling proposition*. A unique selling proposition (USP) is stronger than just a unique proposition (UP). For example, a purple toothpaste is unique, but it probably won't sell.

User Status. Markets can be segmented into groups of nonusers, ex-users, potential users, first-time users, and regular users of a product. Thus blood banks must not rely on only regular donors to supply blood. They must recruit new first-time donors and contact ex-donors, and each will require a different marketing strategy. The company's position in the market will also influence its focus. Market-share leaders will focus on attracting potential users, whereas smaller firms will focus on attracting current users away from the market leader.

TABLE 11-2   Benefit Segmentation of the Toothpaste Market

BENEFIT SEGMENTS	DEMOGRAPHICS	BEHAVIORISTICS	PSYCHOGRAPHICS	FAVORED BRANDS
Economy (low price)	Men	Heavy users	High autonomy, value oriented	Brands on sale
Medicinal (decay prevention)	Large familes	Heavy users	Hypochondriac, conservative	Crest
Cosmetic (bright teeth)	Teens, young adults	Smokers	High sociability, active	Maclean's, Ultra Brite
Taste (good tasting)	Children	Spearmint lovers	High self-involvement, hedonistic	Colgate, Aim

Source: Adapted from Russell J. Haley, "Benefit Segmentation: A Decision Oriented Research Tool," *Journal of Marketing,* July 1963, pp. 30–35.

Usage Rate. Markets can also be segmented into light-, medium-, and heavy-user groups of the product. Heavy users are often a small percentage of the market but account for a high percentage of total consumption. Figure 11-6 shows usage rates for some popular consumer products. Products were divided into two groups, light users and heavy users. Using beer as an example, the figure shows that 41% of the sampled households buy beer. But the heavy users accounted for 87% of the beer consumed—almost seven times as much as the light users. Clearly, a beer company would prefer to attract one heavy user to its brand rather than several light users. Thus, most beer companies target the heavy beer drinker, using appeals such as Schaefer's "the one beer to have when you're having more than one," or Miller Lite's "tastes great, less filling."

A product's heavy users often have common demographics, psychographics, and media habits. The profile of heavy beer drinkers shows the following characteristics: working class; ages 25 to 50; heavy viewers of television, particularly sports programs.[11] These profiles can assist marketers in developing price, message, and media strategies.

Social marketing agencies face a heavy-user dilemma. A family-planning agency would normally target poor families who have many children, but these families are also the most resistant to birth control messages. The National Safety Council would target unsafe drivers, but these drivers are the most resistant to safe-driving appeals. The agencies must consider whether to go after a few highly resistant heavy offenders or many less-resistant light offenders.

Loyalty Status. A market can be segmented by consumer-loyalty patterns. Consumers can be loyal to brands (Coca-Cola), stores (Sears), and other entities. Suppose there are five brands: A, B, C, D, and E. Buyers can be divided into four groups according to their *brand loyalty* status:

◆ *Hard-Core Loyals:* Consumers who buy one brand all the time. Thus a buying pattern of A, A, A, A, A, A might represent a consumer with undivided loyalty to brand A.

FIGURE 11-6
Heavy and Light Users of Common Consumer Products
Source: See Victor J. Cook and William Mindak, "A Search for Constants: The 'Heavy User' Revisited!" *Journal of Consumer Marketing,* Spring 1984, p. 80.

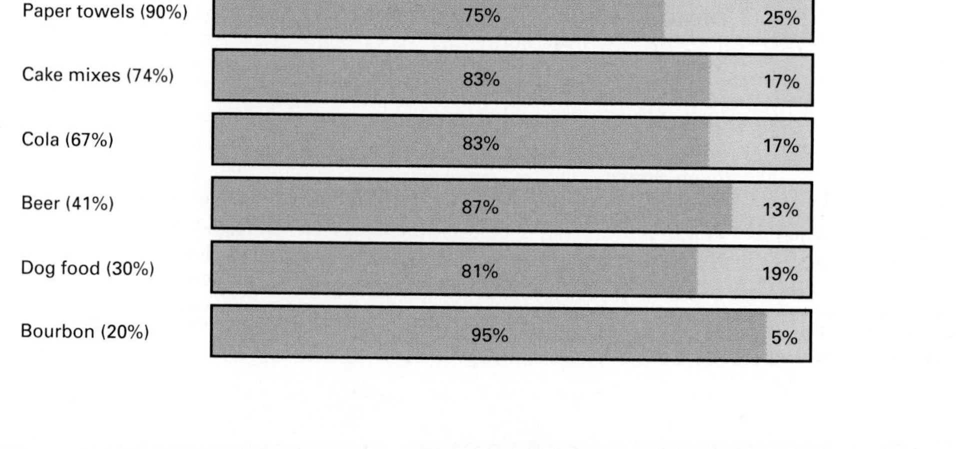

PRODUCT (% USERS)	HEAVY HALF	LIGHT HALF
Soaps and detergents (94%)	75%	25%
Toilet tissue (95%)	71%	29%
Shampoo (94%)	79%	21%
Paper towels (90%)	75%	25%
Cake mixes (74%)	83%	17%
Cola (67%)	83%	17%
Beer (41%)	87%	13%
Dog food (30%)	81%	19%
Bourbon (20%)	95%	5%

- *Split Loyals:* Consumers who are loyal to two or three brands. The buying pattern A, A, B, B, A, B represents a consumer with a divided loyalty between A and B. This group is rapidly increasing. More people now buy from a small set of acceptable brands that are equivalent in their minds.

- *Shifting Loyals:* Consumers who shift from favoring one brand to another. The buying pattern A, A, A, B, B, B would suggest a consumer who is shifting brand loyalty from A to B.

- *Switchers:* Consumers who show no loyalty to any brand. The buying pattern A, C, E, B, D, B would suggest a nonloyal consumer who is either *deal prone* (buys the brand on sale) or *variety prone* (wants something different each time).[12]

Each market consists of different numbers of the four types of buyers. A brand-loyal market is one with a high percentage of hard-core brand-loyal buyers. Thus the toothpaste market and the beer market are fairly high brand-loyal markets. Companies selling in a brand-loyal market have a hard time gaining more market share, and companies that enter such a market have a hard time getting in.

A company can learn a great deal by analyzing loyalty in its market. It should study the characteristics of its own hard-core loyals. Colgate finds that its hard-core loyals are more middle class, have larger families, and are more health conscious. This pinpoints the target market for Colgate.

By studying its split loyals, the company can pinpoint which brands are most competitive with its own. If many Colgate buyers also buy Crest, Colgate can attempt to improve its positioning against Crest, possibly using direct-comparison advertising.

By looking at customers who are shifting away from its brand, the company can learn about its marketing weaknesses and hope to correct them. As for switchers, their numbers are growing. The company can attract them by running frequent sales; however, they may not be worth attracting.

One caution: what appear to be brand-loyal purchase patterns might reflect *habit, indifference, a low price, a high switching cost,* or the *nonavailability* of other brands. The company must examine what is behind the observed purchase patterns.

Buyer-Readiness Stage. A market consists of people in different stages of readiness to buy a product. Some are unaware of the product; some are aware; some are informed; some are interested; some desire the product; and some intend to buy. The relative numbers make a big difference in designing the marketing program. Suppose a health agency wants women to take an annual Pap test to detect possible cervical cancer. At the beginning, most women are unaware of the Pap test. The marketing effort should go into high-awareness-building advertising using a simple message. Later, the advertising should dramatize the benefits of the Pap test and the risks of not taking it, in order to move more women into desiring the test. A special offer might be made of a free health examination to move women into actually signing up. In general, the marketing program should be adapted to the different stages of buyer readiness.

Attitude. Five attitude groups can be found in a market: enthusiastic, positive, indifferent, negative, and hostile. Door-to-door workers in a political campaign use the voter's attitude to determine how much time to spend with the voter. They thank enthusiastic voters and remind them to vote; they reinforce those who are positively disposed; they try to win the votes of indifferent voters; they spend no time trying to change the attitudes of negative and hostile voters. To the extent that attitudes are correlated with demographic descriptors, the political party can more efficiently locate the best prospects.

Bases for Segmenting Business Markets

Business markets can be segmented using many of the same variables employed in consumer market segmentation, such as geography, benefits sought, and usage rate. Yet there are also new variables. Bonoma and Shapiro proposed segmenting the business market with the variables shown in Table 11-3. The demographic variables are the most important, followed by the operating variables—down to the personal characteristics of the buyer.

The table lists major questions that business marketers should ask in determining which segments and customers to serve. Thus a rubber-tire company should first decide which *industries* it wants to serve, noting the following differences:

> Automobile manufacturers vary in their requirements, with luxury-car manufacturers wanting a much higher-grade tire than standard car manufacturers. And the tires needed by aircraft manufacturers have to meet much higher safety standards than tires needed by farm tractor manufacturers.

Within a chosen target industry, a company can further segment by *customer size*. The company might set up separate programs for dealing with large and small

---

TABLE 11-3
Major Segmentation Variables for Business Markets

DEMOGRAPHIC

- *Industry:* Which industries should we focus on?
- *Company size:* What size companies should we focus on?
- *Location:* What geographical areas should we focus on?

OPERATING VARIABLES

- *Technology:* What customer technologies should we focus on?
- *User/nonuser status:* Should we focus on heavy, medium, light users, or nonusers?
- *Customer capabilities:* Should we focus on customers needing many or few services?

PURCHASING APPROACHES

- *Purchasing-function organization:* Should we focus on companies with highly centralized or decentralized purchasing organizations?
- *Power structure:* Should we focus on companies that are engineering dominated, financially dominated, etc.?
- *Nature of existing relationships:* Should we focus on companies with which we have strong relationships or simply go after the most desirable companies?
- *General purchase policies:* Should we focus on companies that prefer leasing? service contracts? systems purchases? sealed bidding?
- *Purchasing criteria:* Should we focus on companies that are seeking quality? service? price?

SITUATIONAL FACTORS

- *Urgency:* Should we focus on companies that need quick and sudden delivery or service?
- *Specific application:* Should we focus on certain applications of our product rather than all applications?
- *Size of order:* Should we focus on large or small orders?

PERSONAL CHARACTERISTICS

- *Buyer-seller similarity:* Should we focus on companies whose people and values are similar to ours?
- *Attitudes toward risk:* Should we focus on risk-taking or risk-avoiding customers?
- *Loyalty:* Should we focus on companies that show high loyalty to their suppliers?

Source: Adapted from Thomas V. Bonoma and Benson P. Shapiro, *Segmenting the Industrial Market* (Lexington, MA: Lexington Books, 1983).

customers. Steelcase, a major manufacturer of office furniture, divides its customers into three groups:

- *National Accounts:* Accounts such as IBM, Prudential, and Standard Oil are handled by national account managers working with field district managers.
- *Field Accounts:* Medium-size accounts are handled by field sales personnel.
- *Dealer Accounts:* Smaller accounts are handled by franchised dealers who sell Steelcase products.

Within a given target industry and customer size, the company can segment by *purchase criteria*:

Laboratories typically differ in their purchase criteria for scientific instruments. Government laboratories need low prices and service contracts. University laboratories need equipment that requires little service. Industrial laboratories need equipment that is highly reliable and accurate.

Business marketers generally identify segments through a sequential segmentation process. Consider an aluminum company:

The aluminum company first undertook *macrosegmentation* consisting of three steps.[13] It looked at which end-use market to serve: automobile, residential, or beverage containers. Choosing the residential market, it needed to determine the most attractive product application: semifinished material, building components, or aluminum mobile homes. Deciding to focus on building components, it considered the best customer size and chose large customers. The second stage consisted of *microsegmentation*. The company distinguished between customers buying on price, service, or quality. Because the aluminum company had a high-service profile, it decided to concentrate on the service-motivated segment of the market.

Even this segmentation scheme postulates a single benefit as driving product choice within each segment. Yet business buyers may seek different benefit bundles. Robertson and Barich identified three business segments based on their stage in the purchase decision process:[14]

1. *First-Time Prospects:* These customers have not yet purchased. They want to buy from a salesperson or vendor who understands their business, who explains things well, and whom they can trust.
2. *Novices:* These customers have already purchased the product. They want easy-to-read manuals, hot lines, a high level of training, and knowledgeable sales reps.
3. *Sophisticates:* These customers want speed in maintenance and repair, product customization, and high technical support.

Robertson and Barich suggest that these segments may have different channel preferences. For example, first-time prospects would prefer to deal with a company salesperson instead of a catalog/direct-mail channel, since the latter provides too little information. But as the market matures, more buyers become sophisticated and may prefer different channels. However, companies that have committed themselves to channels that were effective in the market's early stage will lose flexibility in keeping and satisfying sophisticates.

Robertson and Barich believe that their scheme is highly usable by the salesforce in planning their calls. They complain that senior managers too often get enthusiastic about a nice-sounding strategic segmentation scheme, pour a lot of money into refining it, only to discover that the salesforce cannot use it.

Rangan, Moriarty, and Swartz studied a mature commodity market to test the normal occurrence of two business segments: buyers who prefer a low price and little service and buyers who are willing to pay a higher price for more service.[15] To their surprise, they found four business segments:

1. *Programmed buyers:* These buyers view the product as not very important to their operation. They buy it as a routine purchase item. They usually pay full price and receive below-average service. Clearly this is a highly profitable segment for the vendor.

2. *Relationship buyers:* These buyers regard the product as moderately important and are knowledgeable about competitive offerings. They get a small discount and a modest amount of service and prefer the vendor as long as the price is not far out of line. They are the second most profitable group.

3. *Transaction buyers:* These buyers see the product as very important to their operations. They are price and service sensitive. They receive about a 10% discount and receive above-average service. They are knowledgeable about competitive offerings and are ready to switch for a better price, even at the sacrifice of some service.

4. *Bargain hunters:* These buyers see the product as very important and demand the deepest discount and the highest service. They know the alternative suppliers, bargain hard, and are ready to switch at the slightest dissatisfaction. The company needs these buyers for volume purposes but they are not very profitable.

This segmentation scheme can help a company in a mature commodity industry do a better job of figuring out where to apply price and service increases and decreases, since each segment would react differently.[16]

Developing the Customer Segment Profile

Each customer segment needs to be profiled in more detail. We need further segment descriptors, such as their demographics, psychographics, mediagraphics, attitudes, and behavior. As an example, Smythe reported a benefit segmentation study of coffee drinkers.[17] Coffee drinkers were asked to assign importance ratings to 25 product attributes. The data were factor analyzed, and three clear segments emerged. The segments were named decaffeinated, nondecaffeinated, and ground. Table 11-4 shows a partial profile of the three customer segments. They were approximately equal in size but quite different in benefits desired, use frequency, and demographics. The finding, for example, showed that decaffeinated-coffee drinkers were older, widowed, and so on. Clearly, the marketer hopes to discover different profiles for the segments. In the best case, the segments will differ psychographically and have different demographics and mediagraphics. Thus the results would indicate that a decaffeinated-coffee brand such as Sanka should be placed into heavy distribution where older and widowed people are found, and the brand should be advertised mostly in print media read by these people.

Requirements for Effective Segmentation

There are many ways to segment a market. Not all segmentations, however, are effective. For example, buyers of table salt could be divided into blond and brunet customers. But hair color is not relevant to the purchase of salt. Furthermore, if all salt buyers buy the same amount of salt each month, believe all salt is the same, and want to pay the same price, this market would be minimally segmentable from a marketing point of view.

To be maximally useful, market segments must exhibit five characteristics:

♦ *Measurable:* The size, purchasing power, and profile of the segments can be measured. Certain segmentation variables are difficult to measure. An illustration would be the

TABLE 11-4
Coffee-Market-Segment
Profiles

| NAME | SEGMENT | | |
	Decaffeinated	Nondecaffeinated	Ground
Size	35%	33%	32%
Distinguishing benefits	Decaffeinated	Not decaffeinated	Not prepared quickly
Desired	Not make me nervous, prepared quickly, not wake up, concentrated form	Wake up, convenient package, well-known brand, easy to prepare	Not convenient package, not easy to prepare, special equipment, not concentrated form
Frequency of use	Light users	Medium users	Heavy users
Type usage	Instant	Both	Ground
Brand usage	Sanka, Brim, Taster's Choice, Néscafé	Maxwell House, Folger's	Hills Bros, all others
Demographics	Older, widowed, lower income, more minorities	Average age, divorced, average income, more minorities	Younger, married, higher income, fewer minorities

Source: Robert J. Smythe, *Market Segmentation,* a pamphlet published by NFO Research, Inc., Toledo, Ohio (no date).

size of the segment of teenage smokers who smoke primarily to rebel against their parents.

◆ *Substantial:* The segments are large and profitable enough to serve. A segment should be the largest possible homogeneous group worth going after with a tailored marketing program. It would not pay, for example, for an automobile manufacturer to develop cars for persons who are shorter than four feet.

◆ *Accessible:* The segments can be effectively reached and served. Suppose a perfume company finds that heavy users of its brand are single women who are out late at night and frequent bars. Unless these women live or shop at certain places and are exposed to certain media, they will be difficult to reach.

◆ *Differentiable:* The segments are conceptually distinguishable and respond differently to different marketing-mix elements and programs. If married and unmarried women respond similarly to a sale of fur coats, they do not constitute separate segments.

◆ *Actionable:* Effective programs can be formulated for attracting and serving the segments. A small airline, for example, identified seven market segments, but its staff was too small to develop separate marketing programs for each segment.

Market Targeting

Market segmentation reveals the market-segment opportunities facing the firm. The firm now has to evaluate the various segments and decide how many and which ones to target. We will now look at the tools for market-segment evaluation and selection.

Evaluating the Market Segments

In evaluating different market segments, the firm must look at three factors, namely segment size and growth, segment structural attractiveness, and company objectives and resources.

SEGMENT SIZE AND GROWTH ❖ The first question to ask is whether a potential segment has the right size and growth characteristics. The "right size" is a relative matter. Large companies prefer segments with large sales volumes and often overlook or avoid small segments. Small companies in turn avoid large segments because they require too many resources.

Segment growth is normally a desirable characteristic, since companies generally want growing sales and profits. At the same time, competitors will rapidly enter growing segments and depress their profitability.

SEGMENT STRUCTURAL ATTRACTIVENESS ❖ A segment might have desirable size and growth but lack profit potential. Porter has identified five forces that determine the intrinsic long-run profit attractiveness of a market or segment.[18] His model is shown in Figure 11-7. The company has to appraise the impact on long-run profitability of five groups: *industry competitors*, *potential entrants*, *substitutes*, *buyers*, and *suppliers*. The five threats they pose are as follows:

1. *Threat of Intense Segment Rivalry:* A segment is unattractive if it already contains numerous, strong, or aggressive competitors. The picture is even worse if the segment is stable or declining, if capacity additions are done in large increments, if fixed costs are high, if exit barriers are high, or if competitors have high stakes in staying in the segment. These conditions will lead to frequent price wars, advertising battles, and new-product introductions and will make it expensive for the companies to compete.

2. *Threat of New Entrants:* A segment is unattractive if it is likely to attract new competitors who will bring in new capacity, substantial resources, and a drive for market-share growth. The question boils down to whether new entrants can easily get in. They will find it hard if there are high barriers to entry coupled with sharp retaliation from incumbent firms. The lower the barriers to entry and incumbent willingness to retaliate, the less attractive the segment. A segment's attractiveness varies with the height of the entry and exit barriers.[19] The most attractive segment to be in is one in which entry barriers are high and exit barriers are low (see Figure 11-8). Few new firms can enter the industry, and poor-performing firms can easily exit. When both entry and exit barriers are high, profit potential is high but is usually accompanied by more risk because

FIGURE 11-7
Five Forces Determining Segment Structural Attractiveness
Source: Adapted with permission of The Free Press, a Division of Macmillan, Inc. from *Competitive Advantage: Creating and Sustaining Superior Performance* by Michael E. Porter, p. 235. Copyright © 1985 by Michael E. Porter.

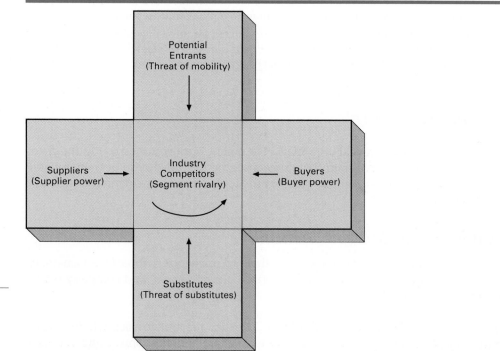

FIGURE 11-8
Barriers and Profitability

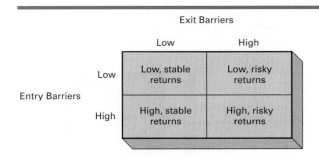

poorer-performing firms stay in and fight it out. When entry and exit barriers are both low, then firms easily enter and leave the industry, and the returns are stable and low. The worst case is when entry barriers are low and exit barriers are high: here firms enter during good times but find it hard to leave during bad times. The result is chronic overcapacity and depressed earnings for all.

3. *Threat of Substitute Products:* A segment is unattractive when there are actual or potential substitutes for the product. Substitutes place a limit on the potential prices and profits that a segment can earn. The company has to watch closely the price trends in the substitutes. If technology advances or competition increases in these substitute industries, prices and profits in the segment are likely to fall.

4. *Threat of Growing Bargaining Power of Buyers:* A segment is unattractive if the buyers possess strong or growing bargaining power. Buyers will try to force prices down, demand more quality or services, and set competitors against each other, all at the expense of seller profitability. Buyers' bargaining power grows when they become more concentrated or organized, when the product represents a significant fraction of the buyers' costs, when the product is undifferentiated, when the buyers' switching costs are low, when the buyers are price sensitive because of low profits, or when the buyers can integrate backward. In defense, sellers might select buyers who possess the least power to negotiate or switch suppliers. A better defense consists of developing superior offers that strong buyers cannot refuse.

5. *Threat of Growing Bargaining Power of Suppliers:* A segment is unattractive if the company's suppliers are able to raise prices or reduce quantity. Suppliers tend to be powerful when they are concentrated or organized, when there are few substitutes, when the supplied product is an important input, when the switching costs are high, and when the suppliers can integrate forward. The best defenses are to build win-win relations with suppliers or use multiple supply sources.

COMPANY OBJECTIVES AND RESOURCES ❖ Even if a segment is large, growing, and structurally attractive, the company needs to consider its own objectives and resources in relation to that segment. Some attractive segments could be dismissed because they do not mesh with the company's long-run objectives. Even if the segment fits the company's objectives, the company must consider whether it possesses the requisite skills and resources to succeed in that segment. Each segment has certain *success requirements*. The segment should be dismissed if the company lacks one or more necessary competences and is in no position to acquire the necessary competences. But even if the company possesses the requisite competences, it needs to develop some superior advantages. It should enter only market segments where it can offer superior value.

Selecting the Market Segments

Having evaluated different segments, the company must now decide which and how many segments to serve. That is the problem of *target market selection*. The company can consider five patterns of target market selection as shown in Figure 11-9.

FIGURE 11-9 Five Patterns of Target Market Selection

Source: Adapted from Derek F. Abell, *Defining the Business: The Starting Point of Strategic Planning* (Englewood Cliffs, NJ: Prentice-Hall, 1980), Chap. 8, pp. 192–96.

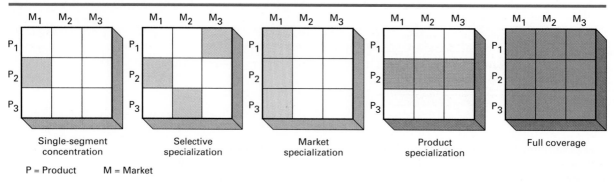

Single-segment concentration   Selective specialization   Market specialization   Product specialization   Full coverage

P = Product   M = Market

SINGLE-SEGMENT CONCENTRATION ❖ In the simplest case, the company selects a single segment. Volkswagen concentrates on the small-car market, and Richard D. Irwin on the economics and business texts market. Through *concentrated marketing*, the firm achieves a strong market position in the segment owing to its greater knowledge of the segment's needs and the special reputation it gains. Furthermore, the firm enjoys operating economies through specializing its production, distribution, and promotion. If it captures leadership in the segment, the firm can earn a high return on its investment.

At the same time, concentrated marketing involves higher than normal risks. The particular market segment can turn sour; for example, when young women suddenly stopped buying sportswear, it caused Bobbie Brooks's earnings to fall sharply. Or a competitor may invade the segment. For these reasons, many companies prefer to operate in more than one segment.

SELECTIVE SPECIALIZATION ❖ Here the firm selects a number of segments, each objectively attractive and appropriate, given the firm's objectives and resources. There may be little or no synergy between the segments, but each segment promises to be a money maker. This strategy of *multisegment coverage* has the advantage of diversifying the firm's risk. Even if one segment becomes unattractive, the firm can continue to earn money in other segments.

PRODUCT SPECIALIZATION ❖ Here the firm concentrates on making a certain product that it sells to several segments. An example would be a microscope manufacturer that sells microscopes to university laboratories, government laboratories, and commercial laboratories. The firm makes different microscopes for these different customer groups but avoids manufacturing other instruments that laboratories might use. Through this strategy, the firm builds up a strong reputation in the specific product area. The downside risk would occur if microscopes were supplanted by an entirely new technology.

MARKET SPECIALIZATION ❖ Here the firm concentrates on serving many needs of a particular customer group. An example would be a firm that sells an assortment of products for university laboratories, including microscopes, oscilloscopes, Bunsen burners, and chemical flasks. The firm gains a strong reputation for specializing in serving this customer group and becomes a channel for all new products that this customer group could feasibly use. The downside risk would occur if university laboratories suddenly had their budgets cut and reduced their purchases.

FULL MARKET COVERAGE ❖ Here a firm attempts to serve all customer groups with all the products that they might need. Only large firms can undertake a full market coverage strategy. Examples would include IBM (computer market), General Motors (vehicle market), and Coca-Cola (drink market).

Large firms can cover a whole market in two broad ways, namely, through undifferentiated marketing or differentiated marketing.

Undifferentiated Marketing. The firm might ignore market-segment differences and go after the whole market with one market offer.[20] It focuses on what is common in the needs of buyers rather than on what is different. It designs a product and a marketing program that will appeal to the broadest number of buyers. It relies on mass distribution and mass advertising. It aims to endow the product with a superior image in people's minds. An example of undifferentiated marketing is the Coca-Cola Company's early marketing of only one drink in one bottle size in one taste to suit everyone.

Undifferentiated marketing is defended on the grounds of cost economies. It is seen as "the marketing counterpart to standardization and mass production in manufacturing."[21] The narrow product line keeps down production, inventory, and transportation costs. The undifferentiated advertising program keeps down advertising costs. The absence of segment research and planning lowers the costs of marketing research and product management. Presumably, the company can turn its lower costs into lower prices to win the price-sensitive segment of the market.

Nevertheless, a growing number of marketers have expressed strong doubts about this strategy. Gardner and Levy, while acknowledging that "some brands have very skillfully built up reputations of being suitable for a wide variety of people," noted that "it is not easy for a brand to appeal to stable lower-middle-class people and at the same time to be interesting to sophisticated, intellectual upper-middle-class buyers. . . . It is rarely possible for a product or brand to be all things to all people."[22]

When several competitors practice undifferentiated marketing, the result is intense competition in the largest market segments and undersatisfaction of the smaller ones. Kuehn and Day have called this tendency to go after the largest market segment the "majority fallacy."[23] The recognition of this fallacy has led firms to increase their interest in entering smaller neglected market segments.

Differentiated Marketing. Here the firm operates in several market segments and designs different programs for each segment. General Motors claims to do this when it says that it produces a car for every "purse, purpose, and personality." And IBM offers many hardware and software packages for different segments in the computer market. Consider the case of the Edison Brothers:

> *Edison Brothers operates nine hundred shoe stores that fall into four different chain categories, each appealing to a different market segment. Chandler's sells higher-priced shoes. Baker's sells moderate-priced shoes. Burt's sells shoes for budget shoppers, and Wild Pair is oriented to the shopper who wants very stylized shoes. Within three blocks on State Street in Chicago are found Burt's, Chandler's, and Baker's. Putting the stores near each other does not hurt them because they are aimed at different segments of the women's shoe market. This strategy has made Edison Brothers the country's largest retailer of women's shoes.[24]*

Differentiated marketing typically creates more total sales than undifferentiated marketing. "It is ordinarily demonstrable that total sales may be increased with a more diversified product line sold through more diversified channels."[25] However, it also increases the costs of doing business. The following costs are likely to be higher:

- *Product Modification Costs:* Modifying a product to meet different market segment requirements usually involves some R&D, engineering, and/or special tooling costs.
- *Manufacturing Costs:* It is usually more expensive to produce, say, ten units of ten different products than 100 units of one product. The longer the production setup time for each product and the smaller the sales volume of each product, the more expensive it becomes. On the other hand, if each model is sold in sufficiently large volume, the higher costs of setup time may be quite small per unit.
- *Administrative Costs:* The company has to develop separate marketing plans for the separate segments of the market. This requires extra marketing research, forecasting, sales analysis, promotion, planning, and channel management.
- *Inventory Costs:* It is more costly to manage inventories containing many products than few products.
- *Promotion Costs:* The company has to reach different market segments with different promotion programs. This increases promotion-planning costs and media costs.

Since differentiated marketing leads to both higher sales and higher costs, nothing can be said in general regarding the profitability of this strategy. Companies should be cautious about *oversegmenting* their market. If this happens, they may want to turn to *countersegmentation* or broadening the customer base.[26] Johnson & Johnson, for example, broadened its target market for its baby shampoo to include adults. And Beecham launched its Aquafresh toothpaste to attract simultaneously three benefit segments: those seeking fresh breath, whiter teeth, and cavity protection.

FIGURE 11-10
Three Alternative Market
Selection Strategies

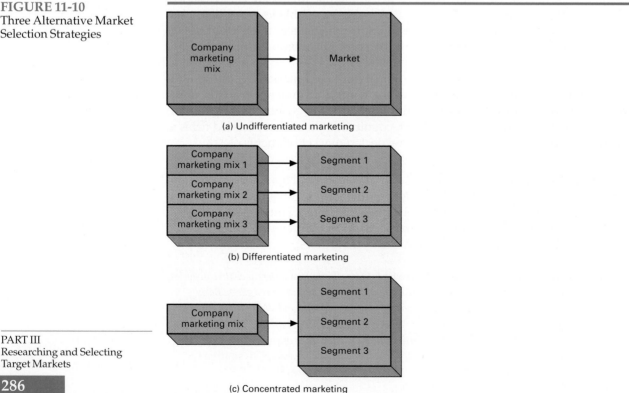

(a) Undifferentiated marketing

(b) Differentiated marketing

(c) Concentrated marketing

Figure 11-10 summarizes the differences among undifferentiated marketing, differentiated marketing, and concentrated marketing.

Additional Considerations in Evaluating and Selecting Segments

Three other considerations must be taken into account in evaluating and selecting segments.

ETHICAL CHOICE OF MARKET TARGETS ❖ Market targeting sometimes generates controversy. The public is concerned when marketers take unfair advantage of vulnerable groups (such as children) or disadvantaged groups (such as inner-city poor people), or promote potentially harmful products. Marketers need to proceed in a socially responsible way when these issues may arise (see Socially Responsible Marketing 11-1).

SEGMENT INTERRELATIONSHIPS AND SUPERSEGMENTS ❖ In selecting more than one segment to serve, the company should pay close attention to *segment interrelationships* on the cost, performance, and technology side. A com-

Socially Responsible Marketing 11-1

Issues in the Choice of Market Targets

Market targeting sometimes generates controversy and concern. Issues usually involve the targeting of vulnerable or disadvantaged consumers with controversial or potentially harmful products.

Over the years, the cereal industry has been heavily criticized for its marketing efforts directed toward children. Critics worry that sophisticated advertising, in which high-powered appeals are presented through the mouths of lovable animated characters will overwhelm children's defenses. Children will be enticed to gobble too much sugared cereal or to eat poorly balanced breakfasts. The marketers of toys and other children's products have been similarly criticized. Some critics have even called for a complete ban on advertising to children. Children cannot understand the selling intent of the advertiser, they reason, so any advertising targeted toward children is inherently unfair. To encourage responsible advertising to children, the Children's Advertising Review Unit, the advertising industry's self-regulatory agency, has published extensive children's advertising guidelines that recognize the special needs of child audiences.

Cigarette, beer, and fast-food marketers have also generated much controversy in recent years by their attempts to target inner-city minority consumers. For example, McDonald's and other chains have drawn criticism for pitching their high-fat, salt-laden fare to low-income, inner-city residents who are much more likely than suburbanites to be heavy consumers. R. J. Reynolds took heavy flak in 1990 when it announced plans to market Uptown, a menthol cigarette targeted toward low-income blacks.

Not all attempts to target children, minorities, or other special segments draw such criticism. For example, Colgate-Palmolive's Colgate Junior toothpaste has special features designed to get children to brush longer and more often. Golden Ribbon Playthings has developed a highly acclaimed and very successful black character doll named "Huggy Bean" targeted toward minority consumers to connect them with their African heritage.

Thus, in market targeting, the issue is not *who* is targeted but rather *how* and for *what*. Socially responsible marketing calls for segmentation and targeting that serve not just the interests of the company, but also the interests of those targeted.

SOURCES: See "Selling Sin to Blacks," *Fortune*, October 21, 1991, p. 100; Martha T. Moore, "Putting on a Fresh Face," *USA Today*, January 3, 1992, pp. B1, B2; Dorothy J. Gaiter, "Black-Owned Firms Are Catching an Afrocentric Wave," *The Wall Street Journal*, January 8, 1992, p. B2; and Maria Mallory, "Waking Up to a Major Market," *Business Week*, March 23, 1992, pp. 70–73.

FIGURE 11-11
Segments and
Supersegments

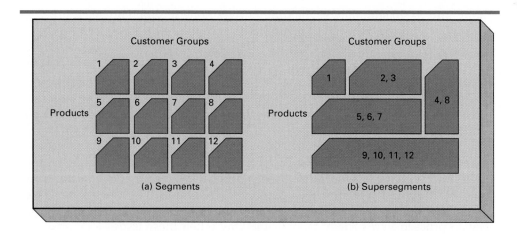

pany carrying a fixed cost (its salesforce, store outlets, and so on) will add products to absorb and share some of the cost. Thus a salesforce will be given additional products to sell, and a fast-food outlet will offer additional dishes. This is a search for *economies of scope*, which can be just as important as economies of scale.

Companies should also identify and try to operate in *supersegments* rather than in isolated segments. Figure 11-11 shows how twelve single segments can be regrouped into five supersegments based on certain synergies, such as using the same raw materials, manufacturing facilities, or distribution channels. The firm would be wise to choose a supersegment rather than a single segment within the supersegment; otherwise, it might be at a competitive disadvantage with those firms that have locked into that supersegment.

SEGMENT-BY-SEGMENT INVASION PLANS ❖ Even if the firm plans to target a supersegment, it is wise to enter one segment at a time and conceal its grand plan. The competitors must not know to what segment(s) the firm will move next. This is illustrated in Figure 11-12. Three firms, A, B, and C, have specialized in adapting computer systems to the needs of airlines, railroads, and trucking companies. Company A has specialized in meeting all the computer needs of airlines. Company B has specialized in selling large computer systems to all three transportation sectors. Company C recently entered this market and has specialized in

FIGURE 11-12
Segment-by-Segment
Invasion Plan

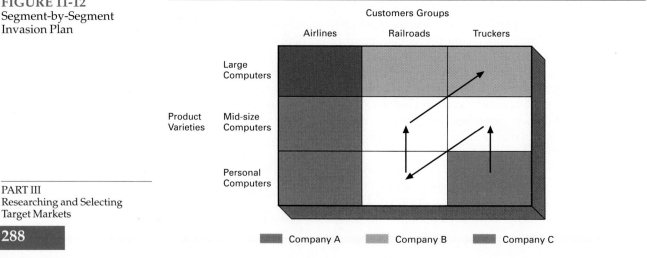

selling personal computers to trucking companies. The question is: Where should company C move next? The arrows have been added to the chart to show the planned sequence of market-segment invasions unknown to company C's competitors. Company C will next offer midsize computers to trucking companies; then to allay company B's concern about its large computer business with trucking companies, company C moves into offering personal computers tailored to railroad needs. Later, it offers midsize computers to railroads. Finally, it launches a full attack on company B's large computer position in trucking companies. Of course, its planned sequence is provisional in that much depends on the competitors' segment moves over time.

Unfortunately, too many companies fail to develop a long-term invasion plan in which they have plotted the sequence and timing of market-segment entries. Pepsi-Cola is an exception in that its attack on Coca-Cola was thought through in grand-plan terms, first attacking Coca-Cola in the grocery market, then in the vending-machine market, then in the fast-food market, and so on. Japanese firms also plot their invasion sequence. They first gain a foothold in a market—say Toyota introduces a small car into the market—and then they expand with more cars, then larger cars, and eventually luxury cars. American firms turn blue when a Japanese firm enters the market, knowing that the Japanese firm will not stop at the first segment but will use it as a launching pad for successive invasions.

At the same time, a company's invasion plans can be thwarted when it confronts *blocked* markets. Then the invader must figure out a way to break into a blocked market (see Global Marketing 11-1).

Global Marketing 11-1

Using Megamarketing to Break Into Blocked Markets

It is one thing to want to do business in a particular market or country and another to be allowed in on reasonable terms. The problem of entering *blocked markets* calls for a *megamarketing* approach, defined as *the strategic coordination of economic, psychological, political, and public-relations skills to gain the cooperation of a number of parties in order to enter and/or operate in a given market*. Pepsi-Cola faced this problem in seeking to enter the Indian market:

> After Coca-Cola was asked to leave India, Pepsi began to lay plans to enter this huge market. Pepsi worked with an Indian business group to seek government approval for its entry over the objections of both domestic soft-drink companies and antimultinational legislators. Pepsi saw the solution to lie in making an offer that the Indian government would find hard to refuse. Pepsi offered to help India export some of its agricultural products in a volume that would more than cover the cost of importing soft-drink concentrate. Pepsi also promised to focus considerable selling effort on rural areas to help in their economic development. Pepsi further offered to transfer food-processing, packaging, and water-treatment technology to India. Clearly, Pepsi's strategy was to bundle a set of benefits that would win the support of various interest groups in India.

Thus Pepsi's marketing problem went beyond the normal four Ps of operating effectively in a market. To enter India, Pepsi faced a six-P marketing problem, with *politics* and *public opinion* constituting the two additional Ps. Winning over the Indian government and public to gain admission is a much tougher challenge.

Once in, a multinational must be on its best behavior, since it is under great scrutiny, and critics abound. This task calls for well-thought-out *civic positioning* of the multinational. Olivetti, for example, enters new markets by building housing for workers, generously supporting local arts and charities, and hiring and training indigenous managers. In this way, it hopes to realize long-run profits by accepting high short-run costs.

SOURCE: See Philip Kotler, "Megamarketing," *Harvard Business Review*, March–April 1986, pp. 117–24.

SUMMARY ❖

Sellers can take three approaches to a market. Mass marketing is the decision to mass produce and mass distribute one product and attempt to attract all kinds of buyers. Product-variety marketing aims to offer a variety of products to broaden the customer base. Target marketing is the decision to distinguish the different groups that make up a market and to develop corresponding products and marketing mixes for each target market. Sellers today are moving away from mass marketing and product differentiation toward target marketing because the latter is more helpful in spotting market opportunities and developing winning products and marketing mixes.

The key steps in target marketing are market segmentation, market targeting, and product positioning. Market segmentation is the act of dividing a market into distinct groups of buyers with different needs or responses. The marketer tries different variables to see which reveal the best segmentation opportunities. For each segment, a customer-segment profile is developed. Segmentation effectiveness depends on arriving at segments that are measurable, substantial, accessible, differentiable, and actionable.

Next, the seller has to target the best market segment(s). The seller must first evaluate the profit potential of each segment, which is a function of segment size and growth, segment structural attractiveness, and company objectives and resources. Then the seller must decide how many segments to serve. The seller can ignore segment differences (undifferentiated marketing), develop different market offers for several segments (differentiated marketing), or go after one or a few market segments (concentrated marketing). In choosing target segments, marketers need to consider segment interrelationships and potential segment invasion plans.

NOTES ❖

1. Laurel Cutler, quoted in "Stars of the 1980s Cast Their Light," *Fortune*, July 3, 1989, p. 76.

2. Andrew A. Boccone, "Speciality Chemicals: In Pursuit of Fast-Growth Niche Markets," *Chemical Week*, April 12, 1989, pp. 32–34.

3. Robert E. Linneman and John L. Stanton, Jr., *Making Niche Marketing Work: How to Grow Bigger by Acting Smaller* (New York: McGraw-Hill, Inc., 1991).

4. Alan R. Andreasen and Russell W. Belk, "Predictors of Attendance at the Performing Arts," *Journal of Consumer Research*, September 1980, pp. 112–20.

5. See Manohar U. Kalwani and Donald G. Morrison, "A Parsimonious Description of the Hendry System," *Management Science*, January 1977, pp. 467–77.

6. See "Marketing's New Look: Campbell Leads a Revolution in the Way Consumer Products Are Sold," *Business Week*, January 26, 1987, pp. 64–69.

7. *American Demographics*, August 1986.

8. Richard P. Coleman, "The Significance of Social Stratification in Selling," in *Marketing: A Maturing Discipline*, ed. Martin L. Bell (Chicago: American Marketing Association, 1961), pp. 171–84.

9. Quoted in Franklin B. Evans, "Psychological and Objective Factors in the Prediction of Brand Choice; Ford versus Chevrolet," *Journal of Business*, October 1959, pp. 340–69.

10. Ralph Westfall, "Psychological Factors in Predicting Product Choice," *Journal of Marketing*, April 1962, pp. 34–40.

11. Frank M. Bass, Douglas J. Tigert, and Ronald T. Lonsdale, "Market Segmentation: Group versus Individual Behavior," *Journal of Marketing Research*, August 1968, p. 276.

12. This classification was adapted from George H. Brown, "Brand Loyalty—Fact or Fiction?" *Advertising Age*, June 1952–January 1953, a series.

13. See Yoram Wind and Richard Cardozo, "Industrial Market Segmentation," *Industrial Marketing Management 3* (1974), pp. 153–66; and James D. Hlavacek and B. C. Ames,

"Segmenting Industrial and High-Tech Markets," *Journal of Business Strategy*, Fall 1986, pp. 39–50.

14. Thomas S. Robertson and Howard Barich, "A Successful Approach to Segmenting Industrial Markets," *Planning Forum*, November/December 1992, pp. 5–11.

15. V. Kasturi Rangan, Rowland T. Moriarty, and Gordon S. Swartz, "Segmenting Customers in Mature Industrial Markets," *Journal of Marketing*, October 1992, pp. 72–82.

16. For another interesting approach to segmenting the business market, see John Berrigan and Carl Finkbeiner, *Segmentation Marketing: New Methods for Capturing Business* (New York: Harper-Business, 1992).

17. Robert J. Smythe, *Market Segmentation*, a pamphlet published by NFO Research, Toledo, Ohio (no date).

18. Michael E. Porter, *Competitive Strategy* (New York: Free Press, 1985), pp. 4–8 and pp. 234–36.

19. Michael E. Porter, *Competitive Strategy* (New York: Free Press, 1980), pp. 22–23.

20. See Wendell R. Smith, "Product Differentiation and Market Segmentation as Alternative Marketing Strategies," *Journal of Marketing*, July 1956, pp. 3–8; and Alan A. Roberts, "Applying the Strategy of Market Segmentation," *Business Horizons*, Fall 1961, pp. 65–72.

21. Smith, "Product Differentiation," p. 4.

22. Burleigh Gardner and Sidney Levy, "The Product and the Brand," *Harvard Business Review*, March–April 1955, p. 37.

23. Alfred A. Kuehn and Ralph L. Day, "Strategy of Product Quality," *Harvard Business Review*, November–December 1962, pp. 101–102.

24. Natalie McKelvy, "Shoes Make Edison Brothers a Big Name," *Chicago Tribune*, February 23, 1979.

25. Roberts, "Applying the Strategy of Market Segmentation," p. 66.

26. Alan J. Resnik, Peter B. B. Turney, and J. Barry Mason, "Marketers Turn to 'Countersegmentation,'" *Harvard Business Review*, September–October, 1979, pp. 100–106.

12

Differentiating and Positioning the Marketing Offer

You should never go into battle before you win the war.

ANONYMOUS

All men can see the tactics whereby I conquer, but what none can see is the strategy out of which victory is evolved.

ANONYMOUS

Suppose a company has researched and selected its target market. If it is the only company serving this target market, it will probably be able to charge a price that will yield a reasonable profit. If it charges too high a price and there are no substantial entry barriers, competitors will enter this market and bring the price down. If several firms pursue this target market and their products are undifferentiated, then most buyers will buy from the lowest price firm. Other firms will be forced to lower their price. The only alternative for the original firm is to differentiate its market offer from the competitors. If it can effectively differentiate its offer, it can charge a price premium. Differentiation allows the firm to get a price premium based on the extra value perceived by and delivered to the customers.

There are four broad ways to think about differentiating a company's offer. The firm can create value by offering something that is better, newer, faster, or cheaper. "Better" means that the company's offer outperforms its rivals. It usually involves improving an existing product in a minor way. "Newer" means developing a solution that didn't exist before. This usually involves higher risk than a simple improvement but also the chance of a higher gain. "Faster" means reducing the performance or delivery time involved in using or buying a product or service. Finally, "cheaper" means getting a similar product for less money.

Companies that rely solely on differentiating their offer by cutting their cost and price may be making a mistake. First, a "cheaper" product than its rivals is often suspect as not being as good, even when it is good. Second, the firm may often cut services in order to keep the price down and this may alienate the buyer. Third, a competitor will usually emerge to offer a still "cheaper" version, based on finding a lower-cost production site. If the firm did not distinguish its offer in any other way than being cheaper, it will succumb to this competitor.

Treacy and Wiersema recently distinguished three strategies that lead to successful differentiation and market leadership.[1] They are:

- *Operational excellence:* providing customers with reliable products or services at competitive prices and easy availability. Examples: Dell Computer, Wal-Mart, American Airlines, Federal Express
- *Customer intimacy:* knowing customers intimately and being able to respond quickly to their specific and special needs. Examples: Home Depot, Staples, Ciba-Geigy, Kraft
- *Product leadership:* offering customers innovative products and services that enhance the customer's utility and outperform competitors' products. Examples: Nike, Apple, Sony

Thus a company can win by operating its business better, knowing its customers better, or consistently making better products.

This chapter will explore specific ways a company can effectively differentiate and position its offer. We will address the following questions:

- How can the firm identify sources of potential competitive advantage?
- What are the major differentiating attributes available to firms?

◆ How can the firm choose an effective positioning in the market?

◆ How can the firm communicate its positioning to the market?

Tools for Competitive Differentiation

In developing its marketing strategy, a company must ask in what specific ways can it obtain a competitive advantage. The number of differentiation opportunities vary with the type of industry. There are industries which present numerous opportunities for differentiation and those which present few opportunities. The Boston Consulting Group distinguished four types of industries based on the number of available competitive advantages and their size (see Figure 12-1). The four industry types are as follows:

◆ *Volume Industry:* A volume industry is one in which companies can gain only a few, but rather large, advantages. An example would be the construction-equipment industry where a company can strive for the low-cost position or the highly differentiated position and win "big" on either basis. Here profitability is correlated with company size and market share.

◆ *Stalemated Industry:* A stalemated industry is one in which there are few potential advantages and each is small. An example would be the steel industry where it is hard to differentiate the product or its manufacturing cost. The companies can try to hire better salespeople, entertain more lavishly, and the like, but these are small advantages. Here profitability is unrelated to company market share.

◆ *Fragmented Industry:* A fragmented industry is one in which companies face many opportunities for differentiation, but each opportunity is small. A restaurant, for example, can differentiate in many ways but end up not gaining a large market share. Profitability is not related to restaurant size: Both small and large restaurants can be profitable or unprofitable.

◆ *Specialized Industry:* A specialized industry is one in which companies face many differentiation opportunities, and each differentiation can have a high payoff. An example would be companies making specialized machinery for selected market segments. Some small companies can be as profitable as some large companies.

Thus not every company faces a plethora of cost-reducing or benefit-building opportunities for gaining competitive advantage. Some companies will find many minor advantages available, but all are highly imitable and therefore perishable. One solution for these companies is to continually identify new potential advantages and introduce them one by one to keep the competitors off balance. These companies need to "routinize" the innovation process, expecting not so much to achieve a major sustainable advantage but rather to gain market share by introducing many little differences over time.

FIGURE 12-1
The New BCG Matrix

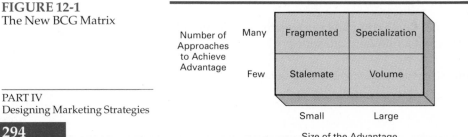

Milind Lele has observed that individual companies differ in their *potential "maneuverability"* along five dimensions: changing their target market, product, place (channels), promotion, or price. The company's freedom of maneuver is affected by the industry structure and the firm's position in the industry. For each possible maneuver, the company needs to estimate the prospective return. Those maneuvers which promise the highest return define the company's *strategic leverage*. Companies in a stalemated industry have by definition very little maneuverability and strategic leverage, and those in specialization industries have great scope for maneuverability and strategic advantage.

We are now ready to examine specific ways in which a company can differentiate its market offer from competitors. A company or market offer can be differentiated along four basic dimensions: *product, services, personnel,* or *image* (see Table 12-1). Let us look at the specific tools more closely.

Product Differentiation

Here we will identify bases for differentiating a physical product. At one extreme we find highly standardized products that allow little variation: chicken, steel, aspirin. Yet even here, genuine variation is possible. Frank Perdue claims that his branded chickens are better—they are tenderer—and he gets a 10% price premium based on this claim. Steel can vary in its consistency and properties. Bayer claims that its aspirin "gets into the bloodstream faster." And Procter & Gamble has successfully differentiated what might appear to be a commodity—namely detergents (see Companies and Industries 12-1).

At the other extreme are products capable of high differentiation, such as automobiles, commercial buildings, and furniture. Here the seller faces an abundance of design parameters. The main product differentiators are *features, performance, conformance, durability, reliability, repairability, style,* and *design.*[2]

FEATURES ❖ *Features are characteristics that supplement the product's basic functioning.* Most products can be offered with varying features. The starting point is a stripped-down, or "bare-bones," version of the product. The company can create additional versions by adding extra features. Thus an automobile manufacturer can offer optional features, such as electric windows, automatic transmission, and air conditioning. The automobile manufacturer needs to decide which features to make standard and which to make optional. Each feature has a chance of capturing the fancy of additional buyers.

Features are a competitive tool for differentiating the company's product. Some companies are extremely innovative in adding new features to their product. One of the key factors in the success of Japanese companies is that they continuously enhance the features in their watches, cameras, automobiles, motorcycles,

PRODUCT	SERVICES	PERSONNEL	IMAGE
Features	Delivery	Competence	Symbol
Performance	Installation	Courtesy	Media
Conformance	Customer Training	Credibility	Atmosphere
Durability	Consulting Service	Reliability	Events
Reliability	Repair	Responsiveness	
Repairability	Miscellaneous	Communication	
Style			
Design			

TABLE 12-1
Differentiation Variables

Nine Ways to Differentiate a White Powder

Procter & Gamble makes nine brands of laundry detergent (Tide, Cheer, Gain, Dash, Bold, Dreft, Ivory Snow, Oxydol, and Era). These P&G brands compete with one another on the same supermarket shelves. But why would P&G introduce several brands in one category instead of concentrating its resources on a single leading brand? The answer lies in the fact that different people want different *mixes of benefits* from the products they buy. Take laundry detergents as an example. To some people, cleaning and bleaching power are most important; to others, fabric softening matters most; still others want a mild, fresh-scented detergent.

Procter & Gamble has identified at least nine important laundry detergent segments and has developed a different brand designed to meet the special needs of each. The nine P&G brands are positioned for different segments as follows:

- *Tide* is "so powerful, it cleans down to the fiber." It's the all-purpose family detergent for extra-tough laundry jobs. "Tide's in, dirt's out."
- *Cheer* with Color Guard gives "outstanding cleaning *and* color protection. So your family's clothes look clean, bright, and more like new."
- *Oxydol* contains bleach. It "makes your white clothes

really white and your colored clothes really bright. So don't reach for the bleach—grab a box of Ox!"
- *Gain*, originally P&G's "enzyme" detergent, was repositioned as the detergent that gives you clean, fresh-smelling clothes—it "freshens like sunshine."
- *Bold* is the detergent with fabric softener. It "cleans, softens, and controls static." Bold liquid adds "the fresh fabric softener scent."
- *Ivory Snow* is "Ninety-nine and forty-four one hundredths percent pure." It's the "mild, gentle soap for diapers and baby clothes."
- *Dreft* is also formulated for baby's diapers and clothes. It contains borax, "nature's natural sweetener" for "a clean you can trust."
- *Dash* is P&G's value entry. It "attacks tough dirt," but "Dash does it for a great low price."
- *Era Plus* has "built-in stain removers." It "gets tough stains out and does a great job on your whole wash too."

Clearly, white powder in a box can be functionally and psychologically differentiated and endowed with distinct brand personalities. By producing several brands, P&G has managed to capture more of the market—in this case 55%—than it could hope for with only one brand.

calculators, videorecorders, and so on. Being first in introducing valued new features is one of the most effective ways to compete.

How can a company identify and select appropriate new features? One answer is for the company to contact recent buyers and ask them a series of questions:

> How do you like the product? Any bad features? Good features? Are there any features that could be added that would improve your satisfaction? What are they? How much would you pay for each feature? How do you feel about the following features that other customers mentioned?

This will provide the company with a long list of potential features. The next task is to decide which ones are worth adding. For each potential feature, the company should calculate its *customer value* versus *company cost*. Suppose an auto manufacturer is considering the three possible improvements shown in Table 12-2. "Rear window defrosting" would cost the company $10 per car to add at the factory level. And the average customer said this feature was worth $20. The company could therefore generate $2 of incremental customer satisfaction for every $1 in incremental company cost. Looking at the other two features, it appears that "power steering" would create the most customer satisfaction per dollar of company cost.

TABLE 12-2   Measuring Customer Effectiveness Value

FEATURE	COMPANY COST (1)	CUSTOMER VALUE (2)	CUSTOMER EFFECTIVENESS (3 = 2 ÷ 1)
Rear window defrosting	$10	$ 20	2
Cruise control	$60	$ 60	1
Power steering	$60	$180	3

These criteria are only a starting point. The company will also consider how many people want each feature, how long it would take to introduce each feature, whether competitors could easily copy the feature, and so on.

Companies must also think in terms of feature bundles or packages. Japanese car companies, for example, often manufacture cars at three "trim levels" rather than allowing the customer to specify all the individual options. This lowers the Japanese car company's manufacturing and inventory-carrying costs and prices. Companies must decide whether to offer feature customization to customers at a higher cost or more standardization to customers at a lower cost.

PERFORMANCE QUALITY ❖ *Performance quality refers to the levels at which the product's primary characteristics operate.* Thus a Digital Equipment midsize computer performs better than a Data General computer if it has speedier processing and a larger memory. Buyers of expensive products normally compare the performance characteristics of different brands. They will pay more for better performance as long as the higher price does not exceed the higher perceived value.

Most products are established initially at one of four performance levels: low, average, high, and superior. The question is: Does higher product performance produce higher profitability? The Strategic Planning Institute studied the impact of higher relative product quality (which is a surrogate for performance and other value-adding factors) and found a significantly positive correlation between relative product quality and return on investment [see Figure 12-2(a)]. In a subsample of 525 midsize business units, those with low relative product quality earned about 17%; medium quality, 20%; and high quality, 27%. Thus the high-quality business units earned 60% more than the low-quality business units. They earned more be-

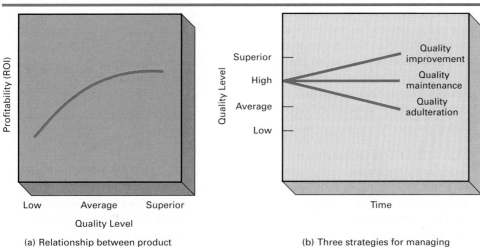

(a) Relationship between product quality and profitability (return on investment – ROI)

(b) Three strategies for managing product quality through time

FIGURE 12-2
Brand-Quality Strategies
and Profitability

CHAPTER 12
Differentiating and Positioning
the Marketing Offer

cause their premium quality enabled them to charge a premium price, they benefited from more repeat purchasing, consumer loyalty, and positive word of mouth, and their costs of delivering more quality were not much higher than for business units producing low quality.

At the same time, this does not mean that the firm should design the highest performance level possible. There are diminishing returns to still higher performance in that fewer buyers are willing to pay for it. Certain products are "overengineered." A person who drives ten blocks to work does not need a Rolls-Royce. The manufacturer must design a performance level appropriate to the target market and competitors' performance level.

A company must also decide how to manage performance quality through time. Three strategies are illustrated in Figure 12-2(b). The first, where the manufacturer continuously improves the product, often produces the highest return and market share. Procter & Gamble is a major practitioner of product-improvement strategy, which combined with the high initial product performance, helps explain its leadership position in many markets. The second strategy is to maintain product quality. Many companies leave their quality unaltered after its initial formulation unless glaring faults or opportunities occur. The third strategy is to reduce product quality through time. Some companies cut the quality to offset rising costs, hoping the buyers will not notice any difference. Others reduce the quality deliberately in order to increase their current profits, although this often hurts their long-run profitability.

CONFORMANCE QUALITY ❖ *Conformance quality is the degree to which a product's design and operating characteristics come close to the target standard*. It reflects whether the various produced units are identically made and meet the specifications. Suppose a Porsche is designed to accelerate to 60 miles an hour within ten seconds. If every Porsche coming off the assembly line does this, the automobile is said to have high conformance quality. However, if Porsches vary greatly in their acceleration time, they have low conformance on this criterion. The problem with low conformance is that the product's promised performance will not be fulfilled for many buyers and they will be disappointed. One of the major reasons for the high-quality reputation enjoyed by Japanese manufacturers is that their products have high conformance. Their automobiles are praised for having good "fit and finish," and people gladly pay for this.

DURABILITY ❖ *Durability is a measure of the product's expected operating life*. For example, Volvo advertises that it has the highest mean life of automobile makes and this justifies its higher price. Buyers will pay more for a more durable product. However, this is subject to some qualifications. The extra price must not be excessive. Furthermore, the product must not be subject to high fashion or technological obsolescence in which case the buyer may not pay more for longer-lived products. Thus advertising that a personal computer or videocamera has the highest durability may have little appeal because their features and performance levels are undergoing rapid change.

RELIABILITY ❖ *Reliability is a measure of the probability that a product will not malfunction or fail within a specified time period*. Thus a Mercedes has more reliability than a Jaguar if its chance of not malfunctioning in some important way within a year is 90% compared to 60%. Buyers are willing to pay a premium for more reliable products. They want to avoid the high costs of breakdowns and repair time. Maytag, which manufactures major home appliances, has an outstanding reputation for reliable appliances and often shows its service person sleeping because he has no work to do. The Japanese have been especially successful in improving the reliability of their products. Here are two examples:

A Japanese firm imported Oster blenders and sold them through 2,500 stores in Japan. The Japanese firm complained about receiving 2% returns because the agitator blade rusted within two years. It told the American manufacturer that it would not accept more than 0.5% returns and that the manufacturer needed to use a higher grade of stainless steel for Japan. The U.S. manufacturer acceded and in time introduced the better blade in the United States as well.

The Mitsubishi company acquired Motorola's Quasar division, which manufactured television receivers. Motorola had experienced 141 defects in every 100 sets; Mitsubishi reduced this to 6 per 100. Buyer complaints fell to one tenth their previous level and the company's warranty liability also dropped to one tenth.

REPAIRABILITY ❖ *Repairability is a measure of the ease of fixing a product that malfunctions or fails*. Thus an automobile made with standard parts that are easily replaced has high repairability. Ideal repairability would exist if users could fix the product themselves with little or no cost or time lost. The buyer might simply remove the defective part and insert a replacement part. As the next best thing, some products include a diagnostic feature that allows service people to correct it over the telephone from a distant location or advise the user how to correct it. Before GE sends its repair person to fix a home appliance, it tries to solve the problem over the phone. In over 50% of the cases, this works and the customer has saved money and feels good about GE. The worst situation is when a product breaks down and requires a service call, and much time elapses before the service people and parts arrive.

STYLE ❖ *Style describes how well the product looks and feels to the buyer*. Thus many car buyers pay a premium for Jaguar automobiles because of their extraordinary look, even though Jaguar's record of reliability is poor. General Motors's Cadillac division hired Pininfarina, an Italian automobile-design firm, to design its high-priced Allanté to give it European styling. Some companies have outstanding styling reputations, such as Herman Miller in office furniture, Olivetti in office machines, Bang & Olufsen in home stereo equipment, Nissan and Mazda in sports cars, and Swatch in watches (see Global Marketing 12-1). Style has the advantage of creating product distinctiveness that is difficult to copy. Therefore it is surprising that more companies have not invested in better styling. Many products are yawn-producing rather than eye-catching. For example, most small kitchen appliances lack styling distinctiveness, with the exceptions of some coffee makers and other small appliances made by Italian and German firms. At the same time, a strong style does not necessarily promise high performance. A chair may look sensational but be extremely uncomfortable.

Under style differentiation, we must include *packaging* as a styling weapon, especially in food products, cosmetics, toiletries, and small consumer appliances. The package provides the buyer's first encounter with the product and is capable of turning the buyer "on" or "off." Packaging is discussed in detail in Chapter 17.

DESIGN: THE INTEGRATING FORCE ❖ All of the foregoing qualities are design parameters. They suggest how difficult the product-design task is, given all the tradeoffs that can be made. The designer has to figure out how much to invest in feature development, performance, conformance, reliability, repairability, style, and so forth. From the company's point of view, a well-designed product would be easy to manufacture and distribute. From the customer's point of view, a well-de-

Using Style to Differentiate a Global Product: The Swatch Watch

The Swiss watch industry, which at one time produced most of the world's watches, reeled precariously from a succession of competitive attacks that all but captured the low-price end of the watch market. First there was Timex, the U.S. company, that successfully introduced simple and reliable low-cost time-keeping pieces. Then the Japanese watch makers introduced their highly accurate electronic digital watches. Still later, Hong Kong manufacturers flooded the world market with cheap imitations of Swiss and Japanese products. The Swiss could only hold on to their high-price fashion jewelry watches such as Rolex, Piaget, Longines, and others.

Then in 1981, ETA, a subsidiary of Switzerland's largest watch company, started a project that resulted in the now-famous Swatch watch. The name itself was a contraction of S'Watch, standing for Swiss Watch, which became Swatch. Swatch is a lightweight, water-resistant, shock-proof electronic analogue watch with a colorful plastic band. It is issued in many different faces and bands, all very colorful and sporty. Prices range from $40 to $100. The watch is designed to appeal as a fashion item to young, active, and trendy people.

The watch is produced on a single fully automated assembly line in a Swiss state-of-the-art factory. It only has 51 components which permits its thin look and low cost. Manufacturing costs have steadily declined over the years to about $5 a watch.

Swatch is sold today in more than 30 countries. The United States accounts for approximately 50% of Swatch sales. Originally placed in jewelry stores and fashion outlets in the United States, Swatches are now also sold in up-scale department stores but not in mass-merchandise outlets. Swatch is even creating "Swatch Shops" within major department stores with the aim of adding ancillary products—sunglasses, eyeglass holders—bearing Swatch designs to sell in a total Swatch environment.

One of Swatch's chief strengths has been its promotional and merchandising skill. Here are some examples:

1. Swatch issues new watches during the year and people eagerly await the new arrivals. Many people own more than one Swatch watch, since they want to wear different colors on different days or occasions. One businessman has 25 Swatch watches and each day selects his suit, tie, shirt, and Swatch watch.

2. Swatch also launches limited editions of "snazzy" watch designs twice a year. Swatch watch collectors have the privilege of bidding to buy one of the limited edition. The catch is that Swatch may produce only 40,000 units and yet receive orders from 100,000 or more collectors. They will sponsor a drawing to choose the 40,000 lucky collectors who can buy the watch.

3. Christies, the auction house, holds periodic auctions of earlier Swatch watches. One collector paid $60,000 for one of the rarer Swatch watches. Given that Swatches only appeared in the last twelve years, they have achieved the status of "classics of our time."

4. In a Lisbon museum, there is an exhibit of rare Swatch watches protected behind bulletproof glass.

5. Swatch operates some of its own retail stores. On the famous Via Monte Napoleone fashion street in Milan, the Swatch store attracts more visitors than any of the famous stores that line the street. Sometimes crowds will form outside of the store and a voice on a loudspeaker will read four digits and only persons whose passport numbers contain the four digits will be allowed into the store to buy watches.

6. Many companies have approached Swatch to issue a Swatch with their company logo. Swatch acceded only once to Coca-Cola but has refused to do this for other companies.

Swatch clearly has written the marketing book on how to build a cult following by applying superior styling, merchandising, and promotion.

SOURCE: See "Swatch: Ambitious," *The Economist*, April 18, 1992, pp. 74–75.

signed product would be pleasant to look at, and also easy to open, install, learn how to use, use, repair, and dispose of. The designer has to take all of this into account and follow the maxim, "form follows function." The designer has to compromise some of the desirable characteristics. Much depends on knowing how the target market perceives and weighs the different benefits and costs.

Unfortunately, too many companies fail to invest in good design. Some companies confuse design with styling and think that design is a matter of making a product and then putting some fancy casing around it. Or they think that reliability is something to catch during inspections rather than designing it into the manufacturing process. They may think of designers as people who pay insufficient attention to cost or who produce designs that are too novel for the market to accept. A design audit instrument to measure a company's design sensitivity and effectiveness would help management gauge whether it is adding sufficient value through design.[3]

As competition intensifies, design will offer one of the most potent ways to differentiate and position a company's products and services. This is particularly true in selling durable equipment, apparel, retail services, and even packaged goods. Design, after all, includes product design, process design, graphics, architectural and interior design, and corporate identification. Certain countries have established themselves as design leaders: Italian design in apparel and furniture; Scandinavian design for functionality, aesthetic, and environmental consciousness; German design for austerity and robustness. Japan currently outspends many other industrial countries in the amount they spend on design.

Does design investment pay off? Both anecdotal evidence and a research study suggests it does. Braun, a German division of Gillette, has elevated design to a high art and has had much success with its various small appliances (electric razors, coffee makers, etc.) (see Companies and Industries 12-2). The Danish firm of Bang & Olufsen has received many kudos for the design of its stereo and TV equipment. Herman Miller, the American office furniture company, has won much admiration for the ergonomic and aesthetic distinctiveness of its furniture. As for research study evidence, consider the following:

> The Design Innovation Group in Great Britain carried out a three-year research study surveying 221 product, engineering, industrial, and graphic design projects. These design projects took place in medium and small UK manufacturing companies and

Companies and Industries 12-2

Braun's Ten Principles of Good Design

Since 1955, top management at Braun AG has given design an equal status with engineering and manufacturing. Designers join product-development teams from the beginning, and, in many cases, ideas coming from designers start a new project, whether a hair dryer, food processor, or electric shaver. Designers will prepare three-dimensional foam models to show the other product-development team members and these models will be used later by market researchers to test customer reactions. Braun's designers stay in touch with the latest materials, and they design the product for easy "manufacturability." Dieter Rams is Braun's chief designer, and he has developed the following ten commandments of good design for his company:

1. Good design is innovative.
2. Good design enhances the usefulness of a product.
3. Good design is aesthetic.
4. Good design displays the logical structure of a product; its form follows its function.
5. Good design is unobtrusive.
6. Good design is honest.
7. Good design is enduring.
8. Good design is consistent right down to details.
9. Good design is ecologically conscious.
10. Good design is minimal design.

Not all designers accept all of these principles. Some critics think they lead to designs that are too austere and functionalist. But it is precisely these principles that have given Braun products their distinctive identity.

were partly supported by government subsidies. The study found that 90% of the projects made a profit with an average payback period of 15 months from product launch. The average design project cost about $100,000 and produced an average sales increase of 41%.

All said, good design can attract attention, improve quality and performance, lower costs, and more strongly communicate value to the intended target market.

Services Differentiation

In addition to differentiating its physical product, the firm can also differentiate the accompanying services. When the physical product cannot easily be differentiated, the key to competitive success often lies in service augmentation and quality. The main service differentiators are *delivery*, *installation*, *customer training*, *consulting service*, *repair*, and a few others.

DELIVERY ❖ Delivery refers to how well the product or service is delivered to the customer. It includes the speed, accuracy, and care attending the delivery process. Deluxe Check Printers, Inc., for example, has built an impressive reputation for shipping out its checks one day after receiving the order—without being late once in twelve years. Buyers will often choose the supplier who has a better reputation for on-time delivery. The choice among rail carriers often hinges on their perceived differences in delivery speed and reliability. (See Marketing Strategies 12-1.)

INSTALLATION ❖ Installation refers to the work done to make a product operational in its planned location. Buyers of heavy equipment expect good installation service from the vendor. Vendors can differ in the quality of their installation service. IBM, for example, delivers all of the purchased equipment to the site at the same time rather than sending in different components at different times, to sit waiting for everything else to arrive. When IBM is asked to move IBM equipment to another location, it is willing to move competitors' equipment and furniture as well.

CUSTOMER TRAINING ❖ Customer training refers to training the customer's employees to use the vendor's equipment properly and efficiently. Thus General Electric not only sells and installs expensive X-ray equipment in hospitals but takes responsibility for training the users of this equipment. McDonald's requires its new franchisees to attend Hamburger University for two weeks to learn how to properly manage their franchise.

CONSULTING SERVICE ❖ Consulting service refers to data, information systems, and advising services that the seller offers free or for a price to buyers. McKesson Corporation, a major drug wholesaler, helps its 12,000 independent pharmacists set up accounting and inventory systems, computer ordering systems, and so forth. McKesson believes that helping its customers compete better will make them more loyal. One of the best providers of value-adding consulting service is Milliken & Company:

> Milliken sells shop towels to industrial launderers who rent them to factories. These towels are physically similar to competitors' towels. Yet Milliken charges a higher price for its towels and enjoys the leading market share. How can it charge more for essentially a commodity? The answer is that Milliken continuously "decommodi-

tizes" this product through continuous service enhancements for its launderer customers. Milliken trains its customers' salespeople; supplies prospect leads and sales-promotional material to them; supplies on-line computer-order-entry and freight-optimization systems; carries on marketing research for customers; sponsors quality-improvement workshops; and lends its salespeople to work with customers on customer action teams. Launderers are more than willing to buy Milliken shop towels and pay a price premium because the extra services improve their profitability.[4]

REPAIR ❖ Repair describes the quality of repair service available to buyers of the company's product. Caterpillar claims to offer better and faster repair service for its heavy-construction equipment anywhere in the world. Automobile buyers are quite concerned with the quality of repair service that they can expect from any dealer from whom they buy.

MISCELLANEOUS SERVICES ❖ Companies can find many other ways to add value through differentiating their customer services and service quality. The company can offer a better product warranty or maintenance contract than its competitors. The company can establish patronage awards as the airlines have done with their frequent-flyer programs. There are virtually an unlimited number of specific services and benefits that companies can offer to differentiate themselves from their competitors.

Personnel Differentiation

Companies can gain a strong competitive advantage through hiring and training better people than their competitors do. Thus Singapore Airlines enjoys an excellent reputation in large part because of the beauty and grace of their flight attendants. The McDonald's people are courteous, the IBM people are professional, and the Disney people are upbeat. The salesforce of such companies as Connecticut General Life and Merck enjoy an excellent reputation.[5] Wal-Mart has differentiated its superstores by assigning at each store a store employee to be a "people greeter," who welcomes shoppers, gives advice on where to find items, marks merchandise carried in for returns or exchanges, and gives small gifts to children.

Better-trained personnel exhibit six characteristics:

- *Competence:* The employees possess the required skill and knowledge.
- *Courtesy:* The employees are friendly, respectful, and considerate.
- *Credibility:* The employees are trustworthy.
- *Reliability:* The employees perform the service with consistency and accuracy.
- *Responsiveness:* The employees respond quickly to customers' requests and problems.
- *Communication:* The employees make an effort to understand the customer and communicate clearly.[6]

Image Differentiation

Even when competing offers look the same, buyers may respond differently to the company or brand images. Consider the success of Marlboro cigarettes. The primary way to account for Marlboro's extraordinary worldwide market share (around 30%) is that Marlboro's "macho cowboy" image has struck a responsive chord with most of the cigarette-smoking public. Marlboro has developed a distinctive "personality."

Turbomarketing: Using Quick Response Time as a Competitive Tool

A company can try to establish a competitive advantage in four ways: It can make a better offer, a newer offer, a cheaper offer, or a faster offer. Many smart companies are placing their bet today on being faster. They are becoming *turbomarketers,* learning the art of *cycle time compression* or *time speedup.* They are applying turbomarketing to four areas: innovation, manufacturing, logistics, and retailing.

Speeding up innovation is essential in an age of shorter product life cycles. Competitors in many industries learn about new technologies and new market opportunities at about the same time. For example, several companies are racing today to achieve a breakthrough treatment for AIDS, to exploit the promising application of superconductivity, and to develop high-definition television. Those companies that first reach practical solutions will enjoy "first-mover" advantages in the market. In auto manufacture, the Japanese have achieved a considerable competitive advantage in being able to design and introduce new car models within three years. Ford is catching up, having designed the 1986 Taurus in four years, while GM still seems to need five years. Being early rather than late pays off. A McKinsey and Company study found that products that came out six months late but on budget earned an average of 33% less profit in their first five years; products that came out on time but 50% over budget cut profit only 4%.

The key to innovation speedup is to eliminate unnecessary delays in the company's new-product-development process. Is the company too slow at gathering new research ideas, screening them, developing and testing new concepts and prototypes, or launching the product? By examining each step of the product development process, the company can usually find ways to reduce innovation time.

Manufacturing is a second area in which great strides have been made in reducing cycle time. Toyota used to take five weeks to build a special-order car; now it can do this in three days. Today a Motorola salesperson can work with a customer to choose features for a customized pager; transmit the order to the factory using his modem; production starts in 17 minutes; shipment takes place in two hours; and the new pagers reach the customers' premises the next day.

Logistics is a third area where alert manufacturers are working hard to develop faster resupply systems. Here are some examples:

Apparel manufacturers such as Levi Strauss, Benetton, and The Limited have adopted *quick response systems* that link the information systems of their suppliers, manufacturing plants, distribution centers, and retailing outlets.

Federal Express's huge success is the result of recognition by its founder, Fred Smith, of the importance that

IDENTITY VERSUS IMAGE ❖ A successful brand personality does not come about by itself. It is the result of a conscious *identity-building program.* The identity-building tools are names, logos, symbols, atmospheres, events. Hopefully this work will create the desired *brand image.* But it is important to distinguish between identity and image. *Identity* comprises the ways that a company aims to identify itself to its publics. *Image* is the way the public perceives the company. The company designs its identity in order to shape the public's image, but other factors intervene to determine each person's image of the company.

One seeks certain characteristics in an image. It must convey a *singular message* that establishes the product's major virtue and positioning. It must convey this message in a *distinctive* way so that it is not confused with similar messages from competitors. It must deliver *emotional power* so that it stirs the hearts as well as the minds of buyers.

Developing a strong image calls for creativity and hard work. The image cannot be implanted in the public's mind overnight nor seeded by one media vehicle alone. The image must be conveyed through every available communication vehi-

households and businesses place on fast and reliable mail delivery. Smith implemented a brilliant logistical hub-and-spoke system that enabled Federal Express to deliver letters and small packages picked up before 5 P.M. to anywhere in the United States before 11 A.M. the next day, or money back. He is now extending this system to worldwide delivery of mail.

Retailing speedup is a fourth frontier for competitive advantage. Years ago, customers waited a week to have a roll of film developed or to receive a new pair of glasses. Today, film is developed in one hour, and a new pair of glasses can be produced in an hour. The key concept has been to convert retail stores into *minifactories*. Today's photo stores now operate film-developing equipment; and optician retailers operate minilaboratories in their stores. The same factory principle is applied by Mrs. Fields, Dunkin Donuts, and others who bake the goods as needed in their stores.

Services are also being speeded up. Mortgage loans typically take several weeks to process before approval; Citicorp, using an expert system, has reduced approval time to 15 minutes. Auto damage insurance claims can also be settled faster. Progressive Insurance dispatches an "office van" equipped with a PC, modem, printer, and fax, which arrives at the scene of an accident within an hour. The adjuster can assess damages, make an offer, and issue a check on the spot.

Home delivery service is also being speeded up.

Domino's Pizza's success is due to its promise to deliver pizza to any customer in its trade area within one-half hour or to supply it free or at a reduced charge. As if this were not fast enough, new competitors will shorten the promised time further by equipping vans with ovens and telephones so that pizzas can be cooked in the van as it is driven to the customer's location.

Not all industries are caught up in the speed frenzy. Some companies rightfully worry that speedups might hurt their quality. They may launch products too quickly without sufficient care, or overtax their distribution system. Smart companies don't let this happen. They redesign their operations to be not only faster but better. All it takes is one company in the industry to find a way to serve customers faster and better to force the others to reexamine their performance on innovation, manufacturing, logistics, and retailing cycle time.

For further reading, see Brian Dumaine, "Speed," *Fortune,* February 17, 1989, pp. 54–59; George Stalk, Jr. and Thomas M. Hout, *Competing Against Time* (New York: The Free Press, 1990); and Stanley Davis and Bill Davidson, *2020 Vision: Transform Your Business Today to Succeed in Tomorrow's Economy* (New York: Simon & Schuster, 1991), Chapter 2.

cle and disseminated continuously. If "IBM means service," this message must be expressed in *symbols, written and audio/visual media, atmosphere,* and *events.*

SYMBOLS ❖ A strong image consists of one or more symbols that trigger company or brand recognition. The company and brand *logos* should be designed for instant recognition. The company might choose some *object* such as the lion (Harris Bank), apple (Apple Computer), or doughboy (Pillsbury) to symbolize a quality of the organization. The company might build a brand around a famous person, as with new perfumes—Passion (Elizabeth Taylor) and Uninhibited (Cher). A further step consists of choosing a *color* identifier such as blue (IBM) or red (Campbell soup) and sometimes a specific piece of *sound/music.*

WRITTEN AND AUDIO/VISUAL MEDIA ❖ The chosen symbols must be worked into *advertisements* that convey the company or brand personality. The ads should convey a storyline, a mood, a performance level—something distinctive. The message should be replicated in other *publications,* such as annual reports, brochures, catalogs. The company's *stationery and business cards* should reflect the same image that the company wants to convey.

ATMOSPHERE ❖ The physical space in which the organization produces or delivers its products and services becomes another powerful image generator. Hyatt Regency hotels developed a distinctive image through its atrium lobbies. A bank that wants to look friendly must choose the right building design, interior design, layout, colors, materials, and furnishings.

EVENTS ❖ A company can build an identity through the type of events it sponsors. Perrier, the bottled water company, came into prominence by laying out exercise tracks and sponsoring health sports events. AT&T and IBM identify themselves as sponsors of cultural events such as symphony performances and art exhibits. Other organizations identify themselves with popular causes: Heinz gives money to hospitals, and General Foods makes donations to MADD (Mothers against Drunk Drivers).

Developing a Positioning Strategy

We have seen that any company or brand can be differentiated. There is no such thing as a *commodity*. Instead of thinking that it is selling a "commodity," the company must see its task as that of converting an "undifferentiated product" into a "differentiated offer." Dermot Dunphy, the CEO of Sealed Air Corporation, which makes plastic bubble wrap said, "The lesson to be learned is that no matter how commonplace a product may appear, it does not have to become a commodity. Every product, every service can be differentiated."[7] Levitt and others have pointed out dozens of ways to differentiate an offer.[8] Part of the answer lies in recognizing that buyers have different needs and are therefore attracted to different offers.

At the same time, not all brand differences are meaningful or worthwhile. Not every difference is a differentiator. Each difference has the potential to create company costs as well as customer benefits. Therefore the company must carefully select the ways in which it will distinguish itself from competitors. A difference is worth establishing to the extent that it satisfies the following criteria:

- ◆ *Important:* The difference delivers a highly valued benefit to a sufficient number of buyers.
- ◆ *Distinctive:* The difference either isn't offered by others or is offered in a more distinctive way by the company.
- ◆ *Superior:* The difference is superior to other ways to obtain the same benefit.
- ◆ *Communicable:* The difference is communicable and visible to buyers.
- ◆ *Preemptive:* The difference cannot be easily copied by competitors.
- ◆ *Affordable:* The buyer can afford to pay for the difference.
- ◆ *Profitable:* The company will find it profitable to introduce the difference.

Many companies have introduced differentiations that failed on one or more of these tests. The Westin Stamford hotel in Singapore advertises that it is the world's tallest hotel; actually this isn't important to many tourists and in fact turns many off. AT&T's Picturevision phones failed, partly because the public did not think that seeing the other person was worth the phone's high cost. Polaroid's Polarvision, which produced instantly developed film, bombed too. Although

Polarvision was distinctive and even preemptive, it was inferior to another way of capturing motion, namely videocameras.

Suppose a heavy-duty-truck manufacturer, say Volvo, worried that truck buyers saw most truck brands as similar and therefore chose their brand mainly on price. Table 12-3A describes this hypothetical situation. In this case, the buyer sees no differences among the trucks. Every truck has an excellent ride (score 9 out of 10), and every truck has only average living features (score 6). Realizing this, Volvo and its three competitors decide to differentiate their truck's physical characteristics.

❖ **Differentiation** *is the act of designing a set of meaningful differences to distinguish the company's offer from competitors' offers.*

The results are shown in Table 12-3B. No truck is superior to all of its competitors on all attributes. Navistar is best at fuel economy, but only average in ride quality. Mack is superior in durability, but it is less distinguished on the other attributes.

We conclude that each truck will appeal to different groups of buyers. Any truck manufacturer can show this *comparison chart* to its target buyers. The column under each brand describes the brand's *total positioning strategy*. This can also be illustrated using perceptual maps (see Marketing Concepts and Tools 12-1).

Each firm will want to promote those few differences that will appeal most strongly to its target market. The firm will want to develop a *focused positioning strategy*. We will simply call this *positioning* and define it as follows:

❖ **Positioning** *is the act of designing the company's offer and image so that it occupies a distinct and valued place in the target customers' minds.*

Positioning calls for the company to decide how many differences and which differences to promote to the target customers.

How Many Differences to Promote?

Many marketers advocate promoting only one benefit to the target market. Rosser Reeves said a company should develop a *unique selling proposition* (USP) for each brand and stick to it.[9] Thus Crest toothpaste consistently promotes its anticavity protection, and Mercedes promotes its great automotive engineering. Ries and Trout also favor one consistent positioning message.[10] Each brand should pick an

			PERFORMANCE RATING			
	ATTRIBUTE	Weight	Navistar	Paccar	Volvo	Mack
A. No Differentiation	Durability	35	7	7	7	7
	Fuel economy	25	8	8	8	8
	Living features	20	6	6	6	6
	Ride	20	9	9	9	9
	Attribute	Weight	Navistar	Paccar	Volvo	Mack
B. Substantial Differentiation	Durability	35	7	7	8	9
	Fuel economy	30	9	8	7	7
	Living features	20	6	9	7	6
	Ride	15	5	7	8	6

TABLE 12-3
Purchase Decision by Customer for Heavy-Duty Trucks

Hypothetical examples.

Source: Robert D. Buzzell and Bradley T. Gale, *The PIMS Principles: Linking Strategy to Performance* (New York: Free Press, 1987), p. 122.

Positioning Theme Parks Using Perceptual Maps

Suppose a theme park company wants to build a new theme park in the Los Angeles area to take advantage of the large number of tourists who come to Los Angeles to see Disneyland and other tourist attractions. Seven theme parks now operate in the Los Angeles area. Management feels that the existing theme parks are quite expensive: A family of four will pay $50 for a day at Disneyland. Management believes it could develop a less-expensive theme park that would appeal to cost-conscious tourists. Management, however, needs to know how consumers view the seven existing theme parks in terms of various satisfactions they seek, including low cost.

The company used the following procedure to develop a perceptual map of Los Angeles's seven major tourist attractions. It presented consumers with a series of triads (for example, the triad Busch Gardens, Japanese Deer Park, and Disneyland) and asked them to choose the two most similar attractions and the two least similar attractions in each triad. A statistical analysis led to the accompanying perceptual map.

This map contains two features. There are seven dots representing the seven major tourist attractions in the Los Angeles area. The closer any two attractions are, the more similar they are; thus Disneyland and Magic Mountain are perceived as similar, whereas Disneyland and Lion Country Safari are perceived as very dissimilar.

The map also contains nine satisfactions that people look for in tourist attractions, indicated by arrows. The standing of each tourist attraction on each attribute can be read. For example, Marineland of the Pacific is perceived by consumers as involving the "least waiting time," so it is furthest along the imaginary line of the "little waiting" arrow, while Magic Mountain is perceived as involving the most waiting time. Consumers think of Busch Gardens as the most economical attraction and Knott's Berry Farm as the most expensive attraction. Evidently, the company will face Busch Gardens as a major competitor if it decides to build a theme park to appeal to cost-conscious tourists. At the same time, management will pay attention to all the other satisfactions consumers seek as it figures out a product concept for the theme park and its positioning strategy in relation to the other theme parks.

The analysis can be improved further by preparing a separate perceptual map for each market segment instead of one map for the total market. Each market segment is likely to perceive the products and benefits somewhat differently.

SOURCES: See Robert V. Stumpf, "The Market Structure of the Major Tourist Attractions in Southern California," *Proceedings of the 1976 Sperry Business Conference* (Chicago: American Marketing Association, pp. 101–6).

---

attribute and tout itself as "number one" on that attribute. Buyers tend to remember "number one" messages, especially in an overcommunicated society (see Marketing Strategies 12-2).

What are some of the "number-one" positions to promote? The major ones are "best quality," "best service," "lowest price," "best value," and "most advanced technology." If a company hammers away at one of these positionings and convincingly delivers on it, it will probably be best known and recalled for this strength.

Not everyone agrees that *single-benefit positioning* is always best. The company can try for *double-benefit positioning*. This may be necessary if two or more firms are claiming to be best on the same attribute. The intention is to find a special niche within the target segment. Steelcase, Inc., a leading office-furniture-systems company, differentiates itself from its competitors on two benefits: best on-time delivery, and best installation support. Volvo positions its automobiles as "safest" and "most durable." Fortunately, these two benefits are compatible. One expects that a very safe car would also be very durable.

There are even cases of successful *triple-benefit positioning*. Beecham promotes its Aquafresh toothpaste as offering three benefits: "anticavity protection," "better

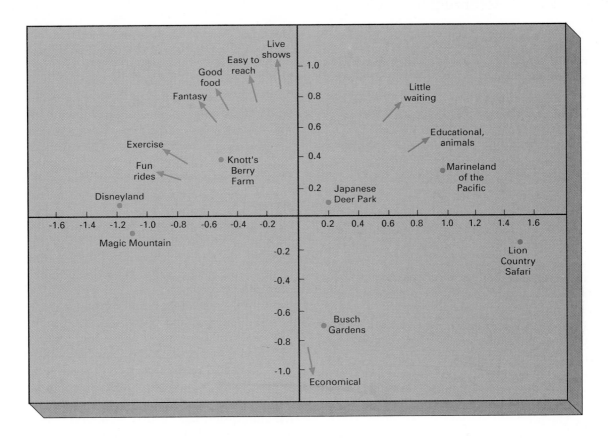

breath," and "whiter teeth." Clearly, many people want all three benefits, and the challenge is to convince them that the brand delivers all three. Beecham's solution was to create a toothpaste that squeezed out of the tube in three colors, thus visually confirming the three benefits. In doing this, Beecham "countersegmented"; that is, it attracted three segments instead of one. In a time when segments are becoming very small, companies are trying to broaden the positioning strategy to appeal to more segments.

However, as companies increase the number of claims for their brand, they risk disbelief and a loss of clear positioning. In general, a company must avoid four major positioning errors:

◆ *Underpositioning:* Some companies discover that buyers have only a vague idea of the brand. Buyers don't really sense anything special about it.

◆ *Overpositioning:* Buyers may have too narrow an image of the brand. Thus a consumer might think that diamond rings at Tiffany start at $5,000 when in fact Tiffany now offers affordable diamond rings starting at $900.

◆ *Confused Positioning:* Buyers might have a confused image of the brand resulting from making too many claims or changing the brand's positioning too frequently.

"Positioning" According to Ries and Trout

The word *positioning* was popularized by two advertising executives, Al Ries and Jack Trout. They see positioning as a creative exercise done with an existing product. Here is their definition:

Positioning starts with a product. A piece of merchandise, a service, a company, an institution, or even a person. . . . But positioning is not what you do to a product. Positioning is what you do to the mind of the prospect. That is, you position the product in the mind of the prospect.

Ries and Trout argue that current products generally have a position in the minds of consumers. Thus Hertz is thought of as the world's largest auto-rental agency, Coca-Cola as the world's largest soft-drink company, Porsche as one of the world's best sports cars, and so on. These brands own those positions and it would be hard for a competitor to steal these positions. A competitor has only three strategy options.

One strategy is to strengthen its own current position in the mind of consumers. Thus Avis took its second position in the auto rental business and made a strong point about it: "We're number two. We try harder." This is believable to the consumer. And 7-Up capitalized on the fact that it was not a cola soft drink by advertising itself as the Uncola.

The second strategy is to search for a new unoccupied position that is valued by enough consumers and to grab it. They call it "Cherchez le creneau," or "Look for the hole." Find the hole in the market and fill it. Thus Milky Way candy wanted to strengthen its market share against Hershey. Its marketers noticed that most candy bars were eaten within a minute once they were opened, but Milky Way lasted longer. So they went after the position "lasts longer," which no competitor owned. As another example, United Jersey Bank was searching for a way to compete against the giant New York banks such as Citibank and Chase. Its marketers noticed that giant banks were usually slower in arranging loans. They positioned United Jersey as "the fast-moving bank," and their success rested on becoming a "fast-moving bank."

The third strategy is to deposition or reposition the competition. Most U.S. buyers of dinnerware thought that Lenox china and Royal Doulton both came from England. Royal Doulton put out ads showing that Lenox china was made in New Jersey, but theirs came from England. In a similar vein, Stolichnaya vodka attacked Smirnoff and Wolfschmidt vodka by pointing out that these brands were made, respectively, in Hartford (Connecticut) and Lawrenceburg (Indiana), but "Stolichnaya is different. It is Russian." As a final example, Wendy's famous commercial, where a 70-year-old woman named Clara looked at a competitor's hamburger and says "Where's the beef?" showed how an attack could destabilize the consumer's confidence in the leader.

Essentially, Ries and Trout outline how similar

♦ *Doubtful Positioning:* Buyers may find it hard to believe the brand claims in view of the product's features, price, or manufacturer.

The advantage of solving the *positioning problem* is that it enables the company to solve the *marketing-mix problem*. The marketing mix—product, price, place, and promotion—is essentially the working out of the tactical details of the positioning strategy. Thus a firm that seizes upon the "high-quality position" knows that it must produce high-quality products, charge a high price, distribute through high-class dealers, and advertise in high-quality magazines. That is the primary way to project a consistent and believable high-quality image.

In searching for a positioning strategy, at least seven positioning strategies are available.[11] They are described below and illustrated for the theme parks in Marketing Concepts and Tools 12-1:

♦ *Attribute Positioning:* Disneyland can advertise itself as the largest theme park in the world. Largeness is a product feature that indirectly implies a benefit, namely, the most entertainment options.

brands can acquire some distinctiveness in an "overcommunicated society" where there is so much advertising that consumers screen out most of the messages. A consumer may know only about seven soft drinks even though there are many more on the market. Even then, the mind often knows them in the form of a *product ladder,* such as Coke/Pepsi/RC Cola or Hertz/Avis/National. Ries and Trout note that the second firm usually enjoys half the business of the first firm, and the third firm enjoys half the business of the second firm. Furthermore, the top firm is remembered best.

People tend to remember *number one.* For example, when asked, "Who was the first person to successfully fly alone over the Atlantic Ocean?" we will answer "Charles Lindberg." When asked, "Who was the second person to do it?" we draw a blank. That is why companies fight for the number-one position. Ries and Trout point out that the "size" position can be held by only one brand. What counts is to achieve a number-one position along some valued attribute, not necessarily "size." Thus 7-Up is the number-one Uncola, Porsche is the number-one small sports car, and Dial is the number-one deodorant soap. The marketer should identify an important attribute or benefit that convincingly can be owned by the brand. In this way, brands get hooked into the mind in spite of the incessant advertising bombardment reaching consumers.

A fourth strategy, not mentioned by Ries and Trout, can be called the exclusive-club strategy. It can be developed by a company when a number-one position along some meaningful attribute cannot be achieved. A company can promote the idea that it is one of the Big Three, Big Eight, and so on. The Big Three idea was invented by the third-largest auto firm, Chrysler, and the Big Eight idea was invented by the eighth-largest accounting firm. (The market leader never invents this concept.) The implication is that those in the club are the "best." A Fortune-500 company financial officer feels safe in choosing any Big Eight accounting firm for auditing; but if the officer chose some other firm and something went wrong, he or she could be criticized for straying out of the Big Eight.

Ries and Trout essentially deal with the psychology of positioning or repositioning a current brand in the consumer's mind. They acknowledge that the positioning strategy might call for changes in the product's name, price, and packaging, but these are "cosmetic changes done for the purpose of securing a worthwhile position in the prospect's mind." Other marketers would add more emphasis to *real positioning* where they work up every tangible aspect of a new product to capture a position. Psychological positioning must be supported by real positioning; it is not just a mind game.

SOURCE: Al Ries and Jack Trout, *Positioning: The Battle for Your Mind* (New York: Warner Books, 1982).

◆ *Benefit Positioning:* Knott's Berry Farm can position itself as a theme park for people seeking a fantasy experience.

◆ *Use/Application Positioning:* Japanese Deer Park can position itself for the tourist who can spend only an hour and wants to catch some quick entertainment.

◆ *User Positioning:* Magic Mountain can advertise itself as the theme park for "thrill seekers," thus defining itself through a user category.

◆ *Competitor Positioning:* Lion Country Safari can advertise that it has a greater variety of animals than the Japanese Deer Park.

◆ *Product Category Positioning:* Marineland of the Pacific can position itself not as a "recreational theme park" but as an "educational institution," thus putting itself into a different product class from the expected one.

◆ *Quality/Price Positioning:* Busch Gardens can position itself as the "best value" for the money (as opposed to such positionings as "high quality/high price" or "lowest price").

TABLE 12-4   Method for Competitive-Advantage Selection

(1) COMPETITIVE ADVANTAGE	(2) COMPANY STANDING (1-10)	(3) COMPETITOR STANDING (1-10)	(4) IMPORTANCE OF IMPROVING STANDING (H-M-L)*	(5) AFFORDABILITY AND SPEED (H-M-L)	(6) COMPETITOR'S ABILITY TO IMPROVE STANDING (H-M-L)	(7) RECOMMENDED ACTION
Technology	8	8	L	L	M	Hold
Cost	6	8	H	M	M	Monitor
Quality	8	6	L	L	H	Monitor
Service	4	3	H	H	L	Invest

*H = High; M = Medium; L = Low

Which Differences to Promote?

Suppose a company has identified four alternative positioning platforms: technology, cost, quality, and service (see Table 12-4). It has one major competitor. Both companies stand at 8 on technology (1 = low score, 10 = high score), which means they both have good technology. The company cannot gain much by improving its technology further, especially given the cost of doing so. The competitor has a better standing on cost (8 instead of 6), and this can hurt the company if the market becomes more price sensitive. The company offers higher quality than its competitors (8 instead of 6). Finally, both companies offer below-average service.

It would seem that the company should go after cost or service to improve its market appeal relative to the competitor. However, other considerations arise. The first is how important to the target customers improvements are in each of these attributes. Column 4 indicates that improvements in cost and service would be of high importance to customers. Next, can the company afford to make the improvements, and how fast can it complete them? Column 5 shows that improving service would have high affordability and speed. But would the competitor also be able to improve service if the company started to do so? Column 6 shows that the competitor's ability to improve service is low, perhaps because the competitor does not believe in service or is strapped for funds. Column 7 then shows the appropriate actions to take with respect to each attribute. The one that makes the most sense is for the company to improve its service and promote the improvement as a secondary benefit. Service is important to customers; the company can afford to improve its service and do it fast; and the competitor probably cannot catch up.

> This was the conclusion that Monsanto reached in one of its chemical markets. Monsanto immediately hired additional technical service people and when they were trained and ready, Monsanto promoted itself as the "technical service leader."

Thus this type of reasoning can help the company choose or add genuine competitive advantages.

Communicating the Company's Positioning

The company must not only develop a clear positioning strategy; it must also communicate it effectively. Suppose a company chooses the "best-in-quality" positioning strategy. Quality is communicated by choosing those physical signs and cues that people normally use to judge quality. Here are some examples:

A designer of fine fur coats sews in expensive silk linings, knowing that women will judge the quality of the fur partly by the quality of the lining.

A lawn-mower manufacturer claims its lawn mower is "powerful" and uses a noisy motor because buyers think noisy lawn mowers are more powerful.

A truck manufacturer undercoats the chassis not because it needs undercoating but because undercoating suggests concern for quality.

A car manufacturer makes cars with good-slamming doors because many buyers slam the doors in the showroom to test how well the car is built.

Ford designed its Mustang to be a "sports car" and communicated this by the car's styling, bucket seats, and leather steering wheel. Yet it was not a true sports car in terms of performance. On the other hand, the BMW is a true sports car but is not designed to look like one.

Quality is also communicated through other marketing elements. A high price usually signals a premium-quality product to buyers. The product's quality image is also affected by the packaging, distribution, advertising, and promotion. Here are some cases where a brand's quality image was hurt:

A well-known frozen-food brand lost its prestige image by being on sale too often.

A premium beer's image was hurt when it switched from bottles to cans.

A highly regarded television receiver lost its quality image when mass-merchandise outlets began to carry it.

Thus the quality of the brand's packaging, channels, promotion, and so on, must collectively communicate and support the brand's image.

The manufacturers' reputation also contributes to the perception of quality. Certain companies are sticklers for quality; consumers expect Nestlé's products and IBM products to be good. To make a quality claim credible, the surest way is to offer "satisfaction or your money back." Smart companies try to communicate their quality to buyers and guarantee that this quality will be delivered or their money will be refunded.

SUMMARY ❖

Positioning is the act of designing the company's offer and image so that the target market understands and appreciates what the company stands for in relation to its competitors. The company's positioning must be rooted in an understanding of how the target market defines value and makes choices among vendors. The positioning tasks consist of three steps. First, the company has to identify possible product, services, personnel, and image differences that might be established in relation to competition. Second, the company has to apply criteria to select the most important differences. Third, the company has to effectively signal to the target market how it differs from its competition. The company's product-positioning strategy will then enable it to take the next step, namely, plan its competitive marketing strategies.

NOTES ❖

1. Michael Treacy and Fred Wiersema, "Customer Intimacy and Other Value Disciplines," *Harvard Business Review*, January-February 1993, pp. 84–93.

2. Some of the following bases are discussed in David A. Garvin, "Competing on the Eight Dimensions of Quality," *Harvard Business Review*, November-December 1987, pp. 101–9.

3. See Philip Kotler, "Design: A Powerful but Neglected Strategic Tool," *Journal of Business Strategy*, Fall 1984, pp. 16–21. Also see Christopher Lorenz, *The Design Dimension* (New York: Basil Blackwell Inc., 1986).

4. Adapted from Tom Peters's description in *Thriving on Chaos* (New York: Knopf, 1987), pp. 56–57.

5. See M. D. Harkavay, *100 Best Companies to Sell For* (New York: Wiley Press, 1989).

6. Adapted from A. Parasuraman, V. A. Zeithaml, and L. L. Berry, "A Conceptual Model of Service Quality and Its Implications for Future Research," *Journal of Marketing*, Fall 1985, pp. 41–50. Also see Chapter 18.

7. Speech to a sales meeting of Sealed Air Corporation, March 19, 1984.

8. Theodore Levitt, "Marketing Success through Differentiation—of Anything," *Harvard Business Review*, January-February, 1980.

9. Rosser Reeves, *Reality in Advertising* (New York: Knopf, 1960).

10. See Al Ries and Jack Trout, *Positioning: The Battle for Your Mind* (New York: Warner Books, 1982).

11. See Yoram J. Wind, *Product Policy: Concepts, Methods and Strategy* (Reading, MA: Addison-Wesley, 1982), pp. 79–81; and David Aaker and J. Gary Shansby, "Positioning Your Product," *Business Horizons*, May-June 1982, pp. 56–62.

13

Developing, Testing, and Launching New Products and Services

Nothing in this world is so powerful as an idea whose time has come.
VICTOR HUGO

While great devices are invented in the laboratory, great products are invented in the Marketing Department.
WILLIAM H. DAVIDOW

Once a company has carefully segmented the market, chosen its target customer groups, and determined the desired market positioning, it is ready to develop and launch appropriate and, it is hoped, successful products. Marketing management plays a key role in this process. Rather than leave it to the R&D department to develop new products, marketing actively participates with other departments in every stage of the product-development process.

Every company must carry on new-product development. Replacement products must be found in order to maintain or build future sales. Furthermore, customers want new products, and competitors will do their best to supply them. In 1992, 16,000 new products were introduced into groceries and drugstores. A Booz, Allen & Hamilton survey reported that 700 companies expected that 31% of their profits would come from new products introduced in the next five years.[1]

A company can add new products through *acquisition* and/or *new-product development*. The acquisition route can take three forms. The company can buy other companies. There has been a flurry of corporate acquisitions in recent years aimed at acquiring new products: Procter & Gamble acquired Richardson-Vicks, Noxell, and several Revlon brands; R. J. Reynolds bought Nabisco; Philip Morris acquired General Foods and Kraft; and General Electric bought RCA. Alternatively, the company can acquire selected patents from other companies. Or it can buy a license or franchise from another company.

The new-product development route can take two forms. The company can develop new products in its own laboratories. Or it can contract with independent researchers or new-product-development firms to develop specific products for the company.

Many companies pursue growth through both acquisition and new-product development. Their managements feel that the best opportunities might lie in acquisition at certain times and new-product development at other times, and they want to be skilled at both.

What do we mean by new products? *New products* for our purposes will include *original products*, *improved products*, *modified products*, and *new brands* that the firm develops through its own R&D efforts. We will also be concerned with whether consumers see them as "new."

Booz, Allen & Hamilton identified six categories of new products in terms of their newness to the company and to the marketplace.[2] They are

- *New-to-the-World Products:* New products that create an entirely new market
- *New-Product Lines:* New products that allow a company to enter an established market for the first time
- *Additions to Existing Product Lines:* New products that supplement a company's established product lines (package sizes, flavors, and so on)
- *Improvements in Revisions to Existing Products:* New products that provide improved performance or greater perceived value and replace existing products
- *Repositionings:* Existing products that are targeted to new markets or market segments
- *Cost Reductions:* New products that provide similar performance at lower cost

A company usually pursues a mix of these new products. An important finding is that only 10% of all new products are truly innovative and new to the world. These products involve the greatest cost and risk because they are new to both the company and the marketplace. Most company new product activity is devoted to improving existing products rather than creating new ones. At Sony, over 80% of new product activity is devoted to improving and modifying existing Sony products.

This chapter will examine the following questions:

♦ What are the main risks in developing new products?
♦ What organizational structures are used in managing new-product development?
♦ How can the stages of the new-product-development process be better managed?
♦ After product launch, what factors affect the rate of consumer adoption and new-product diffusion?

The New-Product-Development Dilemma

Given the intense competition in most markets today, companies that fail to develop new products are exposing themselves to great risk. Their existing products are vulnerable to changing consumer needs and tastes, new technologies, shortened product life cycles, and increased domestic and foreign competition.

At the same time, new-product development is risky. Texas Instruments lost $660 million before withdrawing from the home computer business; RCA lost $575 million on its ill-fated videodisc players; Ford lost $350 million on its ill-fated Edsel; Du Pont lost an estimated $100 million on its synthetic leather called Corfam; and the French Concorde aircraft will never recover its investment.

New products continue to fail at a disturbing rate. The new-product failure rate in packaged goods (consisting mostly of line extensions) is estimated at 80%.[3] Clancy and Shulman believe that the same high failure rate befalls new financial products and services, such as credit cards, insurance plans, and brokerage services.[4] Cooper and Kleinschmidt estimate that about 75% of new products fail at launch.[5] These estimates, of course, depend on how the researcher defines a new-product failure, i.e., whether the product failed to deliver any profit or delivered profits below expectations.

Why do many new products fail? There are several factors. A high-level executive might push a favorite idea through in spite of negative marketing research findings. Or the idea is good, but the market size is overestimated. Or the actual product is not well designed. Or it is incorrectly positioned in the market, not advertised effectively, or overpriced. Often new-product-development costs are higher than expected, or the competitors fight back harder than expected.

Successful new-product development is hindered by many factors:

♦ *Shortage of Important New-Product Ideas in Certain Areas:* There may be few ways left to improve some basic products such as steel, detergents, and so forth.
♦ *Fragmented Markets:* Keen competition is leading to market fragmentation. Companies have to aim their new products at smaller market segments, and this means lower sales and profits for each product.
♦ *Social and Governmental Constraints:* New products have to satisfy public criteria such as consumer safety and ecological compatibility. Government requirements have slowed down innovation in the drug industry and have complicated product-design and advertising decisions in industries such as industrial equipment, chemicals, automobiles, and toys.

- *Costliness of the New-Product-Development Process:* A company typically has to generate many new-product ideas in order to finish with a few good ones. Furthermore, the company has to face rising R&D, manufacturing, and marketing costs.

- *Capital Shortage:* Some companies with good ideas cannot raise the funds needed to research them.

- *Faster Development Time:* Many competitors are likely to get the same idea at the same time, and the victory often goes to the swiftest. Alert companies have to compress development time by using computer-aided design and manufacturing techniques, strategic partners, early concept tests, and advanced marketing planning. Japanese companies see the challenge as "achieving better quality at a cheaper price at a faster speed than competitors."[6]

- *Shorter Product Life Cycle:* When a new product is successful, rivals are so quick to copy it that the new product's life cycle is considerably shortened. Sony used to enjoy a three-year lead time on its new products before they were copied extensively by competitors. Now Matsushista and other competitors will copy the product within six months, hardly leaving enough time for Sony to recoup its investment.

Yet some common elements characterize successful new-product launches (see Marketing Concepts and Tools 13-1). Successful new-product development requires the company to establish an effective organization for managing the new-product-development process. The company must also apply the best analytical tools and concepts in each stage of the new-product-development process. We will look at each in turn.

Effective Organizational Arrangements

Top management is ultimately accountable for the new-product success record. It cannot simply ask the new-product manager to come up with great ideas. New-product-development requires top management to define the business domains and product categories that the company wants to emphasize. In one food company, the new-product manager spent thousands of dollars researching a new snack idea only to hear the president say, "Drop it. We don't want to be in the snack business."

Top management must establish specific criteria for acceptance of new-product ideas, especially in large multidivisional companies where all kinds of projects bubble up as favorites of various managers.

For example, the Gould Corporation established the following acceptance criteria: the product can be introduced within five years; the product has a market potential of at least $50 million and a 15% growth rate; the product will provide at least 30% return on sales and 40% on investment; and the product will achieve technical or market leadership.

A major decision facing top management is how much to budget for new-product development. R&D outcomes are so uncertain that it is difficult to use normal investment criteria for budgeting. Some companies solve this problem by encouraging and financing as many projects as possible, hoping to achieve a few winners. Other companies set their R&D budget by applying a conventional percentage-to-sales figure or by spending what the competition spends. Still other companies decide how many successful new products they need and work backwards to estimate the required R&D investment.

Table 13-1 shows how a company can calculate the investment cost of new-product development. The new-products manager at a large consumer-packaged-goods company reviewed the results of 64 new-product ideas his company considered. Only one in four ideas, or 16, passed the idea-screening stage, and it

Marketing Concepts and Tools 13-1

Key Factors in Launching Successful New Products

Because so many new products fail, companies are eager to learn how to improve their odds of new-product success. One approach is to identify successful new products and determine what is common to them. Cooper and Kleinschmidt have summarized many past studies of new-product success; in addition, they conducted a study of 200 moderate-to-high-technology new-product launches looking for factors that successful products shared in common that were not shared by product failures. They found that the number-one success factor is a *unique superior product* (e.g., higher quality, new features, higher value in use, etc.). Specifically, products with a high product advantage succeed 98% of the time, compared to products with a moderate advantage (58% success) or minimal advantage (18% success). Another key success factor is a *well-defined product concept prior to development*, where the company carefully defined and assessed the target market, product requirements, and benefits before proceeding. Other success factors were *technological and marketing synergy, quality of execution in all stages*, and *market attractiveness*.[1]

Madique and Zirger, in a separate study of successful product launches in the electronics industry (where product success was defined as meeting or exceeding financial break-even), found eight factors accounting for new-product success. Specifically, they found new-product success to be greater: *the deeper the company's understanding of customer needs, the higher the performance-to-cost ratio, the earlier the product is introduced ahead of competition, the greater the expected contribution margin, the greater the development cross-functional teamwork, the more spent on announcing and launching the product, and the greater the top management support.*[2]

SOURCES: 1. Robert G. Cooper and Elko J. Kleinschmidt, *New Products: The Key Factors in Success* (Chicago: American Marketing Association, 1990). 2. Modesto A. Madique and Billie Jo Zirger, "A Study of Success and Failure in Product Innovation: The Case of the U.S. Electronics Industry," *IEEE Transactions on Engineering Management*, November 1984, pp. 192–203.

cost $1,000 per idea reviewed at this stage. Half of these ideas, or eight, survived the concept-testing stage, at a cost of $20,000 each. Half of these, or four, survived the product-development stage, at a cost of $200,000 each. Half of these, or two, did well in the test market, at a cost of $500,000 each. When these two ideas were launched, at a cost of $5,000,000 each, only one was highly successful. Thus the one successful idea had cost the company $5,721,000 to develop. In the process, 63 other ideas fell by the wayside. Therefore the total cost for developing one successful new product was $13,984,400. Unless the company can improve the pass ratios and reduce the costs at each stage, it will have to budget nearly $14,000,000 for each successful new idea it hopes to find. If top management wants four successful new products in the next few years, it will have to budget at least $56,000,000 (= 4× $14,000,000) for new-product development.

A key factor in new-product-development work is to establish effective or-

STAGE	NUMBER OF IDEAS	PASS RATIO	COST PER PRODUCT IDEA	TOTAL COST
1. Idea screening	64	1:4	$ 1,000	$ 64,000
2. Concept test	16	1:2	20,000	320,000
3. Product development	8	1:2	200,000	1,600,000
4. Test marketing	4	1:2	500,000	2,000,000
5. National launch	2	1:2	5,000,000	10,000,000
			$5,721,000	$13,984,000

TABLE 13-1
Estimated Cost of Finding One Successful New Product (Starting with 64 New Ideas)

ganizational structures. Companies handle new-product development in several ways:[7]

- *Product Managers:* Many companies assign responsibility for new-product ideas to their product managers. In practice, this system has several faults. Product managers are usually so busy managing their product lines that they give little thought to new products other than brand modifications or extensions; they also lack the specific skills and knowledge needed to critique and develop new products.

- *New-Product Managers:* General Foods and Johnson & Johnson have new-product managers who report to group product managers. This position professionalizes the new-product function; on the other hand, new-product managers tend to think in terms of product modifications and line extensions limited to their product market.

- *New-Product Committees:* Most companies have a high-level management committee charged with reviewing and approving new-product proposals.

- *New-Product Departments:* Large companies often establish a new-product department headed by a manager who has substantial authority and access to top management. The department's major responsibilities include generating and screening new ideas, working with the R&D department, and carrying out field testing and commercialization.

- *New-Product Venture Teams:* The 3M Company, Dow, Westinghouse, and General Mills often assign major new-product-development work to venture teams. A venture team is a group brought together from various operating departments and charged with developing a specific product or business. They are "intrapreneurs" relieved of their other duties, given a budget, a time frame, and a "skunkworks" setting.

Where companies have poor records of new-product success, the cause often is a lack of organizational teamwork. The traditional model of innovation calls for the R&D department to get a bright idea and research it, then have an engineering team design, which they throw over to the manufacturing department to produce, and then over to sales to sell. But this "sequential product development" approach creates many problems. The manufacturing people often send the design back to the engineers saying they cannot produce it at the targeted cost; the engineers then spend time redesigning the product. When the salesforce later shows the product to customers, they find that it cannot be sold at the targeted price, since consumer needs and wants are not met. The salespeople are mad at the engineers, the R&D people call the salespeople incompetent, and mutual blaming is rife.

The solution is clear. To speed up new-product development, many companies are adopting a team-oriented approach called *simultaneous product development* (see Marketing Concepts and Tools 13-2). Effective product development requires closer *teamwork* among R&D, engineering, manufacturing, purchasing, marketing, and finance from the beginning. The product idea must be researched from a marketing point of view, and a specific cross-functional team must guide the project throughout its development. Studies of Japanese companies show that their new-product success is due in large part to utilizing much more cross-functional teamwork. Also of great importance is that Japanese companies bring customers in at an early stage to get their views.

According to Booz, Allen & Hamilton, the most successful innovating companies have made a consistent commitment of resources to new-product development, have designed a new-product strategy that is linked to their strategic planning process, and have established formal and sophisticated organizational arrangements for managing the new-product-development process.[8]

The most sophisticated tool for managing the innovation process is the *stage-gate system*.[9] It is used by 3M and a number of other companies (see Companies and Industries 13-1). The basic idea is to divide the innovation process into several dis-

Simultaneous Product Development: Getting Better Products to the Market Faster

Philips, the giant Dutch consumer electronics company, marketed the first practical videocassette recorder in 1972, gaining a three-year lead on its Japanese competitors. But in the seven years that it took Philips to develop its second generation of VCR models, Japanese manufacturers had launched at least three generations of new products. A victim of its own creaky product-development process, Philips never recovered from the Japanese onslaught. In today's fast-changing, fiercely competitive world, turning out new products too slowly can result in product failures, lost sales and profits, and crumbling market positions.

Today many companies are moving from a sequential product-development approach to a simultaneous product-development approach. Top management establishes a cross-functional team and challenges it with stiff and seemingly contradictory goals—"turn out carefully planned and superior new products, but do it quickly." The team becomes a driving force that pushes the product forward. In the sequential process, a bottleneck at one phase can seriously slow or even halt the entire project. In the simultaneous approach, if one functional area hits snags, it works to resolve them while the team moves on. Simultaneous development is more like a rugby match than a relay race—team members pass the new product back and forth as they move downfield toward the common goal of a speedy and successful new-product launch.

The Allen-Bradley Company, a maker of industrial controls, provides an example of the tremendous benefits gained by using simultaneous development. All of the company's departments work together to design and develop new products. The company recently developed a new electrical control in just two years; under the old system, it would have taken six years.

The auto industry has discovered the benefits of simultaneous product development. The approach is called "simultaneous engineering" at GM, the "team concept" at Ford, and "process-driven design" at Chrysler. The first American cars built using this process, the Ford Taurus and Mercury Sable, have been major marketing successes. Using simultaneous product development, Ford slashed development time from 60 months to less than 40. It squeezed 14 weeks from its cycle by simply getting the engineering and finance departments to review designs at the same time instead of sequentially. It claims that such actions have helped cut average engineering costs for a project by 35%. In an industry that has typically taken five or six years to turn out a new model, Mazda now brags about two-to-three-year product-development cycles—a feat that would be impossible without simultaneous development.

However, the simultaneous approach has limitations. Super-fast product development can be riskier and more costly than the slower, more orderly sequential approach. And it often creates increased organizational tension and confusion. But in rapidly changing industries facing increasingly shorter product life cycles, the rewards of fast and flexible product development far exceed the risks. Companies that get new and improved products to the market faster than competitors gain a dramatic competitive edge. They can respond more quickly to emerging consumer tastes and charge higher prices for more advanced designs.

SOURCES: Hirotaka Takeuchi and Ikujiro Nonaka, "The New New Product Development Game," *Harvard Business Review,* January–February 1986, pp. 137–46; Bro Uttal, "Speeding New Ideas to Market," *Fortune,* March 2, 1987, pp. 62–65; John Bussey and Douglas R. Sease, "Speeding Up: Manufacturers Strive To Slice Time Needed To Develop New Products," *The Wall Street Journal,* February 23, 1988, pp. 1, 24; and Paul Kunkel, "Competing by Design," *Business Week,* March 25, 1991, pp. 51–63.

tinct stages. At the end of each stage is a gate or checkpoint. The project leader, working with a cross-functional team, must bring a set of known deliverables to each gate before the project can be passed to the next stage. For example, to move from the *business plan* stage into *product development* requires evidence of a convincing market research study of consumer needs and interest, a competitive analysis, and a technical appraisal. Senior managers act as "gatekeepers" and review the criteria at each gate to judge whether the project deserves being moved to the next stage, which always involves higher cost. The gatekeepers make one of four deci-

CHAPTER 13
Developing, Testing, and Launching New Products and Services

3M's Approach to Innovation

Certain companies have earned an outstanding reputation for successful and continuous innovation. Heading most lists is the Minneapolis-based 3M Company—maker of more than 60,000 products including sandpaper, adhesives, floppy discs, contact lenses, overhead projectors, post-it notes, and so on. This $13 billion company's immodest goal is to have each of its 40 divisions generate at least 25% of its income from products introduced within the preceding five years! And more astonishing, they succeed. Each year the company launches more than 200 new products.

3M invests 6.5% of its annual sales in R&D—twice as much as the average company. 3M encourages everyone, not just its engineers, to become "product champions." Anyone who is hot about an idea is encouraged to do some homework to find out what knowledge exists, where the product would be developed in the company, whether it is patentable, and how profitable it might be. The company's renowned "15% rule" allows all employees to spend up to 15% of their time "bootlegging"—working on projects of personal interest. When a promising idea comes along, a venture team is formed with representatives from R&D, manu-facturing, sales, marketing, and legal. Each team is headed by an "executive champion," who nurtures the team and protects it from bureaucratic intrusion. If a "healthy-looking product" is developed, the team stays with it and markets it. If the product fails, each team member returns to his or her previous level. Some teams have tried three or four times to make a success out of an idea and, in several cases, have succeeded.

3M knows that it must try thousands of new-product ideas to hit one big jackpot. One well-worn slogan at 3M is, "You have to kiss a lot of frogs to find a prince." "Kissing frogs" often means making mistakes but 3M accepts blunders and dead ends as a normal part of creativity and innovation. Its philosophy seems to be "if you aren't making mistakes, you probably aren't doing anything."

Each year 3M hands out its Golden Step awards to venture teams whose new product earned more than $2 million in U.S. sales or $4 million in worldwide sales within three years of its commercial introduction. "Intrapreneurship" is the name of the game at 3M, a game that more companies are seeking to master.

sions: go/kill/hold/recycle. The project leader and team know the criteria they must meet at each stage. They are expected to drive the project from its beginning to the time it is launched or killed. This contrasts with companies that move new-product development from department to department, changing leaders all the time. Stage-gate systems bring a number of benefits, including putting strong discipline into the innovation process, making its steps visible to all involved, and clarifying the project leader's and team's responsibilities at each point.

We are now ready to look at the major marketing challenges at each stage of the new-product-development process. Eight stages are involved: *idea generation, screening, concept development and testing, marketing strategy, business analysis, product development, market testing,* and *commercialization.*

Idea Generation

The new-product-development process starts with the search for ideas. The search should not be casual. Top management should define the products and markets to emphasize. It should state the new-product objectives, whether it is high cash flow, market-share domination, or some other objective. It should state how much effort should be devoted to developing breakthrough products, modifying existing products, and copying competitors' products.

Sources of New-Product Ideas

New-product ideas can come from many sources: customers, scientists, competitors, employees, channel members, and top management.

The marketing concept holds that *customers' needs and wants* are the logical place to start in the search for new-product ideas. Hippel has shown that the highest percentage of ideas for new industrial products originate with customers.[10] Technical companies can learn a great deal by studying a special set of their customers, the *lead users*, namely, those customers who make the most advanced use of the company's product and who recognize needed improvements ahead of other customers. Companies can identify customers' needs and wants through customer surveys, projective tests, focused group discussion, and suggestion and complaint letters from customers. Many of the best ideas come from asking customers to describe their problems with current products. Thus an automobile company can ask recent buyers what they like and dislike about the car; what improvements could be made; and how much they would pay for each improvement. This survey will yield numerous ideas for future improvements of the product.

Companies also rely on their *scientists, engineers, designers,* and other *employees* for new-product ideas. Successful companies have established a company culture that encourages every employee to seek new ideas for improving the company's production, products, and services. Toyota claims that its employees submit two million ideas annually, about 35 suggestions per employee, and over 85% of them are implemented. Kodak and some American firms give monetary and recognition awards to their employees who submit the best ideas during the year.

Companies can find good ideas by examining their *competitors'* products and services. They can learn from distributors, suppliers, and sales representatives what competitors are doing. They can find out what customers like and dislike in their competitors' new products. They can buy their competitors' products, take them apart, and build better ones. Their competitive strategy is one of *product imitation and improvement* rather than *product innovation*. The Japanese are masters of this strategy, in that they have licensed or copied many Western products and found ways to improve them.

Company *sales representatives* and *middlemen* are a particularly good source of new-product ideas. They have firsthand exposure to customers' needs and complaints. They often learn first of competitive developments. An increasing number of companies train and reward their sales representatives, distributors, and dealers for finding new ideas. For example: Bill Keefer, chairman of Warner Electric Brake and Clutch, requires his salesforce to list on each monthly call report the three best product ideas they heard on customer visits. He reads these ideas each month and pens notes to his engineers, manufacturing executives, and so on, to follow up the better ideas.

Top management can be another major source of new-product ideas. Some company leaders, like Edwin H. Land, former CEO of Polaroid, take personal responsibility for technological innovation in their companies. That is not always constructive, as when a top executive pushes through a pet idea without thoroughly researching market size or interest. When Land pushed forward his Polavision project (instantly developed movies), it ended as a major product failure, because the market became more interested in videotapes as a way to film action.

New-product ideas can come from other sources as well, including inventors, patent attorneys, university and commercial laboratories, industrial consultants, advertising agencies, marketing research firms, and industrial publications.

Although ideas can flow in from many sources, their chance of receiving serious attention often depends on someone in the organization taking the role of *prod-*

uct champion. Unless someone strongly advocates the product idea, it is not likely to receive serious consideration.

Idea-Generating Techniques

Really good ideas come out of inspiration, perspiration, and techniques. A number of "creativity" techniques can help individuals and groups generate better ideas.

ATTRIBUTE LISTING ❖ This technique calls for listing the major attributes of an existing product and then modifying each attribute in the search for an improved product. Consider a screwdriver.[11] Its attributes: a round, steel shank; a wooden handle, manually operated; and torque provided by twisting action. Now a group considers ways to improve product performance or appeal. The round shank could be made hexagonal so that a wrench could be applied to increase the torque; electric power could replace manual power; the torque could be produced by pushing. Osborn suggested that useful ideas can be found by addressing the following questions to an object and its attributes: *put to other uses? adapt? magnify? minify? substitute? rearrange? reverse? combine?*[12]

FORCED RELATIONSHIPS ❖ Here several objects are considered in relation to each other. An office-equipment manufacturer wanted to design a new desk for executives. Several objects were listed—a desk, television set, clock, computer, copying machine, bookcase, and so on. The result was a fully electronic desk with a console resembling that found in an airplane cockpit.

MORPHOLOGICAL ANALYSIS ❖ This method calls for identifying the structural dimensions of a problem and examining the relationships among them. Suppose the problem is that of "getting something from one place to another via a powered vehicle." The important dimensions are the type of vehicle (cart, chair, sling, bed); the medium (air, water, oil, hard surface, rollers, rails); the power source (pressed air, internal-combustion engine, electric motor). Thus a cart-type vehicle powered by an internal-combustion engine and moving over hard surfaces is the automobile. The hope is to find some novel combinations.[13]

NEED/PROBLEM IDENTIFICATION ❖ The preceding creativity techniques do not require consumer input to generate ideas. Need/problem identification, on the other hand, starts with consumers. Consumers are asked about needs, problems, and ideas. For example, they can be asked about their problems in using a particular product or product category. Here is an illustration:

> The Landis Group, a marketing research firm, uses this technique. For a given product category, it interviews about 1,000 respondents and asks whether they are "completely satisfied," "slightly dissatisfied," "moderately dissatisfied," or "extremely dissatisfied." If they have any degree of dissatisfaction, the respondents describe their problems and complaints in their own words. For example, in a study of users of English muffins, 15% expressed some dissatisfaction, and the largest problems were muffins that were not precut, were too dry or soft, or had poor taste. The demographics revealed that the most dissatisfied users were in the 19-to-29 age group with low incomes. This information can be used by an existing competitor or a new entrant to improve the product and target the most dissatisfied groups. The various problems would be rated for their *seriousness, incidence,* and *cost of remedying* to determine which product improvements to make.

The preceding techniques can be used in reverse. Consumers receive a list of problems and tell which products come to mind as having each problem.[14] Thus the problem: "The package of _____ doesn't fit well on the shelf" might lead consumers to name dog foods and dry breakfast cereals. A food marketer might think of entering these markets with a smaller-size package.

Hippel recommends that industrial marketers can identify new-product ideas best by working with *lead users* rather than *average users* of the product class. Lead users have more advanced needs and face them years before most other users. Thus the Allen-Bradley Company, a leading programmable-controls manufacturer, would pick up "breakthrough" ideas by researching the needs of its most advanced customers.[15]

BRAINSTORMING ❖ Group creativity can be stimulated through brainstorming techniques developed by Alex Osborn. The usual brainstorming group consists of six to ten people. The problem should be specific. The sessions should last about an hour. The chairman starts with, "Remember, we want as many ideas as possible—the wilder the better—and remember, no *evaluation*." The ideas start flowing, one idea sparks another, and within an hour over a hundred or more new ideas may find their way into the tape recorder. For the conference to be maximally effective, Osborn laid down four guidelines:

- *Criticism Is Ruled Out:* Negative comments on ideas must be withheld until later.
- *Freewheeling Is Welcomed:* The wilder the idea, the better; it is easier to tame down than to think up.
- *Quantity Is Encouraged:* The greater the number of ideas, the more the likelihood of useful ideas.
- *Combining and Improving Ideas Is Encouraged:* Participants should suggest how ideas of others can be joined into still newer ideas.[16]

SYNECTICS ❖ William J. J. Gordon felt that Osborn's brainstorming session produced solutions too quickly, before a sufficient number of perspectives had been developed. Gordon decided to define the problem so broadly that the group would have no inkling of the specific problem.

One problem was to design a method of closing vaporproof suits worn by workers who handled high-powered fuels.[17] Gordon kept the specific problem a secret and led a discussion on the general problem of "closure," which led to images of different closure mechanisms, such as birds' nests, mouths, or thread. As the group exhausted the initial perspectives, Gordon gradually introduced facts that refined the problem further. When the group was getting close to a good solution, Gordon described the problem. Then the group started to refine the solution. These sessions would last a minimum of three hours, for Gordon believed that fatigue played an important role in unlocking ideas.

Gordon described five principles underlying the synectics method:

- *Deferment:* Look first for viewpoint rather than solutions.
- *Autonomy of Object:* Let the problem take on a life of its own.
- *Use of the Commonplace:* Take advantage of the familiar as a springboard to the strange.
- *Involvement/Detachment:* Alternate between entering into the particulars of the problem and standing back from them, in order to see them as instances of a universal.
- *Use of Metaphor:* Let apparently irrelevant, accidental things suggest analogies that are sources of new viewpoints.[18]

The main point about idea generation is that any company can attract good ideas by organizing properly. The company should motivate employees to submit ideas. They should be sent to an *idea chairman* whose name and phone number are well known. The ideas should be put in written form and reviewed each week by an *idea committee*. The idea committee should sort the ideas into three groups: promising ideas, marginal ideas, and rejects. Each promising idea should be researched by a committee member who reports back. The surviving promising ideas then move into a full-scale screening process. The company would offer payments or recognition to the employees submitting the best ideas.

Idea Screening

The purpose of idea generation is to create a large number of ideas. The purpose of the succeeding stages is to *reduce* the number of ideas to an attractive, practicable few. The first idea-pruning stage is screening.

In screening ideas, the company must avoid two types of errors. A DROP-error occurs when the company dismisses an otherwise good idea. The easiest thing to do is to find fault with other people's ideas (see Figure 13-1). Some companies shudder when they look back at some ideas they dismissed:

> Xerox saw the novel promise of Chester Carlson's copying machine; IBM and Eastman Kodak did not see it at all. RCA was able to envision the innovative opportunity of radio; the Victor Talking Machine Company could not. Henry Ford recognized the promise of the automobile; yet only General Motors realized the need to segment the automobile market into price and performance categories . . . Marshall Field understood the unique market development possibilities of installment buying;

FIGURE 13-1
Forces Fighting New Ideas
Source: Jerold Panas, Young & Partners, Inc.

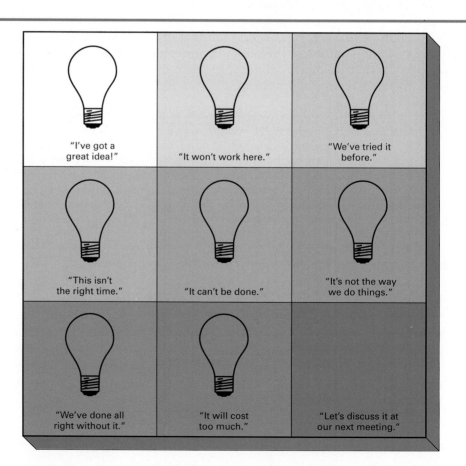

Endicott Johnson did not, calling it "the vilest system yet devised to create trouble." And so it has gone.[19]

If a company makes too many DROP-errors, its standards are too conservative.

A GO-error occurs when the company permits a poor idea to move into development and commercialization. We can distinguish three types of product failures. An *absolute product failure* loses money; its sales do not cover variable costs. A *partial product failure* loses money, but its sales cover all the variable costs and some of the fixed costs. A *relative product failure* yields a profit that is less than the company's target rate of return.

The purpose of screening is to drop poor ideas as early as possible. The rationale is that product-development costs rise substantially with each successive development stage. When products reach later stages, management feels that they have invested so much in developing the product that it should be launched to recoup some of the investment. But this is letting good money chase bad money, and the real solution is to not let poor product ideas get this far.

Product-Idea Rating Devices

Most companies require new-product ideas to be described on a standard form that can be reviewed by a new-product committee. The description states the product idea, the target market, and the competition, and it roughly estimates the market size, product price, development time and costs, manufacturing costs, and rate of return.

The executive committee then reviews each new-product idea against a set of criteria. In the case of the Kao Company of Japan, the committee considers such questions as: Does the product meet a need? Would it offer superior price performance? Can it be distinctively advertised? Figure 13-2 shows a detailed set of questions about whether a product idea meshes well with the company's objectives, strategies, and resources. Ideas that do not satisfy one or more of these questions are dropped.

The surviving ideas can be rated using the weighted-index method shown in Table 13-2. The first column lists factors required for successful product launches. In the next column, management assigns weights to these factors to reflect their relative importance. Thus management believes marketing competence will be very

TABLE 13-2
Product-Idea-Rating Device

PRODUCT SUCCESS REQUIREMENTS	RELATIVE WEIGHT (A)	COMPANY COMPETENCE LEVEL (B)	RATING (A X B)
Company personality and goodwill	.20	.6	.120
Marketing	.20	.9	.180
Research and development	.20	.7	.140
Personnel	.15	.6	.090
Finance	.10	.9	.090
Production	.05	.8	.040
Location and facilities	.05	.3	.015
Purchasing and supplies	.05	.9	.045
Total	1.00		.720*

* Rating scale: .00–.40 poor; .41–.75 fair; .76–1.00 good. Present minimum acceptance rate: .70.

Source: Adapted with modifications from Barry M. Richman, "A Rating Scale for Product Innovation," *Business Horizons*, Summer 1962, pp. 37–44.

FIGURE 13-2
Evaluating a Market
Opportunity in Terms of the
Company's Objectives and
Resources

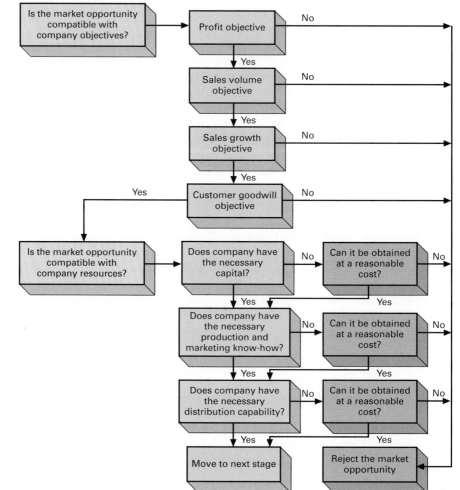

important (.20) and purchasing and supplies competence of minor importance (.05). The next task is to rate the company's competence on each factor on a scale from .0 to 1.0. Here management feels that its marketing competence is very high (.9) and its location and facilities competence low (.3). The final step is to multiply each factor's importance by the company competence level to obtain an overall rating of the company's ability to launch this product successfully. In the example, the product idea scored .72, which places it at the high end of the "fair idea" level.

This basic rating device can be refined further.[20] Its purpose is to promote systematic product-idea evaluation and discussion—it is not supposed to make the decision for management.

Concept Development and Testing

Attractive ideas must be refined into testable product concepts. We can distinguish between a product idea, a product concept, and a product image. A *product idea* is a possible product that the company might offer to the market. A *product concept* is an elaborated version of the idea expressed in meaningful consumer terms. A *product image* is the particular picture that consumers acquire of an actual or potential product.

Concept Development

We shall illustrate concept development with the following situation. A large food processing company gets the idea of producing a powder to add to milk to increase its nutritional value and taste. This is a product idea. Consumers, however, do not buy product ideas; they buy product concepts.

Any product idea can be turned into several product concepts. First, the question, who is to use this product? The powder can be aimed at infants, children, teenagers, or young or middle-aged adults. Second, what primary benefit should be built into this product? Taste, nutrition, refreshment, energy? Third, what is the primary occasion for this drink? Breakfast, midmorning, lunch, midafternoon, dinner, late evening? By asking these questions, a company can form several concepts:

- *Concept 1:* An *instant breakfast drink* for adults who want a quick nutritious breakfast without preparing a breakfast.
- *Concept 2:* A *tasty snack drink* for children to drink as a midday refreshment.
- *Concept 3:* A *health supplement* for older adults to drink in the late evening before retiring.

These represent *category concepts*; that is, they position the idea within a category. An *instant breakfast drink* would compete against bacon and eggs, breakfast cereals, coffee and pastry, and other breakfast alternatives. A *tasty snack drink* would compete against soft drinks, fruit juices, and other tasty thirst quenchers. The category concept and not the product idea defines the product's competition.

Suppose the instant-breakfast-drink concept looks best. The next task is to show where this powdered product would stand in relation to other breakfast products. This is shown in the *product-positioning map*, Figure 13-3(a), using the two dimensions of cost and preparation time. An instant breakfast drink offers the buyer low cost and quick preparation. Its nearest competitor is cold cereal; its most distant competitor is bacon and eggs. These contrasts can be utilized in communicating and promoting the concept to the market.

Next, the product concept has to be turned into a *brand concept*. Figure 13-3(b) is a *brand-positioning map* showing the current positions of three existing brands of instant breakfast drinks. The company needs to decide how much to charge and

FIGURE 13-3 Product and Brand Positioning

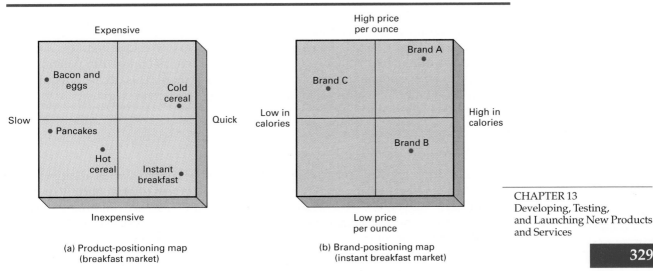

(a) Product-positioning map
(breakfast market)

(b) Brand-positioning map
(instant breakfast market)

Developing Prototypes for Concept Testing Using Stereolithography and Virtual Reality

Concept testing is more dependable the more the tested concepts resemble the final product or experience. Today a firm is able to create a three-dimensional model of a physical product (such as a small appliance, toy, etc.) through a technique known as 3–D printing or "stereolithography." Alternative physical products can be designed on a computer, and a plastic mold of each can be produced in a very short time. Potential consumers can view the plastic molds and then give their comments and reactions.[1]

When a large physical product such as an automobile is involved, it can be tested using a radically new approach called "virtual reality." The researchers use a software package to design a car on a computer, and the car can be manipulated on the computer as if it were a real object. By operating certain controls, the respondent approaches the simulated car, opens the door, sits in the car, starts the engine, hears the sound, drives away, and experiences the ride. The whole experience can be enriched by placing the simulated car in a simulated showroom and having a simulated salesperson approach the customer with a certain manner and words. The respondent, after completing this experience, is asked a series of questions about what he or she liked and disliked, as well as the likelihood of buying such a car. The researchers can vary certain car features and salesroom encounters to see which have the greatest appeal. As expensive as this approach might be, the researchers learn a great deal about designing the right car

before investing millions of dollars in building the real product.[2]

Suppose a major auto company decides to design a car for middle-to high-income people who drive a long distance every day to work. What would such people want in their car? Using focus groups, the auto researchers conclude that people would want the following: a comfortable seat, a tray for beverages, a coin slot for toll road charges, fast acceleration, good mirrors for lane switching, etc. These can be called the *customer attributes* (CAs). Once the CAs are established, the marketing department turns them over to engineers to convert into fundamental *engineering attributes* (EAs), such as horsepower, weight, gear ratios, and wind drag. The job of *customer-driven engineering* is to turn the CAs into EAs and determine the best tradeoffs given the attributes and their costs. At the next step, manufacturing selects tolerance and implements quality control monitoring systems. Then suppliers who can deliver the target tolerances and quality are chosen. This approach, called *quality function deployment*, is used by Japanese companies in designing various manufactured products.[3]

SOURCES: 1. "The Ultimate Widget: 3–D 'Printing' May Revolutionalize Product Design and Manufacturing," *U.S. News & World Report*, July 20, 1992, p. 55. 2. Benjamin Wooley, *Virtual Worlds* (London: Blackwell, 1992). 3. John Hauser, "House of Quality," *Harvard Business Review*, May–June 1988, pp. 63–73.

how calorific to make its drink. The new brand could be positioned in the medium-price, medium-calorie market or in the low-price, low-calorie market. The new brand would gain distinctiveness in either position, as opposed to positioning it next to an existing brand and fighting for market share. This decision requires researching the size and profitability of alternative preference segments in the market.

Concept Testing

Concept testing calls for testing these competing concepts with an appropriate group of target consumers. The concepts can be presented symbolically or physically. At this stage, a word and/or picture description suffices, although the reliability of a concept test increases, the more concrete and physical the stimulus (see Marketing Concepts and Tools 13-3). The consumers are presented with an elaborated version of each concept. Here is concept 1:

A powdered product that is added to milk to make an instant breakfast that gives the person all the breakfast nutrition needed along with good taste and high convenience. The product would be offered in three flavors, chocolate, vanilla, and strawberry and would come in individual packets, six to a box, at 79 cents a box.

Consumers are asked to respond to the following questions about the concept:

1. Are the benefits clear to you and believable?

   This measures the concept's *communicability* and *believability*. If the scores are low, the concept must be refined or revised.

2. Do you see this product as solving a problem or filling a need for you?

   This measures the *need level*. The stronger the need, the higher the expected consumer interest.

3. Do other products currently meet this need and satisfy you?

   This measures the *gap level* between the new product and existing products. The greater the gap, the higher the expected consumer interest. The need level can be multiplied by the gap level to produce a *need-gap score*. The higher the need-gap score, the higher the expected interest. A high need-gap score means that the consumer sees the product as filling a strong need *and* one that is not satisfied by available alternatives.

4. Is the price reasonable in relation to the value?

   This measures *perceived value*. The higher the perceived value, the higher the expected consumer interest.

5. Would you (definitely, probably, probably not, definitely not) buy the product?

   This measures *purchase intention*. We would expect it to be high for consumers who answered the previous three questions positively.

6. Who would use this product, and when and how often will the product be used?

   This provides a measure of *user targets, purchase occasions*, and *purchase frequency*.

The marketer now summarizes the respondents' answers to judge whether the concept has a broad and strong consumer appeal. The need-gap levels and purchase-intention levels can be checked against norms for the product category to see whether the concept appears to be a winner, a long shot, or a loser. One food manufacturer rejects any concept that draws a definitely-would-buy score of less than 40%. If the concept looks good, the information also tells the company what products this new product competes against, what consumers are the best targets, and so on.

Concept development and testing methodology applies to any product, service, or idea, such as an electric car, a new machine tool, a new banking service, or a new health plan. Too many managers think their job is done when they get a product idea. They think the task is to turn the idea into a physical product and sell it. But as Theodore Levitt put it, "Everybody sells intangibles in the marketplace, no matter what is produced in the factory." They forget that all selling is *concept selling*.[21] Later the product encounters all kinds of problems in the marketplace that would have been avoided if the company had done a good job of concept development and testing (see Marketing Concepts and Tools 13-4).

Marketing-Strategy Development

The new-product manager must now develop a marketing-strategy plan for introducing this product into the market. The marketing strategy will undergo further refinement in subsequent stages.

Using Conjoint Analysis to Measure Consumer Preferences

Consumer preferences for alternative product concepts can be measured through *an increasingly popular technique called conjoint analysis.* Conjoint analysis is a method for deriving the utility values that consumers attach to varying levels of an object's attributes. Respondents are shown different hypothetical offers formed by combining varying levels of the attributes. They are asked to rank-order the various offers in terms of preference. The results can be used by management to determine the most appealing offer and the estimated market share and profit the company might realize.

Green and Wind have illustrated this approach in connection with developing a new spot-removing carpet-cleaning agent for home use. Suppose the new-product marketer is considering the following five design elements:

- Three package designs (a, b, c—see figure)
- Three brand names (K2R, Glory, Bissell)
- Three prices ($1.19, $1.39, $1.59)
- A possible Good Housekeeping seal (yes, no)
- A possible money-back guarantee (yes, no)

Although the researcher can form 108 possible product concepts ($3 \times 3 \times 3 \times 2 \times 2$), it would be too much to ask consumers to rank or rate all of these concepts. A sample

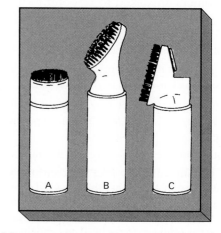

of, say, 18 contrasting product concepts can be chosen, and consumers would find it easy enough to rank them from the most preferred to the least preferred (see last column). The accompanying chart shows how one consumer ranked the 18 product concepts. This consumer ranked product concept 18 the highest, thus preferring package design C, the name Bissell, a price of $1.19, a Good Housekeeping seal, and a money-back guarantee.

From these data, a statistical program can derive the individual consumer's utility functions for the five attributes (see the five figures). Utility is measured by a

One Consumer's Ranking of 18 Stimulus Combinations

CARD	PACKAGE DESIGN	BRAND NAME	PRICE	GOOD HOUSEKEEPING SEAL?	MONEY BACK GUARANTEE?	RESPONDENT'S EVALUATION (RANK NUMBER)
1	A	K2R	$1.19	No	No	13
2	A	Glory	1.39	No	Yes	11
3	A	Bissell	1.59	Yes	No	17
4	B	K2R	1.39	Yes	Yes	2
5	B	Glory	1.59	No	No	14
6	B	Bissell	1.19	No	No	3
7	C	K2R	1.59	No	Yes	12
8	C	Glory	1.19	Yes	No	7
9	C	Bissell	1.39	No	No	9
10	A	K2R	1.59	Yes	No	18
11	A	Glory	1.19	No	Yes	8
12	A	Bissell	1.39	No	No	15
13	B	K2R	1.19	No	No	4
14	B	Glory	1.39	Yes	No	6
15	B	Bissell	1.59	No	Yes	5
16	C	K2R	1.39	No	No	10
17	C	Glory	1.59	No	No	16
18	C	Bissell	1.19	Yes	Yes	1*

* Highest rank

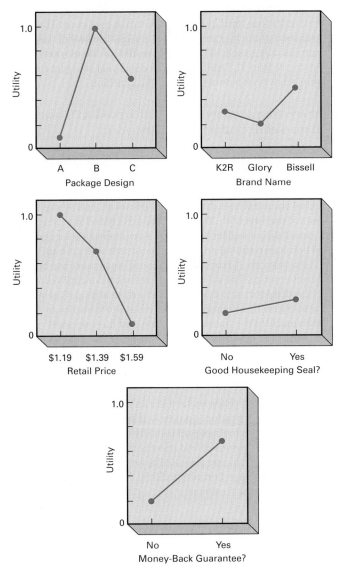

with a Good Housekeeping seal and a money-back guarantee.

We can also determine the relative importance of each attribute to this consumer. An attribute's relative importance is given by the difference between the highest and lowest utility level for that attribute. Clearly this consumer sees price and package design as the most important attributes followed by money-back guarantee, brand name, and last, a Good Housekeeping seal.

When preference data are collected from a large sample of target consumers, the data can be used to estimate the market share that any specific offer is likely to achieve, given any assumptions about competitive response. The company, however, may not launch the market offer that promises to gain the greatest market share because of cost considerations. For example, it may decide that package C, although it adds less utility than package B, might cost considerably less and be more profitable to adopt. The most appealing offer is not always the most profitable offer to make.

Under some conditions, researchers will collect the data not using a *full-profile* description of each offer but rather presenting two factors at a time (called a *tradeoff* approach). For example, respondents may be shown a table with three price levels and three package types and asked which of the nine combinations they would like most, followed by which one they would prefer next, and so on. They would then be shown a further table consisting of tradeoffs between another two variables. The tradeoff approach may be easier to use when there are many variables and possible offers. On the other hand, it is less realistic in that respondents are focusing only on two variables at a time.

Conjoint analysis has become one of the most popular concept development and testing tools, having had several thousand commercial applications. Marriott designed its Courtyard hotel concept with the benefit of conjoint analysis. Other applications have included auto styling, airline travel services, ethical drugs, credit card features, and so on.

SOURCES: The full-profile example was taken from Paul E. Green and Yoram Wind, "New Ways to Measure Consumers' Judgments," *Harvard Business Review* (July–August, 1975), pp. 107–17. Copyright © 1975 by the President and Fellows of Harvard College; all rights reserved. Also see Paul Green, Donald S. Tull, and Gerald Albaum, *Research for Marketing Decisions* (Englewood Cliffs, NJ: Prentice Hall, 1988), pp. 616–31; and Paul E. Green and V. Srinivasan, "Conjoint Analysis in Marketing: New Developments With Implications for Research and Practice," *Journal of Marketing,* October 1990, pp. 3–19.

number that ranges between zero and one; the higher the utility, the stronger the consumer's preference for that level of the attribute. Looking at packaging, for example, we see that Package B is the most favored, followed by C and then A (A hardly has any utility). The preferred names are Bissell, K2R, and Glory, in that order. The consumer's utility varies inversely with price. A Good Housekeeping seal is preferred, but it does not add that much utility and may not be worth the effort to obtain it. A money-back guarantee is strongly preferred. Putting these results together, we can see that the consumer's most desired offer would be package design B, with the brand name Bissell, selling at the price of $1.19,

The marketing-strategy plan consists of three parts. The first part describes the size, structure, and behavior of the target market, the planned product positioning, and the sales, market share, and profit goals sought in the first few years. Thus:

> The target market for the instant breakfast drink is families with children who are receptive to a new, convenient, nutritious, and inexpensive form of breakfast. The company's brand will be positioned at the higher-price, higher-quality end of the market. The company will aim initially to sell 500,000 cases or 10% of the market, with a loss in the first year not exceeding $1.3 million. The second year will aim for 700,000 cases or 14% of the market, with a planned profit of $2.2 million.

The second part of the marketing strategy outlines the product's planned price, distribution strategy, and marketing budget for the first year:

> The product will be offered in a chocolate flavor in individual packets of six to a box at a retail price of 79¢ a box. There will be 48 boxes per case, and the case's price to distributors will be $24. For the first two months, dealers will be offered one case free for every four cases bought, plus cooperative-advertising allowances. Free samples will be distributed door to door. Coupons with 20¢ off will be advertised in newspapers. The total sales-promotional budget will be $2,900,000. An advertising budget of $6,000,000 will be split 50/50 between national and local. Two thirds will go into television and one third into newspapers. Advertising copy will emphasize the benefit concepts of nutrition and convenience. The advertising-execution concept will revolve around a small boy who drinks instant breakfast and grows strong. During the first year, $100,000 will be spent on marketing research to buy store audits and consumer-panel information to monitor the market's reaction and buying rates.

The third part of the marketing-strategy plan describes the long-run sales and profit goals and marketing-mix strategy over time:

> The company intends to win a 25% market share and realize an aftertax return on investment of 12%. To achieve this return, product quality will start high and be improved over time through technical research. Price will initially be set at a skimming level and lowered gradually to expand the market and meet competition. The total promotion budget will be boosted each year about 20%, with the initial advertising/sales promotion split of 65:35 evolving eventually to 50:50. Marketing research will be reduced to $60,000 per year after the first year.

Business Analysis

After management develops the product concept and marketing strategy, it can evaluate the business proposal's attractiveness. Management needs to prepare the sales, cost, and profit projections to determine whether they satisfy the company's objectives. If they do, the product concept can move to the product-development stage. As new information comes in, the business analysis will undergo further revision.

Estimating Sales

Management needs to estimate whether sales will be high enough to yield a satisfactory profit. Sales-estimation methods depend on whether the product is a one-time-purchase product, an infrequently purchased product, or a frequently purchased product. Figure 13-4(a) illustrates the product life-cycle sales that can be

FIGURE 13-4 Product Life-Cycle Sales for Three Types of Products

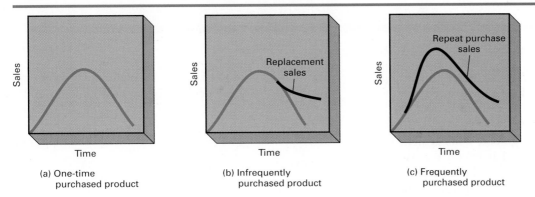

(a) One-time
    purchased product

(b) Infrequently
    purchased product

(c) Frequently
    purchased product

expected for one-time purchased products. Sales rise at the beginning, peak, and later approach zero as the number of potential buyers is exhausted. If new buyers keep entering the market, the curve will not go down to zero.

Infrequently purchased products, such as automobiles, toasters, and industrial equipment, exhibit replacement cycles dictated by either their physical wearing out or their obsolescence associated with changing styles, features, and tastes. Sales forecasting for this product category calls for separately estimating first-time sales and replacement sales [see Figure 13-4(b)].

Frequently purchased products, such as consumer and industrial nondurables, have product life-cycle sales resembling Figure 13-4(c). The number of first-time buyers initially increases and then decreases as fewer are left (assuming a fixed population). Repeat purchases occur soon, providing that the product satisfies some buyers. The sales curve eventually falls to a plateau representing a level of steady repeat-purchase volume; by this time, the product is no longer a new product.

ESTIMATING FIRST-TIME SALES ❖ The first task is to estimate first-time purchases of the new product in each period. Three examples of methods for estimating first-time purchases are shown in Marketing Concepts and Tools 13-5.

ESTIMATING REPLACEMENT SALES ❖ To estimate replacement sales, management has to research the *survival-age distribution* of its product. The low end of the distribution indicates when the first replacement sales will take place. The actual timing of replacement will be influenced by the customer's economic outlook, cash flow, and product alternatives as well as the company's prices, financing terms, and sales effort. Since replacement sales are difficult to estimate before the product is in actual use, some manufacturers base their decision to launch a new product solely on their estimate of first-time sales.

ESTIMATING REPEAT SALES ❖ For a frequently purchased new product, the seller has to estimate repeat sales as well as first-time sales. That is because the unit value of frequently purchased products is low, and repeat purchases take place soon after the introduction. A high rate of repeat purchasing means that customers are satisfied; sales are likely to stay high even after all first-time purchases take place. The seller should note the percentage of repeat purchases that take place in each *repeat-purchase class:* those who rebuy once, twice, three times, and so on. Some products and brands are bought a few times and dropped. It is important to estimate whether the repeat-purchase ratio is likely to rise or fall, and at what rate, with deeper repeat-purchase classes.[22]

Estimating Purchase Rates of New Products

MEDICAL EQUIPMENT ❖ A medical-equipment manufacturer developed a new instrument for analyzing blood specimens. The company identified three market segments—hospitals, clinics, and unaffiliated laboratories. For each segment, management defined the minimum-size facility that would buy this instrument. Then it estimated the number of facilities in each segment. It reduced the number by the estimated purchase probability, which varied from segment to segment. It then summed the remaining number of potential customers and called this the *market potential*. *Market penetration* was then estimated, based on the planned advertising and personal selling per period, the rate of favorable word of mouth, the price of the machine, and the activity of competitors. These two estimates were multiplied to estimate new-product sales.

ROOM AIR CONDITIONERS ❖ Models of epidemics (sometimes called contagion models) provide a useful analogy to the new-product diffusion process. Bass has used an epidemic equation to forecast sales of new appliances, including room air conditioners, refrigerators, home freezers, black-and-white television, and power lawn mowers.[1] He used sales data for the first few years of product introduction to estimate sales for the subsequent years, until replacement demand became a major factor. His sales projection for room air conditioners fit well. The predicted time of peak was 8.6 years as against an actual time of peak of 7.0 years. The predicted magnitude of peak was 1.9 million as against an actual peak of 1.8 million.

CONSUMER NONDURABLES ❖ Fourt and Woodlock developed a first-time sales model that they tested with several new consumer-nondurable products.[2] Their observation of new-product market-penetration rates showed that (1) cumulative sales approached a limiting penetration level of less than 100% of all households and (2) the successive increments of gain declined. Their equation is

$$q_t = r\bar{q}(1-r)^{t-1} \qquad (13\text{-}1)$$

where:

q_t = percentage of total U.S. households expected to try the product in period t
r = rate of penetration of untapped potential
$\bar{q}$ = percentage of total U.S. households expected eventually to try the new product
t = time period

Assume that it is estimated that 40% of all households will eventually try a new product ($\bar{q}=0.4$). Furthermore, in each period 30% of the remaining new-buyer potential is penetrated ($r=0.3$). The percentages of U.S. households trying the product in the first four periods are

$$q_1 = r\bar{q}(1-r)^{1-1} = (0.3)(0.4)(0.7^0) = 0.120$$
$$q_2 = r\bar{q}(1-r)^{2-1} = (0.3)(0.4)(0.7^1) = 0.084$$
$$q_3 = r\bar{q}(1-r)^{3-1} = (0.3)(0.4)(0.7^2) = 0.059$$
$$q_4 = r\bar{q}(1-r)^{4-1} = (0.3)(0.4)(0.7^3) = 0.041$$

As time moves on, the incremental trial percentage moves toward zero. To estimate dollar sales from new buyers in any period, the estimated trial rate for any period is multiplied by the total number of U.S. households times the expected first-purchase expenditure per household of the product.

SOURCES: 1. Frank M. Bass, "A New Product Growth Model for Consumer Durables," *Management Science,* January 1969, pp. 215–17. 2. Louis A. Fourt and Joseph N. Woodlock, "Early Prediction of Market Success for New Grocery Products," *Journal of Marketing,* October 1960, pp. 31–38.

Estimating Costs and Profits

After preparing the sales forecast, management can estimate the expected costs and profits of this venture. The costs are estimated by the R&D, manufacturing, marketing, and finance departments. Table 13-3 illustrates a five-year projection of sales, costs, and profits for the instant-breakfast-drink product.

Row 1 shows the *projected sales revenue* over the five-year period. The company expects to sell $11,889,000 (approximately 500,000 cases at $24 per case) in the first year. Sales are expected to rise around 28% in each of the next two years, in-

TABLE 13-3 Projected Five-Year Cash-Flow Statement (in thousands of dollars)

	YEAR 0	YEAR 1	YEAR 2	YEAR 3	YEAR 4	YEAR 5
1. Sales revenue	0	11,889	15,381	19,654	28,253	32,491
2. Cost of goods sold	0	3,981	5,150	6,581	9,461	10,880
3. Gross margin	0	7,908	10,231	13,073	18,792	21,611
4. Development costs	−3,500	0	0	0	0	0
5. Marketing costs	0	8,000	6,460	8,255	11,866	13,646
6. Allocated overhead	0	1,189	1,538	1,965	2,825	3,249
7. Gross contribution	−3,500	− 1,281	2,233	2,853	4,101	4,716
8. Supplementary contribution	0	0	0	0	0	0
9. Net contribution	−3,500	− 1,281	2,233	2,853	4,101	4,716
10. Discounted contribution (15%)	−3,500	− 1,113	1,691	1,877	2,343	2,346
11. Cumulative discounted cash flow	−3,500	− 4,613	− 2,922	− 1,045	1,298	3,644

crease by 47% in the fourth year, and then slow down to 15% growth in the fifth year. Behind this sales projection is a set of assumptions about the rate of market growth, the company's market share, and the factory-realized price.

Row 2 shows the *cost of goods sold*, which hovers around 33% of sales revenue. This cost is found by estimating the average cost of labor, ingredients, and packaging per case.

Row 3 shows the expected *gross margin*, which is the difference between sales revenue and cost of goods sold.

Row 4 shows anticipated *development costs* of $3.5 million. The development costs consist of three components. The first is the *product-development cost* of researching, developing, and testing the physical product. The second is the *marketing research costs* of fine tuning the marketing program and assessing the market's likely response. It covers the estimated costs of package testing, in-home placement testing, name testing, and test marketing. The third is the *manufacturing-development costs* of new equipment, new or renovated plant, and inventory investment.

Row 5 shows the estimated *marketing costs* over the five-year period to cover advertising, sales promotion, and marketing research and an amount allocated for salesforce coverage and marketing administration. In the first year, marketing costs stand at 67% of sales and by the fifth year are estimated to run at 42% of sales.

Row 6 shows the *allocated overhead* to this new product to cover its share of the cost of executive salaries, heat, light, and so on.

Row 7, the *gross contribution*, is found by subtracting the preceding three costs from the gross margin. Years 0 and 1 involve losses, and thereafter the gross contribution becomes positive and is expected to run as high as 15% of sales by the fifth year.

Row 8, *supplementary contribution*, is used to list any change in income from other company products caused by the introduction of the new product. It has two components. *Dragalong income* is additional income on other company products resulting from adding this product to the line. *Cannibalized income* is the reduced income on other company products resulting from adding this product to the line.[23]

Row 9 shows the *net contribution*, which in this case is the same as the gross contribution.

Row 10 shows the *discounted contribution*, namely, the present value of each future contribution discounted at 15% per annum. For example, the company will not receive $4,716,000 until the fifth year, which means that it is worth only $2,346,000 today if the company can earn 15% on its money.[24]

Finally, row 11 shows the *cumulative discounted cash flow*, which is the cumulation of the annual contributions in row 10. This cash flow is the key series on which management bases its decision on whether to go forward into product development or drop the project. Two things are of central interest. The first is the *maximum investment exposure*, which is the highest loss that the project can create. We see that the company will be in a maximum loss position of $4,613,000 in year 1; this will be the company's loss if it terminates the project. The second is the *payback period*, which is the time when the company recovers all of its investment including the built-in return of 15%. The payback period here is approximately three and a half years. Management therefore has to decide whether to risk a maximum investment loss of $4.6 million and a payback period of three and a half years.

Companies use other financial measures to evaluate the merit of a new-product proposal. The simplest is *break-even analysis*, where management estimates how many units of the product the company would have to sell to break even with the given price and cost structure. If management believed that the company could easily reach the break-even number, it would normally move the project into product development.

The most complex method is *risk analysis*. Here three estimates (optimistic, pessimistic, and most likely) are obtained for each uncertain variable affecting profitability under an assumed marketing environment and marketing strategy for the planning period. The computer simulates possible outcomes and computes a rate-of-return probability distribution, showing the range of possible rates of returns and their probabilities.[25]

Product Development

If the product concept passes the business test, it moves to R&D and/or engineering to be developed into a physical product. Up to now it has existed only as a word description, a drawing, or a crude mockup. This step calls for a large jump in investment, which dwarfs the idea-evaluation costs incurred in the earlier stages. This stage will answer whether the product idea can be translated into a technically and commercially feasible product. If not, the company's accumulated project cost will be lost except for any useful information gained in the process.

The R&D department will develop one or more physical versions of the product concept. It hopes to find a prototype that the consumers see as embodying the key attributes described in the product-concept statement, performs safely under normal use and conditions, and which can be produced within the budgeted manufacturing costs.

Developing a successful prototype can take days, weeks, months, or even years. Designing a new commercial aircraft will take several years of development work. Even developing a new taste formula can take time. For example, the Maxwell House Division of General Foods discovered that consumers wanted a brand of coffee that was "bold, vigorous, deep tasting." Its laboratory technicians spent over four months working with various coffee blends and flavors to formulate a corresponding taste. It turned out to be too expensive to produce, and the company "cost reduced" the blend to meet the target manufacturing cost. The change compromised the taste, however, and the new coffee brand did not sell well in the market.

The lab scientists must not only design the required functional characteristics but also know how to communicate the psychological aspects through *physical cues*.

This requires knowing how consumers react to different colors, sizes, weights, and other physical cues. In the case of a mouthwash, a yellow color supports an "antiseptic" claim (Listerine), a red color supports a "refreshing" claim (Lavoris), and a green color supports a "cool" claim (Scope). Or to support the claim that a lawn mower is powerful, the lab people have to design a heavy frame and a fairly loud engine. Marketers need to supply lab people with information on what attributes consumers seek and how consumers judge whether these attributes are present.

When the prototypes are ready, they must be put through rigorous functional and consumer tests. The *functional tests* are conducted under laboratory and field conditions to make sure that the product performs safely and effectively. The new aircraft must fly; the new snack food must be shelf stable; the new drug must not create dangerous side effects. Functional product testing of new drugs now takes years of laboratory work with animal subjects and then human subjects before the drugs obtain Federal Drug Administration approval. In the case of equipment testing, consider the Bissell Company's experience testing a combination electric vacuum cleaner-floor scrubber:

> . . . four were left with the research and development department for continued tests on such things as water lift, motor lift, effectiveness in cleaning, and dust bag design. The other eight were sent to the company's advertising agency for tests by a panel of fifty housewives. The research and development department found some serious problems in their further tests of the product. The life of the motor was not sufficiently long, the filter bag did not fit properly, and the scrubber foot was not correct. Similarly, the consumer tests brought in many consumer dissatisfactions that had not been anticipated; the unit was too heavy, the vacuum did not glide easily enough, and the scrubber left some residue on the floor after use.[26]

Consumer testing can take a variety of forms, from bringing consumers into a laboratory to giving them samples to use in their homes. *In-home product placement tests* are common with products ranging from ice-cream flavors to new appliances. When Du Pont developed its new synthetic carpeting, it installed free carpeting in several homes in exchange for the homeowners' willingness to report their likes and dislikes about synthetic carpeting. Consumer-preference testing draws on a variety of techniques, such as simple ranking, paired comparisons, and rating scales, each with its own advantages and limitations (see Marketing Concepts and Tools 13-6).

Market Testing

After management is satisfied with the product's functional and psychological performance, the product is ready to be dressed up with a brand name, packaging, and a preliminary marketing program to test it in more authentic consumer settings. (Branding and packaging decisions are discussed in Chapter 17.) The purpose of market testing is to learn how consumers and dealers react to handling, using, and repurchasing the actual product and how large the market is.

Not all companies choose the route of market testing. A company officer of Revlon, Inc., stated:

> In our field — primarily higher-priced cosmetics not geared for mass distribution — it would be unnecessary for us to market test. When we develop a new product, say an improved liquid makeup, we know it's going to sell because we're familiar with the field. And we've got 1,500 demonstrators in department stores to promote it.

Methods for Measuring Consumer Preferences

Suppose a consumer is shown three items—A, B, and C. They might be three automobiles or advertisements or names of political candidates. There are three methods—simple rank ordering, paired comparison, and monadic rating—for measuring an individual's preference for these items.

The *simple-rank-order* method asks the consumer to rank the three items in order of preference. The consumer might respond with A > B > C. This method does not reveal how intensely the consumer feels about each item. The consumer may not like any one of them very much. Nor does it indicate how much the consumer prefers one object to another. Also, this method is difficult to use when there are many objects.

The *paired-comparison* method calls for presenting a set of items to the consumer, two at a time, asking which one is preferred in each pair. Thus the consumer could be presented with the pairs AB, AC, *and* BC and say that he or she prefers A to B, A to C, and B to C.

Then we could conclude that A > B > C. Paired comparisons offer two major advantages. First, people find it easy to state their preference between items taken two at a time. The second advantage is that the paired-comparison method allows the consumer to concentrate intensely on the two items, noting their differences and similarities.

The *monadic-rating* method asks the consumer to rate his or her liking of each product on a scale. Suppose the following seven-point scale is used. Suppose the consumer returns the following ratings: A=6, B=5, C=3. This yields more information than the previous methods. We can derive the individual's preference order (i.e., A > B > C) and even know the qualitative levels of his or her preference for each and the rough distance between preferences. This method is also easy for respondents to use, especially when there is a large set of objects to evaluate.

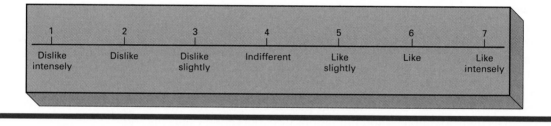

Most companies, however, know market testing can yield valuable information about buyers, dealers, marketing program effectiveness, market potential, and other matters. The main issues are, How much market testing and what kind?

The amount of market testing is influenced by the *investment cost* and *risk* on the one hand, and the *time pressure* and *research cost* on the other. High investment/risk products deserve to be market tested so as not to make a mistake; the cost of the market tests will be an insignificant percentage of the total project cost. High-risk products—those that create new-product categories (first instant breakfast) or have novel features (first fluoride toothpaste)—warrant more market testing than modified products (another toothpaste brand). But the amount of market testing may be severely reduced if the company is under great time pressure because the season is just starting or because competitors are about to launch their brands. The company may therefore prefer the risk of a product failure to the risk of losing distribution or market penetration on a highly successful product. The cost of market testing will also affect how much is done and what kind.

Market-testing methods differ in testing consumer and industrial products. They are described in Marketing Concepts and Tools 13-7.

Market Testing Methods for Consumer and Business Goods

Consumer-Goods Market Testing

In testing consumer products, the company seeks to estimate four variables, namely, *trial, first repeat, adoption,* and *purchase frequency*. The company hopes to find these variables at high levels. In some cases, it will find many consumers trying the product but few rebuying it, showing a lack of product satisfaction. Or it might find high first-time repurchase but then a rapid wearout in the repeat purchase rate. Or it might find high permanent adoption but low purchase frequency (as with "gourmet" frozen foods) because the buyers use the product only on special occasions.

In testing the trade, the company wants to learn how many and what types of retailers will handle the product, under what terms, and with what shelf-position commitments.

The major methods of consumer-goods market testing, from the least to the most costly, are described in the following paragraphs.

SALES-WAVE RESEARCH ❖ In sales-wave research, consumers who initially try the product at no cost are reoffered the product, or a competitor's product, at slightly reduced prices. They might be reoffered the product as many as three to five times (sales waves), the company noting how many customers selected that company's product again and their reported level of satisfaction. Sales-wave research can also include exposing consumers to one or more advertising concepts in rough form to see what impact the advertising has on repeat purchase.

Sales-wave research enables the company to estimate the repeat-purchase rate under conditions where consumers spend their own money and choose among competing brands. The company can also gauge the impact of alternative advertising concepts on producing repeat purchases. Finally, sales-wave research can be implemented quickly, conducted under relative competitive security, and carried out without needing to develop final packaging and advertising.

On the other hand, sales-wave research does not indicate the trial rates that would be achieved with different sales-promotion incentives, since the consumers are preselected to try the product. Nor does it indicate the brand's power to gain distribution and favorable shelf position from the trade.

SIMULATED TEST MARKETING ❖ Simulated test marketing calls for finding 30 to 40 qualified shoppers (at a shopping center or elsewhere) and questioning them about their brand familiarity and preferences in a specific product category. They are then invited to a brief screening of commercials or print ads, including well-known ones and new ones. One ad advertises the new product, but it is not singled out for attention. The consumers receive a small amount of money and are invited into a store where they may buy any items. Even those who did not buy the new brand are given the brand as a free sample. The company notes how many consumers buy the new brand and competing brands. This provides a measure of the ad's relative effectiveness in stimulating trial against competing ads. The consumers are asked the reasons for their purchases or nonpurchases. Some weeks later, they are reinterviewed by phone to determine product attitudes, usage, satisfaction, and repurchase intention and are offered an opportunity to repurchase any products.

This method has several advantages, including the measuring of advertising effectiveness and trial rates (and repeat rates if extended), results that are available in a much shorter time and at a fraction of the cost of using real test markets, and competitive security. The results are usually incorporated into new-product forecasting models to project ultimate sales levels. Marketing research firms report surprisingly accurate predictions of sales levels of products that are subsequently launched in the market.[1]

CONTROLLED TEST MARKETING ❖ Several research firms manage a panel of stores that will carry new products for a fee. The company with the new product specifies the number of stores and geographical locations it wants to test. The research firm delivers the product to the participating stores and controls shelf position, number of facings, displays and point-of-purchase promotions, and pricing, according to plans. Sales results can be measured through electronic scanners at the checkouts. The company can also evaluate the impact of local advertising and promotions during the test.

Controlled test marketing allows the company to test the impact of in-store factors and limited advertising on consumer's buying behavior without involving consumers directly. A sample of consumers can be inter viewed later to gather their impressions of the product. The company does not have to use its own salesforce, give trade allowances, or "buy" distribution. On the other hand, controlled test marketing provides no information on how to sell the trade on carrying the new product. This technique also exposes the product to competitors.

TEST MARKETS ❖ Test markets are the ultimate way to test a new consumer product in a situation resembling the one that would be faced in a full-scale launching of the product. The company usually works with an outside research firm to locate a few representative test cities in which the company's salesforce will try to sell the trade on carrying the product and giving it good shelf exposure. The company will put on a full advertising and promotion campaign in these markets similar to the one that would be used in national marketing. It is a chance to do a dress rehearsal of the total plan. A full-scale test can cost the company over $1 million, depending on the number of cities tested, the duration of the test, and the amount of data the company wants to collect.

Management will face several decisions:

1. *How many test cities?* Most tests use between two and six cities, with an average of four. A larger number of cities should be used, the greater the maximum possible loss, the greater the number of contending marketing strategies, the greater the regional differences, and the greater the chance of calculated test-market interference by competitors.

2. *Which cities?* No city is a perfect microcosm of the nation as a whole. Some cities, however, typify aggregate national or regional characteristics better than others, such as Syracuse, Dayton, Peoria, and Des Moines. Each company develops its own test-city selection criteria. One company looks for test cities that have diversified industry, good media coverage, cooperative chain stores, average competitive activity, and no evidence of being overtested.

3. *Length of test?* Test markets last anywhere from a few months to several years. The longer the product's average repurchase period, the longer the test period necessary to observe repeat-purchase rates. On the other hand, the period should be cut down if competitors are rushing to the market.

4. *What information?* Management must decide on the type of information to collect in relation to its value and cost. *Warehouse shipment data* will show gross inventory buying but will not indicate weekly sales at retail. *Store audits* will show actual retail sales and competitors' market shares but will not reveal the characteristics of the buyers of the different brands. *Consumer panels* will indicate which people are buying which brands and their loyalty and switching rates. *Buyer surveys* will yield in-depth information about consumer attitudes, usage, and satisfaction. Among other things that can be researched are trade attitudes, retail distribution, and the effectiveness of advertising, promotion, and point-of-sale material.

5. *What action to take?* If the test markets show a high trial and high repurchase rate, this indicates a GO-decision. If the test markets show a high trial and a low repurchase rate, the customers are not satisfied, and the product should be redesigned or dropped. If the test markets show a low trial and a high repurchase rate, the product is satisfying, but more people have to try it. This means increasing advertising and sales promotion. Finally, if the trial and repurchase rates are both low, then the product should be dropped.

Test marketing can yield several benefits. Its primary benefit is to yield a *more reliable forecast of future sales.* If product sales fall below target levels in the test market, the company must drop or modify the product or the marketing program.

A second benefit is the *pretesting of alternative marketing plans.* Some years ago Colgate-Palmolive used a different marketing mix in each of four cities to market a new soap product. The four approaches were (1) an average amount of advertising coupled with free samples distributed door to door, (2) heavy advertising plus samples, (3) an average amount of advertising linked with mailed redeemable coupons, and (4) an average amount of advertising with no special introductory offer. The third alternative generated the best profit level, although not the highest sales level.

Other benefits include the following: the company may discover a product fault; the company picks up valuable clues to distribution-level problems; and the company may gain better insight into the behavior of different market segments.

In spite of the benefits of test marketing, many companies question its value today. In this fast-changing marketplace, companies that have spotted an unfulfilled need are eager to get to the market first. Test marketing would slow them down and reveal their plans to competitors who will rush to develop their own rival products. Furthermore, aggressive competitors increasingly take steps to spoil the test markets, making the test results less reliable.

Many large companies today are skipping the test-marketing stage and relying on other market-testing methods.[2] For example, General Mills now prefers to launch the new product in perhaps 25% of the country, an area too large for rivals to disrupt. They review scanner data which tell them within days how the product is doing and what corrective fine-tuning actions they should take. And Colgate-Palmolive often launches a new product in a set of small "lead countries" and keeps rolling it out if it proves successful.[3]

Business-Goods Market Testing

Business goods can also benefit from market testing, the tests varying with the type of goods. Expensive industrial goods and new technologies will normally undergo Alpha and Beta testing. *Alpha testing* refers to the in-company product testing to measure and improve product performance, reliability, design, and operating cost. Following satisfactory results, companies will initiate *Beta testing* which involves inviting potential adopters to permit confidential testing at their sites. Beta testing provides benefits to both the vendors and the test sites. The vendor's technical people observe how these test sites use the product, a practice that often exposes unanticipated problems of safety and servicing and clues the vendor about customer training and servicing requirements. The vendor can also observe how much value the equipment adds to the customer's operation as a clue to subsequent pricing. The vendor will ask the test sites after the test to express their purchase intention and other reactions.

The test sites also benefit in several ways: they can influence the vendor's product design, gain experience with the new product ahead of competitors, receive a price break in return for their cooperation, and enhance their reputation as technological pioneers. At the same time, the vendor has to carefully interpret the Beta test results since only a small number of test sites are used, they are not randomly drawn, and the tests are somewhat customized to each site, therefore limiting generalizability. Another risk is that test sites which are unimpressed may leak unfavorable reports about the product under development.

A second common market-test method is to introduce the new business product at *trade shows*. Trade shows draw a large number of buyers, who view new products in a few concentrated days. The vendor can observe how much interest buyers show in the new product, how they react to various features and terms, and how many express purchase intentions or place orders. The disadvantage is that trade shows reveal the product to competitors; therefore the vendor should be ready to launch the product at that point.

The new industrial product can also be tested in *distributor and dealer display rooms*, where it may stand next to the manufacturer's other products and possibly competitors' products. This method yields preference and pricing information in the normal selling atmosphere for the product. The disadvantages are that the customers might want to place orders that cannot be filled, and those customers who come in might not represent the target market.

Test marketing has been used by some manufacturers. They produce a limited supply of the product and give it to the salesforce to sell in a limited set of geographical areas that receive promotional support, printed catalog sheets, and so on. In this way, management can learn what might happen under full-scale marketing and make a more informed decision about commercializing the product.

SOURCES: 1. The best-known systems are Yankelovich's "Litmus Forecasting Model, Elrick and Lavidge's "COMP," and Management Decision System's "ASSESSOR." For a description of "ASSESSOR," see Alvin J. Silk and Glen L. Urban, "Pre-Test Marketing Evaluation of New Packaged Goods: A Model and Measurement Methodology," *Journal of Marketing Research,* May 1978, pp. 171–91. For a recent assessment, see Allan D. Shocker and William G. Hall, "Pretest Market Models: A Critical Evaluation," *Journal of Product Innovation Management 3* (1986), pp. 86–107. 2. "Spotting Competitive Edges Begets New Product Success," *Marketing News,* December 21, 1984, p. 4; "Testing Time for Test Marketing," *Fortune,* October 29, 1984, pp. 75–76; and Jay E. Klompmaker, G. David Hughes, and Russell I. Haley, "Test Marketing in New Product Development," *Harvard Business Review,* May–June 1976, pp. 128–38. 3. Ibid.

Commercialization

Market testing presumably gives management enough information to decide about whether to launch the new product. If the company goes ahead with commercialization, it will face its largest costs to date. The company will have to contract for manufacture or build or rent a full-scale manufacturing facility. The size of the plant will be a critical decision variable. The company can build a plant smaller than called for by the sales forecast, to be on the safe side. That is what Quaker Oats did when it launched its 100 Percent Natural breakfast cereal. The demand so exceeded the company's sales forecast that for about a year it could not supply enough product to the stores. Although Quaker Oats was gratified with the response, the low forecast cost it a considerable amount of lost profits.

Another major cost is marketing. To introduce a major new consumer packaged good into the national market, the company may have to spend between $20 million and $80 million in advertising and promotion in the first year. In the introduction of new food products, marketing expenditures typically represent 57% of sales during the first year.

When (Timing)

In commercializing a new product, *market-entry timing* can be critical. Suppose a company has almost completed the development work on its new product and hears about a competitor nearing the end of its development work. The company faces three choices:

1. *First Entry:* The first firm entering a market usually enjoys "first mover advantages" consisting of locking up key distributors and customers and gaining reputational leadership. A McKinsey study showed that being first to introduce a new product, even if it is over budget, is better than coming in later, but on budget. On the other hand, if the product is rushed to the market before it is thoroughly debugged, the product can acquire a flawed image.

2. *Parallel Entry:* The firm might time its entry with the competitor. If the competitor rushes to launch, the company does the same. If the competitor takes its time, the company also takes time, using the extra time to refine its product. The company might want the promotional costs of launching to be borne by both of them.

3. *Late Entry:* The firm might delay its launch until after the competitor has entered. There are three potential advantages. The competitor will have borne the cost of educating the market. The competitor's product may reveal faults that the late entrant can avoid. And the company can learn the size of the market. For example, the British company EMI pioneered the CT scan, but GE took over the market because of greater manufacturing excellence and hospital distribution strength.

The timing decision involves additional considerations. If the new product replaces the company's older product, the company might delay the introduction until the old product's stock is drawn down. If the product is highly seasonal, it might be held back until the right season. All said, market-entry timing deserves careful thought. (For further discussion, see Marketing Strategies 14-1 on page 363 on the market pioneer advantage.)

Where (Geographical Strategy)

The company must decide whether to launch the new product in a *single locality*, a *region*, *several regions*, the *national market*, or the *international market*. Few companies have the confidence, capital, and capacity to launch new products into full national or global distribution (see Global Marketing 13-1). They will develop a *planned market rollout* over time. Small companies, in particular, will select an attractive city and put on a blitz campaign to enter the market. They will enter other cities one at a time. Large companies will introduce their product into a whole region and then move to the next region. Companies with national distribution networks, such as auto companies, will launch their new models in the national market.

In rollout marketing, the company has to rate the alternative markets for their attractiveness. The candidate markets can be listed as rows, and rollout attractiveness criteria can be listed as columns. The major rating criteria are *market potential, company's local reputation, cost of filling the pipeline, cost of communication media, influence of area on other areas,* and *competitive penetration.* In this way, the company ranks the prime markets and develops a geographical rollout plan.

The factor of competitive presence is very important. Suppose McDonald's wants to launch a new chain of fast-food pizza parlors. Suppose Pizza Hut, a formidable competitor, is strongly entrenched on the East Coast. Another pizza chain is entrenched on the East Coast but is weak. The Midwest is the battleground between two other chains. The South is open, but Shakey's is planning to move in. We can see that McDonald's faces quite a complex decision in choosing a market rollout strategy.

To Whom (Target-Market Prospects)

Within the rollout markets, the company must target its distribution and promotion to the best prospect groups. Presumably, the company has already profiled the prime prospects. Prime prospects for a new consumer product would ideally have the following characteristics: They would be early adopters; they would be heavy users; they would be opinion leaders; and they could be reached at a low cost.[27] Few groups have all of these characteristics. The company can rate the various prospect groups on these characteristics and target to the best prospect group. The aim is to generate strong sales as soon as possible to motivate the salesforce and attract further prospects.

Global Marketing 13-1

Should New Products Be Designed for the Domestic Market or the World Market?

Most companies design their new products to sell primarily in the domestic market. Then if the product does well, the company considers exporting the product to neighboring countries or the world market, redesigning it if necessary.

Cooper and Kleinschmidt, in their study of industrial products, found that domestic products designed solely for the domestic market tend to show a high failure rate, low market share, and low growth. Yet this is the most popular orientation of companies when they design new products. On the other hand, products that are designed for the world market—or at least to include neighboring countries—achieve significantly more profits, both at home and abroad. Yet only 17% of the products in the Cooper/Kleinschmidt study were designed with this orientation. Their conclusion is that companies would achieve a higher rate of new-product success if they adopted an international focus in designing and developing their new products. They would be more careful in naming the product, choosing materials, designing its features, and so on, and subsequent alterations would be less costly.

SOURCE: Robert G. Cooper and Elko J. Kleinschmidt, *New Products: The Key Factors in Success* (Chicago: American Marketing Association, 1990), pp. 35–38.

Many companies are surprised to learn who really buys their product and why. Microwave ovens began to enjoy explosive growth only after microwave-oven popcorn was developed. Early adopters of VCRs were attracted by the opportunity to watch erotic films.

How (Introductory Market Strategy)

The company must develop an action plan for introducing the new product into the rollout markets. For example:

> In May 1986, Polaroid launched its new Spectra instant camera with a $40 million first-year advertising budget. Billboard ads were put up in 25 markets as part of a teaser campaign, followed by a saturation print and television campaign aiming to generate 25 exposures for 90% of Spectra's target audience.

To sequence and coordinate the many activities involved in launching a new product, management can use network-planning techniques such as *critical path scheduling*.

A summary of the various steps and decisions in the new-product-development process is presented in Figure 13-5.

The Consumer-Adoption Process

The *consumer-adoption process* begins where the firm's *innovation process* leaves off. It describes how potential customers learn about new products, try them, and adopt or reject them. Management must understand this process in order to build an effective strategy for early market penetration. The *consumer-adoption process* is later followed by the *consumer-loyalty process*, which is the concern of the established producer.

Years ago, new-product marketers used a *mass-market approach* in launching their product. They would distribute the product everywhere and advertise it to everyone on the assumption that most people are potential buyers. The mass-market approach, however, has two drawbacks: It calls for heavy marketing expenditures, and it involves many wasted exposures to people who are not potential consumers. These drawbacks led to a second approach, *heavy-user target marketing*, where the product is initially aimed at the heavy users. This approach makes sense, provided that heavy users are identifiable and are early adopters. But even within the heavy-user group, consumers differ in their interest in new products and brands; many heavy users are loyal to their existing brands. Many new-product marketers now aim at those consumers who are early adopters. According to *early-adopter theory*:

- Persons within a target market differ in the amount of elapsed time between their exposure to a new product and their trying it.
- Early adopters share some traits that differentiate them from late adopters.
- Efficient media exist for reaching early adopters.
- Early adopters tend to be opinion leaders and helpful in "advertising" the new product to other potential buyers.

We now turn to the theory of innovation diffusion and consumer adoption, which provides clues to identifying early adopters.

FIGURE 13-5 Summary of the New-Product-Development Decision Process

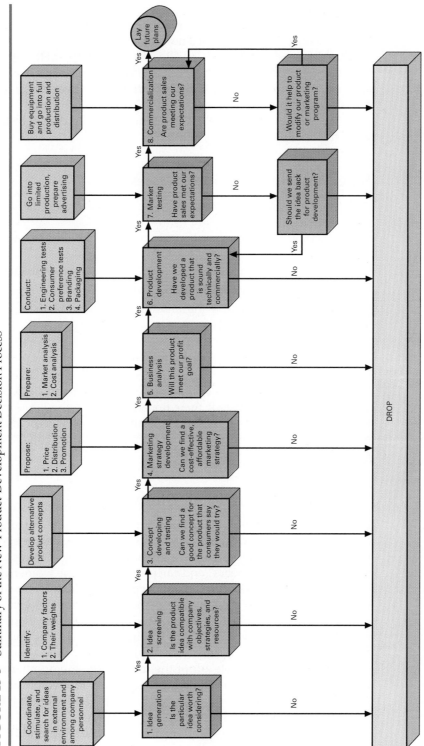

Concepts in Innovation, Diffusion, and Adoption

An *innovation* refers to any good, service, or idea that is *perceived* by someone as new. The idea may have a long history, but it is an innovation to the person who sees it as new.

Innovations take time to spread through the social system. Rogers defines *diffusion process* as "the spread of a new idea from its source of invention or creation to its ultimate users or adopters."[28] The *adoption process*, on the other hand, focuses on "the mental process through which an individual passes from first hearing about an innovation to final adoption." *Adoption* is the decision of an individual to become a regular user of a product.

We will now examine the main generalizations drawn from hundreds of studies of how people accept new ideas.

Stages in the Adoption Process

Adopters of new products have been observed to move through the following five stages:

- *Awareness:* The consumer becomes aware of the innovation but lacks information about it.
- *Interest:* The consumer is stimulated to seek information about the innovation.
- *Evaluation:* The consumer considers whether to try the innovation.
- *Trial:* The consumer tries the innovation to improve his or her estimate of its value.
- *Adoption:* The consumer decides to make full and regular use of the innovation.

This progression suggests that the new-product marketer should aim to facilitate consumer movement through these stages. A portable electric-dishwasher manufacturer might discover that many consumers are stuck in the interest stage; they do not buy because of their uncertainty and the large investment cost. But these same consumers would be willing to use an electric dishwasher on a trial basis for a small monthly fee. The manufacturer should consider offering a trial-use plan with option to buy.

Individual Difference in Innovativeness

People differ markedly in their readiness to try new products. Rogers defines a person's *innovativeness* as "the degree to which an individual is relatively earlier in adopting new ideas than the other members of his social system." In each product area, there are "consumption pioneers" and early adopters. Some women are the first to adopt new clothing fashions or new appliances; some doctors are the first to prescribe new medicines; and some farmers are the first to adopt new farming methods.

Other individuals adopt new products much later. People can be classified into the adopter categories shown in Figure 13-6. The adoption process is represented as a normal distribution when plotted over time. After a slow start, an increasing number of people adopt the innovation, the number reaches a peak, and then it diminishes as fewer nonadopters remain. Innovators are defined as the first 2.5% of the buyers to adopt a new idea; the early adopters are the next 13.5% who adopt the new idea; and so forth.

Rogers sees the five adopter groups as differing in their value orientations. Innovators are *venturesome*; they are willing to try new ideas at some risk. Early adopters are guided by *respect*; they are opinion leaders in their community and adopt new ideas early but carefully. The early majority are deliberate; they adopt new ideas before the average person, although they rarely are leaders. The late ma-

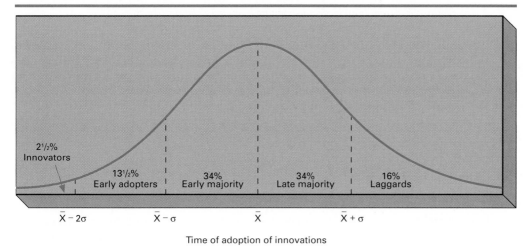

jority are *skeptical*; they adopt an innovation only after a majority of people have tried it. Finally, laggards are *tradition bound*; they are suspicious of changes, mix with other tradition-bound people, and adopt the innovation only when it takes on a measure of tradition itself.

This adopter classification suggests that an innovating firm should research the demographic, psychographic, and media characteristics of innovators and early adopters and direct communications specifically to them. Identifying early adopters is not always easy. No one has demonstrated the existence of a general personality trait called innovativeness. Individuals tend to be innovators in certain areas and laggards in others. We can think of a businessperson who dresses conservatively but who delights in trying unfamiliar cuisines. The marketer's challenge is to identify the characteristics of likely early adopters in its product area. For example, innovative farmers are likely to be better educated and more efficient than noninnovative farmers. Innovative homemakers are more gregarious and usually higher in social status than noninnovative homemakers. Certain communities have a high share of early adopters. Rogers offers the following hypotheses about early adopters:

> The relatively earlier adopters in a social system tend to be younger in age, have higher social status, a more favorable financial position, more specialized operations, and a different type of mental ability from later adopters. Earlier adopters utilize information sources that are more impersonal and cosmopolite than later adopters and that are in closer contact with the origin of new ideas. Earlier adopters utilize a greater number of different information sources than do later adopters. The social relationships of earlier adopters are more cosmopolite than for later adopters, and earlier adopters have more opinion leadership.[29]

Role of Personal Influence

Personal influence plays a large role in the adoption of new products. Personal influence describes the effect of product statements made by one person on another's attitude or purchase probability. According to Katz and Lazarsfeld:

> About half of the women in our sample reported that they had recently made some change from a product or brand to which they were accustomed to something new. The fact that one third of

these changes involved personal influences indicates that there is also considerable traffic in marketing advice. Women consult each other for opinions about new products, about the quality of different brands, about shopping economies and the like.[30]

Although personal influence is an important factor, its significance is greater in some situations and for some individuals than for others. Personal influence is more important in the evaluation stage of the adoption process than in the other stages. It has more influence on late adopters than early adopters. And it is more important in risky situations than in safe situations.

Influence of Product Characteristics on the Rate of Adoption

The characteristics of the innovation affects its rate of adoption. Some products catch on immediately (e.g., frisbees), whereas others take a long time to gain acceptance (e.g., diesel-engine autos). Five characteristics are especially important in influencing the rate of adoption of an innovation. We will consider these characteristics in relation to the rate of adoption of personal computers for home use.

The first is the innovation's *relative advantage*—the degree to which it appears superior to existing products. The greater the perceived relative advantage of using a personal computer, say, in preparing income taxes and keeping financial records, the more quickly personal computers will be adopted.

The second characteristic is the innovation's *compatibility*—the degree to which it matches the values and experiences of the individuals in the community. Personal computers, for example, are highly compatible with the lifestyles found in upper-middle-class homes.

Third is the innovation's *complexity*—the degree to which it is relatively difficult to understand or use. Personal computers are complex and will therefore take a longer time to penetrate into home use.

Fourth is the innovation's *divisibility*—the degree to which it can be tried on a limited basis. The availability of rentals of personal computers with an option to buy increases their rate of adoption.

The fifth characteristic is the innovation's *communicability*—the degree to which the results of its use are observable or describable to others. The fact that personal computers lend themselves to demonstration and description helps them diffuse faster in the social system.

Other characteristics influence the rate of adoption, such as initial costs, ongoing costs, risk and uncertainty, scientific credibility, and social approval. The new-product marketer has to research all these factors and give the key ones maximum attention in designing the new-product and marketing program.[31]

Influence of Organizational Buyers' Characteristics on the Rate of Adoption

Organizations also vary in their readiness to adopt an innovation. Thus the creator of a new teaching method would want to identify innovative schools. The producer of a new piece of medical equipment would want to identify innovative hospitals. Adoption is associated with variables in the organization's environment (community progressiveness, community income), the organization itself (size, profits, pressure to change), and the administrators (education level, age, cosmopoliteness). Once a set of useful indicators is found, it can be used to identify the best target organizations.

SUMMARY ❖

Organizations are increasingly recognizing the necessity and advantages of regularly developing new products and services. Their more mature and declining products must be replaced by newer products.

New products, however, can fail. The risks of innovation are as great as the rewards. The key to successful innovation lies in developing better organizational arrangements for handling new-product ideas and developing sound research and decision procedures at each stage of the new-product-development process.

The new-product-development process consists of eight stages: idea generation, idea screening, concept development and testing, marketing-strategy development, business analysis, product development, market testing, and commercialization. The purpose of each stage is to decide whether the idea should be further developed or dropped. The company wants to minimize the chances that poor ideas will move forward and good ideas will be rejected.

With regard to new products, consumers respond at different rates, depending on the consumer's characteristics and the product's characteristics. Manufacturers try to bring their new products to the attention of potential early adopters, particularly those with opinion-leader characteristics.

NOTES ❖

1. *New Products Management for the 1980s* (New York: Booz, Allen & Hamilton, 1982).

2. Ibid.

3. Cited in Kevin J. Clancy and Robert S. Shulman, *The Marketing Revolution: A Radical Manifesto for Dominating the Marketplace* (New York: Harper Business, 1991), p. 6.

4. Ibid.

5. Robert G. Cooper and Elko J. Kleinschmidt, "New Product Processes at Leading Industrial Firms," *Industrial Marketing Management,* May 1991, pp. 137–47.

6. See "High-Speed Management for the High-Tech Age," *Fortune,* March 5, 1984, pp. 62–68.

7. See David S. Hopkins, *Options in New-Product Organization* (New York: Conference Board, 1974).

8. A good review of other studies of factors associated with new-product success is found in Modesto A. Maidique and Billie Jo Zirger, "A Study of Success and Failure in Product Innovation: The Case of the U.S. Electronics Industry," *IEEE Transactions on Engineering Management*, November 1984, pp. 192–203.

9. See Robert G. Cooper, "Stage-Gate Systems: A New Tool for Managing New Products," *Business Horizons,* May–June 1990, pp. 44–54.

10. Eric von Hippel, "Lead Users: A Source of Novel Product Concepts," *Management Science*, July 1986, pp. 791–805. Also see his *The Sources of Innovation* (New York: Oxford University Press, 1988).

11. See John E. Arnold, "Useful Creative Techniques," in *Source Book for Creative Thinking,* eds. Sidney J. Parnes and Harold F. Harding (New York: Scribner's, 1962), p. 255.

12. See Alex F. Osborn, *Applied Imagination,* 3rd ed. (New York: Scribner's, 1963), pp. 286–87.

13. See Edward M. Tauber, "HIT: Heuristic Ideation Technique—A Systematic Procedure for New Product Search," *Journal of Marketing,* January 1972, pp. 58–70; and Charles L. Alford and Joseph Barry Mason, "Generating New Product Ideas," *Journal of Advertising Research,* December 1975, pp. 27–32.

14. See Edward M. Tauber, "Discovering New Product Opportunities with Problem Inventory Analysis," *Journal of Marketing,* January 1975, pp. 67–70.

15. Eric von Hippel, "Learning from Lead Users," in *Marketing in an Electronic Age,* ed. Robert D. Buzzell (Cambridge, MA: Harvard Business School Press, 1985), pp. 308–17.

16. Osborn, *Applied Imagination,* p. 156.

17. John W. Lincoln, "Defining a Creativeness in People," in *Source Book for Creative Thinking,* pp. 274–75.

18. Ibid., p. 274.

19. Mark Hanan, "Corporate Growth through Venture Management," *Harvard Business Review,* January–February 1969, p. 44.

20. See John T. O'Meara, Jr., "Selecting Profitable Products," *Harvard Business Review,* January–February 1961, pp. 110–18.

21. Theodore Levitt, "Marketing Intangible Products and Product Intangibles," *Harvard Business Review,* May–June, 1981, p. 95.

22. See Robert Blattberg and John Golanty, "Tracker: An Early Test Market Forecasting and Diagnostic Model for New Product Planning," *Journal of Marketing Research,* May 1978, pp. 192–202.

23. See Roger A. Kerin, Michael G. Harvey, and James T. Rothe, "Cannibalism and New Product Development," *Business Horizons*, October 1978, pp. 25–31.

24. The present value (*V*) of a future sum (*I*) to be received *t* years from today and discounted at the interest rate (*r*) is given by $V = I_t / (1 + r)^t$. Thus $\$4,761 / (1.15)^5 = \$2,346$.

25. See David B. Hertz, "Risk Analysis in Capital Investment," *Harvard Business Review,* January–February 1964, pp. 96–106.

26. Ralph Westfall and Harper W. Boyd, Jr., *Cases in Marketing Management* (Homewood, IL: Richard D. Irwin, 1961), p. 365.

27. Philip Kotler and Gerald Zaltman, "Targeting Prospects for a New Product," *Journal of Advertising Research,* February 1976, pp. 7–20.

28. The following discussion leans heavily on Everett M. Rogers, *Diffusion of Innovations* (New York: Free Press, 1962). Also see his third edition, published in 1983.

29. Rogers, *Diffusion of Innovations*, p. 192.

30. Elihu Katz and Paul F. Lazarsfeld, *Personal Influence* (New York: Free Press, 1955), p. 234.

31. For a recent summary of the literature, see Hubert Gatignon and Thomas S. Robertson, "A Propositional Inventory for New Diffusion Research," *Journal of Consumer Research,* March 1985, pp. 849–67.

14

Managing Product Life Cycles and Strategies

Profit is the payment you get when you take advantage of change.
JOSEPH SCHUMPETER

This is one of the saddest days of my life, a sad one for me, for our employees, officers, and directors; indeed, it is sad for the American public. Apparently, there is just not the need for our product in today's scheme of living.
MARTIN ACKERMAN, PRESIDENT OF *THE SATURDAY EVENING POST*

D uring a product's life, a company will normally reformulate its marketing strategy several times. Not only do economic conditions change, and competitors launch new assaults, but, in addition, the product passes through new stages of buyer interest and requirements. Consequently, a company must plan successive strategies appropriate to each stage in the product's life cycle. The company hopes to extend the product's life and profitability even knowing that the product will not last forever.

We will answer three questions in this chapter: What is a product life cycle? What marketing strategies are appropriate at each stage of the product life cycle? How do markets themselves evolve, and what marketing strategies are appropriate?

The Product Life Cycle

The product life cycle (PLC) is an important concept in marketing that provides insights into a product's competitive dynamics. At the same time, the concept can prove misleading if not carefully used. To fully understand PLC, we will first describe its parent concept, the *demand/technology life cycle*.[1]

Demand/Technology Life Cycle

Marketing thinking should not begin with a product, or even a product class, but rather with a need. The product exists as one solution among many to meet a need. For example, the human race has a need for "calculating power," and this need has grown over the centuries. The changing need level is described by a *demand life-cycle curve*, the highest curve shown in Figure 14-1(a). There is a stage of *emergence* (E), followed by stages of *accelerating growth* (G_1), *decelerating growth* (G_2), *maturity* (M), and *decline* (D). In the case of "calculating power," the maturity and decline stages might not have set in yet.

Now a need is satisfied by some technology. The need for "calculating power" was first satisfied by finger counting; then by abacuses; still later by slide rules, adding machines, hand calculators, and computers. Each new technology normally satisfies the need in a superior way. Each exhibits a *demand-technology life cycle*, shown by the curves (T_1 and T_2) under the demand-cycle curve in Figure 14-1(a). Each demand-technology life cycle shows an emergence, rapid growth, slower growth, maturity, and then decline.

Within a given demand-technology cycle, there will appear a succession of product forms that satisfy the specific need at the time. Thus the hand calculator provided a new technology offering "calculating power." Initially, it took the product form of a large plastic box with a small screen and numerical keys, and it could perform only four tasks: adding, subtracting, multiplying, and dividing. This form lasted a few years and was succeeded by smaller hand calculators that could perform additional mathematical operations. Today's product forms include hand calculators no larger than the size of a business card. Figure 14-1(b) shows a succession

FIGURE 14-1 Demand-Technology-Product Life Cycles

Source: H. Igor Ansoff, *Implanting Strategic Management* (Englewood Cliffs, NJ: Prentice-Hall, 1984), p. 41.

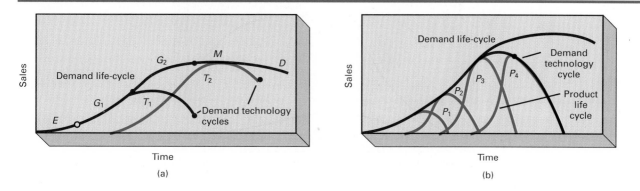

of *product-forms life cycles*, P_1, P_2, P_3, P_4. Later we will show that each product form contains a set of brands with their own *brand life cycles*.

These distinctions suggest that if a company concentrates only on its own brand life cycle, it is missing the bigger picture of what is happening to the product life cycle. Thus a manufacturer of slide rules might have paid attention to the slide-rule brands, but it should actually have worried about a new technology (hand calculators) destroying the slide-rule market.

Companies must decide what demand technology to invest in and when to transit to a new demand technology. Ansoff calls a demand technology a *strategic business area* (*SBA*), namely "a distinctive segment of the environment in which the firm does or may want to do business."[2] Today's companies face many changing technologies but cannot invest in all of them. They have to bet on which demand technology will win. They can bet heavily on one new technology or bet lightly on several. If the latter, they are not likely to become the leader. The pioneering firm that bets heavily on the winning technology is likely to capture leadership. Thus firms must carefully choose the strategic business areas in which they will operate.

Stages in the Product Life Cycle

We can now focus on the product life cycle. The product life cycle portrays *distinct stages* in the *sales history* of a product. Corresponding to these stages are distinct opportunities and problems with respect to marketing strategy and profit potential. By identifying the stage that a product is in, or may be headed toward, companies can formulate better marketing plans.

To say that a product has a life cycle is to assert four things:

- Products have a limited life.
- Product sales pass through distinct stages, each posing different challenges to the seller.
- Profits rise and fall at different stages of the product life cycle.
- Products require different marketing, financial, manufacturing, purchasing, and personnel strategies in each stage of their life cycle.

Most discussions of product life cycle (PLC) portray the sales history of a typical product as following an **S**-shaped curve (see Figure 14-2). This curve is typically divided into four stages, known as *introduction, growth, maturity*, and *decline*.[3]

- *Introduction:* A period of slow sales growth as the product is introduced in the market. Profits are nonexistent in this stage because of the heavy expenses of product introduction.

FIGURE 14-2
Sales and Profit Life Cycles

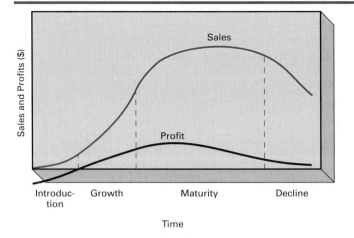

- *Growth:* A period of rapid market acceptance and substantial profit improvement.
- *Maturity:* A period of a slowdown in sales growth because the product has achieved acceptance by most potential buyers. Profits stabilize or decline because of increased marketing outlays to defend the product against competition.
- *Decline:* The period when sales show a downward drift and profits erode.

Designating where each stage begins and ends is somewhat arbitrary. Usually the stages are marked where the rates of sales growth or decline become pronounced. Polli and Cook proposed an operational measure based on a normal distribution of percentage changes in real sales from year to year.[4]

Those planning to use the PLC concept must investigate the extent to which the PLC concept describes product histories in their industry. They should check the normal sequence of stages and the average duration of each stage. Cox found that a typical ethical drug spanned an introductory period of one month, a growth stage of six months, a maturity stage of 15 months, and a very long decline stage—the last because of manufacturers' reluctance to drop drugs from their catalogs. These stage lengths must be reviewed periodically. Intensifying competition is leading to shorter PLCs over time, which means that products must earn their profits in a shorter period.

Product-Category, Product-Form, and Brand Life Cycles

The PLC concept can be used to analyze a product category (liquor), a product form (white goods), a subproduct form (vodka), or a brand (Smirnoff) (see Figure 14-3).

- *Product categories* have the longest life cycles. Many product categories stay in the mature stage for an indefinite duration, since they are highly population related. Some major product categories—cigars, newspapers, coffee—seem to have entered the decline stage of the PLC. Meanwhile some others—facsimile machines, cordless telephones—are clearly in the growth stage.
- *Product forms* exhibit the standard PLC histories more faithfully than do product categories. Thus manual typewriters passed through the stages of introduction, growth, maturity, and decline; their successors—electric typewriters and electronic typewriters—similarly passed through these stages.
- *Branded products* can have a short or long PLC. A Nielsen study found that the life expectancy of new branded products was approximately three years.[5] At the same time,

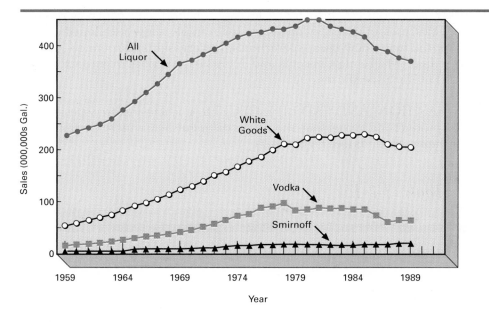

FIGURE 14-3
PLCs for a Product Category,
Product Forms, and Brand
Source: Developed from data supplied by Professor Albert L. Page of the University of Illinois at Chicago.

some *brand names*—such as Ivory, Jello-O, Hershey's—often have a very long PLC and are used to name and launch new products. P&G, for example, believes that it can keep a strong brand name going forever.

Other Shapes of the Product Life Cycle

Not all products exhibit an **S**-shaped PLC. Researchers have identified from six to seventeen different PLC patterns.[6] Three common patterns are shown in Figure 14-4. Figure 14-4(a) shows a "growth-slump-maturity" pattern, often characteristic of small kitchen appliances. For example, the sales of electric knives grew rapidly when first introduced and then fell to a "petrified" level. The petrified level is sustained by late adopters buying the product for the first time and early adopters replacing the product.

The "cycle-recycle" pattern in Figure 14-4(b) often describes the sales of new drugs. The pharmaceutical company aggressively promotes its new drug, and this produces the first cycle. Later sales start declining, and the company gives the drug another promotion push, which produces a second cycle usually of smaller magnitude and duration.

Still another common pattern is the "scalloped" PLC in Figure 14-4(c). Here

FIGURE 14-4   Common Product Life-Cycle Patterns

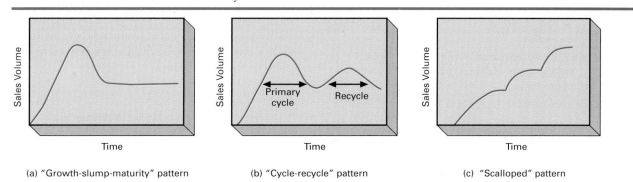

(a) "Growth-slump-maturity" pattern   (b) "Cycle-recycle" pattern   (c) "Scalloped" pattern

sales pass through a succession of life cycles based on the discovery of new-product characteristics, uses, or users. Nylon's sales, for example, show a scalloped pattern because of the many new uses—parachutes, hosiery, shirts, carpeting—discovered over time.[7] Marketing Concepts and Tools 14-1 describes major factors that shape the PLC for a specific product.

STYLE, FASHION, AND FAD LIFE CYCLES ❖ There are three special categories of product life cycles that should be distinguished—those pertaining to styles, fashions, and fads (see Figure 14-5).

Marketing Concepts and Tools 14-1

Forecasting the Shape and Duration of the Product Life Cycle

Goldman and Muller have presented interesting observations on factors influencing the shape and duration of product-specific life cycles. First consider the shape of an ideal product life cycle:

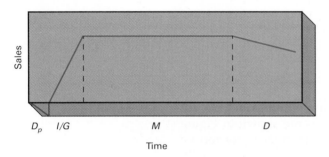

The product-development period (D_p) is short, and therefore the product-development costs are low. The introduction/growth period (I/G) is short, and therefore sales reach their peak quite soon, which means early maximum revenue. The maturity period (M) lasts a long time, which means the company enjoys an extended period of profits. The decline (D) is very slow, which means that profits fall only gradually.

A firm launching a new product should forecast the PLC shape based on factors that influence the length of each stage:

- ◆ *Development time* is shorter and less costly for routine products than for high-tech products.
- ◆ *Introduction and growth time* will be short under the following conditions:

  The product does not require setting up a new infrastructure of distribution channels, transportation, services, or communication.

  The dealers will readily accept and promote the new product.

  Consumers have an interest in the product, will adopt it early, and will give it favorable word of mouth.

- ◆ *Maturity time* will last long to the extent that consumer tastes and product technology are fairly stable and the company maintains leadership in the market. Companies make the most money by riding out a long maturity period. If the maturity period is short, the company might not recover its full investment.
- ◆ *Decline time* is long if consumer tastes and product technology change only slowly. The more brand loyal the consumers, the slower the rate of decline. The lower the exit barriers, the faster some firms will exit, and this will slow down the rate of decline for the remaining firms.

Given these factors, we can see why many high-tech firms fail. They face highly unattractive PLCs. The worst type of PLC would look like this:

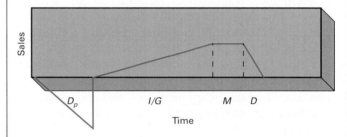

The development time is long, and the development cost is steep; the introduction/growth time is long; the maturity period is short; and the decline is fast. Many high-tech firms must invest a great amount of time and cost to develop their product; they find that it takes a long time to introduce it to the market; the market does not last long; and the decline is steep, owing to the rapid technological change.

SOURCE: Arieh Goldman and Eitan Muller, "Measuring Shape Patterns of Product Life Cycles: Implications for Marketing Strategy," paper, August 1982 Hebrew University of Jerusalem, Jerusalem School of Business Administration.

FIGURE 14-5   Style, Fashion, and Fad Life Cycles

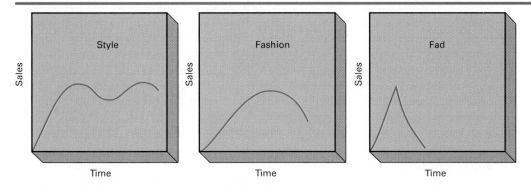

A *style* is a basic and distinctive mode of expression appearing in a field of human endeavor. For example, styles appear in homes (colonial, ranch, Cape Cod); clothing (formal, casual, funky); and art (realistic, surrealistic, abstract). Once a style is invented, it can last for generations, going in and out of vogue. A style exhibits a cycle showing several periods of renewed interest.

A *fashion* is a currently accepted or popular style in a given field. For example, jeans are a fashion in today's clothing, and "country western" is a fashion in today's popular music. Fashions pass through four stages.[8] In the *distinctiveness stage*, some consumers take an interest in something new that sets them apart from other consumers. In the *emulation stage*, other consumers take an interest out of a desire to emulate the fashion leaders. In the *mass-fashion stage*, the fashion has become extremely popular, and manufacturers have geared up for mass production. Finally, in the *decline stage*, consumers start moving toward other fashions that are beginning to catch their attention.

Thus fashions tend to grow slowly, remain popular for a while, and decline slowly. The length of a fashion cycle is hard to predict. Wasson believes that fashions come to an end because they represent a purchase compromise, and consumers start looking for missing attributes. For example, as automobiles become smaller, they become less comfortable, and then a growing number of buyers start wanting larger cars. Furthermore, too many consumers adopt the fashion, thus turning others away. Reynolds suggests that the length of a particular fashion cycle depends on the extent to which the fashion meets a genuine need, is consistent with other trends in the society, satisfies societal norms and values, and does not meet technological limits as it develops.[9] Robinson, however, sees fashions as living out inexorable cycles regardless of economic, functional, or technological changes in society.[10] Sproles has reviewed and compared several theories of fashion cycles.[11]

Fads are fashions that come quickly into the public eye, are adopted with great zeal, peak early, and decline very fast. Their acceptance cycle is short, and they tend to attract only a limited following. They often have a novel or capricious aspect, as when people start buying "pet rocks" or run naked and "streak." Fads appeal to people who are searching for excitement or who want to distinguish themselves from others or want something to talk about to others. Fads do not survive because they do not normally satisfy a strong need or do not satisfy it well. It is difficult to predict whether something will be only a fad, or how long it will last. The amount of media attention, along with other factors, will influence the fad's duration.

Rationale for the Product Life Cycle

Earlier we described the **S**-shaped PLC concept without providing a rationale in marketing terms. The theory of the diffusion and adoption of innovations provides the underlying rationale. When a new product is launched, the company has to stimulate awareness, interest, trial, and purchase. This takes time, and in the introductory stage only a few persons ("innovators") will buy it. If the product is satisfying, larger numbers of buyers ("early adopters") are drawn in. The entry of competitors into the market speeds up the adoption process by increasing the market's awareness and by causing prices to fall. More buyers come in ("early majority") as the product is legitimized. Eventually, the growth rate decreases as the number of potential new buyers approaches zero. Sales become steady at the replacement-purchase rate. Eventually sales decline as new-product classes, forms, and brands appear and divert buyer interest from the existing product. Thus the product life cycle is explained by normal developments in the diffusion and adoption of new products.

Even when the product's sales decline in one country, its sales may be rising in another country. Product adoption occurs throughout the world at different rates. Often a late-adopting country may end up producing the product more economically and become a leader in diffusing the product to other countries. This phenomenon is called the *international product life cycle* (see Global Marketing 14-1).

Global Marketing 14-1

The International Product Life Cycle

One reason why domestic companies must pay attention to foreign market developments lies in the phenomenon of the *international product life cycle*. According to Wells, "Many products go through a trade cycle, during which the United States is initially an exporter, then loses its export markets and may finally become an importer of the product." The four stages of the international product life cycle are

- *U.S. Manufacturers Export Product:* An innovation is launched in the United States and succeeds because of the huge market and the highly developed infrastructure. Eventually, U.S. producers start exporting the product to other countries.

- *Foreign Production Starts:* As foreign manufacturers become familiar with the product, some of them start producing it for their home market. They do this under licensing or joint-venture arrangement or simply by copying the product. Their government often abets their efforts by imposing tariffs or quotas on imports of the product.

- *Foreign Production Becomes Competitive in Export Markets:* By now, foreign manufacturers have gained production experience, and, with their lower costs, they start exporting the product to other countries.

- *Import Competition Begins:* The foreign manufacturers' growing volume and lower costs enable them to export the product to the United States in direct competition with U.S. producers.

The implication is that a U.S. manufacturer's sales in the home market will eventually decline as foreign markets start producing the product and ultimately export it to the United States. The U.S. manufacturers' best defense is to become global marketers. U.S. firms should open production and distribution facilities in other countries with large markets and/or lower costs. Global marketers are able to extend the product life cycle by moving the product into countries that are getting ready to use it.

Some critics feel that it has less validity today because multinational enterprises now operate vast global networks through which they might innovate new products anywhere in the world and move them through various countries not necessarily in the sequence predicted by the original formulation of the international PLC.

SOURCE: See Louis T. Well, Jr., "A Product Life Cycle for International Trade?" *Journal of Marketing,* July 1968, pp. 1–6; Ian H. Giddy, "The Demise of the Product Cycle Model in International Business Theory," *Columbia Journal of World Business,* Spring 1978, p. 92; and Raymond Vernon, "The Product Cycle Hypothesis in a New International Environment," *Oxford Bulletin of Economics and Statistics,* November 1979, pp. 255–67.

We now turn to each stage of the PLC and consider the appropriate marketing strategies.

Introduction Stage

The introduction stage starts when the new product is launched. It takes time to roll out the product in several markets and to fill the dealer pipelines, so sales growth is apt to be slow. Such well-known products as instant coffee, frozen orange juice, and powdered coffee creamers lingered for many years before they entered a stage of rapid growth. Buzzell identified several causes for the slow growth of many processed food products: delays in the expansion of production capacity; technical problems ("working out the bugs"); delays in obtaining adequate distribution through retail outlets; and customer reluctance to change established behaviors.[12] In the case of expensive new products, sales growth is retarded by additional factors: for one thing, the small number of buyers who can afford the new product.

In this stage, profits are negative or low because of the low sales and heavy distribution and promotion expenses. Much money is needed to attract distributors and "fill the pipelines." Promotional expenditures are at their highest ratio to sales "because of the need for a high level of promotional effort to (1) inform potential consumers of the new and unknown product, (2) induce trial of the product, and (3) secure distribution in retail outlets."[13]

There are only a few competitors, and they produce basic versions of the product, since the market is not ready for product refinements. The firms focus their selling on those buyers who are the readiest to buy, usually higher-income groups. Prices tend to be on the high side because "(1) costs are high due to relatively low output rates, (2) technological problems in production may have not yet been fully mastered, and (3) high margins are required to support the heavy promotional expenditures which are necessary to achieve growth."[14]

Marketing Strategies in the Introduction Stage

In launching a new product, marketing management can set a high or a low level for each marketing variable, such as price, promotion, distribution, and product quality. Considering only price and promotion, management can pursue one of the four strategies shown in Figure 14-6.

A *rapid-skimming strategy* consists of launching the new product at a high price and a high promotion level. The firm charges a high price in order to recover as much gross profit per unit as possible. It spends heavily on promotion to convince the market of the product's merits even at the high price. The high promotion acts to accelerate the rate of market penetration. This strategy makes sense under

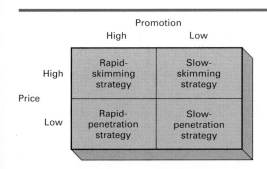

FIGURE 14-6
Four Introductory
Marketing Strategies

CHAPTER 14
Managing Product Life Cycles
and Strategies

361

the following assumptions: a large part of the potential market is unaware of the product; those who become aware are eager to have the product and can pay the asking price; and the firm faces potential competition and wants to build up brand preference.

A *slow-skimming strategy* consists of launching the new product at a high price and low promotion. The high price helps recover as much gross profit per unit as possible, and the low level of promotion keeps marketing expenses down. This combination is expected to skim a lot of profit from the market. This strategy makes sense when the market is limited in size; most of the market is aware of the product; buyers are willing to pay a high price; and potential competition is not imminent.

A *rapid-penetration strategy* consists of launching the product at a low price and spending heavily on promotion. This strategy promises to bring about the fastest market penetration and the largest market share. This strategy makes sense when the market is large; the market is unaware of the product; most buyers are price sensitive; there is strong potential competition; and the company's unit manufacturing costs fall with the scale of production and accumulated manufacturing experience.

A *slow-penetration strategy* consists of launching the new product at a low price and low level of promotion. The low price will encourage rapid product acceptance; and the company keeps its promotion costs down in order to realize more net profit. The company believes that market demand is highly price elastic but minimally promotion elastic. This strategy makes sense when the market is large; the market is highly aware of the product; the market is price sensitive; and there is some potential competition.

A company, especially the *market pioneer*, must choose a launch strategy that is consistent with its intended product positioning. The launch strategy should be the first step in a grand plan for life-cycle marketing. If the pioneer chooses its launch strategy to make a "killing," it will be sacrificing long-run revenue for the sake of short-run gain. Market pioneers have the best chance of retaining market leadership if they play their cards right (see Marketing Strategies 14-1).

The pioneer should visualize the various product markets it could initially enter, knowing that it cannot enter all of them. Suppose market-segmentation analysis reveals the product market segments shown in Figure 14-7. The pioneer should analyze the profit potential of each product market singly and in combination and decide on a market expansion strategy. Thus the pioneer in Figure 14-7 plans first to enter product market P_1M_1, then move the product into a second market (P_1M_2), then surprise competition by developing a second product for the second market (P_2M_2), then take the second product back into the first market (P_2M_1), and then launch a third product for the first market (P_3M_1). If this game plan works,

FIGURE 14-7
Long-Range Product/
Market Expansion Strategy
(P_i = product i;
M_j = market j)

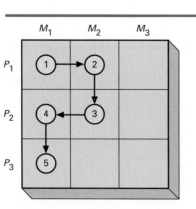

Does the Market Pioneer Enjoy a Long-Term "Advantage"?

Companies that plan to introduce a new product must make a decision about "order of market entry." To be first in the market can be highly rewarding, and yet risky and expensive. To come in later would make sense if the firm can bring superior technology, quality, or brand strength.

Most studies indicate that the market pioneer gains the most advantage. Clearly such pioneering companies as Campbell's, Coca-Cola, Eastman Kodak, Hallmark, and Xerox developed sustained market dominance. Robinson and Fornell studied a broad range of mature consumer and industrial-goods businesses, and found that market pioneers generally enjoy a substantially higher market share than do early followers and late entrants.

Average Market Share (%)		
	Consumer Goods	Industrial Goods
Pioneer	29	29
Early follower	17	21
Late entrant	13	15

Urban's study also found a pioneer advantage: it appears that the second entrant obtained only 71% of the pioneer's market share, and the third entrant obtained only 58%. And Carpenter and Nakamoto found that 19 out of 25 companies who were market leaders in 1923 were still the market leaders in 1983, fifty years later.

What are the sources of the pioneer's advantage? Some advantages are consumer-based. Early users will favor the pioneer's brand because they tried it and it satisfied them. The pioneer's brand also establishes the evaluative attributes that the product class should possess. Because the pioneer's brand normally aims at the middle of the market, it captures more users. There are also producer advantages stemming from economies of scale, technological leadership, ownership of scarce assets, and other barriers to entry.

However, doubts can be raised about the strength or inevitability of the pioneer advantage. One only has to reflect on the fate of Bowmar (hand calculators), Reynolds (ballpoint pens), and Osborne (portable computers), market pioneers who were overtaken by later entrants. Lieberman and Montgomery suggest that later entrants may enjoy such advantages as free-rider effects, technology and customer needs shifts, and incumbency inertia. The pioneer may falter also because of improper market positioning or insufficient resources or investment.

In a recent paper, Golder and Tellis raise further doubts about the pioneer advantage. They distinguish between an *inventor* (first to develop patents in a new-product category), *product pioneer* (first to develop a working model), and a *market pioneer* (first to sell in the new-product category). They also include nonsurviving pioneers in their sample, who were omitted in other studies. With these refinements they conclude that while pioneers may still have an advantage, it is less pronounced than claimed. A larger number of market pioneers fail than has been reported and a larger number of early market leaders (though not pioneers) succeed, especially if they enter decisively and commit substantial resources to obtaining market leadership. Examples of later entrants overtaking market pioneers are IBM over Sperry in mainframe computers, Matshushita over Sony in VCRs, Texas Instruments over Bowmar in hand calculators, and GE over EMI in CT scan equipment. At a minimum, this suggests that under the right circumstances the late entrant can overcome the pioneer advantage. Yet an alert pioneer, according to Robertson and Gatignon, can pursue various strategies to prevent later market entrants from wresting away leadership.

SOURCES: William T. Robinson and Claes Fornell, "Sources of Market Pioneer Advantages in Consumer Goods Industries," *Journal of Marketing Research,* August 1985, pp. 305–17; Glen L. Urban, et al., "Market Share Rewards to Pioneering Brands: An Empirical Analysis and Strategic Implications," *Management Science,* June 1986, pp. 645–59; Gregory S. Carpenter and Kent Nakomoto, "Consumer Preference Formation and Pioneering Advantage," *Journal of Marketing Research,* August 1989, pp. 285–98; Marvin B. Lieberman and David B. Montgomery, "First-Mover Advantages," *Strategic Management Journal,* Vol. 9, 1988, pp. 41–58; Peter N. Golder and Gerald J. Tellis, "Pioneer Advantage: Marketing Logic or Marketing Legend?" *Journal of Marketing Research,* May 1992, pp. 34–46; and Thomas S. Robertson and Hubert Gatignon, "How Innovators Thwart New Entrants into their Market," *Planning Review,* September–October 1991, pp. 4–11, 48.

the market-pioneer firm will own a good part of the first two market segments and serve them with two or three products. Naturally, this game plan may be altered as time passes and new factors emerge. But at least the firm has prepared a total invasion plan for capturing market leadership.

By looking ahead, the pioneer knows that competition will eventually enter and cause prices and its market share to fall. The questions are: When will this happen? What should the pioneer do at each stage? Frey has described five stages of the competitive cycle that the pioneer has to anticipate (see Figure 14-8).[15] Initially, the pioneer is the *sole supplier*, with 100% of the production capacity and sales. The second stage, *competitive penetration*, starts when a new competitor has built production capacity and begins commercial sales. Other competitors enter as well, and the leader's share of production capacity and share of sales fall.

Subsequent competitors enter the market charging a lower price than the leader. As time passes, the perceived relative value of the leader's offer declines, forcing a reduction in the leader's price premium.

Capacity tends to be overbuilt during the rapid growth stage, so that when a cyclical slowdown occurs, industry overcapacity drives down margins to more "normal" levels. New competitors decide not to enter, and existing competitors try to solidify their positions. This leads to the third stage, *share stability*, in which capacity shares and market shares stabilize.

This period is followed by a stage of *commodity competition*. The product is viewed as a commodity, buyers no longer pay a price premium, and the suppliers earn only an average rate of return. At this point, the withdrawal stage begins. The pioneer might decide to build share further as other firms withdraw. As the pioneer moves through the various stages of this competitive cycle, it must continuously formulate new pricing and marketing strategies.

Growth Stage

The growth stage is marked by a rapid climb in sales. The early adopters like the product, and middle-majority consumers start buying the product. New competi-

FIGURE 14-8   Stages of the Competitive Cycle
Source: John B. Frey, "Pricing Over the Competitive Cycle," speech presented at the 1982 Marketing Conference, © 1982, The Conference Board, New York.

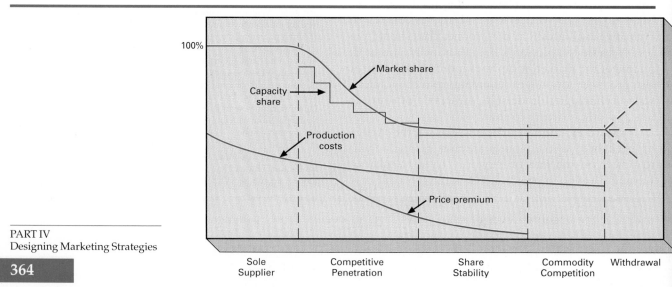

tors enter the market, attracted by the opportunities for large-scale production and profit. They introduce new product features and expand the number of distribution outlets.

Prices remain where they are or fall slightly insofar as demand is increasing quite rapidly. Companies maintain their promotional expenditures at the same or at a slightly increased level to meet competition and to continue to educate the market. Sales rise much faster, causing a decline in the promotion-sales ratio.

Profits increase during this stage as promotion costs are spread over a larger volume, and unit manufacturing costs fall faster than price declines owing to the "experience-curve" effect.

The rate of growth eventually changes from an accelerating rate to a decelerating rate. Firms have to watch for the onset of the decelerating rate in order to prepare new strategies.

Marketing Strategies in the Growth Stage

During this stage, the firm uses several strategies to sustain rapid market growth as long as possible:

- The firm improves product quality and adds new product features and improved styling.
- The firm adds new models and flanker products.
- It enters new market segments.
- It increases its distribution coverage and enters new distribution channels.
- It shifts from product-awareness advertising to product-preference advertising.
- It lowers prices to attract the next layer of price-sensitive buyers.

The firm that pursues these market-expansion strategies will strengthen its competitive position. But this improvement comes at additional cost. The firm in the growth stage faces a tradeoff between high market share and high current profit. By spending money on product improvement, promotion, and distribution, it can capture a dominant position. It forgoes maximum current profit in the hope of making even greater profits in the next stage.

Maturity Stage

At some point, a product's rate of sales growth will slow down, and the product will enter a stage of relative maturity. This stage normally lasts longer than the previous stages, and it poses formidable challenges to marketing management. *Most products are in the maturity stage of the life cycle, and therefore most of marketing management deals with the mature product.*

The maturity stage can be divided into three phases. In the first phase, *growth maturity*, the sales growth rate starts to decline. There are no new distribution channels to fill, although some laggard buyers still enter the market. In the second phase, *stable maturity*, sales flatten on a per capita basis because of market saturation. Most potential consumers have tried the product, and future sales are governed by population growth and replacement demand. In the third phase, *decaying maturity*, the absolute level of sales now starts to decline, and customers start switching to other products and substitutes.

The slowdown in the rate of sales growth creates overcapacity in the industry. This overcapacity leads to intensified competition. Competitors scramble to find and enter niches. They engage in frequent markdowns and off-list pricing. They increase their advertising and trade and consumer deals. They increase their R&D budgets to develop product improvements and flanker products. They make deals to supply private brands. These steps spell some profit erosion. A shakeout period begins, and weaker competitors withdraw. The industry eventually consists of well-entrenched competitors whose basic drive is to gain competitive advantage.

These competitors are of two types (see Figure 14-9). Dominating the industry are a few giant firms that produce a large proportion of the industry's output. These firms serve the whole market and make their profits mainly through high volume and lower costs. These volume leaders are somewhat differentiated in terms of reputations for high quality, high service, or low price. Surrounding these dominant firms are a multitude of market nichers. The nichers include market specialists, product specialists, and customizing firms. The nichers serve and satisfy their small target markets very well and command a price premium. The issue facing a firm in a mature market is whether to struggle to become one of the "big three" and achieve profits through high volume and low cost or to pursue a niching strategy and achieve profits through high margin.

Marketing Strategies in the Mature Stage

In the mature stage, some companies abandon their weaker products. They prefer to concentrate their resources on their more profitable products and on new products. Yet they might be ignoring the high potential that many old products still

FIGURE 14-9
Companies in a Mature
Industry

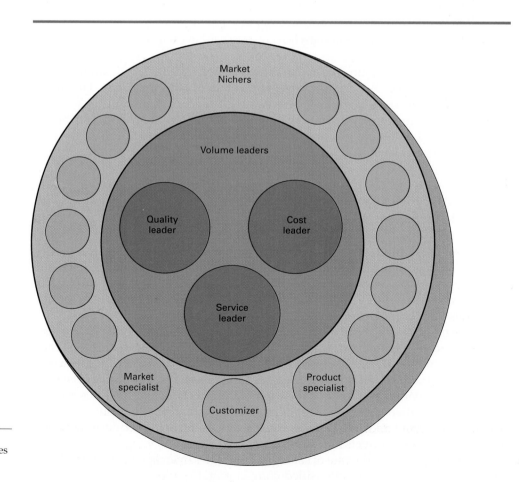

have. Many industries widely thought to be mature—autos, motorcycles, television, watches, cameras—were proved otherwise by the Japanese, who found ways to offer new values to customers. Seemingly moribund brands like Jell-O, Ovaltine, and Arm & Hammer baking soda have achieved major sales revivals several times, through the exercise of marketing imagination. Marketers should systematically consider strategies of market, product, and marketing-mix modification.

MARKET MODIFICATION ❖ The company might try to expand the market for its mature brand by working with the two factors that make up sales volume:

$$\text{Volume} = \text{number of brand users} \times \text{usage rate per user}$$

The company can try to expand the number of brand users in three ways:

- *Convert Nonusers:* The company can try to attract nonusers to the product. For example, the key to the growth of air freight service is the constant search for new users to whom air carriers can demonstrate the benefits of using air freight over ground transportation.
- *Enter New Market Segments:* The company can try to enter new market segments—geographic, demographic, and so on—that use the product but not the brand. For example, Johnson & Johnson successfully promoted its baby shampoo to adult users.
- *Win Competitors' Customers:* The company can attract competitors' customers to try or adopt the brand. For example, Pepsi-Cola is constantly tempting Coca-Cola users to switch to Pepsi-Cola, throwing out one challenge after another.

Volume can also be increased by convincing current brand users to increase their annual usage of the brand. Here are three strategies:

- *More Frequent Use:* The company can try to get customers to use the product more frequently. For example, orange-juice marketers try to get people to drink orange juice on occasions other than breakfast time.
- *More Usage per Occasion:* The company can try to interest users in using more of the product on each occasion. Thus a shampoo manufacturer might indicate that the shampoo is more effective with two rinsings than one.
- *New and More Varied Uses:* The company can try to discover new product uses and convince people to use the product in more varied ways. Food manufacturers, for example, list several recipes on their packages to broaden the consumers' uses of the product.

PRODUCT MODIFICATION ❖ Managers also try to stimulate sales by modifying the product's characteristics. This can take several forms.

A strategy of *quality improvement* aims at increasing the functional performance of the product—its durability, reliability, speed, taste. A manufacturer can often overtake its competition by launching the "new and improved" machine tool, automobile, television set, or detergent. Grocery manufacturers call this a "plus" launch and promote a new additive or advertise something as "stronger," "bigger," or "better." This strategy is effective to the extent that the quality is improved, buyers accept the claim of improved quality, and a sufficient number of buyers will pay for higher quality.

A strategy of *feature improvement* aims at adding new features (e.g., size, weight, materials, additives, accessories) that expand the product's versatility, safety, or convenience. For example, adding electric power to hand lawn mowers increased the speed and ease of cutting grass. Lawn-mower manufacturers then worked on designing better safety features. Some manufacturers have added conversion features so that a power lawn mower doubles as a snow plow.

A strategy of feature improvement has several advantages. New features build an image of company innovativeness. They win the loyalty of certain market segments who value these features. They can be adopted or dropped quickly and made optional to the buyer. They provide an opportunity for free publicity and they generate salesforce and distributor enthusiasm. The chief disadvantage is that feature improvements are highly imitable; unless there is a permanent gain from being first, the feature improvement might not pay.

A strategy of *style improvement* aims at increasing the aesthetic appeal of the product. The periodic introduction of new car models amounts to style competition rather than quality or feature competition. In the case of packaged-food and household products, companies introduce color and texture variations and often restyle the package, treating it as an extension of the product. The advantage of a style strategy is that it might confer a unique market identity and win a loyal following. Yet style competition has some problems. First, it is difficult to predict whether people—and which people—will like a new style. Second, a style change usually requires discontinuing the old style, and the company risks losing customers who liked the old style.

MARKETING-MIX MODIFICATION ❖ Product managers might also try to stimulate sales by modifying one or more marketing-mix elements. They should ask the following questions about the nonproduct elements of the marketing mix in searching for ways to stimulate a mature product's sales:

- *Prices:* Would a price cut attract new triers and users? If so, should the list price be lowered, or should prices be lowered through price specials, volume or early-purchase discounts, freight absorption, or easier credit terms? Or would it be better to raise the price to signal higher quality?

- *Distribution:* Can the company obtain more product support and display in the existing outlets? Can more outlets be penetrated? Can the company introduce the product into new types of distribution channels?

- *Advertising:* Should advertising expenditures be increased? Should the advertising message or copy be changed? Should the media-vehicle mix be changed? Should the timing, frequency, or size of ads be changed?

- *Sales Promotion:* Should the company step up sales promotion—trade deals, cents-off, rebates, warranties, gifts, and contests?

- *Personal Selling:* Should the number or quality of salespeople be increased? Should the basis for salesforce specialization be changed? Should sales territories be revised? Should salesforce incentives be revised? Can sales-call planning be improved?

- *Services:* Can the company speed up delivery? Can it extend more technical assistance to customers? Can it extend more credit?

Marketers often debate which tools are more effective in the mature stage. For example, would the company gain more by increasing its advertising or sales-promotion budget? Some say that sales promotion has more impact at this stage because consumers have reached an equilibrium in their buying habits and preferences, and psychological persuasion (advertising) is not as effective as financial persuasion (sales-promotion deals). In fact, many consumer-packaged-goods companies spend over 60% of their total promotion budget on sales promotion to support mature products. Yet other marketers say that brands should be managed as capital assets and supported by advertising. Advertising expenditures should be treated as a capital investment, not a current expense. Brand managers, however,

Marketing Strategies 14-2

Breaking Through the "Mature-Product" Syndrome

Managers of mature products need a systematic framework for identifying possible "breakthrough" ideas. Professor John A. Weber of Notre Dame developed the following framework, which he calls gap analysis, to guide the search for growth opportunities.

The key idea is to identify possible gaps in the product line, distribution, usage, competition, and so on. Market-structure analysis would prompt the following questions about a mature beverage product such as Kool-Aid:

1. *Natural changes in the size of industry market potential:* Will current birthrates and demographics favor more consumption of Kool-Aid? How will the economic outlook affect Kool-Aid consumption?

2. *New uses or new user segments:* Can Kool-Aid be made to appeal to teenagers, young adult singles, young adult parents, etc?

3. *Innovative product differentiations:* Can Kool-Aid be made in different versions such as low calorie or super-sweet?

4. *Add new product lines:* Can the Kool-Aid name be used to launch a new soft-drink line?

5. *Stimulate nonusers:* Can children be persuaded to try Kool-Aid?

6. *Stimulate light users:* Can children be reminded to drink Kool-Aid daily?

7. *Increase amount used on each use occasion:* Can more Kool-Aid be put in each package at a higher price?

8. *Close existing product and price gaps:* Should new sizes of Kool-Aid be introduced?

9. *Create new product-line elements:* Should Kool-Aid introduce new flavors?

10. *Expand distribution coverage:* Can Kool-Aid distribution coverage be expanded to Alaska, Hawaii, and Europe?

11. *Expand distribution intensity:* Can the percentage of convenience stores in the Midwest that carry Kool-Aid be increased from 70% to 90%?

12. *Expand distribution exposure:* Can offers to the trade get more shelf facings for Kool-Aid?

13. *Penetrate substitute's positions:* Can consumers be convinced that Kool-Aid is a better drink than other types of soft drinks (e.g., soda, milk, etc.)

14. *Penetrate direct competitor's position(s):* Can consumers of other brands be convinced to switch to Kool-Aid?

15. *Defend firm's present position:* Can Kool-Aid satisfy the current users more so that they remain loyal?

Thus Weber's system leads to a large number of marketing ideas. The next step is to identify the best ideas, work out their details, and implement them.

SOURCE: See John A. Weber, *Growth Opportunity Analysis* (Reston, VA: Reston Publishing Co., 1976); and John A. Weber, *Identifying and Solving Marketing Problems with Gap Analysis* (Notre Dame, IN, PO Box 77: Strategic Business Systems, 1986).

---

use sales promotion because its effects are quicker and more visible to their superiors, but excessive sales-promotion activity can hurt the brand's long-run profit performance.

A major problem with marketing-mix modifications is that they are highly imitable by competition, especially price reductions and additional services. The firm may not gain as much as expected, and all firms might experience profit erosion as they step up their marketing attacks on each other.

Marketing Strategies 14-2 presents a framework for finding ideas for rebuilding the sales of mature products.

Decline Stage

The sales of most product forms and brands eventually decline. The sales decline might be slow, as in the case of oatmeal; or rapid, as in the case of the Edsel automobile. Sales may plunge to zero, or they may petrify at a low level.

Sales decline for a number of reasons, including technological advances, consumer shifts in tastes, and increased domestic and foreign competition. All lead to overcapacity, increased price cutting, and profit erosion.

As sales and profits decline, some firms withdraw from the market. Those remaining may reduce the number of product offerings. They may withdraw from smaller market segments and weaker trade channels. They may cut the promotion budget and reduce their prices further.

Unfortunately, most companies have not developed a well-thought-out policy for handling their aging products. Sentiment plays a role:

> But putting products to death—or letting them die—is a drab business, and often engenders much of the sadness of a final parting with old and tried friends. The portable, six-sided pretzel was the first product The Company ever made. Our line will no longer be our line without it.[16]

Logic also plays a role. Management believes that product sales will improve when the economy improves, or when the marketing strategy is revised, or when the product is improved. Or the weak product may be retained because of its alleged contribution to the sales of the company's other products. Or its revenue may cover out-of-pocket costs, and the company has no better use for the money.

Unless strong reasons for retention exist, carrying a weak product is very costly to the firm. The cost is not just the amount of uncovered overhead and profit. Financial accounting cannot adequately convey all the hidden costs: The weak product might consume a disproportionate amount of management's time; it often requires frequent price and inventory adjustment; it generally involves short production runs in spite of expensive setup times; it requires both advertising and salesforce attention that might be better used to make the "healthy" products more profitable; its very unfitness can cause customer misgivings and cast a shadow on the company's image. The biggest cost might well lie in the future. Failing to eliminate weak products delays the aggressive search for replacement products; the weak products create a lopsided product mix, long on "yesterday's breadwinners" and short on "tomorrow's breadwinners"; they depress current profitability and weaken the company's foothold on the future.

Marketing Strategies During the Decline Stage

A company faces a number of tasks and decisions to handle its aging products.

IDENTIFYING THE WEAK PRODUCTS ❖ The first task is to establish a system for identifying weak products. The company appoints a product-review committee with representatives from marketing, R&D, manufacturing, and finance. This committee develops a system for identifying weak products. The controller's office supplies data for each product showing trends in market size, market share, prices, costs, and profits. This information is analyzed by a computer program that identifies dubious products. The criteria include the number of years of sales decline, market-share trends, gross-profit margin, and return on investment. The managers responsible for dubious products fill out rating forms showing where they think sales and profits will go, with and without any changes in marketing strategy. The product-review committee examines this information and makes a recommendation for each dubious product—leave it alone, modify its marketing strategy, or drop it.[17]

DETERMINING MARKETING STRATEGIES ❖ Some firms will abandon declining markets earlier than others. Much depends on the level of the *exit barriers*.[18] The lower the exit barriers, the easier it is for firms to leave the industry, and the more tempting it is for the remaining firms to remain and attract the customers of the withdrawing firms. The remaining firms will enjoy increased sales and profits. For example, Procter & Gamble stayed in the declining liquid-soap business and improved its profits as the others withdrew.

In a study of company strategies in declining industries, Harrigan distinguished five decline strategies available to the firm:

- Increasing the firm's investment (to dominate or strengthen its competitive position)
- Maintaining the firm's investment level until the uncertainties about the industry are resolved
- Decreasing the firm's investment level selectively, by sloughing off unprofitable customer groups, while simultaneously strengthening the firm's investment in lucrative niches
- Harvesting (or milking) the firm's investment to recover cash quickly
- Divesting the business quickly by disposing of its assets as advantageously as possible[19]

The appropriate decline strategy depends on the industry's relative attractiveness and the company's competitive strength in that industry. For example, a company in an unattractive industry but possessing competitive strength should consider shrinking selectively. However, if the company is in an attractive industry and has competitive strength, it should consider strengthening its investment. Procter & Gamble on a number of occasions has taken disappointing brands that were in strong markets and *restaged* them.

> P&G launched a "not oily" hand cream called Wondra that was packaged in an inverted bottle so the cream would flow out from the bottom. Although initial sales were high, repeat purchases were disappointing. Consumers complained that the bottom got sticky and that "not oily" suggested it wouldn't work well. P&G carried out two restagings: First, it reintroduced Wondra in an upright bottle, and later reformulated the ingredients so they would work better. Sales then picked up.

P&G prefers restaging to abandoning brand names. P&G spokespersons like to claim that there is no such thing as a product life cycle, and they point to Ivory, Camay, and many other "dowager" brands that are still thriving.

If the company were choosing between *harvesting* and *divesting*, its strategies would be quite different. Harvesting calls for gradually reducing a product or business's costs while trying to maintain its sales. The first costs to cut are R&D costs and plant and equipment investment. The company might also reduce product quality, salesforce size, marginal services, and advertising expenditures. It would try to cut these costs without tipping off customers, competitors, and employees that it is slowly pulling out of the business. If customers knew that, they would switch suppliers; if competitors knew it, they would tell customers; if employees knew it, they would seek new jobs elsewhere. Thus harvesting is an ethically ambivalent strategy, and it is also difficult to execute. Yet many mature products warrant this strategy. Harvesting can substantially increase the company's current cash flow, provided that sales do not collapse.[20]

Harvesting eventually makes a business worthless. On the other hand, if the firm had decided instead to divest the business, it would have first looked for a buyer. It would have tried to increase the attractiveness of the business, not run it down. Therefore the company must think carefully about whether to harvest or divest the weakening business unit.

THE DROP DECISION ❖ When a company decides to drop a product, it faces further decisions. If the product has strong distribution and residual goodwill, the company can probably sell it to a smaller firm.

> Jeffrey Martin, Inc. bought several "worn-out" brands from Purex Corporation, including Cuticura, Bantron, and Doan's Pills and turned them around. Two Minnesota businessmen bought the *Ipana* toothpaste name and formula from Bristol-Myers; with no promotion, they sold $250,000 in the first seven months of operation.

If the company can't find any buyers, it must decide whether to liquidate the brand quickly or slowly. It must also decide on how much parts inventory and service to maintain for past customers.

Summary and Critique of the Product Life-Cycle Concept

Table 14-1 summarizes the characteristics, marketing objectives, and marketing strategies of the four stages of the PLC.

Some marketers have prescribed more specific strategies during each stage of the PLC. Figure 14-10 displays life-cycle strategies for grocery-product marketing.

The PLC concept is used by marketing managers to interpret product and market dynamics. As a *planning tool*, the PLC concept characterizes the main marketing challenges in each stage and poses major alternative marketing strategies. As a *control tool*, the launched PLC concept allows the company to measure product performance against similar products launched in the past. As a *forecasting tool*, the PLC concept is less useful because sales histories exhibit diverse patterns, and the stages vary in duration.

PLC theory has its share of critics. They claim that life-cycle patterns are too variable in their shape and duration. PLCs lack what living organisms have, namely, a fixed sequence of stages and a fixed length of each stage. Critics charge that marketers can seldom tell what stage the product is in. A product may appear to be mature when actually it has only reached a temporary plateau prior to another upsurge. They charge that the PLC pattern is the result of marketing strategies rather than an inevitable course that sales must follow:

> Suppose a brand is acceptable to consumers but has a few bad years because of other factors — for instance, poor advertising, delisting by a major chain, or entry of a "me-too" competitive product backed by massive sampling. Instead of thinking in terms of corrective measures, management begins to feel that its brand has entered a declining stage. It therefore withdraws funds from the promotion budget to finance R&D on new items. The next year the brand does even worse, panic increases. . . . Clearly, the PLC is a dependent variable which is determined by marketing actions; it is not an independent variable to which companies should adapt their marketing programs.[21]

In other words, if a brand's sales are declining, management should not conclude that the brand is inevitably in the decline stage. If management withdraws funds from the brand, it will create a self-fulfilling prophecy that will continue the brand's decline. Instead, management should examine all the ways it could stimulate sales: modifying the customer mix, the brand's positioning, or the marketing mix. Only when management cannot identify a promising turnaround strategy might it conclude that the brand is in the decline stage of its life cycle. Then it must decide what to do.

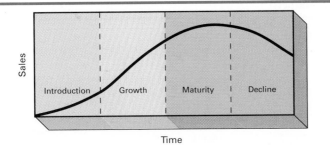

CHARACTERISTICS

	Introduction	Growth	Maturity	Decline
Sales	Low sales	Rapidly rising sales	Peak sales	Declining sales
Costs	High cost per customer	Average cost per customer	Low cost per customer	Low cost per customer
Profits	Negative	Rising profits	High profits	Declining profits
Customers	Innovators	Early adopters	Middle majority	Laggards
Competitors	Few	Growing number	Stable number beginning to decline	Declining number

MARKETING OBJECTIVES

	Introduction	Growth	Maturity	Decline
	Create product awareness and trial	Maximize market share	Maximize profit while defending market share	Reduce expenditure and milk the brand

STRATEGIES

	Introduction	Growth	Maturity	Decline
Product	Offer a basic product	Offer product extensions, service, warranty	Diversify brands and models	Phase out weak items
Price	Use cost-plus	Price to penetrate market	Price to match or best competitors	Cut price
Distribution	Build selective distribution	Build intensive distribution	Build more intensive distribution	Go selective: phase out unprofitable outlets
Advertising	Build product awareness among early adopters and dealers	Build awareness and interest in the mass market	Stress brand differences and benefits	Reduce to level needed to retain hardcore loyals
Sales Promotion	Use heavy sales promotion to entice trial	Reduce to take advantage of heavy consumer demand	Increase to encourage brand switching	Reduce to minimal level

Sources: This table was assembled by the author from several sources: Chester R. Wasson, *Dynamic Competitive Strategy and Product Life Cycles* (Austin, TX: Austin Press, 1978); John A. Weber, "Planning Corporate Growth with Inverted Product Life Cycles," *Long Range Planning*, October 1976, pp. 12–29; and Peter Doyle, "The Realities of the Product Life Cycle," *Quarterly Review of Marketing*, Summer 1976, pp. 1– 6.

FIGURE 14-10   PLC Marketing for Grocery Products

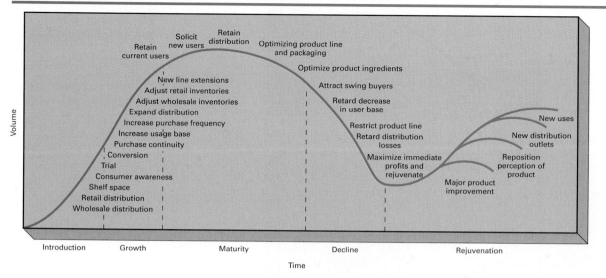

The Concept of Market Evolution

The PLC focuses on what is happening to a particular product or brand rather than on what is happening to the overall market. It yields a product-oriented picture rather than a market-oriented picture. The demand/technology life cycle mentioned earlier reminds us to take a broader look at the whole market. Firms need to anticipate the evolutionary path of a market as it is affected by new needs, competitors, technology, channels, and other developments.

Stages in Market Evolution

A market evolves through four stages: emergence, growth, maturity, and decline. We will describe and illustrate these stages.

EMERGENCE STAGE   ❖   Before a market materializes, it exists as a *latent market*. A latent market consists of people who share a similar need or want for something that does not yet exist. For example, people have wanted a means of more rapid calculation than can be provided by a paper and pencil. Until recently, this need was imperfectly satisfied through abacuses, slide rules, and large adding machines.

Suppose an entrepreneur recognizes this need and imagines a technological solution in the form of a small, hand-size electronic calculator. He now has to determine the product attributes, specifically *physical size* and *number of arithmetic functions*. Being market oriented, he interviews potential buyers and asks them to state their preferred levels on each attribute.

Suppose consumer preferences are represented by the dots in Figure 14-11(a). Evidently target customers vary greatly in their preferences. Some want a four-function calculator (adding, subtracting, multiplying, and dividing) and others want more functions (calculating percentages, square roots, logs, and so forth). Some want a small hand calculator and others want a large one. When buyer preferences scatter evenly in a market, it is called a *diffused-preference market*.

The entrepreneur's problem is to design an optimal product for this market.[22] He has three options:

- The new product can be designed to meet the preferences of one of the corners of the market (*a single-niche strategy*).
- Two or more products can be simultaneously launched to capture two or more parts of the market (*a multiple-niche strategy*).
- The new product can be designed for the middle of the market (*a mass-market strategy*).

For small firms, a single-niche market strategy makes the most sense. A small firm has insufficient resources for capturing and holding the mass market. Larger firms would enter and clobber the small firm. Its best bet is to develop a specialized product and capture a corner of the market that will not attract competitors for a long time.

A large firm might go after the mass market by designing a product that is "medium" in size and number of functions. A product in the center minimizes the sum of the distances of existing preferences from the actual product. A hand calculator designed for the mass market will minimize total dissatisfaction. Assume that the pioneer firm is large and designs its product for the mass market. On launching the product, the *emergence stage* begins.

GROWTH STAGE ❖ If sales are good, new firms will enter the market, ushering in a *market growth stage*. An interesting question is, Where will a second firm enter the market, assuming that the first firm established itself in the center? The second firm has three options:

- It can locate its brand in one of the corners (*a single-niche strategy*).
- It can locate its brand next to the first competitor (*a mass-market strategy*).
- It can launch two or more products in different unoccupied corners (*a multiple-niche strategy*).

If the second firm is small, it will avoid head-on competition with the pioneer and launch its brand in one of the market corners. If the second firm is large, it

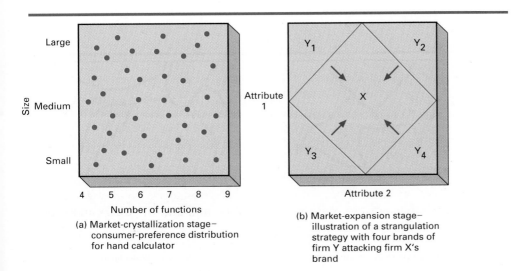

FIGURE 14-11
Market-Space Diagrams

Size

Large

Medium

Small

4   5   6   7   8   9
Number of functions
(a) Market-crystallization stage—
consumer-preference distribution
for hand calculator

Attribute 1

Y_1 Y_2

X

Y_3 Y_4

Attribute 2
(b) Market-expansion stage—
illustration of a strangulation
strategy with four brands of
firm Y attacking firm X's
brand

might launch its brand in the center against the pioneer firm. The two firms can easily end up sharing the mass market almost equally. Or a large second firm can implement a multiniche strategy.

> Procter & Gamble occasionally will enter a market containing a large, entrenched competitor, and instead of launching a me-too product or single-segment product, it introduces a succession of products aimed at different segments. Each entry creates a loyal following and takes some business away from the major competitor. Soon the major competitor is surrounded, its revenue is weakened, and it is too late to launch new brands in outlying segments. P&G, in a moment of triumph, then launches a brand against the major segment. This is called an encirclement strategy and is illustrated in Figure 14-11(b).

MATURITY STAGE ❖ Each firm entering the market will go after some position, locating either next to a competitor or in an unoccupied segment. Eventually, the competitors cover and serve all the major market segments. In fact, they go further and invade each other's segments, reducing everyone's profits in the process. As the market's growth slows down, the market splits into finer segments and a condition of high market fragmentation occurs. This is illustrated in Figure 14-12(a), the letters representing different companies supplying various segments. Note that two segments are unserved because they are too small to yield a profit.[23]

This, however, is not the end of the market's evolution. Market fragmentation is often followed by market consolidation, caused by the emergence of a new attribute that has strong market appeal. Market consolidation took place in the toothpaste market when P&G introduced its new fluoride toothpaste, Crest, which effectively retarded dental decay. Suddenly toothpaste brands that claimed whitening power, cleaning power, sex appeal, taste, or mouthwash effectiveness were pushed into the corners because consumers primarily wanted a dental-protection toothpaste. P&G's Crest won a lion's share of the market, as shown by the X territory in Figure 14-12(b).

But even a consolidated market condition will not last. Other companies will copy the successful brand, and the market will eventually splinter again. Mature markets swing between market fragmentation and market consolidation. The fragmentation is brought about by competition, and the consolidation is brought about by innovation.

FIGURE 14-12
Market-Fragmentation and Market-Reconsolidation Stages

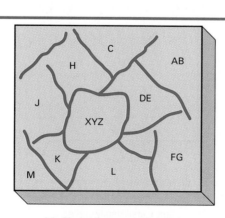

(a) Market-fragmentation stage

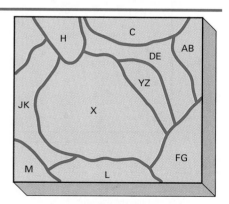

(b) Market-reconsolidation stage

DECLINE STAGE ❖ Eventually, the market demand for the present products will begin to decline. Either the total need level declines or a new technology starts replacing the old. Thus an entrepreneur might invent a mouth-spray substitute that is superior to toothpaste. In this case, the old technology will eventually disappear and a new demand-technology life cycle will emerge.

Dynamics of Attribute Competition

Thus markets emerge and evolve through several stages. Consider the evolution of the paper-towel market. Originally, homemakers used cotton and linen dish cloths and towels in their kitchens. A paper company, looking for new markets, developed paper towels to compete with cloth towels. This development crystallized a new market. Other paper manufacturers entered and expanded the market. The number of brands proliferated and created market fragmentation. Industry overcapacity led manufacturers to search for new features. One manufacturer, hearing consumers complain that paper towels were not absorbent, introduced "absorbent" paper towels and increased its market share. This market consolidation did not last long because competitors came out with their versions of absorbent paper towels. The market became fragmented again. Then another manufacturer heard consumers express a wish for a "superstrength" paper towel and introduced one. It was soon copied by other manufacturers. Another manufacturer introduced a "lint-free" paper towel, which was subsequently copied. Thus paper towels evolved from a single product to one with various absorbencies, strengths, and applications. Market evolution was driven by the forces of innovation and competition.

Competition produces a continuous round of newly discovered product attributes. If a new attribute succeeds, then several competitors soon offer it, and it loses its determinance. To the extent that most banks are now "friendly," friendliness no longer influences consumer choice of a bank. To the extent that most airlines serve in-flight meals, meals are no longer a basis for air-carrier choice. *Customer expectations are progressive.* This underlines the strategic importance of a company's maintaining the lead in introducing new attributes. Each new attribute, if successful, creates a competitive advantage for the firm, leading to temporarily higher-than-average market share and profits. The market leader must learn to *routinize* the innovation process.

A crucial question is: *Can a firm look ahead and anticipate the succession of attributes that are likely to win favor and be technologically feasible?* How can the firm discover new attributes? There are four approaches.

The first approach employs a *customer-survey process* to identify new attributes. The company asks consumers what benefits they would like added to the product and their desire level for each. The firm also examines the cost of developing each new attribute and likely competitive responses. It chooses those attributes promising the highest incremental profit.

The second approach uses an *intuitive process*. Entrepreneurs get hunches and undertake product development without much marketing research. Natural selection determines winners and losers. If a manufacturer has intuited an attribute that the market wants, that manufacturer is considered smart, although from another perspective, it was only luck. This theory offers no guidance as to how to visualize new attributes.

A third approach says that new attributes emerge through a *dialectical process*. Any valued attribute gets pushed to an extreme form through the competitive process. Thus blue jeans, starting out as an inexpensive clothing article, over time became fashionable and more expensive. This unidirectional movement, however, contains the seeds of its own destruction. Eventually some manufacturer introduces a cheaper material for pants, and consumers flock to buy it. Dialectical theory says that innovators should not march with the crowd but rather in the opposite direction toward market segments that are suffering from increasing neglect.

A fourth approach holds that new attributes emerge through a *needs-hierarchy process* (see Maslow's theory, page 185). On this theory, we would predict that the first automobiles would provide basic transportation and be designed for safety. At a later time, automobiles would start appealing to social acceptance and status needs. Still later, automobiles would be designed to help people "fulfill" themselves. The innovator's task is to assess when the market is ready to satisfy a higher-order need.

The actual unfolding of new attributes in a market is more complex than any simple theories would suggest. We should not underestimate the role of technological and societal processes in influencing the emergence of new attributes. For example, the strong consumer interest in compact-size television sets remained unmet until miniaturization technology was sufficiently developed. Technological forecasting attempts to predict the timing of future technological developments that will permit new-attribute offers to consumers. The societal factor also plays a major role in shaping attribute evolution. Developments such as inflation, shortages, environmentalism, consumerism, and new lifestyles create consumer disequilibrium and lead consumers to reevaluate product attributes. For example, inflation increases the desire for a smaller car, and car safety increases the desire for a heavier car. The innovator must use marketing research to gauge the demand potency of different attributes in order to determine the company's best move vis-à-vis competition.

SUMMARY ❖

Products and markets have life cycles that call for changing marketing strategies over time. Every new need follows a demand life cycle that passes through the stages of emergence, accelerating growth, decelerating growth, maturity, and decline. Each new technology that emerges to satisfy that need exhibits a demand-technology life cycle. Particular product forms of a given technology also show a life cycle, as do brands within that product form.

The sales history of many products follows an **S**-shaped curve consisting of four stages. The *introduction* stage is marked by slow growth and minimal profits as the product is pushed into distribution. During this stage, the company has to decide between strategies of rapid skimming, slow skimming, rapid penetration, or slow penetration. If successful, the product enters a *growth* stage marked by rapid sales growth and increasing profits. The company attempts to improve the product, enter new market segments and distribution channels, and reduce its prices slightly. There follows a *maturity* stage in which sales growth slows down and profits stabilize. The company seeks innovative strategies to renew sales growth, including market, product, and marketing-mix modification. Finally, the product enters a *decline* stage in which little can be done to halt the deterioration of sales and profits. The company's task is to identify the truly weak products; develop for each one a strategy of continuation, focusing, or milking; and finally phase out weak products in a way that minimizes the hardship to company profits, employees, and customers.

Not all products pass through an **S**-shaped PLC. Some products show a growth-slump-maturity pattern, others a cycle-recycle shape, and still others a scalloped shape. Researchers have discovered over a dozen PLC shapes, including those describing styles, fashions, and fads. PLC theory has been criticized on the grounds that companies cannot predict the shapes in advance, or know what stage they are in within a given shape, or predict the duration of the stages. Also, PLCs are the result of chosen marketing strategies rather than of an inevitable sales history that is independent of the chosen marketing strategies.

Product life-cycle theory must be broadened by a theory of market evolution. The theory of market evolution holds that new markets *emerge* when a product is created to satisfy an unmet need. The innovator usually designs a product for the mass market. Competitors enter the market with similar products leading to *market growth*. Growth eventually slows down and the market enters *maturity*. The market undergoes increasing *fragmentation* until some firm introduces a powerful new attribute that *consolidates* the market into fewer and larger segments. This stage does not last, because competitors copy the new attributes. There is a cycling back and forth between market consolidation based on innovation and fragmentation based on competition. The market for the present technology will ultimately *decline* upon the discovery of superior technologies.

Companies must try to anticipate new attributes that the market wants. Profits go to those who introduce new and valued benefits early. The search for new attributes can be based on customer survey work, intuition, dialectical reasoning, or needs-hierarchy reasoning. Successful marketing comes through creatively visualizing the market's evolutionary potential.

NOTES ❖

1. This discussion of demand/technology cycles is drawn from H. Igor Ansoff, *Implanting Strategic Management* (Englewood Cliffs, NJ: Prentice Hall, 1984), pp. 37–44.

2. Ibid., p. 38.

3. Some authors distinguished additional stages. Wasson suggested a stage of competitive turbulence between growth and maturity. See Chester R. Wasson, *Dynamic Competitive Strategy and Product Life Cycles* (Austin, TX: Austin Press, 1978). *Maturity* describes a stage of sales growth slowdown and *saturation*, a stage of flat sales after sales have peaked.

4. Rolando Polli and Victor Cook, "Validity of the Product Life Cycle," *Journal of Business*, October 1969, pp. 385–400.

5. *Nielsen Researcher*, no. 1 (Chicago: A. G. Nielsen Co., 1968).

6. See William E. Cox, Jr., "Product Life Cycles as Marketing Models," *Journal of Business*, October 1967, pp. 375–84; John E. Swan and David R. Rink, "Fitting Market Strategy to Varying Product Life Cycles," *Business Horizons*, January–February 1982, pp. 72–76; and Gerald J. Tellis and C. Merle Crawford, "An Evolutionary Approach to Product Growth Theory," *Journal of Marketing*, Fall 1981, pp. 125–34.

7. Jordan P. Yale, "The Strategy of Nylon's Growth," *Modern Textiles Magazine*, February 1964, pp. 32 ff. Also see Theodore Levitt, "Exploit the Product Life Cycle," *Harvard Business Review*, November–December 1965, pp. 81–94.

8. Chester R. Wasson, "How Predictable Are Fashion and Other Product Life Cycles?" *Journal of Marketing*, July 1968, pp. 36–43.

9. William H. Reynolds, "Cars and Clothing: Understanding Fashion Trends," *Journal of Marketing*, July 1968, pp. 44–49.

10. Dwight E. Robinson, "Style Changes: Cyclical, Inexorable and Foreseeable," *Harvard Business Review*, November–December 1975, pp. 121–31.

11. George B. Sproles, "Analyzing Fashion Life Cycles—Principles and Perspectives," *Journal of Marketing*, Fall 1981, pp. 116–24.

12. Buzzell, "Competitive Behavior," p. 51.

13. Ibid.

14. Ibid., p. 52.

15. John B. Frey, "Pricing over the Competitive Cycle," speech presented at the 1982 Marketing Conference, Conference Board, New York.

16. R. S. Alexander, "The Death and Burial of 'Sick Products,'" *Journal of Marketing*, April 1964, p. 1.

17. See Philip Kotler, "Phasing Out Weak Products," *Harvard Business Review*, March–April 1965, pp. 107–18; Paul W. Hamelman and Edward M. Mazze, "Improving Product Abandonment Decisions," *Journal of Marketing*, April 1972,

pp. 20–26; and Richard T. Hise, A. Parasuraman, and R. Viswanathan, "Product Elimination: The Neglected Management Responsibility," *Journal of Business Strategy*, Spring 1984, pp. 56–63.

18. See Kathryn Rudie Harrigan, "The Effect of Exit Barriers upon Strategic Flexibility," *Strategic Management Journal*, 1 (1980), pp. 165–76.

19. Kathryn Rudie Harrigan, "Strategies for Declining Industries," *Journal of Business Strategy*, Fall 1980, p. 27.

20. See Philip Kotler, "Harvesting Strategies for Weak Products," *Business Horizons*, August 1978, pp. 15–22; and Laurence P. Feldman and Albert L. Page, "Harvesting: The Misunderstood Market Exit Strategy," *Journal of Business Strategy*, Spring 1985, pp. 79–85.

21. Nariman K. Dhalla and Sonia Yuspeh, "Forget the Product Life Cycle Concept!" *Harvard Business Review*, January–February 1976, pp. 102–12, here p. 105.

22. This problem is trivial if consumers' preferences are concentrated at one point. If there are distinct clusters of preference, the entrepreneur can design a product for the largest cluster or for the cluster that the company can serve best.

23. The product space is drawn with two attributes for simplicity. Actually, more attributes come into being as the market evolves. The product space grows from a two-dimensional to an n-dimensional space.

15

Designing Marketing Strategies for Market Leaders, Challengers, Followers, and Nichers

"Cheshire Puss," she [Alice] began . . . "would you please tell me which way I ought to go from here?" "That depends on where you want to get to," said the cat.

LEWIS CARROLL

It takes a rough sea to make a great captain.

ANONYMOUS

W̲e will now examine the problem of designing winning marketing strategies that take into account competitors' strategies. Some competitors will be large, others small. Some will have great resources, others will be strapped for funds. According to the Arthur D. Little consulting firm, a firm will occupy one of six competitive positions in the target market:[1]

- *Dominant:* This firm controls the behavior of other competitors and has a wide choice of strategic options.
- *Strong:* This firm can take independent action without endangering its long-term position and can maintain its long-term position regardless of competitors' actions.
- *Favorable:* This firm has a strength that is exploitable in particular strategies and has more than average opportunity to improve its position.
- *Tenable:* This firm is performing at a sufficiently satisfactory level to warrant continuing in business, but it exists at the sufferance of the dominant company and has a less-than-average opportunity to improve its position.
- *Weak*: This firm has unsatisfactory performance but an opportunity exists for improvement and it must change or else exit.
- *Nonviable:* This firm has unsatisfactory performance and no opportunity for improvement.

Further insight can be gained by classifying firms by the role they play in the target market, that of leading, challenging, following, or niching. Suppose a market is occupied by the firms shown in Figure 15-1. Forty percent of the market is in the hands of a *market leader*, the firm with the largest market share. Another 30% is in the hands of a *market challenger*, a runner-up firm that is fighting hard for an increased market share. Another 20% is in the hands of a *market follower*, another runner-up firm that is willing to maintain its market share and not rock the boat. The remaining 10% is in the hands of *market nichers*, firms that serve small market segments not being served by larger firms.

We will examine in this chapter the different marketing challenges and strategies facing market leaders, challengers, followers, and nichers.

Market-Leader Strategies

Many industries contain one firm that is the acknowledged market leader. This firm has the largest market share in the relevant product market. It usually leads the other firms in price changes, new-product introductions, distribution coverage, and promotional intensity. The leader may or may not be admired or respected, but other firms acknowledge its dominance. The leader is an orientation point for competitors, a company to either challenge, imitate, or avoid. Some of the best-known market leaders are General Motors (autos), Kodak (photography), IBM (computers), Xerox (copying), Procter & Gamble (consumer packaged goods), Caterpillar (earth-moving equipment), Coca-Cola (soft drinks), McDonald's (fast food), and Gillette (razor blades).

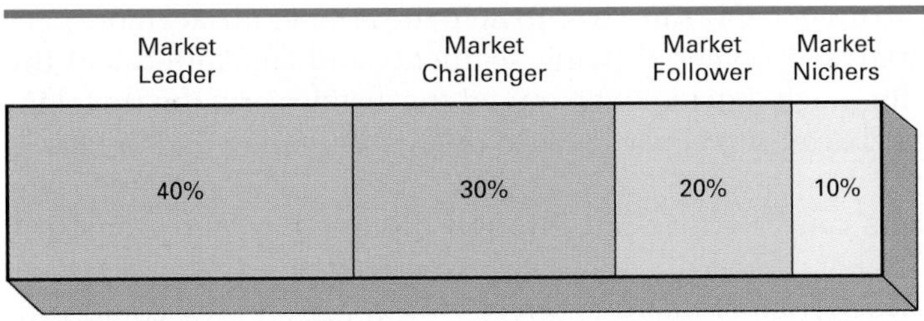

FIGURE 15-1
Hypothetical Market
Structure

Market Leader	Market Challenger	Market Follower	Market Nichers
40%	30%	20%	10%

Unless a dominant firm enjoys a legal monopoly, its life is not altogether easy. It must maintain a constant vigilance. Other firms keep challenging its strengths or trying to take advantage of its weaknesses. The market leader can easily miss a turn in the road and plunge into second or third place. A product innovation may come along and hurt the leader (e.g., Tylenol's nonaspirin painkiller taking over the lead from Bayer Aspirin). The leader might spend conservatively, expecting hard times, while a challenger spends liberally (Montgomery Ward's loss of its retail dominance to Sears after World War II). The dominant firm might look old-fashioned against new and peppier rivals (*Playboy* magazine's fall to second place in newsstand circulation after *Penthouse*). The dominant firm's costs might rise excessively and hurt its profits (Food Fair's decline, resulting from poor cost control).

Dominant firms want to remain number one. This calls for action on three fronts. First, the firm must find ways to expand total market demand. Second, the firm must protect its current market share through good defensive and offensive actions. Third, the firm can try to increase its market share further, even if market size remains constant.

Expanding the Total Market

The dominant firm normally gains the most when the total market expands. If Americans increase their picture taking, Kodak stands to gain the most because it sells over 80% of the country's film. If Kodak can convince more Americans to buy cameras and take pictures, or to take pictures on other occasions besides holidays, or to take more pictures on each occasion, Kodak will benefit considerably. In general, the market leader should look for *new users*, *new uses*, and *more usage* of its products.

NEW USERS ❖ Every product class has the potential of attracting buyers who are unaware of the product or who are resisting it because of its price or lack of certain features. A manufacturer can search for new users among three groups. For example, a perfume manufacturer can try to convince women who do not use perfume to use perfume (*market-penetration strategy*), or convince men to start using perfume (*new-market strategy*), or sell perfume in other countries (*geographical-expansion strategy*).

One of the great successes in developing a new class of users was accomplished by Johnson & Johnson with its baby shampoo. The company became concerned about future sales growth when the birthrate slowed down. Their marketers noticed that other family members occasionally used the baby shampoo for their own hair. Management decided to develop an advertising campaign aimed at adults. In a short time, Johnson & Johnson baby shampoo became the leading brand in the total shampoo market.

In another case, Boeing faced a sharp decline in orders for B-747 jumbo jets when the airlines had acquired enough aircraft to serve existing demand. Boeing concluded that the key to more B-747 sales was to help the airlines attract more people to flying. Boeing analyzed potential flying segments and concluded that the working class did not fly much. Boeing encouraged the airlines and the travel industry to create and sell charter travel packages to unions, churches, and lodges.

NEW USES ❖ Markets can be expanded through discovering and promoting new uses for the product. For example, the average American eats dry breakfast cereal three mornings a week. Cereal manufacturers would gain if they could promote cereal eating on other occasions during the day. Thus some cereals are promoted as snacks to increase their use frequency.

Du Pont's nylon provides a classic story of new-use expansion. Every time nylon became a mature product, Du Pont discovered a new use. Nylon was first used in parachutes; then as a fiber for women's stockings; later, a major material in women's blouses and men's shirts; still later, it entered automobile tires, seat upholstery, and carpeting.[2] Each new use started the product on a new life cycle. Credit goes to Du Pont's continuous R&D program to find new uses.

In even more cases, customers deserve credit for discovering new uses. Vaseline petroleum jelly started out as a lubricant in machine shops, and over the years, users have reported many new uses for the product, including use as a skin ointment, a healing agent, and a hair dressing.

Arm & Hammer, the baking-soda manufacturer, had a product whose sales had been drifting downward for 125 years! Baking soda had a number of uses, but no single use was advertised. Then the company discovered some consumers who used it as a refrigerator deodorant. It launched a heavy advertising and publicity campaign focusing on this single use and succeeded in getting half of the homes in America to place an open box of baking soda in their refrigerator. A few years later, Arm & Hammer discovered consumers who used it to quell kitchen grease fires, and it promoted this use with great results.

The company's task is to monitor customers' uses of the product. This applies to industrial products as well as consumer products. Von Hippel's studies show that most new industrial products were originally suggested by customers rather than by company R&D laboratories.[3] This highlights the importance of systematically collecting customer needs and suggestions to guide new-product development.

MORE USAGE ❖ A third market-expansion strategy is to convince people to *use more of the product per use occasion*. If a cereal manufacturer convinces consumers to eat a full bowl of cereal instead of half a bowl, total sales will increase. Procter & Gamble advises users that its Head & Shoulders shampoo is more effective with two applications instead of one per shampoo.

A creative example of a company that stimulated higher usage per occasion is the Michelin Tire Company (French). Michelin wanted French car owners to drive their cars more miles per year—thus leading to more tire replacement. It conceived the idea of rating French restaurants on a three-star system. They reported that many of the best restaurants were in the South of France, leading many Parisians to consider weekend drives to Provence and the Riviera. Michelin also published guidebooks with maps and sights along the way to further entice travel.

Defending Market Share

While trying to expand total market size, the dominant firm must continuously defend its current business against rival attacks. The leader is like a large elephant being attacked by a swarm of bees. The largest and nastiest bee keeps buzzing around the leader. Coca-Cola must constantly guard against Pepsi-Cola; Gillette against Bic; Hertz against Avis; McDonald's against Burger King; General Motors against Ford; and Kodak against Fuji (see Global Marketing 15-1).

Sometimes there are several large, dangerous bees. AT&T has to defend its telecommunications business against the former Bell regional companies, the connect companies (MCI, Sprint), domestic and foreign equipment producers (Northern Telecom, Siemens), and computer firms moving into telecommunications (IBM, Apple, and so on). Clearly, it cannot defend all of its territory and needs to decide where to draw the battle lines.

What can the market leader do to defend its terrain? Twenty centuries ago, Sun Tzu told his warriors: "One does not rely on the enemy not attacking, but relies on the fact that he himself is unassailable." The most constructive response is *continuous innovation*. The leader refuses to be content with the way things are and leads the industry in developing new products and customer services, distribution effectiveness, and cost cutting. It keeps increasing its competitive effectiveness and value to customers. The leader applies the military principle of the offensive: *The commander exercises initiative, sets the pace, and exploits enemy weaknesses*. The best defense is a good offense.

The market leader, even when it does not launch offensives, must guard all fronts and not leave any major exposed flanks. It must keep its costs down, and its prices must be consonant with the value the customers see in the brand. The leader must "plug holes" so that attackers do not jump in. Thus a consumer-packaged-goods leader will produce its brands in several sizes and forms to meet varying consumer preferences and hold on to as much scarce dealer shelf space as possible.

The cost of "plugging holes" can be high. But the cost of abandoning an unprofitable product/market segment can be higher! General Motors did not want to lose money by making small cars; but it is losing more now because it allowed Japanese car makers to come in strong in the U.S. market. Xerox felt it would lose money making small copier machines, but now it has lost much more by allowing the Japanese to enter and grow in the market.

The real answer is that the market leader must consider carefully which terrains are important to defend even at a loss and which can be given up with little risk. The leader cannot defend all of its positions in the market; it must concentrate its resources where they count. The aim of defensive strategy is to reduce the probability of attack, divert attacks to less threatening areas, and lessen their intensity. Any attack is likely to hurt profits. But the defender's form and speed of response can make an important difference in the profit consequences. Researchers are currently exploring the most appropriate forms of response to price and other attacks (see Marketing Strategies 15-1 for an interesting model called Defender).

The intensified competition that has taken place worldwide in recent years has sparked management's interest in models of military warfare, particularly as described in the writings of Sun-Tsu, Mushashi, von Clausewitz, and Liddell-Hart.[4] Leading companies, like leading nations, have been advised to protect their interests with such strategies as "brinkmanship," "massive retaliation," "limited warfare," "graduated response," "diplomacy of violence," and "threat systems." There are, in fact, six defense strategies that a dominant firm can use. They are illustrated in Figure 15-2 on page 388 and described in the following paragraphs.[5]

POSITION DEFENSE ❖ The most basic idea of defense is to build an impregnable fortification around one's territory. The French built the famous Maginot line in peacetime to protect its territory against possible future German invasion. But this fortification, like all static defense maneuvers, failed. Simply defending one's current position or products is a form of *marketing myopia*. Henry Ford's myopia about his Model-T brought an enviably healthy company with $1 billion in cash reserves to the brink of financial ruin. Even such strong brands as Coca-Cola and

CHAPTER 15
Designing Marketing Strategies
for Market Leaders,
Challengers, Followers,
and Nichers

385

Kodak and Fuji Fight It Out Internationally

For more than 100 years, Eastman Kodak has been known for its easy-to-use cameras, high-quality film, and solid profits. But during the past decade, Kodak's sales have flattened and its profits have declined. Kodak has been outpaced by more innovative competitors, many of whom are Japanese, who introduced or improved upon 35-mm cameras, videocameras, and one-hour film-processing labs. However, when Fuji Photo Film Company moved in on Kodak's bread-and-butter color film business, Kodak took the challenge seriously.

When Fuji entered the U.S. film market, it offered high-quality color films at 10% lower prices than Kodak was offering and beat Kodak to the market with high-speed films. Fuji also pulled off a major marketing coup by outbidding Kodak to become the official film of the 1984 Los Angeles Summer Olympic Games. Fuji's share of the huge U.S. color film market grew to more than 8% in 1984, and it announced its goal of winning a 15% market share. Fuji's U.S. sales were growing at a rate of 20% a year—much faster than the overall market-growth rate.

Kodak fought back fiercely to protect its share of the U.S. film market. It matched Fuji's lower prices and unleashed a series of product improvements that culminated most recently in its Ektar 25, 125, and 1,000 films. Kodak outspent Fuji by 20 to 1 on advertising and promotion, paid $10 million to obtain sponsorship of the 1988 Summer Olympics in Seoul, South Korea, and snapped up the rights to the 1992 Olympics in Barcelona. Through these and other moves, Kodak has successfully defended its U.S. market position. Fuji has not been able to entice many consumers to abandon Kodak's familiar yellow and black film box to reach for Fuji green. By the early 1990s, Kodak's share of the U.S. market had stabilized at a whopping 80%.

But Kodak took the battle a step further—it attacked Japan, Fuji's home turf. Kodak is no stranger to international marketing: 40% of its $17 billion in sales come from 150 countries outside the United States. In fact, Kodak has been selling film in Japan since 1889. But until a few years ago, the company didn't give the Japanese market much attention. Recently, however, Kodak has taken several aggressive steps to increase its Japanese presence and sales. It set up a separate subsidiary—Kodak Japan—and tripled its Japanese staff. It bought out a Japanese distributor and prepared to set up its own Japanese marketing and sales staff. It invested in a new technology center and a large Japanese research facility. Finally, Kodak greatly increased its Japanese promotion and publicity. Kodak Japan now sponsors everything from Japanese television talk shows to sumo wrestling tournaments.

Despite these strong efforts, it may be as hard for Kodak in Japan as for Fuji in the United States. Fuji, with more than $3 billion in annual sales, has the resources to blunt Kodak's attack. The Japanese giant is firmly entrenched with a 70% share of the Japanese market versus Kodak's 15%. Moreover, high tariffs on foreign film protect Fuji's interests. Still, Kodak will gain several benefits from its stepped-up attack on Japan. First, Japan offers big opportunities for increased sales and profits—its $1.5 billion film and photo paper market is second only to that of the United States. Second, much of today's new photographic technology originates in Japan, so a greater presence in Japan will help Kodak keep up with the latest developments. Third, ownership and joint ventures in Japan will help Kodak better understand Japanese manufacturing and obtain new products for the United States and other world markets. Kodak already sells many Japanese-made products under its own name in the United States: Kodak video cameras are made by Matsushita, its video tape by TDK Electronics. Kodak owns 10% of Chinon Industries, which makes the company's 35-mm cameras. Kodak sells film-processing labs made by Japanese manufacturers, and its medium-volume copiers are made by Canon.

Kodak reaps one more important benefit from its attack on the Japanese market: If Fuji must devote heavy resources to defending its Japanese home turf against Kodak's attacks, it will have fewer resources to use against Kodak in the United States.

SOURCES: See James B. Treece, Barbara Buell, and Jane Sasseen, "How Kodak is Trying to Move Mount Fuji," *Business Week*, December 2, 1985, pp. 62–64; Carla Rapoport, "You Can Make Money in Japan," *Fortune*, February 12, 1990, pp. 85–92; Keith H. Hammonds, "A Moment Kodak Wants to Capture," *Business Week*, August 27, 1990, pp. 52–53; Alison Fahey, "Polaroid, Kodak, Fuji Get Clicking," *Advertising Age*, May 20, 1991, p. 18; and Peter Nulty, "The New Look of Photography," *Fortune*, July 1, 1991, pp. 36–41.

Marketing Strategies 15-1

Defense Strategies According to the Defender Model

Professors Hauser, Shugan, and Gaskin have built and tested a model called Defender. The model makes the following assumptions:

1. Consumers share the same product perceptions. (Thus all consumers see Tylenol as high in gentleness per dollar and low in effectiveness per dollar, Excedrin as high in effectiveness but low in gentleness, and so on.)

2. Consumers differ in their preferences for various product characteristics. (Thus some consumers value gentleness more than effectiveness, others show the reverse preference.)

3. Consumers vary in the number of brands they know and will consider.

4. Consumers' choices are affected by product features, price, distribution, advertising, and promotion. (Each marketing tool's effect on sales response is known.)

The Defender model can be illustrated with the history of Datril's price attack on the market leader, Tylenol. Tylenol had gained a large market share based on its perceived gentleness (no stomach upsets) and was achieving outstanding profits. Bristol-Myers then introduced the same product, Datril, and advertised it as "just as good as Tylenol, only cheaper." If consumers believed this, Datril would make deep inroads into Tylenol's market share. How should Tylenol defend itself?

The researchers examined the possible defensive measures available to Tylenol, using the Defender model, and came to the following conclusions:

1. The defender should lower its prices, especially if the market is unsegmented. If the market is segmented, the price might be raised in some of the less vulnerable segments. (The best pricing strategy is independent of what should be done with distribution and advertising; once chosen, however, the pricing strategy will affect distribution and advertising.)

2. The defender should reduce its expenditures on distribution; specifically, it should drop marginal retailers who no longer are profitable to serve.

3. The defender should improve its strong product features even more rather than try to improve along the lines of the attacker's strong product features.

4. The defender should spend less on awareness-building advertising and direct more on repositioning-building advertising.

These conclusions are subject to further qualifications given the restrictive assumptions on which the model was based. For example, price and positioning are interrelated strategically. In some cases, price cuts encourage price wars. To avoid such destructive competition, it is often best to differentiate products in order to compete on product benefits, not price.

What did Tylenol actually do to defend itself from Datril's attack? Tylenol quickly cut its price to match Datril's, and later added the Extra Strength Tylenol brand to capture consumers' interest in effectiveness. Through these steps, Tylenol preserved its position as market leader and prevented Datril from making much of an inroad.

SOURCE: John R. Hauser and Steve M. Shugan, "Defensive Marketing Strategy," *Marketing Science*, Fall 1983, pp. 319–60; John R. Hauser and S. P. Gaskin, "Application of the 'DEFENDER' Consumer Model," *Marketing Science*, Fall 1984, pp. 327–51.

Bayer aspirin cannot be relied on by their companies as the main sources of future growth and profitability. Coca-Cola today, in spite of selling nearly half the soft drinks of the world, has acquired fruit-drink companies and diversified into desalination equipment and plastics. Clearly, leaders under attack would be foolish to put all their resources into building fortifications around their current product.

FLANKING DEFENSE ❖ The market leader should not only guard its territory but also erect outposts to protect a weak front or possibly serve as an invasion base for counterattacking. Here is a good example of a flanking defense:

Jewel Food Store is a leading supermarket food chain store in Chicago. The company believes that supermarkets will continue to remain a dominant force but is flanking its position by strengthening its food-retailing-assortment mix. Jewel is meeting the

FIGURE 15-2   Defense Strategies

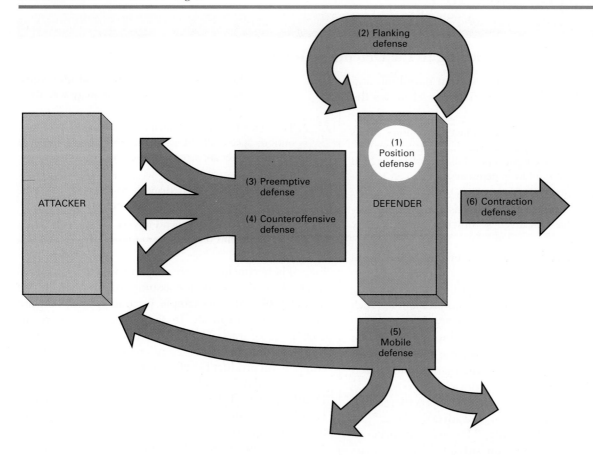

fast-food boom by offering a wide assortment of instant and frozen meals; and it is meeting the discount-food challenge by promoting generic lines. Jewel is tailoring its various stores to suit local demands for such items as fresh bakery products and ethnic foods. Jewel has set up the Jewel-T division, a network of "box" discount stores patterned after pioneer Aldi. To fight "combination stores," Jewel integrated a large number of its supermarkets with its Osco Drug Stores.

The flanking defense is of little value unless it is seriously mounted. This was precisely General Motors' and Ford's mistake when they half-heartedly designed the Vega and Pinto compact cars years ago to ward off the small-car attacks launched by the Japanese and European car makers. The American compacts were poorly made, and they failed to retard the sale of the foreign compact cars. A careful assessment of any potential threat must be made, and if warranted, a relatively serious commitment should be made to a flanking defense.

PREEMPTIVE DEFENSE ❖ A more aggressive defense maneuver is to launch an attack on the enemy *before* it starts its offense against the company. Preemptive defense assumes that an ounce of prevention is worth more than a pound of cure. When Chrysler's market share began rising from 12 to 18% some years ago, one rival marketing executive was overheard to say, "If they [Chrysler] go to 20%, it will be over our dead bodies."

Or a company could wage guerrilla action across the market—hitting one competitor here, another there—and keep everyone off balance. Or the preemptive defense could assume the proportions of a grand market envelopment, as practiced by Seiko with its 2,300 watch models distributed worldwide. Or it could resemble the sustained price attack that Texas Instruments practiced. Sustained, high-pressure strategies aim at retaining the initiative at all times and keeping the competition always on the defensive.

Sometimes the preemptive strike is waged psychologically. The market leader sends out *market signals* to dissuade competitors from attacking.[6] A major U.S. pharmaceutical firm is the leader in a certain drug category. Every time it learns that a competitor might build a factory to produce that drug, the company leaks the news that it is considering cutting the drug price and building another plant. This intimidates the competitor, who decides against entering that product arena. Meanwhile the leader never gets to cutting its price or adding another plant. Of course, this bluff can work only a few times.

Market leaders with strong resources have the capacity to withstand some attacks and may even entice the opponents into costly attacks. Heinz let Hunt's carry out its massive attack in the ketchup market without much counteroffensive; and in the end, this strategy proved very costly to Hunt's. Not reacting to a strong attack, however, calls for great confidence in the ultimate superiority of the company's market offer.

COUNTEROFFENSIVE DEFENSE ❖ Most market leaders, when attacked, will respond with a counterattack. The leader cannot remain passive in the face of a competitor's price cut, promotion blitz, product improvement, or sales-territory invasion. The leader has the strategic choice of meeting the attacker frontally, or maneuvering against the attacker's flank, or launching a pincer movement to cut off the attacking formations from their base of operation. Sometimes the leader's market-share erosion is so rapid that a head-on counterattack is necessary. But a leader enjoying some strategic depth can often weather the initial attack and counterattack effectively at the opportune moment. In many situations, it may be worth minor setbacks to allow the offensive to develop fully before counterattacking. This may seem a dangerous strategy of "wait and see," but there are sound reasons for not barreling into a counteroffensive.

A better response to an attack is to pause and identify a chink in the attacker's armor, namely, a segment gap in which a viable counteroffensive can be launched. Cadillac designed its Seville as an alternative to the Mercedes and pinned its hope on offering a smoother ride, more creature comforts, and a lower price than the Mercedes offered.

When a market leader's territory is attacked, an effective counterattack is to invade the attacker's main territory so that it will have to pull back some of its troops to defend its territory. One of Northwest Airlines' most profitable routes is Minneapolis to Atlanta. A smaller air carrier launched a deep fare cut and advertised it heavily to expand its share in this market. Northwest retaliated by cutting its fares on the Minneapolis/Chicago route, which the attacking airline depended on for its major revenue. With its major revenue source hurting, the attacking airline restored its Minneapolis/Atlanta fare to a normal level.

MOBILE DEFENSE ❖ Mobile defense involves more than the leader aggressively defending its territory. In mobile defense, the leader stretches its domain over new territories that can serve as future centers for defense and offense. It spreads to these new territories not so much through normal brand proliferation as through innovation activity on two fronts, namely, market broadening and market diversification. These moves generate strategic depth for the firm, enabling it to weather continual attacks and launch retaliatory strikes.

Market broadening calls upon a company to shift its focus from the current product to the underlying generic need and get involved in R&D across the whole

CHAPTER 15
Designing Marketing Strategies
for Market Leaders,
Challengers, Followers,
and Nichers

389

range of technology associated with that need. Thus "petroleum" companies sought to recast themselves into "energy" companies. Implicitly, this demands that they dip their research fingers into the oil, coal, nuclear, hydroelectric, and chemical industries. But this market-broadening strategy should not be carried too far or it would fault two fundamental military principles—the *principle of the objective* (pursue a clearly defined and attainable objective) and the *principle of mass* (concentrate your efforts at a point of the enemy's weakness). The objective of being in the energy business is too broad. The energy business is not a single need but a whole range of needs (heating, lighting, propelling, and so on). That leaves very little in the world that is not potentially the energy business. Furthermore, too much broadening would dilute the company's mass in the current competitive theater, and survival today surely must take precedence over the grand battles imagined for tomorrow. The error of *marketing myopia* would be replaced by *marketing hyperopia*, a condition where vision is better for distant than for near objects.

Reasonable broadening, however, makes sense. Armstrong World Industries exemplified a successful market-broadening strategy by redefining its domain from "floor covering" to "decorative room covering" (including walls and ceilings). By recognizing the customer's need to create a pleasant interior through various covering materials, Armstrong expanded into neighboring businesses that were synergistically balanced for growth and defense.

Market diversification into unrelated industries is the other alternative to generating strategic depth. When U.S. tobacco companies like Reynolds and Philip Morris acknowledged the growing curbs on cigarette smoking, they were not content with position defense or even with looking for new substitutes for the cigarette. Instead they moved quickly into new industries, such as beer, liquor, soft drinks, and frozen food.

CONTRACTION DEFENSE ❖ Large companies sometimes recognize that they can no longer defend all of their territory. Their forces are spread too thin, and competitors are nibbling away on several fronts. The best course of action then appears to be planned contraction (also called strategic withdrawal). Planned contraction is not market abandonment but rather giving up the weaker territories and reassigning resources to stronger territories. Planned contraction is a move to consolidate one's competitive strength in the market and concentrate mass at pivotal positions.

> Westinghouse cut its number of refrigerator models from 40 to the 30 that accounted for 85% of sales. General Motors standardized its auto engines and now offers fewer options. Campbell's Soup, Heinz, General Mills, Del Monte, and Georgia-Pacific are among those companies that have significantly pruned their product lines in recent years.

Expanding Market Share

Market leaders can improve their profitability further through increasing their market share. In many markets, one share point is worth tens of millions of dollars. A one-share-point gain in coffee is worth $48 million and in soft drinks, $120 million! No wonder normal competition has turned into marketing warfare.

Some years ago, the Strategic Planning Institute launched a study called *Profit Impact of Market Strategy (PIMS)*, which sought to identify the most important variables affecting profits. Data were collected from hundreds of business units in a variety of industries to identify the most important variables associated with profitability. The key variables included market share, product quality, and several others.

They found that a company's *profitability* (measured by pretax ROI) rises with its *relative market share* of its served market,[7] as shown in Figure 15-3(a).[8] According to a PIMS report, "The average ROI for businesses with under 10% market share was about 9%. . . . On the average, a difference of ten percentage points in market share is accompanied by a difference of about five points in pretax ROI." The PIMS study shows that businesses with market shares above 40% earn an average ROI of 30%, or three times that of those with shares under 10%.[9]

These strong findings have led many companies to pursue market-share expansion and leadership as their objective, since that would produce not only more *profit dollars* but also more *profitability* (return on investment). General Electric, for example, has decided that it must be number one or two in each market or else get out. GE divested its computer business and its air-conditioning business because it could not achieve top-dog position in these industries. Cynics have concluded that GE does not really want to stay in markets where it has to compete!

Various critics have attacked the PIMS study as either weak or spurious. Hammermesh reported finding numerous successful low-share businesses.[10] Woo and Cooper identified 40 low-share businesses that enjoyed pretax ROIs of 20% or more; they were characterized as having high relative product quality, medium-to-low prices, narrow product lines, and low total costs.[11] Most of these companies produced industrial components or supplies.

Some industry studies have yielded a **V**-shaped relationship between market share and profitability. Figure 15-3(b) shows a **V**-curve for agricultural-equipment firms. The industry leader, Deere & Company, earns a high return. However, Hesston and Steiger, small specialty firms, also earn high returns. J. I. Case and Massey-Ferguson are trapped in the valley, and International Harvester commands substantial market share but earns lower returns. Thus such industries have one or a few highly profitable large firms, several profitable small and more-focused firms, and several medium-sized firms with poorer profit performance. According to Roach:

FIGURE 15-3   Relationship between Market Share and Profitability
Source: Strategic Planning Institute (The PIMS Program), 955 Massachusetts Avenue, Cambridge, MA 02139.

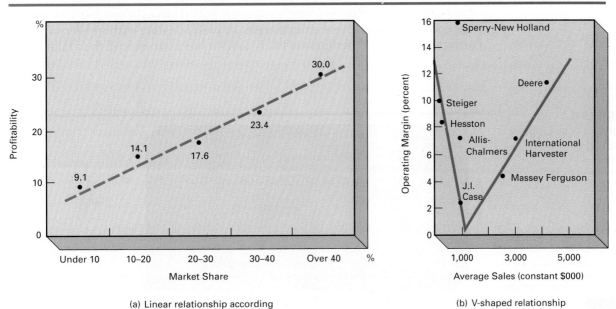

(a) Linear relationship according
to PIMS studies

(b) V-shaped relationship

The large firms on the **V**-curve tend to address the entire market, achieving cost advantages and high market share by realizing economies of scale. The small competitors reap high profits by focusing on some narrower segment of the business and by developing specialized approaches to production, marketing, and distribution for that segment. Ironically, the medium-sized competitors at the trough of the **V**-curve are unable to realize any competitive advantage and often show the poorest profit performance. Trapped in a strategic "No Man's Land," they are too large to reap the benefits of more focused competition, yet too small to benefit from the economies of scale that their larger competitors enjoy.[12]

How can the two graphs in Figure 15-3 be reconciled? The PIMS findings argue that profitability increases as a business gains share relative to its competitors in its *served market*. The **V**-shaped curve ignores market segments and looks at a business's profitability relative to its size in the total market. Thus Mercedes earns high profit because it is a high-share company in its served market of luxury cars even though it is a low-share company in the total auto market. And it has achieved this high share in its served market because it does other things right, such as producing high relative product quality and achieving high asset turnover and good cost control.

Companies must not think, however, that gaining increased market share in their served market will automatically improve their profitability. Much depends on their strategy for gaining increased market share. The cost of buying higher market share may far exceed its revenue value. The company should consider three factors before blindly pursuing increased market share.

The first factor is the possibility of provoking antitrust action. Jealous competitors are likely to cry "monopolization" if a dominant firm makes further inroads on market share. This rise in risk would cut down the attractiveness of pushing market-share gains too far.

The second factor is economic cost. Figure 15-4 shows the possibility that profitability might begin to fall with further market-share gains after some level. In the illustration, the firm's *optimal market share* is 50%, and if the firm pursues a larger share, this move might come at the expense of profitability. That is consistent with the PIMS findings in that PIMS did not show what happens to profitability for different levels within the over-40% category. Basically, the cost of gaining further market share might exceed the value. A company that has, say, 60% of the market must recognize that the "holdout" customers may dislike the company, be loyal to competitive suppliers, have unique needs, or prefer dealing with smaller suppliers. Furthermore, the competitors are likely to fight harder to defend their falling mar-

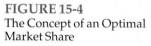

FIGURE 15-4
The Concept of an Optimal
Market Share

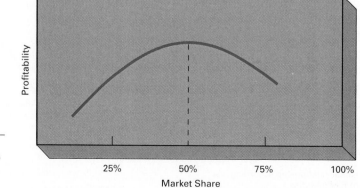

ket share. The cost of legal work, public relations, and lobbying rises with market share. In general, pushing for higher market share is less justified when there are few scale or experience economies, unattractive market segments exist, buyers want multiple sources of supply, and exit barriers are high. The leader might be better off concentrating on expanding market size rather than fighting for further increases in market share. Some dominant marketers have even gained by selectively decreasing their market share in weaker areas.[13]

The third factor is that companies might pursue the wrong marketing-mix strategy in their bid for higher market share and therefore not increase their profit. While certain marketing-mix variables are effective in building market share, not all lead to higher profits (see Marketing Concepts and Tools 15-1). Higher shares tend to produce higher profits under two conditions:

◆ *Unit Costs Fall with Increased Market Share:* Unit costs fall because the leader enjoys cost economies by running larger plants and because it goes down the cost-experience curve faster. This means that one effective marketing strategy for gaining profitable increases in market share is to fanatically pursue the lowest costs in the industry and pass the cost savings to customers through lower prices. That was Henry Ford's strategy for selling autos in the 1920s and Texas Instruments' strategy for selling transistors in the 1960s.

◆ *The Company Offers a Superior-Quality Product and Charges a Premium Price that More than Covers the Cost of Offering Higher Quality:* Crosby, in his book *Quality Is Free*, claims that building more quality into a product does not cost the company more because the company saves in less scrappage, aftersales servicing, and so on.[14] Furthermore, its products are so desired that consumers pay a large premium over cost. This strategy for profitable market-share growth is pursued by IBM, Caterpillar, and Michelin, among others.

Marketing Concepts and Tools 15-1

The Impact of Different Marketing-Mix Variables on Market Share

Some light on the impact of different marketing variables on market share was shed by Buzzell and Wiersema, drawing on the PIMS data base. They found that companies showing market-share gains typically outperformed their competitors in three areas: new-product activity, relative product quality, and marketing expenditures. Specifically:

1. Share-gaining companies typically developed and added more new products to their line.

2. Companies that increased their product quality relative to competitors' enjoyed greater share gains than those whose quality ratings remained constant or declined.

3. Companies that increased their marketing expenditures faster than the rate of market growth typically achieved share gains. Increases in salesforce expenditures were effective in producing share gains for both industrial and consumer markets. Increased advertising expenditures produced share gains mainly for consumer-goods companies. Increased sales-promotion expenditures were effective in producing share gains for all kinds of companies.

4. Companies that cut their prices more deeply than competitors did not achieve significant market-share gains, contrary to expectations. Presumably, enough rivals met the price cuts partly, and others offered other values to the buyers, so that buyers did not switch as much to the price cutter.

The reported study did not investigate whether the market-share gains were worth the cost of achieving them. Evidently companies are able to "buy" a higher market share, but the real issue is whether it will lead to higher profits sooner or later.

SOURCE: Based on Robert D. Buzzell and Frederick D. Wiersema, "Successful Share-Building Strategies," *Harvard Business Review*, January–February, 1981, pp. 135–44.

All said, market leaders who stay on top have learned the art of expanding the total market, defending their current territory, and increasing their market share profitably. Companies and Industries 15-1, on pages 396–97, details the specific principles that two great companies—Procter & Gamble and Caterpillar—use to maintain and expand their leadership in their respective markets.

Market-Challenger Strategies

Firms that occupy second, third, and lower ranks in an industry can be called runner-up, or trailing, firms. Some are quite large in their own right, such as Colgate, Ford, Montgomery Ward, Avis, Westinghouse, and Pepsi-Cola. These runner-up firms can adopt one of two postures. They can attack the leader and other competitors in an aggressive bid for further market share (market challengers). Or they can play ball and not "rock the boat" (market followers).

There are many cases of market challengers that gained ground on the market leader or even overtook the leader: Canon, which was only one tenth the size of Xerox in the mid-1970s, today produces more copier machines than Xerox; Toyota today produces more cars than General Motors; British Airways flies more international passengers than the former leader, Pan Am. These challengers set high aspirations and leveraged their smaller resources while the market leaders ran their businesses as usual.

Dolan found that competitive rivalry and price cutting is most intense in industries with high fixed costs, high inventory costs, and stagnant primary demand, such as steel, auto, paper, and chemicals.[15] We will now examine the competitive attack strategies available to market challengers.[16]

Defining the Strategic Objective and Opponent(s)

A market challenger must first define its strategic objective. The military *principle of objective* holds that *every military operation must be directed toward a clearly defined, decisive, and attainable objective.* The strategic objective of most market challengers is to increase their market shares, thinking that this will lead to greater profitability. Deciding on the objective, whether it is to subdue the competitor or reduce its share, interacts with the question of who the competitor is. Basically, an aggressor can choose to attack one of three types of firms:

- *It Can Attack the Market Leader:* This is a high-risk but potentially high-payoff strategy and makes good sense if the leader is a "false leader" and not serving the market well. The "terrain" to examine is consumer need or dissatisfaction. If a substantial segment is unserved or poorly served, it provides an excellent strategic target. Miller's "lite beer" campaign was successful because it pivoted on discovering many consumers who wanted a "lighter" beer. The alternative strategy is to out-innovate the leader across the whole segment. Thus Xerox wrested the copy market from 3M by developing a better copying process (dry instead of wet copying). Later Canon grabbed a large chunk of Xerox's market by introducing desk copiers.

- *It Can Attack Firms of Its Own Size that Are Not Doing the Job and Are Underfinanced:* Consumer satisfaction and innovation potential need to be examined minutely. Even a frontal attack might work if the other firm's resources are limited.

- *It Can Attack Small Local and Regional Firms that Are Not Doing the Job and Are Underfinanced:* Several of the major beer companies grew to their present size not by stealing each other's customers but by gobbling up the smaller firms, or "guppies."

Thus the issue of choosing the competitors and choosing the objective interact. If the attacking company goes after the market leader, its objective might be to wrest a certain share. Thus Bic is under no illusion that it could topple Gillette in the razor market—it is simply seeking a larger share. If the attacking company goes after a small local company, its objective might be to drive that company out of existence. The important principle remains: *Every military operation must be directed toward a clearly defined, decisive, and attainable objective.*

Choosing an Attack Strategy

Given clear opponents and objectives, how do military strategists view their major options in attacking an enemy? The starting point is known as the *principle of mass*, which holds that *superior combat power must be concentrated at the critical time and place for a decisive purpose*. We can make progress by imagining an opponent who occupies a certain market territory. We distinguish among five attack strategies shown in Figure 15-5.

FRONTAL ATTACK ❖ An aggressor is said to launch a frontal (or "head-on") attack when it masses its forces right up against its opponent. It attacks the opponent's strengths rather than its weaknesses. The outcome depends on who has more strength and endurance. In a pure frontal attack, the attacker matches its opponent's product, advertising, price, and so on. Recently the runner-up razor-blade manufacturer in Brazil attacked Gillette, the market leader. The attacker was asked if it is offering the consumer a better razor blade. "No," was the reply. "A lower

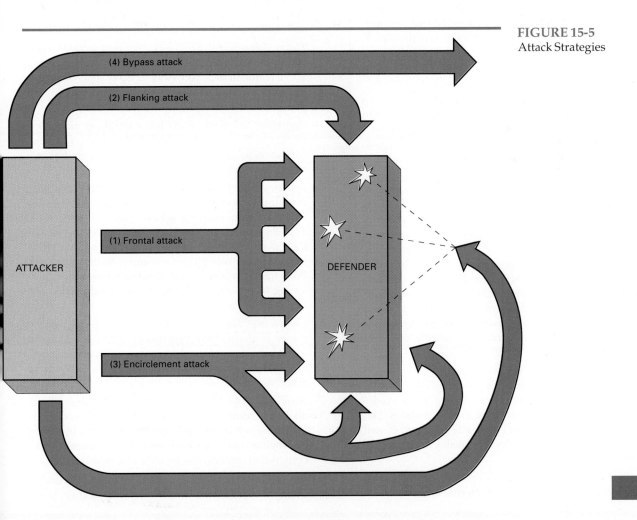

FIGURE 15-5
Attack Strategies

How Procter and Gamble and Caterpillar Maintain Their Market Leadership

The principles of maintaining market leadership are admirably illustrated by companies such as Procter & Gamble, Caterpillar, McDonald's, and Hertz, all of which have shown a remarkable ability to protect their market shares against repeated attacks by able challengers. Their success is based not on doing one thing well but on doing everything well. They do not allow any weaknesses to develop. We will examine the basics behind Procter & Gamble's and Caterpillar's success.

Procter & Gamble (P&G) is widely regarded as the United States' most skilled marketer of consumer packaged goods. It sells the number-one brand in several important categories: automatic dishwashing (Cascade), detergents (Tide), toilet tissue (Charmin), paper towels (Bounty), fabric softeners (Downy), toothpaste (Crest), and shampoo (Head & Shoulders). Its market leadership rests on several principles.

- *Customer Knowledge:* P&G studies its customers— both final consumers and the trade—through continuous marketing research and intelligence gathering. It provides a toll-free 800 number so consumers can call P&G directly with any inquiries, suggestions, or complaints about P&G products.

- *Long-Term Outlook:* P&G takes its time to analyze an opportunity and prepare the best product and then commits itself for the long run to make this product a success. It struggled with Pringles potato chips for almost a decade before achieving marketplace success.

- *Product Innovation:* P&G is an active product innovator and benefit segmenter. It launches brands offering new consumer benefits rather than "me-too" brands backed by heavy advertising. P&G spent ten years researching and developing the first effective anticavity toothpaste, Crest. It spent several years researching the first effective over-the-counter antidandruff shampoo, Head & Shoulders. P&G found that new parents wanted relief from handling and washing diapers and innovated Pampers, an affordable disposable paper diaper. The company thoroughly tests its new products with consumers, and only when real preference is indicated does it launch them in the national market.

- *Quality Strategy:* P&G designs products of above-average quality. Once launched, the product is continuously improved. When P&G announces "new and improved," they mean it. This is in contrast to some companies that, after establishing the quality level, rarely improve it, and to other companies that reduce the quality in an effort to squeeze out more profit.

- *Line-Extension Strategy:* P&G produces its brands in several sizes and forms to satisfy varying consumer preferences. This gives its brand more shelf space and prevents competitors from moving in to satisfy unmet market needs.

- *Brand-Extension Strategy:* P&G will often use its strong brand names to launch new products. For example, the Ivory brand has been extended from a soap to include liquid soap, a dishwashing detergent, and a shampoo. Launching a new product under a strong existing brand name gives the new brand more instant recognition and credibility with much less advertising outlay.

- *Multibrand Strategy:* P&G originated the art of marketing several brands in the same product category. For example, it produces eight brands of hand soap, six shampoo brands, and four brands each of liquid dishwashing detergent, toothpaste, coffee, and floor cleaner. The aim is to design brands that meet different consumer wants and that compete against specific competitors' brands. Each brand manager runs the brand independently and competes for company resources. Having several brands on the shelf, the company "locks up" shelf space and gains more clout with distributors.

- *Heavy Advertising:* P&G is the nation's second largest consumer-packaged-goods advertiser, spending over $2.15 billion in fiscal year 1991. It never stints on spending money to create strong consumer awareness and preference.

- *Aggressive Salesforce:* P&G has a top-flight field salesforce, which is very effective in working with key retail customers to gain shelf space and cooperation in point-of-purchase displays and promotions.

- *Effective Sales Promotion:* P&G has a sales-promotion department to counsel its brand managers on the most effective promotions to achieve particular objectives. The department studies the results of consumer and trade deals and develops an expert sense of their effectiveness under varying circumstances. At the same time, P&G tries to minimize the use of sales promotion, preferring to rely on advertising to build long-term consumer preference.

- *Competitive Toughness:* P&G carries a big stick when it comes to constraining aggressors. P&G is willing to spend large sums of money to outpromote new competitive brands and prevent them from gaining a foothold in the market.

- *Manufacturing Efficiency:* P&G's reputation as a great marketing company is matched by its greatness as a manufacturing company. P&G spends large sums of money developing and improving production operations to keep its costs among the lowest in the industry.

- *Brand-Management System:* P&G originated the brand-management system, in which one executive is responsible for each brand. The system has been copied by many competitors but frequently without the success that P&G has achieved through perfecting its system over the years. In a recent development, P&G modified its general management structure so that each brand category is now run by a general manager with volume and profit responsibility. While this does not replace the independent brand-management system, it helps to sharpen strategic focus on the key consumer needs and competition in the category.

Thus P&G's market leadership is not based on doing one thing well but on the successful orchestration of myriad factors that contribute to market leadership. In 1985, P&G suffered its first profit decline in 33 years, as a result of successful attacks by Colgate, Lever Brothers, Beecham, and Kimberly-Clark on some of its key brands. But P&G bounced back with innovations and product improvements and continues to lead the pack.

Since the 1940s, Caterpillar has dominated the construction-equipment industry. Its tractors, crawlers, and loaders, painted in the familiar yellow, are a common sight at any construction area and account for 50% of the world's sales of heavy construction equipment. Caterpillar has managed to retain leadership in spite of charging a premium price for its equipment and being challenged by a number of able competitors, including John Deere, Massey-Ferguson, J. I. Case, and Komatsu. Several principles combine to explain Caterpillar's success:

- *Premium-Product Quality:* Caterpillar produces high-quality equipment known for its reliability. Reliability is a key buyer consideration in the purchase of heavy industrial equipment. Caterpillar designs its equipment with a heavier gauge of steel than necessary, to convince buyers of its superior quality.

- *Extensive-and-Efficient-Dealership System:* Caterpillar maintains the largest number of independent construction-equipment dealers in the industry. Its 260 dealers throughout the world carry a complete line of Caterpillar equipment. Caterpillar dealers focus their attention on Caterpillar equipment and do not carry other lines. Competitors' dealers, on the other hand, normally lack a full line and carry complementary, noncompeting lines. Caterpillar can choose the best dealers (a new Caterpillar dealership costs the franchisee $5 million) and spends the most money in training, servicing, and motivating them.

- *Superior Service:* Caterpillar has built a worldwide parts and service system second to none in the industry. Caterpillar can deliver replacement parts and service anywhere in the world within 24 hours of equipment breakdown. Competitors cannot match this without making a substantial investment. Any competitor duplicating this service level would only neutralize Caterpillar's advantage rather than score a new advantage.

- *Superior Parts Management:* Thirty percent of Caterpillar's sales volume and over 50% of its profit come from the sale of replacement parts. Caterpillar has developed a superior parts-management system to keep margins high in this end of the business.

- *Premium Price:* Caterpillar charges a 10 to 15% premium over comparable competitors' equipment because of the extra value perceived by buyers.

- *Full-Line Strategy:* Caterpillar produces a full line of construction equipment to enable customers to do one-stop buying.

- *Good Financing:* Caterpillar arranges generous financial terms to customers buying its equipment. This is important because of the high purchase cost.

Recently Caterpillar experienced difficulties because of the depressed global-construction-equipment market and cutthroat competition. Their specific problem has been Komatsu, Japan's number-one construction firm, which adopted the internal slogan "Encircle Caterpillar." Komatsu studies and attacks market niches, continuously enlarges its product line and improves its product quality, and prices its equipment sometimes as much as 40% lower. Caterpillar tells buyers that Komatsu's lower prices reflect lower quality, but not all buyers accept this or are willing to pay more for higher quality.

Caterpillar has fought back by cutting its costs by 27% and meeting Komatsu's prices and sometimes even initiating price cutting. The price wars drove competitors like International Harvester and Clark Equipment near the brink of ruin, and Caterpillar itself lost almost $1 billion in the years 1982–84. But Caterpillar has rebounded strongly, winning back share and profits in its world markets. Komatsu, in the meantime, has had to raise its prices several times and its market share, which was 12% in 1986, dropped to 9%. The long and damaging price wars appear to be coming to an end, with both sides settling for peaceful coexistence and improved profits.

SOURCES: Faye Rice, "The King of Suds Reigns Again," *Fortune*, August 4, 1986, pp. 130–34; Bill Kelley, "Komatsu in Cat Fight," *Sales & Marketing Management*, April 1986, pp. 50–53; and Ronald Henkoff, "This Cat Is Acting Like a Tiger," *Fortune*, December 19, 1988, pp. 71–76.

price?" "No." "A better package?" "No." "A cleverer advertising campaign?" "No." "Better allowances to the trade?" "No." "Then how do you expect to take share away from Gillette?" "Sheer determination" was the reply. Needless to say, its offensive failed.

For a pure frontal attack to succeed, the aggressor needs a strength advantage over the competitor. The *principle of force* says that *the side with the greater manpower (resources) will win the engagement.* This rule is modified if the defender has greater firing efficiency through enjoying a terrain advantage (such as holding a mountain top). The military dogma is that for a frontal attack to succeed against a well-entrenched opponent or one controlling the "high ground," the attacking forces must deploy at least a 3:1 advantage in combat firepower. If the aggressor has a smaller force or poorer firepower than the defender, a frontal attack amounts to a suicide mission and makes no sense. RCA, GE, and Xerox learned this the hard way when they launched frontal attacks on IBM, overlooking its superior defensive position.

As an alternative to a pure frontal attack, the aggressor can launch a modified frontal attack, the most common being to cut its price vis-à-vis the opponent's. Such attacks can take two forms. The more usual ploy is to match the leader's offer on other counts and beat it on price. This can work if the market leader does not retaliate by cutting price, and if the competitor convinces the market that its product is equal to the competitor's, and at a lower price, it is a real value.

> Helene Curtis is a master practitioner of the strategy of convincing the market that its brand is equal in quality but a better value than the higher-priced competitor's brands. Curtis makes low-budget imitations of leading high-priced brands and promotes them with blatant comparative-advertising campaigns: "We do what theirs does for less than half the price," is the message. In 1972 Curtis had a meager 1% share of the shampoo market for its Suave shampoo. It launched its new strategy in 1973. By 1976, it had overtaken Procter & Gamble's Head & Shoulders and Johnson & Johnson's Baby Shampoo to lead the market in volume. Its share hit 16% in 1979.

The other form of price-aggressive strategy involves a heavy investment by the attacker to achieve lower production costs and then an attack on competitors on a price basis. Texas Instruments has had brilliant success in using the price weapon strategically. The Japanese, too, launch modified frontal attacks involving price and cost cutting.

FLANK ATTACK ❖ An enemy's army is strongest where it expects to be attacked. It is necessarily less secure in its flanks and rear. Its weak spots (blind sides), therefore, are natural targets for attack. The major principle of modern offensive warfare is *concentration of strength against weakness*. The aggressor may attack the strong side to tie up the defender's troops but will launch the real attack at the side or rear. This "turning" maneuver catches the defending army off guard. Flank attacks make excellent marketing sense and are particularly attractive to the aggressor possessing fewer resources than the opponent. If the aggressor cannot overwhelm the defender with brute strength, it can outmaneuver the defender with subterfuge.

A flank attack can be directed along two strategic dimensions—geographical and segmental. In a geographical attack, the aggressor spots areas where the opponent is underperforming. For example, some of IBM's rivals chose to set up strong sales branches in medium- and smaller-size cities that were relatively neglected by IBM. For example, Honeywell pursued businesses in smaller cities and towns where it did not have to battle against larger numbers of IBM salespeople.

The other flanking strategy is to spot uncovered market needs not being served by the leaders, as Japanese auto makers did when choosing to serve the growing consumer market for fuel-efficient cars and Miller Brewing Company "discovered" the consumer market for "light" beer.

A flanking strategy is another name for identifying shifts in market segments—which are causing gaps to develop that are not being served by the industry's product profile—and rushing in to fill the gaps and develop them into strong segments. Instead of a bloody battle between two or more companies trying to serve the same market, flanking leads to a fuller coverage of the market's varied needs. Flanking is in the best tradition of modern marketing philosophy, which holds that the purpose of marketing is to *discover needs and satisfy them*. Flank attacks are much more likely to be successful than frontal attacks.

ENCIRCLEMENT ATTACK ❖ The pure flanking maneuver was defined as pivoting on a market need neglected by competitors. The encirclement maneuver, on the other hand, is an attempt to capture a wide slice of the enemy's territory through a comprehensive "blitz" attack. Encirclement involves launching a grand offensive on several fronts, so that the enemy must protect its front, sides, and rear simultaneously. The aggressor may offer the market everything the opponent offers and more, so that the offer is unrefusable. Encirclement makes sense where the aggressor commands superior resources and believes that a swift encirclement will break the opponent's will. Here are two examples:

> Seiko's attack on the watch market illustrates an encirclement strategy.[17] Seiko expanded distribution in every major watch market and overwhelmed its competitors and consumers with an enormous variety of constantly changing models. In the United States, it offers 400 watch models, but its marketing clout is backed by the 2,300 models it makes and sells worldwide. "They hit the mark on fashion, features, user preferences, and everything else that might motivate the consumer," says an admiring vice-president of a U.S. competitor.

> An encirclement attack does not always work. In 1963 Hunt's, with a 19% market share, launched a major encirclement attack to go after Heinz's 27% market share. Hunt's rolled out two new flavors of ketchup to disrupt the consumers' traditional taste preference for Heinz and also to capture more retail shelf space. It lowered its price to 70% of Heinz's price. It offered heavy trade allowances to retailers. It raised its advertising budget to over twice the level of Heinz's. This marketing program meant that Hunt's would lose money during the attack but would make it up by attracting enough new buyers. The strategy failed to work. The Heinz brand continued to enjoy consumer preference; as a result, not enough Heinz users tried or stayed with Hunt's brand. Hunt's finally gave up the attack.

Hunt's debacle underscores our core proposition that segmentation opportunity should be a fundamental basis for attack. If empty niches do not now exist or cannot be created by segment diffusion tactics, then the aggressor's attack is essentially a frontal attack. As such, it would require a three-to-one advantage in resources to succeed.

BYPASS ATTACK ❖ The bypass is the most indirect of assault strategies. It means bypassing the enemy and attacking easier markets to broaden one's resource base. This strategy offers three lines of approach: diversifying into *unrelated products*, diversifying into new *geographical markets*, and leapfrogging into *new technologies* to supplant existing products.

> Colgate's impressive turnaround utilized the first two principles.[18] In the United States, Colgate generally suffered at the hands of P&G. When David Foster took over as CEO in 1971, Colgate had the reputation as a stodgy marketer of soap and detergent. By 1979 Foster had transformed the company into a $4.3 billion conglomerate.

Foster recognized that any head-on battles with P&G were futile. "They outgunned us three to one at the store level," said Foster, "and had three research people to our one." Foster's strategy was simple—increase Colgate's lead abroad and bypass P&G at home by diversifying into non-P&G markets. A string of acquisitions followed in textiles and hospital products, cosmetics, and a range of sporting goods and food products. The outcome: In 1971, Colgate was underdog to P&G in about half of its business. By 1976, in three fourths of its business, it was either comfortably placed against P&G or did not face it at all.

Technological leapfrogging is a bypass strategy practiced typically in high-tech industries. Instead of copying the competitor's product and waging a costly frontal attack, the challenger patiently researches and develops the next technology and launches an attack, shifting the battleground to its territory where it has an advantage. Nintendo's successful attack in the video-game market was precisely about wresting market share by introducing a superior technology and redefining the "competitive space."

GUERRILLA ATTACK ❖ Guerrilla attack is another option available to market aggressors, especially smaller undercapitalized ones. Guerrilla warfare consists of waging small, intermittent attacks on different territories of the opponent, with the aim of harassing and demoralizing the opponent and eventually securing permanent footholds. Liddell-Hart stated the military rationale:

> The more usual reason for adopting a strategy of limited aim is that of awaiting a change in the balance of force—a change often sought and achieved by draining the enemy's force, weakening him by pricks instead of risking blows. The essential condition of such a strategy is that the drain on him should be disproportionately greater than on oneself. The object may be sought by raiding his supplies; by local attacks which annihilate or inflict disproportionate loss on parts of his force; by bringing him into unprofitable attacks; by causing an excessively wide distribution of his force; and, not least, by exhausting his moral and physical energy.[19]

The guerrilla aggressor will use both conventional and unconventional means to attack the opponent. These would include selective price cuts, intense promotional blitzes, and occasional legal actions. The key is to focus the attack on a narrow territory:

> Diamond Crystal Salt had less than a 5% share of the national salt market compared with Morton's 50%. There was no way that it could compete with Morton on a broad front. Diamond decided to focus its attack against Morton in its own core regional market and launched an aggressive marketing campaign. They managed to build a three-to-one lead over Morton.

Normally, guerrilla warfare is practiced by a smaller firm against a larger one. It is a case of David attacking Goliath. Not able to mount a frontal or even an effective flanking attack, the smaller firm launches a barrage of short promotional and price attacks in random corners of the larger opponent's market in a manner calculated to gradually weaken the opponent's market power. Even here, the attacker has to decide between launching a few major attacks or a continual stream of minor attacks. *Military dogma holds that a continual stream of minor attacks usually creates more cumulative impact, disorganization, and confusion in the enemy than a few major ones.* In line with this, the guerrilla attacker would find it more effective to attack small, isolated, weakly defended markets rather than major stronghold markets like New York, Chicago, and Los Angeles, where the defender is better entrenched and more willing to retaliate quickly and decisively. It would be a mistake to think of a guerrilla campaign as only a "low-resource" strategy alternative available to financially weak challengers. Conducting a continual guerrilla campaign can be expensive, although admittedly less expensive than a frontal, encirclement, or even flanking attack. Furthermore, guerrilla war is more a preparation for war than a war itself. Ultimately it must be backed by a stronger attack if the aggressor hopes to "beat" the opponent. Hence, in terms of resources, guerrilla warfare is not necessarily a low-cost operation.

The preceding attack strategies are very broad. The challenger must put together a total strategy consisting of several specific strategies. Marketing Strategies 15-2 lists several specific marketing strategies for attacking competitive positions.

Market-Follower Strategies

Some years ago, Professor Levitt wrote an article entitled "Innovative Imitation" in which he argued that a strategy of *product imitation* might be as profitable as a strategy of *product innovation*.[20] After all, the innovator bears the huge expense of developing the new product, getting it into distribution, and informing and educating the market. The reward for all this work and risk is normally market leadership. However, another firm can come along, copy or improve the new product, and launch it. Although this firm probably will not overtake the leader, the follower can achieve high profits because it did not bear any of the innovation expense.

Many runner-up companies prefer to follow rather than challenge the market leader. The effort to draw away the leader's customers is never taken lightly by the leader. If the challenger's lure is lower prices, improved service, or additional product features, the leader can quickly match these to diffuse the attack. The leader probably has more staying power in an all-out battle. A hard fight might leave both firms worse off, and this means the runner-up firm must think carefully before attacking. Unless the firm can launch a preemptive strike—in the form of a substantial product innovation or distribution breakthrough—it often prefers to follow rather than attack the leader.

Patterns of "conscious parallelism" are common in capital-intensive homogeneous-product industries, such as steel, fertilizers, and chemicals. The opportunities for product differentiation and image differentiation are low; service quality is often comparable; price sensitivity runs high. Price wars can erupt at any time. The mood in these industries is against short-run grabs for market share because that strategy only provokes retaliation. Most firms decide against stealing each other's customers. Instead, they present similar offers to buyers, usually by copying the leader. Market shares show a high stability.

This is not to say that market followers lack strategies. A market follower must know how to hold current customers and win a fair share of new customers. Each follower tries to bring distinctive advantages to its target market—location, services, financing. The follower is a major target of attack by challengers. Therefore, the market follower must keep its manufacturing costs low and its product quality and services high. It must also enter new markets as they open up. Followship is not the same as being passive or a carbon copy of the leader. The follower has to define a growth path, but one that does not invite competitive retaliation. Three broad followership strategies can be distinguished:

- ◆ *Cloner:* The cloner emulates the leader's products, distribution, advertising, and so on. The cloner doesn't originate anything but parasitically lives off the market leader's investments. In the extreme, the cloner is a *counterfeiter* who produces "knockoffs" of the leader's product. Firms such as Apple Computer and Rolex are plagued with the counterfeiter problem, especially in the Far East, and are seeking ways to defeat or police the counterfeiters.

- ◆ *Imitator:* The imitator copies some things from the leader but maintains differentiation in terms of packaging, advertising, pricing, and so on. The leader doesn't mind the imitator as long as the imitator doesn't attack the leader aggressively. The imitator even helps the leader avoid the charge of monopoly.

- ◆ *Adapter:* The adapter takes the leader's products and adapts and often improves them. The adapter may choose to sell to different markets to avoid direct confrontation with the leader. But often the adapter grows into the future challenger, as many Japanese firms have done after adapting and improving products developed elsewhere.

What does a follower firm earn? Although a follower firm doesn't bear innovation expenses, it normally earns less than the leader. For example, a study of food processing companies showed the largest firm averaging a 16% return on investment (ROI); the number-two firm, 6%; the number-three firm, −1%, and number-four firm, −6%. In this case, only the top two firms have profits, and the number-two firm's profits are nothing to brag about. No wonder Jack Welch, CEO of GE, told his business units that each must reach the number-one or -two position in their market or else! This followership is not often a rewarding path to pursue.

Marketing Strategies 15-2

Attack Strategies Available to Challengers

Market challengers can choose among several attack strategies:

1. *Price-Discount Strategy:* The challenger can sell a comparable product at a lower price. (See Figure 19-1, p. 490. Leader in cell 1, challenger in cell 2.) The Fuji Corporation used this strategy to attack Kodak's preeminence in the photographic-paper field. It priced its comparable paper at 10% less than Kodak's. Kodak chose not to lower its price, with the result that Fuji achieved market-share gains. Texas Instruments is the prime practitioner of price cutting. It will offer a comparable-quality product and cut its price progressively to gain market share and gain lower costs of production. Texas Instruments sacrifices profits in the first few years in a drive to gain unchallenged market leadership. It did this with transistors and hand calculators. For a price-discount strategy to work, three assumptions must be fulfilled. First, the challenger must convince buyers that its product and service are comparable to the leader's. Second, the buyers must be sensitive to the price difference and feel comfortable about turning their back on existing suppliers. Third, the market leader must refuse to cut its price in spite of the competitor's attack.

2. *Cheaper-Goods Strategy:* Another strategy is to offer an average- or low-quality product at a much lower price. (See Figure 19-1. Leader in cell 1, challenger in cell 5 or 9.) This works when there is a sufficient segment of buyers who are interested only in price. Firms that establish themselves through this strategy, however, can be attacked by "cheaper-goods" firms whose prices are even lower. In defense, they can try to upgrade their quality over time.

3. *Prestige-Goods Strategy:* A market challenger can launch a higher-quality product and charge a higher price than the leader. (See Figure 19-1. Leader in cell 1, challenger goes to northwest of cell 1.) Mercedes gained on Cadillac in the American market by offering a car of higher quality and higher price. Some prestige-goods firms later roll out lower-price products to take advantage of their charisma.

4. *Product-Proliferation Strategy:* The challenger can attack the leader by launching a larger product variety, thus giving buyers more choice. Hunt went after Heinz in the ketchup market by creating several new ketchup flavors and bottle sizes in contrast with Heinz's reliance on one flavor of ketchup, sold in a limited number of bottle sizes.

Market-Nicher Strategies

An alternative to being a follower in a large market is to be a leader in a small market, or niche. Smaller firms normally avoid competing with larger firms by targeting small markets of little or no interest to the larger firms. But increasingly, even large firms are setting up business units, or companies, to serve niches. Here are three large profitable companies that have pursued niching strategies:

Johnson & Johnson is a $12.4 billion health-care marketer that practices a "grow-and-divide" philosophy. It consists of 166 affiliates and subsidiaries. Each operation is headed by a president. Many of the business units pursue niche markets and more than half of the company's products are in leadership positions in their respective markets.

EG&G is a $2.7 billion industrial-equipment-and-components company consisting of over 175 distinct and autonomous business units, many with less than $10 million in sales in markets worth $25 million. Many business units have their own R&D, manufacturing, and salesforce. EG&G is currently the market or technical leader in 80% of its markets. More astonishing, EG&G ranked second in earnings per share and first in profitability in the *Fortune* 1000. EG&G illustrates how niche marketing may pay larger dividends than mass marketing.

5. *Product-Innovation Strategy:* The challenger might pursue product innovation to attack the leader's position. Polaroid and Xerox are companies whose success is based on continuously introducing innovations in the camera and copying fields, respectively. Miller rose to second place in the beer industry by successfully launching a light beer and introducing "pony-sized" bottles for lighter beer drinkers. The public often gains most from challenger strategies oriented toward product innovation.

6. *Improved-Services Strategy:* The challenger can try to offer new or better services to customers. IBM achieved its success by recognizing that customers were more interested in the software and the service than in the hardware. Avis's famous attack on Hertz, "We're only second. We try harder," was based on promising and delivering cleaner cars and faster service than Hertz.

7. *Distribution-Innovation Strategy:* A challenger might discover or develop a new channel of distribution. Avon became a major cosmetics company by perfecting door-to-door selling instead of battling other cosmetic firms in conventional stores. U.S. Time Company achieved great success by selling its low-price Timex watches through mass-merchandise channels instead of jewelry stores.

8. *Manufacturing-Cost-Reduction Strategy:* The challenger might pursue lower manufacturing costs than its competitors through more efficient purchasing, lower labor costs, and more modern production equipment. The company can use its lower costs to price more aggressively to gain market share. This strategy has been critical to the successful Japanese invasion of world markets.

9. *Intensive Advertising Promotion:* Some challengers attack the leader by increasing their expenditures on advertising and promotion. When Hunt went after Heinz in the ketchup market, it built its annual spending level to $6.4 million as against Heinz's $3.4 million. Miller Beer similarly outspent Budweiser in its attempt to achieve first place in the U.S. beer market. Substantial promotional spending, however, is usually not a sensible strategy unless the challenger's product or advertising message exhibits superiority over competition.

A challenger rarely improves its market share by relying on only one strategy. Its success depends on combining several principles to improve its position over time.

Illinois Tool Works (ITW) manufactures thousands of products including nails, screws, plastic six-pack holders for soda cans, bicycle helmets, backpacks, plastic buckles for pet collars, resealable food packages, and so on. ITW has 90 highly autonomous divisions. When one division commercializes a new product, the product and personnel are spun off into a new entity.

The main point is that firms with low shares of the total market can be highly profitable through smart niching. Recently Clifford and Cavanagh identified over two dozen highly successful midsize companies and studied their success factors.[21] They found that virtually all these companies were nichers. One example is A. T. Cross, which niched itself in the high-price pen-and-pencil market with its famous gold writing instruments that most executives, managers, and professionals own. Instead of manufacturing all types of writing instruments, A. T. Cross has stuck to the high-price niche and enjoyed great sales growth and profit. The consultants discovered other common factors shared by successful midsize companies, including offering high value, charging a premium price, creating new experience curves, and shaping a strong corporate culture and vision.

Why is niching profitable? The main reason is that the market nicher ends up knowing the target customer group so well that it meets their needs better than other firms that are casually selling to this niche. As a result, the nicher can charge a substantial markup over costs because of the added value. The nicher achieves *high margin*, whereas the mass marketer achieves *high volume*.

What characterizes an ideal niche? An ideal market niche would have the following characteristics:

- The niche is of sufficient size and purchasing power to be profitable.
- The niche has growth potential.
- The niche is of negligible interest to major competitors.
- The firm has the required skills and resources to serve the niche in a superior fashion.
- The firm can defend itself against an attacking major competitor through the customer goodwill it has built up.

The key idea in nichemanship is specialization. Marketing Strategies 15-3 describes several specialist roles open to nichers. Consider, for example, end-user specialization:

> *Computer companies are among the newest converts to "end user" specialization, except they call it* vertical marketing. *For years, computer companies sold general hardware and software systems across many markets and the price battles got rough. Smaller companies started to specialize by vertical slices — law firms, medical practices, banks, etc. — studying the specific hardware and software needs of their target group and designing high value-added products that had a competitive advantage over more general products. Their salesforces were trained to understand and service the particular vertical market. Computer companies also worked with independent* value-added resellers (VARs) *who customized the computer hardware and software for individual clients or customer segments and earned a price premium in the process.*[22]

Nichers have three tasks: creating niches, expanding niches, and protecting niches. For example, Nike, the athletic shoe manufacturer, is constantly creating new niches by designing special shoes for different sports and exercises such as hiking, walking, cycling, cheerleading, windsurfing, and so on. After creating a market for a particular use, Nike then expands the niche by designing different versions and brands within that shoe category, such as Nike Air Jordans or Nike

Specialist Roles Open to Market Nichers

◆ *End-User Specialist:* The firm specializes in serving one type of end-use customer. For example, a law firm can specialize in the criminal, civil, or business-law markets.

◆ *Vertical-Level Specialist:* The firm specializes at some vertical level of the production-distribution value chain. For example, a copper firm may concentrate on producing raw copper, copper components, or finished copper products.

◆ *Customer-Size Specialist:* The firm concentrates on selling to either small, medium-size, or large customers. Many nichers specialize in serving small customers who are neglected by the majors.

◆ *Specific-Customer Specialist:* The firm limits its selling to one or a few major customers. Many firms sell their entire output to a single company, such as Sears or General Motors.

◆ *Geographic Specialist:* The firm sells only in a certain locality, region, or area of the world.

◆ *Product or Product-Line Specialist:* The firm produces only one product line or product. Within the laboratory-equipment industry are firms that produce only

microscopes, or even more narrowly, only lenses for microscopes.

◆ *Product-Feature Specialist:* The firm specializes in producing a certain type of product or product feature. Rent-a-Wreck, for example, is a California car-rental agency that rents only "beat-up" cars.

◆ *Job-Shop Specialist:* The firm customizes its products for individual customers.

◆ *Quality/Price Specialist:* The firm operates at the low or high end of the market. For example, Hewlett-Packard specializes in the high-quality, high-price end of the hand-calculator market.

◆ *Service Specialist:* The firm offers one or more services not available from other firms. An example would be a bank that takes loan requests over the phone and hand delivers the money to the customer.

◆ *Channel Specialist:* The firm specializes in serving only one channel of distribution. For example, a soft-drink company decides to make a very large-size soft drink available only in gas stations.

Airwalkers. Finally, Nike must protect its leadership position as new competitors enter the niche.

Niching carries a major risk in that the market niche might dry up or be attacked. For example, Minnetonka, a small Minnesota company, developed a liquid soap in a dispenser that provided aesthetics and convenience in the bathroom. The soap was purchased by some households as a specialty item. But when the larger firms noticed this niche, they invaded it and turned it from a niche into a superseg-ment, and Minnetonka's share suffered.

The firm must recognize that niches can weaken. The firm must continually create new niches. The firm should "stick to its niching" but not necessarily to its niche. That is why *multiple niching* is preferable to *single niching*. By developing strength in two or more niches, the company increases its chances for survival.

Firms entering a market should aim at a niche initially rather than the whole market. Marketing Strategies 15-4 describes the major entry strategies used by several firms that entered markets occupied by incumbents. Most of them chose a niching strategy.

SUMMARY ❖

Marketing strategies are highly dependent on whether the company is a market leader, challenger, follower, or nicher.

A market leader faces three challenges: expanding the total market, protect-

Strategies for Entering Markets Held by Incumbent Firms

What marketing strategies can companies use to enter a market held by incumbent firms? Biggadike examined the strategies of 40 invading firms. He found that ten firms entered at a lower price, nine matched the incumbents' prices, and 21 entered at a higher price. While 28 claimed superior quality, five matched incumbents' quality, and seven reported inferior product quality. Most entrants offered a specialist product line and served a narrower market segment. Less than 20% managed to innovate a new channel of distribution. Over half the entrants offered a higher level of customer service. Over half the entrants spent less than incumbents on salesforce, advertising, and promotion. Thus, the modal marketing mix of entrants was: (1) higher prices and higher quality; (2) narrower product line; (3) narrower market segment; (4) similar distribution channels; (5) superior service; and (6) lower expenditure on salesforce, advertising, and promotion.

Carpenter and Nakamoto examined strategies for launching a new product into a market dominated by one brand such as Jell-O or Federal Express. These brands, which include many market pioneers, are particularly difficult to attack because many are the standard against which others are judged. A slightly different new brand, therefore, can be perceived as less attractive; and a similar one can be seen as offering nothing unique. They identified four strategies that have good profit potential in this situation:

+ *Differentiation*—positioning away from the dominant brand with a parity or premium price and heavy advertising spending to establish the new brand as a credible alternative to the dominant brand. Example: Honda's motorcycle challenges Harley Davidson.

+ *Challenger*—positioning close to the dominant brand with heavy advertising spending and parity or premium price to challenge the dominant brand as the category standard. Examples: Pepsi competing against Coke; Avis competing against Hertz.

+ *Niche*—positioning away from the dominant brand with a high price and a low advertising budget to exploit a profitable, remaining niche. Example: Tom's of Maine all-natural toothpaste competing against Crest.

+ *Premium*—positioning near the dominant brand with little advertising spending but a premium price to move "up market" relative to the dominant brand. Examples: Godiva chocolate and Haagen Daas ice cream competing against standard brands.

SOURCE: See Ralph Biggadike, *Entering New Markets: Strategies and Performance* (Cambridge, MA: Marketing Science Institute, September 1977), pp. 12–20; Gregory S. Carpenter and Kent Nakamoto, "Competitive Strategies for Late Entry into a Market with a Dominant Brand," *Management Science*, October 1990, pp. 1268–78; and Gregory S. Carpenter and Kent Nakamoto, "Competitive Late Mover Strategies," working paper, Northwestern University, 1993.

ing market share, and expanding market share. The market leader seeks to expand the total market because it is the chief beneficiary of any increased sales. To expand market size the leader looks for new users, new uses, and more usage. To protect its existing market share, the market leader has several defenses: position defense, flanking defense, preemptive defense, counteroffensive defense, mobile defense, and contraction defense. The most sophisticated leaders cover themselves by doing everything right, leaving no openings for competitive attack. Leaders can also try to increase their market share. This makes sense if profitability increases at higher market-share levels, and the company's tactics do not invite antitrust action.

A market challenger is a firm that aggressively tries to expand its market share by attacking the leader, other runner-up firms, or smaller firms in the industry. The challenger can choose from a variety of attack strategies, including a frontal attack, flanking attack, encirclement attack, bypass attack, and guerrilla attack.

A market follower is a runner-up firm that chooses not to rock the boat, usually out of fear that it stands to lose more than it might gain. The follower is not without a strategy, however, and seeks to use its particular competences to participate actively in the growth of the market.

A market nicher is a smaller firm that chooses to operate in some specialized part of the market that is unlikely to attract the larger firms. Market nichers often become specialists in some end use, vertical level, customer size, specific customer, geographic area, product or product line, product feature, job-shop approach, quality/price level, service, or channel. Multiple niching is preferable to single niching in order to reduce risk. Many of the most profitable small and medium-size firms owe their success to a niching strategy.

NOTES ❖

1. See Robert V. L. Wright, *A System For Managing Diversity* (Cambridge, MA: Arthur D. Little, December 1974).

2. See Jordan P. Yale, "The Strategy of Nylon's Growth," *Modern Textiles Magazine*, February 1964, pp. 32 ff. Also see Theodore Levitt, "Exploit the Product Life Cycle," *Harvard Business Review*, November–December 1965, pp. 81–94.

3. See Eric von Hippel, "A Customer-Active Paradigm for Industrial Product Idea Generation," working paper, Sloan School of Management, MIT, Cambridge, MA, May 1977.

4. Sun Tsu, *The Art of War* (London: Oxford University Press, 1963); Miyamoto Mushashi, *A Book of Five Rings* (Woodstock, NY: Overlook Press, 1974); Carl von Clausewitz, *On War* (London: Routledge & Kegan Paul, 1908); and B. H. Liddell-Hart, *Strategy* (New York: Praeger, 1967).

5. These six defense strategies, as well as the five attack strategies described on pp. 395–401, are taken from Philip Kotler and Ravi Singh, "Marketing Warfare in the 1980s," *Journal of Business Strategy*, Winter 1981, pp. 30–41. For additional reading, see Gerald A. Michaelson, *Winning the Marketing War: A Field Manual for Business Leaders* (Lanham, MD: Abt Books, 1987); Al Ries and Jack Trout, *Marketing Warfare* (New York: McGraw-Hill, 1986); Jay Conrad Levinson, *Guerrilla Marketing* (Boston, MA: Houghton-Mifflin Co., 1984); and Barrie G. James, *Business Wargames* (Harmondsworth, England: Penguin Books, 1984).

6. See Michael E. Porter, *Competitive Strategy* (New York: Free Press, 1980), Chap. 4.

7. *Relative market share* is the business's market share in its served market relative to the combined market share of its three leading competitors, expressed as a percentage. For example, if this business has 30% of the market and its three largest competitors have 20%, 10%, and 10%: 30/(20 + 10 + 10) = 75%.

8. Sidney Schoeffler, Robert D. Buzzell, and Donald F. Heany, "Impact of Strategic Planning on Profit Performance," *Harvard Business Review*, March–April 1974, pp. 137–45; and Robert D. Buzzell, Bradley T. Gale, and Ralph G. M. Sultan, "Market Share—A Key to Profitability," *Harvard Business Review*, January–February 1975, pp. 97–106.

9. See Buzzell et al., "Market Share," pp. 97, 100. The results held up in more recent PIMS studies where the database now includes 2,600 business units in a wide range of industries. See Robert D. Buzzell and Bradley T. Gale, *The PIMS Principles: Linking Strategy to Performance* (New York: Free Press, 1987).

10. Richard G. Hamermesh, M. J. Anderson, Jr., and J. E. Harris, "Strategies for Low Market Share Businesses," *Harvard Business Review*, May–June 1978, pp. 95–102.

11. Carolyn Y. Woo and Arnold C. Cooper, "The Surprising Case for Low Market Share," *Harvard Business Review*, November–December 1982, pp. 106-13; also see their "Market–Share Leadership—Not Always So Good," *Harvard Business Review*, January–February 1984, pp. 2–4.

12. John D. C. Roach, "From Strategic Planning to Strategic Performance: Closing the Achievement Gap," *Outlook*, published by Booz, Allen & Hamilton, New York, Spring 1981, p. 21. This curve assumes that pretax return on sales is highly correlated with profitability and that company revenue is a surrogate for market share. Michael Porter, in his *Competitive Strategy*, p. 43, shows a similar **V**-shaped curve.

13. Philip Kotler and Paul N. Bloom, "Strategies for High Market-Share Companies," *Harvard Business Review*, November-December 1975, pp. 63–72. Also see Michael E. Porter, *Competitive Advantage* (New York: Free Press, 1985), pp. 221–26.

14. Philip B. Crosby, *Quality Is Free* (New York: McGraw-Hill, 1979).

15. See Robert J. Dolan, "Models of Competition: A Review of Theory and Empirical Evidence," in *Review of Marketing*, ed. Ben M. Enis and Kenneth J. Roering (Chicago: American Marketing Association, 1981), pp. 224–34.

16. For additional reading, see C. David Fogg, "Planning Gains in Market Share," *Journal of Marketing*, July 1974, pp. 30–38; and Bernard Catry and Michel Chevalier, "Market Share Strategy and the Product Life Cycle," *Journal of Marketing*, October 1974, pp. 29–34.

17. See "Seiko's Smash," *Business Week*, June 5, 1978, p. 89.

18. See "The Changing of the Guard," *Fortune*, Sept. 24, 1979; "How to Be Happy Though No. Two," *Forbes*, July 15, 1976, p. 36.

19. Liddell-Hart, *Strategy*, p. 335.

20. Theodore Levitt, "Innovative Imitation," *Harvard Business Review*, September–October 1966, pp. 63 ff.

21. Donald K. Clifford and Richard E. Cavanagh, *The Winning Performance: How America's High- and Midsize Growth Companies Succeed* (New York: Bantam Books, 1985).

22. See Bro Uttal, "Pitching Computers to Small Businesses," *Fortune*, April 1, 1985, pp. 95–104. Also see Stuart Gannes, "The Riches in Market Niches," *Fortune*, April 27, 1987, pp. 227–30.

16

Designing Strategies for the Global Marketplace

A traveler without knowledge is like a bird without wings.

SA'DI, GULISTAN (1258)

There will be two kinds of CEOs who will exist in the next five years: those who think globally and those who are unemployed.

PETER DRUCKER

The 1990s marks the first decade when domestic companies around the world have to start thinking globally. Time and distance are rapidly shrinking with the advent of faster communication, transportation, and financial flows. Products developed in one country—Gucci purses, Monte Blanc pens, McDonald's hamburgers, Japanese sushi, Pierre Cardin suits, German BMWs—are finding enthusiastic acceptance in other countries. We would not be surprised to hear about a German businessman wearing an Italian suit meeting an English friend at a Japanese restaurant who later returns home to drink Russian vodka and watch *Dallas* on TV. A global shopping market is emerging.

True, many companies have been conducting international marketing for decades. Nestlé, Shell, Bayer, Toshiba, and other multinationals are familiar to most consumers around the world. But today global competition is intensifying. Domestic companies that never thought about foreign competitors suddenly find these competitors in their backyard. Newspaper headlines report daily on Japanese victories over U.S. producers in consumer electronics, motorcycles, copying machines, cameras, and watches; the gains of Japanese, German, Swedish, and Korean car imports in the U.S. market; about the French firm Bic's successful attacks on Gillette; on Nestlé's gains in the coffee and candy markets; and on the loss of textile and shoe markets to Third World imports. Such names as Sony, Honda, Nestlé, Perrier, Mercedes-Benz, and Volkswagen are household words. And many companies that are thought to be American firms are really foreign firms: Bantam Books, Baskin-Robbins Ice Cream, Capitol Records, Kiwi Shoe Polish, and Lipton Tea. Americans complain that foreign companies are buying up America: Japanese land purchases in Hawaii, the Japanese purchase of Rockefeller Center, Arab purchases of Manhattan office buildings—and one offer by a Saudi Arabian sheik to buy the Alamo for his son.

Although some would stem the foreign invasion through protective legislation, protectionism in the long run only raises living costs and protects inefficient domestic firms. The right answer is that companies must learn how to enter foreign markets and increase their global competitiveness.

Every government runs an export promotion program, trying to persuade its local companies to export. Denmark pays more than half the salary of marketing consultants who help small and medium-size Danish companies get into exports. Many countries go further and subsidize companies that agree to export by granting preferential land and energy costs, and supplying outright cash so that they can charge lower prices than their foreign competitors.

The more that companies delay taking steps toward internationalizing, the more they risk being shut out of growing markets in Western Europe, Eastern Europe, the Far East, and elsewhere. Today the European Common Market countries are removing barriers to the flow of goods, services, money, and people—they are deregulating business, privatizing some state enterprise, and setting common commercial standards.[1] New opportunities are proliferating in Eastern Europe as these countries struggle to convert from state-planned economies to market-driven economies.

All companies will have to address fundamental questions: What market presence should we try to achieve in our country, on our continent, and globally?

Who will our competitors be and what are their strategies and resources? Where shall we produce or source our product? What strategic alliances should we form with other firms?

Ironically, while companies need to enter and compete in foreign markets, the risks are high. They have several major concerns:

1. *Huge Foreign Indebtedness:* Many countries with otherwise attractive markets have accumulated huge foreign debts on which they cannot even pay the interest. Among these countries are Brazil, Poland, and Bulgaria.

2. *Unstable Governments:* High indebtedness, high inflation, and high unemployment in several countries have resulted in highly unstable governments that expose foreign firms to the risks of expropriation, nationalization, limits to profit repatriation, and so on.

3. *Foreign-Exchange Problems:* High indebtedness and economic and political instability force a country's currency to fluctuate or depreciate in value. Foreign firms want payment in hard currency with profit-repatriation rights, but that is not available in many markets. Foreign investors hesitate to hold much of the foreign currency, and this hesitancy limits trade.

4. *Foreign-Government Entry Requirements and Bureaucracy:* Governments place many regulations on foreign firms, such as requiring joint ventures with the majority share going to the domestic partner; a high number of nationals to be hired; technology transfer; and limits on profit repatriation.

5. *Tariffs and Other Trade Barriers:* Governments often impose high tariffs to protect their industries. They also resort to invisible trade barriers such as slowing down import approval, requiring costly product adjustments, and slowing down inspection or clearance of arriving goods.

6. *Corruption:* Officials in several countries require bribes to cooperate. They award business to the highest briber rather than the lowest bidder. U.S. managers are prohibited by the Foreign Corrupt Practices Act of 1977 from paying bribes, whereas competitors from other countries operate under no such limitation.

7. *Technological Pirating:* A company locating its plant abroad worries about foreign managers learning how to make its product and breaking away to compete openly or clandestinely. This has happened in such diverse areas as machinery, electronics, chemicals, and pharmaceuticals.

8. *High Cost of Product and Communication Adaptation:* A company going abroad must study each foreign market carefully, become sensitive to its economics, laws, politics, and culture, and adapt its products and communications to foreign tastes. Otherwise, it might make serious blunders. It will bear higher costs and must wait longer for its profits to materialize.

One might conclude that companies are doomed whether they stay at home or go abroad. We would argue that companies selling in *global industries* have no choice but to internationalize their operations.

❖ A global industry *is an industry in which the strategic positions of competitors in major geographic or national markets are fundamentally affected by their overall global positions.*[2]

A *global firm* is therefore one that, in operating in more than one country, captures R&D, production, logistical, marketing, and financial advantages in its costs and reputation that are not available to purely domestic competitors. As an example, Ford's "world truck" has a European-made cab, a North American-built chassis, is assembled in Brazil, and imported into the United States for sale. Global firms plan, operate, and coordinate their activities on a worldwide basis.

Domestic firms in global industries must act before the foreign windows close on them, since firms from other countries are globalizing at a rapid rate. This does

FIGURE 16-1 Major Decisions in International Marketing

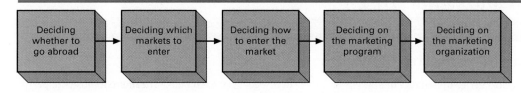

Deciding whether to go abroad → Deciding which markets to enter → Deciding how to enter the market → Deciding on the marketing program → Deciding on the marketing organization

not mean that small and medium-size firms must operate in over a dozen countries to succeed. These firms can practice global nichemanship, as many Scandinavian and Benelux companies do.

In this chapter, we will examine the following questions (see Figure 16-1):

- What factors should a company review before deciding to go abroad?
- How can companies evaluate and select specific foreign markets to enter?
- What are the major alternative ways to enter a foreign market?
- To what extent must the company adapt its products and marketing program to each foreign country?
- How should the company manage and organize its international activities?

Deciding Whether to Go Abroad

Most companies would prefer to remain domestic businesses if their domestic market were large enough. Managers would not need to learn another country's language and laws, deal with strange and volatile currencies, face political and legal uncertainties and harassments, or redesign their products to suit quite different customer needs and expectations. Business would be easier and safer.

Yet there are several factors that might draw a company into the international arena. The company's domestic market might be attacked by global firms offering better products or lower prices. The company might want to counterattack these competitors in their home markets to tie up their resources. The company might discover that some foreign markets present higher profit opportunities than the domestic market. The company might need a larger customer base in order to achieve economies of scale. The company might want to reduce its dependence on any one market so as to reduce its risk. The company's customers might be going abroad and require international servicing.

Before making a decision to go abroad, the company must weigh several risks. The company might not understand foreign customer preferences and fail to offer a competitively attractive product (see Global Marketing 16-1). The company might not understand the foreign country's business culture and know how to deal effectively with foreign nationals. The company might underestimate foreign regulations and incur unexpected costs. The company might realize that it lacks managers with international experience. The foreign country might change its commercial laws in an unfavorable way, might depreciate its currency or introduce exchange control, or might undergo a political revolution and expropriate foreign property.

Because of the competing advantages and risks, companies often don't act until some event thrusts them into the international arena. Someone—a domestic exporter, a foreign importer, a foreign government—solicits the company to sell abroad. Or the company is saddled with overcapacity and must find additional markets for its goods.

Global Marketing 16-1

In Going Abroad, Step Cautiously

Companies venturing abroad can easily make mistakes based on ethnocentric thinking. It is often wiser to assume that the customers abroad are different rather than similar to the home customers. Here are examples of blunders made by some otherwise savvy marketing companies:

> Hallmark cards bombed when they were introduced in France. The French dislike syrupy sentiment and prefer writing their own cards.

> Philips began to earn a profit in Japan only after it had reduced the size of its coffeemakers to fit into the smaller Japanese kitchens and its shavers to fit the smaller Japanese hands.

> Coca-Cola had to withdraw the two-liter bottle in Spain after discovering that few Spaniards owned refrigerators with large enough compartments.

> General Foods' Tang initially failed in France because it was positioned as a substitute for orange juice at breakfast. The French drink little orange juice and almost none at breakfast.

Kellogg's Pop-Tarts failed in Britain because the percentage of British homes with toasters was significantly lower than in the United States, and the product was too sweet for British tastes.

P & G's Crest toothpaste initially failed in Mexico when it used the U.S. campaign. Mexicans did not care as much for the decay prevention benefit, nor did scientifically oriented advertising appeal to them.

General Foods squandered millions trying to introduce Japanese consumers to packaged cake mixes. The company failed to note that only 3% of Japanese homes were equipped with ovens. Then they promoted the idea of baking cakes in Japanese rice cookers, overlooking the fact that the Japanese use their rice cookers throughout the day to keep rice warm and ready.

S. C. Johnson's wax floor polish initially failed in Japan. The wax made the floors too slippery and Johnson had overlooked the fact that Japanese do not wear shoes in their homes.

Deciding Which Markets to Enter

In deciding to go abroad, the company needs to define its *international marketing objectives and policies*. What *proportion of foreign to total sales* will it seek? Most companies start small when they venture abroad. Some plan to stay small, viewing foreign operations as a small part of their business. Other companies have more grandiose plans, seeing foreign business as ultimately equal to, or even more important than, their domestic business.

The company must decide whether to market in a *few countries* or *many countries*. The Bulova Watch Company made the latter choice and expanded into over 100 countries. It spread itself too thin, made profits in only two countries, and lost around $40 million. Generally speaking, it makes sense to operate in fewer countries with a deeper commitment and penetration in each. Ayal and Zif argued that a company should enter fewer countries when

- ◆ Market entry and market control costs are high;
- ◆ Product and communication adaptation costs are high;
- ◆ Population and income size and growth are high in the initial countries chosen; and
- ◆ Dominant foreign firms can establish high barriers to entry.[3]

The company must also decide on the *types of countries* to consider. Country attractiveness is influenced by the product, geographical factors, income and population, political climate, and other factors. The seller might have a predilection for certain groups of countries or parts of the world. Kenichi Ohmae recommends that companies concentrate on selling in the "triad markets"—the United States, Western Europe, and Japan (see Global Marketing 16-2).

Suppose a company has assembled a list of potential export markets. How does it choose among them? Many companies prefer to sell to neighboring countries because they understand these countries better, and they can control their costs better because of the proximity. Thus it is not surprising that the United States' largest market is Canada, or that Swedish companies first sold their goods to their

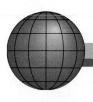

Global Marketing 16-2

Should Multinationals Restrict Their Trade to the Triad Markets?

Some trade strategists have argued that it is not worthwhile to sell in the Third World; the lucrative markets are in North America, Western Europe, and the Far East. Kenichi Ohmae, the head of McKinsey's office in Tokyo, argues this view in his *Triad Power*. He notes that

> *Opportunities are great in booming states such as California, which is bigger than Brazil (in economic terms), and Texas, whose gross state product is bigger than the combined GNP of the Association of Southeast Asian Nations.*

He goes on to say:

> *The "triad" of Japan, Europe, and the United States represents not only the major and fastest growing market for most products but also an increasingly homogeneous one. Gucci bags, Sony Walkmans, and McDonald's hamburgers are seen on the streets of Tokyo, Paris, and New York.*

Ohmae also thinks multinationals make a mistake rushing to Third World countries to produce components just because the wages are lower. Low wages do not necessarily spell lower costs if the labor is inefficient or redundant, or product quality is poorer. With growing automation, labor costs are becoming smaller anyway.

Ohmae also criticizes multinationals for taking too much time to introduce their new products into foreign markets. Swift competitors copy their products and launch them in foreign markets before the pioneer gets there. His solution: A multinational should establish strategic alliances (licenses, joint ventures, consortia, and so forth) with companies that operate in each triad market, so that the multinational could introduce its

new products in all triad markets simultaneously and capture market leadership. This strategy would provide a sufficient-size market to justify larger initial plant investment and lower unit costs. In addition, the multinational need not worry about being kept out by trade barriers, since its partners would be "insiders" in the foreign markets.

While Ohmae's position makes short-run sense—that is, profits are likely to be higher in the triad regions—it can spell a disastrous policy for the world economy in the long run. The triad markets are rich but mature: Companies have to strain their creativity to find growth opportunities in these markets. In contrast, the unmet needs of the developing world represent an ocean of opportunity. They are huge potential markets for food, clothing, shelter, consumer electronics, appliances, and other goods. Unless purchasing power is somehow put into the Third World, the industrial world will remain saddled with excess productive capacity and a very slow growth rate; and the developing economies will be stuck with excess consumer needs that they are unable to satisfy. Somehow various governments and multinationals must find ways to link these two worlds dynamically and synergistically in a mutually beneficial relationship.

SOURCE: See Kenichi Ohmae, *Triad Power* (New York: Free Press, 1985); and Philip Kotler and Nikhilesh Dholakia, "Ending Global Stagnation: Linking the Fortunes of the Industrial and Developing Countries," *Business in the Contemporary World*, Spring 1989, pp. 86–97.

Scandinavian neighbors. At other times, *psychic proximity* rather than *geographical proximity* determines choices. Consider the following example:

> *CMC's market research in the computer field revealed that England, France, West Germany, and Italy offer us significant markets. England, France, and Germany are about equal-size markets, while Italy represents about two-thirds the potential of any one of those countries. . . . Taking everything into consideration, we decided to set up first in England because its market for our products is as large as any and its language and laws are similar to ours. England is different enough to get your feet wet, yet similar enough to the familiar U.S. business environment so that you do not get in over your head.*[4]

Yet one can question whether the reason for selecting England—the compatibility of its language and culture—should have been given this prominence. The candidate countries should be initially rated on three major criteria, namely, *market attractiveness*, *competitive advantage*, and *risk*. Here is an example:

> The International Hough Company manufacturers mining equipment and is evaluating China and four Eastern European countries as possible market opportunities. It first rates the *market attractiveness* of each country, looking at such indicators as GNP/capita, work force in mining, imports of machinery, and population growth. It then rates its own potential *competitive advantage* in each country, looking at such indicators as prior business dealings, whether it would be a low-cost producer, whether its senior management can work comfortably in that country. Finally it rates the *risk level* of each country, looking at such indicators as political stability, currency stability, and repatriation rules (see Global Marketing 16-3). By indexing, weighing, and combining the various numbers, it arrives at the picture shown in Figure 16-2. China appears to present the best opportunity insofar as it rates high on market attractiveness and competitive advantage, and low on risk. Romania, on the other hand, ranks low on market attractiveness, medium on competitive advantage, and high on risk.

Now International Hough must prepare a financial analysis to see what it could earn on its investment. It could turn out that no country promises a sufficient return, or that they all do. Five steps are involved in estimating the probable rate of return on investment:

1. *Estimate of Current Market Potential:* The first step is to estimate total industry sales in each market. This task calls for using published data and primary data collected by the company.
2. *Forecast of Future Market Potential and Risk:* The firm also needs to forecast future industry sales, a difficult task. It requires predicting economic and political developments and their impact on industry sales.
3. *Forecast of Sales Potential:* Estimating the company's sales requires forecasting its probable market share based on its competitive advantage, another difficult task.
4. *Forecast of Costs and Profits:* Costs will depend on the company's contemplated entry strategy. If it exports or licenses, its costs will be spelled out in the contracts. If it locates manufacturing facilities in the country, its cost estimation will require understanding local labor conditions, taxes, trade practices, and so on. The company subtracts estimated costs from estimated sales to derive company profits for each year of the planning horizon.
5. *Estimate of Rate of Return On Investment:* The forecasted income stream should be related to the investment stream to derive the implicit rate of return. This should be high enough to cover the company's normal target return on its investment and the risk of marketing in that country.[5]

Global Marketing 16-3

Assessing Country Risk

The daily news is so filled with reports of unstable governments and faltering economies that business firms are of course hesitant to put their investment at risk in another country. If seemingly secure governments like the shah's regime in Iran and Marcos's regime in the Philippines could topple, can any country be depended on? Since 1960, over 1,500 companies were expropriated in 511 separate actions by 76 nations. Even short of expropriation, a company could lose its investment because of strikes, currency devaluation, blocked currency, and so on.

Analysts distinguish between two types of country risk. The first is *asset protection/investment recovery risk*, which arises from direct action taken by the government or the people that results in destroying, expropriating, or limiting transfer of invested resources. The second is *operational profitability/cash-flow risk*, which arises from economic downturns, currency depreciation, strikes, and so on. Some analysts think of the former risk as political risk and the latter risk as economic risk, but both types often intermingle.

No wonder then that companies buy *political-risk-assessment reports* such as Business International's (BI) Country Assessment Service, BERI, or Frost & Sullivan's World Political Risk Forecasts. Using different models and measurement techniques, these services come up with numerical ratings showing each country's current risk level and, in some cases, their expected risk level three years from now.

Many companies find these estimates interesting but inadequate. They measure the *macrorisk* affecting all foreign companies but not the *microrisk* facing any particular company or industry. For example, a country may present little macrorisk but might be planning to nationalize foreign oil companies. Consequently, companies need to supplement macrorisk estimates with other methods of gaining insight into risk. General Motors and Caterpillar use advisory councils of prominent foreign experts. Gulf Oil has its own political-risk-assessment office staffed with area experts. Many companies send their senior officers on periodic grand tours to various countries where they have or are planning major investments, to talk to government officials and their own staff about recent and expected developments.

SOURCES: See Stephan Kobrin, "Foreign Investment and the Management of Political Risk," *Journal of International Business Studies,* Winter 1981, pp. 128–30; R. J. Rummel and D. A. Heenan, "How Multinationals Analyze Political Risk," *Harvard Business Review,* January-February 1978, pp. 67–76; and Louis Kraar, "The Multinationals Get Smarter about Political Risks," *Fortune,* March 24, 1980, pp. 86–100.

FIGURE 16-2
Evaluating Which Markets to Enter

Market Attractiveness		High	Medium	Low	
	H	China			
	M		Czechoslovakia		L
	L	Eastern Germany			
	H		Poland		
	M			Romania	H
	L				

Competitive Advantage

Risk

Deciding How to Enter the Market

Once a company decides to target a particular country, it has to determine the best mode of entry. Its broad choices are *indirect exporting*, *direct exporting*, *licensing*, *joint ventures*, and *direct investment*. Each succeeding strategy involves more commitment, risk, control, and profit potential. The five market-entry strategies are shown in Figure 16-3 and examined on the following pages.

Indirect Export

The normal way to get involved in a foreign market is through export. *Occasional exporting* is a passive level of involvement where the company exports from time to time on its own initiative or in response to unsolicited orders from abroad. *Active exporting* takes place when the company makes a commitment to expand exports to a particular market. In either case, the company produces all of its goods in the home country. It might or might not adapt them to the foreign market. Exporting involves the least change in the company's product lines, organization, investments, or mission.

Companies typically start with *indirect exporting*; that is, they work through independent middlemen. Four types of middlemen are available to the company:

- *Domestic-Based Export Merchant:* This middleman buys the manufacturer's products and sells them abroad on its own account.
- *Domestic-Based Export Agent:* This agent seeks and negotiates foreign purchases and is paid a commission. Included in the group are trading companies.
- *Cooperative Organization:* A cooperative organization carries on exporting activities on behalf of several producers and is partly under their administrative control. This form is often used by producers of primary products—fruits, nuts, and so on.
- *Export-Management Company:* This middleman agrees to manage a company's export activities for a fee.

Indirect export has two advantages. First, it involves less investment. The firm does not have to develop an export department, an overseas salesforce, or a set of foreign contacts. Second, it involves less risk. International-marketing middlemen bring know-how and services to the relationship, and the seller will normally make fewer mistakes.

Direct Export

Companies eventually may decide to handle their own exports. The investment and risk are somewhat greater, but so is the potential return. The company can carry on direct exporting in several ways:

- *Domestic-Based Export Department or Division:* An export sales manager carries on the actual selling and draws on market assistance as needed. It might evolve into a self-contained export department performing all the activities involved in export and operating as a profit center.
- *Overseas Sales Branch or Subsidiary:* An overseas sales branch allows the manufacturer to achieve greater presence and program control in the foreign market. The sales branch handles sales and distribution and might handle warehousing and promotion as well. It often serves as a display center and customer-service center.

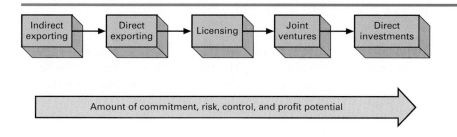

FIGURE 16-3
Five Modes of Entry Into
Foreign Markets

- *Traveling Export Sales Representatives:* The company can send home-based sales representatives abroad to find business.
- *Foreign-Based Distributors or Agents:* The company can hire foreign-based distributors or agents to sell the goods on behalf of the company. They might be given exclusive rights to represent the manufacturer in that country or only general rights.

Licensing

Licensing represents a simple way for a manufacturer to become involved in international marketing. The licensor licenses a foreign company to use a manufacturing process, trademark, patent, trade secret, or other item of value for a fee or royalty. The licensor gains entry into the foreign market at little risk; the licensee gains production expertise or a well-known product or name without having to start from scratch. Gerber introduced its baby foods in the Japanese market through a licensing arrangement. Coca-Cola carries out its international marketing by licensing bottlers around the world—or, more technically, franchising bottlers—and supplies them with the syrup and the training needed to produce, distribute, and sell the product.

Licensing has potential disadvantages in that the firm has less control over the licensee than if it had set up its own production facilities. Furthermore, if the licensee is very successful, the firm has foregone profits, and if and when the contract ends, it might find that it has created a competitor. To avoid creating a future competitor, the licensor usually supplies some proprietary ingredients or components needed in the product. But the main hope is for the licensor to lead in innovation so that the licensee will continue to depend on this licensor.

Companies can enter foreign markets on other bases. A company can sell a *management contract* to manage a foreign hotel, airport, hospital, or other organization for a fee. In this case, the firm is exporting a service instead of a product. Management contracting is a low-risk method of getting into a foreign market, and it yields income from the beginning. The arrangement is especially attractive if the contracting firm is given an option to purchase some share in the managed company within a stated period. On the other hand, the arrangement is not sensible if the company can put its scarce management talent to better uses or if there are greater profits to be made by undertaking the whole venture. Management contracting prevents the company from going into competition with its clients.

Another entry method is *contract manufacturing*, where the firm engages local manufacturers to produce the product. When Sears opened department stores in Mexico and Spain, Sears found qualified local manufacturers to produce many of its products. Contract manufacturing has the drawback of less control over the manufacturing process and the loss of potential profits on manufacturing. On the other hand, it offers the company a chance to start faster, with less risk, and with the opportunity to form a partnership or buy out the local manufacturer later.

Joint Ventures

Foreign investors may join with local investors to create a joint venture in which they share ownership and control. Forming a joint venture might be necessary or desirable for economic or political reasons. The foreign firm might lack the financial, physical, or managerial resources to undertake the venture alone. Or the foreign government might require joint ownership as a condition for entry.

Joint ownership has certain drawbacks. The partners might disagree over investment, marketing, or other policies. One partner might want to reinvest earnings for growth, and the other partner might want to withdraw these earnings. Furthermore, joint ownership can hamper a multinational company from carrying out specific manufacturing and marketing policies on a worldwide basis.[6]

Direct Investment

The ultimate form of foreign involvement is direct ownership of foreign-based assembly or manufacturing facilities. The foreign company can buy part or full interest in a local company or build its own facilities. As a company gains experience in export, and if the foreign market appears large enough, foreign production facilities offer distinct advantages. First, the firm could secure cost economies in the form of cheaper labor or raw materials, foreign-government investment incentives, freight savings, and so on. Second, the firm will gain a better image in the host country because it creates jobs. Third, the firm develops a deeper relationship with government, customers, local suppliers, and distributors, enabling it to adapt its products better to the local marketing environment. Fourth, the firm retains full control over the investment and therefore can develop manufacturing and marketing policies that serve its long-term international objectives. Fifth, the firm assures itself access to the market in case the host country starts insisting that purchased goods have domestic content.

The main disadvantage is that the firm exposes its large investment to risks such as blocked or devalued currencies, worsening markets, or expropriation. The firm will find it expensive to reduce or close down its operations, since the host country might require substantial severance pay to the employees. The firm, however, has no choice but to accept these risks if it wants to operate on its own in the host country.

The Internationalization Process

Many companies show a distinct preference for a particular mode of entry. One company might prefer exporting because it minimizes its risk. Another company might prefer licensing because it is an easy way to make money without investing much capital. Another company might favor direct investment because it wants full control. Yet insisting on one mode of entry is too limiting. Some countries will not permit imports of certain goods nor allow direct investment but will only accept a joint-owned venture with a foreign national. Consequently, companies need to master all of these entry methods. Even though a company might have preferences, it needs to adapt to each situation. Most sophisticated multinationals manage several entry modes simultaneously.

The problem facing most countries is that too few of their companies participate in foreign trade. This keeps the country from earning sufficient foreign exchange to pay for needed imports. Consequently, governments sponsor aggressive export promotion programs. These programs should be based on a deep understanding of how companies become internationalized.

Johanson and his associates have studied the *internationalization process* among Swedish companies.[7] They see firms moving through four stages:

1. No regular export activities
2. Export via independent representatives (agents)
3. Establishment of one or more sales subsidiaries
4. Establishment of production facilities abroad

The first task is to get companies to move from stage 1 to stage 2. This move is helped by studying how firms made their first export decisions.[8] Most firms work with an independent agent, usually in a country posing low psychic barriers to entry. A company then engages further agents to enter additional countries. Later, it establishes an export department to manage its agent relationships. Still later, the company replaces its agents with sales subsidiaries in its larger export markets. This increases the company's investment and risk but also increases its earning potential. To manage these sales subsidiaries, the company replaces the export department with an international department. If certain markets continue to be large and stable, or if the host country insists on local production, the company takes the next step of locating production facilities in those markets, representing a still larger commitment and still larger potential earnings. By this time, the company is operating as a multinational company and reconsidering the best way to organize and manage its global operations.

Deciding on the Marketing Program

Companies that operate in one or more foreign markets must decide how much to adapt their marketing-strategy mix to local conditions. At one extreme are companies that use a *standardized marketing mix* worldwide. Standardization of the product, advertising, distribution channels, and other elements of the marketing mix promises the lowest costs because no major changes have been introduced. At the other extreme is the idea of an *adapted marketing mix*, where the producer adjusts the marketing-mix elements to each target market, bearing more costs but hoping for a larger market share and profit return. Between these two extremes, many possibilities exist. Global Marketing 16-4 describes the main issues. Here we will examine potential adaptations that firms might make of their product, promotion, price, and distribution as they enter foreign markets.

Product

Keegan distinguished five adaptation strategies of product and promotion to a foreign market (see Figure 16-4 on page 422).[9]

Straight extension means introducing the product in the foreign market without any change. Top management instructs its salespeople: "Find customers for the product as it is." The first step, however, should be to determine whether the foreign consumers use that product. Deodorant usage among men ranges from 80% in the United States to 55% in Sweden to 28% in Italy to 8% in the Philippines. In interviewing women in one country about how often they used a deodorant, a typical response was "I use it when I go dancing once a year" which is hardly grounds for introducing the product.

Straight extension has been successful with cameras, consumer electronics, many machine tools, and so on, but a disaster in other cases. General Foods introduced its standard powdered Jell-O in the British market only to find that British

Global Marketing 16-4

Global Standardization or Adaptation?

The marketing concept holds that consumers vary in their needs and that marketing programs will be more effective when tailored to each customer target group. Since this applies within a country, it should apply even more cogently in foreign markets where economic, political, and cultural conditions vary widely.

Yet many multinationals are bothered by what they see as an excessive amount of adaptation. Consider Gillette:

> Gillette sells over 800 products in more than 200 countries. It has fallen into a situation where different brand names are used for the same product in different countries, and where the same brand is formulated differently in different countries. Gillette's Silkience shampoo is called Soyance in France, Sientel in Italy, and Silience in Germany; its formula is the same in some cases but varies in others. Its advertising messages and copy are also varied because each Gillette country manager proposes several changes that he or she thinks will increase sales. Headquarters management feels at a loss to think that it might know more about local conditions than its country managers.

Gillette and other companies would like to impose more standardization, globally or at least regionally. They see this as a way to save costs and to build up global brand power.

They take inspiration from the British advertising firm of Saatchi & Saatchi and Professor Theodore Levitt of Harvard. Saatchi & Saatchi won several advertising accounts on the strength of their claim that they can build single advertising campaigns that will work globally. Meanwhile, Professor Levitt supplied the intellectual rationale for global standardization. He wrote:

> *The world is becoming a common marketplace in which people—no matter where they live—desire the same products and lifestyles. Global companies must forget the idiosyncratic differences between countries and cultures and instead concentrate on satisfying universal drives.*

Levitt believes that new communication and transportation technologies have created a more homogeneous world market. People around the world want the same basic things—things that make life easier and increase their discretionary time and buying power. This convergence of needs and wants has created global markets for standardized products.

According to Levitt, traditional multinational corporations focus on differences between specific markets. They cater to superficial preference differences and produce a proliferation of highly adapted products. Adaptation results in less efficiency and higher prices to consumers.

In contrast, the global corporation sells the same product the same way to all consumers. It focuses on similarities across world markets and aggressively works to "sensibly force suitably standardized products and services on the entire globe." These global marketers realize substantial economies through standardization of production, distribution, marketing, and management. They translate their efficiency into greater value for consumers by offering high quality and more reliable products at lower prices.

Levitt would advise an auto company to make a world car, a shampoo company to make a world shampoo, and a construction company to make a world tractor. In fact, some companies have successfully marketed global products: Coca-Cola, McDonald's hamburgers, Montblanc pens and pencils, and Sony Walkmans. Some products are more global and require less adaptation on the whole. Yet even in these cases, some adaptation takes place. Coca-Cola is less sweet or less carbonated in certain countries; McDonald's uses chili sauce instead of ketchup on its hamburgers in Mexico; and Montblanc pens and pencils have different advertising copy and messages in some countries.

Professor Levitt assumes that global standardization will save a lot of cost, will lead to lower prices, and

consumers prefer the solid wafer or cake form. Campbell Soup lost an estimated $30 million in introducing its condensed soups in England; the consumers saw the small-size cans and did not realize that water needed to be added. Straight extension is tempting because it involves no additional R&D expense, manufacturing retooling, or promotional modification. But it can be costly in the long run.

Product adaptation involves altering the product to meet local conditions or

cause more goods to be snapped up by price-sensitive consumers. But these assumptions are debatable. A company needs to think in terms of incremental revenue versus incremental cost. Consider the following:

> Mattel Toys had successfully sold its Barbie doll in dozens of countries without modification. But in Japan, Barbie did not sell well. Takara, its Japanese licensee, surveyed eighth-grade girls and they (and their parents) thought the doll's breasts were too big and legs were too long. Mattel, however, was reluctant to modify the doll because this would require additional production, packaging, and advertising costs. Finally, Takara prevailed, and within two years, Takara sold two million modified Barbie dolls. Clearly, the incremental revenue far exceeded the incremental cost.

Rather than assuming that the company's domestic product can be introduced as is in another country, the company should review all possible adaptation elements and determine which adaptations would add more revenue than cost. The adaptation elements include the following:

Product features	Colors	Advertising themes
Brand name	Materials	Advertising media
Labeling	Prices	Advertising execution
Packaging	Sales promotion	

One study showed that companies made one or more marketing-mix adaptations in 80% of their foreign-directed products and that the average number of adapted elements was four. It should also be recognized that some host countries require adaptations, independent of whether the company wants to make them. The French do not allow children to be used in ads; the Germans ban the use of the word *best* to describe a product, and so on.

As one example, Kenner Parker Tonka, the toy company, had to make several adaptations within Western Europe. It had to replace PVC plastic in one of its boys' action toys with another plastic because Germany limited the use of PVC. It had to charge a lower price in Holland because Dutch parents spent less on children's toys. It had to change Wish World Kids, a toy for girls, to Les Ali Babettes to convey meaning to the French. In England, it introduced its toys separately to each national retailer, whereas in France it introduced its toys at the annual toy fair because of the large number of independent small retailers.

Thus global standardization is not an all-or-nothing proposition but a matter of degree. Companies are certainly justified in looking for more standardization, regionally if not globally. Goodyear, for example, is trying to bring regional uniformity into its logos, corporate advertising, and product lines in continental Europe so that it will have a more recognizable presence. Resistance typically arises from country managers because regional standardization puts more power into the hands of the regional manager and less in each country manager. And country managers might ask for excessive changes. Yet, companies must remember that while standardization might save some costs, competitors are always ready to offer more of what the customers in each country want. Global marketing, yes; global standardization, not necessarily.

SOURCES: Theodore Levitt, "The Globalization of Markets," *Harvard Business Review,* May-June 1983, pp. 92–102. For an example of the work involved in building a single global campaign, see "Playtex Kicks Off a One-Ad-Fits-All Campaign," *Business Week,* December 16, 1985, pp. 48–49. For a negative assessment of global standardization attempts, see "Marketers Turn Sour on Global Sales Pitch Harvard Guru Makes," *The Wall Street Journal,* May 12, 1988, p. 1. For a well-balanced approach, see John A. Quelch and Edward J. Hoff, "Customizing Global Marketing," *Harvard Business Review,* May–June 1986, pp. 59–68.

preferences. There are several levels of adaptation. A company can produce a *regional version* of its product, such as a Western European version, a North American version, and so on. Or it can produce a *country version*. In Japan, Mister Donut's coffee cup is smaller and lighter to fit the hand of the average Japanese consumer; even the doughnuts are a little smaller. In Australia, Heinz sells a baby food made from strained lamb brains; and in the Netherlands, a baby food made from strained

FIGURE 16-4
Five International Product
and Promotion Strategies

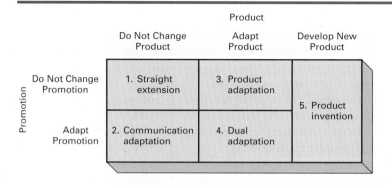

brown beans. General Foods blends different coffees for the British (who drink their coffee with milk), the French (who drink their coffee black), and Latin Americans (who want a chicory taste). A company can produce a *city version* of its product, for instance, a beer to meet Munich tastes or Tokyo tastes. Finally, a company can produce *different retailer versions* of its product, such as a coffee brew for the Migros chain store and another for the Cooperative chain store, both in Switzerland.

Product invention consists of creating something new. It can take two forms. *Backward invention* is reintroducing earlier product forms that are well adapted to a foreign country's needs. The National Cash Register Company reintroduced its crank-operated cash register at half the price of a modern cash register and sold substantial numbers in Latin America and Africa. That illustrates the *international product life cycle* where countries stand at different stages of readiness to accept a particular product. *Forward invention* is creating a new product to meet a need in another country. There is an enormous need in less-developed countries for low-cost, high-protein foods. Companies like Quaker Oats, Swift, and Monsanto are researching the nutrition needs of these countries, formulating new foods, and developing advertising campaigns to gain product trial and acceptance. Product invention is a costly strategy, but the payoffs can be great.

A growing part of international trade is taking place in services. In fact, the world market for services is growing at double the rate of world merchandise trade. The largest firms in accounting, advertising, banking, communications, construction, insurance, law, and management consulting are pursuing global expansion. Arthur Andersen, American Express, Citicorp, Club Med, Hilton, and Thomas Cook are known worldwide. At the same time, many countries have erected entry barriers or regulations that make the exporting of services difficult. Brazil requires all accountants to possess a professional degree from a Brazilian university. Many Western European countries want to limit the use of U.S. television programs. Many U.S. states bar foreign bank branches, and at the same time, the United States is pressuring Korea to open their markets to U.S. banks. GATT wants to see more free trade in international services, but the progress is slow.

Promotion

Companies can run the same advertising and promotion campaigns used in the home market or change them for each local market.

Consider the message. The company can change the message at three different levels. The company can use one message everywhere, only varying the language, name, and colors. Exxon used "Put a tiger in your tank" with minor variations and gained international recognition. Colors might be changed to avoid taboos in some countries. Purple is associated with death in Burma and some Latin American nations; white is a mourning color in Japan; and green is associated with disease in Malaysia. Even names and headlines have to be modified. In Germany, *mist* means "manure," *scotch* (Scotch tape) means "schmuck," and Pepsi's "Come Alive with Pepsi" was translated as "Come Out of the Grave with Pepsi." In Spain, Chevrolet's *Nova* translates as "it doesn't go!" An Electrolux vacuum cleaner ad, translated from Swedish into English, was run in a Korean magazine reading "Nothing sucks like Electrolux." And a laundry soap ad claiming to wash "really dirty parts" was translated in French-speaking Quebec to read "a soap for washing 'private parts.' "

The next possibility is to use the same theme globally but adapt the copy to each local market:

> A Camay soap commercial showed a beautiful woman bathing. In Venezuela, a man was seen in the bathroom; in Italy and France, only a man's hand was seen; and in Japan, the man waited outside.

Finally, some companies encourage or allow their ad agencies to adapt the theme and execution to each local market. Consider the following two examples:

> Kraft uses different ads for Cheez Whiz in different countries, given that household penetration is 95% in Puerto Rico, where the cheese is put on everything; 65% in Canada, where it is spread on toast in the morning breakfast; and 35% in the United States, where it is considered a junk food.

> Renault advertises its car differently in different countries. In France, Renault is described as a little "supercar," which is fun to drive on highways and in the city. In Germany, Renault emphasizes safety, modern engineering, and interior comfort. In Italy, Renault emphasizes road handling and acceleration. And in Finland, Renault emphasizes solid construction and reliability.

The use of media also requires international adaptation because media availability varies from country to country. Norway and Sweden do not permit television advertising. Belgium and France do not allow advertising cigarettes and alcoholic drinks on TV. Austria and Italy regulate TV advertising to children. Saudi Arabia does not want advertisers to use women in ads. India taxes advertising. Magazines vary in their availability and effectiveness; they play a major role in Italy and a minor one in Austria. Newspapers have a national reach in the United Kingdom, but the advertiser can buy only local newspaper coverage in Spain.

Marketers must also adapt their sales-promotion techniques to different markets. Germany and Greece, for example, prohibit coupons, whereas coupons are the leading form of consumer sales promotion in the United States. France prohibits games of chance and limits premiums and gifts to 5% of product value. The result of these varying restrictions is that international companies generally assign sales promotion as a responsibility of local management.

Price

Multinationals face several specific pricing problems when selling abroad. They must deal with price escalation, transfer prices, dumping charges, and gray markets.

When companies sell their goods abroad, they face a *price escalation* problem. A Gucci handbag may sell for $120 in Italy and $240 in the United States. Why? Gucci has to add the cost of transportation, tariffs, importer margin, wholesaler margin, and retailer margin to its factory price. Depending on these added costs, as well as the currency-fluctuation risk, the product might have to sell for two to five times as much in another country to make the same profit for the manufacturer. In addition to this, the cost escalation varies from country to country: the question then is how to set the prices in different countries. Companies have three choices:

1. *Setting a Uniform Price Everywhere:* Thus Coca-Cola might want to charge 40 cents everywhere in the world. But then Coca-Cola would earn quite different profit rates in different countries because of varying escalation costs. Also this would result in the price being too high a price in poor countries and not high enough in rich countries.

2. *Setting a Market-Based Price in Each Country:* Here Coca-Cola would charge what each country could afford. But this ignores differences in the actual cost from country to country. Also it would lead to a situation where middlemen in low-price countries transshipped their Coca-Cola to high-price countries.

3. *Setting a Cost-Based Price in Each Country:* Here Coca-Cola would use a standard markup of its costs everywhere. But this might price Coca-Cola out of the market in countries where its costs are high.

Another problem arises when a company sets a *transfer price* for goods that it ships to its foreign subsidiaries. Consider the following:

> The Swiss pharmaceutical company Hoffman-LaRoche charged its Italian subsidiary only $22 a kilo for Librium in order to make high profits in Italy where the corporate taxes were lower. It charged its British subsidiary $925 per kilo for the same Librium in order to make high profits at home instead of in Britain, where the corporate taxes were high. The British Monopoly Commission sued Hoffman-LaRoche for back taxes and won.

If the company charges too high a price to a subsidiary, it ends up paying higher tariff duties, although it may pay lower income taxes in the foreign country. If the company charges too low a price to its subsidiary, it can be charged with *dumping*. Dumping is indicated when a company either charges less than its costs or less than it charges in its home market. Thus Zenith accused Japanese television manufacturers of dumping their TV sets on the U.S. market. When the U.S. Customs Bureau finds evidence of dumping, it can levy a dumping tariff. Various governments are watching for abuses and often force companies to charge the *arm's-length price*, namely, the price charged by other competitors for the same or similar product.

Many multinationals are plagued by the *gray-market* problem. For example:

> Minolta sold its cameras to dealers in Hong Kong for a lower price than in Germany because of lower transportation costs and tariffs. The Hong Kong dealers worked on smaller margins than the German retailers, who preferred high markups to high volume. Minolta's cameras ended up selling at retail for $174 in Hong Kong and $270 in Germany. Some Hong Kong wholesalers noticed this price difference and shipped Minolta cameras to German dealers for less than they were paying the German distributor. The German distributor couldn't sell his stock and complained to Minolta.

Very often a company finds some enterprising distributors buying more than they can sell in their own country and transshipping goods to another country in competition with the established distributor in order to take advantage of price differences. Multinationals try to prevent gray markets by policing the distributors, or by raising their prices to lower-cost distributors, or by altering the product characteristics or service warranties for different countries.

Distribution Channels

The international company must take a *whole-channel* view of the problem of distributing its products to the final users. Figure 16-5 shows the three major links between the seller and ultimate user. In the first link, *seller's international marketing*

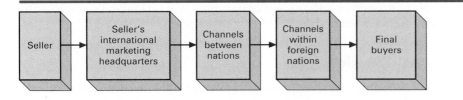

FIGURE 16-5
Whole-Channel Concept for
International Marketing

headquarters, the export department or international division makes decisions on channels and other marketing-mix elements. The second link, *channels between nations*, gets the products to the borders of the foreign nations. It consists of decisions on the types of intermediaries (agents, trading companies, and the like), the type of transportation (air, sea, and so on), and the financing and risk arrangements. The third link, *channels within foreign nations*, gets the products from their foreign entry point to the final buyers and users. Too many American manufacturers think their job is done once the product leaves their factory. They should pay attention to how the product moves within the foreign country.

Within-country channels of distribution vary considerably among countries. There are striking differences in the *number* and *types of middlemen* serving each foreign market. To sell soap in Japan, Procter & Gamble has to work through what is probably the most complicated distribution system in the world. It must sell to a *general wholesaler*, who sells to a *product wholesaler*, who sells to a *product-specialty wholesaler*, who sells to a *regional wholesaler*, who sells to a *local wholesaler*, who finally sells to *retailers*. All these distribution levels can result in the doubling or tripling of the consumers' price over the importer's price.[10] If P&G takes the same soap to tropical Africa, the company might sell to an *import wholesaler*, who sells to several *jobbers*, who sell to *petty traders* (mostly women) working in local markets.

Another difference lies in the *size and character of retail units* abroad. Where large-scale retail chains dominate the U.S. scene, much foreign retailing is in the hands of many small independent retailers. In India, millions of retailers operate tiny shops or sell in open markets. Their markups are high, but the real price is brought down through price haggling. Supermarkets would conceivably bring down prices, but they are difficult to start because of many economic and cultural barriers.[11] People's incomes are low, and they must shop daily for small amounts and are limited to whatever quantity can be carried home on foot or on a bicycle. Also, homes lack storage and refrigeration space to keep food fresh for several days. Packaging costs are kept low in order to keep the prices low. In India, cigarettes are often bought singly. Breaking bulk remains an important function of middlemen and helps perpetuate the long channels of distribution that are a major obstacle to the expansion of large-scale retailing in developing countries.

Deciding on the Marketing Organization

Companies manage their international marketing activities in at least three ways.

Export Department

A firm normally gets into international marketing by simply shipping out the goods. If its international sales expand, the company organizes an export department consisting of a sales manager and a few assistants. As sales increase further, the export department is expanded to include various marketing services so that the company can go after business more aggressively. If the firm moves into joint ventures or direct investment, the export department will no longer be adequate to manage international operations.

International Division

Many companies become involved in several international markets and ventures. A company might export to one country, license to another, have a joint venture in a third, and own a subsidiary in a fourth. Sooner or later it will create an international division to handle all its international activity. The international division is headed by an international-division president, who sets goals and budgets and is responsible for the company's growth in the international market.

International divisions are organized in a variety of ways. The international

Global Marketing 16-5

The World's Champion Marketers: The Japanese

Few dispute that the Japanese have performed an economic miracle since World War II. In a relatively short time, they have achieved global market leadership in industries thought to be "mature" and dominated by impregnable giants: autos, motorcycles, watches, cameras, optical instruments, steel, shipbuilding, musical instruments, zippers, radios, television, video recorders, hand calculators, and so on. Japanese firms are currently moving into the number-two position in computers and construction equipment and making strong inroads into the chemical, rubber tires, pharmaceutical, and machine-tool industries. They are building a stronger position in designer clothing and cosmetics and slowly moving into aircraft manufacture.

Many theories have been offered to explain Japan's global successes. Some point to its unique business practices, such as lifetime employment, quality circles, consensus management, and just-in-time production. Others point to the supportive role of government policies and subsidies, the existence of powerful trading companies, and businesses' access to low-cost bank financing. Still others view Japan's success as based on unfair dumping practices, protected markets, and almost-zero defense industry costs.

One of the main keys to Japan's performance is its skill in marketing-strategy formulation and implementation. The Japanese came to the United States to study marketing and went home understanding its principles better than many U.S. companies did. The Japanese know how to select a market, enter it, build their market share, and protect their leadership position against competitors' attacks.

Selecting Markets

The Japanese government and companies work hard to identify attractive global markets. They favor global industries that are capital intensive and knowledge intensive but that require only small quantities of natural resources. Candidates include consumer electronics, cameras, watches, motorcycles, and pharmaceuticals. They prefer product markets that are in a state of technological evolution. They identify product markets where consumers are dissatisfied. They look for industries where the market leaders are complacent or underfinanced. They adopt a strategic intent to dominate these industries and reduce or destroy competition.

Entering Markets

The Japanese send study teams into the target country to spend several weeks or months evaluating the market and figuring out a strategy. They study and license existing technology from abroad. They manufacture first in Japan and build their base, discouraging foreign competitors from selling in Japan through a variety of tariff and nontariff barriers. They often enter a foreign market by selling their products to a private brander, such as an American department store or manufacturer. Later, they will introduce their own brand—a low-price, stripped-down product, or a product as good as the competitions' but priced lower, or a product exhibiting higher quality or new features or designs. The Japanese proceed to line up good distribution in order to provide reliable service to their customers. They rely on advertising to bring their products to the public's attention. A key

division's corporate staff consists of specialists in marketing, manufacturing, research, finance, planning, and personnel; they plan for and provide services to various operating units. The operating units can be organized according to one or more of three principles. They can be *geographical organizations*. Reporting to the international-division president might be regional vice-presidents for North America, Latin America, Europe, Africa, the Middle East, and the Far East. Reporting to the regional vice-presidents are country managers who are responsible for a salesforce, sales branches, distributors, and licensees in the respective countries. Or the operating units may be *world product groups*, each with an international vice-president responsible for worldwide sales of each product group. The vice-presidents may draw on corporate-staff area specialists for expertise on different geographical areas. Finally, the operating units may be *international subsidiaries*,

characteristic of their entry strategy is to build market share rather than early profits. The Japanese are patient capitalists who will wait even a decade before realizing their profits.

Building Market Share

Once Japanese firms gain a market foothold, they direct their energies toward expanding their market share. They rely on product-development strategies and market-development strategies. They pour money into product improvement, product upgrading, and product proliferation, so that they can offer more and better things than the competition. They spot new opportunities through market segmentation and sequence market development across a number of countries, with the aim of building a network of world markets and production locations. They gain further volume through an aggressive program of buying up competitors or joint venturing with them.

Protecting Market Share

Once the Japanese achieve market domination, they find themselves in the role of defenders rather than attackers. The Japanese defense strategy is a good offense through continuous product development and refined market segmentation. Japanese firms use two market-oriented principles to maintain their leadership. The first is "zero-customer-feedback time," whereby they survey recent customers to find out how they like the product and what improvements they would want. The second is "zero-product-improvement time," whereby they add worthwhile product improvements continuously, so

that the product remains the leader. The Japanese also protect themselves by hiring U.S. lawyers, public relations people, and former public officials to defend their U.S. interests and improve their image.

Responding to the Japanese Competitors

Although U.S. and European firms were slow to respond to Japanese inroads, most of them are now mounting counteroffensives. IBM is adding new products, automatizing its factories, sourcing components from abroad, and entering strategic partnerships with others. Black & Decker is closing product-line gaps, increasing product quality, streamlining manufacturing, and pricing more aggressively. More companies are copying Japanese practices that work — quality control, quality circles, consensus management, just-in-time production — when they fit the company culture. And more companies are entering the Japanese market to compete on their soil. Although getting in and operating successfully in Japan takes a considerable amount of money and patience, several companies have done an outstanding job, including Coca-Cola, McDonald's, Max Factor, Xerox, IBM, and Warner-Lambert.

SOURCE: For further discussion, see Philip Kotler, Liam Fahey, and Somkid Jatusripitak, *The New Competition* (Englewood Cliffs, NJ, Prentice-Hall, 1985).

each headed by a president. The various subsidiary presidents report to the president of the international division.

Many multinationals shift between these three types of organizations because each creates problems. The history of Westinghouse's international operations is illustrative:[12]

> Before 1960, Westinghouse had several foreign subsidiaries that were loosely linked through an international division. To achieve more coordination, Westinghouse established in 1960 a strong international division with regional and country managers. However, several of Westinghouse's product groups found it frustrating to work through the international division, and they pressed for global control over planning and implementation. The corporation acceded in 1971 and disbanded the international division and gave 125 division managers worldwide responsibility. However, the results were not uniformly good. Many product groups did not pay sufficient attention to the international opportunities, since most of their business was domestic; they lacked international expertise; and they failed to coordinate their international operations with each other. Not surprisingly, in 1979 Westinghouse established a matrix organization consisting of an international vice-president who managed four regional managers, who in turn managed country managers, along with an overlay of international product managers from the various product groups. The matrix solution promised to be sensitive both to local area needs and to global product strategy but at greater cost and greater management conflict along the way.

Global Marketing 16-6

Should International Companies Organize Globally, Locally, or "Glocally"?

International corporations face a major strategy tradeoff between standardizing versus localizing their global operations and marketing. The argument for standardizing is that it saves costs and allows the promotion of one central brand or corporate image worldwide. The argument for localizing is that every market is different and victory will go to the competitor who best adapts the offer to the local market.

Clearly the answer is "it all depends." Bartlett and Ghoshal proposed the circumstances under which each approach works best. In their *Managing Across Borders,* they described a number of forces that favor *global integration* (e.g., capital-intensive production, homogeneous demand, and so on) versus *national responsiveness* (e.g., local standards and barriers, strong local preferences). They went on to distinguish three organizational strategies:

1. A *global strategy* treats the world as a single market. This strategy is warranted when the forces for global integration are strong and the forces for national responsiveness are weak. This characterizes consumer electronics, for example, where most buyers around the world will accept a fairly standardized pocket radio, CD player, TV,

and so on. Bartlett and Ghoshal go on to point out that Matsushita has performed better than GE and Philips in the consumer electronics market because Matsushita operates in a more globally coordinated and standardized way.

2. A *multinational strategy* treats the world as a portfolio of national opportunities. This strategy is warranted when the forces favoring national responsiveness are strong and the forces favoring global integration are weak. This characterizes the branded packaged goods business with its food products, cleaning products, and so on. Bartlett and Ghoshal cite Unilever as a better performer than Kao and P&G because Unilever grants more autonomy in decision making to its local branches.

3. A *"glocal" strategy* standardizes certain core elements and localizes other elements. This strategy makes sense for an industry such as telecommunications where each nation requires some adaptation of its equipment but the providing company can also standardize some of the core components. Bartlett and Ghoshal cite Ericsson as balancing these considerations better than NEC (which is too globally oriented) and ITT (which is too locally oriented).

Global Organization

Several firms have passed beyond the international-division stage and have become truly global organizations (see Global Marketing 16-5). They have stopped thinking of themselves as national marketers who have ventured abroad and now think of themselves as global marketers. The top corporate management and staff plan worldwide manufacturing facilities, marketing policies, financial flows, and logistical systems. The global operating units report directly to the chief executive or executive committee, not to the head of an international division. Executives are trained in worldwide operations, not just domestic or international. Management is recruited from many countries; components and supplies are purchased where they can be obtained at the least cost; and investments are made where the anticipated returns are greatest.

Yet companies that operate in many countries face several organizational complexities. For example, when it comes to pricing IBM's AS400 computers to a large banking system in Germany, how much influence should be wielded by IBM's AS400 product manager, IBM's market manager for the banking sector, and IBM's German country manager? This partly boils down to the question of whether the decisions should be made globally with a high degree of standardization, or whether the decisions should be made locally. This is discussed in Global Marketing 16-6.

The message, then, is that international companies must review whether they have organized their international operations and marketing programs appropriately, given the characteristics of the global industry and global market in which they operate.

One of the most successful "glocal" companies is ABB, formed by a merger between the Swedish company ASEA and the Swiss company Brown Boveri. ABB's products are industrial, including power transformers, electrical installations, instrumentation, auto components, air-conditioning equipment, railroad equipment, and so on. With $25 billion in sales and 240,000 employees, ABB is headed by Percy Barnevik, one of Europe's most dynamic CEOs. The company's motto is "ABB is a global company local everywhere." Barnevik established English as the company's official language (all ABB managers must be conversant in English) and all financial results must be reported in dollars. ABB is organized with the aim of reconciling three contradictions: to be global and local; to be big and small; and to be radically decentralized with centralized reporting and control. ABB has only 100 staff people at headquarters, compared to the 3,000 who populate Siemens headquarters. The company's many product lines are organized into eight business segments, 50 business areas, 1,200 companies, and 4,500 profit centers, with the average employee belonging to a profit center of around 50 employees. Managers are regularly rotated among countries and mixed-nationality teams are encouraged. Depending on the type of business, some are treated as superlocal businesses with lots of autonomy and others as superglobal businesses with major central control. Barnevik uses a proprietary software system called Abacus which allows him to review performance data each month in each of the 4,500 profit centers. When the system flags exceptional and deficient performances, he contacts the appropriate country managers, business area managers, and local company presidents. He wants his managers to be locally knowledgeable but also attuned to global considerations in making their decisions.

SOURCE: See Christopher A. Bartlett and Sumantra Ghoshal, *Managing Across Borders* (Cambridge, MA: Harvard Business School Press, 1989); and William Taylor, "The Logic of Global Business: An Interview with ABB's Percy Barnevik," *Harvard Business Review*, March–April 1991, pp. 91–105.

SUMMARY ❖

Companies no longer can pay attention only to their domestic market, no matter how large it is. Many industries are global industries, and their leading firms achieve lower costs and higher brand awareness. Protectionist measures can only slow down the invasion of superior goods; the best company defense is a sound global offense.

At the same time, global marketing is risky because of fluctuating exchange rates, unstable governments, protectionist barriers, high product- and communication-adaptation costs, and several other factors. Yet the international product life cycle suggests that comparative advantage in many industries will move from high-cost to low-cost countries, and companies cannot simply stay domestic and expect to maintain their markets. Given the potential gains and risks of international marketing, companies need a systematic way to make sound international marketing decisions.

The first step is to understand the international marketing environment, particularly the international trade system. In considering a particular foreign market, its economic, political, legal, and cultural characteristics must be assessed. Second, the company must consider what proportion of foreign to total sales to seek, whether to do business in a few or many countries, and what types of countries to enter. The third step is to decide which particular markets to enter, and this calls for evaluating the probable rate of return on investment against the level of risk. Fourth, the company has to decide how to enter each attractive market. Many companies start as indirect or direct exporters and then move to licensing, joint ventures, and finally direct investment; this company evolution has been called the internationalization process. Companies must next decide on the extent to which their products, promotion, price, and distribution should be adapted to individual foreign markets. Finally, the company must develop an effective organization for pursuing international marketing. Most firms start with an export department and graduate to an international division. A few become global companies, which means that top management plans and organizes on a global basis.

NOTES ❖

1. See John A. Quelch, Robert D. Buzzell, and Eric R. Salama, *The Marketing Challenge of 1992* (Boston: Addison-Wesley, 1990).

2. Michael E. Porter, *Competitive Strategy* (New York: Free Press, 1980), p. 275.

3. Igal Ayal and Jehiel Zif, "Market Expansion Strategies in Multinational Marketing," *Journal of Marketing,* Spring 1979, pp. 84–94.

4. James K. Sweeney, "A Small Company Enters the European Market," *Harvard Business Review,* September–October 1970, pp. 127–28.

5. See David S. R. Leighton, "Deciding When to Enter International Markets," in *Handbook of Modern Marketing,* ed. Victor P. Buell (New York: McGraw-Hill, 1970), sec. 20, pp. 23-28.

6. However, see J. Peter Killing, "How to Make a Global Joint Venture Work," *Harvard Business Review,* May–June 1982, pp. 120–27.

7. See Jan Johanson and Finn Wiedersheim-Paul, "The Internationalization of the Firm," *Journal of Management Studies,* October 1975, pp. 305–22.

8. See Stan Reid, "The Decision Maker and Export Entry and Expansion," *Journal of International Business Studies,* Fall 1981, pp. 101–12; Igal Ayal, "Industry Export Performance: Assessment and Prediction," *Journal of Marketing,* Summer 1982, pp. 54–61; and Somkid Jatusripitak, *The Exporting Behavior of Manufacturing Firms* (Ann Arbor,MI: University of Michigan Press, 1986).

9. Warren J. Keegan, *Multinational Marketing Management,* 4th ed. (Englewood Cliffs, NJ: Prentice Hall, 1989), pp. 378–81.

10. See William D. Hartley, "How Not to Do It: Cumbersome Japanese Distribution System Stumps U.S. Concerns," *The Wall Street Journal,* March 2, 1972.

11. See Arieh Goldman, "Outreach of Consumers and the Modernization of Urban Food Retailing in Developing Countries," *Journal of Marketing,* October 1974, pp. 8–16.

12. See Christopher A. Bartlett, "How Multinational Organizations Evolve," *Journal of Business Strategy,* Summer 1982, pp. 20–32. Also see Christopher A. Bartlett and Sumantra Ghoshal, *Managing Across Borders: The Transnational Solution* (Boston: Harvard Business School Press, 1989).

17

Managing Product Lines, Brands, and Packaging

In the factory, we make cosmetics; in the store, we sell hope.

CHARLES REVSON

Any damn fool can put on a deal, but it takes genius, faith, and perseverance to create a brand.

DAVID OGILVY

W|e are now ready to examine each marketing-mix element in detail. We will begin with product, the most important element in the marketing mix. We will address the following questions in this chapter:

- What is a product?
- How can a company build and manage its product mix and product lines?
- How can a company make better brand decisions?
- How can packaging and labeling be used as a marketing tool?

What Is a Product?

We define *product* as follows:

❖ A product *is anything that can be offered to a market for attention, acquisition, use, or consumption that might satisfy a want or need.*

Products that are marketed include *physical goods* (e.g., automobiles, books), *services* (e.g., haircuts, concerts), *persons* (e.g., Michael Jordan, Barbra Streisand), *places* (e.g., Hawaii, Venice), *organizations* (e.g., American Heart Association, Girl Scouts), and *ideas* (e.g., family planning, safe driving).

Five Levels of a Product

In planning its market offer or product, the marketer needs to think through five product levels (see Figure 17-1).[1] The most fundamental level is the *core benefit*, namely the fundamental service or benefit that the customer is really buying. In the case of a hotel, the night guest is buying "rest and sleep." In the case of drills, the purchasing agent is buying "holes." Marketers must see themselves as benefit providers.

The marketer has to turn the core benefit into a *generic product*, namely a basic version of the product. Thus a hotel consists of a building with rooms to rent. In the same way, we can recognize other generic products — a toaster, a sheet of steel, a concert, a medical examination.

At the third level, the marketer prepares an *expected product*, namely a set of attributes and conditions that buyers normally expect and agree to when they purchase this product. Hotel guests, for example, expect a clean bed, soap and towels, plumbing fixtures, a telephone, clothes closet, and a relative degree of quiet. Since most hotels can meet this minimum expectation, the traveler normally will have no preference and will settle for whichever hotel is most convenient.

At the fourth level, the marketer prepares an *augmented product*, namely one that includes additional services and benefits that distinguish the company's offer from competitors' offers. A hotel, for example, can augment its product by including a television set, shampoo, fresh flowers, rapid check-in, express checkout, fine

FIGURE 17-1
Five Product Levels

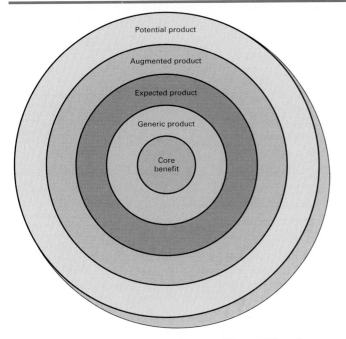

dining and room service, and so on. Elmer Wheeler once observed, "Don't sell the steak—sell the sizzle."

Today's competition essentially takes place at the product-augmentation level. (In less-developed countries, competition takes place mostly at the expected product level.) Product augmentation leads the marketer to look at the buyer's total *consumption system*: "The way a purchaser of a product performs the total task of whatever it is that he or she is trying to accomplish when using the product."[2] In this way, the marketer will recognize many opportunities for augmenting its offer in a competitively effective way. According to Levitt:

> The new competition *is not between what companies produce in their factories, but between what they add to their factory output in the form of packaging, services, advertising, customer advice, financing, delivery arrangements, warehousing, and other things that people value.*[3]

However, some things should be noted about product-augmentation strategy. First, each augmentation costs the company money. The marketer has to ask whether customers will pay enough to cover the extra cost. Second, augmented benefits soon become expected benefits. Thus hotel guests now expect a television set, shampoo, and other amenities in their room. This means that competitors will have to search for still further features and benefits to add to their offer. Third, as companies raise the price of their augmented product, some competitors can revert to offering a "stripped-down" product at a much lower price. Thus alongside the growth of fine hotels like Four Seasons, Westin, and Hyatt we see the emergence of lower-cost hotels and motels catering to clients who simply want the basic product.

At the fifth level stands the *potential product*, namely all of the augmentations and transformations that this product might ultimately undergo in the future. Whereas the augmented product describes what is included in the product today, the potential product points to its possible evolution. Here is where companies search aggressively for new ways to satisfy customers and distinguish their offer. The recent emergence of all-suite hotels where the guest occupies a set of rooms represents an innovative transformation of the traditional hotel product.

Some of the most successful companies add benefits to their offer that not only *satisfy* customers but also *delight* them. Delighting is a matter of adding *unexpected surprises* to the offer. Thus the hotel guest finds candy on the pillow, or a bowl of fruit, or a videorecorder with optional videotapes. The company is saying that we want to treat you in a special way.

Product Hierarchy

Each product is related to certain other products. Product hierarchies stretch from basic needs to particular items that satisfy these needs. We can identify seven levels of the product hierarchy. Here they are defined and illustrated for life insurance:

1. *Need Family:* The core need that underlies the product family. Example: security.
2. *Product Family:* All the product classes that can satisfy a core need with reasonable effectiveness. Example: savings and income.
3. *Product Class:* A group of products within the product family recognized as having a certain functional coherence. Example: financial instruments.
4. *Product Line:* A group of products within a product class that are closely related because they function in a similar manner or are sold to the same customer groups or are marketed through the same types of outlets or fall within given price ranges. Example: life insurance.
5. *Product Type:* Those items within a product line that share one of several possible forms of the product. Example: term life.
6. *Brand:* The name associated with one or more items in the product line that is used to identify the source or character of the item(s). Example: Prudential.
7. *Item:* A distinct unit within a brand or product line that is distinguishable by size, price, appearance, or some other attribute. The item is called a *stockkeeping unit*, or product variant. Example: Prudential renewable term life insurance.

Another example: the need "hope" gives rise to a product family called toiletries and a product class within that family called cosmetics, of which one line is lipstick, which has different product forms, such as tube lipstick, which is offered as a brand called Revlon in a particular type, such as "frosted."

Two other terms frequently arise. A *product system* is a group of diverse but related items that function in a compatible manner. For example, the Nikon Company sells a basic 35mm camera along with an extensive set of lenses, filters, and other options that constitute a product system. A *product mix* (or product assortment) is the set of all products and items that a particular seller makes available to the buyers.

Product Classifications

Marketers have traditionally classified products on the basis of varying product characteristics. The thought is that each product type has an appropriate marketing-mix strategy. Marketing Concepts and Tools 17-1 presents the major classifications of consumer and industrial goods and their marketing-strategy implications.

With this background, we are ready to examine company decisions regarding the product mix, product lines, and individual products.

Product-Mix Decisions

We will first consider product-mix decisions.

❖ A product mix *(also called* product assortment*) is the set of all product lines and items that a particular seller offers for sale to buyers.*

For example, Kodak's product mix consists of two strong lines: information and image products. NEC's (of Japan) basic product mix consists of communication and computer products. Michelin has three product lines: tires, maps, and restaurant-rating services.

A company's product mix will have a certain width, length, depth, and consistency. These concepts are illustrated in Table 17-1 for selected Procter & Gamble consumer products.

The *width* of P&G's product mix refers to how many different product lines the company carries. Table 17-1 shows a product-mix width of five lines. (In fact, P&G produces many additional lines — hair-care products, health-care products, personal-hygiene products, beverages, food, and so on.)

The *length* of P&G's product mix refers to the total number of items in its product mix. In Table 17-1, it is 26. We can also talk about the average length of a line at P&G. This is obtained by dividing the total length (here 26) by the number of lines (here 5), or an average product length of 5.17.

The *depth* of P&G's product mix refers to how many variants are offered of each product in the line. Thus if Crest comes in three sizes and two formulations (regular and mint), Crest has a depth of six. By counting the number of variants within each brand, the average depth of P&G's product mix can be calculated.

The *consistency* of the product mix refers to how closely related the various product lines are in end use, production requirements, distribution channels, or some other way. P&G's product lines are consistent insofar as they are consumer goods that go through the same distribution channels. The lines are less consistent insofar as they perform different functions for the buyers.

These four dimensions of the product mix provide the handles for defining the company's product strategy. The company can expand its business in four ways. The company can add new product lines, thus widening its product mix. The company can lengthen each product line. The company can add more product variants to each product and deepen its product mix. Finally, the company can pursue more product-line consistency or less, depending upon whether it wants to acquire a strong reputation in a single field or participate in several fields.

Product-mix planning is largely the responsibility of the company's strategic planners. They must assess, with information supplied by the company marketers, which product lines to grow, maintain, harvest, and divest.

TABLE 17-1 Product-Mix Width and Product-Line Length for Procter & Gamble Products (Including Dates of Introduction)

	PRODUCT-MIX WIDTH				
	Detergents	Toothpaste	Bar Soap	Disposable Diapers	Paper Tissue
PRODUCT-LINE LENGTH	Ivory Snow 1930 Dreft 1933 Tide 1946 Cheer Oxydol 1952 Dash 1954 Bold 1965 Gain 1966 Era 1972 Solo 1979	Gleem 1952 Crest 1955 Denquel 1980	Ivory 1879 Kirk's 1885 Lava 1893 Camay 1926 Zest 1952 Safeguard 1963 Coast 1974	Pampers 1961 Luvs 1976	Charmin 1928 White Cloud 1958 Puffs 1960 Banner 1982

Product Classifications and Their Marketing-Strategy Implications

Durable Goods, Nondurable Goods, and Services

Products can be classified into three groups according to their durability or tangibility:

- *Nondurable Goods:* Nondurable goods are tangible goods that normally are consumed in one or a few uses. Examples include beer, soap, and salt. Since these goods are consumed fast and purchased frequently, the appropriate strategy is to make them available in many locations, charge only a small markup, and advertise heavily to induce trial and build preference.

- *Durable Goods:* Durable goods are tangible goods that normally survive many uses. Examples include refrigerators, machine tools, and clothing. Durable products normally require more personal selling and service, command a higher margin, and require more seller guarantees.

- *Services:* Services are activities, benefits, or satisfactions that are offered for sale. Examples include haircuts and repairs. Services are intangible, inseparable, variable, and perishable. As a result, they normally require more quality control, supplier credibility, and adaptability.

Consumer-Goods Classification

Consumers buy a vast array of goods. These goods can be classified on the basis of *consumer shopping habits.* We can distinguish between convenience, shopping, specialty, and unsought goods.

- *Convenience Goods:* Goods that the customer usually purchases frequently, immediately, and with a minimum of effort. Examples include tobacco products, soaps, and newspapers.

Convenience goods can be further divided into staples, impulse goods, and emergency goods. *Staples* are goods that consumers purchase on a regular basis. For example, one buyer might routinely purchase Heinz ketchup, Crest toothpaste, and Ritz crackers. *Impulse goods* are purchased without any planning or search effort. These goods are usually displayed widely. Thus candy bars and magazines are placed next to checkout counters because shoppers may not have thought of buying them until spotting them. *Emergency goods* are purchased when a need is urgent—umbrellas during a rainstorm, boots and shovels during the first winter snowstorm. Manufacturers of emergency goods will place them in many outlets so as to capture the sale when the customer needs these goods.

- *Shopping Goods:* Goods that the customer, in the process of selection and purchase, characteristically compares on such bases as suitability, quality, price, and style. Examples include furniture, clothing, used cars, and major appliances.

Shopping goods can be divided into homogeneous and heterogeneous goods. The buyer sees *homogeneous shopping goods* as similar in quality but different enough in price to justify shopping comparisons. The seller has to "talk price" to the buyer. But in shopping for clothing, furniture, and other *heterogeneous shopping goods*, product features are often more important to the consumer than the price. The seller of heterogeneous shopping goods must therefore carry a wide assortment to satisfy individual tastes and must have well-trained salespeople to provide information and advice to customers.

- *Specialty Goods:* Goods with unique characteristics and/or brand identification for which a significant group of buyers are habitually willing to make a special purchasing effort. Examples include specific brands and types of fancy goods, cars, stereo components, photographic equipment, and men's suits.

A Mercedes, for example, is a specialty good because interested buyers will travel far to buy one. Specialty goods do not involve the buyer in making comparisons; buyers invest time only to reach dealers carrying the wanted products. The dealers do not need convenient locations; however, they must let prospective buyers know their locations.

- *Unsought Goods:* Goods that the consumer does not know about or knows about but does not normally think of buying. New products, such as smoke detectors and food processors, are unsought goods until the consumer is made aware of them through advertising. The classic examples of known but unsought goods are life insurance, cemetery plots, gravestones, and encyclopedias.

Unsought goods require substantial marketing effort in the form of advertising and personal selling. Some of the most sophisticated personal-selling techniques have developed from the challenge to sell unsought goods.

Industrial-Goods Classification

Organizations buy a vast variety of goods and services. A useful industrial-goods classification would suggest appropriate marketing strategies in the industrial market. Industrial goods can be classified in terms of *how they enter the production process and their relative costliness*. We can distinguish three groups: materials and parts, capital items, and supplies and services.

- *Materials and Parts:* Goods that enter the manufacturer's product completely. They fall into two classes: raw materials and manufactured materials and parts.

Raw materials fall into two major classes: *farm products* (e.g., wheat, cotton, livestock, fruits, and vegetables) and *natural products* (e.g., fish, lumber, crude petroleum, iron ore). Each is marketed somewhat differently. *Farm products* are supplied by many producers who turn them over to marketing intermediaries who provide assembly, grading, storage, transportation, and selling services. Farm products are somewhat expandable in the long run but not in the short run. Farm products' perishable and seasonal nature gives rise to special marketing practices. Their commodity character results in relatively little advertising and promotional activity, with some exceptions. From time to time, commodity groups will launch campaigns to promote the consumption of their product—potatoes, prunes, milk. And some producers brand their product—Sunkist oranges, Chiquita bananas.

Natural products are highly limited in supply. They usually have great bulk and low unit value and require substantial transportation to move them from producer to user. There are fewer and larger producers, who often market them directly to industrial users. Because the users depend on these materials, long-term-supply contracts are common. The homogeneity of natural materials limits the amount of demand-creation activity. Price and delivery reliability are the major factors influencing the selection of suppliers.

Manufactured materials and parts are exemplified by *component materials* (e.g., iron, yarn, cement, wires) and *component parts* (e.g., small motors, tires, castings). *Component materials* are usually fabricated further—for example, pig iron is made into steel, and yarn is woven into cloth. The standardized nature of component materials usually means that price and supplier reliability are the most important purchase factors. *Component parts* enter the finished product completely with no further change in form, as when small motors are put into vacuum cleaners, and tires are put on automobiles. Most manufactured materials and parts are sold directly to industrial users, with orders often placed a year or more in advance. Price and services are the major marketing considerations, and branding and advertising tend to be less important.

- *Capital Items:* Long-lasting goods that facilitate developing and/or managing the finished product. They include two groups: installations and equipment.

Installations consist of *buildings* (e.g., factories and offices) and *equipment* (e.g., generators, drill presses, computers, elevators). Installations are major purchases. They are usually bought directly from the producer, with the typical sale preceded by a long negotiation period. The producers use a top-notch salesforce, which often includes sales engineers. The producers have to be willing to design to specification and to supply postsale services. Advertising is used but is much less important than personal selling.

Equipment comprises *portable factory equipment and tools* (e.g., hand tools, lift trucks) and *office equipment* (e.g., typewriters, desks). These types of equipment do not become part of the finished product. They simply help in the production process. They have a shorter life than installations but a longer life than operating supplies. Although some equipment manufacturers sell direct, more often they use middlemen, because the market is geographically dispersed, the buyers are numerous, and the orders are small. Quality, features, price, and service are major considerations in vendor selection. The salesforce tends to be more important than advertising, although the latter can be used effectively.

- *Supplies and Services:* Short-lasting goods that facilitate developing and/or managing the finished product at all.

Supplies are of two kinds: *operating supplies* (e.g., lubricants, coal, typing paper, pencils) and *maintenance and repair items* (paint, nails, brooms). Supplies are the equivalent of convenience goods in the industrial field, as they are usually purchased with a minimum effort on a straight rebuy basis. They are normally marketed through intermediaries because of the great number of customers, their geographical dispersion, and the low unit value of these goods. Price and service are important considerations, since suppliers are quite standardized, and brand preference is not high.

Business services include *maintenance and repair services* (e.g., window cleaning, typewriter repair) and *business advisory services* (e.g., legal, management consulting, advertising). Maintenance and repair services are usually supplied under contract. Maintenance services are often provided by small producers, and repair services are often available from the manufacturers of the original equipment. Business advisory services are normally new task-buying situations, and the industrial buyer will choose the supplier on the basis of the supplier's reputation and people.

Thus we see that a product's characteristics will have a major influence on marketing strategy. At the same time, marketing strategy will also depend on other factors, such as the product's life-cycle stage, competitors' strategies, and economic conditions.

SOURCE: For some definitions, see *Marketing Definitions: A Glossary of Marketing Terms* (Chicago: American Marketing Association, 1960). Also see Patrick E. Murphy and Ben M. Enis, "Classifying Products Strategically," *Journal of Marketing*, July 1986, pp. 24–42.

Product-Line Decisions

A product mix consists of various product lines.

❖ *A product line is a group of products that are closely related because they perform a similar function, are sold to the same customer groups, are marketed through the same channels, or make up a particular price range.*

Each product line is usually managed by a different executive. In General Electric's Consumer Appliance Division, there are product-line managers for refrigerators, stoves, washing machines, and other appliances. At Northwestern University, there are separate academic deans for the medical school, law school, business school, engineering school, music school, speech school, journalism school, and liberal arts.

Product-Line Analysis

Product-line managers need to know the sales and profits of each item in their line and how their product line compares with competitors' product lines.

PRODUCT-LINE SALES AND PROFITS ❖ The product-line manager needs to know the percentage of total sales and profits contributed by each item in the line. Figure 17-2 shows an example for a five-item product line.

The first item accounts for 50% of total sales and 30% of total profits. The first two items account for 80% of total sales and 60% of total profits. If these two items were suddenly hurt by a competitor, the product line's sales and profitability would collapse. A high concentration of sales in a few items means line vulnerability. These items must be carefully monitored and protected. At the other end, the last item constitutes only 5% of the product line's sales and profits. The product-line manager may even consider dropping this slow-selling item from the line unless it has strong growth potential.

PRODUCT-LINE MARKET PROFILE ❖ The product-line manager must also review how the product line is positioned against competitors' product lines. Consider a paper company with a product line consisting of paper board.[4] Two of

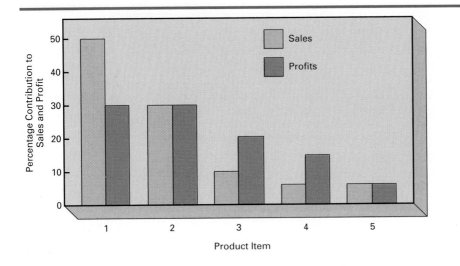

the major attributes of paper board are paper weight and finish quality. Paper weight is usually offered at standard levels of 90, 120, 150, and 180 weight. Finish quality is offered at three standard levels. Figure 17-3 shows the location of the various product-line items of company X and four competitors, A, B, C, and D. Competitor A sells two product items in the extra-high weight class ranging from medium to low finish quality. Competitor B sells four items that vary in weight and finish quality. Competitor C sells three items in which the greater their weight, the greater their finish quality. Competitor D sells three items, all lightweight but varying in finish quality. Finally, company X offers three items that vary in weight and finish quality.

This product-item mapping is useful for designing product-line marketing strategy. It shows which competitors' items are competing against company X's items. For example, company X's low-weight/medium-quality paper competes against competitor D's and B's papers. But its high-weight/medium-quality paper has no direct competitor. The map also reveals possible locations for new-product items. For example, no manufacturer offers a high-weight/low-quality paper. If company X estimates a strong unmet demand and can produce and price this paper right, it could consider adding this item to its line.

Another benefit of product mapping is that it identifies market segments. Figure 17-3 shows the types of paper, by weight and quality, preferred by the general printing industry, the point-of-purchase display industry, and the office-supply industry, respectively. The map shows that company X is well positioned to serve the needs of the general printing industry but is less effective in serving the other two industries and might consider bringing out more paper types that meet these needs.

Product-Line Length

An issue facing product-line managers is optimal product-line length. A product line is too short if the manager can increase profits by adding items; the line is too long if the manager can increase profits by dropping items.

The issue of product-line length is influenced by company objectives. Companies seeking high market share and market growth will carry longer lines. They are less concerned when some items fail to contribute to profits. Companies that emphasize high profitability will carry shorter lines consisting of "cherry-picked" items.

FIGURE 17-3
Product Map for a Paper-
Product Line
Source: Benson P. Shapiro, *Industrial
Product Policy: Managing the Existing
Product Line* (Cambridge, MA:
Marketing Science Institute,
September 1977), p. 101.

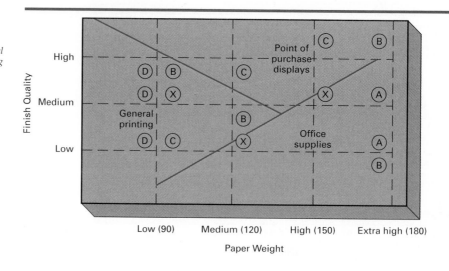

Product lines tend to lengthen over time. Excess manufacturing capacity puts pressure on the product-line manager to develop new items. The salesforce and distributors also pressure for a more complete product line to satisfy their customers. The product-line manager will add items in pursuit of greater sales and profits.

But as items are added, several costs rise: design and engineering costs, inventory-carrying costs, manufacturing-changeover costs, order-processing costs, transportation costs, and new-item promotional costs. Eventually someone calls a halt to the mushrooming product line. Top management may freeze things because of insufficient funds or manufacturing capacity. The controller may question the line's profitability and call for a study. The study will probably show a large number of money-losing items. These items will be dropped in a major effort to increase profitability. A pattern of undisciplined product-line growth followed by massive product pruning will repeat itself many times.

A company can enlarge the length of its product line in two ways: by line stretching and line filling.

LINE-STRETCHING DECISION ❖ Every company's product line covers a certain part of the total possible range. For example, BMW automobiles are located in the upper price range of the automobile market. *Line stretching* occurs when a company lengthens its product line beyond its current range. The company can stretch its line downward, upward, or both ways.

DOWNWARD STRETCH ❖ Many companies initially locate at the upper end of the market and subsequently stretch their line downward.

> IBM historically operated in the large-mainframe end of the computer market, leaving minicomputer manufacture to other firms, such as Digital Equipment and Data General. However, the slowdown in growth of the large-batch-oriented data-processing units led IBM to enter minicomputer manufacture as an avenue to further growth. IBM's interest in minicomputers was further stimulated by its growing interest in computer networks and distributed data-processing systems. This led IBM to stretch further downward into manufacturing personal computers.

Companies often add models to the lower end of their line in order to advertise their brand as starting at a low price. Thus Sears may advertise room air conditioners "starting at $240," and General Motors may advertise a new Chevrolet at

$7,000. These "fighter" or "promotional" models are used to draw in customers on a price basis. The customers, upon seeing the better models, often trade up. This strategy must be used carefully. The "promotional" brand, although stripped, must support the brand's quality image. The seller must also stock the promotional model when it is advertised. Consumers must not feel they were "baited and switched."

A company might stretch downward for any of the following reasons:

- The company is attacked by a competitor at the high end and decides to counterattack by invading the competitor's low end.
- The company finds that slower growth is taking place at the high end.
- The company initially entered the high end to establish a quality image and intended to roll downward.
- The company adds a low-end unit to plug a market hole that would otherwise attract a new competitor.

In making a downward stretch, the company faces risks. The new low-end item might *cannibalize* higher-end items. Consider the following:

> General Electric's Medical Systems Division is the market leader in CT scanners, those expensive diagnostic machines used in hospitals. GE learned that a Japanese competitor was planning to attack its market. GE's guess was that the Japanese model would be smaller, more electronic, and less expensive. The best GE defense would be to introduce a similar machine before the Japanese model entered the market. But some GE executives were concerned that this lower-price version would hurt the sales and higher profit margin on their large CT scanner. But one manager settled the issue by saying: "Aren't we better off to cannibalize ourselves than to let the Japanese do it?"

Or the low-end item might provoke competitors to counteract by moving into the higher end. Or the company's dealers may not be willing or able to handle the lower-end products because they are less profitable or dilute their image. Harley Davidson's dealers neglected the small motorcycles that Harley finally designed to compete with the Japanese.

A major miscalculation of several American companies has been their failure to plug holes in the lower end of their markets. General Motors resisted building smaller cars, and Xerox resisted building smaller copying machines. Japanese companies spotted a major opening and moved in quickly.

UPWARD STRETCH ❖ Companies in the lower end of the market might contemplate entering the higher end. They might be attracted by a higher growth rate, higher margins, or simply the chance to position themselves as full-line manufacturers.

An upward-stretch decision can be risky. Not only are the higher-end competitors well entrenched, but they may counterattack by going downmarket. Prospective customers may not believe that the lower-end company can produce high-quality products. Finally, the company's sales representatives and distributors may lack the talent and training to serve the higher end of the market.

TWO-WAY STRETCH ❖ Companies serving the middle market might decide to stretch their line in both directions. Texas Instruments (TI) introduced its first calculators in the medium-price/medium-quality end of the market. Gradually, it added calculators at the lower end, taking market shares away from Bowmar; and it introduced high-quality calculators selling at lower prices than Hewlett-Packard calculators, which had dominated the high end. This two-way stretch won TI early market leadership in the hand-calculator market.

The Marriott Hotel group also has performed a two-way stretch of its hotel product line. Alongside its medium-price hotels, it added the Marriott Marquis line to serve the upper end of the market, the Courtyard line to serve a lower end of the market, and Fairfield Inns to serve the economy end of the market. Each branded hotel line is aimed at a different target market. Marriott Marquis aims to attract and please top executives; Marriotts, middle managers; Courtyards, salespeople; and Fairfield Inns, vacationers and others on a low travel budget. (See Figure 17-4.) The major risk with this strategy is that some travelers will trade down after finding the lower-price hotels in the Marriott chain have pretty much everything they want. But it is still better for Marriott to capture its customers who move downward than to lose them to competitors.

Line-filling decision. A product line can also be lengthened by adding more items within the present range of the line. There are several motives for line filling: reaching for incremental profits; trying to satisfy dealers who complain about lost sales because of missing items in the line; trying to utilize excess capacity; trying to be the leading full-line company; and trying to plug holes to keep out competitors.

Line filling is overdone if it results in cannibalization and customer confusion. The company needs to differentiate each item in the consumer's mind. Each item should possess a *just-noticeable difference.* According to Weber's law, customers are more attuned to relative than to absolute difference.[5] They will perceive the difference between boards 2 and 3 feet long and boards 20 and 30 feet long but not between boards 29 and 30 feet long. The company should make sure that new-product items have a noticeable difference.

The company should check that the proposed item meets a market need and is not being added simply to satisfy an internal need.

> The famous Edsel automobile, on which Ford lost $350 million, met Ford's internal positioning needs but not the market's needs. Ford noticed that Ford owners would trade up to General Motors cars like Oldsmobile or Buick rather than step up to Ford's Mercury or Lincoln. Ford decided to create a steppingstone car to fill its line. The Edsel was created, but it failed to meet a market need because many similar cars were available, and many buyers were turning to smaller cars.

FIGURE 17-4
Two-Way Product-Line
Stretch: Marriott Hotels

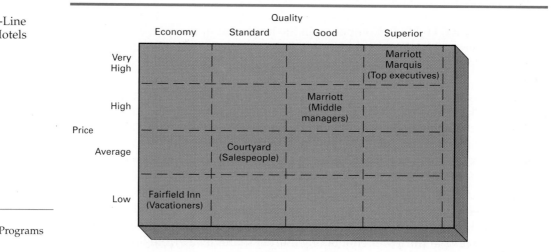

Once the product-line manager decides to add another item to sell at a certain price, the design task is turned over to the company engineers. The planned price will dictate how the item is designed, rather than the design dictating the price that will be charged.

Line-Modernization Decision

Even when product-line length is adequate, the line might need to be modernized. For example, a company's machine tools might have a 1950s look and lose out to newer-styled competitors' lines.

The issue is whether to overhaul the line piecemeal or all at once. A piecemeal approach allows the company to see how customers and dealers take to the new style. Piecemeal modernization is less draining on the company's cash flow. A major disadvantage of piecemeal modernization is that it allows competitors to see changes and start redesigning their own line.

In rapidly changing product markets, product modernization is carried on continuously. Companies plan product improvements to encourage *customer migration* to higher-valued, higher-priced items. A major issue is timing the product improvements so they do not come out too early (thus damaging sales of the current product line) or too late (after competition has established a strong reputation for more advanced equipment).

Line-Featuring Decision

The product-line manager typically selects one or a few items in the line to feature. Managers might feature low-end promotional models to serve as "traffic builders." Thus Sears will announce a special low-price sewing machine to attract customers. And Rolls Royce announced an economy model selling for only $178,000—in contrast to its high-end model selling for $310,000—to attract new buyers.

At other times, managers will feature a high-end item to lend prestige to the product line. Stetson promotes a man's hat selling for $150, which few men buy but which acts as a "flagship" or "crown jewel" to enhance the line's image.

Sometimes a company finds one end of its line selling well and the other end poorly. The company may try to boost demand for the slower sellers, especially if they are produced in a factory that is idled by the lack of demand. This situation faced Honeywell when its medium-size computers were not selling as well as its large computers. But things are not this simple. It could be argued that the company should promote the items that sell well rather than trying to prop up weak demand.

Line-Pruning Decision

Product-line managers must periodically review items for pruning. There are two occasions for pruning. One is when the product line includes deadwood that is depressing profits. The weak items can be identified through sales and cost analysis. RCA cut down its color television sets from 69 to 44 models, and a chemical company cut down its products from 217 to the 93 with the largest volume, the largest contribution to profits, and the greatest long-term potential. Many companies have implemented major prunings to achieve stronger long-term profits.

The other occasion for product pruning is when the company is short of production capacity. The manager should concentrate on producing the higher-margin items. Companies typically shorten their lines in periods of tight demand and lengthen their lines in periods of slow demand.

Brand Decisions

In developing a marketing strategy for individual products, the seller has to confront the branding decision. Branding is a major issue in product strategy. On the one hand, developing a branded product requires a great deal of long-term investment spending, especially for advertising, promotion, and packaging. It would be easier for manufacturers to make the product for others to brand. This is the course taken by Taiwanese manufacturers, who make a great amount of the world's clothing, consumer electronics, and computers but not under Taiwanese brand names.

On the other hand, these manufacturers eventually learn that the power lies with the brand-name companies. Brand-name companies can replace their Taiwanese manufacturing sources with cheaper sources in Malaysia and elsewhere. Japanese and South Korean companies did not make this mistake. They spent liberally to build up brand names such as Sony, Toyota, Goldstar, and Samsung for their products. Even when these companies can no longer afford to manufacture their products in their homeland, the brand names continue to command customer loyalty.

What Is a Brand?

Perhaps the most distinctive skill of professional marketers is their ability to create, maintain, protect, and enhance brands. The American Marketing Association defines a brand as follows:

❖ A brand *is a name, term, sign, symbol, or design, or a combination of them, intended to identify the goods or services of one seller or group of sellers and to differentiate them from those of competitors.*

Thus, a brand identifies the seller or maker. Under trademark law, the seller is granted exclusive rights to the use of the brand name in perpetuity. This differs from other assets such as patents and copyrights which have expiration dates.

A brand is essentially a seller's promise to consistently deliver a specific set of features, benefits, and services to the buyers. The best brands convey a warranty of quality. But a brand is even a more complex symbol.[6] A brand can convey up to six levels of meaning:

- *Attributes:* A brand first brings to mind certain attributes. Thus, Mercedes suggests expensive, well built, well engineered, durable, high prestige, high resale value, fast, and so on. The company may use one or more of these attributes to advertise the car. For years Mercedes advertised, "Engineered like no other car in the world." This served as the positioning platform for projecting other attributes of the car.
- *Benefits:* A brand is more than a set of attributes. Customers are not buying attributes; they are buying benefits. Attributes need to be translated into functional and/or emotional benefits. The attribute durable could translate into the functional benefit, "I won't have to buy a new car every few years." The attribute expensive might translate into the emotional benefit, "The car helps me feel important and admired." The attribute well-built might translate into the functional and emotional benefit, "I am safe in case of an accident."
- *Values:* The brand also says something about the producer's values. Thus, Mercedes stands for high performance, safety, prestige, and so on. The brand marketer must figure out the specific groups of car buyers who would be seeking these values.
- *Culture:* The brand may additionally represent a certain culture. The Mercedes represents German culture: organized, efficient, high quality.
- *Personality:* The brand can also project a certain personality. If the brand were a per-

son, an animal, or an object, what would come to mind? Mercedes may suggest a no-nonsense boss (person), a reigning lion (animal), or an austere palace (object). Sometimes it might take on the personality of an actual well-known person or spokesman.

♦ *User:* The brand suggests the kind of consumer who buys or uses the product. We would be surprised to see a 20-year-old secretary driving a Mercedes. We would expect instead to see a 55-year-old top executive behind the wheel. The users will be those who respect the values, culture, and personality of the product.

All this suggests that a brand is a complex symbol. If a company treats a brand only as a name, it misses the point of branding. The challenge in branding is to develop a deep set of meanings for the brand. When the audience can visualize all six dimensions of a brand, we call it a *deep brand*; otherwise it is a *shallow brand*. A Mercedes is a deep brand because we understand its meaning along all six dimensions. An Audi is a brand with less depth, since we may not grasp as easily its specific benefits, personality, and user profile.

Given these six levels of a brand's meanings, marketers must decide at which level(s) to deeply anchor the brand's identity. One mistake would be to promote only the brand's attributes. First, the buyer is not interested in the brand attributes so much as the brand benefits. Second, competitors can easily copy the attributes. Third, the current attributes may be devalued later, hurting a brand that is too tied to specific attributes.

Even promoting the brand on one or more of its benefits can be risky. Suppose Mercedes touts its main benefit as "high performance." Suppose several competitive brands emerge with high or higher performance. Or suppose car buyers start placing less importance on high performance as compared to other benefits. Mercedes would need the freedom to maneuver into a new benefit positioning.

The most enduring meanings of a brand are its values, culture, and personality. They define the brand's essence. The Mercedes stands for "high technology, performance, success," and so on. This is what Mercedes must project in its brand strategy. It would be a mistake for Mercedes to market an inexpensive car bearing the name Mercedes. This would dilute the value and personality that Mercedes has built up over the years.

The Concept and Measurement of Brand Equity

Brands vary in the amount of power and value they have in the marketplace. At one extreme are brands that are not known by most buyers in the marketplace. Then there are brands for which buyers have a fairly high degree of *brand awareness* (measured either by brand recall or recognition). Beyond this are brands that have a high degree of *brand acceptability* in that most customers would not resist buying them. Then there are brands which enjoy a high degree of *brand preference*. They would be selected over the others. Finally there are brands that command a high degree of *brand loyalty*. Tony O'Reilly, CEO of H. J. Heinz, proposed this test of brand loyalty: "My acid test . . . is whether a housewife, intending to buy Heinz tomato ketchup in a store, finding it to be out of stock, will walk out of the store to buy it elsewhere or switch to an alternative product."

A powerful brand is said to have high *brand equity*. According to Aaker, brand equity is higher, the higher the brand loyalty, name awareness, perceived quality, strong brand associations, and other assets such as patents, trademarks, and channel relationships.[7] The point is that a brand is an asset insofar as it can be sold or bought for a price. Certain companies are basing their growth on acquiring and building rich *brand portfolios*. Grand Metropolitan acquired various Pillsbury brands, Green Giant vegetables, Haagen-Dazs ice cream, and Burger King. Nestlé acquired Rowntree (UK), Carnation (US), Stouffer (US), Buitoni-Perugina (Italy), and Perrier (France), making it the world's largest food company. In fact, Nestlé paid $4.5 billion to buy Rowntree, or five times more than its book value. These companies do not normally list brand equity on their balance sheet because of the somewhat arbitrariness of the estimate. Yet when Grand Metropolitan bought Heublein, it added $800 million to its assets to reflect the value of Smirnoff and other names.

Measuring the actual equity of a brand name is somewhat arbitrary. Aaker describes five different approaches, including basing it on the price premium, the stock value, the brand replacement value, and so on. For example, one measure of brand equity value is the price premium the brand commands times the extra volume it moves over what an average brand would command.[8]

The world's top ten brand superpowers, according to Interbrand, are (in rank order): Coca-Cola, Kellogg's, McDonald's, Kodak, Marlboro, IBM, American Express, Sony, Mercedes Benz, and Nescafé.[9] According to one estimate, the brand equity of Marlboro is $31 billion, Coca-Cola $24 billion, and Kodak $13 billion. But it should be noted that different potential acquirers would leverage the brand in different ways and would accordingly pay more or less for these brands.

High brand equity provides a number of competitive advantages to a company. The company will enjoy reduced marketing costs because of the high level of consumer brand awareness and loyalty. The company will have more trade leverage in bargaining with distributors and retailers since the customers expect them to carry the brand. The company can charge a higher price than its competitors because the brand has higher perceived quality. The company can more easily launch brand extensions since the brand name carries high credibility. Above all, the brand offers the company some defense against the fierce price competition.

As an asset, a brand name needs to be carefully managed so that its brand equity doesn't depreciate. This requires maintaining or improving over time brand awareness, brand perceived quality and functionality, positive brand associations, and so on. These require continuous R&D investment, skillful advertising, excellent trade and consumer service, and other measures. Some companies, such as Canada Dry and Colgate-Palmolive, have appointed "brand equity managers" to guard the brand's image, associations, and quality, and prevent short-term tactical actions from hurting the brand. They have to lean against brand managers who overpromote the brand in order to produce short-term profits at the expense of long-term equity.

Leading companies do not believe that well-managed brands need to be subject to a brand life cycle. Many brand leaders of 70 years ago are still today's brand leaders: Kodak, Del Monte, Wrigley's, Gillette, Coca-Cola, and Campbell's.

Such companies as Procter & Gamble, Caterpillar, IBM, and Sony have achieved outstanding *company brand strength*, as measured by the proportion of product/markets where the company is the brand leader or co-leader. Thus, P&G's impressive marketing reputation in the United States rests on the fact that it markets the leading brand in 19 of the 39 categories in which it competes, and one of the top three brands in 34 of its categories. Its average market share is close to 25%.

Some analysts see brands as outlasting a company's specific products and facilities. They see brands as the major enduring asset of a company. Yet every powerful brand really represents a set of loyal customers. Therefore, the fundamental asset underlying brand equity is *customer equity*. This suggests that the proper focus of marketing planning is that of extending *loyal customer lifetime value* with brand management serving as a major marketing tool.

Branding poses challenging decisions to the marketer. The key decisions are shown in Figure 17-5 and discussed in the following paragraphs.

FIGURE 17-5
An Overview of Branding
Decisions

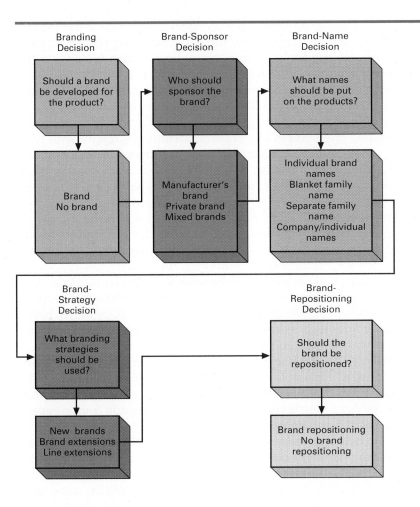

Branding Decision

The first decision is whether the company should develop a brand name for its product. In the past, most products went unbranded. Producers and middlemen sold their goods out of barrels, bins, and cases, without any supplier identification. Buyers would have to depend on the seller's integrity. The earliest signs of branding were in the efforts of medieval guilds to require craftspeople to put trademarks on their products to protect themselves and consumers against inferior quality. In the fine arts, too, branding began with artists signing their works.

Today, branding is such a strong force that hardly anything goes unbranded. Salt is packaged in distinctive manufacturers' containers, oranges are stamped with growers' names, common nuts and bolts are packaged in cellophane with a distributor's label, and automobile components — spark plugs, tires, filters — bear separate brand names from the auto makers. Fresh food products — such as chicken, turkey, and salmon — are increasingly being sold under strongly advertised brand names.

In some cases, there has been a return to "no branding" of certain staple consumer goods and pharmaceuticals. Correfours, the originator of the French hypermarché, introduced a line of "no brands" in its stores in the early 1970s. In 1977, the Jewel Food Stores in Chicago introduced a 40-item "generic" line. *Generics* are unbranded, plainly packaged, less expensive versions of common products such as spaghetti, paper towels, and canned peaches. They offer standard or lower quality at a price that may be as much as 20% to 40% lower than nationally advertised brands and 10% to 20% lower than retailer private-label brands. The lower price is made possible by lower-quality ingredients, lower-cost labeling and packaging, and minimal advertising. Nevertheless, generics are sufficiently satisfying so that over 70% of consumers who have purchased generics said they would buy them again. Generic products in the food, household goods, and pharmaceutical industries present a major challenge to high-priced brands and weaker brands.

National brands have fought generics in a number of ways. Ralston-Purina increased its quality and targeted pet owners who identified strongly with their pets and cared most about quality. Procter & Gamble introduced its Banner paper products, a line offering less quality than its higher lines but greater quality than generics at a competitive price. Other companies simply have cut their prices to compete with generics.[10]

Why do sellers prefer to brand their products when it clearly involves a cost—packaging, labeling, advertising, legal protection—and a risk if the product should prove unsatisfying to the user? It turns out that branding gives the seller several advantages.

First, the brand name makes it easier for the seller to process orders and track down problems. Thus Anheuser-Busch receives an order for a hundred cases of Michelob eight-ounce beer instead of an order for "some of your better beer." Furthermore, the seller finds it easier to trace the order if it is misshipped, or to determine why the beer was rancid if consumers complain.

Second, the seller's brand name and trademark provide legal protection of unique product features, which would otherwise be copied by competitors.

Third, branding gives the seller the opportunity to attract a loyal and profitable set of customers. Brand loyalty gives sellers some protection from competition and greater control in planning their marketing program.

Fourth, branding helps the seller segment markets. Instead of P&G's selling a simple detergent, it can offer eight detergent brands, each formulated differently and aimed at specific benefit-seeking segments.

Fifth, good brands help build the corporate image. By carrying the company's name, they help advertise the quality and size of the company.

There is evidence that distributors want manufacturers' brand names as a means of making the product easier to handle, identifying suppliers, holding production to certain quality standards, and increasing buyer preference. Consumers want brand names to help them identify quality differences and shop more efficiently.

Brand-Sponsor Decision

A manufacturer has several options with respect to brand sponsorship. The product may be launched as a *manufacturer brand* (sometimes called a national brand), a *distributor brand* (also called retailer, store, or private brand), or a *licensed brand name* (see Marketing Strategies 17-1). Or the manufacturer may produce some output under its own name and some under distributor labels. Kellogg's, John Deere & Company, and IBM sell virtually all of their output under their own brand names. Hart Schaffner & Marx sells some of its manufactured clothes under licensed names such as Christian Dior, Pierre Cardin, and Johnny Carson. Whirlpool produces output both under its own name and under distributors' names.

Although manufacturers' brands tend to dominate, large retailers and wholesalers have been developing their own brands. Sears has created several names—Diehard batteries, Craftsman tools, Kenmore appliances—that command brand preference and even brand insistence. An increasing number of department stores, supermarkets, and drugstores feature store brands.

Why do middlemen bother with sponsoring their own brands? They have to

Marketing Strategies 17-1

Licensing Brand Names for Royalties

Manufacturers or retailers may take years and spend millions to develop consumer preference for their brands. An alternative is to "rent" names that hold magic for consumers. The names or symbols previously created by other manufacturers, the names of well-known celebrities, the characters introduced in popular movies and books—for a fee, any of these can provide a manufacturer's product with an instant and proven brand name. Name and character licensing has become a big business in recent years. Retail sales of licensed products jumped from $4 billion in 1977 to $67 billion in 1991.

Apparel and accessories sellers are the largest users, accounting for about 35% of all licensing. Producers and retailers pay sizable royalties to adorn their products with the names of such fashion innovators as Bill Blass, Calvin Klein, Pierre Cardin, Gucci, and Halston, all of whom license their names or initials for everything from blouses to ties and linens to luggage. In recent years, designer labels have become so common that many retailers are discarding them in favor of their own store brands in order to regain exclusivity, pricing freedom, and higher margins. Even less fashionable names can bring astounding success. Coca-Cola clothes by Murjani rang up $100 million in retail sales in just two years. Other consumer products companies jumped quickly into corporate fashion licensing—Hershey, Jell-O, Burger King, McDonald's, and others.

Sellers of children's toys, games, food, and other products also make extensive use of name and character licensing. The list of characters attached to children's clothing, toys, school supplies, linens, dolls, lunchboxes, cereals, and other items is almost endless. It ranges from such classics as Mickey Mouse, Peanuts, and Barbie to Batman, the Teenage Mutant Ninja Turtles, and the Simpsons.

The newest form of licensing is corporate licensing—renting a corporate trademark or logo made famous in one category and using it in a related category. Currently successful examples include Singer sewing supplies, Caterpillar work clothes, Fabergé costume jewelry, Winnebago camping equipment, and Coppertone swimwear and sunglasses. Harley-Davidson is now licensing its name for consumer products. One toy manufacturer now markets the Harley-Davidson Big Wheel tricycle, and the company has authorized other products that meet appropriate standards of quality and taste—products ranging from wine coolers, to chocolates, to cologne.

SOURCES: See John A. Quelch, "How to Build a Product Licensing Program," *Harvard Business Review,* May–June 1985, pp. 186 ff.; Teresa Carson and Amy Dunkin, "What's in a Name? Millions If It's Leased," *Business Week,* April 8, 1985, pp. 97–98; Michael Gates, "Creative Licensing," *Incentive,* April 1989, pp. 32–36; Cyndee Miller, "Corporate Licensing Grows as Firms Seek 'Risk-Free' Products," *Marketing News,* April 29, 1991, pp. 1, 8; and Kate Fitzgerald, "Licensing: Safe Bet in Recession," *Advertising Age,* June 17, 1991, p. 46.

hunt down qualified suppliers who can deliver consistent quality. They have to order large quantities and tie up their capital in inventories. They have to spend money promoting their private label. They have to take the chance that if their private-label product is not good, the customer will develop a negative attitude toward their other products.

In spite of these potential disadvantages, middlemen develop private brands because they can be profitable. They search for manufacturers with excess capacity who will produce the private label at a low cost. Other costs, such as advertising and physical distribution, may also be low. This means that the private brander is able to charge a lower price and often make a higher profit margin. The private brander may be able to develop strong store brands that draw traffic into its stores.

The competition between manufacturers' and middlemen's brands is called the *battle of the private-label brands.* In this confrontation, middlemen have many advantages. Retail shelf space is scarce. Many supermarkets now charge a slotting fee as a condition before accepting a new brand, presumably to cover the cost of listing it and stocking it.[11] They also charge separately for special display space and in-store advertising space. Middlemen give more prominent display to their own brands and make sure they are better stocked. Middlemen are now building better quality in their store brands, thus building consumers' satisfaction. Many shoppers know that the store brand is often manufactured by one of the larger manufacturers anyway. Store brands often are priced lower than comparable manufacturers' brands, thus appealing to budget-conscious shoppers, especially in times of inflation or recession.

As a result, the former dominance of manufacturers' brands is weakening. Consider the following case:

> Loblaw Cos., the Canadian supermarket chain, is increasing the number of its house brands. Loblaw now sells the leading cookie brand in Canada, its President's Choice Decadent Chocolate Chip Cookie, which tastes better and costs less than Nabisco's Chips Ahoy brand. It has captured 14% of the market, mostly from Nabisco. Loblaw also introduced its private-label cola, called President's Choice cola, which racked up 50% of Loblaw's canned cola sales.

Manufacturers of national brands are very frustrated by the growing power of the retailers. Kevin Price put it well: "A decade ago, the retailer was a chihuahua nipping at the manufacturer's heels—a nuisance, yes, but only a minor irritant; you fed it and it went away. Today it's a pit bull and it wants to rip your arms and legs off. You'd like to see it roll over, but you're too busy defending yourself to even try."[12] Some marketing commentators predict that middlemen's brands will eventually knock out all but the strongest manufacturers' brands.

In years past, consumers saw the brands in any category arranged as a *brand ladder*, with their favorite brand at the top and remaining brands in descending order of preference. There are increasing signs now that this ladder is disappearing and being replaced with a consumer perception of *brand parity*, namely, that many brands are equivalent. These consumers are ready to buy whichever acceptable brand is on sale that week. As stated by Joel D. Weiner, former Kraft executive, "People don't think the world will come to a screeching halt if they use Tide instead of Cheer." A 1990 study by DDB Needham Worldwide reported that the percentage of packaged-goods consumers saying that they bought only well-known brands fell from 77% to 62% between 1975 and 1990. A Grey Advertising Inc. study reported that 66% of consumers said they were trading down to lower-priced brands, particularly store brands.

This weakening in brand preeminence is due to many factors. Consumers, hard pressed to spend more wisely, are more sensitive to quality, price, and value. They are noting more quality equivalence as competing manufacturers as well as national retailers copy and duplicate the qualities of the best brands. The continuous barrage of coupons and price specials is training a generation of consumers to buy on price. The fact that companies have reduced their advertising to 30% of their total promotion budget has hurt their brand support. The endless stream of brand extensions and line extensions has blurred brand identity and led to a confusing amount of product proliferation. Store brands have been improving in quality, and given the increasing confidence consumers are placing in their store chains, this is posing a strong challenge to manufacturer-owned brands. In the United States, the shares of the top three manufacturer-owned grocery brands has dropped precipitously in some categories.[13]

Manufacturers react by spending substantial amounts of money on consumer-directed advertising and promotion to maintain strong brand preference. Their price has to be somewhat higher to cover this promotion. At the same time, the mass distributors put considerable pressure on them to put more of their promotional money into trade allowances and deals if they want adequate shelf space. Once manufacturers start giving in, they have less to spend on consumer promotion and advertising, and their brand leadership starts slipping. This is the national brand manufacturers' dilemma.

To maintain their power vis-à-vis the trade, leading brand marketers need to apply the following strategies. They must invest in R&D to bring out new brands, features, and continuous quality improvements. They must sustain a strong advertising program to maintain high brand awareness and insistence. They must find ways to "partner" with major mass distributors in a joint search for logistical economies and competitive strategies that improve their joint performance. For example, P&G has assigned 20 of its managers to work at Wal-Mart headquarters in Bentonville, Arkansas, alongside Wal-Mart managers in a search for ways to reduce their joint cost and improve their competitive performance.

Brand-Name Decision

Manufacturers who brand their products face further choices. Four brand-name strategies are used:

1. *Individual Brand Names:* This policy is followed by General Mills (Bisquick, Gold Medal, Betty Crocker, Nature Valley).
2. *A Blanket Family Name for All Products:* This policy is followed by Heinz and General Electric.
3. *Separate Family Names for All Products:* This policy is followed by Sears (Kenmore for appliances, Craftsman for tools, and Homart for major home installations).
4. *Company Trade Name Combined with Individual Product Names:* This policy is followed by Kellogg's (Kellogg's Rice Krispies, Kellogg's Raisin Bran, and Kellogg's Corn Flakes).

What are the advantages of an individual-brand-names strategy? A major advantage is that the company does not tie its reputation to the product's acceptance. If the product fails or appears to have low quality, it does not hurt the company's name. A manufacturer of good-quality watches, such as Seiko, can introduce a lower-quality line of watches (called Pulsar) without diluting the Seiko name. The individual-brand-names strategy permits the firm to search for the best name for each new product. A new name permits the building of new excitement and conviction.

A blanket family name also has advantages. The development cost is less because there is no need for "name" research or for heavy advertising expenditures to create brand-name recognition. Furthermore, sales will be strong if the manufacturer's name is good. Thus Campbell's introduces new soups under its brand name with extreme simplicity and achieves instant recognition. On the other hand, Philips in Europe puts its name on many of its products, but since its products vary from high quality to average quality, most people expect only average quality in a Philips product. This hurts the sales of its superior products.

Where a company produces quite different products, it is not desirable to use one blanket family name. Swift and Company developed separate family names for its hams (Premium) and fertilizers (Vigoro). When Mead Johnson developed a diet supplement for gaining weight, it created a new family name, Nutriment, to avoid confusion with its family-brand weight-reducing products, Metrecal. Companies will often invent different family names for different quality lines within the same product class. Thus A&P food stores sell a first-grade, second-grade, and third-grade set of brands —Ann Page, Sultana, and Iona, respectively.

Finally, some manufacturers tie their company name with an individual brand name for each product. The company name legitimizes, and the individual name individualizes, the new product. Thus Quaker Oats in *Quaker Oats Cap'n*

Crunch taps the company's reputation in the breakfast-cereal field, and Cap'n Crunch individualizes and dramatizes the new product.

Once a company decides on its brand-name strategy, it faces the task of choosing a specific brand name. The company could choose the name of a person (Honda, Estée Lauder), location (American Airlines, Kentucky Fried Chicken), quality (Safeway stores, Duracell), lifestyle (Weight Watchers, Healthy Choice), or artificial name (Exxon, Kodak). Among the desirable qualities for a brand name are the following:[14]

1. *It Should Suggest Something About the Product's Benefits:* Examples: Coldspot, Beautyrest, Craftsman, Accutron.
2. *It Should Suggest Product Qualities Such as Action or Color:* Examples: Duz, Sunkist, Spic and Span, Firebird.
3. *It Should Be Easy to Pronounce, Recognize, and Remember:* Short names help. Examples: Tide, Crest, Puffs.
4. *It Should Be Distinctive:* Examples: Mustang, Kodak, Exxon.
5. *It Should Not Carry Poor Meanings in Other Countries and Languages:* Example: *Nova* is a poor name for a car to be sold in Spanish-speaking countries; it means "doesn't work."

Normally, companies choose brand names by developing a list, debating the merits of different names, and making a choice. Today companies prefer to hire a marketing research firm to develop names and test them. Name-research procedures include *association tests* (What images come to mind?), *learning tests* (How easily is the name pronounced?), *memory tests* (How well is the name remembered?), and *preference tests* (Which names are preferred?). One of the best-known specialists in the "name game" is NameLab, Inc., which is responsible for such brand names as Acura, Compaq, and Zapmail.

Many firms strive to build a unique brand name that eventually will become intimately identified with the product category. Such brand names as Frigidaire, Kleenex, Levis, Jell-O, Scotch Tape, and Fiberglas have succeeded in this way. However, their very success may threaten the exclusive rights to the name. Cellophane, shredded wheat, and the 386 chip are now names in the common domain.

Given the rapid growth of the global marketplace, companies should choose brand names with an eye to their global reach. These names should be meaningful and pronounceable in other languages. Otherwise companies will find that they cannot use well-known local brand names as they geographically expand. (See Global Marketing 17-1.)

Brand-Strategy Decisions

A company has four choices when it comes to brand strategy (see Figure 17-6). The company can introduce *line extensions* (existing brand name extended to new sizes, flavors, and so on in the existing product category), *brand extensions* (brand names extended to new-product categories), *multibrands* (new brand names introduced in the same product category), and *new brands* (new brand name for a new category product). According to *Gorman's New Product News*, of the 6,125 new products accepted by groceries in the first five months of 1991, 89% were line extensions, 6% were brand extensions, and only 5% bore new brand names (both multibrands and new brands). Here we will examine the rationale underlying each brand strategy.

LINE EXTENSIONS ❖ Line extensions occur when a company introduces additional items in the same product category under the same brand name such as

How Far Should Global Branding Be Pushed?

In the past, most companies established new brand names that made sense in their local country. When they later attempted to introduce their brand into foreign markets, some companies discovered that the existing brand name was not appropriate. The name was difficult to pronounce, offensive, funny, meaningless, or already coopted by someone else. The company would be forced to develop a new brand name for the same product when it was introduced in other countries. P&G had to create a different brand name for its Pert Plus shampoo when it introduced it in Japan (called Rejoy) and the United Kingdom (called Vidal Sassoon). Some companies market the very same product under a dozen different names in different countries. Using different local brand names for the same product comes at a high cost, however. The company has to prepare different labels, packaging, and advertising.

The trend today is toward a shrinking global market, a "borderless world." This is especially evident in Europe where custom duties, border delays, and other impediments to deter European trade are rapidly diminishing. Companies operating in Europe are eager to launch new brands initially as Eurobrands. P&G successfully launched its detergent Ariel as a Eurobrand. Other companies are bent on folding existing brand names into one Eurobrand name. Mars has replaced its Treets and Bonitas brand names with M&M's worldwide and changed its third largest United Kingdom brand—Marathon—to the Snickers name that it uses in the United States and other parts of Europe. Taking a cue, Unilever is now seeking to market its various detergent brands—All, Omo, Persil, Presto, Skip, and Via—under fewer labels.

Clearly some brand names have gained worldwide acceptance. Such companies as Kodak, McDonald's, IBM, Sony, and Coca-Cola would not think of using different brand names as they enter additional countries. Levitt and others believe that the world's population is growing more homogeneous in their tastes, thanks to modern communication and travel, and will increasingly respond to global brands.

What are the advantages of a global brand name? One main advantage is economy of scale in preparing standard packaging, labels, promotions, and advertising. In the case of advertising, economies result from both standardized ads and the fact that media coverage increasingly overlaps between countries, especially in Europe. Another advantage is that sales may increase because travelers will see their favorite brands advertised and distributed in other markets. Third, trade channels are more ready to accept a global brand which has been advertised in their market. Finally, a worldwide recognized brand name is a power in itself, especially when the country-of-origin associations are highly respected. Japanese companies have developed a global reputation for high technology and quality and their names on products give instant confidence to buyers that they are getting good value.

But there are also costs and risks to global branding. A single brand name may not be as appealing as locally chosen names. If the company replaced a well-regarded local name with a global name, the changeover cost can be substantial. The company will have to inform millions of people that their brand still exists but under another name. Even the company's local managers may resist the name change ordered from headquarters. The overcentralization of brand planning and programming may dissipate local creativity that might have produced even better ideas for marketing the product.

Some critics charge that global standardization ignores the great differences not only between countries but within regions of each country. At a time when domestic marketers are increasingly calling for local area marketing within their country, the call for global standardization appears misguided.

Even when a company has promoted its global brand name worldwide, it is difficult to standardize its brand associations in all countries. Heineken beer, for example, is viewed as a high-quality beer in the United States and France; a grocery beer in the United Kingdom; and a cheap beer in Belgium. Cheez Whiz, a Kraft company cheese spread, is viewed as a "junk food" in the United States; a toast spread in Canada; and a coffee flavorer in Puerto Rico.

The major inference to draw from this is that wise companies will globalize those elements that make or save substantial sums of money and localize those that competitive positioning and success require.

FIGURE 17-6
Four Brand Strategies

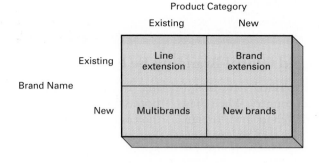

new flavors, forms, colors, added ingredients, package sizes, and so on. Thus, Dannon Company recently introduced several Dannon line extensions including seven new yogurt flavors, a fat-free yogurt, and a large economy-size yogurt. The line extensions may be *innovative* ("nonfat yogurt"), *"me-too"* (to copy a competitor), or *"filling in"* (another package size).

The vast majority of new-product activity consists of line extensions. Excess manufacturing capacity often drives a company to introduce additional items. The company might want to meet the consumers' desire for variety. The company might recognize a latent consumer want and try to capitalize on it. The company may want to match a competitor's successful line extension. Many companies introduce line extensions primarily to command more shelf space from resellers.

Many companies are now introducing *branded variants*, which are specific lines of a brand that are supplied to specific retailers or channels of distribution. They result from the pressure that retailers put on manufacturers to enable the retailers to provide distinctive offerings to their customers. Thus, a camera company may supply its low-end cameras to mass merchandisers while limiting its higher-priced items to specialty camera shops. Or Valentino may design and supply different lines of its suits and jackets to different department stores.[15]

Line extension involves risks. There is the chance that the brand name will lose its specific meaning; Ries and Trout call this the "line-extension trap."[16] When a person asked for a Coke in the past, she received a six-ounce bottle. Today the vendor will have to ask: New, Classic, or Cherry Coke? Regular or diet? Caffeine or caffeine free? Bottle or can? The other risk is that many line extensions will not sell enough to cover their development and promotion costs. Furthermore, even when they sell enough, the sales may come at the expense of other items in the line. A line extension works best when it takes sales away from competing brands, not when it "cannibalizes" the company's other items. According to *Progressive Grocer*:

> *The question is, do line extensions build incremental volume, or is there a point of diminishing returns at which they only cannibalize existing sales? . . . Many retailers and manufacturers too are beginning to suspect that, in too many cases, it is the latter.*[17]

BRAND EXTENSIONS ❖ A company may decide to use an existing brand name to launch a product in a new category. Armour used its Dial brand name to launch a variety of new products that would not easily have obtained distribution without the strength of the Dial name. Honda uses its company name to cover such different products as its automobiles, motorcycles, snowblowers, lawnmowers, marine engines, and snowmobiles. This allows Honda to advertise that it can fit "six Hondas in a two-car garage." Hershey recently launched its first product in the peanut butter category, using one of its existing candy brand names, Reese. Pierre Cardin has licensed its name to cover a variety of apparel and home furnishings categories (recall Marketing Strategies 17-1 on page 449).

Brand-extension strategy offers a number of advantages. A well-regarded brand name gives the new product instant recognition and earlier acceptance. It enables the company to enter new-product categories more easily. Sony puts its name on most of its new electronic products and this establishes an instant conviction that each new product is of high quality. Brand extension saves considerable advertising cost that would normally be required to familiarize consumers with a new brand name. Because of these advantages, it is highly probable that brand-extension strategy will increasingly be used in the 1990s.

At the same time, brand-extension strategy involves risks. The new product might disappoint buyers and damage their respect for the company's other products. The brand name may be inappropriate to the new product—consider buying Standard Oil ketchup, Drano milk, or Boeing cologne. The brand name may lose its special positioning in the consumer's mind through overextension. *Brand dilution* is said to occur when consumers no longer associate a brand with a specific product or highly similar products. Consider the contrast between how Hyatt and Marriott hotels are named:

> Hyatt practices a brand-extension strategy. Hyatt's name appears in every hotel variation, that is, Hyatt Resorts, Hyatt Regency, Hyatt Suites, and Park Hyatt. Marriott, in contrast, practices multibranding. Its various types of hotels are called Marriott Marquis, Marriott, Residence Inn, Courtyard, and Fairfield Inns. It is harder for Hyatt guests to know the differences between Hyatt hotel types, whereas Marriott more clearly aims its hotels at different segments and builds distinct brand names and images for each.

Transferring an existing brand name to a new category requires great care. For example, S. C. Johnson's popular shaving cream is called Edge. This name was successfully extended to its aftershave lotion. The name Edge probably could also be used to introduce a brand of razor blades. However, the risk would increase in using the name Edge to launch a new shampoo or toothpaste. Then Edge would lose its meaning as a name for shaving products.

Companies that are tempted to transfer their brand name must research how well the brand's associations fit the new product. The best result would occur when the brand name builds the sales of both the new product and the existing product. An acceptable result would be where the new product sells well without affecting the sales of the existing product. The worst result would be where the new product fails and hurts the sales of the existing product.

MULTIBRANDS ❖ A company will often introduce additional brands in the same category. There are various motives for doing this. Sometimes the company sees this as a way to establish different features and/or appeal to different buying motives. Thus, P&G produces nine different brands of detergents. This also enables the company to lock up more distributor shelf space. Or the company may want to protect its major brand by setting up *flanker brands*. For example, Seiko establishes different brand names for its higher-priced (Seiko Lasalle) and lower-priced watches (Pulsar) to protect its flanks. Sometimes the company inherits different brand names in the process of acquiring competitor companies and each brand name has a loyal following. Thus, Electrolux, the Swedish multinational, owns a stable of acquired brand names (Frigidaire, Kelvinator, Westinghouse, Zanussi, White, Gibson) for its appliance lines.

A major pitfall in introducing multibrand entries is that each might obtain only a small market share, and none may be particularly profitable. The company will have dissipated its resources over several brands instead of building a few brands to a highly profitable level. These companies should weed out the weaker brands and establish tighter screening procedures for choosing new brands. Ideally, a company's brands should cannibalize the competitors' brands and not each other. Or at least the net profits with the multibrand strategy should be larger even if some cannibalism occurs.[18]

NEW BRANDS ❖ When a company launches products in a new category, it may find that none of its current brand names are appropriate. Thus, if Timex decides to make toothbrushes, it is not likely to call them Timex toothbrushes. This could hurt its present brand image and not help the new product. Companies are better off creating new brand names. For example, Sears established separate family names for different product categories. Finally, the company might believe that the power of its existing brand name is waning and a new brand name is needed.

In deciding whether to introduce a new brand name rather than using an existing one, the manufacturer should consider several questions. For example, the 3M Company asks: Is the venture large enough? Will it last long enough? Is it best to avoid using the 3M name in case the product fails? Does the product need the boost power of the 3M name? Will the cost of establishing a new brand name be covered by the probable sales and profits? Companies are naturally wary about the high cost of imprinting a new brand name in the public's mind. Establishing a new brand name in the U.S. marketplace for a mass consumer good can cost anywhere from $50 million to $100 million.

Brand-Repositioning Decision

However well a brand is positioned in a market, the company may have to reposition it later. A competitor may launch a brand next to the company's brand and cut into its market share. Or customer preferences may shift, leaving the company's brand with less demand.

A classic story of successful brand repositioning is the Seven-Up campaign. Seven-Up was one of several soft drinks bought primarily by older people who wanted a bland, lemon-flavored drink. Research indicated that while a majority of soft-drink consumers preferred a cola, they did not prefer it all the time, and many other consumers were noncola drinkers. Seven-Up went for leadership in the noncola market by executing a brilliant campaign, calling itself the Uncola. The Uncola was featured as a youthful and refreshing drink, the one to reach for instead of a cola. Seven-Up created a new way for consumers to view the soft-drink market, as consisting of colas and uncolas, with Seven-Up leading the uncolas.

The problem of repositioning a brand can be illustrated for Hamm's beer. Figure 17-7 shows beer-brand perceptions and taste preferences on two attributes: lightness and mildness. The dots show the perceived positions of the brands, and the circles represent locations of consumer preference. The larger circles represent more intense demand. This map reveals that Hamm is not meeting the preferences of any distinct segment.

To remedy this problem, Hamm needs to identify the best preference cluster in which to reposition. Preference cluster #1 would be a poor choice, because Schlitz and Budweiser are serving this segment. Preference cluster #2 seems like a good choice because of its size and the presence of only one competitor, Miller. Preference cluster #9 would be another possibility, although it is relatively small. Hamm can also think about a long-shot repositioning toward the supercluster #3, #5, and #8 or the supercluster #4 and #6.

Management must weigh two factors in making its choice. The first is the cost of repositioning the brand to that segment. The cost includes changing the prod-

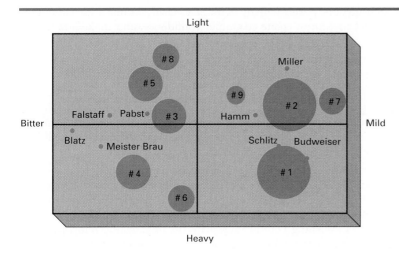

uct's qualities, packaging, advertising, and so on. In general, the repositioning cost rises with the repositioning distance. Hamm would need more money to reposition its brand in segment #8 than in segment #2. Hamm might be better off creating a new brand for segment #8 than repositioning its present brand.

The other factor is the revenue that the brand would earn in the new position. The revenue depends on the number of consumers in the preference segment, their average purchase rate, the number and strength of competitors in that segment, and the price charged by brands in that segment. Hamm must make its decision by comparing likely revenues and costs of each repositioning alternative.

Packaging and Labeling Decisions

Many physical products going to the market have to be packaged and labeled. Packaging can play a minor role (e.g., inexpensive hardware items) or a major role (e.g., cosmetics). Some packages—such as the Coke bottle and the L'eggs container—are world famous. Many marketers have called packaging a fifth P, along with price, product, place, and promotion. Most marketers, however, treat packaging as an element of product strategy.

We define *packaging as the activities of designing and producing the container or wrapper for a product.* The container or wrapper is called the package. The package might include up to three levels of material. Thus, Old Spice After-Shave Lotion is in a bottle (*primary package*) that is in a cardboard box (*secondary package*) that is in a corrugated box (*shipping package*) containing six dozen boxes of Old Spice.

In recent times, packaging has become a potent marketing tool. Well-designed packages can create convenience value for the consumer and promotional value for the producer.

Various factors have contributed to packaging's growing use as a marketing tool:

◆ *Self-Service*: An increasing number of products are sold on a self-service basis in supermarkets and discount houses. In an average supermarket, which stocks 15,000 items, the typical shopper passes by some 300 items per minute. Given that 53% of all purchases are made on impulse, the effective package operates as a "five-second commercial." The package must perform many of the sales tasks. It must attract attention, describe the product's features, create consumer confidence, and make a favorable overall impression.

- *Consumer Affluence:* Rising consumer affluence means consumers are willing to pay a little more for the convenience, appearance, dependability, and prestige of better packages.

- *Company and Brand Image:* Companies are recognizing the power of well-designed packages to contribute to instant recognition of the company or brand. The Campbell Soup Company estimates that the average shopper sees its familiar red and white can 76 times a year, creating the equivalent of $26 million worth of advertising.

- *Innovation Opportunity:* Innovative packaging can bring large benefits to consumers and profits to producers. Toothpaste pump dispensers have captured 12% of the toothpaste market because for many consumers, they are more convenient and less messy. Chesebrough-Pond's increased its overall nail-polish sales by 22% after introducing its novel Aziza Polishing Pen for fingernails. Kraft is testing retort pouches, which are foil-and-plastic containers, as a successor to cans. The first companies to put their soft drinks in pop-top cans and their liquid sprays in aerosol cans attracted many new customers. Now wine makers are experimenting with pop-top cans and bag-in-the-carton forms of packaging.

Developing an effective package for a new product requires several decisions. The first task is to establish the *packaging concept*. The packaging concept defines what the package should basically *be* or *do* for the particular product. Should the package's main function(s) be to offer superior product protection, introduce a novel dispersing method, suggest certain qualities about the product or the company, or something else?

> General Foods developed a new dog-food product in the form of meatlike patties. Management decided that the unique and palatable appearance of these patties demanded maximum visibility. *Visibility* was defined as the basic packaging concept. Management considered various alternatives and finally chose a tray with a film covering.

Decisions must be made on additional packaging elements —*size*, *shape*, *materials*, *color*, *text*, and *brand mark*. Decisions must be made on much or little text, cellophane or other transparent films, a plastic or a laminate tray, and so on. Decisions must be made on "tamperproof" devices where a product safety issue is involved. The various packaging elements must be harmonized. Size interacts with materials, colors, and so on. The packaging elements must also be harmonized with decisions on pricing, advertising, and other marketing elements.

After the packaging is designed, it must be tested. *Engineering tests* are conducted to ensure that the package stands up under normal conditions; *visual tests*, to ensure that the script is legible and the colors harmonious; *dealer tests*, to ensure that dealers find the packages attractive and easy to handle; and *consumer tests*, to ensure favorable consumer response.

In spite of these precautions, a packaging design occasionally gets through with some basic flaw:

> *Sizzl-Spray, a pressurized can of barbecue sauce developed by Heublein . . . had a potential packaging disaster that was discovered in the market tests. . . . "We thought we had a good can, but fortunately we first test marketed the product in stores in Texas and California. It appears as soon as the cans got warm they began to explode. Because we hadn't gotten into national distribution, our loss was only $150,000 instead of a couple of million."* [19]

Developing effective packaging may cost several hundred thousand dollars and take from a few months to a year. The importance of packaging cannot be overemphasized, considering the functions it performs in attracting and satisfying customers. Companies must pay attention, however, to the growing environmental and safety concerns about packaging and make decisions that serve society's interests as well as immediate customer and company objectives.[20]

Sellers must label their products. The label may be a simple tag attached to the product or an elaborately designed graphic that is part of the package. The label might carry only the brand name or a great deal of information. Even if the seller prefers a simple label, the law may require additional information.

Labels perform several functions. The label *identifies* the product or brand, for instance, the name Sunkist stamped on oranges. The label might also *grade* the product; thus canned peaches are grade labeled A, B, and C. The label might *describe* the product: who made it, where it was made, when it was made, what it contains, how it is to be used, and how to use it safely. Finally, the label might *promote* the product through its attractive graphics. Some writers distinguish between identification labels, grade labels, descriptive labels, and promotional labels.

Labels eventually become outmoded and need freshening up. The label on Ivory soap has been redone 18 times since the 1890s, with gradual changes in the size and design of the letters. The label on Orange Crush soft drink was substantially changed when its competitors' labels began to picture fresh fruits, thereby pulling in more sales. Orange Crush developed a label with new symbols to suggest freshness and with much stronger and deeper colors.

There is a long history of legal concerns surrounding labels, as well as packaging and products in general. Socially Responsible Marketing 17-1 describes the sensitivities that marketers should have in making product and packaging decisions.

SUMMARY ❖

Product is the first and most important element of the marketing mix. Product strategy calls for making coordinated decisions on product mixes, product lines, brands, packaging, and labeling.

A product can be looked at on five levels. The core benefit is the essential service or benefit that the buyer is buying. The generic product is the basic product recognized as such. The expected product is the set of attributes and conditions that the buyer normally expects in buying the product. The augmented product is additional services and benefits that the seller adds to distinguish the offer from competitors. The potential product is the set of possible new features and services that might eventually be added to the offer.

All products can be classified according to their durability (nondurable goods, durable goods, and services). Consumer goods are usually classified according to customer shopping habits (convenience, shopping, specialty, and unsought goods). Industrial goods are classified according to how they enter the production process (materials and parts, capital items, and supplies and services).

Most companies handle more than one product. Their product mix can be described as having a certain width, length, depth, and consistency. These four dimensions are the tools for developing the company's product strategy. The various lines making up the product mix must be periodically reevaluated for their prof-

Socially Responsible Marketing 17-1

Issues in Product and Packaging Decisions

Product and packaging decisions are attracting increasing public attention. When making such decisions, marketers should carefully consider the following issues and regulations.

Product Decisions and Public Policy

PRODUCT ADDITIONS AND DELETIONS ❖ Under the Antimerger Act, the government may prevent companies from adding products through acquisitions if the effect threatens to lessen competition. Companies dropping products must be aware that they have legal obligations, written or implied, to their suppliers, dealers, and customers who have a stake in the discontinued product.

PATENT PROTECTION ❖ A firm must obey the U.S. patent laws when developing new products. A company cannot make its product "illegally similar" to another company's established product. An example is Polaroid's successful suit to prevent Kodak from selling its new instant-picture camera on the grounds that it infringed on Polaroid's instant-camera patents.

PRODUCT QUALITY AND SAFETY ❖ Manufacturers must comply with specific laws regarding product quality and safety. The Federal Food, Drug, and Cosmetic Act protects consumers from unsafe and adulterated food, drugs, and cosmetics. Various acts provide for the inspection of sanitary conditions in the meat- and poultry-processing industries. Safety legislation has been passed to regulate fabrics, chemical substances, automobiles, toys, and drugs and poisons. The Consumer Product Safety Act of 1972 established a Consumer Product Safety Commission, which has the authority to ban or seize potentially harmful products and set severe penalties for violation of the law. If consumers have been injured by a product that has been defectively designed, they can sue manufacturers or dealers. Product liability suits are now occurring at the rate of over one million per year, with individual awards often running in the millions of dollars. This phenomenon has resulted in huge increases in product-liability insurance premiums, causing big problems in some industries. For example, the cost of liability insurance for producers of children's car seats rose from $50,000 in 1984 to over $750,000 in 1986. Some companies pass these higher rates along to consumers by raising prices. Others are forced to discontinue high-risk product lines.

PRODUCT WARRANTIES ❖ Many manufacturers offer written product warranties to convince customers of their product's quality. But these warranties are often limited and written in a language the average consumer does not understand. Too often, consumers learn that they are not entitled to services, repairs, and replacements that seem to be implied. To protect consumers, Congress passed the Magnuson-Moss Warranty Act in 1975. The act requires that full warranties meet certain minimum standards, including repair "within a reasonable time and without charge" or a replacement or full refund if the product does not work "after a rea-

itability and growth potential. The company's better lines should receive disproportionate support; weaker lines should be phased down or out; and new lines should be added to fill the profit gap.

Each product line consists of product items. The product-line manager should study the sales and profit contributions of each product item as well as the way the items are positioned against competitors' items. This provides information for making product-line decisions. Line stretching involves the question of whether a particular line should be extended downward, upward, or both ways; line filling—whether items should be added within the present range of the line; line modernization—whether the line needs a new look and whether it should be installed piecemeal or all at once; line featuring—which features to use in promoting the line; and line pruning—how to detect and remove weaker product items from the line.

sonable number of attempts" at repair. Otherwise, the company must make it clear that it is offering only a limited warranty. The law has led several manufacturers to switch from full to limited warranties and others to drop warranties altogether as a marketing tool.

Packaging Decisions and Public Policy

FAIR PACKAGING AND LABELING ❖ The public is concerned about false and potentially misleading packaging and labeling. The Federal Trade Commission Act of 1914 held that false, misleading, or deceptive labels or packages constitute unfair competition. Consumers are also concerned about confusing package sizes and shapes that make price comparisons difficult. The Fair Packaging and Labeling Act, passed by Congress in 1967, set mandatory labeling requirements, encouraged voluntary industry packaging standards, and allowed federal agencies to set packaging regulations in specific industries. The Food and Drug Administration has required processed-food producers to include nutritional labeling that clearly states the amounts of protein, fat, carbohydrates, and calories contained in products, as well as their vitamin and mineral content as a percentage of the recommended daily allowance. The FDA has recently launched a drive to control health claims in food labeling by taking action against the potentially misleading use of such descriptions as "light," "high fiber," "no cholesterol," and others. Consumerists have lobbied for additional labeling laws to require *open dating* (to describe product freshness), *unit pricing* (to state the product cost in standard measurement units), *grade labeling* (to rate the quality level of certain consumer goods), and *percentage labeling* (to show the percentage of each important ingredient).

SCARCE RESOURCES AND POLLUTION ❖ The growing concern over shortages of paper, aluminum, and other materials suggests that marketers should try harder to reduce their packaging. For example, the growth of nonreturnable glass containers has resulted in using up to 17 times as much glass as with returnable containers. As much as 40% of the total solid waste in this country is made up of package material. Many packages end up as broken bottles and crumpled cans littering the streets and countryside. All of this packaging creates a major problem in solid waste disposal, requiring huge amounts of labor and energy.

These packaging questions have mobilized public interest in new packaging laws. Marketers must be equally concerned. They must try to design fair, economical, and ecological packages for their products.

SOURCES: See Michael Brody, "When Products Turn," *Fortune*, March 3, 1986, pp. 20–24; "Marketers Feel Product-Liability Pressure," *Advertising Age*, May 12, 1986, pp. 3, 75; Marisa Manley, "Product Liability: You're More Exposed Than You Think," *Harvard Business Review*, September-October 1987, pp. 28–40; and John E. Calfee, "FDA's Ugly Package," *Advertising Age*, March 16, 1992, p. 25.

Companies need to develop brand policies for the individual product items in their lines. They must decide whether to brand at all, whether to do producer or distribution branding, whether to use family or individual brand names, whether to extend the brandname to new products, whether to create multiple brands, and whether to reposition any brand.

Physical products require packaging decisions to create such benefits as protection, economy, convenience, and promotion. Marketers have to develop a packaging concept and test it functionally and psychologically to make sure it achieves the desired objectives and is compatible with public policy. Physical products also require labeling for identification and possible grading, description, and promotion of the product. Sellers may be required by law to present certain information on the label to inform and protect consumers.

NOTES ❖

1. This discussion is adapted from Theodore Levitt, "Marketing Success through Differentiation— of Anything," *Harvard Business Review,* January-February 1980, pp. 83–91. The first level, core benefit, has been added to Levitt's discussion.

2. See Harper W. Boyd, Jr., and Sidney J. Levy, "New Dimensions in Consumer Analysis," *Harvard Business Review,* November–December 1963, pp. 129–40.

3. Theodore Levitt, *The Marketing Mode* (New York: McGraw-Hill, 1969), p. 2.

4. This illustration is found in Benson P. Shapiro, *Industrial Product Policy: Managing the Existing Product Line* (Cambridge, MA: Marketing Science Institute, September 1977), pp. 3–5, 98–101.

5. See Steuart Henderson Britt, "How Weber's Law Can Be Applied to Marketing," *Business Horizons,* February 1975, pp. 21–29.

6. The following scheme benefitted from a presentation by Larry Light, former international division chairman of Ted Bates Advertising, at the Kellogg School, Northwestern University, where he spoke of four dimensions: attributes, benefits, values, and personality; and the scheme of Jean-Noel Kapferer called the *prism of identity* in which he outlined six dimensions of a brand, though not all the same six dimensions described here. See Jean-Noel Kapferer, *Strategic Brand Management: New Approaches to Creating and Evaluating Brand Equity* (London: Kogan Page, 1992), pp. 38ff.

7. David A. Aaker, *Managing Brand Equity* (New York: The Free Press, 1991).

8. Ibid., pp. 21–30. Also see Patrick Barwise, et al., *Accounting for Brands* (London: Institute of Chartered Accountants in England and Wales, 1990); and Peter H. Farquhar, Julia Y. Han, and Yuji Ijiri, "Brands on the Balance Sheet," *Marketing Management,* Winter 1992, pp. 16–22. Brand equity should reflect not only the capitalized value of the incremental profits from the current use of the brand name but also the value of its potential extensions to other products.

9. See Interbrand, *World's Greatest Brands* (New York: John Wiley & Son, 1992). Landor Associates also studies top brands in different countries using two measures: the "share-of-mind score," which is a measure of brand recall, and "esteem," which is a measure of favorable opinion about the brand. The scores on the two measures are averaged to develop the brand's rank or image power. The top brands differ in each country and region. For example, the top five brands in Europe are Coca-Cola, Sony, Mercedes-Benz, BMW, and Philips; and the top five brands in Japan are Sony, National, Mercedes-Benz, Toyota, and Taskashimaya. For more reading, see Cathy Taylor, "Consumers Know Native Brands Best," *Adweek,* September 17, 1990, p. 31; Kathleen Deveny, "More Brand Names Gain Recognition Around the World," *The Wall Street Journal,* September 13, 1990, p. B7; R. Craig Endicott, "The Top 200 Brands," *Advertising Age,* May 21, 1990, pp. 25–27; and "Hard Sellers: The Leading Advertisers," *The Wall Street Journal,* March 21, 1991, p. B4.

10. For further reading, see Brian F. Harris and Roger A. Strang, "Marketing Strategies in the Age of Generics," *Journal of Marketing,* Fall 1985, pp. 70–81.

11. Slotting fees are payments required or demanded by retailers to stock new products and find "slots" for them on the shelves. Thus Safeway required a payment of $25,000 from a small pizza roll manufacturer to stock its product.

12. Quoted in "Trade Promotion: Much Ado About Nothing," *Promo,* October 1991, p. 37.

13. See Gretchen Morgenson, "The Trend is Not Their Friend," *Forbes,* September 16, 1991; and "What's In a Name? Less and Less," *Business Week,* July 8, 1991.

14. See Kim Robertson, "Strategically Desirable Brand Name Characteristics," *Journal of Consumer Marketing,* Fall 1989, pp. 61–70.

15. See Steven M. Shugan, "Branded Variants," *1989 AMA Educators' Proceedings* (Chicago: American Marketing Association, 1989), pp. 33–38.

16. Al Ries and Jack Trout, *Positioning: The Battle For Your Mind* (New York: McGraw-Hill, 1981).

17. *Progressive Grocer,* October 1990, pp. 113–14.

18. See Mark B. Taylor, "Cannibalism in Multibrand Firms," *Journal of Business Strategy,* Spring 1986, pp. 69–75.

19. "Product Tryouts: Sales Tests in Selected Cities Help Trim Risks of National Marketing," *The Wall Street Journal,* August 10, 1962.

20. See Alicia Swasy, "Sales Lost Their Vim? Try Repackaging," *The Wall Street Journal,* October 11, 1989, p. B1.

18

Managing Service Businesses and Ancillary Services

There are no such things as service industries. There are only industries whose service components are greater or less than those of other industries. Everybody is in service.

THEODORE LEVITT

The four Ps of services marketing: people, people, people, and people.

RICHARD DOW

Marketing thinking developed initially in connection with selling physical products such as toothpaste, cars, steel, and equipment. Yet one of the major megatrends has been the phenomenal growth of services. In the United States, service jobs now account for 77% of total employment and 70% of GNP and are expected to provide 90% of all new jobs in the next ten years. This has led to a growing interest in the special problems of marketing services.[1] We will look at the issues here.

Service industries are quite varied. The *government sector*, with its courts, employment services, hospitals, loan agencies, military services, police and fire departments, post office, regulatory agencies, and schools, is in the service business. The *private nonprofit sector*, with its museums, charities, churches, colleges, foundations, and hospitals, is in the service business. A good part of the *business sector*, with its airlines, banks, computer-service bureaus, hotels, insurance companies, law firms, management consulting firms, medical practices, motion picture companies, plumbing-repair companies, and real-estate firms, is in the service business. Many workers in the *manufacturing sector* are really service providers, such as the computer operators, accountants, and legal staff. In fact, they make up a "service factory" providing services to the "goods factory."

Not only are there traditional service industries, but new types keep popping up all the time:

> *For a fee, there are now companies that will balance your budget, babysit your philodendron, wake you up in the morning, drive you to work or find you a new home, job, car, wife, clairvoyant, cat feeder, or gypsy violinist. Or perhaps you want to rent a garden tractor? A few cattle? Some original paintings? Or maybe some hippies to decorate your next cocktail party? If it is business services you need, other companies will plan your convention and sales meetings, design your products, handle your data processing, or supply temporary secretaries or even executives.*[2]

In this chapter, we will examine the following questions:

- How are services defined and classified?
- What are the distinctive characteristics of services as opposed to goods?
- How can service firms improve their differentiation, quality, and productivity?
- How can goods-producing companies improve their customer-support services?

Nature and Classification of Services

We define a service as follows:

❖ A service *is any act or performance that one party can offer to another that is essentially intangible and does not result in the ownership of anything. Its production may or may not be tied to a physical product.*

A company's offer to the marketplace usually includes some services. The service component can be a minor or a major part of the total offer. In fact, the offer can range from a pure good on the one hand to a pure service on the other. Five categories of offer can be distinguished:

1. *A Pure Tangible Good:* Here the offer consists primarily of a tangible good such as soap, toothpaste, or salt. No services accompany the product.

2. *A Tangible Good with Accompanying Services:* Here the offer consists of a tangible good accompanied by one or more services to enhance its consumer appeal. For example, an automobile manufacturer must sell more than an automobile. Levitt observes that "the more technologically sophisticated the generic product (e.g., cars and computers), the more dependent are its sales on the quality and availability of its accompanying customer services (e.g., display rooms, delivery, repairs and maintenance, application aids, operator training, installation advice, warranty fulfillment). In this sense, General Motors is probably more service intensive than manufacturing intensive. Without its services, its sales would shrivel."[3] In fact, many manufacturers are now discovering opportunities to sell their services as a separate profit center (see Marketing Strategies 18-1).

3. *A Hybrid:* Here the offer consists of equal parts of goods and services. Restaurants, for example, are patronized both for their food and their service.

4. *A Major Service with Accompanying Minor Goods and Services:* Here the offer consists of a major service along with additional services and/or supporting goods. For example, airline passengers are buying transportation service. They arrive at their destinations without anything tangible to show for their expenditure. However, the trip includes some tangibles, such as food and drinks, a ticket stub, and an airline magazine. The service requires a capital-intensive good—an airplane—for its realization, but the primary item is a service.

5. *A Pure Service:* Here the offer consists primarily of a service. Examples include babysitting, psychotherapy, and massages. The psychoanalyst provides a pure service, with the only tangible elements an office and a couch.

As a consequence of this varying goods-to-service mix, it is difficult to generalize about services unless further distinctions are made.

First, services vary as to whether they are *equipment based* (automated car washes, vending machines) or *people based* (window washing, accounting services). People-based services vary by whether they are provided by unskilled, skilled, or professional workers.

Some services require the *client's presence*. Thus brain surgery involves the client's presence, but a car repair does not. If the client must be present, the service provider has to be considerate of his or her needs. Thus beauty shop operators will invest in their shop's decor, play background music, and engage in light conversation with the client.

Services differ as to whether they meet a *personal need* (personal services) or a *business need* (business services). Physicians will price physical examinations differently for private patients versus company employees on a retainer. Service providers typically develop different marketing programs for personal and business markets.

Finally, *service providers differ in their objectives* (profit or nonprofit) and *ownership* (private or public). These two characteristics, when crossed, produce four quite different types of service organizations. Clearly, the marketing programs of a private investor hospital will differ from those of a private charity hospital or a Veterans' Administration hospital.[4]

Manufacturers Learn to Sell Services

As many companies experience shrinking profit margins on the products they sell, they are forced to pay more attention to trying to make money on their services. They sometimes charge fees for services which they formerly gave away with the product. In other cases, they are pricing their services more carefully. Auto dealers today make most of their profit on selling financing, insurance, and repair services and contracts, not on selling automobiles. In still other cases, companies are creating service businesses alongside their product businesses. In some instances, their service businesses are growing faster and are more profitable than the company's product businesses.

Here are six ways that manufacturers can create service businesses:

1. *Repackaging their product into a system solution.* A company can be satisfied selling only its products—chemicals, computers, machine tools—or embed them into service programs that meet more of the customers' needs. Thus, a service-minded fertilizer company can offer to customize the fertilizer for each individual farm and even spread the fertilizer with its own equipment.

2. *Packaging the company's internal services into saleable external services.* Some companies, in developing an internal competence, recognize that they can sell this competence to other companies. For example, Xerox developed a highly effective internal salesforce training program and subsequently decided to launch Xerox Learning Systems to sell its sales training system to other companies. Today Xerox is so proficient at *benchmarking* that it could easily package its system for sale to other companies.

3. *Servicing other companies from the company's physical facilities.* Companies that manage a physical facility often find that they can sell the facility's services to other companies. Kimberly-Clark, located in Neenah, Wisconsin, operates and maintains its own fleet of corporate aircraft. It has expanded the facility to provide and sell maintenance and overhaul services to other companies operating corporate aircraft.

4. *Offering to manage other companies' physical facilities.* A major growth area is *contract management* of such facilities as lawns, cafeterias, data processing centers, and so on. Thus Scott, the seed company, also operates a lawn maintenance business; and S. C. Johnson, which sells insect sprays, also manages a major extermination service business called BBBK.

5. *Selling financial services.* Equipment companies often discover that they can profit from financing the customers' purchases. GE Credit Corporation originally financed only GE customers and dealers, but today finances commercial and home loans, auto leases, dealer inventories, and other areas.

6. *Moving into distribution services.* Manufacturers can also integrate forward into owning and operating retailing outlets for their products. Hart Schaffner and Marx is essentially a clothing manufacturer which also operates a series of retail clothing chains. And Quaker Oats, the cereal manufacturer, manages several restaurant chains.

All this is to say that manufacturers should not think of themselves as strictly manufacturers when some of their best opportunities may lie in creating service businesses.

SOURCES: See Irving D. Canton, "Learning to Love the Service Economy," *Harvard Business Review*, May–June 1984, pp. 89–97; and Mack Hanan, *Profits Without Products: How to Transform Your Product Business into a Service* (New York: AMACOM, 1992).

Characteristics of Services and Their Marketing Implications

Services have four major characteristics that greatly affect the design of marketing programs.

Intangibility

Services are intangible. Unlike physical products, they cannot be seen, tasted, felt, heard, or smelled before they are bought. The person getting a "face lift" cannot see the results before the purchase, and the patient in the psychiatrist's office cannot predict the outcome.

To reduce uncertainty, buyers will look for signs or evidence of the service quality. They will draw inferences about service quality from the place, people, equipment, communication material, symbols, and price that they see.

Therefore, the service provider's task is to "manage the evidence," to "tangibilize the intangible."[5] Whereas product marketers are challenged to add abstract ideas, service marketers are challenged to put physical evidence and imagery on their abstract offers. Consider the following tangible images: "You are in good *hands* with Allstate"; "I've got a piece of the *Rock*." (Prudential).

Suppose a bank wants to position itself as the "fast" bank. It could "tangibilize" this positioning strategy through a number of tools:

1. *Place:* The bank's physical setting must connote quick service. The bank's exterior and interior should have clean lines. The layout of the desks and the traffic flow should be planned carefully. Queues should not get overly long.

2. *People:* The bank's personnel should be busy. There should be a sufficient number of employees to manage the workload.

3. *Equipment:* The bank's equipment—computers, copying machines, desks—should be and look "state of the art." A customer would think twice if all the typewriters were 1940-vintage Remingtons.

4. *Communication Material:* The bank's communication material—text and photos—should suggest efficiency and speed.

5. *Symbols:* The bank should choose a name and symbol suggesting its fast service. It could adopt the Greek god Mercury as a pictorial symbol.

6. *Price:* The bank could advertise that it will deposit $5 in the account of any customer who waits in line for more than five minutes.

Inseparability

Services are typically produced and consumed simultaneously. This is not true of physical goods that are manufactured, put into inventory, distributed through multiple resellers, and consumed still later. If the service is rendered by a person, then the provider is part of the service. Since the client is also present as the service is produced, provider-client interaction is a special feature of services marketing. Both the provider and the client affect the service outcome.

In the case of entertainment and professional services, buyers are highly interested in the specific provider. It is not the same concert if Kenny Rogers is indisposed and replaced by Marie Osmond, or if a legal defense will be supplied by John Nobody because F. Lee Bailey is unavailable. When clients have strong provider preferences, price is raised to ration the preferred provider's limited time.

Several strategies exist for getting around this limitation. The service provider can learn to work with larger groups. Psychotherapists have moved from one-on-one therapy to small-group therapy to groups of over 300 people in a large hotel ballroom who are getting simultaneously "therapized." The service provider can learn to work faster—the psychotherapist can spend 30 minutes with each patient instead of 50 minutes and can see more patients. The service organization can train more service providers and build up client confidence, as H&R Block has done with its national network of trained tax consultants.

Variability

Services are highly variable, since they depend on who provides them and when and where they are provided. A Dr. Christiaan Barnard heart transplant was of higher quality than one performed by a less-experienced surgeon. And Dr. Barnard's heart transplants varied with his energy and mental set at the time of each operation. Service buyers are aware of this high variability and frequently talk to others before selecting a service provider.

Service firms can take three steps toward quality control. The first is investing in good personnel selection and training. Airlines, banks, and hotels spend substantial sums to train their employees in providing good service. Thus one should find the same friendly and helpful personnel in every Hyatt Hotel.

The second step is standardizing the service-performance process throughout the organization. This is helped by preparing a *service blueprint* which depicts the service events and processes in a flow chart, with the objective of recognizing potential service fail points. Figure 18-1 shows a service blueprint for a nationwide floral-delivery organization.[6] The customer's experience is limited to dialing the phone, making choices, and placing an order. Behind the scenes, the floral organization gathers the flowers, places them in a vase, delivers them, and collects payment.

The third step is monitoring customer satisfaction through suggestion and complaint systems, customer surveys, and comparison shopping, so that poor service can be detected and corrected.[7]

Perishability

Services cannot be stored. The reason many doctors charge patients for missed appointments is that the service value existed only at the point when the patient should have shown up. The perishability of services is not a problem when demand is steady because it is easy to staff the services in advance. When demand fluctuates, service firms have difficult problems. For example, public-transportation companies have to own much more equipment because of rush-hour demand than they would if demand were even throughout the day.

Sasser has described several strategies for producing a better match between demand and supply in a service business.[8]

On the demand side:

♦ *Differential Pricing* will shift some demand from peak to off-peak periods. Examples include low early-evening movie prices and weekend discount prices for car rentals.

♦ *Nonpeak Demand Can Be Cultivated:* McDonald's opened its Egg McMuffin breakfast service, and hotels developed their minivacation weekends.

♦ *Complementary Services* can be developed during peak time to provide alternatives to waiting customers, such as cocktail lounges to sit in while waiting for a table and automatic tellers in banks.

♦ *Reservation Systems* are a way to manage the demand level, and airlines, hotels, and physicians employ them extensively.

On the supply side:

♦ *Part-Time Employees* can be hired to serve peak demand. Colleges add part-time teachers when enrollment goes up, and restaurants call in part-time waitresses when needed.

♦ *Peak-Time Efficiency Routines* can be introduced. Employees perform only essential tasks during peak periods. Paramedics assist physicians during busy periods.

♦ *Increased Consumer Participation* in the tasks can be encouraged, as when consumers fill out their own medical records or bag their own groceries.

♦ *Shared Services* can be developed, as when several hospitals share medical-equipment purchases.

♦ *Facilities for Future Expansion* can be developed, as when an amusement park buys surrounding land for later development.

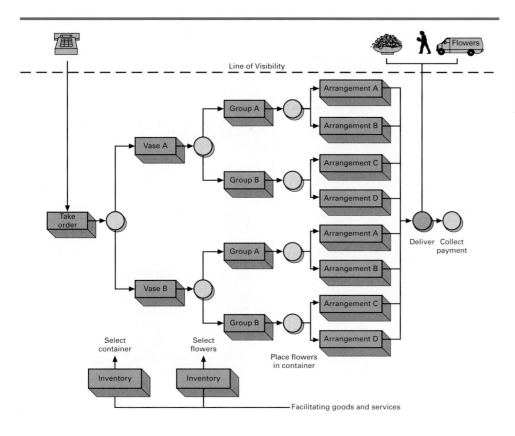

FIGURE 18-1
A Service-Performance-
Process Map: Nationwide
Floral Delivery
Source: G. Lynn Shostack, "Service
Positioning Through Structural
Change," *Journal of Marketing*,
January 1987, p. 39.

Marketing Strategies for Service Firms

Until recently, service firms lagged behind manufacturing firms in their use of marketing. Many service businesses are small (shoe repair, barbershops) and do not use formal management or marketing techniques. There are also professional service businesses (law and accounting firms) that formerly believed it was unprofessional to use marketing. Other service businesses (colleges, hospitals) faced so much demand until recently that they saw no need for marketing.

Furthermore, service businesses are more difficult to manage using a *traditional marketing* approach. In a product business, the product is fairly standardized and sits on a shelf, waiting for the customer to reach for it, pay, and leave. In a service business, there are more elements (see Figure 18-2). Consider a customer visiting a bank to get a loan (service X). The customer sees other customers waiting for this and other services. The customer also sees a physical environment consisting of a building, interior, equipment, and furniture. In addition, the customer sees contact personnel and deals with a loan officer. All this is visible to the customer. Not visible is a whole "backroom" production process and organization system that supports the visible service business. Thus the service outcome is influenced by a host of variable elements.

In view of this complexity, Gronroos has argued that service marketing requires not only external marketing but also internal and interactive marketing (see Figure 18-3).[9] *External marketing* describes the normal work done by the company to prepare, price, distribute, and promote the service to customers. *Internal marketing* describes the work done by the company to train and motivate its employees to serve customers well. Berry has argued that the most important contribution the marketing department can make is to be "exceptionally clever in getting everyone

CHAPTER 18
Managing Service Businesses
and Ancillary Services

FIGURE 18-2
Elements in a Service
Encounter
Source: Slightly modified from P.
Eiglier and E. Langeard, "A
Conceptual Approach of the Service
Offering," in *Proceedings of the
EAARM X Annual Conference,* eds. H.
Hartvig Larsen and S. Heede,
Copenhagen School of Economics
and Business Administration, 1981.

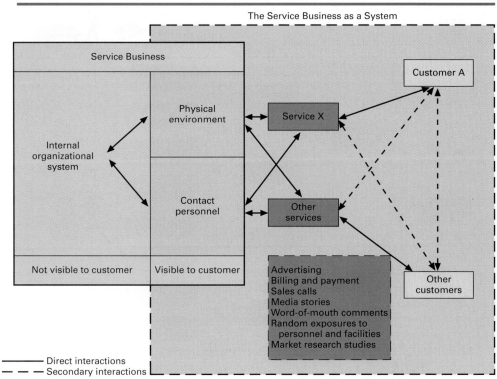

else in the organization to practice marketing."[10] (See Marketing Strategies 18-2.)

Interactive marketing describes the employees' skill in serving the client. The client judges service quality not only by its *technical quality* (e.g., Was the surgery successful?) but also by its *functional quality* (e.g., Did the surgeon show concern and inspire confidence?).[11] Professionals along with other service providers must deliver "high touch" as well as "high tech."[12]

In fact, there are some services where the customers cannot judge the technical quality even after they have received the services! Figure 18-4 arrays various products and services according to their difficulty of evaluation.[13] At the left are

FIGURE 18-3
Three Types of Marketing
in Service Industries

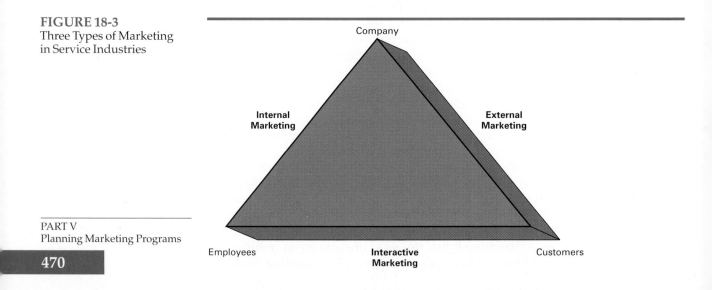

goods high in *search qualities*, namely, characteristics that the buyer can evaluate before purchase. In the middle are goods and services high in *experience qualities*, namely, characteristics that the buyer can evaluate after purchase. At the right are goods and services high in *credence qualities*, namely, characteristics that the buyer normally finds hard to evaluate even after consumption.

Since services are generally higher in experience and credence qualities, consumers feel more risk in their purchase. That has several consequences. First, service consumers generally rely more on word of mouth than on service-firm advertising. Second, they rely heavily on price, personnel, and physical cues to judge the service quality. Third, they are highly loyal to the service provider when satisfied.

As services competition intensifies, more marketing sophistication will be needed. One of the main agents of change will be product marketers who move into service industries. Sears moved into services marketing years ago—insurance, banking, income-tax consulting, car rentals. Gerber Products runs nursery schools and insurance companies.[14]

Service companies face three tasks—increasing their *competitive differentiation*, their *service quality*, and their *productivity*. Although these interact to some extent, we will examine each separately.

Managing Differentiation

Service marketers frequently complain about the difficulty of differentiating their services from those of competitors. The deregulation of several major service industries—communications, transportation, energy, banking—precipitated intense price competition. The early success of People's Express airline showed that many commuters cared more about travel costs than service. The great success of Charles Schwab in the discount brokerage service showed that many customers had little loyalty to the more established brokerage houses when they could save money. To the extent that customers view a service as fairly homogeneous, they care less about the provider than the price.

CHAPTER 18
Managing Service Businesses
and Ancillary Services

471

FIGURE 18-4 Continuum of Evaluation for Different Types of Products

Source: Valarie A. Zeithaml, "How Consumer Evaluation Processes Differ between Goods and Services," in *Marketing of Services*, eds. James H. Donnelly and William R. George (Chicago: American Marketing Association, 1981).

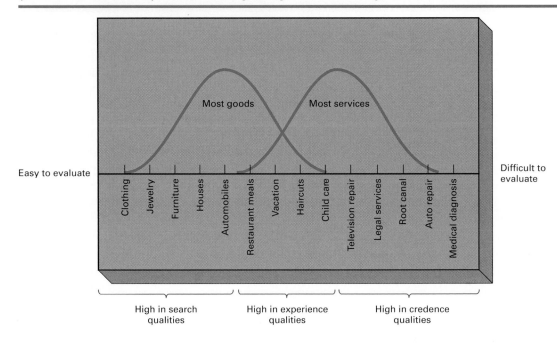

The solution to price competition is to develop a differentiated offer, delivery, and image. The *offer* can include *innovative features* to distinguish it from competitor offers. What the customer expects is called the *primary service package*, and to this can be added *secondary service features*. In the airline industry, various carriers have introduced such secondary service features as movies, advanced seating, merchandise for sale, air-to-ground telephone service, and frequent-flyer award programs. Hertz recently added an innovative secondary service feature to differentiate its auto rental service, namely, its #1 Club Gold service for its Club Gold members:

> The Hertz customer is picked up by a Hertz courtesy shuttle bus and taken directly to the preassigned car. The keys will be in the ignition and the trunk is open, ready to receive the luggage. The preprinted invoice will be hanging from the rear-view mirror and the customer simply shows his or her driver's license to the security guard on the way out.

The major problem is that most service innovations are easily copied. Few of them are preemptive in the long run. Still, the service company that regularly researches and introduces service innovations will gain a succession of temporary advantages over its competitors, and through earning a reputation for innovation, may retain customers who want to go with the best. Thus Citicorp enjoys the reputation as being a lead innovator in the banking industry in aggressively creating or furthering such innovations as automatic teller machines, nationwide banking, broad-spectrum financial accounts and credit cards, and floating prime rates.

The service company can differentiate its *service delivery* in three ways, namely, through *people*, through *physical environment*, and through *process* (the 3Ps of service marketing). A service company can distinguish itself by having more able and reliable customer-contact people than its competitors. A service company can develop a more attractive physical environment in which the service is delivered. Finally, a service company can design a superior delivery process, such as home banking.

Service companies can also work on differentiating their *image*, specifically through symbols and branding. The Harris Bank of Chicago adopted the lion as its symbol and uses it on its stationery, in its advertising, and even as stuffed animals offered to new depositors. As a result, the Harris lion is well known and confers an image of strength to the bank. Several hospitals have attained "megabrand" reputations for being the best in their field, such as the Mayo Clinic, Massachusetts General, and Sloane-Kettering. Any of these hospitals could open clinics in other cities and attract patients on the strength of their "brand power." Several highly branded service companies have developed successful international operations (see Global Marketing 18-1).

Global Marketing 18-1

Expanding a Service Business Internationally: Club Med

Club Med, a subsidiary of the French firm, Club Méditerranée, S.A., managed to achieve exceptional marketing and financial success in its short 40-year history. Gilbert Trigano opened the first Club Med "village" in Greece in 1955, and today Club Med operates more than 104 villages in 30 countries.

The Club Med formula is simple: provide a vacation that removes people from everyday pressures, where they don't have to make many decisions, where they can dress casually, meet, play, and dine with other people, and enjoy beautiful warm weather. For a few memorable weeks, the vacationers escape from the competitive world and enter into a simpler, more cooperative existence.

The Club Med villages are located mostly in warm-weather areas such as the Caribbean, Oceania, Pacific Basin, and the Malaysia/Indonesian area. Guests prepay for their whole stay and use beads instead of money in the village. Club Med rooms are identical and there are no locks on the door nor room telephones to connect people with the outside world. The guests, called GMs (gentils membres) are assisted by the staff members, called GOs (gentils organisateurs). The GOs, of whom there may be 100 in a village, work long hours and act as the guests' instructors, entertainers, and friends. The villages are located in picturesque settings and are fully equipped with tennis courts, discotheques, and excellent food service.

Club Med earns an attractive profit stemming from the guests' fees and other areas of savings. The Club earns millions in interest by receiving and depositing guests' prepayments weeks in advance of the guests' visits. Club Med is able to buy air transportation at wholesale rates because of its large volume, while charging retail rates to the guests. In addition, substantial money for building new villages comes from the host countries, which are eager to build their tourism industry.

Until recently, Club Med applied a standard approach to the design and operation of its villages. Today it is introducing more adaptations in the effort to attract and satisfy more target markets. Club Med has created some villages to appeal to more mature customers who are married and have children. The Club has established computer workshops in some villages to appeal to more business-oriented guests. The Club has increased the number of non-French GOs as a way to further internationalize the villages. New villages have been located more conveniently to guests traveling from the northeastern United States. Advertising places less emphasis now on selling Club Med as a place for singles who are pursuing sun, fun, and beautiful physiques. All said, Club Med is moving from standardized global marketing to adaptive global marketing.

Source: See, for example, "A New Course for Club Med," *Asian Business*, January 1991, pp. 96–98.

Managing Service Quality

One of the major ways to differentiate a service firm is to deliver consistently higher-quality service than competitors. The key is to meet or exceed the target customers' service-quality expectations. Their expectations are formed by their past experiences, word of mouth, and service-firm advertising. The customers choose providers on this basis and, after receiving the service, they compare the *perceived service* with the *expected service*. If the perceived service falls below the expected service, customers lose interest in the provider. If the perceived service meets or exceeds their expectations, they are apt to use the provider again. (See Companies and Industries 18-1.)

Parasuraman, Zeithaml, and Berry formulated a service-quality model that highlights the main requirements for delivering the expected service quality.[15] The model, shown in Figure 18-5, identifies five gaps that cause unsuccessful service delivery. They are described in the following paragraphs.

1. *Gap Between Consumer Expectation and Management Perception:* Management does not always perceive correctly what customers want. Hospital administrators may think that patients want better food, but patients may be more concerned with nurse responsiveness.

2. *Gap Between Management Perception and Service-Quality Specification:* Management might correctly perceive the customers' wants but not set a specified performance standard. Hospital administrators may tell the nurses to give "fast" service without specifying it quantitatively.

FIGURE 18-5
Service-Quality Model
Source: A. Parasuraman, Valarie A. Zeithaml, and Leonard L. Berry, "A Conceptual Model of Service Quality and Its Implications for Future Research," *Journal of Marketing*, Fall 1985, p. 44.

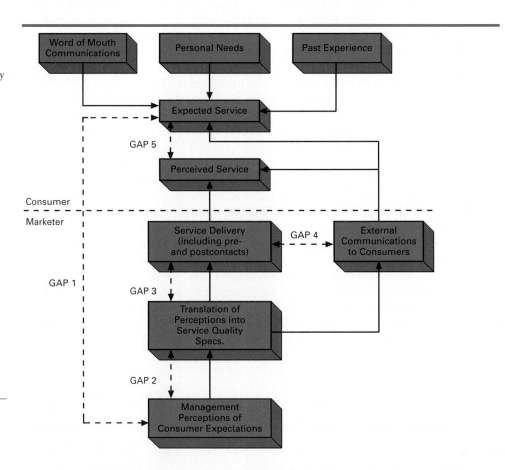

Companies and Industries 18-1

What Car Buyers Think of Auto Dealers

Theodore R. Cunningham, Chrysler's executive vice-president of sales and marketing, recently shared this with a reporter from *The Wall Street Journal:* "In a recent survey, new-car buyers said they'd rather visit their dentist for a root canal than have to go through the process of buying a car again. We're out to change the entire dealership culture."

Every car buyer has had the experience of entering a showroom, being approached immediately by an overly aggressive or overly friendly salesperson, who either couldn't answer certain questions or obviously faked the answers, who couldn't cite the rock-bottom price without going to the boss, who returned saying that fortunately the boss is in a good mood and could meet the price, and then during the contract signing, the salesperson tried to sell additional options on equipment, rustproofing, warranties, with the customer growing more and more exhausted. A few days later, when picking up the car, the salesperson didn't remember the customer, and didn't return phone calls promptly when the customer's new car didn't start. "Call the service department," was the normal answer from the salesforce.

No wonder that a growing number of car buyers would prefer to buy their car by mail rather than step into a dealer showroom. And the fault is not entirely the dealers. Auto manufacturers put so much pressure on their dealers to move cars, and the incentives are all locked up with the volume sold, that dealer salespeople understandably get pushy.

Of course, there have always been auto dealerships that do offer exceptional service quality. Carl Sewell, who runs one of America's largest and most successful dealerships, provides matchless service for his Dallas customers. He follows the rule: "If the customer asks, the answer is always yes." His Cadillac loan car fleet numbers 150 cars. His dealership has a service technician on call 24 hours a day, seven days a week. Customers who break their key in their lock or whose car stalls will be rescued by his service people at no charge. If his service people fail to repair a car right the first time, the dealership will drive a "loaner" to the customer and pick up the customer's car at no charge. When the customer's car is ready, the customer receives a complimentary gift. Sewell isn't satisfied just selling a car once to a customer. His philosophy is aptly summed up in his best-selling book, *Customers for Life: How to Turn That One-Time Buyer into a Lifetime Customer.*

But the occasional Carl Sewell isn't who is beginning to turn around auto manufacturers' thinking about dealerships. It's what a few new car makers have done with their dealerships. The pace has been set by the Japanese when Toyota franchised its Lexus dealerships and Nissan franchised its Infinity dealerships. Both companies spent almost as much time designing the dealership philosophy and setting as designing their new cars. The new showrooms are physically attractive and expansive. The customer enters and is offered coffee by the receptionist, and then brought to look at any car. A salesperson arrives and introduces the customer to the sales manager. The customer is then given a tour of the service bays (normally empty of cars). The customer is offered a generous test drive. Throughout, the interaction with the salesperson is quiet, calm, and cordial with the salesperson supplying accurate technical information. There is no high pressure selling. If the customer leaves without ordering a car, there will be one or two follow-up calls that are brief and polite. If the customer decides to buy the car, there is no haggling over price.

Seeing this new model of dealer performance, General Motors copied it as "best practice" in setting up the Saturn dealerships. Now Chrysler, in launching its new LH model, will spend $30 million to reeducate the 100,000 people working in its dealerships—from owners to sales managers to service personnel to switchboard operators. Ford is also attempting to install "relationship marketing" in its dealerships. All of these auto companies are realizing that a retained customer may be worth something like $325,000 over a lifetime, if they do the job right.

SOURCES: Bradley A. Stertz, "For LH Models, Chrysler Maps New Way to Sell," *The Wall Street Journal*, June 30, 1992, p. B1. Carl Sewell and Paul B. Brown, *Customers for Life: How to Turn That One-Time Buyer into a Lifetime Customer* (New York: Pocket Books, 1990).

3. *Gap Between Service-Quality Specifications and Service Delivery:* The personnel might be poorly trained or overworked and incapable or unwilling to meet the standard. Or they may be held to conflicting standards, such as taking time to listen to customers and serving them fast.

4. *Gap Betweeen Service Delivery and External Communications:* Consumer expectations are affected by statements made by company representatives and ads. If a hospital brochure shows a beautiful room but the patient arrives and finds the room to be cheap and tacky looking, then the external communications have distorted the customer's expectations.

5. *Gap Between Perceived Service and Expected Service:* This gap occurs when the consumer measures the company's performance in a different way and misperceives the service quality. The physician may keep visiting the patient to show care, but the patient may interpret this as an indication that something really is wrong.

The same researchers found that there are five determinants of service quality. These are presented in the order of their importance as rated by customers (an allocation of 100 points):[16]

1. *Reliability:* The ability to perform promised service dependably and accurately. (32)

2. *Responsiveness:* The willingness to help customers and to provide prompt service. (22)

3. *Assurance:* The knowledge and courtesy of employees and their ability to convey trust and confidence. (19)

4. *Empathy:* The provision of caring, individualized attention to customers. (16)

5. *Tangibles:* The appearance of physical facilities, equipment, personnel, and communication materials. (11)

Various studies show that excellently managed service companies share a number of common practices. Among them are the following:

1. *A Strategic Concept:* Top service companies are "customer obsessed." They have a clear sense of their target customers and the customer needs they are trying to satisfy. They have developed a distinctive strategy for satisfying these needs that wins enduring customer loyalty.

2. *A History of Top-Management Commitment to Quality:* Companies such as Marriott, Disney, Delta, and McDonald's have thorough commitments to quality. Their management looks not only at financial performance on a monthly basis but also at service performance. Ray Kroc of McDonald's insisted on continually measuring each McDonald's outlet on its conformance to QSCV: quality, service, cleanliness, and value. Franchises that failed to conform were dropped.

3. *The Setting of High Standards:* The best service providers set high service-quality standards. Swissair, for example, aims for having 96% or more of its passengers rate its service as good or superior; otherwise it takes action. Citibank aims to answer phone calls within ten seconds and customer letters within two days. The standards must be set *appropriately* high. A 98% accuracy standard may sound good but it would result in Federal Express losing 64,000 packages a day, ten words would be misspelled on each page, 400,000 prescriptions would be misfilled daily, and drinking water would be unsafe eight days a year. Companies can be distinguished between those offering "merely good" service and those offering "breakthrough" service aiming at 100% defect-free service.[17]

4. *Systems for Monitoring Service Performance:* The top service firms audit service performance, both their own and competitors', on a regular basis. They use a number of devices to measure performance: *comparison shopping, ghost shopping, customer surveys, suggestion and complaint forms, service-audit teams,* and *letters to the president.* General Electric sends out 700,000 response cards a year to households to rate its service people's performance. Citibank checks continuously on measures of ART, namely, *accuracy, responsiveness,* and *timeliness.* It does "ghost shopping" to find out if its employees deliver good service. The First Chicago Bank employs a Performance Measurement Program consisting of charting on a weekly basis its performance on a large number of customer-sensitive issues. Figure 18-6 shows a typical chart used by the bank to track

FIGURE 18-6   Tracking Customer Service Performance

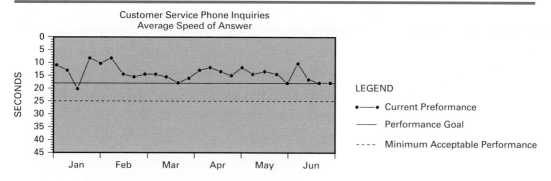

its speed in answering customer service phone inquiries. It will take action whenever its performance falls below the minimum acceptable performance level. It also raises its performance goal over time. Marketing Concepts and Tools 18-1 describes a tool called *importance-performance analysis* for rating the various elements of the service bundle and identifying what actions are required.

5. *Systems for Satisfying Complaining Customers:* Well-run service businesses respond quickly and generously to customer complaints. Timothy Firnstahl, who runs a Seattle restaurant chain called Satisfaction Guaranteed Eateries, Inc., set down these service recovery guidelines: "When guests have to wait more than ten minutes beyond their reservation time, but less than twenty, we suggest free drinks. If they wait more than twenty minutes, the entire meal may be free. If the bread arrives more than five minutes after the guests sit down, we suggest free chowder"[18] (see Marketing Concepts and Tools 18-2).

6. *Satisfying the Employees as Well as the Customers*: Excellently managed service companies believe that employee relations will reflect on customer relations. Management carries out internal marketing and creates an environment of employee support and rewards for good service performance. Management regularly audits employees' satisfaction with their jobs. At one time, Citibank set a customer satisfaction goal of 90% and an employee satisfaction goal of 70%. But the question was raised whether Citibank could deliver 90% customer satisfaction if 30% of their employees are unhappy. Karl Albrecht observed that unhappy employees can be "terrorists." Rosenbluth and Peters, in *The Customer Is Number Two,* go so far as to say that the company's employees, not the company's customers, have to be made number one if the company hopes to truly satisfy its customers.[19]

Companies and Industries 18-2 illustrates how one great service marketer, Disney, combines a number of excellent practices that provide a continuing high level of customer satisfaction with its theme parks.

Managing Productivity

Service firms are under great pressure to increase productivity. Since service businesses are highly labor intensive, costs have been rising rapidly. There are six approaches to improving service productivity.

The first is to have service providers work harder or more skillfully. Working harder is not a likely solution, but working more skillfully can occur through better selection and training procedures.

The second is to increase the quantity of service by surrendering some quality. Doctors working for HMOs have moved toward handling more patients and giving less time to each patient.

Importance-Performance Analysis

Services can be usefully rated according to their *customer importance* and *company performance*. The accompanying table shows how customers rated 14 service elements (attributes) of an automobile dealer's service department on importance and performance.

Importance was rated on a four-point scale of "extremely important," "important," "slightly important," and "not important." Dealer performance was rated on a four-point scale of "excellent," "good," "fair," and "poor." For example, "Job done right the first time" received a mean importance rating of 3.83 and a mean performance rating of 2.63, indicating that customers felt it was highly important but was not being performed well.

The ratings of the 14 elements are displayed in the figure and are divided into four sections. Quadrant A shows important service elements that are not being performed at the desired levels; they include elements 1, 2, and 9. The dealer should concentrate on improving the service department's performance on these elements. Quadrant B shows important service elements where the department is performing well; its job is to maintain the high performance. Quadrant C shows minor service elements that are being delivered in a mediocre way but do not need any attention, since they are not very important. Quadrant D shows that a minor service element, "Send out maintenance notices," is being performed in an excellent manner, a case of possible overkill. Measuring service elements according to their importance and performance tells marketers where to focus their efforts.

SOURCE: John A. Martilla and John C. James, "Importance–Performance Analysis," *Journal of Marketing*, January 1977, pp. 77–79.

ATTRIBUTE NUMBER	ATTRIBUTE DESCRIPTION	MEAN IMPORTANCE RATING*	MEAN PERFORMANCE RATING+
1	Job done right the first time	3.83	2.63
2	Fast action on complaints	3.63	2.73
3	Prompt warranty work	3.60	3.15
4	Able to do any job needed	3.56	3.00
5	Service available when needed	3.41	3.05
6	Courteous and friendly service	3.41	3.29
7	Car ready when promised	3.38	3.03
8	Perform only necessary work	3.37	3.11
9	Low prices on service	3.29	2.00
10	Clean up after service work	3.27	3.02
11	Convenient to home	2.52	2.25
12	Convenient to work	2.43	2.49
13	Courtesy buses and cars	2.37	2.35
14	Send out maintenance notices	2.05	3.33

*Ratings obtained from a four-point scale of "extremely important," "important," "slightly important," and "not important."

+Ratings obtained from a four-point scale of "excellent," "good," "fair," and "poor." A "no basis for judgment" category was also provided.

Systems for Complaint Handling and Service Recovery

Studies of customer dissatisfaction show that customers are dissatisfied with their purchases about 25% of the time. How often do they complain? The surprising finding is that only about 5% complain. The other 95% either feel that it is not worth the effort to complain, or that they don't know how or to whom to complain.

Of the 5% of customers who complain, only about 50% report a satisfactory problem resolution. Yet the need to resolve a customer problem in a satisfactory manner is critical. Whereas, on average, a satisfied customer tells three people about a good product experience, a dissatisfied customer gripes to 11 people. If each of them tells still other people, the number of people exposed to bad word of mouth may grow exponentially.

Often the customers who are most upset are the company's best customers. Another finding is that customers whose complaints are satisfactorily resolved often become more company-loyal than customers who were never dissatisfied. About 34% of customers who register major complaints will buy again from the company if their complaint is resolved, and this rises to 52% for minor complaints. If the complaint is resolved quickly, between 52% (major complaints) and 95% (minor complaints) will buy again from the company.

Therefore, companies need to develop a *service recovery* program. The first requirement is that companies make it easy for dissatisfied customers to complain. This can be accomplished by providing customer satisfaction forms and prominently featuring an 800 number "hot line." The second requirement is that the company's employees who receive complaints are well trained and empowered to resolve customer problems speedily and satisfactorily. Studies show that the faster the company responds to the complaint, the higher the amends offered, and the better the attitude, the higher the customer's satisfaction with the company. The third requirement is to go beyond satisfying particular customers and discovering and correcting the root causes of frequent problems. By studying the pattern of complaints, the company can correct system failures which are typically the source of these problems.

SOURCES: See John Goodman, Technical Assistance Research Programs (TARP), U.S. Office of Consumer Affairs Study on Complaint Handling in America, 1986; Karl Albrecht and Ron Zemke, *Service America!* (Homewood, IL: Dow-Jones Irwin, 1985); Leonard L. Berry and A. Parasuraman, *Marketing Services* (New York: The Free Press, 1991); and Roland T. Rust, Bala Subramanian, and Mark Wells, "Making Complaints a Management Tool," *Marketing Management*, 1, no. 3, 1992, 41–45.

The third is to "industrialize the service" by adding equipment and standardizing production. Levitt recommended that companies adopt a "manufacturing attitude" toward producing services as represented by McDonald's assembly-line approach to fast-food retailing, culminating in the "technological hamburger."[20] Shouldice Hospital near Toronto, Canada only operates on patients with hernias and has reduced patient stay from the typical seven days to half that time by industrializing the service. Although its doctors are paid less than in private practice and its nurses attend more patients than in a normal hospital, patient satisfaction is unbelievably high.[21]

The fourth is to reduce or make obsolete the need for a service by inventing a product solution, the way television substituted for out-of-home entertainment, the wash-and-wear shirt reduced the need for commercial laundries, and certain antibiotics reduced the need for tuberculosis sanitariums.

The fifth is to design a more effective service. How-to-quit-smoking clinics and jogging may reduce the need for expensive medical services later on. Hiring paralegal workers reduces the need for expensive legal professionals.

The sixth is to present customers with incentives to substitute their own labor for company labor. For example, business firms that are willing to sort their own mail before delivering it to the post office pay lower postal rates. A restaurant that features a self-service salad bar is replacing "waitering" work with customer work.[22]

CHAPTER 18
Managing Service Businesses
and Ancillary Services

Walt Disney Enterprises—A Highly Responsive Organization

Service companies—hotels, hospitals, colleges, banks, and others—are increasingly recognizing the importance of a fifth P, namely, the people. Service companies' employees are in constant contact with consumers and can create good or bad impressions.

Organizations are eager to learn how to "turn on" their inside people (employees) to serve their outside people (customers). Here is what the Disney organization does to market "positive customer attitudes" to its employees:

1. Disney's staff extends a special welcome to new employees. These employees are supplied with written instructions on what to expect—where to report, what to wear, and how long each training phase will be.

2. On the first day, new employees report to Disney University for an all-day orientation session. They sit four to a table, receive name tags, and are served coffee, juice, and pastry while they introduce themselves and get acquainted. Each new employee immediately knows three other people and feels part of a group.

3. The employees are introduced to the Disney philosophy and operations through an audiovisual presentation. They learn that they are in the entertainment business. They are "cast members" whose job it is to be enthusiastic, knowledgeable, and professional in serving Disney's "guests." They learn how they will each play a role in producing the "show." Then they are treated to lunch, tour the park, and are shown the recreational area set aside for the employees' exclusive use. That area consists of a lake, recreation hall, picnic area, boating and fishing facilities, and a large library.

4. The next day, the new employees report to their assigned jobs, such as security hosts (police), transportation hosts (drivers), custodial hosts (street cleaners), or food-and-beverage hosts (restaurant workers). They will receive a few days of additional training before they go "on stage." When they have learned their function,

they receive their "theme costumes" and are ready to perform.

5. The new employees receive additional training on how to answer questions guests frequently ask about the park. When they don't have the answer, they can dial switchboard operators who are armed with thick fact books and stand ready to answer any question.

6. The employees receive a Disney newspaper called *Eyes and Ears*, which features news of activities, employment opportunities, special benefits, educational offerings, and so on. Each issue contains a generous number of pictures of high-achieving employees.

7. Each Disney manager spends a week each year in "cross-utilization," namely, leaving the desk and heading for the front line, such as taking tickets, selling popcorn, or loading or unloading rides. In this way, management stays in touch with running the park and maintaining service quality to satisfy the millions of visitors. All managers and employees wear name badges and address each other on a first-name basis, regardless of rank.

8. All exiting employees answer a questionnaire on how they felt about working for Disney and any dissatisfactions they might have. In this way, Disney's management can measure its success in producing employee satisfaction and, ultimately, customer satisfaction.

No wonder the Disney people are so successful in satisfying their "guests." Management's attention to its employees helps the latter feel important and personally responsible for the "show." The employees' sense of "owning this organization" spills over to the millions of visitors with whom they come in contact.

SOURCE: See N. W. Pope, "Mickey Mouse Marketing," *American Banker*, July 25, 1979; and "More Mickey Mouse Marketing," *American Banker*, September 12, 1979.

Companies must avoid pushing productivity so hard that they reduce perceived quality. Some productivity steps, by standardizing quality, increase customer satisfaction. Other productivity steps lead to too much standardization and rob the customer of customized service. "High touch" is replaced by "high tech." Burger King challenged McDonald's by running a "Have it your way" campaign, where customers could get a "customized" hamburger sandwich even though this reduced Burger King's productivity somewhat.

Managing Product Support Services

Thus far we have focused our attention on service industries. No less important are product-based industries that must provide a service bundle to their customers. Manufacturers of equipment—small appliances, office machines, tractors, mainframes, airplanes—all have to provide the buyers with *product support services*. In fact, product support service is becoming a major battleground for competitive advantage. Some equipment companies, such as Caterpillar Tractor and John Deere, make more than 50% of their profits from product support services. On the other hand, companies that make a good product but provide poor local product support will be seriously disadvantaged. This is a major obstacle for foreign companies who cannot develop a good local product support system.

Firms that provide high-quality service will undoubtedly outperform their less service-oriented competitors. Table 18-1 provides evidence. The Strategic Planning Institute sorted out the top third and the bottom third of 3,000 business units according to ratings of "relative perceived service quality." The table shows that the high-service businesses managed to charge more, grow faster, and make more profits on the strength of their superior service quality.

The company must define customer needs carefully in designing both the product and the product support system. What customers are most concerned about is an interruption of the service that they expect from the product. Customers have three worries.[23] One is *failure frequency*, namely, how often in a given period is the product likely to break down. This is a measure of the product's *reliability*. A farmer may tolerate a combine that will break down once a year, but not two or three times. A company might claim that its average failure frequency is once a year but the average neglects the fact that some percentage of the customers will experience two, three, or more breakdowns per year. These customers will abandon and badmouth the company.

Next the customer is worried about the *downtime duration*. The longer the downtime, the higher the user cost, especially if a crew is idled. A construction manager, for example, can tolerate a few hours downtime of an excavator but the manager's impatience rises at an increasing rate as more hours pass. The customer counts on the seller's *service dependability*, namely, the seller's ability to fix the machine quickly, or at least provide a loaner so that work can resume.

The third worry is the *out-of-pocket costs of maintenance and repair service*. How much does the customer have to spend on regular maintenance, repair service costs, and so on?

An intelligent buyer will take all of these factors into consideration in choosing a vendor. The buyer will want to estimate the offer's *expected life-cycle costs*. Expected life-cycle cost is *the purchase cost plus the discounted cost of maintenance and*

TABLE 18-1   Contribution of Service Quality to Relative Performance

	HIGH THIRD IN SERVICE QUALITY	LOW THIRD IN SERVICE QUALITY	DIFFERENCE IN % POINTS
Price index relative to competition	7%	−2%	+ 9%
Change in market share per annum	6%	−2%	+ 8%
Sales growth per annum	17%	8%	+ 9%
Return on sales	12%	1%	+11%

Source: Phillip Thompson, Glenn Desourza, and Bradley T. Gale, "The Strategic Management of Service and Quality," *Quality Progress,* June 1985, p. 24.

repair less the discounted salvage value. Buyers have a right to ask for hard data in choosing among vendors.

The importance of reliability, service dependability, and maintenance will vary among different products and product users. A one-computer office will need higher product reliability and faster repair service than an office where there are other computers available if one breaks down. An airline needs 100% reliability in the air but can tolerate less than this when the engine is being started on the ground. (See Marketing Strategies 18-3.)

A necessary step requires the manufacturer to identify the services that customers value most and their relative importance. In the case of expensive equipment, such as medical imaging equipment, manufacturers offer *facilitating services,* such as *equipment installation, staff training, maintenance and repair services,* and *financing.* They may also add *value-augmenting services.* Herman Miller, a major

Marketing Strategies 18-3

Offering Warranties, Guarantees, and Service Contracts to Promote Sales

Any seller is legally responsible for fulfilling the normal or reasonable expectations of the buyer of goods. The seller's responsibility may be expressed or implied. *Warranties* are formal statements of expected product performance by the manufacturer. Products under warranty can be returned to the manufacturer or designated repair center for repair, replacement, or refund. Warranties, whether expressed or implied, are legally enforceable.

The seller will not always include a formal warranty with the product. Nevertheless, a company selling toasters is delivering an implied warranty that the toasters will toast bread, be safe in use, and will work for a reasonable length of time. The buyer, however, may also ask the seller for an express warranty that the product will be fit for a particular purpose. If the seller says that a pair of boots are fit for a particular purpose, say mountain climbing, and they fail in this purpose, the buyer can return the boots and not pay the bill or he can claim a refund. The Uniform Commercial Code defines the conditions under which implied or express warranties are enforceable.

Many sellers will go further and offer *guarantees.* Guarantees are general assurances that the product can be returned if its performance is unsatisfactory. An example would be a "money-back" guarantee. Guarantees serve as a sales tool. They may be advertised and further embodied in a printed warranty furnished with the product. Guarantees work best when the terms are clearly stated and devoid of loopholes. The customer should find it easy to act upon, and the company's redress should be swift. Otherwise, buyers will be dissatisfied, and this dissatisfaction can lead to no further purchases, bad word of mouth, and a potential lawsuit.

Today most companies are in the business of satisfying their customers. Many even promise "general or complete satisfaction" without being more specific. Thus, Procter & Gamble advertises: "If you are not satisfied for any reason, return for replacement, exchange, or refund." Some companies go beyond a general guarantee of satisfaction to a special or extraordinary promise setting them apart from their competition. Here are examples of the creative use of guarantees:

- Xerox recently promised that if any of its customers are dissatisfied with a Xerox product within three years of its purchase, Xerox will replace it until the customer is fully satisfied.

- L. L. Bean, the outdoors furnishings company, promises its customers "100% satisfaction in every way, forever." For example, if a customer buys a pair of boots and two months later finds that they scuff easily, L. L. Bean will take them back and refund the money or replace them with another brand.

- A. T. Cross guarantees its Cross pens and pencils for life. Thus, the customer whose pen stops working simply mails it to A. T. Cross (mailing envelopes are provided at stores selling Cross writing instruments) and the pen is repaired or replaced at no charge.

- Federal Express won its place in the minds and hearts of mailers by promising next-day delivery "absolutely, positively by 10:30 A.M."

office-furniture company, offers buyers the Herman Miller promise: (1) five-year product warranties; (2) quality audits after project installation; (3) guaranteed move-in dates; (4) trade-in allowances on systems products.

Companies need to plan their product design and service-mix decisions in tandem. Design and quality-assurance managers should be part of the new-product development team. Good product design will reduce the amount of subsequent servicing needed. The Canon home copier uses a disposable toner cartridge that greatly reduces the need for service calls. Kodak and 3M are designing equipment allowing the user to "plug in" to a central diagnostic facility that performs tests, locates the trouble, and fixes the equipment over the telephone lines. Thus, a key to successful service strategy is to design the products so that they rarely break down and, if they do, are easily and rapidly fixed with minimal service expense.

- Deluxe Corporation, the leading printer of checkbooks, guarantees a "48-hour turnaround, zero defects."

- BBBK, a pest extermination company, offers the following guarantee: (1) no payment until all pests are eradicated; (2) if the effort fails, the customer receives a full refund and fees to pay the next exterminator; (3) if guests on the client's premises spot a pest, BBBK will pay for the guest's room and send an apology letter; and (4) if the client's facility is closed down, BBBK will pay all fines, lost profits, and $5,000. For this high level of guarantee, BBBK is able to charge up to ten times more than its competitors, enjoys a high market share, and has paid out only 0.4% of sales in guarantees.

- Wells Fargo banks will automatically deposit $5 in the account of any customer who has waited longer than five minutes in line.

- Domino's Pizza owes much of its meteoric success to the promise that it could deliver a pizza to a home within a half-hour or, if late, the household would get it free.

In deciding to offer specific guarantees as a marketing tool, the company has to make certain decisions. First, the guarantee should distinguish the company's offer from its competitors. Second, the guarantee should have a convincing and compelling character. Third, the guarantee should state the remedy for failure: goods replacement, repair, exchange, or refund.

Guarantees are an effective marketing tool in two specific situations. One is where the company and/or the product is not well known. For example, a company might develop and offer a liquid that claims to remove the toughest spots from carpeting. A "money-back guarantee if not satisfied" would provide buyers with some confidence in purchasing the product.

A second situation is where the product's quality is superior to competition. Here the company can gain by guaranteeing superior performance as a competitive tool to attract more buyers and/or charge higher prices.

Another sales tool, beyond warranties and guarantees, is the *service contract* (also called an *extended warranty*). The buyer may want to insure receiving maintenance and repair service beyond the normal guaranteed period offered by the seller. Service contracts are contracts offered by the seller to provide free maintenance and repair service for a specified period of time at a specified contract price. In the case of buying an automobile, nearly half of new car buyers will purchase a service contract, at a cost ranging between $500 and $800. Why? Because the buyer knows that one repair problem can cost that much. Although assured by the salesperson that the car is incredibly reliable, now the buyer decides to buy "peace of mind." The service contract cost seems a small additional amount to pay in relation to the total price of the car.

For additional reading, see "More Firms Pledge Guaranteed Service," *The Wall Street Journal*, July 17, 1991, p. B1, B6.

Postsale Service Strategy

Manufacturers must decide how they want to offer aftersales service to customers, including maintenance and repair services, training services, and the like. They have four alternatives:

1. The manufacturer could provide these services through a customer service department (see Marketing Concepts and Tools 18-3).
2. The manufacturer could make arrangements with distributors and dealers to provide these services.
3. The manufacturer could leave it to independent service-specialist firms to provide these services.
4. The manufacturer could leave it to customers to service their own equipment.

Consider the supplying of maintenance and repair services. Manufacturers usually start out adopting the first alternative. They want to stay close to the equipment and know its problems. They also find it expensive to train others, and this takes time. They also discover that they can make good money running the parts-and-service business. As long as they are the only supplier of the needed parts, they can charge a premium price. In fact, many equipment manufacturers price their equipment low and compensate by charging high prices for parts and service. Some equipment manufacturers make over half of their profits in aftersale service. This also explains why competitors emerge who manufacture the same or similar

---

Marketing Concepts and Tools 18-3

How to Run a Customer Service Department

Every company must make provisions for presale and postsale service to its customers. This is handled by the customer service department. The quality of these customer service departments varies greatly. At one extreme are customer service departments that simply turn over customer calls to the appropriate person or department for action, with little follow-up as to whether the customer's request was satisfied. At the other extreme are customer service departments eager to receive customer requests, suggestions, and even complaints and handle them expeditiously. Companies such as P&G, GE, and Merck fall in the latter category.

P&G prints a toll-free number on every product and receives nearly a million calls a year. Included are calls requesting information on how to use a product, or suggestions on how to improve a product, or complaints about a defective product. P&G welcomes all of these calls, which provide a basis for constantly improving its operations.

GE annually spends $10 million to operate the GE Answer Center 24 hours a day, 365 days a year. It handles three million calls a year. At the heart of the system is a giant database that provides the center's Customer Representatives (CRs) with instant access to 750,000 answers concerning 8,500 models in 120 product lines. Only about 15% of the calls are complaints. GE has discovered that when they handle a complaint in a satisfactory manner, over 80% of the complainers will buy again from GE. GE selects and trains its CRs thoroughly and arms them with one of the largest databases containing a file of more than 750,000 answers.

Merck runs a Medical Question Answering Service for physicians. A physician can call Merck for information about a certain illness and Merck's librarians will mail or fax important articles clarifying that illness. Although this service is expensive to operate, it undoubtedly builds a strong image of Merck in the physician's mind.

SOURCE: For further reading, see Ross M. Scovotti, "Customer Service . . . A Tool for Growing Increased Profits," *Teleprofessional*, September 1991, pp. 22-27.

parts and sell them to customers or middlemen for less. Manufacturers warn customers of the danger of using competitor-made parts, but they are not always convincing.

Over time, manufacturers switch more of the maintenance and repair service to authorized distributors and dealers. These middlemen are closer to the customers, operate in more locations, and can offer quicker if not better service. Manufacturers still make a profit on selling the parts but leave the servicing profit to their middlemen.

Still later, independent service firms emerge. Over 40% of the auto-service work is now done outside the franchised automobile dealerships, by independent garages and chains such as Midas Muffler, Sears, and J. C. Penney's. Independent service organizations have emerged to handle mainframes, telecommunications equipment, and a variety of other equipment lines. They typically offer a lower price and/or faster service than the manufacturer or authorized middlemen.

Ultimately, some large customers take over responsibility for handling their own maintenance and repair services. Thus a company with several hundred personal computers, printers, and related equipment might find it cheaper to have its own service personnel on site. These companies typically press the manufacturer for an "unbundled" price, since they are providing their own services.

Lele has noted the following major trends in the product support area:[24]

1. Equipment manufacturers are building more reliable and more easily fixable equipment. One reason is the shift from electromechanical equipment to electronic equipment, which has fewer breakdowns and is more repairable. Also, companies are adding modularity and disposability to facilitate self-servicing.

2. Customers are becoming more sophisticated about buying product-support services and are pressing for "services unbundling." They want separate prices quoted for each service element and the right to shop for the service elements they want.

3. Customers increasingly dislike having to deal with a multitude of service providers handling their different types of equipment. Some third-party service organizations now service a greater range of equipment.[25]

4. Service contracts are an "endangered species." Because of the increase in disposable and/or never-fail equipment, customers are less inclined to pay anywhere from 2% to 10% of the purchase price every year for a service.

5. Customer service choices are increasing rapidly, and this is holding down prices and profits on service. Equipment manufacturers increasingly have to figure out how to make money on pricing their equipment independent of service contracts.

SUMMARY ❖

As the United States moves increasingly toward a service economy, marketers need to know more about marketing service products. Services are activities or benefits that one party can offer to another and do not result in the ownership of anything. Services are intangible, inseparable, variable, and perishable. Each characteristic poses problems and requires strategies. Marketers have to find ways to "tangibilize" the intangible; to increase the productivity of providers who are inseparable from the product; to standardize the quality in the face of variability; and to influence demand movements and supply capacities in the face of service perishability.

Service industries have typically lagged behind manufacturing firms in adopting and using marketing concepts, but this is now changing. Services marketing strategy calls not only for external marketing but also for internal marketing, to motivate the employees, and interactive marketing, to create skills in the service providers. Customers will use technical and functional criteria to judge the quality of services. To succeed, service marketers must create competitive differentiation, offer high service quality, and find ways to increase service productivity.

Even product-based companies must provide and manage a service bundle for their customers; in fact, their services bundle may be more critical than the product in winning customers. The service mix includes presale services such as technical advice and dependable delivery, as well as postsale services such as prompt repair, and personnel training. The marketer has to decide on the mix, quality, and source of various product-support services that customers require.

NOTES ❖

1. See G. Lynn Shostack, "Breaking Free from Product Marketing," *Journal of Marketing*, April 1977, pp. 73–80; Leonard L. Berry, "Services Marketing Is Different," *Business*, May–June 1980, pp. 24–30; Eric Langeard, John E. G. Bateson, Christopher H. Lovelock, and Pierre Eiglier, *Services Marketing: New Insights from Consumers and Managers* (Cambridge, MA: Marketing Science Institute, 1981); Karl Albrecht and Ron Zemke, *Service America! Doing Business in the New Economy* (Homewood, IL: Dow-Jones-Irwin, 1985); and Karl Albrecht, *At America's Service* (Homewood, IL: Dow-Jones-Irwin, 1988).

2. "Services Grow While the Quality Shrinks," *Business Week*, October 30, 1971, p. 50.

3. Theodore Levitt, "Production-Line Approach to Service," *Harvard Business Review*, September–October 1972, pp. 41–42.

4. Further classifications of services are described in Christopher H. Lovelock, *Services Marketing* (Englewood Cliffs, NJ: Prentice-Hall, 1984). Also see John E. Bateson, *Managing Services Marketing: Text and Readings* (Hinsdale, IL: Dryden Press, 1989).

5. See Theodore Levitt, "Marketing Intangible Products and Product Intangibles," *Harvard Business Review*, May–June 1981, pp. 94–102; and Berry, "Services Marketing Is Different."

6. See G. Lynn Shostack, "Service Positioning Through Structural Change," *Journal of Marketing*, January 1987, pp. 34–43.

7. For a good discussion of quality-control systems at the Marriott Hotel chain, see G. M. Hostage, "Quality Control in a Service Business," *Harvard Business Review*, July–August 1975, pp. 98–106.

8. See W. Earl Sasser, "Match Supply and Demand in Service Industries," *Harvard Business Review*, November–December 1976, pp. 133–40.

9. Christian Gronroos, "A Service Quality Model and Its Marketing Implications," *European Journal of Marketing*, 18, no. 4 (1984), 36–44. Gronroos's model is one of the most thoughtful contributions to service-marketing strategy.

10. Leonard Berry, "Big Ideas in Services Marketing," *Journal of Consumer Marketing*, Spring 1986, pp. 47–51.

11. Gronroos, "Service Quality Model, pp. 38–39.

12. See Philip Kotler and Paul N. Bloom, *Marketing Professional Services* (Englewood Cliffs, NJ: Prentice-Hall, 1984).

13. See Valarie A. Zeithaml, "How Consumer Evaluation Processes Differ between Goods and Services," in *Marketing of Services*, eds. James H. Donnelly and William R. George (Chicago: American Marketing Association, 1981), pp. 186–90.

14. The argument that product-based companies face substantial opportunities in the service sector is presented in Irving D. Canton, "Learning to Love the Service Economy," *Harvard Business Review*, May–June 1984, pp. 89–97.

15. A. Parasuraman, Valarie A. Zeithaml, and Leonard L. Berry, "A Conceptual Model of Service Quality and Its Implications for Future Research," *Journal of Marketing*, Fall 1985, pp. 41–50.

16. Leonard L. Berry and A. Parasuraman, *Marketing Services: Competing Through Quality* (New York: The Free Press, 1991), p. 16.

17. See James L. Heskett, W. Earl Sasser, Jr., and Christopher W. L. Hart, *Service Breakthroughs* (New York: Free Press, 1990).

18. Timothy W. Firnstahl, "My Employees Are My Service Guarantee," *Harvard Business Review*, July–August 1989, pp. 29–34.

19. See Hal F. Rosenbluth and Diane McFerrin Peters, *The Customer Comes Second* (New York: William Morrow & Co., 1992).

20. Theodore Levitt, "Production-Line Approach to Service," *Harvard Business Review*, September–October 1972, pp. 41–52; also see his "Industrialization of Service," *Harvard Business Review*, September–October 1976, pp. 63–74.

21. See William H. Davidow and Bro Uttal, *Total Customer Service: The Ultimate Weapon* (New York: Harper & Row, 1989).

22. Christopher H. Lovelock and Robert F. Young, "Look to Consumers to Increase Productivity," *Harvard Business Review*, May–June 1979.

23. See Milind M. Lele and Uday S. Karmarkar, "Good Product Support Is Smart Marketing," *Harvard Business Review*, November–December 1983, pp. 124–32.

24. Milind M. Lele, "How Service Needs Influence Product Strategy," *Sloan Management Review*, Fall 1986, pp. 63–70.

25. However, see Ellen Day and Richard J. Fox, "Extended Warranties, Service Contracts, and Maintenance Agreement—A Marketing Opportunity?" *Journal of Consumer Marketing*, Fall 1985, pp. 77–86.

19

Designing Pricing Strategies and Programs

There ain't no brand loyalty that two-cents-off can't overcome.

ANONYMOUS

The real issue is value, not price.

ROBERT T. LINDGREN

A ll profit organizations and many nonprofit organizations set prices on their products or services. Price goes by many names:

Price is all around us. You pay rent *for your apartment,* tuition *for your education, and a* fee *to your physician or dentist. The airline, railway, taxi, and bus companies charge you a* fare; *the local utilities call their price a* rate; *and the local bank charges you* interest *for the money you borrow. The price for driving your car on Florida's Sunshine Parkway is a* toll, *and the company that insures your car charges you a* premium. *The guest lecturer charges an* honorarium *to tell you about a government official who took a* bribe *to help a shady character steal* dues *collected by a trade association. Clubs or societies to which you belong may make a special* assessment *to pay unusual expenses. Your regular lawyer may ask for a* retainer *to cover her services. The "price" of an executive is a* salary, *the price of a salesperson may be a* commission, *and the price of a worker is a* wage. *Finally, although economists would disagree, many of us feel that* income taxes *are the price we pay for the privilege of making money.* [1]

How are prices set? Through most of history, prices were set by buyers and sellers negotiating with each other. Sellers would ask for a higher price than they expected to receive, and buyers would offer less than they expected to pay. Through bargaining, they would arrive at an acceptable price.

Setting one price for all buyers is a relatively modern idea. It was given impetus by the development of large-scale retailing at the end of the nineteenth century. F. W. Woolworth, Tiffany and Co., John Wanamaker, and others advertised a "strictly one-price policy," because they carried so many items and supervised so many employees.

Through most of history, price has operated as the major determinant of buyer choice. That is still the case in poorer nations, among poorer groups, and with commodity-type products. However, nonprice factors have become relatively more important in buyer-choice behavior in recent decades. Yet price still remains one of the most important elements determining company market share and profitability.

Price is the only element in the marketing mix that produces revenue; the other elements produce costs. Price is also one of the most flexible elements of the marketing mix, in that it can be changed quickly, unlike product features and channel commitments. At the same time, pricing and price competition are the number-one problems facing many marketing executives. Yet many companies do not handle pricing well. The most common mistakes are these: Pricing is too cost oriented; price is not revised often enough to capitalize on market changes; price is set independent of the rest of the marketing mix rather than as an intrinsic element of market-positioning strategy; and price is not varied enough for different product items, market segments, and purchase occasions.

Companies handle pricing in a variety of ways. In small companies, prices are often set by top management rather than by marketing or salespeople. In large companies, pricing is typically handled by division and product-line managers. Even here, top management sets the general pricing objectives and policies and often approves the prices proposed by lower levels of management. In industries where pricing is a key factor (aerospace, railroads, oil companies), companies will often establish a pricing department to set prices or assist others in determining appropriate prices. This department reports either to the marketing department, finance department, or top management. Others who exert an influence on pricing include sales managers, production managers, finance managers, and accountants.

This chapter will examine three questions: How should a price be set on a product or service for the first time? How should the price be adapted over time and space to meet varying circumstances and opportunities? When should the company initiate a price change, and how should it respond to a competitor's price change?

Setting the Price

Pricing is a problem when a firm has to set a price for the first time. This happens when the firm develops or acquires a new product, when it introduces its regular product into a new distribution channel or geographical area, and when it enters bids on new contract work.

The firm must decide where to position its product on quality and price. A company can position its product in the middle of the market or at three levels above or three levels below the middle. The seven levels are as follows:

Segment	Example (Automobiles)
Ultimate	Mercedes-Benz
Luxury	Audi
Special Needs	Volvo
Middle	Buick
Ease/Convenience	Escort
Me Too, But Cheaper	Hyundai
Price Alone	Yugo

Thus, in many markets, there is an ultimate brand (the *gold standard*), here the Mercedes-Benz automobile. Just below the ultimate are luxury brands, such as Audi, Lincoln, Lexus, and so on. Below them are brands that meet a special need: Volvo (safety) or Porsche (high performance). In the middle are a large number of brands, including Buick, Renault, and so on. One step below the middle are brands that provide mainly the functional benefit sought such as an Escort automobile. Below them are cheaper brands that nevertheless perform satisfactorily, such as the Hyundai. At the bottom are brands whose only appeal is price, such as the Yugo, a car that is not only cheap but cheaply made.

This scheme suggests that the seven positioning levels of products don't compete with each other, but only compete within each group. Yet there can be competition between price-quality segments. Figure 19-1 shows nine possible price-quality strategies. The diagonal strategies 1, 5, and 9 can all coexist in the same market; that is, one firm offers a high-quality product at a high price, another firm offers an average-quality product at an average price, and still another firm offers a low-quality product at a low price. All three competitors can coexist as long as the market consists of three groups of buyers, those who insist on quality, those who insist on price, and those who balance the two considerations.

Positioning strategies 2, 3, and 6 represent ways to attack the diagonal positions. Strategy 2 says, "Our product has the same high quality as product 1 but we charge less." Strategy 3 says the same thing and offers an even greater saving. If

FIGURE 19-1
Nine Price/Quality
Strategies

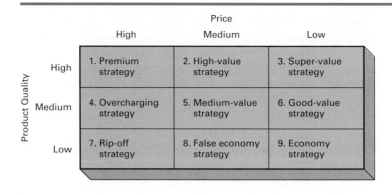

quality-sensitive customers believe these competitors, they will sensibly buy from them and save money (unless firm 1's product has acquired snob appeal). (See Marketing Strategies 19-1.)

Positioning strategies 4, 7, and 8 amount to overpricing the product in relation to its quality. The customers will feel "taken" and will probably complain or spread

Marketing Strategies 19-1

Lexus Challenges Mercedes

Toyota is a master at implementing value creation. Toyota recognized that a substantial number of consumers around the world wanted and could afford an expensive car. Within this group were many consumers who would like to buy a Mercedes but who thought that it was overpriced. They would be ready to buy a car that had Mercedes performance but was priced more reasonably. This gave Toyota the idea of developing a new car that could be convincingly compared to a Mercedes but could be positioned as a better value. The buyer would get the feeling that he or she was a "smart" buyer, not one who throws away money just to gain status.

Toyota designers and engineers proceeded to develop a car that they named Lexus and to market it with a multiple warhead attack. The new car had a sculptured look with fine fit and finish and plush interior. Toyota advertised the Lexus with a picture showing it next to a Mercedes with the headline reading: "The First Time in History That Trading a $73,000 Car For a $36,000 Car Could Be Considered Trading Up." Toyota proceeded to set up a separate dealership to sell the Lexus. Toyota took pains to select highly competent dealers and paid as much attention to designing the showrooms and the sales procedures as to designing the car. The showrooms had generous space, flowers and plants, free coffee, and professional salespeople. Dealers developed a list of

prospects and sent them a handsome package containing a 12-minute videotape dramatizing Lexus's performance features. For example, the videotape showed an engineer placing a glass of water on the engine blocks of a Mercedes and Lexus. When the car engines were turned on, the water shook on the Mercedes engine block but not on the Lexus engine block, suggesting that the Lexus automobile had a smoother engine and offered a smoother ride. Lexus's superior stability was further dramatized by placing a glass of water on the car's dashboard and sharply turning the street corner: the glass remained upright. Those early buyers who bought the Lexus were not only satisfied—they were *delighted*. The buyers raved to their friends and became the best (unpaid) salespeople for the new Lexus.

Meanwhile Mercedes had to reconsider its whole value-positioning strategy. If Mercedes lowered its prices, it was admitting that its car had been overpriced. If it kept the same prices, it would continue to lose sales to Lexus. The most sensible strategy might be for Mercedes to raise its prices and add generous guarantees and services, such as free repairs for six years, and so on. By raising its prices further, Mercedes would be saying that it is the "rich man's" car and not at all in the same class as Lexus.

bad word of mouth about the company. These strategies should be avoided by professional marketers.

The firm has to consider many factors in setting its pricing policy. In the following paragraphs, we will describe a six-step procedure for price setting: (1) selecting the pricing objective, (2) determining demand, (3) estimating costs, (4) analyzing competitors' prices and offers, (5) selecting a pricing method, and (6) selecting the final price.

Selecting the Pricing Objective

The company first has to decide what it wants to accomplish with the particular product. If the company has selected its target market and market positioning carefully, then its marketing-mix strategy, including price, will be fairly straightforward. For example, if a recreational-vehicle company wants to produce a luxurious truck camper for affluent customers, this implies charging a high price. Thus pricing strategy is largely determined by the prior decision on market positioning.

At the same time, the company might pursue additional objectives. The clearer a firm's objectives, the easier it is to set price. Each possible price will have a different impact on such objectives as profits, sales revenue, and market share. This is shown in Figure 19-2 for a hypothetical product. If the company wants to maximize pretax profits, it should charge $97. If it wants to maximize sales revenue, it should charge $86. If it wants to maximize market share, it should set an even lower price.

A company can pursue any of six major objectives through its pricing.

SURVIVAL ❖ Companies pursue survival as their major objective if plagued with overcapacity, intense competition, or changing consumer wants. To keep the plant operating and the inventories turning over, they will often cut prices. Profits are less important than survival. As long as prices cover variable costs and some fixed costs, the companies stay in business. However, survival is only a short-run objective. In the long run, the firm must learn how to add value or face extinction.

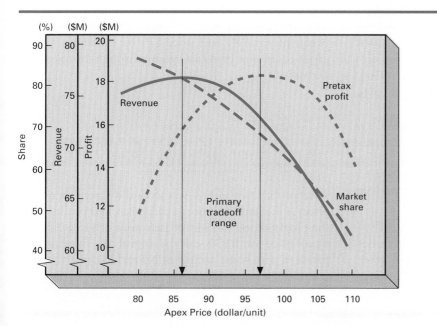

FIGURE 19-2
Relation Between Price, Revenue, Market Share, and Profits
Source: Decision Making in Marketing (New York: The Conference Board, 1971). Figure is by Franz Edelman.

MAXIMUM CURRENT PROFIT ❖ Many companies try to set the price that will maximize current profits. They estimate the demand and costs associated with alternative prices and choose the price that produces maximum current profit, cash flow, or rate of return on investment. (See Marketing Concepts and Tools 19-1 for theory of profit-maximization pricing.)

There are problems associated with current profit maximization. It assumes that the firm has knowledge of its demand and cost functions; in reality, they are difficult to estimate. Also, the company is emphasizing current financial performance rather than long-run performance. Finally, the company is ignoring the effects of other marketing-mix variables, competitors' reactions, and legal restraints on price.

MAXIMUM CURRENT REVENUE ❖ Some companies will set a price to maximize sales revenue. Revenue maximization requires only estimating the demand function. Many managers believe that revenue maximization will lead to long-run profit maximization and market-share growth.

MAXIMUM SALES GROWTH ❖ Other companies want to maximize unit sales. They believe that a higher sales volume will lead to lower unit costs and higher long-run profit. They set the lowest price, assuming the market is price sensitive. This is called *market-penetration pricing*. Texas Instruments (TI) is a prime practitioner of market-penetration pricing. TI will build a large plant, set its price as

Marketing Concepts and Tools 19-1

Finding the Profit-Maximizing Price

Economists have worked out a simple model for pricing to maximize current profits. The model assumes that the firm has knowledge of its demand and cost functions for the product in question. The demand function describes the estimated quantity (Q) that would be purchased per period at various prices (P) that might be charged. Suppose the firm determines through statistical demand analysis that its *demand equation* is

$$Q = 1,000 - 4P \qquad (19\text{-}1)$$

This equation expresses the law of demand—less will be bought per period at higher prices.

The cost function describes the total cost (C) of producing any quantity per period (Q). In the simplest case, the total cost function is described by the linear equation $C = F + cQ$ where F is total fixed cost and c is unit variable cost. Suppose the company estimated the following *cost equation* for its product:

$$C = 6,000 + 50Q \qquad (19\text{-}2)$$

Management needs two more equations, both definitional, to determine the profit-maximizing price. First, *total revenue* (R) is equal to price times quantity sold:

$$R = PQ \qquad (19\text{-}3)$$

Second, *total profits* (Z) is the difference between total revenue and total cost:

$$Z = R - C \qquad (19\text{-}4)$$

The company can now determine the relationship between profits (Z) and price (P) by starting with the profit equation $(19\text{-}4)$ and going through the following derivation:

$$Z = R - C$$
$$Z = PQ - C$$
$$Z = PQ - (6,000 + 50Q)$$
$$Z = P(1,000 - 4P) - 6,000 - 50(1,000 - 4P)$$
$$Z = 1,000P - 4P^2 - 6,000 - 50,000 + 200P$$
$$Z = -56,000 + 1,200P - 4P^2$$

Total profits turn out to be a second-degree function of price. It is a hatlike figure (a parabola), and profits reach their highest point ($34,000) at a price of $150. The optimal price of $150 can be found by drawing the parabola with some sample prices and locating the high point, or by using calculus.

low as possible, win a large market share, experience falling costs, and cut its price further as costs fall.

The following conditions favor setting a low price: (1) the market is highly price sensitive, and a low price stimulates more market growth; (2) production and distribution costs fall with accumulated production experience; and (3) a low price discourages actual and potential competition.

MAXIMUM MARKET SKIMMING ❖ Many companies favor setting high prices to "skim" the market. Du Pont is a prime practitioner of *market-skimming pricing*. With each innovation—cellophane, nylon, Teflon, and so on—it estimates the highest price it can charge given the comparative benefits of its new product versus the available substitutes. The company sets a price that makes it just worthwhile for some segments of the market to adopt the new material. Each time sales slow down, Du Pont lowers the price to draw in the next price-sensitive layer of customers. In this way, Du Pont skims a maximum amount of revenue from the various market segments. As another example, Polaroid also practices market skimming. It first introduces an expensive version of a new camera and gradually introduces simpler, lower-price models to draw in new price-sensitive segments.

Market skimming makes sense under the following conditions: (1) a sufficient number of buyers have a high current demand; (2) the unit costs of producing a small volume are not so much higher that they cancel the advantage of charging what the traffic will bear; (3) the high initial price does not attract more competitors; (4) the high price communicates the image of a superior product.

PRODUCT-QUALITY LEADERSHIP ❖ A company might aim to be the product-quality leader in the market. Maytag, a prime example, builds high-quality washing machines and prices them at roughly $100 more than competitors' washing machines. Maytag uses the slogan "Built to last longer," and its ads feature "Ol' Lonely," the Maytag repairman, who is asleep at the phone because no one ever calls him for service. Maytag's premium quality/premium price strategy has earned it a consistently higher-than-average rate of return in its industry.

OTHER PRICING OBJECTIVES ❖ Nonprofit and public organizations may adopt a number of other pricing objectives. A university aims for *partial cost recovery*, knowing that it must rely on private gifts and public grants to cover the remaining costs. A nonprofit hospital may aim for *full cost recovery* in its pricing. A nonprofit theater company may price its productions to fill the maximum number of theater seats. A social service agency may set a *social price* geared to the varying income situations of different clients.

Determining Demand

Each price that the company might charge will lead to a different level of demand and will therefore have a different impact on its marketing objectives. The relation between the current price charged and the resulting current demand is captured in the familiar *demand schedule* (see Figure 19-3[a]). The demand schedule shows the number of units the market will buy in a given time period at alternative prices that might be charged during the period. In the normal case, demand and price are inversely related, that is, the higher the price, the lower the demand (and conversely).

In the case of prestige goods, the demand curve is sometimes positively sloped. A perfume company found that by raising its price, it sold more perfume rather than less! Some consumers take the higher price to signify a better or more expensive perfume. However, if too high a price is charged, the level of demand will be lower.

FIGURE 19-3
Inelastic and Elastic
Demand

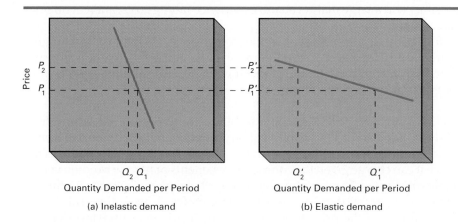

Quantity Demanded per Period

(a) Inelastic demand

Quantity Demanded per Period

(b) Elastic demand

FACTORS AFFECTING PRICE SENSITIVITY ❖ The demand curve shows the market's purchase rate at alternative prices. It sums the reactions of many individuals who have different price sensitivities. The important first step is to understand the factors that affect buyers' price sensitivity. Nagle has identified nine factors:

1. *Unique-Value Effect:* Buyers are less price sensitive when the product is more unique.
2. *Substitute-Awareness Effect:* Buyers are less price sensitive when they are less aware of substitutes.
3. *Difficult-Comparison Effect:* Buyers are less price sensitive when they cannot easily compare the quality of substitutes.
4. *Total-Expenditure Effect:* Buyers are less price sensitive the lower the expenditure is to their income.
5. *End-Benefit Effect:* Buyers are less price sensitive the less the expenditure is to the total cost of the end product.
6. *Shared-Cost Effect:* Buyers are less price sensitive when part of the cost is borne by another party.
7. *Sunk-Investment Effect:* Buyers are less price sensitive when the product is used in conjunction with assets previously bought.
8. *Price-Quality Effect:* Buyers are less price sensitive when the product is assumed to have more quality, prestige, or exclusiveness.
9. *Inventory Effect:* Buyers are less price sensitive when they cannot store the product.[2]

METHODS OF ESTIMATING DEMAND SCHEDULES ❖ Most companies make some attempt to measure their demand schedules. In researching the demand schedule, the investigator needs to make assumptions about competitive behavior. There are two ways to estimate demand. One is to assume that competitors' prices remain constant regardless of the price charged by the company. The other is to assume that competitors charge a different price for each price the company might set. We will assume the former and defer the question of competitors' price reactions until later.

To measure a demand schedule requires varying the price. A study can be done in a laboratory setting asking subjects to state how many units they would buy at different possible prices.[3] Bennett and Wilkinson used an in-store method of estimating the demand schedule. They systematically varied the prices of several products sold in a discount store and observed the results.[4]

In measuring the price/demand relationship, the market researcher must control or allow for other factors that might affect demand. If a company increased its advertising expenditures at the same time that it lowered its price, we would not know how much of the increased demand was due to the lower price versus the increased advertising. Economists show the impact of nonprice factors on demand by shifts of the demand curve rather than movements along the demand curve. Nagle has presented an excellent summary of the various methods used to measure price sensitivity and demand.[5]

PRICE ELASTICITY OF DEMAND ❖ Marketers need to know how responsive demand would be to a change in price. Consider the two demand curves in Figure 19-3. In (a), a price increase from P_1 to P_2 leads to a relatively small decline in demand from Q_1 to Q_2. In (b), the same price increase leads to a substantial drop in demand from Q_1' to Q_2'. If demand hardly changes with a small change in price, we say the demand is inelastic. If demand changes considerably, demand is elastic. Specifically, the price elasticity of demand is given by the following formula:

$$\text{Price elasticity of demand} = \frac{\%\ \text{Change in quantity demanded}}{\%\ \text{Change in price}}$$

Suppose demand falls by 10% when a seller raises the price by 2%. Price elasticity of demand is therefore -5 (the minus sign confirms the inverse relation between price and demand). If demand falls by 2% with a 2% increase in price, then elasticity is -1. In this case, the seller's total revenue stays the same. The seller sells fewer items but at a higher price that preserves the same total revenue. If demand falls by 1% when price is increased by 2%, then elasticity is -0.5. The less elastic the demand, the more it pays for the seller to raise the price.

What determines the price elasticity of demand? Demand is likely to be less elastic under the following conditions: (1) There are few or no substitutes or competitors; (2) buyers do not readily notice the higher price; (3) buyers are slow to change their buying habits and search for lower prices; (4) buyers think the higher prices are justified by quality improvements, normal inflation, and so on.

If demand is elastic rather than inelastic, sellers will consider lowering the price. A lower price will produce more total revenue. This makes sense as long as the costs of producing and selling more units do not increase disproportionately.

Various studies of price elasticity have been reported; for example, the price elasticity of automobiles, -1.0 to -2.2; coffee, -5.3; yogurt, -1.2; and confectionery, -2.0.[6] But one must be careful in using these estimates. Price elasticity depends on the magnitude and direction of the contemplated price change. It may be negligible, with a small price change, and substantial, with a large price change. It may differ for a price cut versus a price increase. Finally, long-run price elasticity is apt to differ from short-run elasticity. Buyers may continue with their current supplier after a price increase, because they do not notice the increase, or the increase is too small, or they are distracted by other concerns, or find choosing a new supplier takes time, but they may eventually switch suppliers. In this case, demand is more elastic in the long run than in the short run. Or the reverse may happen: Buyers drop a supplier after being notified of a price increase but return later. The distinction between short-run and long-run elasticity means that sellers will not know the total effect of their price change until time passes.

Estimating Costs

Demand largely sets a ceiling to the price that the company can charge for its product. And company costs set the floor. The company wants to charge a price that covers its cost of producing, distributing, and selling the product, including a fair return for its effort and risk.

TYPES OF COSTS ❖ A company's costs take two forms, fixed and variable. *Fixed costs* (also known as overhead) are costs that do not vary with production or sales revenue. Thus a company must pay bills each month for rent, heat, interest, executive salaries, and so on, whatever the company's output. Fixed costs go on regardless of the production level.

Variable costs vary directly with the level of production. For example, each hand calculator produced by Texas Instruments (TI) involves a cost of plastic, microprocessing chips, packaging, and the like. These costs tend to be constant per unit produced. They are called variable because their total varies with the number of units produced.

Total costs consist of the sum of the fixed and variable costs for any given level of production. Management wants to charge a price that will at least cover the total production costs at a given level of production.

COST BEHAVIOR AT DIFFERENT LEVELS OF PRODUCTION PER PERIOD ❖ To price intelligently, management needs to know how its costs vary with different levels of production.

Take the case where a company such as TI has built a fixed-size plant to produce 1,000 hand calculators a day. Figure 19-4(a) shows the typical **U**-shaped behavior of the short-run average cost curve (SRAC). The cost per unit is high if few units are produced per day. As production approaches 1,000 units per day, average cost falls. The reason is that the fixed costs are spread over more units, with each one bearing a smaller fixed cost. TI can try to produce more than 1,000 units per day but at increasing costs. Average cost increases after 1,000 units, because the plant becomes inefficient: Workers have to queue for machines, machines break down more often, and workers get in each other's way.

If TI believes that it could sell 2,000 units per day, it should consider building a larger plant. The plant will use more efficient machinery and work arrangements, and the unit cost of producing 2,000 units per day will be less than the unit cost of producing 1,000 units per day. This is shown in the long-run average cost curve in Figure 19-4(b). In fact, a 3,000-capacity plant would be even more efficient according to Figure 19-4(b). But a 4,000-daily production plant would be less efficient because of increasing diseconomies of scale: There are too many workers to manage, paperwork slows things down, and so on. Figure 19-4(b) indicates that a 3,000-daily production plant is the optimal size to build, if demand is strong enough to support this level of production.

COST BEHAVIOR AS A FUNCTION OF ACCUMULATED PRODUCTION ❖ Suppose TI runs a plant that produces 3,000 hand calculators per day. As TI gains experience producing hand calculators, it learns how to do it better. The workers learn shortcuts, the flow of materials is improved, procurement costs are cut, and so on. The result is that average cost tends to fall with accumulated production experience. This is shown in Figure 19-5. Thus the average cost of producing the first 100,000 hand calculators is $10 per calculator. When the company has produced the first 200,000 calculators, the average cost has fallen to $9. After its accumulated production experience doubles again to 400,000, the average cost is $8. This decline in the average cost with accumulated production experience is called the *experience curve* (sometimes *learning curve*).

Now suppose three firms compete in this industry, TI, A, and B. TI is the lowest-cost producer at $8, having produced 400,000 units in the past. If all three firms sell the calculator for $10, TI makes $2 profit per unit, A makes $1 and B breaks even. The smart move for TI would be to lower its price to $9. This will drive B out of the market, and even A will consider leaving. TI will pick up the business that would have gone to B (and possibly A). Furthermore, price-sensitive customers

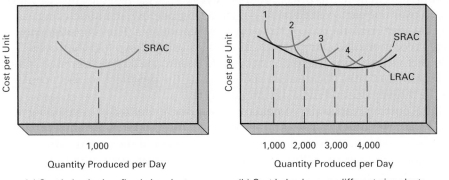

FIGURE 19-4
Cost per Unit at Different
Levels of Production per
Period

Cost per Unit | SRAC

1,000

Quantity Produced per Day

(a) Cost behavior in a fixed-size plant

Cost per Unit | 1 2 3 4 SRAC LRAC

1,000 2,000 3,000 4,000

Quantity Produced per Day

(b) Cost behavior over different-size plants

will enter the market at the lower price. TI's costs will drop still further and faster and more than restore its profits, even at a price of $9. TI has used this aggressive pricing strategy repeatedly to gain market share and drive others out of the industry.

Experience-curve pricing nevertheless carries major risks. The aggressive pricing might give the product a cheap image. The strategy also assumes that the competitors are weak and not willing to fight it out. Finally, the strategy leads the company into building more plants to meet the demand while a competitor might innovate a lower-cost technology and obtain lower costs than the market leader, who is now stuck with the old technology.

Most experience-curve pricing has focused on the behavior of manufacturing costs. But all costs, including marketing costs, are subject to learning improvements. Thus if three firms are each investing a large sum of money trying out telemarketing, the firm that has used it the longest might achieve the lowest telemarketing costs. This firm can charge a little less for its product and still earn the same return, all other costs being equal.[7]

TARGET COSTING ❖ We have seen that costs change with production scale and experience. They can also change as a result of a concentrated effort by the company's designers, engineers, and purchasing agents to reduce them. The Japanese in particular use a method called target costing.[8] They use market research to establish a new product's desired functions. Then they determine the price at which the product must sell given its appeal and competitors' prices. They deduct the de-

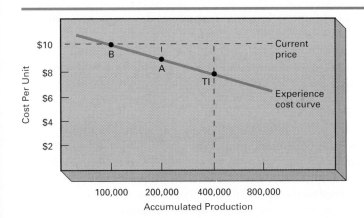

Cost Per Unit

$10 — — — — — — — — — — Current price
B
$8 — A
TI
$6 — Experience cost curve
$4 —
$2 —

100,000   200,000   400,000   800,000

Accumulated Production

sired profit margin from this price, and this leaves the target cost they must achieve. They then examine each cost element—design, engineering, manufacturing, sales, and so on—and break them down into further components. They consider ways to reengineer components, eliminate functions, and bring down supplier costs. The whole objective is to bring the final cost projections into the target cost range. If they can't succeed, they may decide against developing the product because it couldn't sell for the target price and make the target profit.

Target costing is an improvement over the normal method of developing new products which is to design the product, estimate its costs, and then determine its price. Target costing instead focuses on taking costs out of the product during the planning and design stage, rather than trying to reengineer costs after the product has been introduced.

Analyzing Competitors' Costs, Prices, and Offers

While market demand might set a ceiling and the company's costs set a floor to pricing, competitors' costs, prices, and possible price reactions help the firm establish where its prices might be set. The company needs to benchmark its costs against its competitors' costs to learn whether it is operating at a cost advantage or disadvantage. The company also needs to learn the price and quality of competitors' offers. The firm can send out comparison shoppers to price and assess competitors' offers. The firm can acquire competitors' price lists and buy competitors' equipment and take it apart. The firm can ask buyers how they perceive the price and quality of each competitor's offer.

Once the company is aware of competitors' prices and offers, it can use them as an orienting point for its own pricing. If the firm's offer is similar to a major competitor's offer, then the firm will have to price close to the competitor or lose sales. If the firm's offer is inferior, the firm will not be able to charge more than the competitor. If the firm's offer is superior, the firm can charge more than the competitor. The firm must be aware, however, that competitors might change their prices in response to the firm's price. Basically, the firm will use price to position its offer vis-à-vis competitors.

Selecting a Pricing Method

Given the three Cs—the customers' demand schedule, the cost function, and competitors' prices—the company is now ready to select a price. The price will be somewhere between one that is too low to produce a profit and one that is too high to produce any demand. Figure 19-6 summarizes the three major considerations in price setting. Costs set a floor to the price. Competitors' prices and the price of substitutes provide an orienting point that the company has to consider in setting its price. Customers' assessment of unique product features in the company's offer establish the ceiling price.

Companies resolve the pricing issue by selecting a pricing method that includes one or more of these three considerations. The pricing method will then lead to a specific price. We will examine the following price-setting methods: markup pricing, target-return pricing, perceived-value pricing, value pricing, going-rate pricing, and sealed-bid pricing.

MARKUP PRICING ❖ The most elementary pricing method is to add a standard markup to the product's cost. Construction companies submit job bids by estimating the total project cost and adding a standard markup for profit. Lawyers, accountants, and other professionals typically price by adding a standard markup to their costs. Some sellers tell their customers they will charge their cost plus a

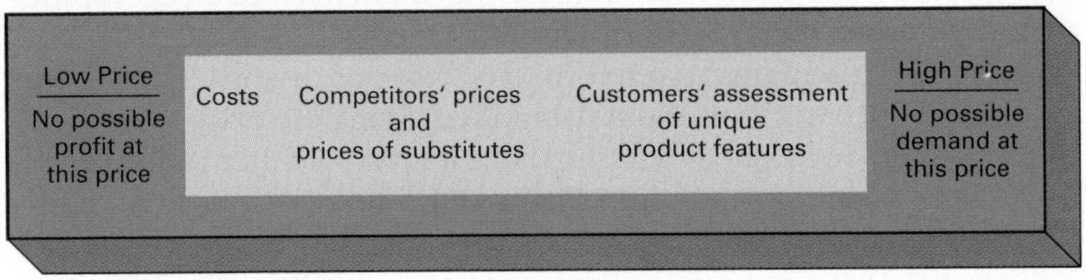

FIGURE 19-6
The Three Cs Model
for Price Setting

specified markup; for example, aerospace companies price this way to the government.

To illustrate markup pricing, suppose a toaster manufacturer had the following costs and sales expectations:

Variable cost	$10
Fixed cost	$300,000
Expected unit sales	$50,000

Therefore, the manufacturer's unit cost is given by:

$$\text{Unit cost} = \text{variable cost} + \frac{\text{fixed costs}}{\text{unit sales}} = \$10 + \frac{\$300,000}{50,000} = \$16$$

Now assume the manufacturer wants to earn a 20% markup on sales. The manufacturer's markup price is given by:

$$\text{Markup price} = \frac{\text{unit cost}}{(1 - \text{desired return on sales})} = \frac{\$16}{1 - 0.2} = \$20$$

The manufacturer would charge dealers $20 per toaster and make a profit of $4 per unit. The dealers in turn will mark up the toaster. If dealers want to earn 50% on sales, they will mark up the toaster to $40. This is equivalent to a cost markup of 100% (= $20/20).

Markups vary considerably among different goods. Common markups (on price, not cost) in supermarkets are 9% on baby foods, 14% on tobacco products, 20% on bakery products, 27% on dried foods and vegetables, 37% on spices and extracts, and 50% on greeting cards.[9] Quite a lot of dispersion is found around the averages. Within the spices-and-extracts category, markups on retail price range from 19% to 57%. Markups are generally higher on seasonal items (to cover the risk of not selling), specialty items, slower moving items, items with high storage and handling costs, and demand-inelastic items.

Does the use of standard markups to set prices make logical sense? Generally, no. Any pricing method that ignores current demand, perceived value, and competition is not likely to lead to the optimal price. Suppose the toaster manufacturer discussed earlier charged $20 but only sold 30,000 toasters instead of 50,000. Then the manufacturer's unit cost would have been higher, since the fixed costs are spread over fewer units, and its realized percentage markup on sales would have been lower. Markup pricing works only if that price actually brings in the expected level of sales.

Companies introducing a new product often price it high hoping to recover their costs as rapidly as possible. But a high-markup strategy could be fatal if a competitor is pricing low. This happened to Philips in pricing its videodisc players. Philips wanted to make a profit on each videodisc player. Meanwhile, Japanese competitors priced low and succeeded in building their market share rapidly, which in turn pushed down their costs substantially.

Still, markup pricing remains popular for a number of reasons. First, sellers have more certainty about costs than about demand. By tying the price to cost, sellers simplify their own pricing task; they do not have to make frequent adjustments as demand changes. Second, where all firms in the industry use this pricing method, their prices tend to be similar. Price competition is therefore minimized, which would not be the case if firms paid attention to demand variations when they priced. Third, many people feel that cost-plus pricing is fairer to both buyers and sellers. Sellers do not take advantage of buyers when the latter's demand becomes acute; yet the sellers earn a fair return on their investment.

TARGET-RETURN PRICING ❖ Another cost-pricing approach is *target-return pricing*. The firm determines the price that would yield its target rate of return on investment (ROI). Target pricing is used by General Motors, which prices its automobiles to achieve a 15 to 20% ROI. This pricing method is also used by public utilities that are constrained to make a fair return on their investment.

Suppose the toaster manufacturer discussed previously has invested $1 million in the business and wants to set a price to earn a 20% ROI, namely $200,000. The target-return price is given by the following formula:

$$\text{Target-return price} = \text{unit cost} + \frac{\text{desired return} \times \text{invested capital}}{\text{unit sales}}$$

$$= \$16 + \frac{.20 \times \$1,000,000}{\$50,000} = \$20$$

The manufacturer will realize this 20% ROI provided its costs and estimated sales turn out to be accurate. But what if sales do not reach 50,000 units? The manufacturer can prepare a *break-even chart* to learn what would happen at other sales levels. Figure 19-7 shows the break-even chart. Fixed costs are $300,000 regardless of sales volume. Variable costs are superimposed on the fixed costs and rise linearly with volume. The total revenue curve starts at zero and rises linearly with each unit sold. The slope of the total revenue curve reflects the price of $20 per unit.

The total revenue and total cost curve cross at 30,000 units. This is the *break-even volume*. It can be verified by the following formula:

$$\text{Break-even volume} = \frac{\text{fixed cost}}{\text{price} - \text{variable cost}} = \frac{\$300,000}{\$20 - \$10}$$

The manufacturer, of course, is hoping that the market will buy 50,000 units at $20, in which case it earns $200,000 on its $1 million investment. But much depends on the price elasticity and competitors' prices. Unfortunately, target-return pricing tends to ignore these considerations. The manufacturer should consider different prices and estimate their probable impacts on sales volume and profits. The manufacturer should also search for ways to lower its fixed and/or variable costs, because lower costs will lower its required break-even volume.

PERCEIVED-VALUE PRICING ❖ An increasing number of companies are basing their price on the product's *perceived value*. They see the buyers' perceptions of value, not the seller's cost, as the key to pricing. They use the nonprice variables in the marketing mix to build up perceived value in the buyers' minds. Price is set to capture the perceived value.[10]

Perceived-value pricing fits well with product-positioning thinking. A com-

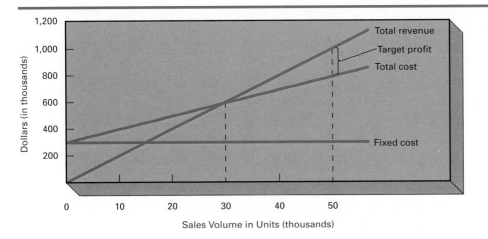

pany develops a product concept for a particular target market with a planned quality and price. Then management estimates the volume it hopes to sell at this price. The estimate indicates the needed plant capacity, investment, and unit costs. Management then figures out whether the product will yield a satisfactory profit at the planned price and cost. If the answer is yes, the company goes ahead with product development. Otherwise, the company drops the idea.

Du Pont and Caterpillar are two major practitioners of perceived-value pricing. Du Pont anchors its price not on its cost but on customer value. When Du Pont developed its new synthetic fiber for carpets, it demonstrated to carpet manufacturers that they could afford to pay Du Pont as much as $1.40 per pound for the new fiber and still make their current profit. Du Pont calls this the *value-in-use price*. Du Pont recognized, however, that pricing the new material at $1.40 per pound would leave the carpet manufacturers indifferent. So it set the price lower than $1.40 to provide a purchase inducement to adopt the new fiber. Du Pont did not use its manufacturing cost to set the price but only to judge whether there was enough profit to go ahead in the first place.

As another example of Du Pont value-in-use pricing, Du Pont will price a certain chemical at both a standard price and a premium price, where the latter includes added values. Consider the following pricing example:

ATTRIBUTE	STANDARD LEVEL	PREMIUM LEVEL	ADDED VALUE
Quality	Impurities less than ten parts per million	Impurities less than one part per million	$1.40
Delivery	Within two weeks	Within one week	.15
System	Supply chemical only	Supply total system	.80
Innovation	Little R&D support	High level R&D support	2.00
Retraining	Train initially	Retrain on request	.40
Service	Through home office purchases	Locally available	.25
Price	$100/pound	$105/pound	5.00

The customer who wants the premium offer pays $105 instead of $100 a pound. Du Pont has measured the perceived value of each added benefit and this amounts to a $5 premium per pound. This is sometimes called *component-value pricing*. The customer may end up requesting a few but not all of the added values and try to secure a price per pound between the standard and the premium price. This depends upon whether Du Pont is willing to *unbundle* its premium offer.

Caterpillar uses perceived value to set prices on its construction equipment. It might price its tractor at $100,000, although a similar competitor's tractor might be priced at $90,000. And Caterpillar will sell more than the competitor! When a prospective customer asks a Caterpillar dealer why he should pay $10,000 more for the Caterpillar tractor, the dealer answers:

$ 90,000	tractor's price if it is only equivalent to the competitor's tractor
7,000	price premium for superior durability
6,000	price premium for superior reliability
5,000	price premium for superior service
2,000	price premium for the longer warranty on parts
110,000	is the price to cover the value package
− 10,000	discount
$100,000	final price

Thus, the Caterpillar dealer is able to put a price or value on each component making up the offer (called *component-value pricing*). The stunned customer learns that although he is asked to pay a $10,000 premium for the Caterpillar tractor, he is actually getting a $10,000 discount! He ends up choosing the Caterpillar tractor because he is convinced that its *lifetime operating costs* will be lower.

The key to perceived-value pricing is to accurately determine the market's perception of the offer's value. Sellers with an inflated view of their offer's value will overprice their product. Sellers with an underestimated view will charge less than they could. Market research is needed to establish the market's perception of value as a guide to effective pricing. Methods for estimating perceived value are described in Marketing Concepts and Tools 19-2. Methods for estimating a price around the estimated perceived value are described in Marketing Concepts and Tools 19-3.

VALUE PRICING ❖ In recent years, several companies have adopted *value pricing* by which they charge a low price for a high-quality offering. Lexus is a good example because Toyota could have priced Lexus, given its extraordinary quality, much closer to the Mercedes price. Mercedes pricing represents a "more for more" pricing philosophy. Below this would be a "more for the same" pricing philosophy, which is embraced by discounters. Below this would be a "more for less" pricing philosophy, which is represented by Lexus.

Value pricing is not the same as perceived-value pricing. The latter is really a "more for more" pricing philosophy. It says that the company should price at a level that captures what the buyer thinks the product is worth. Value pricing, on the other hand, says that the price should represent an extraordinary bargain for consumers.

Here are other examples of value-pricing marketers:[11]

Wal-Mart charges everyday low prices at the same time it offers a great assortment of brands and excellent services and guarantees. Not surprisingly, it has become the world's largest retailer.

Southwest Airlines charges about one third of what its competitors charge but provides a very comfortable flight and extremely friendly service, though one without frills. Southwest is one of the only U.S. airlines to post profits.

Dell Computer, the direct-marketing computer company, offers buyers high-quality personal computers and excellent service while charging lower prices than its retail-

Methods of Estimating Perceived Value—An Illustration

Three companies, A, B, and C, produce rapid-relay switches. Industrial buyers are asked to examine and rate the respective companies' offers. Here are three alternative methods:

- *Direct Price-Rating Method:* Here the buyers estimate a price for each switch that they think reflects the total value of buying the switch from each company. For example, they may assign $2.55, $2.00, and $1.52, respectively.

- *Direct Perceived-Value-Rating Method:* Here the buyers allocate 100 points to the three companies to reflect the total value of buying the switch from each company. Suppose they assign 42, 33, and 25, respectively. If the average market price of a relay switch is $2.00, the three firms could charge, respectively, $2.55, $2.00, and $1.52, to reflect the variation in perceived value.

- *Diagnostic Method:* Here the buyers rate the three offers on a set of attributes. They allocate 100 points to the three companies with regard to each attribute. They also allocate 100 points to reflect the relative importance of the attributes. Suppose the results are as follows:

IMPORTANCE WEIGHT	ATTRIBUTE	PRODUCTS		
		A	B	C
25	Product durability	40	40	20
30	Product reliability	33	33	33
30	Delivery reliability	50	25	25
15	Service quality	45	35	20
100	(Perceived value)	(41.65)	(32.65)	(24.9)
	(Equilibrium price)	$2.55	$2.00	$1.52

By multiplying the importance weights against each company's ratings, we find that company A's offer is perceived to be above average (at 42), company B's offer is average (at 33), and company C's offer is below average (at 25).

Company A can set a high price for its switches because buyers perceive a better offer. If A wants to price proportionally to its perceived value, it can charge around $2.55 (= $2.00 for an average quality switch × 42/33). If all three companies set their price proportional to their perceived value, they will all enjoy some market share, since they all offer the same perceived value-to-price.

If a company prices at less than its perceived value, it will gain a higher-than-average market share because buyers will be getting extra value for their money. This is illustrated in the accompanying figure.

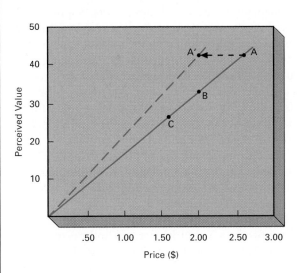

The three offers, A, B, and C, initially lie on the same value/price line. Respective market shares will depend on the relative density of ideal points (not shown) surrounding the three offers. Now suppose company A lowers its price to A'. Its value/price will be on a higher line (the dashed line), and it will pull market share away from both B and C, particularly B, because it offers more value at the same price as B. In self-defense, B will either lower its price or raise its perceived value by adding more service reliability, and so on. If the cost of increasing its perceived value is less than the revenue loss resulting from a lower price, B should strengthen its perceived value.

For an empirical study of nine methods used by companies to assess customer value, see James C. Anderson, Dipak C. Jain, and Pradeep K. Chintagunta, "Customer Value Assessment in Business Markets: A State-of-Practice Study," *Journal of Business-to-Business Marketing,* vol. 1(1), 1993, pp. 3–29.

Methods for Establishing a Price Around a Perceived Value

Companies cannot always depend on their customers' recognizing the value of their offer against their competitors' offers. Each competitor's offer may not only differ in price but in its impact on the customer's operating costs, working capital costs, ordering costs, set-up costs, financing costs, and disposal costs. Sophisticated industrial companies use a tool called *economic value to the customer* (EVC) to build up their customers' perception of value. EVC is calculated by comparing their product's total costs against the benefits of the product the customer is currently using (reference product). This is an effective way of analyzing pricing policy for industrial goods where the purchase price represents only a portion of the lifetime costs to the customer.

The accompanying figure illustrates how EVC is determined. Suppose a company is developing two products, Y and Z, to compete with product X, currently being used by the customer.

New product Y performs the same function as the reference product X, but its start-up and postpurchase costs are only $400, yielding a $300 savings. Because the customer's current product X has life-cycle costs of $1,000, the economic value that new product Y offers the customer is $600 ($1,000 minus $400). Thus the customer might be willing to pay up to $600 for product Y.

New product Z has more features or performance characteristics than product X or Y. These extra features of Z have a perceived incremental value of $300 when compared with the reference product. So compared to the current product, Z saves $100 in postpurchase costs and has an incremental value of $300, resulting in an economic value of $700 to the customer. Thus Z provides a higher EVC than Y despite its higher postpurchase costs because it provides additional customer value.

The firm should set its price at a point between its costs and the EVC that is perceived by the customer. If the firm priced Y at $400, the customer would save $200 compared with X, despite paying $100 more for Y. The firm's profit depends on its cost of supplying Y. If Y costs $250 to supply, the firm will make $150 ($=400-250).

The firm can use EVC to determine which market segments to enter. It should enter segments where its price would create more economic value than the customers are getting from their current product.

SOURCE: This exhibit was condensed by the author from John L. Forbis and Nitin T. Mehta, "Economic Value to the Customer," *McKinsey Staff Paper* (Chicago: McKinsey & Co., Inc., February 1979), pp. 1–10.

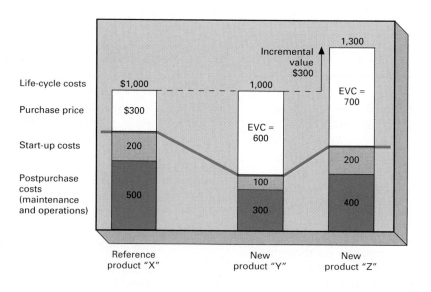

oriented competitors. Its sales and profits have grown at a far faster rate than its competitors.

Taco Bell reengineered its fast-food operations and lowered its prices significantly to reintroduce the notion of value pricing to its fast-food customers.

Nucor Steel, through running highly efficient mini-mill operations, has been able to offer steel customers high-quality steel at substantially lower prices than Bethlehem and other steel makers can charge.

Value pricing is not a matter of simply setting lower prices on one's products compared to competitors. It is a matter of reengineering the company's operations to truly become the low-cost producer without sacrificing quality, and to lower one's prices significantly in order to attract a large number of value-conscious customers.

GOING-RATE PRICING ❖ In *going-rate pricing*, the firm bases its price largely on competitors' prices with less attention paid to its own cost or demand. The firm might charge the same, more, or less than its major competitor(s). In oligopolistic industries that sell a commodity such as steel, paper, or fertilizer, firms normally charge the same price. The smaller firms "follow the leader." They change their prices when the market leader's prices change rather than when their own demand or cost changes. Some firms may charge a slight premium or slight discount, but they preserve the amount of difference. Thus minor gasoline retailers usually charge a few cents less than the major oil companies, without letting the difference increase or decrease.

Going-rate pricing is quite popular. Where costs are difficult to measure or competitive response is uncertain, firms feel that the going price represents a good solution. The going price is thought to reflect the industry's collective wisdom as to the price that would yield a fair return and not jeopardize industrial harmony.

SEALED-BID PRICING ❖ Competitive-oriented pricing is common where firms bid for jobs. The firm bases its price on expectations of how competitors will price rather than on a rigid relation to the firm's costs or demand. The firm wants to win the contract, and winning normally requires submitting a lower price than competitors.

Yet the firm cannot set its price below a certain level. It cannot price below cost without worsening its position. On the other hand, the higher it sets its price above its costs, the lower its chance of getting the contract.

The net effect of the two opposite pulls can be described in terms of the bid's *expected profit* (see Table 19-1). Suppose a bid of $9,500 would yield a high chance of getting the contract, say .81, but only a low profit, say $100. The expected profit with this bid is therefore $81. If the firm bid $11,000, its profit would be $1,600, but its chance of getting the contract might be reduced, say to .01. The expected profit would be only $16. One logical bidding criterion would be to bid the price that

TABLE 19-1
Effect of Different Bids on Expected Profit

COMPANY'S BID	COMPANY'S PROFIT	PROBABILITY OF GETTING AWARD WITH THIS BID (ASSUMED)	EXPECTED PROFIT
$ 9,500	$ 100	0.81	$ 81
10,000	600	0.36	216
10,500	1,100	0.09	99
11,000	1,600	0.01	16

would maximize the expected profit. According to Table 19-1, the best bid would be $10,000, for which the expected profit is $216.

Using expected profit as a criterion for setting price makes sense for the firm that makes many bids. In playing the odds, the firm will achieve maximum profits in the long run. The firm that bids only occasionally or that needs a particular contract badly will not find it advantageous to use the expected-profit criterion. This criterion, for example, does not distinguish between a $1,000 profit with a 0.10 probability and a $125 profit with an 0.80 probability. Yet the firm that wants to keep production going would prefer the second contract to the first.

Selecting the Final Price

The preceding pricing methods narrow the price range from which to select the final price. In selecting the final price, the company must consider additional factors.

PSYCHOLOGICAL PRICING ❖ Sellers should consider the psychology of prices in addition to their economics. Many consumers use price as an indicator of quality. When Fleischmann raised its price of gin from $4.50 to $5.50, its liquor sales went up, not down. Image pricing is especially effective with ego-sensitive products such as perfumes and expensive cars. A $100 bottle of perfume might contain $10 worth of scent, but giftgivers pay $100 to communicate their high regard for the receiver.

A study of the relationship between price and quality perceptions of cars found the relationship to be operating in a reciprocal manner.[12] Higher-priced cars were perceived to possess (unwarranted) high quality. Higher-quality cars were likewise perceived to be higher priced than they actually were. When alternative information about true quality is available, price becomes a less significant indicator of quality.[13] When this information is not available, price acts as a quality signal.

Sellers often manipulate *reference prices* in pricing their product. Buyers carry in their minds a reference price when looking at a particular product. The reference price might have been formed by noticing current prices, past prices, or the buying context. For example, a seller can place its product among expensive products to imply that it belongs in the same class. Department stores will display women's apparel in separate departments differentiated by price; dresses found in the more expensive department are assumed to be of better quality. Reference-price thinking is also created by stating a high manufacturer's suggested price, or by indicating that the product was priced much higher originally, or by pointing to a competitor's high price.

Many sellers believe that prices should end in an odd number. Newspaper ads are dominated by prices ending in odd numbers. Thus a stereo amplifier is priced at $299 instead of $300. Many customers see this as a price in the $200 range rather than $300 range. Another explanation is that odd endings convey the notion of a discount or bargain. But if a company wants a high-price image instead of a low-price image, it should avoid the odd-ending tactic.

THE INFLUENCE OF OTHER MARKETING-MIX ELEMENTS ON PRICE ❖ The final price must take into account the brand's quality and advertising relative to competition. Farris and Reibstein examined the relationship between relative price, relative quality, and relative advertising for 227 consumer businesses and found the following results:

1. Brands with average relative quality but high relative advertising budgets were able to charge premium prices. Consumers apparently were willing to pay higher prices for known products than for unknown products.

2. Brands with high relative quality and high relative advertising obtained the highest prices. Conversely, brands with low quality and low advertising charged the lowest prices.

3. The positive relationship between high prices and high advertising held most strongly in the later stages of the product life cycle, for market leaders, and for low-cost products.[14]

COMPANY PRICING POLICIES ❖ The contemplated price must be consistent with company pricing policies. Many companies set up a pricing department to develop pricing policies and establish or approve pricing decisions. Their aim is to insure that the salespeople quote prices that are reasonable to customers and profitable to the company.

IMPACT OF PRICE ON OTHER PARTIES ❖ Management must also consider the reactions of other parties to the contemplated price. How will the *distributors and dealers* feel about it? Will the *company salesforce* be willing to sell at that price or complain that the price is too high? How will *competitors* react to this price? Will *suppliers* raise their prices when they see the company's price? Will the *government* intervene and prevent this price from being charged? In the last case, marketers need to know the laws affecting price and make sure that their pricing policies are defensible (see Socially Responsible Marketing 19-1).

Adapting the Price

Companies do not set a single price but rather a pricing structure that reflects variations in geographical demand and costs, market-segment requirements, purchase timing, order levels, and other factors. As a result of offering discounts, allowances, and promotional support, a company rarely realizes the same profit from each unit of a product that it sells (see Marketing Concepts and Tools 19-4). Here we will examine several price-adaptation strategies: geographical pricing, price discounts and allowances, promotional pricing, discriminatory pricing, and product-mix pricing.

Geographical Pricing

Geographical pricing involves the company in deciding how to price its products to customers in different locations and countries. Should the company charge higher prices to distant customers to cover the higher shipping costs and risk losing their business? Should the company entertain countertrade proposals instead of direct monetary payment when dealing with certain foreign buyers? Many companies will have to give serious consideration to barter and countertrade arrangements if they want to win the business of certain buyers (see Global Marketing 19-1).

Price Discounts and Allowances

Most companies will modify their basic price to reward customers for such acts as early payment, volume purchases, and off-season buying. Descriptions of these price adjustments—called discounts and allowances—follow.

CASH DISCOUNTS ❖ A cash discount is a price reduction to buyers who promptly pay their bills. A typical example is, "2/10, net 30," which means that

Issues in Pricing

Setting prices is an important element of a competitive marketplace, and many federal and state laws govern the rules of fair play in pricing. The most important pieces of legislation affecting pricing are the Sherman, Clayton, and Robinson-Patman Acts, initially adopted to curb the formation of monopolies and to regulate business practices that might unfairly restrain trade. Because these federal statutes can be applied only to interstate commerce, some states have adopted similar provisions for companies that operate locally. Public policy on pricing centers on three potentially damaging pricing practices: price fixing, price discrimination, and deceptive pricing.

Price Fixing. Federal legislation on price fixing states that sellers must set prices without talking to competitors. Otherwise, price collusion is suspected. Price fixing is illegal per se—that is, the government does not accept any excuses for price fixing.

Price Discrimination. The Robinson-Patman Act seeks to ensure that sellers offer the same price terms to a given level of trade. For example, every retailer is entitled to the same price terms whether the retailer is Sears or the local bicycle shop. However, price discrimination is allowed if the seller can prove that its costs are different when selling to different retailers—for example, that it costs less per unit to sell a large volume of bicycles to Sears than to sell a few bicycles to a local dealer. Or the seller can discriminate in its pricing if the seller manufactures different qualities of the same product for different retailers. The seller has to prove that these differences are proportional. Price differentials may also be used to "match competition" in "good faith," provided that the firm is trying to meet competitors at its own level of competition and that the price discrimination is temporary, localized, and defensive rather than offensive.

Deceptive Pricing. Deceptive pricing occurs when a seller states prices or price savings that are not actually available to consumers. Some such deceptions are difficult for consumers to discern, as when an airline adver-

tises a low one-way fare that is available only with the purchase of a round-trip ticket, or when a retailer sets artificially high "regular" prices, then announces "sale" prices close to its previous everyday prices. Many federal and state statutes regulate against deceptive pricing practices. For example, the Automobile Information Disclosure Act requires automakers to attach a statement to new-car windows stating the manufacturer's suggested retail price, the prices of optional equipment, and the dealer's transportation charges. The FTC issues its *Guides Against Deceptive Pricing,* warning sellers not to advertise a price reduction unless it is a saving from the usual retail price, not to advertise "factory" or "wholesale" prices unless such prices are what they are claimed to be, and not to advertise comparable value prices on imperfect goods. Many states have developed retail advertising guidelines to ensure that locally advertised prices are accurately stated and clearly understood by consumers.

Other Regulated Pricing Practices. Sellers are also prohibited from using *predatory pricing*—selling below cost with the intention of destroying competition. Wholesalers and retailers in over half the states face laws requiring a minimum percentage markup over their cost of merchandise plus transportation. These laws attempt to protect small sellers from larger ones who might sell items below cost to attract customers. *Resale price maintenance* is also prohibited—a manufacturer cannot require dealers to charge a specified retail price for its product. Although the seller can propose a manufacturer's *suggested* retail price to dealers, it cannot refuse to sell to a dealer who takes independent pricing action, nor can it punish the dealer by shipping late or denying advertising allowances.

SOURCES: For more on public policy and pricing, see Louis W. Stern and Thomas L. Eovaldi, *Legal Aspects of Marketing Strategy* (Englewood Cliffs, NJ: Prentice Hall, 1984), Chap. 5; and Robert J. Posch, *The Complete Guide to Marketing and the Law* (Englewood Cliffs, NJ: Prentice Hall, 1988), Chap. 28.

payment is due within 30 days but the buyer can deduct 2% by paying the bill within ten days. The discount must be granted to all buyers who meet these terms. Such discounts are customary in many industries and serve the purpose of improving the sellers' liquidity and reducing credit-collection costs and bad debts.

QUANTITY DISCOUNTS ❖ A quantity discount is a price reduction to buyers who buy large volumes. A typical example is, "$10 per unit for less than 100 units; $9 per unit for 100 or more units." Quantity discounts must be offered equally to all customers and must not exceed the cost savings to the seller associated with selling large quantities. These savings include reduced expenses of selling, inventory, and transportation. They can be offered on a noncumulative basis (on each order placed) or a cumulative basis (on the number of units ordered over a given period). Discounts provide an incentive to the customer to order more from a given seller rather than buying from multiple sources.

FUNCTIONAL DISCOUNTS ❖ Functional discounts (also called trade discounts) are offered by the manufacturer to trade-channel members if they will perform certain functions, such as selling, storing, and record keeping. Manufacturers may offer different functional discounts to different trade channels because of their varying functions, but manufacturers must offer the same functional discounts within each trade channel.

SEASONAL DISCOUNTS ❖ A seasonal discount is a price reduction to buyers who buy merchandise or services out of season. Seasonal discounts allow the seller to maintain steadier production during the year. Ski manufacturers will offer sea-

Marketing Concepts and Tools 19-4

Using Transaction Pricing to Improve Profit Margins

Many companies are so ready to grant discounts, allowances, and special terms to their dealers and customers that they may fail to realize how little profit may be left. Consider the following situation:

Dealer list price	$6.00
Order size discount	.10
Competitive discount	.12
Invoice price	$5.78
Payment terms discount	.30
Annual volume discount	.37
Off-invoice promotions	.35
Co-op advertising	.20
Freight	.19
Pocket price	$4.47

Here the manufacturer quoted a $6.00 list price to a dealer but deducted an order size discount and a competitive discount, leaving an invoice price of $5.78. However, this did not represent the manufacturer's pocket price (that is, what is left in the manufacturer's pocket) because of further costs, resulting in the manufacturer realizing a pocket price of $4.47, which is 22.7% less than the dealer list price.

Marn and Rosiello label this a *pocket price waterfall* because each element represents a revenue leak. The pocket prices for any specific product, when formed into a *pocket price band*, may vary as much as several hundred percent between the lowest and highest pocket price.

Marn and Rosiello argue that companies normally fail to recognize the profit deterioration caused by the special terms offered to dealers and customers. They further note that not all revenue leaks equally affect the customer's purchase decision. Companies should measure the cost of granting each element against its impact on making the sale. Then they should establish better policies as to what should be granted to customers in bidding for their business.

Beyond this, the authors argue that pricing has a larger impact on profitability than other *profit levers*. A 1% improvement in price creates an operating profit improvement of 11.1%, whereas other 1% improvements would have the following leverage on profits: variable costs, 7.8%, volume, 3.3%, and fixed cost, 2.3%. Therefore, they contend that managing transaction pricing more effectively can substantially improve a company's profitability.

SOURCE: See Michael V. Marn and Robert L. Rosiello, "Managing Price, Gaining Profit," *Harvard Business Review*, September–October 1992, pp. 84–94.

Global Marketing 19-1

How Nations Use Countertrade

Most international trade involves cash transactions. The buyer agrees to pay the seller in cash within a certain stated time period. Yet many nations today lack sufficient hard currency to pay for their purchases from other nations. They want to offer other items in payment, and this has led to a growing practice called countertrade. Although most companies dislike countertrade deals, they might have no choice if they want the business.

Countertrade takes several forms:

- *Barter:* Barter involves the direct exchange of goods, with no money and no third party involved. For example, the West Germans agreed to build a steel plant in Indonesia in exchange for Indonesian oil.

- *Compensation Deal:* Here the seller receives some percentage of the payment in cash and the rest in products. A British aircraft manufacturer sold planes to Brazil for 70% cash and the rest in coffee.

- *Buyback Arrangement:* The seller sells a plant, equipment, or technology to another country and agrees to accept as partial payment products manufactured with the equipment supplied. For example, a U.S. chemical company built a plant for an Indian company and accepted partial payment in cash and the remainder in chemicals to be manufactured at the plant.

- *Offset:* The seller receives full payment in cash but agrees to spend a substantial amount of money in that country within a stated time period. For example, Pepsi-Cola sells its cola syrup to Russia for rubles and agrees to buy Russian vodka at a certain rate for sale in the United States.

More complex countertrade deals involve more than two parties. For example, Daimler-Benz agreed to sell 30 trucks to Romania and accept in exchange 150 Romanian-made jeeps, which it sold in Ecuador for bananas, which in turn were sold to a West German supermarket chain for deutschmarks. Through this circuitous transaction, Daimler-Benz finally achieved payment in German currency. Various barter houses and countertrade specialists have emerged to assist the parties to these transactions. Everyone agrees that international trade would be more efficient if carried out in cash, but too many nations lack sufficient hard currency. Sellers have no choice but to learn the intricacies of countertrade, which is a growing phenomenon in world trade.

SOURCE: For further reading, see John W. Dizard, "The Explosion of International Barter," *Fortune*, February 7, 1983; Leo G. B. Welt, *Trade Without Money: Barter and Countertrade* (New York: Harcourt Brace Jovanovich, 1984); and Christopher M. Korth, ed., *International Countertrade* (New York: Quorum Books, 1987).

---

sonal discounts to retailers in the spring and summer to encourage early ordering. Hotels, motels, and airlines will offer seasonal discounts in their slow selling periods.

ALLOWANCES ❖ Allowances are other types of reductions from the list price. For example, *trade-in allowances* are price reductions granted for turning in an old item when buying a new one. Trade-in allowances are most common in the automobile industry and are also found in other durable-goods categories. *Promotional allowances* are payments or price reductions to reward dealers for participating in advertising and sales-support programs.

Promotional Pricing

Under certain circumstances, companies will temporarily price their products below the list price and sometimes even below cost. Promotional pricing takes several forms.

- *Loss-Leader Pricing:* Here supermarkets and department stores drop the price on well-known brands to stimulate additional store traffic. But manufacturers typically disapprove of their brands being used as loss leaders because this can dilute the brand image as well as cause complaints from other retailers who charge the list price. Manufacturers have tried to restrain middlemen from loss-leader pricing through retail-price-maintenance laws, but these laws have been revoked.

◆ *Special-Event Pricing:* Sellers will establish special prices in certain seasons to draw in more customers. Thus linens are promotionally priced every January to attract shopping-weary customers into the stores.

◆ *Cash Rebates:* Consumers are offered cash rebates to encourage their purchasing the manufacturer's product within a specified time period. The rebates can help the manufacturer clear inventories without cutting the list price. Auto manufacturers have offered rebates several times in recent years to stimulate sales. The initial rebates were effective, but, when repeated, they seemed to lose their effectiveness. They may have given a price break to those who intended to buy a car without stimulating others to think about buying a car. Rebates also appear in consumer-packaged-goods marketing. They stimulate sales without costing the company as much as would cutting the price. The reason is that many buyers buy the product but fail to mail in the coupon for a refund.

◆ *Low-Interest Financing:* Instead of lowering the price, the company can offer customers low-interest financing. Auto makers announced 3% financing and in one case 0% financing to attract customers. Since many auto buyers finance their auto purchases, low-interest financing is appealing. However, although low-interest financing attracts customers to auto showrooms, many don't buy when they learn that a large down payment is required; the loan must be paid back in 30 months instead of 60 months; the car price is not discounted much with this kind of loan; and the loan may apply only to expensive cars.

◆ *Warranties and Service Contracts:* The company can promote sales by adding a free warranty offer or service contract. Instead of charging for the warranty or service contract, it offers it free or at a reduced price if the customer will buy. This is a way of reducing the "price."

◆ *Psychological Discounting:* This involves putting an artificially high price on a product and then offering it at substantial savings; for example, "Was $359, now $299." Illegitimate discount tactics are fought by the Federal Trade Commission and Better Business Bureaus. On the other hand, discounts from normal prices are a legitimate form of promotional pricing.

Companies must research these promotional pricing tools and make sure that they are lawful in the particular country. If they work, the problem is that competitors will copy them rapidly, and they lose their effectiveness for the individual company. If they do not work, they waste company money that could have been put into longer-impact marketing tools, such as building up product quality and service and improving the product image through advertising.

Discriminatory Pricing

Companies will often modify their basic price to accommodate differences in customers, products, locations, and so on. *Discriminatory pricing* occurs when a company sells a product or service at two or more prices that do not reflect a proportional difference in costs. Discriminatory pricing takes several forms:

◆ *Customer-Segment Pricing:* Here different customer groups are charged different prices for the same product or service. Museums will charge a lower admission fee to students and senior citizens.

◆ *Product-Form Pricing:* Here different versions of the product are priced differently but not proportionately to their respective costs. SCM Corporation prices its most expensive Proctor-Silex steam/dry iron at $54.95, $5 above its next most expensive iron. The top model has a light that signals when the iron is ready. Yet the extra feature costs less than $1 to make. As another example, Evian prices an eight-ounce bottle of its mineral water at 56 cents. Evian takes the same water and packages an ounce in a moisturizer spray for $5. Through product-form pricing, Evian manages to charge $5 an ounce for water.

♦ *Image Pricing:* Some companies will price the same product at two different levels based on image differences. Thus a perfume manufacturer can put the perfume in one bottle, give it a name and image, and price it at $10 an ounce; and in a fancier bottle with a different name and image and price it at $30 an ounce.

♦ *Location Pricing:* Here locations are priced differently even though the cost of offering each location is the same. A theater varies its seat prices according to audience preferences for different locations.

♦ *Time Pricing:* Here prices are varied by season, day, or hour. Public utilities vary their energy rates to commercial users by time of day and weekend versus weekday.

For price discrimination to work, certain conditions must exist. First, the market must be segmentable, and the segments must show different intensities of demand. Second, members of the lower price segment must not be able to resell the product to the higher price segment. Third, competitors must not be able to undersell the firm in the higher price segment. Fourth, the cost of segmenting and policing the market must not exceed the extra revenue derived from price discrimination. Fifth, the practice must not breed customer resentment and ill will. Sixth, the particular form of price discrimination must not be illegal.

As a result of deregulation in several industries, competitors have increased their use of discriminatory pricing. An airline, for example, will charge different fares to passengers on the same flight depending on the seating class; the time of day (morning or night coach); the day of the week (workday or weekend); the season; the person's company, past business or status (youth, military, senior citizen); and so on. Airlines call this system *yield management*, which is an exercise in trying to realize as much revenue as possible in filling the plane's seats.

Product-Mix Pricing

Price-setting logic has to be modified when the product is part of a product mix. In this case, the firm searches for a set of prices that maximizes the profits on the total product mix. Pricing is difficult because the various products have demand and cost interrelationships and are subject to different degrees of competition. We can distinguish six situations.

PRODUCT-LINE PRICING ❖ Companies normally develop product lines rather than single products. For example, Panasonic offers five different color video sound cameras, ranging from a simple one weighing 4.6 pounds, to a complex one weighing 6.3 pounds that includes auto focusing, fade control, and two-speed zoom lens. Each successive camera offers additional features, permitting *premium pricing*. Management must decide on the *price steps* to establish between the various cameras. The price steps should take into account cost differences between the cameras, customer evaluations of the different features, and competitors' prices. If the price difference between two successive cameras is small, buyers will often buy the more advanced camera, and this will increase company profits if the price difference is greater than the cost difference. If the price difference is large, customers will buy the less advanced camera.

In many lines of trade, sellers use well-established *price points* for the products in their line. Thus a men's clothing store might carry men's suits at three price levels: $150, $250, and $350. The customers will associate low-, average-, and high-quality suits with the three price "points." Even if the three prices are all raised, men will normally buy suits at their preferred price point. The seller's task is to establish perceived-quality differences that justify the price differences.

OPTIONAL-FEATURE PRICING ❖ Many companies offer optional products or features along with their main product. The automobile buyer can order electric window controls, defoggers, and light dimmers. However, pricing these options is a sticky problem. Automobile companies must decide which items to include in the price and which to offer as options. General Motors' normal pricing strategy is to advertise a stripped-down model for $8,000 to pull people into the showrooms and devote most of the showroom space to feature-loaded cars at $10,000 or up. The economy model is stripped of so many comforts and features that most buyers will reject it. When GM launched its new front-wheel-drive J-cars, it took a clue from the Japanese auto makers and included in the sticker price a number of popular options. Now the advertised price represented a well-equipped car. Unfortunately, the price was high, and many car shoppers balked.

Restaurants face a similar pricing problem. Restaurant customers can order liquor in addition to the meal. Many restaurants price their liquor high and their food low. The food revenue covers the food and other restaurant costs, and the liquor produces the profit. This explains why waiters press hard to get customers to order drinks. Other restaurants price their liquor low and food high to draw in a drinking crowd.

CAPTIVE-PRODUCT PRICING ❖ Some products require the use of ancillary or captive products. Examples of captive products are razor blades and camera film. Manufacturers of the main products (razors and cameras) often price them low and set high markups on the supplies. Thus Kodak prices its cameras low because it makes its money on selling film. Those camera makers who do not sell film have to price their cameras higher in order to make the same overall profit.

There is a danger, however, in pricing the captive product too high. Caterpillar, for example, makes high profits in the aftermarket by pricing high its parts and service. It marks up its equipment by 30% and its parts sometimes by 300%. This has given rise to "pirates," who counterfeit these parts and sell them to "shady tree" mechanics, who install them, sometimes without passing on the cost savings to the customers. Meanwhile Caterpillar loses these sales. Caterpillar attempts to control this problem by exhorting equipment owners to use only authorized dealers if they want guaranteed performance. But clearly the problem is created by the high prices that manufacturers charge for their aftermarket products.[15]

TWO-PART PRICING ❖ Service firms often charge a fixed fee plus a variable usage fee. Thus telephone users pay a minimum monthly fee plus charges for calls beyond the minimum number. Amusement parks charge an admission fee plus fees for rides over a certain minimum. The service firm faces a problem similar to captive-product pricing, namely, how much to charge for the basic service and how much for the variable usage. The fixed fee should be low enough to induce purchase of the service, and the profit can be made on the usage fees.

BYPRODUCT PRICING ❖ In producing processed meats, petroleum products, and other chemicals, there are often byproducts. If the byproducts have little value and are in fact costly to dispose of, that will affect the pricing of the main product. The manufacturer should accept any price that covers more than the cost of disposing of them. If the byproducts have value to a customer group, then they should be priced on their value. Any income earned on the byproducts will make it easier for the company to charge a lower price on its main product if forced to by competition.

PRODUCT-BUNDLING PRICING ❖ Sellers will often bundle their products at a set price. Thus an auto manufacturer might offer an option package at less than the cost of buying all the options separately. A theater company will price a season subscription at less than the cost of buying all the performances separately. Since customers may not have planned to buy all of the components, the savings on the price bundle must be substantial enough to induce them to buy the bundle.[16]

Some customers will want less than the whole bundle. Suppose a medical equipment supplier's offer includes free delivery and training. A particular customer might ask to forego the free delivery and training in order to get a lower price. The customer is asking the seller to "unbundle" its offer. The seller could actually increase its profit through unbundling if it saves more in cost than the price reduction that it offers to the customer for the particular items which are eliminated. Thus, if the supplier saves $100 by not supplying delivery and it reduces the customer's price by $80, for example, the supplier has increased its profit by $20.

Initiating and Responding to Price Changes

After developing their pricing strategies, companies will face situations where they may need to cut or raise prices.

Initiating Price Cuts

Several circumstances might lead a firm to cut its price. One circumstance is *excess capacity*. Here the firm needs additional business and cannot generate it through increased sales effort, product improvement, or other measures. It may abandon "follow-the-leader" pricing and resort to "aggressive" pricing to boost its sales. But in initiating a price cut, the company might trigger a price war, as competitors try to hold on to their market shares.

Another circumstance is a *declining market share*. Several American industries —automobiles, consumer electronics, cameras, watches, and steel—have been losing market share to Japanese competitors. To stem the losses, some American companies have resorted to more aggressive pricing action. General Motors, for example, cut its subcompact car prices by 10% on the West Coast, where Japanese competition is strongest.

Companies will also initiate price cuts in a *drive to dominate the market through lower costs*. Either the company starts with lower costs than its competitors or it initiates price cuts in the hope of gaining market share, which would lead to falling costs through larger volume and more experience. People Express waged an aggressive low-price strategy and gained a large market share. But this strategy also involves high risks.

1. *Low-Quality Trap:* Consumers will assume that the quality is below that of the higher-priced competitors.
2. *Fragile-Market-Share Trap:* A low price buys market share but not market loyalty. Customers will shift to another lower-price firm that comes along.
3. *Shallow-Pockets Trap:* The higher-priced competitors may cut their prices and may have longer staying power because of deeper cash reserves.

People Express some years later fell into these traps.

Companies may have to cut their prices in a period of *economic recession*. Fewer consumers are willing to buy higher-price versions of a product. Marketing Strategies 19-2 shows several ways in which a seller of a high-price product can adjust its price and/or marketing mix in facing a declining demand situation.

Initiating Price Increases

Many companies need to raise their prices. A successful price increase can increase profits considerably. For example, if the company's profit margin is 3% of sales, a 1% price increase will increase profits by 33% if sales volume is unaffected. This is illustrated in the following table where we assume that a company charged $10 and sold 100 units and had costs of $970, leaving a profit of $30, or 3% on sales. By raising its price by 10¢ (1% price increase), it boosted its profits by 33%, assuming the same sales volume.

	BEFORE	AFTER	
Price	$ 10	$10.10	(a 1% price increase)
Units sold	100	100	
Revenue	$1,000	$1,010	
Costs	− 970	− 970	
Profit	$ 30	$ 40	(a $33\frac{1}{3}$% profit increase)

A major circumstance provoking price increases is *cost inflation*. Rising costs unmatched by productivity gains squeeze profit margins and lead companies to regular rounds of price increases. Companies often raise their prices by more than the cost increase in anticipation of further inflation or government price controls; this is called *anticipatory pricing*. Companies hesitate to make long-run price commitments to customers, fearing that cost inflation will erode their profit margins.

Another factor leading to price increases is *overdemand*. When a company cannot supply all of its customers, it can raise its prices, put customers on allocation, or both. The "real" price can be increased in several ways, each with a different impact on buyers. The following price adjustments are common:

- *Adoption of Delayed Quotation Pricing:* The company does not set its final price until the product is finished or delivered. Delayed quotation pricing is prevalent in industries with long production lead times, such as industrial construction and heavy-equipment manufacture.

- *Use of Escalator Clauses:* The company requires the customer to pay today's price and all or part of any inflation increase that takes place before delivery. An escalator clause in the contract bases price increases on some specified price index, such as the cost-of-living index. Escalator clauses are found in many contracts involving industrial projects of long duration.

- *Unbundling of Goods and Services:* The company maintains its price but removes or prices separately one or more elements that were part of the former offer, such as free delivery or installation. IBM, for example, now offers training as a separately priced service. Many restaurants have shifted from dinner pricing to à la carte pricing. A joke in Brazil is that the current price of a car no longer includes the tires and steering wheel.

- *Reduction of Discounts:* The company instructs its salesforce not to offer its normal cash and quantity discounts.

A company might also have to decide whether to raise the price sharply on a one-time basis or to raise it by small amounts several times. For example, when costs rose for Supercut stores (a franchised chain of hairdressers), management debated between raising the haircut price immediately from $6 to $8 or raising the price to $7 this year and $8 the following year. Generally, consumers prefer small

Analyzing the Marketing-Mix Alternatives Facing a Firm in an Economic Recession

Here we will describe an actual but disguised situation involving two competing appliance manufacturers. Company A's appliances are perceived to be of higher quality and higher prices than company B's appliances. The perceived positions of the two brands are shown in Figure (a) along the dimensions of *perceived quality* and *price*. Note that the two brands lie on the same quality-to-price line. This means that consumers feel they would get approximately the same value per dollar whether they bought brand A or B. Those who want more quality would buy A if they could afford it. Those who want to spend less would buy B.

The dots in Figure (a) represent the preferences of potential buyers for quality/price combinations. Buyers whose preferences are nearest to A will buy A; the same goes for B. Clearly, each brand has a substantial market, and both are likely to enjoy good market shares.

An economic recession now occurs. There are fewer buyers and their preferences shift toward the cheaper appliance B (see Figure [b]). The number of buyers willing to buy the higher-price appliance diminishes. If company A does nothing about this, its market share will shrink.

Company A must identify its marketing alternatives and choose among them. At least seven marketing alternatives exist. They are illustrated in Figure (c) and described on the next page.

At the right are various strategic options, their reasoning, and consequences.

STRATEGIC OPTIONS	REASONING	CONSEQUENCES
1. Maintain price and perceived quality. Engage in selective customer pruning.	Firm has high customer loyalty. It is willing to lose poorer customers to competitors.	Smaller market share. Lower profitability.
2. Raise price and perceived quality.	Raise price to cover rising costs. Improve quality to justify higher prices.	Smaller market share. Maintained profitability.
3. Maintain price and raise perceived quality.	It is cheaper to maintain price and raise perceived quality.	Smaller market share. Short-term decline in profitability. Long-term increase in profitability.
4. Cut price partly and raise perceived quality.	Must give customers some price reduction but stress higher value of offer.	Maintained market share. Short-term decline in profitability. Long-term maintained profitability.
5. Cut price fully and maintain perceived quality.	Discipline and discourage price competition.	Maintained market share. Short-term decline in profitability.
6. Cut price fully and reduce perceived quality.	Discipline and discourage price competition and maintain profit margin.	Maintained market share. Maintained margin. Reduced long-term profitability.
7. Maintain price and reduce perceived quality.	Cut marketing expense to combat rising costs.	Smaller market share. Maintained margin. Reduced long-term profitability.

price increases on a regular basis to sharp price increases. In passing price increases on to customers, the company needs to avoid the image of a price gouger. Customer memories are long, and they will turn against the price gougers when the market softens. The price increases should be accompanied by company communications explaining why prices are being increased. The company's salesforce should help customers find ways to economize.

There are other ways that the company can respond to high costs or demand without raising prices. The possibilities include the following:

- Shrinking the amount of product instead of raising the price. (Hershey Foods maintained its candy bar price but trimmed its size. Nestlé maintained its size but raised the price.)

Company A might consider launching an economy model located close to company B's model so that it can capture the increased number of economy-minded customers (a modification of alternative 6). The economy model may be launched under the same brand name or a new brand name. By offering a prestige and an economy model, company A can hold or increase its market share.

Company A should first try to increase perceived quality rather than lower its price. Perceived quality can be increased by adding free services, new features, and so on. If successful, this typically reduces the company's profits less than lowering its prices does.

The choice of a marketing strategy hinges on a number of considerations, including company A's current market share, current and planned capacity, market growth rate, customer price sensitivity and perceived-value sensitivity, market-share/profitability relationship, and competitors' probable strategic responses and initiatives. The company needs to forecast the impact of each marketing strategy on its sales, market share, costs, profit, and long-run investment.

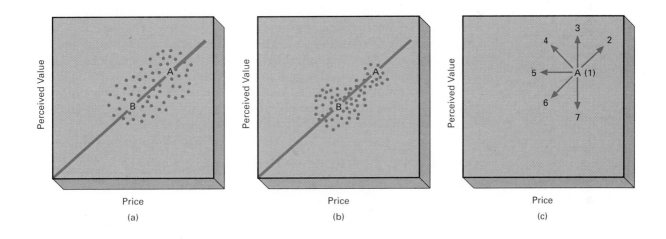

- Substituting less-expensive materials or ingredients. (Many candy-bar companies substituted synthetic chocolate for real chocolate to fight the price increases in cocoa.)
- Reducing or removing product features to reduce cost. (Sears engineered down a number of its appliances so they could be priced competitively with those sold in discount stores.)
- Removing or reducing product services, such as installation, free delivery, or long warranties.
- Using less-expensive packaging material or promoting larger package sizes to keep down packaging cost.
- Reducing the number of sizes and models offered.
- Creating new economy brands. (The Jewel Food Stores introduced 170 generic items selling at 10 to 30% less than national brands to offer to price-conscious consumers.)

The best action to take is not always obvious. Quaker Oats produces the successful cereal called Quaker Oats Natural, which contains several ingredients, such as almonds and raisins, whose prices jumped during a recent inflation. Quaker Oats saw two choices, namely, raising the price, or cost-reducing the ingredients by including fewer almonds and raisins, or finding cheaper substitutes. It decided against changing the ingredients and raised the price. But the price elasticity was high, and sales fell. This forced the company to reconsider ways to cost-reduce the ingredients, knowing that such a move also involves a risk.

Customers' Reactions to Price Changes

Any price change can affect customers, competitors, distributors, and suppliers and may provoke government reaction as well. Here we will consider customers' reactions.

Customers do not always put a straightforward interpretation on price changes.[17] A price cut can be interpreted in the following ways: The item is about to be replaced by a new model; the item is faulty and is not selling well; the firm is in financial trouble and may not stay in business to supply future parts; the price will come down even further, and it pays to wait; or the quality has been reduced.

A price increase, which would normally deter sales, may carry some positive meanings to customers: The item is "hot" and might be unobtainable unless it is bought soon; the item represents an unusually good value; or the seller is greedy and is taking advantage of customers.

Customers are most price sensitive to products that cost a lot and/or are bought frequently, whereas they hardly notice higher prices on low-cost items that they buy infrequently. In addition, some buyers are less concerned with the product's *price* than the *total costs* of obtaining, operating, and servicing the product over its lifetime. A seller can charge more than competitors and still get the business if the customer can be convinced that the total lifetime costs are lower.

Competitors' Reactions to Price Changes

A firm contemplating a price change has to worry about competitors' as well as customers' reactions. Competitors are most likely to react where the number of firms is small, the product is homogeneous, and the buyers are highly informed.

How can the firm anticipate the likely reactions of its competitors? Assume that the firm faces one large competitor. The competitor's reaction can be estimated from two vantage points. One is to assume that the competitor reacts in a set way to price changes. In this case, its reaction can be anticipated. The other is to assume that the competitor treats each price change as a fresh challenge and reacts according to self-interest at the time. In this case, the company will have to figure out what lies in the competitor's self-interest. The competitor's current financial situation should be researched, along with recent sales and capacity, customer loyalty, and corporate objectives. If the competitor has a market-share objective, it is likely to match the price change. If it has a profit-maximization objective, it may react on some other strategy front, such as increasing the advertising budget or improving the product quality. The challenge is to read the competitor's mind by using inside and outside sources of information.

The problem is complicated because the competitor can put different interpretations on, say, a company price cut: The competitor can surmise that the company is trying to steal the market, that the company is doing poorly and trying to boost its sales, or that the company wants the whole industry to reduce prices to stimulate total demand.

When there are several competitors, the company must estimate each close competitor's likely reaction. If all competitors behave alike, this estimate amounts to an analysis of a typical competitor. If the competitors do not react uniformly because of critical differences in size, market shares, or policies, then separate analyses are necessary. If some competitors will match the price change, there is good reason to expect that the rest will also match it. Marketing Concepts and Tools 19-5 shows how a major chemical company analyzed the probable reactions of various parties to a contemplated price reduction.

Marketing Concepts and Tools 19-5

Using Decision Theory to Assess Competitors' Probable Reactions to a Contemplated Price Cut

A large chemical company had been selling a plastic substance to industrial users for several years and enjoyed a 40% market share. The management became worried about whether its current price of $1.00 per pound could be maintained for much longer. The main source of concern was the rapid build-up of capacity by its three competitors and the possible attraction of further competitors by the current price. Management saw that the solution to possible oversupply lay in further market expansion. The key opportunity for market expansion lay in an important market segment that was closely held by a substitute plastic product produced by six firms. This substitute product was not as good, but it was priced lower. Management thought of displacing the substitute product through a price reduction. If it could penetrate this segment, there was a good chance it could also penetrate three other segments.

The first task was to develop a decision model for the problem. This required defining the objectives, price alternatives, and key uncertainties. The chosen objective was to maximize the present value of future profits over the next five years. Management considered four price alternatives: maintaining the price at $1.00 or reducing the price to 93¢, 85¢, or 80¢. The key uncertainties were the following:

- How much penetration in the key segment would take place without a price reduction?
- How would the six firms producing the substitute plastic react to each possible price reduction?
- How much key-segment penetration would take place for each possible price reaction by the suppliers of the substitute plastic?
- How much would key-segment penetration speed up penetration of the other three segments?

- If the key segment was not penetrated, what is the probability that the company's competitors would initiate a price reduction soon?
- How would a price reduction affect the decision of existing competitors to expand their capacity and potential competitors to enter the industry?

The data-gathering phase consisted of asking sales personnel to place subjective probabilities on the possible states of the key uncertainties. For example, one question asked for the probability that the substitute product producers would retaliate if the company reduced its price to 93¢ per pound. On the average, the sales personnel felt that there was a 5% probability of a full match, a 60% probability of a half match, and a 35% probability of no retaliation. They were also asked for probabilities if price were reduced to 85¢ and to 80¢. The sales personnel indicated, as expected, that the probability of retaliation increased with the size of the price reduction.

The next step was to estimate the payoff associated with each price alternative. A decision-tree analysis revealed over 400 possible outcomes. The results indicated that all price reductions had a higher expected payoff than no price reduction, and a price reduction to 80¢ had the highest expected payoff. To check the sensitivity of these results, they were recomputed for alternative assumptions about the rate of market growth and the cost of capital. The ranking of the strategies was not affected by changes in assumptions. The analysis confirmed the desirability of a price reduction.

SOURCE: See Paul E. Green, "Bayesian Decision Theory in Pricing Strategy," *Journal of Marketing*, January 1963, pp. 5–14.

Responding to Price Changes

Here we reverse the question and ask how a firm should respond to a price change initiated by a competitor. In markets characterized by high product homogeneity, the firm has little choice but to meet a competitor's price cut. The firm should search for ways to enhance its augmented product, but if it cannot find any, it will have to meet the price reduction.

When a competitor raises its price in a homogeneous-product market, the other firms might not match it. They will comply if the price increase will benefit the industry as a whole. But if one firm does not think that it or the industry would gain, its noncompliance can make the leader and the others rescind the price increases.

In nonhomogeneous-product markets, a firm has more latitude in reacting to a competitor's price change. Buyers choose the vendor on a multiplicity of considerations: service, quality, reliability, and other factors. These factors desensitize buyers to minor price differences.

Before reacting, the firm needs to consider the following issues: (1) Why did the competitor change the price? Is it to steal the market, to utilize excess capacity, to meet changing cost conditions, or to lead an industrywide price change? (2) Does the competitor plan to make the price change temporary or permanent? (3) What will happen to the company's market share and profits if it does not respond? Are other companies going to respond? and (4) What are the competitor's and other firms' responses likely to be to each possible reaction?

Market leaders frequently face aggressive price cutting by smaller firms trying to build market share. Using price, Fuji attacks Kodak, Bic attacks Gillette, and Datril attacks Tylenol. IBM's personal computers are under great attack today from dozens of lower-priced computers. When the attacking firm's product is comparable to the leaders, its lower price will cut into the leader's share. The leader at this point has several options.

- *Maintain Price:* The leader might maintain its price and profit margin, believing that (a) it would lose too much profit if it reduced its price; (b) it would not lose much market share; and (c) it could regain market share when necessary. The leader believes that it could hold on to good customers, giving up the poorer ones to the competitor. The argument against price maintenance is that the attacker gets more confident as its sales increase, the leader's salesforce gets demoralized, and the leader loses more share than expected. The leader panics, lowers price to regain share, and finds it more difficult and costly than expected.

- *Raise Perceived Quality:* The leader could maintain price but strengthen the value of its offer. It could improve its product, services, and communications. It could stress the relative quality of its product over that of the low-price competitor. The firm may find it cheaper to maintain price and spend money to improve its perceived quality than to cut price and operate at a lower margin.

- *Reduce Price:* The leader might drop its price to the competitor's price. It might do so because (a) its costs fall with volume; (b) it would lose market share because the market is price sensitive; and (c) it would be hard to rebuild market share once it is lost. This action will cut its profits in the short run. Some firms will reduce their product quality, services, and marketing communications to maintain profits but this will ultimately hurt their long-run market share. The company should try to maintain its quality as it cuts prices.

- *Increase Price and Improve Quality:* The leader might raise its price and introduce new brands to bracket the attacking brand. Heublein, Inc. used this strategy when its Smirnoff's vodka, which had 23% of the American vodka market, was attacked by another brand, Wolfschmidt, priced at $1 less a bottle. Instead of lowering the price of Smirnoff by $1, Heublein raised the price by $1 and put the increased revenue into its advertising. At the same time, Heublein introduced another brand, Relska, to compete

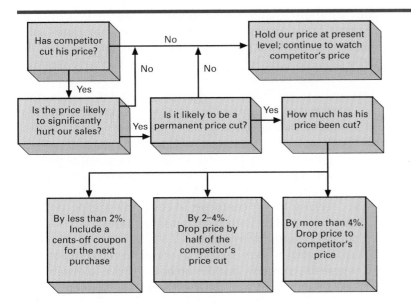

with Wolfschmidt and still another, Popov, to sell for less than Wolfschmidt. This strategy effectively bracketed Wolfschmidt and gave Smirnoff an even more elite image.

♦ *Launch Low-Price Fighter Line:* One of the best responses is to add lower-price items to the line or to create a separate lower-price brand. This is necessary if the particular market segment being lost is price sensitive, since it will not respond to arguments of higher quality.

The best response varies with the particular situation. The company under attack has to consider the product's stage in the life cycle, its importance in the company's product portfolio, the intentions and resources of the competitor, the price and quality sensitivity of the market, the behavior of costs with volume, and the company's alternative opportunities.

An extended analysis of company alternatives is not always feasible when the attack occurs. The competitor might have spent considerable time in preparing this decision, but the company may have to react decisively within hours or days. About the only way to reduce price-reaction time is to anticipate possible competitors' price changes and to prepare contingent responses. Figure 19-8 shows a company price-reaction program to be used if a competitor cuts prices. Reaction programs for meeting price changes find their greatest application in industries where price changes occur with some frequency and where it is important to react quickly. Examples can be found in the meat-packing, lumber, and oil industries.

SUMMARY ❖

In spite of the increased role of nonprice factors in the modern marketing process, price remains a critical element and is especially challenging in markets characterized by monopolistic competition or oligopoly.

In setting the price of a product, the company should follow a six-step procedure. First, the company carefully establishes its marketing objective(s), such as survival, maximum current profit, maximum current revenue, maximum sales growth, maximum market skimming, or product-quality leadership. Second, the company determines the demand schedule, which shows the probable quantity purchased per period at alternative price levels. The more inelastic the demand, the higher the company can set its price. Third, the company estimates how its costs vary at different output levels and with different levels of accumulated production experience. Fourth, the company examines competitors' prices as a basis for positioning its own price. Fifth, the company selects one of the following pricing methods: markup pricing, target-return pricing, perceived-value pricing, value pricing, going-rate pricing, and sealed-bid pricing. Sixth, the company selects its final price, expressing it in the most effective psychological way, coordinating it with the other marketing-mix elements, checking that it conforms to company pricing policies, and making sure it will find acceptance with distributors and dealers, company salesforce, competitors, suppliers, and government.

Companies will adapt the price to varying conditions in the marketplace. One is geographical pricing, where the company decides on how to price to distant customers. A second is price discounts and allowances, where the company establishes cash discounts, quantity discounts, functional discounts, seasonal discounts, and allowances. A third is promotional pricing, where the company decides on loss-leader pricing, special-event pricing, cash rebates, low-interest financing, and psychological discounting. A fourth is discriminatory pricing, where the company establishes different prices for different customer segments, product forms, brand images, places, and times. A fifth is product-mix pricing, where the company decides on the price zones for several products in a product line and on the pricing of optional features, captive products, byproducts, and product bundles.

When a firm considers initiating a price change, it must carefully consider customers' and competitors' reactions. Customers' reactions are influenced by the meaning customers see in the price change. Competitors' reactions flow from either a set reaction policy or from a fresh appraisal of each situation. The firm initiating the price change must also anticipate the probable reactions of suppliers, middlemen, and government.

The firm facing a price change initiated by a competitor must try to understand the competitor's intent and the likely duration of the change. If swiftness of reaction is desirable, the firm should preplan its reactions to different possible price actions by competitors.

NOTES ❖

1. David J. Schwartz, *Marketing Today: A Basic Approach*, 3rd ed. (New York: Harcourt Brace Jovanovich, 1981), p. 271.

2. Thomas T. Nagle, *The Strategy and Tactics of Pricing* (Englewood Cliffs, NJ: Prentice Hall, 1987), Chap. 3. This is an excellent reference book for making pricing decisions.

3. John R. Nevin, "Laboratory Experiments for Estimating Consumer Demand—A Validation Study," *Journal of Marketing Research*, August 1974, pp. 261–68.

4. See Sidney Bennett and J. B. Wilkinson, "Price-Quantity Relationships and Price Elasticity Under In-Store Experimentation," *Journal of Business Research*, January 1974, pp. 30–34.

5. Nagle, *Strategy and Tactics of Pricing*, Chap. 11.

6. For a summary of elasticity studies, see Dominique M. Hanssens, Leonard J. Parsons, and Randall L. Schultz, *Market Response Models: Econometric and Time Series Analysis* (Boston: Kluwer Academic Publishers, 1990), pp. 187–91. For methods of estimating elasticity, see Leonard J. Parsons and Randall L. Schultz, *Marketing Models and Econometric Research* (New York: North-Holland, 1976).

7. See William W. Alberts, "The Experience Curve Doctrine Reconsidered," *Journal of Marketing*, July 1989, pp. 36–49.

8. See "Japan's Smart Secret Weapon," *Fortune*, August 12, 1991, p. 75.

9. "Supermarket 1984 Sales Manual," *Progressive Grocer*, July 1984.

10. See Daniel A. Nimer, "Pricing the Profitable Sale Has a Lot to Do with Perception," *Sales Management*, May 19, 1975, pp. 13–14.

11. See "Value Marketing," *Business Week*, November 11, 1991, pp. 54–60; and "What Intelligent Consumers Want," *Fortune*, December 28, 1992, pp. 56–60.

12. Gary M. Erickson and Johny K. Johansson, "The Role of Price in Multi-Attribute Product-Evaluations," *Journal of Consumer Research*, September 1985, pp. 195–99.

13. George J. Szybillo and Jacob Jacoby, "Intrinsic versus Extrinsic Cues as Determinants of Perceived Product Quality," *Journal of Applied Psychology*, February 1974, pp. 74–78.

14. Paul W. Farris and David J. Reibstein, "How Prices, Expenditures, and Profits Are Linked," *Harvard Business Review*, November–December 1979, pp. 173–84.

15. See Robert E. Weigand, "Buy In-Follow On Strategies for Profit," *Sloan Management Review*, Spring 1991, pp. 29–37.

16. See Gerald J. Tellis, "Beyond the Many Faces of Price: An Integration of Pricing Strategies," *Journal of Marketing*, October 1986, pp. 146–60, here p. 155. This excellent article also analyzes and illustrates other pricing strategies.

17. For an excellent review, see Kent B. Monroe, "Buyers' Subjective Perceptions of Price," *Journal of Marketing Research*, February 1973, pp. 70–80.

20

Selecting and Managing Marketing Channels

The middleman is not a hired link in a chain forged by a manufacturer, but rather an independent market, the focus of a large group of customers for whom he buys.

PHILLIP MCVEY

Adversarial power relationships work only if you never have to see or work with the bastards again.

PETER DRUCKER

In today's economy, most producers do not sell their goods directly to the final users. Between them and the final users stand a host of marketing intermediaries performing a variety of functions and bearing a variety of names. Some intermediaries—such as wholesalers and retailers—buy, take title to, and resell the merchandise; they are called *merchant middlemen*. Others—such as brokers, manufacturers' representatives, and sales agents—search for customers and may negotiate on behalf of the producer but do not take title to the goods; they are called *agent middlemen*. Still others—such as transportation companies, independent warehouses, banks, and advertising agencies—assist in the performance of distribution but neither take title to goods nor negotiate purchases or sales; they are called *facilitators*.

Marketing-channel decisions are among the most critical decisions facing management. *The company's chosen channels intimately affect all the other marketing decisions.* The company's pricing depends on whether it uses mass merchandisers or high-quality boutiques. The firm's salesforce and advertising decisions depend on how much training and motivation the dealers need. In addition, the company's channel decisions *involve relatively long-term commitments to other firms.* When an auto maker signs up independent dealers to sell its automobiles, the auto maker cannot buy them out the next day and replace them with company-owned outlets. When a drug manufacturer relies on independent retail druggists to sell its products, the drug manufacturer must heed them when they object to its selling through mass-distribution outlets. Corey observed:

> A distribution system . . . is a key external resource. Normally it takes years to build, and it is not easily changed. It ranks in importance with key internal resources such as manufacturing, research, engineering, and field sales personnel and facilities. It represents a significant corporate commitment to large numbers of independent companies whose business is distribution—and to the particular markets they serve. It represents, as well, a commitment to a set of policies and practices that constitute the basic fabric on which is woven an extensive set of long-term relationships.[1]

Thus there is a powerful inertial tendency in channel arrangements. Therefore management must choose channels with an eye on tomorrow's likely selling environment as well as today's.

In this chapter, we address the following questions: What is the nature of marketing channels? What decisions do companies face in designing, managing, evaluating, and modifying their channels? What trends are taking place in channel dynamics? How can channel conflict be managed? In the next chapter we will examine marketing-channel issues from the perspective of retailers, wholesalers, and physical-distribution agencies.

The Nature of Marketing Channels

Most producers work with marketing intermediaries to bring their products to market. The marketing intermediaries make up a *marketing channel* (also called trade channel or distribution channel). We will use Stern and El-Ansary's definition of a marketing channel:

❖ Marketing channels *can be viewed as sets of interdependent organizations involved in the process of making a product or service available for use or consumption.*[2]

Why Are Marketing Intermediaries Used?

Why is the producer willing to delegate some of the selling job to intermediaries? The delegation means relinquishing some control over how and to whom the products are sold. The producer appears to be placing the firm's destiny in the hands of intermediaries. On the other hand, producers gain several of the following advantages.

Many producers lack the financial resources to carry out direct marketing. For example, General Motors sells its automobiles through more than 10,000 dealer outlets; even General Motors would be hard pressed to raise the cash to buy out its dealers.

Direct marketing would require many producers to become middlemen for the complementary products of other producers in order to achieve mass-distribution economies. For example, the Wm. Wrigley Jr. Company would not find it practical to establish small retail gum shops throughout the country or to sell gum door to door or by mail order. It would have to sell gum along with many other small products and would end up in the drugstore and grocery store business. Wrigley finds it easier to work through the extensive network of privately owned distribution organizations.

Producers who can afford to establish their own channels can often earn a greater return by increasing their investment in their main business. If a company earns a 20% rate of return on manufacturing and foresees only a 10% return on retailing, it will not want to undertake its own retailing.

Some producers, however, will set up a partially owned distribution system. Thus McDonald's owns over one fifth of all its outlets. The advantages are that the company learns about managing retail outlets, can rapidly and flexibly test new products and ideas, provides a model for operator-owned outlets, and uses owned outlets to benchmark the performance of operator-owned outlets. The disadvantages are that operator-owners may resent the competition coming from company-owned outlets and fear that the company will eventually buy out the operators. Dual distribution often creates channel conflict.

The use of middlemen largely boils down to their superior efficiency in making goods widely available and accessible to target markets. Marketing intermediaries, through their contacts, experience, specialization, and scale of operation, offer the firm more than it can usually achieve on its own.

From the point of view of the economic system, the basic role of marketing intermediaries is to transform the heterogeneous supplies found in nature into assortments of goods that people want to buy. According to Stern and El-Ansary:

Intermediaries smooth the flow of goods and services. . . . This procedure is necessary in order to bridge the discrepancy between the assortment of goods and services generated by the producer and the assortment demanded by the consumer. The discrepancy results from the fact that manufacturers typically produce a large quantity of a limited variety of goods, whereas consumers usually desire only a limited quantity of a wide variety of goods.[3]

Wroe Alderson made the same point: "The goal of marketing is the matching of segments of supply and demand."[4]

Figure 20-1 shows one major source of economies effected by using middle-

FIGURE 20-1
How a Distributor Effects an
Economy of Effort

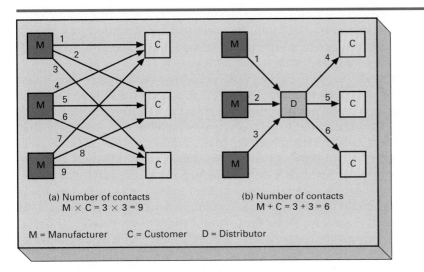

(a) Number of contacts
M × C = 3 × 3 = 9

(b) Number of contacts
M + C = 3 + 3 = 6

M = Manufacturer   C = Customer   D = Distributor

men. Part (a) shows three producers, each using direct marketing to reach three customers. This system requires nine different contacts. Part (b) shows the three producers working through one distributor, who contacts the three customers. This system requires only six contacts. In this way, middlemen reduce the amount of work that must be done.

Marketing-Channel Functions and Flows

A marketing channel performs the work of moving goods from producers to consumers. It overcomes the time, place, and possession gaps that separate goods and services from those who would use them. Members in the marketing channel perform a number of key functions and participate in the following marketing flows:

- *Information:* The collection and dissemination of marketing research information about potential and current customers, competitors, and other actors and forces in the marketing environment.
- *Promotion:* The development and dissemination of persuasive communications about the offer designed to attract customers.
- *Negotiation:* The attempt to reach final agreement on price and other terms so that transfer of ownership or possession can be effected.
- *Ordering:* The backward communication of intentions to buy by the marketing-channel members to the manufacturer.
- *Financing:* The acquisition and allocation of funds required to finance inventories at different levels of the marketing channel.
- *Risk Taking:* The assumption of risks connected with carrying out the channel work.
- *Physical Possession:* The successive storage and movement of physical products from raw materials to the final customers.
- *Payment:* Buyers paying their bills through banks and other financial institutions to the sellers.
- *Title:* The actual transfer of ownership from one organization or person to another.

These functions and flows are listed in the normal order in which they arise between any two channel members. Some of these flows are *forward flows* (physical, title, and promotion); others are *backward flows* (ordering and payment); and still others move in *both directions* (information, negotiation, finance, and risk taking). Five of these flows are illustrated in Figure 20-2 for the marketing of forklift trucks. If all of these flows were superimposed in one diagram, the tremendous complexity of even simple marketing channels would be apparent.

The question is not *whether* these functions need to be performed—they must be—but rather *who* is to perform them. All of the functions have three things in common: They use up scarce resources; they can often be performed better through specialization; and they are shiftable among channel members. To the extent that the manufacturer performs the functions, the manufacturer's costs go up, and its prices must be higher. When some functions are shifted to middlemen, the producer's costs and prices are lower, but the middlemen must add a charge to cover their work. If the middlemen are more efficient than the manufacturer, the prices faced by consumers should be lower. Consumers might decide to perform some of the functions themselves, in which case they should enjoy lower prices. The issue of who should perform various channel tasks is one of relative efficiency and effectiveness.

Marketing functions, then, are more basic than the institutions that at any given time perform them. Changes in channel institutions largely reflect the discovery of more efficient ways to combine or separate economic functions that must be carried on to provide meaningful assortments of goods to target customers.

Number of Channel Levels

Marketing channels can be characterized by the number of channel levels. Each middleman that performs work in bringing the product and its title closer to the

FIGURE 20-2 Five Different Marketing Flows in the Marketing Channel for Forklift Trucks

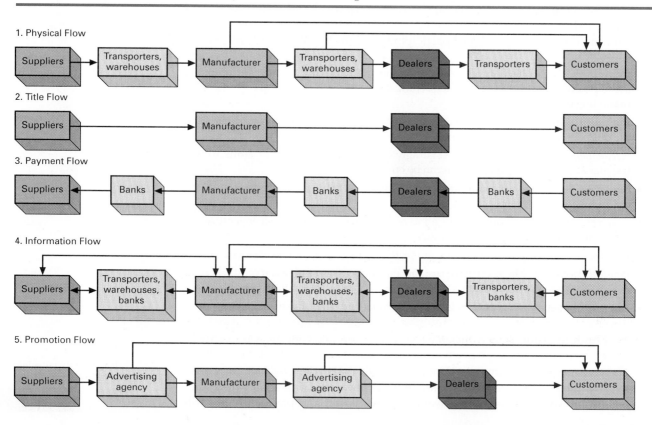

FIGURE 20-3
Consumer and Industrial Marketing Channels

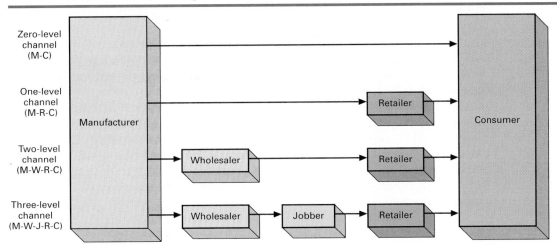

(a) Consumer marketing channels

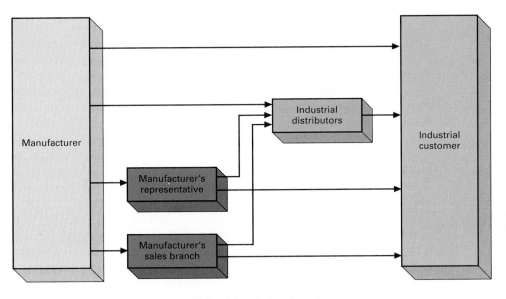

(b) Industrial marketing channels

final buyer constitutes a *channel level*. Since the producer and the final customer both perform work, they are part of every channel. We will use the number of *intermediary levels* to designate the *length* of a channel. Figure 20-3(a) illustrates several consumer-goods marketing channels of different lengths.

A *zero-level channel* (also called a *direct-marketing channel*) consists of a manufacturer selling directly to the final customer. The major ways of direct marketing are door to door, home parties, mail order, telemarketing, TV selling, and manufacturer-owned stores. Avon's sales representatives sell cosmetics to women on a door-to-door basis; Tupperware representatives sell kitchen goods through home parties; Franklin Mint sells collectible objects through mail order; Shearson-Lehman brokers use the telephone to prospect for new customers; some manufacturers of exercise equipment sell through TV commercials or documentaries; and Singer sells its sewing machines through its own stores.

A *one-level channel* contains one selling intermediary, such as a retailer. A *two-*

level channel contains two intermediaries. In consumer markets, they are typically a wholesaler and a retailer. A *three-level channel* contains three intermediaries. For example, in the meat-packing industry, wholesalers sell to jobbers, who sell to small retailers.

Higher-level marketing channels are also found. In Japan, food distribution may involve as many as six levels. From the producer's point of view, the problem of obtaining information about the end users and exercising control increases with the number of channel levels.

Figure 20-3(b) shows channels commonly used in industrial marketing. An industrial-goods manufacturer can use its salesforce to sell directly to industrial customers. Or it can sell to industrial distributors who sell to the industrial customers. Or it can sell through manufacturer's representatives or its own sales branches directly to industrial customers, or use them to sell through industrial distributors. Thus zero-, one-, and two-level marketing channels are quite common in industrial marketing channels.

Channels normally describe a forward movement of products. One can also talk about *backward channels*. According to Zikmund and Stanton:

> The recycling of solid wastes is a major ecological goal. Although recycling is technologically feasible, reversing the flow of materials in the channel of distribution—marketing trash through a "backward" channel—presents a challenge. Existing backward channels are primitive, and financial incentives are inadequate. The consumer must be motivated to undergo a role change and become a producer—the initiating force in the reverse distribution process.[5]

Several middlemen play a role in backward channels, including manufacturers' redemption centers, community groups, traditional middlemen such as soft-drink middlemen, trash-collection specialists, recycling centers, modernized "rag and junk men," trash-recycling brokers, and central-processing warehousing. Using various backward channels, Reynolds Metal Company paid over $77 million in 1985 to retrieve over seven billion used cans.

Channels in the Service Sector

The concept of marketing channels is not limited to the distribution of physical goods. Producers of services and ideas also face the problem of making their output *available* and *accessible* to target populations. They develop "educational-dissemination systems" and "health-delivery systems." They must figure out agencies and locations for reaching a spatially distributed population:

> Hospitals must be located in geographic space to serve the people with complete medical care, and we must build schools close to the children who have to learn. Fire stations must be located to give rapid access to potential conflagrations, and voting booths must be placed so that people can cast their ballots without expending unreasonable amounts of time, effort, or money to reach the polling stations. Many of our states face the problem of locating branch campuses to serve a burgeoning and increasingly well educated population. In the cities we must create and locate playgrounds for the children. Many overpopulated countries must assign birth control clinics to reach the people with contraceptive and family planning information.[6]

Marketing channels also are used in "person" marketing. Before 1940, professional comedians could reach audiences through seven channels: vaudeville houses, special events, nightclubs, radio, movies, carnivals, and theaters. In the 1950s, television emerged as a strong channel, and vaudeville disappeared. Politicians also must find cost-effective channels—mass media, rallies, coffee hours—for distributing their messages to voters.[7]

Channel-Design Decisions

We will now examine several channel-decision problems facing manufacturers. In designing marketing channels, manufacturers have to struggle between what is ideal, what is feasible, and what is available. A new firm typically starts as a local operation selling in a limited market. Since it has limited capital, it usually uses existing middlemen. The number of middlemen in any local market is apt to be limited: a few manufacturer's sales agents, a few wholesalers, several established retailers, a few trucking companies, and a few warehouses. Deciding on the best channels might not be a problem. The problem might be to convince one or a few available middlemen to handle their line.

If the new firm is successful, it might branch out to new markets. Again, the manufacturer will tend to work through the existing intermediaries, although that might mean using different types of marketing channels in different areas. In the smaller markets, the firm might sell directly to retailers; in the larger markets, it might sell through distributors. In rural areas, it might work with general-goods merchants; in urban areas, with limited-line merchants. In one part of the country, it might grant exclusive franchises because the merchants normally work this way; in another, it might sell through all outlets willing to handle the merchandise. Thus the manufacturer's channel system evolves in response to local opportunities and conditions.

Designing a channel system calls for analyzing customer needs, establishing channel objectives, identifying the major channel alternatives, and evaluating them.

Analyzing Service Output Levels Desired by Customers

Understanding what, where, why, when, and how target customers buy is the first step in designing the marketing channel. The marketer must understand the *service output levels* desired by the target customers. Channels produce five service outputs:

- *Lot Size:* The lot size is the number of units that the marketing channel permits a typical customer to buy on a buying occasion. In buying cars for its fleet, Hertz prefers a channel from which it can buy a large lot size; and a household wants a channel that would permit buying a lot size of one. Obviously different channels must be set up for fleet car buyers and household buyers. The smaller the lot size, the greater the service output level that the channel must provide.

- *Waiting Time:* Waiting time is the average time that customers of that channel wait for receipt of the goods. Customers normally prefer fast delivery channels. Faster service requires a greater service output level.

- *Spatial Convenience:* Spatial convenience expresses the degree to which the marketing channel makes it easy for customers to purchase the product. Chevrolet, for example, offers greater spatial convenience than Cadillac, in that there are a much greater number of Chevrolet dealers. Chevrolet's greater market decentralization helps customers save on transportation and search costs in buying and repairing an automobile. Spatial convenience is being further augmented by the use of direct marketing.

- *Product Variety:* Product variety represents the assortment breadth provided by the marketing channel. Normally customers prefer greater assortment breadth because it increases the chance of exactly meeting their need. Thus car buyers would rather buy from a dealership carrying multiple manufacturer brands than only one manufacturer's brand.

♦ *Service Backup:* Service backup represents the add-on services (credit, delivery, installation, repairs) provided by the channel. The greater the service backup, the greater the work provided by the channel.[8]

The marketing-channel designer must know the service outputs desired by the target customers. Providing increased levels of service outputs means increased costs for the channel and higher prices for customers. The success of discount stores indicates that many consumers are willing to accept lower-service outputs when this translates into lower prices.

Establishing the Channel Objectives and Constraints

The channel objectives should be stated in terms of targeted service output levels. According to Bucklin, under competitive conditions, channel institutions should arrange their functional tasks so as to minimize total channel costs with respect to desired levels of service outputs.[9] Usually, several segments can be identified that desire differing service output levels. Effective channel planning requires determining which market segments to serve and the best channels to use in each case. Each producer develops its channel objectives in the face of several constraints.

Channel objectives vary with product characteristics. *Perishable* products require more direct marketing because of the dangers associated with delays and repeated handling. *Bulky* products, such as building materials or soft drinks, require channels that minimize the shipping distance and the number of handlings in the movement from producer to consumers. *Nonstandardized* products, such as custom-built machinery and specialized business forms, are sold directly by company sales representatives because middlemen lack the requisite knowledge. Products requiring installation and/or maintenance services are usually sold and maintained by the company or exclusively franchised dealers. *High unit value* products are often sold through a company salesforce rather than through middlemen.

Channel design must take into account the strengths and weaknesses of different types of intermediaries. For example, manufacturers' reps are able to contact customers at a low cost per customer because the total cost is shared by several clients. But the selling effort per customer is less intense than if the company's sales reps did the selling. Channel design is also influenced by the competitors' channels.

Channel design must adapt to the larger environment. When *economic conditions* are depressed, producers want to move their goods to market in the most economical way. This means using shorter channels and dispensing with inessential services that add to the final price of the goods. *Legal regulations and restrictions* also affect channel design. The law looks unfavorably upon channel arrangements that "may tend to substantially lessen competition or tend to create a monopoly."

Identifying the Major Channel Alternatives

After a company has defined its target market and desired positioning, it should identify its channel alternatives. A channel alternative is described by three elements: the *types of business intermediaries*, the *number of intermediaries*, and the *terms and responsibilities of each channel participant*.

TYPES OF INTERMEDIARIES ❖ The firm needs to identify the types of intermediaries available to carry on its channel work. Here are two examples:

A test-equipment manufacturer developed an audio device for detecting poor mechanical connections in machines with moving parts. The company executives felt that this product would sell in all industries where electric, combustion, or steam engines were used, such as aviation, automobiles, railroads, food canning, construction, and oil. The company's salesforce was small. The problem was how to reach these diverse industries effectively. The following channel alternatives were identified:

◆ *Company Salesforce:* Expand the company's direct salesforce. Assign sales representatives to territories to contact all prospects in the area. Or develop separate salesforces for the different industries.

◆ *Manufacturer's Agency:* Hire manufacturer's agencies in different regions or end-use industries to sell the new test equipment.

◆ *Industrial Distributors:* Find distributors in the different regions and/or end-use industries who will buy and carry the audio device. Give them exclusive distribution, adequate margins, product training, and promotional support.

A consumer electronics company produces FM car radios. It identified the following channel alternatives:

◆ *OEM Market:* The company could sell its radios to automobile manufacturers to be installed as original equipment. OEM stands for *original equipment manufacture*.

◆ *Auto-Dealer Market:* The company could sell its radios to auto dealers for replacement sales when they service cars.

◆ *Retail Automotive-Parts Dealers:* The company could sell its radios to retail automotive-parts dealers. They could reach these dealers through a direct salesforce or through distributors.

◆ *Mail-Order Market:* The company could advertise its radios in mail-order catalogs.

Companies should search for innovative marketing channels. The Conn Organ Company merchandised organs through department and discount stores, thus drawing more attention to organs than they ever enjoyed in small music stores. The Book-of-the-Month Club merchandised books through the mails. Other sellers followed with record-of-the-month clubs, candy-of-the-month clubs, and dozens of others.

Sometimes a company chooses an unconventional channel because of the difficulty or cost of working with the dominant channel. The decision sometimes turns out extremely well. The advantage of the unconventional channel is that the company will encounter a lesser degree of competition during the initial move into this channel. Here are two examples:

The U.S. Time Company originally tried to sell its inexpensive Timex watches through regular jewelry stores. But most jewelry stores refused to carry them. The company searched for other channels and placed its watches into mass-merchandise outlets. This turned out to be a great decision because of the rapid growth of mass merchandising.

Avon chose door-to-door selling because it was not able to break into regular department stores. They not only mastered door-to-door selling but made more money than most cosmetics firms that sold through department stores.

NUMBER OF INTERMEDIARIES ❖ Companies have to decide on the number of middlemen to use at each channel level. Three strategies are available.

Exclusive Distribution. *Exclusive distribution* involves severely limiting the number of intermediaries handling the company's goods or services. It applies where the producer wants to maintain a great deal of control over the service level and service outputs offered by the resellers. Often it involves *exclusive dealing* where the resellers must not carry competing brands. It requires a greater partnership between the seller and reseller. Through granting exclusive distribution, the producer hopes to obtain more aggressive and knowledgeable selling. Exclusive distribution tends to enhance the product's image and allow higher markups. It is found in the distribution of new automobiles, some major appliances, and some women's apparel brands.

Selective Distribution. *Selective distribution* involves the use of more than a few but less than all of the intermediaries who are willing to carry a particular product. It is used both by established companies and by new companies seeking to obtain distributors by promising them selective distribution. The company does not have to dissipate its efforts over many outlets, including many marginal ones. It can develop a good working relation with the selected middlemen and expect a better than average selling effort. Selective distribution enables the producer to gain adequate market coverage with more control and less cost than intensive distribution.

Intensive Distribution. A strategy of *intensive distribution* is characterized by placing the goods or services in as many outlets as possible. When the consumer requires a great deal of location convenience, it is important to offer greater intensity of distribution. This strategy is generally used for convenience items such as tobacco products, gasoline, soap, snack foods, and bubble gum.

Manufacturers are constantly tempted to move from exclusive or selective distribution to more intensive distribution to increase their coverage and sales. This may help their short-term performance but often hurts their long-term performance. Suppose a fashion goods manufacturer such as Liz Claiborne were to drive for more intensive distribution. As the company expanded from its current high-end retailers to mass merchandisers, it would lose some control over the display arrangements, the accompanying service levels, and the pricing. As the product entered more retail outlets with differing overheads, some retailers would be in a position to undercut other retailers, resulting in a price war. Buyers would attach less prestige to Liz Claiborne apparel and the manufacturer's ability to command premium prices would be reduced.

TERMS AND RESPONSIBILITIES OF CHANNEL MEMBERS ❖ The producer must determine the conditions and responsibilities of the participating channel members. The main elements in the "trade-relations mix" are *price policies, conditions of sale, territorial rights,* and *specific services to be performed by each party.*

Price policy calls for the producer to establish a price list and schedule of discounts. The middlemen must see these as equitable and sufficient.

Conditions of sale refer to payment terms and producer guarantees. Most producers grant cash discounts to their distributors for early payment. Producers might also guarantee distributors against defective merchandise or price declines. A guarantee against price declines induces distributors to buy larger quantities.

Distributors' territorial rights are another element in the trade-relations mix. Distributors want to know where the producer will enfranchise other distributors. They would also like to receive full credit for all sales taking place in their territory, whether or not they did the selling.

Mutual services and responsibilities must be carefully spelled out, especially in franchised and exclusive-agency channels. For example, McDonald's provides franchisees with a building, promotional support, a record-keeping system, training, and general administrative and technical assistance. In turn, franchisees are expected to satisfy company standards regarding physical facilities, cooperate with new promotional programs, furnish requested information, and buy specified food products.

Evaluating the Major Channel Alternatives

Suppose a producer has identified several channel alternatives and wants to determine the best one. Each alternative needs to be evaluated against *economic*, *control*, and *adaptive criteria*. Consider the following situation:

> A Memphis furniture manufacturer wants to sell its line to retailers on the West Coast. The manufacturer is trying to decide between two alternatives:

1. One alternative calls for hiring ten new *sales representatives*, who would operate out of a sales office in San Francisco. They would receive a base salary plus commissions.

2. The other alternative would use a San Francisco manufacturer's *sales agency* that has extensive contacts with retailers. The agency has 30 sales representatives, who would receive a commission based on their sales.

ECONOMIC CRITERIA ❖ Each channel alternative will produce a different level of sales and costs. The first question is whether more sales will be produced through a company salesforce or through a sales agency. Most marketing managers believe that a company salesforce will sell more. Company sales representatives concentrate entirely on the company's products; they are better trained to sell the company's products; they are more aggressive because their future depends on the company's success; they are more successful because many customers prefer to deal directly with the company.

On the other hand, the sales agency could conceivably sell more than a company salesforce. First, the sales agent has 30 sales representatives, not just ten. Second, the agency's salesforce might be just as aggressive as a direct salesforce. That depends on how much commission the company offers. Third, some customers prefer dealing with agents who represent several manufacturers rather than with salespersons from one company. Fourth, the agency has extensive contacts and marketplace knowledge, whereas a company salesforce would need to build these from scratch, which would be a difficult, costly, and long-term task.

The next step is to estimate the costs of selling different volumes through each channel. The cost schedules are shown in Figure 20-4. The fixed costs of engaging a sales agency are lower than those of establishing a company sales office. But costs rise faster through a sales agency because sales agents get a larger commission than company salespeople.

There is one sales level (S_B) at which selling costs are the same for the two

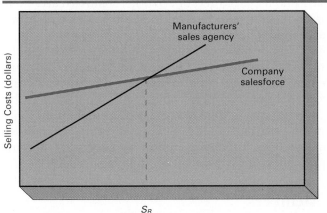

FIGURE 20-4
Break-Even Cost Chart for the Choice between a Company Salesforce and a Manufacturer's Sales Agency

channels. The sales agency is the preferred channel for any sales volume below S_B, and the company sales branch is preferred at any volume higher than S_B. Not surprisingly, sales agents tend to be used by smaller firms, or by large firms in their smaller territories wherever the sales volume is too low to warrant a company salesforce.

CONTROL CRITERIA ❖ Channel evaluation must be broadened to include control issues. Using a sales agency poses a control problem. A sales agency is an independent business firm seeking to maximize its profits. The agents may concentrate on the customers who buy the most, not necessarily of the manufacturer's goods. Furthermore, the agents might not master the technical details of the company's product or handle its promotion materials effectively.

ADAPTIVE CRITERIA ❖ In order to develop a channel, the channel members must make some degree of commitment to each other for a specified period of time. Yet these commitments invariably lead to a decrease in the producer's ability to respond to a changing marketplace. In rapidly changing, volatile, or uncertain product markets, the producer needs to seek channel structures and policies that maximize control and ability to swiftly change marketing strategy.

Channel-Management Decisions

After a company has chosen a channel alternative, individual middlemen must be *selected*, *motivated*, and *evaluated*. Also, channel arrangements must be modified over time.

Selecting Channel Members

Producers vary in their ability to attract qualified middlemen within the chosen channel. Some producers have no trouble recruiting middlemen. For example, Toyota was able to attract many new dealers for its new Lexus. In some cases, the promise of exclusive or selective distribution will draw a sufficient number of applicants.

At the other extreme are producers who have to work hard to get qualified middlemen. When Polaroid started, it could not get photographic-equipment stores to carry its new cameras and was forced to use mass-merchandising outlets. Small food producers normally find it hard to get supermarket chains to carry their products. Equipment manufacturers often find it hard to locate qualified distributors and dealers (see Companies and Industries 20-1).

Whether producers find it easy or difficult to recruit middlemen, they should at least determine what characteristics distinguish the better middlemen. They will want to evaluate the middlemen's number of years in business, the other lines carried, growth and profit record, solvency, cooperativeness, and reputation. If the middlemen are sales agents, producers will want to evaluate the number and character of other lines carried and the size and quality of the salesforce. If the middlemen are department stores that want exclusive distribution, the producer will want to evaluate the stores' locations, future growth potential, and type of clientele.

Motivating Channel Members

Middlemen must be continuously motivated to do their best job. The terms that lead them to join the channel provide some motivation, but these must be supple-

Companies and Industries 20-1

Building a Distributor Team for Epson Products

Japan's Epson Corporation, a leading manufacturer of computer printers, was preparing to add computers to its product line. Not happy with its current distributors nor trusting their ability to sell to new types of retail outlets, Epson's general manager, Jack Whalen, decided to quietly recruit new distributors to replace the existing ones. Whalen hired Hergenrather & Company, a recruiting company, and gave the following instructions:

- Search for applicants who have two-step distribution experience (factory to distributor to dealer) in either brown goods (TVs, and so on) or white goods (refrigerators, and so on).

- The applicants have to be CEO types who would be willing and able to set up their own distributorships.

- They will be offered $80,000 yearly salary plus bonus, and $375,000 to help them set up in business; each will add $25,000 of his or her own money, and each will get equity in the business.

- They will handle only Epson products but may stock other companies' software. Each distributor will hire a training manager and run a fully equipped service center.

The recruiting firm had a hard time finding qualified and motivated prospects. Their want ads in *The Wall Street Journal* (which did not mention the company's name) pulled almost 1,700 letters but mostly from unqualified people looking for jobs. Then the firm used the Yellow Pages to get the names of existing distributors and phoned the second-in-command managers. It arranged interviews and, after much work, produced a list of highly qualified individuals. Whalen interviewed them and chose the 12 most qualified candidates for his 12 distributor areas. The recruiting agency was paid $250,000 for its recruiting effort.

The final step called for terminating Epson's existing distributors. These distributors had no inkling of this development, since the recruitment was conducted in secrecy. Jack Whalen gave them a 90-day notice of the changeover. They were shocked, having worked with Epson as its first distributors. But they had no contracts. Whalen knew they lacked the ability to handle Epson's expanded computer product line and reach the target number of dealers. He saw no other solution.

SOURCE: Arthur Bragg, "Undercover Recruiting: Epson America's Sly Distributor Switch," *Sales and Marketing Management,* March 11, 1985, pp. 45–49.

---

mented by training, supervision, and encouragement. The producer must not only sell through the middlemen but to them.

Stimulating channel members to top performance must start with understanding of the middlemen's needs and wants. McVey listed the following propositions to help understand middlemen:

> [The middleman often acts] as a purchasing agent for his customers and only secondarily as a selling agent for his suppliers. . . . He is interested in selling any product which these customers desire to buy from him. . . .

> The middleman attempts to weld all of his offerings into a family of items which he can sell in combination, as a packaged assortment, to individual customers. His selling efforts are directed primarily at obtaining orders for the assortment, rather than for individual items. . . .

> Unless given incentive to do so, middlemen will not maintain separate sales records by brands sold. . . . Information that could be used in product development, pricing, packaging, or promotion planning is buried in nonstandard records of middlemen, and sometimes purposely secreted from suppliers.[10]

Producers vary greatly in how they manage their distributors. Essentially, they can draw on different types of power to gain cooperation (see Marketing Concepts and Tools 20-1). They can aim for achieving a relationship based on *cooperation*, *partnership*, or *distribution programming*.[11]

Most producers see the problem as that of gaining middlemen *cooperation*.

Five Bases of Power for Managing Channel Relationships

Manufacturers need to draw on some source of power to gain middleman cooperation. *Power* is the ability of one channel member to get another channel member to do something that might not be done otherwise. French and Raven distinguished among five bases of power: coercive, reward, legitimate, expert, and referent.

Coercive power would be represented by the manufacturer's threatening to withdraw a resource or terminate the relationship if the middlemen fail to cooperate. This power is quite effective if the middlemen are highly dependent upon the manufacturer. But the exercise of coercive power produces resentment and can lead the middlemen to organize countervailing power. While coercive power may be effective in the short run, it is usually the least effective type of power to use in the long run.

Reward power would occur if the manufacturer offers an extra benefit for the performance of specific acts by middlemen. Reward power typically produces better results than coercive power but can be overrated. The middlemen are conforming to the manufacturer's wishes not out of intrinsic conviction but because of an external benefit. They will grow to expect a reward every time the manufacturer wants a certain behavior to occur. If the reward is later withdrawn, the middlemen feel cheated.

Legitimate power is wielded when the manufacturer requests a behavior as warranted by the hierarchical relationship and contract. Thus General Motors may insist that its dealers carry certain inventory levels as part of the franchise agreement. The manufacturer feels it has this right and the middleman has this obligation. As long as the middlemen view the manufacturer as a legitimate leader, legitimate power works.

Expert power can be applied by the manufacturer, who has special knowledge that is valued by the middlemen. For example, a manufacturer may have a sophisticated system for locating leads for middlemen or giving expert training to the middlemen's salesforces. This is an effective form of power, since the middlemen would perform poorly if they couldn't get this help from the manufacturer. The problem is that once the expertise is passed on to the middlemen, this basis of power weakens. The solution is that the manufacturer must continue to develop new expertise so that the middlemen will be eager to continue cooperating with the manufacturer.

Referent power occurs when the manufacturer is so highly respected that middlemen are proud to be identified with him. Companies such as IBM, Caterpillar, McDonald's, and Neiman-Marcus have high referent power, and middlemen are normally ready to go along with their wishes.

To the extent possible, manufacturers will gain cooperation best if they cultivate referent power, expert power, legitimate power, and reward power, in that order, and generally avoid the use of coercive power.

SOURCE: These bases of power were identified in John R. P. French and Bertram Raven, "The Bases of Social Power," in *Studies in Social Power,* ed. Dorwin Cartwright. (Ann Arbor, MI: University of Michigan Press, 1959) pp. 150–67.

They will use the carrot-and-stick approach. They will use positive motivators, such as higher margins, special deals, premiums, cooperative advertising allowances, display allowances, and sales contests. At times they will apply negative sanctions, such as threatening to reduce the margins, slow down delivery, or terminate the relationship. The weakness of this approach is that the producer has not really studied the middlemen's needs, problems, strengths, and weaknesses. Instead, the producer applies miscellaneous motivators based on crude stimulus-response thinking. McCammon notes that many manufacturer programs "consist of hastily improvised trade deals, uninspired dealer contests, and unexamined discount structures."[12]

More sophisticated companies try to forge a long-term *partnership* with their distributors. The manufacturer develops a clear sense of what it wants from its distributors in the way of market coverage, inventory levels, marketing development, account solicitation, technical advice and services, and marketing information. The manufacturer seeks distributor agreement with these policies and may introduce a *functional compensation plan* for adhering to the policies:

> A dental supply company, instead of paying a straight 35% sales commission to its distributors, pays 20% for carrying out its basic sales work, another 5% for carrying a 60-day inventory, another 5% for paying its bills on time, and another 5% for reporting customer purchase information.

Distribution programming is the most advanced arrangement. McCammon defines this as building a planned, professionally managed, vertical marketing system that incorporates the needs of both the manufacturer and the distributors.[13] The manufacturer establishes a department within the company called *distributor-relations planning*, and its job is to identify the distributors' needs and build up merchandising programs to help each distributor operate as optimally as possible. This department and the distributors jointly plan the merchandising goals, inventory levels, space and visual merchandising plans, sales-training requirements, and advertising and promotion plans. The aim is to convert the distributors from thinking that they make their money primarily on the buying side (through tough negotiation with the manufacturer) to seeing that they make their money on the selling side by being part of a sophisticated vertical marketing system.

Kraft provides a good example of distribution programming. Kraft is able to tailor its offering not only to each supermarket chain but also to each individual store within each chain. It can develop micromerchandising programs that fit the types of shoppers that patronize each store, whether they are full-margin shoppers, commodity shoppers, dine-out shoppers, and so on. The Kraft trade marketing team at headquarters has developed a database on each store and chain and has trained and empowered their local salesforces to use this database to provide each store with the optimal Kraft product mix.

Too many manufacturers think of their distributors and dealers as their customers rather than their working partners. Marketing Strategies 20-1 describes the various mechanisms progressive manufacturers use to convert their distributors into partners.

Evaluating Channel Members

The producer must periodically evaluate middlemen's performance against such standards as sales-quota attainment, average inventory levels, customer delivery time, treatment of damaged and lost goods, cooperation in promotional and training programs, and middlemen services owed to the customer.

The producer will discover on occasion that too much is being paid to particular middlemen for what they are actually doing. One manufacturer discovered that he was compensating a distributor for holding inventories in his warehouse but the inventories were actually being held in a public warehouse at the manufacturer's expense. Producers should set up functional discounts in which they pay specified amounts for the trade channel's performance of each agreed-upon service. Underperforming middlemen need to be counseled, retrained, or remotivated. If they do not shape up, however, it might be better to terminate their services.

Modifying Channel Arrangements

A producer must do more than design a good channel system and set it into motion. The system will require periodic modification to meet new conditions in the mar-

Marketing Strategies 20-1

Turning Industrial Distributors into Business Partners

Narus and Anderson interviewed several manufacturers who enjoyed excellent working relations with their distributors to discover the channel attitudes and practices that contributed to the successful relations. Here are some of the partner-building practices they found:

1. Timken Corporation (roller bearings) has its sales representatives make *multilevel calls* on distributors, including their general managers, purchasing managers, and sales personnel.

2. Square D (circuit breakers, switchboards) has its sales representatives spend a day with each distributor, *"working the counter"* in order to understand the distributor's business.

3. Du Pont has established a *Distributor Marketing Steering Committee*, which meets to regularly discuss problems and trends.

4. Dayco Corporation (engineered plastics and rubber products) runs an *annual week-long retreat* with 20 young distributors' executives and 20 young Dayco executives interacting in seminars and outings.

5. Parker Hannifin Corporation (fluid-power products) sends out an *annual mail survey* asking its distributors to rate the corporation's performance on key dimensions. It also informs its distributors about new products and applications through *newsletters* and *videotapes*. It collects and analyzes *photocopies of distributors' invoices* and advises distributors on how to improve their sales.

6. Cherry Electrical Products (electrical switches and electronic keyboards) appointed a distributor marketing manager who works with distributors to produce *formal distributor marketing plans*. The company also operates a *rapid response system* to distributor calls by assigning two inside salespeople to each distributor.

These are a few ways that progressive manufacturers have successfully turned their distributors into working partners.

SOURCE: See James A. Narus and James C. Anderson, "Turn Your Industrial Distributors into Partners," *Harvard Business Review*, March–April 1986, pp. 66–71.

---

ketplace. Modification becomes necessary when consumer buying patterns change, market expands, product matures, new competition arises, and new, innovative distribution channels emerge (see Marketing Strategies 20-2).

This fact struck a large appliance manufacturer who had been marketing exclusively through franchised dealers and was losing market share. Several distribution developments had taken place since the original channel was designed:

♦ An increasing share of major-brand appliances was being merchandised through discount houses.

♦ An increasing share of major appliances was being sold as department-store private brands.

♦ Tract home builders increasingly wanted to buy directly from manufacturers.

♦ Door-to-door selling and direct mail were increasingly being used by dealers and competitors.

♦ The only strong independent dealers were located in small towns, but rural families were increasingly making their purchases in large cities.

These developments led this manufacturer to undertake a major overhaul of his channels.

In competitive markets with low entry barriers, the optimal channel structure will inevitably change over time. The current channel structure will no longer produce the most efficient service outputs for the given costs. As a result, the current structure will necessarily change in the direction of the optimal structure. Three levels of channel adaptation can be distinguished. The change could involve *adding*

Marketing Strategies 20-2

Smart Companies Change Their Marketing Channels Over the Product Life Cycle

No marketing channel can be trusted to remain competitively dominant over the whole product life cycle. Early adopters might be willing to pay for high value-added channels, but later buyers will switch to lower-cost channels. Thus small office copiers were first sold by manufacturers' direct salesforces, later through office-equipment dealers, still later through mass merchandisers, and now by mail-order firms. Insurance companies that persist in using independent agents and auto companies that use independent dealers will face strong competition from new, lower-cost channels, and their reluctance to change might prove fatal in the long run.

Miland Lele developed the following grid to show how marketing channels have changed for PCs and designer apparel at different stages in the product life cycle:

- *Introductory Stage:* Radically new products or fashions tend to enter the market through specialist channels (such as hobbyist shops, boutiques) that spot trends and attract early adopters.

- *Rapid Growth Stage:* As buyers' interest grows, higher-volume channels appear (dedicated chains, department stores) that offer services but not as many as the previous channels offered.

- *Maturity Stage:* As growth slows down, some competitors move their product into lower-cost channels (mass merchandisers).

- *Decline Stage:* As the decline begins, even lower-cost channels emerge (mail-order houses, off-price discounters).

The earliest channels face the challenge of market creation; they are high cost because they must search for and educate buyers. They are followed by channels that expand the market and offer sufficient services. In the maturity stage, many buyers want lower costs, and they patronize lower value-added channels. Finally, the remaining potential buyers can be reached only by creating very low prices in low, value-added channels.

SOURCE: See Miland M. Lele, *Creating Strategic Leverage* (New York: John Wiley & Sons, 1992), pp. 249–51.

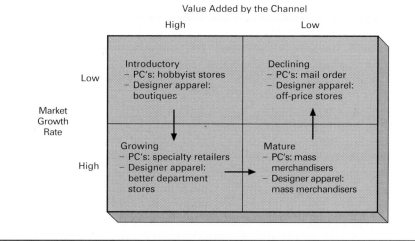

or dropping individual channel members, adding or dropping particular market channels, or developing a totally new way to sell goods in all markets.

Adding or dropping specific middlemen requires an incremental analysis. What would the firm's profits look like with and without this middleman? An automobile manufacturer's decision to drop a dealer would require subtracting the dealer's sales and estimating the possible loss or gain of sales to the manufacturer's other dealers.

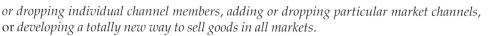

CHAPTER 20
Selecting and Managing
Marketing Channels

Modifying Existing Distribution Systems Toward the Ideal

Distribution channels clearly get outmoded with the passage of time. A gap arises between a seller's *existing distribution system* and the *ideal system* that would satisfy target customers' needs and desires. Examples of this abound: Avon's door-to-door system for selling cosmetics had to be modified as more women entered the workforce; IBM's exclusive reliance on a field salesforce had to be modified with the introduction of low-valued personal computers.

Yet distribution systems, in contrast to advertising budgets, prices, and sales-promotion programs, are very difficult to change. The company has built up long-standing relations with distributors and dealers, and replacing them is bound to meet resistance if not sabotage. To deal with this problem, Stern and Sturdivant have outlined an eight-step process for moving an obsolescent distribution system closer to target customers' ideal system.

The first step calls for finding out what target customers want in the way of channel services if no constraints existed. Customers would specify the lot size, convenience, amount of time they were willing to wait, product variety, and service backup they want. They would indicate the importance of various services and the tradeoffs they would make.

Step two consists of conceiving alternative distribution systems that would provide these services. Thus investors might be asked to evaluate buying stock through brokers, over the phone, through a computer linkup, and so on. Their responses will provide a picture of which distribution systems are favored by which customer segments.

Step three requires evaluating the feasibility and cost of the alternative distribution systems. It might be discovered, for example, that offering a computer-linked system of stock trading would cost too much or be unsupportable by current technologies.

Step four involves gathering company executives' objectives for the company's distribution system. At this point, some executives will insist on certain principles that must be observed: a brokerage company should not offer discount brokerage; an auto company should not compromise independent franchised dealerships; a paper company should not circumvent longstanding relationships with paper merchants in order to sell directly to discount chains.

Sometimes a producer contemplates dropping all middlemen whose sales are below a certain amount. For example, Navistar noted at one time that 5% of its dealers were selling fewer than three or four trucks a year. It cost the company more to service these dealers than their sales were worth. However, the decision to drop these dealers could have large repercussions on the system as a whole. The unit costs of producing trucks would be higher, since the overhead would be spread over fewer trucks; some employees and equipment would be idled; some business in these markets would go to competitors; and other dealers might become insecure. All of this would have to be taken into account.

The most difficult decision involves revising the overall channel strategy.[14] For example, an automobile manufacturer might replace independent dealers with company-owned dealers; a soft-drink manufacturer might consider replacing local franchised bottlers with centralized bottling and direct sales. These decisions would require revising most of the marketing mix and would have profound consequences (see Marketing Concepts and Tools 20-2).

Channel Dynamics

Distribution channels do not stand still. New wholesaling and retailing institutions emerge, and new channel systems evolve. Here we will look at the recent growth of

Step five calls for comparing the available options given management's criteria on the one hand and the customer ideal distribution system on the other. One of three situations could emerge. The best would be where the ideal system, the management-bounded system, and the existing system closely resemble each other, in which case any customer dissatisfaction is probably the fault of poor implementation rather than poor distribution-system design. A second possibility is that the existing and management-bounded systems are similar but differ substantially from the ideal. If the gap is to be closed, then management must reconsider its constraints. A third possibility is that all three systems may differ substantially. In this case, there are two gaps to close before the distribution system can become customer driven.

The sixth step is to ask management and selected experts to review management's key assumptions. Management should know the costs of their assumptions and constraints as well as the gains and risks of changing them.

The seventh step calls for asking management to confront the gap between the existing and the ideal management system and to agree on what changes they are willing to make.

The eighth step involves preparing a plan to implement the agreed-upon changes. If possible, changes on a small scale might be introduced to identify any positive or negative effects that might have been overlooked.

This eight-step process will not necessarily lead to modifying the company's existing distribution system. It might even convince management that the existing system and set of management constraints are necessary and desirable. But most of the time, this process will result in modifying the company's distribution system toward the ideal. The key point is that customers will switch to those distribution systems that deliver the sought-after benefits and services. Managers who protect outmoded distribution systems will lose in the marketplace.

SOURCE: See Louis W. Stern and Frederick D. Sturdivant, "Customer-Driven Distribution Systems," *Harvard Business Review*, July–August 1987, pp. 34–41. For more elaboration of each step along with examples, see Louis W. Stern and Adel I. El-Ansary, *Marketing Channels*, 4th ed. (Englewood Cliffs, NJ: Prentice-Hall, 1992), pp. 205–27.

vertical, horizontal, and multichannel marketing systems and see how these systems cooperate, conflict, and compete.

Growth of Vertical Marketing Systems

One of the most significant recent channel developments consists of *vertical marketing systems*, which have emerged to challenge *conventional marketing channels*. A conventional marketing channel comprises an independent producer, wholesaler(s), and retailer(s). Each is a separate business entity seeking to maximize its own profits, even if it reduces profit for the system as a whole. No channel member has complete or substantial control over the other members. McCammon characterizes conventional channels as "highly fragmented networks in which loosely aligned manufacturers, wholesalers, and retailers have bargained with each other at arm's length, negotiated aggressively over terms of sale, and otherwise behaved autonomously."[15]

A vertical marketing system (VMS), by contrast, comprises the producer, wholesaler(s), and retailer(s) acting as a unified system. One channel member owns the others or franchises them or has so much power that they all cooperate. The vertical marketing system can be dominated by the producer, the wholesaler, or the retailer. McCammon characterizes VMSs as "professionally managed and centrally programmed networks, pre-engineered to achieve operating economies and maximum market impact."[16] VMSs came into being to control channel behavior and eliminate the conflict that results when independent channel members pursue their own objectives. They achieve economies through their size, bargaining power, and elimination of duplicated services. VMSs have become the dominant mode of distribution in the U.S. consumer marketplace, serving between 70 and 80% of the total market. The three types of VMSs—corporate, administered, and contractual—are described in Market Environment and Trends 20-1.

Many independent retailers, if they have not joined VMSs, have developed specialty stores that serve market segments that are not attractive to the mass merchandisers. The result is a polarization in retailing between large vertical marketing organizations, on the one hand, and specialty independent stores, on the other. This development creates a problem for manufacturers. They are strongly tied to independent middlemen, whom they cannot easily give up. But they must eventually realign themselves with the high-growth vertical marketing systems on less attractive terms. Vertical marketing systems constantly threaten to bypass large manufacturers and set up their own manufacturing. *The new competition in retailing is no longer between independent business units but between whole systems of centrally programmed networks (corporate, administered, and contractual) competing against each other to achieve the best cost economies and customer response.*

Marketing Environment and Trends 20-1

Major Forms of Vertical Marketing Systems

CORPORATE VMS ❖ A *corporate VMS* combines successive stages of production and distribution under single ownership. Vertical integration is favored by companies that desire a high level of control over the channels. Vertical integration can be achieved by backward or forward integration. Consider some examples. Sears obtains over 50% of the goods it sells from companies that it partly or wholly owns. Sherwin-Williams makes paint but also owns and operates 2,000 retail outlets. Giant Food Stores operates an ice-making facility, a soft-drink bottling operation, an ice-cream-making plant, and a bakery that supplies Giant stores with everything from bagels to birthday cakes. And Gallo, the world's largest wine maker, does much more than simply turn grapes into wine.

> The [Gallo] brothers own Fairbanks Trucking Company, one of the largest intrastate truckers in California. Its 200 semis and 500 trailers are constantly hauling wine out of Modesto and raw materials back in—including . . . lime from Gallo's quarry east of Sacramento. Alone among wine producers, Gallo makes bottles—two million a day—and its Midcal Aluminum Co. spews out screw tops as fast as the bottles are filled. Most of the country's 1,300 or so wineries concentrate on production to the neglect of marketing. Gallo, by contrast, participates in

> every aspect of selling short of whispering in the ear of each imbiber. The company owns its distributors in about a dozen markets and probably would buy many . . . more . . . if the laws in most states did not prohibit doing so.[1]

ADMINISTERED VMS ❖ An *administered VMS* coordinates successive stages of production and distribution not through common ownership but through the size and power of one of the parties. Manufacturers of a dominant brand are able to secure strong trade cooperation and support from resellers. Thus Kodak, Gillette, Procter & Gamble, and Campbell Soup are able to command unusual cooperation from their resellers in connection with displays, shelf space, promotions, and price policies.

CONTRACTUAL VMS ❖ A *contractual VMS* consists of independent firms at different levels of production and distribution integrating their programs on a contractual basis to obtain more economies and/or sales impact than they could achieve alone. Johnston and Lawrence have called them "value-adding partnerships" (VAPs).[2] Contractual VMSs have expanded the most in recent years and constitute one of the most significant developments in the economy. Contractual VMSs are of three types.

Growth of Horizontal Marketing Systems

Another channel development is the readiness of two or more nonrelated companies to put together resources or programs to exploit an emerging marketing opportunity. Each company lacks the capital, know-how, production, or marketing resources to venture alone; or it is afraid of the risk; or it sees a substantial synergy in joining with another company. The companies might work with each other on a temporary or permanent basis or create a separate company. Adler calls this *symbiotic marketing*.[17] Here are examples:

> Pillsbury and Kraft Foods Company have set up an arrangement where Pillsbury makes and advertises its line of refrigerated dough products, while Kraft uses its expertise to sell and distribute these products to the stores.

> H&R Block and Hyatt Legal Services formed a joint venture in which Hyatt's legal clinics are housed in H&R Block's tax-preparation offices. Hyatt pays a fee for office space, secretarial assistance, and office-equipment usage, and enjoys a chance for accelerated market penetration through locating in H&R Block's nationwide office network. Meanwhile H&R Block benefits from renting its facilities, which otherwise have a highly seasonal pattern.

Wholesaler-Sponsored Voluntary Chains. Wholesalers organize voluntary chains of independent retailers to help them compete with large chain organizations. The wholesaler develops a program in which independent retailers standardize their selling practices and achieve buying economies that enable the group to compete effectively with chain organizations.

Retailer Cooperatives. Retailers might take the initiative and organize a new business entity to carry on wholesaling and possibly some production. Members concentrate their purchases through the retailer co-op and plan their advertising jointly. Profits are passed back to members in proportion to their purchases. Non-member retailers might also buy through the co-op but do not share in the profits.

Franchise Organizations. A channel member called a franchisor might link several successive stages in the production-distribution process. Franchising has been the fastest growing and most interesting retailing development in recent years. Although the basic idea is an old one, some forms of franchising are quite new. Three forms of franchises can be distinguished.

The first is the *manufacturer-sponsored retailer franchise system*, exemplified by the automobile industry. Ford, for example, licenses dealers to sell its cars, the dealers being independent businesspeople who agree to meet various conditions of sales and services.

The second is the *manufacturer-sponsored wholesaler franchise system*, which is found in the soft-drink industry. Coca-Cola, for example, licenses bottlers (wholesalers) in various markets who buy its syrup concentrate and then carbonate, bottle, and sell it to retailers in local markets.

The third is the *service-firm-sponsored retailer franchise system*. Here a service firm organizes a whole system for bringing its service efficiently to consumers. Examples are found in the auto-rental business (Hertz, Avis), fast-food-service business (McDonald's, Burger King), and motel business (Howard Johnson, Ramada Inn).

SOURCES: 1. Jaclyn Fierman, "How Gallo Crushes the Competition," *Fortune*, September 1, 1986, p. 27. 2. Russell Johnston and Paul R. Lawrence, "Beyond Vertical Integration—the Rise of the Value-Adding Partnership," *Harvard Business Review*, July–August 1988, pp. 94–101.

The Lamar Savings Bank of Texas arranged with Safeway Stores, Inc. to locate its savings offices and automated teller machines in Safeway stores. Lamar gained accelerated entry at a low cost, and Safeway was able to offer in-store banking convenience to its customers.

Growth of Multichannel Marketing Systems

In the past, many companies sold to a single market through a single channel. Today, with the proliferation of customer segments and channel possibilities, more companies have adopted multichannel marketing. *Multichannel marketing* occurs when a single firm uses two or more marketing channels to reach one or more customer segments (see Marketing Strategies 20-3).

By adding more channels, companies can gain three important benefits: *increased market coverage*, *lower channel cost*, and *more customized selling*. Companies often add a channel in order to reach a customer segment which its current channels can't reach (e.g., adding rural agents to reach sparsely located farmer-customers). Or companies may add a new channel to lower their cost of selling to an existing customer group (e.g., selling by phone rather than personally visiting small customers). Or companies may add a channel whose selling features fit the customer requirements better (e.g., using a technical salesforce to sell more complex equipment).

The gains from adding new channels, however, come at a price. New channels typically introduce *conflict* and *control problems*. Conflict occurs when two or more company channels end up competing for the same customers. Control problems occur insofar as the new channels are more independent and cooperation is more difficult (see Marketing Strategies 20-4).

Clearly companies need to think through their channel architecture in advance. Moriarty and Moran propose using a *hybrid grid* to plan the channel architecture.[18] The hybrid grid is shown in Figure 20-5 with three marketing channels portrayed.

The hybrid grid is based on the proposition that *marketing tasks*, not marketing channels, are the fundamental building blocks for channel architecture. Successful

FIGURE 20-5
The Hybrid Grid
Source: Rowland T. Moriarty and Ursula Moran, "Marketing Hybrid Marketing Systems," *Harvard Business Review*, November–December 1990, p. 150.

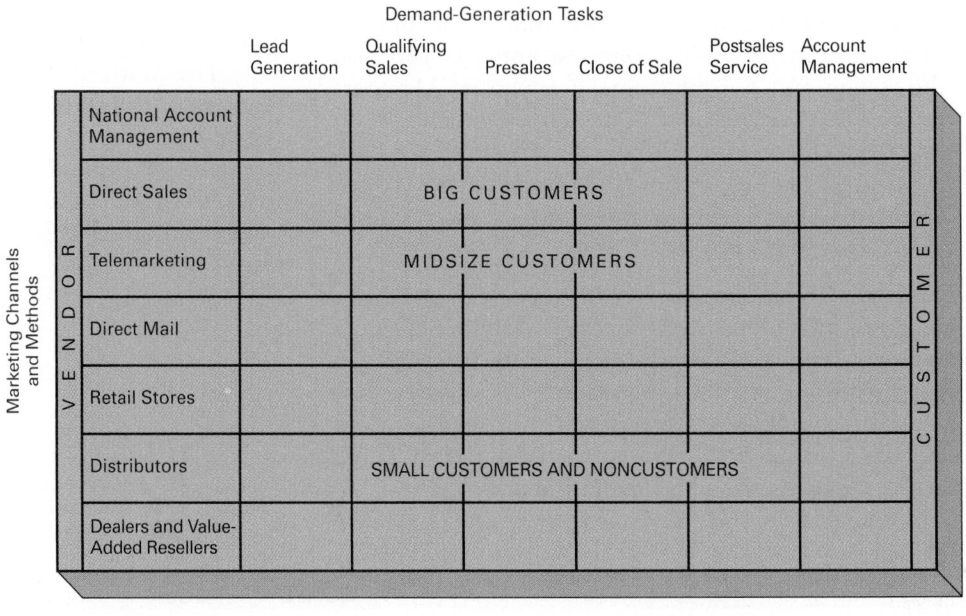

Multichannel Marketing Comes to Financial Services

Companies that employ a single channel to sell different products to different customers will find themselves increasingly vulnerable to companies that build more appropriate channels. This can be illustrated with the following *offering grid* shown in Figure (a).

The bottom of the grid shows products ranging from commodities to customized products; the vertical axis shows levels of distribution-value-added service ranging from low to high. Thus pension fund management is located at the upper left: pension funds are customized and require a high level of personal service, information, and execution. At the other extreme is Trade-Plus, a service of C. D. Anderson of San Francisco, which permits a person to do stock trading at home using a personal computer; in this case, the product is extremely simple, and there is hardly any value added by the channel.

Now consider Merrill Lynch's offerings, which fall horizontally on the offering grid. Merrill Lynch offers several services through a fairly high value-added, full-service brokerage distribution channel consisting of its local-office account executives and home-office researchers. By sticking with only one channel, Merrill Lynch has allowed other competitors to appear, such as Charles Schwab & Company, which offers discount brokerage service. Schwab's customers phone Schwab's customer-service representatives, who take orders but provide no investment advice or research.

The point is that each cell on the diagonal represents a potential opportunity if there is sufficient demand. Companies that use only one channel for several products and customer groups will inevitably face increased competition. As customers become more knowledgeable about a service and as technology permits further mechanization, more channels will open up in the lower-right-hand cells of the grid, presenting competition to higher distribution-value-added channels.

Citibank recognized this trend and has created the set of services shown in Figure (b). Private Banking consists of customized asset-management services aimed at wealthy customers and delivered through personal bankers in gracious surroundings. Focus provides banking and investment services through an account officer who is available by phone. Citi-One Account Banking permits simple banking transactions to be executed through automated teller machines. Clearly, Citibank is building differentiated products and channels for different customer groups.

SOURCE: This discussion is adapted from *Distribution: A Competitive Weapon,* published in 1985 by The MAC Group, 1430 Massachusetts Avenue, Cambridge, MA 02138, pp. 14–18.

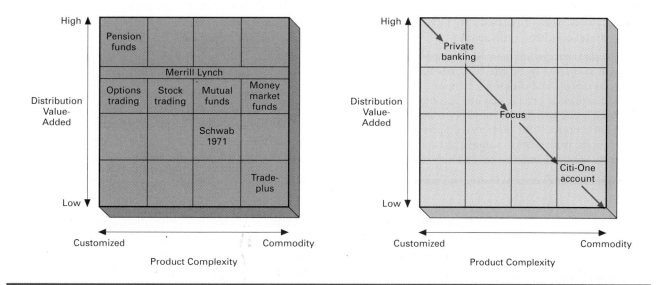

The Downside of Multichannel Marketing: Channel Conflict at IBM

Until 1981, IBM used only its direct salesforce to sell all of its equipment. When IBM added personal computers to its product line in the late 1970s, it could no longer afford to sell them through its only channel, its expensive direct salesforce. In no less than ten years, IBM added 18 new channels to reach its customers, including dealers, value-added resellers (VARs), catalog operations, direct mail, and telemarketing.

IBM's aim was to utilize a range of the most cost-effective channels to reach different target buyer segments. To illustrate the underlying logic, suppose IBM used only its field salesforce to reach all markets regardless of their size or profit potential. IBM's costs would be given by the selling-cost line A in the following figure, which rises for larger customers because the salesforce spends more time with them. Now suppose the company divides its pool of prospects into very large, large, medium, and small (urban and rural) customers. Suppose the company assigns *national account managers* to handle the very large accounts; *field salespeople* to call on large customers; *telemarketers* to phone medium-size customers for orders; *dealers* to sell to small urban customers; and *agents* to sell to small rural customers. This arrangement results in sharply reducing the selling cost of serving smaller customers, as shown by selling-cost line B. Now there is more profit available from each customer group.

But there is also bad news. By adding indirect channels, IBM faced a situation of *channel conflict*. Its field salesforce was displeased. In fact, the following three channel conflicts could arise:

1. *Conflict between the national account managers and field salesforce.* To be effective, national account managers rely on field salespeople to make calls to the plants and offices of certain national account customers located in the salesperson's territory, sometimes on a moment's notice. The territory salesperson may receive requests from several national account managers to make such calls and this can seriously disrupt the sales-person's normal call schedule and hurt his or her commissions. Salespeople may not cooperate with national account managers when it conflicts with their interests.

2. *Conflict between the field salesforce and the telemarketers.* Salespeople often resent their company setting up a tele-marketing operation to sell to smaller customers. They want the right to call on small customers in their territory and earn commissions. They don't want the company to turn over these customers to an inside telemarketing operation. Yet the company will tell the salespeople that this frees up their time to sell to larger accounts on which they can earn more commission. But the salespeople object. To gain salesforce cooperation, many companies will offer token commission or credit to the salespeople for any telephone sales made to small accounts in their territories.

3. *Conflict between the field salesforce and the dealers.* Dealers include *value-added resellers,* who buy computers from IBM and add specialized software needed by the target buyer, and *computer retail stores,* which are an excellent channel for selling small equipment to walk-in traffic and small business. In principle, these dealers are supposed to pursue only small customers, but many have chased larger accounts. They frequently can offer specialized software installation and training, better service, and even lower prices than IBM's direct salesforce. The direct salesforce becomes angry when these dealers go after their accounts and view them as "competition." They see these resellers as disrupting relationships with their accounts. They want IBM to refuse to sell through dealers who try to sell to large accounts against them. But IBM would lose a lot of business if it dropped these successful resellers. As an alternative, IBM has decided to give booking credit to salespeople for business sold to their accounts by aggressive re-sellers. IBM has tried hard to harmonize these two channels, hoping that they would "partner" to sell the account rather than compete.

When a company such as IBM finds that a significant percentage of its revenues are in conflict, it needs to establish clear *channel boundaries.* Boundaries can be

selling calls for performing six marketing tasks: *lead generation, qualifying sales, presales, close of sales, postsales service,* and *account management.* These six tasks may be performed by a single channel, as when a company's salespeople are individually responsible for finding and qualifying leads, preselling and closing sales, and serving and managing accounts.

One common practice is for companies to establish different channels to sell to

established on the basis of *customer characteristics, geography*, or *products*. For example, IBM can require its value-added resellers who prepare software systems for hospitals to limit their selling to hospitals of under 200 beds (a customer boundary). It can use agents in rural areas and computer dealers in large cities. It could supply a modified personal computer to sell through dealerships as opposed to selling advanced PCs through its direct salesforce. Clear channel boundaries will reduce some conflict, but there will remain debate over who should handle certain ambiguous account categories, such as small but fast-growing accounts and large accounts with decentralized purchasing units.

SOURCE: For further reading, see Frank V. Cespedes and E. Raymond Corey, "Managing Multiple Channels," *Business Horizons*, July–August 1990, pp. 67–77.

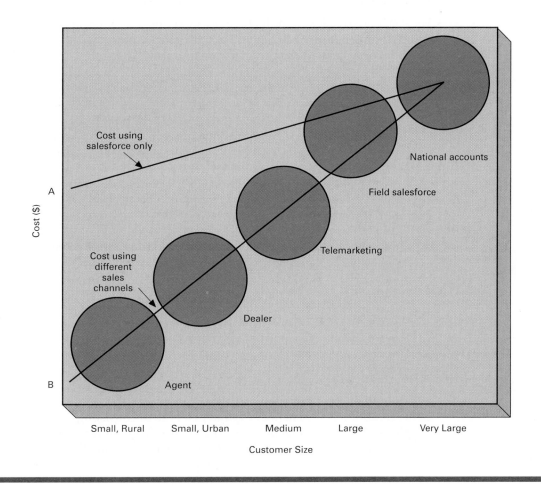

different customer size groups. The example in the hybrid grid shows direct sales handling large customers, telemarketing handling midsize customers, and distributors handling small customers and noncustomers. This looks like an attractive solution insofar as the company can serve more customers at an appropriate cost and customization level for each. But these gains are offset by an increased level of conflict over who has *account ownership*.

Moriarty and Moran believe that there is a better way to design and manage a hybrid marketing system than the three-channel solution shown in Figure 20-5. They advocate establishing a Marketing and Sales Productivity System (MSP).[19] This system establishes a centralized marketing database containing information about customers, prospects, products, marketing programs, and methods. All the marketing units pass their data through this system. Prospect leads are generated by ads and direct mail featuring an 800 number. Interested prospects are sent a catalog and are phoned later by an inside sales representative. If the prospect welcomes further contact and information, this is turned over to the appropriate channel for preselling and closing the sale. Service is handled through telemarketing. Account management is handled by the appropriate channels. In this way, the company has succeeded in putting together a hybrid channel architecture and management system which aims to optimize on cost, coverage, customization, conflict, and control.

Roles of Individual Firms in a Channel

Vertical, horizontal, and multichannel marketing systems underscore the dynamic and changing nature of channels. Each firm in an industry has to define its role in the channel system. McCammon has distinguished five roles:

- *Insiders* are members of the dominant channel, who enjoy access to preferred sources of supply and high respect in the industry. They want to perpetuate the existing channel arrangements and are the main enforcers of the industry code.

- *Strivers* are firms seeking to become insiders. They have less access to preferred sources of supply, which can handicap them in periods of short supply. They adhere to the industry code because of their desire to become insiders.

- *Complementors* are not part of the dominant channel. They perform functions not normally performed by others in the channel, or serve smaller segments of the market, or handle smaller quantities of merchandise. They usually benefit from the present system and respect the industry code.

- *Transients* are outside the dominant channel and do not seek membership. They go in and out of the market and move around as opportunities arise. They have short-run expectations and little incentive to adhere to the industry code.

- *Outside Innovators* are the real challengers and disrupters of the dominant channels. They develop a new system for carrying out the marketing work of the channel; if successful, they force major channel realignments. They are companies like McDonald's, Avon, and Dell Computer, which doggedly develop new systems to challenge the old.[20]

Another important channel role is that of *channel captain*. The channel captain is the dominant member of a particular channel, the one who leads it. For example, General Motors is the channel captain of a system consisting of a huge number of suppliers, dealers, and facilitators. The channel captain is not always a manufacturer, as the examples of McDonald's and Sears indicate. Some channels do not have a channel captain in that each firm proceeds on its own.

Channel Cooperation, Conflict, and Competition

No matter how well channels are designed and managed, there will be some conflict, if for no other reason than the interests of independent business entities don't always coincide. Here we examine three questions: What types of conflict arise in channels? What are the major causes of channel conflict? What can be done to resolve situations of conflict?

Types of Conflict and Competition

Suppose a manufacturer sets up a vertical channel consisting of wholesalers and retailers. The manufacturer hopes for *channel cooperation* in that cooperation normally produces greater total channel profits than if each channel member acted only on self-interest. By cooperating, the channel members can more effectively sense, serve, and satisfy the target market.

Yet vertical, horizontal, and multichannel conflict can occur. *Vertical channel conflict* exists when there is conflict between different levels within the same channel. For example, General Motors came into conflict with its dealers years ago in trying to enforce policies on service, pricing, and advertising. And Coca-Cola came into conflict with those of its bottlers who agreed to also bottle Dr Pepper. (See Companies and Industries 20-2.)

Horizontal channel conflict exists when there is conflict between members at the same channel level within the channel. Some Ford car dealers in Chicago complained about other Ford Chicago dealers advertising and pricing too aggressively. Some Pizza Inn franchisees complained about other Pizza Inn franchisees cheating on the ingredients, maintaining poor service, and hurting the overall Pizza Inn image. Benetton has been accused of franchising too many stores near to each other, depressing their profits. In these cases, the *channel captain* must establish clear and enforceable policies and take quick action to control this type of conflict.

Multichannel conflict exists when the manufacturer has established two or more channels that compete with each other in selling to the same market. When Levi Strauss agreed to distribute its jeans through Sears and Penney in addition to its normal specialty-store channel, it was highly resented by the specialty stores. When several clothing manufacturers—Ralph Lauren, Liz Claiborne, and Anne Klein—opened their own stores, the department stores who carried their clothes were mad. When Zenith agreed to sell its television sets through some mass merchandisers, it was resented by its independent radio and TV appliance stores. Multichannel conflict is likely to be especially intense when the members of one channel either get a lower price (based on larger volume purchases) or are willing to work with a lower margin.

Causes of Channel Conflict

It is important to distinguish the different causes that might produce channel conflict. Some causes are easy to resolve, others more difficult.

A major cause is *goal incompatibility*. For example, the manufacturer may want to achieve rapid market growth through a low-price policy. The dealers, on the other hand, may prefer to work with high margins and pursue short-run profitability. This is a difficult conflict to solve.

Sometimes the conflict arises from *unclear roles and rights*. IBM sells personal computers to large accounts through its own salesforce, and its licensed dealers are also trying to sell to large accounts. Territory boundaries, credit for sales, and so forth are grounds for conflict.

The conflict can also stem from *differences in perception*. The manufacturer may be optimistic about the near-term economic outlook and want dealers to carry higher inventory. But the dealers may be pessimistic about the near-term outlook.

The conflict might arise because of the *great dependence* of the middlemen on the manufacturer. Exclusive dealers, such as auto dealers, have their fortunes inti-

Vertical Channel Conflict in the Consumer Packaged-Goods Industry

For many years, large consumer packaged-goods manufacturers enjoyed high market power relative to retailers. Much of this was based on the pull strategies where manufacturers spent huge amounts on advertising to build brand preference, and as a consequence, retailers were obliged to carry their brands. But several developments have been shifting power to retailers relative to the manufacturers:

1. The growth of giant retailers and their concentrated buying power. (In Switzerland, two retailers—Migros and the Coop—account for almost 70% of all the retail food sales.)

2. Retailer development of well-regarded lower-price store brands to compete with manufacturers' brands.

3. The lack of sufficient shelf space to accommodate all the new brands being offered. (The average U.S. supermarket carries 24,000 items and 10,000 new items are being offered by manufacturers each year.)

4. The insistence of giant retailers for more trade-promotion money from manufacturers if they want their brands to enter or remain in the store and receive store support.

5. The reduced funds available to manufacturers to spend on advertising, and the erosion of mass audiences for advertising.

6. The retailers' growing marketing and information sophistication. (The use of bar codes, scanner data, electronic data interchange, and direct product profitability.)

The growing power of retailers is manifested by the levying of *slotting fees* upon manufacturers wishing to get new products into the stores; *display fees* to cover space costs; *fines* for late deliveries and incomplete orders; and *exit fees* to cover the cost of returning terminated merchandise to the manufacturers.

Manufacturers are also discovering that if their brand isn't one of the top two or three national brand leaders, they might as well drop out. In the food industry, the number-one brand earns about an 18% return on investment, the number-two brand, 6%, the number-three brand, 1%, and the number-four brand loses 6%.[1] Since the retailer wants to offer no more than four brands within a food category, and supplies two of its own, only the two top national brands will make money. The exiting minor brands will be driven to produce the store brands.

---

mately affected by the product design and pricing decisions of the manufacturer. This creates a high potential for conflict.

Managing Channel Conflict

Certain channel conflict can be constructive. It can lead to more dynamic adaptation to a changing environment. At the same time, too much conflict is dysfunctional. The problem is not one of eliminating conflict but of managing it better. There are several mechanisms for effective conflict management.[21]

Perhaps the most important solution is the adoption of *superordinate goals*. The channels members somehow come to an agreement on the fundamental goal they are jointly seeking, whether it is survival, market share, high quality, or customer satisfaction. This often takes place when the channel faces an outside threat, such as a more efficient competing channel, an adverse piece of legislation, or a shift in consumer desires. Working closely together might eliminate the threat. There is also the chance that the intense cooperation might have taught the parties a permanent lesson on the value of working toward the same end.

A useful conflict management device is the *exchange of persons* between two or

All of this has challenged manufacturers to figure out how they could regain or hold on to their power vis-à-vis retailers. Clearly manufacturers can't set up their own retail outlets. Nor do manufacturers want to continue to spend so much money on trade promotion and thus weaken their brand-building spending ability. Market share leaders are resorting to the following strategies to maintain their power in the channel:

1. Focus on the brands which have a chance of being number one or two in their category and commit to continuous research to improve their quality, features, packaging, and so on.

2. Maintain an active program of line extensions and a careful program of brand extensions. As part of this, develop fighter brands to compete with retailers' store brands.

3. Spend as much as possible on targeted advertising to build and maintain brand franchise.

4. Treat each major retail chain as a distinct target market, recognize their separate needs, and adjust offers and sales systems to serve each target retailer profitably. Treat them as strategic partners and be ready to customize products, packaging, services, benefits, electronic linkups, and cost savings.

5. Provide a high level of service quality and new services: on-time accurate delivery of complete orders, order cycle time reduction, emergency delivery capability, merchandising advice, inventory management support, simplicity of order processing and billing, and access to information regarding order/shipment status.

6. Consider adopting everyday low pricing as an alternative to trade dealing which leads to large forecasting errors, forward buying, and geographical diverting of merchandise.

7. Employ referent power, legitimate power, expert power, reward power, in that order, and avoid coercive power.

8. Support traditional retailers and aggressively expand into alternative retail outlets such as warehouse membership clubs, discount merchandisers, convenience stores, and some direct marketing.

SOURCE: For additional reading, see "Not Everyone Loves a Supermarket Special: P&G Moves to Banish Wildly Fluctuating Prices That Boosts Its Costs," *Business Week*, February 17, 1992, pp. 64–68. 1. Reported in Quaker 1986 Annual Report, derived from PIMS database, Strategic Planning Institute, Cambridge, MA. After-tax return divided by invested capital.

more channel levels. For example, General Motors executives might agree to work in some dealerships, and some dealership owners might work at General Motors in their dealer policy area. Presumably, each will grow to appreciate the other's point of view and carry more understanding when returning to their position.

Cooptation is an effort by one organization to win the support of the leaders of another organization by including them in advisory councils, boards of directors, and the like, so that they feel that their opinions are being heard. As long as the initiating organization treats the leaders of the other organization seriously, cooptation can work to reduce conflict. But the initiating organization also pays a price in that it may have to compromise its policies and plans in order to win the support of the other side.

Much can be accomplished by encouraging *joint membership in and between trade associations*. For example, there is good cooperation between the Grocery Manufacturers of America and the Food Marketing Institute representing most of the food chains; this cooperation led to the development of the Universal Product Code. Presumably, the associations can consider issues between the food manufacturers and retailers and put them through an orderly process of resolution.

When conflict is chronic or acute, the parties may have to resort to diplomacy, mediation, or arbitration. *Diplomacy* takes place when each side sends a person or group to meet with their counterpart from the other side to resolve the conflict. It makes sense to assign diplomats to work more or less continuously with each other to avoid the flaring up of conflicts. *Mediation* means resorting to a neutral third party who brings skills in conciliating the interests of the two parties. *Arbitration* occurs when the two parties agree to present their arguments to a third party (one or more arbitrators) and accept the arbitration decision.

Given the potential for channel conflict in all channel arrangements, channel members would be wise to develop in advance agreed-upon methods of resolving channel conflict. Socially Responsible Marketing 20-1 describes the legal and ethical sensitivities that marketers should have in dealing with their distribution partners.

Socially Responsible Marketing 20-1

Issues in Channel Relations

For the most part, companies are legally free to develop whatever channel arrangements suit them. In fact, the laws affecting channels seek to prevent the exclusionary tactics of companies that might keep other companies from using a desired channel. Of course, this means that the company must itself avoid using such exclusionary tactics. Most channel law deals with the mutual rights and duties of the channel members once they have formed a relationship.

Exclusive Dealing

Many producers and wholesalers like to develop exclusive channels for their products. When the seller allows only certain outlets to carry its products, this strategy is called *exclusive distribution*. When the seller requires that these dealers not handle competitors' products, its strategy is called *exclusive dealing*. Both parties benefit from exclusive arrangements: The seller obtains more loyal and dependable outlets, and the dealers obtain a steady source of supply and stronger seller support. But exclusive arrangements exclude other producers from selling to these dealers. This situation brings exclusive dealing contracts under the scope of the Clayton Act of 1914. They are legal as long as they do not substantially lessen competition or tend to create a monopoly and as long as both parties enter into the agreement voluntarily.

Exclusive Territories

Exclusive dealing often includes exclusive territorial agreements. The producer may agree not to sell to other dealers in a given area, or the buyer may agree to sell only in its own territory. The first practice is normal under franchise systems as a way to increase dealer enthusiasm and commitment. It is also perfectly legal—a seller has no legal obligation to sell through more outlets than it wishes. The second practice, whereby the producer tries to keep a dealer from selling outside its territory, has become a major legal issue.

Tying Agreements

Producers of a strong brand sometimes sell it to dealers only if the dealers will take some or all of the rest of the line. This is called *full-line forcing*. Such tying agreements are not necessarily illegal, but they do violate the Clayton Act if they tend to lessen competition substantially. The practice may prevent consumers from freely choosing among competing suppliers of these other brands.

Dealers' Rights

Producers are free to select their dealers, but their right to terminate dealers is somewhat restricted. In general, sellers can drop dealers "for cause." But they cannot drop dealers if, for example, the dealers refuse to cooperate in a doubtful legal arrangement, such as exclusive dealing or tying agreements.

SUMMARY ❖

Marketing-channel decisions are among the most complex and challenging decisions facing the firm. Each channel system creates a different level of sales and costs. Once a firm chooses a marketing channel, it must usually remain with it for a substantial period. The chosen channel will significantly affect and be affected by the other elements in the marketing mix.

Middlemen are used when they are able to perform channel functions more efficiently than the manufacturers can. The most important channel functions and flows are information, promotion, negotiation, ordering, financing, risk taking, physical possession, payment, and title. These marketing functions are more basic than the particular retail and wholesale institutions that may exist at any time.

Manufacturers face many channel alternatives for reaching a market. They can sell direct or use one, two, three, or more intermediary-channel levels. Channel design calls for determining the service outputs (lot size, waiting time, spatial convenience, product variety, service backup), establishing the channel objectives and constraints, identifying the major channel alternatives (types and number of intermediaries, specifically intensive, exclusive, or selective distribution), and the channel terms and responsibilities. Each channel alternative has to be evaluated according to economic, control, and adaptive criteria.

Channel management calls for selecting particular middlemen and motivating them with a cost-effective trade-relations mix. The aim is to build a "partnership" feeling and joint-distribution programming. Individual channel members must be periodically evaluated against their own past sales and other channel members' sales. Channel modification must be performed periodically because of the continuously changing marketing environment. The company has to evaluate adding or dropping individual middlemen or individual channels and possibly modifying the whole channel system.

Marketing channels are characterized by continuous and sometimes dramatic change. Three of the most significant trends are the growth of vertical, horizontal, and multichannel marketing systems.

All channel systems have a potential for vertical, horizontal, and multichannel conflict stemming from such sources as goal incompatibility, unclear roles and rights, differences in perception, and high dependence. Managing these conflicts can be sought through superordinate goals, exchange of persons, cooptation, joint membership in trade associations, diplomacy, mediation, and arbitration.

NOTES ❖

1. E. Raymond Corey, *Industrial Marketing: Cases and Concepts* (Englewood Cliffs, NJ: Prentice Hall, 1976), p. 263.

2. Louis W. Stern and Adel I. El-Ansary, *Marketing Channels*, 4th ed. (Englewood Cliffs, NJ: Prentice Hall, 1992), p. 1.

3. Ibid., pp. 5–6.

4. Alderson, "The Analytical Framework for Marketing," *Proceedings—Conference of Marketing Teachers from Far Western States* (Berkeley: University of California Press, 1958).

5. William G. Zikmund and William J. Stanton, "Recycling Solid Wastes: A Channels-of-Distribution Problem," *Journal of Marketing*, July 1971, p. 34.

6. Ronald Abler, John S. Adams, and Peter Gould, *Spatial Organizations: The Geographer's View of the World* (Englewood Cliffs, NJ: Prentice-Hall, 1971), pp. 531–32.

7. See Irving Rein, Philip Kotler, and Martin Stoller, *High Visibility* (New York: Dodd, Mead, 1987).

8. Louis P. Bucklin, *Competition and Evolution in the Distributive Trades* (Englewood Cliffs, NJ: Prentice-Hall, 1972).

9. Louis P. Bucklin, *A Theory of Distribution Channel Structure* (Berkeley: Institute of Business and Economic Research, University of California, 1966).

10. Philip McVey, "Are Channels of Distribution What the Textbooks Say?" *Journal of Marketing*, January 1960, pp. 61–64.

11. See Bert Rosenbloom, *Marketing Channels: A Management View*, 4th ed. (Hinsdale, IL: Dryden Press, 1991), pp. 287–301.

12. Bert C. McCammon, Jr., "Perspectives for Distribution Programming," in *Vertical Marketing Systems*, ed. Louis P. Bucklin (Glenview, IL: Scott, Foresman, 1970), p. 32.

13. Ibid, p. 43.

14. For an excellent report on this issue, see Howard Sutton, *Rethinking the Company's Selling and Distribution Channels*, research report no. 885, Conference Board, 1986, 26 pp.

15. McCammon, "Perspectives for Distribution Programming," pp. 32–51.

16. Ibid.

17. Lee Adler, "Symbiotic Marketing," *Harvard Business Review*, November–December 1966, pp. 59–71; and P. "Rajan" Varadarajan and Daniel Rajaratnam, "Symbiotic Marketing Revisited," *Journal of Marketing*, January 1986, pp. 7–17.

18. See Rowland T. Moriarty and Ursula Moran, "Marketing Hybrid Marketing Systems," *Harvard Business Review*, November–December 1990, pp. 146–155.

19. For more on MSP, see Gordon S. Swartz and Rowland T. Moriarty, "Marketing Automation Meets the Capital Budgeting Wall," *Marketing Management*, 1, no. 3, 1992.

20. Bert C. McCammon, Jr., "Alternative Explanations of Institutional Change and Channel Evolution," in *Toward Scientific Marketing*, ed. Stephen A. Greyser (Chicago: American Marketing Association, 1963), pp. 477–90.

21. This section draws on Stern and El-Ansary, *Marketing Channels*, Chap. 6.

21

Managing Retailing, Wholesaling, and Physical-Distribution Systems

When is a refrigerator not a refrigerator? . . . when it is in Pittsburgh at the time it is desired in Houston.

J. L. HESKETT, N. A. GLASKOWSKY, AND R. M. IVIE

I n the preceding chapter, we examined marketing intermediaries from the viewpoint of manufacturers who wanted to build and manage marketing channels. In this chapter, we view these intermediaries—retailers, wholesalers, and physical-distribution organizations—as requiring and forging their own marketing strategies. Instead of producing *form utility*, these intermediaries produce *place*, *time*, and *possession utility*. Some of these intermediaries are so large and powerful that they dominate the manufacturers who deal with them. Many are using strategic planning, advanced information systems, and marketing tools. They are measuring performance more on a return-on-investment basis than on a profit-margin basis. They are segmenting their markets and improving their market targeting and positioning. They are aggressively pursuing market expansion and diversification strategies.

We will ask the following questions about each sector (retailers, wholesalers, and physical-distribution firms): What is the nature and importance of this sector? What major types of organizations occupy this sector? What marketing decisions do organizations in this sector make? What are the major trends in this sector?

Retailing

Nature and Importance of Retailing

Retailing includes all the activities involved in selling goods or services directly to final consumers for their personal, nonbusiness use. Any organization that does this selling—whether a manufacturer, wholesaler, or retailer—is doing retailing. It does not matter *how* the goods or services are sold (by person, mail, telephone, or vending machine) or *where* they are sold (in a store, on the street, or in the consumer's home). On the other hand, a *retailer* or *retail store* is any business enterprise whose sales volume comes primarily from retailing.

Types of Retailers

Retail organizations exhibit great variety and new forms keep emerging. Several classifications have been proposed. For our purposes, we will discuss store retailers, nonstore retailing, and retail organizations.

STORE RETAILERS ❖ Consumers today can shop for goods and services in a wide variety of stores. Marketing Environment and Trends 21-1 describes the most important retail-store types, many of which are found in most countries.

Retail-store types, like products, pass through stages of growth and decline that can be described as the *retail life cycle*.[1] A retail-store type emerges, enjoys a period of accelerated growth, reaches maturity, and then declines. Older retail forms took many years to reach maturity, but newer retail forms reach their maturity much earlier. The department store took 80 years to reach maturity, whereas warehouse retail outlets, a more modern form, reached their maturity in ten years.

Major Retailer Types

Here are brief descriptions of the most important store types.

SPECIALTY STORE ❖ A specialty store carries a narrow product line with a deep assortment within that line. Examples of specialty retailers are apparel stores, sporting-goods stores, furniture stores, florists, and bookstores. Specialty stores can be subclassified by the degree of narrowness in their product line. A clothing store would be a *single-line store;* a men's clothing store would be a *limited-line store;* and a men's custom-shirt store would be a *superspecialty store.* Some analysts contend that, in the future, superspecialty stores will grow the fastest to take advantage of increasing opportunities for market segmentation, market targeting, and product specialization. Current examples are Athlete's Foot (sport shoes only) and Tall Men (tall-men's clothing).

DEPARTMENT STORE ❖ A department store carries several product lines, typically clothing, home furnishings, and household goods, where each line is operated as a separate department managed by specialist buyers or merchandisers. Sears is a good example. *Specialty department stores* are also found, carrying only clothing, shoes, cosmetics, gift items, and luggage; examples are Saks Fifth Avenue and I. Magnin.

In some cities and countries, department stores are in the declining stage of the *retail life cycle.* They face increased competition from discount houses, specialty-store chains, and warehouse retailers, and the heavy traffic, poor parking, and deterioration of central cities, which have made downtown shopping less appealing.

Department stores are waging a "comeback" war. Many have opened branches in suburban shopping centers, where there are better parking facilities and higher family incomes. Others are running more frequent sales, remodeling their stores, "going boutique," leasing departments, and experimenting with mail-order and telemarketing. Some department stores are retrenching on the number of employees, product lines, and customer services, such as delivery and credit, but this strategy may hurt their major appeal, namely, better service.

Ironically, department stores in some parts of the world are thriving. Japanese department stores such as Takashimaya and Mitsukoshi attract numerous shoppers. These stores feature art galleries, cooking classes, and children playgrounds. The El Cortes Ingles department store chain in Spain draws crowds of Spanish shoppers.

SUPERMARKET ❖ A supermarket is a relatively large, low-cost, low-margin, high-volume, self-service operation designed to serve the consumer's total needs for food, laundry, and household-maintenance products. Supermarkets earn an operating profit of only about 1% on their sales and 10% on their net worth.

Supermarkets have been hit hard by a number of innovative competitors, such as convenience food stores, discount food stores, and superstores. Another challenge has been the rapid growth of out-of-home eating, with Americans now spending nearly 40% of their food budgets outside the food stores.

Supermarkets have moved in several directions to improve their competitiveness. They have opened *larger stores,* with today's selling space occupying approximately 25,000 square feet. Supermarkets carry a large *number* and *variety of items,* typically over 12,000 items. The largest increase has been in nonfood items, which now account for 25% of total supermarket sales. Many supermarkets are moving into prescriptions, appliances, records, sporting goods, hardware, garden supplies, and even cameras, hoping to find high-margin lines to improve profitability. Supermarkets are also *upgrading their facilities* through more expensive locations, larger parking lots, carefully planned architecture and decor, longer store hours and Sunday openings, and a broad variety of customer services, such as check cashing, restrooms, and background music. Supermarkets have also increased their *promotional budgets.* They have also moved heavily into *private brands* to reduce their dependence on national brands and increase their profit margins.

"Supermarketing" as a method of doing business has recently spread to other types of business, particularly in the drug, home-improvement, toy, and sporting-goods fields.

CONVENIENCE STORE ❖ Convenience food stores are relatively small stores that are located near residential areas, are open long hours and seven days a week, and carry a limited line of high-turnover convenience products. Their long hours and their use by consumers mainly for "fill-in" purchases make them relatively high-price operations. Many have added sandwiches, coffee, and pastry for takeout. They fill an important consumer need, and people seem willing to pay for the convenience.

SUPERSTORE, COMBINATION STORE, AND HYPERMARKET ❖ *Superstores* average 35,000 square feet of selling space and aim at meeting the consumers' total needs for routinely purchased food and nonfood items. They usually offer services such as laundry, dry cleaning, shoe repair, check cashing and bill paying, and bargain lunch counters. *Combination stores* represent a diversification of the supermarket store into the growing drug-and-prescription field. Combination food and drug stores average 55,000 square feet of selling space. *Hypermarkets* are even larger, ranging between 80,000 and 220,000 square feet. The hypermarket combines supermarket, discount, and warehouse retailing principles. Its product assortment goes beyond routinely purchased goods and includes furniture, large and small appliances, clothing items, and many other items. The basic approach is bulk display and minimum handling by store personnel, with discounts offered to customers who are willing to carry heavy appliances and furniture out of the store.

DISCOUNT STORE ❖ A discount store sells standard merchandise at lower prices by accepting lower margins and selling higher volumes. The use of occasional discounts or specials does not make a discount store. A true discount store *regularly* sells its merchandise at lower prices, offering mostly national brands, not inferior goods. Early discount stores cut expenses by operating in warehouselike facilities in low-rent but heavily traveled districts. They slashed prices, advertised widely, and carried a reasonable breadth and depth of products.

In recent years, many discount retailers have "traded up." They have improved decor, added new lines and services, and opened suburban branches—all of which has led to higher costs and prices. And as some department stores have cut their prices to compete with discounters, the distinction between many discount and department stores has blurred.

Discount retailing has moved beyond general merchandise into specialty merchandise stores, such as discount sporting-goods stores, electronics stores, and bookstores.

OFF-PRICE RETAILERS ❖ When the major discount stores traded up, a new wave of *off-price retailers* moved in to fill the low-price, high-volume gap. Ordinary discounters buy at regular wholesale prices and accept lower margins to keep prices down. Off-price retailers, on the other hand, buy at less than regular wholesale prices and charge consumers less than retail. They tend to carry a changing and unstable collection of higher-quality merchandise, often leftover goods, overruns, and irregulars obtained at reduced prices from manufacturers or other retailers. Off-price retailers have made the biggest inroads in clothing, accessories, and footwear.

There are three main types of off-price retailers— *factory outlets, independents,* and *warehouse clubs.* *Factory outlets* are owned and operated by manufacturers and normally carry the manufacturer's surplus, discontinued, or irregular goods. Such outlets increasingly group together in *factory outlet malls,* where dozens of

One reason that new store types emerge to challenge old store types is given by the *wheel-of-retailing* hypothesis.[2] Conventional store types typically offer many services to their customers and price their merchandise to cover the cost. This provides an opportunity for new store forms to emerge—for example, discount stores—which offer lower prices, less service, and less status but have lower operating costs. A large number of shoppers use the conventional stores for deciding what to buy and then drive to the discount stores to make the actual purchase. As these discount stores increase their market share, they offer more services and upgrade their facilities. Their increased costs, however, force them to raise their prices until they start to resemble the conventional outlets they displaced. As a consequence, they become vulnerable to newer types of low-cost, low-margin operations. This hypothesis partly explains the initial success and current troubles of department stores and, more recently, discount stores.

New store types emerge to meet widely different consumer preferences for

outlet stores offer prices as much as 50% below retail on a broad range of items. The number of factory outlet malls has doubled in the past four years, standing today at 275, making them one of the hottest growth areas in retailing. The malls are moving upscale and now feature brands such as Esprit and Liz Claiborne, causing department stores to protest since they have to charge more, given their higher costs. The manufacturers counter that they send last year's merchandise and seconds to the factory outlet malls, not to be confused with the new merchandise they supply to the department stores. The malls are also located far from urban areas, making travel more difficult. Still, the department stores are concerned about the growing number of shoppers willing to make weekend trips to stock up on branded merchandise at substantial savings.

Independent off-price retailers either are owned and run by entrepreneurs or are divisions of larger retail corporations.

Warehouse clubs (or *wholesale clubs*) sell a limited selection of brand-name grocery items, appliances, clothing, and a hodgepodge of other goods at deep discounts to members who pay $25 to $50 annual membership fees. Starting in the mid-1970s to serve small businesses, warehouse clubs also serve group members coming from government agencies, nonprofit organizations, and some large corporations. These wholesale clubs operate in huge, low-overhead, warehouselike facilities and offer few frills. Their costs are lower because they buy on deals and use less labor for stocking. Such clubs make no home deliveries and accept no credit cards. But they do offer rock-bottom prices—typically 20% to 40% below supermarket and discount-store prices. Given their significantly lower prices, they are causing supermarkets much concern about retaining their food customers. Led by such chains as Wal-Mart-owned Sam's, Price Club, and Costco, warehouse clubs reported a 26% increase in sales in 1990.

CATALOG SHOWROOM ❖ A *catalog showroom* sells a broad selection of high-markup, fast-moving, brand-name goods at discount prices. These include jewelry, power tools, cameras, luggage, small appliances, toys, and sporting goods. Catalog showrooms make their money by cutting costs and margins to provide low prices that will attract a higher volume of sales. Catalog showrooms have been struggling in recent years to hold their share of the retail market.

SOURCE: For further reading, see Laura Zinn, "Who Will Survive," *Business Week*, November 26, 1990, pp. 134–44; Alison Fahey, "Department Store Outlook," *Advertising Age*, January 28, 1991, p. 23; Julie Liesse Erickson, "Supermarket Chains Work to Fill Tall Order," *Advertising Age*, April 28, 1986, pp. S1–S2; Christy Fisher, "Convenience Chains Pump for New Life," *Advertising Age*, April 23, 1990, p. 80; Todd Mason, "The Return of the Amazing Colossal Store," *Business Week*, August 22, 1988, pp. 59–61; Adrienne Ward, "New Breed of Mall Knows: Everyone Loves a Bargain," *Advertising Age*, January 27, 1992; "No-Frills Warehouses: Retailing for Hard Times," *Newsweek*, August 5, 1991, p. 65; Kevin Helliker, "Thriving Factory Outlets Anger Retailers as Store Suppliers Turn Into Competitors," *The Wall Street Journal*, October 8, 1991, pp. B1, B6; and Jack G. Kaikati, "Don't Discount Off-Price Retailers," *Harvard Business Review*, May–June 1985, pp. 85–92.

service levels and specific services. Thus, in the past, most consumers purchased shoes in shoe stores, where they were waited on by fitters. Today, most shoes are bought in mass-merchandise outlets where consumers take them off the shelf, and an increasing number of shoes are purchased through the mail. It turns out that retailers in most product categories can position themselves as offering one of four levels of service:

- ◆ *Self-Service Retailing:* Used in many retailing operations, especially for obtaining convenience goods and, to some extent, shopping goods. Self-service is the cornerstone of all discount operations. Many customers are willing to carry out their own locate-compare-select process to save money.

- ◆ *Self-Selection Retailing:* Involves customers in finding their own goods, although they can ask for assistance. Customers complete their transactions by paying a salesperson for the item. Self-selection organizations have higher operating expenses than self-service operations because of the additional staff requirements.

- *Limited-Service Retailing:* Provides more sales assistance because these stores carry more shopping goods, and customers need more information. The stores also offer services, such as credit and merchandise-return privileges, not normally found in less service-oriented stores and hence they have higher operating costs.
- *Full-Service Retailing:* Provides salespeople who are ready to assist in every phase of the locate-compare-select process. Customers who like to be waited on prefer this type of store. The high staffing cost, along with the higher proportion of specialty goods and slower-moving items (fashions, jewelry, cameras), the more liberal merchandise-return policies, various credit plans, free delivery, home servicing of durables, and customer facilities such as lounges and restaurants, results in high-cost retailing.

By combining these different service levels with different assortment breadths, we can distinguish four broad positioning strategies available to retailers as shown in Figure 21-1 on page 564.

1. Bloomingdale's typifies stores that feature a broad product assortment and high value added. Stores in this quadrant pay close attention to store design, product quality, service, and image. Their profit margin is high, and if they are fortunate enough to have high volume, they will be very profitable.

Marketing Environment and Trends 21-2

Major Types of Nonstore Retailing

DIRECT SELLING ❖ Direct selling—which started centuries ago with itinerant peddlers—has burgeoned into a $9 billion industry, with over 600 companies selling *door to door, office to office,* or at *home sales parties.* The pioneers include the Fuller Brush Company (brushes, brooms, and the like), Electrolux (vacuum cleaners), Southwestern Company of Nashville (Bibles), and World Book (encyclopedias). Door-to-door selling improved considerably with Avon's entry into the industry, with the concept of the homemakers' friend and beauty consultant—the Avon lady. Its army of nearly a million representatives worldwide produced over $2 billion in sales in 1985, making it the world's largest cosmetics firm and the number-one door-to-door marketer. Tupperware, on the other hand, helped popularize the home-sales-parties method of selling, in which several friends and neighbors are invited to a party in someone's home where Tupperware products are demonstrated and sold.[1]

A variant of direct selling is called *multilevel marketing,* whereby companies such as Amway or Shaklee recruit independent businesspeople who act as distributors for their products, who in turn recruit and sell to subdistributors, who eventually recruit others to sell their products, usually in customer homes. A distributor's compensation includes a percentage of the sales to the entire sales group that the distributor recruited as well as earnings on any direct sales to retail customers. This system has also been called "pyramid selling," but the Direct Selling Education Foundation says that pyramid selling describes fraudulent schemes where the money is made by those initiating the scheme and the products rarely reach and satisfy final consumers.[2]

Direct selling is expensive (the salesperson gets a 20 to 50% commission), and there are the costs of hiring, training, managing, and motivating the salesforce. To motivate its salesforce of over 50,000 women, Mary Kay Cosmetics tempts them with prizes of diamonds, minks, and the right to drive one of 125 pink Cadillacs for an entire year. The future of direct selling is somewhat uncertain, with more women at work during the day.

DIRECT MARKETING ❖ Direct marketing has its roots in mail-order marketing but today includes reaching people in other ways than visiting their homes or offices, including telemarketing, television direct-response marketing, and electronic shopping. It is more fully described in Chapter 24, pp. 654–64.

AUTOMATIC VENDING ❖ Automatic vending has been applied to a considerable variety of merchandise, including impulse goods with high convenience

2. Tiffany typifies stores that feature a narrow product assortment and high value added. Such stores cultivate an exclusive image and tend to operate on a high margin and low volume.

3. Kinney Shoe typifies stores that feature a narrow line and low value added. Such stores, often referred to as specialty mass merchandisers, appeal to price-conscious consumers. They keep their costs and prices low through designing similar stores and centralizing buying, merchandising, advertising, and distribution.

4. K mart typifies stores that feature a broad line and low value added. They focus on keeping prices low so that they have an image of being a place for good buys. They make up for their low margin by achieving a high volume.

NONSTORE RETAILING ❖ Although the overwhelming majority of goods and services is sold through stores, *nonstore retailing* has been growing much faster than store retailing, amounting to more than 12% of all consumer purchases. Some observers foresee as much as a third of all general-merchandise retailing being done through nonstore channels by the end of the century. Several types of nonstore retailing are described in Marketing Environment and Trends 21-2.

value (cigarettes, soft drinks, candy, newspapers, hot beverages) and other products (hosiery, cosmetics, food snacks, hot soups and food, paperbacks, record albums, film, T-shirts, insurance policies, shoeshines, and even fishing worms). In Japan, vending machines have advanced further and dispense jewelry, frozen beef, fresh flowers, whiskey, and even names of prospective dating partners. Vending machines are found in factories, offices, large retail stores, gasoline stations, hotels, restaurants, and many other venues. Vending machines offer customers the advantages of 24-hour selling, self-service, and unhandled merchandise.

At the same time, automatic vending is a relatively expensive channel, and prices of vended merchandise are often 15 to 20% higher. Vendor costs are high because of frequent restocking at widely scattered locations, frequent machine breakdowns, and the high pilferage rate in certain locations. For the customer, the biggest irritations are machine breakdowns, out-of-stocks, and the fact that merchandise cannot be returned.

Vending machines are increasingly supplying entertainment services—pinball machines, slot machines, juke boxes, and the new electronic computer games. A highly specialized vending machine is the *automatic teller machine (ATM)*, which allows bank customers 24-hour service on checking, savings, withdrawals, and transfer of funds from one account to another. Industry trends include "debit card" vending, where a person's account is immediately debited upon purchasing, and "prepaid card" vending, where a person's card value is reduced for each purchase until the card is exhausted.

BUYING SERVICE ❖ A buying service is a storeless retailer serving specific clienteles—usually the employees of large organizations, such as schools, hospitals, unions, and government agencies. The organization's members become members of the buying service and are entitled to buy from a selective list of retailers who have agreed to give discounts to buying service members. Thus a customer seeking a video camera would get a form from the buying service, take it to an approved retailer, and buy the appliance at a discount. The retailer would then pay a small fee to the buying service. United Buying Service, for example, offers its 900,000 members the opportunity to buy merchandise at "cost plus 8%."

SOURCES: 1. See "New Hustle for an Old Product," *Newsweek*, August 26, 1985, p. 48. 2. See Peter Clothier, *Multi-Level Marketing: A Practical Guide to Successful Network Selling* (London: Kogan Page, 1990).

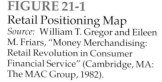

FIGURE 21-1
Retail Positioning Map
Source: William T. Gregor and Eileen
M. Friars, "Money Merchandising:
Retail Revolution in Consumer
Financial Service" (Cambridge, MA:
The MAC Group, 1982).

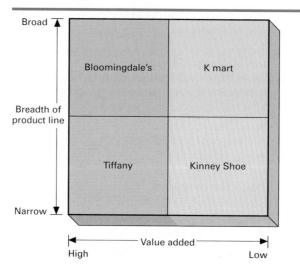

RETAIL ORGANIZATIONS ❖ Although many retail stores are independently owned, an increasing number are falling under some form of corporate retailing. The five types of corporate retailing are *corporate chains, voluntary chain and retailer cooperatives, consumer cooperatives, franchise organizations*, and *merchandising conglomerates*. They are described in Marketing Environment and Trends 21-3. See also Companies and Industries 21-1 on page 567.

Retailer Marketing Decisions

Retailers today are anxious to find new marketing strategies to attract and hold customers. In the past, they held customers by having special or unique assortments of goods, by offering greater or better services than competitors, by offering store credit cards to enable their buyers to buy on credit, or simply by being closer and more convenient. All of this has changed. Today, many stores offer similar assortments: National brands such as Calvin Klein, Izod, and Levi are now found in most department stores, mass-merchandise outlets, and off-price discount stores. The national brand manufacturers, in their drive for volume, placed their branded goods everywhere. The result was that retail stores and assortments looked more and more alike.

Service differentiation also has eroded. Many department stores trimmed their services, and many discounters increased their services. Customers became smarter shoppers and more price sensitive. They did not see a reason to pay more for identical brands, especially when service differences were diminishing. Nor did they need to get credit from a particular store, as bank credit cards became increasingly accepted by all stores.

For all these reasons, many retailers today are rethinking their marketing strategy.[3] We will now examine the marketing decisions faced by retailers in the areas of target market, product assortment and procurement, services and store atmosphere, price, promotion, and place.

TARGET-MARKET DECISION ❖ A retailer's most important decision concerns the target market. Should the store focus on upscale, midscale, or downscale shoppers? Do the target shoppers want variety, assortment depth, or convenience? Until the target market is defined and profiled, the retailer cannot make consistent

Major Types of Retail Organizations

CORPORATE CHAIN ❖ *Chain stores* are two or more outlets that are commonly owned and controlled, employ central buying and merchandising, and sell similar lines of merchandise. Corporate chains appear in all types of retailing, but they are strongest in department stores, variety stores, food stores, drugstores, shoe stores, and women's clothing stores.

Corporate chains gain many advantages over independents. Their size allows them to buy in large quantities at lower prices. They can afford to hire corporate-level specialists to deal with such areas as pricing, promotion, merchandising, inventory control, and sales forecasting. Chains gain promotional economies because their advertising costs are spread over many stores and a large sales volume. And some chains permit their local units to meet variations in consumer preferences and competition in local markets.

VOLUNTARY CHAIN AND RETAILER COOPERATIVE ❖ The growing competition from corporate chains led independent retailers to form two types of associations. One is the *voluntary chain*, which consists of a wholesaler-sponsored group of independent retailers engaged in bulk buying and common merchandising. Examples include the Independent Grocers Alliance (IGA) in groceries and True Value in hardware. The other is the *retailer cooperative*, which consists of independent retailers who set up a central buying organization and conduct joint promotion efforts. Examples include Associated Grocers in groceries and ACE in hardware. These organizations, through achieving the needed merchandising economies, have become effective in meeting the price challenge of the corporate chains.

CONSUMER COOPERATIVE ❖ A consumer cooperative (or co-op) is any retail firm owned by its customers. Consumer co-ops are started by community residents who feel that local retailers are not serving them well, either charging too high prices or providing poor-quality products. The residents contribute money to open their own store, and they vote on its policies and elect a group to manage it. The store might set its prices low or, alternatively, set normal prices with members receiving a patronage dividend based on their individual level of purchases.

FRANCHISE ORGANIZATION ❖ A franchise organization is a contractual association between a franchiser (a manufacturer, wholesaler, or service organiza-

tion) and franchisees (independent businesspeople who buy the right to own and operate one or more units in the franchise system). Franchise organizations are normally based on some unique product, service, or method of doing business, or on a trade name, or patent, or on goodwill that the franchiser has developed. Franchising has been prominent in fast foods, video stores, health/fitness centers, hair cutting, auto rentals, motels, travel agencies, real estate, and dozens of other product and service areas.[1]

The franchiser's compensation can consist of the following elements: an initial fee, a royalty on gross sales, rental and lease fees on equipment and fixtures supplied by the franchiser, a share of the profits, and sometimes a regular license fee. In a few cases, franchisers have also charged management consulting fees, but usually the franchisee is entitled to this service as part of the total package.

One of the most successful franchise systems of all time is McDonald's. McDonald's franchisees may invest as much as $600,000 in initial start-up costs for a franchise. McDonald's then charges a 3.5% service fee and a rental charge of 8.5% of the franchisee's volume. It also requires franchisees to attend "Hamburger University" for three weeks to learn how to manage the business. The franchisees must also adhere to certain procedures in buying materials and in preparing and selling the product. With 11,000 outlets in 50 countries and more than $17.5 billion in annual sales, McDonald's doubles the sales of its nearest rival, Burger King, and triples those of third-place Wendy's. Nineteen million customers pass through the famous golden arches each day. McDonald's now serves 145 hamburgers per second. McDonald's opens a new store every 15 hours. In January 1990, McDonald's opened its first outlet in Moscow, a 700-seat restaurant, and rang up 30,000 meals on 27 cash registers, breaking the opening-day record for McDonald's worldwide.

Subway Sandwich Shops may have been the fastest growing franchise system in the last five years—its franchises growing from 1,750 to 7,000 worldwide. One factor in its success is its low start-up fee of between $45,000–$70,000, which is lower than 70% of other franchise system start-up fees. Another factor is its aggressive recruiting program using the services of development agents (mostly other franchisees) who get commissions for recruiting and setting up new franchisees. Subway holds the premise leases and sublets the shops. They receive an 8% royalty on the franchisee's revenue and another 2.5% for advertising. Subway has been criticized for not maintaining high quality control as a result of its soaring growth and also for its agents exaggerating probable earnings to prospective franchisees. Within a three-year period, about 40% of Subway franchises either closed, were never opened, relocated, or changed hands. There is typically a conflict between the franchise system owners who benefit from growth and the franchisees, who benefit only when they can make a decent living.[2]

McDonald's, Subway, and other fast-food franchisers are currently facing rising labor costs and food costs, forcing them to raise their prices. New competitors continue to emerge, popularizing ethnic foods, such as tacos and gyros. Some major franchisers are now opening units in smaller towns, where there is less competition. Others are moving into large factories, office buildings, colleges, and even hospitals. Others are experimenting with new products that they hope will appeal to consumers and be profitable to the firm.

MERCHANDISING CONGLOMERATE ❖ Merchandising conglomerates are free-form corporations that combine several diversified retailing lines and forms under central ownership, along with some integration of their distribution-and-management function.[3] For example, F. W. Woolworth, in addition to its variety stores, operates Kinney Shoe Stores, Afterthoughts (costume jewelry and handbag specialty stores), Herald Square Stationers, Frame Scene, and Kids Mart. In the future, diversified retailing is likely to be adopted by more corporate chains. The major question is whether diversified retailing produces superior management systems and economies that benefit all of the separate retail lines.

SOURCES: 1. See "Why Franchising is Taking Off," *Fortune*, February 12, 1990, p. 124. 2. Barbara Marsh, "Franchise Realities: Sandwich-Shop Chain Surges, But to Run One Can Take Heroic Effort," *The Wall Street Journal*, September 16, 1992, p. 1, A5. 3. See Rollie Tillman, "Rise of the Conglomerchant," *Harvard Business Review*, November–December 1971, pp. 44–51.

decisions on product assortment, store decor, advertising messages and media, price levels, and so on.

Too many retailers have not clarified their target market or are trying to satisfy too many markets, satisfying none of them well. Even Sears, which serves so many different people, must define better which groups to make its major target customers so that it can fine-tune its product assortment, prices, locations, and promotions to these groups.

Some retailers have defined their target markets quite well. Here are two prime examples whose founders are among the richest men in America:

Leslie H. Wexner borrowed $5,000 in 1963 to create *The Limited Inc.*, which started as a single store targeted to young, fashion-conscious women. All aspects of the store—clothing assortment, fixtures, music, colors, personnel—were orchestrated to match the target consumer. He continued to open more stores, but a decade later his original customers were no longer in the "young" group. To catch the new "youngs," he started the Limited Express. Over the years, he started or acquired other targeted store chains, including Lane Bryant, Victoria's Secret, Sizes Unlimited, Lerners, and so on. Today, The Limited operates 4,494 stores in 14 retailing divisions. Sales totaled $6.1 billion in 1991.

The late Sam Walton and his brother opened the first *Wal-Mart* discount store in Rogers, Arkansas in 1962. It was a big, flat, warehouse-type store aimed at selling everything from apparel to automotive supplies to small appliances at the lowest possible prices to small-town America. More recently, Wal-Mart has been building stores in larger cities. Today, Wal-Mart operates 1,600 stores in 35 states and produces more than $32 billion in annual sales, making it America's largest retailer. Wal-Mart's secret: target small-town America, listen to the customers, treat the employees as partners, purchase carefully, and keep a tight rein on expenses. Signs reading "Satisfaction Guaranteed" and "We Sell for Less" hang prominently at each store's entrance, and customers are often welcomed by a "people greeter" eager to lend a helping hand. Wal-Mart spends considerably less than Sears and K mart in advertising, and yet its sales are growing at the rate of 30% a year. Sam Walton also launched a successful new set of stores called Sam's Wholesale Club, which provides members (small businesses, government employees, and so forth) with superdiscounts on furniture, appliances, supplies, and food products.

Retailers should conduct periodic marketing research to ensure that they are reaching and satisfying their target customers. Consider a store that seeks to attract affluent consumers but whose image is shown by the solid line in Figure 21-2. The store's image does not appeal to its target market. The store has to either serve the mass market or redesign itself into a "classier store." Suppose it decides on the latter. Some time later, the store interviews customers again. The store image is now shown by the dashed line in Figure 21-2. The store has succeeded in realigning its image closer to its target market.

At the same time, a retailer's positioning must be somewhat elastic, especially if it manages outlets in locations with different socioeconomic patterns. A bank had

Companies and Industries 21-1

Pizza Hut Tries to Manage Its Franchises

Franchise systems pose a formidable management challenge to the franchiser. Coca-Cola has come into conflict with some of its bottlers on many occasions. Supercut, a franchised chain of haircutting salons, had to handle a franchisee revolt against its policies. The fact is that the interests of the franchiser and the franchisees often diverge.

Consider the case of Pizza Hut. Pizza Hut has 7,000 units, of which 47% are owned by the company and the remainder are in the hands of franchisees. Suppose Pizza Hut wants to introduce three new policies:

1. Pizza Hut wants its units to offer pizza delivery in addition to dining facilities.

2. Pizza Hut wants to advertise lower prices nationwide.

3. Pizza Hut wants to add new food products to its menus.

Note first that all three policies will impose new costs on the franchisees. They would have to buy delivery vehicles and new equipment for the new-product lines. This means that their bottom line will be hurt in the short run.

Some franchisees positively don't want to comply with any of these policies. Consider a franchisee operating a successful Pizza Hut in a small town. The townspeople are perfectly satisfied with dining at Pizza Hut or using its carry-out services; home delivery service is less relevant. Or consider a powerful franchisee who owns several units who is planning to retire soon, and is very satisfied with the wealth he has accumulated with his franchises. He is more interested in wealth preservation than in further growth.

In most franchise systems, the franchisees appoint a representative to negotiate for them with the franchiser. This representative has a difficult job, not only because he or she faces the franchiser, but also because the franchisees have so many conflicting interests among themselves. The franchisees vary in how much competition they face, their resources, their time horizons, and so on.

All said, managing a franchised system is a never-ending challenge.

FIGURE 21-2 A Comparison Between the Old and New Image of a Store Seeking to Appeal to a Class Market

Source: Adapted from David W. Cravens, Gerald E. Hills, and Robert B. Woodruff, *Marketing Decision Making: Concepts and Strategy* (Homewood, IL: Richard D. Irwin, 1976), p. 234. © 1976 by Richard D. Irwin, Inc.

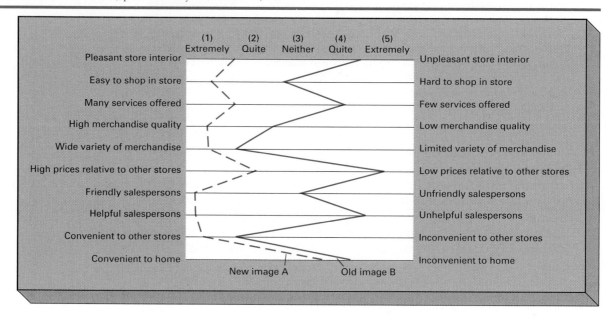

located three branches in different parts of a city. It recognized that each branch needed to respond to a different key driver, as follows:

BRANCH	KEY DRIVER
Branch A (high income, professional)	Timeliness
Branch B (middle income, housewives)	Friendliness
Branch C (low income)	Competence

PRODUCT-ASSORTMENT-AND-PROCUREMENT DECISION ❖ The retailer's *product assortment* must match the shopping expectations of the target market. In fact, it becomes a key element in the competitive battle among similar retailers. The retailer has to decide on product-assortment *breadth* (narrow or wide) and *depth* (shallow or deep). Thus in the restaurant business, a restaurant can offer a narrow and shallow assortment (small lunch counters), a narrow and deep assortment (delicatessen), a broad and shallow assortment (cafeteria), or a broad and deep assortment (large restaurants). Another product-assortment dimension is the quality of the goods. The customer is interested in product quality as well as product range.

The retailer's real challenge begins after the store's product assortment and quality level have been defined. There will always be competitors with similar assortments and quality. The challenge is to develop a product-differentiation strategy. Wortzel suggests several product-differentiation strategies for retailers:

1. *Feature Some Exclusive National Brands Which Are Not Available at Competing Retailers:* Thus Saks might get exclusive rights to carry the dresses of a well-known international designer.

2. *Feature Mostly Private Branded Merchandise:* The Limited designs most of the clothes carried in its stores.

3. *Feature Blockbuster Distinctive Merchandise Events:* Bloomingdale's will run month-long shows featuring the goods of another country, such as India or China, throughout its store.

4. *Feature Surprise or Ever-Changing Merchandise:* Benetton changes some portion of its merchandise every month so that customers will want to drop in frequently. Loehmann's offers surprise assortments of distress merchandise, overstocks, and closeouts.

5. *Feature the Latest or Newest Merchandise First:* The Sharper Image will lead other retailers in introducing the newest electronic appliances from around the world.

6. *Offer Merchandise Customizing Services:* Harrod's of London will make custom-tailored suits, shirts, and ties for customers, in addition to their ready-made men's wear.

7. *Offer a Highly Targeted Assortment:* Lane Bryant carries goods for the larger woman. Brookstone offers unusual tools and gadgets for the person who wants to shop in an "adult toy store."[4]

Once the retailer decides on the product-assortment strategy, the retailer must decide on procurement sources, policies, and practices. In small businesses, the owner usually handles merchandise selection and buying. In large firms, buying is a specialized function and full-time job.

Consider supermarkets. In the corporate headquarters of a supermarket chain, specialist buyers (sometimes called merchandise managers) are responsible for developing brand assortments and listening to new-brand presentations by salespersons. In some chains, these buyers have the authority to accept or reject new items. In other chains, they are limited to screening "obvious rejects" and "obvious accepts"; they bring other items to the chain's buying committee for approval. Borden found that the buyer's recommendation carries a lot of influence in the committee decision.[5]

Even when an item is accepted by a chain-store buying committee, individual stores in the chain may not carry it. According to one supermarket chain executive: "No matter what the sales representatives sell or buyers buy, the person who has the greatest influence on the final sale of the new item is the store manager." In the nation's chain and independent supermarkets, two thirds of the new items accepted at the warehouse are ordered on the store manager's own decision, and only one third represent forced distribution.

Thus, producers face a major challenge trying to get their new items onto store shelves. They offer the nation's supermarkets between 150 and 250 new items each week, and store space does not permit more than 10% to be accepted.

Producers are clearly interested in knowing the acceptance criteria used by buyers, buying committees, and store managers. A. C. Nielsen Company asked store managers to rank on a three-point scale the importance of different elements in influencing their decision to accept a new item. They found that buyers are most influenced, in order of importance, by strong evidence of consumer acceptance, a well-designed advertising and sales-promotion plan, and generous financial incentives to the trade.

The role of supermarket buyers, buying committees, and store managers characterize, with some variation, the buying organizations of other reseller enterprises. Large department store chains use buyers who specialize by line of merchandise and have great authority to select the merchandise to be featured. The buyers are aided by assistant buyers who assist in demand forecasting, stock control, and merchandising. Individual store managers then make future decisions with respect to which goods to order and which to display prominently.

Resellers are rapidly improving their procurement skills. They are mastering the principles of demand forecasting, merchandise selection, stock control, space allocation, and display. They are using computers to track inventory, compute eco-

CHAPTER 21
Managing Retailing,
Wholesaling, and
Physical-Distribution
Systems

569

A New Tool for Resellers: Direct Product Profitability (DPP)

Resellers are making increased use of a tool to evaluate new-product profits, called *direct product profitability* (DPP). DPP enables resellers to measure a product's handling costs from the time it reaches their warehouse until a customer buys it and takes it out of their retail store. DPP measures only the direct costs associated with handling the product—receiving, moving to storage, paperwork, selecting, checking, loading, and space cost. Resellers who have adopted DPP learn to their surprise that the gross margin on a product often has little correlation with the direct product profit. For example, some high-volume products may have such high handling costs that they are less profitable and deserve less shelf space than some low-volume products.

The Food Marketing Institute (FMI) is standard-izing this tool and promoting its widespread use. DPP can make a number of contributions. First, DPP can help resellers improve the management of their space. Second, DPP will bring about joint manufacturer-reseller actions to lower handling costs, for instance, improving package and case design and size or changing delivery methods. Third, DPP permits testing the profitability of alternative store-shelving plans and locations.

Some manufacturers feel threatened by this tool because it gives resellers a powerful argument for selecting or rejecting existing or new products. Smart manufacturers, however, are studying this tool and using it to help resellers reduce their costs, thus gaining greater trade acceptance in the process.

---

nomic order quantities, prepare orders, and generate printouts of dollars spent on vendors and products. They are learning to measure direct product profitability (see Marketing Concepts and Tools 21-1).

Thus, vendors are facing increasingly sophisticated reseller buyers, and this accounts for some of the shifting of power from manufacturers to resellers. Vendors need to understand the resellers' changing requirements and to develop competitively attractive offers that help resellers serve their customers better. Table 21-1 lists several marketing tools used by vendors to improve their attractiveness to resellers. Companies and Industries 21-2 shows how one vendor, GE, took the initiative to establish higher service and profitability for its dealers.

SERVICES AND STORE ATMOSPHERE DECISION ❖ Retailers must also decide on the *services mix* to offer customers. The old "mom and pop" grocery stores offered home delivery, credit, and conversation, services that today's supermarkets have completely eliminated. Table 21-2 lists some major services that full-

---

TABLE 21-1
Vendor Marketing Tools
Used with Resellers

Cooperative advertising, where vendor agrees to pay a portion of the retailer's advertising costs for the vendor's product

Preticketing, where the vendor places a tag on each product listing its price, manufacturer, size, identification number, and color; these tags help the reseller reorder merchandise as it is sold

Stockless purchasing, where the vendor carries the inventory and delivers goods to the reseller on short notice

Automatic reordering systems, where the vendor supplies forms and computer links for the automatic reordering of merchandise by the reseller

Advertising ads, such as glossy photos, broadcast scripts

Special prices for storewide promotion

Return and exchange privileges for the reseller

Allowances for merchandise markdowns by the reseller

Sponsorship of in-store demonstrations

General Electric Adopts a "Virtual Inventory" System to Support Its Dealers

Before the late 1980s, GE operated a traditional system of trying to load its dealers with GE appliances on the premise that a "loaded" dealer is a "loyal" dealer. The dealer would have less space to feature other brands and would recommend GE appliances to reduce its high inventory. To load its dealers, GE would offer the lowest price when the dealer ordered a full truckload of GE appliances.

GE subsequently realized that this approach created problems, especially for smaller independent appliance dealers who could ill afford to carry a large stock. These dealers were hard pressed to meet the price competition of the larger multibrand dealers. Rethinking its strategy from the point of view of creating dealer satisfaction and profitability, GE invented an alternative model called the Direct Connect system. Under this system, GE dealers carry only display models. They rely on a "virtual inventory" to fill orders. Dealers can access GE's order-processing system 24 hours a day, check on model availability, and place orders for next-day delivery. Furthermore, dealers get GE's best price, GE financing from GE Credit, and no interest charge for the first 90 days.

The dealers benefit by having much lower inventory costs and yet having available a large virtual inventory to satisfy their customers. In exchange for this benefit, the dealers must commit to selling nine major GE product categories; generating 50% of their sales in GE products; opening their books to GE for review; and paying GE every month through electronic funds transfer. The net result is that dealers' profit margins have skyrocketed.

GE also has benefitted. The dealers are more committed and dependent on GE. The new order-entry system has saved GE substantial clerical costs. And GE now knows the actual sales of its goods at the retail level, which helps it schedule its production more accurately. It now is able to produce in response to demand rather than to meet inventory replenishment rules. And it has been able to simplify its warehouse locations so as to be able to deliver appliances throughout 90% of the United States within 24 hours.

SOURCE: See Michael Treacy and Fred Wiersema, "Customer Intimacy and Other Discipline Values," *Harvard Business Review,* pp. 84–93.

---

service retailers can offer. The services mix is one of the key tools for differentiating one store from another.

The *store's atmosphere* is another element in its arsenal. Every store has a physical layout that makes it hard or easy to move around. Every store has a "look"; one store is dirty, another is charming, a third is palatial, a fourth is somber. The store must embody a planned atmosphere that suits the target market and draws consumers toward purchase. A funeral parlor should be quiet, somber, and peaceful, and a discothèque should be bright, loud, and vibrating. The Banana Republic

PREPURCHASE SERVICES	POSTPURCHASE SERVICES	ANCILLARY SERVICES
1. Accepting telephone orders	1. Delivery	1. Check cashing
2. Accepting mail orders	2. Regular wrapping	2. General information
3. Advertising	3. Gift wrapping	3. Free parking
4. Window display	4. Adjustments	4. Restaurants
5. Interior display	5. Returns	5. Repairs
6. Fitting rooms	6. Alterations	6. Interior decorating
7. Shopping hours	7. Tailoring	7. Credit
8. Fashion shows	8. Installations	8. Rest rooms
9. Trade-ins	9. Engraving	9. Baby-attendant service

TABLE 21-2
Typical Retail Services

CHAPTER 21
Managing Retailing, Wholesaling, and Physical-Distribution Systems

Source: Carl M. Larson, Robert E. Weigand, and John S. Wright, *Basic Retailing,* 2nd ed. (Englewood Cliffs, NJ: Prentice-Hall, 1976), p. 384. Reprinted by permission of Prentice-Hall, Inc., Englewood Cliffs, NJ.

Travel & Safari Clothing stores work on the concept of "retail theater"; customers feel they are shopping in an African bazaar or hunting lodge. Supermarkets have found that varying the tempo of music affects the average time spent in the store and the average expenditures; and supermarkets are exploring ways to release aromas through sticker displays on store shelves to stimulate hunger or thirst. Some fine department stores vaporize perfume fragrances in certain departments. The New Otani Hotel in Singapore features an $8 million waterfall that rises and falls to music. "Packaged environments" are designed by creative people who combine visual, aural, olfactory, and tactile stimuli aimed at achieving some customer objective.[6] (See Marketing Strategies 21-1.)

PRICE DECISION ❖ The retailer's prices are a key positioning factor and must be decided in relation to the target market, the product-and-service assortment mix, and competition. All retailers would like to charge high markups and achieve high volumes, but usually the two do not go together. Most retailers fall into the *high-markup, lower-volume group* (fine specialty stores) or the *low-markup, higher-volume group* (mass merchandisers and discount stores). Within each of these groups, there are further gradations. Thus Bijan's on Rodeo Drive in Beverly Hills prices suits starting at $1,000 and shoes at $400, far in excess of the prices of fine department stores. At the other extreme, 47th Street Photo in New York City is a super-discounter of well-known branded merchandise, pricing below even normal discounters and catalog houses.

Retailers must also pay attention to pricing tactics. Most retailers will put low prices on some items to serve as *traffic builders* or *loss leaders*. They will run storewide sales on occasion. They will plan markdowns on slower-moving merchandise: for example, shoe retailers expect to sell 50% of their shoes at the normal markup, 25% at a 40% markup, and the remaining 25% at cost. (For more on price decision, see Marketing Strategies 21-2 on page 574.)

PROMOTION DECISION ❖ The retailer must use promotion tools that support and reinforce its image positioning. Fine stores will place tasteful full-page ads in magazines such as *Vogue* and *Harper's*. Discount retailers will place loud ads on radio, television, and newspapers touting low prices and specials. Fine stores will carefully train their salespeople in how to greet customers, interpret their needs, and handle their doubts and complaints. Discounters will use less well-trained salespeople and use a whole range of sales-promotion tools to generate traffic.

PLACE DECISION ❖ Retailers are accustomed to saying that the three keys to success are "location, location, and location." For example, customers primarily choose the nearest bank and gas station. Department-store chains, oil companies, and fast-food franchisers must exercise great care in selecting locations. The problem breaks down into selecting regions of the country in which to open outlets, then particular cities, and then particular sites. A supermarket chain, for example, might decide to operate in the Midwest and Southeast; within the Midwest, in the cities of Chicago, Milwaukee, and Indianapolis; and within Chicago, in 14 locations, mostly suburban.

Large retailers must wrestle with the problem of whether to locate several small stores in many locations or larger stores in fewer locations. Generally speaking, the retailer should locate enough stores in each city to gain promotion and distribution economies. The larger the individual stores, the greater their trading area or reach.

Retailers have a choice of locating their stores in the central business district, a regional shopping center, a community shopping center, or a shopping strip.

Marketing Strategies 21-1

Today's Retailing Takes Its Cues from Broadway

Richard Melman, 50, is Chicago's preeminent restaurateur. Each of his 32 restaurants is thematic: Tucci Benucch resembles an outdoor Italian village cafe; Ed Debevic is a 1950s kitsch diner; R. J. Grunts is a burger-and-chili hangout; Ambria is an elegant crystal, table-cloth, and candle restaurant. According to food-industry consultant Ronald N. Paul, "Rich Melman is the Andrew Lloyd Webber of the restaurant industry. He doesn't just produce food, he produces theatre."[1]

Turning retail establishments into theater isn't limited to restaurants. F.A.O. Schwarz opened a three-story toy store on Chicago's upscale North Michigan Avenue that has lines of customers waiting to get in. Once in, customers have to take an escalator to the third floor and make their way down through various boutiques where crowds gather around spectacular Lego exhibits, Barbie Doll departments, giant stuffed zoo animals, a talking tree, and so on. F.A.O. Schwarz's "theater" is in stark contrast to the numbing rows of shelves and high stacked boxes in the typical Toys "Я" Us store where nothing much seems to happen with the 15,000 toys, except lower prices.

Just a few blocks south of F.A.O. Schwarz stands four-story Niketown, which is now attracting more visitors than Chicago's famed Museum of Science and Industry. Niketown is the ultimate testimony to niche-manship: every room is dedicated to a different sport where one can see and buy the appropriate outfits and shoes that belong to that sport. The teenager would-be-basketball star heads for the second floor where he spots a giant picture of Michael Jordan, a whole array of basketball shoes and clothing, and even a basketball court where he can try on the shoes, shoot a few baskets, and sense how they help his performance.

Next door to Niketown is more staid theater in the form of the Sony Showroom, where various Sony products are set up to be touched, activated, and demonstrated. On the second floor, one experiences the future home theater with its giant screen and full-theater sound. On the first floor, one spots the televised image of a beautiful bouquet of flowers being shot through a Sony Handycam videocamera and televised through high-definition television, with the picture almost exceeding the beauty of the original flowers.

Perhaps the quintessential sign of the conversion of stores into theater is the Mall of America near Minneapolis—a superregional mall plus destination theme park. Anchored by four major department stores—Nordstrom's, Macy's, Bloomingdales', and Sears—the giant complex contains another 800 specialty stores. One of the stores, Oshman Supersports USA, features a basketball court, a boxing gym, a base-ball batting cage, a 50-foot archery range, and a simulated ski slope. The retail stores surround a seven-acre amusement park called Knott's Camp Snoopy, which consists of 26 rides, an ice skating rink, a miniature golf course on two levels, and a walk-through 1.2 million gallon aquarium featuring hundreds of marine specimens and a dolphin show. The mall owners expect the mall to attract as many as 40 million visitors a year from as far away as Japan.

All of this confirms that people don't just buy products. They buy services. And one of the most potent services in the future of retailing is entertainment itself.

SOURCES: See "Why Rich Melman Is Really Cooking," *Business Week,* November 2, 1992, pp. 127–28; and Howard Rudnitsky, "Battle of the Malls," *Forbes,* March 30, 1992.

- ◆ *Central Business Districts:* represent the oldest and most heavily trafficked city area, often known as downtown. Store and office rents are normally high. But a number of downtowns, such as Detroit's, have been hit by a flight to the suburbs with resulting deterioration of downtown retailing facilities and a changing shopper mix.

- ◆ *Regional Shopping Centers:* are large suburban malls containing 40 to over 100 stores and drawing from a five-mile to ten-mile radius. Typically, the malls feature one or two nationally known anchor stores, such as Sears or Marshall Fields, and a great number of smaller stores, many under franchise operation. Malls are attractive because of generous parking, one-stop shopping, restaurants, and recreational facilities. Successful malls charge high rents but in return generate high shopper density.

Marketing Strategies 21-2

Does an "Everyday-Low-Prices" Strategy Make More Sense Than a "Promotional Pricing" Strategy?

Many companies charge list prices and then run price-off sales from time to time. In this way, most of their customers pay the full price while deal-prone customers willing to wait for sales pay less than the full price. The full-price customers essentially subsidize the promotional-price customers.

Sears used this traditional pricing strategy. But Sears and other companies have recently had to reconsider their pricing strategy in the face of discounters. Historically, Sears set its prices lower than upscale department stores and attracted almost everyone to its stores to buy something. Sears ran frequent sales on seasonal items, special-purchased items, and items accumulating in inventory.

In recent years, Sears has seen growing competition from discount merchants such as K mart and Wal-Mart, who feature *everyday low prices* and run far fewer sales. A growing number of Sears customers have been switching many of their purchases to these discount merchants.

Sears found itself facing a critical pricing-strategy decision. In the spring of 1989, it announced the biggest pricing change in its 102-year history. Scrapping its weekly-sales approach, Sears adopted an *everyday low-price* strategy. Sears closed all of its 824 stores for 42 hours and retagged every piece of merchandise, slashing prices by as much as 50%! During the next three weeks, Sears aired its biggest-ever advertising campaign to announce: "We've lowered our prices on over 50,000 items!"

Sears expected to benefit in a number of ways. It would retain its present customers and attract some old customers back; the higher volume would compensate for the reduced margins. Sears would save the high advertising, inventory, and personnel costs involved in running weekly sales.

A year later, Sears found that its everyday-low-price strategy did not seem to be working. Their volume was not building up and their margins were lower. Sears apparently did not lower its prices significantly; many shoppers reported that Sears's "low" prices were still higher than competitors. One reason was that Sears's selling and administrative expenses ran about 30% of sales, as compared with about 23% at rival K mart. In order to be successful with everyday low *prices*, Sears first had to achieve everyday low *costs*. Another problem was that Sears's customers were conditioned to "hold out" for its traditional price-off sales and still expected them. Recently, Sears has begun to run price-off sales again and it is not clear whether they will maintain the claim of everyday low prices.

Coughlan and Vilcassim believe that in a duopolistic retail market with no real differentiation, a promotional-price retailer will eventually be forced to change to everyday low prices if facing a competitor who runs everyday low prices. Both firms would be unable to make above-normal profits because of competitive price pressures. Both firms will be tempted to run occasional sales in the hope of gaining a temporary advantage.

SOURCE: See Anne T. Coughlan and Naufel J. Vilcassim, "Retail Marketing Strategies: An Investigation of Everyday Low Pricing vs. Promotional Pricing Policies," working paper, Northwestern University, Kellogg Graduate School of Management, December 1989.

- ◆ *Community Shopping Centers:* are smaller malls with typically one anchor store and between 20 and 40 smaller stores.
- ◆ *Shopping Strips:* contain a cluster of stores serving a neighborhood's normal needs for groceries, hardware, laundry, and gasoline. They serve people within a five-minute to ten-minute driving range.

In view of the tradeoff between high traffic and high rents, retailers must decide on the most advantageous locations for their outlets. They can use a variety of methods to assess locations, including traffic counts, surveys of consumer shopping habits, analysis of competitive locations, and so on.[7] Several models for site location have also been formulated.[8]

Retailers can assess a particular store's sales effectiveness by looking at four indicators:

1. Number of people passing by on an average day
2. Percentage who enter the store
3. Percentage of those entering who buy
4. Average amount spent per sale

A store that is doing poorly might be in a poorly trafficked location; or not enough passerbys drop in; or too many drop-ins browse but do not buy; or the buyers do not buy very much. Each problem can be remedied. Traffic is remedied by a better location; drop-ins are increased by better window displays and sales announcements; and the number buying and the amount purchased are largely a function of merchandise quality, prices, and salesmanship.

Trends in Retailing

At this point, we can summarize the main developments that retailers need to take into account as they plan their competitive strategies:

1. *New Retail Forms:* New retail forms constantly emerge to threaten established retail forms. A New York bank will deliver money to its important customers' offices or homes. Adelphi College offers "commuter train classroom education" in which businesspeople commuting between Long Island and Manhattan can earn credits toward an M.B.A. degree. American Bakeries started Hippopotamus Food Stores to allow customers to buy institutional-size packages at savings of 10 to 30%.

2. *Shortening Retail Life Cycles:* New retail forms are facing a shortening life span.

3. *Nonstore Retailing:* Over the past decade, mail-order sales increased at twice the rate of in-store sales. The electronic age has significantly increased the growth for nonstore retailing. Consumers receive sales offers over their televisions, computers, and telephones to which they can immediately respond by calling a toll-free number.

4. *Increasing Intertype Competition:* Competition today is increasingly intertype, or between different types of outlets. Thus we see competition between store and nonstore retailers. Discount stores, catalog showrooms, and department stores all compete for the same consumers.

5. *Polarity of Retailing:* Increasing intertype competition has produced retailers positioning themselves on extreme ends of the number of product lines carried. High profitability and growth have been achieved by mass merchandisers like K mart and specialty stores like Radio Shack and Toys "Я" Us.

6. *Giant Retailers:* Superpower retailers are emerging who through their superior information systems and buying power are able to offer strong price savings to consumers, while causing havoc among their suppliers and rival retailers (see Companies and Industries 21-3).

7. *Changing Definition of One-Stop Shopping:* Specialty stores in malls are becoming increasingly competitive with large department stores in offering one-stop shopping. Customers park once and have a variety of specialty shops available.

8. *Growth of Vertical Marketing Systems:* Marketing channels are increasingly becoming professionally managed and programmed. As large corporations extend their control over marketing channels, independent small stores are being squeezed out.

9. *Portfolio Approach:* Retail organizations are increasingly designing and launching new store formats targeted to different lifestyle groups. They are not sticking to one format, such as department stores, but are moving into a mix of businesses that appears promising.

CHAPTER 21
Managing Retailing,
Wholesaling, and
Physical-Distribution
Systems

575

Superpower Retailers Are Riding High

Retailers such as Wal-Mart, K mart, Toys "Я" Us, Circuit City Stores, Target Stores, Home Depot, and Costco are striking terror in the hearts of their competitors and in their manufacturer-suppliers as well. Why? Because these superpower retailers are using sophisticated marketing information and logistical systems to deliver good service and immense volumes of product at appealing prices to masses of consumers. They are crowding out smaller manufacturers and retailers in the process. Whereas total retailing is growing at about 5.25% annually, the sales of superpower retailers are growing at rates between 15% and 47%.

These superpower retailers believe they are in a better position than manufacturers to determine what customers want. They are beginning to tell even the most powerful manufacturers what to make, in what sizes, colors, and packaging, how to price and promote the goods, when and how to ship them, and even how to reorganize and improve their production and management.

These manufacturers have little choice but to agree. Otherwise they will cut themselves out of a possible 10% to 30% of the market. They know that their competitors are eagerly waiting in the wings to replace them. So they have to accept a much thinner profit margin for the sake of moving massive volumes through these retailers.

And they have to accept many other demands from these powerful retailers. Costco—a warehouse club giant—demands special package sizes from its suppliers. Home Depot—a giant home improvement chain—requires lumber companies to place bar-code stickers on every piece of wood. Toys "Я" Us—the nation's largest toy retailer—gets exclusives such as a Barbie for President doll from Mattel. In addition, giant retailers will fine manufacturers for defective goods and late deliveries. They also will demand special discounts for new store openings and other occasions.

All of this is revolutionizing the retail scene for large manufacturers, small manufacturers, other retailers, and consumers. Large manufacturers are working more closely with these retailers to meet their needs. P&G now has a special liaison team of 20 employees working with Wal-Mart. In developing a new line of power tools, Black & Decker solicited Home Depot's advice on the name, color, and warranty to be sure that Home Depot found the line acceptable. Borden decided to collapse its eight sales organizations into one after Wal-Mart complained about having to deal with 28 different Borden people in ordering from Borden.

10. *Growing Importance of Retail Technology:* Retail technologies are becoming critically important as competitive tools. Progressive retailers are using computers to produce better forecasts, control inventory costs, order electronically from suppliers, send electronic mail between stores, and even sell to customers within stores. They are adopting checkout scanning systems, electronic funds transfer, in-store television, and improved merchandise-handling systems.

11. *Global Expansion of Major Retailers:* Retailers with unique formats and strong brand positioning are increasingly moving into other countries (see Global Marketing 21-1 on pp. 578–79).[9]

Wholesaling

Nature and Importance of Wholesaling

Wholesaling includes *all activities involved in selling goods or services to those who buy for resale or business use.* It excludes manufacturers and farmers because they are engaged primarily in production, and it excludes retailers.

Small manufacturers, on the other hand, are shrinking in number as a consequence of giant retailism. The giant retailers prefer to deal with fewer suppliers and prefer the larger ones. Small retailers don't have the budgets to meet demands for customized products and packages, to invest in electronic linkups, to make frequent delivery, or to advertise heavily their brand names. Those small manufacturers who do get into Wal-Marts and K marts make it big but find that they continuously have to expand their investment and quality and drop their prices. So much of their business is dedicated to one retailer that they are extremely vulnerable. For example, Murray Becker Industries, which supplied 80% of its framed pictures to K mart, is now suing K mart for $2 million in damages on the grounds they were wrongfully terminated.

Powerful retailers are forcing smaller retailers out of business. This is especially happening with "category killers," retailers who concentrate on a single product category—Toys "Я" Us (toys), Home Depot (home improvement), Circuit City Stores (electronics), Office Depot (business supplies). They avoid large shopping centers and locate instead in accessible but less expensive facilities, offering low prices and wide selections. They end up grabbing a lion's share of retailing in the specific product category and force a reduction in the number of manufacturers. As a result of Toys "Я" Us controlling 20% of toy retailing, today six toy manufacturers dominate the industry where ten years ago no toy manufacturer controlled more than 5%.

Does anyone benefit besides the giant retailers? The consumers, of course. The giant retailers' relentless drive for efficiency leads to savings passed on to consumers in the form of lower prices or better service. For example, Wal-Mart's operating and selling expenses are 15% compared to 28% for Sears. At the same time, while consumers are benefitting today, they eventually can be hurt in two ways. The closing down of smaller manufacturers may reduce innovation and product variety. And as the giants dominate their respective industries, they may lose some efficiency and raise their prices. But even here, there may be limits to the giant retailers' ability to raise prices. Although Toys "Я" Us managed to put its largest rival, Child World, out of business last year, it now faces increased competition from Wal-Mart, K mart, and Target Stores that have decided to increase their toy business, forcing Toys "Я" Us to keep the lid on its prices.

SOURCE: "Clout! More and More, Retail Giants Rule the Marketplace," *Business Week,* December 21, 1992, pp. 66–73.

Wholesalers (also called *distributors*) differ from retailers in a number of ways. First, wholesalers pay less attention to promotion, atmosphere, and location because they are dealing with business customers rather than final consumers. Second, wholesale transactions are usually larger than retail transactions, and wholesalers usually cover a larger trade area than retailers. Third, the government deals with wholesalers and retailers differently in regard to legal regulations and taxes.

Why are wholesalers used at all? Manufacturers could bypass them and sell directly to retailers or final consumers. The answer lies in several efficiencies that wholesalers bring about. First, small manufacturers with limited financial resources cannot afford to develop direct-selling organizations. Second, even manufacturers with sufficient capital might prefer to use their funds to expand production rather than carry out wholesaling activities. Third, wholesalers are likely to be more efficient at wholesaling because of their scale of operation, their wider number of customer contacts, and their specialized skills. Fourth, retailers who carry many lines often prefer to buy assortments from a wholesaler rather than buy directly from each manufacturer.

CHAPTER 21
Managing Retailing,
Wholesaling, and
Physical-Distribution
Systems

577

Global Marketing 21-1

Three Outstanding European Global Retailers: Benetton, Ikea, and Marks & Spencer

Over the years, several giant American retailers—McDonald's, The Limited, Gap, Toys "Я" Us—have become globally prominent as a result of their great marketing prowess. Many European retailers also deserve citation for their brilliant marketing and management practices. Among the outstanding European retailers are Benetton, Ikea, and Marks & Spencer.

Benetton

Within a short period of 24 years, a one-store Italian apparel manufacturer managed to become one of the world's leaders in the production and retailing of high fashion casual wear, particularly knitware. Today Benetton operates more than 5,000 franchised clothing outlets in over 80 countries. About 80% of its manufacturing is subcontracted to regional factories on four continents.

Benetton's key innovation is the ability to produce what consumers want when they need it. Prior to Benetton, knit goods were made from predyed yarns, which meant that manufacturers had to guess what colors and designs would sell. Wrong guesses meant inventory gluts and large markdowns.

The company's founder, Luciano Benetton, developed a process of dyeing knit goods after production, basing the colors on incoming retail orders. Benetton's retailers are equipped with point-of-sales devices that transmit current sales information instantly by satellite to headquarters, indicating the hot selling colors and styles. This permits Benetton to conduct more accurate production planning and shipment. Benetton will ship different merchandise assortments to Benetton retailers within the same city because of differences within the local population's preferences and shopping habits. Benetton achieves a major advantage over its competition because of its ability to "micromarket" to individual retailers on a "quick-response," "just-in-time" basis. Benetton's logistical advantage results in much lower inventories and warehousing costs, and its profits are 30% higher than the U.S. apparel industry average. Benetton owes a large part of its success to its high investment in *information power.*

Benetton's explosive growth has created problems such as franchising too many stores within the same urban area, resulting in some retailers losing money. Benetton also has been criticized for its "United Colors of Benetton" advertising campaign, which confronts viewers with strong and jarring pictures capturing a priest kissing a nun, a black woman nursing a white baby, a young man dying of AIDS, and others, few of which have any direct connection with their product—sweaters. Yet this campaign, directed at highlighting mankind's burning social issues, have established the Benetton brand name worldwide.

Ikea

Ikea, the large Swedish furniture company, demonstrates that a locally developed retail format can be exported successfully to other countries. Having opened its first store outside of Scandinavia in 1973, Ikea stores now operate in 25 countries, with sales totaling over $4 billion, making it the world's largest furniture retailer.

Thus retailers and manufacturers have reasons to use wholesalers. Wholesalers are used when they are more efficient in performing one or more of the following functions:

- *Selling and Promoting:* Wholesalers provide a salesforce enabling manufacturers to reach many small-business customers at a relatively low cost. The wholesaler has more contacts and is often more trusted by the buyer than is the distant manufacturer.

- *Buying and Assortment Building:* Wholesalers are able to select items and build assortments needed by their customers, thus saving the customers considerable work.

- *Bulk Breaking:* Wholesalers achieve savings for their customers through buying in carload lots and breaking the bulk into smaller units.

Ikea's success is based on the exceptional "value message" it sends out to buyers. Shoppers enter a spacious store (about the size of three football fields) laid out with dozens of model rooms displaying everything from furniture to housewares to kitchen cabinets (about 6,000 items are stocked in the average store). Ikea's headquarters staff members design all its products with a Scandinavian esthetic. The products are manufactured in various locations under contract. The furniture consists of "knock-down" pieces which can be packaged "flat" and brought home for self-assembly to keep prices low. The pieces are typically more stylish than those found in cheap furniture outlets.

Ikea stores are "user friendly." In addition to the showroom space, they feature supervised children's playrooms and a self-service restaurant with good food at low prices. Instead of just appealing to low-income families, the stores attract a large contingent of middle-class shoppers looking for value.

Ikea entered Britain in 1987 and now operates five British outlets with sales per square foot at more than 2.5 times the industry average. It entered the U.S. market in 1985 in suburban Philadelphia where, in the first week, 150,000 people bought more than $1 million worth of furniture. It now has seven stores in the United States and plans eventually to open 60 stores.

Ikea offers a vivid example of a "category killer," namely a giant retailer threatening to destroy the competition by specializing in a single product category and offering high product quality and service at a remarkably low price.

Marks & Spencer

The great British retailer, Marks & Spencer (M&S), started out as a penny bazaar in 1884, grew into a chain of variety stores, and today operates over 300 specialty department stores found throughout Britain and with branches on the Continent. M&S carries primarily apparel, household textiles, and foods in its stores. Its early social mission was to make available well-designed, high-quality clothing to working-class people at affordable prices. It has successfully branded its clothing under its famous St. Michael label. After World War II, M&S added food to its line with the same formula of offering high-quality food at an affordable price. Today shoppers will find some of the best food available in Britain in M&S's food department, including many specially developed versions of fruits, vegetables, and poultry products that have been grown for freshness and consistency.

M&S's success is the result of several strengths. It applies a thoroughgoing customer orientation in conducting its operations, using customers' definitions of quality, service, and value. It selects its suppliers carefully and assists them in developing efficient production and quality-control techniques. It simplifies its operating procedures and fosters good human relations with its employees. All of these contribute to M&S's ability to offer quality, service, and value while keeping its costs among the lowest in the industry.

For further reading, see "Benetton Learns to Darn," *Forbes*, October 3, 1988, pp. 122–26; and "Benetton Strips Back Down to Sportswear," *Business Week*, March 5, 1990, p. 42.

- ◆ *Warehousing:* Wholesalers hold inventories, thereby reducing the inventory costs and risks to suppliers and customers.
- ◆ *Transportation:* Wholesalers provide quicker delivery to buyers because they are closer than the manufacturer.
- ◆ *Financing:* Wholesalers finance their customers by granting credit, and they finance their suppliers by ordering early and paying their bills on time.
- ◆ *Risk Bearing:* Wholesalers absorb some risk by taking title and bearing the cost of theft, damage, spoilage, and obsolescence.
- ◆ *Market Information:* Wholesalers supply information to their suppliers and customers regarding competitors' activities, new products, price development, and so on.

CHAPTER 21
Managing Retailing,
Wholesaling, and
Physical-Distribution
Systems

579

◆ *Management Services and Counseling:* Wholesalers often help retailers improve their operations by training their sales clerks, helping with stores' layouts and displays, and setting up accounting and inventory-control systems. They may help their industrial customers by offering training and technical services.

Growth and Types of Wholesaling

Wholesaling has grown in the U.S. at a compound growth rate of 5.8% over the past ten years.[10] A number of factors have contributed to wholesaling's growth: the growth of larger factories located some distance from the principal buyers; the growth of production in advance of orders rather than in response to specific orders; an increase in the number of levels of intermediate producers and users; and the increasing need for adapting products to the needs of intermediate and final users in terms of quantities, packages, and forms.

Wholesalers fall into four groups: *merchant wholesalers, brokers and agents, manufacturers' and retailers' branches and offices,* and *miscellaneous wholesalers* (see Marketing Environment and Trends 21-4).

Wholesaler Marketing Decisions

Wholesaler-distributors have experienced mounting competitive pressures in recent years. They have faced new sources of competition, demanding customers, new technologies, and more direct-buying programs by large industrial, institutional, and retail buyers. As a result, they have had to develop appropriate strategic responses. One major drive has been to increase asset productivity by managing better their inventories and receivables. And they have had to improve their strategic decisions on target markets, product assortment and services, pricing, promotion, and place.

TARGET-MARKET DECISION ❖ Wholesalers need to define their target markets and not try to serve everyone. They can choose a target group of customers according to size criteria (e.g., only large retailers), type of customer (e.g., convenience food stores only), need for service (e.g., customers who need credit), or other criteria. Within the target group, they can identify the more profitable customers and design stronger offers and build better relationships with them. They can propose automatic reordering systems, set up management-training and advisory systems, and even sponsor a voluntary chain. They can discourage less profitable customers by requiring larger orders or adding surcharges to smaller ones.

PRODUCT-ASSORTMENT-AND-SERVICES DECISION ❖ The wholesalers' "product" is their assortment. Wholesalers are under great pressure to carry a full line and maintain sufficient stock for immediate delivery. But this can kill profits. Wholesalers today are reexamining how many lines to carry and are choosing to carry only the more profitable ones. They are grouping their items on an ABC basis, with A standing for the most-profitable items and C for the least profitable. Inventory-carrying levels are varied for the three groups. Wholesalers are also examining which services count most in building strong customer relationships and which ones should be dropped or charged for. The key is to find a distinct mix of services valued by their customers.

PRICING DECISION ❖ Wholesalers usually mark up the cost of goods by a conventional percentage, say 20%, to cover their expenses. Expenses may run 17%

Major Wholesaler Types

Merchant Wholesalers

Merchant wholesalers are independently owned businesses that take title to the merchandise they handle. In different trades they are called jobbers, distributors, or mill supply houses. Merchant wholesalers can be subclassified into full-service wholesalers and limited-service wholesalers.

FULL-SERVICE WHOLESALERS ❖ Full-service wholesalers provide such services as carrying stock, maintaining a salesforce, offering credit, making deliveries, and providing management assistance. They include two types: wholesale merchants and industrial distributors.

Wholesale Merchants. Wholesale merchants sell primarily to retailers and provide a full range of services. *General-merchandise wholesalers* carry several merchandise lines, while *general-line wholesalers* carry one or two lines in greater depth. *Specialty wholesalers* specialize in carrying only part of a line. (Examples are health-food wholesalers, seafood wholesalers, and so on.)

Industrial Distributors. Industrial distributors are merchant wholesalers who sell to manufacturers rather than to retailers. They provide several services, such as carrying stock, offering credit, and providing delivery. They may carry a broad range of merchandise, a general line, or a specialty line. Industrial distributors may concentrate on such lines as MRO items (maintenance, repair, and operating supplies), OEM items (original-equipment supplies such as ball bearings, motors), or equipment (such as hand and power tools, fork trucks).

LIMITED-SERVICE WHOLESALERS ❖ Limited-service wholesalers offer fewer services to their suppliers and customers. There are several types.

Cash-and-Carry Wholesalers. Cash-and-carry wholesalers have a limited line of fast-moving goods and sell to small retailers for cash and normally do not deliver.

Truck Wholesalers. Truck wholesalers perform a selling and delivery function primarily. They carry a limited line of semiperishable merchandise (such as milk, bread, snack foods), which they sell for cash as they make their rounds of supermarkets, small groceries, hospitals, restaurants, factory cafeterias, and hotels.

Drop Shippers. Drop shippers operate in bulk industries, such as coal, lumber, and heavy equipment. They do not carry inventory or handle the product. Upon receiving an order, they select a manufacturer, who ships the merchandise directly to the customer on the agreed terms and time of delivery. The drop shipper assumes title and risk from the time the order is accepted to its delivery to the customer.

Rack Jobbers. Rack jobbers serve grocery and drug retailers, mostly in the area of nonfood items. They send delivery trucks to stores, and the delivery person sets up toys, paperbacks, hardware items, health and beauty aids, and so on. They price the goods, keep them fresh, set up point-of-purchase displays, and keep inventory records. Rack jobbers sell on consignment, which means that they retain title to the goods and bill the retailers only for the goods sold to consumers. Thus they provide such services as delivery, shelving, inventory carrying, and financing. They do little promotion because they carry many branded items that are highly advertised.

Producers' Cooperatives. Producers' cooperatives are owned by farmer members and assemble farm produce to sell in local markets. Their profits are distributed to members at the end of the year. They often attempt to improve product quality and promote a co-op brand name, such as Sun Maid raisins, Sunkist oranges, or Diamond walnuts.

Mail-Order Wholesalers. Mail-order wholesalers send catalogs to retail, industrial, and institutional customers featuring jewelry, cosmetics, specialty foods, and other small items. Their main customers are businesses in small outlying areas. No salesforce is maintained to call on customers. The orders are filled and sent by mail, truck, or other efficient means of transportation.

Brokers and Agents

Brokers and agents differ from merchant wholesalers. They do not take title to goods, and they perform only a few functions. Their main function is to facilitate buying and selling, and for this they will earn a commission of anywhere from 2 to 6% of the selling price. They generally specialize by product line or customer types.

BROKERS ❖ The chief function of a broker is to bring buyers and sellers together and assist in negotiation. They are paid by the party who hired them. They do not carry inventory, get involved in financing, or assume risk. The most familiar examples are food brokers, real-estate brokers, insurance brokers, and security brokers.

AGENTS ❖ Agents represent either buyers or sellers on a more permanent basis. There are several types.

Manufacturers' Agents. Manufacturers' agents represent two or more manufacturers of complementary lines. They enter into a formal written agreement with each manufacturer covering pricing policy, territories, order-handling procedure, delivery service and warranties, and commission rates. They know each manufacturer's product line and use their wide contacts to sell the manufacturer's products. Manufacturers' agents are used in such lines as apparel, furniture, and electrical goods. Most manufacturers' agents are small businesses, with only a few employees, who are skilled salespeople. They are hired by small manufacturers who cannot afford to maintain their own field salesforces and by large manufacturers who want to use agents to open new territories or to represent them in territories that cannot support full-time salespeople.

Selling Agents. Selling agents are given contractual authority to sell a manufacturer's entire output. The manufacturer either is not interested in the selling function or feels unqualified. The selling agent serves as a sales department and has significant influence over prices, terms, and conditions of sale. The selling agent normally has no territorial limits. Selling agents are found in such product areas as textiles, industrial machinery and equipment, coal and coke, chemicals, and metals.

Purchasing Agents. Purchasing agents generally have a long-term relationship with buyers and make purchases for them, often receiving, inspecting, warehousing, and shipping the merchandise to the buyers. One type consists of *resident buyers* in major apparel markets, who look for suitable lines of apparel that can be carried by small retailers located in small cities. They are knowl-edgeable and provide helpful market information to clients as well as obtaining the best goods and prices available.

Commission Merchants. Commission merchants (or houses) are agents who take physical possession of products and negotiate sales. Normally, they are not employed on a long-term basis. They are used most often in agricultural marketing by farmers who do not want to sell their own output and do not belong to producers' cooperatives. A commission merchant would take a truckload of commodities to a central market, sell it for the best price, deduct a commission and expenses, and remit the balance to the producer.

Manufacturers' and Retailers' Branches and Offices

The third major type of wholesaling consists of wholesaling operations conducted by sellers or buyers themselves rather than through independent wholesalers. There are two types.

SALES BRANCHES AND OFFICES ❖ Manufacturers often set up their own sales branches and offices to improve inventory control, selling, and promotion. *Sales branches* carry inventory and are found in such industries as lumber and automotive equipment and parts. *Sales offices* do not carry inventory and are most prominent in dry-goods and notions industries.

PURCHASING OFFICES ❖ Many retailers set up purchasing offices in major market centers such as New York and Chicago. These purchasing offices perform a role similar to that of brokers or agents but are part of the buyer's organization.

Miscellaneous Wholesalers

A few specialized types of wholesalers are found in certain sectors of the economy, such as agricultural assemblers, petroleum bulk plants and terminals, and auction companies.

of the gross margin, leaving a profit margin of approximately 3%. In grocery wholesaling, the average profit margin is often less than 2%. Wholesalers are beginning to experiment with new approaches to pricing. They might cut their margin on some lines in order to win important new customers. They will ask suppliers for a special price break when they can turn it into an opportunity to increase the supplier's sales.

PROMOTION DECISION ❖ Wholesalers rely primarily on their salesforce to achieve promotional objectives. Even here, most wholesalers see selling as a single salesperson talking to a single customer instead of a team effort to sell, build, and service major accounts. As for nonpersonal promotion, wholesalers would benefit from adopting some of the image-making techniques used by retailers. They need to develop an overall promotion strategy involving trade advertising, sales promotion, and publicity. They also need to make greater use of supplier promotion materials and programs.

PLACE DECISION ❖ Wholesalers typically locate in low-rent, low-tax areas and put little money into their physical setting and offices. Often the materials-handling systems and order-processing systems lag behind the available technologies. To meet rising costs, progressive wholesalers have been making time and motion studies of materials-handling procedures. The ultimate development is the *automated warehouse*. Orders are fed into a computer and items are picked up by mechanical devices and conveyed on a belt to the shipping platform, where they are assembled. Most wholesalers now use computers to carry out accounting, billing, inventory control, and forecasting. For example, Grainger, a major distributor, developed a local inventory-inquiry system to connect its 188 distribution branches. A Grainger branch can quickly locate whether items not in stock are available in another branch. This has greatly reduced customer-response time and has boosted customer sales.

Trends in Wholesaling

Manufacturers always have the option of bypassing wholesalers or of replacing inefficient wholesalers with better ones. Manufacturers' major complaints against wholesalers are as follows: They do not aggressively promote the manufacturer's product line, acting more like order takers; they do not carry enough inventory and therefore fail to fill customers' orders fast enough; they do not supply the manufacturer with up-to-date market and competitive information; they do not attract high-caliber managers and bring down their own costs; and they charge too much for their services.

Progressive wholesaler-distributors, on the other hand, are those who adapt their services to meet the changing needs of their suppliers and target customers. They recognize that the rationale for their existence comes from adding value to the channel. They are constantly improving their services and/or reducing their costs. (See Marketing Strategies 21-3 for core strategies used by high-performance wholesaler-distributors.)

Narus and Anderson interviewed leading industrial distributors and identified four ways they strengthened their relationships with manufacturers:

1. They sought a clear agreement with their manufacturers about their expected functions in the marketing channel.
2. They gained insight into the manufacturers' requirements by visiting their plants and attending manufacturer association conventions and trade shows.
3. They fulfilled their commitments to the manufacturer by meeting the volume targets, promptly paying their bills, and feeding back customer information to their manufacturers.
4. They identified and offered value-added services to help their suppliers.[11]

CHAPTER 21
Managing Retailing,
Wholesaling, and
Physical-Distribution
Systems

583

Strategies of High-Performance Wholesaler-Distributors

McCammon, Lusch, and their colleagues studied 97 high-performance wholesaler-distributors to uncover their core strategies for gaining a sustained competitive advantage. The study identified the following 12 core strategies that were transforming the structure of distribution.

1. *Mergers and Acquisitions:* At least a third of the sampled wholesalers made new acquisitions which were aimed at entering new markets, at strengthening their position in existing markets, and/or at diversifying or vertically integrating.

2. *Asset Redeployment:* At least 20 of the 97 wholesalers sold or liquidated one or more marginal operations in order to strengthen their core businesses.

3. *Corporate Diversification:* Several wholesalers diversified their portfolio of businesses in order to reduce their firm's cyclical exposure.

4. *Forward and Backward Integration:* Several wholesalers increased their vertical integration in order to improve their margins.

5. *Proprietary Brands:* A third of the companies increased their proprietary-brand programs.

6. *Expansion into International Markets:* At least 26 wholesalers operated on a multinational basis and planned to increase their penetration into Western Europe and East Asia.

7. *Value-Added Services:* Most wholesalers increased their value-added services including "red flag" delivery service, customized packaging operations, and computerized management information systems. McKesson, the large drug wholesaler, established direct computer links with 32 drug manufacturers, a computerized accounts-receivable program for pharmacists, and computer terminals for drugstores for ordering inventories.

8. *Systems Selling:* More wholesalers offered turnkey merchandising programs to their buyers, posing a threat to those wholesalers who remained off-the-shelf suppliers.

9. *New Game Strategies:* Some wholesalers spotted new customer groups and created new turnkey merchandising programs for them.

10. *Niche Marketing:* Some wholesalers have specialized in one or few product categories, carrying extensive inventories, and in high service and rapid delivery, to satisfy special markets neglected by larger competitors.

11. *Multiplex Marketing:* Multiplex marketing occurs when firms manage to simultaneously serve multiple market segments in a cost-effective and competitively superior way. Several wholesalers have added new market segments to their core segments, hoping to achieve larger economies of scale and competitive strength. Thus membership warehouse clubs, in addition to wholesaling to small and medium-size business customers, obtain additional sales from consumers. Some drug wholesalers, in addition to serving hospitals, have created programs for doctor clinics, ethical pharmacies, and health maintenance organizations.

12. *New Technologies of Distribution:* High-performance wholesalers have improved their systems for computerized order entry, inventory control, and warehouse automation. In addition, they are making increased use of direct-response marketing and telemarketing.

SOURCE: See Bert McCammon, Robert F. Lusch, Deborah S. Coykendall, and James M. Kenderdine, *Wholesaling in Transition* (Norman: University of Oklahoma, College of Business Administration, 1989).

A recent Arthur Andersen & Company study concluded that wholesale-distributors will need to undergo "aggressive restructuring" in the 1990s:

Competitive pressures will keep sales prices in check, resulting in stable or, in many instances, shrinking gross margins. Consolidation will reduce significantly the number of firms in the industry, while the remaining larger firms will use new technology-driven services to increase market share and technology-driven operating techniques to improve productivity. Wholesaler-distributors will need new sources of capital to fund these investments in technology and market expansion. The challenge for companies in the industry will be to generate and balance the investment needed to capture growth in a maturing market with those needed to improve value-added services.[12]

Physical Distribution

Producers of physical products and services must decide on the best way to store and move their goods and services to their market destinations. They typically need to engage the services of physical-distribution firms—warehouses and transportation companies—to assist in this task. Producers know that their physical-distribution effectiveness will have a major impact on customer satisfaction and company costs. A poor distribution system can destroy an otherwise good product.[13]

Here we will examine the nature, objectives, systems, and organizational aspects of physical distribution (also called *market logistics*).

Nature of Physical Distribution

Physical distribution *involves planning, implementing, and controlling the physical flows of materials and final goods from points of origin to points of use to meet customer requirements at a profit.* The aim of physical distribution is to manage *supply chains*, that is, value-added flows from suppliers to ultimate users, as follows:

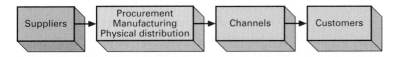

Thus, the logistical task is to coordinate the activities of suppliers, purchasing agents, marketers, channel members, and customers.

Companies manage their supply chains through information. Major gains in logistical efficiency have resulted from information technology advances, particularly computers, point-of-sale terminals, uniform product codes, satellite tracking, electronic data interchange (EDI), and electronic funds transfer (EFT). These developments have made it possible for companies to make or require promises such as "the product will be at dock 25 at 10 a.m. tomorrow," and controlling this promise through information. (See Companies and Industries 21-4.)

Physical distribution involves several activities (see Figure 21-3). The first is sales forecasting, on the basis of which the company schedules production and inventory levels. The production plans indicate the materials that the purchasing department must order. These materials arrive through inbound transportation, enter the receiving area, and are stored in raw-material inventory. Raw materials are converted into finished goods. Finished-goods inventory is the link between the customers' orders and the company's manufacturing activity. Customers' orders draw down the finished-goods inventory level, and manufacturing activity builds it up. Finished goods flow off the assembly line and pass through packing, in-plant warehousing, shipping-room processing, outbound transportation, field warehousing, and customer delivery and servicing.

Management has become concerned about the total cost of physical distribution, which can amount in some cases to 30–40% of the product's cost. Considering that advertising costs less than 3% of sales, marketing executives would undoubtedly be well rewarded if they could find ways to reduce physical-distribution costs.

Wal-Mart Gains Logistical Superiority Through Information Technology Investments

One of the major keys to distribution efficiency is information. Wal-Mart was one of the first retailers to make heavy investments in information technology. It equipped its stores with computerized scanning equipment for cash registers. Thus, when a teenager bought a size 10 Reebock running shoe, this information went directly to Reebock's computer to trigger replacement or production.

This system enables Wal-Mart to know what customers are buying and therefore to tell manufacturers what to produce and where to ship the goods. Wal-Mart requires its suppliers to ship their goods tagged and hung, so that they can be moved directly into the store's selling space, thus reducing warehousing and data-processing costs. As a result, Wal-Mart stores use only 10% of their space for goods storage, compared to the 25% average nonselling space in competitor stores.

Another result of Wal-Mart's computerized ordering system is that Wal-Mart insists on linking its computers directly to its manufacturers, bypassing brokers and other middlemen, and passing on the savings to their customers.

SOURCE: See Rita Koselka, "Distribution Revolution," *Forbes,* May 25, 1992, pp. 54–62.

Lowered physical-distribution costs will permit lower prices or yield higher profit margins.

The main elements of total physical-distribution costs are transportation (37%), inventory carrying (22%), warehousing (21%), and order processing/customer service/distribution administration (20%).[14] Experts believe that substantial savings can be effected in the physical-distribution area, which has been described as "the last frontier for cost economies" and "the economy's dark continent."

Physical distribution is not only a cost; it is a potent tool in competitive marketing. Companies can attract additional customers by offering better service, faster cycle time, or lower prices through physical-distribution improvements. Companies lose customers when they fail to supply goods on time. In the summer of 1976, Kodak launched its national advertising campaign for its new instant camera before it had delivered enough cameras to the stores. Customers found that it was not available and bought Polaroids instead.

Traditional physical-distribution thinking starts with goods at the plant and tries to find low-cost solutions to get them to customers. Marketers prefer *market-logistics* thinking that starts with the marketplace and works backward to the factory. Here is an example of market-logistics thinking:

> At one time, German consumers purchased individual bottles of soft drinks. A soft-drink manufacturer decided to test a six-pack. Consumers responded positively. Retailers responded positively because the bottles could be loaded faster on the shelves, and more bottles would be purchased per occasion. The manufacturer designed the six-packs to fit on the store shelves. Then cases and pallets were designed for bringing these six-packs efficiently to the store's receiving rooms. Factory operations were redesigned to produce the new six-packs. The purchasing department let out bids for the new needed materials. Once implemented, the manufacturer's market share rose substantially.

Logistical thinking clearly not only addresses the problem of *outbound distribution* (goods moving from the factory to the customers) but also the problem of *inbound*

FIGURE 21-3 Major Activities Involved in Physical Distribution

Source: Redrawn, with modifications, from Wendell M. Stewart, "Physical Distribution: Key to Improved Volume and Profits," *Journal of Marketing*, January 1965, p. 66.

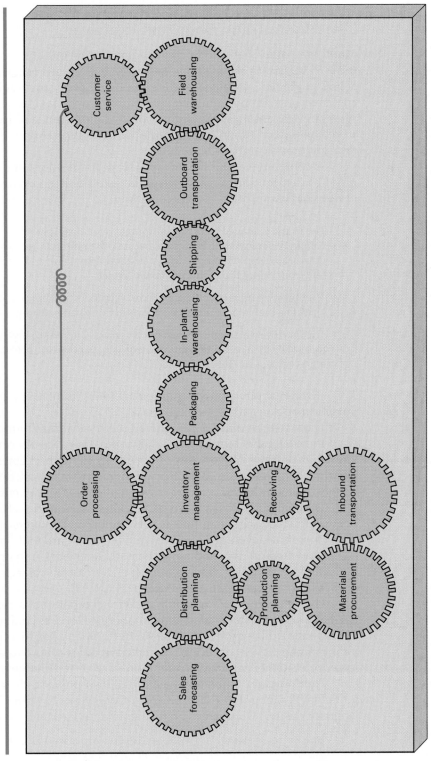

distribution (goods moving from suppliers to the factory). In leading-edge logistics firms, the logistics executives handle both inbound and outbound distribution.

The Physical-Distribution Objective

Many companies state their physical-distribution objective as *getting the right goods to the right places at the right time for the least cost*. Unfortunately, this provides little actual guidance. No physical-distribution system can simultaneously maximize customer service and minimize distribution cost. Maximum customer service implies large inventories, premium transportation, and multiple warehouses, all of which raise distribution cost. Minimum distribution cost implies cheap transportation, low stocks, and few warehouses.

A company cannot achieve physical-distribution efficiency by asking each physical-distribution manager to minimize his or her own costs. Physical-distribution costs interact, often in an inverse way:

> The traffic manager favors rail shipment over air shipment because this reduces the company's freight bill. However, because the railroads are slower, rail shipment ties up working capital longer, delays customer payment, and might cause customers to buy from competitors offering faster service.

> The shipping department uses cheap containers to minimize shipping costs. This leads to a high rate of damaged goods in transit and customer ill will.

> The inventory manager favors low inventories to reduce inventory cost. However, this policy increases stockouts, back orders, paperwork, special production runs, and high-cost fast-freight shipments.

Given that physical-distribution activities involve strong tradeoffs, decisions must be made on a total system basis.

The starting point for designing the physical-distribution system is to study what the customers require and what competitors are offering. Customers are interested in on-time delivery, supplier willingness to meet emergency needs, careful handling of merchandise, supplier willingness to take back defective goods and resupply them quickly, and supplier willingness to carry inventory for the customer.

The company has to research the relative importance of these service outputs. For example, service-repair time is very important to buyers of copying equipment. Xerox therefore developed a service-delivery standard that "can put a disabled machine anywhere in the continental United States back into operation within three hours after receiving the service request." Xerox runs a service division consisting of 12,000 service and parts personnel.

The company must take into account competitors' service standards. It will normally want to offer at least the same service level as competitors. But the objective is to maximize profits, not sales. The company has to look at the costs of providing higher levels of service. Some companies offer less service and charge a lower price. Other companies offer more service and charge a premium price.

The company ultimately has to establish physical-distribution objectives to guide its planning. For example, Coca-Cola wants to "put Coke within an arm's length of desire." Companies go further and define standards for each service factor.

> One appliance manufacturer has established the following service standards: to deliver at least 95% of the dealer's orders within seven days of order receipt, to fill the dealer's orders with 99% accuracy, to answer dealer inquiries on order status within three hours, and to ensure that damage to merchandise in transit does not exceed 1%.

Given the physical-distribution objectives, the company must design a physical-distribution system that will minimize the cost of achieving these objectives. Each possible physical-distribution system will lead to the following cost:

$$D = T + FW + VW + S \qquad (21\text{-}1)$$

where:

D = total distribution cost of proposed system
T = total freight cost of proposed system
FW = total fixed warehouse cost of proposed system
VW = total variable warehouse costs (including inventory) of proposed system
S = total cost of lost sales due to average delivery delay under proposed system

Choosing a physical-distribution system calls for examining the total distribution cost associated with different proposed systems and selecting the system that minimizes total distribution cost. Alternatively, if it is hard to measure S in (21-1), the company should aim to minimize the distribution cost $T + FW + VW$ of reaching a *target level of customer service*.

We will now examine four major decision issues: (1) How should orders be handled? (*order processing*); (2) Where should stocks be located? (*warehousing*); (3) How much stock should be held? (*inventory*); and (4) How should goods be shipped? (*transportation*).

Order Processing

Physical distribution begins with a customer order. A key need in companies today is to shorten the *order-to-remittance cycle*, that is, the elapsed time between an order placement and payment. This cycle involves many steps, including transmission of the order by the salesperson, order entry and customer credit check, inventory and production scheduling, order and invoice shipment, and receipt of payment. The longer this cycle takes, the lower the customer's satisfaction and the company's profits.

Companies are making great progress in speeding up order handling, thanks to computers. General Electric operates a computer-oriented system that upon receipt of a customer's order, checks the customer's credit standing and whether and where the items are in stock. The computer issues an order to ship, bills the customer, updates the inventory records, sends a production order for new stock, and relays the message back to the sales representative that the customer's order is on its way—all in less than 15 seconds.

Warehousing

Every company has to store its finished goods until they are sold. A storage function is necessary because production and consumption cycles rarely match. Many agricultural commodities are produced seasonally, whereas demand is continuous. The storage function overcomes discrepancies in desired quantities and timing.

The company must decide on a desirable number of stocking locations. More stocking locations means that goods can be delivered to customers more quickly. Warehousing costs go up, however. The number of stocking locations must strike a balance between customer-service levels and distribution costs.

Some inventory is kept at or near the plant, and the rest is located in warehouses around the country. The company might own *private warehouses* and rent space in *public warehouses*. Companies have more control in owned warehouses, but they tie up their capital and face some inflexibility if desirable locations change. Public warehouses, on the other hand, charge for the rented space and provide ad-

CHAPTER 21
Managing Retailing,
Wholesaling, and
Physical-Distribution
Systems

589

ditional services (at a cost) for inspecting goods, packaging them, shipping them, and invoicing them. In using public warehouses, companies have a broad choice of locations and warehouse types, including those specializing in cold storage, commodities only, and so on.

Companies use storage warehouses and distribution warehouses. *Storage warehouses* store goods for moderate-to-long periods of time. *Distribution warehouses* receive goods from various company plants and suppliers and move them out as soon as possible. For example, Wal-Mart Stores, Inc. operates four distribution centers. One center covers 400,000 square feet on a 93-acre site. The shipping department loads 50 to 60 trucks daily, delivering merchandise on a twice-weekly basis to its retail outlets. This is less expensive than supplying each retail outlet from each plant directly.

The older multistoried warehouses with slow elevators and inefficient materials-handling procedures are receiving competition from newer single-storied *automated warehouses* with advanced materials-handling systems under the control of a central computer. The computer reads store orders and directs lift trucks and electric hoists to gather goods according to their bar codes, move them to loading docks, and issue invoices. These warehouses have reduced worker injuries, labor costs, pilferage, and breakage, and have improved inventory control. When the Helene Curtis Company replaced its six antiquated warehouses with a new $32 million facility, it managed to cut its distribution costs by 40%.[15]

Inventory

Inventory levels represent a major physical-distribution decision affecting customer satisfaction. Salespeople would like their companies to carry enough stock to fill all customer orders immediately. However, it is not cost effective for a company to carry this much inventory. *Inventory cost increases at an increasing rate as the customer-service level approaches 100%.* Management would need to know by how much sales and profits would increase as a result of carrying larger inventories and promising faster order-fulfillment times.

Inventory decision making involves knowing when to order and how much to order. As inventory draws down, management must know at what stock level to place a new order. This stock level is called the *order (or reorder) point*. An order point of 20 means reordering when the stock falls to 20 units. The order point should be higher, the higher the order lead time, the usage rate, and the service standard. If the order lead time and customer-usage rate are variable, the order point should be set higher to provide a *safety stock*. The final order point should balance the risks of stockout against the costs of overstock.

The other decision is how much to order. The larger the quantity ordered, the less frequently an order has to be placed. The company needs to balance order-processing costs and inventory-carrying costs. Order-processing costs for a manufacturer consist of *setup costs* and *running costs* for the item. If setup costs are low, the manufacturer can produce the item often, and the cost per item is quite constant and equal to the running costs. If setup costs are high, however, the manufacturer can reduce the average cost per unit by producing a long run and carrying more inventory.

Order-processing costs must be compared with inventory-carrying costs. The larger the average stock carried, the higher the inventory-carrying costs. These carrying costs include storage charges, cost of capital, taxes and insurance, and depreciation and obsolescence. Inventory-carrying costs might run as high as 30% of inventory value. This means that marketing managers who want their companies to carry larger inventories need to show that the larger inventories would produce incremental gross profit that would exceed incremental inventory-carrying costs.

The optimal order quantity can be determined by observing how order-processing costs and inventory-carrying costs sum up at different order levels. Figure 21-4 shows that the order-processing cost per unit decreases with the number of units ordered because the order costs are spread over more units. Inventory-carrying charges per unit increase with the number of units ordered because each unit remains longer in inventory. The two cost curves are summed vertically into a total-cost curve. The lowest point on the total-cost curve is projected down on the horizontal axis to find the optimal order quantity Q^*.[16]

The growing interest in *just-in-time production methods* promises to change inventory-planning practices. Just-in-time production consists of arranging for supplies to come into the factory at the rate that they are needed. If the suppliers are dependable, then the manufacturer can carry much lower levels of inventory and still meet customer-order-fulfillment standards.

More companies are attempting to move from an *anticipatory-based supply chain* to a *response-based supply chain*.[17] The former involves the company producing the amount called for by a sales forecast. The company builds and holds stock at various supply points such as the plant, distribution centers, and retail outlets. Each supply point reorders automatically when their order point is reached. When sales are slower than anticipated, the company tries to draw down its inventories by sponsoring deals and promotions. An example of this system is the American auto industry which produces cars far in advance of demand and these cars often sit for months in inventory until the companies undertake aggressive promotion.

A response-based supply chain is customer-triggered in that there is continuous production and replacement of stock as orders arrive. The company produces what is currently selling. For example, Japanese car makers take orders for cars and produce and ship them within four days. Some manufacturers of large appliances, such as Whirlpool and GE, are moving to this system. Benetton, the Italian fashion house, works on a *quick-response system*, dyeing its sweaters in the colors that are currently selling instead of attempting to guess long in advance which colors people will want. Producing for order rather than for forecast substantially cuts down inventory costs and risks.

Transportation

Marketers need to be concerned with their company's transportation decisions. Transportation choices will affect product pricing, on-time delivery performance,

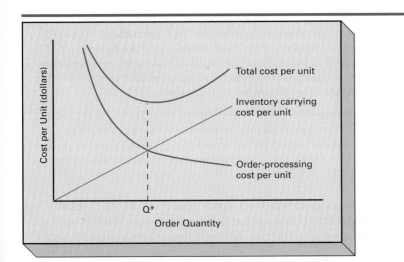

FIGURE 21-4
Determining Optimal Order Quantity

and the condition of the goods when they arrive, all of which will affect customer satisfaction.

In shipping goods to its warehouses, dealers, and customers, the company can choose among five transportation modes: rail, air, trucks, waterways, and pipelines. Shippers consider such criteria as *speed, frequency, dependability, capability, availability,* and *cost*. If a shipper seeks speed, air and truck are the prime contenders. If the goal is low cost, then water and pipeline are the prime contenders. Trucks stand high on most of the criteria, and that accounts for their growing share.

Shippers are increasingly combining two or more transportation modes, thanks to containerization. *Containerization* consists of putting the goods in boxes or trailers that are easy to transfer between two transportation modes. *Piggyback* describes the use of rail and trucks; *fishyback*, water and trucks; *trainship*, water and rail; and *airtruck*, air and trucks. Each coordinated mode of transportation offers specific advantages to the shipper. For example, piggyback is cheaper than trucking alone and yet provides flexibility and convenience.

In choosing transportation modes, shippers can decide between private, contract, and common carriers. If the shipper owns its own truck or air fleet, the shipper becomes a *private carrier*. A *contract carrier* is an independent organization selling transportation services to others on a contract basis. A *common carrier* provides services between predetermined points on a schedule basis and is available to all shippers at standard rates.

Transportation decisions must consider the complex tradeoffs between various transportation modes and their implications for other distribution elements, such as warehousing and inventory. As transportation costs change over time, companies need to reanalyze their options in the search for optimal physical-distribution arrangements.[18]

Organizational Responsibility for Physical Distribution

We see that decisions on warehousing, inventory, and transportation require the highest degree of coordination. A growing number of companies have set up a permanent committee composed of managers responsible for different physical-distribution activities. This committee meets periodically to develop policies for improving overall distribution efficiency. Some companies have appointed a vice-president of physical distribution, who reports to the marketing or manufacturing vice-president or the president. Here are two examples:

> The Burroughs Corporation organized the Distribution Services Department to centralize control over its physical-distribution activities. This department reported to the marketing vice-president because of the great importance Burroughs attached to good customer service. Within two and one-half years following the reorganization, the company achieved savings of over $2 million annually (on $200 million of sales), plus a higher level of service to field branches and customers.

> Heinz created a new department of coordinate stature with marketing and production, which was headed by a vice-president of distribution. Heinz felt that this arrangement would guarantee respect for the department, develop a greater degree of professionalism and objectivity, and avoid partisan domination by marketing or production.

The location of the physical-distribution department within the company is a secondary concern. The important thing is that the company coordinates its physical-distribution and marketing activities in order to create high customer satisfaction at a reasonable cost.

SUMMARY ❖

Retailing and wholesaling consist of many organizations involved in bringing goods and services from the point of production to the point of use.

Retailing includes all the activities involved in selling goods or services directly to final consumers for their personal, nonbusiness use. Retailers can be classified in terms of store retailers, nonstore retailing, and retail organizations.

Store retailers include many types, such as specialty stores, department stores, supermarkets, convenience stores, superstores/combination stores/hypermarkets, discount stores, warehouse stores, and catalog showrooms. These store forms have had different longevities and are at different stages of the retail life cycle. Depending on the wheel of retailing, some will go out of existence because they cannot compete on a quality, service, or price basis.

Nonstore retailing is growing more rapidly than store retailing. It includes direct marketing, direct selling (door-to-door and party selling), automatic vending, and buying services.

Much of retailing is in the hands of large retail organizations such as corporate chains, voluntary chain and retailer cooperatives, consumer cooperatives, franchise organizations, and merchandising conglomerates. More retail chains are now sponsoring diversified retailing lines and forms instead of sticking to one form, such as the department store.

Retailers, like manufacturers, must prepare marketing plans that include decisions on target markets, product assortment and services, pricing, promotion, and place. Retailers are showing strong signs of improving their professional management and their productivity, in the face of such trends as shortening retail life cycles, new retail forms, increasing intertype competition, new retail technologies, and so on.

Wholesaling includes all the activities involved in selling goods or services to those who are buying for the purpose of resale or for business use. Wholesalers help manufacturers deliver their products efficiently to the many retailers and industrial users across the nation. Wholesalers perform many functions, including selling and promoting, buying and assortment building, bulk breaking, warehousing, transporting, financing, risk bearing, supplying market information, and providing management services and counseling. Wholesalers fall into four groups: merchant wholesalers; agents and brokers; manufacturers' and retailers' branches and offices; and miscellaneous wholesalers.

Wholesalers, too, must make decisions on their target market, product assortment and services, pricing, promotion, and place. Wholesalers who fail to carry adequate assortments and inventory and provide satisfactory service are likely to be bypassed by manufacturers. Progressive wholesalers, on the other hand, are adapting marketing concepts and streamlining their costs of doing business.

The marketing concept calls for paying increased attention to physical distribution. Physical distribution is an area of potentially high cost savings and improved customer satisfaction. When order processors, warehouse planners, inventory managers, and transportation managers make decisions, they affect each other's costs and demand-creation capacity. The physical-distribution concept calls for treating all these decisions within a unified framework. The task becomes that of designing physical-distribution arrangements that minimize the total cost of providing a desired level of customer service.

CHAPTER 21
Managing Retailing,
Wholesaling, and
Physical-Distribution
Systems

593

NOTES ❖

1. William R. Davidson, Albert D. Bates, and Stephen J. Bass, "Retail Life Cycle," *Harvard Business Review* (November–December 1976), pp. 89–96.

2. Stanley C. Hollander, "The Wheel of Retailing," *Journal of Marketing,* July 1960, pp. 37–42.

3. For a fuller discussion, see Lawrence H. Wortzel, "Retailing Strategies for Today's Marketplace," *Journal of Business Strategy,* Spring 1987, pp. 45–56; Also see Roger D. Blackwell and W. Wayne Talarzyk, "Life-Style Retailing: Competitive Strategies for the 1980s," *Journal of Retailing,* Winter 1983, pp. 7–26.

4. Wortzel, *Retailing Strategies.*

5. Neil H. Borden, Jr., *Acceptance of New Food Products by Supermarkets* (Boston: Division of Research, Graduate School of Business Administration, Harvard University, 1968).

6. For more discussion, see Philip Kotler, "Atmospherics as a Marketing Tool," *Journal of Retailing,* Winter 1973–74, pp. 48–64; and Mary Jo Bitner, "Servicescapes: The Impact of Physical Surroundings on Customers and Employees," *Journal of Marketing,* April 1992, pp. 57–71.

7. R. L. Davies and D. S. Rogers, eds., *Store Location and Store Assessment Research* (New York: John Wiley, 1984).

8. David L. Huff, "Defining and Estimating a Trading Area," *Journal of Marketing,* July 1964, pp. 34–38; David A. Gautschi, "Specification of Patronage Models for Retail Center Choice," *Journal of Marketing Research,* May 1981, pp. 162–74; Sara L. McLafferty, *Location Strategies for Retail and Service Firms* (Lexington, MA: Lexington Books, 1987).

9. For further discussion of retail trends, see Eleanor G. May, C. William Ress, and Walter J. Salmon, *Future Trends in Retailing* (Cambridge, MA: Marketing Science Institute, February 1985); and Louis W. Stern and Adel I. El-Ansary, *Marketing Channels,* 4th ed. (Englewood Cliffs, NJ: Prentice Hall, 1992).

10. See Bert McCammon, Robert F. Lusch, Deborah S. Coykendall, and James M. Kenderdine, *Wholesaling in Transition* (Norman: University of Oklahoma, College of Business Administration, 1989).

11. James A. Narus and James C. Anderson, "Contributing as a Distributor to Partnerships with Manufacturers," *Business Horizons,* September–October 1987. Also see James D. Hlavecek and Tommy J. McCuistion, "Industrial Distributors—When, Who, and How," *Harvard Business Review,* March–April 1983, pp. 96–101.

12. Arthur Andersen & Co., *Facing the Forces of Change: Beyond Future Trends in Wholesale Distribution* (Washington, DC: Distribution Research and Education Foundation, 1987), p. 7. This report is an excellent source of information on the wholesaling industry.

13. See Rita Koselka, "Distribution Revolution," *Forbes,* May 25, 1992, pp. 54–62.

14. See "Know Your Distribution Costs," *Distribution,* April 1987, p. 36.

15. Koselka, "Distribution Revolution," *Forbes.*

16. The optimal order quantity is given by the formula $Q^* = 2DS/IC$ where D = annual demand, S = cost to place one order, and I = annual carrying cost per unit. Known as the economic-order quantity formula, it assumes a constant ordering cost, a constant cost of carrying an additional unit in inventory, a known demand, and no quantity discounts. For further reading on this subject, see Charles D. Mecimore, *Techniques in Inventory Management and Control* (Montvale, NJ: National Association of Accountants, 1987).

17. From an address by Professor Donald J. Bowersox at Michigan State University on August 5, 1992.

18. For a study of the characteristics of 117 leading edge logistics companies, see Donald J. Bowersox, et al., *Leading Edge Logistics Competitive Positioning for the 1990's* (Oak Brook, IL: Council of Logistics Management, 1989).

22

Designing Communication and Promotion-Mix Strategies

People no longer buy shoes to keep their feet warm and dry. They buy them because of the way the shoes make them feel — masculine, feminine, rugged, different, sophisticated, young, glamorous, "in." Buying shoes has become an emotional experience. Our business now is selling excitement rather than shoes.

FRANCIS C. ROONEY

odern marketing calls for more than developing a good product, pricing it attractively, and making it accessible to target customers. Companies must also communicate with their present and potential customers. Every company is inevitably cast into the role of communicator and promoter.

What is communicated, however, should not be left to chance. To communicate effectively, companies hire advertising agencies to develop effective ads; sales-promotion specialists to design buying-incentive programs; direct-marketing specialists to build databases and interact with customers and prospects by mail and telephone; and public-relations firms to supply product publicity and develop the corporate image. They train their salespeople to be friendly and knowledgeable. For most companies, the question is not whether to communicate but rather what to say, to whom, and how often.

A modern company manages a complex marketing communications system. The company communicates with its middlemen, consumers, and various publics. Its middlemen communicate with their consumers and various publics. Consumers engage in word-of-mouth communication with other consumers and publics. Meanwhile, each group provides communication feedback to every other group.

The marketing communications mix (also called the promotion mix) consists of five major tools:

- *Advertising:* Any paid form of nonpersonal presentation and promotion of ideas, goods, or services by an identified sponsor.
- *Direct Marketing:* Use of mail, telephone, and other nonpersonal contact tools to communicate with or solicit a response from specific customers and prospects.
- *Sales Promotion:* Short-term incentives to encourage trial or purchase of a product or service.
- *Public Relations* and *Publicity*: A variety of programs designed to promote and/or protect a company's image or its individual products.
- *Personal Selling:* Face-to-face interaction with one or more prospective purchasers for the purpose of making sales.[1]

Table 22-1 lists numerous specific tools that fall within these categories. At the same time, communication goes beyond these specific communication/promotion tools. The product's styling, its price, the package's shape and color, the salesperson's manner and dress, the place of business, the company's stationery—all communicate something to the buyers. The whole marketing mix, not just the promotional mix, must be orchestrated for maximum communication impact.

This chapter examines three major questions: How does communication work? What are the major steps in developing an effective marketing communications program? Who should be responsible for marketing communication planning? Chapter 23 deals with advertising; Chapter 24, with direct marketing, sales promotion, and public relations; and Chapter 25, with the salesforce.

TABLE 22-1 Common Communication/Promotion Tools

ADVERTISING	SALES PROMOTION	PUBLIC RELATIONS	PERSONAL SELLING	DIRECT MARKETING
Print and broadcast ads	Contests, games, sweepstakes, lotteries	Press kits	Sales presentations	Catalogs
Packaging-outer	Premiums and gifts	Speeches	Sales meetings	Mailings
Packaging inserts	Sampling	Seminars	Incentive programs	Telemarketing
Motion pictures	Fairs and trade shows	Annual reports	Samples	Electronic shopping
Brochures and booklets	Exhibits	Charitable donations	Fairs and trade shows	TV shopping
Posters and leaflets	Demonstrations	Sponsorships		
Directories	Couponing	Publications		
Reprints of ads	Rebates	Community relations		
Billboards	Low-interest financing	Lobbying		
Display signs	Entertainment	Identity media		
Point-of-purchase displays	Trade-in allowances	Company magazine		
Audiovisual material	Trading stamps	Events		
Symbols and logos	Tie-ins			

The Communication Process

Marketers need to understand how communication works. A communication model answers (1) who (2) says what (3) in what channel (4) to whom (5) with what effect. Figure 22-1 shows a communication model with nine elements. Two elements represent the major parties in a communication—*sender* and *receiver*. Two represent the major communication tools—*message* and *media*. Four represent major communication functions—*encoding*, *decoding*, *response*, and *feedback*. The last element is *noise* in the system.

The model underscores the key factors in effective communication. Senders must know what audiences they want to reach and what responses they want. They encode their messages in a way that takes into account how the target audience usually decodes messages. The sender must transmit the message through efficient media that reach the target audience. Senders must develop feedback channels so that they can know the receiver's response to the message.

For a message to be effective, the sender's encoding process must mesh with the receiver's decoding process. Messages are essentially signs that must be familiar to the receiver. The more the sender's field of experience overlaps with that of the receiver, the more effective the message is likely to be. "The source can encode, and the destination can decode, only in terms of the experience each has had."[2] This puts a burden on communicators from one social stratum (such as advertising people) who want to communicate effectively with another stratum (such as factory workers).

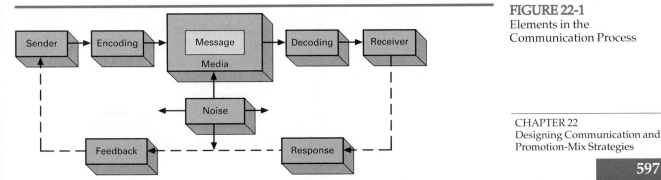

FIGURE 22-1
Elements in the Communication Process

CHAPTER 22
Designing Communication and
Promotion-Mix Strategies

The sender's task is to get his or her message through to the receiver. There is considerable noise in the environment—people are bombarded by several hundred commercial messages a day. The target audience may not receive the intended message for any of three reasons. The first is *selective attention* in that they will not notice all of the stimuli. The second is *selective distortion* in that they will twist the message to hear what they want to hear. The third is *selective recall* in that they will retain in permanent memory only a small fraction of the messages that reach them.

The communicator must design the message to win attention in spite of surrounding distractions. The likelihood that a potential receiver will attend to a message is given by[3]

$$\text{Likelihood of attention} = \frac{\text{Perceived reward strength} - \text{Perceived punishment strength}}{\text{Perceived expenditure of effort}}$$

Selective attention explains why ads with bold headlines promising something, such as "How to Make a Million," along with an arresting illustration and little copy, have a high likelihood of grabbing attention. For very little effort, the receiver might gain a great reward.

As for selective distortion, receivers have set attitudes, which lead to expectations about what they will hear or see. They will hear what fits into their belief system. As a result, receivers often add things to the message that are not there (*amplification*) and do not notice other things that are there (*leveling*). The communicator's task is to strive for message simplicity, clarity, interest, and repetition to get the main points across to the audience.

As for selective recall, the communicator aims to get the message into the receiver's long-term memory. Long-term memory holds all the information one has ever processed. In entering the receiver's long-term memory, the message can modify the receiver's beliefs and attitudes. But first the message has to enter the receiver's short-term memory, which is a limited-capacity store that processes incoming information. Whether the message passes from the receiver's short-term memory to his or her long-term memory depends on the amount and type of *message rehearsal* by the receiver. Rehearsal is not simply message repetition; rather, the receiver elaborates on the meaning of the information in a way that brings related thoughts from the receiver's long-term memory into his or her short-term memory. If the receiver's initial attitude toward the object is positive and he or she rehearses support arguments, the message is likely to be accepted and have high recall. If the receiver's initial attitude is negative and the person rehearses counterarguments, the message is likely to be rejected but to stay in long-term memory. Counterarguing inhibits persuasion by making an opposing message available. Much of persuasion requires the receiver's rehearsal of his or her own thoughts. Much of what is called persuasion is self-persuasion.[4]

Communicators have been looking for audience traits that correlate with their degree of persuasibility. People of high education and/or intelligence are thought to be less persuasible, but the evidence is inconclusive. Women have been found to be more persuasible than men, although this is mediated by a woman's acceptance of the prescribed female role. Women who value traditional sex roles are more influenceable than women who are less accepting of the traditional roles.[5] Persons who accept external standards to guide their behavior and who have a weak self-concept appear to be more persuasible. Persons who are low in self-confidence are also thought to be more persuasible. However, research by Cox and Bauer showed a curvilinear relation between self-confidence and persuasibility, with those moderate in self-confidence being the most persuasible.[6] The communicator should look for audience traits that correlate with persuasibility and use them to guide message and media development.

Fiske and Hartley have outlined factors that moderate the effect of a communication:

1. The greater the monopoly of the communication source over the recipient, the greater the change or effect in favor of the source over the recipient.
2. Communication effects are greatest where the message is in line with the existing opinions, beliefs, and dispositions of the receiver.
3. Communication can produce the most effective shifts on unfamiliar, lightly felt, peripheral issues, which do not lie at the center of the recipient's value system.
4. Communication is more likely to be effective where the source is believed to have expertise, high status, objectivity, or likability, but particularly where the source has power and can be identified with.
5. The social context, group, or reference group will mediate the communication and influence whether or not it is accepted.[7]

Steps in Developing Effective Communications

We will now examine the major steps in developing a total communication and promotion program. The marketing communicator must (1) identify the target audience, (2) determine the communication objectives, (3) design the message, (4) select the communication channels, (5) allocate the total promotion budget, (6) decide on the promotion mix, (7) measure the promotion's results, and (8) manage and coordinate the total marketing communication process.

Identifying the Target Audience

A marketing communicator must start with a clear target audience in mind. The audience could be potential buyers of the company's products, current users, deciders, or influencers. The audience could be individuals, groups, particular publics, or the general public. The target audience will critically influence the communicator's decisions on what to say, how to say it, when to say it, where to say it, and to whom to say it.

IMAGE ANALYSIS ❖ A major part of audience analysis is to assess the audience's current image of the company, its products, and its competitors. People's attitudes and actions toward an object are highly conditioned by their beliefs about the object. *Image* is the *set of beliefs, ideas,* and *impressions that a person holds of an object.*

The first step is to measure the target audience's knowledge of the object, using the following *familiarity scale:*

NEVER HEARD OF	HEARD OF ONLY	KNOW A LITTLE BIT	KNOW A FAIR AMOUNT	KNOW VERY WELL

If most respondents circle only the first two categories, then the company's challenge is to build greater awareness.

Respondents who are familiar with the product can be asked how they feel toward it, using the following *favorability scale:*

VERY UNFAVORABLE	SOMEWHAT UNFAVORABLE	INDIFFERENT	SOMEWHAT FAVORABLE	VERY FAVORABLE

If most respondents check the first two categories, then the organization must overcome a negative image problem.

The two scales can be combined to develop insight into the nature of the communication challenge. To illustrate, suppose area residents are asked about their familiarity with and attitudes toward four local hospitals, A, B, C, and D. Their responses are averaged and shown in Figure 22-2. Hospital A has the most positive image: Most people know it and like it. Hospital B is less familiar to most people, but those who know it like it. Hospital C is viewed negatively by those who know it, but fortunately for the hospital, not too many people know it. Hospital D is seen as a poor hospital, and everyone knows it!

Clearly, each hospital faces a different communication task. Hospital A must work at maintaining its good reputation and high community awareness. Hospital B must gain the attention of more people, since those who know it consider it a good hospital. Hospital C must find out why people dislike it and must take steps to improve its performance while keeping a low profile. Hospital D should lower its profile (avoid news), improve its quality, and then seek public attention again.

Each hospital needs to go further and research the specific content of its image. The most popular tool for this research is the *semantic differential*.[8] It involves the following steps:

1. *Developing a Set of Relevant Dimensions:* The researcher asks people to identify the dimensions they would use in thinking about the object. People could be asked, "What things do you think of when you consider a hospital?" If someone suggests "quality of medical care," this would be turned into a bipolar adjective scale — say, "inferior medical care" at one end and "superior medical care" at the other. It could be rendered as a five- or seven-point scale. A set of additional dimensions for a hospital are shown in Figure 22-3.

2. *Reducing the Set of Relevant Dimensions:* The number of dimensions should be kept small to avoid respondent fatigue in having to rate *n* objects on *m* scales. There are essentially three types of scales:

   ♦ evaluation scales (good-bad qualities)
   ♦ potency scales (strong-weak qualities)
   ♦ activity scales (active-passive qualities)

   Using these scales as a guide, the researcher can remove redundant scales that fail to add much information.

FIGURE 22-2
Familiarity-Favorability
Analysis

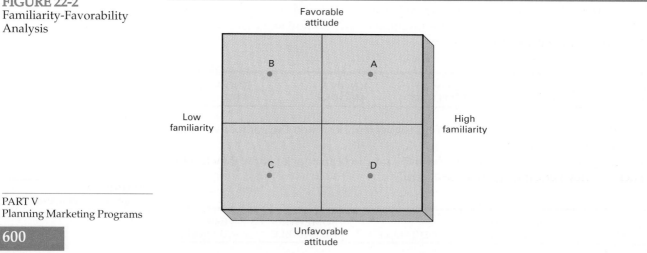

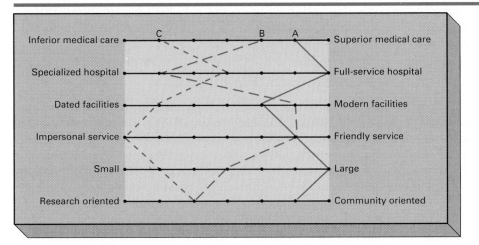

FIGURE 22-3
Images of Three Hospitals
(Semantic Differential)

3. *Administering the Instrument to a Sample of Respondents:* The respondents are asked to rate one object at a time. The bipolar adjectives should be randomly arranged so as not to list all of the unfavorable adjectives on one side.

4. *Averaging the Results:* Figure 22-3 shows the results of averaging the respondents' pictures of hospitals A, B, and C (hospital D is left out). Each hospital's image is represented by a vertical "line of means" that summarizes the average perception of that hospital. Thus hospital A is seen as a large, modern, friendly, and superior hospital. Hospital C, on the other hand, is seen as a small, dated, impersonal, and inferior hospital.

5. *Checking on the Image Variance:* Since each image profile is a line of means, it does not reveal how variable the image actually is. Did everyone see hospital B exactly as shown, or was there considerable variation? In the first case, we would say that the image is highly *specific*; and in the second case, highly *diffused*. An organization might not want a very specific image. Some organizations prefer a diffused image so that different groups will see the organization in different ways.

The management should now propose a *desired image* in contrast to the *current image*. Suppose hospital C would like the public to view more favorably the quality of the hospital's medical care, facilities, friendliness, and so on. Management must decide which image gaps it wants to close first. Is it more desirable to improve the hospital's friendliness (through staff training programs) or the quality of its facilities (through renovation)? Each image dimension should be reviewed in terms of the following questions:

♦ What contribution to the organization's overall favorable image would be made by closing that particular image gap to the extent shown?

♦ What strategy (combination of real changes and communication changes) would help close the particular image gap?

♦ What would be the cost of closing that image gap?

♦ How long would it take to close that image gap?

An organization seeking to improve its image must have great patience. Images are "sticky." They persist long after the organization has changed. Thus a famous hospital's medical care might have deteriorated, and yet it continues to be highly regarded in the public mind. Image persistence is explained by the fact that once people have a certain image of an object, they selectively perceive further data. They perceive what is consistent with their image. It will take highly disconfirming information to raise doubts and open their minds to new information. Thus an image enjoys a life of its own, especially when people do not have continuous or new firsthand experiences with the changed object.

Determining the Communication Objectives

Once the target market and its characteristics are identified, the marketing communicator must decide on the desired audience response. The ultimate response, of course, is purchase and satisfaction. But purchase behavior is the end result of a long process of consumer decision making. The marketing communicator needs to know how to move the target audience to higher states of readiness to buy.

The marketer can be seeking a *cognitive*, *affective*, or *behavioral* response from the target audience. That is, the marketer might want to put something into the consumer's mind, change the consumer's attitude, or get the consumer to act. Even here, there are different models of consumer-response stages. Figure 22-4 shows the four best-known *response hierarchy models*.

All of these models assume that the buyer passes through a cognitive, affective, and behavioral stage, in that order. This sequence is the "learn-feel-do" sequence and is appropriate when the audience has high involvement with a product category perceived to have high differentiation, as is the case in purchasing an automobile. An alternative sequence is the "do-feel-learn" sequence, when the audience has high involvement but perceives little or no differentiation within the product category, as in purchasing aluminum siding. Still a third sequence is the "learn-do-feel" sequence, when the audience has low involvement and perceives little differentiation within the product category, as is the case in purchasing salt. By understanding the appropriate sequence, the marketer can do a better job of planning communications.[9]

Here we will assume that the buyer has high involvement with the product category and perceives high differentiation within the category. Therefore we will

FIGURE 22-4
Response Hierarchy Models
SOURCES: (a) E. K. Strong, *The Psychology of Selling* (New York: McGraw-Hill, 1925), p. 9; (b) Robert J. Lavidge and Gary A. Steiner, "A Model for Predictive Measurements of Advertising Effectiveness," *Journal of Marketing*, October 1961, p. 61; (c) Everett M. Rogers, *Diffusion of Innovations* (New York: Free Press, 1962), pp. 79-86; (d) various sources.

Stages	"AIDA" Model[a]	"Hierarchy-of-Effects" Model[b]	"Innovation-Adoption" Model[c]	"Communications" Model[d]
Cognitive stage	Attention	Awareness ↓ Knowledge	Awareness	Exposure ↓ Reception ↓ Cognitive response
Affective stage	Interest ↓ Desire	Liking ↓ Preference ↓ Conviction	Interest ↓ Evaluation	Attitude ↓ Intention
Behavior stage	Action	Purchase	Trial ↓ Adoption	Behavior

work with the "hierarchy-of-effects" model (learn, feel, do) and describe the six buyer-readiness states—awareness, knowledge, liking, preference, conviction, and purchase.

AWARENESS ❖ If most of the target audience is unaware of the object, the communicator's task is to build awareness, perhaps just name recognition. This can be accomplished with simple messages repeating the name. Even then, building awareness takes time. Suppose a small Iowa college named Pottsville seeks applicants from Nebraska but has no name recognition in Nebraska. And suppose there are 30,000 high school seniors in Nebraska who may potentially be interested in Pottsville College. The college might set the objective of making 70% of these students aware of Pottsville's name within one year.

KNOWLEDGE ❖ The target audience might have company or product awareness but not know much more. Pottsville may want its target audience to know that it is a private four-year college with excellent programs in English and the language arts. Pottsville College thus needs to learn how many people in the target audience have little, some, or much knowledge about Pottsville. The college may then decide to select product knowledge as its first communication objective.

LIKING ❖ If target members know the product, how do they feel about it? If the audience looks unfavorably on Pottsville College, the communicator has to find out why and then develop a communication campaign to shore up favorable feelings. If the unfavorable view is based on real problems of the college, then a communication campaign alone cannot do the job. Pottsville will have to fix its problems and then communicate its renewed quality. Good public relations call for "good deeds followed by good words."

PREFERENCE ❖ The target audience might like the product but not prefer it to others. In this case, the communicator must try to build consumer preference. The communicator will promote the product's quality, value, performance, and other features. The communicator can check on the campaign's success by measuring audience preferences again after the campaign.

CONVICTION ❖ A target audience might prefer a particular product but not develop a conviction about buying it. Thus some high school seniors may prefer Pottsville but may not be sure they want to go to college. The communicator's job is to build conviction that going to college is the right thing to do.

PURCHASE ❖ Finally, some members of the target audience might have conviction but not quite get around to making the purchase. They may wait for more information or plan to act later. The communicator must lead these consumers to take the final step. Actions might include offering the product at a low price, offering a premium, or letting consumers try it on a limited basis. Thus Pottsville might invite selected high school students to visit the campus and attend some classes. Or it might offer scholarships to deserving students.

Determining the target response is critical in developing a communication program. Marketing Concepts and Tools 22-1 shows how the communicator can determine simultaneously both the target audience and the target response.

Designing the Message

Having defined the desired audience response, the communicator moves to developing an effective message. Ideally, the message should gain *attention*, hold *interest*,

Determining the Target Audience and Sought Response

Communication objectives depend heavily on how many people already know about a product and may have tried it. Ottesen developed a device called a *market map* to be used in choosing the target audience and eliciting the sought response. The market map follows.

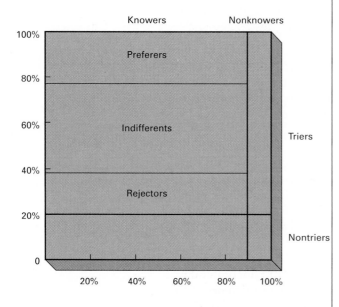

The horizontal dimension shows the current percentage of the market that knows the brand, here 90%. The vertical dimension shows the percentage of the market that has tried the brand, here 80%. From these two measures, we know that the brand is mature. The knowers-triers further divide into those who prefer (23%), are indifferent (39%), and have rejected (18%) the brand. The knowers-nontriers can also be assumed to divide into those who have a positive, indifferent, and negative attitude toward the brand (not shown).

The task is to set communication objectives for this brand. Since 90% of the target market already know the brand, it would not make sense to build awareness in the remaining 10%. The 10% who do not know this brand consist of persons who are unaware of many things and probably do not have much income. It is expensive to reach these people and is seldom worth it.

What about getting more knowers-nontriers to try the product? That is a worthwhile objective and can best be accomplished through sales promotion (free samples, cents-off coupons, and so on) rather than through additional advertising or personal selling. Since 23% of the current triers prefer the brand, we cannot expect that more than 23% of the new triers will stay with the brand. The marketer should calculate whether achieving this number of new-trier preferers would be worth the cost of the sales-promotion campaign.

Another plausible communication objective is to increase the proportion of triers who prefer this brand to other brands. This is difficult because consumer attitude is a function of how the consumer experiences the brand's performance and price of the brand. If the company wants to increase preference, what is required is product improvement and lower prices rather than more advertising.

The following conclusions can be drawn about the three trier groups. Communication to those who already prefer the brand is usually not very productive unless there is high consumer forgetfulness or a high level of competitors' expenditure aimed at preferers. Communication directed to the rejectors is probably wasted because the rejectors are not likely to pay attention to the advertising and probably would not retry the brand. Communication directed to the indifferents will probably be effective in attracting some proportion of their purchases, especially if the advertising makes some strong point to this audience.

Thus the communication objectives depend very much on the readiness states of the market. When a brand is new, there are few knowers and triers, and communication can be very effective in increasing their number. When the brand is mature, it makes sense to try to convert nontriers into triers through sales promotion and to fight for a normal share of the indifferent triers. It makes less sense to try to increase the percentage of knowers to reinforce preferers, or to try to get rejectors to retry the brand.

SOURCE: See Otto Ottesen, "The Response Function," in *Current Theories in Scandinavian Mass Communications Research*, ed. Mie Berg (Grenaa, Denmark: G.M.T., 1977).

arouse *desire*, and elicit *action* (AIDA model). In practice, few messages take the consumer all the way from awareness through purchase, but the AIDA framework suggests the desirable qualities.

Formulating the message will require solving four problems: what to say (*message content*), how to say it logically (*message structure*), how to say it symbolically (*message format*), and who should say it (*message source*).

MESSAGE CONTENT ❖ The communicator has to figure out what to say to the target audience to produce the desired response. This process has been variously called the *appeal, theme, idea,* or *unique selling proposition* (USP). It amounts to formulating some kind of benefit, motivation, identification, or reason why the audience should think about or investigate the product. Three types of appeals can be distinguished. *Rational appeals* appeal to the audience's self-interest. They show that the product will produce the claimed benefits. Examples would be messages demonstrating a product's quality, economy, value, or performance. It is widely believed that industrial buyers are most responsive to rational appeals. They are knowledgeable about the product class, trained to recognize value, and accountable to others for their choice. Consumers, when they buy certain big-ticket items, also tend to gather information and compare alternatives. They will respond to quality, economy, value, and performance appeals.

Emotional appeals attempt to stir up negative or positive emotions that will motivate purchase. Communicators have worked with *fear, guilt*, and *shame appeals* in getting people to do things they should (e.g., brushing teeth, taking an annual health checkup) or stop doing things they shouldn't (e.g., smoking, overimbibing, drug abuse, overeating). Fear appeals are effective up to a point, but if the audience anticipates too much fear in the message, they will avoid it (see Marketing Strategies 22-1 on page 606). Communicators also use positive emotional appeals such as *humor, love, pride,* and *joy.* Evidence has not established that a humorous message, for example, is necessarily more effective than a straight version of the same message. Humorous messages probably attract more attention and create more liking and belief in the sponsor, but humor can also detract from comprehension.[10]

Moral appeals are directed to the audience's sense of what is right and proper. They are often used to exhort people to support social causes, such as a cleaner environment, better race relations, equal rights for women, and aid to the disadvantaged. An example is the March of Dimes appeal: "God made you whole. Give to help those He didn't." Moral appeals are less often used in connection with everyday products.

Some advertisers believe that messages are maximally persuasive when they are moderately discrepant with what the audience believes. Messages that only state what the audience believes attract less attention and at best only reinforce audience beliefs. But if the messages are too discrepant with the audience's beliefs, they will be counterargued in the audience's mind and be disbelieved. The challenge is to design a message that is moderately discrepant and avoids the two extremes.

MESSAGE STRUCTURE ❖ A message's effectiveness depends on its structure as well as its content. Hovland's research at Yale has shed much light on conclusion drawing, one- versus two-sided arguments, and order of presentation.

Conclusion drawing raises the question as to whether the communicator should draw a definite conclusion for the audience or leave it to them. Some early experiments supported the greater efficacy of stating conclusions for the audience. Recent research, however, indicates that the best ads ask questions and allow read-

Marketing Strategies 22-1

Do Fear Appeals Work?

For many years marketing communicators believed that a message's effectiveness increased with the level of fear produced. Actually study findings indicate that neither extremely strong nor extremely weak fear appeals are as effective as moderate ones in producing adherence to a recommendation. Ray and Wilkie explained the finding by hypothesizing two types of effects as fear increases:

> First, there are the facilitating effects that are most often overlooked in marketing. If fear can heighten drive, there is the possibility of greater attention and interest in the product and message than if no drive were aroused. . . . But fear also brings the important characteristic of inhibition into the picture. . . . If fear levels are too high, there is the possibility of defensive avoidance of the ad, denial of the threat, selective exposure or distortion of the ad's meaning, or a view of the recommendations as being inadequate to deal with so important a fear.

Source credibility moderates the effectiveness of a fear appeal. When source credibility is high, a fear appeal induces attitude change. American Express, a high-credibility source, uses a fear appeal in its campaign to admonish consumers to carry American Express traveler's checks. If the fear message is to be effective, the communication should promise to relieve, in a believable and efficient way, the fear it arouses: otherwise buyers will ignore or minimize the threat.

SOURCES: Michael L. Ray and William L. Wilkie, "Fear: The Potential of an Appeal Neglected by Marketing," *Journal of Marketing,* January 1970, pp. 55–56; Brian Sternthal and C. Samuel Craig, "Fear Appeals: Revisited and Revised," *Journal of Consumer Research,* December, 1974, pp. 22–34; John J. Burnett and Richard L. Oliver, "Fear Appeal Effects in the Field: A Segmentation Approach," *Journal of Marketing Research,* May 1979, pp. 181–90; and Lynette S. Unger and James M. Stearns, "The Use of Fear and Guilt Messages in Television Advertising: Issues and Evidence," in *1983 Educators' Proceedings,* ed. Patrick E. Murphy (Chicago: American Marketing Association, 1983), pp. 16–20.

ers and viewers to form their own conclusions.[11] Conclusion drawing might cause negative reactions in the following situations:

- If the communicator is seen as untrustworthy, the audience might resent the attempt to influence them.
- If the issue is simple or the audience is intelligent, they might be annoyed at the attempt to explain the obvious.
- If the issue is highly personal, the audience might resent the communicator's attempt to draw a conclusion.

Drawing too explicit a conclusion can limit a product's acceptance. If Ford had hammered away on the point that the Mustang was for young people, this strong definition might have blocked other age groups who were attracted to it. *Stimulus ambiguity* can lead to a broader market definition and more spontaneous uses of certain products. Conclusion drawing seems better suited for complex or specialized products where a single and clear use is intended.

One- or two-sided arguments raises the question of whether the communicator should only praise the product or also mention some of its shortcomings. One would think that one-sided presentations would be the most effective. Yet the answer is not clear-cut. Here are some findings:[12]

- One-sided messages work best with audiences that are initially predisposed to the communicator's position, and two-sided arguments work best with audiences who are opposed.
- Two-sided messages tend to be more effective with better-educated audiences.
- Two-sided messages tend to be more effective with audiences that are likely to be exposed to counterpropaganda.

Order of presentation raises the question of whether a communicator should present the strongest arguments first or last. In the case of a one-sided message, presenting the strongest argument first has the advantage of establishing attention and interest. This is important in newspapers and other media where the audience does not attend to the whole message. However, it means an anticlimactic presentation. With a captive audience, a climactic presentation might be more effective. In the case of a two-sided message, the issue is whether to present the positive argument first (*primacy effect*) or last (*recency effect*). If the audience is initially opposed, the communicator might start with the other side's argument. This will disarm the audience and allow concluding with his or her strongest argument. Neither the primacy nor recency effect dominates in all situations.[13]

MESSAGE FORMAT ❖ The communicator must develop a strong format for the message. In a print ad, the communicator has to decide on the headline, copy, illustration, and color. If the message is to be carried over the radio, the communicator has to carefully choose words, voice qualities (speech rate, rhythm, pitch, articulation), and vocalizations (pauses, sighs, yawns). The "sound" of an announcer promoting a used automobile has to be different from one promoting a new Cadillac. If the message is to be carried on television or in person, then all of these elements plus body language (nonverbal clues) have to be planned. Presenters have to pay attention to their facial expressions, gestures, dress, posture, and hair style. If the message is carried by the product or its packaging, the communicator has to pay attention to color, texture, scent, size, and shape.

> Color plays an important communication role in food preferences. When women sampled four cups of coffee that had been placed next to brown, blue, red, and yellow containers (all the coffee was identical, unknown to the women), 75% felt that the coffee next to the brown container tasted too strong; nearly 85% judged the coffee next to the red container to be the richest; nearly everyone felt that the coffee next to the blue container was mild and that the coffee next to the yellow container was weak.

MESSAGE SOURCE ❖ Messages delivered by attractive sources achieve higher attention and recall. Advertisers often use celebrities as spokespeople, such as Michael Jordan for Nike, O. J. Simpson for Hertz, and Ed McMahon for Alpo dog food. Celebrities are likely to be effective when they personify a key product attribute. Thus O. J. Simpson is a good spokesperson for Hertz because he is known for his speed. But what is equally important is that the spokesperson has credibility. Messages delivered by highly credible sources are more persuasive. Pharmaceutical companies want doctors to testify about their products' benefits because doctors have high credibility. Antidrug crusaders will use ex-drug addicts to warn high school students against drugs because ex-addicts have higher credibility than teachers.

But what factors underlie source credibility? The three factors most often identified are expertise, trustworthiness, and likability.[14] *Expertise* is the specialized knowledge the communicator possesses to back the claim. Doctors, scientists, and professors rank high on expertise in their respective fields. *Trustworthiness* is related to how objective and honest the source is perceived to be. Friends are trusted more than strangers or salespeople. *Likability* describes the source's attractiveness to the audience. Such qualities as candor, humor, and naturalness make a source more likable. The most highly credible source, then, would be a person who scored high on all three dimensions.

If a person has a positive attitude toward a source and a message, or a negative attitude toward both, a state of congruity is said to exist. What happens if the person holds one attitude toward the source and the opposite toward the message? Suppose a homemaker hears a likable celebrity praise a brand that she dislikes. Osgood and Tannenbaum posit that *attitude change will take place in the direction of increasing the amount of congruity between the two evaluations.*[15] The homemaker will end up respecting the celebrity somewhat less or respecting the brand somewhat more. If she encounters the same celebrity praising other disliked brands, she will eventually develop a negative view of the celebrity and maintain her negative attitudes toward the brands. The *principle of congruity* says that communicators can use their good image to reduce some negative feelings toward a brand but in the process might lose some esteem with the audience.

Selecting the Communication Channels

The communicator must select efficient channels of communication to carry the message. Communication channels are of two broad types, *personal* and *nonpersonal*. Within each are found many subchannels (see Companies and Industries 22-1).

PERSONAL COMMUNICATION CHANNELS ❖ Personal communication channels involve two or more persons communicating directly with each other. They might communicate face to face, person to audience, over the telephone, or through the mails. Personal communication channels derive their effectiveness through the opportunities for individualizing the presentation and feedback.

A further distinction can be drawn between advocate, expert, and social channels of communication. *Advocate channels* consist of company salespeople contacting buyers in the target market. *Expert channels* consist of independent experts making statements to target buyers. *Social channels* consist of neighbors, friends, family members, and associates talking to target buyers.

Many companies are becoming acutely aware of the power of the "talk factor" or "word of mouth" coming from expert and social channels in generating new business. They are seeking ways to stimulate these channels to provide recommendations for their products and services. Here are two examples:

Companies and Industries 22-1

Pharmaceutical Companies Use a Whole Battery of Communication Channels to Get Their Message to Physicians

Pharmaceutical companies have a problem. Their salespeople, who are highly paid college graduates, can rarely wrest more than ten minutes time from a busy physician. Their presentation must be crisp, quick, and convincing. This makes pharmaceutical sales calls extremely expensive and the industry has had to amplify its battery of communication channels. These include placing *journal ads,* sending *direct mail* (including audio and videotapes), passing out *free samples,* and even *telemarketing.* Pharmaceutical companies sponsor *clinical conferences* to which they invite and pay for a large number of physicians to spend a weekend listening in the morning to leading physicians extol certain drugs, followed by an afternoon of golf or tennis. Salespeople will arrange evening *teleconferences* where physicians are invited to be at their phone to discuss a common problem with an expert. And salespeople will sponsor *small group lunches and dinners* with physicians. All of these approaches are undertaken in the hope of building physician preference for a branded therapeutic agent that may not differ much from its generic counterpart.

Regis McKenna advises a software company launching a new product to initially promote it to the trade press, opinion luminaries, financial analysts, and others who can supply favorable word of mouth; then to dealers; and finally to customers.[16]

Professionals will often encourage their clients to recommend their services to others. Dentists, for example, can ask satisfied patients to recommend friends and acquaintances and subsequently thank them for their recommendations (see Marketing Concepts and Tools 22-2).

Personal influence carries especially great weight in two situations. One is with products that are expensive, risky, or purchased infrequently. Here buyers are likely to be high information seekers and go beyond mass-media information to seek the recommendations of experts and social acquaintances. The other situation

Marketing Concepts and Tools 22-2

Developing Word-of-Mouth Referral Channels to Build Business

There are hundreds of occasions when people will ask others—friends, acquaintances, professionals—for a recommendation. These include times when someone is seeking a physician, electrician, hotel, hospital, lawyer, management consultant, insurance agent, architect, interior decorator, and so on. If we have confidence in the recommender, we will normally act on the referral. In such cases, the recommender has potentially benefitted the service provider as well as the service seeker.

The recommender, of course, must be prudent in making the recommendation. If the service seeker acts on the recommendation and is dissatisfied, he or she could lose confidence in the recommender. He or she may even stop patronizing the recommender or in extreme cases, start bad-mouthing or suing the recommender.

Given these risks, why would anyone take the responsibility of recommending anyone? There are three potential benefits. First, the recommender may feel good about having helped the client or friend. Second, the client or friend may now be bonded even more strongly to the recommender. Third, the recommender may receive some tangible benefit from the service provider.

In the last case, the benefit may take one of four forms. First, the service provider might reciprocate by referring business to the recommender. Second, the service provider might give the recommender enhanced service, a discounted price, or on-premise advertising. Third, the service provider, in gratitude, may send small gifts to the recommender, such as tickets to sporting events, subscriptions, or holiday gifts. Last, the service

provider may pay a commission, kickback, or finder's fee. This is clearly illegal or unethical in some professions but occurs in other cases; for example, car dealers can accept commissions on the loans they send to banks.

From the point of view of service providers, they clearly have a strong interest in building *referral channels*. Service providers not only promote their organization directly to potential customers but also to potential *referral sources*. Thus, architects know that they might get recommendations from lawyers, accountants, building contractors, banks, and interior decorators. Child psychiatrists know that they might get recommendations from school counselors, clergy, social workers, and physicians. The challenge is to locate high-yield referral sources and take active measures to cultivate their support. Service providers build relationships with referral sources by sending them newsletters, taking them to lunch, offering free consultation, and so on. When service providers get new clients on recommendations, they would be wise to send an acknowledging note appreciating the referral; and after serving the client, they would be wise to notify the recommender of the service outcome. All said, service providers must view potential referral sources as another target market requiring a specific marketing plan for cultivating their support.

SOURCES: For additional reading, see Scott R. Herriott, "Identifying and Developing Referral Channels," *Management Decision*, 30-1, 1992, pp. 4–9; Peter H. Reingen and Jerome B. Kernan, "Analysis of Referral Networks in Marketing: Methods and Illustration," *Journal of Marketing Research*, November 1986, pp. 370–78; and Jerry R. Wilson, *Word-of-Mouth Marketing* (New York: John Wiley & Sons, Inc., 1991).

is where the product suggests something about the user's status or taste. Here buyers will consult others in order to avoid embarrassment.

Companies can take several steps to stimulate personal influence channels to work on their behalf:

- *Identify Influential Individuals and Companies and Devote Extra Effort to Them:* In industrial selling, the entire industry might follow the market leader in adopting innovations. Early sales efforts should focus on the market leader.
- *Create Opinion Leaders by Supplying Certain People with the Product on Attractive Terms:* A new tennis racket might be offered initially to members of high school tennis teams at a special low price. The company would hope that these star high school tennis players would "talk up" their new racket to other high schoolers.
- *Work Through Community Influentials Such as Local Disc Jockeys, Class Presidents, and Presidents of Women's Organizations:* When the Ford Thunderbird was introduced, invitations were sent to executives offering them a free car to drive for the day. Of the 15,000 who took advantage of the offer, 10% indicated that they would become buyers, while 84% said they would recommend it to a friend.
- *Use Influential People in Testimonial Advertising:* Pepsi-Cola paid Michael Jackson several million dollars to make Pepsi commercials; golf and tennis companies always use well-known players to endorse their equipment.
- *Develop Advertising That Has High "Conversation Value":* Wendy's "Where's the Beef?" campaign (showing an elderly lady named Clara questioning where the hamburger was hidden in all that bread) created high conversation value.[17]

NONPERSONAL COMMUNICATION CHANNELS ❖ Nonpersonal communication channels carry messages without personal contact or interaction. They include media, atmospheres, and events.

Media consist of print media (newspapers, magazines, direct mail), broadcast media (radio, television), electronic media (audiotape, videotape, videodisc), and display media (billboards, signs, posters). Most nonpersonal messages come through paid media.

Atmospheres are "packaged environments" that create or reinforce the buyer's leanings toward product purchase. Thus law offices are decorated with Oriental rugs and oak furniture to communicate "stability" and "experience."[18] A luxury hotel will incorporate elegant chandeliers, marble columns, and other tangible signs of luxury.

Events are occurrences designed to communicate particular messages to target audiences. Public-relations departments arrange news conferences, grand openings, and sport sponsorships to achieve specific communication effects with a target audience.

Although personal communication is often more effective than mass communication, mass media might be the major means to stimulate personal communication. Mass communications affect personal attitudes and behavior through a *two-step flow-of-communication process.* "Ideas often flow from radio and print to opinion leaders and from these to the less active sections of the population."[19]

This two-step communication flow has several implications. First, the influence of mass media on public opinion is not as direct, powerful, and automatic as supposed. It is mediated by *opinion leaders,* persons who belong to primary groups and whose opinions are sought in one or more product areas. Opinion leaders are more exposed to mass media than those they influence. They carry messages to people who are less exposed to media, thus extending the influence of the mass media; or they may carry altered messages or none at all, thus acting as *gatekeepers.*

Second, the hypothesis challenges the notion that people's consumption styles are primarily influenced by a "trickle-down" effect from higher-status classes. To the contrary, people primarily interact within their own social class and acquire their fashion and other ideas from people like themselves who are opinion leaders.[20]

A third implication is that mass communicators would be more efficient by directing their messages specifically to opinion leaders, letting the latter carry the message to others. Thus pharmaceutical firms try to promote their new drugs to the most influential physicians first. More recent research indicates that both opinion leaders and the general public are affected by mass communication. Opinion leaders are prompted by the mass media to spread information, while the general public seeks information from the opinion leaders.

Communication researchers are moving toward a social-structure view of interpersonal communication.[21] They see society as consisting of *cliques*, small social groups whose members interact with each other more frequently than with others. Clique members are similar, and their closeness facilitates effective communication but also insulates the clique from new ideas. The challenge is to create more system openness whereby cliques exchange more information with others in the society. This openness is helped by persons who function as liaisons and bridges. A *liaison* is a person who connects two or more cliques without belonging to either. A *bridge* is a person who belongs to one clique and is linked to a person in another clique. Word-of-mouth communications flow most readily within cliques, and the problem is to facilitate communication between cliques and to create a diffusion network.

Establishing the Total Promotion Budget

One of the most difficult marketing decisions facing companies is how much to spend on promotion. John Wanamaker, the department-store magnate, said, "I know that half of my advertising is wasted, but I don't know which half."

Thus it is not surprising that industries and companies vary considerably in how much they spend on promotion. Promotional expenditures might amount to 30 to 50% of sales in the cosmetics industry and only 10 to 20% in the industrial equipment industry. Within a given industry, low- and high-spending companies can be found. Philip Morris is a high spender. When it acquired the Miller Brewing Company, and later the Seven-Up Company, it substantially increased total promotion spending. The additional spending at Miller's raised its market share from 4 to 19% within a few years.

How do companies decide on their promotion budget? We will describe four common methods used to set a promotion budget.

AFFORDABLE METHOD ❖ Many companies set the promotion budget at what they think the company can afford. One executive explained this method as follows: "Why it's simple. First, I go upstairs to the controller and ask how much they can afford to give us this year. He says a million and a half. Later, the boss comes to me and asks how much we should spend and I say 'Oh, about a million and a half.'"[22]

This method of setting budgets completely ignores the role of promotion as an investment and the immediate impact of promotion on sales volume. It leads to an uncertain annual promotion budget, which makes long-range market communication planning difficult.

PERCENTAGE-OF-SALES METHOD ❖ Many companies set their promotion expenditures at a specified percentage of sales (either current or anticipated) or of the sales price. A railroad company executive said: "We set our appropriation for each year on December 1 of the preceding year. On that date we add our passenger revenue for the next month, and then take 2% of the total for our advertising appropriation for the new year."[23] Automobile companies typically budget a fixed percentage for promotion based on the planned car price. Oil companies set the appropriation at a fraction of a cent for each gallon of gasoline sold under their own label.

A number of advantages are claimed for the percentage-of-sales method. First, it means that promotion expenditures would vary with what the company can "afford." This satisfies the financial managers, who feel that expenses should bear a close relation to the movement of corporate sales over the business cycle. Second, it encourages management to think in terms of the relationship between promotion cost, selling price, and profit per unit. Third, it encourages competitive stability to the extent that competing firms spend approximately the same percentage of their sales on promotion.

In spite of these advantages, the percentage-of-sales method has little to justify it. It uses circular reasoning in viewing sales as the cause of promotion rather than as the result. It leads to a budget set by the availability of funds rather than by market opportunities. It discourages experimenting with countercyclical promotion or aggressive spending. The promotion budget's dependence on year-to-year sales fluctuations interferes with long-range planning. The method does not provide a logical basis for choosing the specific percentage, except what has been done in the past or what competitors are doing. Finally, it does not encourage building up the promotion budget by determining what each product and territory deserves.

COMPETITIVE-PARITY METHOD ❖ Some companies set their promotion budget to achieve *share-of-voice* parity with their competitors. This thinking is illustrated by the executive who asked a trade source, "Do you have any figures which other companies in the builders' specialties field have used which would indicate what proportion of gross sales should be given over to advertising?"[24] This executive believes that by spending the same percentage of his sales on advertising as his competitors, he will maintain his market share.

Two arguments are advanced for this method. One is that the competitors' expenditures represent the collective wisdom of the industry. The other is that maintaining a competitive parity helps prevent promotion wars.

Neither argument is valid. There are no grounds for believing that competition knows better what should be spent on promotion. Company reputations, resources, opportunities, and objectives differ so much that their promotion budgets are hardly a guide. Furthermore, there is no evidence that budgets based on competitive parity discourage promotional wars from breaking out.

OBJECTIVE-AND-TASK METHOD ❖ The objective-and-task method calls upon marketers to develop their promotion budgets by defining their specific objectives, determining the tasks that must be performed to achieve these objectives, and estimating the costs of performing these tasks. The sum of these costs is the proposed promotion budget.

Ule showed how the objective-and-task method could be used to establish an advertising budget. Suppose Helene Curtis wants to launch a new woman's anti-dandruff shampoo, Clear.[25] The steps are as follows:

1. *Establish the Market-Share Goal:* The company estimates that there are 50 million potential users and sets a target of attracting 8% of the market, that is, 4 million users.

2. *Determine the Percent of the Market that Should Be Reached by Clear Advertising:* The advertiser hopes to reach 80% (40 million prospects) with the advertising message.

3. *Determine the Percent of Aware Prospects that Should Be Persuaded to Try the Brand:* The advertiser would be pleased if 25% of aware prospects (10 million) tried Clear. This is because they estimate that 40% of all triers, or 4 million persons, would become loyal users. That is the market goal.

4. *Determine the Number of Advertising Impressions Per 1% Trial Rate:* The advertiser estimates that 40 advertising impressions (exposures) for every 1% of the population would bring about a 25% trial rate.

5. *Determine the Number of Gross Rating Points that Would Have to Be Purchased:* A gross rating point is one exposure to 1% of the target population. Since the company wants to achieve 40 exposures to 80% of the population, it will want to buy 3,200 gross rating points.

6. *Determine the Necessary Advertising Budget on the Basis of the Average Cost of Buying a Gross Rating Point:* To expose 1% of the target population to one impression costs an average of $3,277. Therefore, 3,200 gross rating points would cost $10,486,400 (= $3,277 × 3,200) in the introductory year.

This method has the advantage of requiring management to spell out its assumptions about the relationship between dollars spent, exposure levels, trial rates, and regular usage.

A major question is how much weight should promotion receive in the total marketing mix (as opposed to product improvement, lower prices, more services, and so on). The answer depends on where the company's products are in their life cycles, whether they are commodities or highly differentiable products, whether they are routinely needed or have to be "sold," and other considerations. In theory, the total promotional budget should be established where the marginal profit from the last promotional dollar just equals the marginal profit from the last dollar in the best nonpromotional use. Implementing this principle, however, is not easy.

Deciding on the Promotion Mix

Companies face the task of distributing the total promotion budget over the five promotional tools—advertising, sales promotion, direct marketing, public relations, and salesforce. Within the same industry, companies can differ considerably in how they allocate their promotional budget. Avon concentrates its promotional funds on personal selling, while Revlon spends heavily on advertising. In selling vacuum cleaners, Electrolux spends heavily on a door-to-door salesforce, while Hoover relies more on advertising. Thus it is possible to achieve a given sales level with varying promotional mixes.

Companies are always searching for ways to gain efficiency by substituting one promotional tool for another as its economics become more favorable. Many companies have replaced some field sales activity with ads, direct mail, and telemarketing. Other companies have increased their sales-promotion expenditures in relation to advertising, to gain quicker sales. The substitutability among promotional tools explains why marketing functions need to be coordinated in a single marketing department.

Designing the promotion mix is further complicated when one tool can be used to promote another. Thus when McDonald's decides to run a Million Dollar Sweepstakes program in its fast-food outlets (a form of sales promotion), it has to take out newspaper ads to inform the public. When General Mills develops a consumer advertising campaign to launch a new cake mix, it has to also develop a trade-channel campaign to win their support.

Is there a logical sequence for building up the promotion budget? Usually the salesforce cost is established first because much of this is a fixed cost. Then there is the question of whether to set the sales-promotion budget or the advertising budget next. Brand managers in consumer package goods companies increasingly set the trade-promotion budget first, because the trade is powerful enough to demand a certain amount of trade-promotion money. Then they set the consumer-promotion budget to make sure that consumers come in and buy enough of the promoted products. Finally, they decide on the advertising budget (see Companies and Industries 22-2).

Companies and Industries 22-2

How Do Companies Actually Set Their Promotion Budgets?

Although companies can benefit by using marketing theories and models to set their marketing budgets—and some do—most companies go through a process which is partly rational, partly political, partly expedient. Low and Mohr carried out in-depth interviews with 21 managers at consumer products firms to learn how they set and allocated marketing communication budgets. The issue was how brand managers set the total promotion budget and its allocation to advertising, consumer promotion, and trade promotion. They found that these companies developed their budgets through a *brand team* approach. The teams included managers from sales, trade marketing, manufacturing, accounting, and marketing research, as well as the brand manager, brand assistants, and a category manager (if this position exists).

First the brand team does an extensive situation analysis in the course of developing the annual marketing plan. Based on this analysis, the team establishes marketing objectives and a broad strategy. Then the brand manager forecasts the brand sales and profits based on the broad strategy. This is followed by developing an initial allocation of the budget to advertising, consumer promotion, and trade promotion. Some companies treat trade promotion as a given, and then allocate the balance to advertising and consumer promotion, based on historical precedent. The allocation is then adjusted further in the light of competitors' promotional activity and other factors. For example, if the competitor is expected to increase trade promotion, the brand manager would switch more money to trade promotion.

Now the brand plan is presented to senior management—the company president, marketing vice president, group managers, sales vice president, and a senior financial manager. At this stage, senior managers may require or advise changes, partly reflecting what they think this brand deserves in relation to the other brands under review. The revised plan is then implemented.

During the year, the brand manager will adjust the allocations in response to competitive and economic developments. Toward the end of the period, brand managers will often cut advertising when the brand is not meeting its profit objectives, since this money falls to the bottom line without hurting short-term sales. At the end of the year, companies should—though many don't—do a post-mortem to evaluate the previous year's spending in order to improve the manager's ability to use marketing tools more effectively in the future.

Given this budget setting process, we can see that it follows a rational sequence of steps which involves political negotiation, the use of traditional promotion allocation rules, and reactive last-minute adjustments to marketplace events.

Low and Mohr then examined factors that would influence the relative allocation of funds to the different promotional tools. Here are some of their findings:

1. More money is put into advertising—compared to sales promotion—in the introduction and growth stages of the product life cycle, especially if the market growth rate is strong. Companies with the largest market share, profit margin, and/or product differentiation also spend relatively more on advertising.

2. More money is put into sales promotion the greater the competition, the more the short-term focus of management, the more the political influence of the firm's salesforce, and the more the retailers' strength.

3. Relative to trade and consumer promotion, advertising tends to have a positive effect on consumer attitudes and long-term market share but a negative effect on short-term market share.

4. Relative to advertising, consumer and trade promotion tend to have a negative effect on consumer attitudes and long-term market share but a positive effect on short-term market share.

SOURCE: See George S. Low and Jakki J. Mohr, "The Advertising Sales Promotion Trade-Off: Theory and Practice," (Cambridge, MA: Marketing Science Institute, Report Number 92-127, October 1992).

Many factors influence the marketer's choice and mix of promotional tools. We will examine these factors in the following paragraphs.

NATURE OF EACH PROMOTIONAL TOOL ❖ Each promotional tool has its own unique characteristics and costs. Marketers have to understand these characteristics in selecting them.[26]

Advertising.   Because of the many forms and uses of advertising, it is difficult to make all-embracing generalizations about its distinctive qualities as a component of the promotional mix. Yet the following qualities can be noted:

- *Public Presentation:* Advertising is a highly public mode of communication. Its public nature confers a kind of legitimacy on the product and also suggests a standardized offering. Because many persons receive the same message, buyers know that their motives for purchasing the product will be publicly understood.
- *Pervasiveness:* Advertising is a pervasive medium that permits the seller to repeat a message many times. It also allows the buyer to receive and compare the messages of various competitors. Large-scale advertising by a seller says something positive about the seller's size, power, and success.
- *Amplified Expressiveness:* Advertising provides opportunities for dramatizing the company and its products through the artful use of print, sound, and color. Sometimes, however, the tool's very success at expressiveness may dilute or distract from the message.
- *Impersonality:* Advertising cannot be as compelling as a company sales representative. The audience does not feel obligated to pay attention or respond. Advertising is able to carry on only a monologue, not a dialogue, with the audience.

On the one hand, advertising can be used to build up a long-term image for a product (Coca-Cola ads), and on the other, to trigger quick sales (a Sears ad for a weekend sale). Advertising is an efficient way to reach numerous geographically dispersed buyers at a low cost per exposure. Certain forms of advertising, such as TV advertising, can require a large budget, while other forms, such as newspaper advertising, can be done on a small budget. Advertising might have an effect on sales simply through its presence. Consumers might believe that a heavily advertised brand must offer "good value"; otherwise, why would advertisers spend so much money touting the product?

Sales Promotion.   Although sales-promotion tools—coupons, contests, premiums, and the like—are highly diverse, they have three distinctive characteristics:

- *Communication:* They gain attention and usually provide information that may lead the consumer to the product.
- *Incentive:* They incorporate some concession, inducement, or contribution that gives value to the consumer.
- *Invitation:* They include a distinct invitation to engage in the transaction now.

Companies use sales-promotion tools to create a stronger and quicker response. Sales promotion can be used to dramatize product offers and to boost sagging sales. Sales-promotion effects are usually short run, however, and not effective in building long-run brand preference.

Direct Marketing.   Although direct marketing has several forms— direct mail, telemarketing, electronic marketing, and so on—it has a few distinctive characteristics:

- *Nonpublic:* The message is normally addressed to a specific person and does not reach others.
- *Customized:* The message can be customized to appeal to the addressed individual.
- *Up to date:* A message can be prepared very quickly for delivery to an individual.

Public Relations and Publicity. The appeal of public relations is based on its three distinctive qualities:

- *High Credibility:* News stories and features seem more authentic and credible to readers than ads do.
- *Off Guard:* Public relations can reach many prospects who might avoid salespeople and advertisements. The message gets to the buyers as news rather than as a sales-directed communication.
- *Dramatization:* Public relations has, like advertising, a potential for dramatizing a company or product.

Marketers tend to underuse public relations or use it as an afterthought. Yet a well-thought-out public-relations program coordinated with the other promotion-mix elements can be extremely effective.

Personal Selling. Personal selling is the most cost-effective tool at later stages of the buying process, particularly in building up buyers' preference, conviction, and action. The reason is that personal selling, when compared with advertising, has three distinctive qualities:

- *Personal Confrontation:* Personal selling involves an alive, immediate, and interactive relationship between two or more persons. Each party is able to observe each other's needs and characteristics at close hand and make immediate adjustments.
- *Cultivation:* Personal selling permits all kinds of relationships to spring up, ranging from a matter-of-fact selling relationship to a deep personal friendship. Effective sales representatives will normally keep their customers' interests at heart if they want long-run relationships.
- *Response:* Personal selling makes the buyer feel under some obligation for having listened to the sales talk. The buyer has a greater need to attend and respond, even if the response is a polite "thank you."

These distinctive qualities come at a cost. A salesforce represents a greater long-term cost commitment than advertising. Advertising can be turned on and off, but the size of a salesforce is more difficult to alter.

FACTORS IN SETTING THE PROMOTION MIX ❖ Companies consider several factors in developing their promotion mix. An examination of these factors follows.

Type of Product Market. The rated importance of promotional tools varies between consumer and industrial markets (see Figure 22-5). Consumer-goods companies rate advertising, sales promotion, personal selling, and public relations in that order. Industrial-goods companies rate personal selling, sales promotion, advertising, and public relations in that order. In general, personal selling is more heavily used with complex, expensive, and risky goods and in markets with fewer and larger sellers (hence, industrial markets).

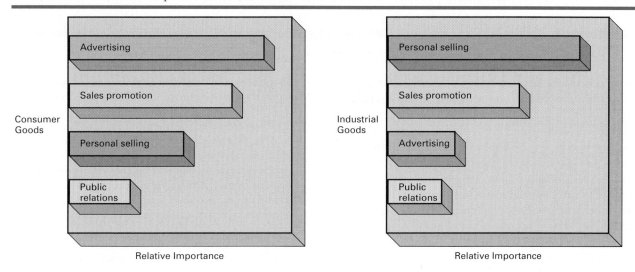

While advertising is less important than sales calls in industrial markets, it still plays a significant role. Advertising can perform the following functions:

- *Awareness Building:* Prospects who are not aware of the company or product might refuse to see the sales representative. Furthermore, the sales representative might have to take a lot of time describing the company and its products.

- *Comprehension Building:* If the product embodies new features, some of the burden of explaining them can be effectively undertaken by advertising.

- *Efficient Reminding:* If prospects know about the product but are not ready to buy, reminder advertising would be more economical than sales calls.

- *Lead Generation:* Advertisements offering brochures and carrying the company's phone number are an effective way to generate leads for sales representatives.

- *Legitimation:* Sales representatives can use tear sheets of the company's ads in leading magazines to legitimize their company and products.

- *Reassurance:* Advertising can remind customers how to use the product and reassure them about their purchase.

Advertising's important role in industrial marketing is underscored in a number of studies. Morrill showed in his study of industrial-commodity marketing that advertising combined with personal selling increased sales 23% over what they were with no advertising. The total promotional cost as a percentage of sales was reduced by 20%.[27] Freeman developed a formal model for dividing promotional funds between advertising and personal selling on the basis of the selling tasks that each performs more economically.[28] Levitt's research also showed the important role that advertising can play in industrial marketing (see Marketing Strategies 22-2). Lilien carried out a series of investigations in a project called ADVISOR in which he sought to determine and critique the practices used by industrial marketers to set their marketing communication budgets (see Marketing Concepts and Tools 22-3 on page 619).

Conversely, personal selling can make a strong contribution in consumer-goods marketing. Some consumer marketers play down the role of the salesforce, using them mainly to collect weekly orders from dealers and to see that sufficient

CHAPTER 22
Designing Communication and
Promotion-Mix Strategies

Marketing Strategies 22-2

Role of Corporate Advertising in Industrial Marketing

Professor Theodore Levitt sought to determine the relative contribution of the company's reputation (built mainly by advertising) and the company's sales presentation (personal selling) in producing industrial sales. Purchasing agents were shown filmed sales presentations of a new but fictitious technical product for use as an ingredient in making paint. The variables were the quality of the sales presentation and whether the salesperson came from a well-known company, a less-known but credible company, or an unknown company. Purchasing-agent reactions were collected after viewing the films and again five weeks later. The findings were as follows:

1. A company's reputation improves the chances of getting a favorable first hearing and an early adoption of the product. Therefore, corporate advertising that can build up the company's reputation (other factors also shape its reputation) will help the company's sales representatives.

2. Sales representatives from well-known companies have an edge in getting the sale if their sales presentations are adequate. If a sales representative from a lesser-known company makes a highly effective sales presentation, that can overcome the disadvantage. Smaller companies should use their limited funds to select and train good sales representatives rather than spend the money on advertising.

3. Company reputations help most where the product is complex, the risk is high, and the purchasing agent is less professionally trained.

SOURCE: Theodore Levitt, *Industrial Purchasing Behavior: A Study in Communication Effects* (Boston: Division of Research, Harvard Business School, 1965).

stock is on the shelf. The common feeling is that "salespeople put products on shelves and advertising takes them off." Yet even here an effectively trained salesforce can make three important contributions:

- *Increased Stock Position:* Sales representatives can persuade dealers to take more stock and devote more shelf space to the company's brand.
- *Enthusiasm Building:* Sales representatives can build dealer enthusiasm for a new product by dramatizing the planned advertising and sales-promotion backup.
- *Missionary Selling:* Sales representatives can sign up more dealers to carry the company's brands.

Push Versus Pull Strategy. The promotional mix is heavily influenced by whether the company chooses a push or pull strategy to create sales. The two strategies are contrasted in Figure 22-6. A *push strategy* involves manufacturer mar-

FIGURE 22-6
Push versus Pull Strategy

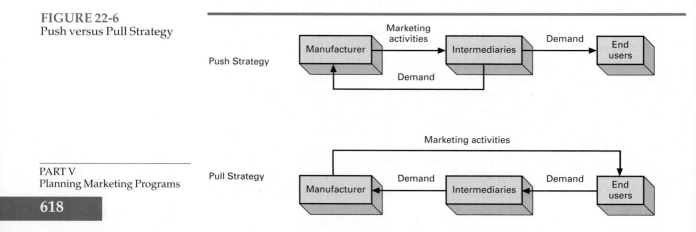

The ADVISOR Project Probes into How Industrial Marketers Set Their Marketing Budgets

Professor Gary L. Lilien directed a five-year study called the ADVISOR project, which examined how industrial marketers set their advertising budgets. ADVISOR ultimately consisted of two projects—ADVISOR 1 and ADVISOR 2.

Data on various marketing factors were collected on 66 industrial products from 12 companies. The study sought to develop marketing expenditure norms for industrial marketers. Industrial marketers tended to make a two-step decision in setting their advertising budgets. They decided, first, how much to spend on total marketing as a percentage of sales (the M/S ratio) and, second, how much to spend on advertising as a percentage of the marketing budget (the A/M ratio). When these ratios are multiplied, they give the A/S ratio, namely the advertising-to-sales ratio.

The data yielded the following norms:

	ADVERTISING	A/S	M/S	A/M
Median:	$92,000	0.6%	6.9%	9.9%
Range for 50% of products:	$16,000–$272,000	0.1%–1.8%	3%–14%	5%–19%

Thus the average industrial company in the sample spent $92,000 on advertising each product, and in 50% of the cases, this figure ranged from $16,000 to $272,000. The average industrial company spent only 0.6% of its sales on advertising; it budgeted about 7% of its sales for total marketing; and it budgeted about 10% of its total marketing budget for advertising. The table also shows the 50% ranges for each ratio.

A company could use this table to check whether its M/S and A/M ratios are within a 50% range of most companies. If one or both ratios are outside of the range, either too low or too high, then management should ask why. If good reasons cannot be found, the advertising and marketing budgets should be revised.

There could be good reasons for spending outside of the typical range. Lilien investigated a large number of factors suggested by marketing managers that would lead them to spend more or less than the normal amount on advertising and/or marketing. He found six factors that had a major influence on marketing budgets:

- The M/S ratio fell as the product life cycle progressed.

- The higher the purchase frequency, the greater the A/M.
- The higher the product quality or uniqueness, the higher the A/M.
- The higher the market share, the lower the M/S.
- The higher the customer concentration, the lower the M/S ratio.
- The higher the customer growth rate, the higher the M/S and A/M ratios.

Next ADVISOR investigated how industrial companies allocated their advertising budgets to the following four media:

- *Space:* trade, technical press, and house journals (41%)
- *Direct Mail:* leaflets, brochures, catalogs, and other direct-mail pieces (24%)
- *Shows:* trade shows and industrial films (11%)
- *Promotion:* sales promotion (24%)

The numbers show the median percentage that industrial companies spent on the four media. Lilien tested four variables that influence the allocation percentages and found:

- The higher the sales volume, the more the use of shows and sales promotion and the less the use of space and direct mail.
- With products in later stages of the life cycle, more is spent on direct mail and less on sales promotion.
- The higher the customer concentration, the more for sales promotion and the less for trade shows.
- The greater the number of customers, the less the use of direct mail.

Subsequently, ADVISOR 2 was launched with a larger sample, and it confirmed the earlier results. ADVISOR 2 led to the building of optimization models for setting marketing and advertising budgets.

SOURCES: Gary L. Lilien and John D. C. Little, "The ADVISOR Project: A Study of Industrial Marketing Budgets," *Sloan Management Review,* Spring 1976, pp. 17–31, by permission of the publisher. Copyright © 1976 by the Sloan Management Review Association. All rights reserved; and Gary L. Lilien, "ADVISOR 2: Modeling the Marketing Mix Decision for Industrial Products," *Management Science,* February 1979, pp. 191–204. Copyright © 1979 The Institute of Management Science.

keting activities (primarily salesforce and trade promotion) directed at channel intermediaries to induce them to order and carry the product and promote it to end users. A *pull strategy* involves marketing activities (primarily advertising and consumer promotion) directed at end users to induce them to ask intermediaries for the product and thus induce the intermediaries to order the product from the manufacturer. Companies in the same industry may differ in their emphasis on push or pull. For example, Lever Brothers relies more heavily on push, and Procter & Gamble on pull.

Buyer-Readiness Stage.   Promotional tools vary in their cost effectiveness at different stages of buyer readiness. Figure 22-7 shows the relative cost effectiveness of three promotional tools. Advertising and publicity play the most important roles in the awareness stage, more than is played by "cold calls" from sales representatives or by sales promotion. Customer comprehension is primarily affected by advertising and personal selling. Customer conviction is influenced mostly by personal selling and less by advertising and sales promotion. Closing the sale is influenced mostly by personal selling and sales promotion. Reordering is also affected mostly by personal selling and sales promotion, and somewhat by reminder advertising. Clearly, advertising and publicity are most cost effective at the early stages of the buyer decision process, and personal selling and sales promotion are most effective at the later stages.

Product-Life-Cycle Stage.   Promotional tools also vary in their cost effectiveness at different stages of the product life cycle. Figure 22-8 offers a speculative view of their relative effectiveness.

In the introduction stage, advertising and publicity have high cost effectiveness, followed by sales promotion to induce trial and personal selling to gain distribution coverage.

In the growth stage, all the tools can be toned down because demand has its own momentum through word of mouth.

In the maturity stage, sales promotion, advertising, and personal selling all grow more important, in that order.

In the decline stage, sales promotion continues strong, advertising and publicity are reduced, and salespeople give the product only minimal attention.

Company Market Rank.   Top ranking brands derive more benefit from advertising than sales promotions. This is shown in Figure 22-9. For the top three brands,

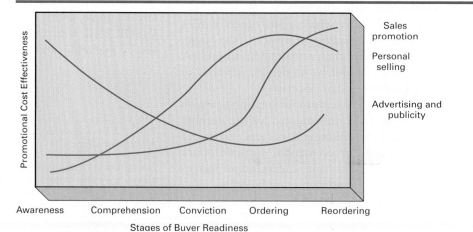

FIGURE 22-7
Cost Effectiveness of Different Promotional Tools at Different Buyer-Readiness Stages

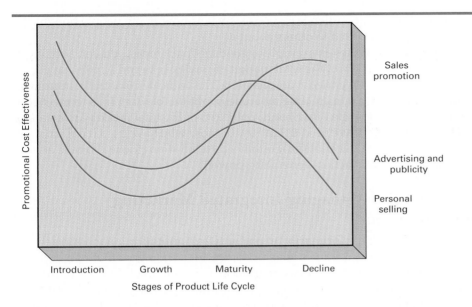

ROI rises with a rising ratio of advertising spending to sales promotion. The only exception is for brands ranked fourth or worse, where profitability decreases in moving from low to high advertising.

Measuring Promotion's Results

After implementing the promotional plan, the communicator must measure its impact on the target audience. This involves asking the target audience whether they recognize or recall the message, how many times they saw it, what points they recall, how they felt about the message, and their previous and current attitudes toward the product and company. The communicator would also want to collect

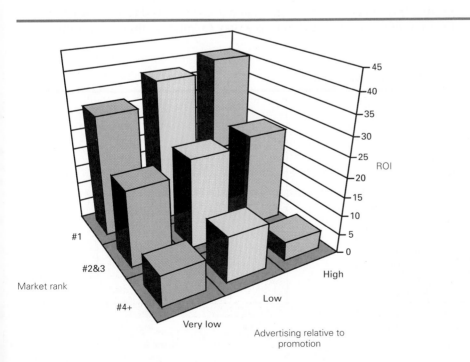

FIGURE 22-9
How Market Rank and the
Advertising/Promotion
Ratio Affects Profitability
Source: Bradley T. Gale,
"Power Brands: The
Essentials," an unpublished
paper, November 1991, p. 2.

CHAPTER 22
Designing Communication and
Promotion-Mix Strategies

behavioral measures of audience response, such as how many people bought the product, liked it, and talked to others about it.

Figure 22-10 provides an example of good feedback measurement. Looking at brand A, we find that 80% of the total market are aware of brand A, 60% have tried it, and only 20% who have tried it are satisfied. This indicates that the communication program is effective in creating awareness, but the product fails to meet consumer expectations. On the other hand, only 40% of the total market are aware of brand B, and only 30% have tried it, but 80% of those who have tried it are satisfied. In this case, the communication program needs to be strengthened to take advantage of the brand's satisfaction-generating power.

Organizing and Managing Integrated Marketing Communications

Many companies still rely primarily on one or two communication tools to achieve their communication aims. This is in spite of the great changes taking place in the market economy, specifically the disintegration of mass markets into a multitude of minimarkets, each requiring its own communication approach, the proliferation of new types of media, and the growing sophistication of consumers. The wide range of communication tools, messages, and audiences makes it imperative that companies give thought to a fresher and fuller use and orchestration of communication tools.

Today, a growing number of companies are adopting the concept of *integrated marketing communications (IMC)*. As defined by the American Association of Advertising Agencies (4 As), IMC is:

> . . . *a concept of marketing communications planning that recognizes the added value of a comprehensive plan that evaluates the strategic roles of a variety of communications disciplines—for example, general advertising, direct response, sales promotion and public relations—and combines these disciplines to provide clarity, consistency, and maximum communications' impact through the seamless integration of discrete messages.*

A 1991 study of the attitudes of top management and marketing executives in large consumer products companies indicated that over 70% favored the concept of integrated marketing communications as a way to improve their communications

FIGURE 22-10   Current Consumer States for Two Brands

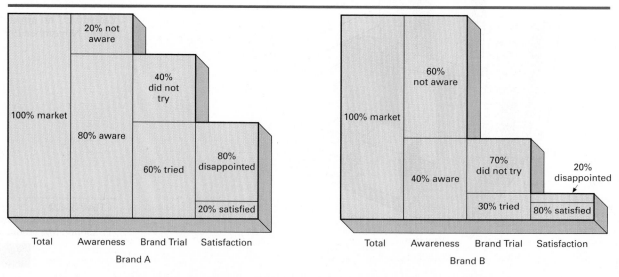

impact. And several large advertising agencies—Ogilvy & Mather, Young & Rubicam, Saatchi and Saatchi—quickly acquired major agencies specializing in sales promotion, public relations, and direct marketing in order to provide one-stop shopping. To their disappointment, their clients by and large have not bought their integrated marketing communications package, preferring to deal with separate agencies for the specific required communication programs.

Why the resistance? In part, large companies employ different communication specialists to consult their brand managers. Each communication specialist will fight for more budget. The sales manager will want to hire two extra sales representatives for $80,000, while the advertising manager will want to spend the same money on a prime-time television commercial. The public-relations manager sincerely believes that a publicity program will work wonders, while telemarketing and direct-mail program specialists believe they have the answer.

Brand managers themselves are poorly trained in the various forms of marketing communications, perhaps having only traditional experience in media advertising. They know very little about direct marketing, sales promotion, or public relations. The head of each functional communication tool knows little about the other communication tools. Furthermore, the communication heads have allied with their favorite outside specialist agencies and oppose turning over their communication responsibilities to one superadvertising agency. They argue that the company should choose the best specialist agency for each purpose, not second- and third-rate agencies just because they belong to the superadvertising agency. They are convinced that the advertising agency doesn't have its act together either, with each department in the agency operating as a separate profit center. They believe that the ad agency will still put most of the advertiser's money into the advertising budget.

To correct this situation, the following must be done:

◆ The chief executive officer must champion IMC and appoint a marketing communications director who has overall responsibility for the company's marketing communications efforts.

◆ The company must work out a philosophy of the capabilities and cost effectiveness of each communication tool.

◆ The company must track all promotional expenditures by product, promotional tool, stage of product life cycle, and observed effect, as a basis for improving further use of these tools.

◆ Brand managers must be retrained to think IMC. And all the communication specialists must be retrained in IMC, while keeping their specialist skills.

Integrated marketing communications will produce more message consistency and greater sales impact. It places a responsibility in someone's hand—where none existed before—to unify the company and brand images and messages as they come through thousands of company activities. IMC will improve the company's ability to reach the right customers with the right messages at the right time and in the right place. [29]

SUMMARY ❖

Marketing communications is one of the four major elements of the company's marketing mix. Marketers must know how to use advertising, sales promotion, direct marketing, public relations, and personal selling to communicate the product's existence and value to the target customers.

The communication process itself consists of nine elements: sender, receiver, encoding, decoding, message, media, response, feedback, and noise. Marketers must know how to get through to the target audience in the face of the audience's tendencies toward selective attention, distortion, and recall.

Developing the promotion program involves eight steps. The communicator must first identify the target audience and its characteristics, including the image that the audience has of the product. Next the communicator has to define the communication objective, whether it is to create awareness, knowledge, liking, preference, conviction, or purchase. Then a message must be designed containing an effective content, structure, format, and source. Then communication channels—both personal and nonpersonal—must be selected. Next the total promotion budget must be established. Four common methods are the affordable method, the percentage-of-sales method, the competitive-parity method, and the objective-and-task method. The promotion budget must be divided among the main promotional tools, as affected by such factors as push versus pull strategy, buyer-readiness stage, and product-life-cycle stage. The communicator must then monitor to see how much of the market becomes aware of the product, tries it, and is satisfied in the process. Finally, all of the communication must be managed and integrated for consistency, good timing, and cost effectiveness.

NOTES ❖

1. The definitions are adapted from Peter D. Bennett, *Dictionary of Marketing Terms* (Chicago: American Marketing Association, 1988).

2. Wilbur Schramm, "How Communication Works," in *The Process and Effects of Mass Communication*, eds. Wilbur Schramm and Donald F. Roberts (Urbana: University of Illinois Press, 1971), p. 4.

3. Ibid., p. 32.

4. See Brian Sternthal and C. Samuel Craig, *Consumer Behavior, An Information Processing Perspective* (Englewood Cliffs, NJ: Prentice-Hall, 1982), pp. 97–102.

5. See Alice H. Eagly, "Sex Differences in Influenceability," *Psychological Bulletin*, January 1978, pp. 86–116.

6. Donald F. Cox and Raymond A. Bauer, "Self-confidence and Persuasibility in Women," *Public Opinion Quarterly*, Fall 1964, pp. 453–66; and Raymond L. Horton, "Some Relationships between Personality and Consumer Decision-Making," *Journal of Marketing Research*, May 1979, pp. 233–46.

7. See John Fiske and John Hartley, *Reading Television* (London: Methuen, 1980), p. 79.

8. The semantic differential was developed by C. E. Osgood, C. J. Suci, and P. H. Tannenbaum, *The Measurement of Meaning* (Urbana: University of Illinois Press, 1957).

9. See Michael L. Ray, *Advertising and Communications Management* (Englewood Cliffs, NJ: Prentice-Hall, 1982).

10. See Brian Sternthal and C. Samuel Craig, "Humor in Advertising," *Journal of Marketing*, October 1973, pp. 12–18; and John Koten, "After the Serious '70s, Advertisers Are Going for Laughs Again," *The Wall Street Journal*, February 23, 1984, p. 31.

11. See James F. Engel, Roger D. Blackwell, and Paul W. Minard, *Consumer Behavior*, 5th ed. (Hinsdale, IL: Dryden Press, 1986), p. 477.

12. See C. I. Hovland, A. A. Lumsdaine, and F. D. Sheffield, *Experiments on Mass Communication*, vol. 3 (Princeton, NJ: Princeton University Press, 1948), Chap. 8. For an alternate viewpoint, see George E. Belch, "The Effects of Message Modality on One- and Two-Sided Advertising Messages," in *Advances in Consumer Research*, eds. Richard P. Bagozzi and Alice M. Tybout (Ann Arbor, MI: Association for Consumer Research, 1983), pp. 21–26.

13. See Sternthal and Craig, *Consumer Behavior*, pp. 282–84.

14. Herbert C. Kelman and Carl I. Hovland, "Reinstatement of the Communication in Delayed Measurement of Opinion Change," *Journal of Abnormal and Social Psychology* 48 (1953), 327–35.

15. C. E. Osgood and P. H. Tannenbaum, "The Principles of Congruity in the Predicition of Attitude Change," *Psychological Review* 62 (1955), 42–55.

16. See Regis McKenna, *The Regis Touch* (Reading, MA: Addison-Wesley, 1985); and Regis McKenna, *Relationship Marketing* (Reading, MA: Addison-Wesley, 1991).

17. Also see Thomas S. Robertson, *Innovative Behavior and Communication* (New York: Holt, Rinehart & Winston, 1971), Chap. 9.

18. See Philip Kotler, "Atmospherics as a Marketing Tool," *Journal of Retailing*, Winter 1973–1974, pp. 48–64.

19. P. F. Lazarsfeld, B. Berelson, and H. Gaudet, *The People's Choice*, 2nd ed. (New York: Columbia University Press, 1948), p. 151.

20. See George P. Moschis, "Social Comparison and Informal Group Influence," *Journal of Marketing Research*, August 1976, pp. 237–44.

21. See Evertt M. Rogers, *Diffusion of Innovations*, 3rd ed. (New York: Free Press, 1983).

22. Quoted in Daniel Seligman, "How Much for Advertising?" *Fortune*, December 1956, p. 123. For a good discussion of setting promotion budgets, see Michael L. Rothschild, *Advertising* (Lexington, MA: D. C. Heath, 1987), Chap. 20.

23. Albert Wesley Frey, *How Many Dollars for Advertising?* (New York: Ronald Press, 1955), p. 65.

24. Ibid., p. 49.

25. G. Maxwell Ule, "A Media Plan for 'Sputnik' Cigarettes," *How to Plan Media Strategy* (American Association of Advertising Agencies, 1957 Regional Convention), pp. 41–52.

26. For the characteristics of advertising and salesforce described, see Sidney J. Levy, *Promotional Behavior* (Glenview, IL: Scott, Foresman, 1971), Chap. 4.

27. *How Advertising Works in Today's Marketplace: The Morrill Study* (New York: McGraw-Hill, 1971), p. 4.

28. Cyril Freeman, "How to Evaluate Advertising's Contribution," *Harvard Business Review,* July–August 1962, pp. 137–48.

29. See Don E. Shultz, Stanley I. Tannenbaum, and Robert F. Lauterborn, *Integrated Marketing Communications: Putting It Together and Making It Work* (Lincolnwood, IL: NTC Business Books, 1992); Ernan Roman, *Integrated Direct Marketing* (New York: McGraw-Hill, 1989); and Mary L. Koelle, "Integrated Marketing Communications: Barriers to the Dream," *Integrated Marketing Communications*, June 19, 1991, pp. 7–9.

23

Designing Effective Advertising Programs

If you think advertising doesn't pay — we understand there are twenty-five mountains in Colorado higher than Pike's Peak. Can you name one?
THE AMERICAN SALESMAN

dvertising is one of the five major tools companies use to direct persuasive communications to target buyers and publics. We define *advertising* as any paid form of nonpersonal presentation and promotion of ideas, goods, or services by an identified sponsor. The spenders include not only business firms but museums, professionals, and social organizations that advertise their causes to various target publics. Advertising is employed in all the countries of the world, including socialist countries. Advertising is a cost-effective way to disseminate messages, whether it is to build brand preference for Coca-Cola or to motivate a developing nation's consumers to drink milk or to practice birth control.

Organizations obtain their advertising in different ways. In small companies, advertising is handled by someone in the sales or marketing department, who works with an advertising agency. A large company will set up its own advertising department, whose manager reports to the vice-president of marketing. The advertising department's job is to develop the total budget, help develop advertising strategy, approve advertising agency ads and campaigns, and handle direct-mail advertising, dealer displays, and other forms of advertising not ordinarily performed by the agency. Most companies use an outside advertising agency to help them create advertising campaigns and to select and purchase media (see Companies and Industries 23-1).

In developing an advertising program, marketing managers must always start by identifying the *target market* and *buyer motives*. Then they can proceed to make the five major decisions in developing an advertising program, known as the five Ms:

- What are the advertising objectives? *(mission)*
- How much can be spent? *(money)*
- What message should be sent? *(message)*
- What media should be used? *(media)*
- How should the results be evaluated? *(measurement)*

These decisions are further described in Figure 23-1 and in the following sections.

Setting the Advertising Objectives

The first step in developing an advertising program is to set the advertising objectives. These objectives must flow from prior decisions on the target market, market positioning, and marketing mix. The marketing-positioning and marketing-mix strategies define the job that advertising must do in the total marketing program.

Many specific communication and sales objectives can be assigned to advertising. Colley lists 52 possible advertising objectives in his well-known *Defining Advertising Goals for Measured Advertising Results*.[1] He outlines a method called DAGMAR (after the book's title) for turning advertising objectives into specific

How Does an Advertising Agency Work?

Madison Avenue is a familiar name to most Americans. It is a street in New York City where several major advertising agency headquarters are located. But most of the nation's 10,000 agencies are found outside New York, and almost every city has at least one agency, even if it is a one-person shop. Some ad agencies are huge—the largest U.S. agency, Young & Rubicam, has annual billings of over $7.5 billion. Dentsu, a Japanese agency, is the world's largest agency with billings of more than $10 billion.

Agencies employ specialists who generally can perform advertising tasks better than a company's own staff. Agencies also bring an outside point of view to solving a company's problems, along with years of experience from working with different clients and situations. And because the firm can dismiss its agency, an agency works hard to do a good job.

Advertising agencies usually have four departments: *creative,* which develops and produces ads; *media,* which selects media and places ads; *research,* which studies audience characteristics and wants; and *business,* which handles the agency's business activities. Each account is supervised by an account executive, and people in each department are usually assigned to work on one or more accounts.

Agencies often attract new business through their reputation or size. Generally, a client invites a few agencies to make a presentation for its business and then selects one of them.

Ad agencies have traditionally been paid through commissions and some fees. Under this system, the agency usually receives 15% of the purchased media cost as a rebate. Suppose the agency buys $60,000 of magazine space for a client. The magazine bills the advertising agency for $51,000 ($60,000 less 15%), and the agency bills the client for $60,000, keeping the $9,000 commission. If the client bought space directly from the magazine, it would have paid $60,000 because commissions are paid only to recognized advertising agencies.

However, both advertisers and agencies have become increasingly unhappy with the commission system. Large advertisers complain that they pay more for the same services received by small ones simply because they place more advertising. Advertisers also believe that the commission system drives agencies away from low-cost media and short advertising campaigns. Agencies are unhappy because they provide many extra services for an account without earning more. As a result, the trend is now toward paying either a straight fee or a combination commission and fee. And some large advertisers are tying agency compensation to the performance of the agency's advertising campaigns. Campbell's is happy to pay a 15% commission if the advertising campaign is excellent; if the campaign is only good, the agency gets 13%; and if the campaign is poor, the agency gets 13% and a warning. Philip Morris prefers to pay its agencies 15% and then add a bonus if the campaign is especially effective. The key problem with these pay-for-performance schemes is how to judge whether the campaign is excellent, good, fair, or poor. Sales and communication measures can both be misleading.

Another trend: In recent years, as growth in advertising spending has slowed, many agencies have tried to keep growing by buying other agencies, thus creating huge agency holding companies. The largest of these agency "megagroups," WPP Group, includes several large agencies—Ogilvy & Mather; J. Walter Thompson; Scali, McCabe, Sloves; Fallon McElligott; and others—with combined billings exceeding $18 billion.

Many agencies have also sought growth by diversifying into related marketing services. These new "superagencies" offer a complete menu of marketing and promotion services under one roof, including advertising, sales promotion, public relations, direct marketing, and marketing research. Some observers argue that the future of advertising agencies in the face of declining network advertising revenue and the proliferation of new media rests precisely on offering their clients *integrated marketing communications.* At the same time, many clients still prefer to pick and choose their own specialty communications agencies rather than rely on the total services of one superagency.

SOURCES: See Walecia Konrad, "A Word from the Sponsor: Get Results—Or Else," *Business Week,* July 4, 1988, p. 66; Anthony Ramirez, "Do Your Ads Need a Superagency?" *Fortune,* April 27, 1987, pp. 84–89; "U.S. and Foreign Advertising Agency Income Report," a special issue of *Advertising Age,* March 29, 1989; and Faye Rice, "A Cure for What Ails Advertising?" *Fortune,* December 16, 1991, pp. 119–22.

FIGURE 23-1   Major Decisions in Advertising Management

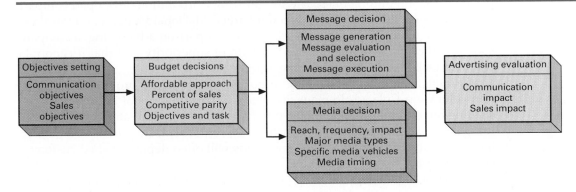

measurable goals. An *advertising goal* is a specific communication task and achievement level to be accomplished with a specific audience in a specific period of time. Colley provides an example:

> To increase among 30 million homemakers who own automatic washers the number who identify brand X as a low-sudsing detergent and who are persuaded that it gets clothes cleaner—from 10% to 40% in one year.

Advertising objectives can be classified as to whether their aim is to inform, persuade, or remind. Table 23-1 lists examples of these objectives.

Informative advertising figures heavily in the pioneering stage of a product category, where the objective is to build *primary demand*. Thus the yogurt industry initially had to inform consumers of yogurt's nutritional benefits and many uses.

Persuasive advertising becomes important in the competitive stage, where a company's objective is to build *selective demand* for a particular brand. Most advertising falls into this category. For example, Chivas Regal attempts to persuade consumers that it delivers more status than any other brand of Scotch whisky. Some persuasive advertising has moved into the category of *comparison advertising*, which seeks to establish the superiority of one brand through specific comparison with one or more other brands in the product class.[2] Comparison advertising has

TO INFORM	
Telling the market about a new product.	Describing available services.
Suggesting new uses for a product.	Correcting false impressions.
Informing the market of a price change.	Reducing buyers' fears.
Explaining how the product works.	Building a company image.

TO PERSUADE	
Building brand preference.	Persuading buyers to purchase now.
Encouraging switching to your brand.	Persuading buyers to receive a sales call.
Changing buyers' perception of product attributes.	

TO REMIND	
Reminding buyers that the product may be needed in the near future.	Keeping it in buyers' minds during off seasons.
Reminding buyers where to buy it.	Maintaining its top-of-mind awareness.

TABLE 23-1
Possible Advertising
Objectives

CHAPTER 23
Designing Effective
Advertising Programs

been used in such product categories as deodorants, fast-food hamburgers, tooth-pastes, tires, and automobiles. The Burger King Corporation developed comparison advertising for its franchise when it battled McDonald's in a war over flame broiling versus frying hamburgers. In using comparison advertising, a company should make sure that it can prove its claim of superiority and that it cannot be counterattacked in an area where the other brand is stronger.

Reminder advertising is highly important with mature products. Expensive four-color Coca-Cola ads in magazines have the purpose not of informing or persuading but of reminding people to purchase Coca-Cola. A related form of advertising is *reinforcement advertising*, which seeks to assure current purchasers that they have made the right choice. Automobile ads will often depict satisfied customers enjoying special features of their new car.

The choice of the advertising objective should be based on a thorough analysis of the current marketing situation. For example, if the product class is mature, and the company is the market leader, and if brand usage is low, the proper objective should be to stimulate more brand usage. On the other hand, if the product class is new, and the company is not the market leader, but its brand is superior to the leader, then the proper objective is to convince the market of the brand's superiority.

Deciding on the Advertising Budget

After determining advertising objectives, the company can proceed to establish its advertising budget for each product. The role of advertising is to shift the product's demand curve upward. The company wants to spend the amount required to achieve the sales goal. But how does a company know if it is spending the right amount? If the company spends too little, the effect is insignificant, and the company is, paradoxically, spending too much. On the other hand, if the company spends too much on advertising, then some of the money could have been put to better use. Some critics charge that large consumer-packaged-goods firms tend to overspend on advertising, and industrial companies generally underspend on advertising:[3]

> Large consumer-packaged-goods companies use image advertising extensively and are uncertain about its effect, since it doesn't produce immediate sales. They overspend as a form of "insurance" against not spending enough. In addition, their advertising agencies have a vested interest in convincing the companies to put most of their promotional funds into advertising. Finally, the companies get low efficiency out of their dollars by doing too little front-end work (marketing research and strategic positioning) and too much back-end work (copy testing).

> Industrial companies rely heavily on their salesforces to bring in orders. They do not spend enough on advertising to build customer awareness and comprehension. They underestimate the power of company and product image in preselling industrial customers.

A possible counterargument to the charge that consumer-packaged-goods companies spend too much is that advertising has a carryover effect that lasts beyond the current period. Although advertising is treated as a current expense, part of it is really an investment that builds up an intangible value called goodwill (or brand equity). When $5 million is spent on capital equipment, it is treated as, say, a five-year depreciable asset and only one fifth of the cost is written off in the first year. When $5 million is spent on advertising to launch a new product, the entire cost must be written off in the first year. This treatment of advertising as a complete expense limits the number of new-product launches that a company can undertake in any one year.

How much impact does advertising really have on inducing brand switching or brand loyalty? Tellis analyzed household purchases of 12 key brands of a frequently purchased consumer product and drew these conclusions:

> *Advertising appears effective in increasing the volume purchased by loyal buyers but less effective in winning new buyers. For loyal buyers, high levels of exposure per week may be unproductive because of a leveling off of ad effectiveness. . . . Advertising appears unlikely to have some cumulative effect that leads to loyalty. . . . Features, displays, and especially price have a stronger impact on response than does advertising.*[4]

These findings did not sit well with the advertising community, and several people attacked his data and methodology. A set of controlled experiments by the research firm IRI found advertising-producing sales gains during the test year that lasted two to three years later. They concluded that advertising's impact is grossly underestimated when only a one-year perspective is employed. The whole subject of advertising effectiveness is still poorly understood and awaiting evidence from further carefully designed empirical studies.

Four commonly used methods for setting the advertising budget were described earlier in Chapter 22, pp. 611–13. We favored the *objective-and-task method* because it requires the advertiser to define the advertising campaign's specific objectives and then to estimate the costs of the activities needed to achieve these objectives. Here we will describe specific factors to consider when setting the advertising budget:[5]

- ◆ *Stage in the Product Life Cycle:* New products typically receive large advertising budgets to build awareness and to gain consumer trial. Established brands usually are supported with lower budgets as a ratio to sales.
- ◆ *Market Share and Consumer Base:* High-market-share brands usually require less advertising expenditures as a percentage of sales to maintain their share. To build share by increasing market size requires larger advertising expenditures. Additionally, on a cost-per-impression basis, it is less expensive to reach consumers of a widely used brand than to reach consumers of low-share brands.
- ◆ *Competition and Cluster:* In a market with a large number of competitors and high advertising spending, a brand must advertise more heavily to be heard above the noise in the market. Even simple clutter from advertisements not directly competitive to the brand creates a need for heavier advertising.
- ◆ *Advertising Frequency:* The number of repetitions needed to put across the brand's message to consumers also determines the advertising budget.
- ◆ *Product Substitutability:* Brands in a commodity class (e.g., cigarettes, beer, soft drinks) require heavy advertising to establish a differential image. Advertising is also important when a brand can offer unique physical benefits or features.

Marketing scientists have built a number of advertising-expenditure models that take into account these and other factors. One of the best early models was developed by Vidale and Wolfe.[6] Essentially, the model called for a larger advertising budget, the higher the sales-response rate, the higher the sales-decay rate (i.e., the rate at which customers forget the advertising and brand), and the higher the untapped sales potential. On the other hand, this model leaves out other important factors, such as the rate of competitive advertising and the effectiveness of the company's ads.

Professor John Little proposed an adaptive-control method for setting the advertising budget.[7] Suppose the company has set an advertising-expenditure rate based on its most current information on the sales-response function. It spends this rate in all markets except in a subset of $2n$ markets randomly drawn. In n test markets the company spends at a lower rate, and in the other n it spends at a higher rate. This will yield information on the average sales created by low, medium, and high rates of advertising that can be used to update the parameters of the sales-response function. The updated function is used to determine the best advertising-expenditure rate for the next period. If this experiment is conducted each period, advertising expenditures will closely track optimal advertising expenditures.[8]

Deciding on the Advertising Message

Advertising campaigns differ in their creativity. As William Bernbach observed: "The facts are not enough.... Don't forget that Shakespeare used some pretty hackneyed plots, yet his message came through with great execution." Consider the following:[9]

> McDonald's spent $185.9 million on television in 1983, over twice the spending rate of its rival, Burger King. Yet viewers said they remembered and liked better Burger King ads over McDonald's.

> The best known and liked TV advertising in 1983 was Miller Lite beer commercials showing sports figures and celebrities arguing over whether Miller's advantage was "great taste" or "less filling." This campaign outperformed all the other beer commercials even though several spent more money.

Clearly, the effect of the creativity factor in a campaign can be more important than the number of dollars spent. Only after gaining attention can a commercial help to increase the brand's sales. The advertising adage is, "Until it's compelling, it isn't selling."

Advertisers go through three steps to develop a creative strategy: message generation, message evaluation and selection, and message execution.

Message Generation

In principle, the product's message should be decided as part of developing the product concept; it expresses the major benefit that the brand offers. Yet even within this concept, there may be latitude for a number of possible messages. And over time, the marketer might want to change the message without even changing the product, especially if consumers are seeking new or different "benefits" from the product.

Creative people use several methods to generate possible advertising appeals. Many creative people proceed *inductively* by talking to consumers, dealers, experts, and competitors. Consumers are the major source of good ideas. Their feelings about the strengths and shortcomings of existing brands provide important clues to creative strategy. Leo Burnett advocates "in-depth interviewing where I come realistically face to face with the people I am trying to sell. I try to get a picture in my mind of the kind of people they are—how they use this product and what it is."[10] A leading hair-spray company carries out continuous consumer research to determine consumer satisfaction with existing brands and attributes. If consumers want stronger holding power, the company considers reformulating its product and using this new appeal.

Some creative people use a *deductive* framework for generating advertising messages. Maloney proposed one framework (see Table 23-2).[11] He saw buyers as expecting one of four types of reward from a product: *rational*, *sensory*, *social*, or *ego*

TABLE 23-2 Examples of Twelve Types of Appeals

TYPES OF POTENTIALLY REWARDING EXPERIENCE WITH A PRODUCT	POTENTIAL TYPE OF REWARD			
	Rational	Sensory	Social	Ego Satisfaction
Results-of-Use Experience	1. Get clothes cleaner	2. Settles stomach upset completely	3. When you care enough to serve the best	4. For the skin you deserve to have
Product-in-Use Experience	5. The flour that needs no sifting	6. Real gusto in a great light beer	7. A deodorant to guarantee social acceptance	8. The store for the young executive
Incidental-to-Use Experience	9. The plastic pack keeps the cigarette fresh	10. The portable television that's lighter in weight, easier to lift	11. The furniture that identifies the home of modern people	12. Stereo for the man with discriminating taste

Source: Adapted from John C. Maloney, "Marketing Decisions and Attitude Research," in *Effective Marketing Coordination*, ed. George L. Baker, Jr. (Chicago: American Marketing Association, 1961), pp. 595–618.

satisfaction. And buyers might visualize these rewards from *results-of-use experience*, *product-in-use experience*, or *incidental-to-use experience.* Crossing the four types of rewards with the three types of experience generates twelve types of advertising messages.

The advertiser can generate a theme for each of the twelve cells as possible messages for the product. For example, the appeal "gets clothes cleaner" is a rational-reward promise following results-of-use experience; and the phrase "real gusto in a great light beer" is a sensory-reward promise connected with product-in-use experience.

How many alternative ad themes should the advertiser create before making a choice? The more ads that are independently created, the higher the probability of finding an excellent one. Yet the more time spent on creating ads, the higher the costs. There must be an optimal number of alternative ads that an agency should create and test for the client. Under the present commission system, typically 15%, the agency does not like to go to the expense of creating and pretesting many ads.[12] In an ingenious study, Gross concluded that agencies generally create too few ad alternatives for their clients.[13] He estimates that advertising agencies spend from 3% to 5% of their media income on creating and testing ads, whereas he believes they should spend closer to 15%. He even proposes that a company hire competing advertising agencies to create ads, from which the best one is selected.

Message Evaluation and Selection

The advertiser needs to evaluate the alternative messages. A good ad normally focuses on one core selling proposition. Twedt suggested that messages be rated on *desirability*, *exclusiveness*, and *believability*.[14] The message must first say something desirable or interesting about the product. The message must also say something exclusive or distinctive that does not apply to every brand in the product category. Finally, the message must be believable or provable.

For example, the March of Dimes searched for an advertising theme to raise money for its fight against birth defects.[15] Several messages came out of a brainstorming session. A group of young parents was asked to rate each message for interest, distinctiveness, and believability, assigning up to 100 points for each (see Figure 23-2). For example, "700 children are born each day with a birth defect" scored 70, 62, and 80 on interest, distinctiveness, and believability, while "Your next baby could be born with a birth defect" scored 58, 51, and 70. The first message outperformed the second on all accounts.

FIGURE 23-2
Advertising Message
Evaluation
Source: William A. Mindak and
H. Malcolm Bybee, "Marketing's
Application to Fund Raising,"
Journal of Marketing, July 1971,
pp. 13–18.

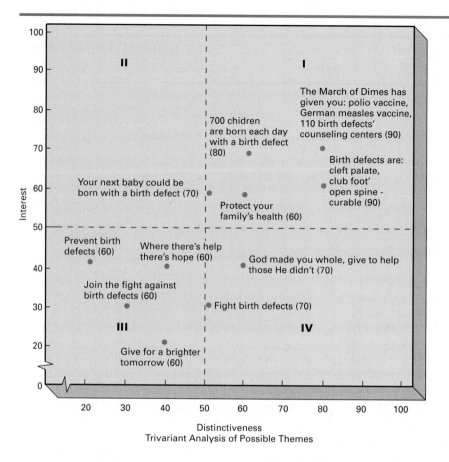

Distinctiveness
Trivariant Analysis of Possible Themes

The advertiser should pretest the ads to determine which appeal has the strongest behavioral impact. For example, the Washington State Apple Commission was trying to decide whether to advertise the various *uses* of apples or the *healthful* qualities of apples.[16] An experiment was carried out in 72 self-service food stores in six midwestern cities for 16 weeks. The results showed that the apple-use theme significantly outperformed the other theme in promoting sales.

Message Execution

The message's impact depends not only upon what is said but also on how it is said. Some ads aim for *rational positioning* and others for *emotional positioning.* American ads typically present an explicit feature or benefit designed to appeal to the rational mind: "Gets clothes cleaner," "Brings relief faster," and so on. Japanese ads are more indirect and appeal to the emotional mind: an example was Nissan's Infiniti car ad, which showed not the car but beautiful scenes from nature aimed at producing an emotional association and response.

The choice of headlines, copy, and so on, can make a difference in the ad's impact:

Lalita Manrai reported a study in which she created two ads for the same car. The first ad carried the headline "A New Car"; the second, the headline "Is This Car for You?" The second headline utilized an advertising strategy called *labeling,* in which the consumer is labeled as the type of person who is interested in that type of product. The two ads also differed in that the first ad described the car's features and the second described the car's benefits. In the test, the second ad far outperformed the first

ad in terms of overall impression of the product, reader interest in buying the product, and likelihood of recommending it to a friend.[17]

Message execution can be decisive for those products that are highly similar, such as detergents, cigarettes, coffee, and vodka. Consider the success of Absolut Vodka:

> Vodka is generally viewed as a commodity product. Yet the amount of brand preference and loyalty in the vodka market is astonishing. Most of it is based on selling an image, not the product. When the Swedish brand Absolut entered the U.S. market in 1979, the company sold a disappointing 7,000 cases that year. By 1991, sales had soared to over 2,000,000 cases. Absolut became the largest selling imported vodka in America, with 65% of the market. Its sales are also skyrocketing globally. Its secret weapon: a targeting, packaging, and advertising strategy. Absolut aims for sophisticated, upwardly mobile, affluent drinkers. The vodka is in a distinctive odd-shaped bottle suggestive of Swedish austerity. The bottle has become an icon and is used as the centerpiece of every ad, accompanied by puns such as "Absolut Magic" or "Absolut Larceny." Well-known artists—Warhol, Haring, Scharf—have designed many Absolut ads and the bottle image always figures in a clever way in the ad. Absolut has won more industry awards than any advertising campaign in history.

In preparing an ad campaign, the advertiser usually prepares a *copy strategy statement* describing the objective, content, support, and tone of the desired ad. Here is the strategy statement for a Pillsbury product called 1869 Brand Biscuits:

> The *objective* of the advertising is to convince biscuit users that now they can buy a canned biscuit that's as good as homemade—Pillsbury's 1869 Brand Biscuits. The *content* consists of emphasizing the following product characteristics: they look like homemade biscuits; they have the same texture as homemade biscuits; and they taste like homemade biscuits. *Support* for the "good as homemade" promise will be twofold: (1) 1869 Brand Biscuits are made from a special kind of flour (soft wheat flour) used to make homemade biscuits but never before used in making canned biscuits, and (2) the use of traditional American biscuit recipes. The *tone* of the advertising will be a news announcement, tempered by a warm, reflective mood emanating from a look back at traditional American baking quality.

Creative people must now find a *style, tone, words,* and *format* for executing the message. All of these elements must deliver a cohesive image and message. Since few people read body copy, the picture and headline must summarize the selling proposition.

Any message can be presented in different *execution styles:*

- ◆ *Slice of Life:* This shows one or more persons using the product in a normal setting. A family seated at the dinner table might express satisfaction with a new biscuit brand.
- ◆ *Lifestyle:* This emphasizes how a product fits in with a lifestyle. A Scotch whisky ad shows a handsome middle-aged man holding a glass of Scotch whisky in one hand and steering his yacht with the other.
- ◆ *Fantasy:* This creates a fantasy around the product or its use. Revlon's ad for Jontue features a barefoot woman wearing a chiffon dress. She comes out of an old French barn, crosses a meadow, and confronts a handsome young man on a white steed, who carries her away.
- ◆ *Mood or Image:* This builds an evocative mood or image around the product, such as beauty, love, or serenity. No claim is made about the product except through suggestion. Many cigarette ads, such as those for Salem and Newport cigarettes, create moods.

- *Musical:* This uses background music or shows one or more persons or cartoon characters singing a song involving the product. Many cola ads have used this format.
- *Personality Symbol:* This creates a character that personifies the product. The character might be *animated* (Jolly Green Giant, Pillsbury Doughboy, Mr. Clean) or *real* (Marlboro man, Morris the Cat).
- *Technical Expertise:* This shows the company's expertise and experience in making the product. Thus Hills Brothers shows one of its buyers carefully selecting the coffee beans, and Italian Swiss Colony emphasizes its many years of experience in winemaking.
- *Scientific Evidence:* This presents survey or scientific evidence that the brand is preferred or outperforms other brands. For years, Crest toothpaste has featured scientific evidence to convince toothpaste buyers of Crest's superior cavity-fighting properties.
- *Testimonial Evidence:* This features a highly credible, likable, or expert source endorsing the product. It could be a celebrity like O. J. Simpson (Hertz Rent-a-Car) or ordinary people saying how much they like the product (see Marketing Strategies 23-1).

The communicator must also choose an appropriate *tone* for the ad. Procter & Gamble is consistently positive in its tone; its ads say something superlatively positive about the product. Humor is avoided so as not to take attention away from the message. On the other hand, Volkswagen's ads for its famous "Beetle" typically took on a humorous and self-deprecating tone ("the Ugly Bug").

Marketing Strategies 23-1

Celebrity Endorsements as a Strategy

Marketers have used celebrities from time immemorial to endorse their products. A well-chosen celebrity can at the very least draw attention to a product or brand, as when Ed McMahon promotes Alpo dog food or Publishers Clearing House. Or the celebrity's mystique can transfer over to the brand—Catherine Deneuve in an ad for Chanel No 5. Or the celebrity's expertise and authority transfers to the brand—Chris Evert endorsing a Wilson tennis racquet.

The choice of the right celebrity is critical. The celebrity should have high recognition, high positive affect, and high appropriateness to the product. Howard Cossell has high recognition but negative affect among many groups. Sylvester Stallone has high recognition and high positive affect but might not be appropriate for advertising a World Peace Conference. Alan Alda, Paul Newman, and Bill Cosby could successfully advertise a large number of products because they have extremely high ratings for well-knownness and likability (known as the *Q* factor in the entertainment industry).

Athletes are a particularly effective endorsing group, especially for athletic products, beverages, and apparel. Joe Namath advertises Brut and Joe Montana advertises Pepsi. Michael Jordan, star of the Chicago Bulls, earns about $4 million a year endorsing Nike, Wilson, Coca-Cola, Johnson Products, and McDonald's. Nike sold $110 million worth of "Air Jordan" basketball shoes and apparel in its first year with Jordan as its representative. Not only does the celebrity's image appear in ads but the message is multiplied in the sales of T-shirts, toys and games, and hundreds of additional merchandise items.

The marketer's chief worry in selecting a celebrity is that the additional sales more than cover the costs. The marketer also hopes that the celebrity won't endorse too many other products and wear thin. Beyond this, they pray that the celebrity doesn't get involved in a scandal (as when Pepsi dropped Madonna because of an anti-Christian song), get sick, injured, or die. They cover these last risks with insurance.

SOURCE: See Irving Rein, Philip Kotler, and Martin Stoller, *High Visibility: How Executives, Politicians, Entertainers, Athletes, and Other Professionals Create, Market, and Achieve Successful Images* (New York: Dodd, Mead, 1987).

Memorable and attention-getting *words* must be found. The following themes listed on the left would have had much less impact without the creative phrasing on the right:[18]

Theme	Creative Copy
7-Up is not a cola.	"The Un-Cola."
Let us drive you in our bus instead of driving your car.	"Take the bus, and leave the driving to us."
Shop by turning the pages of the telephone directory.	"Let your fingers do the walking."
If you drink a beer, Schaefer is a good beer to drink.	"The beer to have when you're having more than one."
We don't rent as many cars, so we have to do more for our customers.	"We try harder."
Red Roof Inns offer inexpensive lodging.	"Sleep cheap at Red Roof Inns."

Creativity is especially required for headlines. There are six basic types of headlines: *news* ("New Boom and More Inflation Ahead . . . and What You Can Do About It"); *question* ("Have You Had It Lately?"); *narrative* ("They Laughed When I Sat Down at the Piano, but When I Started to Play!"); *command* ("Don't Buy Until You Try All Three"); *1-2-3 ways* ("12 Ways to Save on Your Income Tax"); and *how-what-why* ("Why They Can't Stop Buying"). Look at the care exercised by airlines to find the right way to describe their planes as safe without mentioning safety: "The Friendly Skies of United" (United); "The Wings of Man" (Eastern); and "The World's Most Experienced Airline" (Pan American).

Format elements such as ad size, color, and illustration will make a difference in an ad's impact as well as its cost. A minor rearrangement of mechanical elements within the ad can improve its attention-getting power. Larger-size ads gain more attention, though not necessarily by as much as their difference in cost. Four-color illustrations instead of black and white increase ad effectiveness and ad cost. By planning the relative dominance of different elements of the ad, optimal delivery can be achieved. New electronic eye movement studies show that consumers can be led through an ad by strategic placement of the ad's dominant elements.

A number of researchers into print advertisements report that the *picture*, *headline*, and *copy* are important, in that order. The reader first notices the picture, and it must be strong enough to draw attention. Then the headline must be effective in propelling the person to read the copy. The copy itself must be well composed. Even then, a really outstanding ad will be noted by less than 50% of the exposed audience; about 30% of the exposed audience might recall the headline's main point; about 25% might remember the advertiser's name; and less than 10% will have read most of the body copy. Ordinary ads, unfortunately, do not achieve even these results.

An industry study listed the following characteristics for ads that scored above average in recall and recognition: innovation (new product or new uses), "story appeal" (as an attention-getting device), before-and-after illustration, demonstrations, problem solution, and the inclusion of relevant characters that become emblematic of the brand (these may be cartoon figures, such as the Jolly Green Giant, or actual people, including celebrities).[19]

The questions are often raised: Why do so many ads look alike? Why aren't advertising agencies more creative? Norman W. Brown, former head of the advertising agency of Foote, Cone & Belding, answers that in many cases the advertisers, and not their agencies, are to blame. When his agency develops a highly creative

Socially Responsible Marketing 23-1

Issues in the Use of Advertising

Most marketers work hard to communicate openly and honestly with consumers. Still, abuses may occur, and public policy makers have developed a substantial body of laws and regulations to govern advertising.

By law, companies must avoid false or deceptive advertising. Advertisers must not make false claims, such as stating that a product cures something when it does not. They must avoid false demonstrations, such as using sand-covered plexiglass instead of sandpaper in a commercial to demonstrate that a razor blade can shave sandpaper.

Advertisers must not create ads that have the capacity to deceive, even though no one may actually be deceived. A floor wax cannot be advertised as giving six months' protection unless it does so under typical conditions, and a diet bread cannot be advertised as having

fewer calories simply because its slices are thinner. The problem is how to tell the difference between deception and "puffery"—simple acceptable exaggerations not intended to be believed.

Sellers must avoid bait-and-switch advertising that attracts buyers under false pretenses. For example, suppose a seller advertises a sewing machine at $79. When consumers try to buy the advertised machine, the seller cannot then refuse to sell it, downplay its features, show a faulty one, or promise unreasonable delivery dates in order to switch the buyer to a more expensive machine.

SOURCE: For further reading, see Louis W. Stern and Thomas I. Eovaldi, *Legal Aspects of Marketing Policy* (Englewood Cliffs, NJ: Prentice Hall, 1984); and Robert J. Posch, *The Complete Guide to Marketing and the Law* (Englewood Cliffs, NJ: Prentice Hall, 1988).

---

campaign, the brand manager or higher management levels worry about the risk and either reject it or ask for so many modifications that it loses its force. His conclusion: "Many ads aren't creative because many companies want comfort, not creativity."

At the same time, advertisers and their agencies must make sure that their "creative" advertising doesn't overstep social and legal norms (see Socially Responsible Marketing 23-1).

Deciding on the Media

The advertiser's next task is to choose advertising media to carry the advertising message. The steps are deciding on desired reach, frequency, and impact; choosing among major media types; selecting specific media vehicles; deciding on media timing; and deciding on geographical media allocation.

Deciding on Reach, Frequency, and Impact

Media selection is the *problem of finding the most cost-effective media to deliver the desired number of exposures to the target audience.* But what do we mean by the desired number of exposures? Presumably, the advertiser is seeking a certain response from the target audience, for example, a certain level of *product trial*. Now the rate of product trial will depend, among other things, on the level of audience brand awareness. Suppose the rate of product trial increases at a diminishing rate with the level of audience awareness, as shown in Figure 23-3(a). If the advertiser seeks a product trial rate of (say) T^*, it will be necessary to achieve a brand awareness level of A^*.

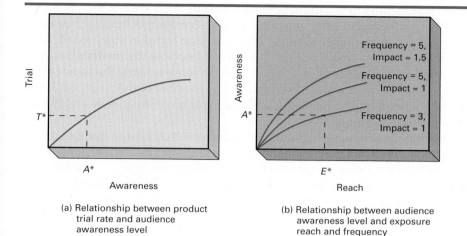

(a) Relationship between product
    trial rate and audience
    awareness level

(b) Relationship between audience
    awareness level and exposure
    reach and frequency

The next task is to find out how many exposures, E^*, will produce a level of audience awareness of A^*. The effect of exposures on audience awareness depends on the exposures' reach, frequency, and impact:

- *Reach (R):* The number of different persons or households exposed to a particular media schedule at least once during a specified time period.
- *Frequency (F):* The number of times within the specified time period that an average person or household is exposed to the message.
- *Impact (I):* The qualitative value of an exposure through a given medium (thus a food ad in *Good Housekeeping* would have a higher impact than in the *Police Gazette*).

Figure 23-3(b) shows the relationship between audience awareness and reach. Audience awareness will be greater, the higher the exposures' reach, frequency, and impact. The media planner recognizes important tradeoffs between reach, frequency, and impact. Suppose the media planner has an advertising budget of $1,000,000 and the cost per thousand exposures of average quality is $5. This means that the advertiser can buy 200,000,000 exposures ($= \$1,000,000 \div \$5/1,000$). If the advertiser seeks an average exposure frequency of 10, then the advertiser can reach 20,000,000 people ($= 200,000,000 \div 10$) with the given budget. Now if the advertiser wants higher-quality media costing $10 per thousand exposures, the advertiser will be able to reach only 10,000,000 people unless it is willing to lower the desired exposure frequency.

The relationship between reach, frequency, and impact is captured in the following concepts:

- *Total Number of Exposures (E):* This is the reach times the average frequency; that is, $E = R \times F$. This measure is referred to as the *gross rating points* (GRP). If a given media schedule reaches 80% of the homes with an average exposure frequency of 3, the media schedule is said to have a GRP of 240 ($= 80 \times 3$). If another media schedule has a GRP of 300, it is said to have more weight, but we cannot tell how this weight breaks down into reach and frequency.
- *Weighted Number of Exposures (WE):* This is the reach times average frequency times average impact, that is $WE = R \times F \times I$.

The media planning tradeoff is as follows. With a given budget, what is the most cost-effective combination of reach, frequency, and impact? *Reach* is more important when launching new products, flanker brands, well-known brands, or infrequently purchased brands, or going after an undefined target market. *Frequency* is more important where there are strong competitors, a complex story to tell, high consumer resistance, or a frequent-purchase cycle.[20] Suppose the media planner is willing to use average-impact media. It would make sense to settle the issue of frequency first. How many exposures does an average member of the target audience need for the advertising to trigger behavior? Once this target frequency is decided, then reach will be determined.

Many advertisers believe that a target audience needs a large number of exposures for the advertising to work. Too few repetitions can be a waste, since they will hardly be noticed. Others doubt the value of high ad frequency. They feel that after people see the same ad a few times, they either act on it, get irritated by it, or stop noticing it. Krugman asserted that three exposures to an advertisement might be enough:

> *The first exposure is by definition unique. As with the initial exposure to anything, a "What is it?" type of cognitive response dominates the reaction. The second exposure to a stimulus . . . produces several effects. One may be the cognitive reaction that characterized the first exposure, if the audience missed much of the message the first time around. . . . More often, an evaluative "What of it?" response replaces the "What is it?" response. . . . The third exposure constitutes a reminder, if a decision to buy based on the evaluations has not been acted on. The third exposure is also the beginning of disengagement and withdrawal of attention from a completed episode.*[21]

Krugman's thesis favoring three exposures has to be qualified. He means three actual *advertising exposures* — i.e., the person sees the ad three times. This should not be confused with *vehicle exposures*. If only half the readers look at magazine ads, or if the readers look at ads only every other issue, then the advertising exposure is only half of the vehicle exposures. Most research services estimate vehicle exposures, not ad exposures. A media strategist would have to buy more vehicle exposures than three in order to achieve Krugman's three "hits."[22]

Another factor arguing for advertising repetition is that of forgetting. The job of advertising repetition is partly to put the message back into memory. The higher the forgetting rate associated with that brand, product category, or message, the higher the warranted level of repetition.

But repetition is not enough. Ads wear out and viewers tune out. Advertisers should not coast on a tired ad but insist on fresh executions by their advertising agency. For example, Duracell can choose from more than 40 different versions of its basic ad.

Choosing Among Major Media Types

The media planner has to know the capacity of the major media types to deliver reach, frequency, and impact. The major advertising media along with their costs, advantages, and limitations are profiled in Table 23-3.

Media planners make their choice among these media categories by considering several variables, the most important ones being the following:

- ◆ *Target-Audience Media Habits:* For example, radio and television are the most effective media for reaching teenagers.
- ◆ *Product:* Women's dresses are best shown in color magazines, and Polaroid cameras are best demonstrated on television. Media types have different potentials for demonstration, visualization, explanation, believability, and color.

TABLE 23-3 Profiles of Major Media Types

MEDIUM	VOLUME IN BILLIONS	PERCENTAGE	EXAMPLE OF COST	ADVANTAGES	LIMITATIONS
Newspapers	30.4	24.1	$29,800 for one page, weekday *Chicago Tribune*	Flexibility; timeliness; good local market coverage; broad acceptance; high believability	Short life; poor reproduction quality; small "pass-along" audience
Television	27.4	21.7	$1,500 for 30 seconds of prime time in Chicago	Combines sight, sound, and motion; appealing to the senses; high attention; high reach	High absolute cost; high clutter; fleeting exposure; less audience selectivity
Direct mail	24.4	19.3	$1,520 for the names and addresses of 40,000 veterinarians	Audience selectivity; flexibility; no ad competition within the same medium; personalization	Relatively high cost; "junk mail" image
Radio	8.5	6.7	$700 for one minute of drive time (during commuting hours, A.M. and P.M.) in Chicago	Mass use; high geographic and demographic selectivity; low cost	Audio presentation only; lower attention than television; nonstandardized rate structures; fleeting exposure
Magazines	6.5	5.2	$84,390 for one page, four-color in *Newsweek*	High geographic and demographic selectivity; credibility and prestige; high-quality reproduction; long life; good pass-along readership	Long ad purchase lead time; some waste circulation; no guarantee of position
Outdoor	1.1	0.8	$25,500 per month for 71 billboards in metropolitan Chicago	Flexibility; high repeat exposure; low cost; low competition	No audience selectivity; creative limitations
Other	28.1	22.2			
Total	126.4	100.0			

Source: Columns 2 and 3 are from Robert J. Coen, "How Bad a Year for Ads Was 1991?" *Advertising Age,* May 4, 1992, pp. 3, 51.

- *Message:* A message announcing a major sale tomorrow will require radio or newspapers. A message containing a great deal of technical data might require specialized magazines or mailings.
- *Cost:* Television is very expensive, whereas newspaper advertising is inexpensive. What counts is the cost-per-thousand exposures rather than the total cost.

Ideas about media impact and cost must be reexamined regularly. For a long time, television enjoyed the dominant position in the media mix, and other media were neglected. Then media researchers began to notice television's reduced effectiveness, which was due to increased commercial clutter (advertisers beamed shorter and more numerous commercials at the television audience, resulting in poorer audience attention and impact), increased "zipping and zapping" of commercials, and lowered commercial TV viewing owing to the growth in cable TV and VCRs. Furthermore, television advertising costs rose faster than other media costs. Several companies found that a combination of print ads and television commercials often did a better job than television commercials alone. This illustrates that advertisers must periodically review the different media to determine their best buys. Another reason for review is the continuous emergence of *new media* (see Marketing Environment and Trends 23-1).

Given the abundant media and their characteristics, the media planner must decide on how to allocate the budget to the major media types. For example, in launching its new biscuit, Pillsbury might decide to allocate $3 million to daytime

The Ceaseless Search for New Media

Media, like other products and services, pass through clearly identified life-cycle stages. Each new medium— newspapers, magazines, radio, motion pictures, television—has a period of dominance followed by decline. The older media don't die but petrify at some level, although experiencing from time to time new surges of interest. Today new media are being invented faster and their cycle of ascendancy and decline may be shorter.

As network television costs soar and audiences shrink, advertisers are driven to invent or discover new targeted advertising media. Advertisers are shifting larger portions of their budgets to media that cost less and target more effectively.

Two media benefiting most from this shift are outdoor advertising and cable television. Advertisers have increased their spending on outdoor media by 25% in the last four years, to $1.1 billion annually. Outdoor advertising provides an excellent way to reach important local consumer segments. As for cable television, today it reaches more than 59% of all U.S. households and produces an advertising revenue exceeding $3 billion a year. Cable systems allow narrow programming formats such as all sports, all news, nutrition programs, arts programs, and others that target select groups.

Another promising media site is the store itself. Older promotional in-store vehicles, such as end-aisle displays and special price tags, are being supplemented by a flurry of new media vehicles. Some supermarkets are selling space on their tiled floors for company logos. They are experimenting with *talking shelves,* where shoppers get information as they pass certain food sections. One company has introduced the *videocart,* which contains a computerized screen that carries consumer-benefit information ("cauliflower is rich in vitamin C") 70% of the time and advertiser promotions ("20¢ off on

White Star Tuna this week") 30% of the time.

New media are also being created for other special locations. The most inventive media creator is Christopher Whittle, who has targeted both physician waiting rooms and school lunchrooms. His company places copies of *Special Reports* in cooperating doctors' waiting rooms, which carry feature articles on family, health, and money matters along with full-page ads from Kraft, P&G, and other major advertisers. He seeks agreement from physicians to carry no more than two other magazines in their waiting rooms and boasts of 25 million readers who, he claims, are four times more likely to remember ads in *Special Reports* than those in traditional women's service magazines. He also donates television sets to school lunchrooms, provided they carry his Channel One news show, which also carries commercials of special interest to young people. In this area, he has met a lot of resistance.

Others are pushing for ads to appear in best-selling paperback books and in movie videotapes. Written material such as annual reports, data sheets, catalogs, and newsletters are increasingly carrying ads. Many companies sending out monthly bills (credit card companies, department stores, oil companies, airlines, and the like) are including inserts in the envelope that advertise products. Some companies mail audiotapes or videotapes to prospects that advertise their products. As the productivity of more standard media declines, the search for new media will grow unabated.

SOURCES: Betsy Sharkey, "Shopping Cart Videos: A New Medium for Ads?" *Adweek*, January 8, 1990; "Whittle's Advertisers Are Getting Tired of Waiting," *Business Week*, January 22, 1990, p. 33; and "Alternative Media," *PROMO*, December 1990, pp. 6, 7, 14, 24.

network television, $2 million to women's magazines, and $1 million to daily newspapers in 20 major markets.

Selecting Specific Media Vehicles

Now the media planner searches for the most cost-effective media vehicles. The media planner faces an incredible number of choices:

In the magazine field, there are over 4,000 special-interest magazines. This means that advertisers can easily reach special-interest groups but will find it hard to reach general-audience groups. The only remaining large-circulation magazines are *TV Guide* and *Reader's Digest*, both with 17 million circulation, and then *Time*, *Newsweek*, and so on, with 4 million to 5 million circulation.

In the television field, there are over 1,000 commercial and 300 public TV stations. Beyond this, there are thousands of program vehicles to consider. The favorites used to be prime-time network shows. Yet network TV, which reached 90% of homes during prime time in 1980, is now reaching just over 60%. The inroads are being made by cable and pay-per-view TV, videorecorders, compact disc players, computers, and other entertainment forms that at present offer little opportunity for advertising. Advertisers are experimenting with both old and new media to offset the decline of network TV.[23]

In the radio field, there are nearly 9,000 radio stations; and in the newspaper field, over 17,000 daily newspapers. All of this spells a condition of extreme *media fragmentation*, which may allow advertisers to reach special-interest groups more effectively but raises the cost of reaching general audiences for such products as soaps, food products, and small appliances.

For example, the advertiser who decides to buy 30 seconds of advertising on network television can pay $100,000 for a popular prime-time TV program, $380,000 for an especially popular program like *The Cosby Show*, or $550,000 for an event like the Super Bowl. How does the media planner make choices among the rich array of media? The media planner relies on media-measurement services that provide estimates of audience size, composition, and media cost. Audience size has several possible measures:

- *Circulation:* The number of physical units carrying the advertising.
- *Audience:* The number of people who are exposed to the vehicle. (If the vehicle has pass-on readership, then the audience is larger than circulation.)
- *Effective Audience:* The number of people with the target's characteristics who are exposed to the vehicle.
- *Effective Ad-Exposed Audience:* The number of people with the target's characteristics who actually saw the ad.

THE COST-PER-THOUSAND CRITERION ❖ Media planners calculate the *cost per thousand persons reached* by a vehicle. If a full-page, four-color ad in *Newsweek* costs $84,000 and *Newsweek's* estimated readership is three million people, the cost of exposing the ad to 1,000 persons is approximately $28. The same ad in *Business Week* may cost $30,000 but reach only 775,000 persons—at a cost per thousand of $39. The media planner would rank each magazine by cost per thousand and favor those magazines with the lowest cost per thousand for reaching target consumers.

Several adjustments have to be applied to this initial measure. First, the measure should be adjusted for *audience quality*. For a baby lotion advertisement, a magazine read by one million young mothers would have an exposure value of one million, but if read by one million old men it would have a zero exposure value. Second, the exposure value should be adjusted for the *audience-attention probability*. Readers of *Vogue*, for example, pay more attention to ads than do readers of *Newsweek*. Third, the exposure value should be adjusted for the *editorial quality* (prestige and believability) that one magazine might have over another. Fourth, the exposure value should be adjusted for the magazine's ad placement policies and extra services (such as regional or occupational editions and lead time requirements).

Media planners are increasingly using more sophisticated measures of media effectiveness and employing them in mathematical models for arriving at the best media mix. Many advertising agencies use a computer program to select the initial media and then make further improvements based on subjective factors omitted in the model.[24]

Deciding on Media Timing

The advertiser faces a macroscheduling problem and a microscheduling problem.

MACROSCHEDULING PROBLEM ❖ The advertiser has to decide how to schedule the advertising in relation to seasonal and business-cycle trends. Suppose 70% of a product's sales occur between June and September. The firm has three options. The firm can vary its advertising expenditures to follow the seasonal pattern, to oppose the seasonal pattern, or to be constant throughout the year. Most firms pursue a policy of seasonal advertising. Yet consider this:

> Some years ago, one of the soft-drink manufacturers put more money into off-season advertising. This resulted in increased nonseasonal consumption of its brand, while not hurting the brand's seasonal consumption. Other soft-drink manufacturers started to do the same, with the net result that a more-balanced consumption pattern occurred. The previous seasonal concentration of advertising had created a self-fulfilling prophecy.

Forrester has proposed using his "industrial dynamics" methodology to test cyclical advertising policies.[25] He sees advertising as having a lagged impact on consumer awareness; awareness has a lagged impact on factory sales; and factory sales have a lagged impact on advertising expenditures. These time relationships can be studied and formulated mathematically into a computer-simulation model. Alternative timing strategies would be simulated to assess their varying impacts on company sales, costs, and profits. Rao and Miller also developed a lag model to relate a brand's share to advertising and promotional expenditures on a market-by-market basis. They tested their model successfully with five Lever brands in 15 districts relating market share to dollars spent on TV, print, price-off, and trade promotions.[26]

Kuehn developed a model to explore how advertising should be timed for frequently purchased, highly seasonal, low-cost grocery products.[27] Kuehn showed that the appropriate timing pattern depends on the *degree of advertising carryover* and the *amount of habitual behavior in customer brand choice*. *Carryover* refers to the rate at which the effect of an advertising expenditure wears out with the passage of time. A carryover of 0.75 per month means that the current effect of a past advertising expenditure is 75% of its level in the previous month. *Habitual behavior* indicates how much brand holdover occurs independent of the level of advertising. High habitual purchasing, say 0.90, means that 90% of the buyers repeat their brand choice in the next period.

Kuehn found that when there is no advertising carryover or habitual purchasing, the decision maker is justified in using a percentage-of-sales rule to budget advertising. The optimal timing pattern for advertising expenditures coincides with the expected seasonal pattern of industry sales. But if there is advertising carryover and/or habitual purchasing, the percentage-of-sales budgeting method is not optimal. It would be better to time advertising to lead sales. Advertising expenditures should peak before sales peak. Lead time should be greater, the higher the carryover. Furthermore, the advertising expenditures should be steadier, the greater the habitual purchasing.

MICROSCHEDULING PROBLEM ❖ The microscheduling problem calls for allocating advertising expenditures within a short period to obtain the maximum impact. Suppose the firm decides to buy 30 radio spots in the month of September.

Figure 23-4 shows several possible patterns. The left side shows that advertising messages for the month can be concentrated in a small part of the month ("burst" advertising), dispersed continuously throughout the month, or dispersed intermittently throughout the month. The top side shows that the advertising messages can be beamed with a level, rising, falling, or alternating frequency.

The most effective pattern depends upon the communication objectives in relation to the nature of the product, target customers, distribution channels, and other marketing factors. Consider the following cases:

> A *retailer* wants to announce a preseason sale of ski equipment. She recognizes that only certain people are interested in skis. She thinks that the target buyers need to hear the message only once or twice. Her objective is to maximize reach, not frequency. She decides to concentrate the messages on sale days at a level rate but to vary the time of day to avoid the same audiences. She uses pattern (1).

> A *muffler manufacturer-distributor* wants to keep his name before the public. Yet he does not want his advertising to be too continuous because only 3 to 5% of the cars on the road need a new muffler at any given time. He chooses to use intermittent advertising. Furthermore, he recognizes that Fridays are paydays, so he sponsors a few messages on a midweek day and more messages on Friday. He uses pattern (12).

The timing pattern should consider three factors. *Buyer turnover* expresses the rate at which new buyers enter the market; the higher this rate, the more continuous the advertising should be. *Purchase frequency* is the number of times during the period that the average buyer buys the product; the higher the purchase frequency, the more continuous the advertising should be. The *forgetting rate* is the rate at which the buyer forgets the brand; the higher the forgetting rate, the more continuous the advertising should be.

In launching a new product, the advertiser has to choose between ad continuity, concentration, flighting, and pulsing. *Continuity* is achieved by scheduling exposures evenly throughout a given period. But high advertising costs and seasonal variations in sales discourage continuous advertising. Generally, advertisers use

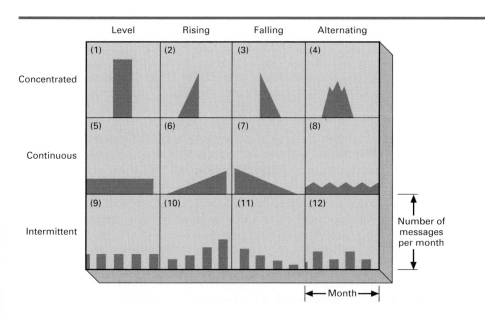

FIGURE 23-4
Classification of Advertising Timing Patterns

continuous advertising in expanding market situations, with frequently purchased items, and in tightly defined buyer categories. *Concentration* calls for spending all the advertising dollars in a single period. This makes sense for products with only one selling season or holiday. *Flighting* calls for advertising for some period, followed by a hiatus with no advertising, and then followed by a second flight. It is used when funding is limited, the purchase cycle is relatively infrequent, or with seasonal items. *Pulsing* is continuous advertising at low weight levels reinforced periodically by waves of heavier activity. Pulsing draws upon the strength of continuous advertising and flights to create a compromise scheduling strategy. Those who favor pulsing feel that the audience will learn the message more thoroughly, and money can be saved.

> *Anheuser-Busch's research indicated that Budweiser could suspend advertising in a particular market and experience no adverse sales effect for at least a year and a half. Then the company could introduce a six-month burst of advertising and restore the previous growth rate. This analysis led Budweiser to adopt a pulsing advertising strategy.*[28]

Deciding on Geographical Media Allocation

A company has to decide how to allocate its advertising budget over space as well as over time. The company makes "national buys" when it places ads on national TV networks or in nationally circulated magazines. It makes "spot buys" when it buys TV time in just a few TV markets or regional editions of magazines. In these cases, the ads reach a market 40 to 60 miles from a city center, called Areas of Dominant Influence (ADIs) or Designated Marketing Areas (DMAs). Finally, the company makes "local buys" when they advertise in local newspapers, radio, or outdoor.

As an example of the geographical allocation issues that arise, consider the following:

> Pizza Hut levies a 4% advertising fee on its franchisees. It spends 2% of its budget on national media and 2% on regional and local media. Some of the national advertising is wasted because of Pizza Hut's low penetration in certain areas. Thus, even though Pizza Hut may have a 30% share of the franchised pizza market nationally, this may vary from a 5% share in some cities to a 70% share in other cities. The franchisees in the higher market share cities want much more advertising money spent in these areas. But if Pizza Hut spent its whole budget on regional media, there would only be enough money to cover half of the nation. Regional spending involves greater production costs and a larger number of creative executions to match local situations, instead of only one creative execution for the national market. Thus, national advertising offers efficiency but fails to effectively address the different local situations. Ironically, companies vary their sales promotion regionally, but normally spend much of their advertising money nationally.

Evaluating Advertising Effectiveness

Good planning and control of advertising depend critically on measures of advertising effectiveness. Yet the amount of fundamental research on advertising effectiveness is appallingly small. According to Forrester:

> *I doubt that there is any other function in industry where management bases so much expenditure on such scanty knowledge. The advertising industry spends 2 or 3% of its gross dollar volume on what it calls "research," and even if this were really true research, the small amount*

would be surprising. However, I estimate that less than a tenth of this amount would be considered research plus development as these terms are defined in the engineering and product research departments of companies . . . probably no more than ⅕ of 1% of total advertising expenditure is used to achieve an enduring understanding of how to spend the other 99.8%.[29]

Most measurement of advertising effectiveness is of an applied nature, dealing with specific ads and campaigns. Most of the money is spent by agencies on *pretesting* ads, and much less is spent on *postevaluating* their effects. Many companies develop an advertising campaign, put it into the national market, and then evaluate its effectiveness. It would be better to limit the campaign to one or a few cities first and evaluate its impact before rolling a campaign throughout the country with a very large budget. One company tested its new campaign first in Phoenix. The campaign bombed, and the company saved all the money that it would have spent going national.

Most advertisers try to measure the *communication effect* of an ad, that is, its potential effect on awareness, knowledge, or preference. They would like to measure the *sales effect* but often feel it is too difficult to measure. Yet both can be researched.

Communication-Effect Research

Communication-effect research seeks to determine whether an ad is communicating effectively. Called *copy testing*, it can be done before an ad is put into media and after it is printed or broadcast.

There are three major methods of advertising pretesting. The first is a *direct rating method*, which asks consumers to rate alternative ads. These ratings are used to evaluate an ad's attention, read-through, cognitive, affective, and behavior strengths (see Figure 23-5). Although an imperfect measure of an ad's actual impact, a high rating indicates a potentially more effective ad. *Portfolio tests* ask consumers to view and/or listen to a portfolio of advertisements, taking as much time as they need. Consumers are then asked to recall all the ads and their content, aided or unaided by the interviewer. Their recall level indicates an ad's ability to stand out and to have its message understood and remembered. *Laboratory tests* use equipment to measure consumers' physiological reactions—heartbeat, blood pressure, pupil dilation, perspiration—to an ad. These tests measure an ad's attention-getting power but reveal nothing about its impact on beliefs, attitudes, or intentions. (Marketing Concepts and Tools 23-1 describes specific advertising research techniques.)

Advertisers are also interested in posttesting the overall communication im-

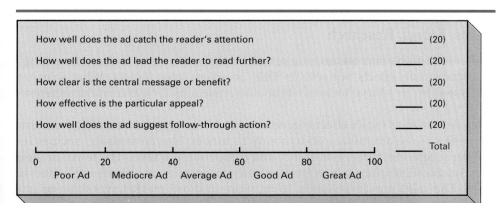

FIGURE 23-5
Simplified Rating Sheet
for Ads

Advertising Research Techniques

There are several methods of ad pretesting.

PRINT ❖ Starch and Gallup & Robinson, Inc. are two widely used print pretesting services in which test ads are placed into magazines. The magazines are then circulated to consumers. These consumers are contacted later and interviewed concerning the magazines and their advertising. Recall and recognition tests are used to determine advertising effectiveness. In Starch's case, three readership scores are prepared: (a) *noted*, the percentage of readers who recall seeing the ad in the magazine; (b) *seen/associated*, the percentage who correctly identify the product and advertiser with the ad; and (c) *read most*, the percentage who say they read more than half of the written material in the ad. Starch also furnishes adnorms showing the average scores for each product class for the year, and separately for men and women for each magazine, to enable advertisers to compare their ad's impact to competitors' ads.

BROADCAST SERVICES ❖ Four broadcast pretest methods are available:

♦ *In-Home Tests:* A small-screen projector is taken into the homes of target consumers. These consumers then view the commercials. The technique gains a subject's complete attention but creates an unnatural viewing situation.

♦ *Trailer Tests:* To get closer to the consumers' actual decision point, pretesting is conducted in a trailer in a shopping center. Shoppers are shown the test products and given an opportunity to select a series of brands in a simulated shopping situation. Consumers then view a series of commercials. They are then given coupons to be used in the shopping center. By evaluating redemption, advertisers can estimate the commercial's influence on purchase behavior.

♦ *Theater Tests:* Consumers are invited to a theater to view a potential new television series along with some commercials. Before the show begins, the consumers indicate their preferred brands in different categories. After the viewing, consumers are again asked to choose their preferred brands in various categories. Preference changes are assumed to measure the persuasive power of the commercials.

♦ *On-Air Tests:* These tests are conducted on a regular TV channel. Respondents are recruited to watch the program during the test commercial or are selected based on their having viewed the program. They are asked questions about their commercial recall. This technique creates a real-world atmosphere in which to evaluate commercials.

pact of a completed advertising campaign. To what extent did the ad campaign increase brand awareness, brand comprehension, stated brand preference, and so on? Assuming that the advertiser had measured these levels before the campaign, the advertiser can draw a random sample of consumers after the campaign to assess the communication effects. If a company hoped to increase brand awareness from 20% to 50% and only succeeded in increasing it to 30%, then something is wrong: the company is not spending enough, its ads are poor, or some other factor is missing.

Sales-Effect Research

Communication-effect advertising research helps advertisers assess advertising's communication effects but reveals little about its sales impact. What sales are generated by an ad that increases brand awareness by 20% and brand preference by 10%?

Advertising's sales effect is generally harder to measure than its communication effect. Sales are influenced by many factors besides advertising, such as the product's features, price, availability and competitors' actions. The fewer or more controllable these other factors are, the easier it is to measure advertising's effect on sales. The sales impact is easiest to measure in direct-marketing situations and hardest to measure in brand or corporate-image-building advertising.

Companies are generally interested in finding out whether they are overspending or underspending on advertising. One approach is to work with the following formulation:

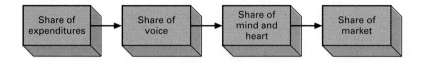

In other words, a company's share of advertising expenditures produces a share of voice that earns a share of their minds and hearts and ultimately a share of market. Peckham studied the relationship between share of voice and share of market for several consumer products over a number of years and found a 1-to-1 ratio for established products and a 1.5-2.0 to 1.0 ratio for new products.[30] Using this information, suppose we observed the following data for three well-established firms selling an almost identical product at an identical price:

	ADVERTISING EXPENDITURE	SHARE OF VOICE	SHARE OF MARKET	ADVERTISING EFFECTIVENESS
A	$2,000,000	57.1	40.0	70
B	1,000,000	28.6	28.6	100
C	500,000	14.3	31.4	220

Firm A spends $2,000,000 of the industry's total expenditures of $3,500,000; so its share of voice is 57.1%. Yet its share of market is only 40%. By dividing its share of market by its share of voice, we get an advertising-effectiveness ratio of 70, suggesting that firm A is either overspending or misspending. Firm B is spending 28.6% of total advertising expenditures and has a 28.6 market share; the conclusion is that it is spending its money efficiently. Firm C is spending only 14.3% of the total and yet achieving a market share of 31.4%; the conclusion is that it is spending its money superefficiently and should probably increase its expenditures.

Researchers try to measure the sales impact through analyzing either historical or experimental data. The *historical approach* involves correlating past sales to past advertising expenditures on a current or lagged basis using advanced statistical techniques. Palda studied the effect of advertising expenditures on the sales of Lydia Pinkham's Vegetable Compound between 1908 and 1960.[31] He calculated the short-term and long-term marginal sales effects of advertising. The marginal advertising dollars increased sales by only 50¢ in the short term, suggesting that Pinkham spent too much on advertising. But the long-term marginal sales effect was three times as large. Palda calculated a posttax marginal rate of return on company advertising of 37% over the whole period.

Montgomery and Silk estimated the sales effectiveness of three communication tools used in the pharmaceutical industry.[32] A drug company spent 38% of its communication budget on direct mail, 32% on samples and literature, and 29% on journal advertising. Yet the sales-effects research indicated that journal advertising, the least-used communication tool, had the highest long-run advertising elasticity, here .365; samples and literature had an elasticity of .108; and direct mail had an elasticity of only .018. They concluded that the company spent too much on direct mail and too little on journal advertising.

Other researchers use *experimental design* to measure the sales impact of advertising. Instead of spending the normal percentage of advertising to sales in all

FIGURE 23-6
Experimental Design for
Testing the Effect of Three
Levels of Advertising
Expenditure on Market
Share
Source: From p. 166, *Mathematical
Models and Marketing Management*,
by Robert Buzzell. Boston: Division
of Research, Graduate School of
Business Administration, Harvard
University, 1968. Reprinted by
permission.

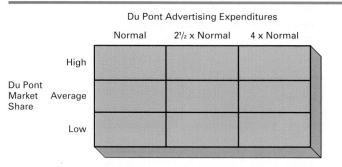

territories, the company spends more in some territories and less in others. These tactics are called *high-spending tests* and *low-spending tests*. If the high-spending tests produce substantial sales increases, it appears that the company has been underspending. If they fail to produce more sales and if low-spending tests do not lead to sales decreases, then the company has been overspending. These tests, of course, must be accompanied by good experimental controls and last sufficiently long to capture lagged effects of changed advertising-expenditure levels.

> Du Pont was one of the first companies to design advertising experiments. Du Pont's paint division divided 56 sales territories into high, average, and low market-share territories. Du Pont spent the normal amount for advertising in one third of the group; in another third, two and one-half times the normal amount; and in the remaining third, four times the normal amount (see Figure 23-6). At the end of the experiment, Du Pont estimated how much extra sales were created by higher levels of advertising expenditure. Du Pont found that higher advertising expenditure increased sales at a diminishing rate, and that the sales increase was weaker in Du Pont's high market-share territories.[33]

Another approach to allocating an advertising budget geographically is to use a model that considers the differences between geographic areas in terms of their market size, advertising response, media efficiency, competition, and profit margins. Urban developed a media allocation model that relies upon these geographic variables to allocate the advertising budget.[34]

In general, a growing number of companies are striving to measure the sales effect of advertising expenditures instead of settling only for communication-effect measures.

SUMMARY ❖

Advertising—the use of paid media by a seller to communicate persuasive information about its products, services, or organization—is a potent promotional tool. Advertising takes on many forms (national, regional, local; consumer, industrial, retail; product, brand, institutional; and so on) designed to achieve a variety of objectives (immediate sales, brand recognition, preference, and so on).

Advertising decision making is a five-step process consisting of objectives setting, budget decision, message decision, media decision, and ad-effectiveness evaluation. Advertisers need to establish clear goals as to whether the advertising is supposed to inform, persuade, or remind buyers. The advertising budget can be established on the basis of what is affordable, as a percentage of sales, on the basis of competitors' expenditures, or on the basis of objectives and tasks; and more advanced decision models are available. The message decision calls for generating messages, evaluating and selecting among them, and executing them effectively. The media decision calls for defining the reach, frequency, and impact goals; choosing among major media types; selecting specific media vehicles; and scheduling the media. Finally, campaign evaluation calls for evaluating the communication and sales effects of advertising, before, during, and after the advertising.

NOTES ❖

1. See Russell H. Colley, *Defining Advertising Goals for Measured Advertising Results* (New York: Association of National Advertisers, 1961).

2. See William L. Wilkie and Paul W. Farris, "Comparison Advertising: Problem and Potential," *Journal of Marketing,* October 1975, pp. 7–15.

3. For a good discussion, see David A. Aaker and James M. Carman, "Are You Overadvertising?" *Journal of Advertising Research,* August–September 1982, pp. 57–70.

4. Gerald J. Tellis, "Advertising Exposure, Loyalty, and Brand Purchase: A Two-Stage Model of Choice," *Journal of Marketing Research,* May 1988, pp. 134–44.

5. See Donald E. Schultz, Dennis Martin, and William P. Brown, *Strategic Advertising Campaigns* (Chicago: Crain Books, 1984), pp. 192–97.

6. M. L. Vidale and H. R. Wolfe, "An Operations-Research Study of Sales Response to Advertising," *Operations Research,* June 1957, pp. 370–81.

7. John D. C. Little, "A Model of Adaptive Control of Promotional Spending," *Operations Research,* November 1966, pp. 1075-97.

8. For additional models for setting the advertising budget, see Gary L. Lilien, Philip Kotler, and K. Sridhar Moorthy, *Marketing Models* (Englewood Cliffs, NJ: Prentice-Hall, 1992), Chap. 6.

9. See John Koten, "Creativity, Not Budget Size, Is Vital to TV-Ad Popularity," *The Wall Street Journal,* March 1, 1984, p. 25.

10. See "Keep Listening to That Wee, Small Voice," in *Communications of an Advertising Man* (Chicago: Leo Burnett Co., 1961), p. 61.

11. John C. Maloney, "Marketing Decisions and Attitude Research," in *Effective Marketing Coordination,* ed. George L. Baker, Jr. (Chicago: American Marketing Association, 1961), pp. 595–618.

12. At this time, fortunately, the expense of creating rough ads is rapidly falling with the advance of computer desktop publishing techniques. An ad agency's creative department can compose many alternative ads in a short time by drawing from computer files containing different still and video images, typesets, and so on.

13. Irwin Gross, "An Analytical Approach to the Creative Aspect of Advertising Operations" (Ph.D. dissertation, Case Institute of Technology, November 1967).

14. Dik Warren Twedt, "How to Plan New Products, Improve Old Ones, and Create Better Advertising," *Journal of Marketing,* January 1969, pp. 53–57.

15. See William A. Mindak and H. Malcolm Bybee, "Marketing Application to Fund Raising," *Journal of Marketing,* July 1971, pp. 13–18.

16. See Peter L. Henderson, James F. Hind, and Sidney E. Brown, "Sales Effect of Two Campaign Themes," *Journal of Advertising Research,* December 1961, pp. 2–11.

17. Lalita Manrai, "Effect of Labeling Strategy in Advertising: Self-Referencing versus Psychological Reactance" (Ph.D. dissertation, Northwestern University, 1987).

18. L. Greenland, "Is This the Era of Positioning?" *Advertising Age,* May 29, 1972.

19. David Ogilvy and Joel Raphaelson, "Research on Advertising Techniques That Work—and Don't Work," *Harvard Business Review,* July–August 1982, pp. 14–18.

20. Schultz et al., *Strategic Advertising Campaigns,* p. 340.

21. See Herbert E. Krugman, "What Makes Advertising Effective?" *Harvard Business Review,* March–April 1975, pp. 96–103, here p. 98.

22. See Peggy J. Kreshel, Kent M. Lancaster, and Margaret A. Toomey, "Advertising Media Planning: How Leading Advertising Agencies Estimate Effective Reach and Frequency" (Urbana: University of Illinois, Department of Advertising, paper no. 20, January 1985). Also see Jack Z. Sissors and Lincoln Bumba, *Advertising Media Planning,* 3rd ed. (Lincolnwood, IL: NTC Business Books, 1988), Chap. 9.

23. See "As Network TV Fades, Many Advertisers Try Age-Old Promotions: They Switch to Direct Mail, Coupon and PR Ploys," *The Wall Street Journal,* August 26, 1986, p. 1.

24. See Roland T. Rust, *Advertising Media Models: A Practical Guide* (Lexington, MA: Lexington Books, 1986).

25. See Jay W. Forrester, "Advertising: A Problem in Industrial Dynamics," *Harvard Business Review,* March–April 1959, pp. 100–110.

26. See Amber G. Rao and Peter B. Miller, "Advertising/Sales Response Functions," *Journal of Advertising Research,* April 1975, pp. 7–15.

27. See Alfred A. Kuehn, "How Advertising Performance Depends on Other Marketing Factors," *Journal of Advertising Research,* March 1962, pp. 2–10.

28. Philip H. Dougherty, "Bud `Pulses' the Market," *The New York Times,* February 18, 1975.

29. Forrester, "Advertising," p. 102.

30. See J. O. Peckham, *The Wheel of Marketing* (Scarsdale, NY: privately printed, 1975), pp. 73–77.

31. Kristian S. Palda, *The Measurement of Cumulative Advertising Effect* (Englewood Cliffs, NJ: Prentice-Hall, 1964), p. 87.

32. David B. Montgomery and Alvin J. Silk, "Estimating Dynamic Effects of Market Communications Expenditures," *Management Science,* June 1972, pp. 485–501.

33. See Robert D. Buzzell, "E. I. Du Pont de Nemours & Co.: Measurement of Effects of Advertising," in his *Mathematical Models and Marketing Management* (Boston: Division of Research, Graduate School of Business Administration, Harvard University, 1964), pp. 157–79.

34. See Glen L. Urban, "Allocating Ad Budgets Geographically," *Journal of Advertising Research,* December 1975, pp. 7–16.

24

Designing Direct-Marketing, Sales-Promotion, and Public-Relations Programs

Gifts are like hooks.

MARTIAL (86 A.D.)

We despise no source that can pay us a pleasing attention.

MARK TWAIN

In this chapter, we will describe the nature and use of three promotional tools—direct marketing, sales promotion, and public relations. These tools are often viewed as secondary to the major ones of advertising and personal selling. Yet they can contribute strongly to marketing performance and are playing a growing role. Direct marketing, sales promotion, and public relations are not well understood by marketing practitioners, nor are marketing departments typically organized to handle them effectively. The first companies in their industries to learn to use these tools more effectively could gain a significant competitive edge.

Direct Marketing

Most companies rely primarily on advertising, sales promotion, and personal selling to move their products and services. They use advertising to create awareness and interest, sales promotion to provide an incentive to buy, and personal selling to close the sale. Direct marketing attempts to compress these elements to lead to a direct sale without using an intermediary. The person exposed to an ad—in a catalog, direct-mail piece, phone call, magazine, newspaper, TV, or radio program—can call a toll-free 800 number and charge the order to a credit-card number, or respond by mail and either write in the credit card number or enclose a check.

Although direct marketing first emerged in the form of direct-mail and mail-order catalogs, it has taken on several more forms in recent years, including telemarketing, direct-response radio and television, electronic shopping, and the like. What is common to these diverse marketing vehicles is that they are used to obtain direct orders from targeted customers or prospects. This is in contrast to mass advertising, which reaches an unspecified number of people, most of whom are not in the market for the product and will not make a purchase decision at a retail outlet until some future occasion.

Although direct marketing has boomed in recent years, a large number of companies still relegate it to a minor role in their promotion mix. The company's advertising, sales-promotion, and salesforce departments receive most of the promotion dollars and jealously guard their budgets (although some of these budgets are used for direct marketing). Many advertising agencies still don't offer direct-marketing services because they are unfamiliar with this new discipline or believe they can make more money developing and running advertising campaigns. Still, most large advertising agencies have acquired direct-marketing capabilities and are increasingly offering their clients more varied communication resources.

The salesforce has its own reasons for resistance. According to Roman:

> If salespeople hear "direct marketing," they instinctively feel that their turf is threatened and that accounts will be taken away from them by direct writing of orders. Even if the program is as benign as lead generation and qualification to produce better leads, and hence higher sales, for the field sales force, there is likely to be resentment based on a perceived loss of control of the selling process.[1]

There are, of course, company exceptions. Citicorp, AT&T, IBM, Ford, and American Airlines have used direct marketing to build profitable relations with customers over the years. Colgate-Palmolive, Procter & Gamble, Quaker Oats, General Foods, and other packaged-goods marketers began using direct-marketing techniques in the late 1980s to sample products, retain customer loyalty, and win over targeted users of competitive brands. Retailers like Saks Fifth Avenue, and Bloomingdale's regularly send out catalogs to supplement their in-store sales. Direct-marketing companies like L. L. Bean, Lands' End, Eddie Bauer, Spiegel's, Franklin Mint, and Sharper Image have built fortunes in the direct-marketing mail-order and phone-order business. Several have opened retail stores after establishing strong brand names as direct marketers.

Nature, Growth, and Advantages of Direct Marketing

The term *direct marketing* has taken on new meanings over the years. Originally, it was simply a form of marketing in which products or services moved from producer to consumer without the use of any middleman. In this sense, companies that use salespeople to sell direct to end users or that operate factory outlets are using direct marketing. Later, the term described marketing done through the mails, whether catalog marketing or direct-mail marketing. As the telephone and other media came into heavy use to promote offers directly to customers, direct marketing was redefined by the Direct Marketing Association (DMA):

❖ Direct marketing *is an interactive system of marketing which uses one or more advertising media to effect a measurable response and/or transaction at any location.*

In this definition, the emphasis is on marketing undertaken to get a measurable response, typically an order from a customer. (It can be called *direct-order marketing*.)

Today, many users of direct marketing visualize it as playing a broader role (which can be called *direct-relationship marketing*).[2] These direct marketers use *direct-response advertising media* to make a sale and learn about a *customer* whose name and profile are entered in a *customer database*, which is used to build a continuing and enriching *relationship*. The emphasis is on building preferred customer relationships. Airlines, hotels, and others are building strong customer relationships through frequency award programs and are using their customer database to target their offers to individual customers. They are making offers to those customers and prospects most able, willing, and ready to buy the product or service. To the extent that they succeed, they will gain much higher response rates to their promotions.

Sales produced through direct-marketing channels have been growing at a rapid rate. While retail sales grow around 6% annually, catalog/direct-mail sales are growing at around 10%. Sales through catalog/direct mail were estimated at $164 billion in 1988.[3] Marketing Concepts and Tools 24-1 lists the more common advertising media used in direct marketing.

Direct marketing is used by manufacturers, retailers, service companies, catalog merchants, and nonprofit organizations. Its growth in the consumer market is largely a response to the "demassification" of the market, in which there is an ever-multiplying number of market niches with highly individualized needs and preferences. People in these markets have credit cards and known mailing addresses and telephone numbers, which facilitate reaching and transacting with them. Households have less time to shop because of the substantial number of women who have entered the workforce. The higher costs of driving, traffic congestion, parking headaches, the shortage of retail sales help and queues at the checkout

Major Tools of Direct Marketing

CATALOG MARKETING ❖ Catalog marketers mail annually over 12.4 billion copies of more than 8,500 different catalogs. The average household receives at least 50 catalogs per year. Catalogs are sent by huge general-merchandise retailers—J. C. Penney, Spiegel—that carry a full line of merchandise. Specialty department stores, such as Neiman-Marcus and Saks Fifth Avenue, send catalogs to cultivate an upper-middle-class market for high-priced, often exotic merchandise such as "his and her" bathrobes, designer jewelry, and gourmet foods. Several major corporations have also acquired or developed mail-order divisions. Xerox offers children's books; Avon sells women's apparel; W. R. Grace sells cheese; American Airlines offers luggage; General Foods offers needlework kits; and General Mills sells sports shirts. There are thousands of smaller enterprises in the mail catalog business, typically issuing catalogs in specialty-goods areas, such as consumer electronics, lawn and garden equipment, women's wear, household ware, and so on. Among the most innovative mail catalog houses are Lands' End (sportswear), L. L. Bean (sportswear), and Sharper Image (consumer electronics). These catalog houses lead in developing attractive product assortments and illustrating them in fine four-color photographed layouts. They provide a 24-hour toll-free number, payment by credit card, and early shipment of merchandise.

The success of a mail-order business depends greatly on the company's ability to manage its mailing and customer lists, to control its inventory carefully, to offer quality merchandise, and to project a distinctive customer-benefiting image. Some catalog companies distinguish themselves by adding literary or information features to their catalogs, sending swatches of materials, operating a special hotline to answer questions, sending gifts to the best customers, and donating a percent of profits to good causes. A handful of the more successful catalog houses—Sharper Image, Lands' End—have opened retail outlets to attract their existing customers and newcomers into another channel for doing business with them. Some catalog houses—Neiman-Marcus, Spiegel—are experimenting with video catalogs that they mail to their best customers and prospects.

DIRECT-MAIL MARKETING ❖ Direct-mail marketing is a huge business that runs into the tens of billions of dollars. Direct marketers send single mail pieces—letters, flyers, foldouts, and other "salespeople on wings." Some direct marketers have been mailing audiotapes, videotapes, and even computer diskettes. An exercise-equipment company mails a video demonstrating the use and health advantages of an expensive home exercise machine called the Nordic Track Cardiovascular Exerciser. Ford sends a computer diskette called a Disk Drive Test Drive to consumers responding to its car ads in computer publications. The diskette's menu allows the consumer to read persuasive copy, get technical specifications, view attractive graphics about the car, and get answers to frequently asked questions.

In general, direct-mail marketers hope to sell a product or service, collect or qualify leads for the salesforce, communicate interesting news, or reward loyal customers with a gift. The names might be selected from a list compiled by the company or from lists purchased from mailing-list brokers. These brokers are able to sell lists of any description—the superwealthy, mobile-home owners, classical-music lovers, and so on. Direct marketers typically buy a subsample of names from a potential list and do a test mailing to see if the response rate is high enough.

Direct mail is becoming increasingly popular because it permits high target-market selectivity, can be personalized, is flexible, and allows early testing and measuring of results. While the cost per thousand people reached is higher than with mass media, the people reached are much better prospects. Over 45% of Americans purchased something through direct mail in 1991. Direct mail has proved very successful in promoting books, magazine subscriptions, and insurance, and is increasingly being used to sell novelty and gift items, clothing, gourmet foods, and industrial items. Direct mail is also used heavily by charities, which raised $49 billion (24% of total charity money raised) in 1990 and accounted for about 25% of all direct-mail revenues.

TELEMARKETING ❖ Telemarketing has become a major direct-marketing tool. In 1991, marketers spent an estimated $234 billion in telephone charges to help sell their products and services. Telemarketing blossomed in the late 1960s with the introduction of inbound and outbound Wide Area Telephone Service (WATS). With IN WATS, marketers can offer customers and prospects toll-free 800 numbers to place orders for goods or services stimulated by print or broadcast ads, direct mail or catalogs, or to make complaints and suggestions. With OUT WATS, they can use the phone to sell directly to consumers and businesses, generate or qualify sales leads, reach more distant buyers, or service current customers or accounts.

The average household receives 19 telephone calls each year and makes 16 calls to place orders. Some telemarketing systems are fully automated. For example, automatic-dialing and recorded-message players (ADRMPs) can dial numbers, play a voice-activated advertising message, and take orders from interested customers on an answering-machine device or by forwarding the call to an operator. Telemarketing is increasingly used in business marketing as well as consumer marketing. For example, Raleigh Bicycles used telemarketing to reduce the amount of personal selling needed for contacting its dealers. In the first year, salesforce travel costs were reduced by 50%, and sales in a single quarter were up 34%.

TELEVISION DIRECT-RESPONSE MARKETING ❖ Television is a growing medium for direct marketing both through network and cable channels. Television is used in two ways to market products directly to consumers. The first is through *direct-response advertising*. Direct-response marketers air television spots, often 60 or 120 seconds long, that persuasively describe a product and give customers a toll-free number for ordering. Direct-response advertising works well for magazines, books, small appliances, records and tapes, collectibles, and many other products. One of the best examples is Dial Media's ads for Ginsu knives, which ran for seven years and sold almost three million sets of knives worth over $40 million in sales. Recently, some companies have prepared 30-minute "infomercials," which resemble documentaries—on quitting smoking, curing baldness, or losing weight—and carries testimony from satisfied users of the product or service, and includes a toll-free number for ordering or getting further information.

Another television marketing approach is *at-home shopping channels* where an entire television program—or whole channel—is dedicated to selling goods and services. The largest is the Home Shopping Network (HSN), which broadcasts 24 hours a day. The program's hosts offer bargain prices on products ranging from jewelry, lamps, collectible dolls, and clothing to power tools and consumer electronics—usually obtained by HSN at closeout prices. The show is upbeat, with the hosts honking horns, blowing whistles, and praising viewers for their good taste. Viewers call an 800 number to order goods. Handling more than 1,200 incoming lines, 400 operators enter orders directly into computer terminals. Orders are shipped within 48 hours.

RADIO, MAGAZINE, AND NEWSPAPER DIRECT-RESPONSE MARKETING ❖ Magazines, newspapers, and radios are also used to present direct-response offers to customers. The person hears or reads about an offer and dials a toll-free number to place an order.

ELECTRONIC SHOPPING ❖ Electronic shopping takes two forms. The first, videotex, is a two-way system that links consumers' television sets with the seller's computer data banks by cable or telephone lines. The videotex service consists of a computerized catalog of products offered by producers, retailers, banks, travel organizations, and others. Consumers use an ordinary television set that has a special keyboard device connected to the system by two-way cable.

The other form involves the use of personal computers with a modem through which consumers dial a service such as Prodigy or CompuServe. For a monthly charge or usage charge, these services allow consumers to order goods from local or national retailers; do their banking with local banks; book airline, hotel, and car rental reservations; get headline news and movie reviews; and send messages to others. The number of users of electronic home shopping is still quite small but is likely to grow as more consumers acquire cable television and personal computers.

KIOSK SHOPPING ❖ Some companies have designed "customer-order-placing machines" (in contrast to vending machines) and placed them in stores, airports, and other locations. For example, the Florsheim Shoe Company includes a machine in several of their stores on which the customer indicates the type of shoe he wants (dress, sport), and the color and size. Pictures of Florsheim shoes appear on the screen that meet his criteria. If the particular shoes are not available in the store, the customer can dial an attached phone and type in his credit-card information and where the shoes should be delivered. In another application, Hosts USA is a kiosk found in airports. The traveler sees a video screen with text describing categories such as executive gifts, action gifts, kids' gifts, spirits. The traveler touches the screen to indicate a category of interest. Within the category, if she is interested in, say, Samsonite luggage, a video comes on dramatizing the benefits of Samsonite luggage. If she wants to order it, she touches the screen again to indicate whether she wants it gift wrapped, with or without a personal note, and next-day or regular delivery. A phone next to the screen rings and she puts her credit card into a slot. This completes the transaction, and the product is then mailed to the indicated address.

SOURCES: For more reading, see Janice Steinberg, "Cacophony of Catalogs Fill All Niches," *Advertising Age*, October 26, 1987, pp. S1–2; Rudy Oetting, "Telephone Marketing: Where We've Been and Where We Should Be Going," *Direct Marketing*, February 1987, p. 8; Arthur Bragg, "TV's Shopping Shows: Your New Move?" *Sales & Marketing Management*, October 1987, pp. 85–89; Alison Fahey, "Prodigy Videotex Expands Its Reach," *Advertising Age*, April 24, 1989, p. 75.

counter all encourage *at-home shopping*. In addition, many chain stores have dropped slower-moving specialty items, thus creating an opportunity for direct marketers to promote these items. The development of toll-free phone numbers and the willingness of direct marketers to accept telephone orders at night or on Sundays have boosted this form of selling. Another major factor is the growth of 24-hour and 48-hour delivery via Federal Express, Airborne, DHL, and other carriers. Finally, the growth of computer power has allowed direct marketers to build enhanced customer databases from which they can single out the best prospects for any product they wish to advertise.

Direct marketing has also grown rapidly in business-to-business marketing. A major reason is the high and increasing costs of reaching business markets through the salesforce. Table 24-1 shows the typical cost per contact in reaching business markets with different media. Clearly, if out-of-town personal sales calls cost $250 per contact, they ought to be made only to customers and prospects who are virtually ready to buy. Lower cost-per-contact media, such as telemarketing, direct mail, and selective and mass advertising, should be used to identify prime prospects before visiting them.

TABLE 24-1

Typical Cost per Contact of Reaching Business Markets with Different Media Vehicles

Personal sales calls	$250	(out of town)
	52	(local)
Seminars, trade show exhibits	40	
Salesperson writes a single letter	25	
Showroom or counter selling	16	
Yellow Pages large display ad	16	
Telephone order desk	9	(800 number)
	6	(local)
Mass phoning program	8	(national with WATS)
	4	(local)
Direct mail	.30	
Selective media	.15	(ad in trade publication)
Mass media	.01–.05	(radio, newspaper, TV)

Source: John Klein & Associates, Inc., Cleveland, Ohio, 1988.

Direct marketing provides a number of benefits to customers. Consumers who buy from mail-order channels say that mail-order shopping is fun, convenient, and hassle-free. It saves them time. They can do comparative shopping from their armchairs by browsing through their catalogs. It introduces them to a larger selection of merchandise and to new lifestyles. They can order gifts to be sent directly to intended recipients without having to leave their homes. Industrial customers also attest to a number of advantages, specifically learning about many products and services without tying up time in meeting salespeople.

Direct marketing provides a number of advantages to sellers. It allows greater prospect *selectivity*. A direct marketer can buy a mailing list containing the names of almost any group: left-handed people, overweight people, millionaires, newborn babies, and so on. The message can be *personalized* and *customized*. Eventually, according to Pierre Passavant, "We will store hundreds . . . of messages in memory. We will select ten thousand families with twelve or twenty or fifty specific characteristics and send them very individualized laser-printed letters."[4] Furthermore, the direct marketer can build a *continuous relationship* with each customer. The mother of the newborn baby will receive regular mailings describing new clothes, toys, and other goods that the growing baby will need. Direct marketing can be *timed* more precisely to reach prospects at the right moment. Direct-marketing material receives *higher readership*, since it reaches more interested prospects. Direct marketing permits *testing* of alternative media and messages (headlines, salutations, benefits, prices, and the like) in the search for the most cost-effective approach. Direct marketing permits *privacy* in that the direct marketer's offer and strategy are not visible to competitors. Finally, the direct marketer knows whether the campaign has been profitable because of *response measurement*.

The Development of Integrated Direct Marketing

Most direct marketers rely on a single advertising vehicle and a "one-shot" effort to reach and sell a prospect. An example of a *single vehicle, single-stage campaign* would be sending a one-time mailing offering a cookware item. A *single vehicle, multiple-stage campaign* would involve sending successive mailings to a prospect to trigger purchase. Magazine publishers, for example, send about four notices to a household to get reluctant subscribers to renew.

A more powerful approach is to execute a *multiple vehicle, multiple-stage campaign*. Roman calls this technique *integrated direct marketing* (IDM). Consider the following sequence:

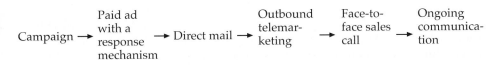

For example, a computer company may launch a new computer by first arranging news stories to stir interest. Then the company can place full-page ads to create further awareness and interest. The ads would contain an offer of a free booklet. The company would then mail the brochure and an offer to sell the computer at a special price. Those who do not buy are then phoned. Some prospects will place an order; others might request a face-to-face sales call. Even if the prospect is not ready to buy, there is ongoing communication. Roman says that this use of *response compression*, whereby multiple media are deployed within a tightly defined time frame, increases impact and awareness of the message. The underlying idea is to deploy select media with precise timing to generate greater incremental sales that exceed incremental costs.

As an example, Roman cites a Citicorp campaign to market home equity loans. Instead of using only "mail plus an 800 number," Citicorp used "mail plus coupon plus 800 number plus outbound telemarketing plus print advertising." Although the second campaign cost more, it resulted in a 15% increase in the number of new accounts compared with direct mail alone. Roman concluded:

> When a mailing piece which might generate a 2% response on its own is supplemented by a tollfree 800-number ordering channel, we regularly see response rise by 50-125%. A skillfully integrated outbound telemarketing effort can add another 500% lift in response. Suddenly our 2% response has grown to 13% or more by adding interactive marketing channels to a "business as usual" mailing. The dollars and cents involved in adding media to the integrated media mix is normally marginal on a cost-per-order basis because of the high level of responses generated. . . . Adding media to a marketing program will raise total response . . . because different people are inclined to respond to different stimuli.[5]

Rapp and Collins developed a very useful model—they call it *maximarketing*—that makes direct-marketing techniques the driving force in the general marketing process.[6] Their model recommends the creation of a customer database and advocates making direct-contact marketing a full partner in the marketing process. Maximarketing consists of a comprehensive set of steps for reaching the prospect, making the sale, and developing the relationship. (See Marketing Concepts and Tools 24-2.)

Developing a Database Marketing System

Most companies have not yet moved into *database marketing*, which goes far beyond simple *direct marketing*. Database marketing uses database technology and sophisticated analytical techniques combined with direct-marketing methods to elicit a desired, measurable response in target groups and individuals. Many companies still confuse a *customer list* with a *marketing database*. A customer list is simply a set of names, addresses, and telephone numbers, whereas a marketing database contains individual's demographics, psychographics, mediagraphics, past sales by recency, frequency, monetary amount, and other relevant descriptors:

❖ A marketing database *is an organized collection of comprehensive data about individual customers, prospects, or suspects that is current, accessible, and actionable for such marketing purposes as lead generation, lead qualification, sale of a product or service, or maintenance of customer relationships.*

At the present time, mass marketers generally know little about individual customers. Retailers know some things about their charge-account customers but almost nothing about their cash or other credit-card customers. Banks develop customer databases in each separate product area but typically fail to tie this information together in a complete profile of the customer that could be used for cross-selling purposes or relationship pricing.

Well-trained field salespeople, on the other hand, normally develop effective customer databases. Using a laptop computer, they record pertinent facts about their individual customers: their purchase volume, prices, needs, buying criteria, hobbies, food preferences, family names, birthdays, and so on. Following each sales call, the salesperson enters information on when to make the next call, special customer concerns and questions, and so on. Knowing a lot about each customer gives salespeople a distinct competitive advantage.

Building a marketing database involves investing in central and remote computer hardware, data-processing software, information-enhancement programs,

Marketing Concepts and Tools 24-2

The "Maximarketing" Model for Integrated Marketing

Rapp and Collins's maximarketing model consists of the nine steps described here.

1. *Maximized targeting* calls upon the marketer to define and identify the best target prospects for the offer. The marketer either buys appropriate mailing lists or searches the customer database for characteristics that point to high interest, ability to pay, and readiness to buy. Additional "best customer" criteria include those who buy with some frequency, don't return many orders, don't complain, and pay on time. Mass marketers can go "fishing" for prospects with direct-response advertising in such mass media as television, newspaper supplements, and magazine insert cards.

2. *Maximized media* leads the direct marketer to examine the exploding variety of media and choose those which allow for convenient two-way communication and measurement of results.

3. *Maximized accountability* calls for evaluating campaigns on the basis of cost per prospect response rather than cost per thousand exposures as is used in mass advertising.

4. *Maximized awareness* involves searching for messages that will break through the clutter and reach the hearts and minds of the prospects by means of "whole brain" advertising, appealing to a person's rational and emotional sides.

5. *Maximized activation* emphasizes that advertising must trigger purchase or at least advance prospects to a measurably higher stage of buying readiness. Activation devices include statements like "Send for more information" and "Reply coupon must be returned by September 30."

6. *Maximized synergy* involves finding ways of doing double duty with the advertising, for instance, combining awareness building with direct response, promoting other distribution channels, and sharing costs with other advertisers.

7. *Maximized linkage* calls for linking the advertising to the sale by concentrating on the better prospects and spending more of the total budget to convert them, rather than spending money simply to send an awareness message to the world at large.

8. *Maximized sales* through database building calls upon the marketer to continue to market directly to known customers by cross-selling, upgrading, and introduction of new products. The marketer keeps enhancing the customer database with more customer information and ends up with a rich private advertising medium. Many marketers today are getting as interested in the loyalty-building process as they are in the customer-acquisition process, with the aim of maximizing lifetime customer value.

9. *Maximized distribution* involves the marketer in building additional channels to reach prospects and customers—for instance, when the direct marketer opens retail stores or obtains shelf space in existing retail stores, or when the retailer issues a catalog or a manufacturer such as General Foods decides to sell a premium brand of coffee directly to the consumer.

SOURCE: Summarized from Stan Rapp and Thomas L. Collins, *Maximarketing* (New York: McGraw-Hill, 1987).

---

communication links, personnel to capture data, user-training costs, design of analytical programs, and so forth. The system should be user friendly and available to various marketing groups, such as those in product and brand management, new-product development, advertising and promotion, direct mail, telemarketing, field sales, order fulfillment, and customer service. Building a marketing database takes time and involves much cost, but when it runs properly, the selling company will achieve much higher marketing productivity. Consider the following:

A General Electric customer database indicates each customer's geodemographics, psychographics, mediagraphics, appliance purchasing history, and so on. GE direct marketers can determine which past customers might be ready to replace their washing machines, for instance, those who bought their GE washing machines six years ago and have large families. They can determine which customers would be interested in a new GE videorecorder based on their history of buying other GE consumer electronic products. They can identify the heaviest past GE purchasers and send them

$30 gift certificates to apply against their next purchase of a GE appliance. Clearly, a rich customer database allows a company to anticipate customer needs, locate good prospects, and reward loyal customers.

Major Decisions in Direct Marketing

In preparing a direct-marketing campaign, marketers must decide on their objectives, targets, offer strategy, various tests, and measures of campaign success. Here we will review these decisions.

OBJECTIVES ❖ The direct marketer normally aims to secure immediate purchases from prospects. The campaign's success is judged by the response rate. A response rate of 2% is normally considered good in direct-marketing sales campaigns. Yet this rate also implies that 98% of the campaign effort was wasted.

That is not necessarily the case. The direct marketing presumably had some effect on awareness and intention to buy at a later date. Furthermore, not all direct marketing aims to produce an immediate sale. One major use of direct marketing is to produce prospect leads for the salesforce. Direct marketers also send communications to strengthen brand image and company preference; examples include banks that mail birthday greeting cards to their best customers and department stores that send gifts to their best customers. Some direct marketers run campaigns to inform and educate their customers to prepare them for later purchase; thus Ford sends out booklets on "How to Take Good Care of Your Car." Given the variety of direct-marketing objectives, the direct marketer needs to carefully spell out the campaign objectives.

TARGET CUSTOMERS ❖ Direct marketers need to figure out the characteristics of customers and prospects who would be most able, willing, and ready to buy. Bob Stone recommends applying the R-F-M formula (recency, frequency, monetary amount) for rating and selecting customers from a list.[7] The best customer targets are those who bought most recently, who buy frequently, and who spend the most. Points are established for varying R-F-M levels, and each customer is scored; the higher the score, the more attractive the customer.

Direct marketers can use segmentation criteria in targeting prospects. Good prospects can be identified on the basis of such variables as age, sex, income, education, previous mail-order purchases, and so forth. Occasions also provide a good segmentation departure point. New mothers will be in the market for baby clothes and baby toys; college freshmen will buy typewriters, computers, television sets, and clothing; and newly marrieds will be looking for housing, furniture, appliances, and bank loans. Another good segmentation departure point is consumer lifestyles. There are consumers who are computer buffs, cooking buffs, outdoor buffs, and so forth; some successful catalog marketers have targeted these groups and won their hearts and minds.

Once the target market is defined, the direct marketer needs to obtain names of good prospects in the target market. Here is where *list acquisition and management skills* come into play. The direct marketer's best list is typically the house list of past customers who have bought the company's products. The direct marketer can buy additional lists from list brokers. Names on these lists are priced at so much a name. But external lists have problems, including name duplication, incomplete data, obsolete addresses, and so on. The better lists include overlays of demographic and psychographic information, in addition to simple addresses. The main point is that the direct marketer needs to test lists in advance to know their worth.

OFFER STRATEGY ❖ Direct marketers have to figure out an effective offer strategy to meet the target market's needs. Nash sees the offer strategy as consisting of five elements—the product, the offer, the medium, the distribution method, and the creative strategy.[8] Fortunately, all of these elements can be tested.

Each medium has its own rules for effective use. Consider direct mail. In developing a package mailing, the direct marketer has to decide on five components. Each component can help or hurt the overall response rate. The *outside envelope* will be more effective if it contains an illustration, preferably in color, and/or a catchy reason to open the envelope, such as the announcement of a contest, premium, or benefit to the recipient. Envelopes are more effective—but more costly—when they contain a colorful commemorative stamp, when the address is handtyped or handwritten, and when the envelope differs in size or shape from standard envelopes.

The *sales letter* should use a personal salutation and start with a headline in bold type in the form of a newslead, a how/what/why statement, a narrative, or a question to gain attention. The letter should be printed on good-quality paper and run for as many pages as are necessary to make the sale, with some indented paragraphs and underlining of pertinent phrases and sentences. A computer-type letter usually outpulls a printed letter, and the presence of a pithy P.S. at the letter's end increases the response rate, as does the signature of someone whose title is appropriate and impressive. A colorful *circular* accompanying the letter will also increase the response rate in most cases by more than its cost. The *reply form* should feature an 800 toll-free number and contain a perforated receipt stub and guarantee of satisfaction. The inclusion of a postage-free *reply envelope* will dramatically increase the response rate.

Consider, on the other hand, a telemarketing campaign. Effective telemarketing depends on choosing the right telemarketers, training them well, and incentivizing them. Telemarketers should have pleasant voices and project enthusiasm. Women are more effective than men for many products. The telemarketers should initially train with a script and eventually move toward more improvisation. The opening lines are critical: They should be brief and lead with a good question that catches the listener's interest. The telemarketer needs to know how to end the conversation if the prospect seems to be a poor one. The call should be made at the right time, which is late morning and afternoon to reach business prospects, and the evening hours between 7 to 9 to reach households. The telemarketing supervisor can build up telemarketer enthusiasm by offering prizes to the first one who gets an order or to the top performer. Given the higher cost per contact for telemarketing, and privacy issues, precise list selection and targeting is critical.

Clearly, other media, such as catalog mail order, TV home shopping, and so on, have their own rules for effective use.

TESTING DIRECT-MARKETING ELEMENTS ❖ One of the great advantages of direct marketing is the ability to test under real marketplace conditions the efficacy of different components of the offer strategy. Direct marketers can test product features, copy, prices, media, mailing lists, and the like. Although direct-marketing response rates are at the single-digit level, testing these components can add substantially to the overall response rate and profitability.

The response rate to a direct-marketing campaign typically understates the long-term impact of the campaign. Suppose only 2% of recipients of a direct-mail piece advertising Samsonite luggage place an order. A much larger percentage became aware (direct mail has high readership), and some percentage formed an intention to buy at a later date (the purchase will occur at a retail outlet). Furthermore, some percentage of the audience may mention Samsonite luggage to others as a result of seeing the promotion. Some companies are now measuring the impact of direct marketing on awareness, intention to buy, and word of mouth to derive a larger estimate of the promotion's impact than is measured by the response rate alone.

MEASURING THE CAMPAIGN'S SUCCESS ❖ By adding up the planned campaign costs, the direct marketer can figure out in advance the needed break-even response rate. This rate must be net of returned merchandise and bad debts. Returned merchandise can kill an otherwise effective campaign. The direct marketer needs to analyze the main causes of returned merchandise, such as late arrival, defective merchandise, damage in transit, not as advertised, incorrect order fulfillment.

By carefully analyzing past campaigns, direct marketers can steadily improve their performance. Even when a specific campaign fails to break even, it might still be profitable.

> Suppose a membership organization spends $10,000 on a new-member campaign and attracts 100 new members, each paying $70. It appears that the campaign has lost $3,000 (= $10,000 − $7,000). But if 80% of new members renew their membership in the second year, the organization gets another $5,600 without any effort. It has now received $12,600 (= $7,000 + $5,600) for its investment of $10,000. To figure out the long-term break-even rate, one needs to figure out not only the initial response rate but the percentage who renew each year and for how many years they renew.

This example introduces the concept of *customer lifetime value*. The ultimate value of a customer is not revealed by the customer's purchase during a particular mailing. Rather the customer's ultimate value is the profit made on all the customer's purchases over time less the customer acquisition and maintenance costs. For an average customer, one would calculate the average customer longevity, average customer annual expenditure, and average gross margin, properly discounted for the opportunity cost of money, less the average customer acquisition cost. The formula would be adjusted for nonaverage customers whose expected lifetime value the company wants to assess.

After assessing customer lifetime values, the company can focus its communication efforts on the more attractive customers. These efforts include sending communications that may not even sell the customer anything—but maintain the customer's interest in the company and its products. Such communications include free newsletters, tips, and birthday greetings, all serving to build a stronger customer relationship.

Direct marketing has spawned a growing body of theory, measurement, and competent practice. It adds a number of communication concepts and capabilities to the marketers' toolbox. When tied to a carefully developed customer database, it can increase sales and profit yields and strengthen customer relationships. It can provide more accurate prospect leads and trigger new sales at a lower cost. Ultimately, marketers will make direct marketing and database marketing an integral part of their marketing strategy and planning.[9] Yet they must do this responsibly (see Socially Responsible Marketing 24-1).

Sales Promotion

Sales promotion *consists of a diverse collection of incentive tools, mostly short term, designed to stimulate quicker and/or greater purchase of particular products/services by consumers or the trade.* Examples are found everywhere:

Issues in the Use of Direct Marketing

Direct marketers and their customers usually enjoy mutually rewarding relationships. Occasionally, however, a darker side emerges. Concerns include simple excesses that irritate consumers, instances of unfairness, cases of outright deception and fraud, and invasion-of-privacy issues.

Irritation

Many people find the increasing number of hard-sell solicitations to be a nuisance. They dislike direct-response TV commercials that are too loud, too long, and too insistent. Especially bothersome are dinner-time or late-night phone calls, poorly trained callers, and computerized calls placed by an ADRMP (auto-dial recorded message player).

Unfairness

Some direct marketers take unfair advantage of impulsive or less sophisticated buyers. TV shopping shows and program-long "infomercials" may be the worst culprits. They feature smooth-talking hosts, elaborately staged demonstrations, claims of drastic price reductions, "while they last" time limitations, and unexcelled ease of purchase to capture buyers who have low sales resistance.

Deception and Fraud

Some direct marketers design mailers and write copy intended to mislead buyers. They may exaggerate product size, performance claims, or the "retail price." Political fund raisers sometimes use gimmicks such as "look-alike" envelopes that resemble official documents, simulated newspaper clippings, and fake honors and awards. Some nonprofit organizations pretend to be conducting research surveys when they are actually asking leading questions to screen or persuade consumers.

The Federal Trade Commission receives thousands of complaints each year about fraudulent investment scams or phoney charities. By the time buyers realize that they have been bilked and alert the authorities, the thieves are usually somewhere else plotting new schemes.

Invasion of Privacy

Invasion of privacy is perhaps the toughest public-policy issue now confronting the direct-marketing industry. It seems that almost every time consumers order products by mail or telephone, enter a sweepstakes, apply for a credit card, or take out a magazine subscription, their names, addresses, and purchasing behavior are entered into some company's already bulging database. Using sophisticated computer technologies, direct marketers can use these databases to effectively "microtarget" their selling efforts. Consumers often benefit from such database marketing—they receive more offers that are closely matched to their interests. However, direct marketers sometimes find it difficult to walk the fine line between their desires to reach carefully targeted audiences and consumer rights to privacy. Many critics worry that marketers may know *too* much about consumers' lives, and that they may use this knowledge to take unfair advantage of consumers. They ask: Should AT&T be allowed to sell marketers the names of customers who frequently call the 800 numbers of catalog companies? Is it right for credit bureaus to compile and sell lists of people who have recently applied for credit cards—people who are considered prime direct-marketing targets because of their spending behavior? Or is it right for states to sell the names and addresses of driver's license holders, along with height, weight, and gender information, allowing apparel retailers to target tall or overweight people with special clothing offers?

The direct-marketing industry is working to address issues of ethics and public policy. They know that, left untended, such problems will lead to increasingly negative consumer attitudes, lower response rates, and calls for greater state and federal legislation to further restrict direct-marketing practices. More importantly, in the last analysis, most direct marketers want the same thing that consumers want: honest and well-designed marketing offers targeted only toward consumers who will appreciate and respond to them. Direct marketing is just too expensive to waste on consumers who don't want it.

SOURCE: Portions adapted from Terrence H. Witkowski, "Self-Regulation Will Suppress Direct Marketing's Downside," *Marketing News*, April 24, 1989, p. 4.

A coupon in the Sunday newspaper clearly indicates a 40-cent savings on brand X coffee. The end-of-the-aisle display confronts an impulse buyer with a wall of snack foods. A family buys a camcorder and gets a free traveling case or buys a car and gets a check for a $500 rebate. An appliance retailer is given a 10% manufacturer discount on January's orders if the retailer advertises the product in the local newspaper.[10]

Whereas advertising offers a *reason* to buy, sales promotion offers an *incentive* to buy. Sales promotion includes tools for *consumer promotion* (e.g., samples, coupons, cash refund offers, prices off, premiums, prizes, patronage rewards, free trials, warranties, demonstrations, contests); *trade promotion* (e.g., buying allowances, free goods, merchandise allowances, cooperative advertising, advertising and display allowances, push money, dealer sales contests); and *salesforce promotion* (e.g., bonuses, contests, sales rallies).

Sales-promotion tools are used by most organizations, including manufacturers, distributors, retailers, trade associations, and nonprofit organizations. As examples of the last, churches often sponsor bingo games, theater parties, testimonial dinners, and raffles.

Rapid Growth of Sales Promotion

A decade ago, the *advertising-to-sales-promotion ratio* was about 60:40. Today, in many consumer-packaged-goods companies, the picture is reversed, with sales promotion accounting for between 60% to 70% of the combined budget. Sales-promotion expenditures have been increasing 12% annually, compared with advertising's increase of 7.6%. Total sales promotion is estimated at $100 billion.[11] And the fast growth rate is expected to continue.

Several factors contributed to the rapid growth of sales promotion, particularly in consumer markets.[12] Internal factors include the following: Promotion is now more accepted by top management as an effective sales tool; more product managers are qualified to use sales-promotion tools; and product managers are under greater pressure to increase their current sales. External factors include the following: The number of brands has increased; competitors use promotions frequently; many brands are at parity; consumers are more deal oriented; the trade has demanded more deals from manufacturers; and advertising efficiency has declined because of rising costs, media clutter, and legal restraints.

The rapid growth of sales-promotion media (coupons, contests, and the like) has created a situation of *promotion clutter*, similar to advertising clutter. There is a danger that consumers will start tuning out, in which case coupons and other media will weaken in their ability to trigger purchase. Manufacturers will have to find ways to rise above the clutter, for instance, by offering larger coupon-redemption values or using more dramatic point-of-purchase displays or demonstrations.

Purpose of Sales Promotion

Sales-promotion tools vary in their specific objectives. A free sample stimulates consumer trial, while a free management-advisory service cements a long-term relationship with a retailer.

Sellers use incentive-type promotions to attract new triers, to reward loyal customers, and to increase the repurchase rates of occasional users. New triers are of three types—users of another brand in the same category, users in other categories, and frequent brand switchers. Sales promotions often attract the brand switchers, because users of other brands and categories do not always notice or act on a promotion. Brand switchers are primarily looking for low price, good value, or premiums. Sales promotions are unlikely to turn them into loyal brand users. Sales promotions used in markets of high brand similarity produce a high sales response in the short run but little permanent gain in market share. In markets of high brand dissimilarity, sales promotions can alter market shares more permanently.

Sellers often think of sales promotion as designed to break down brand loyalty, and advertising as designed to build up brand loyalty. Therefore, an important issue for marketing managers is how to divide the budget between sales promotion and advertising. Ten years ago marketing managers would decide what they needed to spend on advertising and put the rest into sales promotion. Today, marketing managers first estimate what they need to spend in trade promotion, then what they need to spend in consumer promotion, andwhatever is left they will budget for advertising.

There is a danger, however, in letting advertising take a back seat to sales promotion. When a brand is price promoted too much of the time, the consumer begins to think of it as a cheap brand and often will only buy it on deal. No one knows when this happens, but there is risk in putting a well-known brand leader on promotion more than 30 percent of the time.[13] Dominant brands use dealing less frequently, since most of it would only subsidize current users.

Most observers feel that dealing activities do not build long-term consumer loyalty, as does advertising. Brown's study of 2,500 instant coffee buyers concluded that:

- Sales promotions yield faster and more measurable responses in sales than advertising does.
- Sales promotions do not tend to yield new, long-term buyers in mature markets because they attract mainly deal-prone consumers who switch among brands as deals become available.
- Loyal brand buyers tend not to change their buying patterns as a result of competitive promotion.
- Advertising appears to be capable of increasing the "prime franchise" of a brand.[14]

There is also evidence that price promotions do not permanently build total category volume. They usually build short-term volume that is not maintained. Small-share competitors find it advantageous to use sales promotion, because they cannot afford to match the large advertising budgets of the market leaders. Nor can they obtain shelf space without offering trade allowances or stimulate consumer trial without offering consumer incentives. Price competition is often used by a small brand seeking to enlarge its share, but it is less effective for a category leader whose growth lies in expanding the entire category.[15]

The upshot is that many consumer-packaged-goods companies feel that they are forced to use more sales promotion than they would like. Kellogg, Kraft, and other market leaders have announced that they will put a growing emphasis on the pull side of the business and increase their advertising budgets. They blame the heavy use of sales promotion for causing decreasing brand loyalty, increasing consumer price sensitivity, brand-quality-image dilution, and a focus on short-run marketing planning.

Farris and Quelch, however, dispute this.[16] They argue that the heavy use of sales promotion is a symptom and not a cause of these problems. They point to more fundamental causes, such as slower population growth, more educated consumers, industry overcapacity, the diminishing effectiveness of advertising, the growth of trade power, and the great pressure in the U.S. for short-run profit performance.

Farris and Quelch counter that sales promotion provides a number of benefits that are important to manufacturers as well as consumers. Sales promotions enable manufacturers to adjust to short-term variations in supply and demand. They enable manufacturers to charge a higher list price to test "how high is up." They induce consumers to try new products instead of never straying from their current ones. They lead to more varied retail formats, such as the *everyday-low-price store* and the *promotional-pricing store*, giving consumers more choice. They promote greater consumer awareness of prices. They permit manufacturers to sell more than they would normally sell at the list price, and to the extent that there are economies of scale, this reduces the unit costs. They help the manufacturer adapt programs to different consumer segments. Consumers themselves enjoy some satisfaction from being smart shoppers when they take advantage of price specials.

Major Decisions in Sales Promotion

In using sales promotion, a company must establish the objectives, select the tools, develop the program, pretest the program, implement and control it, and evaluate the results. We will examine these steps in the following paragraphs.

ESTABLISHING THE SALES-PROMOTION OBJECTIVES ❖ Sales-promotion objectives are derived from broader *promotion objectives*, which are derived from more basic *marketing objectives* developed for the product. The specific objectives set for sales promotion will vary with the type of target market. For *consumers*, objectives include encouraging purchase of larger-size units, building trial among nonusers, and attracting switchers away from competitors' brands. For *retailers*, objectives include inducing retailers to carry new items and higher levels of inventory, encouraging off-season buying, encouraging stocking of related items, offsetting competitive promotions, building brand loyalty of retailers, and gaining entry into new retail outlets. For the *salesforce*, objectives include encouraging support of a new product or model, encouraging more prospecting, and stimulating off-season sales.

SELECTING THE SALES-PROMOTION TOOLS ❖ Many sales-promotion tools are available to accomplish these objectives. The promotion planner should take into account the type of market, sales-promotion objectives, competitive conditions, and cost effectiveness of each tool. We will now consider the main sales-promotion tools used for consumer promotion, trade promotion, and business promotion.

Consumer-Promotion Tools. The main consumer-promotion tools are listed in Marketing Concepts and Tools 24-3. We can distinguish between *manufacturer promotions* and *retailer promotions* to consumers. The former is illustrated by the auto industry's frequent use of rebates, gifts to motivate test drives and purchases, and high-value trade-in credit. The latter includes price cuts, feature advertising, retailer coupons, and retailer contests/premiums. We can also distinguish between those sales-promotion tools that are "consumer-franchise building" and those that are not. The former imparts a selling message along with the deal, as in the case of free samples, coupons when they include a selling message, and premiums when they are related to the product. Sales-promotion tools that are not consumer-franchise building include price-off packs, consumer premiums not related to a product, contests and sweepstakes, consumer refund offers, and trade allowances. Sellers should use consumer-franchise-building promotions, because they reinforce the consumer's brand understanding.

Sales promotion seems most effective when used together with advertising. "In one study, point-of-purchase displays related to current TV commercials were found to produce 15% more sales than similar displays not related to such advertis-

Major Consumer-Promotion Tools

SAMPLES ❖ Samples are offers of a free amount of a product or service. The sample might be delivered door to door, sent in the mail, picked up in a store, found attached to another product, or featured in an advertising offer. Sampling is the most effective and most expensive way to introduce a new product. For example, Lever Brothers had so much confidence in its new Surf detergent that it distributed free samples to four out of five American households at a cost of $43 million.

COUPONS ❖ Coupons are certificates entitling the bearer to a stated saving on the purchase of a specific product. Coupons can be mailed, enclosed in other products or attached to them, or inserted in magazine and newspaper ads. The redemption rate varies with the mode of distribution; newspaper coupons are redeemed about 2% of the time, direct-mail-distributed coupons about 8% of the time, and pack-distributed about 17% of the time. Coupons can be effective in stimulating sales of a mature brand and inducing early trial of a new brand. Experts believe that coupons should provide a 15% to 20% saving to be effective. P&G broke into the Pittsburgh market with its Folger brand by offering a 35¢ *discount coupon* on a one-pound can mailed to area homes and a *coupon in can* for 10¢ off.

CASH REFUND OFFERS (REBATES) ❖ Cash refund offers provide a price reduction after the purchase rather than at the retail shop. The consumer sends a specified "proof of purchase" to the manufacturer, who "refunds" part of the purchase price by mail. Toro ran a clever preseason promotion on specific snowblower models, offering a rebate if the snowfall in the buyer's market area was below average; competitors were not able to match this offer on such short notice. On the other hand, automobile rebates have become so common that many car buyers postpone purchasing until a rebate is announced. Since most auto companies match each other on the rebates, little is gained.

PRICE PACKS ❖ Price packs (also called cents-off deals) are offers to consumers of savings off the regular price of a product, flagged on the label or package. They can take the form of a *reduced-price pack*, which is single packages sold at a reduced price (such as two for the price of one), or a *banded pack*, which is two related products banded together (such as a toothbrush and toothpaste). Price packs are very effective in stimulating short-term sales, even more than coupons.

PREMIUMS ❖ Premiums (or gifts) are merchandise offered at a relatively low cost or free as an incentive to purchase a particular product. A *with-pack premium* accompanies the product inside (in-pack) or on (on-pack) the package. Quaker Oats ran a promotion where it inserted $5 million in gold and silver coins in bags of Ken-L Ration dog food. The package itself, if a *reusable container*, can serve as a premium. A *free in-the-mail premium* is an item mailed to consumers who send in a proof of purchase, such as a box top. A *self-liquidating premium* is an item sold below its normal retail price to consumers who request it. Manufacturers now offer consumers all kinds of premiums bearing the company's name: The Budweiser consumer can order T-shirts, hot-air balloons, and hundreds of other items with Bud's name on them.

PRIZES (CONTESTS, SWEEPSTAKES, GAMES) ❖ Prizes are offers of the chance to win cash, trips, or merchandise as a result of purchasing something. A *contest* calls for consumers to submit an entry—a jingle, estimate, suggestion—to be examined by a panel of judges who will select the best entries. A *sweepstake* calls for consumers to submit their names in a drawing. A *game* presents consumers with something every time they buy—bingo numbers, missing letters—which might or might not help them win a prize. All of these tend to gain more attention than do coupons or small premiums. The chance of a trip to Hawaii generates much more interest and excitement. A British cigarette company included a lottery ticket in each pack providing the chance to win up to $10,000 if the lottery ticket won. Sometimes the prize is a person, as when Canada Dry offered the winner either $1 million or dinner with actress Joan Collins (cash won out in this case).

PATRONAGE AWARDS ❖ Patronage awards are values in cash or in other forms that are proportional to one's patronage of a certain vendor or group of vendors. Most airlines offer "frequent-flyer plans," providing points for miles traveled that can be turned in for free airline trips. The Marriott Hotels has adopted an "honored guest" plan that awards points for users of their hotels. Cooperatives pay their members dividends according to their annual patronage. Trading stamps also represent patronage rewards in that customers receive stamps when they buy from certain merchants and can redeem them for merchandise at stamp redemption centers or through mail-order catalogs.

FREE TRIALS ❖ Free trials consist of inviting prospective purchasers to try the product without cost in the hope that they will buy the product. Thus auto dealers encourage free test drives to stimulate purchase interest.

PRODUCT WARRANTIES ❖ Product warranties are an important promotional tool, especially as consumers become more quality sensitive. When Chrysler offered a five-year car warranty, substantially longer than GM's or Ford's, customers took notice. They inferred that Chrysler quality must be good. And Sears's offer of a lifetime warranty on its auto batteries certainly screams quality to the buyers. Companies must make a number of decisions before featuring a warranty. Is the product quality high enough? Should the product quality be improved further? Can competitors offer the same warranty? How long should the warranty be? What should it cover (replacement, repair, cash)? How much should be spent to advertise the warranty so that potential consumers know about it and consider it? Clearly, companies must carefully estimate the sales-generating value of the proposed warranty against its potential costs.

TIE-IN PROMOTIONS ❖ Tie-in promotions involve two or more brands or companies that team up on coupons, refunds, and contests to increase their pulling power. Companies pool funds with the hope of broader exposure, while several salesforces push these promotions to retailers, giving them a better shot at extra display and ad space.

CROSS-PROMOTIONS ❖ Cross-promotions involve using one brand to advertise another noncompeting brand. For example, Nabisco cookies might advertise that they contain Hershey chocolate chips and the box may even contain a coupon to buy a Hershey product.

POINT-OF-PURCHASE (POP) DISPLAYS AND DEMONSTRATIONS ❖ POP displays and demonstrations take place at the point of purchase or sale. A five-foot-high cardboard figure of Cap'n Crunch next to Cap'n Crunch cereal boxes or at the end of an aisle is an example. Unfortunately, many retailers do not like to handle the hundreds of displays, signs, and posters they receive from manufacturers. Manufacturers are responding by creating better POP materials, tying them in with television or print messages, and offering to set them up. The L'eggs pantyhose display is one of the most creative in the history of POP materials and a major factor in the success of this brand.

---

ing. In another, a heavy sampling approach along with TV advertising proved more successful than either TV alone or TV with coupons in introducing a product."[17]

Many large companies have a sales-promotion manager whose job is to help brand managers choose the right promotional tool. The following example shows how one firm determined the appropriate sales-promotion tool:

> A firm launched a new product and achieved a 20% market share within six months. Its penetration rate is 40% (i.e., the percentage of the target market that purchased the brand at least once). Its repurchase rate is 10% (the percentage of the first-time triers who repurchased the brand one or more times). This firm needs to create more loyal users. An in-pack coupon would be appropriate to build more repeat purchase. But if the repurchase rate had been high, say 50 percent, then the company should try to attract more new triers. Here a media-mailed coupon might be appropriate.

Trade-Promotion Tools. Manufacturers use a number of trade-promotion tools (see Marketing Concepts and Tools 24-4). Surprisingly, more sales-promotion dollars are directed to the trade (58%) than to consumers (42%)![18] Manufacturers seek four objectives in awarding money to the trade:

Marketing Concepts and Tools 24-4

Major Trade-Promotion Tools

PRICE-OFF ❖ A price-off (also called off-invoice or off-list) is a straight discount off the list price on each case purchased during a stated time period. The offer encourages dealers to buy a quantity or carry a new item that they might not ordinarily buy. The dealers can use the buying allowance for immediate profit, advertising, or price reductions.

ALLOWANCE ❖ An allowance is an amount offered in return for the retailer's agreeing to feature the manufacturer's products in some way. An *advertising allowance* compensates retailers for advertising the manufacturer's product. A *display allowance* compensates them for carrying a special product display.

FREE GOODS ❖ Free goods are offers of extra cases of merchandise to middlemen who buy a certain quantity or who feature a certain flavor or size. Manufacturers might offer *push money*, which is cash or gifts to dealers or their salesforce to push the manufacturer's goods. Manufacturers might offer free *specialty advertising items* to the retailers that carry the company's name, such as pens, pencils, calendars, paperweights, memo pads, and ashtrays.

1. *Trade Promotion Can Persuade the Retailer or Wholesaler to Carry the Brand:* Shelf space is so scarce that manufacturers often have to offer price-offs, allowances, buy-back guarantees, free goods, or outright payments (called slotting allowances) to get on the shelf, and once there, to stay on the shelf.

2. *Trade Promotion Can Persuade the Retailer or Wholesaler to Carry More Goods Than the Normal Amount:* Manufacturers will offer volume allowances to get the trade to carry more in their warehouses and stores. Manufacturers believe that the trade will work harder when they are "loaded" with the manufacturer's product.

3. *Trade Promotion Can Induce the Retailers to Promote the Brand by Featuring, Display, and Price Reductions:* Manufacturers might seek an end-of-aisle display or increased shelf facings or price reduction stickers and obtain them by offering the retailers allowances paid on "proof of performance."

4. *Trade Promotion Can Stimulate Retailers and Their Sales Clerks to Push the Product:* Manufacturers compete for retailer sales effort by offering push money, sales aids, recognition programs, premiums, and sales contests.

Manufacturers probably spend more on trade promotion than they would freely choose to spend. The increased concentration of buying power in the hands of fewer and larger retailers has increased the trade's ability to demand manufacturers' financial support at the expense of consumer promotion and advertising. In fact, the trade has come to depend on promotion money from the manufacturers: It is estimated that grocery stores received $12.6 billion in 1984 from packaged-goods manufacturers, three times as much as their entire reported profits. If this money were withdrawn, grocery prices would increase substantially. Nor can any manufacturer unilaterally stop offering trade allowances without losing retailer support. In some countries, the retailers have become the major advertisers, using mostly the promotional allowances extracted from their suppliers.

Food retailers strongly prefer trade deals to consumer deals. They are unhappy about the amount of consumer deals they have to handle. According to Chevalier and Curhan:

> *Retailers view promotional efforts initiated by manufacturers as encouraging profitless brand switching rather than increasing sales or profits. Manufacturers, on the other hand, complain that retailer-initiated promotions sometimes damage brand franchises which have been care-*

fully and expensively nurtured over many years. Worse yet, manufacturers complain that retailers frequently take advantage of them by "absorbing" deals without passing their benefits along to consumers.[19]

As the number of competitive sales promotions has increased, friction has been created between the company's salesforce and its brand managers. The salesforce says that the retailers will not keep the company's products on the shelf unless they receive more trade-promotion money, while the brand managers want to spend the limited funds on consumer promotion and advertising. Some company sales vice-presidents are insisting that they control the budget for consumer promotion and especially trade promotion, since they know the local market better than a brand manager sitting at headquarters. Some companies have given a substantial part of the sales-promotion budget to the salesforce or local marketing managers to handle.

Manufacturers have other problems with trade promotions. First, they find it difficult to police retailers to make sure that they are doing what they agreed to do. Retailers do not always convert the buying allowances into reduced prices for consumers, and they might not provide extra shelving or display even after receiving merchandise or display allowances. Manufacturers are increasingly insisting on proof of performance before paying these allowances. Second, more retailers are doing "forward buying," namely, buying a greater quantity of the brand during the deal period than they can sell during the deal period. Retailers might respond to a 10% off-case allowance by buying a 12-week or longer supply. The manufacturer finds that it has to schedule more production than planned and bear the costs of extra work shifts and overtime.

Third, retailers are doing more "diverting," namely, buying more cases than needed in a region in which the manufacturer offered a deal and shipping the surplus to nondeal regions. Manufacturers are trying to handle forward buying and dealing by limiting the amount they will sell at a discount, or producing and delivering less than the full order in an effort to smooth production.[20]

All said, manufacturers feel that trade promotion has become a nightmare. It contains layers of deals (off-invoice, street money, lump-sum funds, market development funds), is complex to administer, and the manufacturers lose money for the most part. Kevin Price describes trade promotion in the following way:

> *A decade ago, the retailer was a chihuahua nipping at the manufacturer's heels — a nuisance, yes, but only a minor irritant; you fed it and it went away. Today it's a pit bull and it wants to rip your arms and legs off. You'd like to see it roll over, but you're too busy defending yourself to even try . . . Today management of trade promotions is a president-level issue.*[21]

Business-Promotion Tools. Companies spend billions of dollars on business-promotion tools (see Marketing Concepts and Tools 24-5). These tools are used to gather business leads, impress and reward customers, and stimulate the salesforce to greater effort. Companies typically develop budgets for each business-promotion tool that stay fairly close from year to year.

DEVELOPING THE SALES-PROMOTION PROGRAM ❖ The marketer must make further decisions to define the full promotion program. Increasingly, marketers are blending several media into a total campaign concept. Kerry E. Smith describes the following:

> *A sports trivia game to create pull-through at taverns for a premium beer brand would use TV to reach consumers, direct mail to incentivize distributors, point-of-purchase for retail support, telephones for consumer call-ins, a service bureau for call processing, live operators*

Major Business-Promotion Tools

TRADE SHOWS AND CONVENTIONS ❖ Industry associations organize annual trade shows and conventions. Firms selling products and services to the particular industry buy space and set up booths and displays to demonstrate their products at the trade show. Over 5,600 trade shows take place every year, drawing approximately 80 million attendees. Trade show attendance can range from a few thousand people to over 70,000 for large shows held by the restaurant or hotel-motel industries. The participating vendors expect several benefits, including generating new sales leads, maintaining customer contacts, introducing new products, meeting new customers, selling more to present customers, and educating customers with publications, motion pictures, and audiovisual materials. Here are some findings:

- Trade shows help companies reach many prospects not reached through their salesforces. About 90% of a trade show's visitors see a company salesperson for the first time.

- The average attendee spends 7.8 hours viewing exhibits over a two-day period and spends an average of 22 minutes at each exhibit visited. Of those attending, 85% make a final purchase decision for one or more products displayed.

- The average cost per visitor reached (including exhibits, personnel travel, living and salary expenses, and preshow promotion costs) is $200. The Trade Show Bureau estimates that this is much lower than the cost of generating a sale from a sales call.

Business marketers may spend as much as 35% of their annual promotion budget on trade shows. They face a number of decisions, including which trade shows to participate in, how much to spend on each trade show, how to build dramatic exhibits that attract attention, and how to effectively follow up on sales leads. Trade shows can benefit greatly from professional management.

SALES CONTESTS ❖ A *sales contest* is a contest involving the salesforce or dealers, aimed at inducing them to increase their sales results over a stated period, with prizes going to those who succeed. A majority of companies sponsor annual or more frequent sales contests for their salesforce. Called incentive programs, they serve to motivate and to give recognition to good company performance. The good performers may receive trips, cash prizes, or gifts. Some companies award points for performance, which the receiver can turn into any of a variety of prizes. An unusual though not very expensive prize may often work better than much more costly prizes. Incentives work best when they are tied to measurable and achievable sales objectives (such as finding new accounts, reviving old accounts) where employees feel they have an equal chance. Otherwise, employees who do not think the goals are reasonable will not take up the challenge.

SPECIALTY ADVERTISING ❖ Specialty advertising consists of useful, low-cost items given by salespeople to prospects and customers without obligation and which bear the company's name and address and sometimes an advertising message. Common items are ballpoint pens, calendars, cigarette lighters, and memo pads. The item keeps the company's name before the prospect and creates goodwill because of the item's utility. One survey indicated that over 86% of manufacturers supply their salespeople with specialty items.

SOURCES: For trade shows, see Thomas V. Bonoma, "Get More Out of Your Trade Shows," *Harvard Business Review,* January–February 1983, pp. 75–83; and Jonathan M. Cox, Ian K. Sequeira, and Lori L. Bock, "Show Size Grows: Audience Quality Stays High," *Business Marketing,* May 1988, pp. 84–88. For sales contests, see C. Robert Patty and Robert Hite, *Managing Sales People,* 3rd ed. (Englewood Cliffs, NJ: Prentice Hall, 1988), pp. 313–27. For specialty advertising, see George M. Zinkham and Lauren A. Vachris, "The Impact of Selling Aids on New Prospects," *Industrial Marketing Management* 13 (1984), 187–93; and Ernest F. Cooke, Louise W. Smith, and Doris C. Van Doren, "Manufacturing Companies Try to Become 'Special' by Using Specialty Advertising," *Journal of Business & Industrial Marketing,* Summer/Fall 1989, pp. 43–48.

---

for data entry, and computer software and hardware to tie it all together . . . . Companies use telepromotions not only to pull product through at retail but also to identify customers, generate leads, build databases and deliver coupons, product samples and rebate offers.[22]

In this context, there are specific tasks. The marketer has to determine *the size of the incentive* to offer. A certain minimum incentive is necessary if the promotion is

CHAPTER 24
Designing Direct-Marketing, Sales-Promotion, and Public-Relations Programs

to succeed. A higher incentive level will produce more sales response but at a diminishing rate.

Conditions for participation have to be established. Incentives might be offered to everyone or to select groups. A premium might be offered only to those who turn in box tops or proof-of-purchase seals. Sweepstakes might not be offered in certain states or to families of company personnel or to persons under a certain age.

The marketer has to decide on the *duration of promotion*. If the sales-promotion period is too short, many prospects will not be able to take advantage, since they might not be repurchasing at the time. If the promotion runs too long, the deal will lose some of its "act now" force. According to one researcher, the optimal frequency is about three weeks per quarter, and optimal duration is the length of the average purchase cycle.[23] Of course, the optimal promotion cycle varies by product category and even by specific product.

The marketer must choose a *distribution vehicle*. A fifteen-cents-off coupon can be distributed in the package, store, mail, or advertising media. Each distribution method involves a different level of reach, cost, and impact.

The *timing of promotion* must be established. For example, brand managers develop calendar dates for the annually planned promotions. The dates are used by production, sales, and distribution. On-the-spot promotions will also be needed and will require cooperation on a short notice.

Finally, the marketer must determine the *total sales-promotion budget*. The sales-promotion budget can be developed in two ways. It can be built from the ground up, where the marketer chooses the individual promotions and estimates their total cost. The cost of a particular promotion consists of the *administrative cost* (printing, mailing, and promoting the deal) and the *incentive cost* (cost of premium or cents-off, including redemption costs), multiplied by the *expected number of units* that will be sold on the deal.

> Suppose a brand of after-shave lotion will be marked down $.09 for a limited period. The item regularly sells for $1.09, of which $.40 represents a contribution to the manufacturer's profit before marketing expense. The brand manager expects a million bottles to be sold under this deal. Thus the incentive cost of the deal will be $90,000 ($= 0.09 \times 1,000,000$). Suppose the administrative cost is estimated at $10,000. Then the total cost is $100,000. In order to break even on this deal, the company will have to sell 250,000 ($= \$100,000 \div 0.40$) more units than would have occurred over the same period without the deal.

In the case of a coupon deal, the cost would take into account the fact that only a fraction of the consumers will redeem the coupons. As for an in-pack premium, the deal cost must include the procurement cost and packaging of the premium, offset by any price increase on the package.

The more common way to develop the sales-promotion budget is to use a conventional percentage of the total promotion budget. For example, toothpaste might get a sales-promotion budget of 30% of the total promotion budget, whereas shampoo might get 50%. These percentages vary for different brands in different markets and are influenced by the stages of the product life cycle and competitive expenditures on promotion.

Multiple-brand companies should coordinate their sales-promotion activities, such as making single mailings of multiple coupons to consumers. Strang, in his study of company sales-promotion practices, found three major budgeting inadequacies:

- ◆ Lack of consideration of cost effectiveness.

- Use of simplistic decision rules, such as extensions of last year's spending, percentage of expected sales, maintenance of a fixed ratio to advertising, and the "left-over approach," where promotion gets what is left after advertising is set.
- Advertising and promotional budgets being prepared independently.[24]

PRETESTING THE SALES-PROMOTION PROGRAM ❖ Although sales-promotion programs are designed on the basis of experience, pretests should be conducted to determine if the tools are appropriate, the incentive size optimal, and the presentation method efficient. A survey by the Premium Advertisers Association indicated that less than 42% of premium offers were ever tested for their effectiveness.[25] Strang maintains that promotions can usually be tested quickly and inexpensively and that some large companies test alternative strategies in selected market areas with each national promotion.[26]

Sales promotions directed at consumer markets can be readily pretested. Consumers can be asked to rate or rank different possible deals. Or trial tests can be run in limited geographical areas.

IMPLEMENTING AND CONTROLLING THE SALES-PROMOTION PROGRAM ❖ Implementation and control plans should be prepared for each individual promotion. Implementation planning must cover lead time and sell-in time. Lead time is the time necessary to prepare the program prior to launching it.

> It covers initial planning, design, and approval of package modifications or material to be mailed or distributed to the home, preparation of conjunctive advertising and point-of-sale materials, notification of field sales personnel, establishment of allocations for individual distributors, purchasing and printing of special premiums or packaging materials, production of advance inventories and staging at distribution centers in preparation for release at a specific date, and finally, the distribution to the retailer.[27]

Sell-in time begins with the launch and ends when approximately 95% of the deal merchandise is in the hands of consumers, which can take one to several months, depending on the deal duration.

EVALUATING THE SALES-PROMOTION RESULTS ❖ Evaluation is a crucial requirement, and yet, according to Strang, "evaluation of promotion programs receives . . . little attention. Even where an attempt is made to evaluate a promotion, it is likely to be superficial. . . . Evaluation in terms of profitability is even less common."[28]

Manufacturers can use four methods to measure sales-promotion effectiveness. The most common method is to examine the *sales data* before, during, and after a promotion. Suppose a company has a 6% market share in the prepromotion period, which jumps to 10% during the promotion, falls to 5% immediately after the promotion, and rises to 7% in the postpromotion period (see Figure 24-1). The promotion evidently attracted new triers and also stimulated more purchasing by existing customers. After the promotion, sales fell as consumers worked down their inventories. The long-run rise to 7% indicates that the company gained some new users. Sales promotions work best, in general, when they attract competitors' customers to try a superior product and these customers permanently switch as a result.

If the company's product is not superior, the brand's share is likely to return to its prepromotion level. The sales promotion only altered the time pattern of demand rather than the total demand. The promotion may have covered its costs but

FIGURE 24-1
Effect of Consumer Deal
on Brand Share

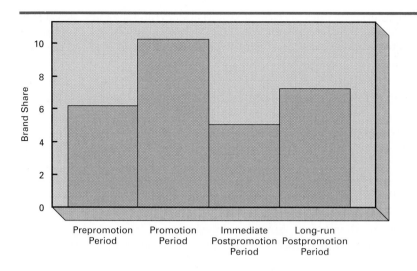

more likely did not. One study of more than 1,000 promotions concluded that only 16% paid off.[29]

Consumer-panel data would reveal the kinds of people who responded to the promotion and what they did after the promotion.[30] If more information is needed, *consumer surveys* can be conducted to learn how many recall the promotion, what they thought of it, how many took advantage of it, and how the promotion affected their subsequent brand-choice behavior. Sales promotions can also be evaluated through *experiments* that vary such attributes as incentive value, duration, and distribution media.

Beyond these methods of evaluating the results of specific promotions, management must recognize other potential costs and problems. First, promotions might decrease long-run brand loyalty by making more consumers deal prone rather than advertising prone. Second, promotions can be more expensive than they appear. Some are inevitably distributed to the wrong consumers (nonswitchers, always switchers, and the company's own customers, who get a free subsidy). Furthermore, there are hidden costs of special production runs, extra salesforce effort, and handling requirements. Third, certain promotions irritate retailers, and they demand extra trade allowances or refuse to cooperate in the promotion.

In spite of these problems, sales promotion will continue to play a growing role in the total promotion mix. Its effective use will require defining the sales-promotion objectives, selecting the appropriate tools, constructing the sales-promotion program, pretesting it, implementing it, and evaluating the results.[31]

Public Relations

Public relations (PR) is another important marketing tool. Not only must the company relate constructively to its customers, suppliers, and dealers, but it must also relate to a large set of interested publics. We define a public as:

❖ A public *is any group that has an actual or potential interest or impact on a company's ability to achieve its objectives.*

A public can facilitate or impede a company's ability to achieve its objectives. The wise company takes concrete steps to manage successful relations with its key publics. Most companies operate a public relations department to plan these relations. The PR department monitors the attitudes of the organization's publics and distributes information and communications to build goodwill. When negative publicity breaks out, the PR department acts as a troubleshooter. The best PR departments spend time counseling top management to adopt positive programs and to eliminate questionable practices so that negative publicity does not arise in the first place.

PR has generally been treated as a marketing stepchild, an afterthought to more serious promotion planning. The public-relations department is typically located at corporate headquarters; and its staff is so busy dealing with various publics—stockholders, employees, legislators, the media, community leaders, and action groups—that PR support for marketing objectives tends to be neglected. PR departments perform the following five activities, not all of which support marketing objectives:

- *Press Relations:* The aim of press relations is to place newsworthy information into the news media to attract attention to a person, product, service, or organization.
- *Product Publicity:* Product publicity involves various efforts to publicize specific products.
- *Corporate Communication:* This activity covers internal and external communications and promotes understanding of the organization.
- *Lobbying:* Lobbying involves dealing with legislators and government officials to promote or defeat legislation and regulation.
- *Counseling:* Counseling involves advising management about public issues and company positions and image.[32]

In addition, marketing managers and PR practitioners do not always talk the same language. One major difference is that marketing managers are much more bottom-line oriented, whereas PR practitioners see their job as preparing and disseminating communications. But this is changing. Companies are setting up a *marketing public-relations group* (MPR) to directly support corporate/product promotion and image making. Thus MPR, like financial PR and community PR, would serve a special constituency, namely the marketing department.[33]

The old name for MPR was *publicity*, which was seen as the task of securing editorial space—as opposed to paid space—in print and broadcast media to promote or "hype" a product, place, or person. But MPR goes beyond simple publicity. MPR can contribute to the following tasks:

- *Assist in the Launch of New Products:* The amazing commercial success of Cabbage Patch Kids was due not so much to the paltry advertising budget of $500,000 but to clever publicity, including donating the dolls to children in hospitals, sponsoring Cabbage Patch Kids adoption parties for schoolchildren, and so on.
- *Assist in Repositioning a Mature Product:* New York City had an extremely bad press in the seventies until the "I Love New York" campaign began, bringing millions of additional tourists to the city.
- *Build Up Interest in a Product Category:* Companies and trade associations have used PR to rebuild interest in declining commodities like eggs, milk, and potatoes and to expand consumption of such products as tea and orange juice.
- *Influence Specific Target Groups:* McDonald's sponsors special neighborhood events in Hispanic and black communities for good causes and in turn builds up a good company image.
- *Defend Products That Have Encountered Public Problems:* Johnson & Johnson's masterly use of PR was a major factor in saving Tylenol from extinction.

- *Build the Corporate Image in a Way That Projects Favorably on Its Products:* Iaccoca's speeches and his autobiography created a whole new winning image for the Chrysler Corporation.

As the power of mass advertising weakens owing to rising media costs, increasing clutter, and smaller audiences, marketing managers are turning more to MPR. In a survey of 286 U.S. marketing managers, three fourths reported that their companies were using MPR. They found it particularly effective in building awareness and brand knowledge, for both new and established products. MPR is particularly effective in blanketing local communities and reaching specific ethnic and other groups. In several cases, MPR proved more cost effective than advertising. Nevertheless, it must be planned jointly with advertising. MPR needs a larger budget, and the money might have to come from advertising.[34]

Marketing managers will need to acquire more skill in using PR resources. The Gillette company requires each brand manager to have a budget line for MPR and to justify *not* using it if they do not. A brand manager might ask the MPR professional how many cases $100,000 for MPR would move. But that is a hard question to answer. MPR is even more difficult to evaluate than advertising. Advertising is much more under the control of the company, and the measurement tools are better developed. Therefore, MPR people find it hard to recommend a budget level; much depends on coming up with good MPR ideas and then convincing others that the favorable results would far exceed their cost.

Clearly, public relations can potentially impact public awareness at a fraction of the cost of advertising. The company does not pay for the space or time obtained in the media. It pays for a staff to develop and circulate the stories and manage certain events. If the company develops an interesting story, it could be picked up by all the news media and be worth millions of dollars in equivalent advertising. The Body Shop, for example, has never spent money on advertising; its success has been entirely due to publicity. In general, MPR carries more credibility than advertising. Some experts say that consumers are five times more likely to be influenced by editorial copy than by advertising.

Major Decisions in Marketing PR

In considering when and how to use MPR, management should establish the marketing objectives, choose the PR messages and vehicles, and evaluate the PR results. The main tools of MPR are described in Marketing Concepts and Tools 24-6.

ESTABLISHING THE MARKETING OBJECTIVES ❖ MPR can contribute to the following objectives:

- *Build Awareness:* PR can place stories in the media to bring attention to a product, service, person, organization, or idea.
- *Build Credibility:* PR can add credibility by communicating the message in an editorial context.
- *Stimulate the Salesforce and Dealers:* PR can help boost salesforce and dealer enthusiasm. Stories about a new product before it is launched will help the salesforce sell it to retailers.
- *Hold Down Promotion Costs:* PR costs less than direct mail and media advertising. The smaller the company's promotion budget, the stronger the case for using PR to gain share of mind.

Specific objectives should be set for every MPR campaign. The Wine Growers of California hired the public-relations firm of Daniel J. Edelman, Inc., to develop a

Major Tools in Marketing PR

PUBLICATIONS ❖ Companies rely extensively on communication materials to reach and influence their target markets. These include annual reports, brochures, articles, audiovisual materials, and company newsletters and magazines. Chrysler's annual report almost serves as a sales brochure, promoting each new car to the stockholders. Brochures can play an important role in informing target customers about what a product is, how it works, and how it is to be assembled. Thoughtful articles written by company executives can draw attention to the company and its products. Company newsletters and magazines can help build up the company's image and convey important news to target markets. Audiovisual material, such as films, slides-and-sound, and video and audio cassettes, are coming into increasing use as promotion tools. The cost of audiovisual materials is usually greater than the cost of printed material, but so is the impact. Today, it is common for colleges to hire a professional firm to prepare an attractive video that can be shown on recruiting trips or sent to applicants to encourage their choosing the college.

EVENTS ❖ Companies can draw attention to new products or other company activities by arranging special events. These include news conferences, seminars, outings, exhibits, contests and competitions, anniversaries, and sport and cultural sponsorships that will reach the target publics. Sponsoring a sports event, such as the Coors International Bicycle Class or the Volvo International Tennis Tournament, gives these companies a chance to invite and host their suppliers, distributors, and customers as well as to bring repeated attention to their name and products.

NEWS ❖ One of the major tasks of PR professionals is to find or create favorable news about the company, its products, and its people. News generation requires skill in developing a story concept, researching it, and writing a press release. But the PR person's skill must go beyond preparing news stories. Getting the media to accept press releases and attend press conferences calls for marketing and interpersonal skills. A good PR media director understands the press's needs for stories that are interesting and timely and for press releases that are well written and attention getting. The media director needs to build favorable relations with editors and reporters. The more the press is cultivated, the more likely it is to give more and better coverage to the company.

SPEECHES ❖ Speeches are another tool for creating product and company publicity. Iaccoca's charismatic talks before large audiences helped Chrysler sell its cars. Increasingly, company executives must field questions from the media or give talks at trade associations or sales meetings, and these appearances can build or hurt the company's image. Companies are choosing their spokespersons carefully and using speech writers and coaches to help improve the public speaking of their spokespersons.

PUBLIC-SERVICE ACTIVITIES ❖ Companies can improve public goodwill by contributing money and time to good causes. A large company typically will ask executives to support community affairs where their offices and plants are located. In other instances, companies will donate a certain amount of money to a specified cause out of consumer purchases. Called *cause-related marketing*, it is used by a growing number of companies to build public goodwill. General Foods offered to pay 5¢ to the Muscular Dystrophy Association for every redeemed General Foods cents-off coupon and 10¢ to Mothers Against Drunk Driving for every redeemed Tang coupon. Procter & Gamble and Publishers' Clearing House jointly coordinated a promotion to aid the Special Olympics. Product coupons were included in the Publishers' Clearing House mailing, and Procter & Gamble donated 10¢ per coupon redeemed to the Special Olympics program.

IDENTITY MEDIA ❖ Normally, a company's materials acquire separate looks, which creates confusion and misses an opportunity to create and reinforce a corporate identity. In an overcommunicated society, companies have to compete for attention. They should strive to create a visual identity that the public immediately recognizes. The visual identity is carried by the company's logos, stationery, brochures, signs, business forms, business cards, buildings, uniforms and dress codes, and rolling stock.

SOURCE: For further reading on cause-related marketing, see P. Rajan Varadarajan and Anil Menon, "Cause-Related Marketing: A Co-Alignment of Marketing Strategy and Corporate Philanthropy," *Journal of Marketing*, July 1988, pp. 58–74.

publicity campaign to convince Americans that wine drinking is a pleasurable part of good living and to improve the image and market share of California wines. The following publicity objectives were established: (1) develop magazine stories about wine and get them placed in top magazines (*Time, House Beautiful*) and in newspapers (food columns, feature sections); (2) develop stories about wine's many health values and direct them to the medical profession; and (3) develop specific publicity for the young adult market, college market, governmental bodies, and various ethnic communities. These objectives were refined into specific goals so that final results could be evaluated.

CHOOSING THE PR MESSAGES AND VEHICLES ❖ The MPR practitioner next identifies or develops interesting stories to tell about the product. Suppose a relatively unknown college wants more visibility. The MPR practitioner will search for possible stories. Do any faculty members have unusual backgrounds, or are any working on unusual projects? Are any new and unusual courses being taught? Are any interesting events taking place on campus? Usually this search will uncover scores of stories that can be fed to the press. The chosen stories should reflect the image this college wants.

If the number of stories is insufficient, the MPR practitioner should propose newsworthy events that the college could sponsor. Here the challenge is to *create news* rather than *find news*. PR ideas include hosting major academic conventions, inviting expert or celebrity speakers, and developing news conferences. Each event is an opportunity to develop a multitude of stories directed at different audiences.

Event creation is a particularly important skill in publicizing fund-raising drives for nonprofit organizations. Fund-raisers have developed a large repertoire of special events, including *anniversary celebrations, art exhibits, auctions, benefit evenings, bingo games, book sales, cake sales, contests, dances, dinners, fairs, fashion shows, parties in unusual places, phonathons, rummage sales, tours,* and *walkathons.* No sooner is one type of event created, such as a walkathon, than competitors spawn new versions, such as readathons, bikathons, and jogathons.[35]

For-profit organizations also use various events to call attention to their products and services. Humana, Inc., a hospital chain that had virtually no national name recognition in 1984, achieved 16% name recognition in the American public by February 1985 as a result of sponsoring a series of artificial heart implants, which received national news coverage. Fuji Photo Film Company flew its blimp over the renovated Statue of Liberty during its massive celebration, scoring over its rival Kodak, which had mounted a permanent photo exhibit at the site. Anheuser-Busch sponsored a Black World Championship Rodeo in Brooklyn, attracting more than 5,000 spectators.

MPR practitioners are able to find or create stories on behalf of even mundane products. Here are two examples:

> Some years ago the Potato Board financed a publicity campaign to encourage more potato consumption. A national attitude-and-usage study indicated that many consumers perceived potatoes as fattening, nonnutritious, and a poor source of vitamins and minerals. These attitudes were disseminated by various opinion leaders, such as food editors, diet advocates, and doctors. Actually, potatoes have far fewer calories than most people imagine, and they contain several important vitamins and minerals. The Potato Board decided to develop separate publicity programs for consumers, doctors and dieticians, nutritionists, home economists, and food editors. The consumer program consisted of disseminating many stories about the potato for network television and women's magazines, developing and distributing *The Potato Lover's Diet Cookbook,* and placing articles and recipes in food editors' columns. The food editors' program consisted of food-editor seminars conducted by nutrition experts.

One of the top brands of cat food is Star-Kist Foods' 9-Lives. Its brand image revolves around Morris the Cat. The advertising agency of Leo Burnett, which created Morris for its ads, wanted to make him more of a living, breathing, real-life feline to whom cat owners and cat lovers could relate. It hired a public-relations firm, which then proposed and carried out the following ideas: (1) launch a Morris "look-alike" contest in nine major markets; (2) write a book called *Morris, an Intimate Biography;* (3) establish a coveted award called The Morris, a bronze statuette given to the owners of award-winning cats at local cat shows; (4) sponsor an "Adopt-a-Cat Month," with Morris as the official "spokescat"; and (5) distribute a booklet called "The Morris Method" on cat care. These publicity steps strengthened the brand's market share in the cat-food market.

IMPLEMENTING THE MPR PLAN ❖ Implementing publicity requires care. Take the matter of placing stories in the media. A great story is easy to place. But most stories are less than great and might not get past busy editors. One of the chief assets of publicists is their personal relationship with media editors. Public-relations practitioners are often ex-journalists who know many media editors and know what they want. PR people look at media editors as a market to satisfy so that these editors will continue to use their stories.

Publicity requires extra care when it involves staging special events, such as testimonial dinners, news conferences, and national contests. PR practitioners need a good head for detail and for coming up with quick solutions when things go wrong.

EVALUATING THE MPR RESULTS ❖ MPR's contribution is difficult to measure, because it is used along with other promotional tools. If it is used before the other tools come into action, its contribution is easier to evaluate.

Exposures. The easiest measure of MPR effectiveness is the number of *exposures* carried by the media. Publicists supply the client with a clippings book showing all the media that carried news about the product and a summary statement such as the following:

> *Media coverage included 3,500 column inches of news and photographs in 350 publications with a combined circulation of 79.4 million; 2,500 minutes of air time of 290 radio stations and an estimated audience of 65 million; and 660 minutes of air time on 160 television stations with an estimated audience of 91 million. If this time and space had been purchased at advertising rates, it would have amounted to $1,047,000.[36]*

This exposure measure is not very satisfying. There is no indication of how many people actually read, heard, or recalled the message and what they thought afterward. There is no information on the net audience reached, since publications overlap in readership. Because publicity's goal is reach, not frequency, it would be useful to know the number of unduplicated exposures.

Awareness/Comprehension/Attitude Change. A better measure is the change in product *awareness/comprehension/attitude* resulting from the MPR campaign (after allowing for the effect of other promotional tools). For example, how many people recall hearing the news item? How many told others about it (a measure of word of mouth)? How many changed their minds after hearing it? The Potato Board learned, for example, that the number of people who agreed with the statement "Potatoes are rich in vitamins and minerals" went from 36% before the campaign to 67% after the campaign, a significant improvement in product comprehension.

Sales-and-Profit Contribution. Sales-and-profit impact is the most satisfactory measure, if obtainable. For example, 9-Lives sales had increased 43% by the end of the Morris the Cat PR campaign. However, advertising and sales promotion had also been stepped up, and their contribution has to be allowed for. Suppose total sales have increased $1,500,000, and management estimates that MPR contributed 15% of the total sales increase. Then the return on MPR investment is calculated as follows:

Total sales increase	$1,500,000
Estimated sales increase due to PR (15%)	225,000
Contribution margin on product sales (10%)	22,500
Total direct cost of MPR program	− 10,000
Contribution margin added by PR investment	12,500
Return on MPR investment ($12,500/$10,000)	125%

In the years ahead, we can expect more joint strategy planning of advertising, PR, and the other promotional tools. Major advertising agencies have recognized the growing leverage obtained from PR by recently acquiring major PR firms: For example, Young & Rubicam acquired Burson-Marsteller, and J. Walter Thompson acquired Hill and Knowlton. The acquired PR firms will benefit from the highly disciplined methods of the ad agencies, and the ad agencies will benefit from the expanded areas of creativity afforded by PR.

SUMMARY ❖

Direct marketing, sales promotion, and public relations are three tools of growing importance in marketing planning.

Direct marketing is an interactive system of marketing, which uses one or more advertising media (direct mail, catalogs, telemarketing, electronic shopping, and so forth) to effect a measurable response and/or transaction at any location. It has been growing at a more rapid rate than store marketing and is used by manufacturers, retailers, service companies, and other types of organizations. Among its advantages are selectivity, personalization, continuity, better timing, high readership, testability, and privacy. There are strong trends toward integrated direct marketing, maximarketing, and database marketing.

Sales promotion covers a wide variety of short-term incentive tools designed to stimulate consumer markets, the trade, and the organization's own salesforce. Sales-promotion expenditures now exceed advertising expenditures and are growing at a faster rate. Consumer-promotion tools include samples, coupons, cash refund offers, price packs, premiums, prizes, patronage awards, free trials, product warranties, tie-in promotions, and point-of-purchase displays and demonstrations. Trade-promotion tools include price-off, advertising and display allowances, free goods, push money, and specialty advertising items. Business-promotion tools include trade shows/conventions, sales contests, and specialty advertising. Sales-promotion planning calls for establishing the sales-promotion objectives, selecting the tools, developing, pretesting and implementing the sales-promotion program, and evaluating the results.

Public relations is another important communication/promotion tool. Although less utilized, it has great potential for building awareness and preference in the marketplace, repositioning products, and defending them. The major PR tools are publications, events, news, speeches, public-service activities, written material, audiovisual material, corporate-identity media, and telephone information services. Public-relations planning involves establishing the PR objectives, choosing the appropriate messages and vehicles, and evaluating the PR results.

NOTES ❖

1. Ernan Roman, *Integrated Direct Marketing* (New York: McGraw-Hill, 1989), p. 108.

2. The terms *direct-order marketing* and *direct-relationship marketing* were suggested as subsets of direct marketing by Stan Rapp and Tom Collins in *The Great Marketing Turnaround* (Englewood Cliffs, NJ: Prentice Hall, 1990).

3. This estimate is provided by Arnold Fishman in *1988 Guide to Mail Order Sales*. Also see Mary Lou Roberts and Paul D. Berger, *Direct Marketing Management* (Englewood Cliffs, NJ: Prentice Hall, 1989), pp. 11–15.

4. Pierre A. Passavant, "Where Is Direct Marketing Headed in the 1990s?," an address in Philadelphia, May 4, 1989.

5. Roman, *Integrated Direct Marketing*, p. 3. As another illustration, LaTour and Manrai reported the following results for the percentage of people who came to a blood drive: no direct mail, no telephone, 2.0%; direct mail only, 4.4%; telephone only, 7.4%; direct mail followed by telephone, 21.9%. See Stephen A. LaTour and Ajay K. Manrai, "Interactive Impact of Informational and Normative Influence on Donations," *Journal of Marketing Research*, August 1989, pp. 327–35.

6. Stan Rapp and Thomas L. Collins, *Maximarketing* (New York: McGraw-Hill, 1987).

7. Bob Stone, *Successful Direct Marketing Methods* (Chicago: NTC Books, 1993).

8. Edward Nash, *Direct Marketing*, 2nd ed. (New York: McGraw-Hill, 1986), p. 16.

9. For further reading, see Robert C. Blattberg and John Deighton, "Interactive Marketing: Exploiting the Age of Addressability," *Sloan Management Review*, Fall 1991, pp. 5–14.

10. From Robert C. Blattberg and Scott A. Neslin, *Sales Promotion: Concepts, Methods, and Strategies* (Englewood Cliffs, NJ: Prentice Hall, 1990). This text provides the most comprehensive and analytical treatment of sales promotion to date.

11. Len Strawzeweski, "Promotion 'Carnival' Gets Serious," *Advertising Age*, May 2, 1988, pp. S1–2.

12. Roger A. Strang, "Sales Promotion—Fast Growth, Faulty Management," *Harvard Business Review*, July–August 1976, pp. 115–24, here pp. 116–19.

13. For a good summary of the research on whether promotion erodes the consumer franchise of leading brands, see Blattberg and Neslin, *Sales Promotion*, pp. 471–75.

14. Robert George Brown, "Sales Response to Promotions and Advertising," *Journal of Advertising Research*, August 1974, pp. 33–39, here pp. 36–37.

15. F. Kent Mitchel, "Advertising/Promotion Budgets: How Did We Get Here, and What Do We Do Now?" *Journal of Consumer Marketing*, Fall 1985, pp. 405–47.

16. See Paul W. Farris and John A. Quelch, "In Defense of Price Promotion," *Sloan Management Review*, Fall 1987, pp. 63–69.

17. Strang, "Sales Promotion," p. 124.

18. *Advertising Age*, August 15, 1985, p. 19.

19. See Michel Chevalier and Ronald C. Curhan, *Temporary Promotions as a Function of Trade Deals: A Descriptive Analysis* (Cambridge, MA: Marketing Science Institute, 1975), p. 2.

20. See "Retailers Buy Far in Advance to Exploit Trade Promotions," *The Wall Street Journal*, October 9, 1986, p. 35.

21. "Trade Promotion: Much Ado About Something," *PROMO*, October 1991, pp. 15, 37, 40.

22. Quoted from Kerry E. Smith, "Media Fusion," *PROMO*, May 1992, p. 29.

23. Arthur Stern, "Measuring the Effectiveness of Package Goods Promotion Strategies" (Paper presented to the Association of National Advertisers, Glen Cove, NY, February 1978).

24. Strang, "Sales Promotion," p. 119.

25. Russell D. Bowman, "Merchandising and Promotion Grow Big in Marketing World," *Advertising Age*, December 1974, p. 21.

26. Strang, "Sales Promotion," p. 120.

27. Kurt H. Schaffir and H. George Trenten, *Marketing Information Systems* (New York: Amacom, 1973), p. 81.

28. Strang, "Sales Promotion," p. 120.

29. See Magid M. Abraham and Leonard M. Lodish, "Getting the Most Out of Advertising and Promotion," *Harvard Business Review*, May–June 1990, pp. 50–60.

30. See Joe A. Dodson, Alice M. Tybout, and Brian Sternthal, "Impact of Deals and Deal Retraction on Brand Switching," *Journal of Marketing Research*, February 1978, pp. 72–81. They found that deals generally increase brand switching, the rate depending on the type of deal. Media-distributed coupons induce substantial switching, cents-off deals induce somewhat less switching, and package coupons hardly affect brand switching. Furthermore, consumers generally return to their preferred brands after the deal.

31. Books on sales promotion include John A. Quelch, *Sales Promotion Management* (Englewood Cliffs, NJ: Prentice Hall, 1989); and John C. Totten and Martin P. Block, *Analyzing Sales Promotion: Text and Cases* (Chicago: Commerce Communications, 1987). For an expert systems approach to sales promotion, see John W. Keon and Judy Bayer, "An Expert Approach to Sales Promotion Management," *Journal of Advertising Research*, June–July 1986, pp. 19–26.

32. Adapted from Scott M. Cutlip, Allen H. Center, and Glen M. Brown, *Effective Public Relations*, 6th ed. (Englewood Cliffs, NJ: Prentice-Hall, 1985), pp. 7–17.

33. For an excellent account, see Thomas L. Harris, *The Marketer's Guide to Public Relations* (New York: John Wiley & Sons, 1991).

34. Tom Duncan, *A Study of How Manufacturers and Service Companies Perceive and Use Marketing Public Relations* (Muncie, IN: Ball State University, December 1985).

35. See Dwight W. Catherwood and Richard L. Van Kirk, *The Complete Guide to Special Event Management* (New York: John Wiley & Sons, 1992).

36. Arthur M. Merims, "Marketing's Stepchild: Product Publicity," *Harvard Business Review*, November–December 1972, pp. 111–12. Also see Katerine D. Paine, "There Is a Method for Measuring PR," *Marketing News*, November 6, 1987, p. 5.

25

Managing the Salesforce

I don't know who you are.
I don't know your company.
I don't know your company's product.
I don't know what your company stands for.
I don't know your company's customers.
I don't know your company's record.
I don't know your company's reputation.
Now — what was it you wanted to sell me?

McGraw-Hill Publications

obert Louis Stevenson observed that "everyone lives by selling something."
U.S. firms spend over $140 billion annually on personal selling—more than
they spend on any other promotional method. Over 8 million Americans are
employed in sales and related occupations.[1] Salesforces are found in nonprofit as
well as profit organizations. College recruiters are the university's salesforce arm
for attracting new students. Churches use membership committees to attract new
members. The U.S. Agricultural Extension Service sends agricultural specialists to
sell farmers on using new farming methods. Hospitals and museums use fund raisers to contact and raise money from donors. Selling is one of the world's oldest professions.

The term *sales representative* covers a broad range of positions in our economy,
where the differences are often greater than the similarities. McMurry devised the
following classification of sales positions:

1. *Deliverer:* Positions where the salesperson's job is predominantly to deliver the product (e.g., milk, bread, fuel, oil)

2. *Order Taker:* Positions where the salesperson is predominantly an inside order taker
   (e.g., the haberdashery salesperson standing behind the counter) or outside order
   taker (e.g., the soap salesperson calling on the supermarket manager)

3. *Missionary:* Positions where the salesperson is not expected or permitted to take an
   order but is called on only to build goodwill or to educate the actual or potential user
   (e.g., the medical "detailer" representing an ethical pharmaceutical house)

4. *Technician:* Positions where the major emphasis is placed on technical knowledge
   (e.g., the engineering salesperson who is primarily a consultant to the "client" companies)

5. *Demand Creator:* Positions that demand the creative sale of tangible products (e.g.,
   vacuum cleaners, refrigerators, siding, and encyclopedias) or of intangibles (e.g., insurance, advertising services, or education)[2]

The positions range from the least to the most creative types of selling. The
first jobs call for servicing accounts and taking new orders, while the latter require
seeking prospects and influencing them to buy. Our discussion will focus on the
more creative types of selling.

This chapter examines three major questions related to the salesforce: What
decisions do companies make in designing a salesforce? How can the planned
salesforce be implemented and managed? What tools can the salesforce use to improve its sales effectiveness? The components of these decisions are shown in
Figure 25-1 and discussed in the following sections.

Designing the Salesforce

Sales personnel serve as the company's personal link to the customers. The sales
representative is the company to many of its customers and in turn brings back to
the company much needed intelligence about the customer. Therefore, the com-

FIGURE 25-1   Steps in Designing and Managing the Salesforce

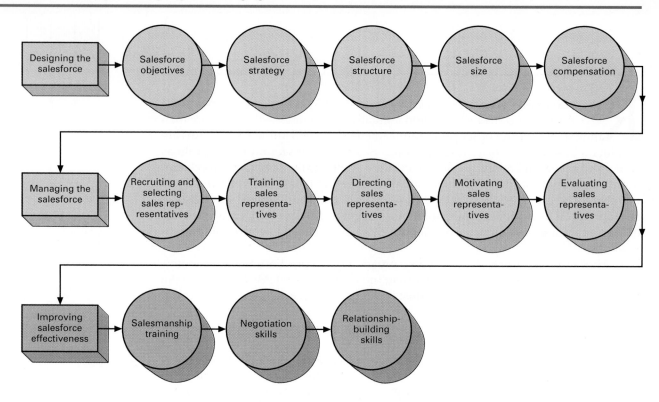

pany needs to give its deepest thought to issues in salesforce design, namely, developing salesforce objectives, strategy, structure, size, and compensation.

Salesforce Objectives

Salesforce objectives must be based on the character of the company's target markets and the company's desired position in these markets. The company must consider the unique role that personal selling can play in the marketing mix to serve customer needs in a competitively effective way. Personal selling happens to be the most expensive contact and communication tool used by the company. Given that the average cost of a personal sales call is $250, and closing a sale typically requires four calls, the total cost to close a sale is $1,000.[3]

On the other hand, personal selling is also the most effective tool at certain stages of the buying process, such as the buyer-education, negotiation, and sales-closing stages. It is important that the company carefully consider when and how to use sales representatives to facilitate the marketing task.

Companies typically set different objectives for their salesforces. IBM's sales representatives are responsible for *selling, installing,* and *upgrading* customer computer equipment; AT&T sales representatives are responsible for *developing, selling,* and *protecting* accounts. Sales representatives perform one or more of the following tasks for their companies:

- ◆ *Prospecting:* Sales representatives find and cultivate new customers.
- ◆ *Targeting:* Sales representatives decide how to allocate their scarce time among prospects and customers.
- ◆ *Communicating:* Sales representatives skillfully communicate information about the company's products and services.

- *Selling:* Sales representatives know the art of "salesmanship"—approaching, presenting, answering objections, and closing sales.
- *Servicing:* Sales representatives provide various services to the customers—consulting on their problems, rendering technical assistance, arranging financing, and expediting delivery.
- *Information Gathering:* Sales representatives conduct market research and intelligence work and fill in call reports.
- *Allocating:* Sales representatives decide on which customers to allocate scarce products to during product shortages.

Companies typically define specific salesforce objectives. One company wants its sales representatives to spend 80% of their time with current customers and 20% with prospects, and 85% of their time on established products and 15% on new products. If norms are not established, sales representatives might spend most of their time selling established products to current accounts and neglect new products and new prospects.

The sales representative's mix of tasks varies with the state of the economy. During product shortages, sales representatives find themselves with nothing to sell. Some companies jump to the conclusion that fewer sales representatives are needed. But this thinking overlooks the salesperson's other roles—allocating the product, counseling unhappy customers, communicating company plans on remedying shortages, and selling the company's other products that are not in short supply.

As companies move toward a stronger market orientation, their salesforces need to become more market focused and customer oriented. The traditional view is that salespeople should worry about volume and sell, sell, sell, and that the marketing department should worry about marketing strategy and profitability. The newer view is that salespeople should know how to produce customer satisfaction and company profit. They should know how to analyze sales data, measure market potential, gather market intelligence, and develop marketing strategies and plans. Sales representatives need analytical marketing skills, and this becomes especially critical at the higher levels of sales management. Marketers believe that salesforces will be more effective in the long run if they understand marketing as well as selling.

Salesforce Strategy

Companies compete with other companies to get orders from customers. They must deploy their salesforces strategically so that they call on the right customers at the right time and in the right way. Sales representatives work with customers in several ways:

- *Sales Representative to Buyer:* A sales representative discusses issues with a prospect or customer in person or over the phone.
- *Sales Representative to Buyer Group:* A sales representative gets to know as many members of the buyer group as possible.
- *Sales Team to Buyer Group:* A company sales team works closely with the members of the customer's buying group.
- *Conference Selling:* The sales representative brings company resource people to discuss a major problem or opportunity.
- *Seminar Selling:* A company team conducts an educational seminar for the customer company about state-of-the-art developments.

Thus today's sales representative often acts as the "account manager," who arranges contacts between various people in the buying and selling organizations. Selling increasingly calls for teamwork, requiring the support of other personnel, such as *top management,* who are increasingly involved in the sales process, especially when *national accounts* or *major sales* are at stake;[4] *technical people,* who supply technical information and service to the customer before, during, or after product purchase; *customer-service representatives,* who provide installation, maintenance, and other services to the customer; and an *office staff,* consisting of sales analysts, order expediters, and secretaries.

Once the company decides on a desirable selling approach, it can use either a direct or a contractual salesforce. A *direct (or company) salesforce* consists of full- or part-time paid employees who work exclusively for the company. This salesforce includes *inside sales personnel,* who conduct business from their office using the telephone and receiving visits from prospective buyers, and *field sales personnel,* who travel and visit customers. A *contractual salesforce* consists of manufacturers' reps, sales agents, or brokers, who are paid a commission based on their sales.

Salesforce Structure

The salesforce strategy will have implications for structuring the salesforce. If the company sells one product line to one end-using industry with customers in many locations, the company would use a territorial salesforce structure. If the company sells many products to many types of customers, it might need a product or market salesforce structure (see Marketing Concepts and Tools 25-1 for alternative salesforce structures).

A good illustration of the problem of designing a salesforce structure is provided by Wilkinson Sword USA which had a 7.9% U.S. market share in 1974 but lost most of it in subsequent years.[5] In 1984 Wilkinson decided to rebuild its U.S. market share by setting a goal of recruiting 34 new salespeople. Here are the steps it took:

1. *Account identification:* Wilkinson identified 25 leading supermarket chains and hired two *national account managers* to handle them out of Wilkinson's Atlanta headquarters (for a discussion of national account managers, see Marketing Strategies 25-1).

2. *Geographical territories:* The United States was partitioned into three divisions—East, West, and Central. Each division was divided into roughly five areas, and each area further subdivided into a few territories.

3. *Staffing and training:* Wilkinson looked for people with five or more years of selling experience in top health-and-beauty aid companies and offered them a competitive package. The first year was spent in staffing and training.

4. *Trade relations:* Wilkinson hired a vice-president of trade relations as well as retail merchandisers to handle stocking and stockouts, monitor prices, and so on.

On the other hand, established companies need to periodically revise their salesforce structure as market and economic conditions change. Xerox is a good case in point:

> Xerox managed several salesforces, the main one selling copier/duplicator equipment, and others selling printing systems, office systems, and so on. With the move to the electronic office, Xerox decided to merge salesforces so that different Xerox salespeople would not all call upon the same customers and confuse them with arguments for different office products and systems. Xerox divided the new salesforce into four groups:
>
> ♦ *NAMs:* national account managers serving major companies with dispersed multiple locations

Alternative Structures for the Salesforce

TERRITORIAL-STRUCTURED SALESFORCE
❖ In the simplest sales organization, each sales representative is assigned an exclusive territory in which to represent the company's full line. This sales structure has a number of advantages. First, it results in a clear definition of the salesperson's responsibilities. As the only salesperson working the territory, he or she bears the credit or blame for area sales to the extent that personal selling effort makes a difference. Second, territorial responsibility increases the sales representative's incentive to cultivate local business and personal ties. These ties contribute to the sales representative's selling effectiveness and personal life. Third, travel expenses are relatively small, since each sales representative travels within a small geographical area.

Territorial sales organization is often supported by many levels of sales-management positions. For example:

> Campbell Soup has changed from a product salesforce structure to a territorial one in which each salesperson is responsible for selling all Campbell Soup products. Starting at the bottom of the organization, *sales merchandisers* report to *sales representatives,* who report to *retail supervisors,* who report to *directors of retail sales operations,* who report to one of 22 *regional sales managers.* Regional sales managers are headed by one of four *general sales managers* (West, Central, South, and East), who report to a *vice-president and general sales manager.*[1]

Each higher-level sales manager takes on increasing marketing and administrative work in relation to the time available for selling. In fact, sales managers are paid for their management skills rather than their selling skills. The new sales trainee, in looking ahead, can expect to become a sales representative and then a district manager and, depending on his or her ability and motivation, may move to higher levels of sales or general management.

In designing territories, the company seeks certain territorial characteristics: The territories are easy to administer; their sales potential is easy to estimate; they reduce total travel time; and they provide a sufficient and equitable workload and sales potential for each sales representative. These characteristics are achieved through deciding on territory size and shape.

Territory Size. Territories can be designed to provide either *equal sales potential* or *equal workload.* Each principle offers advantages at the cost of some dilemmas. Territories of *equal potential* provide each sales representative with the same income opportunities and provide the company with a means to evaluate performance. Persistent differences in sales yield by territory are assumed to reflect differences in ability or effort of individual sales representatives. Salespersons are encouraged to work at their top capacity.

But because customer density varies by territory, territories with equal potential can vary widely in size. The potential for selling drill presses in Chicago is larger than in several western states. A sales representative assigned to Chicago can cover the same sales potential with much less effort than the sales representative who sells in the Far West. The sales representative assigned to the larger and sparser territory is going to end up with either fewer sales and less income for equal effort or equal sales through extraordinary effort. One solution is to pay the western sales representatives more compensation for the extra effort. But this reduces the profits on sales in the western territories. Another solution is to acknowledge that territories differ in attractiveness and assign the better or more senior sales representatives to the better territories.

Alternatively, territories could be designed to *equalize the sales workload.* Each sales representative can then cover his or her territory adequately. This principle, however, results in some variation in territory sales potentials. That does not concern a salesforce on straight salary. But where sales representatives are compensated partly on their sales, territories will vary in their attractiveness even though their workloads are equal. A lower compensation rate can be paid to sales representatives in the territories with the higher sales potential, or the territories with the better potential can go to the higher performers.

Territory Shape. Territories are formed by combining smaller units, such as counties or states, until they add up to a territory of a given sales potential or workload. Territorial design must take into account the location of natural barriers, the compatibility of adjacent areas, the adequacy of transportation, and so forth. Many companies prefer a certain territory shape because the shape can influence the cost and ease of coverage and the sales representatives' job satisfaction. Most common are circular, cloverleaf, and wedge-shaped territories. Today, companies can use computer programs to design sales territories that optimize such criteria as compactness, equalization of workload or sales potential, and minimal travel time.

PRODUCT-STRUCTURED SALESFORCE ❖

The importance of sales representatives' knowing their products, together with the development of product divisions and product management, has led many companies to structure their salesforces along product lines. Product specialization is particularly warranted where the products are technically complex, highly unrelated, or very numerous. For example, Kodak uses different salesforces for its film products and its industrial products. The film-products salesforce deals with simple products that are intensively distributed, while the industrial-products salesforce deals with complex products that require technical understanding. As might be expected, the film salesforce is paid a salary, while the industrial salesforce works on a salary and commission plan.

The mere existence of different company products, however, is not a sufficient argument for specializing the salesforce by product. Such specialization might not be the best course if the company's separate product lines are bought by the same customers. For example, Baxter has several product divisions, each with its own salesforce. It is conceivable that several Baxter sales representatives might visit the same hospital on the same day. Much cost could be saved by sending only one Baxter salesperson to represent Baxter's whole product line to that hospital.

MARKET-STRUCTURED SALESFORCE ❖

Companies often specialize their salesforces along industry or customer lines. Separate salesforces can be set up for different industries and even different customers. For example, IBM set up a sales office for finance and brokerage customers in New York, another for GM in Detroit, and still another for Ford in nearby Dearborn.

The most obvious advantage of market specialization is that each salesforce can become knowledgeable about specific customer needs. At one time, General Electric's sales representatives specialized in products (fan motors, switches, and so forth), but it later changed to specialization in industries, such as the air-conditioning industry and auto industry, because that is how customers saw the purchase of fan motors, switches, and so forth. A market-specialized salesforce can sometimes reduce total salesforce costs. A pump manufacturer at one time used highly trained sales engineers to sell to both original-equipment manufacturers (who needed to deal with technical representatives) and jobbers (who did not need to deal with technical representatives). Later, the company split its salesforce and staffed the jobber salesforce with lower-paid, less-technical sales personnel. The major disadvantage of market-structured salesforces arises when the various types of customers are scattered throughout the country. This requires extensive travel by each salesforce.

COMPLEX SALESFORCE STRUCTURES. ❖

When a company sells a wide variety of products to many types of customers over a broad geographical area, it often combines several principles of salesforce structure. Sales representatives can be specialized by territory-product, territory-market, product-market, and so on. A sales representative might then report to one or more line managers and staff managers.

SOURCES: 1. See Rayna Skolnik, "Campbell Stirs Up Its Salesforce," *Sales and Marketing Management,* April 1986, pp. 56–58. 2. See Andris A. Zoltners and Prabhakant Sinha, "Sales Territory Alignment: A Review and Model," *Management Science,* November 1983, pp. 1237–56; and Leonard M. Lodish, "Sales Territory Alignment to Maximize Profits," *Journal of Marketing Research,* February 1975, pp. 30–36.

- ◆ *MAMs:* major account managers serving major accounts with one or two other accounts in the region
- ◆ *ARs:* account representatives serving standard commercial accounts with potential of $5,000-$10,000
- ◆ *MRs:* marketing representatives serving all others

Each sales group faces a different selling cycle and is rewarded under a different compensation plan. In taking this step, Xerox put its salesforce through a deep and

Marketing Strategies 25-1

National Account Management—What It Is and How It Works

When a company sells to many small accounts, it uses a territory-based salesforce. However, large accounts (called key accounts, major accounts, house accounts) are often singled out for special attention and handling. If the account is a large company with many divisions operating in many parts of the country and subject to many buying influences (such as Sears or General Motors), it is likely to be handled as a *national account* and assigned to a specific individual or sales team. If the company has several such accounts, it is likely to organize a *national account management (NAM) division*. The company will then sell to these larger customers through this division. A company such as Xerox handles about 250 national accounts through its NAM division.

National account management is growing for a number of reasons. As buyer concentration increases through mergers and acquisitions, fewer buyers account for a larger share of a company's sales. Thus the largest 20% of accounts might account for more than 80% of a company's sales. Another factor is that many buyers are centralizing their purchases of certain items instead of leaving those purchases to the local units. This gives them more bargaining power with the sellers. The sellers in turn need to devote more attention to these major buyers. Still another factor is that as products become more complex, more groups in the buyer's organization become involved in the purchase process, and the typical salesperson might not have the skill, authority, or coverage to be effective in selling to the large buyer.

In organizing a national account program, a company faces a number of issues, including how to select national accounts; how to manage them; how to develop, manage, and evaluate national account managers; how to organize a structure for national account management; and where to locate national account management in the organization.

Essentially a company wants its national account managers to be good at a number of things. They must be able to reach all of the buying influences in the buyer's organization. They must be able to reach all the groups in their own organization—salespeople, R&D staff, manufacturing people, and so on—to coordinate them in meeting the buyer's requirements. Thus national account managers link all the parts of their company with all the parts of the buying company. In many organizations they are, in fact, called "relationship managers."

SOURCES: For further discussion, see the working papers on National Account Management prepared by Benson P. Shapiro and Rowland T. Moriarty under the sponsorship of the Marketing Science Institute, Cambridge, MA, published in 1980–83. Also see Linda Cardillo Platzer, *Managing National Accounts* (New York: Conference Board, 1984), report no. 850.

---

long sales retraining program because each sales rep needed to learn how to represent all of Xerox's product lines to the customer. At the same time, each sales rep could call in Xerox experts in particular product lines to help make the sale. Xerox used a team approach to sell which they called Team Xerox.[6]

Salesforce Size

Once the company clarifies its salesforce strategy and structure, it is ready to consider salesforce size. Sales representatives are one of the company's most productive and expensive assets. Increasing their number will increase both sales and costs.

Once the company establishes the number of customers it wants to reach, it can use a *workload approach* to establish salesforce size. This method consists of the following steps:

1. Customers are grouped into size classes according to their annual sales volume.
2. The desirable call frequencies (number of sales calls on an account per year) are established for each class.

3. The number of accounts in each size class is multiplied by the corresponding call frequency to arrive at the total workload for the country, in sales calls per year.
4. The average number of calls a sales representative can make per year is determined.
5. The number of sales representatives needed is determined by dividing the total annual calls required by the average annual calls made by a sales representative.

Suppose the company estimates that there are 1,000 A accounts and 2,000 B accounts required in the nation; and A accounts require 36 calls a year and B accounts 12 calls a year. This means the company needs a salesforce that can make 60,000 sales calls a year. Suppose the average sales representative can make 1,000 calls a year. The company would need 60 full-time sales representatives.

Salesforce Compensation

To attract sales representatives, the company has to develop an attractive compensation package. Sales representatives would like income regularity, extra reward for an above-average performance, and fair payment for experience and longevity. On the other hand, management would like to achieve control, economy, and simplicity. Management objectives, such as economy, will conflict with sales representatives' objectives, such as financial security. No wonder that compensation plans exhibit a tremendous variety among industries and even within the same industry.

Management must determine the level and components of an effective compensation plan. The *level of compensation* must bear some relation to the "going market price" for the type of sales job and required abilities. For example, the average earnings of an experienced salesperson in 1988 amounted to $38,900.[7] If the market price for salespeople is well defined, the individual firm has little choice but to pay the going rate. To pay less would bring forth less than the desired quantity or quality of applicants, and to pay more would be unnecessary. The market price for salespeople, however, is seldom well defined. For one thing, sales compensation plans differ in the importance of fixed and variable salary elements, fringe benefits, and expense allowances. And data on the average take-home pay of competitors' sales representatives can be misleading because of significant variations in the average seniority and ability levels of the competitors' salesforces. Published data on industry salesforce compensation levels are infrequent and generally lack sufficient detail.

The company must next determine the *components of compensation*—a fixed amount, a variable amount, expenses, and fringe benefits. The *fixed amount*, which might be salary or a drawing account, is intended to satisfy the sales representatives' need for income stability. The *variable amount*, which might be commissions, bonus, or profit sharing, is intended to stimulate and reward greater effort. *Expense allowances* enable the sales representatives to meet the expenses involved in travel, lodging, dining, and entertaining. And *fringe benefits*, such as paid vacations, sickness or accident benefits, pensions, and life insurance, are intended to provide security and job satisfaction.

Sales management must decide on the relative importance of these components in the compensation plan. A popular rule favors making about 70% of the salesperson's total income fixed and allocating the remaining 30% among the other elements. But the variations around this average are so pronounced that it can hardly serve as a guide. Fixed compensation receives more emphasis in jobs with a high ratio of nonselling to selling duties and in jobs where the selling task is technically complex and involves teamwork. Variable compensation receives more emphasis in jobs where sales are cyclical or depend on salesforce initiative.

Fixed and variable compensation give rise to three basic types of salesforce compensation plans—straight salary, straight commission, and combination salary and commission. A recent study of salesforce compensation plans showed that about 14% paid straight salary, 19% paid straight commission, 37% paid salary plus commission, 26% paid salary plus bonus, and 10% paid salary plus commission plus bonus.[8]

Managing the Salesforce

Having established the salesforce's objectives, strategy, structure, size, and compensation, the company has to move to recruiting, selecting, training, directing, motivating, and evaluating sales representatives. Various policies and procedures guide these decisions.

Recruiting and Selecting Sales Representatives

IMPORTANCE OF CAREFUL SELECTION ❖ At the heart of a successful salesforce operation is the selection of effective sales representatives. The performance difference between an average and a top sales representative can be considerable. One survey revealed that the top 27% of the salesforce brought in over 52% of the sales. Beyond the differences in sales productivity are the great wastes in hiring the wrong persons. The average annual salesforce turnover rate for all industries is almost 20%. When a salesperson quits, the costs of finding and training a new salesperson—plus the cost of lost sales—can run as high as $50,000 to $75,000. And a salesforce with many new people is less productive.[9]

The financial loss due to turnover is only part of the total cost. The new sales representative who remains with the company receives a direct income averaging around half of the direct selling cost. If he or she receives $20,000 a year, another $20,000 goes into fringe benefits, expenses, supervision, office space, supplies, and secretarial assistance. Consequently, the new sales representative needs to produce sales on which the gross margin at least covers the selling expenses of $40,000. If the gross margin is 10%, the new salesperson will have to sell at least $400,000 for the company to break even.

WHAT MAKES A GOOD SALES REPRESENTATIVE? ❖ Selecting sales representatives would be simple if one knew what traits to look for. One good starting point is to ask customers what traits they like and prefer in salespeople. Most customers say they want the sales representative to be honest, reliable, knowledgeable, and helpful. The company should look for these traits when selecting candidates.

Another approach is to look for traits common to the most successful salespeople in the company. Charles Garfield, in his study of superachievers, concluded that supersales performers exhibit the following traits: risk taking, powerful sense of mission, problem-solving bent, care for the customer, and careful call planners.[10] Robert McMurry wrote: "It is my conviction that the possessor of an *effective* sales personality is a *habitual 'wooer,' an individual who has a compulsive need to win and hold the affection of others.*"[11] He listed five additional traits of the supersalesperson: "A high level of energy, abounding self-confidence, a chronic hunger for money, a well-established habit of industry, and a state of mind that regards each objection, resistance, or obstacle as a challenge."[12] Mayer and Greenberg offered one of the shortest lists of traits; they concluded that the effective salesperson has two basic qualities: *empathy,* the ability to feel as the customer does; and *ego drive,* a strong personal need to make the sale.[13]

In defining a desirable sales profile, the company must consider the characteristics of the specific sales job. Is there a lot of paperwork? Does the job call for much travel? Will the salesperson confront a high proportion of rejections?

RECRUITMENT PROCEDURES ❖ After management develops its selection criteria, it must recruit. The personnel department seeks applicants by various means, including soliciting names from current sales representatives, using employment agencies, placing job ads, and contacting college students. As for college students, companies have found it hard to sell them on selling. Few students want to go into selling as a career.[14] The reluctant ones gave such reasons as, "Selling is a job and not a profession," "It calls for deceit if the person wants to succeed," and "There is insecurity and too much travel." To counter these objections, company recruiters emphasize starting salaries, income opportunities, and the fact that one fourth of the presidents of large U.S. corporations started out in marketing and sales.

APPLICANT-RATING PROCEDURES ❖ Recruitment procedures, if successful, will attract many applicants, and the company will need to select the best ones. The selection procedures can vary from a single informal interview to prolonged testing and interviewing, not only of the applicant but of the applicant's spouse.[15]

Many companies give formal tests to sales applicants. Although test scores are only one information element in a set that includes personal characteristics, references, past employment history, and interviewer reactions, they are weighted quite heavily by such companies as IBM, Prudential, Procter & Gamble, and Gillette. Gillette claims that tests have reduced turnover by 42% and have correlated well with the subsequent progress of new sales representatives in the sales organization.

Training Sales Representatives

Many companies send their new sales representatives into the field almost immediately after hiring them. They are supplied with samples, order books, and a description of their territory. And much of their selling is ineffective. A vice-president of a major food company spent one week watching 50 sales presentations to a busy buyer for a major supermarket chain. Here is what he observed:

> *The majority of salesmen were ill prepared, unable to answer basic questions, uncertain as to what they wanted to accomplish during the call. They did not think of the call as a studied professional presentation. They didn't have a real idea of the busy retailer's needs and wants.*[16]

Today's customers cannot put up with inept salespeople. The customers are more demanding and face many more suppliers. Customers expect salespeople to have deep product knowledge, to add ideas to improve the customer's operations, and to be efficient and reliable. This has required a much higher investment in training.

Training programs, of course, are costly. They involve large outlays for instructors, materials, and space; paying a person who is not yet selling; and losing opportunities because he or she is not in the field. Yet they are essential. Today's new sales representatives may spend a few weeks to several months in training. The median training period is 28 weeks in industrial-products companies, 12 in service companies, and four in consumer-products companies. Training time varies with the complexity of the selling task and the type of person recruited into the sales organization. At IBM, new sales representatives are not on their own for two years! And IBM expects its sales representatives to spend 15% of their time each year in additional training.

The training programs have several goals:

- *Sales Representatives Need to Know and Identify with the Company:* Most companies devote the first part of the training program to describing the company's history and objectives, the organization and lines of authority, the chief officers, the company's financial structure and facilities, and the chief products and sales volumes.

- *Sales Representatives Need to Know the Company's Products:* Sales trainees are shown how the products are produced and how they function in various uses.

- *Sales Representatives Need to Know Customers' and Competitors' Characteristics:* Sales representatives learn about the different types of customers and their needs, buying motives, and buying habits. They learn about the company's and competitors' strategies and policies.

- *Sales Representatives Need to Know How to Make Effective Sales Presentations:* Sales representatives receive training in the principles of selling. In addition, the company outlines the major sales arguments for each product and may provide a sales script.

- *Sales Representatives Need to Understand Field Procedures and Responsibilities:* Sales representatives learn how to divide time between active and potential accounts; how to use the expense account, prepare reports, and route effectively.

New methods of training are continually emerging. Among the instructional approaches are role playing, sensitivity training, cassette tapes, videotapes, programmed learning, and films on selling and on company products.

> *One of the latest training methods is exemplified by a self-study system that IBM uses called Info-Window. Info-Window combines a personal computer and a laser videodisc. A sales trainee can practice sales calls with an on-screen actor who portrays a manager in a particular industry. The actor responds differently depending on what the sales trainee says. The trainee is filmed during this interactive session on a VCR linked to Info-Window.[17]*

Training departments need to collect evidence of the effect of different training approaches on sales performance. There should be a measurable impact on salesforce turnover, sales volume, absenteeism, average sale size, calls-to-close ratio, customer complaints and compliments, new accounts per time unit, and volume of returned merchandise. The substantial costs of company training programs raise the question of whether a company could do better by hiring experienced sales representatives away from other companies. The gain is often illusory, however, because the experienced salesperson is brought in at a higher salary. Some of the representatives' specific training and company experience are wasted when they transfer to other companies. Within some industries, companies tacitly agree not to hire sales personnel away from each other.

Directing Sales Representatives

New sales representatives are given more than a territory, a compensation package, and training—they are given supervision. Supervision is the fate of everyone who works for someone else. It is the expression of the employers' natural and continuous interest in the activities of their agents. Through supervision, employers hope to direct and motivate the salesforce to do a better job.

Companies vary in how closely they direct their sales representatives. Sales representatives who are paid mostly on commission generally receive less supervision. Those who are salaried and must cover definite accounts are likely to receive substantial supervision.

DEVELOPING NORMS FOR CUSTOMER CALLS ❖ In 1989, the average salesperson made 4.2 sales calls a day.[18] This was down from five daily sales calls in the early 1980s. The downward trend is due to the increased use of the phone and fax machines, the increased reliance on automatic ordering systems, and the drop in cold calls owing to better market research information for pinpointing prospects.

Companies also decide on how many calls to make a year on particular-size accounts. Most companies classify customers into A, B, and C accounts, reflecting the sales volume, profit potential, and growth potential of the account. A accounts might receive nine calls a year; B, six calls; and C, three calls. The call norms depend on competitive call norms and expected account profitability.

The real issue is how much sales volume could be expected from a particular account as a function of the annual number of calls. Magee described an experiment where similar accounts were randomly split into three sets.[19] Sales representatives were asked to spend less than five hours a month with accounts in the first set, five to nine hours a month with those in the second set, and more than nine hours a month with those in the third set. The results demonstrated that additional calls produced more sales, leaving only the question of whether the magnitude of sales increase justified the additional cost.

DEVELOPING NORMS FOR PROSPECT CALLS ❖ Companies often specify how much time their salesforces should spend prospecting for new accounts. Spector Freight wants its sales representatives to spend 25% of their time prospecting and to stop calling on a prospect after three unsuccessful calls.

Companies set up prospecting standards for a number of reasons. If left alone, many sales representatives will spend most of their time with current customers. Current customers are better-known quantities. Sales representatives can depend upon them for some business, whereas a prospect might never deliver any business. Unless sales representatives are rewarded for opening new accounts, they might avoid new-account development. Some companies rely on a missionary salesforce to open new accounts.

USING SALES TIME EFFICIENTLY ❖ Sales representatives need to know how to use their time efficiently. One tool is the *annual call schedule* showing which customers and prospects to call on in which months and which activities to carry out.

> Sales representatives of Bell Telephone companies plan their calls and activities around three concepts. The first is *market development*—various efforts to educate customers, cultivate new business, and gain greater visibility in the buying community. The second is *sales-generating activities*—direct efforts to sell particular products to customers on particular calls. The third is *market-protection activities*—various efforts to learn what competition is doing and to protect relations with existing customers. The salesforce aims for balance among these activities, so that the company does not achieve high current sales at the expense of long-run market development.

Another tool is *time-and-duty analysis*. The sales representative spends time in the following ways:

- *Travel:* In some jobs, travel time amounts to over 50% of total time. Travel time can be cut down by using faster means of transportation—recognizing, however, that this will increase costs. Companies encourage air travel for their salesforce, to increase their ratio of selling to total time.

- *Food and Breaks:* Some portion of the salesforce's workday is spent in eating and taking breaks.

- *Waiting:* Waiting consists of time spent in the outer office of the buyer. This is dead time unless the sales representative uses it to plan or to fill out reports.

- *Selling:* Selling is the time spent with the buyer in person or on the phone. It breaks down into "social talk" and "selling talk."

- *Administration:* This consists of the time spent in report writing and billing, attending sales meetings, and talking to others in the company about production, delivery, billing, sales performance, and other matters.

No wonder actual face-to-face selling time can amount to as little as 25% of total working time![20] If it could be raised from 25% to 30%, this would be a 20% improvement. Companies are constantly seeking ways to improve salesforce productivity. Their methods take the form of training sales representatives in the use of "phone power," simplifying record-keeping forms, and using the computer to develop call and routing plans and to supply customer and competitive information.

To reduce time demands on their *outside salesforce,* many companies have increased the size and responsibilities of their *inside salesforce.* In a survey of 135 electronics distributors, Narus and Anderson found that an average of 57% of the salesforce members were inside salespeople.[21] Managers gave as reasons the escalating cost of outside sales calls and the growing use of computers and innovative telecommunications equipment. These managers think the proportion of inside salesforce members will reach two thirds in the 1990s.

Inside salespeople include three types. There are *technical-support persons,* who provide technical information and answers to customers' questions. There are *sales assistants,* who provide clerical backup for the outside salespersons. They call ahead and confirm appointments, carry out credit checks, follow up on deliveries, and answer customers' questions when they cannot reach the outside sales rep. And there are *telemarketers,* who use the phone to find new leads, qualify them, and sell to them. A telemarketer can call up to 50 customers a day compared to the four that an outside salesperson can contact. They can be effective in the following ways: cross-selling the company's other products; upgrading orders; introducing new company products; opening new accounts and reactivating former accounts; giving more attention to neglected accounts; and following up and qualifying direct-mail leads.

The inside salesforce frees the outside sales reps to spend more time selling to major accounts, identifying and converting new major prospects, placing electronic ordering systems in customers' facilities, and obtaining more blanket orders and systems contracts. Meanwhile, the inside salespeople spend more time in checking inventory, following up orders, phoning smaller accounts, and so on. The outside sales reps are paid largely on an incentive-compensation basis, and the inside reps on a salary or salary plus bonus pay.

Another dramatic breakthrough in improving salesforce productivity is provided by new technological equipment—desktop and laptop computers, videocassette recorders, videodiscs, automatic dialers, electronic mail, fax machines, teleconferencing. The salesperson has truly gone "electronic." Not only is sales and inventory information transferred much faster, but specific computer-based decision support systems have been created for sales managers and sales representatives (see Marketing Environment and Trends 25-1).

Motivating Sales Representatives

Some sales representatives will put forth their best effort without any special coaching from management. To them, selling is the most fascinating job in the world. They are ambitious and self-starters. But the majority of sales representatives require encouragement and special incentives to work at their best level. This is especially true of field selling, for the following reasons:

- *The Nature of the Job:* The selling job is one of frequent frustration. Sales representatives usually work alone; their hours are irregular; and they are often away from home. They confront aggressive, competing sales representatives; they have an inferior status relative to the buyer; they often do not have the authority to do what is necessary to win an account; they lose large orders that they have worked hard to obtain.
- *Human Nature:* Most people operate below capacity in the absence of special incentives, such as financial gain or social recognition.
- *Personal Problems:* Sales representatives are occasionally preoccupied with personal problems, such as sickness in the family, marital discord, or debt.

The problem of motivating sales representatives has been studied by Churchill, Ford, and Walker.[22] The basic model follows.

Marketing Environment and Trends 25-1

Salespeople Use Computers as a Productivity Tool

Companies have been struggling with the twin problems of containing salesforce costs and improving information circulation between headquarters and field offices. *Sales automation* has been making inroads on both problems. The key idea is to help salespeople improve the speed with which they can find and qualify leads, gather information prior to a customer presentation, reduce their paperwork, and report new sales to the company. The laptop computer has provided the answer.

Here is how sales automation works at Shell Chemical Company. The company developed a laptop-computer-based software package consisting of several applications. The salesforce first responded to the *automatic-expense-statement* program because they could more easily and accurately record expenses and get earlier reimbursement. Soon the salesforce increased their use of the *sales-inquiry* function, which allowed them to retrieve the latest account-specific information, including phone numbers, addresses, recent developments and prices. *Electronic mail* allowed the sales reps to rapidly receive and send messages to others. Various *business forms,* such as territory work plans and sales call reports could be filled out faster and sent electronically. The salesforce automation package also included an *appointment-calendar,* a *to-do list* function, a *spreadsheet,* and a *graphics software* package, which proved very helpful for salespeople to prepare charts and graphs for customer presentations.

Many of the *Fortune* 500 companies that have equipped their salesforces with laptops report sharp increases in the productivity of their sales reps. Some companies report increases of 5 to 10% in a salesperson's selling time because of less travel and paperwork, better call planning, and more effective calls. National Life Insurance believes that as much as 50% of its recent sales gains may be attributable to their salesforce's use of their laptop-computer-based sales-support system.

SOURCES: See Kate Bertrand, "Sales Management Software Tackles Toughest Customers," *Business Marketing,* May 1988, pp. 57–64; "Computer-Based Sales Support: Shell Chemical's System" (New York: Conference Board, Management Briefing: Marketing, April–May 1989), pp. 4–5; Thayer C. Taylor, "Computers in Sales and Marketing: S & MM's Survey Results," *Sales & Marketing Management,* May 1987, pp. 50–53; "If Only Willy Loman Had Used a Laptop," *Business Week,* October 12, 1987, p. 137; and Louis A. Wallis, *Computer-Based Sales Force Support* (New York: The Conference Board, Report No. 953, 1990).

Motivation → Effort → Performance → Rewards → Satisfaction

This says that the higher the salesperson's motivation, the greater his or her effort; greater effort will lead to greater performance; greater performance will lead to greater rewards; greater rewards will lead to greater satisfaction; and greater satisfaction will reinforce motivation. This model implies the following:

1. *Sales managers must be able to convince salespeople that they can sell more by working harder or by being trained to work smarter.* But if sales are determined largely by economic conditions or competitive actions, this linkage is somewhat undermined.

2. *Sales managers must be able to convince salespeople that the rewards for better performance are worth the extra effort.* But if the rewards seem to be set arbitrarily or are too small or of the wrong kind, this linkage is undermined.

The researchers went on to measure the importance of different possible rewards. The reward with the highest value was *pay,* followed by *promotion, personal growth,* and *sense of accomplishment.* The least-valued rewards were *liking* and *respect, security,* and *recognition.* In other words, salespeople are highly motivated by pay and the chance to get ahead and satisfy their intrinsic needs, and less motivated by compliments and security. But the researchers also found that the importance of motivators varied with the salespersons' demographic characteristics:

1. Financial rewards were mostly valued by older, longer-tenured salespeople and those who had large families.

2. Higher-order rewards (recognition, liking and respect, sense of accomplishment) were more valued by young salespeople who were unmarried or had small families and usually more formal education.

We discussed compensation as a motivator earlier. Here we will examine sales quotas and supplementary motivators.

SALES QUOTAS ❖ Many companies set sales quotas prescribing what their sales representatives should sell during the year and by product. Compensation is often tied to the degree of quota fulfillment.

Sales quotas are developed from the annual marketing plan. The company first prepares a sales forecast. This forecast becomes the basis for planning production, workforce size, and financial requirements. Then management establishes sales quotas for its regions and territories, which typically add up to more than the sales forecast. Sales quotas are set higher than the sales forecast in order to stretch sales managers and salespeople to perform at their best level. If they fail to make their quotas, the company nevertheless might make its sales forecast.

Each area sales manager divides the area's quota among the area's sales representatives. There are three schools of thought on quota setting. The *high-quota school* sets quotas higher than what most sales representatives will achieve but that are attainable. Its adherents believe that high quotas spur extra effort. The *modest-quota school* sets quotas that a majority of the salesforce can achieve. Its adherents feel that the salesforce will accept the quotas as fair, attain them, and gain confidence. The *variable-quota school* thinks that individual differences among sales representatives warrant high quotas for some, modest quotas for others. According to Heckert:

Actual experience with sales quotas, as with all standards, will reveal that sales representatives react to them somewhat differently, particularly at first. Some are stimulated to their highest efficiency, others are discouraged. Some sales executives place considerable emphasis upon this human element in setting their quotas. In general, however, good men will in the long run respond favorably to intelligently devised quotas, particularly when compensation is fairly adjusted to performance.[23]

Quotas can be set on dollars sales, unit volume, margin, selling effort or activity, and product type. One general view is that a salesperson's quota should be at least equal to the person's last year's sales plus some fraction of the difference between territory sales potential and last year's sales, the fraction being higher, the more the salesperson reacts favorably to pressure.

SUPPLEMENTARY MOTIVATORS ❖ Companies use additional motivators to stimulate sales-force effort. Periodic *sales meetings* provide a social occasion, a break from routine, a chance to meet and talk with "company brass," and a chance to air feelings and to identify with a larger group. Sales meetings are an important communication and motivational tool.[24]

Companies also sponsor *sales contests* to spur the salesforce to a special selling effort above what would normally be expected. The awards could be cars, vacations, cash, or recognition. The contest should present a reasonable opportunity for enough salespeople to win. At IBM, about 70% of the salesforce qualifies for the 100% Club. Their reward is a three-day trip that includes a recognition dinner and a blue and gold pin. If only a few salespersons can win or almost everyone can win, it will fail to spur additional effort. The sales contest period should not be announced in advance, or else some salespersons will defer some sales to the beginning of the period; also some may pad their sales during the period with customer promises to buy that do not materialize after the contest period ends.

Evaluating Sales Representatives

We have been describing the *feed-forward* aspects of sales supervision—how management communicates what the sales representatives should be doing and motivates them to do it. But good feed-forward requires good *feedback*. And good feedback means getting regular information from sales representatives to evaluate their performance.

SOURCES OF INFORMATION ❖ Management obtains information about its sales representatives in several ways. The most important source is sales reports. Additional information comes through personal observation, customers' letters and complaints, customer surveys, and conversations with other sales representatives.

Sales reports are divided between *activity plans* and *writeups of activity results*. The best example of the former is the *salesperson's work plan*, which sales representatives submit a week or month in advance. The plan describes intended calls and routing. This report leads the salesforce to plan and schedule their activities, informs management of their whereabouts, and provides a basis for comparing their plans and accomplishments. Sales representatives can be evaluated on their ability to "plan their work and work their plan."

Many companies require their sales representatives to develop an annual *territory marketing plan* in which they outline their program for developing new accounts and increasing business from existing accounts. This type of report casts sales representatives into the role of market managers and profit centers. Their sales managers study these plans, make suggestions, and use them to develop sales quotas.

Sales representatives write up their completed activities on *call reports*. Call reports inform sales management of the salesperson's activities, indicate the status of specific customer accounts, and provide useful information for subsequent calls. Sales representatives also submit expense reports, new-business reports, lost-business reports, and reports on local business and economic conditions.

These reports provide raw data from which sales managers can extract key indicators of sales performance. The key indicators are (1) average number of sales calls per salesperson per day, (2) average sales call time per contact, (3) average revenue per sales call, (4) average cost per sales call, (5) entertainment cost per sales call, (6) percentage of orders per hundred sales calls, (7) number of new customers per period, (8) number of lost customers per period, and (9) salesforce cost as a percentage of total sales. These indicators answer several useful questions: Are sales representatives making too few calls per day? Are they spending too much time per call? Are they spending too much on entertainment? Are they closing enough orders per hundred calls? Are they producing enough new customers and holding on to the old customers?

FORMAL EVALUATION OF PERFORMANCE ❖ The salesforce's reports along with other observations supply the raw materials for evaluating members of the salesforce. Formal evaluation procedures lead to at least three benefits. First, management has to communicate their standards for judging sales performance. Second, management needs to gather comprehensive information about each salesperson. And third, sales representatives know they will have to sit down one morning with the sales manager and explain their performance or failure to achieve certain goals.

SALESPERSON-TO-SALESPERSON COMPARISONS ❖ One type of evaluation is to compare and rank the sales performance of the various sales representatives. Such comparisons, however, can be misleading. Relative sales performances are meaningful only if there are no variations in territory market potential, workload, competition, company promotional effort, and so forth. Furthermore, current sales are not the only success indicator. Management should also be interested in how much each sales representative contributes to current net profits; this requires examining each sales representative's mix of products sold and sales expenses. Even more important is finding out how satisfied the salesperson's customers are with his or her service.

CURRENT-TO-PAST SALES COMPARISONS ❖ A second type of evaluation is to compare a sales representative's current performance and past performance. An example is shown in Table 25-1.

The sales manager can learn many things about John Smith from this table. Smith's total sales increased every year (line 3). This does not necessarily mean that Smith is doing a better job. The product breakdown shows that he has been able to push the sales of product B further than the sales of product A (lines 1 and 2). According to his quotas for the two products (lines 4 and 5), his success in increasing product B sales could be at the expense of product A sales. According to gross profits (lines 6 and 7), the company earns more selling A than B. Smith might be pushing the higher-volume, lower-margin product at the expense of the more profitable product. Although he increased total sales by $1,100 between 1992 and 1993 (line 3), the gross profits on his total sales actually decreased by $580 (line 8).

Sales expense (line 9) shows a steady increase, although total expense as a percentage of total sales seems to be under control (line 10). The upward trend in Smith's total dollar expense does not seem to be explained by any increase in the number of calls (line 11), although it might be related to his success in acquiring new customers (line 14). There is a possibility that in prospecting for new cus-

TABLE 25-1
Form for Evaluating
Sales Representative's
Performance

	TERRITORY: MIDLAND SALES REPRESENTATIVE: JOHN SMITH			
	1990	1991	1992	1993
1. Net sales product A	$251,300	$253,200	$270,000	$263,100
2. Net sales product B	423,200	439,200	553,900	561,900
3. Net sales total	674,500	692,400	823,900	825,000
4. Percent of quota product A	95.6	92.0	88.0	84.7
5. Percent of quota product B	120.4	122.3	134.9	130.8
6. Gross profits product A	$ 50,260	$ 50,640	$ 54,000	$ 52,620
7. Gross profits product B	42,320	43,920	55,390	56,190
8. Gross profits total	92,580	94,560	109,390	108,810
9. Sales expense	$ 10,200	$ 11,100	$ 11,600	$ 13,200
10. Sales expense to total sales (%)	1.5	1.6	1.4	1.6
11. Number of calls	1,675	1,700	1,680	1,660
12. Cost per call	$ 6.09	$ 6.53	$ 6.90	$ 7.95
13. Average number of customers	320	324	328	334
14. Number of new customers	13	14	15	20
15. Number of lost customers	8	10	11	14
16. Average sales per customer	$ 2,108	$ 2,137	$ 2,512	$ 2,470
17. Average gross profit per customer	$ 289	$ 292	$ 334	$ 326

tomers, he is neglecting present customers, as indicated by an upward trend in the annual number of lost customers (line 15).

The last two lines show the level and trend in Smith's sales and gross profits per customer. These figures become more meaningful when they are compared with overall company averages. If John Smith's average gross profit per customer is lower than the company's average, he could be concentrating on the wrong customers or not spending enough time with each customer. A review of his annual number of calls (line 11) shows that Smith might be making fewer annual calls than the average salesperson. If distances in his territory are similar to other territories, this could mean that he is not putting in a full workday, he is poor at sales planning and routing, or he spends too much time with certain accounts.

CUSTOMER-SATISFACTION EVALUATION ❖ John Smith might be quite effective in producing sales but not rate high with his customers. Perhaps he is slightly better than the competitors' salespeople, or his product is better, or he keeps finding new customers to replace others who don't like to deal with him. An increasing number of companies are measuring customer satisfaction not only with their product and customer-support service but with their salespeople. The customers' opinion of the salesperson, product, and service can be measured by mail questionnaires or telephone calls. Company salespeople who score high on satisfying their customers can be given special recognition, awards, or bonuses.

QUALITATIVE EVALUATION OF SALES REPRESENTATIVES ❖ Evaluations can also assess the salesperson's knowledge of the company, products, customers, competitors, territory, and responsibilities. Personality characteristics can be rated, such as general manner, appearance, speech, and temperament. The sales manager can also review any problems in motivation or compliance. The sales manager can check that the sales representative knows and observes the law (see Socially Responsible Marketing 25-1). Each company must decide what would be most useful to know. It needs to communicate these criteria to the sales representa

Socially Responsible Marketing 25-1

Issues in Selling

Companies that market products directly through their own salesforces must ensure that their salespeople follow the rules of "fair competition." Most states have enacted deceptive sales acts that spell out what is not allowed. For example, salespeople may not lie to consumers or mislead them about the advantages of buying a product. To avoid bait-and-switch practices, salespeople's statements must match advertising claims.

From a public-policy viewpoint, different rules apply to consumers who are called upon at home versus those who go to a store in search of a product. Because people who are called upon at home may be taken by surprise and may be especially vulnerable to high-pressure selling techniques, the Federal Trade Commission (FTC) has adopted a *three-day cooling off rule* to give special protection to customers who are not seeking products. Under this rule, customers who agree in their own homes to buy something costing more than $25 have 72 hours in which to cancel a contract or return merchandise and get their money back, no questions asked.

Much personal selling involves business-to-business trade. In selling to businesses, salespeople may not offer bribes to purchasing agents or others influencing a sale. They may not obtain or use technical or trade secrets of competitors through bribery or industrial espionage. Finally, salespeople must not disparage competitors or competing products by suggesting things that are not true.

SOURCE: For further reading, see Louis W. Stern and Thomas I. Eovaldi, *Legal Aspects of Marketing Policy* (Englewood Cliffs, NJ: Prentice Hall, 1984); and Robert J. Posch, *The Complete Guide to Marketing and the Law* (Englewood Cliffs, NJ: Prentice Hall, 1988).

tives so that they know how their performance is judged and can make an effort to improve it.

Principles of Personal Selling

We turn now from designing and managing a salesforce to the purpose of a salesforce, namely, to sell. Personal selling is an ancient art. It has spawned a large literature and many principles. Effective salespersons have more than instinct; they are trained in a method of analysis and customer management. Selling today is a profession that involves mastering and applying a whole set of principles. There are many different styles of personal selling, some consistent with the marketing concept and some antithetical to the spirit of the marketing concept. We will examine three major aspects of personal selling: salesmanship, negotiation, and relationship marketing.

Selling

Today's companies spend hundreds of millions of dollars each year to train their salespeople in the art of selling. Over a million copies of books, cassettes, and videotapes on selling are purchased annually, with such tantalizing titles as *How to Outsell the Born Salesman, How to Sell Anything to Anybody, How Power Selling Brought Me Success in 6 Hours, Where Do You Go from No. 1?* and *1000 Ways a Salesman Can Increase His Sales*. One of the most enduring books is Dale Carnegie's *How to Win Friends and Influence People*.

All of the sales-training approaches try to convert a salesperson from being a passive *order taker* to an active *order getter*. *Order takers* operate on the following assumptions: Customers know their needs; they resent attempts at influence;

and they prefer courteous and self-effacing salespersons. An example of an order-taking mentality would be a Fuller Brush salesperson who knocks on dozens of doors each day, simply asking consumers if they need any brushes.

In training salespersons to be *order getters,* there are two basic approaches, a *sales-oriented approach* and a *customer-oriented approach*. The first one trains the salesperson in *high-pressure selling techniques,* such as those used in selling encyclopedias or automobiles. The techniques include exaggerating the product's merits, criticizing competitive products, using a slick presentation, selling yourself, and offering some price concession to get the order on the spot. This form of selling assumes that the customers are not likely to buy except under pressure, that they are influenced by a slick presentation and ingratiating manners, and that they will not be sorry after signing the order, or if they are, it doesn't matter.

The other approach trains salespeople in *customer problem solving*. The salesperson learns how to listen and question in order to identify customer needs and come up with good product solutions. Presentation skills are made secondary to customer-need analysis skills. The approach assumes that customers have latent needs that constitute company opportunities, that they appreciate constructive suggestions, and that they will be loyal to sales representatives who have their long-term interests at heart. The problem solver is a much more congruent concept for the salesperson under the marketing concept than the hard seller or order taker.

No sales approach works best in all circumstances (see Marketing Concepts and Tools 25-2). Yet most sales-training programs agree on the major steps involved in any effective sales process. These steps are shown in Figure 25-2 and discussed next.[25]

PROSPECTING AND QUALIFYING ❖ The first step in the selling process is to identify prospects. Although the company will try to supply leads, sales representatives need skill in developing their own leads. Leads can be developed in the following ways:

- Asking current customers for the names of prospects
- Cultivating other referral sources, such as suppliers, dealers, noncompeting sales representatives, bankers, and trade association executives
- Joining organizations to which prospects belong
- Engaging in speaking and writing activities that will draw attention
- Examining data sources (newspapers, directories) in search of names
- Using the telephone and mail to find leads
- Dropping in unannounced on various offices (cold canvassing)

Sales representatives need skill in screening out poor leads. Prospects can be qualified by examining their financial ability, volume of business, special requirements, location, and likelihood of continuous business. The salesperson might phone or write to prospects before deciding whether to visit them. The leads can be categorized as hot leads, warm leads, and cool leads.

FIGURE 25-2 Major Steps in Effective Selling

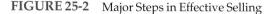

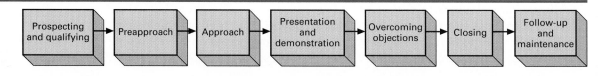

The Variety of Selling Styles and Buying Styles

Blake and Mouton distinguish selling styles along two dimensions, the salesperson's *concern for the sale* and *concern for the customer*. These two dimensions give rise to the following *sales grid,* which describes five types of salespersons. Type 1, 1 is very much the order taker and 9, 1 is the hard seller. Type 5, 5 is a soft seller, while the 1, 9 is "sell myself." Type 9, 9 is the problem-solving mentality, which is most consistent with the marketing concept.

Blake and Mouton argue that no one selling style is effective with all buyers. Furthermore, buying styles are just as varied. Buyers vary in their concern for the purchase and concern for the salesperson. Some buyers couldn't care less; some are defensive; some will only listen to salespersons from well-known companies.

Effective selling depends on matching the seller's style to the buyer's style. Evans sees selling as a *dyadic process,* where the outcome depends on the match of *buyer* and *seller characteristics* as well as on *buying and selling styles.* He found that people bought insurance from people very much like themselves in such factors as age, height, income, political opinions, religious beliefs, and smoking. What mattered was the perceived similarity more than the actual similarity. Evans proposed that insurance companies should hire all types of salespersons if they want to achieve broad market penetration. The only requirement is that they exhibit the intelligence and abilities effective in selling insurance.

SOURCES: Robert R. Blake and Jane S. Mouton, *The Grid for Sales Excellence: Benchmarks for Effective Salesmanship* (New York: McGraw-Hill, 1970), p. 4. For additional reading, see Franklin B. Evans, "Selling as a Dyadic Relationship—a New Approach," *American Behavioral Scientist,* May 1963, pp. 76–79; Harry L. Davis and Alvin J. Silk, "Interaction and Influence Processes in Personal Selling," *Sloan Management Review,* Winter 1972, pp. 59–76; and Barton A. Weitz, Harish Sujan, and Mita Sujan, "Knowledge, Motivation, and Adaptive Behavior: A Framework for Improving Selling Effectiveness," Marketing Science Institute, working paper, November 1985.

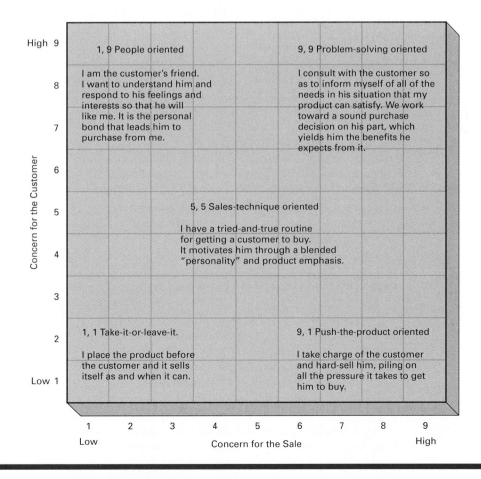

PREAPPROACH ❖ The salesperson needs to learn as much as possible about the prospect company (what it needs, who is involved in the purchase decision) and its buyers (their personal characteristics and buying styles). The salesperson can consult standard sources (*Moody's, Standard and Poor, Dun and Bradstreet*), acquaintances, and others to learn about the company. The salesperson should set *call objectives,* which might be to qualify the prospect or gather information or make an immediate sale. Another task is to decide on the best *approach,* which might be a personal visit, a phone call, or a letter. The best *timing* should be thought out because many prospects are busy at certain times. Finally, the salesperson should plan an *overall sales strategy* for the account.

APPROACH ❖ The salesperson should know how to greet the buyer to get the relationship off to a good start. This involves the salesperson's appearance, the opening lines, and the follow-up remarks. The salesperson might consider wearing clothes similar to what buyers wear (for instance, in Texas the men wear open shirts and no ties); show courtesy and attention to the buyer; and avoid distracting mannerisms, such as pacing the floor or staring at the customer. The opening line should be positive; for example, "Mr. Smith, I am Alice Jones from the ABC Company. My company and I appreciate your willingness to see me. I will do my best to make this visit profitable and worthwhile for you and your company." This might be followed by key questions and active listening to understand the buyer and his or her needs better.

PRESENTATION AND DEMONSTRATION ❖ The salesperson now tells the product "story" to the buyer, following the AIDA formula of gaining *attention,* holding *interest,* arousing *desire,* and obtaining *action.* The salesperson emphasizes throughout customer benefits, bringing in product features as evidence of these benefits. A benefit is any advantage, such as lower cost, less work, or more profit for the buyer. A feature is a product characteristic, such as weight or size. A common selling mistake is to dwell on product features (a product orientation) instead of customer benefits (a market orientation).

Companies have developed three different styles of sales presentation. The oldest is the *canned approach,* which is a memorized sales talk covering the main points. It is based on stimulus-response thinking; that is, the buyer is passive and can be moved to purchase by the use of the right stimulus words, pictures, terms, and actions. Thus an encyclopedia salesperson might describe the encyclopedia as "a once-in-a-lifetime buying opportunity" and focus on beautiful four-color pages of sports pictures, hoping to trigger desire for the encyclopedia. Canned presentations are used primarily in door-to-door and telephone selling. The *formulated approach* is also based on stimulus-response thinking but identifies early the buyer's needs and buying style and then uses a formulated approach to this type of buyer. The salesperson initially draws the buyer into the discussion in a way that reveals the buyer's needs and attitudes. Then the salesperson moves into a formulated presentation that shows how the product will satisfy the buyer's needs. It is not canned but follows a general plan.

The *need-satisfaction approach* starts with a search for the customer's real needs by encouraging the customer to do most of the talking. This approach calls for good listening and problem-solving skills. The salesperson takes on the role of a knowledgeable *business consultant* hoping to help the customer save money or make more money. It is well described by an IBM sales representative: "I get inside the business of my key accounts. I uncover their key problems. I prescribe solutions for them, using my company's systems and even, at times, components from other suppliers.

I prove beforehand that my system will save money or make money for my accounts. Then I work with the account to install the system and make it prove out."[26]

Sales presentations can be improved with demonstration aids such as booklets, flip charts, slides, movies, audio and video cassettes, and actual product samples. To the extent that the buyer can see or handle the product, he or she will better remember its features and benefits. During the demonstration, the salesperson can draw on five influence strategies:[27]

- *Legitimacy:* The salesperson emphasizes the reputation and experience of his or her company.
- *Expertise:* The salesperson shows deep knowledge of the buyer's situation and company's products, doing this without being overly "smart."
- *Referent Power:* The salesperson builds on any shared characteristics, interests, and acquaintances.
- *Ingratiation:* The salesperson provides personal favors (a free lunch, promotional gratuities) to strengthen affiliation and reciprocity feelings.
- *Impression Management:* The salesperson manages to convey favorable impressions of himself or herself.

OVERCOMING OBJECTIONS ❖ Customers almost always pose objections during the presentation or when asked for the order. Their resistance can be psychological or logical. *Psychological resistance* includes resistance to interference, preference for established supply sources or brands, apathy, reluctance to giving up something, unpleasant associations about the other person, predetermined ideas, dislike of making decisions, and neurotic attitude toward money. *Logical resistance* might consist of objections to the price, delivery schedule, or certain product or company characteristics. To handle these objections, the salesperson maintains a positive approach, asks the buyer to clarify the objection, questions the buyer in a way that the buyer has to answer his or her own objection, denies the validity of the objection, or turns the objection into a reason for buying. The salesperson needs training in the broader skills of negotiation, of which handling objections is a part.

CLOSING ❖ Now the salesperson attempts to close the sale. Some salespeople do not get to this stage or do not do it well. They lack confidence or feel uncomfortable about asking for the order or do not recognize the right psychological moment to close the sale. Salespersons need to know how to recognize closing signals from the buyer, including physical actions, statements or comments, and questions. Salespersons can use one of several closing techniques. They can ask for the order, recapitulate the points of agreement, offer to help the secretary write up the order, ask whether the buyer wants A or B, get the buyer to make minor choices such as the color or size, or indicate what the buyer will lose if the order is not placed now. The salesperson might offer the buyer specific inducements to close, such as a special price, an extra quantity at no charge, or a token gift.

FOLLOW-UP AND MAINTENANCE ❖ This last step is necessary if the salesperson wants to ensure customer satisfaction and repeat business. Immediately after closing, the salesperson should complete any necessary details on delivery time, purchase terms, and other matters. The salesperson should schedule a follow-up call when the initial order is received, to make sure there is proper installation, instruction, and servicing. This visit would detect any problems, assure the buyer of the salesperson's interest, and reduce any cognitive dissonance that might have arisen. The salesperson should develop an account maintenance plan to make sure that the customer is not forgotten or lost.

Negotiation

Much of business-to-business selling involves negotiating skills. The two parties need to reach agreement on the price and the other terms of sale. Salespersons need to win the order without making deep concessions that will hurt profitability.

NEGOTIATION DEFINED ❖ Marketing is concerned with exchange activities and the manner in which the terms of exchange are established. In *routinized exchange*, the terms are established by administered programs of pricing and distribution. In *negotiated exchange*, price and other terms are set via bargaining behavior. Arndt observed that a growing number of markets are coming under negotiated exchange, in which two or more parties negotiate long-term binding agreements (e.g., joint ventures, franchises, subcontracts, vertical integration). These markets are moving from being highly competitive to being highly "domesticated," that is, being less available to competitors.[28]

Although price is the most frequently negotiated issue, other issues include contract completion time; quality of goods and service offered; purchase volume; responsibility for financing, risk taking, promotion, and title; and product safety. The number of negotiation issues is virtually unlimited.

Bargaining, or *negotiation*, which we will use interchangeably, has the following features:

- ◆ At least two parties are involved.
- ◆ The parties have a conflict of interest with respect to one or more issues.
- ◆ The parties are at least temporarily joined together in a special kind of voluntary relationship.
- ◆ Activity in the relationship concerns the division or exchange of one or more specific resources and/or the resolution of one or more intangible issues among the parties or among those they represent.
- ◆ The activity usually involves the presentation of demands or proposals by one party and evaluation of these by the other, followed by concessions and counter proposals. The activity is thus sequential rather than simultaneous.[29]

Marketers who find themselves in bargaining situations need certain traits and skills to be effective. The most important traits are preparation and planning skill, knowledge of subject matter being negotiated, ability to think clearly and rapidly under pressure and uncertainty, ability to express thoughts verbally, listening skill, judgment and general intelligence, integrity, ability to persuade others, and patience. These will help the marketer in knowing when to negotiate and how to negotiate.[30]

WHEN TO NEGOTIATE ❖ Lee and Dobler have listed the following circumstances where negotiation is an appropriate procedure for concluding a sale:

1. When many factors bear not only on price, but also on quality and service.
2. When business risks cannot be accurately predetermined.
3. When a long period of time is required to produce the items purchased.
4. When production is interrupted frequently because of numerous change orders.[31]

Negotiation is appropriate whenever a *zone of agreement* exists.[32] A zone of agreement exists when there are simultaneously overlapping acceptable outcomes for the parties. This concept is illustrated in Figure 25-3. Suppose two parties are negotiating a price, and each privately establishes a *reservation price*. The seller has a

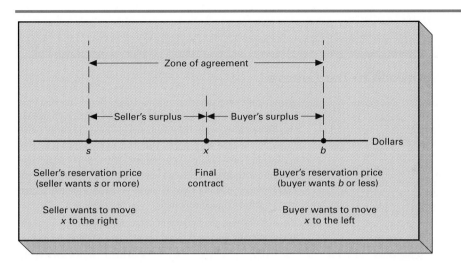

FIGURE 25-3
The Zone of Agreement

Source: Reprinted by permission of the publishers from *The Art and Science of Negotiation,* by Howard Raiffa, Cambridge, MA: The Belknap Press of Harvard University Press, copyright © 1982 by the President and Fellows of Harvard College.

reservation price, *s,* which is the *minimum* he will accept. Any final-contract value, *x,* that is below *s,* is worse than not reaching an agreement at all. For any $x > s$, the seller receives a surplus. Obviously, the seller desires as large a surplus as possible while maintaining good relations with the buyer. Likewise, the buyer has a reservation price, *b,* that is the *maximum* he will pay; any *x* above *b* is worse than no agreement. For any $x < b$, the buyer receives a surplus. If the seller's reservation price is below the buyer's, that is, $s < b$, then a zone of agreement exists, and the final price will be determined through bargaining.

There is an obvious advantage in knowing the other party's reservation price and in making one's own reservation price seem higher (for a seller) or lower (for a buyer) than it really is. However, the openness with which buyers and sellers reveal their reservation prices depends upon the bargainers' personalities, the negotiation circumstances, and the expectation about future relations.

FORMULATING A BARGAINING STRATEGY ❖ Bargaining involves preparing a strategic plan before bargaining begins and making good tactical decisions during the bargaining sessions. A bargaining strategy *can be defined as a commitment to an overall approach that has a good chance of achieving the negotiator's objectives.* For example, some negotiators pursue a "hard" strategy with opponents, while others maintain that a "soft" strategy yields more favorable results. Fisher and Ury propose another strategy, that of "principled negotiation." (See Marketing Concepts and Tools 25-3.)[33]

BARGAINING TACTICS DURING NEGOTIATIONS ❖ Negotiators use a variety of tactics when bargaining. Bargaining tactics can be defined as maneuvers to be made at specific points in the bargaining process. Threats, bluffs, last-chance offers, hard initial offers, and other tactics occur in bargaining (see Marketing Strategies 25-2).

Fisher and Ury have offered tactical advice that is consistent with their strategy of principled negotiation. Their first piece of tactical advice concerns what should be done if the other party is more powerful. The best tactic is to know one's BATNA—Best Alternative to a Negotiated Agreement. By identifying one's alternatives if a settlement is not reached, it sets a standard against which any offer can be measured. It protects one from being pressured into accepting unfavorable terms from a more powerful opponent.

Another tactic comes into play when the opposing party insists on arguing his

---

The Principled-Negotiation Approach to Bargaining

In a research program known as the Harvard Negotiation Project, Roger Fisher and William Ury arrived at four points for conducting "principled negotiations."

1. *Separate the People from the Problem:* Because people are involved in the bargaining, it is easy for emotions to become entangled with the objective merits of the issue being negotiated. Framing negotiation issues in terms of the personalities involved rather than the interests of the parties can lead to ineffective bargaining. Negotiation deteriorates when it becomes a test of wills instead of a joint problem-solving activity. Separating the people from the problem first involves making accurate perceptions. Each party must understand empathetically the opponent's viewpoint and try to feel the level of emotion with which they hold it. Second, emotions brought into or evolving out of negotiations should be made explicit and acknowledged as legitimate. Openly discussing emotions of both parties while not reacting to an emotional outburst helps keep negotiations from degenerating into unproductive name-calling sessions. Third, clear communications must exist between parties. Listening actively, acknowledging what is being said, communicating about problems rather than the opponent's shortcomings, and directly addressing interests will improve the chances of reaching a satisfactory solution.

2. *Focus on Interests, Not Positions:* The difference between positions and interests is that one's position is something one decided upon, while one's interests are what caused one to adopt the position. Thus a bargaining *position* may be that a contract must include a stiff penalty for late shipment; but the party's *interest* is to maintain an unbroken flow of raw materials. Reconciling interests works better because for every interest there usually exist several possible positions that could satisfy that interest.

3. *Invent Options for Mutual Gain:* Inventing options for mutual gain involves searching for a larger pie rather than arguing over the size of each slice. Looking for options that offer mutual gain helps identify shared interests.

4. *Insist on Objective Criteria:* When an opposing negotiator is intransigent and argues his position rather than his interests, a good strategy is to insist that the agreement must reflect fair objective criteria independent of the position of either side. By discussing objective criteria instead of stubbornly held positions, neither party is yielding to the other; both are yielding to a fair solution. Such objective criteria may be market value, depreciated book value, competitive prices, replacement costs, wholesale price index, and so on.

SOURCE: Adapted from Roger Fisher and William Ury, *Getting to Yes: Negotiating Agreement Without Giving In* (Boston: Houghton Mifflin Co., 1981), p. 57.

---

or her *position* instead of his or her *interests* and attacks one's proposals or person. While the tendency is to push back hard when pushed, the better tactic is to deflect the attack from the person and direct it against the problem. Look at the interests that motivated the opposing party's position and invent options that can satisfy both parties' interests. Invite the opposing party's criticism and advice ("If you were in my position, what would you do?").

Another set of bargaining tactics are responses to opposition tactics that are intended to deceive, distort, or otherwise influence the bargaining to their own advantage. What tactic should be used when the other side uses a threat, or a take-it-or-leave-it tactic, or seats the other party on the side of the table with the sun in his eyes? A negotiator should recognize the tactic, raise the issue explicitly, and question the tactic's legitimacy and desirability—in other words, negotiate over it. Negotiating the use of the tactic follows the same principled negotiation procedure: Question the tactic, ask why the tactic is being used, or suggest alternative courses of action to pursue. If this fails, resort to one's BATNA and terminate the negotiation until the other side ceases to employ these tactics. Meeting these tactics by defending principles is more productive than counterattacking with tricky tactics.

Classic Bargaining Tactics

Here are several standard bargaining tactics:

- *Acting Crazy:* Put on a good show by visibly demonstrating your emotional commitment to your position. This increases your credibility and may give the opponent a justification to settle on your terms.

- *Big Pot:* Leave yourself a lot of room to negotiate. Make high demands at the beginning. After making concessions, you'll still end up with a larger payoff than if you started too low.

- *Get a Prestigious Ally:* The ally can be a person or a project that is prestigious. You try to get the opponent to accept less because the person/object he or she will be involved with is prestigious.

- *The Well Is Dry:* Take a stand and tell the opponent you have no more concessions to make.

- *Limited Authority:* You negotiate in good faith with the opponent, and when you're ready to sign the deal, you say, "I have to check with my boss."

- *Whipsaw/Auction:* You let several competitors know you're negotiating with them at the same time. Schedule competitors' appointments with you for the same time and keep them all waiting to see you.

- *Divide and Conquer:* If you're negotiating with the opponent's team, sell one member of the team on your proposals. That person will help you sell the other members of the team.

- *Get Lost/Stall for Time:* Leave the negotiation completely for a while. Come back when things are getting better and try to renegotiate then. Time period can be long (say you're going out of town) or short (go to the bathroom to think).

- *Wet Noodle:* Give no emotional or verbal response to the opponent. Don't respond to his or her force or pressure. Sit there like a wet noodle and keep a "poker face."

- *Be Patient:* If you can afford to outwait the opponent, you'll probably win big.

- *Let's Split the Difference:* The person who first suggests this has the least to lose.

- *Trial Balloon:* You release your decision through a so-called reliable source before the decision is actually made. This enables you to test reactions to your decision.

- *Surprises:* Keep the opponent off balance by a drastic, dramatic, sudden shift in your tactics. Never be predictable—keep the opponent from anticipating your moves.

SOURCE: From a list of over 200 tactics prepared by Professor Donald W. Hendon of the University of North Alabama in his seminar "How to Negotiate and Win."

Relationship Marketing

The principles of personal selling and negotiation as described are *transaction oriented*; that is, their aim is to help salespeople close a specific sale with a customer. But in many cases, the company is not seeking simply a sale: it has targeted a major customer account that it would like to win and serve. The company would like to demonstrate to the account that it has the capabilities to serve the account's needs in a superior way, particularly if a *committed relationship* can be formed. The type of selling to establish a long-term collaborative relationship is more complex than that described earlier. Neil Rackham sees the selling process as involving four stages: preliminaries, investigating, demonstrating capability, and obtaining commitment. He notes that obtaining commitment involves many more agreements than simply closing the sale.[34]

More companies today are moving their emphasis from transaction marketing to relationship marketing (see Chapter 2, pp. 48-52). The days of the "lone salesperson" working his or her territory and being guided only by a sales quota and a compensation plan are numbered. Today's customers are large and often global.

They prefer suppliers who can sell and deliver a coordinated set of products and services to many locations; who can quickly solve problems that arise in their different locations; and who can work closely with customer teams to improve products and processes. Unfortunately, most companies are not set up to meet these requirements. Their products are sold by separate salesforces that don't easily work together. Their national account managers may be turned down when requesting help from a district salesperson. The company's technical people may not be willing to spend time to educate a customer.

Companies recognize that sales teamwork will increasingly be the key to winning and maintaining accounts. Yet they recognize that asking their people for teamwork doesn't produce it. They need to revise their compensation system to give credit for work on shared accounts; they must set up better goals and measures for their salesforce; and they must emphasize the importance of teamwork in their training programs, while at the same time also honoring the importance of individual initiative.[35]

Marketing Strategies 25-3

When—and How— to Use Relationship Marketing

Barbara Jackson argues that relationship marketing is not effective in all situations but is extremely effective in the right situations. She sees transaction marketing as more appropriate with customers who have a short time horizon and low switching costs, such as buyers of commodities. A customer buying steel can buy from one of several steel suppliers and choose the one offering the best terms. The fact that one steel supplier has been particularly attentive or responsive does not automatically earn it the next sale; its terms have to be competitive. Jackson calls these *always-a-share customers*.

On the other hand, relationship marketing investments pay off handsomely with customers who have long time horizons and high switching costs, such as buyers of office automation systems. Presumably, the customer for a major system carefully researches the competing suppliers and chooses one to work with from whom it can expect good long-term service and state-of-the-art technology. Both the customer and the supplier invest a lot of money and time in the relationship. The customer would find it costly and risky to switch to another vendor, and the seller would find that losing this customer would be a major loss. Jackson calls these *lost-for-good customers,* and here relationship marketing has the greatest payoff.

In "lost-for-good" situations, the challenge is different for the in-supplier versus out-supplier. The in-supplier's strategy is to make switching difficult for the customer. The in-supplier will develop product systems that are incompatible with competitive products and will install proprietary ordering systems that facilitate inventory management and delivery. On the other hand, the out-supplier will design product systems that are compatible with the customer's system, are easy to install and learn, save the customer a lot of money, and promise to improve through time.

Anderson and Narus believe that transaction versus relationship marketing is not so much an issue of the type of industry as it is an issue of the wishes of the particular customer. Some customers value a high service bundle and will stay with that supplier for a long time. Other customers want to cut their costs and will switch suppliers for lower costs. In this case, the company can still try to retain the customer by agreeing to reduce the price provided the customer is willing to accept fewer services; for example, the customer may forego free delivery, some training, and so on. This customer would be treated on a transaction basis rather than on a relationship-building basis. As long as the company cuts its own costs by as much or more than its price reduction, the "transaction-oriented" customer will still be profitable.

Clearly, relationship marketing is not appropriate with all customers in that heavy relationship investments will not always pay off. But it is extremely effective with the right type of customers, who get heavily committed to a specific system and expect consistent and timely service.

SOURCES: Barbara Bund Jackson, *Winning and Keeping Industrial Customers: The Dynamics of Customer Relationships* (Lexington, MA: Heath, 1985); and James C. Anderson and James A. Narus, "Partnering as a Focused Market Strategy," *California Management Review,* Spring 1991, pp. 95–113.

Relationship marketing is based on the premise that important accounts need focused and continuous attention. Salespeople working with key customers must do more than call when they think customers might be ready to place orders. They should call or visit at other times, taking customers to dinner, making useful suggestions about their business, and so on. They should monitor these key accounts, know their problems, and be ready to serve them in a number of ways.

Here are the main steps in establishing a relationship marketing program in a company:

- *Identify the Key Customers Meriting Relationship Marketing:* The company can choose the five or ten largest customers and designate them for relationship marketing. Additional customers can be added who show exceptional growth.

- *Assign a Skilled Relationship Manager to Each Key Customer:* The salesperson servicing the customer should receive training in relationship marketing.

- *Develop a Clear Job Description for Relationship Managers:* It should describe their reporting relationships, objectives, responsibilities, and evaluation criteria. The relationship manager is responsible for the client, is the focal point for all information about the client, and is the mobilizer of company services for the client. Each relationship manager will have only one or a few relationships to manage.

- *Appoint an Overall Manager to Supervise the Relationship Managers:* This person will develop job descriptions, evaluation criteria, and resource support to increase relationship managers' effectiveness.

- *Each Relationship Manager Must Develop Long-Range and Annual Customer-Relationship Plans:* The annual relationship plan will state objectives, strategies, specific actions, and required resources.

When a relationship management program is properly implemented, the organization will begin to focus as much on managing its customers as on managing its products. At the same time, companies should realize that while there is a strong and warranted move toward relationship marketing, it is not effective in all situations. Ultimately, companies must judge which segments and which specific customers will respond profitably to relationship management. (See Marketing Strategies 25-3.)

SUMMARY ❖

Most companies use sales representatives, and many companies assign them the pivotal role in the marketing mix. Sales people are very effective in achieving certain marketing objectives. At the same time, they are very costly. Management must carefully design and manage its personal-selling resources.

Salesforce design calls for decisions on objectives, strategy, structure, size, and compensation. Salesforce objectives include prospecting, communicating, selling and servicing, information gathering, and allocating. Salesforce strategy involves deciding what types and mix and selling approaches are most effective (solo selling, team selling, and so on). Salesforce structure involves organizing by territory, product, market, or some hybrid combination and developing the right territory size and shape. Salesforce size involves estimating the total workload and how many sales hours—and hence salespersons—would be needed. Salesforce compensation involves determining pay level and pay components, such as salary, commission, bonus, expenses, and fringe benefits.

Managing the salesforce involves recruiting and selecting sales representatives and training, directing, motivating, and evaluating them. Sales representatives must be recruited and selected carefully to hold down the high costs of hiring the wrong persons. Sales-training programs familiarize new salespeople with the company's history, its products and policies, the characteristics of the market and competitors, and the art of selling. Salespeople need direction on such matters as developing customer and prospect targets and call norms and using their time efficiently. Salespeople need encouragement through economic and personal rewards and recognition, because they must make tough decisions and are subject to many frustrations. The key idea is that appropriate salesforce motivation will lead to more effort, better performance, higher reward, higher satisfaction, and more motivation. The last management step calls for periodically evaluating each salesperson's performance to help the person do a better job.

The purpose of the salesforce is to sell, and selling is an art. Selling is a seven-step process: prospecting and qualifying, preapproach, approach, presentation and demonstration, overcoming objections, closing, and follow-up and maintenance. Another aspect of selling is negotiation, the art of arriving at transaction terms that satisfy both parties. A third aspect is relationship marketing, the art of creating a closer working relation and interdependence between the people in two organizations.

NOTES ❖

1. See Carlton A. Pederson, Milburn D. Wright, and Barton A. Weitz, *Selling: Principles and Methods*, 9th ed. (Homewood, IL: Irwin, 1988), p. 11; and Douglas J. Dalrymple, *Sales Management: Text and Cases*, 4th ed. (New York: Wiley, 1991).

2. Adapted from Robert N. McMurry, "The Mystique of Super-Salesmanship," *Harvard Business Review*, March–April 1961, p. 114. Also see William C. Moncrief, III, "Selling Activity and Sales Position Taxonomies for Industrial Salesforces," *Journal of Marketing Research*, August 1986, pp. 261–70.

3. For estimates of the cost of sales calls, see "1989 Survey of Selling Costs," *Sales and Marketing Management*, February 20, 1989. Also see *Salesforce Compensation* (Chicago: Dartnell's 27th Survey, 1992).

4. Roger M. Pegram, *Selling and Servicing the National Account* (New York: Conference Board, 1972); William H. Kaven, *Managing the Major Sale* (New York: American Management Association, 1971); Benson P. Shapiro and Ronald S. Posner, "Making the Major Sale," *Harvard Business Review*, March–April 1976, pp. 68-78; and Mack Hanan, *Key Account Selling* (New York: Amacom, 1982).

5. Source: See Rayna Skolnik, "The Birth of a Sales Force," *Sales and Marketing Management*, March 10, 1986, pp. 42–44.

6. See Thayer C. Taylor, "Xerox's Sales Force Learns a New Game," *Sales and Marketing Management*, July 1, 1986, pp. 48–51; and Taylor, "Xerox's Makeover," *Sales and Marketing Management*, June 1987, p. 68.

7. For estimates of the cost of sales calls, see "1989 Survey of Selling Costs," *Sales and Marketing Management*, February 20, 1989. Also see *Salesforce Compensation* (Chicago: Dartnell's 27th Survey, 1992).

8. Ibid. The percentages total to more than 100% because some companies use more than one type of plan. For further reading, see Anne T. Couglan and Subrata K. Sen, "Salesforce Compensation: Theory and Managerial Implications," *Marketing Science*, Fall 1989, pp. 324–42.

9. George H. Lucas, Jr., A. Parasuraman, Robert A. Davis, and Ben M. Enis, "An Empirical Study of Salesforce Turnover," *Journal of Marketing*, July 1987, pp. 34–59.

10. See Charles Garfield, *Peak Performers: The New Heroes of American Business* (New York: Avon Books, 1986); "What Makes a Supersalesperson?" *Sales & Marketing Management*, August 23, 1984, p. 86; "What Makes a Top Performer?" *Sales & Marketing Management*, May 1989; and Timothy J. Trow, "The Secret of a Good Hire: Profiling," *Sales & Marketing Management*, May 1990, pp. 44–55.

11. McMurry, "Super-Salesmanship," p. 117.

12. Ibid., p. 118.

13. David Mayer and Herbert M. Greenberg, "What Makes a Good Salesman?" *Harvard Business Review*, July–August 1964, pp. 119–25.

14. John C. Crawford and James R. Lumpkin, "The Choice of Selling as a Career," *Industrial Marketing Management*, October 1983, pp. 257–61.

15. James M. Comer and Alan J. Dubinsky, *Managing the Successful Sales Force* (Lexington, MA: Lexington Books, 1985), pp. 5–25.

16. From an address given by Donald R. Keough at the 27th Annual Conference of the Super-Market Institute, Chicago, April 26-29, 1964.

17. Patricia Sellers, "How IBM Teaches Techies to Sell," *Fortune*, June 6, 1988, pp. 141 ff.

18. *Sales Force Compensation* (Chicago: Dartnell's 25th Survey, 1989) p. 13.

19. See John F. Magee, "Determining the Optimum Allocation of Expenditures for Promotional Effort with Operations Research Methods," in *The Frontiers of Marketing Thought and Science*, ed. Frank M. Bass (Chicago: American Marketing Association, 1958), pp. 140–56.

20. "Are Salespeople Gaining More Selling Time?" *Sales and Marketing Management*, July 1986, p. 29.

21. James A. Narus and James C. Anderson, "Industrial Distributor Selling: The Roles of Outside and Inside Sales," *Industrial Marketing Management* 15 (1986), 55–62.

22. See Gilbert A. Churchill, Jr., Neil M. Ford, and Orville C. Walker, Jr., *Sales Force Management: Planning Implementation and Control* (Homewood, IL: Irwin, 1985).

23. J. B. Heckert, *Business Budgeting and Control* (New York: Ronald Press, 1946), p. 138.

24. Richard Cavalier, *Sales Meetings That Work* (Homewood, IL: Dow Jones-Irwin, 1983).

25. Some of the following discussion is based on W. J. E. Crissy, William H. Cunningham, and Isabella C. M. Cunningham, *Selling: The Personal Force in Marketing* (New York: John Wiley, 1977), pp. 119–29.

26. Mark Hanan, "Join the Systems Sell and You Can't Be Beat," *Sales and Marketing Management*, August 21, 1972, p. 44. Also see Hanan, James Cribbin, and Herman Heiser, *Consultative Selling* (New York: American Management Association, 1970).

27. See Rosann L. Spiro and William D. Perreault, Jr., "Influence Use by Industrial Salesmen: Influence Strategy Mixes and Situational Determinants," paper, Graduate School of Business Administration, University of North Carolina, 1976.

28. Johan Arndt, "Toward a Concept of Domesticated Markets," *Journal of Marketing*, Fall 1979, pp. 69–75.

29. Jeffrey Z. Rubin and Bert R. Brown, *The Social Psychology of Bargaining and Negotiation* (New York: Academic Press, 1975), p. 18.

30. For additional reading, see Howard Raiffa, *The Art and Science of Negotiation* (Cambridge, MA: Harvard University Press, 1982); Samuel B. Bacharach and Edward J. Lawler, *Bargaining: Power, Tactics, and Outcome* (San Francisco: Jossey-Bass, 1981); Herb Cohen, *You Can Negotiate Anything* (New York: Bantam Books, 1980); and Gerard I. Nierenberg, *The Art of Negotiating* (New York: Pocket Books, 1984).

31. Lamar Lee and Donald W. Dobler, *Purchasing and Materials Management* (New York: McGraw-Hill, 1977), pp. 146–47.

32. This discussion of zone of agreement is fully developed in Raiffa, *Art and Science of Negotiation*.

33. Roger Fisher and William Ury, *Getting to Yes: Negotiating Agreement Without Giving In* (Boston: Houghton Mifflin, 1981).

34. Neil Rackham, *SPIN Selling* (New York: McGraw-Hill, 1988).

35. See Frank V. Cespedes, Stephen X. Doyle, and Robert J. Freedman, "Teamwork for Today's Selling," *Harvard Business Review*, March–April 1989, pp. 44–54, 58.

26

Organizing and Implementing Marketing Programs

Vision without action is a daydream. Action without vision is a nightmare.
JAPANESE PROVERB

The first place a marketing person has to sell is on the inside — and that's the hardest of all.
ANONYMOUS

We now turn from the *strategic* and *tactical* tasks of marketing to the *administrative* tasks to examine how firms organize, implement, and control their marketing activities. In this chapter, we will ask: What trends are occurring in company organization? How are marketing and sales organized in various companies? What is the marketing department's relation to each key business function? What steps can a company take to build a stronger market-focused orientation? How can a company improve its marketing-implementation skills? In the next chapter, we will examine concepts and tools for evaluating and controlling marketing performance.

Company Organization

Companies need fresh concepts on how to organize their business and marketing in response to significant changes that have occurred in the business environment in recent years. Advances in computers and telecommunication, global competition, increasing buyer requirements for speed and customization, the growing importance of service, and several other forces are requiring companies to reconsider how to organize their business.

In response to these changes, companies have restructured along several lines. Companies are increasingly focusing on developing their core businesses and core competences. In the 1960s and 1970s, many companies diversified into totally unrelated industries. Although the industries looked promising, the companies lacked the appropriate skills and knowledge to compete. Prime examples are Mobil's purchase of Montgomery Ward and Exxon's venture into the office-equipment business.

Large companies realized that while they were good at scaling up existing businesses, they were less effective in starting new businesses. Small entrepreneurs did the latter. So companies began to cultivate "intrapreneurship" by giving more freedom to their executives to produce ideas and take some risk. If 3M could do it, so could they.

Companies also "downsized" and "delayered": they reduced the number of organizational levels in order to get closer to the customer. At one time, AT&T had 19 organizational levels. Clearly, top management was too far removed from customers to fully understand their changing needs. One corrective was to advise managers at all levels to do more "Managing By Walking Around." But a more fundamental corrective was to flatten the organization. Tom Peters proposed that no well-managed organization would have more than five hierarchical levels. The implication was that each manager needed to manage more people. The key to doing this was to train more employees to be self-managers.

Hierarchy also has been giving way to *networking*. With more companies using computers, electronic mail, and fax machines, messages increasingly pass between people at different levels of the organization. Companies encourage more teamwork centered around core business processes, trying to break down departmental walls.

In this context, we will now look at how marketing departments are organized.

Marketing Organization

Over the years, marketing has evolved from a simple sales function to a complex group of activities, not always well-integrated themselves or in relation to the firm's nonmarketing activities. Questions abound concerning the relationship between marketing managers at headquarters and salespeople in the field; about the future of brand management; about the need for a corporate vice-president of marketing; about marketing's relations to manufacturing, R&D, and finance; and so on. To gain some understanding, we will examine how marketing departments evolved in companies, how they are organized, and how they interact with other company departments.

The Evolution of the Marketing Department

The modern marketing department is the product of a long evolution. At least five stages can be distinguished, and companies are found in each stage.

SIMPLE SALES DEPARTMENT ❖ All companies start out with five simple functions. Someone must raise and manage capital (finance), hire people (personnel), produce the product or service (operations), sell it (sales), and keep the books (accounting). The selling function is headed by a sales vice-president, who manages a salesforce and also does some selling. When the company needs marketing research or advertising, the sales vice-president also handles those functions [see Figure 26-1(a)].

SALES DEPARTMENT WITH ANCILLARY MARKETING FUNCTIONS ❖ As the company expands to serve new types of customers or new geographical areas, it needs to strengthen certain marketing functions other than sales. For example, an East Coast firm that plans to open in the West will first have to conduct marketing research to learn about customer needs and market potential. If it opened business in the West, it will have to advertise its name and products in the area. The sales vice-president will need to hire specialists to handle these other marketing activities. The sales vice-president might decide to hire a *marketing director* to manage these functions [see Figure 26-1(b)].

SEPARATE MARKETING DEPARTMENT ❖ The continued growth of the company increases the productive potential of investments in other marketing functions—marketing research, new-product development, advertising and sales promotion, customer service—relative to salesforce activity. Yet the sales vice-president normally continues to give disproportionate time and resources to the salesforce. The marketing director will appeal for more resources but will usually get less than needed. Sometimes the marketing director will quit out of frustration.

Eventually the company president will see the advantage of establishing a separate marketing department [see Figure 26-1(c)]. The marketing department will be headed by a marketing vice-president, who reports, along with the sales vice-president, to the president or executive vice-president. At this stage, sales and marketing are separate functions in the organization that are expected to work closely together.

This arrangement is used by many industrial companies. It permits the com-

FIGURE 26-1 Stages in the Evolution of the Marketing Department

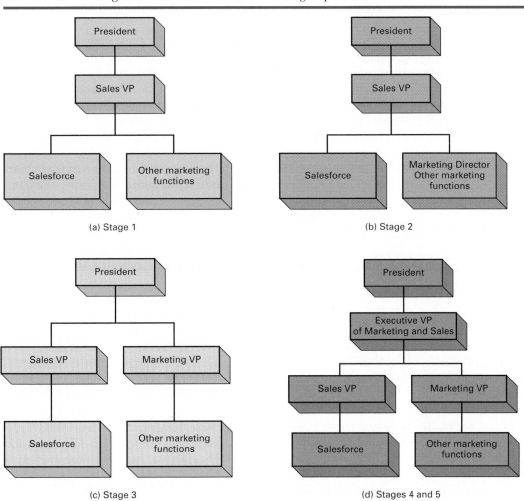

(a) Stage 1

(b) Stage 2

(c) Stage 3

(d) Stages 4 and 5

pany president to get a more balanced view of company opportunities and problems. Suppose sales are falling and the company president asks the sales vice-president for solutions. The sales vice-president might recommend hiring more salespeople, raising sales compensation, running a sales contest, providing more sales training, or cutting the price so that the product will be easier to sell. The company president then asks the marketing vice-president for solutions. The marketing vice-president is less ready to suggest immediate price and salesforce solutions. The marketing vice-president will see the question more from the customer's point of view. Is the company going after the right customers? How do the target customers see the company and its products relative to competitors? Are there changes in product features, styling, packaging, services, distribution, other forms of promotion, and so on, that are warranted? In general, there will be more effort to understand the problem rather than trying to solve it with a pure selling push.

MODERN MARKETING DEPARTMENT ❖ Although the sales and marketing vice-presidents are supposed to work harmoniously, their relationship is occasionally strained and marked by distrust. The sales vice-president resents efforts to make the salesforce less important in the marketing mix; and the marketing vice-president seeks a larger budget for nonsalesforce activities. The sales vice-president is short-run oriented and preoccupied with achieving current sales. The marketing vice-president is more long-run oriented and preoccupied with planning the right products and marketing strategy to meet the customers' long-run needs (see Marketing Concepts and Tools 26-1).

If there is too much disharmony between sales and marketing, the company president might place marketing activities back under the sales vice-president, or instruct the executive vice-president to handle conflicts that arise, or place the marketing vice-president in charge of everything, including the salesforce. This last solution forms the basis of the modern marketing department, a department headed by a marketing and sales executive vice-president with managers reporting from every marketing function, including sales management [see Figure 26-1(d)].

MODERN MARKETING COMPANY ❖ A company can have a modern marketing department and yet not operate as a modern marketing company. The latter

Marketing Concepts and Tools 26-1

Marketers and Salespeople: A Clash of Cultures

Marketing people are the new kids on the block. They are not to be confused with salespeople, although many of them came from sales. But promoting a salesperson into a marketing position does not necessarily make him or her a marketer. In fact, there is quite a difference in the orientation of the two professions.

Technically, the marketing manager's task is to identify opportunities and prepare marketing strategies and plans for guiding products and programs toward these opportunities. Salespeople are responsible for implementing these programs.

Trouble arises in two ways. If the marketer failed to solicit the salespeople's views toward the opportunity and plan, there is a good chance that he or she failed to sell them on implementing it. If, after implementation, the marketer doesn't listen and learn from the salespeople about actual conditions and problems with the plan, the marketer may fail to adjust it for optimal effectiveness.

Basically marketers and salespeople acquire different perspectives as shown here:

Each group carries an image of the other group. Marketers often see salespeople as having several positive traits (people oriented, good communicators, hard working) and some shortcomings (short-term orientation, nonstrategic, and nonanalytical). Salespeople often see marketers as having some positive traits (well educated, data oriented) and some shortcomings (less experienced, not streetwise, nonrisk taking, less intuitive).

Too many companies ignore these differences and promote a top-flight sales manager into a top marketing management position. But many sales managers are impatient with marketing research and marketing planning, preferring to meet customers. Such a company has fooled itself into thinking that marketing is being run by a marketer.

The main objective is for the two groups to reach mutual understanding and respect. In companies where the two groups lack respect, the results inevitably are bad. In companies where the two groups appreciate each other's talents and contributions, the results can be exceptional.

Marketers	Salespeople
Rely on marketing research	Rely on street experiences
Try to identify and understand segments	Try to understand each individual buyer
Spend time in planning	Spend time in face-to-face selling
Think long term	Think short term
Aim to produce profits and gains in market share	Aim to produce sales

depends upon how the other company managers view the marketing function. If they view marketing as primarily a selling function, they are missing the point. If they point to the marketing department and say, "They do the marketing," they are missing the point. All the departments must work for the customer. Everyone is in marketing. Marketing is not only a department but a thorough-going company philosophy. Only then does a company turn into a modern marketing company.

Ways of Organizing the Marketing Department

Modern marketing departments take on numerous forms. All marketing organizations must accommodate to four dimensions of marketing activity: *functions, geographical areas, products, and customer markets.*

FUNCTIONAL ORGANIZATION ❖ The most common form of marketing organization consists of functional-marketing specialists reporting to a marketing vice-president, who coordinates their activities. Figure 26-2 shows five specialists. Additional specialists might include a customer-service manager, a marketing-planning manager, and a physical-distribution manager.

The main advantage of a functional-marketing organization is its administrative simplicity. On the other hand, this form loses effectiveness as the company's products and markets increase. First, there is inadequate planning for specific products and markets, since no one has full responsibility for any product or market. Products that are not favored by anyone are neglected. Second, each functional group competes to gain more budget and status vis-à-vis the other functions. The marketing vice-president has to constantly weigh the claims of competing functional specialists and faces a difficult coordination problem.

GEOGRAPHICAL ORGANIZATION ❖ A company selling in a national market often organizes its salesforce (and sometimes other functions) along geographical lines. The national sales manager may supervise four regional sales managers, who each supervise six zone managers, who in turn supervise eight district sales managers, who supervise ten salespeople. The span of control increases as we move from the national sales manager down toward the district sales managers. Shorter spans allow managers to give more time to subordinates and are warranted when the sales task is complex, the salespersons are highly paid, and the salesperson's influence on profits is substantial.

Several companies are now adding *area market specialists* (regional or local marketing managers) to support the sales efforts in high-volume, distinctive markets. The local market specialist for Los Angeles, for example, would know Los Angeles's customer and trade makeup in great detail and help headquarters marketing managers adjust their marketing mix for Los Angeles to take maximum advantage of the opportunities. The local market specialist would prepare annual and

FIGURE 26-2 Functional Organization

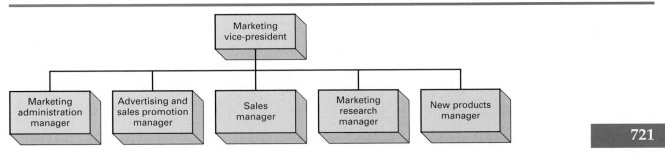

long-range plans for selling all the company's products in Los Angeles and would act as liaison between the headquarters marketing staff and the local salesforce (for more, see Marketing Environment and Trends 26-1).

PRODUCT AND BRAND MANAGEMENT ORGANIZATION ❖ Companies producing a variety of products and brands often establish a product (or brand) management organization. The product management organization does not replace the functional management organization but serves as another layer of management. The product management organization is headed by a products manager, who supervises product category managers, who supervise specific product and brand managers.

A product management organization makes sense if the products are quite different, or if the sheer number of products exceeds the ability of a functional-marketing organization to handle.

Product management first appeared in the Procter & Gamble Company in 1927. A new company soap, Camay, was not doing well, and one of the young executives, Neil H. McElroy (later president of P&G), was assigned to give his exclu-

Marketing Environment and Trends 26-1

Regionalization—A Passing Fad or the New Marketing Era?

For most of this century, major consumer-products companies have held fast to two mass-marketing principles—product standardization and national brand identification. They have marketed the same set of products in about the same way all across the country. But recently, Campbell Soup, Procter & Gamble, General Foods, H. J. Heinz, Kraft, and other companies have tried a new approach—*regionalization*. Instead of marketing in the same way nationally to all customers, they are tailoring their products, advertising, sales promotions, and personal selling efforts to suit the needs and tastes of specific regions, cities, and even neighborhoods. Some national companies have developed micromerchandising programs for different regional chain customers and units within a chain.

Several factors have fueled the move toward regionalization. First, the American mass market for most products has slowly subdivided into a profusion of minimarkets: baby boomers, senior citizens, Hispanics, blacks, single mothers—the list goes on. Today, marketers find it difficult to create a single product or program that appeals to all of these diverse groups. Second, improved information and marketing research technologies have also spurred regionalization. For example, data from retail-store scanners allow instant tracking of product sales from store to store, helping companies pinpoint local problems and opportunities that might call for localized marketing actions. A third important

factor is the increasing power of retailers. Scanners give retailers mountains of market information, and this information gives them power over manufacturers. Furthermore, competition has increased dramatically in recent years for the precious shelf space controlled by retailers. The average supermarket now carries over 300,000 stockkeeping units, and about ten new products are introduced each day. Retailers are often lukewarm about large, national marketing campaigns aimed at masses of consumers. They strongly prefer local programs tied to their own promotion efforts and aimed at consumers in their own cities and neighborhoods. Thus, to keep retailers happy and to get shelf space for their products, manufacturers must now allot more of their marketing budgets to local, store-by-store promotions.

Campbell Soup, a pioneer in regionalization, has jumped in with both feet. For starters, Campbell has created many successful regional brands. It sells its spicy Ranchero beans in the Southwest, Creole soup in the South, and red bean soup in Hispanic areas. For Northwesterners, who like their pickles very sour, it created Zesty pickles. These and other brands appealing to regional tastes add substantially to Campbell's annual sales. But perhaps more significantly, Campbell has reorganized its entire marketing operation to suit its regional strategy. It has divided its market into 22 regions, each with new responsibility for planning local marketing programs, and each with its own advertising and promo-

sive attention to developing and promoting this product. He did it successfully, and the company soon added other product managers.

Since then, many firms have established product management organizations. General Foods, for example, uses a product management organization in its Post Division. There are separate product category managers in charge of cereals, pet food, and beverages. Within the cereal product group, there are separate product managers for nutritional cereals, children's presweetened cereals, family cereals, and miscellaneous cereals. In turn, the nutritional-cereal product manager supervises brand managers.

The product manager's role is to develop product plans, see that they are implemented, monitor the results, and take corrective action. This responsibility breaks down into six tasks:

- Developing a long-range and competitive strategy for the product
- Preparing an annual marketing plan and sales forecast
- Working with advertising and merchandising agencies to develop copy, programs, and campaigns

tion budget. The company has allocated 15% to 20% of its total marketing budget to support local marketing; this allocation may eventually rise to 50%.

Within each region, Campbell sales managers and salespeople now have the authority to create advertising and promotions geared to local market needs and conditions. They use local appeals and choose whatever local advertising media work best in their areas, ranging from newspapers and radio to shopping carts and church bulletins. And they work closely with local retailers on displays, coupon offers, price specials, and local promotional events. For example, one sales manager recently offered Campbell's Pork & Beans at a 50-year-old price (5¢) to help a local retailer celebrate its fiftieth anniversary. Such localized efforts win retailer support and boost consumer sales.

Regionalization may be accompanied by a move toward branchising. *Branchising* means empowering the company's districts or local stores offices to operate more like a franchise. Instead of headquarters tightly regulating the activities of its branches, it gives local management more scope to run their business. IBM recently told its branch manager to "make it your business." Thus, the branches resemble profit centers and local managers have more strategy latitude and incentive.

Although regionalization offers much promise, it also requires making a number of tough decisions. How

many regional managers will be needed? Should they report to national marketing or to local sales management? What is their proper training? How much authority should they have for regional decision making? Where should the budget come from to support this added layer of management? Will regional marketing management reduce headquarters' effort to achieve marketing continuity, consistency, and efficiency? Will the gains more than cover the increased manufacturing and marketing costs?

Regionalization is still in its infancy. Some marketers view it as a fad—they think companies will quickly find that the extra sales will not cover the additional costs. But others think that regionalization will revolutionize the way consumer products are marketed. Gone are the days, they say, when a company can effectively mass market a single product using a single ad campaign all across the country. To these marketers, regionalization signals the start of a new marketing era.

SOURCES: See Christine Dugas, Mark N. Vamos, Jonathan B. Levine, and Matt Rothmann, "Marketing's New Look," *Business Week,* January 26, 1987, pp. 64–69; Al Urbanski, "Repackaging the Brand Manager," *Sales & Marketing Management,* April 1987, pp. 42–45; Scott Hume, "Execs Favor Regional Approach," *Advertising Age,* November 2, 1987, p. 36; "National Firms Find that Selling to Local Tastes Is Costly, Complex," *The Wall Street Journal,* February 9, 1987, p. B1; and Shawn McKenna, *The Complete Guide to Regional Marketing* (Homewood, IL: Business One Irwin, 1992).

- Stimulating support of the product among the salesforce and distributors
- Gathering continuous intelligence on the product's performance, customer and dealer attitudes, and new problems and opportunities
- Initiating product improvements to meet changing market needs

These basic functions are common to both consumer- and industrial-product managers. Yet there are differences in their jobs and emphases. Consumer-product managers typically manage fewer products than industrial-product managers. They spend more time on advertising and sales promotion. They spend more time working with others in the company and various agencies and little time with customers. They are often younger and more educated. Industrial-product managers, by contrast, think more about the technical aspects of their product and possible design improvements. They spend more time with laboratory and engineering personnel. They work more closely with the salesforce and key buyers. They pay less attention to advertising, sales promotion, and promotional pricing. They emphasize rational product factors over emotional ones.

The product management organization introduces several advantages. First, the product manager can concentrate on developing a cost-effective marketing mix for the product. Second, the product manager can react more quickly to problems in the marketplace than a committee of functional specialists. Third, smaller brands are less neglected, because they have a product advocate. Fourth, product manage

FIGURE 26-3
The Product Manager's Interactions

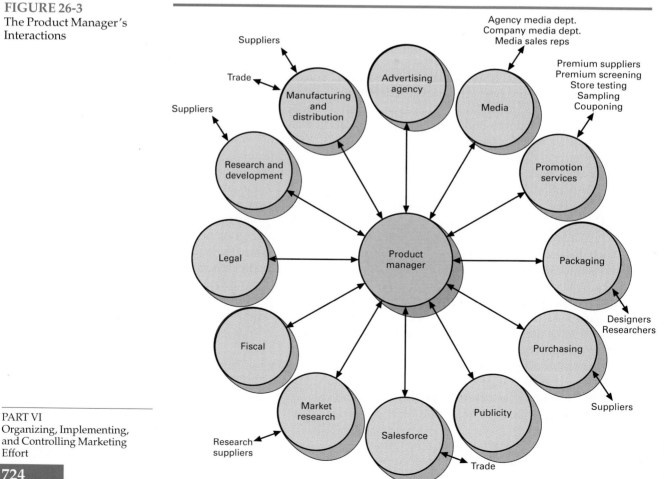

ment is an excellent training ground for young executives, for it involves them in almost every area of company operations (see Figure 26-3).

But a price is paid for these advantages. First, product management creates some conflict and frustration. Typically, product managers are not given enough authority to carry out their responsibilities effectively. They have to rely on persuasion to get the cooperation of advertising, sales, manufacturing, and other departments. They are told they are "minipresidents" but are often treated as low-level coordinators. They are burdened with a great amount of "housekeeping" paperwork. They often have to go over the heads of others to get something done.

Second, product managers become experts in their product but rarely become experts in any of the functions. They vacillate between posing as experts and being cowed by real experts. This is unfortunate when the product depends on a specific type of expertise, such as advertising.

Third, the product management system often turns out to be costlier than anticipated. Originally, one person is appointed to manage each major product. Soon product managers are appointed to manage even minor products. Each product manager, usually overworked, pleads for and gets an *associate brand manager*. Later, both overworked, they persuade management to give them an *assistant brand manager*. With all these people, payroll costs climb. In the meantime, the company continues to increase its functional specialists in copy, packaging, media, sales promotion, market surveys, statistical analysis, and so on. The company becomes saddled with a costly structure of product management people and functional specialists.

Fourth, brand managers normally manage their brand for only a short time. Either product managers move up in a few years to another brand or product, or they transfer to another company, or they leave product management altogether. Their short-term involvement with the brand leads to short-term marketing planning and plays havoc with building up the brand's long-term strengths.

Pearson and Wilson have suggested five steps to make the product management system work better:[1]

- *Clearly Delineate the Limits of the Product Manager's Role and Responsibility for the Product.* They are essentially proposers, not deciders.

- *Build a Strategy-Development-and-Review Process to Provide an Agreed-to Framework for the Product Manager's Operations.* Too many companies allow product managers to get away with shallow marketing plans featuring a lot of statistics but little strategic rationale.

- *Take into Account Areas of Potential Conflict between Product Managers and Functional Specialists when Defining their Respective Roles.* Clarify which decisions are to be made by the product manager, which by the expert, and which will be shared.

- *Set Up a Formal Process that Forces to the Top all Conflict-of-Interest Situations between Product Management and Functional Line Management.* Both parties should put the issues in writing and forward them to general management for settlement.

- *Establish a System for Measuring Results Consistent with the Product Manager's Responsibilities.* If product managers are accountable for profit, they should be given more control over the factors that affect profitability.

A second alternative is to switch from a product-manager to a product-team approach. In fact, there are three types of product-team structures in product management (see Figure 26-4).

- *Vertical Product Team:* This consists of a product manager, associate product manager, and product assistant [Figure 26-4(a)]. The product manager is the leader and primarily deals with other managers to gain their cooperation. The associate product man-

FIGURE 26-4
Three Types of Product
Teams

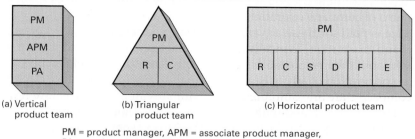

(a) Vertical
product team

(b) Triangular
product team

(c) Horizontal product team

PM = product manager, APM = associate product manager,
PA = product assistant, R = market researcher,
C = communication specialist, S = sales manager,
D = distribution specialist, F = finance/accounting specialist,
E = engineer

ager assists in these tasks and also does some paperwork. The product assistant carries out most of the paperwork and routine analysis.

♦ *Triangular Product Team:* This consists of a product manager and two specialized product assistants, one who takes care of (say) marketing research and the other, marketing communications [Figure 26-4(b)]. This design is used at the Illinois Central Railroad, where three-person teams manage different commodities. Also, the Hallmark Company uses a "marketing team" consisting of a market manager (the leader), a marketing manager, and a distribution manager.

♦ *Horizontal Product Team:* This consists of a product manager and several specialists from marketing and other functions [Figure 26-4(c)]. The 3M Company divided its commercial tape division into nine business-planning teams, each team consisting of a team leader and representatives from sales, marketing, laboratory, engineering, accounting, and marketing research. Instead of a product manager's bearing the entire responsibility of product planning, he or she shares it with representatives from key departments in the company. Their input is critical in the marketing-planning process, and furthermore each team member can bring influence to bear in his or her own department. The ultimate step after a horizontal product team is to form a product division around the product.

A third alternative is to eliminate product-manager positions for minor products and assign two or more products to each remaining product manager. This is feasible especially where two or more products appeal to a similar set of needs. Thus a cosmetics company does not need separate product managers because cosmetics serve one major need—beauty—whereas a toiletries company needs different managers for headache remedies, toothpaste, soap, and shampoo, because these products differ in their use and appeal. (For recent changes in product/brand management, see Marketing Environment and Trends 26-2, pp. 728–29.)

MARKET MANAGEMENT ORGANIZATION ❖ Many companies sell their products to a diverse set of markets. For example, Canon sells its facsimile machines to consumer, business, and government markets. U.S. Steel sells its steel to the railroad, construction, and public-utility industries. When customers fall into different user groups with distinct buying preferences and practices, a market management organization is desirable. A *markets manager* supervises several *market managers* (also called market development managers, market specialists, or industry specialists). The market managers draw upon functional services as needed. Market managers of important markets might even have functional specialists reporting to them.

Market managers are staff, not line, people, with duties similar to those of product managers. Market managers develop long-range and annual plans for their markets. They must analyze where their market is going and what new products their company should offer to this market. Their performance is often judged by their contribution to market-share growth rather than to current profitability in their market. This system carries many of the same advantages and disadvantages of product-management systems. Its strongest advantage is that the marketing activity is organized to meet the needs of distinct customer groups rather than focusing on marketing functions, regions, or products per se.

Many companies are reorganizing along market lines. Hanan calls these companies *market-centered organizations* and argues that "the only way to ensure being market oriented is to put a company's organizational structure together so that its major markets become the centers around which its divisions are built."[2] Xerox has converted from geographical selling to selling by industry. The Mead Company has clustered its marketing activities around home building and furnishings, education, and leisure markets.

One of the most dramatic changes to market centeredness has occurred at the Heinz Company. Heinz was organized around a brand management system, with separate brand managers for soups, condiments, puddings, and so on. Each brand manager was responsible for both grocery sales and institutional sales. Then Heinz created a separate marketing organization for institutional sales because institutional sales were growing faster than grocery sales but were not as well understood by the brand managers. Later, Heinz created three broad market groups: groceries, commercial restaurants, and institutions. Each group contains further market specialists. For example, the institutional division contains market specialists for schools, colleges, hospitals, and prisons.

> The prison market manager's job is to visit prison kitchen managers and learn about their food needs and budgets. Then this manager proposes reformulations of Heinz ketchup, soup, mustard, and other products to make them cost effective and competitive with the offers of other suppliers. Thus Heinz will use a lower grade of tomato and package its ketchup in bulk in order to compete for prison business, which happens to be a growth market as well as a "captive" market!

PRODUCT MANAGEMENT/MARKET MANAGEMENT ORGANIZATION ❖ Companies that produce many products flowing into many markets face a dilemma. They could use a product management system, which requires product managers to be familiar with highly divergent markets. Or they could use a market management system, which means that market managers would have to be familiar with highly divergent products bought by their markets. Or they could install both product and market managers, that is, a *matrix organization*.

Du Pont as a company has done the latter (see Figure 26-5). Its textile fibers de-

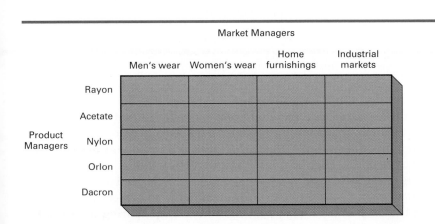

	Market Managers			
Product Managers	Men's wear	Women's wear	Home furnishings	Industrial markets
Rayon				
Acetate				
Nylon				
Orlon				
Dacron				

FIGURE 26-5
Product/Market Management System

What's the Future of Brand Management?

Brand management has become a well-established practice in consumer-packaged-goods companies. Yet the environment in which it was created and thrived is drastically altered today, and observers are questioning whether it provides the best system for managing brands in the new environment.

Today's brand managers are in a double bind: they are under great pressure to produce increased profits while being given less latitude for achieving them. Companies are wondering if they need all the group brand managers, brand managers, associate brand managers, and assistant brand managers. Companies are facing three new environmental forces that challenge the concept of brand managers:

1. *Growing Bargaining Power of the Distribution Channels and Growing Importance of Sales Promotion:* The major distributors of consumer packaged goods—supermarket chains and mass merchandisers—are growing more powerful and are demanding better terms from consumer-packaged-goods companies in exchange for scarce shelf space. These distributors are primarily interested in generating more store traffic, and they are pressing manufacturers for more trade deals. The heat is felt by the manufacturers' salesforces, who tell the brand managers that they cannot get or keep shelf space without more trade deals. The result is that the brand managers shift more money into sales promotion and have less funds to build their brand franchises.

   Furthermore, giant retailers are demanding more multibrand and multicategory promotion deals from each manufacturer. They want customized multibrand deals that would enable them to compete better. These deals have to be worked out at higher levels of management than the brand level. But the brand managers have to be taxed to support these deals, sometimes by giving up some percentage of their budget. Brand managers are being left with less control over their sales-promotion funds.

   As sales promotion becomes more important, the manufacturers are realizing that they are not organized to handle it efficiently. Originally, sales promotion was handled individually by each brand manager. Some companies later appointed a sales-promotion specialist to help brand managers choose good premiums and couponing schemes for consumer sales promotion. Meanwhile, the company's salesforce keeps pressing for more trade-promotion money. The question becomes: How much should be spent on sales promotion out of the total budget and how should this money be split between trade and consumer promotion? Unfortunately, the decisions are being made politically rather than rationally.

2. *Declining Cost Effectiveness of Mass Advertising:* Brand managers are finding that they have less money to spend on advertising, the one tool they know best. Furthermore, mass advertising—particularly network television—is becoming less cost effective. There are fewer people watching network television, and many are not in the market for the advertised products. The money can be spent more effectively by studying category and brand interest levels market by market. But brand managers do not know the individual markets that well. Companies are increasingly using area marketing specialists to develop area marketing plans.

3. *Declining Level of Customer Brand Loyalty:* Consumers have been exposed to so much dealing that a growing number are deal prone rather than brand prone. The consumers' set of acceptable brands is increasing. As more consumers switch their brands each week depending on the deals, brand shares become more volatile. A brand's weekly or monthly market share means less and becomes less useful in deciding how much money to allocate to each brand. Higher levels of management have to decide how much funds to allocate to each brand.

These developments are forcing consumer-packaged-goods companies to rethink how they should develop and manage their brands. There are two competing solutions:

partment consists of separate product managers for rayon, acetate, nylon, orlon, and dacron; and separate market managers for men's wear, women's wear, home furnishings, and industrial markets. The product managers plan the sales and profits of their respective fibers. Their aim is to expand the use of their fiber. They ask market managers to estimate how much of their fiber they can sell in each market. The market managers, on the other hand, are more interested in meeting the needs of their market rather than pushing a particular fiber. In preparing their market

1. *Changing the Job Emphasis of the Brand Manager:* One line of thought is that the brand manager should spend less time creating the promotion plans and become more involved in product improvement and production. Normally, the brand manager has little time to think about creating flankers and brand extensions, and this has forced companies to appoint new-product specialists within brand or category groups to do this work. And the brand manager does not become very involved in knowing the production and logistics steps and how to find cost improvements. Therefore, it might be argued that brand managers should have their responsibilities shifted more to product improvement and production/distribution efficiency concerns.

2. *Introducing Category Management:* Another line of thought is that a company should introduce a stronger category focus in managing its brands. P&G found too much internal competition among its own brands within each category: Its Puritan and Crisco oils both fought for a budget increase, although one deserved it more than the other; its Cheer brand started to copy the same claim as its Tide brand, thus diluting Tide's positioning. P&G's answer: The brand managers are now accountable to a new corps of category managers, who resolve conflicts, protect positionings, allocate budgets, and develop new brands for the category. Category management is also partly a response to the fact that supermarkets are reorganizing by category buyers rather than company buyers.

Nabisco took a different route. Instead of several cookie brand managers, it has three cookie-category management teams: adult rich cookies, children's cookies, and nutritional cookies. Each category team manages several brands with specialists handling advertising, sales promotion, packaging, line extension, and business development. The net result is to reduce the number of middle managers, thus creating a leaner organization.

In reducing the number of brand managers, their counterparts in advertising agencies—namely, account executives—might also be reduced. Many consumer-packaged-goods companies are pressing advertising agencies to lower their costs, especially considering the reduced effectiveness of mass advertising. These companies normally prepare their own brand marketing plans and simply want a good creative plan and media plan from their advertising agency. They wonder why they have to work through account executives and their assistants. Some companies are telling their advertising agencies they are going to pay less or else switch agencies, thus forcing these agencies to reconsider their own organizing patterns and the role of the account executives.

Making changes in the brand management system will not be easy. Everyone involved in brand management will fight changes, since these changes will destroy the normal promotion ladder in the organization. Any company that is rumored to be thinking about abandoning brand management will lose some of its best people before it can reorganize, and the transition will be difficult.

Yet changes are called for. The fact is that brand management is a sales-driven, not a customer-driven, system. Brand managers focus on pushing out their brands to anyone and everyone. Even category management is limited in that it is a product-focused system, cookies if not Oreos. Colgate recently has moved from *brand management* (Colgate toothpaste) to *category management* (toothpaste) to a new stage, *customer-need management* (oral health). This last step finally gets the organization to focus on a customer need.

SOURCES: For further reading, see Robert Dewar and Don Schultz, "The Product Manager, An Idea Whose Time Has Gone," *Marketing Communications*, May 1989, pp. 28–35; "The Marketing Revolution at Procter & Gamble," *Business Week*, July 25, 1988, pp. 72–76; and Kevin T. Higgins, "Category Management: New Tools Changing Life for Manufacturers, Retailers," *Marketing News*, September 25, 1989, pp. 2, 19.

plans, they ask each product manager about planned prices and availabilities of the different fibers. The final sales forecasts of the market managers and the product managers should add to the same grand total.

A matrix organization would seem desirable in a multiproduct, multimarket company. The rub is that this system is costly and conflictual. There is the cost of supporting all three managers. There are also questions about where authority and responsibility should reside. Here are two of many dilemmas:

- *How Should the Salesforce Be Organized?* Should there be separate salesforces for rayon, nylon, and the other fibers? Or should the salesforces be organized according to men's wear, women's wear, and other markets? Or should the salesforce not be specialized?

- *Who Should Set the Prices for a Particular Product/Market?* Should the nylon product manager have final authority for setting nylon prices in all markets? What happens if the men's-wear market manager feels that nylon will lose out in this market unless special price concessions are made on nylon?

Most managers feel that only the more important products and markets justify separate managers. Some are not upset about the conflicts and cost and believe that the benefits of product and market specialization outweigh the costs.[3]

CORPORATE/DIVISIONAL ORGANIZATION ❖ As multiproduct/multimarket companies grow in size, they often convert their larger product and/or market groups into separate divisions. The divisions set up their own departments and services. This raises the question of what marketing services and activities should be retained at corporate headquarters.

Divisionalized companies have reached different answers to this question. Corporate marketing staffs follow one of three models:

- *No Corporate Marketing:* Some companies lack a corporate marketing staff: They don't see any useful function for marketing to perform at the corporate level. Each division has its own marketing department.

- *Moderate Corporate Marketing:* Some companies have a small corporate marketing staff that performs a few functions, primarily (a) assisting top management with overall opportunity evaluation, (b) providing divisions with consulting assistance on request, (c) helping divisions that have little or no marketing, and (d) promoting the marketing concept to other departments of the company.

- *Strong Corporate Marketing:* Some companies have a corporate marketing staff that in addition to the preceding activities, also provides various marketing services to the divisions. The corporate marketing staff might provide specialized *advertising services* (e.g., coordination of media buying, institutional advertising, review of division advertising from a taste and image standpoint, auditing of advertising expenditures), *sales-promotion services* (e.g., companywide promotions, central buying of promotional materials), *marketing research services* (e.g., advanced mathematical analysis, research on marketing development cutting across divisional lines), *sales-administration services* (e.g., counsel on sales organization and sales policies, development of common sales-reporting systems, management of salesforces selling to common customers), and miscellaneous services (e.g., counseling of marketing planning, hiring, and training of marketing personnel).[4]

The question arises as to whether companies favor one of these models. The answer is no. Some companies have recently installed a corporate marketing staff for the first time; others have expanded their corporate marketing department; others have reduced its size and scope; and still others have eliminated it altogether.

The potential contribution of a corporate marketing staff varies in different stages of the company's evolution. Most companies begin with weak marketing in their divisions and often establish a corporate marketing staff to bring stronger marketing into the divisions through training and other services. Some members of the corporate marketing staff might be hired away to head divisional marketing departments. As the divisions become strong in their marketing, corporate marketing has less to offer them. Some companies might decide that corporate marketing has done its job and proceed to eliminate the department.

A corporate marketing staff generally has three justifications. The first is to serve as a corporate focus for review and leadership of overall company marketing activities and opportunities. The second is to offer certain marketing services that can be provided more economically on a centralized basis than by being duplicated in the different divisions. The third is to take responsibility for educating divisional managers, sales managers, and others in the company on the need for, and implementation of, the marketing concept.[5]

Marketing's Relations with Other Departments

In principle, all the functions of a business should interact harmoniously to pursue the overall objectives of the firm. In practice, interdepartmental relations are often characterized by deep rivalries and distrust. Some interdepartmental conflict stems from differences of opinion as to what is in the company's best interests, some from real tradeoffs between departmental well-being and company well-being, and some from unfortunate departmental stereotypes and prejudices.

In the typical organization, each business function has a potential influence on customer satisfaction. Under the marketing concept, all departments need to "think customer" and work together to satisfy customer needs and expectations. The marketing department must drive this point home. The marketing vice-president has two tasks: to coordinate the company's internal marketing activities and to coordinate marketing with finance, operations, and the other company functions, in the interests of the customers.

Yet there is little agreement on how much influence and authority marketing should have over other departments to bring about coordinated marketing. Typically, the marketing vice-president must work through persuasion rather than authority.

> This situation is well illustrated in the case of the marketing vice-president of a major European airline. His mandate is to build up his airline's market share. Yet he has no authority over other functions that affect customer satisfaction:
>
> ◆ He can't hire or train the cabin crew (personnel department).
> ◆ He can't determine the type or quality of food (catering department).
> ◆ He can't enforce cleanliness standards on the plane (maintenance department).
> ◆ He can't determine schedules (operations department).
> ◆ He can't establish the fares (finance department).
>
> What does he control? He controls marketing research, the salesforce, advertising, and promotion. But he must work through the other departments to shape key determinants of customer satisfaction.

Other departments often resist bending their efforts to meet the customers' interests. Just as marketing stresses the customer's point of view, other departments stress the importance of their tasks. Inevitably, departments define company problems and goals from their point of view. As a result, conflicts of interest are unavoidable. Table 26-1 summarizes the main differences in orientation between marketing and other departments. We will briefly examine the typical concerns of each department.

R&D ❖ The company's drive for successful new products is often thwarted by poor working relations between R&D and marketing. In many ways, these groups represent two different cultures in the organization. The R&D department is staffed with scientists and technicians who pride themselves on scientific curiosity and detachment, like to work on challenging technical problems without much concern for immediate sales payoffs, and prefer to work without much supervision or ac-

TABLE 26-1
Organizational Conflicts Between Marketing and Other Departments

DEPARTMENT	THEIR EMPHASIS	MARKETING'S EMPHASIS
R&D	Basic research	Applied research
	Intrinsic quality	Perceived quality
	Functional features	Sales features
Engineering	Long design lead time	Short design lead time
	Few models	Many models
	Standard components	Custom components
Purchasing	Narrow product line	Broad product line
	Standard parts	Nonstandard parts
	Price of material	Quality of material
	Economical lot sizes	Large lot sizes to avoid stockouts
	Purchasing at infrequent intervals	Immediate purchasing for customer needs
Manufacturing	Long production lead time	Short production lead time
	Long runs with few models	Short runs with many models
	No model changes	Frequent model changes
	Standard orders	Custom orders
	Ease of fabrication	Aesthetic appearance
	Average quality control	Tight quality control
Finance	Strict rationales for spending	Intuitive arguments for spending
	Hard and fast budgets	Flexible budgets to meet changing needs
	Pricing to cover costs	Pricing to further market development
Accounting	Standard transactions	Special terms and discounts
	Few reports	Many reports
Credit	Full financial disclosures by customers	Minimum credit examination of customers
	No credit risk	Some credit risk
	Tough credit terms	Easy credit terms
	Tough collection procedures	Easy collection procedures

countability for research costs. The marketing/sales department is staffed with business-oriented persons who pride themselves on a practical understanding of the marketplace, like to see many new products with sales features that can be promoted to customers, and feel compelled to pay attention to costs. Each group often carries negative stereotypes of the other group. Marketers see the R&D people as seeking to discover or maximize technical qualities rather than design for customer requirements, while R&D people see marketers as gimmick-oriented hucksters who are more interested in sales than in the technical features of the product. These stereotypes get in the way of productive teamwork.

Companies vary as to whether they are technology driven, market driven, or balanced. In *technology-driven companies*, the R&D staff researches fundamental problems, looks for major breakthroughs, and strives for technical perfection in product development. R&D expenditures are high, and the new-product success rate tends to be low, although R&D occasionally comes up with major new products.

In *market-driven companies*, the R&D staff designs products to meet specific market needs, much of it involving product modification and the application of existing technologies. A higher ratio of new products succeeds, but this represents mainly product modifications with relatively short product lives.

A *balanced company* is one in which R&D and marketing share responsibility for successful market-oriented innovation. The R&D staff takes responsibility not for invention alone but for successful innovation. The marketing staff takes responsibility not for new sales features alone but also for helping identify new ways to satisfy needs.

Gupta, Raj, and Wilemon concluded that a balanced R&D-marketing coordination is strongly correlated with innovation success.[6] R&D-marketing cooperation can be facilitated in several ways:[7]

- Joint seminars are sponsored to build understanding and respect for each other's goals, working styles, and problems.
- Each new project is assigned to functional teams including an R&D person and a marketing person, who work together through the life of the project. R&D and marketing jointly establish the development goals and marketing plan.
- R&D's participation continues into the selling period, including involvement in preparing technical manuals, participating in trade shows, carrying out postintroductory marketing research with customers, and even doing some selling.
- Conflicts are worked out by higher management, following a clear procedure. In one company, R&D and marketing both report to the same vice-president.

ENGINEERING ❖ Engineering is responsible for finding practical ways to design new products and new production processes. Engineers are interested in achieving technical quality, cost economy, and manufacturing simplicity. They come into conflict with marketing executives when the latter want several models to be produced, often with product features requiring custom rather than standard components. Engineers see marketers as wanting "bells and whistles" on the products rather than intrinsic quality. They think of marketing people as inept technically, as continually changing priorities, and as not fully credible or trustworthy. These problems are less pronounced in companies where marketing executives have engineering backgrounds and can communicate effectively with engineers.

PURCHASING ❖ Purchasing executives are responsible for obtaining materials and components in the right quantities and quality at the lowest possible cost. They see marketing executives pushing for several models in a product line, which requires purchasing small quantities of many items rather than large quantities of a few items. They think that marketing insists on too high a quality of ordered materials and components. They dislike marketing's forecasting inaccuracy; it causes them to place rush orders at unfavorable prices and at other times to carry excessive inventories.

MANUFACTURING ❖ Manufacturing people are responsible for the smooth running of the factory to produce the right products in the right quantities at the right time for the right cost. They have spent their lives in the factory, with its attendant problems of machine breakdowns, inventory stockouts, and labor disputes. They see marketers as having little understanding of factory economics or politics. Marketers will complain about insufficient plant capacity, delays in production, poor quality control, and poor customer service. Yet marketers often turn in inaccurate sales forecasts, recommend product features that are difficult to manufacture, and promise more factory service than is reasonable.

Marketers do not see the factory's problems, but rather they see the problems of their customers, who need the goods quickly, who receive defective merchandise, and who cannot get factory service. Marketers often don't show enough concern for the extra factory costs involved in helping a customer. The problem is not only poor communication but an actual conflict of interest.

Companies settle these conflicts in different ways. In *manufacturing-driven companies*, everything is done to ensure smooth production and low costs. The company prefers simple products, narrow product lines, and high-volume production. Sales campaigns calling for a hasty production buildup are kept to a minimum. Customers on back order have to wait.

Other companies are *marketing driven*, in that the company goes out of its way to satisfy customers. In one large toiletries company, the marketing personnel call the shots, and the manufacturing people have to fall in line, regardless of overtime costs, short runs, and so on. The result is high and fluctuating manufacturing costs, as well as variable product quality.

Companies need to develop a *balanced orientation*, in which manufacturing and marketing codetermine what is in the best interests of the company. Solutions include joint seminars to understand each other's viewpoint, joint committees and liaison personnel, personnel exchange programs, and analytical methods to determine the most profitable course of action.[8]

Company profitability is greatly dependent on achieving successful manufacturing-marketing working relations. Marketers need to understand the marketing implications of new manufacturing strategies—the flexible factory, automation and robotization, just-in-time production, quality circles, and so on. If the company wants to win through being the low-cost producer, that will call for one manufacturing strategy; if the company wants to win through excelling at high quality or high variety or high service, each calls for different manufacturing strategies. Manufacturing design and capacity decisions must take their cues from the manufacturing targets set by marketing strategy with respect to planned output, cost, quality, variety, and service.

Manufacturing should be viewed partly as a marketing tool. Before buyers choose a vendor, they often want to visit the factory to assess how well it is managed. Thus manufacturing personnel and plant layout become important marketing tools.

FINANCE ❖ Financial executives pride themselves on being able to evaluate the profit implications of different business actions. When it comes to marketing expenditures, they feel frustrated. Marketing executives ask for substantial budgets for advertising, sales promotions, and salesforce, without being able to prove how many sales will be produced by these expenditures. Financial executives suspect that the marketers' forecasts are self-serving. They think that marketing people do not spend enough time relating expenditures to sales and shifting their budgets to more profitable areas. They think that marketers are too quick to slash prices to win orders, instead of pricing to make a profit.

Marketing executives, on the other hand, often see financial people as controlling the purse strings too tightly and refusing to invest funds in long-term market development. Financial people see all marketing expenditures as expenses rather than investments. They seem overly conservative and risk averse, causing many opportunities to be lost. The solution lies in giving marketing people more financial training and giving financial people more marketing training. Financial executives need to adapt their financial tools and theories to support strategic marketing.

ACCOUNTING ❖ Accountants see marketing people as lax in providing their sales reports on time. They dislike the special deals that salespeople make with customers because these require special accounting procedures. Marketers, on the other hand, dislike the way accountants allocate fixed-cost burdens to different products in the line. Brand managers may feel that their brand is more profitable than it looks, the problem being high overhead assigned to it. They would also like accounting to prepare special reports on sales and profitability by channels, territories, order sizes, and so on.

CREDIT ❖ Credit officers evaluate the credit standing of potential customers and deny or limit credit to the more doubtful ones. They think that marketers will sell to anyone, including those from whom payment is doubtful. Marketers, on the other hand, often feel that credit standards are too high. They think that "zero bad debts" really means that the company lost a lot of sales and profits. They feel they work too hard to find customers to hear that they are not good enough to sell to.

Strategies for Building a Companywide Marketing Orientation

Only a handful of American companies—P&G, Marriott, McDonald's—are truly market and customer driven. They see marketing as not a function of the marketing department alone but of every department. The best marketing department in the world cannot compensate for other departments lacking a customer orientation. Table 26-2 shows an audit instrument to evaluate which of the company's departments are truly customer driven.

Unfortunately, too many companies are sales driven, product driven, or technology driven. These companies sooner or later experience some market shock. They may lose a major market, experience slow growth or low profitability, or find themselves facing formidable competitors.

> General Motors's substantial market-share decline is largely attributed to its chronic sales orientation. In the past, it produced a variety of cars and sold them successfully primarily because it had twice as many sales and service dealerships as its next largest competitor. But it didn't pay attention to a changing market of smaller cars, higher-quality foreign cars, more service-minded competitor dealerships, and so on. Its management was inside focused, not outside focused. In 1991, it suffered the largest corporate loss in U.S. history, $23.5 billion.[9]

> Sears is another company that failed to recognize and respond to the changing market forces. They underestimated the lower costs and better values offered by the new mass merchandisers, category killers, and specialty retailers. They failed to define and orient their operations toward a target customer, thinking that everyone would shop at Sears. After losing $3.9 billion in 1992, they announced plans to spend $4 billion to remake themselves. They will renovate their stores, increase their advertising of Sears as a brand name, eliminate their catalog operation, and sell some businesses. They have decided on their target customer: the working woman between ages 35-64 with an annual family income from $16,000 to $45,000. It is still an open question whether these changes go far enough in understanding today's customers and the new competitive environment.[10]

These and other companies are now undertaking steps to become "market driven." Yet in many cases, they don't succeed. Why?

In some companies, their CEOs do not really understand marketing and confuse it with promotion. They want their organizations to sell and advertise more aggressively and miss the point that promotion is wasted if their products and prices don't give value to their target customers.

Some CEOs oversimplify the task of changing their company's culture. They think that making speeches about everyone "working for the customer" and running marketing training seminars are sufficient to produce the desired results. They underestimate the resistance to change, especially in the absence of new incentives. When performance doesn't improve within a year or two, they lose patience and turn their attention to another theme, such as a companywide productivity drive.

What steps must a company take if it hopes to successfully grow a marketing culture? Here are the main steps:

1. *Convince Other Managers of the Need to Become Customer Driven:* Here the CEO's leadership and commitment is key. The CEO must convince the company's top managers that becoming more market focused and customer centered would pay off. The CEO

TABLE 26-2   Are the Company's Departments Customer Driven?

R&D
- _____ They spend time meeting customers and listening to their problems.
- _____ They welcome the involvement of marketing, manufacturing, and other departments on each new project.
- _____ They benchmark competitors' products and seek "best of class" solutions.
- _____ They solicit customer reactions and suggestions as the project progresses.
- _____ They continuously improve and refine the product on the basis of market feedback.

PURCHASING
- _____ They proactively search for the best suppliers rather than choose only from those who solicit their business.
- _____ They build long-term relations with fewer but more reliable high-quality suppliers.
- _____ They don't compromise quality for price savings.

MANUFACTURING
- _____ They invite customers to visit and tour their plants.
- _____ They visit customer plants to see how customers use the company's products.
- _____ They willingly work overtime when it is important to meet promised delivery schedules.
- _____ They continuously search for ways to produce goods faster and/or at lower costs.
- _____ They continuously improve product quality, aiming for zero defects.
- _____ They meet customer requirements for "customization" where this can be done profitably.

MARKETING
- _____ They study customer needs and wants in well-defined market segments.
- _____ They allocate marketing effort in relation to the long-run profit potential of the targeted segments.
- _____ They develop winning offers for each target segment.
- _____ They measure company image and customer satisfaction on a continuous basis.
- _____ They continuously gather and evaluate ideas for new products, product improvements, and services to meet customers' needs.
- _____ They influence all company departments and employees to be customer centered in their thinking and practice.

SALES
- _____ They have specialized knowledge of the customer's industry.
- _____ They strive to give the customer "the best solution."
- _____ They make only promises that they can keep.
- _____ They feed back customers' needs and ideas to those in charge of product development.
- _____ They serve the same customers for a long period of time.

LOGISTICS
- _____ They set a high standard for service delivery time and they meet this standard consistently.
- _____ They operate a knowledgeable and friendly customer service department that can answer questions, handle complaints, and resolve problems in a satisfactory and timely manner.

ACCOUNTING
- _____ They prepare periodic "profitability" reports by product, market segment, geographic areas (regions, sales territories), order sizes, and individual customers.
- _____ They prepare invoices tailored to customer needs and answer customer queries courteously and quickly.

FINANCE
- _____ They understand and support marketing expenditures (e.g., image advertising) that represent marketing investments that produce long-term customer preference and loyalty.
- _____ They tailor the financial package to the customers' financial requirements.
- _____ They make quick decisions on customer creditworthiness.

PUBLIC RELATIONS
- _____ They disseminate favorable news about the company and they "damage control" unfavorable news.
- _____ They act as an internal customer and public advocate for better company policies and practices.

OTHER CUSTOMER CONTACT PERSONNEL
- _____ They are competent, courteous, cheerful, credible, reliable, and responsive.

must give frequent speeches to employees, suppliers, and distributors about the importance of delivering quality and value to customers. The CEO must personally exemplify strong customer commitment and reward those in the organization who do likewise.

2. *Appoint a Top Marketing Officer and a Marketing Task Force:* The company should hire a top marketing officer and establish a marketing task force to assist in developing programs for bringing modern marketing thinking and practices into the company. The task force should include the CEO, and the vice-presidents of sales, R&D, purchasing, manufacturing, finance, personnel, and a few other key individuals.

3. *Get Outside Help and Guidance:* The marketing task force would benefit from outside consulting expertise in building a company marketing culture. Consulting firms have considerable experience in helping companies move toward a marketing orientation.

4. *Change the Reward Structures in the Company:* The company will have to change department reward structures if it expects departmental behavior to change. As long as purchasing and manufacturing are rewarded for keeping costs low, they will resist accepting some costs required to serve customers better. As long as finance focuses on short-term profit performance, finance will oppose major marketing investments designed to build more satisfied and loyal customers.

5. *Hire Strong Marketing Talent:* The company should consider hiring well-trained marketing talent from outside, preferably from leading marketing companies. When Citibank got serious about marketing some years ago, it hired away several marketing managers from General Foods. The company will need a strong marketing vice-president who not only manages the marketing department but gains respect and influence with the other vice-presidents. A multidivisional company would benefit from establishing a strong corporate marketing department to consult and strengthen divisional marketing programs.

6. *Develop Strong In-House Marketing Training Programs:* The company should design well-crafted marketing training programs for top corporate management, divisional general managers, marketing and sales personnel, manufacturing personnel, R&D personnel, and so on. These programs should deliver marketing knowledge, skills, and attitudes to company managers and employees.

7. *Install a Modern Marketing-Planning System:* An excellent way to train managers in marketing thinking is to install a modern market-oriented planning system. The planning format will require managers to think about the market environment, marketing opportunities, competitive trends, and other outside forces. These managers would then prepare marketing strategies and sales and profit forecasts for specific products and segments and be accountable for performance.

8. *Establish an Annual Marketing Excellence Recognition Program:* The company should encourage business units that believe they have developed a great marketing plan to submit a description of the plan and results. A special committee would review these plans, select the best plans, and reward the winning teams at a special ceremony. These plans would be disseminated to the other business units as "models of marketing thinking." Such programs are carried on by Arthur Andersen, Becton-Dickinson, and Du Pont.

9. *Consider Reorganizing from a Product-Centered Company to a Market-Centered Company:* Many companies consist of product divisions, with each product division selling in many markets. Thus, six GE divisions may independently sell products to the auto industry. Becoming market centered means setting up an organization that will focus on the needs of specific industries (the auto industry, for example) and coordinate the planning and providing of the company's various products for each industry.

Du Pont exemplifies a company that successfully made the transition from an inward-looking to an outward-looking orientation. Under Richard Heckert's CEO leadership, Du Pont undertook a number of initiatives to build a "marketing community." Several divisions were reorganized along market lines. Du Pont held a series of marketing management training seminars, which were ultimately attended by 300 senior people, 2,000 middle managers, and 14,000 employees. Du Pont established a corporate marketing excellence recognition program and honored 32 Du Pont employees from around the world who had developed innovative marketing strategies, service improvements, and so on.[11]

Hewlett-Packard also launched a drive to become more market oriented. Hewlett-Packard conducted deep studies of customer need and satisfaction; introduced a major total-quality-improvement program; developed better links and teamwork between marketing and other departments; and created a system of measurements of market-oriented performance.

SAS, British Air, Ford, and other major companies also showed that achieving a marketing culture is both possible and profitable. It takes a great amount of planning and patience to get managers to accept the fact that customers are the foundation of the company's business and future. But it can be done.

Marketing Implementation

We now turn to the question of how marketing managers can effectively implement marketing plans. A brilliant strategic marketing plan counts for little if it is not implemented properly. Consider the following example:

> A chemical company decided that customers were not getting good service from any of the competitors. The company decided that it would make customer service its strategic thrust. When this strategy failed, a postmortem revealed a number of implementation failures. The customer-service department continued to be held in low regard by top management; it was undermanned; and it was used as a dumping ground for weak managers. Furthermore, the company's reward system continued to focus on cost containment and current profitability. The company had failed to make the changes required to carry out its strategy.

We define marketing implementation as follows:

❖ Marketing implementation *is the process that turns marketing plans into action assignments and ensures that such assignments are executed in a manner that accomplishes the plan's stated objectives.*

Whereas strategy addresses the *what* and *why* of marketing activities, implementation addresses the *who, where, when,* and *how.* Strategy and implementation are closely related in that one "layer" of strategy implies certain tactical implementation assignments at a lower level. For example, top management's strategic decision to "harvest" a product must be translated into specific actions and assignments.

Bonoma identified four skills related to the effective implementation of marketing programs:

- ◆ Skills in recognizing and diagnosing a problem
- ◆ Skills in assessing the company level where the problem exists
- ◆ Skills in implementing plans
- ◆ Skills in evaluating implementation results[12]

We will examine these skills in the following paragraphs.

Diagnostic Skills

The close interrelationship between strategy and implementation can pose difficult diagnostic problems when marketing programs do not fulfill their expectations. Was the low sales rate the result of poor strategy or poor implementation? Moreover, is the issue to determine what the problem *is* (diagnosis) or what should be *done* about it (action)? Each problem calls for specific management tools and solutions.

Company Levels

Marketing implementation problems can occur at three levels. One level is that of carrying out a *marketing function* successfully. For example, how can the company get more creative advertising from its advertising agency? Another level is that of implementing a *marketing program* that has to blend marketing functions into a coherent whole. This problem arises in launching a new product into the marketplace. A third level is that of implementing a *marketing policy*. For example, the company might want every employee to treat the customer as number one.

Marketing Implementation Skills

A set of skills must be practiced at each company level—functions, programs, policies—to achieve effective implementation. The four skills are allocating, monitoring, organizing, and interacting.

Allocating skills are used by marketing managers in budgeting resources (time, money, and personnel) to functions, programs, and policies; for example, determining how much money to spend on trade shows (functions level) or what warranty work to perform on "marginal" products (policies level) are problems requiring allocation skills.

Monitoring skills are used in managing a system of controls to evaluate the results of marketing actions. Controls can be of four types: annual-plan control, profitability control, efficiency control, and strategic control (see Chapter 27).

Organizing skills are used in developing an effective working organization. Understanding the informal as well as formal marketing organization is important to carrying out effective implementation.

Interacting skills refer to the ability of managers to get things done by influencing others. Marketers must not only motivate the company's own people but must also motivate outsiders—marketing research firms, ad agencies, dealers, wholesalers, agents—whose objectives might differ from the company's.

Good market results do not necessarily prove that there was good marketing implementation. Perhaps the product or the strategy was exceptional, not the implementation. Better implementation may have produced even better results. Clearly, companies must do their best to excel at both strategy and implementation.

SUMMARY ❖

This chapter examined how marketing is organized, how it relates to other company functions, and how marketing strategies must be implemented to succeed in the marketplace.

The modern marketing department evolved through several stages. It started as a sales department and later took on ancillary functions, such as advertising and marketing research. As the ancillary functions grew in importance, many companies created a separate marketing department to manage them. Sales and marketing people generally worked well together. Eventually, the two departments were merged into a modern marketing department headed by a marketing and sales vice-president. A modern marketing department, however, does not automatically create a modern marketing company unless all the other departments and employees accept and practice a customer orientation.

Modern marketing departments are organized in a number of ways. A functional marketing organization is one in which marketing functions are headed by separate managers reporting to the marketing vice-president. A product management organization is one in which products are assigned to product managers, who work with functional specialists to develop and implement their plans. A market management organization is one in which major markets are assigned to market managers, who work with functional specialists to develop and implement their plans. Some large companies use a combined product and market management organization called a matrix organization. Finally, multidivisional companies have to decide whether to establish a corporate marketing department as well as divisional marketing departments.

Marketing must work harmoniously with the other company departments. In its pursuit of customers' interests, marketing often comes into conflict with R&D, engineering, purchasing, manufacturing, inventory, finance, accounting, credit, and other functions. These conflicts can be reduced when the company president commits the company to a customer orientation and when the marketing vice-president learns to work effectively with the other executives. Acquiring a modern marketing orientation requires presidential support, a marketing task force, outside marketing consulting help, a corporate marketing department, in-house marketing seminars, marketing talent hired from the outside and promoted inside, and a market-oriented marketing-planning system.

Those responsible for the marketing function must develop effective strategies and also implement them successfully. Marketing implementation is the process of turning plans into action assignments describing who does what, when, and how. Effective implementation requires skills in allocating, monitoring, organizing, and interacting at the level of marketing functions, programs, and policies.

NOTES ❖

1. Andrall E. Pearson and Thomas W. Wilson, Jr., *Making Your Organization Work* (New York: Association of National Advertisers, 1967), pp. 8–13.

2. Mark Hanan, "Reorganize Your Company Around Its Markets," *Harvard Business Review,* November–December 1974, pp. 63–74.

3. See B. Charles Ames, "Dilemma of Product/Market Management," *Harvard Business Review,* March–April 1971, pp. 66–74.

4. See Watson Snyder, Jr. and Frank B. Gray, *The Corporate Marketing Staff: Its Role and Effectiveness in Multi-Division Companies* (Cambridge, MA: Marketing Science Institute, April 1971).

5. For further reading on marketing organization, see Nigel Piercy, *Marketing Organization: An Analysis of Information Processing, Power and Politics* (London: George Allen & Unwin, 1985); Robert W. Ruekert, Orville C. Walker, and Kenneth J. Roering, "The Organization of Marketing Activities: A Contingency Theory of Structure and Performance," *Journal of Marketing,* Winter 1985, pp. 13–25; and Tyzoon T. Tyebjee, Albert V. Bruno, and Shelby H. McIntyre, "Growing Ventures Can Anticipate Marketing Stages," *Harvard Business Review,* January–February 1983, pp. 2–4.

6. Askok K. Gupta, S. P. Raj, and David Wilemon, "A Model for Studying R&D-Marketing Interface in the Product Innovation Process," *Journal of Marketing,* April 1986, pp. 7–17.

7. See William E. Souder, *Managing New Product Innovations* (Lexington, MA: Heath, 1987), Chaps. 10–11; and William L. Shanklin and John K. Ryans, Jr., "Organizing for High-Tech Marketing," *Harvard Business Review,* November–December 1984, pp. 164–71.

8. See Benson P. Shapiro, "Can Marketing and Manufacturing Coexist?" *Harvard Business Review,* September–October 1977, pp. 104–14. Also see Robert W. Ruekert and Orville C. Walker, Jr., "Marketing's Interaction with Other Functional Units: A Conceptual Framework and Empirical Evidence," *Journal of Marketing,* January 1987, pp. 1–19.

9. See J. Patrick Wright, *On a Clear Day You Can See General Motors* (New York: Avon Books, 1979), Chap. 8.

10. See Stephanie Strom, "Sears to Spend $4 Billion to Remake Itself as Retailer," *The New York Times*, February 12, 1993, pp. C1, C15.

11. Edward E. Messikomer, "DuPont's `Marketing Community,'" *Business Marketing,* October 1987, pp. 90–94.

12. Thomas V. Bonoma, *The Marketing Edge: Making Strategies Work* (New York: Free Press, 1985). Much of this section is based on Bonoma's work.

Evaluating and Controlling Marketing Performance

Having lost sight of our objective, we redoubled our efforts.

OLD ADAGE

If anything can go wrong, it will.

MURPHY'S LAW

The marketing department's job is to plan and control marketing activity. Because many surprises will occur during the implementation of marketing plans, the marketing department has to continuously monitor and control marketing activities. In spite of this need, many companies have inadequate control procedures. This conclusion was reached in a study of 75 companies of varying sizes in different industries. The main findings were these:

- Small companies have poorer controls than large companies. They do a poorer job of setting clear objectives and establishing systems to measure performance.
- Fewer than half of the companies know the profitability of their individual products. About one third of the companies have no regular review procedures for spotting and deleting weak products.
- Almost half of the companies fail to compare their prices with competition, to analyze their warehousing and distribution costs, to analyze the causes of returned merchandise, to conduct formal evaluations of advertising effectiveness, and to review their salesforce call reports.
- Many companies take four to eight weeks to develop control reports, and they are occasionally inaccurate.

Four types of marketing control can be distinguished (Table 27-1). We now turn to these four types of marketing control.

Annual-Plan Control

The purpose of annual-plan control is to ensure that the company achieves the sales, profits, and other goals established in its annual plan. The heart of annual-plan control is *management by objectives*. Four steps are involved (see Figure 27-1). First, management sets monthly or quarterly goals. Second, management monitors its performance in the marketplace. Third, management determines the causes of serious performance deviations. Fourth, management takes corrective action to close the gaps between its goals and performance. This could require changing the action programs or even changing the goals.

This control model applies to all levels of the organization. Top management sets sales and profit goals for the year. These goals are elaborated into specific goals for each lower level of management. Thus each product manager is committed to

FIGURE 27-1
The Control Process

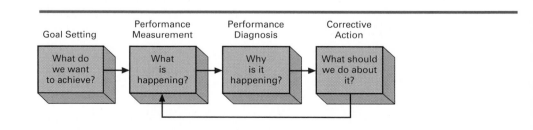

Goal Setting	Performance Measurement	Performance Diagnosis	Corrective Action
What do we want to achieve?	What is happening?	Why is it happening?	What should we do about it?

TABLE 27-1
Types of Marketing Control

TYPE OF CONTROL	PRIME RESPONSIBILITY	PURPOSE OF CONTROL	APPROACHES
I. Annual-plan control	Top management Middle management	To examine whether the planned results are being achieved	Sales analysis Market-share analysis Sales-to-expense ratios Financial analysis Satisfaction tracking
II. Profitability control	Marketing controller	To examine where the company is making and losing money	Profitability by: product territory customer segment trade channel order size
III. Efficiency control	Line and staff management Marketing controller	To evaluate and improve the spending efficiency and impact of marketing expenditures	Efficiency of: salesforce advertising sales promotion distribution
IV. Strategic control	Top management Marketing auditor	To examine whether the company is pursuing its best opportunities with respect to markets, products, and channels	Marketing-effectiveness rating instrument Marketing audit Marketing excellence review Company ethical and social responsibility review

attaining specified levels of sales and costs. Each regional and district sales manager and each sales representative is also committed to specific goals. Each period, top management reviews and interprets the results and ascertains whether any corrective action is needed.

Managers use five tools to check on plan performance: sales analysis, market-share analysis, marketing expense-to-sales analysis, financial analysis, and customer-satisfaction tracking.

Sales Analysis

Sales analysis consists of measuring and evaluating actual sales in relation to sales goals. There are two specific tools in this connection.

Sales-variance analysis measures the relative contribution of different factors to a gap in sales performance. Suppose the annual plan called for selling 4,000 widgets in the first quarter at $1 per widget, or $4,000. At quarter's end, only 3,000 widgets were sold at $.80 per widget, or $2,400. The sales performance variance is $1,600, or 40% of expected sales. The question arises, How much of this underperformance is due to the price decline and how much to the volume decline? The following calculation answers this question:

$$
\begin{array}{lll}
\text{Variance due to price decline} & = (\$1.00 - \$.80)(3,000) = & \$\ 600 \quad 37.5\% \\
\text{Variance due to volume decline} & = (\$1.00)(4,000 - 3,000) = & \underline{\$1,000} \quad \underline{62.5\%} \\
& & \$1,600 \quad 100.0\%
\end{array}
$$

Almost two thirds of the sales variance is due to a failure to achieve the volume target. The company should look closely at why it failed to achieve its expected sales volume.[1]

Microsales analysis may provide the answer. *Microsales analysis* looks at specific products, territories, and so forth, that failed to produce expected sales. Suppose the company sells in three territories and expected sales were 1,500 units, 500 units, and 2,000 units, respectively, adding up to 4,000 widgets. The actual sales volume was 1,400 units, 525 units, and 1,075 units, respectively. Thus territory 1 showed a 7% shortfall in terms of expected sales; territory 2, a 5% surplus; and territory 3, a 46% shortfall! Territory 3 is causing most of the trouble. The sales vice-president can check into territory 3 to see which hypothesis explains the poor performance: Territory 3's sales representative is loafing or has a personal problem; a major competitor has entered this territory; or GNP is depressed in this territory.

Market-Share Analysis

Company sales do not reveal how well the company is performing relative to competitors. For this purpose, management needs to track its market share (see Marketing Concepts and Tools 27-1). If the company's market share goes up, the

Marketing Concepts and Tools 27-1

Defining and Measuring Market Share

The first step in using market-share analysis is to define which measure(s) of market share will be used. Four different measures are available.

◆ *Overall Market Share:* The company's overall market share is its sales expressed as a percentage of total market sales. Two decisions are necessary to use this measure. The first is whether to use unit sales or dollar sales to express market share. The other decision has to do with defining the total market. For example, Harley Davidson's share of the American motorcycle market depends on whether motor scooters and motorized bikes are included. If yes, then Harley Davidson's share will be smaller.

◆ *Served Market Share:* The company's served market share is its sales expressed as a percentage of the total sales to its served market. Its served market is all the buyers who would be able and willing to buy its product. If Harley Davidson only produces and sells expensive motorcycles on the East Coast, its served market share would be its sales as a percentage of the total sales of expensive motorcycles sold on the East Coast. A company's served market share is always larger than its overall market share. A company could capture 100% of its served market and yet have a relatively small share of the total market. A company's first task is to win the lion's share of its served market. As it approaches this goal, it should add new product lines and territories to enlarge its served market.

◆ *Relative Market Share (to Top Three Competitors):* This involves expressing the company's sales as a percentage

of the combined sales of the three largest competitors. If the company has 30% of the market, and the next two largest competitors have 20% and 10%, then this company's relative market share is 50% = 30/60. If each of the three companies had $33\frac{1}{3}$% of the market, then any company's relative market share would be $33\frac{1}{3}$%. Relative market shares above 33% are considered to be strong.

◆ *Relative Market Share (to Leading Competitor):* Some companies track their shares as a percentage of the leading competitor's sales. A relative market share greater than 100% indicates a market leader. A relative market share of exactly 100% means that the firm is tied for the lead. A rise in the company's relative market share means that it is gaining on its leading competitor.

After choosing which market-share measure(s) to use, the company must collect the necessary data. Overall market share is normally the most available measure, since it requires only total industry sales, and these are often available in government or trade association publications. Estimating served market share is harder; it will be affected by changes in the company's product line and geographical market coverage, among other things. Estimating relative market shares is still harder because the company will have to estimate the sales of specific competitors, who guard these figures. The company has to use indirect means, such as learning about competitors' purchase rate of raw materials or the number of shifts they are operating. In the consumer-goods area, individual brand shares are available through syndicated store and consumer panels.

company is gaining on competitors; if it goes down, the company is losing relative to competitors.

These conclusions from market-share analysis, however, are subject to certain qualifications:

- *The Assumption That Outside Forces Affect All Companies in the Same Way Is Often Not True:* The U.S. Surgeon General's Report on the harmful consequences of cigarette smoking caused total cigarette sales to falter but not equally for all companies. Companies with better filters were hurt less.
- *The Assumption That a Company's Performance Should Be Judged Against the Average Performance of All Companies Is Not Always Valid:* A company's performance should be judged against the performance of its closest competitors.
- *If a New Firm Enters the Industry, Then Every Existing Firm's Market Share Might Fall:* A decline in a company's market share might not mean that the company is performing any worse than other companies. A company's share loss will depend on the degree to which the new firm hits the company's specific markets.
- *Sometimes a Market-Share Decline Is Deliberately Engineered by a Company to Improve Profits:* For example, management might drop unprofitable customers or products to improve its profits.
- *Market Share Can Fluctuate for Many Minor Reasons:* For example, market share can be affected by whether a large sale occurs on the last day of the month or at the beginning of the next month. Not all shifts in market share have marketing significance.[2]

Managers must carefully interpret market-share movements by product line, customer type, region, and other breakdowns. A useful way to analyze market-share movements is in terms of four components:

$$\begin{array}{c}\text{Overall}\\\text{Market}\\\text{Share}\end{array} = \begin{array}{c}\text{Customer}\\\text{penetration}\end{array} \times \begin{array}{c}\text{Customer}\\\text{loyalty}\end{array} \times \begin{array}{c}\text{Customer}\\\text{selectivity}\end{array} \times \begin{array}{c}\text{Price}\\\text{selectivity}\end{array} \qquad (27\text{-}1)$$

where:

- *Customer penetration* is the percentage of all customers who buy from this company.
- *Customer loyalty* is the purchases from this company by its customers expressed as a percentage of their total purchases from all suppliers of the same products.
- *Customer selectivity* is the size of the average customer purchase from the company expressed as a percentage of the size of the average customer purchase from an average company.
- *Price selectivity* is the average price charged by this company expressed as a percentage of the average price charged by all companies.

Now suppose the company's dollar market share falls during the period. Equation 27-1 provides four possible explanations. The company lost some of its customers (lower customer penetration). Existing customers are buying a smaller share of their total supplies from this company (lower customer loyalty). The company's remaining customers are smaller in size (lower customer selectivity). The company's price has slipped relative to competition (lower price selectivity).

By tracking these factors through time, the company can diagnose the underlying cause of market-share changes. Suppose at the beginning of the period, customer penetration was 60%; customer loyalty, 50%; customer selectivity, 80%; and price selectivity, 125%. According to 27-1, the company's market share was 30%. Suppose that at the end of the period, the company's market share fell to 27%. In checking, the company finds customer penetration at 55%, customer loyalty at 50%, customer selectivity at 75%, and price selectivity at 130%. Clearly, the market-share decline was due mainly to a loss of customers (fall in customer penetration) who normally made larger-than-average purchases (fall in customer selectivity). The manager can now investigate why these customers were lost.

Marketing Expense-to-Sales Analysis

Annual-plan control requires making sure that the company is not overspending to achieve its sales goals. The key ratio to watch is *marketing expense-to-sales*. In one company, this ratio was 30% and consisted of five component expense-to-sales ratios: *salesforce-to-sales* (15%); *advertising-to-sales* (5%); *sales promotion-to-sales* (6%); *marketing research-to-sales* (1%); and *sales administration-to-sales* (3%).

Management needs to monitor these marketing-expense ratios. They will normally exhibit small fluctuations that can be ignored. But fluctuations outside of the normal range are a cause for concern. The period-to-period fluctuations in each ratio can be tracked on a *control chart* (Figure 27-2). This chart shows that the advertising expense-to-sales ratio normally fluctuates between 8% and 12%, say 99 out of 100 times. In the fifteenth period, however, the ratio exceeded the upper control limit. One of two hypotheses can explain this occurrence:

- *Hypothesis A:* The company still has good expense control, and this situation represents one of those rare chance events.

- *Hypothesis B:* The company has lost control over this expense and should find the cause.

If hypothesis A is accepted, no investigation is made to determine whether the environment has changed. The risk in not investigating is that some real change might have occurred, and the company will fall behind. If hypothesis B is accepted, the environment is investigated at the risk that the investigation will uncover nothing and be a waste of time and effort.

The behavior of successive observations even within the control limits should be watched. Note that the level of the expense-to-sales ratio rose steadily from the ninth period onward. The probability of encountering six successive increases in

FIGURE 27-2
The Control-Chart Model

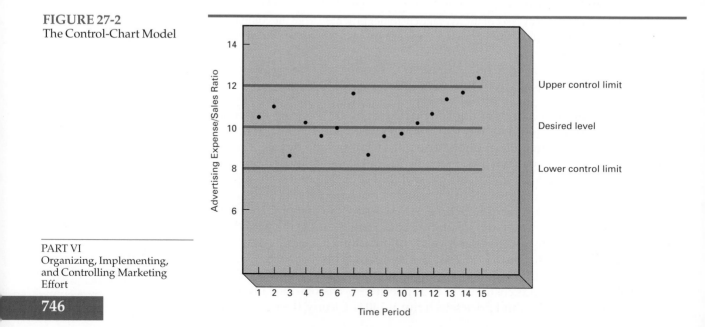

what should be independent events is only 1 in 64.[3] This unusual pattern should have led to an investigation sometime before the fifteenth observation.

When an expense-to-sales ratio gets out of control, disaggregative data are needed to track down the problem. An *expense-to-sales deviation chart* can be used. Figure 27-3 shows the performances of different sales districts in terms of their sales-quota attainment and expense attainment in percentages. For example, district D achieved its sales quota close to the expected expense level. District B exceeded its quota, and its expenses are proportionately higher. The most troubling districts are in the second quadrant. For example, district J achieved less than 80% of its quota, and its expenses are disproportionately high. The next step is to prepare a chart for each deviant district showing sales representatives' standings. Within district J, for example, the poor performance might be associated with one or a few specific sales representatives.

Financial Analysis

The expenses-to-sales ratios should be analyzed in an overall financial framework to determine how and where the company is making its money. Marketers are increasingly using financial analysis to find profitable strategies and not just sales-building strategies.

Financial analysis is used by management to identify the factors that affect the company's *rate of return on net worth.*[4] The main factors are shown in Figure 27-4, along with illustrative numbers for a large chain-store retailer. The retailer is earning a 12.5% return on net worth. The return on net worth is the product of two ratios, the company's *return on assets* and its *financial leverage.* To improve its return on net worth, the company must either increase the ratio of its net profits to its assets or increase the ratio of its assets to its net worth. The company should analyze the composition of its assets (i.e., cash, accounts receivable, inventory, and plant and equipment) and see if it can improve its asset management.

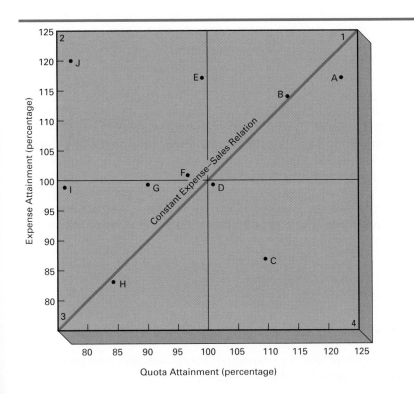

FIGURE 27-3
Comparison of Expense and Revenue Deviations by District
Source: Adapted from D. M. Phelps and J. H. Westing, *Marketing Management*, 3rd ed. (Homewood, IL: Richard D. Irwin, Inc., 1968), p. 754. ©1968 by Richard D. Irwin, Inc.

CHAPTER 27
Evaluating and Controlling Marketing Performance

FIGURE 27-4
Financial Model of Return
on Net Worth

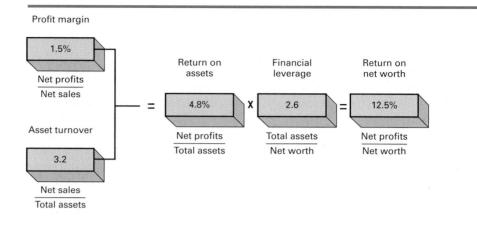

The return on assets is the product of two ratios, namely, the *profit margin* and the *asset turnover*. The profit margin seems low, while the asset turnover is more normal for retailing. The marketing executive can seek to improve performance in two ways: (1) to increase the profit margin by increasing sales or cutting costs; and (2) to increase the asset turnover by increasing sales or reducing the assets (e.g., inventory, receivables) that are held against a given level of sales.[5]

Customer-Satisfaction Tracking

The preceding control measures are largely financial and quantitative in character. They are important but not sufficient. Needed are qualitative measures that provide early warnings to management of impending market-share changes. Alert companies set up systems to monitor the attitudes and satisfaction of customers, dealers, and other stakeholders. By monitoring changing levels of customer preference and satisfaction before they affect sales, management can take earlier action. The main customer-satisfaction tracking systems were described in Chapter 2, pp. 41-42.

Corrective Action

When performance deviates too much from the plan's goals, management needs to undertake corrective action. Normally the company undertakes minor corrective actions, and if they fail to work, the company adopts more drastic measures. When a large fertilizer company's sales continued to decline, the company resorted to an increasingly drastic set of remedies. First the company ordered cutbacks in production. Then it cut its prices selectively. Next it put more pressure on its salesforce to meet their quotas. The company then cut the budgets for personnel hiring and training, advertising, public relations, and research and development. Soon it introduced personnel cuts through layoffs and early retirement. Next it cut investment in plant and equipment. The company then sold some of its businesses to other companies. Finally, the company sought a buyer.

Profitability Control

Here are some disconcerting findings from a bank profitability study:

We have found that anywhere from 20 to 40 percent of an individual institution's products are unprofitable, and up to 60 percent of their accounts generate losses.

Our research has shown that, in most firms, more than half of all customer relationships are not profitable, and 30 to 40 percent are only marginally so. It is frequently a mere 10 to 15 percent of a firm's relationships that generate the bulk of its profits.

Our profitability research into the branch system of a regional bank produced some surprising results . . . 30 percent of the bank's branches were unprofitable.[6]

Companies clearly need to measure the profitability of their various products, territories, customer groups, trade channels, and order sizes. This information will help management determine whether any products or marketing activities should be expanded, reduced, or eliminated.

Methodology of Marketing-Profitability Analysis

We will illustrate the steps in marketing-profitability analysis with the following example:

The marketing vice-president of a lawnmower company wants to determine the profitability of selling its lawnmower through three types of retail channels: hardware stores, garden supply shops, and department stores. Its profit-and-loss statement is shown in Table 27-2.

STEP 1: IDENTIFYING THE FUNCTIONAL EXPENSES ❖ Assume that the expenses listed in Table 27-2 are incurred to sell the product, advertise it, pack and deliver it, and bill and collect for it. The first task is to measure how much of each expense was incurred in each activity.

Suppose that most salary expense went to sales representatives and the rest went to an advertising manager, packing and delivery help, and an office accountant. Let the breakdown of the $9,300 be $5,100, $1,200, $1,400, and $1,600, respectively. Table 27-3 shows the allocation of the salary expense to these four activities.

Table 27-3 also shows the rent account of $3,000 as allocated to the four activities. Since the sales representatives work away from the office, none of the building's rent expense is assigned to selling. Most of the expenses for floor space and

Sales		$60,000
Cost of goods sold		39,000
Gross margin		$21,000
Expenses		
Salaries	$9,300	
Rent	3,000	
Supplies	3,500	
		15,800
Net profit		$ 5,200

TABLE 27-2
A Simplified Profit-and-Loss Statement

NATURAL ACCOUNTS	TOTAL	SELLING	ADVERTISING	PACKING AND DELIVERY	BILLING AND COLLECTING
Salaries	$ 9,300	$5,100	$1,200	$1,400	$1,600
Rent	3,000	—	400	2,000	600
Supplies	3,500	400	1,500	1,400	200
	$15,800	$5,500	$3,100	$4,800	$2,400

TABLE 27-3
Mapping Natural Expenses into Functional Expenses

rented equipment are in connection with packing and delivery. A small portion of the floor space is used by the advertising manager and office accountant.

Finally, the supplies account covers promotional materials, packing materials, fuel purchases for delivery, and home-office stationery. The $3,500 in this account is reassigned to the functional uses made of the supplies. Table 27-3 summarizes how the natural expenses of $15,800 were translated into functional expenses.

STEP 2: ASSIGNING THE FUNCTIONAL EXPENSES TO THE MARKETING ENTITIES ❖ The next task is to measure how much functional expense was associated with selling through each type of channel. Consider the selling effort. The selling effort is indicated by the number of sales made in each channel. This number is found in the selling column of Table 27-4. Altogether, 275 sales calls were made during the period. Since the total selling expense amounted to $5,500 (see Table 27-4), the selling expense per call averaged $20.

Advertising expense can be allocated according to the number of ads addressed to the different channels. Since there were 100 ads altogether, the average ad cost $31.

The packing and delivery expense is allocated according to the number of orders placed by each type of channel; this same basis was used for allocating billing and collection expense.

STEP 3: PREPARING A PROFIT-AND-LOSS STATEMENT FOR EACH MARKETING ENTITY ❖ A profit-and-loss statement can now be prepared for each type of channel. The results are shown in Table 27-5. Since hardware stores ac-

TABLE 27-4
Bases for Allocating Functional Expenses to Channels

CHANNEL TYPE	SELLING	ADVERTISING	PACKING AND DELIVERY	BILLING AND COLLECTING
Hardware	200	50	50	50
Garden supply	65	20	21	21
Department stores	10	30	9	9
	275	100	80	80
Functional expense	$5,500	$3,100	$4,800	$2,400
No. of Units	275	100	80	80
Equals	$20	$31	$60	$30

TABLE 27-5
Profit-and-Loss Statements for Channels

	HARDWARE	GARDEN SUPPLY	DEPT. STORES	WHOLE COMPANY
Sales	$30,000	$10,000	$20,000	$60,000
Cost of goods sold	19,500	6,500	13,000	39,000
Gross margin	$10,500	$ 3,500	$ 7,000	$21,000
Expenses				
Selling ($20 per call)	$ 4,000	$ 1,300	$ 200	$ 5,500
Advertising ($31 per advertisement)	1,550	620	930	3,100
Packing and delivery ($60 per order)	3,000	1,260	540	4,800
Billing ($30 per order)	1,500	630	270	2,400
Total Expenses	$10,050	$ 3,810	$ 1,940	$15,800
Net profit or loss	$ 450	$ (310)	$ 5,060	$ 5,200

counted for one half of total sales ($30,000 out of $60,000), this channel is charged with half the cost of goods sold ($19,500 out of $39,000). This leaves a gross margin from hardware stores of $10,500. From this must be deducted the proportions of the functional expenses that hardware stores consumed. According to Table 27-4, hardware stores received 200 out of 275 total sales calls. At an imputed value of $20 a call, hardware stores have to be charged with a $4,000 selling expense. Table 27-4 also shows that hardware stores were the target of 50 ads. At $31 an ad, the hardware stores are charged with $1,550 of advertising. The same reasoning applies in computing the share of the other functional expenses to charge to hardware stores. The result is that hardware stores gave rise to $10,500 of the total expenses. Subtracting this from the gross margin, the profit of selling through hardware stores is only $450.

This analysis is repeated for the other channels. The company is losing money in selling through garden supply shops and makes virtually all of its profits in selling through department stores. Notice that the gross sales through each channel are not a reliable indicator of the net profits being made in each channel.

Determining the Best Corrective Action

It would be naive to conclude that garden supply shops and possibly hardware stores should be dropped in order to concentrate on department stores. The following questions would need to be answered first:

- To what extent do buyers buy on the basis of the type of retail outlet versus the brand? Would they seek out the brand in those channels that were not eliminated?
- What are the trends with respect to the importance of these three channels?
- Have company marketing strategies directed at the three channels been optimal?

On the basis of the answers, marketing management can evaluate a number of alternative actions:

- *Establish a Special Charge for Handling Smaller Orders:* This move assumes that small orders are a cause of the relative unprofitability of dealing with garden supply shops and hardware stores.
- *Give More Promotional Aid to Garden Supply Shops and Hardware Stores:* This assumes that the store managers could increase their sales with more training or promotional materials.
- *Reduce the Number of Sales Calls and the Amount of Advertising Going to Garden Supply Shops and Hardware Stores:* This assumes that some costs can be saved without seriously hurting sales in these channels.
- *Do Nothing:* This assumes that current marketing efforts are optimal and either that marketing trends point to an imminent profit improvement in the weaker channels or that dropping any channel would reduce profits because of repercussions on production costs or on demand.
- *Do Not Abandon Any Channel as a Whole but Only the Weakest Retail Units in Each Channel:* This assumes that a detailed cost study would reveal many profitable garden shops and hardware stores whose profits are concealed by the poor performance of other stores in these categories.

In general, marketing-profitability analysis indicates the relative profitability of different channels, products, territories, or other marketing entities.[7] It does not prove that the best course of action is to drop the unprofitable marketing entities, nor does it capture the likely profit improvement if these marginal marketing entities are dropped.

Direct versus Full Costing

Like all information tools, marketing-profitability analysis can lead or mislead marketing executives, depending upon the degree of their understanding of its methods and limitations. The example showed some arbitrariness in the choice of bases for allocating the functional expenses to the marketing entities being evaluated. Thus the "number of sales calls" was used to allocate selling expenses, when in principle, "number of sales working-hours" is a more accurate indicator of cost. The former base was used because it involves less record keeping and computation. These approximations might not involve too much inaccuracy, but marketing executives should acknowledge this judgmental element in determining marketing costs.[8]

Far more serious is another judgmental element affecting profitability analysis. The issue is whether to allocate *full costs* or only *direct and traceable costs* in evaluating the performance of a marketing entity. The preceding example sidestepped this problem by assuming only simple costs that fit in with marketing activities. But the question cannot be avoided in the actual analysis of profitability. Three types of costs have to be distinguished:

♦ *Direct Costs:* These are costs that can be assigned directly to the proper marketing entities. For example, sales commissions are a direct cost in a profitability analysis of sales territories, sales representatives, or customers. Advertising expenditures are a direct cost in a profitability analysis of products to the extent that each advertisement promotes only one company product. Other direct costs for specific purposes are salesforce salaries, supplies, and traveling expenses.

♦ *Traceable Common Costs:* These are costs that can be assigned only indirectly, but on a plausible basis, to the marketing entities. In the example, rent was analyzed in this way. The company's floor space was needed for three different marketing activities, and an estimate was made of how much floor space supported each activity.

♦ *Nontraceable Common Costs:* These are costs whose allocation to the marketing entities is highly arbitrary. Consider "corporate image" expenditures. To allocate them equally to all products would be arbitrary, because all products do not benefit equally from corporate image making. To allocate them proportionately to the sales of the various products would be arbitrary because relative product sales reflect many factors besides corporate image making. Other typical examples of difficult-to-assign common costs are top management salaries, taxes, interest, and other types of overhead.

No one disputes including direct costs in marketing cost analysis. There is a small amount of controversy about including traceable common costs. Traceable common costs lump together costs that would change with the scale of marketing activity and costs that would not change. If the lawnmower company drops garden supply shops, it will probably continue to pay the same rent for contractual reasons. In this event, its profits would not rise immediately by the amount of the present loss in selling to garden supply shops ($310). The profit figures are more meaningful when traceable costs can be eliminated.

The major controversy concerns whether the nontraceable common costs should be allocated to the marketing entities. Such allocation is called the *full-cost approach*, and its advocates argue that all costs must ultimately be imputed in order to determine true profitability. But this argument confuses the use of accounting for financial reporting with its use for managerial decision making. Full costing has three major weaknesses:

♦ The relative profitability of different marketing entities can shift radically when one arbitrary way to allocate nontraceable common costs is replaced by another. This weakens confidence in the tool.

- The arbitrariness demoralizes managers, who feel that their performance is judged adversely.
- The inclusion of nontraceable common costs could weaken efforts at real cost control. Operating management is most effective in controlling direct costs and traceable common costs. Arbitrary assignments of nontraceable common costs can lead them to spend their time fighting the arbitrary cost allocations rather than managing their controllable costs well.

Companies are showing a growing interest in using *activity-based cost accounting* (ABC) in interpreting the true profitability of different activities. According to Cooper and Kaplan, this tool "can give managers a clear picture of how products, brands, customers, facilities, regions, or distribution channels both generate revenues and consume resources."[9] To improve profitability, the managers can then examine ways to reduce the resources required to perform various activities, or make the resources more productive or acquire them at a lower cost. Alternatively, management may raise prices on products that consume heavy amounts of support resources. The contribution of ABC is to refocus management's attention away from using only labor or material standard costs to allocate full cost to capturing the actual costs of supporting individual products, customers, and other entities.

Efficiency Control

Suppose a profitability analysis reveals that the company is earning poor profits in connection with certain products, territories, or markets. The question is whether there are more efficient ways to manage the salesforce, advertising, sales promotion, and distribution in connection with these poorer-performing marketing entities.

Some companies have established a *marketing controller* position to assist marketing personnel to improve marketing efficiency. Marketing controllers work out of the controller's office but are specialized in the marketing side of the business. At companies such as General Foods, Du Pont, and Johnson & Johnson, they perform a sophisticated financial analysis of marketing expenditures and results. Specifically, they examine adherence to profit plans, help prepare brand managers' budgets, measure the efficiency of promotions, analyze media production costs, evaluate customer and geographic profitability, and educate marketing personnel on the financial implications of marketing decisions.[10]

Salesforce Efficiency

Sales managers need to monitor the following key indicators of salesforce efficiency in their territory:

- Average number of sales calls per salesperson per day
- Average sales-call time per contact
- Average revenue per sales call
- Average cost per sales call
- Entertainment cost per sales call
- Percentage of orders per 100 sales calls
- Number of new customers per period
- Number of lost customers per period
- Salesforce cost as a percentage of total sales

These indicators raise such useful questions as the following: Are sales representatives making too few calls per day? Are they spending too much time per call? Are they spending too much on entertainment? Are they closing enough orders per hundred calls? Are they producing enough new customers and holding onto the old customers?

When a company starts investigating salesforce efficiency, it can often find areas for improvement. General Electric reduced the size of one of its divisional salesforces after discovering that its salespeople were calling on customers too often. When a large airline found that its salespeople were both selling and servicing, they transferred the servicing function to lower-paid clerks. Another company conducted time-and-duty studies and found ways to reduce the ratio of idle-to-productive time.

Advertising Efficiency

Many managers feel that it is almost impossible to measure what they are getting for their advertising dollars. But they should try to keep track of at least the following statistics:

◆ Advertising cost per thousand target buyers reached by media vehicle
◆ Percentage of audience who noted, saw/associated, and read most of each print ad
◆ Consumer opinions on the ad content and effectiveness
◆ Before-after measures of attitude toward the product
◆ Number of inquiries stimulated by the ad
◆ Cost per inquiry

Management can undertake a number of steps to improve advertising efficiency, including doing a better job of positioning the product, defining advertising objectives, pretesting messages, using the computer to guide the selection of advertising media, looking for better media buys, and doing advertising posttesting.

Sales-Promotion Efficiency

Sales promotion includes dozens of devices for stimulating buyer interest and product trial. To improve sales-promotion efficiency, management should record the costs and sales impact of each sales promotion. Management should watch the following statistics:

◆ Percentage of sales sold on deal
◆ Display costs per sales dollar
◆ Percentage of coupons redeemed
◆ Number of inquiries resulting from a demonstration.

If a sales-promotion manager is appointed, that manager can analyze the results of different sales promotions and advise product managers on the most cost-effective promotions to use.

Distribution Efficiency

Management needs to search for distribution economies. Several tools are available for improving inventory control, warehouse locations, and transportation modes. One problem that frequently arises is that distribution efficiency might decline when the company experiences strong sales increases. Peter Senge describes a situation where a strong sales surge causes the company to fall behind in meeting its promised delivery dates.[11] This leads customers to bad-mouth the company and eventually sales fall. Management responds by increasing salesforce incentives to secure more orders. The salesforce succeeds but once again the company slips in meeting its promised delivery dates. Management needs to perceive the real bottleneck and invest in more production and distribution capacity. The situation is mapped in Figure 27-5. The left loop shows how sales surges are transformed into sales declines because of delivery delays. The right loop shows the fundamental problem, which is the failure of management to invest in additional production and distribution capacity to meet substantial increases in sales.

Strategic Control

From time to time, companies need to undertake a critical review of their overall marketing goals and effectiveness. Marketing is an area where rapid obsolescence of objectives, policies, strategies, and programs is a constant possibility. Each company should periodically reassess its strategic approach to the marketplace. Two tools are available, namely, a *marketing-effectiveness rating review* and a *marketing audit*.

Marketing-Effectiveness Rating Review

Here is an actual situation.

The president of a major industrial-equipment company reviewed the annual business plans of various divisions and found several division plans lacking in marketing substance. He called in the corporate vice-president of marketing and said:

I am not happy with the quality of marketing in our divisions. It is very uneven. I want you to find out which of our divisions are strong, average, and weak in marketing. I want to know if they understand and are practicing customer-oriented marketing. I want a marketing score for each division. For each marketing-deficient division, I want a plan for improving its marketing effectiveness over the next several years. I want evidence next year that each marketing-deficient division is improving its market capabilities.

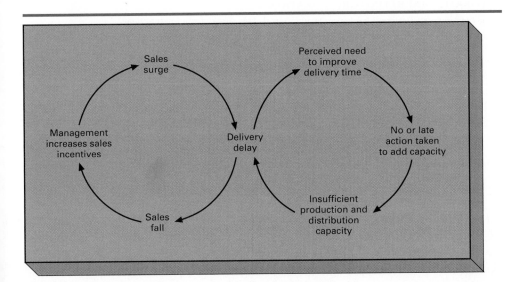

FIGURE 27-5
Dynamic Interactions Between Sales Orders and Distribution Efficiency
Source: Adapted from Peter M. Senge, *The Fifth Discipline.* © 1990 by Peter M. Senge. Used by permission of Doubleday, a division of Bantam Doubleday Dell Publishing Group, Inc.

The corporate marketing vice-president agreed, recognizing that it was a formidable task. His first inclination was to base the evaluation of marketing effectiveness on each division's performance in sales growth, market share, and profitability. His thinking was that high-performing divisions had good marketing leadership and poor-performing divisions had poor marketing leadership.

Marketing effectiveness is not necessarily revealed by current sales and profit performance. Good results could be due to a division's being in the right place at the right time, rather than having effective marketing management. Improvements in that division's marketing might boost results from good to excellent. Another division might have poor results in spite of excellent marketing planning. Replacing the present marketing managers might only make things worse.

The marketing effectiveness of a company or division is reflected in the degree to which it exhibits five major attributes of a marketing orientation: *customer philosophy, integrated marketing organization, adequate marketing information, strategic orientation, and operational efficiency.* Each attribute can be measured. Table 27-6 pre-

TABLE 27-6
Marketing-Effectiveness Rating Instrument (Check One Answer to Each Question)

CUSTOMER PHILOSOPHY

A. Does management recognize the importance of designing the company to serve the needs and wants of chosen markets?

0 ☐ Management primarily thinks in terms of selling current and new products to whomever will buy them.

1 ☐ Management thinks in terms of serving a wide range of markets and needs with equal effectiveness.

2 ☐ Management thinks in terms of serving the needs and wants of well-defined markets and market segments chosen for their long-run growth and profit potential for the company.

B. Does management develop different offerings and marketing plans for different segments of the market?

0 ☐ No.

1 ☐ Somewhat.

2 ☐ To a large extent.

C. Does management take a whole marketing system view (suppliers, channels, competitors, customers, environment) in planning its business?

0 ☐ No. Management concentrates on selling and servicing its immediate customers.

1 ☐ Somewhat. Management takes a long view of its channels although the bulk of its effort goes to selling and servicing the immediate customers.

2 ☐ Yes. Management takes a whole marketing systems view, recognizing the threats and opportunities created for the company by changes in any part of the system.

INTEGRATED MARKETING ORGANIZATION

D. Is there high-level marketing integration and control of the major marketing functions?

0 ☐ No. Sales and other marketing functions are not integrated at the top and there is some unproductive conflict.

1 ☐ Somewhat. There is formal integration and control of the major marketing functions but less than satisfactory coordination and cooperation.

2 ☐ Yes. The major marketing functions are effectively integrated.

E. Does marketing management work well with management in research, manufacturing, purchasing, physical distribution, and finance?

0 ☐ No. There are complaints that marketing is unreasonable in the demands and costs it places on other departments.

1 ☐ Somewhat. The relations are amicable although each department pretty much acts to serve its own interests.

2 ☐ Yes. The departments cooperate effectively and resolve issues in the best interest of the company as a whole.

F. How well organized is the new-product development process?

0 ☐ The system is ill-defined and poorly handled.

1 ☐ The system formally exists but lacks sophistication.

2 ☐ The system is well-structured and operates on teamwork principles.

TABLE 27-6 (cont.)

ADEQUATE MARKETING INFORMATION

G. *When were the latest marketing research studies of customers, buying influences, channels, and competitors conducted?*

0 ☐ Several years ago.

1 ☐ A few years ago.

2 ☐ Recently.

H. *How well does management know the sales potential and profitability of different market segments, customers, territories, products, channels, and order sizes?*

0 ☐ Not at all.

1 ☐ Somewhat.

2 ☐ Very well.

I. *What effort is expended to measure and improve the cost effectiveness of different marketing expenditures?*

0 ☐ Little or no effort.

1 ☐ Some effort.

2 ☐ Substantial effort.

STRATEGIC ORIENTATION

J. *What is the extent of formal marketing planning?*

0 ☐ Management conducts little or no formal marketing planning.

1 ☐ Management develops an annual marketing plan.

2 ☐ Management develops a detailed annual marketing plan and a strategic long-range plan that is updated annually.

K. *How impressive is the current marketing strategy?*

0 ☐ The current strategy is not clear.

1 ☐ The current strategy is clear and represents a continuation of traditional strategy.

2 ☐ The current strategy is clear, innovative, data based, and well reasoned.

L. *What is the extent of contingency thinking and planning?*

0 ☐ Management does little or no contingency thinking.

1 ☐ Management does some contingency thinking although little formal contingency planning.

2 ☐ Management formally identifies the most important contingencies and develops contingency plans.

OPERATIONAL EFFICIENCY

M. *How well is the marketing strategy communicated and implemented?*

0 ☐ Poorly.

1 ☐ Fairly.

2 ☐ Successfully.

N. *Is management doing an effective job with its marketing resources?*

0 ☐ No. The marketing resources are inadequate for the job to be done.

1 ☐ Somewhat. The marketing resources are adequate but they are not employed optimally.

2 ☐ Yes. The marketing resources are adequate and are employed efficiently.

O. *Does management show a good capacity to react quickly and effectively to on-the-spot developments?*

0 ☐ No. Sales and market information is not very current and management reaction time is slow.

1 ☐ Somewhat. Management receives fairly up-to-date sales and market information; management reaction time varies.

2 ☐ Yes. Management has installed systems yielding highly current information and fast reaction time.

TOTAL SCORE

The instrument is used in the following way. The appropriate answer is checked for each question. The scores are added—the total will be somewhere between 0 and 30. The following scale shows the level of marketing effectiveness:

0-5 = None	11-15 = Fair	21-25 = Very good
6-10 = Poor	16-20 = Good	26-30 = Superior

CHAPTER 27
Evaluating and Controlling
Marketing Performance

Source: Philip Kotler, "From Sales Obsession to Marketing Effectiveness," *Harvard Business Review,* November–December 1977, pp. 67–75.

sents a *marketing-effectiveness rating instrument* based on these five attributes. This instrument is filled out by marketing and other managers in the division. The scores are then summarized.

The instrument has been tested in a number of companies, and very few achieve scores within the superior range of 26 to 30 points. The few include well-known master marketers such as Procter & Gamble, McDonald's, IBM, and Nike. Most companies and divisions receive scores in the fair-to-good range, indicating that their own managers see room for marketing improvement. Low attribute scores indicate that the attribute needs attention. Divisional management can then establish a plan for correcting its major marketing weaknesses.[12]

The Marketing Audit

Those companies that discover marketing weaknesses through applying the marketing-effectiveness rating review should undertake a more thorough study known as a *marketing audit*.[13] We define *marketing audit* as follows:

❖ A marketing audit *is a comprehensive, systematic, independent, and periodic examination of a company's—or business unit's—marketing environment, objectives, strategies, and activities with a view to determining problem areas and opportunities and recommending a plan of action to improve the company's marketing performance.*

Let us examine the marketing audit's four characteristics:

- ◆ *Comprehensive:* The marketing audit covers all the major marketing activities of a business, not just a few trouble spots. It would be called a functional audit if it covered only the salesforce or pricing or some other marketing activity. Although functional audits are useful, they sometimes mislead management as to the real source of its problem. Excessive salesforce turnover, for example, could be a symptom not of poor salesforce training or compensation but of weak company products and promotion. A comprehensive marketing audit usually is more effective in locating the real source of the company's marketing problems.

- ◆ *Systematic:* The marketing audit involves an orderly sequence of diagnostic steps covering the organization's macro- and micromarketing environment, marketing objectives and strategies, marketing systems, and specific marketing activities. The diagnosis indicates the most needed improvements. They are incorporated in a corrective-action plan involving both short-run and long-run steps to improve the organization's overall marketing effectiveness.

- ◆ *Independent:* A marketing audit can be conducted in six ways: self-audit, audit from across, audit from above, company auditing office, company task-force audit, and outsider audit. Self-audits, where managers use a checklist to rate their own operations, can be useful, but most experts agree that self-audits lack objectivity and independence.[14] The 3M Company has made good use of a corporate auditing office, which provides marketing audit services to divisions on request.[15] Generally speaking, however, the best audits are likely to come from outside consultants who have the necessary objectivity, broad experience in a number of industries, some familiarity with this industry, and the undivided time and attention to give to the audit.

- ◆ *Periodic:* Typically, marketing audits are initiated only after sales have turned down, salesforce morale has fallen, and other company problems have occurred. Ironically, companies are thrown into a crisis partly because they failed to review their marketing operations during good times. A periodic marketing audit can benefit companies in good health as well as those in trouble. "No marketing operation is ever so good that it cannot be improved. Even the best can be made better. In fact, even the best *must* be better, for few if any marketing operations can remain successful over the years by maintaining the status quo."[16]

MARKETING AUDIT PROCEDURE ❖ A marketing audit starts with a meeting between the company officer(s) and the marketing auditor(s) to work out an agreement on the objectives, coverage, depth, data sources, report format, and the time period for the audit. A detailed plan as to who is to be interviewed, the questions to be asked, the time and place of contact, and so on, is carefully prepared so that auditing time and cost are kept to a minimum. The cardinal rule in marketing auditing is: Don't rely solely on the company's managers for data and opinion. Customers, dealers, and other outside groups must be interviewed. Many companies do not really know how their customers and dealers see them, nor do they fully understand customer needs and value judgments.

When the data-gathering phase is over, the marketing auditor presents the main findings and recommendations. A valuable aspect of the marketing audit is the process that the managers go through to assimilate, debate, and develop new concepts of needed marketing action.

COMPONENTS OF THE MARKETING AUDIT ❖ The marketing audit examines six major components of the company's marketing situation. The major auditing questions are listed in Table 27-7.

TABLE 27-7
Components of a Marketing Audit

PART I. MARKETING-ENVIRONMENT AUDIT

Macroenvironment

A. Demographic	What major demographic developments and trends pose opportunities or threats to this company? What actions has the company taken in response to these developments and trends?
B. Economic	What major developments in income, prices, savings, and credit will affect the company? What actions has the company been taking in response to these developments and trends?
C. Ecological	What is the outlook for the cost and availability of natural resources and energy needed by the company? What concerns have been expressed about the company's role in pollution and conservation, and what steps has the company taken?
D. Technological	What major changes are occurring in product and process technology? What is the company's position in these technologies? What major generic substitutes might replace this product?
E. Political	What changes in laws and regulations might affect marketing strategy and tactics? What is happening in the areas of pollution control, equal employment opportunity, product safety, advertising, price control, and so forth, that affects marketing strategy?
F. Cultural	What is the public's attitude toward business and toward the company's products? What changes in customer lifestyles and values might affect the company?

Task Environment

A. Markets	What is happening to market size, growth, geographical distribution, and profits? What are the major market segments?
B. Customers	What are the customers' needs and buying processes? How do customers and prospects rate the company and its competitors on reputation, product quality, service, salesforce, and price? How do different customer segments make their buying decisions?
C. Competitors	Who are the major competitors? What are their objectives, strategies, strengths, weaknesses, sizes, and market shares? What trends will affect future competition and substitutes for this product?
D. Distribution and Dealers	What are the main trade channels for bringing products to customers? What are the efficiency levels and growth potentials of the different trade channels?
E. Suppliers	What is the outlook for the availability of key resources used in production? What trends are occurring among suppliers?

TABLE 27-7 (cont.)

F. Facilitators and Marketing Firms	What is the cost and availability outlook for transportation services, warehousing facilities, and financial resources? How effective are the company's advertising agencies and marketing research firms?
G. Publics	Which publics represent particular opportunities or problems for the company? What steps has the company taken to deal effectively with each public?

PART II. MARKETING-STRATEGY AUDIT

A. Business Mission	Is the business mission clearly stated in market-oriented terms? Is it feasible?
B. Marketing Objectives and Goals	Are the company and marketing objectives and goals stated clearly enough to guide marketing planning and performance measurement? Are the marketing objectives appropriate, given the company's competitive position, resources, and opportunities?
C. Strategy	Has the management articulated a clear marketing strategy for achieving its marketing objectives? Is the strategy convincing? Is the strategy appropriate to the stage of the product life cycle, competitors' strategies, and the state of the economy? Is the company using the best basis for market segmentation? Does it have clear criteria for rating the segments and choosing the best ones? Has it developed accurate profiles of each target segment? Has the company developed an effective positioning and marketing mix for each target segment? Are marketing resources allocated optimally to the major elements of the marketing mix? Are enough resources or too many resources budgeted to accomplish the marketing objectives?

PART III. MARKETING-ORGANIZATION AUDIT

A. Formal Structure	Does the marketing vice-president have adequate authority and responsibility for company activities that affect customers' satisfaction? Are the marketing activities optimally structured along functional, product, segment, end-user, and geographical lines?
B. Functional Efficiency	Are there good communication and working relations between marketing and sales? Is the product management system working effectively? Are product managers able to plan profits or only sales volume? Are there any groups in marketing that need more training, motivation, supervision, or evaluation?
C. Interface Efficiency	Are there any problems between marketing and manufacturing, R&D, purchasing, finance, accounting, and legal that need attention?

PART IV. MARKETING-SYSTEMS AUDIT

A. Marketing Information System	Is the marketing intelligence system producing accurate, sufficient, and timely information about marketplace developments with respect to customers, prospects, distributors and dealers, competitors, suppliers, and various publics? Are company decision makers asking for enough marketing research, and are they using the results? Is the company employing the best methods for market measurement and sales forecasting?
B. Marketing Planning Systems	Is the marketing planning system well conceived and effectively used? Do marketers have decision support systems available? Does the planning system result in acceptable sales targets and quotas?
C. Marketing Control System	Are the control procedures adequate to ensure that the annual-plan objectives are being achieved? Does management periodically analyze the profitability of products, markets, territories, and channels of distribution? Are marketing costs and productivity periodically examined?
D. New-Product Development System	Is the company well organized to gather, generate, and screen new-product ideas? Does the company do adequate concept research and business analysis before investing in new ideas? Does the company carry out adequate product and market testing before launching new products?

PART V. MARKETING-PRODUCTIVITY AUDIT

A. Profitability Analysis	What is the profitability of the company's different products, markets, territories, and channels of distribution? Should the company enter, expand, contract, or withdraw from any business segments?
B. Cost-Effectiveness Analysis	Do any marketing activities seem to have excessive costs? Can cost-reducing steps be taken?

TABLE 27-7 (cont.)

PART VI. Marketing-Function Audits

A. Products	What are the product-line objectives? Are they sound? Is the current product line meeting the objectives? Should the product line be stretched or contracted upward, downward, or both ways? Which products should be phased out? Which products should be added? What are the buyers' knowledge and attitudes toward the company's and competitors' product quality, features, styling, brand names, and so on? What areas of product and brand strategy need improvement?
B. Price	What are the pricing objectives, policies, strategies, and procedures? To what extent are prices set on cost, demand, and competitive criteria? Do the customers see the company's prices as being in line with the value of its offer? What does management know about the price elasticity of demand, experience-curve effects, and competitors' prices and pricing policies? To what extent are price policies compatible with the needs of distributors and dealers, suppliers, and government regulation?
C. Distribution	What are the distribution objectives and strategies? Is there adequate market coverage and service? How effective are distributors, dealers, manufacturers' representatives, brokers, agents, and others? Should the company consider changing its distribution channels?
D. Advertising, Sales Promotion, and Publicity	What are the organization's advertising objectives? Are they sound? Is the right amount being spent on advertising? Are the ad themes and copy effective? What do customers and the public think about the advertising? Are the advertising media well chosen? Is the internal advertising staff adequate? Is the sales-promotion budget adequate? Is there effective and sufficient use of sales-promotion tools such as samples, coupons, displays, and sales contests? Is the public-relations staff competent and creative? Is the company making enough use of direct and database marketing?
E. Salesforce	What are the salesforce objectives? Is the salesforce large enough to accomplish the company's objectives? Is the salesforce organized along the proper principles of specialization (territory, market, product)? Are there enough (or too many) sales managers to guide the field sales representatives? Does the sales-compensation level and structure provide adequate incentive and reward? Does the salesforce show high morale, ability, and effort? Are the procedures adequate for setting quotas and evaluating performances? How does the company's salesforce compare to competitors' salesforces?

EXAMPLE OF A MARKETING AUDIT[17] ❖ O'Brien Candy Company is a medium-size candy company located in the Midwest. In the past two years, its sales and profits have barely held their own. Top management feels that the trouble lies with the salesforce; they don't "work hard or smart enough." To correct the problem, management plans to introduce a new incentive-compensation system and hire a salesforce trainer to train the salesforce in modern merchandising and selling techniques. Before doing this, however, they decide to hire a marketing consultant to carry out a marketing audit. The auditor interviews managers, customers, sales representatives, and dealers and examines various data. Here are the auditor's findings:

> The company's product line consists primarily of 18 products, mostly candy bars. Its two leading brands are mature and account for 76% of total sales. The company has looked at the fast-developing markets of chocolate snacks and candies but has not made any moves yet.

> The company recently researched its customer profile. Its products appeal especially to lower-income and older people. Respondents who were asked to assess O'Brien's chocolate products in relation to competitors' products described them as "average quality and a bit old-fashioned."

> O'Brien sells its products to candy jobbers and large supermarkets. Its salesforce calls on many of the small retailers reached by the candy jobbers, to fortify displays and provide ideas; its salesforce also calls on many small retailers not covered by jobbers. O'Brien enjoys good penetration of small retailing, although not in all segments, such as the fast-growing restaurant area. Its major approach to middlemen is a "sell-in"

strategy: discounts, exclusive contracts, and stock financing. At the same time O'Brien has not adequately penetrated the mass-merchandise chains. Its competitors rely more heavily on mass-consumer advertising and in-store merchandising and are more successful with the mass merchandisers.

O'Brien's marketing budget is set at 15% of its total sales, compared with competitors' budgets of close to 20%. Most of the marketing budget supports the salesforce, and the remainder supports advertising; consumer promotions are very limited. The advertising budget is spent primarily in reminder advertising for the company's two leading products. New products are not developed often, and when they are, they are introduced to retailers by using a "push" strategy.

The marketing organization is headed by a sales vice-president. Reporting to the sales vice-president is the sales manager, the marketing research manager, and the advertising manager. Having come up from the ranks, the sales vice-president is partial to salesforce activities and pays less attention to the other marketing functions. The salesforce is assigned to territories headed by area managers.

The marketing auditor concluded that O'Brien's problems would not be solved by actions taken to improve its salesforce. The salesforce problem was symptomatic of a deeper company malaise. The auditor prepared a report to management consisting of the findings and recommendations shown in Table 27-8.

TABLE 27-8
Summary of Marketing Auditor's Findings and Recommendations for O'Brien Candy Company

FINDINGS

The company's product lines are dangerously unbalanced. The two leading products accounted for 76% of total sales and have no growth potential. Five of the 18 products are unprofitable and have no growth potential.

The company's marketing objectives are neither clear nor realistic.

The company's strategy is not taking changing distribution patterns into account or catering to rapidly changing markets.

The company is run by a sales organization rather than a marketing organization.

The company's marketing mix is unbalanced, with too much spending on salesforce and not enough on advertising.

The company lacks procedures for successfully developing and launching new products.

The company's selling effort is not geared to profitable accounts.

SHORT-TERM RECOMMENDATIONS

Examine the current product line and weed out marginal performers with limited growth potential.

Shift some marketing expenditures from supporting mature products to supporting more recent ones.

Shift the marketing-mix emphasis from direct selling to national advertising, especially for new products.

Conduct a market-profile study of the fastest growing segments of the candy market and develop a plan to break into these areas.

Instruct the salesforce to drop some of the smaller outlets and not to take orders for under 20 items. Also, cut out the duplication of effort of sales representatives and jobbers calling on the same accounts.

Initiate sales-training programs and an improved compensation plan.

MEDIUM- TO LONG-TERM RECOMMENDATIONS

Hire an experienced marketing vice-president from the outside.

Set formal and operational marketing objectives.

Introduce the product manager concept in the marketing organization.

Initiate effective new-product-development programs.

Develop strong brand names.

Find ways to market its brands to the chain stores more effectively.

Increase the level of marketing expenditures to 20% of sales.

Reorganize the selling function by specializing sales representatives by distribution channels.

Set sales objectives and base sales compensation on gross profit performance.

Source: Adapted with permission from Dr. Ernst A. Tirmann, "Should Your Marketing Be Audited?" *European Business,* Autumn 1971.

The Marketing Excellence Review

Companies can use another instrument to rate their performance in relation to the "best practices" of high-performing businesses. The three columns in Table 27-9 distinguish between poor, good, and excellent business and marketing practice. Management can place a check on each line as to their perception of where the business stands. The resulting profile then exposes the business's weaknesses and strengths. It highlights where the company might move to become a truly outstanding player in the marketplace.

The Company Ethical and Social Responsibility Review

Companies need to use a final instrument to evaluate whether they are truly practicing ethical and socially responsible marketing. We believe that business success and continually satisfying the customer and other stakeholders is intimately tied up with adopting and implementing high standards of business and marketing conduct. The most admired companies in the world abide by a code of serving people's interests, not only their own.

The practices of business are often under attack because business situations routinely pose tough dilemmas as to what is right. One can go back to Howard Bowen's classic questions about the responsibilities of businesspeople:

> Should he conduct selling in ways that intrude on the privacy of people, for example, by door-to-door selling. . .? Should he use methods involving ballyhoo, chances, prizes, hawking, and other tactics which are at least of doubtful good taste? Should he employ "high pressure" tactics in persuading people to buy? Shoud he try to hasten the obsolescence of goods by bringing out an endless succession of new models and new styles? Should he appeal to and attempt to strengthen the motives of materialism, invidious consumption, and "keeping up with the Joneses."[18]

POOR	GOOD	EXCELLENT
Product Driven	Market Driven	Market Driving
Mass-Market Oriented	Segment Oriented	Niche Oriented and Customer Oriented
Product Offer	Augmented Product Offer	Customer Solutions Offer
Average Product Quality	Better Than Average	Legendary
Average Service Quality	Better Than Average	Legendary
End-Product Oriented	Core-Product Oriented	Core-Competency Oriented
Function Oriented	Process Oriented	Outcome Oriented
Reacting to Competitors	Benchmarking Competitors	Leapfrogging Competitors
Supplier Exploitation	Supplier Preference	Supplier Partnership
Dealer Exploitation	Dealer Support	Dealer Partnership
Price Driven	Quality Driven	Value Driven
Average Speed	Better Than Average	Legendary
Hierarchy	Network	Teamwork
Vertically Integrated	Flattened Organization	Strategic Alliances
Stockholder Driven	Stakeholder Driven	Societally Driven

TABLE 27-9
The Marketing Excellence Review: Best Practices

FIGURE 27-6 Major Marketing Decision Areas Posing Legal or Ethical Questions

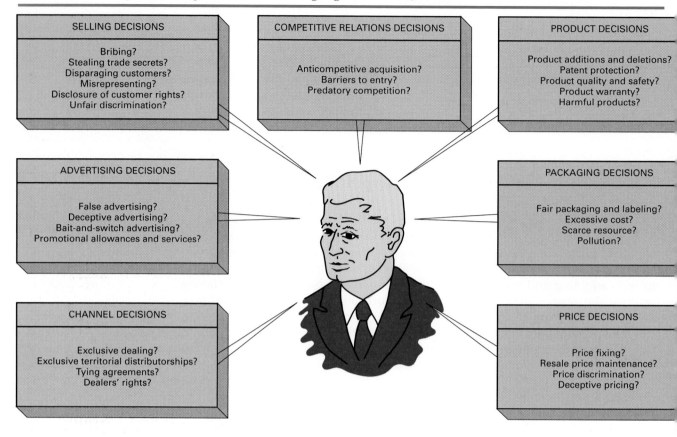

SELLING DECISIONS

Bribing?
Stealing trade secrets?
Disparaging customers?
Misrepresenting?
Disclosure of customer rights?
Unfair discrimination?

COMPETITIVE RELATIONS DECISIONS

Anticompetitive acquisition?
Barriers to entry?
Predatory competition?

PRODUCT DECISIONS

Product additions and deletions?
Patent protection?
Product quality and safety?
Product warranty?
Harmful products?

ADVERTISING DECISIONS

False advertising?
Deceptive advertising?
Bait-and-switch advertising?
Promotional allowances and services?

PACKAGING DECISIONS

Fair packaging and labeling?
Excessive cost?
Scarce resource?
Pollution?

CHANNEL DECISIONS

Exclusive dealing?
Exclusive territorial distributorships?
Tying agreements?
Dealers' rights?

PRICE DECISIONS

Price fixing?
Resale price maintenance?
Price discrimination?
Deceptive pricing?

Specific issues are further highlighted in Figure 27-6. Many were reviewed in earlier chapters. Clearly the company's bottom line cannot be the sole measure of corporate performance.

Raising the level of socially responsible marketing calls for a three-pronged attack. First, society must use the law to define, as clearly as possible, those practices which are illegal, antisocial, or anticompetitive. Second, companies must adopt and disseminate a written code of ethics, build a company tradition of ethical behavior, and hold their people fully responsible for observing the ethical and legal guidelines. Third, individual marketers must practice a "social conscience" in their specific dealings with customers and various stakeholders.

The future holds a wealth of opportunities for companies as they move into the twenty-first century. Technological advances in solar energy, home computers, cable television, modern medicine, transportation, recreation, and communication promise to change the world as we know it. At the same time, forces in the socioeconomic, cultural, and natural environments will impose new limits on marketing and business practice. Companies that are able to innovate new solutions and values in a socially responsible way are the most likely to succeed.

SUMMARY ❖

Marketing control is the natural sequel to marketing planning, organization, and implementation. Companies need to carry out four types of marketing control.

Annual-plan control consists of monitoring the current marketing effort and results to ensure that the annual sales and profit goals will be achieved. The main tools are sales analysis, market-share analysis, marketing expense-to-sales analysis, financial analysis, and customer-satisfaction tracking. If underperformance is detected, the company can implement several corrective measures, including cutting production, changing prices, increasing salesforce pressure, and cutting fringe expenditures.

Profitability control calls for determining the actual profitability of the firm's products, territories, market segments, and trade channels. Marketing-profitability analysis reveals the weaker marketing entities, although it does not indicate whether the weaker units should be bolstered or phased out.

Efficiency control is the task of increasing the efficiency of such marketing activities as personal selling, advertising, sales promotion, and distribution. Managers must watch certain key ratios that indicate how efficiently these functions are being performed.

Strategic control is the task of ensuring that the company's marketing objectives, strategies, and systems are optimally adapted to the current and forecasted marketing environment. One tool, known as the marketing-effectiveness rating instrument, profiles a company's or a division's overall marketing effectiveness in terms of customer philosophy, marketing organization, marketing information, strategic planning, and operational efficiency. Another tool, the marketing audit, is a comprehensive, systematic, independent, and periodic examination of the organization's marketing environment, objectives, strategies, and activities. The marketing audit seeks to identify marketing problem areas and recommends short-run and long-run actions to improve the organization's overall marketing effectiveness. The marketing excellence review helps a company grade its practices in relation to the "best practices" of high-performing companies. Finally, the company ethical and social responsibility review helps the company assess the quality of its performance along ethical and social responsibility lines.

NOTES ❖

1. For further discussion, see James M. Hulbert and Norman E. Toy, "A Strategic Framework for Marketing Control," *Journal of Marketing,* April 1977, pp. 12–20.

2. See Alfred R. Oxenfeldt, "How to Use Market-Share Measurement," *Harvard Business Review,* January–February 1969, pp. 59–68.

3. There is a one-half chance that a successive observation will be higher or lower. Therefore, the probability of finding six successively higher values is given by $(1/2)^6 = 1/64$.

4. Alternatively, companies need to focus on the factors affecting *shareholder value.* The goal of marketing planning is to take the steps that will increase shareholder value. Shareholder value is the *present value* of the future income stream created by the company's present actions. *Rate-of-return analysis* usually focuses on only one year's results. See Alfred Rapport, *Creating Shareholder Value* (New York: Free Press, 1986), pp. 125–30.

5. For additional reading on financial analysis, see Peter L. Mullins, *Measuring Customer and Product Line Profitability* (Washington, DC: Distribution Research and Education Foundation, 1984).

6. The MAC Group, *Distribution: A Competitive Weapon* (Cambridge, MA: 1985), p. 20.

7. For another example, see Leland L. Beik and Stephen L. Buzby, "Profitability Analyses by Market Segments," *Journal of Marketing,* June 1973, pp. 48–53.

8. For common bases of allocation, see Charles H. Sevin, *Marketing Productivity Analysis* (New York: McGraw-Hill, 1965).

9. See Robin Cooper and Robert S. Kaplan, "Profit Priorities from Activity-Based Costing," *Harvard Business Review*, May–June 1991, pp. 130–35.

10. Sam R. Goodman, *Increasing Corporate Profitability* (New York: Ronald Press, 1982), Chap. 1.

11. See Peter M. Senge, *The Fifth Discipline: The Art & Practice of the Learning Organization* (New York: Doubleday Currency, 1990), Chapter 7.

12. For further discussion of this instrument, see Philip Kotler, "From Sales Obsession to Marketing Effectiveness," *Harvard Business Review*, November–December 1977, pp. 67–75.

13. See Philip Kotler, William Gregor, and William Rodgers, "The Marketing Audit Comes of Age," *Sloan Management Review*, Winter 1977, pp. 25–43.

14. However, useful checklists for a marketing self-audit can be found in Aubrey Wilson, *Aubrey Wilson's Marketing Audit Checklists* (London: McGraw-Hill, 1982); and Mike Wilson, *The Management of Marketing* (Westmead, England: Gower Publishing, 1980). Also a marketing audit software program is described in Ben M. Enis and Stephen J. Garfein, "The Computer-Driven Marketing Audit," *Journal of Management Inquiry*, December 1992, pp. 306–18.

15. Kotler, Gregor, and Rodgers, "Marketing Audit Comes of Age," p. 31.

16. Abe Shuchman, "The Marketing Audit: Its Nature, Purposes, and Problems," in *Analyzing and Improving Marketing Performance*, eds. Alfred Oxenfeldt and Richard D. Crisp (New York: American Management Association, 1950), report no. 32, pp. 16–17.

17. This case is adapted with permission from the excellent article by Dr. Ernst A. Tirmann, "Should Your Marketing Be Audited?" *European Business*, Autumn 1971, pp. 49–56.

18. Howard R. Bowen, *Social Responsibilities of the Businessman* (New York: Harper & Row, 1953), p. 215.

Author Index

Brown, James R., 206, 222*n*2
Brown, Norman W., 637
Brown, Paul B., 475
Brown, Robert George, 667, 683*n*14
Brown, Sidney E., 634, 651*n*16
Brown, William P., 254, 262*n*4, 631, 651*n*5
Bruno, Albert V., 731, 740*n*5
Bucklin, Louis P., 532, 556*n*8, 9
Bumba, Lincoln, 640, 651*n*22
Burdick, Richard K., 209, 222*n*9
Burke, Raymond R., 148, 149*n*19
Burlingham, Bo, 30, 33*n*22
Burnett, John J., 606
Burnett, Leo, 632
Bussey, John, 321
Buzby, Stephen L., 751, 765*n*7
Buzzell, Robert D., 56, 60*n*11, 307, 361, 391, 393, 407*n*8, 9, 409, 430*n*1, 650, 652*n*33
Bybee, H. Malcolm, 633, 634, 651*n*15

C

Calder, Bobby J., 188, 202*n*17
Camp, Robert C., 234, 235
Campanelli, Melissa, 176
Canton, Irving D., 466, 471, 486*n*14
Cardozo, Richard N., 219, 222*n*22, 279, 290*n*13
Cardwell, John J., 121, 122*n*9
Carlson, Chester, 326
Carlzon, Jan, 25
Carman, James M., 630, 651*n*3
Carpenter, Gregory S., 363, 406
Carson, Patrick, 161
Carson, Rachel, 159, 168
Carson, Teresa, 449
Catherwood, Dwight W., 680, 683*n*35
Catry, Bernard, 394, 407*n*16
Cattin, P.J., 189
Cavalier, Richard, 700, 715*n*24
Cavanagh, Richard E., 404, 407*n*21
Celente, Gerald, 152, 171*n*1
Center, Allen H., 677, 683*n*32
Cespedes, Frank V., 549, 712, 715*n*35
Chevalier, Michel, 394, 407*n*16, 671, 672, 683*n*19
Chintagunta, Pradeep K., 503
Choate, Robert, 169
Churchill, Gilbert A., Jr., 134, 149*n*5, 208, 222*n*7, 698, 715*n*22
Clancy, Kevin J., 143, 317, 351*n*3
Clark, Bruce H., 26, 33*n*18
Clarke, Roberta N., 31, 34*n*29
Clausing, Don, 57
Clemons, Eric K., 215
Clifford, Donald K., 404, 407*n*21
Clothier, Peter, 563

Coen, Robert J., 641
Cohen, Herb, 708, 715*n*30
Cohen, Joel B., 196, 202*n*26
Cohen, William A., 229
Coleman, Richard P., 177, 273, 290*n*8
Colley, Russell H., 627, 629, 651*n*1
Collins, Thomas L., 655, 660, 661, 683*n*2, 6
Comer, James M., 694, 714*n*15
Cook, Victor J., 276, 356, 379*n*4
Cooke, Ernest F., 673
Cooper, Arnold C., 391, 407*n*11
Cooper, Robert G., 317, 319, 320, 345, 351*n*5, 9
Cooper, Robin, 753, 766*n*9
Corey, E. Raymond, 1, 525, 549, 555*n*1
Cosby, Bill, 636
Cossell, Howard, 636
Coughlan, Anne T., 574, 693, 714*n*8
Cox, Donald F., 598, 624*n*6
Cox, Jonathan M., 673
Cox, William E., Jr., 356, 357, 379*n*6
Coykendall, Deborah S., 580, 584, 594*n*10
Craig, C. Samuel, 145, 598, 605, 606, 607, 624*n*4, 10
Cravens, David W., 568
Crawford, C. Merle, 357, 379*n*6
Crawford, John C., 694, 714*n*14
Cribbin, James, 707, 715*n*26
Crissy, W.J.E., 704, 715*n*25
Crosby, Philip B., 57, 393, 407*n*14
Cross, James, 218
Crutchfield, Richard S., 188, 202*n*18
Cunningham, Isabella C.M., 704, 715*n*25
Cunningham, Theodore R., 475
Cunningham, William H., 704, 715*n*25
Curhan, Ronald C., 671, 672, 683*n*19
Cutler, Laurel, 268, 290*n*1
Cutlip, Scott M., 677, 683*n*32

D

Dalgleish, Julie Gordon, 31, 34*n*31
Dalkey, Norman, 259, 262*n*7
Dalrymple, Douglas J., 685, 714*n*1
Davidow, William H., 6, 33*n*3, 305, 315, 479, 486*n*21
Davidson, William R., 558, 594*n*1
Davies, R.L., 574, 594*n*7
Davis, Harry L., 179, 202*n*6, 705
Davis, Robert A., 693, 714*n*9
Davis, Stanley M., 87, 90*n*18, 266, 267, 305
Dawson, Leslie M., 29, 33*n*21
Day, Ellen, 485, 486*n*25
Day, Ralph L., 199, 200, 203*n*34, 285, 291*n*23
Deal, Terrence E., 87, 90*n*18
Deighton, John, 664, 683*n*9
Dempsey, William A., 217, 222*n*17
Denenberg, Herbert S., 169

Derrick, Frederick W., 181
Desatnick, Robert L., 6, 33*n*3
Desouza, Glenn, 481
Deveny, Kathleen, 446, 462*n*9
Dewar, Robert, 729
Dhalla, Nariman K., 372, 380*n*21
Dholakia, Nikhilesh, 413
Dichter, Ernest, 184, 185, 202*n*13, 210, 222*n*12
Dietvorst, Thomas F., 200, 201, 203*n*41
Dizard, John W., 510
Dobler, Donald W., 708, 715*n*31
Dodson, Joe A., 676, 683*n*30
Dolan, Robert J., 394, 407*n*15
Donnelly, James H., Jr., 52, 60*n*7, 200, 203*n*40
Dorfman, Robert, 119, 122*n*6
Dougherty, Philip H., 646, 651*n*28
Douglas, Susan P., 145
Dowst, Somerby, 215
Doyle, Peter, 207, 222*n*6, 373
Doyle, Stephen X., 712, 715*n*35
Drazen, Erica, 64
Drucker, Peter, 1, 2, 18, 33*n*11, 37, 66, 88, 90*n*4, 408, 524
Dubashi, Jagannath, 267
Dubinsky, Alan J., 694, 714*n*15
Dugas, Christine, 723
Dumaine, Brian, 305
Duncan, Tom, 678, 683*n*34
Dunphy, Dermot, 306

E

Eagly, Alice H., 598, 624*n*5
Edelman, Franz, 491
Edison, Thomas, 92
Eiglier, Pierre, 464, 470, 486*n*1
El-Ansary, Adel I., 526, 543, 555*n*2, 576, 594*n*9
Eliashberg, Jehoshua, 148, 149*n*19
Emerson, Ralph Waldo, 16, 33*n*7
Emery, Albert W., 223
Emery, C. William, 28, 33*n*20
Emshoff, James R., 115, 122*n*2
Endicott, R. Craig, 446, 462*n*9
Engel, James F., 193, 202*n*22, 606, 624*n*11
Enis, Ben M., 438, 693, 714*n*9, 758, 766*n*14
Eovaldi, Thomas L., 508, 638, 703
Erickson, Gary M., 506, 523*n*12
Erickson, Julie Liesse, 561
Erickson, Tamara J., 64, 89*n*2
Evans, Franklin B., 274, 290*n*9, 705
Evans, Philip, 83, 90*n*14
Exter, Thomas, 176

F

Fahey, Alison, 386, 561, 658
Fahey, Liam, 427

Company/Brand Index

Black & Decker, 152, 427, 576
Bloomingdale's, 562, 569, 573, 655
BMW, 153, 313, 409, 440, 462n9
Bobbie Brooks, 284
Body Shop, The, 30, 40, 153, 678
Boeing, 49, 265, 383–84
Boeing 767, 3
Bold, 296, 435
Book-of-the-Month Club, 533
Booz, Allen & Hamilton, 316, 320
Borden, 576
Boston Consulting Group, 70–72, 294
Bounty, 396
Bowmar, 363, 441
BrainJam, 152
BrainReserve, 152
Brand Renewal, 152
Braun AG, 301
Bridgestone, 62, 86
Brim, 281
Bristol-Myers, 372, 387
British Airways, 394, 738
Brookstone, 569
Brown Boveri, 429
Brut, 636
Budweiser, 403, 646, 669
Budweiser beer, 456
Buick, 225, 264, 442, 489
Buick City, 215
Buitoni-Perugina, 446
Bulova Watch Company, 412
Burger King Corporation, 18, 50, 385, 446, 449, 480, 545, 565, 630, 632
Burroughs Corporation, 592
Burson-Marsteller, 682
Busch Gardens, 308, 311
Business International's (BI) Country Assessment Service, 415

C

C.A.C.I., Inc., 255
C.D. Anderson, 547
Cabbage Patch dolls, 152
Cabbage Patch Kids, 677
Cadillac Division of General Motors, 54, 299, 389, 402, 475, 531, 562, 607
Calvin Klein, 564
Camay, 423, 435, 722
Camels, 272
Campbell Soup Company, 45, 217, 271, 305, 363, 390, 420, 446, 451, 458, 544, 628, 689, 722–23
Campbell's Pork & Beans, 723
Canada Dry, 446, 669
Canon, 24, 67, 84, 224, 394, 483
Capitol Records, 409
Cap'n Crunch, 670
Carnation, 446

Carrier, 69
Cascade, 396
Caterpillar, 10, 37, 38–39, 68, 212, 228, 303, 382, 393, 394, 396, 397, 415, 446, 449, 481, 501, 502, 513, 538
Chanel No 5, 636
Channel One, 642
Charles Schwab & Company, 471, 547
Charmin, 396, 435
Chase Econometric, 259
Chase Manhattan Bank, 310
Cheer detergent, 296, 435, 450, 729
Cheez Whiz, 423, 453
Cherry Electrical Products, 540
Chesbrough-Ponds, 458
Chevrolet, 199, 239, 274, 423, 440, 531
Child World, 577
Chinon Industries, 386
Chiquita, 437
Chivas Regal Scotch, 180, 629
Christian Dior, 448
Christies, 300
Chrysler Corporation, 2–3, 67, 144, 211, 311, 321, 388, 475, 670, 678, 679
Chrysler LH model, 475
Ciba-Geigy, 155, 293
Circuit City Stores, 576, 577
Citibank, 21, 87, 152, 310, 476, 477, 547, 737
Citicorp, 305, 422, 655, 660
Citi-One Account Banking, 547
Civic, 67
Claritas, 255
Clark Equipment, 228
Club Med, 24, 422, 473
Club Meditérranée, S.A., 151, 473
ClusterPlus, 255
CMC International, 414
Coast soap, 435
Coca-Cola Company, 30, 125, 175, 224, 276, 285, 289, 300, 310, 363, 367, 382, 384, 385, 387, 406, 412, 417, 420, 424, 427, 446, 449, 453, 462n9, 545, 551, 567, 588, 615, 627, 630, 636
Coke soda, 311
Coldspot, 452
Colgate Junior toothpaste, 287
Colgate-Palmolive Company, 228, 229, 275, 277, 287, 342, 343, 394, 399–400, 446, 655, 729
Columbia Pictures, 69
Compaq, 174, 184, 195, 452
CompuServe, 657
Concorde, 317
Conference Board, 110
Connecticut General Life, 303
Conn Organ Company, 533
Continental Bank, 29
Coop, 552
Cooper Industries, 86
Coors, 679
Corfam, 317

Corning, 155
Corvair, 169
Costco, 561, 576
Council of American Survey Research Organizations, 144
Courtyards by Marriott, 52, 268, 442, 455
Craftsman tools, 448, 451, 452
Cray Research, 240
Creole soup, 722
Cressida, 269
Crest toothpaste, 275, 277, 307, 376, 396, 406, 412, 435, 436, 452, 636
CRG Marketing Group, 102
Crib Jiminy, 272
Crisco, 729
Cummins Engine, 235
Curtis Candy Company, 275
Custom Research Incorporated (CRI), 54
Cuticura, 372
Cycle 1, 2, 3, and 4, 272

D

Daimler-Benz, 510
Daniel J. Edelman, Inc., 678–80
Dannon Company, 454
Dash, 296, 435
Data General, 297, 440
Data Resources, 259
Datril, 387, 520
Dayco Corporation, 540
DDB Needham Worldwide, 450
Deere & Company, 391
Deer Park, 308
Dell Computer, 41, 174, 195, 232, 293, 502, 550
Del Monte, 390, 446
Delta Airlines, 24, 476
Delta Steamship Lines, Inc., 69
Deluxe Check Printers, Inc., 302
Deluxe Corporation, 483
Denquel, 435
Dentsu, 628
Design Innovation Group, 301
DHL, 658
Dial Media, 657
Dial soap, 311, 454
Diamond Crystal Salt, 400
Diamond walnuts, 581
Diehard batteries, 448
Digital Equipment, 297, 440
Digital vax, 87
Disney. See Walt Disney Enterprises
Disneyland, 308, 310
Doan's Pills, 372
Dodge Colt, 3
Domino's Pizza, 68, 305, 483
Donnelly Marketing Information Services, 255
Dow Chemical, 26, 67, 161, 320
Downy, 396

Hills Brothers, 281, 636
Hilton, 422
Hippopotamus Food Stores, 575
Hoffman-LaRoche, 152, 424
Holiday Inns, Inc., 40, 69
Homart, 451
Home Depot, 293, 576, 577
Honda Motor Company, 3, 35, 67, 225, 247, 406, 409, 452, 454
Honeywell, Inc., 82, 443
Hoover Vacuum Cleaner Company, 125, 613
Hot Wings, 252
Howard Johnson, 545
H&R Block, 87, 467, 545
Hudson Institute, 256
Huggy Bean, 287
Humana, Inc., 220, 680
Hunt's Foods, 389, 399, 402, 403
Hyatt Hotel, 50, 433, 455, 468
Hyatt Legal Services, 87, 545
Hyatt Regency, 306, 455
Hyatt Resorts, 455
Hyatt Suites, 455
Hyster, 228
Hyundai, 264, 489

I

I. Magnin, 559
IBM Corporation, 5, 6, 19, 21, 22, 42, 54, 68, 86, 87, 94, 151, 174, 187, 188, 195, 232, 234, 240, 279, 285, 302, 303, 305, 306, 313, 326, 363, 382, 385, 393, 398, 403, 427, 429, 440, 446, 448, 453, 515, 520, 538, 542, 548–49, 551, 655, 690, 694, 695, 700, 706, 723, 758
Ikea, 24, 578–79
Illinois Central Railroad, 726
Illinois Tool Works (ITW), 404
Independent Grocers Alliance (IGA), 565
Infinity, 475
Information Resources, Inc., 130, 134, 141
Institute for the Future, 256
Interbrand, 462n9
International Harvester, 85
International Hough Company, 414
Iona, 451
Ipana toothpaste, 372
Italian Swiss Colony, 636
ITT (International Telephone & Telegraph Corp.), 428
Ivory Snow detergent, 296, 435
Ivory Soap, 357, 435
Izod, 564

J

J.C. Penney, 18, 485, 656
J.D. Powers, 41
J.I. Case, 391
J. Walter Thompson, 628, 682
Jaguar, 239, 299
Japanese Deer Park, 311
Jeffrey Martin, Inc., 372
Jell-O, 357, 367, 406, 419, 449, 452
Jerold Panas, Young & Partners, Inc., 326
Jewel Food Stores, 387–88, 447, 517
John Deere & Company, 189, 448, 481
John Klein & Associates, Inc., 658
Johnny Carson, 448
Johnson & Johnson, 239, 286, 320, 383, 403, 677, 753
Johnson & Johnson Baby Shampoo, 398
Johnson Products, 636

K

Kao Company of Japan, 327, 428
Kasle Steel, 215
Kellogg Company, 412, 446, 448, 451, 667
Kellogg's Corn Flakes, 451
Kellogg's Raisin Bran, 451
Kellogg's Rice Krispies, 451
Kelvinator, 455
Ken-L Ration, 669
Kenmore Appliances, 448
Kenner Parker Tonka, 421
Kentucky Fried Chicken, 252, 452
Kevlar, 16
Kids Mart, 566
Kimberly-Clark, 125, 466
Kinney Shoe Stores, 563, 566
Kirk's soap, 435
Kiwi Shoe Polish, 409
Kleenex, 125, 452
K mart Corp., 59, 563, 574, 575, 576, 577
Knott's Berry Farm, 308, 311
Knott's Camp Snoopy, 573
Kodak. *See* Eastman Kodak
Kodak Japan, 386
Komatsu, 37, 38, 39, 189, 228
Kool-Aid, 369
Kraft Foods Company, 293, 316, 423, 450, 453, 458, 539, 545, 642, 667, 722

L

L.L. Bean, Inc., 22, 36, 234, 482, 655, 656
Lamar Savings Bank, 546
Lamborghini, 158–59
Landis Group, 324

Landor Associates, 462n9
Lands' End, 655, 656
Lane Bryant, 566, 569
Lava, 435
Lavoris, 339
L'eggs, 670
Lego, 573
Lenox china, 310
Lerners, 566
Lever Brothers, 228, 229, 620, 644, 669
Levi Strauss Company, 45, 46, 304, 452, 551, 564
Lexus, 4, 475, 489, 490, 502, 536
The Limited, Inc., 24, 304, 566, 568, 578
Limited Express, 566
Lincoln (car), 442, 489
Lincoln Electric, 218
Lion Country Safari, 308, 311
Lipton Tea, 409
Listerine, 339
Liz Claiborne, 534, 551, 561
Lladro, 51
Loblaw Cos., 450
Loehmann's, 569
Longines, 300
Luvs, 435
Lydia Pinkham's Vegetable Compound, 261, 649
Lyric Opera Company of Chicago, 31

M

McCabe, 628
McCann-Erickson, 183
McDonald's Corporation, 24, 36, 66, 87, 161, 175, 176, 252, 287, 302, 303, 345, 382, 385, 396, 409, 413, 420, 427, 446, 449, 453, 468, 476, 479, 480, 526, 534, 538, 545, 550, 565, 566, 578, 613, 630, 632, 636, 677, 735, 758
McGraw-Hill Research, 258
MCI, 385
McKesson Corporation, 52, 302, 584
McKinsey and Company, 304, 344, 413
Mack Truck, 85, 307
Maclean's toothpaste, 275
Macy's, 573
Magic Mountain, 308, 311
Magnavox Consumer Electronics, 67, 105, 107
Marathon, 453
March of Dimes, 605, 633
Marineland of the Pacific, 308, 311
Market Research & Information Center (MRIC), 127
Marks & Spencer, 24, 36, 578, 579
Marlboro cigarettes, 303, 446
Marriott Hotels, 23, 24, 50, 52, 268, 442, 455, 476, 669, 735
Mars candy, 453
Marshall Field, 326, 573

Q

Quaker Oats, 112, 344, 422, 451, 466, 518, 655, 669
Quasar Division of Motorola, 299

R

R.J. Grunts, 573
R.J. Reynolds Company, 271, 287, 316, 363, 390
Radford (Ill.) Community Hospital, 471
Radio Shack, 575
Raleigh Bicycles, 657
Ralph Lauren, 551
Ralston-Purina, 448
Ramada Inns, Inc., 545
Ranchero beans, 722
RCA Corporation, 5, 6, 67, 316, 317, 326, 398, 443
RC Cola, 311
Red Roof Inns, 637
Reebok, 586
Reese's candy, 454
Rejoy, 453
Relska, 520–21
Remingtons, 467
Renault, 225, 423, 489
Rent-a-Wreck, 405
Residence Inns, 268, 455
Retail Index Services, 134
Revlon, Inc., 69, 239, 339, 613, 635
Reynolds. *See* R.J. Reynolds Company
Reynolds Metal Company, 530
Rheingold, 212
Richard D. Irwin, 284
Richardson-Vicks, 316
Ritz-Carlton Hotel, 54
Ritz crackers, 436
Rockwell International, 221
Rolex Watches, 300, 402
Rolls-Royce, 298, 443
Rowntree, 446
Royal Doulton, 310
Rubbermaid, Inc., 58–59, 152
RX-7 (car), 18

S

S.C. Johnson, 412, 455, 466
Saab, 234
Saatchi & Saatchi, 420, 623
Sable (car), 321
Safeguard soap, 435
Safeway Stores, Inc., 452, 462*n*11, 546
Saks Fifth Avenue, 559, 568, 655, 656
Salem cigarettes, 635

Salvation Army, 31
SAMI/Burke, 131, 134
Samsonite, 658, 663
Samsung, 444
Sam's Wholesale Club, 561, 567
Sanka coffee, 280, 281
Satisfaction Guaranteed Eateries, Inc., 477
Saturn (car), 475
Save the Rainforest, 30
Scali, 628
Scandinavian Airlines (SAS), 25, 738
Scantrack, 134
Schaefer beer, 276, 637
Schering-Plough, 239
Schlitz beer, 456
SCM Corporation, 511
Scope, 339
Scotch Tape, 423, 452
Scott, 466
Sealed Air Corporation, 306
Sears, 5–6, 24, 45, 80, 151, 161, 175, 176, 229, 230, 256, 276, 383, 405, 417, 440, 443, 448, 456, 471, 485, 508, 550, 551, 566, 567, 573, 574, 577, 615, 670, 691, 735
Seiko, 399, 451
Seiko Lasalle, 455
Seventh Day Adventists, 255
Seven-Up Company, 310, 311, 456, 611, 637
Shakey's, 345
Shaklee, 562
Sharper Image, 569, 655, 656
Shearson-Lehman, 529
Shell Chemical Company, 75, 409, 698
Sherwin-Williams, 544
Shiseido, 50
Shouldice Hospital, 479
Siemens, 86, 385, 429
Sientel, 420
Sierra Club, 159
Silience, 420
Silkience, 420
Simmons Market Research Bureau (MRB Group), 134
Sindlinger and Company, 258
Singapore Airlines, 57, 66, 303
Singer Company, 24, 158, 449, 529
Sisters of Charity Hospital, 220
Sizes Unlimited, 566
Sizzl-Spray, 458
Skip, 453
Sloane-Kettering, 473
Sloves, 628
Smirnoff vodka, 310, 356, 446, 520–21
Snickers candy, 453
Solo, 435
Sony Corporation, 18, 24, 32, 36, 68, 105, 224, 225, 293, 317, 318, 363, 409, 413, 420, 444, 446, 453, 455, 462*n*9, 573
Southwest Airlines, 502

Southwestern Bell, 176
Southwestern Company of Nashville, 562
Soyance, 420
Spector Freight, 696
Spectra, 346
Sperry Corporation, 363
Spic and Span detergent, 452
Spiegel's, 655, 656
Sprint, 385
Square D, 540
Standard Oil, 69, 279
Standard Rate & Data Service, 134
Stanford Research Institute, 182
Stanley Tools, 86
Staples, 293
Starch Pretesting Service, 134, 648
Star-Kist Foods, 681
Steelcase, Inc., 308
Steiger, 391
Stetson, 443
Stolichnaya vodka, 310
Stouffer, 446
Strategic Planning Institute, 297
Suave shampoo, 255, 398
Subway Sandwich Shops, 565–66
Sultana, 451
Sunkist, 437, 452, 459, 581
Sun Maid raisins, 581
Supercut stores, 515, 567
Swatch Watch, 299, 300
Swift and Company, 422, 451
Swissair, 476

T

Taco Bell, 505
Takara, 421
Talky Rattle, 272
Tall Men Shops, 559
Tandy, 195
Tang, 412
Target Stores, 576, 577
Taskashimaya, 462*n*9
Taster's Choice, 281
Taurus (car), 304
TDK Electronics, 386
Teenage Mutant Ninja Turtles, 87
Texas Instruments (TI), 16, 54, 81–82, 84, 88, 230, 233, 317, 363, 389, 393, 398, 402, 441, 496–97
Thomas Cook, 422
3M Company, 67, 86, 87, 161, 320, 322, 394, 456, 483, 726, 758
Thunderbird (car), 264, 610
Tide detergent, 296, 396, 435, 450, 452, 729
Tiffany and Co., 309, 488, 563
Timex watches, 403, 456, 533
Timken Corporation, 540
Tom's of Maine, 406
Topol, 228, 229
Toshiba Corporation, 195, 409

Subject Index

C

Call reports, 700–701
Calls, sales representative, 696, 700–701, 706
Canned sales approach, 706
Cannibalization of products, 441
Capital items, 437
Captive-product pricing, 513
"Caring capitalism," 30
Carriers, 592
Carryover effect, advertising, 644
Cash-and-carry wholesalers, 581
Cash cows (growth-share cell), 71, 72
Cash discounts, 507–8
Cash refund offers (rebates), 511, 669
Catalog marketing, 654, 655, 656
Catalog showroom, 561
Category concepts, 329
Category management, 729
Cause-related marketing, 30, 679
Celebrity endorsements, 189, 607–8, 636
Census of Manufacturers, 251
Census tracts, 254
Central business districts, 573
Centralized purchasing, 212
Cents-off deal, 669
CEOs, 735–36
Chain-ratio method, 250
Chain stores, 545, 565, 566–67
Challengers, market, 382, 394–401, 402–3
Channel boundaries, 548–49
Channel captain, 550, 551
Channels, communication, 608–11
Channels, marketing. *See* Marketing channels
Cheaper-goods strategy, 402
Chernobyl nuclear disaster, 5
Child Protection Act (1966), 165
Circular, 663
Civic positioning, 289
Class, social. *See* Social class
Clayton Act (1914), 164, 508
Clinical conferences, 608
Cliques, 611
Closed-end questions, 137, 138
Closing of sale, 707
Club marketing programs, 50–51
Cluster analysis, 147, 269
Cluster marketing enterprises, 153
Coercive power, 538
Coffee-market-segment profiles, 280, 281
Cold War, challenges after end of, 2
Colloquy (newsletter), 50
Combination store, 560
Commercial data, 134
Commercialization, 344–45
Commission merchants, 582
Commission system, 628, 692
Common carrier, 592

Communication(s): adaptation for foreign market, 410; of company's positioning strategy, 312–13; determining objectives of, 602–3, 604; integrated marketing, 622–23, 628; programs, 59; steps in developing effective, 599–623
Communication channels, selecting, 608–11
Communication-effect research, 647–48
Communication process, 597–99; elements in, 597; managing and coordinating, 622–23
Communications mix: deciding on, 613–21; major tools of, 596, 597, 615–16; *See also* Advertising; Personal selling; Public relations (PR); Sales promotion
Communications model, 602
Community influentials, 610
Community shopping centers, 574
Company: channel design and characteristics of, 532; ethical and social responsibility review by, 763–64; history, 66; new view of firm, 5–6; objectives and resources of, 283, 328
Company brand strength, 446
Company culture, 40
Company demand and demand function, 249
Company organization, 717–18
Company orientations toward marketplace, 15–30, 240–42, 735–38; marketing concept, 18–28; product concept, 16–17; production concept, 15–16; selling concept, 16–17, 19; societal marketing concept, 28–30
Company potential, 250
Company pricing policies, 507
Company sales forecast, 249–50
Comparison advertising, 629–30
Compensation, salesforce, 692–93, 699
Compensation deal, 510
Competences, distinctive, 66, 67, 79, 81–83
Competition: advertising budget and, 631; attribute, dynamics of, 377–78; channel, 550–51; channel design and, 532; differentiation and, tools for, 294–306; fair, 703; industry concept of, 225–28; intertype, 575; market concept of, 228; monopolistic, 227; pure, 227; in retailing, 544; in services, 471–72
Competitive advantage, 80, 239, 294, 312, 414
Competitive attack strategies, 394–401, 402–3
Competitive cycle, stages of, 364
Competitive depositioning, 197

Competitive equilibrium, 236, 237
Competitive intelligence system, designing, 237–38
Competitive-parity promotion budget method, 612
Competitive position, 72–75; classification of, 382–407
Competitive scopes, 67–68
Competitive situation, marketing plan, 105
Competitor-centered company, 240–41, 242
Competitor myopia, 224–25
Competitors, 223–43; acquisition of, 86; choosing, 394–95; customer satisfaction with, 40–41; identifying, 224–28; identifying strategies of, 228–31; intelligence gathering on, 237–38; Japanese, 427; objectives of, determining, 231–32; prices and offers, analyzing, 498; product life cycle stages and, 360, 365–66; reaction patterns of, estimating, 236–37; reactions to price changes, 518–19; responding to price changes of, 519–20; as source of new-product ideas, 323; strengths and weaknesses of, assessing, 233–36, 239; types of, 236, 239–40
Complaint and suggestion systems, 41, 476
Complaint handling, 479
Complementors, 550
Complex buying behavior, 190
Complex salesforce structures, 690
Component materials, 437
Component parts, 437
Component-value pricing, 501–2
Composite of salesforce opinions, 258–59
Computers, 154; planning effective resource allocation using, 112–22; salesforce productivity and, 697, 698; warehousing and, 583, 584, 590
Computer workstations, 146
Concentrated marketing, 284, 286
Concentration, advertising, 646
Concentric diversification strategy, 78
Concept development, 328–30
Concept selling, 331
Concept testing, 330–31
Conclusion drawing, 605–6
Conferences, clinical, 608
Conference selling, 687
Conflict, channel, 546, 548–49, 550–54
Conformance quality, 298
Conglomerate, merchandising, 566

Feedback, 58, 87–89, 597; from sales representatives, 700; *See also* Control
Film market, 386
Final price, selecting, 506–7
Finance department, 734
Financial analysis, 747–48; to evaluate foreign markets, 414
Financial benefits added to customer relationship, 49
Financial leverage, 747
Financial objectives, 107
Financial services, multichannel marketing in, 547
Financing, low-interest, 511
Finite resources, 159–60
Firm. *See* Company
First-time sales, estimating, 335, 336
Fishyback, 592
Fixed costs, 496
Flank attack, 398–99
Flanker brands, 455
Flanking defense, 387–88
Flighting, 646
Focus-group research, 135
Focus strategy, 84; *See also* Positioning
Follower strategies, 382, 401–2
Follow-up on sale, 707
Force, principle of, 398
Forced relationships, 324
Forecasts and forecasting: company, 249–50; future demand, 256–61; macroenvironmental, 256–57; market, 248; product life cycle concept as tool in, 372; shape and duration of product life cycle, 358
Foreign-exchange problems, 410
Foreign (international) subsidiaries, 86, 424, 427–28
Foreign marketing. *See* Global markets and marketing
Foreign markets, data on, 145
Forgetting rate, 27–28, 645
Format for message, 607
Formulated sales approach, 706
Fortune magazine, 58
Forward buying, 672
Forward integration strategy, 78, 584
Fragile-market-share trap, 514
Fragmented industry, 294
Franchise organizations, 545, 565–66
Fraud in direct marketing, 665
Free goods, trade promotion with, 671
Free Trade Agreement with Canada, 3
Free trials, 670
Frequency marketing programs (FMP), 50
Frequency of ad exposure, 638–40, 645
Freudian motivation theory, 184–85
Frontal attack, 394–98
Full-cost approach, 752–53
Full demand, 15
Full-line forcing, 554

Full market coverage, 285–87
Full-profile approach to preference measurement, 333
Full-service retailing, 562
Full-service wholesalers, 581
Functional compensation plan, 539
Functional discounts, 509
Functional expenses, 749–50
Functional-marketing organization, 721
Functional tests, 339
Fund-raising drives, nonprofit, 680
Future demand, estimating, 256–61
Future profit potential, assessment of, 62
Future Shock (Toffler), 162
Futurist research firms, 256

G

Galvanometers, 137
Games, 669
Game theory, 147
Gap analysis, 369
Gatekeepers, 210, 610
Gender segmentation, 272
General Agreement on Tariff and Trade (GATT), 422
General Electric approach, 72–75
Generalization, 187
Generics, 432, 447–48
Geodemographic analysis, 255
Geographical marketing organization, 721–22
Geographical scope, 68, 79
Geographical shifts in population, 157
Geographic markets, 11
Geographic segmentation, 270–71; commercialization and, 344–45; pricing strategy, 507; shifts in population and, 157
Ghost shopping, 42
Gifts, 669
Global business networks, 3
Global industries, 228, 410
Global interdependence, 154
Globalization, 59
Globalized economy, 2–4
Global markets and marketing, 408–30, 584; blunders, 412; choosing markets to target, 412–15; decision to go abroad, 411; environment of, forces and trends in, 155; expansion into, 584; Japanese performance in, 426–27; market-entry strategies, 416–19, 426–27; marketing engineering and, 102–3; marketing-strategy mix for, 419–25; organization for, 425–29; rapidly changing, doing business in, 2–6; risks in, 410, 414, 415
Global organization, 429

"Glocal" strategy, 428–29
Goal incompatibility, 551
Goals: formulation of, 83–84; in mission statements, 67; superordinate, 552; *See also* Objectives
GO error, 327
Going-rate pricing, 505
Good Housekeeping seal, 332, 333
Goods, classification of industrial, 436–38
Goodwill (brand equity), 445–46, 630
Government: constraints, 317; environmental protection role of, 162; foreign, global marketing and, 410; regulation by, 164–66, 532
Government market, 12, 220–21
Government publications, 134
Government sector, 464
Grade labeling, 461
Gray-market problem, 424
Green consciousness, 59
Greenhouse effect, 159
"Green" products, 160–61
Gross contribution margin per unit, 113
Gross profit function, 115–16
Growth: diversification, 77, 78; integrative, 76, 78; intensive, 76, 77–78; market growth rate, 71
Growth-share matrix, 70–72
Growth stage: in market evolution, 375–76; in product life cycle, 356, 364–65, 541, 620
Guarantees, 482–83
Guerrilla attack, 400–401

H

Habitual buying behavior, 191–92, 644
Hard selling, 17
Harper's magazine, 572
Harvesting strategy, 72, 90*n*11, 371
Heart share, rating competitors', 233, 235
Heightened attention, 194
Heterogeneous shopping goods, 436
Heuristic model, 147
Hierarchy: of attributes, 269–70; of needs, 185–86, 378; of objectives, 83
Hierarchy-of-effects model, 602, 603
High-performance businesses, nature of, 63–65
High-pressure selling techniques, 704
High-spending tests, 650
Hispanic consumers, 175
Historical approach to sales impact, 649

Vertical marketing system (VMS), 404, 543–45, 575
Vertical product team, 725–26
Vertical scope, 68, 79
Videocart, 642
"Virtual inventory" system, 571
Virtual reality, developing prototypes for concept testing using, 330
Visual tests, 458
Vogue magazine, 572, 643
Volume, break-even, 500
Volume industry, 294
Voluntary chain, 565

W

Waiting time, 531
Wall Street Journal, 130
Wants, consumer, 7, 10, 30
Warehousing, 583, 584, 589–90

Warranties, 460–61, 482–83, 511, 670
Water transportation, 592
Weaknesses, analysis of, 107
Weak products, identifying, 370
Weighted-index method, 327
Wheeler-Lea Act (1938), 164
Wheel-of-retailing hypothesis, 560
Whole channel concept for international marketing, 424–25
Wholesalers, 529, 577; marketing strategies of, 580–83, 584; trade promotion to, 670–72; types of, 525, 580, 581–82, 584
Wholesaler-sponsored voluntary chains, 545
Wholesaling, 576–85
Wholesome Meat Act of 1967, 168
Wide Area Telephone Service (WATS), 656
Width of product mix, 435
Women, car buying and, 179, 180

Word-of-mouth influence, 608, 609
Workload approach salesforce size, 691–92
World-class quality, 189
World population explosion, 155–56

Y

Yankelovich Monitor, 167
Yield management, 512
Yuppies (young urban professionals), 167, 273

Z

Zero-based budgeting, 121
Zero-level channel, 529
ZIP-code centers and data, 254, 255
Zone of agreement, 708–9